Donated by
Ian Thomson

Not for loan

ENERGY LAW IN EUROPE

ENERGY LAW IN EUROPE

National, EU and International Law and Institutions

Edited by

Martha M. Roggenkamp

Anita Rønne

Catherine Redgwell

Iñigo Del Guayo

OXFORD
UNIVERSITY PRESS

OXFORD
UNIVERSITY PRESS

Great Clarendon Street, Oxford OX2 6DP

Oxford University Press is a department of the University of Oxford.
It furthers the University's objective of excellence in research, scholarship,
and education by publishing worldwide in

Oxford New York

Athens Auckland Bangkok Bogotá Buenos Aires Cape Town
Chennai Dar es Salaam Delhi Florence Hong Kong Istanbul Karachi
Kolkata Kuala Lumpur Madrid Melbourne Mexico City Mumbai Nairobi
Paris São Paulo Shanghai Singapore Taipei Tokyo Toronto Warsaw

with associated companies in Berlin Ibadan

Oxford is a registered trade mark of Oxford University Press
in the UK and in certain other countries

Published in the United States
by Oxford University Press Inc., New York

First published 2001

British Library Cataloguing in Publication Data
Data available

Library of Congress Cataloging in Publication Data
Data available

ISBN 0–19–826068–7

1 3 5 7 9 10 8 6 4 2

Typeset by Hope Services (Abingdon) Ltd.
Printed in Great Britain
on acid-free paper by
Biddles Ltd.,
Guildford & King's Lynn

FOREWORD

It is a great pleasure for me to write a Foreword for this collective book. First of all *Energy Law in Europe* is the result of a European effort in a true sense, the end of a long-term project rooted in intensive cooperation between researchers from several European Universities including Almería, Bochum, Bologna, Copenhagen, Dundee, Göttingen, Leiden, Nottingham and Oslo. Secondly, as I see it, it is a crucial step towards the creation of a true European *Corpus Iuris* for Energy.

The backbone of this *Corpus Iuris* is the rapid development of the Internal Energy Market, despite a number of obstacles, the lack of a comprehensive European Energy Policy being just one among others. There is no doubt that both the Electricity and Gas Directives are two milestones on which future steps must be taken. The European Commission is working with governments, regulators, energy companies and energy consumers to define these steps. We want the process to be as transparent and democratic as possible. I believe that any progress towards a common European energy policy should be the result of a conscious decision including subsidiarity concerns. In this respect, *Energy Law in Europe*, a source of precious objective thinking afar from political debates, provides an important contribution to presenting the facts and challenges which need to be at the heart of any political decision.

At the time I write this Foreword the Commission has just launched a strategic debate on energy policy throughout the European Union with a new Green Paper, '*Towards a European strategy for the security of energy supply*'. Today 50 per cent of our energy needs are imported. Tomorrow, 70 per cent will be, if nothing is done. This growing dependence, together with the fight against climate change, will dramatically change the face of energy policy in the European Union. The new policies which will inevitably have to be set in place will in turn shape energy law in a new direction. This is why I would like to encourage the authors to stick together, to associate in their enterprise a representative of each of those countries whose legal system is not analysed in this book, including candidate countries, and to publish a new edition of *Energy Law in Europe* in a few years' time.

In the meantime, and as a key tool to fuel the debate, I am pleased to recommend *Energy Law in Europe* in my capacity as Vice-President of the European Commission and Commissioner for Energy and Transport, not only to students, but to all those who are involved in designing the future of energy policy in Europe.

Loyola de Palacio Valle-Lersundi
Vice-President of the European Commission
Commissioner for Energy and Transport

PREFACE

This book is the result of long-standing collaboration among nine European institutions where energy law forms a part of the legal curriculum, namely, the University of Almería (Spain), the University of Bochum (Germany), the University of Bologna (Italy), the Centre for Energy, Petroleum and Mineral Law & Policy of the University of Dundee (Scotland), the University of Nottingham (England), the University of Copenhagen (Denmark), the University of Göttingen (Germany), the International Institute of Energy Law of the University of Leiden (the Netherlands), and the Institute of Petroleum Law of the University of Oslo (Norway). What initially brought these institutions together was the teaching of energy law and participation in the European Commission-funded Erasmus (now Socrates) programme on international energy law. In addition the members of the editorial team have had the opportunity to collaborate together in the work of the Academic Advisory Group of the Section on Energy and Natural Resources Law of the International Bar Association. Further collaboration at the research level arose out of mutual recognition of the need for a monograph addressing and comparing key energy jurisdictions in Europe within their international and EC law context. In addition to contributions representing all the national systems participating in the Socrates scheme, further invited contributions ensure representative coverage of key energy jurisdictions in Europe and of key regional and international developments.[1]

Although the original impetus for the book was to provide a suitable text on energy law for the students in the Erasmus/Socrates exchange programme, the idea was further developed to broaden the horizon of interested readers. The result is a book which we believe provides a useful tool for anyone interested in European energy law and its developments, including students and practising lawyers within and outside Europe.

The concept for this book first emerged in the summer of 1995 and was brought to fruition over the ensuing five-year period. Although not originally conceived of as a 'millennium project', inevitably in a major collaborative work of this size it has taken some time to finalize the project. In addition, these last few years have seen developments within the energy sector occurring more rapidly than ever before. The Internal Energy Market programme which was launched in

[1] It was not possible to include a French University in this project; we are thus very grateful indeed for the participation of the French Ministry of Industry and Economic Affairs.

1988 saw considerable results at the end of the 1990s with the publication of the Hydrocarbons Licensing Directive, the Electricity Directive, and most recently the Gas Directive. All these developments have been taken into account by the authors with the law as at 1 October 2000, though in some places it has been possible to take into account later developments.

The project has been guided by a four-person editorial team comprising Martha Roggenkamp (University of Leiden), with Anita Rønne (University of Copenhagen), Catherine Redgwell (University of Nottingham, since 1999 University of Oxford), and Iñigo del Guayo (University of Almería). Over the past three years the editorial board has met several times to discuss the chapters in progress, and to return annotated chapters to the authors to ensure both individual comprehensiveness and also comparability between chapters in terms of depth and coverage. These meetings have been very intense but also very stimulating. It has been interesting to note in our discussions the differences between the Member States' legal systems. This has truly been a learning process for all of those involved in the project. Special mention should be made of the wonderful hospitality of the University of Copenhagen in hosting our meetings, for which we are most grateful. It is undoubtedly the case that without such hospitality editing the book would have been a much more difficult and less pleasant task. We would also like to express our gratitude to staff at our respective institutions and to Chris Rycroft and Rebecca Allen of Oxford University Press for their support and encouragement over the last few years.

Leiden
November 2000
Martha Roggenkamp, Anita Rønne,
Catherine Redgwell, Iñigo del Guayo

LIST OF CONTRIBUTORS

Finn Arnesen

Professor dr juris Finn Arnesen heads the Centre for European Law at the University of Oslo. He has published widely within the fields of EU-law, petroleum law and legal reasoning, albeit mainly in the Norwegian language.

Craig S. Bamberger

Mr Craig S. Bamberger has been the Legal Counsel of the International Energy Agency in Paris since 1992; he previously served as international and emergency preparedness counsel for the US Energy Department, and was a partner in a Washington, DC law firm. Mr. Bamberger chaired during 1992–94 the panel of lawyers that advised the negotiating conference for, and assisted in the drafting of, the Energy Charter Treaty, a subject on which he since has published and spoken widely. He received his legal education at Harvard, where he was Note Editor of the International Law Journal, holds an MA from the Fletcher School of Law & Diplomacy, and graduated Phi Beta Kappa from the University of Alabama.

Eugene Daniel Cross

Mr Eugene D. Cross, BA, JD, MFn, LLM, is a senior research fellow at the International Institute of Energy Law of the University of Leiden Faculty of Law in the Netherlands. He is the sole author of several books and articles on energy law, including *Electric Utility Regulation in the European Union* (John Wiley 1996). He has served as a legal adviser to numerous energy regulatory agencies and government ministries on the development and reform of legislative/regulatory frameworks relating to electricity, gas, renewable energy, energy efficiency, cogeneration and district heating.

Stephen R. Dow

Mr Stephen R. Dow, LLB, LLM, DipLP, NP is Lecturer in Energy Law at the Centre for Energy, Petroleum and Mineral Law and Policy at the University of Dundee. He is a qualified solicitor and has advised governments on liberalization of electricity and gas industries. He has worked on both legislative reform and the development of contractual structures to support liberalization. He is the author of several articles on liberalization of the energy sector, and a regular contributor to seminars and workshops on electricity reform.

Iñigo del Guayo

Mr Iñigo del Guayo is Professor in Administrative Law at the University of Almería (Spain). He got his two Law Degees (LLM and PhD) at the University of Navarre (Pamplona, Spain). He is member of the Foundation for Economic Regulation Studies (Madrid), and Head of its Gas Division. In the academic year 1999–2000 he was Director of the Spanish National Institute for Public Administration (Madrid). His main areas of interest are Energy Law and Public Economic Law, together with the judicial review of administrative action within the Economy, in which he has published widely. He is a member of the Academic Advisory Group of the International Bar Association, Section on Energy and Natural Resources Law.

Ulf Hammer

Ulf Hammer is researcher at the Scandinavian institute of Maritime Law since January 2000. Before that he was senior executive officer in the Ministry of Petroleum and Energy (1983–88), Assistant judge (1988–90), legal counsel in Norsk Hydro (1990-95), and research fellow at the Scandinavian Institute of Maritime Law (1995–2000). His main area of research is energy law. Ulf Hammer wrote his doctoral thesis on the regulation of the Norwegian electricity market. He is co-author of a book on the Norwegian Petroleum Act, and has published several articles on petroleum law, electricity law, and EU-law. He is a member of the Academic Advisory Group of the International Bar Association, Section on Energy and Natural Resources Law.

Fabienne Helvin

Fabienne Helvin is a legal and public finance adviser of DGEMP (the Directorate General of Energy and Raw Materials) in the French Ministry of Economy, Finance and Industry. She wrote the first drafts of the decrees implementing the new Electricity Act 2000 and the budget of the French Regulatory Authority. She monitored the legal aspects of the French 'EOLE 2005' programme to favour the use of wind energy in France.

Per Håkon Høisveen

Mr Per Håkon Høisveen is Director General in the Norwegian Ministry of Petroleum and Energy. He is inter alia responsible for the administration of the energy and water resources law. Mr Høisveen was in charge of the preparation for the Norwegian Energy Act of 1990 and for the Water Resources Act of 2000. He is the author of articles and studies on energy law and of a commentary edition to the Energy Act. Mr Høisveen has been a lecturer in water resources law and in energy law and he has been examiner in energy law at the University of Oslo. He is an officer of the Water Law Committee in the IBA Section on Energy and Natural Resources Law.

Knut Kaasen

Dr juris Knut Kaasen is a Professor of Law at the Scandinavian Institute of Maritime Law, a part of the Faculty of Law at the University of Oslo. He is head of the Institute's Department of Petroleum Law, and has served as Associate Dean of the Faculty of Law. Before joining the Institute in 1989, Kaasen served as an assistant district judge and as a counsel in the legal department of Norsk Hydro. He has been heavily involved in the development of agreed forms of contract for the Norwegian petroleum industry, and is frequently engaged as arbitrator and mediator in commercial disputes. He has published books and articles on inter alia safety regulations, licensing systems, joint operating agreements, construction contracts and international law aspects of offshore petroleum activities, and is an editor of the journal 'PetrIus'. He is a member of the Academic Advisory Group of the International Bar Association, Section on Energy and Natural Resources Law.

Hans-Martin Koopmann

Dr Hans-Martin Koopmann was born in 1969 at Leer of Frisia. Studied Law and Theology in Bochum, Copenhagen, Hamburg and Stockholm. LLM in European Community Law (Stockholm 1998). Former appointment at the Institut für Berg- und Energierecht in Bochum as a research associate (1993–97). Participation in various European projects. Specialized in European Public Law with focus on the regulation on business and industry.

Heike Krieger

Dr iur Heike Krieger, *Rechtsassessorin,* works as a *Wissenschaftliche Assistentin* (research fellow) at the Institute for International Law of the University of Göttingen in Germany. Her research interests lie in public international law as well as in public law.

Jan Linehan

Australian Department of Foreign Affairs; formerly Legal Adviser, Energy Charter Secretariat, Brussels (the chapter represents solely the personal views of the author and not necessarily those of the Energy Charter Secretariat or Conference).

Fabrizio Nocera

Mr Fabrizio Nocera is a Legal Adviser of ENEA (the Governmental Agency for New Technologies, Energy and the Environment), and Secretary General to the Italian Center for the Study of Energy Law (CISDEN). He is a member of international and national Working Groups and member of the Italian delegation for the negotiation of international treaties. He is the author of articles, studies, commentaries and compilations in the energy law field.

Dagfinn Nygaard

Lic jur Dagfinn Nygaard is Senior Legal Counsel in Norske Conoco AS, an affiliate of Conoco Inc. Before this, he was senior executive officer in the Ministry of Petroleum and Energy (1983–88) and associate lawyer in Simonsen & Musæus (Oslo) (1988–89). His career began at Norske Conoco in 1989 where he has also been Manager governmental affairs and Manager strategy & portofolio management. He was a guest researcher at the Scandinavian Institute of Maritime Law (1993–95) where he wrote his thesis on third party use of offshore oil installations. He has been a member of both the Industry Policy Committee (1990–93) and of the Legal Committee (1995–2000) in the Norwegian Oil Industry Association (OLF) and served as leader of the Legal Committee (1997–99). He has been a member and leader of several work groups within OLL reporting on a range of petroleum law issues and industrial policy matters including negotiation of environmental agreements. He has published articles on petroleum law.

Johan-Christian Pielow

Mr Johan-Christian Pielow is an Akademischer Oberrat (senior researcher) at the Institute of Energy and Mining Law of the Ruhr University Bochum (since 1993). 'Habilitation' (prof. degree = Privatdozent): June 1998. He has been 'substituting' chairs of public law in several German universities: Bonn (1998), Cologne (1999) and Munich (autumn 1999–October 2000). His main research areas are national and international public economic law and comparative studies of administrative law.

Catherine Redgwell

Catherine Redgwell is a Reader in Public International Law and the Yamani Fellow at St Peter's College, University of Oxford (formerly Senior Lecturer in Law at the University of Nottingham). Her research interests lie primarily in public international law, particularly international environmental law, treaty law and international energy law. She has published widely in leading academic journals and is the author of the monograph *Intergenerational Trusts and Environmental Protection* (MUP/Juris, 1999) as well as serving as the International Law Contributing Editor for Daintith & Willoughby UK Oil & Gas Law (Sweet & Maxwell). She is a member of the Academic Advisory Group of the IBA's section on energy and natural resources law.

Martha M. Roggenkamp

Martha Roggenkamp has been a senior research fellow at the International Institute of Energy Law at the University of Leiden in the Netherlands since 1986. In 1998 she also became a Member of the Energy Group of Nolst Trenité, Lawyers in Rotterdam. She defended her PhD on the 'Legal Regime of Pipelines in the Petroleum Industry' at the University of Leiden in February 1999. Her research lies mainly in the field of energy law. She has written the monograph 'Oil and Gas: Netherlands Law and Practice' and several articles on issues of petroleum law, gas law, pipeline regulation networkbound energy and transit. In addition, Martha Roggenkamp is the chairperson of the editorial board of the series 'Energie & Recht' as well as a member of the editorial board of the *International Energy Law and Taxation Review*. She is also a member of the IBA's section on energy and natural resources law.

Anita Rønne

Anita Rønne is an Assistant Professor in Energy Law with the Faculty of Law, University of Copenhagen, Denmark. She is the Vice-Chairman of the Institute of Legal Science, Sec. B. Her research interests lie in energy law. She has served as the legal adviser to the Danish Energy Agency and foreign government agencies on the development of regulatory frameworks for the energy sector. From 1995 to 1996 she was appointed by the World Bank as a Regulatory Consultant and Project Co-ordinator of the ESMAP project on establishing an Energy Regulatory Authority in Poland. From 1993 to 1995 she was appointed by the EU Commission as the legal adviser to the Polish Government as a member of the Energy Restructuring Group. From 1981 to 1985. Anita Rønne served as Head of Section for Oil and Gas Exploration in the Danish Ministry of Energy. She is a member of the Academic Advisory Group of the International Bar Association, Section on Energy and Natural Resources Law, chair of the Danish Society for Energy Law, and member of the International Committee at the Law Faculty at the University of Copenhagen.

Piet Jan Slot

Professor Dr Piet Jan Slot was appointed to the chair of Economic Law at the University of Leiden in 1982. He is Chairman of the International Institute of Energy Law and Director of the Europa Institute (both part of the Law Faculty of the University of Leiden), as well as an editor of the *Common Market Law Review* and Chairman of the Competition Law Group. He is Honorary Fellow of the Institute of Advanced Legal Studies, University of London. He is a member of the Board of the European Maritime Law Organisation, the European Air Law Association and of the International Bar Association. Professor Slot has been the visiting Jean Monnet professor at the Reinische Friedrich Wilhelms University, Bonn, Germany and a visiting professor at Paris II, Pantheon-Assas. He has published widely, notably in the areas of competition law, state aids (he is co-author of a textbook on state aids), transport and energy law.

Thomas Wälde

Mr Thomas Wälde (Law Degree (Frankfurt). Dr iur (Frankfurt), LLM (Harvard) is Professor of International Economic, Energy and Natural Resources Law at the

Centre for Energy, Petroleum and Mineral Law & Policy, University of Dundee, Scotland, UK. He is Jean Monnet Chair for European Economic and Energy Law; served as professeur invite at the Institut des Hautes Etudes Internationales (U de Paris II—Pantheon-Assas), and visiting professor, American University (Washington DC). He is editor of the *Journal of Energy and Natural Resources Law*; the *CEPMLP Internet Journal*, the Kluwer Series on International Energy/Resources Law, Corresponding Editor of *International Legal Materials (Energy & Investment)* and Director of the CEPMLP internet forum ENATRES and the *Journal of Mineral Policy*. Earlier, he served as the principal UN Interregional Adviser on Natural Resources, Energy and Investment Law. He has published and edited books in international economic, investment, energy, natural resources, mining and environmental law, legal and regulatory reform and advises multinational companies, governments and international organizations in his field of expertise throughout the world.

CONTENTS—SUMMARY

CONTENTS

8. Energy Law in Germany

IV CONCLUSIONS

ABBREVIATIONS

ADEME	Agence française de l'environnement et de la maîtrise de l'énergie (French Environment and Energy Conservation Agency)
AFME	Agence française de la maîtrise de l'énergie (Energy Conservation Agency)
AGRICE	Agriculture for Chemistry and Energy Association
AIE	Agencia industrial del estado (State Agency for Industry)
AJIL	American Journal of International Law
ANDRA	Agence nationale des déchets radioactifs (National Agency for Radioactive Waste Management)
ANPA	Agency for the Protection of the Environment
ANRED	Agence nationale pour la récupération et l'élimination des déchets (Non-Nuclear Waste Agency)
APEC	Asian Pacific Economic Co-operation
APX	Amsterdam Power Exchange
AQA	Agence pour la qualité de l'air (Air Quality Agency)
ATIC	Association technique pour l'importation du charbon (Technical Association for Coal Importation)
bcm	billion cubic metres
BIT	Bilateral Investment Treaty
BP	British Petroleum
Campsa	Compañia Arrendataria del Monopolio de Petróleos, Sociedad Anónima (Operator Company of the Oil Monopoly)
CCGTs	combined cycle gas turbines
CDF	Charbonnages de France
CDM	clean development mechanism
CEA	Commissariat à l'énergie atomique (Atomic Energy Commission)
CEECs	Central & Eastern European Countries
CeERM	co-ordinated emergency response measures
CEN	Comité européen de normalisation (European Committee for Standardization)
CENELEC	Comité européen de normalisation electrotechnique (European Committee for Electro-technical Standardization)
Cepsa	Compañia Española de Petróleos (Spanish Oil Company)
CERN	European Organization for Nuclear Research
CHP	Combined Heat and Power

CIEMAT	Centro de Investigaciones Energéticas, Medioambientales y Tecnológicas (Centre for Energy, Environmental, and Technology Research)
CIES	Comité des investissements économiques et sociaux (Economic and Social Investment Committee)
CIPE	Inter-Ministerial Council for Economic Planning
CLC	1969 International Convention on Civil Liability for Oil Pollution Damage
CLH	Compañia Logística de Hidrocarburos (Hydrocarbons Company for Logistics)
CLR	Commonwealth Law Reports (Australia)
CNEN	Comitato Nazionale per l'Energia Nucleare (National Committee for Nuclear Energy)
CNRS	Centre national de la recherche scientifique (National Centre for Scientific Research)
CO_2	carbon dioxide
COGEMA	Compagnie générale des matières nucléaires (Nuclear Materials Company)
CPSSP	Comité professionnel des stocks pétroliers stratégiques (Professional Strategic Petroleum Stocks Committee)
CRAMRA	1988 Convention on the Regulation of Antarctic Mineral Resource Activities
CRE	Commission de régulation de l'électricité (Electricity Regulatory Commission)
CS	continental shelf
CSS	Commodity Services System
CTC	Costes de Transición a la Competencia (Stranded costs)
DAM	day-ahead market
DGEMP	Direction générale de l'énergie et des matières (Directorate General for Energy and Raw Materials)
DHYCA	Direction des Hydrocarbures (Hydrocarbon Directorate)
DIGEC	Direction du gaz, de l'électricité et du charbon (Gas, Electricity, and Coal Directorate)
DIMAH	Hydrocarbons and Raw Material Directorate
DKK	Danish Kroner
DL	Decree-Law
Dlgov	Legislative Decree
DM	Ministerial Decree
DOM-TOM	Départements et Territoires d'outre-mer (Overseas Départements and Territories)
DONG	National Oil and Gas Company of Denmark
DPCM	Prime Ministerial Decree

DPR	Decree of the President of the Republic
DRIRE	Directions régionales de l'industrie, de la recherche et de l'environnement (Regional Directorates for Industry, Research, and Environment)
DSC	Direction de la sécurité publique (Public Safety Directorate)
DSIN	Direction de la sûreté des installations nucléaires (French Nuclear Regulatory Directorate)
DSU	dispute settlement understanding (WTO)
Dtc	Dienst toezicht en uitvoering Energie (authority monitoring compliance with the Electricity Act and the Gas Act)
DUC	Danish Underground Consortium
DUP	Déclaration d'utilité publique (declaration in the public interest)
DVO	Disputed Variation Order
EA	Electricity Act
EBN	Energie Beheer Nederland (Dutch State participant in the petroleum industry)
EBRD	European Bank for Reconstruction and Development
EC	European Community
ECE	Economic Commission for Europe
ECJ	European Court of Justice
ECOSOC	Economic and Social Council (UN)
ECR	European Court Reports
ECSC	European Coal and Steel Community
ECT	Energy Charter Treaty
EdF	Electricité de France
EEA	European Economic Area
EEC	European Economic Community
EEP	Energy Research Programme
EEZ	Exclusive Economic Zone
EFTA	European Free Trade Association
EGS	Russian unified gas system
EIA	Economic Integration Agreement (chapter 4)
EIA	Environmental Impact Assessment (chapter 9)
EIB	European Investment Bank
ELF	Entreprise de lubrifiants français (French Oil Company)
EMPL	Europe Maghreb Pipeline Ltd
Enagas	Empresa Nacional del Gas (National Gas Undertaking)
Endesa	Empresa Nacional de Electricidad, Sociedad Anónima (National Electricity Undertaking)
ENEA	Comitato nazionale per la ricera e per lo svilupo dell' energia nucleare e delle energie alternativa (National Committee for Nuclear and Renewable Energy)

ENEL	Ente Nazionale per l'Energia Elettrica (National Board for Electricity)
ENI	Ente Nazionale Idrocarburi (National Entity for Hydrocarbons)
Enresa	Empresa Nacional de Residuos (National Undertaking for Radioactive Waste)
Enusa	Empresa Nacional del Uranio, Sociedad Anónima (National Undertaking for Uranium)
EPON	NV Elektriciteits-Produktiemaatschappij Oost en Noord Nederland (electricity production company in the north-east of the Netherlands)
EPS	Energy Performance Standard
EPZ	NV Elektriciteits-Produktiemaatschappij Zuid-Nederland (electricity production company in the south of the Netherlands)
ETSI	European Telecommunications Standards Institute
EU	European Union
EURATOM	European Atomic Energy Community
EVE	Ente Vasco de la Energia (Basque Energy Entity)
EZH	Elektriciteitsbedrijf Zuid Holland NV (electricity company in the western part of the Netherlands)
FACE	Fonds d'amortissement des charges d'électrification (Fund for the Amortization of Electrification Costs)
FAO	Food and Agricultural Organization
FCCC	UN Framework Convention on Climate Change (chapter 3)
FF	French franc
FSU	Former Soviet Union
FU	Supply Committee
GATT	General Agreement on Tariffs and Trade
GdF	Gaz de France
GDP	gross domestic product
GEF	Global Environment Facility
GFU	Gas Negotiation Committee
GPB	Grootschalig Produktiebedrijf (major electricity production company)
GRT	Gestionnaire du réseau de transport (Public Transmission Grid Management Division)
GW	gigawatt
GWh	gigawatt hours
HNG	Hovedstadens Naturgasselskab
HNS	hazardous and noxious substances
IAEA	International Atomic Energy Agency
ICG	Irish Continental Group

ICPE	Installations classées pour la protection de l'environnement (Facilities deemed classified for the purpose of protecting the environment)
ICSID	International Centre for Settlement of Investment Disputes
IDAE	Instituto de Diversificación y Ahorro Energéticos (Diversification and Energy Saving Institute)
IEA	International Energy Agency
IFP	Institut français du pétrole (French Petroleum Institute)
IGS	Integrated Electricity System
ILM	International Legal Materials
IMF	International Monetary Fund
IMO	International Maritime Organization
INB	Installations nucléaires de base
INH	Instituto Nacional de Hidrocarburos (National Institute for Hydrocarbons)
INI	Instituto Nacional de Industria (National Institute for Industry)
INM	Installations nucléaires de base (basic nuclear facilities)
Innst O	Parliament Committee Recommendation
IOPC	International Oil Pollution Compensation Fund
IPF	Indicative project funding
IPP	Independent Power Producers
IPS	Independent Electricity System
IPSN	Institut de protection et de sûreté nucléaire (Nuclear Protection and Safety Institute)
ITGME	Instituto Tecnológico Geominero de España (Spanish Geological and Mineral Technology Institute)
ITO	International Trade Organization
JOA	Joint Operating Agreement
JV	joint venture
JWT	Journal of World Trade
Km	kilometre
KV	kilovolt
KW	kilowatt
KWh	kilowatt hour
LC	1972 London Convention on the Prevention of Marine Pollution by Dumping of Wastes and Other Matter
LNG	liquified natural gas
LOF	Lloyds Open Form
LRTAP	1979 UN/ECE Convention on Long-Range Transboundary Air Pollution
LTA	Long-term agreement
MA	Maritime Act

MAI	Multilateral Agreement on Investment
MAP	Milieu Actie Plan (environmental action plan)
MECU	million ECU
MFN	most favoured nation
ML	Model Licence
MPE	Minister of Petroleum and Energy
Mt	megatonnes
Mtoe	millions of metric tons of oil equivalent.
MW	megawatt
MWh	megawatt hour
NAFTA	North American Free-Trade Agreement
NAM	NV Nederlandse Aardolie Maatschappij (Dutch Oil Company) joint venture of Shell and Exxon—the Groningen concession)
NCS	Norwegian Continental Shelf
NEA	Nuclear Energy Agency
NEP	National Energy Plan
NERSA	Neutron European Reactor sa
NES	National Electricity System
NESRA	National Electricity System Regulation Act 1994
NETA	New Electricity Trading Arrangements
Neth Ybk Int'l	Netherlands Yearbook of International Law
NF 92	Norwegian Fabrication Contract
NGF	Naturgas Fyn
NGMN	Naturgas Midt-Nord
NGS	Naturgas Syd
NGSJ	Naturgas Sjælland
NGT	Noordgastransport (one of the offshore gas pipelines)
Nm^3	Normal cubic metre
NMa	Nederlandse Mededingingsauthoriteit (Dutch Competition Authority)
NOK	Norwegian Kroner
NPD	Norwegian Petroleum Directorate
NPT	Non-Proliferation Treaty
NTP	Nuclear Non-Proliferation Treaty
NTPA	negotiated third-party access
Nucmar	Nuclear material at sea
NVE	Norwegian Water Resources and Energy Directorate
Nw J Int'l L	Northwest Journal of International Law
OECD	Organization for Economic Co-operation and Development
OFICO	Oficina de Compensaciones Eléctricas (Electricity Compensation Office)
OGLTR	Oil and Gas Law and Taxation Review

OJ	Official Journal
OLADE	Organ of Latin American Countries
OPRC	1990 International Convention on Oil Pollution Preparedness, Response, and Co-operation
OPRI	Office de protection contre les rayonnements ionisants (Office for Protection against Ionizing Radiation)
ORSEC	Organisation des secours (Rescue Organization)
OSPAR	1992 Convention for the Protection of the Marine Environment of the Northeast Atlantic
Ott prp	Government Bill to Parliament
P & I Club	Protection and Indemnity Club
PA	Petroleum Act
PCA	EU–Russia Partnership & Co-operation Agreement (1974)
PDO	Plan for Development and Operation
PEN	Piano Energetico Nazionale (National Energy Plan)
Petromed	Petróleos del Mediterráneo (Mediterranean Oil Products Company)
PJ	petajoule
PKB	Planologische Kernbeslissing (National Planning Decision)
PP	Partido Popular (Popular Party)
PPI	Programmation pluriannuelle des investissements (pluri-annual programming of investments)
PSOE	Partido Socialiste Obrero Español (Spanish Socialist Workers Party)
PSOs	public service obligations
PTA	Petroleum Taxation Act
PWR	pressurised water reactor
RD	Royal Decree
RDCM	departmental and local tax on mines
RDL	Royal Decree-Law
RE	Renewable Energy
REB	Regulerende energiebelastung (regulatory energy tax)
REC	regional electricity companies
REE	Red Eléctrica de España (Spanish Electricity Grid Company)
SA	Subsoil Act
SB	single buyer
SC	Sea Containers Ltd
Scm oe	standard cubic metre oil equivalent
SDFI	State direct financial interest
SDR	Special Drawing Rights (IMF)
SEA	Single European Act
SEP	NV Samenwerkende Elektriciteits-Produktiebedrijven (Electricity Generators' Co-operative)

SEPI	Sociedad Estatal de Participaciones Industriales (State Company for Industrial Shares)
SNET	'Société nationale d'électricité et de thermique' (National Thermal and Electricity Generation Company)
SO	system operator
SOEC	Statistical Office of the European Community
SOLAS	Safety of Life at Sea Convention (1974)
SpA	Società per azione (joint stock limited liability company)
SSP	Stena Sealink Ports
Stb	Staatsblad (Official Journal)
Stc	Staatscourant (Official Gazette)
St mld	Government report to Parliament
St prp	Government report to Parliament (budget matter)
TBL	Federation of Norwegian Engineering Industries
TEN	Trans European Networks
Tex Int'l L J	Texas International Law Journal
TGAP	General Tax on Polluting Activities
TJ	terajoule
Toe	tons of oil equivalent
TPA	third-party access
TRIMS	trade related investment measures
TW	terawatt
TWh	terawatt hour
UCD	Unión del Centre Democrático (Union of the Democratic Centre)
UCTE	Union pour la Coordination du Transport de l'Electricité (Union for the Co-ordination of Transmission of Electricity)
UN	United Nations
UNA	NV Energieproduktiebedrijf UNA (electricity production company in the central part of the Netherlands)
UNCC	UN Compensation Commission
UNCLOS	UN Convention on the Law of the Sea
UNEP	UN Environment Programme
Unesa	Unidad Eléctrica (Electricity Companies Association)
UNFCC	UN Framework Convention on Climate Change (chapter 2)
UNICITRAL	United Nations Commission on International Trade Law
UNTS	United Nations Treaty Series
USAID	US Agency for International Development
UVE	Renewable Energy Development Programme
VAT	value added tax
VO	Variation Order
VOC	Volatile Organic Compounds

VOR	Variation Order Request
WGT	Westgastransport (one of the offshore gas pipelines)
WHO	World Health Organization
WMO	World Meteorological Organization
WPC	Working Party in Coal
WPE	Working Party in Electric Power
WPG	Working Party in Gas
WTO	World Trade Organization

TABLES OF CASES

European Court of Justice and Court of First Instance

Alphabetical

Numerical

European Court of Human Rights

International Cases

European Commission

National

Australia

Denmark

France

Germany

Italy

The Netherlands

Spain

United Kingdom

TABLES OF LEGISLATION

National

Canada

Denmark

France

Germany

Ireland

Italy

The Netherlands

Norway

Portugal

Spain

United Kingdom

Notices

Recommendations

Resolutions

Treaties and Conventions

International Legislation

Part I

INTRODUCTION

1

INTRODUCTION

Catherine Redgwell, Martha M Roggenkamp, Anita Rønne, and Iñigo del Guayo

A. Introduction

As outlined in the Preface, this book is the product of collaboration between nine European institutions where energy law is taught within the law school curriculum, with further invited contributions to ensure representative coverage of key energy jurisdictions in Europe and of key regional and international developments.[1] The result seeks to fill a gap in the existing literature on energy law by addressing eight national systems (Denmark, France, Germany, Italy, the Netherlands, Norway, Spain, and the United Kingdom) which are then compared in a concluding comparative chapter. At the outset these national systems are located in their EC and international law contexts with separate chapters on each of these systems. The importance of international institutions in the energy law field is highlighted in the chapter on international organizations, which includes a case study of the International Energy Agency by a former director of that Agency. A recent international development of significance to the European energy sector is highlighted in Chapter 4 below, on the establishment and development of the Energy Charter Treaty. **1.01**

It is the purpose of this introductory chapter briefly to set the stage for the ensuing discussion of national, EC, and international energy laws, including an **1.02**

[1] While it was not possible to include the participation of a Belgian institution in this volume, we welcome the prospect of future collaboration with the recently established Institute of Environmental and Energy Law at the University of Leuven (Belgium).

overview of the current energy picture in Europe. A subsidiary task is to locate energy law solidly as an academic discipline which, as the collaborative teaching which has taken place under the Erasmus/Socrates exchange amply attests, is increasingly finding a deserved place on law school curricula. Of course this is not to ignore the practical importance of energy law for practitioners in the field; indeed, to adopt Bradbrook's terminology,[2] this is intended as a work of both pure and applied energy law.

B. Sources of Energy

1.03 This book focuses upon energy resources, the most important sources of which in the European context are oil and gas, coal, nuclear, hydro, and combustible renewables. Indeed, a similar picture emerges in terms of global energy resources, though with some variation in terms of relative importance.[3] This book is not concerned with the broader category of 'natural resources', which typically includes water, fish, and forests, as well as energy resources.

1.04 Energy resources comprise both finite, exhaustible sources, and renewable forms of energy the consumption of which does not lead to their depletion. Within the former category may be found 'traditional' sources of energy, namely oil, gas, and coal. Of these, reliance on coal has declined in recent years as a result both of the depletion of resources and of the environmental consequences of its use. Gas, on the other hand, has seen its status shift from an expendable by-product of oil-field development to a major source of electricity and heat generation. The peaceful use of nuclear energy was a particular feature of the immediate post-war era in Europe (and the US) which has experienced more public resistance of late, whilst since the oil crises of the 1970s there has been increased reliance upon alternative and renewable forms of energy such as wind power, hydroelectric power, and biofuels. Other sources not yet relied upon to any great extent in Europe, or still at the experimental stage, include solar energy, wave and tidal energy, and ocean thermal energy conversion (OTEC).

1.05 The table opposite, based on International Energy Agency statistics, provides an overview of total primary energy supply by energy sources for each of the eight States considered here.

Regulating Energy Resource Activities: the Development of Energy Law

1.06 With traditional energy sources such as oil, gas, and coal, the legal regime governs every stage of activity from defining rights over the resources, to prospecting and

[2] AJ Bradbrook, 'Energy Law as an Academic Discipline' (1996) 14:2 JERL 194, 206.
[3] See further EE Smith *et al*, *International Petroleum Transactions* (2nd edn, 2000) ch 1.

Key Energy Indicators in 1998[a]

	Oil	Gas	Coal	Nuclear	Hydro	Combustible renewables[b]	Other[c]
Denmark	45.2%	9.9%	26.5%			7.2%	1.2%
France	35.5%	12.8%	6.4%	39.8%	2.0%	4.3%	0.1%
Germany	40.6%	21.1%	24.3%	12.2%	0.4%	1.2%	0.1%
Italy	56.9%	31.1%	7.2%		2.2%	1.0%	1.7%
Netherlands	37.5%	48.6%	12.0%	1.4%		1.4%	0.1%
Norway	34.0%	17.1%	4.3%		39.5%	5.0%	
Spain	54.7%	10.3%	15.4%	13.7%	2.6%	3.2%	0.1%
UK	35.9%	34.2%	17.5%	11.3%	0.2%	0.8%	

[a] Source: IEA, *Key Energy Indicators in 1998*, at http://www.iea.org/stats. Also provided are statistics for carbon emissions expressed in million tonnes of CO_2. Arranged in ascending order from lowest to highest quantity of CO_2 emissions these are: Norway 31.62; Denmark 72.32; the Netherlands 186.40; Spain 235.57; France 384.30; Italy 419.96; UK 582.80; and Germany 904.68.

[b] This IEA category comprises biomass and animal products, municipal waste, and industrial waste.

[c] This includes geothermal, solar, wind, tide, wave energy, and heat.

exploration, through to exploitation, production, storage, transport, trade, and end use. The manner in which these diverse sources of energy are converted into use is a further aspect conditioning the substantive scope of energy law. Conversion to electricity and heat gives rise to a further set of legal issues arising from generation, transmission, distribution, and trade. By-products of generation, including pollution of watercourses, land, and air and the related issue of waste transport and/or disposal, likewise give rise to the need for legal regulation. With recent trends towards liberalization, competition law is of major importance to energy sectors, particularly in Europe, a process deriving considerable impetus from EC law since the launch of the internal energy market programme in 1988.[4] This is aided and abetted by the wave of commercialization and privatization which has taken place within the worldwide energy sector, leading energy lawyers to turn their attention increasingly to legal regulation of the entities carrying out energy activities. Protection of consumer interests is an ever more important component of energy regulation. Moreover, since the 1970s energy savings and conservation have led to new policies and laws designed to reduce energy consumption and/or to encourage more sustainable energy use, including less environmentally harmful sources. Fiscal and economic instruments may be employed, turning attention to matters such as taxes and royalties. In the renewables

[4] For discussion of what constitutes 'European Community Energy Law' see ch 5 below; and DS MacDougall and TW Waelde, *European Community Energy Law: Selected Topics* (1994) esp ch 1.

sector, subsidies have been employed to facilitate market access for new and initially expensive sources for heat and electricity generation.

1.07 Paradoxically, therefore, the energy lawyer finds herself both a specialist and a generalist, for energy law constitutes the sum of diverse parts: public and private law, international law, trade and investment, project financing, intellectual property, aboriginal land rights, tax law, company law, competition law, consumer law, contract law, environmental law, administrative law, constitutional law, and EC law. Historically some writers have compared the development of energy law to environmental law;[5] not a flower child of the 1960s but a modern creation of the 1970s, spurred to development by the energy crisis of 1973 in particular. This crisis was caused by restrictions in oil supply imposed by petroleum-exporting countries which in 1960 established their own organization, OPEC,[6] to counter the influence of large, vertically integrated[7] oil companies referred to as 'The Seven Sisters'.[8] The severe shortages of the 1970s have not been repeated due to a number of factors, including an emphasis on the security and diversity of supply in States previously acutely dependent on imported oil. Increases in supply and tumbling oil prices are further factors militating against a repeat of the crises of the 1970s. In the 1990s, scarcity of supply issues are only one component of energy policies which now reflect broader concerns regarding the structure and regulation of the industry (whether public or private) and the environmental consequences of energy production and use. Given the fundamental changes which have occurred in the ownership and operation of the European energy industry in the past decade, it is no exaggeration to suggest that the changes of the 1990s have been as momentous as those of the 1970s, though more incremental in character owing to the trigger of environmental and commercial considerations rather than a crisis as such.

1.08 In focusing on the catalytic effect of the 1973 energy crisis it is not intended to suggest of course that no laws regulating energy production and use existed previously. Prior to the early 1970s we might have spoken of oil and gas law (especially in the US), or of mining law (certainly going back some centuries in Europe). However, it was only with the heightened concern for security and diversity of supply provoked by the energy crisis that energy policy, and with it energy law as a discrete if

[5] See JP Tomain, *Energy Law* (1981) xix.

[6] The Organization of Petroleum Exporting Countries. Although petroleum-exporting countries, the United Kingdom and Norway are not eligible for membership of OPEC because it is a condition of membership that petroleum is the main export commodity. See further http://www.opec.org.

[7] That is, the company and/or its subsidiaries controlled all aspects of petroleum operations from exploration through to production, transportation, refining, and sale at the petrol pump.

[8] For a fascinating account see A Sampson, *The Seven Sisters: the great oil companies and the world they made* (1975). The companies are Gulf, Texaco, Mobil, Standard Oil (Chevron), Exxon, Shell, and BP.

interrelated discipline, emerged. Such emergence may also be traced institutionally with the establishment of national ministries of energy echoed on the international plane by the establishment of the International Energy Agency. The growth of energy law as an academic discipline may also be dated from this period.

C. Energy Law as an Academic Discipline

1.09 One of the writers recently exploring the nature of energy law as an academic discipline is Bradbrook. He defines energy law as:

> the allocation of rights and duties concerning the exploitation of all energy resources between individuals, between individuals and the government, between governments and between states.[9]

He provides eight 'social considerations' and seven 'jurisprudential considerations' as justifications for energy law as a separate legal discipline.[10]

1.10 Social considerations are: (i) energy law is a multi-disciplinary subject, enhancing its value as an academic discipline and countering professional/discipline isolationism; (ii) it offers new topics for the emerging law and technology field; (iii) the 'overwhelming social importance' of energy; (iv) the contribution of energy policies to achieving sustainable development; (v) security factors, including the destabilizing effect of resource dependence and resource conflicts, and the risks posed by reliance upon nuclear energy (accident, theft, nuclear proliferation); (vi) the moral and ethical dimension, including the intergenerational consequences of depleting energy resources in the present, and of radioactive waste disposal; (vii) the role of government, particularly in the context of privatization of many previously publicly owned energy enterprises; and (viii) individual attitudes to energy issues, of particular relevance in the context of regulatory and non-regulatory techniques to influence consumer energy choice.

1.11 Jurisprudential considerations, on the other hand, relate to the legal characteristics of energy law as interdisciplinary, interjurisdictional (e.g. national/international), its practical and theoretical applications, the dynamism inherent in the subject, the rate of change and law reform, and the interrelationship with economic and with environmental issues.

The multi-disciplinary feature of energy law is clearly illustrated by the academic programmes offered by the above-mentioned universities. In addition to the administrative and regulatory aspects of energy law, the focus can be on

[9] Above, n 2, 194. The latter is designed to include constitutional issues such as the allocation of rights and duties between governments within a federal State, and between States in a treaty arrangement such as the 1997 Amsterdam Treaty or the 1994 Energy Charter Treaty.

[10] ibid, 206–16.

international, EC, or national law and/or limit itself to one energy resource or include the full range of primary and secondary energy resources. Whereas some programmes include an analysis of the most important administrative and contractual aspects of energy law, other institutions may instead include further analysis of the consequences of the exploitation and use of energy for the environment. Although energy law is gradually developing as an academic discipline in Europe it is still very diverse in its approach. Nevertheless, developments at EC level may lead to a more common approach to and standardization in this field.

D. The Structure of the National Chapters

1.12 Given the differences in the energy profile of each of the States considered in this book, it is clearly impossible to adhere strictly to an identical structure for each national chapter. To take two examples, it would be futile to insist on an analysis of nuclear energy law in Denmark, or of the onshore petroleum regime in Norway. None the less, it has been possible to adhere to a similar general structure within each chapter whilst permitting national variations to emerge. This general approach is essential both for comparative purposes and for ease of reference for the reader interested in, say, legal regulation of the electricity sector in each of the national systems. The comparative chapter adheres to the same broad categories as the national chapters.

1.13 Thus each chapter begins with a brief overview of the constitutional and legal structure of that particular national system. It is important for an appreciation of energy regulation to be aware of the basic nature of the legal system in which it operates: federal or unitary, written or unwritten constitution, allocation of energy competences, and so on. This ensures that the legal significance of the sources of energy law may be appreciated, as well as the mechanisms for change and reform. Attention is also paid to the institutional framework. For example, is there a Department or Ministry of Energy, and is it combined with, say, trade and industry or with the environment? Do separate/independent energy regulators exist? The introductory section of each chapter also contains a brief historical overview of the energy sector in that State, and provides a brief sketch of the general pattern of national energy demand and supply.

1.14 There follows a treatment of energy law by sector, in most cases commencing with oil and gas exploration and production onshore and/or offshore, then coal production, followed by consideration of gas and electricity supply issues (generation, transmission, and distribution), and finally renewables. Heat as well as electricity generation is addressed where relevant for the particular national system, e.g. where combined heat and power (CHP) is a component of national energy mix (Denmark and the Netherlands, for example). In addition, each chapter addresses the environmental regulation relevant to the energy sector, in particular energy conservation and efficiency measures. Within each of these categories the extent of treatment necessarily varies according to the energy mix of each State and the extent of legal regulation of each sector. Moreover, unique features of the national system will, by definition, not find their counterpart in the other national chapters, an example being the Norwegian treatment of fabrication contracts. Some mention is made of fiscal matters, but extensive treatment of tax and royalties systems is beyond the compass of this work. To provide the reader with further access to information, a bibliography for further reading and a list of the most relevant laws is included as well as a list of the websites of the most relevant ministries and international organizations.

Part II

INTERNATIONAL AND EUROPEAN REGULATION OF THE ENERGY SECTOR

2

INTERNATIONAL REGULATION OF ENERGY ACTIVITIES

Catherine Redgwell

A. Introduction

This chapter is concerned with the international regulation of energy activities. It is divided into eight parts. Following this introduction, the second part provides a general introduction to public international law necessary for an appreciation of the international legal regulation of energy activities. In particular, it considers the general principles of jurisdiction and control which States may exercise over their territory and their nationals (including companies) in carrying out energy activities. Discussion of the exercise of jurisdiction by States pursuant to the 1982 United Nations Convention on the Law of the Sea (LOSC) is also included in this second part. There follows analysis in Part three of the specific rules of international law applicable to the exploration and exploitation of oil and gas, with **2.01** further particular reference to the substantive provisions of the LOSC. Matters addressed include the definition, extent, and delimitation of the continental shelf and the substantive rules in respect of abandonment and disposal of offshore energy installations offshore. Part four continues the maritime theme with consideration of the maritime transport of petroleum and the consequent need to regulate internationally pollution from oil tankers, in particular liability and compensation for pollution damage. Part five moves from the petroleum sector to consider international regulation of the nuclear sector, focusing on liability and compensation issues as well as notification, assistance, and nuclear safety. Part six considers certain cross-sectoral and transboundary issues of relevance to the international regulation of the environmental impact of energy activities, ranging from environmental impact assessment to the reduction of greenhouse gases under the 1992 Framework Convention on Climate Change. The penultimate part briefly considers the broad topic of energy trade and investment, before moving to the final part which draws some conclusions regarding future trends. Within the compass of a single chapter it is only possible to provide an outline of the breadth and depth of international regulation of relevance to the energy sector, with indications of further reading for the reader wishing to pursue in greater depth the topics covered here.[1] One of the most important recent developments in the international regulation of energy activities, the conclusion of the Energy Charter Treaty, is addressed separately in Chapter 4 in express acknowledgement of its importance to international and, more particularly, European energy activities. Fuller discussion of the international organizations relevant to energy activities is to be found in Chapter 3.

B. International Law and the Energy Sector

(1) What is Public International Law?

2.02 The regulation of energy activities at the global and regional levels is a task for public international law, which is the system of law governing relations between States.[2] International law governs nearly every aspect of inter-State relations, including matters such as jurisdiction, claims to territory, use of the oceans, and

[1] Topics outside the scope of this chapter include energy and the law of armed conflict (see further J Gardam, 'Energy and the Law of Armed Conflict' (1997) 15:2 JENRL 87) and the energy-relevant activities of the United Nations Compensation Commission (UNCC), established in 1991 following the 1990 Gulf War (see further E. Patton, 'Gulf War: After Effects and Legal Consequences' (1993) 11:2 JENRL 98 and the UNCC website at http://www.unorg.ch/uncc/). A further growing field is the intersection of energy law and human rights: see eg the cases under the European Convention on Human Rights such as *Balmer-Schafroth and Others v Switzerland*, Application No 22110/03, (1997) 25 EHRR 598 (judgment 26 August 1997).

[2] See generally I Brownlie, *Principles of Public International Law* (5th edn, 1998); DJ Harris, *Cases and Materials on International Law* (5th edn, 1998); R Jennings and A Watts (eds), *Oppenheim's International Law* vol. I (9th edn, 1996); M Shaw, *International Law* (4th edn, 1997); P Malanczuk, *Akehurst's Modern Introduction to International Law* (7th rev edn, 1997). Other

State responsibility. International obligations relating to energy activities are not found solely within a specific area of public international law called 'international energy law'; rather, they draw upon the rules of international law applicable to a wide range of activities carried out by States in energy and other sectors.[3] Of particular concern in this chapter is the extent to which international law sets standards in respect of energy activities and their consequences, and the enforcement of those standards by or against States.[4]

(2) The Sources of International Law

Introduction

2.03 The most important sources of international law[5] are treaty law and customary international law, treaties being a particularly rich source of State obligations relevant to energy activities. Less relevant are general principles of international law, while judicial decisions[6] and the writings of publicists are subsidiary sources of international law. Both treaty law and customary international law constitute 'hard' law, that is,

non-State actors may possess legal personality, such as international organizations (see further Ch 2, below). For discussion of the international legal personality of a proposed Central Asian Pipeline Organization, see J Carver and G Englefield, 'An International Pipeline Authority: The Case for the Central Asian Pipeline Organisation' (1995) 13:8 Oil and Gas Law and Taxation Review 291, esp. 297–9.

[3] In the petroleum context Ikenna observes that 'there is *stricto senso* no distinct "petroleum" body of law with its own separate sources and methods of law-making deriving from rules and principles exclusive to petroleum matters': NE Ikenna, ' "International Petroleum Law" as a Distinct Legal Discipline' (1996) 8:2 African Journal of International and Comparative Law 428. Nonetheless, the title 'international energy law' is widely applied to indicate the transnational character of energy activities which necessarily transcend regulation by a single, exclusively national, system of law.

[4] For a discussion of the role of international organizations and of individuals as participants in the international legal system, see R Higgins, *Problems & Process: International Law and How We Use It* (1994) ch 3.

[5] Article 38(1) of the Statute of the International Court of Justice sets forth the sources of international law upon which the Court may rely as follows:

(a) international conventions, whether general or particular, establishing rules expressly recognized by the contesting States;
(b) international custom, as evidence of a general practice accepted as law;
(c) the general principles of law recognized by civilized nations;
(d) . . . judicial decisions and the teachings of the most highly qualified publicists of the various nations, as subsidiary means for the determination of rules of law.

[6] This includes the decisions of the International Court of Justice, the judicial organ of the United Nations, and of arbitral tribunals. The case-law of the Court has not addressed substantive energy issues, apart from a series of decisions on maritime boundary delimitations which in some instances have touched on non-living resource allocation. See further below, para 2.37. Only States may appear before the International Court of Justice in contentious proceedings. Disputes between States and private actors, especially in the commercial law sphere, may result in *ad hoc* arbitrations such as the *Aramco* case (*Saudi Arabia v Arabian American Oil Co* (1958) 27 ILR 117) or through the establishment of *ad hoc* standing tribunals such as the Iran–US Claims Tribunal, established in 1981 to deal with a large number of cases arising after the Islamic revolution in Iran. Arbitration is a common method for the determination of commercial disputes, including investment disputes,

their rules are firm and binding upon the States which accept them. Both impose binding legal obligations upon States for the breach of which State responsibility[7] may attach. However, in the international law field there is another important category of rules, referred to as 'soft' law.[8] This consists primarily of declarations and recommendations made by international conferences, institutions, and organizations which regulate the conduct of States but for the breach of which the traditional enforcement mechanisms of international law will not apply. A good example is the IMO's Guidelines and Standards for the Removal of Offshore Installations and Structures on the Continental Shelf.[9] Since codes of conduct may well form the basis of national legislation, or be transformed into binding principles through treaty implementation[10] or into customary international law as a result of State practice (that is to say, 'hardened') the role of codes of conduct and guidelines as contributors to the international law-making process is potentially a highly significant one.[11]

2.04 Unlike treaties and customary international law, soft law may be 'instantly applicable'[12] (at least on this voluntary basis) if States choose to make it so. Also unlike

which may bring a mix of private and public law matters, whether by the contract choice of the parties concerned or in consequence of the establishment of organizations such as the International Centre for the Settlement of International Disputes (ICSID). See generally JG Merrills, *International Dispute Settlement* (3rd edn, 1999).

[7] In general, an act or omission which breaches a rule of treaty or customary law entails State responsibility. This principle was expressed in the *Chorzow Factory* case (1928) PCIJ Ser A, No 17, 21, as follows: 'it is a principle of international law that the breach of an engagement involves an obligation to make reparation in an adequate form . . .' The standard of care imposed on States will vary according to the nature of the activity causing harm and the degree of harm caused to other States. There are three types of liability: absolute, strict, and fault-based liability. To the extent that liability from energy activities has been addressed in international treaties, the standard has generally been one of strict liability. See further the discussion of oil pollution and nuclear liability below. For criticism of the operation of the traditional rules of State responsibility in the environmental sphere, see Birnie and Boyle, *International Law & the Environment* (1992) ch 3.

[8] See further C Chinkin, 'The Challenge of Soft Law' (1989) 38 *ICLQ* 850; D Van Hoof, *Re-Thinking the Sources of International Law* (1983).

[9] See further discussion below. However, Article 60(3) of the 1982 LOSC requires States to take into account any generally accepted international standards established by the competent international organization, which clearly encompasses the 1989 IMO Guidelines. Thus, whilst the Guidelines are not directly binding as such, the States Parties to the 1982 LOSC have a treaty obligation thereunder to take them into account.

[10] For example, the 1989 Basel Convention on the Transboundary Movement of Hazardous Wastes and their Disposal was preceded by the 1985 UNEP Cairo Guidelines and it was UNEP which worked on the draft of the Basel Convention subsequently adopted by a diplomatic conference of States in 1989. A further example of the dynamic of institutions and the 'hardening' of soft law is the decision to prohibit dumping at sea of low-level radioactive waste, first agreed as a voluntary moratorium in 1983 by the Conference of the Parties to the global 1972 London (Dumping) Convention (LDC) but subsequently adopted as a binding treaty amendment with effect from 1994.

[11] For analysis of the contribution made by resolutions of international organizations to the law-making process (ie to 'hard' law), see further Higgins, above n 4, 22–8.

[12] It is generally recognized that customary international law may take some time to evolve through State practice, although in some areas this development is very rapid. See Bin Cheng, 'United Nations Resolutions on Outer Space: "Instant" International Customary Law' (1965) 5 Indian Journal of International Law 23.

treaty and custom, both of which focus on norm-generation by States,[13] there is generally greater scope for the participation of non-State actors in generating soft law. For example, non-State actors may fill the gap left by the slow pace of entry into force of provisions of international treaties, and may have a particular interest in doing so where the conduct of non-State actors is sought to be regulated. An example is the industry-sponsored agreements TOVALOP and CRISTAL, which were put in place pending the anticipated lengthy process of the entry into force of the Civil Liability and Fund Conventions providing for liability and compensation for oil pollution damage. These treaties are discussed further below in paras 2.96–2.99.

Treaty law

Treaties are agreements between States pursuant to which States undertake **2.05** specific obligations; generally such obligations are binding only upon the States which have indicated their consent to be bound through ratification, acceptance, approval, accession, or succession. Treaties are the traditional method for rule-making at international law, and have increased in importance in this regard since World War II. A 'treaty' is defined in Article 2(1) of the 1969 Vienna Convention on the Law of Treaties[14] to mean 'an international agreement concluded between States in written form and governed by international law, whether embodied in a single instrument or in two or more related instruments and whatever its particular designation' (eg agreement, covenant, charter, treaty, convention, protocol). A treaty is only binding on States party to it once the treaty has entered into force.[15] Most treaties stipulate the number of States which must become parties before the treaty enters into force, an essential safeguard of the effectiveness of the treaty.[16] Treaties may also specify that non-State entities may participate; thus the EC is a party to a number of international agreements which allow for the participation

[13] Note, however, that international organizations possess limited legal personality and may enter into treaty arrangements (see further Ch 2 below). See the 1986 Convention on the Law of Treaties between States and International Organizations or between International Organizations, 25 ILM (1986) 543.

[14] Which entered into force in 1980.

[15] Article 18 of the Vienna Convention on the Law of Treaties imposes the generally recognized obligation upon States not to act inconsistently with the object and purpose of the treaty after becoming a party thereto pending its timely entry into force.

[16] In addition, international agreements concluded under the auspices of the International Maritime Organization generally require a minimum number of States Parties representing a minimum percentage of global registered tonnage of merchant ships. For example, the recently concluded 1997 Protocol to MARPOL 73/78 (the 1973 International Convention for the Prevention of Pollution from Ships, as modified by a 1978 Protocol), which will form a new Annex VI 'Regulations for the Prevention of Air Pollution from Ships', will enter into force 12 months after the date on which not less than 15 States, the combined tonnage of which shall be not less than 50% of the gross tonnage of the world's merchant fleet, have become Parties to the Protocol. MARPOL itself has been ratified by 100 States representing 93% of the world's tonnage of merchant shipping. See further paras 2.85–2.91 below.

of a 'regional economic integration organization' or equivalent.[17] Note that it is the EC, not the EU, which has international legal personality and which may thus enter into treaty relations with States.[18] For example, fourteen EC Member States have ratified the 1982 LOSC,[19] as has the EC, whose participation is catered for in Annex IX of the Convention.

2.06 The range of subject matter of such treaties (also called conventions) is virtually limitless.[20] A treaty may be concluded between two States (a bilateral treaty), such as the Frigg Treaty between the United Kingdom and Norway[21] or the 1987 Bilateral Investment Treaty (BIT) between Hungary and the United Kingdom;[22] or between a group of States, perhaps in a particular region, such as the 1997 Amsterdam Treaty,[23] the 1992 North American Free Trade Agreement,[24] or the 1992 Convention for the Protection of the Marine Environment of the North-East Atlantic (OSPAR);[25] or multilaterally, with virtually global participation, such as the 1992 Framework Convention on Climate Change[26] or the 1994 GATT/WTO Agreement.[27] Treaties may also be constitutive, establishing an international organization such as the International Energy Agency (discussed in Chapter 2, below), the United Nations (the UN Charter, which is a treaty), the International Maritime Organization (IMO),[28] or the International Atomic Energy Agency (IAEA).[29]

2.07 There are some drawbacks to the embodiment of international standards in treaty form, however. First, the unanimity or consensus requirement of treaty negotiating conferences can sometimes lead to agreement based on a median or even the

[17] See, for example, Annex IX of the 1982 United Nations Convention on the Law of the Sea, 'Participation by International Organizations'.

[18] See further Article 281 [210] EC and D McGoldrick, *International Relations Law of the European Union* (1997) ch 2; see also Ch 2 below.

[19] At the time of writing only Denmark has not ratified the LOSC.

[20] One limitation, however, is with respect to peremptory norms of general international law (*jus cogens*). Any treaty inconsistent with such a norm at the time of its conclusion is void; any treaty which is inconsistent with a new peremptory norm is likewise void and terminates. These consequences are set forth in Articles 53 and 64 of the 1969 Vienna Convention on the Law of Treaties. For present purposes, it is interesting to note Brownlie's assertion (above, n 2) that the principle of permanent sovereignty over natural resources is *jus cogens*: 515.

[21] St prp nr 183 (1975–76); this was revised in 1998.

[22] UKTS 3, (1988) Cmd 281. See generally JW Salacuse, 'BIT by BIT: The Growth of Bilateral Investment Treaties and their Impact on Foreign Investment in Developing Countries' (1990) 24 *International Lawyer* 655.

[23] OJ 1997, C 340.

[24] 32 ILM (1993) 605.

[25] 32 ILM (1993) 1068.

[26] 31 ILM (1992) 849.

[27] 33 ILM (1994) 28.

[28] 289 UNTS 48 (1948 IMO Convention).

[29] 276 UNTS 4 (1956 IAEA Statute).

lowest common denominator;[30] and the time-period for the entry into force of treaty obligations can stretch from two years to a decade or more. For example, the LOSC was concluded in 1982 but did not enter into force until 16 November 1994 following the deposit of the sixtieth instrument of ratification.[31] Treaty negotiation and implementation can be a cumbersome process and is not always well suited to a dynamic field such as energy law. This difficulty can be addressed through the more imaginative use of treaties with attached protocols, where changing technical standards are embodied in protocols (or annexes) subject to simplified amendment procedures. An excellent example of this approach is provided by the MARPOL 73/78 and its six annexes, the substance of which is discussed below (paras 2.85–2.91). The Energy Charter Treaty is another good example of the use of the flexible mechanism of further protocols.[32] Moreover, energy choice is closely associated with the sovereignty of States and there is ample evidence of a reluctance to relinquish control over energy choice to external bodies. Thus the vast bulk of energy regulation is concerned with facilitating energy commercial activities, and with mitigating the negative transboundary effects of energy extraction and use, rather than impacting on sovereign energy choices.[33]

The impact of treaties in national law varies from one legal system to the next. For **2.08**
example, the United Kingdom is a dualist State, meaning that treaty obligations entered into by the United Kingdom require domestic implementation or 'transformation' into national law. Other States are monist, considering international law to be a part of the domestic legal system. The Netherlands is an example. Even in monist States, however, some degree of transformation via national legislation or subsidiary regulation may be required, particularly in the case of treaty provisions which are not self-executing but require further elaboration for their

[30] For a thorough analysis of a number of treaty regimes see PM Haas, RO Kcohanc, and MA Levy (eds), *Institutions for the Earth: Sources of effective international environmental protection* (1993).

[31] Crucial to its entry into force was the conclusion of the 1994 Agreement Relating to the Implementation of Part XI of the United Nations Convention on the Law of the Sea of 10 December 1982, reproduced at 33 ILM (1994) 1309. See further D Anderson, 'Legal Implications of the Entry into Force of the United Nations Convention on the Law of the Sea' (1995) 44:2 *ICLQ* 313; and *passim* (1995) 55 ZaoRV (proceedings of a symposium on the entry into force of the LOSC).

[32] See Ch 4, below. On the use of flexible approaches to treaty-making in the environmental field, including MARPOL 73/78, see C Redgwell, 'Multilateral Environmental Treaty-Making' in V Gowlland-Debbas (ed), *Multilateral Treaty-Making* (2000).

[33] Article 175 [130s] EC is a good example. Originally added to the EC Treaty in 1987 with the entry into force of the Single European Act, and further modified in 1993 with the entry into force of the Maastricht Treaty, and more recently the Amsterdam Treaty, this article provides a distinctive legal base for EC environmental legislation and adopts qualified majority voting as the norm save for three reserved areas where unanimity is still required in the Council of Ministers for a legal measure to be adopted. All three reserved areas are closely linked to sovereign concerns—land use, taxing powers, and 'measures significantly affecting a Member State's choice between different energy sources and the general structure of its energy supply'.

effective implementation. In both systems, rules of statutory interpretation generally seek to avoid conflicts between domestic legislative provisions and international obligations.

Customary international law

2.09 Customary international law comprises general State practice combined with *opinio juris sive necessitas*, the notion that States consider that certain action, or inaction, is legally required of them at international law.[34] Customary law thus embodies both an objective element (the general and consistent practice of States) and a subjective element (that States so act or refrain from acting in recognition that such (in)action is legally required of them). The process of customary law generation can therefore require a considerable time, though this will vary according to the nature of the rule in question.[35] It is also possible, through the process of persistent objection, to opt out of the application of an emerging rule of customary international law, as the United States did for a time in respect of any extension of the territorial sea beyond three nautical miles (the 1982 Law of the Sea Convention provides for a twelve-mile territorial sea).[36] Customary law and treaty law may also overlap,[37] either where a treaty text embodies rule(s) already recognized as customary international law, or where a treaty text adopts new rules which come to be regarded as reflective of customary law. An example of the former is the codification by the 1958 Geneva Convention on the High Seas of existing traditional high seas freedoms;[38] examples of the latter are the twelve-mile territorial sea limit just mentioned and the concept of the exclusive economic zone in the 1982 United Nations Convention on the Law of the Sea, which in fact passed into the corpus of customary international law even before the Convention entered into force.[39] Another example is the sovereign rights asserted by States

[34] See generally Akehurst, 'Custom as a Source of International Law' (1974–5) XLVII British Year Book of International Law 1. The International Court of Justice has set forth the requirements for customary law formation in several key judgments; see, for example, the *Asylum* case (1950) ICJ Rep. 266, the *Anglo-Norwegian Fisheries* case (1951) ICJ Rep. 116, and the *North Sea Continental Shelf* cases (1969) ICJ Rep. 3.

[35] See further n 12 above.

[36] The role of customary international law and persistent objection is lucidly described in R Churchill and AV Lowe, *The Law of the Sea* (3rd edn, 1999) 8–9. By 1982 (when the LOSC was concluded) the US had accepted the legality of claims to a territorial sea of up to 12 miles: ibid, 9.

[37] As Higgins observes, 'the sources of international law are not compartmentalized': above n 4, 32.

[38] Indeed, the 1958 Geneva Convention on the High Seas, replaced by the 1982 United Nations Convention on the Law of the Sea which entered into force on 16 November 1994, expressly states in the preamble that it is 'generally declaratory of established principles of international law'. As such it was viewed largely as a codification of existing rules of customary law.

[39] In the *Libya/Malta Continental Shelf* case, the International Court of Justice observed that it was 'incontestible that . . . the EEZ . . . is shown by the practice of States to have become part of customary international law': [1985] ICJ Reports 13, 33. Churchill and Lowe (n 36 above) observe that this includes parts of Articles 56 and 58: 161. Other provisions have not been found to have

over the continental shelf, first asserted unilaterally in the 1940s and rapidly transforming into a permissive rule of customary law and then to codification in Article 2 of the 1958 Geneva Convention on the Continental Shelf.

Implementation and enforcement of international standards

International regulatory measures followed by international organizations and established by treaties comprise a third dimension to classical public international law, operating below the level of hard (ie treaty law and customary law) and soft law, collectively described as 'transnational administrative law'. Three typical techniques of transnational law-making may be identified, standard-setting, licensing, and auditing, which in practice are interdependent.[40] For example, permits or licences are not commonly issued at the international level but are left, or delegated, for individual States to issue.[41] The 'international oil pollution prevention certificates' required for oil tankers over a prescribed tonnage are issued by national authorities under Annex I of the 1973 International Convention for the Prevention of Pollution from Ships, as modified by a 1978 Protocol (MARPOL 73/78). Similarly, waste disposal permits are issued under the 1992 Convention for the Protection of the Marine Environment of the Northeast Atlantic (OSPAR) and the 1972 London Convention on the Prevention of Marine Pollution by Dumping of Wastes and Other Matter, according to black (prohibited) and grey (licence required) lists of substances contained in Annexes to the Conventions. The 1989 Basel Convention on the Control of Transboundary Movement of Hazardous Wastes and Their Disposal provides for waste-export notifications and authorizations, issued by national authorities. These licensing regimes depend on mutual recognition (or reciprocity) for their effective functioning, and they are intended to ensure national implementation of international standards at the administrative level. Moreover, since most international standards are established without a regulatory or judicial body authorized to impose sanctions for breach 2.10

achieved this status, most notably Article 6 of the 1958 Geneva Convention on the Continental Shelf, which embodied the equidistance rule in respect of continental shelf delimitation but which the International Court of Justice did not find reflective of customary international law: *North Sea Continental Shelf Cases* [1969] ICJ Reports 3, para 69 (Article 6 'did not embody or crystallize any pre-existing or emerging rule of customary international law'). Higgins observes that while Article 6 prescribed a 'mandatory technique' (equidistance for continental shelf delimitation), the EEZ provisions of the 1982 Law of the Sea Convention are 'jurisdictional entitlements allowed to states in certain maritime areas' and thus more willingly embraced in the practice of States: (n 4 above) 31.

[40] PH Sand, *Lessons Learned in Global Environmental Governance* (1990). Although Sand confines his remarks to environmental law, his classification is broadly applicable to other spheres of transnational administrative activity, including the energy sector.

[41] Exceptions arise in areas subject to common property or common heritage regimes, including the licensing of mining on the deep sea bed under the 1982 LOSC, for example.

of international standards,[42] compliance with international treaty standards is generally achieved through auditing and reporting requirements. At the international level this is generally achieved through annual reports, which are designed, *inter alia*, to have a deterrent effect upon States contemplating a breach of international standards. This method of compliance control is evident in a number of spheres of international regulation, including human rights, trade, and the environment. Energy-related requirements in this last sphere include the requirement under one of the Protocols to the 1979 Geneva Convention on Long-Range Transboundary Air Pollution for annual reports on national programmes, policies, and strategies directed towards the reduction of sulphur emissions.[43] Compiling and reporting upon national inventories of greenhouse gas sources and sinks is a key obligation of all parties to the 1992 Framework Convention on Climate Change.[44] The 1994 Nuclear Safety Convention relies largely on contracting States' scrutiny of national reports to ensure conformity with stipulated nuclear safety requirements.[45] Reporting requirements are also a key device employed under EC law, with directives requiring notification of transformation and often imposing further reporting requirements in respect of implementation, though in the EC context buttressed by the possibility of enforcement action by the European Commission.[46] Increasingly other mechanisms for compliance are being examined, including stipulated consequences for failure to comply with specified treaty obligations (non-compliance procedures). These were pioneered by the 1987 Montreal Protocol to the 1985 Ozone Layer Convention and have since been adopted in a number of forums, including active consideration of such mechanisms under the 1997 Kyoto Protocol to the 1992 United Nations Framework Convention on Climate Change.[47]

[42] It is rare for multilateral agreements to provide for compulsory international adjudication of disputes. An exception is the 1982 LOSC, which contains innovative provisions on dispute settlement, including compulsory conciliation and the establishment of an International Tribunal on the Law of the Sea (ITLOS) sited in Hamburg. See generally JG Merrills, *International Dispute Settlement* (3rd edn, 1999). The International Court of Justice does not have compulsory jurisdiction unless States have accepted such jurisdiction. However, it is always open to States to modify their acceptance of the International Court of Justice's compulsory jurisdiction by making a reservation excepting general or specific matters, as Canada did in respect of its 1970 Arctic Waters Pollution Prevention Act and, more recently, in connection with its Coastal Fisheries Protection Act (as amended in 1994). The first was untested, but the latter was recently successfully invoked by Canada to resist the jurisdiction of the Court in a dispute brought by Spain regarding the arrest of a Spanish trawler outside the Canadian EEZ pursuant to this legislation. See the *Fisheries Jurisdiction (Spain v Canada)* case: on 4 December 1998 the Court held that it did not have jurisdiction over the dispute, at http://www.icj-cij.org/.

[43] See below, paras 2.116–2.117.

[44] Article 4(1)(a) UNFCCC. For the text of national reports see the climate change website at http://www.unfccc.de.

[45] See further below, para 2.111.

[46] For specific examples such as the Transit Directive see below, Ch 4.

[47] See further this author, 'Non-Compliance Procedures and the Climate Change Convention' in B Chambers (ed), *Global Climate Governance: Inter-linkages between the Kyoto Protocol and other multilateral regimes* (1998) ch 3.

(3) *The Exercise of State Jurisdiction over Energy Resources and Energy Resource Activities*

Jurisdictional competences and sovereignty

International law determines the jurisdiction and control which States exercise over their natural resources. Jurisdiction is the capacity of States under international law to prescribe and to enforce a rule of law.[48] Bowett describes jurisdiction as 'a manifestation of State sovereignty',[49] while Brownlie regards jurisdiction as referring 'to particular aspects of the general legal competence of states often referred to as "sovereignty". Jurisdiction is an aspect of sovereignty and refers to juridical, legislative and administrative competence.'[50] As a manifestation of State sovereignty, prescriptive (or legislative) jurisdiction is absolute and exclusive within the State's own territory in respect of matters therein, except for applicable general rules of international law (eg jurisdictional immunities such as diplomatic and State immunity).[51] The enactment of minerals legislation, a tax code, or abandonment regulations would constitute the exercise of the prescriptive jurisdiction of the State, which may apply its national law to matters arising inside and beyond its territory (where jurisdiction is generally based on the nationality principle, discussed in the following section). **2.11**

Problems of jurisdiction tend to arise where a State seeks to regulate persons and/or activities which are not exclusively of domestic or internal concern.[52] International law is *not* generally concerned with internal matters of jurisdiction within a State, eg whether certain State organs have jurisdiction over a particular energy matter, whether a court has jurisdiction over persons or proceedings, nor indeed whether another body, such as an energy board, has jurisdiction over particular persons or subject matter. These matters are exclusively for the domestic law of the State concerned, save for whatever general or particular rules of **2.12**

---

[48] 'State jurisdiction is the power of a state under international law to govern persons and property by its municipal law. It includes both the power to prescribe rules (prescriptive jurisdiction) and the power to enforce them (enforcement jurisdiction). The latter includes both executive and judicial powers of enforcement. Jurisdiction may be concurrent with the jurisdiction of other states or it may be exclusive. It may be civil or criminal. The rules of state jurisdiction identify the persons and property within the permissible range of a state's law and its procedures for enforcing that law. They are not concerned with the content of a state's law except in so far as it purports to subject a person to it or to prescribe procedures for enforcing that law.' Harris (above, n 2) 264.

[49] Bowett, 'Jurisdiction: Changing patterns of authority over activities and resources' (1982) 53 BYIL 1. This link causes problems in regulating activities beyond the territory of the State, particularly in areas of global commons not subject to State sovereignty (considered further below, paras 2.21 and 2.39).

[50] (Above, n 2) 301.

[51] Such jurisdiction may also be curtailed by specific agreement, eg status of forces agreements.

[52] Mann, 'The Doctrine of Jurisdiction in International Law' (1964–I) 113 Recueil de Cours 9, 14. A good example of such difficulties in the energy context is the Siberian Gas Pipeline controversy: see below, para 2.22.

international law may constrain such internal exercises of jurisdictional competence where non-nationals are concerned.

Expropriation

2.13 International law *is* concerned with intra-State matters where a 'foreign element' is present, or where the State fails to comply with its international obligations. A classic example of direct relevance to the energy context are the international rules regulating expropriation by a State of a foreign national's assets.[53] It is now generally accepted that the taking of foreign property[54] is not unlawful *per se*;[55] less settled are the conditions which must be met,[56] including the standard of compensation payable and the method of valuation to be adopted. The right to expropriate is recognized in, *inter alia*, the 1962 United Nations General Assembly Resolution on Permanent Sovereignty over Natural Resources[57] and the 1974 Charter of Economic Rights and Duties of States.[58] Moreover, the 1962 Resolution reflects the widely accepted principle of the permanent sovereignty of States over their natural resources. A number of arbitral awards recognize the 1962 Resolution as reflective of customary international law;[59] however, the provisions on expropriation contained in the 1974 Charter are not generally considered to be reflective of customary international law. Owing to the connection between expropriation and the assertion of permanent sovereignty over natural resources, it is not surprising that so many of the cases involve the expropriation,

[53] It is beyond the scope of this chapter to address the law on expropriation in detail. See generally: Harris (above, n 2) 548 *et seq*; Brownlie (above, n 2) 533 *et seq*; id, *The Rule of Law in International Affairs* (1998) ch X (also contained in (1995) 255 *Recueil des Cours* 228); Malanczuk, (above, n 2) 235 *et seq*; Jennings and Watts (above, n 2) 911 *et seq*; E Paasivirta, 'Internationalization and Stabilization of Contracts versus State Sovereignty' (1989) 60 BYIL 315; S Asante, 'International Law and Foreign Investment: A Reappraisal' (1988) 37A. ICLQ 588; Mouri, *The International Law of Expropriation as Reflected in the Work of the Iran–US Claims Tribunal* (1994); RB Lillich and DB Magraw (eds), *The Iran–United States Claims Tribunal: Its contribution to the law of state responsibility* (1998).

[54] For discussion of what constitutes a taking of property see *Starrett Housing Corp v Iran (Interlocutory Award)* (*US v Iran*) 4 Iran-USCT 122; 23 ILM (1984) 1090 (which examines, *inter alia*, 'creeping' or 'constructive' expropriation). Also considered is what constitutes 'property'. It is now settled that 'property'Encompasses intangible property rights, including contractual rights: see the *Amoco* case (below, n 59) para 108.

[55] There are of course exceptions, such as a provision safeguarding against this in an internationalized contract: see *Texaco Overseas Petroleum Co and California Asiatic Oil Co v Government of the Libyan Arab Republic* (*Texaco v Libya*) (1975/77) 53 ILR 389, 468.

[56] With some exceptions, there is broad support in the case-law for a requirement of public purpose for the expropriation in order for it to be considered lawful. Non-discrimination is also said to be a (related) requirement: see eg the *Aramco* case (above, n 6) para 142. This is particularly so if the requirement is flexibly interpreted: see further Pellonpaa and Fitzmaurice (1988) 19 NYIL 53, 67.

[57] GARes 1803 (XVII), GAOR, 17th Session, Supp. 17, 15.

[58] GARes 3281 (XXIX), reproduced in 14 ILM 251 (1975).

[59] See, for example, *Texaco v Libya*; above, n 55); *Kuwait v American Independent Oil Co* (the *Aminoil* case); and *Amoco International Finance Corp v Iran* (*US v Iran*), 15 Iran-USTR 189.

including the nationalization, of foreign oil company assets.[60] One area of controversy has been the standard of compensation available. Developed States have long adhered to the 1938 formulation of US Secretary of State Hull, expressed in a note to the Mexican Government on its expropriation of foreign oil interests:

> the right to expropriate property is coupled with and conditioned on the obligation to make adequate, effective and prompt compensation. The legality of an expropriation is in fact dependent upon the observance of this requirement.[61]

The 1962 Declaration uses general language ('appropriate compensation . . . in accordance with international law') whilst Article 2(2)(c) of the 1974 Charter suggests 'appropriate' will be judged against local, not international, law and circumstances. The 1962 Declaration provides a middle ground between the Hull formula and the Charter, neither of which have enjoyed widespread support. However, recent recognition has been afforded to the Hull formula in the Energy Charter Treaty provisions on compensation for expropriation, the first multilateral treaty to adopt the prompt, adequate, and effective standard for compensation.[62]

By and large, however, these are not matters of jurisdiction but of the application of other substantive rules of international law, eg the international rules regarding treatment of aliens and their property. In such instances the question is not whether the State has jurisdiction to regulate, say, property matters within its territory (clearly it does) but whether it may properly subject foreign sovereign property to execution proceedings or take foreign property without compensation. In the main these are not questions of jurisdiction but of whether a violation of a substantive norm of international law has been committed by the territorial sovereign. **2.14**

Bases of jurisdiction

There are five recognized bases for the exercise of State jurisdiction under international law, namely: **2.15**

(i) territorial principle: jurisdiction is determined by reference to the place where the action takes place;

[60] For an assessment of the contemporary relevance of the new international economic order of which the Charter forms a part, see T Waelde, 'A Requiem for the New International Economic Order' in N Al-Nauimi and R Meese (eds), *International Legal Issues Arising under the United Nations Decade of International Law* (1995); see also SK Chatterjee, 'The Charter of Economic Rights and Duties of States: An evaluation 15 years on' (1991) 40:3 ICLQ 669.

[61] 3 Hackworth 662.

[62] PM Norton, 'Back to the Future: Expropriation and the Energy Charter Treaty' in TW Waelde (ed), *The Energy Charter Treaty* (1996) 366. For a good overview of the ECT see Bamberger's contribution, ibid, and Ch 4 below; see also M Sornorajah, 'Compensation for Nationalization: The Provisions in the Energy Charter Treaty' in Waelde (ed), 386.

(ii) nationality principle: jurisdiction is determined by reference to the nationality of the actor;
(iii) protective principle: jurisdiction is determined by reference to the national interest affected by the act or omission;
(iv) passive personality principle: jurisdiction is determined by reference to the nationality of the victim;
(v) universality principle: all States have jurisdiction over persons in their custody who are alleged to have committed acts considered particularly heinous and harmful to humanity (eg piracy).

2.16 Situations involving concurrent jurisdiction frequently arise in practice,[63] though in certain contexts international law allocates exclusive jurisdiction over certain matters to the State.[64] Of most relevance to the energy sector are territoriality, nationality, and the protective principle. The other bases of jurisdiction, the passive personality and universality principles, have evolved primarily in the context of the exercise of criminal jurisdiction by States whose nationals are injured, or where crimes against humanity, eg genocide,[65] have been perpetrated. These are not further addressed here. This section concludes with an analysis of the jurisdiction exercised by States under the 1982 LOSC, which is of fundamental importance for offshore energy activities.

Territorial principle

2.17 A State has jurisdiction over all matters arising within its territory. Territory is defined under international law to include land territory and internal waters, as well as territorial waters and the airspace above these areas. In practice most civil and criminal jurisdiction is exercised by States according to the territorial principle, the strongest of the jurisdictional principles.

2.18 States exercise exclusive jurisdiction over the natural resources within their territory. This is reflected in the well established principle of international law recognizing the permanent sovereignty of States over their natural resources, more recently reiterated in Principle 2 of the 1992 Rio Declaration on Environment and Development and in the Energy Charter Treaty.[66] Where a State seeks to control activities beyond its territory, either in the territory of other States or beyond

[63] Jurisdiction is thus concerned with 'what has been described as one of the fundamental functions of public international law, viz. the function of regulating and delimiting the respective competences of States': Mann (above, n 52) 15 (who also observes, at 10, that legislative jurisdiction is to a large extent concurrent rather than exclusive).

[64] Bowett (above, n 49) 14, n 62.

[65] All States have jurisdiction to try offences under the universality principle, whether or not the offender is a national of the State concerned, and irrespective of where the offence occurred. At customary law both piracy and war crimes are recognized as crimes of universal jurisdiction. To this list must now be added a significant number of acts where international treaties confer on States Parties jurisdiction in respect of the crimes enumerated therein, eg the 1988 Rome Convention for the Suppression of Unlawful Acts against the Safety of Maritime Navigation, 27 ILM (1988) 668.

[66] See generally N Schrijver, *Sovereignty over Natural Resources: balancing rights and duties* (1997).

the territorial jurisdiction of any State (eg on the high seas), this is referred to as extraterritorial jurisdiction.

Nationality principle

States exercise jurisdiction over their nationals wherever they may be. 'Nationals' include not only individuals but companies[67] (eg Shell or BP), ships[68] (including oil tankers), and aircraft.[69] Generally speaking it is up to States to stipulate the criteria for the grant of nationality—in other words, the matter is one for municipal, not international, law.[70] **2.19**

States may prescribe the conduct of their nationals abroad, subject to certain limits: for example a State may not require acts which constitute delicts or crimes (ie illegal conduct) abroad. Furthermore, the general principles of non-intervention in the domestic affairs of other States and the sovereign equality of States constrain the exercise of jurisdiction over nationals while in the territory of other States, particularly in respect of those matters viewed as properly regulated by the territorial sovereign. Criminal jurisdiction, for example, is very closely linked with the territory of the State and only rarely will criminal jurisdiction be exercised with extraterritorial effect. **2.20**

A good example of nationality-based jurisdiction is the regulation by States of the conduct of their nationals on the high seas or in Antarctica. In the case of Antarctica, nationality-based jurisdiction overcomes the difficulty with the exercise of territorial jurisdiction which raises the spectre of disputes over territorial sovereignty. In other cases of disputed sovereignty, such as joint development zones, nationality-based jurisdiction has also proved a useful device for putting territorial questions on hold whilst the resources in a zone of disputed maritime jurisdiction are exploited.[71] In respect of areas beyond the territory of the State **2.21**

[67] *Barcelona Traction Power & Light Case (Second Phase)* [1970] ICJ Reports 3.

[68] See, for example, Arts 5 and 6 of the 1958 Geneva Convention on the High Seas and Arts 9–12 of the 1982 LOSC; and the 1986 UNCTAD Convention on the Conditions for the Registration of Ships (not yet in force).

[69] See, for example, Arts 17 and 18 of the 1944 Chicago Convention on International Civil Aviation.

[70] International law does, however, require a genuine link between the individual and the State for the purposes of the grant of nationality (see the *Nottebohm* case, (1955) ICJ Reports 4), a requirement also of ships and of aircraft under the relevant conventions.

[71] See generally H Fox (ed), *Joint Development of Offshore Oil and Gas* (1989/90, 2 volumes), and GH Blake *et al* (eds), *The Peaceful Management of Transboundary Resources* (1995) (chs 1–7 examine hydrocarbons and minerals). There is an extensive literature on specific zones of co-operation. See, for example, an analysis of the zone of co-operation in the Timor Gap established by Treaty between Australia and Indonesia in 1989 by P Reid and C Nolan [1992] 10:7 OGLTR 183; see also D Ong, 'Alternative Joint Development Regimes: A comparison of the Malaysia/Thailand Joint Development Agreement and the Australia/Indonesia Timor Gap Zone of Co-operation Treaty' [1992] 10:8 OGLTR; id, 'Joint Development of the Spratly Islands' Marine Resources' [1993] 11: 5 OGLTR 158; and HHL Roque, 'China's Claim to the Spratly Islands under International Law' (1997) 15:3 JENRL 189.

(sometimes referred to as 'beyond national jurisdiction'), jurisdiction may be exercised on the basis of nationality. This is reflected in the general principle of the exclusivity of flag-State jurisdiction on the high seas. However, such exclusivity may be waived by bilateral or other agreement, such as the 1969 Convention relating to Intervention on the High Seas in Cases of Oil Pollution Casualties, which enables a State to respond where its coastline is threatened even where the (foreign) vessel in question is on the high seas and not within coastal State jurisdiction. This coastal State right achieved swift recognition following British action against the *Torrey Canyon* in 1967.

Protective principle

2.22 States may exercise jurisdiction in respect of activities outside of their territory which have a harmful effect upon the State's welfare, security or economy. A good example in the energy context is the United Kingdom's aerial bombardment of the *Torrey Canyon*, an action subsequently placed on a treaty basis by the 1969 Intervention Convention already mentioned.[72] This was also one of the principles relied upon by Canada in exercising enforcement jurisdiction over the activities of a foreign fishing vessel outside of its EEZ in order to protect fish stocks straddling that zone and the high seas;[73] and by States anxious to ensure that nuclear-powered vessels and vessels carrying hazardous or noxious cargoes are restricted from navigating coastal waters.[74] These latter examples test the limits of existing international law. In the energy context, a well known example of the exercise of extraterritorial jurisdiction on the basis of the protective principle[75] is the attempt under the US Export Administration Act to prevent the European subsidiaries of US companies from selling goods and technology of US origin to Eastern Bloc countries. The legislation applied to companies supplying equipment for the Siberian gas pipeline.[76] Under these controls it was possible for, say, a United Kingdom company to be penalized under US law for trading lawfully in the United Kingdom. The rationale for the United States' extraterritorial application of US law to the conduct outside US territory of foreign companies is the alleged effect upon US trade.[77] Similar controversies have erupted more recently in con-

[72] The 1969 Convention relating to Intervention on the High Seas in Cases of Oil Pollution Casualties, 1975 UKTS 77, extended by a 1973 Protocol to substances other than oil, 1313 UNTS 3.

[73] See the *Fisheries Jurisdiction* case (*Spain v Canada*) above, n 42.

[74] On this issue see Van Dyke, 'Sea Shipment of Japanese Plutonium under International Law' (1993) 24 *Ocean Development and International Law* 399; and id, 'Applying the Precautionary Principle to Ocean Shipments of Radioactive Waste' (1996) 27 *Ocean Development and International Law* 379.

[75] Also referred to here as the 'effects doctrine', to connote that activities by foreign nationals beyond the territory of another State may still have 'effects' within that State.

[76] See discussion in Lowe 'Problems of Extraterritorial Jurisdiction' (1985) 34 ICLQ 724.

[77] The response of some States was to pass 'blocking legislation', such as the United Kingdom's Protection of Trading Interests Act 1980. During the course of a US Congressional Committee's

sequence of the 1996 Helms-Burton Act.[78] Such assertions of extraterritorial jurisdiction remain controversial.

Problems of terminology and of jurisdiction

There is considerable terminological confusion surrounding the terms 'sovereignty', 'sovereign rights', 'jurisdiction', and 'control'. A cursory glance at the 1982 United Nations Convention on the Law of the Sea reveals that all four terms are used: States have sovereignty over the territorial sea, exercise sovereign rights over the living and non-living resources of the exclusive economic zone, and jurisdiction and control over activities undertaken there. Once activities extend beyond the territory of the State, the potential for concurrent jurisdictions and conflict between them arises. Competing jurisdictions may also arise where resources straddle a boundary, or where the boundary has not been determined; disputes over territory, particularly the delimitation of land and/or maritime boundaries, often underlay such conflicts. A number of international agreements have been concluded to facilitate energy activities even in zones of disputed jurisdiction.[79] **2.23**

Areas beyond national jurisdiction—for example the deep sea bed[80] and the moon[81]—are also regulated by agreement, as is Antarctica, where contested claims to territorial sovereignty have been frozen by the 1959 Antarctic Treaty. This did not prevent the negotiation of a sophisticated minerals agreement for Antarctica, the 1988 Convention on the Regulation of Antarctic Mineral Resource Activities **2.24**

---

consideration of reauthorizing and amending the US export control legislation, the EC sent a letter outlining its opposition, which read in part as follows:

> 'US claims to jurisdiction over European subsidiaries of US companies and over goods and technology of US origin located outside the US are contrary to the principles of international law and can only lead to clashes of both a political and legal nature. These subsidiaries, goods and technology must be subject to the laws of the country where they are located.'

Reproduced in AV Lowe, *Extraterritorial Jurisdiction: An Annotated Collection of Legal Materials* (1983).

[78] The Cuban Liberty and Democratic Solidarity Act of 1996 (the Helms-Burton Act) contains provisions under which those who 'traffick' in property confiscated by the Cuban Government on or after 1 January 1959 can be sued for damages in US courts; foreign nationals 'trafficking' in such property can be denied entry to the US. Criticism of this action has been made in, *inter alia*, the WTO Council for Trade in Goods (EC protesting the extraterritorial application of US law). The Act was passed in retaliation for the shooting down of two US registered aircraft by Cuba. Blocking legislation has been enacted in some jurisdictions; see, for example, the United Kingdom's Protection of Trading Interests (US Cuban Assets Control Regulation) Order 1992, SI 1992/2449, made pursuant to the Protection of Trading Interests Act 1980, ibid.

[79] See above, n 71.

[80] Regulated under the 1982 LOSC, read with the 1994 Agreement on Implementation of Part XI.

[81] See further the 1967 Treaty on Principles Governing the Activities of States in the Exploration and Use of Outer Space, Including the Moon and Celestial Bodies, and the 1979 Agreement Governing the Activities of States on the Moon and Other Celestial Bodies.

(CRAMRA). In consequence of the 1991 Protocol to the Antarctic Treaty, however, a moratorium on mining has been imposed for at least fifty years and it is unlikely that CRAMRA will enter into force. The close link between sovereignty and the exercise of territorial jurisdiction is underscored by the need in Antarctica frequently to resort to nationality as the basis for the exercise of jurisdiction to regulate activities in, *inter alia*, the unclaimed portion of Antarctica.

The exercise of jurisdiction by States under the LOSC

2.25 Since both the continental shelf and the exclusive economic zone (EEZ) are theoretically beyond the territory of a State, it might be thought that any exercise of jurisdiction by the coastal State on the basis of the seaward extension of its territorial jurisdiction is extraterritorial in effect. In practice, however, a legal fiction is employed by most States which amounts to the assimilation of the continental shelf and land territory for jurisdictional purposes.[82] For example, the United Kingdom has legislated in respect of activities on the continental shelf, and in respect of enforcement it treats acts and omissions there as if they had occurred within United Kingdom territory. The Continental Shelf Act 1964,[83] which enabled the UK to ratify the 1958 Geneva Convention on the Continental Shelf (GCCS), fills a lacuna in that Convention which is also found in the 1982 Law of the Sea Convention. Both Article 2 GCCS and Article 77(1) LOSC recognize the exclusive sovereign rights of the coastal State for the purpose of exploring and exploiting continental shelf resources, but are silent on the *manner* in which the necessary jurisdiction to assert those exclusive rights would be exercised. Nor do the 1958 or 1982 Conventions convey title to the resources to the coastal State, whereas under national law title to land-based resources, particularly to petroleum resources, is frequently vested in the State. Offshore, coastal States enjoy the exclusive right or entitlement to explore and exploit the resources of the continental shelf but do not own the resources; it is this entitlement which is conferred on licensees, title passing only when the recovered resources are reduced to possession.[84]

2.26 Moreover, and crucially, it is not jurisdiction over all matters which is extended to the continental shelf: coastal States enjoy only a functional sovereignty over the

[82] Bowett observes: 'It is equally clear that States have relied essentially on the territorial principle to support the jurisdiction necessary to protect their interests in resources located outside their territory but conceded by international law to be within the control of the state. The continental shelf doctrine, for example, developed as an assertion of new territorial rights' (above, n 49, 6).

[83] Since replaced in part by the 1998 Petroleum Act, discussed in ch 10 below.

[84] Higgins, above, n 4, 138. Thus under North Sea offshore petroleum licences title passes only at the well head, whilst in respect of onshore licences title can be conveyed by the licence. As explored in, for example, *Daintith and Willoughby United Kingdom Oil & Gas Law* (1999) this has led to lending institutions employing various sophisticated financial devices to get round the problem that the offshore licensee cannot use unrecovered (and hence unowned) resources as collateral.

continental shelf, limited to the exploration and exploitation of the resources there. Any laws extended to the continental shelf must thus relate to exploration and exploitation of the resources of the continental shelf. As Higgins observes, this can give rise to some interesting jurisdictional issues regarding such matters as the ability of a coastal State to tax a company not registered within its jurisdiction but operating on the continental shelf, or the liability in tax to the coastal State of service companies providing food or other services to offshore rigs.[85]

In respect of the EEZ, the same process of assimilation of the EEZ with land territory for jurisdictional purposes may be employed, but only in respect of the limited jurisdictional purposes accorded by international law to the coastal State within the EEZ. This does not mean that installations are part of the land territory: clearly they are not. Rather, it is an expression of the functional jurisdiction which coastal States exercise over resource activities. Artificial islands and offshore installations may be assimilated to territory for the purposes of the exercise of jurisdiction thereover by the coastal State. Note, however, that whilst an offshore structure may be assimilated to land territory for the purposes of the extension of prescriptive and enforcement jurisdiction in a range of civil and criminal matters, installations, even where fixed, may also be assimilated to aircraft or ships for other purposes, such as the international regulation of dumping.[86] In such cases jurisdiction is exercised not on the basis of territoriality, but on the basis of nationality. **2.27**

A further limitation is placed on coastal States in respect of submarine cables and pipelines. Both the 1958 Geneva Convention (Article 4) and the 1982 LOSC (Article 79) require the coastal State to permit other States to lay submarine cables or pipelines on its continental shelf, subject to reasonable conditions (for example concerning the course of the pipeline or the prevention of pollution). In this sense that high seas freedom, retained under the LOSC within the 200-mile EEZ, is closely regulated. Article 79(4) further provides that the coastal State may exercise jurisdiction over such cables and pipelines constructed on or used in connection with exploitation of the resources of the shelf. In practice, where the pipeline has been laid by another State, a regime of concurrent jurisdiction may be agreed.[87] **2.28**

[85] See further Higgins, above, n 4, ch 8, 'Natural Resources and International Law Norms'.

[86] See, for example, the Oslo Convention for the Prevention of Marine Pollution by Dumping from Ships and Aircraft 1972, which defined ships and aircraft to include, *inter alia*, fixed and floating platforms (Art 19(2)). In contrast, the Paris Convention for the Prevention of Marine Pollution from Land-Based Sources 1974 defined land-based pollution to include pollution from man-made structures in the maritime area covered by the Convention (Art 3(c)(iii)). Both these Conventions have been replaced by the 1992 Convention for the Protection of the Marine Environment of the North-East Atlantic, Annex III of which addresses the prevention and elimination of pollution from offshore sources, which encompasses offshore installations and pipelines, and is discussed further below.

[87] See the 1976 Agreement between Norway and the United Kingdom relating to the Exploitation of the Frigg Field Reservoir and the Transmission of Gas therefrom to the United Kingdom, in particular Arts 13–21. This Agreement was updated in 1998. See generally Roggenkamp, below, n 120.

C. Exploration and Exploitation of Oil and Gas

(1) The 1982 United Nations Convention on the Law of the Sea

Introduction

2.29 The 1982 Law of the Sea Convention entered into force on 16 November 1984, with 60 ratifications. As of 16 October 2000 the Convention had 135 Parties, including the European Community.[88] A number of European States were amongst the handful of States which did not sign the Convention upon its conclusion in 1982; however, subsequent developments, including the conclusion in 1994 of an Implementation Agreement[89] addressing a number of industrialized countries' concerns regarding the deep seabed mining provisions of the Convention, paved the way for accession by these States. The legal effect of ratification is that the Convention now prevails, as between States Parties thereto, over the four Geneva Conventions on the Law of the Sea of 29 April 1958.[90] This is certainly the case for most Member States of the European Union. However, a second and different legal regime will apply to States such as Denmark, which has not ratified the 1982 Convention but has ratified the 1958 Geneva Convention on the Continental Shelf, for example. Here the obligations of the 1958 Convention will continue to apply as between Denmark and other parties to the 1958 Conventions. Some provisions will also apply as a matter of customary international law, a point applicable to both the 1958 and the 1982 Conventions.

2.30 The four Geneva Conventions were the product of the First United Nations Conference on the Law of the Sea held at Geneva in 1958 and are based on drafts produced by the International Law Commission, which devoted nine years to the task.[91] Notwithstanding such thorough preparation, a number of issues were left unresolved in 1958, most notably the breadth of the territorial sea and of the exclusive fishing zone. A Second United Nations Conference on the Law of the Sea,

---

[88] All the Member States of the EC and Norway are parties to the LOSC except Denmark, which has signed but not ratified. This is also the case for the 1994 Implementation Agreement, which entered into force on 28 July 1996 and as at 16 October 2000 had 99 Contracting Parties. For status see http://www.un.org/Depts/los.

[89] Agreement Relating to the Implementation of Part XI of The United Nations Convention on the Law of the Sea of 10 December 1982 adopted by General Assembly Resolution 48/263 on 28 July 1994: for text see UN Division for Ocean Affairs and the Law of the Sea, Office of Legal Affairs, *Law of the Sea Bulletin*, Special Issue IV, 16 November 1994. The Agreement was the result of informal consultations undertaken by the United Nations Secretary General from 1990 to 1994 to review the difficulties with Part XI of the 1982 Convention which were widely perceived as preventing widespread ratification of the Convention by developed States.

[90] Art 311 LOSC. Art 309 prohibits reservations to the Convention, a reflection of the 'package deal' and consensus approach to negotiations which spanned 1973–82.

[91] See Johnson, 'The Preparation of the 1958 Geneva Conference on the Law of the Sea' (1958) 8 ICLQ 122.

convened in Geneva in 1960, failed narrowly to reach agreement on this issue, and no treaty text resulted. The Third United Nations Conference on the Law of the Sea (UNCLOS) took place from 1973 to 1982, culminating in the adoption of the 1982 LOSC. It was negotiated as a 'package deal'; in consequence, no reservations are permitted to the Convention.[92]

In 320 Articles and nine Annexes the 1982 Convention regulates all ocean space, from the baselines separating internal from territorial waters through to the deep seabed.[93] It settled for the first time that the maximum outer limit of the territorial sea is twelve miles, and that a new zone, the exclusive economic zone, may be claimed up to 188 miles beyond a twelve-mile territorial sea. Under the LOSC it is possible for all States to enjoy sovereign rights over the living and non-living resources of the seabed, subsoil, and superjacent waters to an outer limit of 200 miles, irrespective of the physical presence of a continental shelf. In other words, a distance criterion replaces the criterion of natural prolongation, at least within the 200-mile limit. Beyond this distance the physical presence of a continental shelf is necessary for the exercise of resource rights beyond 200 miles, with Article 76 LOSC further specifying delimitation criteria for the outer limit of the continental shelf. Beyond the continental shelf is the 'Area', the resources of which are declared to be the common heritage of mankind (Art 136). **2.31**

Whilst largely incorporating the provisions of the 1958 Convention, the 1982 Convention departs significantly from it in defining the juridical nature and outer limits of the continental shelf and in regulating the exploitation of non-living shelf resources beyond 200 nautical miles. Articles 76 (definition) and 82 (payments and contributions in respect of continental shelf exploitation beyond 200 nautical miles) proved particularly contentious during the negotiation of the treaty text. Annex II provides for the establishment of a Commission on the Limits of the Continental Shelf whose recommendations will form the basis for delimitation under Article 76 of the outer limits of the continental shelf where it extends beyond 200 nautical miles; Article 82 provides for a system of revenue-sharing in respect of mineral exploitation on the continental shelf beyond 200 nautical miles. Under the 1982 Convention coastal States also enjoy greater control over submarine pipelines on their continental shelf. **2.32**

In the event of a dispute regarding the interpretation or application of the Convention, Part XV on settlement of disputes will apply. States are free to choose **2.33**

[92] For discussion of the novel approach of UNCLOS III, see AW Koers, 'The Third United Nations Conference on the Law of the Sea: Some remarks on its contribution towards the making of international law' in WP Heere (ed), *International Law and its Sources: Liber Amicorum Maarten Bos* (1989).

[93] For a broad overview of the general provisions of the LOSC, see JA Thomas, 'New Developments in the International Legal Regime for the Offshore Oil and Gas Industry' [1994] 12:4 OGLTR 110.

one or more of the following means for dispute settlement by written declaration made on accession or ratification, or at any time thereafter: (i) the International Tribunal on the Law of the Sea based at Hamburg; (ii) the International Court of Justice; (iii) an arbitral tribunal established under Annex VII of the Convention; and/or (iv) a special arbitral tribunal established in accordance with Annex VIII (for disputes regarding fisheries, preservation of the marine environment, marine scientific research, and navigation, including pollution from vessels and by dumping). It is further open to States Parties to exclude certain matters, including maritime boundary delimitations under Articles 15 (territorial sea), 74 (EEZ), and 83 (continental shelf), from the compulsory procedures for dispute settlement contained in the Convention. Save for recourse to the International Court of Justice, all of these methods for dispute resolution are also open to international organizations party to the Convention (eg the EC).

The jurisdictional provisions of the LOSC

2.34 The provisions regarding the regime of the continental shelf, set forth in Part VI of the Convention (Arts 76 to 85) are of particular relevance to energy activities. Part VI completes that part of the Convention, comprising Articles 2–85, which addresses sea areas subject to coastal State jurisdiction. Thus, unlike the 1958 Geneva Convention on the Continental Shelf, the 1982 Convention fully integrates the continental shelf regime into the legal regulation of the seas as a whole. Such integration is evident in, for example, the cross-referencing to particular EEZ provisions which apply *mutatis mutandis* to the continental shelf. Where a coastal State has proclaimed an exclusive economic zone, the provisions of Part V (EEZ) and Part VI (CS) will together regulate the rights and duties of States within 200 nautical miles of the coast. This complementarity was recognized by the International Court of Justice in the 1985 *Libya/Malta Continental Shelf* case:

> Although the institutions of the continental shelf and the exclusive economic zone are different and distinct, the rights which the exclusive economic zone entails over the sea-bed of the zone are defined by reference to the régime laid down for the continental shelf. Although there can be a continental shelf where there is no exclusive economic zone, there cannot be an exclusive economic zone without a corresponding continental shelf.[94]

Definition and extent of the continental shelf

2.35 For centuries States have exercised functional jurisdiction over adjacent maritime zones for a variety of purposes, including natural resource exploitation. However, the concept of continental shelf jurisdiction is of more recent vintage. Its origins lie in the immediate post-war era, in particular with the September 1945 Proclamation by US President Truman claiming jurisdiction and control over the

[94] [1985] ICJ Rep. 13, 33.

natural resources of the continental shelf appurtenant to the United States.[95] The legal status of the superjacent waters was left unaffected, and the geographic extent of the rights enjoyed was limited to the distance where water depth reaches 200 metres. Prompted by the need to protect and to exploit near-shore reserves of petroleum, this statement *de lege ferenda* swiftly passed into the corpus of customary international law. The concept of the continental shelf was soon codified, following deliberations by the International Law Commission, culminating in the adoption of four conventions in 1958, including the Continental Shelf Convention. Article 1 defined the shelf and the nature of the coastal State rights thereover, while Article 5 addressed the principal resource rights. It is largely of historic interest now since it has been replaced by the provisions of the 1982 United Nations Convention on the Law of the Sea (LOSC),[96] but the latter does not depart significantly from the continental shelf regime first laid down in 1958. Moreover, in 1969 the International Court of Justice observed that Articles 1–3 of the Continental Shelf Convention were identical in content with the customary rules on the continental shelf.[97]

Both the 1958 Geneva Convention on the Continental Shelf and the 1982 Convention define the term 'continental shelf' to mean the sea bed and subsoil of the submarine areas which extend beyond the territorial sea. In defining the outer limit of the continental shelf, however, there is a significant departure in the 1982 Convention. The 1958 Convention adopted a legal definition of the term 'continental shelf' at variance with the geological definition, using water depth and exploitability which would permit the extension of coastal State jurisdiction over the continental shelf to a water depth of 200 metres or to the limits of exploitability. The 1982 Convention adopts a new definition of the continental shelf, employing a geomorphological criterion of the outer edge of the continental margin and a distance criterion of 200 nautical miles from the baselines of the territorial sea where the margin does not extend to that distance. This distance criterion is an explicit acknowledgement of the close link between the regime of the continental shelf and the EEZ. As noted above, the International Court of Justice in the *Libya/Malta* case confirmed the customary international law status of Article 76(1). **2.36**

Further guidance in delimiting the outer extent of the continental shelf is provided in Article 76 LOSC. It provides a complicated set of formulae for calculating the outer limits of the continental margin beyond 200 nautical miles, up to a

[95] 327 *Dept of State Bulletin* 485, reproduced in (1946) 40 AJIL (Supp.) 45.

[96] By operation of Article 311, the 1982 LOSC prevails over the 1958 Geneva Conventions for States Parties to both. The 1958 Conventions will be of continuing relevance for States which have not ratified the 1982 LOSC, and as between States where the 1958 Conventions are the common treaty regime between them (eg where State A has ratified both the 1958 and 1982 Conventions, but States B and C have only ratified the 1958 Conventions).

[97] Cf n 110 below.

maximum of 350 nautical miles where the shelf extends to this distance. A Commission on the Outer Limits of the Continental Shelf[98] has been established to make recommendations regarding delimitations pursuant to the criteria set forth in Article 76.[99] In respect of the exploitation of resources beyond 200 miles to the outer limit of the continental shelf, the shelf State is obliged to share in the proceeds of such exploitation through payments or contributions in kind.[100] In this sense exploitation of outer continental shelf resources reflects in part the common heritage of mankind principle which has influenced the development of the legal regime in respect of the resources of the deep sea bed. A further link is that such payments or contributions are made through the body also responsible for deep sea-bed mining, the International Seabed Authority. These provisions reflect the fact that it is the outer limit of the continental shelf which separates the shelf from the 'Area', ie 'the sea-bed and ocean floor and subsoil thereof, beyond the limits of national jurisdiction' (Art 1(1)). Article 136 declares '[t]he Area and its resources are the common heritage of mankind'. It will be recalled that one reason for the delayed ratification of the Convention by a significant minority of developed States was concern regarding Part XI of the Convention regulating exploitation of the resources of the Area. A number of concerns were addressed in the 1994 Implementation Agreement, paving the way for widespread ratification of the Convention.[101]

Delimitation of the continental shelf between opposite and adjacent States

2.37 Where the continental shelves of opposite or adjacent States overlap, delimitation of the shelf between them may be necessary. In the European context, a number of bilateral agreements have been agreed between States, particularly but not exclusively in the North Sea. For example, bilateral agreements have been concluded between the United Kingdom and Denmark,[102] the Netherlands,[103] Germany,[104]

[98] Elected by the Contracting Parties to the LOSC in March 1997 to a 5-year term, the 21-member Commission includes members from France, Germany, Ireland, and Norway.

[99] To date 7 sessions of the Commission have taken place (June 1997–May 2000). At its fifth meeting in May 1999 the Commission adopted the final text of the Scientific and Technical Guidelines, which are aimed at assisting coastal States in preparing their submissions regarding the outer limits of their continental shelves. See the Statement of the Chairman of the Commission on the Outer Limits of the Continental Shelf on the Progress of Work of the Commission, for each session at http://www.un.org/Depts/los/tempclcs/docs/clcsdocs.htm.

[100] Art 82 LOSC, which provides a formula for calculating such contributions based on a percentage of the volume or value of production, up to a ceiling of 7%, with a 5-year grace period in respect of such payments or contributions in kind.

[101] See further Anderson, above, n 31.

[102] 1967 UKTS 35, Cmnd 3278 and 1973 UKTS 6, Cmnd 5193.

[103] 1967 UKTS 123, Cmnd 5193.

[104] 1973 UKTS 7, Cmnd 5192.

Ireland,[105] France,[106] and Belgium.[107] In 1965 the United Kingdom and Norway delimited by agreement the continental shelf between them.[108] This led subsequently to an international unitization agreement between Norway and the United Kingdom to exploit the Frigg Field Reservoir which straddled the boundary thus agreed.[109]

Such delimitation agreements are consistent with the 1958 Geneva Convention on the Continental Shelf, Article 6(1) of which provides for the delimitation of the boundary of the continental shelf between opposite States by agreement. In the absence of agreement, and unless another boundary is justified by special circumstances, the boundary is to be the median line. In the 1969 *North Sea Continental Shelf* cases,[110] joined cases between Denmark and Germany and the Netherlands and Germany, the International Court of Justice was asked to determine which 'principles and rules of international law are applicable to the delimitation as between the Parties of the areas of continental shelf in the North Sea which appertain to each of them beyond the partial boundary [already] determined'. The 'equidistance—special circumstances rule' of the 1958 Convention was not considered by the Court to reflect customary international law; rather, 'delimitation must be the object of agreement between the States concerned, and ... such agreement must be arrived at in accordance with equitable principles'.[111] Negotiation of the delimitation provisions of the 1982 Convention proved difficult, with no agreement between the 'equitable principles' and 'equidistance/special circumstances' groups. In consequence, Article 83 of the 1982 Law of the Sea Convention is widely perceived to have failed both to endorse any particular method of delimitation, and to adduce legal certainty to the area. Indeed, maritime boundary claims form a significant portion of the docket of the International Court of Justice, a number of delimitation cases having been **2.38**

[105] 1967 UKTS 23, Cmnd 3253, as amended by a 1972 Protocol.

[106] Delimitation between the UK and France is partly by agreement: see the *Anglo-French Continental Shelf Arbitration* (1977–78) Cmnd 7438, 18 ILM (1979) 397 and Agreements of 24 June 1982, 1983 UKTS 20, Cmnd 8859 and of 23 July 1991, Cmnd 1732.

[107] 1991, Cmnd 1735.

[108] 1965 UKTS 71, Cmnd 2757, amended by Protocol of 22 December 1978, 1980 UKTS 31, Cmnd 7853.

[109] The Frigg Field Reservoir Agreement (1976), Cmnd 6491, subsequently updated in 1998.

[110] 1969 ICJ Rep. 3.

[111] ibid, para 85; see also the *Tunisia/Libya Continental Shelf* case [1982] ICJ Rep. 18, 37. In the *North Sea* cases, the Court held: delimitation is to be effected by agreement in accordance with equitable principles, and taking account of all the relevant circumstances, in such a way as to leave as much as possible to each Party all those parts of the continental shelf that constitute a natural prolongation of its land territory into and under the sea, without encroachment on the natural prolongation of the land territory of the other; if, in the application of the preceding sub-paragraph, the delimitation leaves to the Parties areas that overlap, these are to be divided between them in agreed proportions or, failing agreement, equally, unless they decide on a regime of joint jurisdiction, user, or exploitation for the zones of overlap or any part of them. The factors to be taken into account include the natural resources of the continental shelf areas involved.

referred to it, as well as international arbitrations such as the Anglo-French Continental Shelf Arbitration.[112]

The continental shelf and the Area

2.39 As stated above, one of the functions of Article 76 of the 1982 Law of the Sea Convention is to delimit the boundary between the continental margin, subject to national jurisdiction, and the 'Area', ie 'the sea-bed and ocean floor and subsoil thereof, beyond the limits of national jurisdiction' (Art 1(1)). The resources of the Area are declared the common heritage of mankind (Art 136). Article 82 is concerned with revenue-sharing in respect of the exploitation of the non-living resources of the continental shelf beyond 200 nautical miles. It constitutes a compromise between those States with broad continental margins and those States which opposed the extension of the continental shelf regime beyond 200 nautical miles. The compromise solution is an element of revenue-sharing in respect of resource exploitation beyond 200 nautical miles. Payments or contributions in kind are to be made through the International Seabed Authority (see Arts 156 et seq.) after the first five years of production, based on 1 per cent of the value or volume of production, and increasing from 1 per cent each subsequent year to a maximum of 7 per cent in the twelfth year (Art 82(2)). 'Production' is not defined, although it is made clear that it does not include resources used in connection with exploitation (Art 82(2)). Nor is it clear how value will be calculated (presumably prevailing market prices at the time of production), in what currency payments will be made (presumably a freely usable currency—see Annex III, Art 13(12)), nor the modalities for sale of 'contributions in kind'. Developing States which are net importers of mineral resources produced from the continental shelf are exempt from these requirements (Art 82(3)). The payments or contributions are to be distributed to all States Parties—an expression of the common heritage principle—'taking into account the interests and needs of developing States, particularly the least developed and land-locked among them'. Equitable sharing criteria are to be applied by the Authority in distributing payments or contributions in kind. Further guidance on equitable sharing will come from the Assembly of the Authority (Art 160(2)(f)(i)).

2.40 Article 142 addresses resources straddling the continental margin and the Area. Due regard shall be paid 'to the rights and legitimate interests of any coastal State across whose jurisdiction such deposits lie' (Art 142(1)). Consultation with and prior notification to the State concerned is required before exploitation of such resources, as well as the consent of the coastal State for any exploitation in the Area which may result in the exploitation of resources within national jurisdiction (Art 142(2)). Coastal States' rights to respond to grave and imminent pol-

[112] Above, n 106.

lution threats or damage to their coastline from activities in the Area are preserved (Art 142(3)).

(2) The Rights of the Coastal State

Drilling

Although drilling is one of the principal methods by which exploration for and exploitation of the non-living resources of the continental shelf takes place, there was no express mention of it in the 1958 Geneva Convention on the Continental Shelf. This is remedied in the 1982 Convention, which confers on coastal States the exclusive right to authorize and regulate drilling for 'all purposes', ie not only drilling in connection with the exploration for and exploitation of the natural resources of the continental shelf referred to in Article 77(1).[113] Much drilling takes place from artificial islands, installations, and structures, which are regulated by Articles 60 and 80. Drilling is subject to the provisions of Article 208 concerning the prevention, reduction, and control of pollution of the marine environment from sea-bed activities subject to national jurisdiction. Coastal States shall enact laws and regulations to this end, which 'shall be no less effective than international rules, standards and recommended practices and procedures' (Art 208(3)). Article 214 regulates the enforcement of laws and regulations adopted in accordance with Article 208. **2.41**

Installations and structures

The coastal State has the exclusive right to authorize and to regulate the construction, operation, and use of installations and structures. So provides Article 60 of the 1982 Convention,[114] which draws upon the language of Article 5 of the 1958 Geneva Convention on the Continental Shelf, but is considerably broader in scope. Thereunder the coastal State has the exclusive right to construct and to authorize and regulate the construction, operation, and use of all artificial islands (an innovation of the 1982 Convention) and other installations and structures in the EEZ (or on the continental shelf). The exercise of coastal State rights over installations and structures (but not artificial islands, where jurisdiction is not restricted) must be linked with the purposes set forth in Article 56, namely, the economic exploitation of the zone and its natural resources, or where such installations and structures may interfere with the exercise of the rights of the coastal State in the zone. Thus installations and structures serving no economic purpose, **2.42**

[113] Moreover, a coastal State may withhold consent for marine scientific research by another State or competent international organization if it 'involves drilling into the continental shelf, the use of explosives or the introduction of harmful substances into the marine environment' (Art 246(5)(b)).

[114] Though Art 60 is found in Part V concerning the EEZ, Art 80 extends it to natural resource activities on the continental shelf, both within and beyond 200 nautical miles to the outer limit of the shelf.

and those that are not likely to interfere with the coastal State's rights in the zone, fall outwith the scope of Article 60.[115]

2.43 Neither 'installations' nor 'structures' are defined in the Convention.[116] It seems clear that production platforms are included, as are such associated production devices as the well itself, pipelines from the well to the platform, offshore oil storage terminals, and single buoy moorings. Excluded are pipelines to the shore. Less clear is the position in respect of drillships and semi-submersible drilling units. Such ships or units may be regulated by the State of registration through the jurisdictional link of nationality (see Art 91); it is less clear whether the provisions on establishing safety zones, etc, may be applied by the coastal State over such ships or units on its continental shelf.[117]

2.44 In addition to exclusive jurisdiction over artificial islands, installations, and structures, Article 79(4) provides for coastal State jurisdiction over cables and pipelines constructed or used in connection with exploration and exploitation activities on its continental shelf. The list of matters which may be regulated—fiscal, immigration, health, customs, and safety—is indicative rather than exhaustive. Jurisdiction here includes not only the power to prescribe in civil and/or criminal matters, but also the power to enforce. Coastal States may establish 'reasonable' safety zones around artificial islands, installations, and structures for the purpose of ensuring their safety and that of navigation. This is reinforced by paragraph 7, which enjoins the siting of artificial islands, installations, and structures, and their safety zones, in recognized sea lanes where interference with international navigation would occur. Since navigation may be regulated within safety zones, 'regulations against other incompatible activities would also seem permissible for the coastal State; the Convention, however, does not make that clear'.[118] Other appropriate measures to ensure the safety of artificial islands, installations, and structures might include military protection of installations in designated areas. The purposes of designation must be reasonably related to the nature and function of the artificial islands, installations, or structures. The maximum breadth is 500 metres from their outer edge, with the obligation to give due notice of the extent

[115] On acceding to the Convention the United Kingdom made a declaration indicating, *inter alia*, its objection to other States' declarations incompatible with Arts 309 (no reservations or exceptions permitted) and 310 (declarations and statements permitted) including 'those which are not in conformity with the provisions of the Convention relating to the exclusive economic zone or the continental shelf, including those which claim coastal state jurisdiction over all installations and structures in the exclusive economic zone or on the continental shelf'.

[116] This may be contrasted with the 1992 OSPAR Convention, discussed below at paras 2.66–2.84, and with Decision 98/3 thereunder, which provides detailed definitions of concrete and steel platforms.

[117] State practice has been to designate such zones where necessary. See, for example, the United Kingdom's Petroleum Act 1987, ss 21–4.

[118] SV Nandan, S Rosenne, and NR Grandy (eds), *The United Nations Convention on the Law of the Sea 1982: A Commentary*, vol II (1993) 586.

of safety zones. Further latitude is given where generally recognized international standards may depart from this maximum breadth. The IMO has not adopted any such standards and has in fact endorsed 500 metres as a suitable maximum.[119] Such islands, installations, and structures do not generate a territorial sea, continental shelf, or EEZ of their own (as 'real' islands may do—Art 121(2)) nor may they be used as baselines for the purposes of delimiting the maritime zones of the coastal State (see Art 7(1)). Article 121(1) reinforces this exclusion in defining an island as 'a naturally formed area of land . . .', thereby excluding from its scope artificial islands, installations, and structures.

Submarine cables and pipelines

Whilst all States continue to enjoy the freedom to lay submarine cables and pipelines on the continental shelf, this is subject to greater coastal State control under the 1982 Convention, including the right to prevent, reduce, and control pollution and to give consent to the delineation of the course of a pipeline (although not a cable). The laying of submarine cables and pipelines is regulated by Article 79, which reaffirms the right of all States to lay submarine cables and pipelines, with several restrictions. First, coastal State consent is required in respect of the delineation of the course of a pipeline (but not a cable) across the continental shelf (Art 79(3)). Secondly, Article 79 reaffirms the right of the coastal State to establish conditions for submarine cables and pipelines entering the territorial sea, and its jurisdiction over their operation and use on the continental shelf. Finally, Article 79 requires due regard to be paid to the position of existing submarine cables and pipelines and access for their repair. Limitations are also maintained on the coastal State, most notably the requirement in Article 79(2) for the coastal State not to impede the laying or maintenance of submarine cables and pipelines. However, once again rights and duties of coastal and other States are carefully balanced and restrictions upon the coastal State must be balanced against the coastal State's right to take reasonable measures to explore and exploit the natural resources of the continental shelf. **2.45**

The provisions of Part VI on the continental shelf are harmonized with the high seas and EEZ provisions of the Convention in relation to, *inter alia*, the laying of submarine cables and pipelines. Therefore while Article 87 of the Convention reaffirms the high seas freedom to lay submarine cables and pipelines, it makes the exercise of this freedom subject to the provisions of Part VI on the continental shelf, ie Article 79. Thus, for example, the consent of the coastal State is required for the delineation of the course of a pipeline on the continental shelf where it extends beyond 200 nautical miles and where the legal status of the superjacent waters is high seas. Similarly, Article 58 preserves the high seas freedom to lay **2.46**

[119] Report of the UN Secretary General A/41/742 para 35.

submarine cables and pipelines in the EEZ, subject to the provisions of Part VI on the continental shelf. This is consistent with Article 56, which provides that coastal States' rights over the sea bed and subsoil of the EEZ are to be exercised in accordance with the continental shelf provisions of Part VI.

2.47 Where submarine cables and pipelines are laid on the bed of the high seas beyond the continental shelf, then the provisions of Articles 112–15 apply. Article 112 reaffirms the high seas freedom of immersion, namely the right to lay submarine cables and pipelines on the bed of the high seas. Article 112(2) provides that this right is subject to the due regard provisions of Article 79(5), though the exercise of all high seas freedoms is subject to the requirement to have due regard for the interests of other States in the exercise of the freedoms of the high seas (Art 87(2)). This is undoubtedly also a rule of customary international law. Article 87(2) adds the further requirement of due regard for the rights under the Convention with respect to activities in the Area. Articles 113–15 address damage to a submarine cable or pipeline. States are required to legislate for ships flying their flag and for persons under their jurisdiction in respect of any breaking or injury of a submarine cable or pipeline caused wilfully or through 'culpable negligence' (Art 113). States must also adopt laws and regulations in respect of injury or breakage of submarine cables or pipelines caused by laying or repairing other cables or pipelines owned by persons under the jurisdiction of the coastal State (Art 114). Articles 113 and 114 both rely on the exercise of nationality-based jurisdiction over persons or ships in respect of activities taking place beyond national jurisdiction and thus *a fortiori* beyond the territorial jurisdiction of any State. Article 115 requires States to legislate for indemnification by cable and pipeline owners of shipowners who have lost fishing gear, nets, or an anchor in an effort to avoid injuring a submarine cable or pipeline. If a coastal State has not declared an EEZ, then the provisions of Articles 113–15 apply to cables and pipelines on the continental shelf.[120]

Abandonment

2.48 International law further regulates the obligations of the coastal State in respect of abandoned or disused installations and pipelines.[121] There are two aspects to this

[120] Nelson, 'Submarine Cables and Pipelines' in Dupuy and Vignes (eds), *A Handbook on the New Law of the Sea* (1991), vol 2, 987. For discussion of North Sea practice, with particular focus upon transportation, and inter- and intra-field pipelines, see MM Roggenkamp, 'Petroleum Pipelines in the North Sea: Questions of Jurisdiction and Practical Status' (1998) 16:1 JENRL 92. On the Caspian and Black Seas, see B Sas, 'Legal Issues in the Control of the Construction and Operation of Pipelines and the Issue of Transit in the Caspian and Black Sea Regimes' [1995] 13:7 OGLTR 274.

[121] For a general overview see Higgins, 'Abandonment of Energy Sites and Facilities: Relevant International Law' (1993) 11 JENRL 6; Side, Baines, and Young, 'Current controls for abandonment and disposal of offshore installations at sea' (1993) 17:5 *Marine Policy* 354; Igiehon, 'The Abandonment Controversy: From Development of International Law to the Brent Spar Incident—

issue: (1) legal requirements in respect of abandonment; and (2) legal restrictions on disposal, or dumping, of the installation or pipeline or part thereof thus removed. In respect of the first requirement, the 1958 Continental Shelf Convention required complete removal,[122] a reflection of the importance of concerns about freedom of navigation in the 1950s and the absence of deep-water exploitation of petroleum which only came onstream in the 1970s. The 1982 LOSC recognizes these changed circumstances in Article 60(3), which provides as follows:

> Due notice must be given of the construction of such artificial islands, installations or structures, and permanent means for giving warning of their presence must be maintained. Any installations or structures which are abandoned or disused shall be removed to ensure safety of navigation, taking into account any generally accepted international standards established in this regard by the competent international organisation. Such removal shall also have due regard to fishing, the protection of the marine environment and the rights and duties of other States. Appropriate publicity shall be given to the depth, position, and dimensions of any installations or structures not entirely removed.[123]

Thus, whilst Article 60(3) regards the general obligation as one of entire removal, it also expressly contemplates partial removal or leaving the structure *in situ* after production ceases. The entire removal obligation remained in the negotiating text at UNCLOS III until the ninth session in 1980, when the United Kingdom submitted an informal proposal upon which Article 60(3) is based. Removal would be required where a threat to navigation or other legitimate uses of the sea or to the environment was posed by the installation or structure in question. Further modifications were accepted at the final (eleventh) session in 1982, and resulted in the present text of Article 60(3). **2.49**

In 1989 the IMO produced a set of non-binding 'Guidelines and Standards for the Removal of Offshore Installations and Structures on the Continental Shelf and in the Exclusive Economic Zone'. Although not directly binding, States Parties to the 1982 LOSC have an obligation under Article 60(3) to take these **2.50**

"Economy" Overshadowing Environmental Protection?' [1996] 7 *Oil and Gas Law and Taxation Law Review* 298; Z Gao, 'Current Issues of International Law on Offshore Abandonment, with Special Reference to the United Kingdom' (1997) 28 *Ocean Development & International Law* 59 (an updated version of which is found as ch 4 of Z Gao (ed), *Environmental Regulation of Oil and Gas* (1998); and Picton-Turbervill, 'Decommissioning of Offshore Installations: The Legal Aspects' [1998] 6 *Oil and Gas Law and Taxation Law Review* 196.

[122] Art 5(5) of the 1958 Geneva Convention on the Continental Shelf provided that due notice must be given of the construction of any installations, and permanent means for giving warning of their presence must be maintained. Any installations which are abandoned or disused must be entirely removed. For legal arguments regarding the applicability of this provision before the entry into force of the 1982 Law of the Sea Convention see Higgins, n 121 above.

[123] For the drafting history of this provision, see Nandan *et al.*, n 118 above. The IMO is the 'competent international organization' for the purposes of Art 60(3), and for a number of other provisions in the LOSC which adopt this phrase.

Guidelines into account when considering the decommissioning of offshore installations. The Guidelines require an evaluation of six factors:

- any potential effect on navigation and other users of the sea;
- the rate of deterioration of the material and possible future effects upon the marine environment;
- the potential effects upon the marine environment;
- the risk that the material may shift from its present position over time;
- the costs, technical feasibility, and risk to personnel in removing the installation or structure; and
- the other uses to which the installation or structure may be put, or other justifications for leaving it intact, in whole or in part.[124]

2.51 The Guidelines further stipulate that lightweight structures (4,000 tonnes or less) in shallower waters (75 metres depth or shallower) must be entirely removed. Where partial remains are left *in situ*, clearance of 55 metres must be provided in the interests of safety of navigation, in particular submarine navigation. Any installations emplaced after 1 January 1998 must be capable of total removal.[125]

2.52 These Guidelines are reinforced through implementation in national policy and legislation, and through regional agreements. Thus, for example, the 1992 OSPAR Convention for the Protection of the Marine Environment of the North-East Atlantic (see para 2.74) amplifies these obligations in Annex III, which explicitly addresses a further feature of decommissioning, namely disposal of the remains. With effect from 9 February 1999, a further decision of the OSPAR Parties on decommissioning is binding on the Parties (Decision 98/3). In general terms, therefore, State practice has followed the lead of the 1982 Convention. Indeed, it is doubtful whether the entire removal obligation (without exception) presently enjoys support at customary international law. For example, the OSPAR Convention provisions, in particular Decision 98/3, provide for exceptions from entire removal while the 1989 IMO Guidelines expressly contemplate partial removal. Despite this recognition of partial removal, the OSPAR regime will increasingly restrict exceptions to entire removal and the IMO Guidelines specifically require that any installations emplaced after 1 January 1998 must be capable of entire removal. Thus State practice appears to be moving towards entire removal as the ultimate objective, though this is not yet achievable for technical, environmental, safety, and economic reasons.

---

[124] For good discussion see Side, Baines, and Young, above n 121.

[125] The immense Norwegian Troll platform was emplaced well before this deadline, which in effect allowed for a 9-year period from agreement on the Guidelines to the implementation of this particular obligation in order for such orders placed before this restriction to be fulfilled and for larger structures to be emplaced.

(3) Marine Pollution from Continental Shelf Exploration and Exploitation[126]

Marine pollution from offshore petroleum activities may arise in a number of ways: deliberate disposal from offshore installations of domestic and industrial debris (discussed under Dumping, below); operational discharges of oily or chemical drilling wastes; accidental blow-outs such as the 1977 blow-out of the Ekofisk oil platform in the North Sea; collisions between installations and ships; or the rupture of pipelines from normal wear or as a result of damage caused by trawling activities. In addition to the general provisions of the LOSC discussed above, specific regional arrangements have addressed some of these sources of marine pollution arising from continental shelf exploration and exploitation. In the North Sea, the 1969 Agreement for Co-operation in Dealing with Pollution of the North Sea by Oil, replaced in 1983 by an updated agreement which also extended to harmful substances other than oil, addresses oil pollution emergencies.[127] Dumping from ships and from installations in the North Sea and the North-East Atlantic is now regulated by the 1992 OSPAR Convention, considered in more detail below. In the Mediterranean, there is the 1976 Convention for the Protection of the Mediterranean Sea against Pollution, updated in 1995, with an accompanying 1976 Protocol concerning Co-operation in Combating Pollution of the Mediterranean Sea by Oil and other Harmful Substances in Cases of Emergency.[128] This calls for the establishment of contingency plans and monitoring for emergencies, supported by the establishment of a Regional Oil Combatting Centre for the Mediterranean in Malta.[129] **2.53**

(4) Dumping

Introduction

Ocean dumping contributes approximately 10 per cent of total marine pollution. The main substances directly dumped at sea are: dredged material from harbours and rivers (constituting approximately 80 per cent of total sea disposal); sewage sludge (a by-product of municipal sewage treatment plants); chemical waste (a by-product of industrial activities); construction debris; and other sources such as food processing materials and pharmaceuticals.[130] Additionally, sea-bed disposal of radioactive waste and of offshore installations and pipelines is also regulated, and forms the focus of the following discussion. **2.54**

[126] Pollution can also arise from deep sea-bed mining activities, the impact of which is presently being studied by the International Seabed Authority under the LOSC. See further http://www.isa.org.jm.

[127] Cmnd 4205 (1969).

[128] 15 ILM (1976) 285.

[129] Similar provision is found in the other UNEP Regional Seas Conventions. For further discussion see Churchill and Lowe, n 36 above, ch 15.

[130] See *IMO Briefing*, 6 November 1992.

2.55 International regulation of dumping activities is found in both global and regional conventions. Both levels of regulation, with the important reinforcement of effective national regulation, are recognized in Article 210 of the 1982 Law of the Sea Convention. This very general provision adds little to existing international law on the subject.[131] In addition to obliging States to adopt laws and regulations to prevent, reduce, and control pollution of the marine environment by dumping, Article 210 provides that States shall 'endeavour to establish global and regional rules, standards and recommended practices and procedures' to this end. National laws and regulations must ensure that dumping is not carried out without the permission of the competent authorities of States, and may be no less effective in preventing, reducing, and controlling such pollution than global rules and standards.[132] It is therefore necessary to look to specific international and regional treaties regulating dumping to obtain a clear picture of the substantive rules binding on States in this connection. Whether the rules are international or regional in nature, ultimately it is national authorities which have responsibility for permitting dumping activities even in areas beyond national jurisdiction, such as the designated dump sites in the North-East Atlantic located outside shipping lanes and areas of high marine biological activity.[133]

2.56 Some further elaboration is contained in Articles 194 and 216 LOSC. In connection with dumping Article 194 imposes the further obligation on States to take measures 'designed to minimise to the fullest possible extent', *inter alia*, 'the release of toxic, harmful or noxious substances, especially those which are persistent, from land-based sources, from or through the atmosphere or by dumping'.[134] Article 216 LOSC addresses the enforcement of laws and regulations and applicable international rules and standards adopted in respect of pollution by dumping. The coastal State has jurisdiction to enforce within its territorial sea, exclusive economic zone, and its continental shelf; a flag State may exercise enforcement jurisdiction in respect of vessels flying its flag or vessels or aircraft of its registry; and any State may exercise jurisdiction by virtue of the loading of waste within its territory or at an offshore terminus.

[131] But cf Art 192, the first treaty recognition of a general obligation of States to protect and preserve the marine environment.

[132] Art 210, paras (3) and (6).

[133] Art 210(5) LOSC provides that the permitting coastal State shall give 'due consideration of the matter with other States which by reason of their geographical situation may be adversely affected thereby'.

[134] Art 194(3)(a) LOSC. Art 194 also reiterates the obligation found in Principle 21 of the Stockholm Declaration not to transfer pollution beyond the areas where they exercise sovereign rights under the Convention (para 2).

Global regulation of dumping

The 1972 London Convention on the Prevention of Marine Pollution by Dumping of Wastes and Other Matter ('LC') regulates dumping activities globally. The 1972 London Dumping Convention (LDC—since 1993 the LC) entered in force on 30 August 1975. As of 1 January 2000 there were 78 Contracting Parties. The IMO acts as the Secretariat.[135] The LC comprises a preamble, twenty-two articles, and three annexes, subsequently amended on several occasions by amendments adopted by the regular Meetings of the Contracting Parties. In 1996 a Protocol was concluded which significantly strengthens the Convention, but it has not yet entered into force (see further below). **2.57**

The LC was the first attempt to control dumping at sea of land-generated wastes, with the London Conference convened only four months after the 1972 Stockholm Conference on the Human Environment. 'Dumping' is defined in Article III as: **2.58**

(i) any deliberate disposal at sea of wastes or other matter from vessels, aircraft, platforms or other man-made structures at sea;
(ii) any deliberate disposal at sea of vessels, aircraft, platforms or other man-made structures at sea.

Contracting Parties must take 'all practical steps' to prevent pollution of the sea by the dumping of wastes or other matter likely to create hazards to human health, harm living resources and marine life, damage amenities, or interfere with other legitimate uses of the sea. Global in scope, its geographic area of application is beyond the internal waters of Contracting Parties, ie the territorial sea and beyond. The LC does not apply to disposal at sea through the normal operations of ships (cf MARPOL, for example) nor to pollution arising from the exploitation of sea-bed minerals. **2.59**

The LC regulates the disposal of waste at sea. It divides substances into three categories. Annex I material is the most dangerous, whose disposal at sea is prohibited (high-level nuclear materials, organohalogen compounds, cadmium, mercury, persistent plastics, crude oil, materials produced for biological or chemical warfare, and since 1994, low-level radioactive waste). There is an emergency exception to this prohibition, provided that the IMO and other States likely to be affected are consulted. Annex II material is less dangerous, but dumping at sea is only permissible when authorized by a prior special permit with stringent conditions (eg wastes containing significant amounts of arsenic, lead, pesticides, or bulky wastes which may pose hazards to navigation and fishing—low-level radioactive waste formerly Annex II until 1994). Annex III substances are not dangerous but dumping them in certain quantities and/or in particular locations **2.60**

[135] For further details see the IMO's website at: http://www.imo.org/ (links to http://www.londonconvention.org/).

may have an adverse impact on the marine environment, hence a prior general permit is required for dumping at sea. The substances disposed of under Annex III must be fully characterized as to their nature; disposed of in a carefully selected site; and rigorously monitored. Together these annexes are sometimes referred to as the 'black', 'grey', and 'white' lists of materials. Licensing (permitting) is carried out by the flag State or by the loading State.[136] Enforcement is by the flag State or the coastal State within its territorial jurisdiction (the latter encompassing port/loading State). Parties to the LC are obliged to keep records and to monitor, individually or collectively, conditions of the seas.

2.61 On 20 February 1994 an important amendment to the LC 72 came into force which, *inter alia*, bans the dumping at sea of low-level radioactive waste[137] (now an Annex I material). A voluntary moratorium on such dumping had been in effect since the 7th Consultative Meeting in 1983. This formal ban was agreed at the 16th Consultative Meeting of the Contracting Parties to the LC held 8–12 November 1993, but only after this contentious matter was put to the vote. Of the forty-two Contracting Parties present at the Meeting, thirty-seven voted in favour of the ban and five abstained: Belgium, China, France, the Russian Federation, and the UK. The amendment entered into force 100 days later, with only one of the abstaining States, the Russian Federation, making a declaration of non-acceptance of the amendment, though indicating an intention to apply it voluntarily. The Russian statement highlights the economic importance of listing under the LC, since not all States have land disposal sites.[138]

[136] In 1997, at the 19th Consultative Meeting, the LC Contracting Parties adopted revised 'Guidelines for Assessment of Wastes or other Matter that may be Considered for Dumping' to apply both to the LC and to the 1996 Protocol when it enters into force.

[137] The amendment was adopted on 12 November 1993. The amendment defines low-level radioactive waste as follows: 'Low-level radioactive waste includes wastes from nuclear power production and from the industrial, medical and research uses of radioisotopes. The wastes can include broken machinery and equipment as well as old clothing. The wastes are normally incorporated into concrete-filled drums to ensure that they reach the seabed intact.'

In addition, two further amendments were adopted by consensus in 1993 which:

—phased out the dumping of industrial wastes by 31 December 1995 (an amendment not accepted by Argentina; Australia indicated that it would continue to dump jarosite, a by-product of zinc production, until 31 December 1997 at the latest); and

—banned the incineration at sea of industrial wastes from 21 February 1994 (stopped in practice from 1991).

All three—dumping of low-level radioactive waste and of industrial wastes, and incineration of the latter at sea—were permitted under the original LDC. Attitudes have changed towards pollution of the marine environment, as have perceptions of its assimilative capacity.

[138] At the 19th meeting of the Contracting Parties to the LC in 1997, the Russian delegation indicated that it would soon be in a position to accept the 1993 amendments in consequence of the anticipated completion in March 1998 of land-based facilities to process such waste from the Russian ice-breaker fleet and the decommissioning of Russian navy submarines. This was accomplished through, *inter alia*, technical and financial assistance from Norway and from the United States, and with the processing of liquid radioactive waste at facilities in Finland. Australia has also indicated that it will accept in full the 1993 amendments with the expiration of a permit for sea-disposal of jarosite from a zinc smelter in Tasmania.

Since the full effects upon the marine environment of low-level radioactive waste disposal at sea are not known, the Contracting Parties in the amendment agree to conduct scientific studies of the effects after twenty-five years, and thereafter at twenty-five-year intervals. This is a concrete expression of the precautionary principle the application of which to the LC was expressly confirmed by the Contracting Parties at their 14th Consultative Meeting in 1991.[139] 2.62

On 7 November 1996 the most significant change to the LC since 1972 was agreed with the adoption of the 1996 Protocol to the 1972 LC.[140] It will enter into force upon the 26th ratification, which must include fifteen ratifications by Contracting Parties to the 1972 LC. In addition to rendering the precautionary approach mandatory (Art 3(1)), the Protocol adopts a much more stringent threshold for dumping. Article 4 states that Contracting Parties 'shall prohibit the dumping of any wastes or other matter with the exception of those listed in Annex I'. One exception[141] listed is 'vessels and platforms or other man-made structures at sea'. The Scientific Group of Contracting Parties to the LC is presently drafting specific waste assessment guidance in respect of Annex I items. Thus the 1996 Protocol adopts a 'prohibited unless permitted' approach, rather than the 1972 LC approach of 'permitted unless prohibited'. In conjunction with the mandatory application of the precautionary approach, this effectively shifts the burden of proof onto the party wishing to carry out dumping to demonstrate that the proposed dumping operations will be safe.[142] 2.63

Derogation from the general prohibition on dumping, outwith these exceptions, is only permitted in cases of *force majeure* or where danger to human life or a real threat to vessels exists. Annexes II and III address assessment of wastes and arbitral procedures, respectively, and are subject to the tacit amendment procedure for amendment. Article 11 requires compliance procedures to be established by the Conference of the Parties two years after the entry into force of the Protocol. Article 5 reinforces the amendment prohibiting incineration at sea, while Article 6 addresses the problem of prohibited waste under the LC being transferred to 2.64

---

[139] Resolution LDC.44(14) 'The Application of a Precautionary Approach in Environmental Protection within the Framework of the London Dumping Convention'.

[140] See E Kirk, 'The 1996 Protocol to the London Dumping Convention and the Brent Spar' (1997) 46:4 International and Comparative Law Quarterly 826. As of 1 January 2000 there were only 12 Contracting States to the Protocol.

[141] The full list of Annex I exceptions is: 1. dredged material; 2. sewage sludge; 3. fish waste, or material resulting from industrial fish processing operations; 4. vessels and platforms or other man-made structures at sea; 5. inert, inorganic geologic material; 6. organic material of natural origin; and 6. bulky items primarily comprising iron, steel, concrete and similar non-harmful materials for which the concern is physical impact and limited to those circumstances where such wastes are generated at location, such as small islands with isolated communities, having no practicable access to disposal options other than dumping.

[142] The Protocol also applies the polluter pays principle, and discourages pollution transfer.

non-Contracting Parties by prohibiting such transfer: 'Contracting Parties shall not allow the export of wastes or other matter to other countries for dumping or incineration at sea'. Article 26 provides a phase-in period of five years for new Contracting Parties, and for technical assistance.

Regional regulation of dumping

2.65 A number of regional conventions regulate dumping. For example, UNEP's Regional Seas Programme, which has generated framework conventions for nine regional seas areas, includes in three instances protocols which explicitly address dumping: the 1976 Barcelona Convention for the Protection of the Mediterranean Sea Against Pollution (in force 1978),[143] with, *inter alia*, a 1976 Protocol on Dumping (in force 1978); the 1986 Noumea Convention for the Protection of Natural Resources and Environment of the South Pacific Region (in force 1990) with, *inter alia*, a 1986 Protocol on Dumping (in force 1990);[144] and the 1989 Paipa Protocol for the Protection of the South-East Pacific against Radioactive Pollution.[145] Other regional seas are regulated outside of UNEP's Regional Seas Programme, including the North-East Atlantic and North Sea, the Baltic Region,[146] the Black Sea,[147] and the Southern Ocean (Antarctica).[148] See also the 1985 Rarotonga South Pacific Nuclear Free Zone Treaty, which prohibits dumping of radioactive waste within the Zone (in force 1986).[149]

[143] The Barcelona Convention was amended in 1995: see the Convention for the Protection of the Marine Environment and Coastal Region of the Mediterranean, adopted 10 June 1995, amending the 1976 Convention. Six Protocols have been added to the Convention, addressed to hazardous waste (1996), pollution from continental shelf exploration and exploitation (1994), specially protected areas (1982), land-based pollution (1980), oil and other harmful substances in emergencies (1976), and dumping (1976). The Barcelona Convention has been viewed as a prototype for the other regional seas agreements concluded under UNEP's regional seas programme. See generally P Sand, *Marine Environment Law in the United Nations Environment Programme: An Emergent Eco-Regime* (1988).

[144] Reproduced in I Rummel-Bulska and S Osafo (eds), *Selected Multilateral Treaties in the Field of the Environment* (1991), vol II, 381 (Treaty No. 46).

[145] Reproduced in (1990) 15 Law of the Sea Bulletin 41–6.

[146] The 1974 Helsinki Convention has been updated by the 1992 Helsinki Convention on the Protection of the Marine Environment of the Baltic Sea Area, Art 11 of which addresses dumping.

[147] See the 1992 Convention on the Protection of the Black Sea Against Pollution, with Protocol on Dumping, reproduced in 32 ILM 1101 (1993).

[148] In particular, the 1991 Environmental Protocol to the 1959 Antarctic Treaty, reproduced at 30 ILM (1991) 455. In the same year an Arctic Environmental Protection Strategy was adopted for this region which, unlike Antarctica, falls within the sovereign land or marine territory of 8 Arctic States, reproduced at 30 ILM (1991) 624. See further DR Rothwell, *The Polar Regions and the Development of International Law* (1996).

[149] Reproduced in 24 ILM 1142 (1985).

The 1992 Convention for the Protection of the Environment of the North-East Atlantic[150]

The Convention for the Prevention of Marine Pollution by Dumping of Wastes and Other Matter 1972 ('the Oslo Convention') and the 1974 Paris Convention on Land-Based Sources have been replaced by the 1992 Convention for the Protection of the Environment of the Northeast Atlantic (OSPAR),[151] which entered into force on 25 March 1998. There are presently sixteen parties to the OSPAR Convention, including the EC.[152] The Convention builds on the general provisions of Article 60(3) of the 1982 United Nations Convention on the Law of the Sea and the non-binding Guidelines set forth by the IMO in 1989, though the OSPAR provisions go further. At the 1998 Ministerial Meeting of the OSPAR Commission in Sintra, Portugal, on 22–3 July 1998, Decision 98/3 on the Disposal of Disused Offshore Installations was adopted and entered into force on 9 February 1999. A Statement (the 'Sintra Statement') was also concluded which addresses, *inter alia*, decommissioning. Thus the key provisions of OSPAR pertaining to decommissioning must be read in the light of these subsequent developments. Further discussion of Decision 98/3 and of the Sintra Statement follow below. **2.66**

To a significant extent the OSPAR Convention builds upon the texts and decisions of the previous Paris and Oslo Conventions, and reflects in law the co-operation which had emerged in practice between the two regimes. Despite replacing these Conventions, Article 31 specifically provides that all decisions, recommendations, and all other agreements adopted under these Conventions will continue to apply to the extent compatible with, and unless replaced by, new OSPAR measures.[153] It was an essential prerequisite for the effectiveness of the Convention that all States bordering the region became parties, and that the parties to the previous Conventions came on board the new OSPAR Convention to provide legal consistency and continuity. Both objectives were achieved with the requirement for entry into force in Article 29 that all the Contracting Parties to the Oslo and Paris Conventions become parties to OSPAR before its entry into force. The geographic scope of the Convention is defined in Article 1 in both inclusive and exclusive terms. Included are all waters, ie from internal waters out to **2.67**

[150] This section relies in part on material previously published in *Daintith and Willoughby United Kingdom Oil & Gas Law* (3rd edn, 1999).

[151] For further details visit the OSPAR home page at: http://www.ospar.org/.

[152] The other parties are Belgium, Denmark, Finland, France, Germany, Iceland, Ireland, Luxembourg, the Netherlands, Norway, Portugal, Spain, Sweden, Switzerland, and the UK, ie all the Contracting Parties to the Oslo and Paris Conventions, plus Luxembourg and Switzerland.

[153] At the first Ministerial Meeting of the OSPAR Commission in July 1998, a Decision was adopted which clarifies which decisions, recommendations, and other agreements of the Oslo and Paris Commissions remain in force as the basis of the work of the OSPAR Commission. See the OSPAR website, n 151 above.

the high seas, including the sea bed and subsoil, within geographic co-ordinates set forth in Article 1(a), covering principally the North Sea, parts of the Arctic Ocean, and the North-East Atlantic. Excluded are sea areas already encompassed within existing regional sea programmes for the Arctic, Baltic, and Mediterranean Seas.[154]

2.68 The Convention addresses all forms of marine pollution in the North-East Atlantic, including both the land-based sources addressed in the previous Paris Convention and dumping at sea regulated under the Oslo Convention. It clearly reflects the trend in environmental treaties of the 1990s towards a holistic approach to environmental protection.[155] The Convention comprises 34 articles in the main treaty text with three annexes on the prevention and elimination of pollution from land-based sources (Annex I), from dumping or incineration (Annex II), and from offshore sources (Annex III), and a fourth annex on the assessment of the quality of the marine environment (Annex IV). A fifth annex on the protection and conservation of ecosystems and biological diversity of the maritime area was added at the first meeting of the Parties in 1998.[156] In addition, two appendices to the Convention amplify: (i) the techniques referred to in Article 2 of the Convention, ie best environmental practice (BEP) and best available techniques (BAT);[157] (ii) the criteria to be employed in setting priorities and in assessing the nature and extent of programme measures and their time-scales under Annexes I and III (eg toxicity, persistence, transboundary significance, etc); and (iii) criteria for identifying human activities for the purpose of Annex V. Under Article 14 of the Convention, the annexes and appendices form an integral part of the Convention, the latter being confined to matters of a technical, scientific, or administrative nature.

2.69 Thus the real detail of the OSPAR Convention is contained in its annexes and appendices, which are more flexibly amended and modified than the Convention

[154] Art 1(a)(i)(1) and (2) OSPAR.

[155] Similar trends have taken place within national systems, eg the holistic approach of the 1990 Environmental Protection Act in the UK. The OSPAR Convention might be described as a 'one-stop shop' for the protection of the marine environment of the North-East Atlantic; however, ship-source pollution (governed by the IMO under conventions such as MARPOL 73/78), atmospheric pollution (governed by the 1979 UN/ECE Convention on Long-Range Transboundary Air Pollution, 'LRTAP'), and fisheries management (regulated by regional and international agreements) are expressly outwith the OSPAR regime. Nonetheless, co-operation with LRTAP to reduce land-based sources of marine pollution, and with the IMO, is specifically noted in the Sintra Statement (paras 27 and 28).

[156] This reflects the increased scope of the Convention beyond mere pollution prevention to the protection of the marine environment from the adverse effects of human activities, as stated in Article 2(1)(a) (general obligations). For further discussion see L de la Fayette, 'The OSPAR Convention Comes into Force: Continuity and Progress' (1999) 14:2 International Journal of Marine and Coastal Law 247, 252–3. As at 5 October 2000 8 States had indicated their consent to be bound by Annex V and Appendix 3.

[157] The Sintra Statement reaffirms the Parties' commitment to the identification of BAT, BEP, and, where appropriate, clean technology (para 6).

text itself. This permits the Convention more readily to grow and adapt to changing scientific and other data. The main body of the Convention is concerned with definitions, the establishment of basic principles, and with establishing the institutional framework of the treaty. Article 1 defines key terms, whilst Article 2 sets forth the general obligations of the Contracting Parties. The latter establishes the general *raison d'être* of the Convention,[158] which is to prevent and eliminate pollution, to conserve marine ecosystems, and to restore marine areas which have been adversely affected. The general principles to apply in implementing these treaty obligations include the precautionary and the polluter pays principles, which are defined for the purposes of the Convention as follows:

> (a) the precautionary principle, by virtue of which preventive measures are to be taken when there are reasonable grounds for concern that substances and energy introduced, directly or indirectly, into the marine environment may bring about hazards to human health, harm living resources and marine ecosystems, damage amenities or interfere with other legitimate uses of the sea,[159] even when there is no conclusive evidence of a causal relationship between the inputs and the effects;
> (b) the polluter pays principle, by virtue of which the costs of pollution prevention, control and reduction measures are to be borne by the polluter.[160]

Both definitions reflect strong versions of the principle, unqualified by 'should' or 'may'.[161] In particular, the precautionary principle as applied in the light of the Convention's provisions requires neither that *irreversible* harm be threatened nor that preventive measures be assessed according to their cost-effectiveness.[162] Article 2 also requires the Contracting Parties to put in place 'sunset provisions', ie programmes which, where appropriate, encompass 'time limits for completion and which take full account of the latest technological developments'. As such, best available techniques (BAT) and best environmental practices (BEP) (including clean technology) are mandated, and further elaborated upon in Appendix 1.[163] **2.70**

The Convention addresses in Articles 3–7 the pollution and environmental assessment matters covered in detail in the separate annexes. These provisions **2.71**

[158] See also the Preamble which, though not directly legally binding upon the Parties, indirectly provides assistance in interpreting the substantive provisions of the Treaty.

[159] This language draws very closely on the definition of pollution in Art 1 OSPAR, which in turn closely reflects the definition in Art 1 of the 1982 Law of the Sea Convention.

[160] The Sintra Statement reaffirms the Parties' commitment to these principles (para 6).

[161] Unlike Principle 16 of the non-binding 1992 Rio Declaration, which states that 'the polluter should, in principle, bear the cost of pollution. . .'

[162] Unlike Principle 15 of the non-binding 1992 Rio Declaration, which provides that lack of full scientific certainty shall not be used as a reason to postpone cost-effective preventive measures where serious or irreversible damage is threatened. In contrast, the OSPAR formulation requires preventive measures to be taken where hazards to the marine environment are posed even where there is no conclusive evidence of a causal relationship between inputs and their effects. As de la Fayette summarizes, the OSPAR formulation is an active one, it does not require serious or irreversible damage to be threatened, only 'hazard' (not damage) is required, and there is no requirement of the cost-effectiveness of preventive measures taken: n 156 above, 254–5.

[163] See n 157 above.

require Contracting Parties to take all necessary steps, whether individually or jointly, to comply with the substantive provisions of the annexes. Procedural obligations to promote scientific and technical research, including joint programmes,[164] and to provide for access to information, are addressed in Articles 8 and 9.[165] The remainder of the treaty is concerned with establishing the institutional framework, with a Commission and Secretariat, including provision for observer participation in meetings of the Commission (Arts 10–12), providing for the legal effect of decisions and recommendations (Art 13), establishing the mechanisms for amendment and modification of the Convention, and for the amendment, modification, and adoption of annexes and appendices (Arts 15–20).

2.72 There is no enforcement machinery as such for the Convention, apart from Article 32, which reiterates the classical forms of inter-State dispute settlement. There is a special provision for negotiation, consultation, and reaching agreement in the case of transboundary pollution in Article 21, though this does little more than restate customary law obligations to notify, consult, and negotiate in good faith. A nascent form of compliance system may be seen in the obligation imposed on Contracting Parties by Article 22 to report at regular intervals to the Commission on implementation measures taken (including problems encountered), and the obligation then imposed on the Commission under Article 23 to assess compliance by Contracting Parties with the treaty provisions and decisions. Little detail is as yet established, leaving only the framework of Article 23 which simply refers to 'steps to bring about full compliance' including 'measures to assist a Contracting Party to carry out its obligations'. It seems doubtful that the Contracting Parties to this regional agreement will find it necessary to adopt compliance mechanisms analogous to those developed under the 1987 Montreal Protocol to the 1985 Ozone Layer Convention, or currently under discussion within the 1997 Kyoto Protocol to the 1992 Climate Change Convention, but clearly a legal basis exists for such development. If and when membership expands under the OSPAR Convention to include, eg, the Russian Federation,[166] issues of

[164] Quality Status Reports on the marine environment of the North-East Atlantic, which were adopted at the June 2000 COP, are being produced for publication late in 2000. These, in conjunction with the Joint Assessment and Monitoring Programme, will form the scientific basis for further developments under the OSPAR regime. Annex IV requires co-operation in assessment and monitoring, and the submission of data to the Commission, further buttressing the information network under the Convention.

[165] Art 9 is concerned with access to information within national systems, without the requesting party being required to demonstrate an interest. However, para 3 enshrines the traditional safeguards found in access to information regimes, including EC Directive 90/313/EC on the freedom of access to environmental information, and thus permits the preservation of confidential and other data from public access. See further n 267 below.

[166] Paragraph 26 of the Sintra Statement observes only the necessity to co-operate with other States within the catchment area of the North-East Atlantic, especially the Czech Republic and the Russian Federation.

compliance may arise more acutely, particularly if it is recalled that the object of non-compliance measures may be facilitative or coercive.

There is some implicit recognition of common but differentiated responsibilities in the Convention, at least in so far as its wide geographic coverage may necessitate distinguishing between regions in terms of compliance. Thus Article 24 permits the Commission to establish different timetables for implementation for different maritime areas 'having regard to the differences between ecological and economic conditions in the various regions covered by the Convention'. Moreover, Article 2(5) permits Contracting Parties, individually or jointly, to derogate upward from the provisions of the Convention and establish 'more stringent measures with respect to the prevention and elimination of pollution of the maritime area or with respect to the protection of the maritime area against the adverse effects of maritime activities'. Both techniques—common but differentiated responsibility and upward derogation—are found in EC environmental law provisions, for example.[167] **2.73**

Annex III: On the prevention and elimination of pollution from offshore sources

For the offshore oil and gas sector Annex III is of particular interest, as it sets out the substantive standards to be applied to offshore installations and pipelines located within the geographic scope of the Convention. 'Offshore sources' are defined in Article 1 of the Convention to mean 'offshore installations and offshore pipelines from which substances or energy reach the maritime area'. Each of these three key expressions—offshore installations, offshore pipelines, and maritime area—is defined in Article 1. 'Maritime area' is discussed above;[168] 'offshore installation' means 'any man-made structure, plant, or vessel thereof, whether floating or fixed to the seabed, placed within the maritime area for the purpose of . . . activities', while 'offshore pipeline' means 'any pipeline which has been placed in the area for the purposes of offshore activities'.[169] Annex III addresses offshore sources both as creators of waste and as waste constituents themselves through abandonment. Thus Article 4 addresses discharges from offshore sources, while Article 5 addresses the dumping of disused offshore installations and pipelines. The latter includes total and partial removal as well as leaving the remains *in situ*. Article 8 addresses placement for uses other than those for which the installation or pipeline was originally designed or constructed.[170] In each case authorization or **2.74**

[167] See, for example, Arts 175 and 176 (formerly Arts 130s and 130t) of the 1997 Amsterdam Treaty.

[168] See n 154 above.

[169] Art 1(l) and (m). 'Offshore activities' are also defined to mean 'activities carried out in the maritime area for the purposes of exploration, appraisal and exploitation of liquid and gaseous hydrocarbons' (Art 1(j)).

[170] The Commission is specifically charged with, *inter alia*, the duty to draw up criteria for the prevention and elimination of pollution from disused offshore installations and disused offshore pipelines emplaced under Art 8 (Art 10(d)). At the time of writing this had not yet been undertaken.

regulation by the competent authority of the relevant Contracting Party is required, such authorization or regulation to be made in accordance with any decisions, recommendations, or other agreement adopted under the Convention. In consequence of the adoption of Decision 98/3 in July 1998, Annex III must now be read in the light of the provisions of this Decision, discussed further below. A key feature of the abandonment provisions in Annex III is the emphasis on taking a case-by-case approach to the dumping of offshore installations and pipelines. This is a necessary consequence of the diverse physical circumstances of the region encompassed by the Convention, which renders total removal possible in the shallow waters of the Netherlands' continental shelf but highly problematic in the deeper regions of the northern North Sea areas of the Norwegian and United Kingdom continental shelves. In adopting programmes and measures to implement the obligations under Annex III, States must employ BAT and BEP, as well as the criteria set forth in Annex IV. No permit shall be granted where the disused installation or pipeline contains substances which result, or are likely to result, in hazards to human health, marine resources, or marine ecosystems, damage to amenities, or interference with other legal uses of the sea (Art 5(2)). There is a requirement to inform other Contracting Parties of the intention to permit dumping of disused installations or pipelines emplaced after 1 January 1998,[171] to allow time for consultation. For these purposes the Commission acts as a conduit for information, as well as requiring that Contracting Parties keep and report to it records of dumped remains or those left *in situ*, including dates and methods of dumping (Annex III, Art 5(3), 5(4)). Exceptions to the prohibition on dumping of wastes from offshore installations and on the dumping of disused offshore installations or pipelines without prior permission are contained in Article 6, and include when human life or the safety of an offshore installation is threatened.

2.75 In addition to establishing *ex ante* criteria for permitting disposal of disused offshore installations and pipelines, Annex III is also concerned with ongoing obligations in respect of remains left *in situ*, dumped, or emplaced elsewhere. In addition to the record-keeping and reporting obligations already mentioned, Article 7 requires Contracting Parties to take appropriate measures to prevent and eliminate pollution resulting from the abandonment of offshore installations in the maritime area caused by accidents, whilst Articles 4 and 9 place the task of enforcing the requirements and prohibitions of Annex III squarely on the Contracting Parties—the Commission does not have a formal enforcement role as such. The Contracting Parties must provide for a system of monitoring and inspection to ensure compliance with the permitting requirements in respect of discharges from offshore sources (Art 4) and, more generally, must ensure that maritime inspection or similar services report any instances of suspected contravention of the requirements of

[171] The date after which the IMO Guidelines require that any installations emplaced on the sea bed must be capable of total removal.

Annex III (Art 9). Upon receipt of such reports Contracting Parties are under an obligation to inform any other Contracting Party concerned.

Finally, in addition to imposing obligations on Contracting Parties, Annex III clearly sets forth specific duties for the Commission which amplify the tasks set for it in the body of the Convention (Art 10(2)). These include information gathering to provide a list of substances used in offshore operations and, on the basis of this list, to agree lists of substances for the purposes of the assessment required in Annex III Article 5(2) and to list substances which are toxic, persistent, and liable to bioaccumulation, and to prepare measures for their reduction and/or phasing out. In addition, the Commission is charged with establishing criteria, guidelines, and procedures for the prevention and elimination of pollution from disused offshore installations and disused offshore pipelines, whether disposed of under Article 6 or Article 8. **2.76**

The 1998 Sintra Statement

In addition to Annex III, which addresses the abandonment of offshore installations, a decision was adopted at the 1998 Ministerial meeting of the OSPAR Commission in Sintra, Portugal on 22–3 July 1998 which fulfils the obligation of the Commission under Article 10(c) and (d) of Annex III, namely OSPAR Decision 98/3 on the Disposal of Disused Offshore Installations. Pursuant to paragraph 8 of the Decision, it entered into force on 9 February 1999 when it replaced Decision 95/1 of the Oslo Commission concerning the Disposal of Offshore Installations.[172] The Sintra Statement was issued by Ministers, which addresses, *inter alia*, offshore oil and gas. Ministers confirm the general policy of preventing dumping of waste at sea, whether from sea or from land-based activities. The Statement reiterates the key points of the Decision, under which all dumping of steel platforms is prohibited, with only limited derogations for larger steel platforms and for concrete installations (see below). Instead, where safe and practicable to do so, steel platforms will be returned to land for recycling and disposal. No new concrete installations will be emplaced, unless technical or safety reasons require it. This is in line with the IMO Guidelines which require all platforms emplaced after 1 January 1998 to be capable of entire removal, with similar technological and safety exceptions. The Commission is to review the Decision from time to time in the light of subsequent developments, the general objective being to reduce reliance on the exceptions to the general ban on sea disposal. In pursuit of this general objective, the Parties agree to promote research and development, including by industry, into techniques for reusing and dismantling offshore installations and returning them to land for recycling or final **2.77**

[172] The OSPAR Convention stipulates in Art 13 the entry into force requirements for Decisions; however, this Decision was adopted unanimously and provided within its text for an entry into force date.

disposal.[173] Contracting Parties, operators, and contractors are encouraged to exchange such information; collaboration between operators under Joint Operating Agreements to decommission installations is likewise encouraged.

2.78 The Statement also confirmed that the Commission would adopt a strategy for setting environmental goals for the offshore oil and gas industry, and the management mechanisms to achieve such goals. This was done in June 1999 when a fifth strategy was added to the environmental goals of the offshore industry,[174] joining existing strategies addressed to, *inter alia*, radioactive substances, and the use and discharge of hazardous substances.[175] The Sintra Statement also addresses, *inter alia*, discharges of oil from offshore installations (including oil in produced water), and the reduction of emissions of air polluting substances.[176]

2.79 Finally, of relevance to the nuclear sector is the statement adopted at Sintra by the Ministerial Meeting of the OSPAR Commission which, *inter alia*, confirms the French and United Kingdom Governments' decision to abandon the possibility of future exceptions under the Convention in respect of the dumping of low- and intermediate-level radioactive wastes. This had been provided for in Article 3(3)(b) of Annex II to the Convention, which addresses the prolongation of an initial fifteen-year ban on the dumping of such wastes binding on all Contracting Parties. Essentially this OSPAR provision preserved the possibility for France and the United Kingdom to opt out of a continuation of the ban when it came up for consideration at a future date, a possibility now removed by unanimous decision of the Contracting Parties at Sintra.

OSPAR Decision 98/3 on the disposal of offshore installations

2.80 Decision 98/3 is divided into a nine-paragraph main text with four attached annexes addressed to categories of installations where derogations may be considered (Annex 1), the framework for the assessment of proposals for the disposal at sea of disused offshore installations (Annex 2), a consultation procedure (Annex 3), and permit conditions and reports (Annex 4). As with the main treaty text, the Decision commences in Paragraph 1 with definitions. Definitions are provided of concrete and steel installations and of component parts, namely topsides and

[173] Sintra Statement, para 23.

[174] Strategy on Environmental Goals and Management Mechanisms for Offshore Activities (1999–2012). Addressed are oil discharges from offshore facilities; the use and discharge of chemicals (with a 1996 trial scheme to be placed on a permanent footing); and the protection of marine species and habitats.

[175] Another section of the Statement is addressed to hazardous substances, and sets a target of the year 2020 for achieving zero discharges, emissions, and losses of hazardous substances. The overall objective is to return to normal background levels for naturally occurring substances and close to zero for man-made synthetic substances (para 10). Measures for the use and discharge of hazardous substances from offshore sources are to be consistent with the Strategy with Regard to Hazardous Substances (para 24).

[176] ibid, para 24.

footings. 'Disused installation' is also defined, in both inclusive and exclusive terms, to mean 'an offshore installation which is neither (a) serving the purpose of offshore activities for which it was originally placed within the maritime area, nor (b) serving another legitimate purpose in the maritime area authorised or regulated by the competent authority of the relevant Contracting Party'. Specifically excluded from the definition is 'any part of an offshore installation which is located below the surface of the sea-bed or . . . any concrete anchor-base associated with a floating installation which does not, and is not likely to, result in interference with other legitimate uses of the sea'. Moreover, as the title of the Decision confirms, it is addressed to installations and does not cover pipelines.

In common with the general approach of the OSPAR Convention, Decision 98/3 takes a 'prohibited unless permitted' approach to regulating decommissioning. Thus paragraph 2 prohibits the dumping, and the leaving wholly or partly in place, of any disused offshore installations within the maritime area encompassed by the Convention. Any such dumping or leaving partly or wholly *in situ* is addressed solely as a derogation from the basic prohibition. Such derogation shall only be granted by decision of the relevant authority of the Contracting Party following an assessment conducted in accordance with Annex 2, applying the criteria in Annex 1, and following consultation with the other Contracting Parties in accordance with Annex 3 of the Decision. Any resulting permits must be issued in compliance with Annex 4. **2.81**

Annex 1 sets forth four categories of disused offshore installations (excluding topsides, where land disposal is required) in respect of which derogations may be considered, namely: (1) steel platforms weighing more than 10,000 tonnes in air;[177](2) gravity-based concrete installations; (3) floating concrete installations; and (4) any concrete anchor-base which results, or is likely to result, in interference with other legitimate uses of the sea. Derogation is not automatic; Annex 1 merely sets forth a technical threshold for consideration on a case-by-case basis, following which the other provisions of the annexes must be complied with before derogation, namely a permit for offshore disposal, will be granted. This includes stipulation of the information required for, and the required approach to the assessment of, proposals for sea disposal; consultation; and the requirements of form in Annex 4 regarding the issuance of a disposal permit. In essence, therefore, all structures weighing less than 10,000 tonnes should be totally removed and concrete gravity platforms will no longer be emplaced except where strictly necessary for safety or technical reasons. Exceptionally, the footings of steel installations weighing more than 10,000 tonnes will be permitted to remain in place but the **2.82**

[177] The UK Offshore Operators Association (UKOOA) estimates that this will require the removal of at least 80% of North Sea structures: UKOOA Press Release, 23 July 1998, available at http://www.oilandgas.org.uk.

Sintra Statement emphasizes that such derogations will be avoided wherever possible by returning to land for recycling and disposal (para 22).[178]

2.83 In addition, there are specific reporting obligations under the Decision, with the expressly stated purpose of supplying information on decommissioning experience as the basis for reducing the scope of permitted derogations under Annex 1. The OSPAR Commission is charged with the task of seeking unanimous approval for amendments with this effect, for consideration by the Commission at its meeting in 2003 and at regular intervals thereafter (para 7). Implementation Reports must be supplied by OSPAR Contracting Parties to the Commission at the time of issuing the permit (para 9). Such reports must set forth the reasons for the decision and expressly indicate the extent to which views provided during the consultation required under Annex 3 have been incorporated (Annex 4, para 3). A copy of the permit must also be supplied. A further report must be provided within six months of the disposal setting forth the steps by which the disposal was carried out, an indication of any immediately observable consequences of the disposal, and an indication of the measures in place to ensure compliance with any management, monitoring, or publication obligations in the permit.

2.84 The Sintra Statement confirms that Decision 98/3 will be kept under review by the OSPAR Commission with the express aim of reducing the derogations from the general ban on sea disposal. Further legislative activity under the Convention may therefore be forthcoming, with 2003 the target set for the Commission's first attempt to achieve unanimous support for further amendments to Annex 1 reducing the scope of permitted derogations. As indicated above, Decision 98/3 is addressed only to installations: the decommissioning of disused pipelines remains a gap in the international guidance with respect to offshore decommissioning.

D. Maritime Transport of Petroleum

(1) Prevention of Marine Pollution from Oil Tankers[179]

2.85 Pollution of the sea by petroleum from tanker accidents has been the subject of a great deal of regulation as a highly visible yet relatively unimportant source of

[178] In UK waters there are 60 large steel structures, 140 small steel structures, and 11 concrete gravity-based structures. The UKOOA expressed concern regarding Decision 98/3, in particular the decision to require removal of all structures weighing less than 10,000 tonnes rather than preserving individual assessments based on a case-by-case approach: UKOOA Press Release, 23 July 1998, available at http://www.oilandgas.org.uk.

[179] See generally Brubaker, *Marine Pollution and International Law* (1993); Abecassis and Jarashow, *Oil Pollution from Ships* (2nd edn, 1985); and SV Vinogradov and JP Wagner, 'International Legal Regime for the Protection of the Marine Environment Against Operational Pollution from Offshore Petroleum Activities' in Z Gao (ed), *Environmental Regulation of Oil and Gas* (1998).

marine pollution.[180] Indeed, oil pollution from ships was the subject of the very first global convention on marine pollution, the 1954 Oil Pollution Convention (OILPOL). This was updated and replaced in 1983 with the entry into force of the 1973 International Convention for the Prevention of Pollution by Ships and the 1978 Protocol of the same name (MARPOL 1973/78).[181] There are now six annexes to MARPOL addressing different forms of vessel source pollution, as well as oil.[182] These annexes are frequently reviewed to ensure that the technical and other standards remain current.[183] An expedited amendment procedure is utilized for this purpose to ensure the timely entry into force of technical amendments in particular.[184] Annexes I (oil)[185] and II (noxious liquid substances in bulk, eg chemicals) are mandatory; Annex I entered into force on 2 October 1983, Annex II on

[180] A 1990 Joint Group of Experts on the Scientific Aspects of Marine Environmental Protection (GESAMP) Report on the *State of the Marine Environment* identifies maritime transport as responsible for only 12% of marine pollution. Land-based sources of marine pollution are estimated to be responsible for as much as 70–80% of marine pollution yet have received little attention at the international level. This may no doubt be attributed to both the high profile of oil tanker casualties, and the difficulty of regulating the diverse activities on land which contribute to contamination of the marine environment. See also GESAMP Reports and Studies No 50, *Impact of oil and related chemicals and wastes on the marine environment* (1993).

[181] 12 ILM (1973) 1319 and 17 ILM (1978) 246.

[182] Disposal of land-generated waste at sea was left out of MARPOL in consequence of the conclusion one year earlier of the 1972 London Dumping Convention, for which the IMO acts as Secretariat.

[183] For example, further amendments to Protocols I, II, III, and V were adopted in November 1994, and came into force on 3 March 1996. These are technical amendments designed to improve implementation of the Protocols by making it possible for ships to be inspected while in the ports of other Parties to the Convention to ensure that crews are able to carry out the shipboard procedures essential to prevent marine pollution. This goes beyond existing port State inspection procedures, which have been limited primarily to checking certificates and to examining the physical condition of the ship. Given that crew error has been implicated in a number of maritime casualties, this is a positive step in the effective implementation and enforcement of IMO Conventions. It has been co-ordinated with amendments taken in respect of crew safety requirements under the 1974 SOLAS Convention.

[184] The 'tacit acceptance' procedure ensures that once an amendment to the Annexes has been adopted by the Conference of the Parties, it enters into force automatically on the date fixed in the Conference (the minimum period is 16 months) unless rejected within 10 months of adoption by either one-third of the Contracting Parties *or* by Contracting Parties whose combined merchant shipping fleets represent at least 50% of world gross tonnage. This replaces the widespread but cumbersome treaty practice of requiring a two-thirds majority of Contracting Parties expressly to accept an amendment before it enters into force, a requirement further complicated by the tonnage requirements typically found in IMO Conventions.

[185] Since 1998 the IMO has been reviewing the status of tankers used as Floating Production Storage and Offloading Units (FPSOs) and Floating Storage Units (FSUs) under Annex I. Tankers used as such units are presently subject to the less stringent criteria applied to 'other platforms' under the definition of 'drilling rigs and other platforms' rather than the discharge criteria for oil tankers: see discussion in the Marine Environment Protection Committee, 41st session, 30 March–3 April 1998. Also raised in this session was a proposal by Japan that the present definition of 'oil' in Annex I as 'crude oil' and 'other oil' be replaced by a tripartite classification of 'crude oil', 'persistent refined oil', and 'other refined oil'. If adopted, this would have the effect of expanding the scope of Annex I beyond tankers to product carriers carrying persistent refined oil: *IMO Briefing 4*, 8 April 1998, available at http://www.imo.org/.

6 April 1987.[186] As of 31 October 2000 there were 112 States Parties to MARPOL Annex I/II, representing 94.23 per cent of world tonnage. Annex I sets forth, *inter alia*, oil discharge and tanker design criteria (eg load on top and segregated ballast tanks).[187] States must provide adequate reception facilities for oily residues.[188] A key regulatory device is the International Oil Pollution Prevention Certificate, which must be issued to tankers of 150 grt (gross registered tonnage) or more and to other ships of over 400 grt, after the ship has been surveyed and then for no longer than a period of five years (the interval for periodical inspections).[189] This is supplemented by a requirement for tankers and other ships to carry an Oil Record Book itemizing all operations involving oil.[190] In addition to the requirement that this record may be inspected by any other party to MARPOL, it is these documents which in certain circumstances coastal and port States are entitled to inspect under the 1982 Law of the Sea Convention, whether or not a party to MARPOL.[191] This enhancement of port State control was one of the major jurisdictional innovations of the 1982 Law of the Sea Convention in the marine pollution field. Coastal State enforcement powers are also enhanced, including the power to investigate, inspect, and in limited circumstances to arrest vessels navigating in the EEZ when a violation of applicable international rules and standards for the prevention, reduction, and control of pollution from vessels,

186 Of the remaining annexes, which are less relevant in the energy context, Annex V (garbage) entered into force on 31 December 1988 and as at 31 October 2000 had 98 Parties representing 85.98% of world tonnage. Annex III (harmful substances carried in packages) entered into force on 1 July 1992 with 94 Parties constituting 79.39% of world tonnage as at 31 October 2000. Of the 5 original annexes, only Annex IV (sewage) has not yet entered into force, with 78 ratifications constituting 43.44% of world tonnage as of 31 October 2000. Revision of this Annex to facilitate wider participation is likely.

187 See, for example, Regulations 9 and 10 (discharge) and 13–15 (construction).

188 Regulations 10 and 12. Adequate reception facilities are a requirement under 5 of MARPOL's 6 annexes (Annex III is the exception) and are a crucial factor in successfully reducing marine discharges. See further S Tromans, 'Chicken and Egg: Marine Oil Pollution, MARPOL and Port Reception Facilities' [1996] 14:2 OGLTR 513 (which examines the Red Sea and Gulf areas in particular).

189 Regulations 5 (survey) and 8 (duration).

190 Moreover, larger ships (more than 10,000 grt, called very large crude carriers, or VLCCs) must be equipped with, *inter alia*, oil discharge monitoring and control systems (Regulation 15).

191 See in particular Article 218 ('enforcement by port States'). This permits States Parties to the LOSC to institute proceedings against vessels voluntarily in port in respect of discharges from that vessel which have occurred on the high seas (ie outside the internal waters, territorial sea, or EEZ of the port State) in violation of 'applicable international rules and standards established through the competent international organization or general diplomatic conference' (Art 218(1)). Such proceedings may be brought in respect of discharges within the maritime zones of other States at their request, or at the request of the flag State, or by other States which have suffered or been threatened damage in consequence of the discharge (Art 218(2)). Art 220(1) permits enforcement by the coastal State against vessels voluntarily in port for the violation both of national laws and of applicable international rules and standards for the prevention, reduction, and control of pollution from vessels.

eg MARPOL 73/78, has occurred which threatens or causes environmental damage.[192]

On 6 July 1995 important new amendments to MARPOL 73/78 came into effect which, *inter alia*, provide for an enhanced programme of inspection applicable to all oil tankers aged five years or more; and changes to the construction requirements for tankers aged 25 years or older, including mandatory fitting of double hulls or an equivalent design once existing tankers reach this age (Regulation 13G). Double hulls are compulsory for new tankers from 1994 (Regulation 13F). These changes were adopted for existing tankers in March 1992 and took over three years to enter into force. The enhanced inspection programme requires that the hull and other elements be checked for soundness (an examination should be sufficient 'to discover substantial corrosion, significant deformation, fractures, damages or other structural deterioration') during the annual and periodic surveys already required under MARPOL 73/78. The purpose behind the new requirements for construction of ageing tankers is to close the 'quality gap' between new and old tankers in respect of construction requirements, in recognition of the ageing of existing fleets of oil tankers, the majority of which were built before MARPOL 73/78 became mandatory.[193] It addresses concerns that shipowners may have been deferring new tanker orders for which (more expensive) double hulls are mandatory and keeping older vessels in business. In April 2001 further amendments are expected to be adopted which will set forth a programme for the accelerated phasing-out of single-hull oil tankers. **2.86**

A new annex to MARPOL 73/78 on air pollution from ships was adopted on 26 September 1997. It will form Annex VI to MARPOL 73/78, which will enter into force upon receipt of the 15th ratification representing a minimum of 50 per cent of gross registered tonnage. The Protocol limits sulphur and nitrogen oxide emissions and prohibits deliberate emission of ozone-depleting substances. The latter brings MARPOL 73/78 into line with the 1987 Montreal Protocol (as amended) to the 1985 Vienna Convention on the Protection of the Ozone Layer. Under scrutiny are vessel exhaust emissions which contribute approximately 5–7 per cent of global nitrogen oxide and sulphur oxide emissions. Regulations, *inter alia*, limit the sulphur content of vessel fuel to no more than 4.5 per cent; in 'SO_2 Emission Control Areas' this is reduced to 1.5 per cent *or* ships must fit an exhaust **2.87**

[192] Art 220, especially paragraphs (3), (5), and (6). Coastal States may also institute proceedings against vessels voluntarily within port in respect of violations both of national laws (consistent with the LOSC) and of applicable international rules and standards for the prevention, reduction, and control of pollution from vessels—eg MARPOL 73/78—where such violation occurs within its territorial sea or EEZ (Art 220(1)). Similar powers may be exercised within the territorial sea in respect of violations which take place there (Art 220(2)).

[193] Of which there are more than 620 according to the International Association of Independent Tanker Owners (INTERTANKO): *IMO Briefing 4*, 8 April 1998.

gas cleaning or other system. The Baltic Sea is the only area designated in the Protocol, reflecting strong representations made during the negotiations.[194]

2.88 On 1 February 1999 North-West European waters became a 'special area' under Regulation 10 of Annex I of MARPOL (following a 1997 amendment). In consequence, from 1 August 1999 more stringent oil discharge criteria will apply in this area. Waters covered include the North Sea and its approaches,[195] the Irish Sea and its approaches, the Celtic Sea, the English Channel and its approaches, and the north-east Atlantic to the west of Ireland. Within these areas discharging into the sea oil or oily mixtures from any oil tanker or ship over 400 grt is prohibited.[196] Other special areas include the Mediterranean and Baltic Seas areas, the Antarctic Area, the Red Sea Area, and the Gulf of Aden Area.

2.89 Following the *Exxon Valdez* spill in 1989, the IMO sponsored a further convention, the 1990 International Convention on Oil Pollution Preparedness, Response and Co-operation (the OPRC Convention), which entered into force on 13 May 1995 with seventeen ratifications constituting 12.06 per cent of world tonnage.[197] It is designed to ensure that States have in place contingency plans and response mechanisms in the event of oil pollution incidents caused by ships, offshore installations, and port-handling facilities. There was agreement in 1998/99 to review the OPRC Convention in terms of extending it to hazardous and noxious substances (liability for which will be regulated under the 1996 International Convention on Liability and Compensation for Damage in Connection with the Carriage of Hazardous and Noxious Substances (HNS), when it enters into force).[198]

2.90 Two problems exist with respect to implementation of existing IMO treaties: (1) obtaining the necessary State consent to the standard-setting treaty; and (2) implementing and enforcing those standards. The first problem is to ensure that States become parties to the standard-setting conventions laying down applicable international rules and standards. The open registry (or 'flag of convenience') State of Liberia, for example, has ratified MARPOL 73/78 Annexes I and II, III, and V; Panama, on the other hand, has ratified all the Annexes. Barbados has ratified I, II, III, and V; Cyprus, I, II, and V. Haiti is not a party to MARPOL 73/78 at all. However, even a State which is not a party to a standard-setting IMO Convention or Annex thereto can be held to that standard either as a consequence

[194] *IMO News*, No 4 1995 and No 1 1996, 19–20 (paper submitted by Sweden on behalf of the Baltic States suggesting 1.5% emissions).

[195] The North Sea has enjoyed special area status under MARPOL since 1991.

[196] (1997) 4 *IMO News* 5.

[197] As of 31 October 2000 there were 55 Contracting Parties representing 48.51% of world tonnage.

[198] In March 2000 a new protocol to the OPRC Convention addressed to pollution incidents involving hazardous and noxious substances (chemicals) was adopted.

of another treaty obligation, eg Article 211 of the 1982 LOSC,[199] or as a consequence of the enforcement of those standards by port States in the exercise of their jurisdiction over vessels in their port. This is a new development provided for in Article 218[200] of the 1982 LOSC, namely, the concept of the port State, and the enforcement of IMO and other relevant standards against vessels in port, regardless of flag and regardless of whether the port State is a party to the relevant convention. Regional steps to reinforce IMO conventions have also been taken, most notably in the 1982 Paris Memorandum of Port State Control (MOU).[201] This is a non-legally binding agreement by Governments to inspect 25 per cent of ships entering their ports to ensure that the requirements of international treaties—mostly IMO treaties—are met. There is regional co-operation between port authorities to avoid needless duplication. Similar schemes have been set up in the Asia-Pacific Region (the 1993 Tokyo Memorandum); Latin America (the 1992 Vina del Mar Agreement); the Caribbean region, in 1996; and, in June 1998, an Indian Ocean MOU was agreed by fifteen States in the region. In July 1997 a Mediterranean MOU was agreed at Malta encompassing southern States not party to the Paris MOU[202] with the observers from the Paris MOU, the IMO, and the EC. There is a two-year transition period during which the IMO, with EC assistance, is training inspectors and surveyors.

Implementation problems arising out of lax flag State enforcement were further addressed by the IMO in 1993 through the establishment of a new subcommittee on flag State implementation. This was necessary because a wide range of international treaties depend upon the jurisdictional link of nationality, generally the flag State in the case of ships, for their effective enforcement. In 1997 'Guidelines to assist flag States in the implementation of IMO instruments' were adopted, with particular emphasis upon improving the implementation of four key conventions: the International Convention for the Safety of Life at Sea (SOLAS), 1974; MARPOL 73/78; the International Convention on Load Lines (LL), **2.91**

[199] Art 211(2) provides (emphasis added): 'States shall adopt laws and regulations for the prevention, reduction and control of pollution of the marine environment from vessels flying their flag or of their registry. *Such laws and regulations shall at least have the same effect as that of generally accepted international rules and standards established through the competent international organisation or general diplomatic conference.*' For general discussion of the innovative marine pollution provisions of the LOSC, see AE Boyle, 'Marine Pollution under the Law of the Sea Convention' (1985) 79 AJIL 347.

[200] See discussion at n 191 above; and GC Kasoulides, *Port State Control and Jurisdiction* (1993).

[201] Text available at 21 ILM 1 (1982). Parties to the agreement are: Belgium, Denmark, Finland, France, Germany, Greece, Ireland, Italy, the Netherlands, Norway, Poland, Portugal, Spain, Sweden, the United Kingdom, and Canada (ie all Member States of the European Union save for land-locked Luxembourg, plus Poland and Canada).

[202] Algeria, Cyprus, Egypt, Israel, Malta, Morocco, Tunisia, and Turkey, with provision for participation by further Mediterranean States.

1966; and the International Convention on Standards of Training, Certification and Watchkeeping for Seafarers (STCW), 1978.[203]

(2) Liability and Compensation for Oil Pollution Damage

2.92 There has been extensive international regulation of liability and compensation for oil pollution damage, partly in response to a series of catastrophic oil tanker casualties, including the *Torrey Canyon* (1967),[204] which caused damage to the coasts of the UK and France, and the *Amoco Cadiz* (1978), which contaminated the coast of Brittany. The 1969 International Convention on Civil Liability for Oil Pollution Damage (the CLC Convention)[205] governs the liability of shipowners for damage caused by oil pollution. The shipowner will normally be entitled to limit his or her liability arising from such damage to an amount linked to the tonnage of the vessel concerned, up to a maximum of US $22 million (14 million SDRs). Liability for oil pollution is strict under the CLC Convention where oil from a ship causes damage on the territory or territorial sea of a Contracting Party. It is the shipowner who is liable, both for the damage caused and for any preventive measures taken. Liability is strict, so there is no need to prove fault; however, some defences are available, such as civil war, *force majeure*, sabotage, or negligence by the government authority responsible for maintaining navigational aids. Thus the channelling and limiting of claims—processes familiar in other contexts, such as nuclear liability (discussed below)—is effected through the CLC which: (a) permits claims from a single pollution incident affecting a number of States to be brought in one Convention Party; (b) permits the limitation of liability by shipowners according to the tonnage of the vessel; (c) limits the defences available to shipowners, liability being strict; and (d) makes insurance against this liability compulsory.

2.93 However, unless the pollution is the fault of the shipowner, liability is limited under the Civil Liability Convention, although the supplementary 1971 International Convention on the Establishment of an International Fund for Compensation for Oil Pollution Damage (the Fund Convention)[206] may apply

---

[203] IMO Assembly Resolution A.847(20). This replaced interim guidelines issued in 1993 (Resolution A.740(18)).

[204] This incident also led directly to the conclusion of the 1969 Intervention on the High Seas Convention, subsequently extended by protocol to substances other than oil in 1973, reproduced at 9 ILM (1970) 25 and UNTS 27 (1983), respectively.

[205] Reprinted in 9 ILM (1970) 45. As of 31 October 2000 there were 63 parties to the 1969 CLC and 65 parties to the 1992 CLC Protocol. For the replacement of the 1969 CLC, see n 206 below. For further discussion of the Convention see G Gauci, *Oil Pollution at Sea* (1997); Z Ozcayir, *Liability for Oil Pollution and Collision* (1997); C de la Rue (ed), *Liability for Damage to the Marine Environment* (1993); C de la Rue and CB Anderson, *Shipping and the Environment* (1998), part V (Pollution Prevention); and DW Abecassis and RL Jarashow, *Oil Pollution from Ships* (2nd edn, 1985).

[206] Reprinted in 11 ILM (1971) 284. The Convention received its 76th ratification on 10 March 1998 (Guyana) but will be replaced by the 1992 Fund (discussed further below). As States become parties to the 1992 Fund Protocol, denunciation of the earlier CLC and Fund Conventions is

where the Civil Liability Convention does not. The Fund Convention establishes the IOPC Fund (not part of the IMO but a separate intergovernmental organization), which provides supplementary compensation in cases where the compensation by the shipowner (or insurer) is insufficient, he or she cannot pay, or one of the above defences under the CLC Convention applies.[207] It is financed by a levy on oil-importing States, ie those IOPC Fund Member States receiving crude and heavy fuel oil transported by sea. The contribution is paid by individual receivers, ie the oil industry, and not by the Member States, which report on an annual basis the amount of oil received in their ports. This places financial responsibility on oil cargo interests; oil companies establish and maintain funds in each State Party to the Convention to cover claims of this kind. Under the Fund the maximum amount payable in respect of any one claim is approximately £51 million (60 million SDRs), including the amount paid by the shipowner or insurer under the 1969 CLC. Thus cargo owners share in the burden of liability for oil pollution claims. Between its establishment in October 1978 and 31 December 1998 the IOPC Fund was involved in 92 incidents and paid out over £191 million in compensation to Government and other authorities involved in clean-up operations and to private bodies or individuals who suffered damage (eg fishing interests, hoteliers).[208] The only jurisdictional link necessary is that the damage is suffered within the territory, including the territorial sea, of a Contracting Party (ie it is independent of the flag of the vessel, the ownership of the oil, and the place where the incident occurred).

In 1984 Protocols to the CLC and Fund Conventions were negotiated which were designed to increase the level of compensation available as well as to increase the geographic coverage of the Conventions. However, these Protocols will not enter into force, partly because the United States has not ratified them, notwithstanding a vigorous stance in negotiation of the Protocols. In response to the 1989 *Exxon Valdez* oil spill in Alaska, the United States passed the federal Oil Pollution Act (OPA) in 1990, which provides a comprehensive oil pollution response, liability, and compensation regime.[209] **2.94**

required. Accordingly, the number of 1971 Fund Member States was expected to reduce from 76 to 44 by the end of 1999: *International Oil Pollution Compensation Funds Annual Report 1998* (1999) 3. In fact, as at 31 October 2000 there were only 39 parties to the 1971 Fund Convention representing 11.83% of world tonnage.

[207] See further Schiano di Pepe, 'The International Oil Pollution Compensation Funds: The Transitional Period and Beyond' [1998] 6:3 *Environmental Liability* 85.

[208] *Report on the Activities of the International Oil Pollution Compensation Funds in 1998* (1999). Annual reports are issued by the Funds, which may be contacted at iopc.fund@dircon.co.uk.

[209] The Act does not apply to US tankers overseas. See further Wagner, 'The Oil Pollution Act of 1990: An Analysis' (1990) 21 *Journal of Maritime Law and Commerce* 569–87; and CB Bonde, 'Liability for Pollution Damage and Legal Assessment of Damage to the Marine Environment' (1993) 11:2 JENRL 105.

2.95 New protocols to the CLC and Fund Conventions were concluded in 1992 which entered into force on 30 May 1996,[210] and which have the legal effect of superseding the 1984 Protocols. There are no major differences between the 1984 and 1992 Protocols, though the latter sets a lower threshold for entry into force.[211] The 1992 Protocols increase the ceiling on compensation to £115 million (135 million SDRs), including the sum actually paid by the shipowner and insurer, in respect of any one incident under the CLC. The geographic scope of the Conventions is extended to include the EEZ. Substantively the 1992 Protocols extend coverage to spills of persistent oil from unladen tankers, and permit the recovery of expenses for preventive measures even if no oil spill occurs. However, such recovery is limited to circumstances where there is a grave and imminent danger of pollution damage. Pollution damage is defined in the Protocols as:[212]

> loss or damage caused outside the ship by contamination resulting from the escape of discharge of oil from the ship, wherever such escape or discharge may occur, provided that compensation for impairment of the environment shall be limited to costs of reasonable measures of reinstatement actually undertaken or to be undertaken.[213]

2.96 Additional industry schemes mirroring the CLC and Fund Conventions, the 1969 Tanker Owners' Voluntary Agreement concerning Liability for Oil Pollution (TOVALOP)[214] and the 1971 Contract Regarding an Interim Supplement to Tanker Liability for Oil Pollution (CRISTAL),[215] operated until 20 February 1997.[216] These were voluntary agreements conceived as an interim measure to 'plug the gap' pending the entry into force of the CLC and Fund Conventions. Under TOVALOP the shipowner was contractually obliged (eg through a TOVALOP clause in the charter party) to respond immediately to an oil spill, to pay compensation, and to carry certificates as proof of the shipowner's ability to pay response costs and damages. The agreement achieved widespread participation by tankers: 97 per cent of tankers, some 6,800 in total, were covered

---

210 On this date a new organization, the 1992 Fund, came into existence which administers both the 1971 Fund under the 1978 Convention and the 1992 Fund under the 1992 Protocol.

211 As at 31 October 2000 62 States representing 85.78% of world tonnage had become party to the 1992 Fund Convention. The 1992 Fund replaced the 1971 Fund on 15 May 1998, with the 1992 Fund Convention requiring denunciation of both the 1971 CLC and Fund Conventions once a threshold (750 million tonnes of contributing oil under the 1992 Fund) has been reached.

212 See further C Redgwell, 'Compensation for oil pollution damage: quantifying environmental harm' (1992) *Marine Policy* 90–9; and EHP Brans, 'The *Braer* and the Admissibility of Claims for Pollution Damage under the 1992 Protocols to the Civil Liability and the Fund Convention' [1995] 3:4 *Environmental Liability* 61–9.

213 This definition excludes environmental damage *per se*, as well as loss of use of the environment: see further Gauci, 'Protection of the Marine Environment through the International Ship-Source Oil Pollution Compensation Regimes' (1999) 8:1 RECIEL 29.

214 Reprinted in 8 ILM (1969) 497.

215 Reprinted in 10 ILM (1971) 137.

216 Both are described and reproduced in JH Bates and C Benson, *Marine Environmental Law* (1993–), ch 4.

by TOVALOP. However, since the vast majority of claims are now settled under the international conventions and the widespread adoption of the 1992 Protocols is seen as in the best interests of industry, TOVALOP and CRISTAL were discontinued as of 20 February 1997.[217]

Further changes were effected by the 1989 International Convention on Salvage, which addresses remuneration for salvors where an oil spill has been averted or the adverse pollution effects thereof mitigated through the salvor's efforts. Salvage service may be defined as: **2.97**

> a voluntary service which saves, or helps to save, maritime property from any of the multitude of perils which are incident to navigation at sea. . . . A salvage reward is payable by the owner of maritime property which has been preserved by, or received a benefit from, salvage services notwithstanding that he did not enter into any contract for those services.[218]

The 1989 International Convention on Salvage (ICOS) was adopted in April 1989 at a conference convened by the IMO. It entered into force on 14 July 1996, having acquired the requisite fifteen ratifications for entry into force.[219] It replaces the earlier 1910 Brussels Convention on Salvage, which operated under the 'no cure, no pay' principle. This meant that a salvor would only be remunerated ('rewarded') for his/her services if the voluntary salvage operation was successful. Efforts at pollution prevention and control were not adequately taken into account. For example, a salvor might avert a more serious pollution incident by towing a stricken tanker away from shore (as the tug *Pacific* sought to do with the *Amoco Cadiz* in 1978) but without saving the ship or any cargo. The no cure, no pay principle gave salvors no incentive to attempt pollution prevention and control which was unlikely to be rewarded because of their small chance of success.[220] **2.98**

---

[217] Where an injured State is not a party to the CLC and Fund Conventions (such as the US and Iran, two major oil trading States) and/or the spill occurs in waters of a State not party to the Conventions, there will no longer be the safety net of private contractual arrangements whereby shipowners respond to the spill while legal, particularly jurisdictional, arguments take place. Choice of law questions may become more common. On the other hand, ratification of the Protocols may become more widespread, with significant advantages in claims for oil pollution compensation.

[218] Sheen, 'Convention on Salvage' (1983) 57 Tulane Law Review 1387. For further general discussion see C Hill, *Maritime Law* (5th edn, 1998); E Vincenzi, *International Salvage Law* (1992); G Brice, *Maritime Law of Salvage* (3rd edn, 1999); and C de la Rue and CB Anderson, *Shipping and the Environment* (1998), part IV.

[219] As of 31 October 2000 there were 32 Parties to the Convention, representing 29.21% of world tonnage. For background, see C Redgwell, 'The Greening of Salvage Law' (1990) *Marine Policy* 142.

[220] The fate of the salvors of the *Torrey Canyon* (1967) is instructive: 'On this occasion they suffered a double misfortune. First, one of their experienced men lost his life in the engine-room of the *Torrey Canyon.* Second, at a time when it seemed probable that the salvors were nearing success, the public outcry arising from the pollution of the English coastline was such that the government ordered the ship and the remainder of her cargo to be destroyed by fire. She was bombed by naval planes so that the oil burnt. For the salvors this inevitably meant that there was no cure': Sheen, 'Convention on Salvage' (1983) 57 Tulane Law Review 1387, 1395.

2.99 The approach adopted in the Salvage Convention is to create an 'environmental safety net' for salvors, already in practice under Lloyd's Open Form 1980[221] in relation to tankers laden with oil. This allows for the provision of security by shipowners or their insurers, coupled with a safety net related to an ascertainable amount, namely salvors' 'expenses', or a multiple thereof. Thus the salvor would receive 'a finite, quantifiable return even if his[/her] efforts failed to produce an adequate salved value in respect of ship and cargo out of which he could be remunerated'.[222] Salvors may apply for security from P&I clubs for their special compensation claims, which gives them some assurance that their pollution expenses will be met.[223] The first case to interpret the special compensation or 'safety net' provisions of Article 14 is *Semco Salvage and Marine Pte Ltd v Lancer Navigation Co (The Nagasaki Spirit)*,[224] and has led to pressure to revise the Convention.[225] The case turned on whether an element of profit could be included in the calculation of salvage award under the heading 'fair rate for equipment and personnel actually and reasonably used in the salvage operation'. The House of Lords determined that this was not intended to include an element of profit but only remuneration for actual and reasonable expenses incurred.

E. Nuclear Energy[226]

(1) Introduction

2.100 The nuclear energy sector has been the subject of considerable regulatory activity at the international level. The first international agreements, at both global and

[221] LOF 80 made limited inroads into the 'no cure, no pay' formula in respect of oil tankers fully or partly laden with potentially polluting oil. A 'safety net' award might be made against the owner of the ship where the salvor uses his/her best endeavours to prevent the escape of oil from the vessel whilst undertaking salvage operations; that in so doing the salvor is not negligent; and the salvors are not or only partially successful, or the salvor is prevented from completing the service (eg *Torrey Canyon*). LOF 90 replaced LOF 80 to take into account the changes brought about by the ICOS. In 1995 Lloyd's updated the form to coincide with the application of ICOS under English law from 1 January 1995. Such standard form contracts for salvage operations have been in use since 1892 and are periodically updated and revised.

[222] Sheen (n 220 above) 1425.

[223] In 1996 a Code of Practice was agreed between the International Salvage Union and the P&I Clubs regarding future salvage services to which Art 14 of ICOS may be applicable.

[224] [1997] 2 WLR 299; [1997] 1 Lloyd's Rep. 323 (HL); for comment see SD Girvin [1997] 3 Lloyd's Maritime and Commercial LQ 321.

[225] From the salvage industry, which had hoped for a higher reward with the element of profit included, and from the shipowners' insurers (the P&I Clubs) responsible for meeting claims under the Article 14 mechanism, notwithstanding the favourable outcome in *The Nagasaki Spirit*: see further Girvin, n 224 above, 327–38.

[226] This section is only concerned with the peaceful use of nuclear energy, and does not consider the international rules governing nuclear weapons or their use. For discussion of nuclear energy and the environment, see E Molodtsova, 'Nuclear Energy Law and International Environmental Law: An Integrated Approach' (1995) 13:4 JENRL 275.

regional level, were concerned with regulating liability and compensation for nuclear damage. However, following the Chernobyl accident in 1986, further international treaties were agreed which address early notification and assistance in the event of an international nuclear incident. In 1994 a Convention on Nuclear Safety was concluded which concerns the safe operation of land-based nuclear power plants. Given that nuclear energy activities are ultra-hazardous in character, with potentially devastating transboundary implications, this degree of international regulatory activity is unsurprising. It has been facilitated by the work of two key international organizations of relevance to the nuclear sector: the International Atomic Energy Authority (IAEA),[227] which has sponsored a number of international treaties as well as producing a number of soft law guidelines,[228] and the Nuclear Energy Agency (NEA) of the Organization for Economic Co-operation and Development (OECD), which also plays an active role in nuclear law and policy.[229]

(2) Liability and Compensation

The first generation of nuclear treaties addressed liability and compensation with a view to rendering a fledgling energy industry commercially viable. This also reflects the unsatisfactory nature of the general customary international law principles in respect of State responsibility,[230] as well as the magnitude of the potential harm. The first international treaty in the field was a regional one, concluded under the auspices of the OECD: the 1960 Paris Convention on Third Party Liability in the Field of Nuclear Energy.[231] It must be read in conjunction with the **2.101**

[227] For further discussion of this international organization, see below, Ch 3; see also the IAEA home page at http://www.iaea.org/worldatom/. Other treaties concluded under IAEA auspices not considered further here include the 1980 Convention on the Physical Protection of Nuclear Material (in force 8 February 1987, as at 18 October 2000 with 68 parties, including all EU Member States and Norway), which requires States to protect nuclear material transported in their territory and/or aboard their ships or aircraft, and the 1997 Joint Convention on the Safety of Spent Nuclear Fuel Management and the Safety of Radioactive Waste Management with 23 parties as of 14 November 2000. It requires 25 ratifications to enter into force, including 15 States each with an operational nuclear power plant.

[228] See, for example, the IAEA Regulation for the Safe Transport of Radioactive Material (1996, revised) and the IAEA Code of Practice on the International Transboundary Movement of Radioactive Waste (1990). The International Maritime Organization also has a role to play in the maritime transport of nuclear material: see, for example, the IMO Code of Safety for Nuclear Merchant Ships (1981) and the IMO Code for the Safe Carriage of Irradiated Nuclear Fuel, Plutonium and High Level Radioactive Waste in Flasks on Board Ships (the INF Code) (1993).

[229] See further the NEA website at http://www.nea.fr with useful links to national websites of the OECD Member States. The Legal Affairs Section of the NEA is responsible for the publication of the biannual *Nuclear Law Bulletin*, which analyses legislative and other developments at the national and international levels. Past issues from 1968–97, complete with index, are also available on the NEA website.

[230] See further n 7 above.

[231] See the OECD's Nuclear Energy Agency website at http://www.nea.fr/ or the mirror site at http://www.oecd.nea.org.

supplementary 1963 Brussels Convention (as amended).[232] The original Paris Convention entered into force on 1 April 1968 and at the end of 1995 had fourteen Parties;[233] the Brussels Supplementary Convention entered into force on 4 December 1974 and as of 1995 had eleven Parties.[234] These Conventions, prepared by the OECD's Nuclear Agency, are regional in scope, with participation limited to Western Europe. In addition, a global regime was established in 1963 under the auspices of the IAEA, the 1963 Vienna Convention on Civil Liability for Nuclear Damage. Similar in structure to the OECD regime, it is discussed further below.

2.102 The 'Paris/Brussels' regime is designed to elaborate and harmonize legislation relating to third-party liability to ensure that adequate compensation is paid for persons suffering nuclear damage, whilst at the same time ensuring that the development and use of nuclear energy is not thereby hindered. It achieves these two-fold aims through channelling and limiting liability. Channelling liability facilitates recovery for harm arising from nuclear activities, whilst limiting liability ensures the viability of the nuclear industry with the assurance of a quantifiable (and hence insurable) risk. The regime provides that the operator (a private entity or a State) of a nuclear installation shall be liable for damage to or loss of life of any person and for damage to or loss of any property caused by a nuclear accident in a nuclear installation or during transport of nuclear substances to and from installations.[235] Operators are held strictly[236] and exclusively liable for such damage and must be insured or have financial security sufficient to meet the minimum compensation limits set forth in the Conventions. In allocating risk the basic principle is that the polluter pays; though in practice it would be more accurate to state that the risk is spread between the risk-creator (the operator), the Government, and ultimately the public.[237] Read together, the Paris/Brussels regime sets out

[232] The Paris Convention and the Brussels Supplementary Convention have both been amended by Additional Protocols adopted in 1964 and in 1982. As discussed below, further amending protocols were adopted in 1997 which significantly improve the liability regime for nuclear damage.

[233] All EU members except for Luxembourg, Austria, and Ireland, plus Norway and Turkey.

[234] As for the Brussels Convention, save for Greece, Portugal, and Turkey.

[235] For this reason, both the Paris/Brussels and Vienna regimes are supplemented by the 1971 Convention Relating to Civil Liability in the Field of Maritime Carriage of Nuclear Material which, in relation to maritime transport, excludes from liability any person who might be held liable thereunder for damage caused by a nuclear accident where the nuclear operator is liable under the Paris or Vienna Conventions. Both the Paris and Vienna Conventions make provision for ascertaining whether it is the sending or the receiving operator which is liable.

[236] Some sources refer to liability as absolute but this is not strictly accurate since the Conventions provide for limited exculpation: a nuclear occurrence in consequence of an armed attack.

[237] See *Merlin v British Nuclear Fuels Limited* [1990] 3 WLR 383; 3 All ER 711, where the Merlins bore the economic loss occasioned by intangible damage caused to their property, a head of damage held unrecoverable under the UK legislation implementing the Paris/Brussels regime, the 1965 Nuclear Installations Act. The case was distinguished on its facts by the English Court of Appeal in *Blue Circle Industries plc v Ministry of Defence* [1999] Env LR 22.

three layers of compensation and thus spreads the risk between three tiers: (1) the nuclear operator (variable national limits but with a minimum of 5 million SDRs[238]); (2) the installation State (up to a cumulative total of 175 million SDRs); and (3) all Contracting Parties (up to a cumulative total of 300 million SDRs). As indicated, financial liability limits are set at each level—the last set by comparing GNP with number of reactors within the territory.[239] Thus in the event of a serious accident to which the Convention applies the burden of compensation would ultimately be shared across the community of nuclear States. However, there has not yet been a serious test of these compensation provisions within Western Europe. The regime did not apply to the Chernobyl incident because the Soviet Union was not a party to the Convention in 1986 (nor was the Russian Federation at the end of 2000) and the Paris Convention does not apply to nuclear incidents occurring in the territory of non-Contracting States nor to damage suffered there.[240]

In respect of routine, non-catastrophic but accidental, discharges of radiation, the regime has provided little relief to claimants. The twin hurdles of proving causation (damage caused by radiation from the installation in question) and surmounting the threshold of harm (does the harm suffered fall within the definition of damage) are difficult for litigants to surmount.[241] Moreover, the Paris Convention establishes a basic limitation period of only ten years from the nuclear occurrence in respect of bringing of claims for compensation for damage caused by a nuclear occurrence, though there is the possibility for upward derogation (Art 8(a)).[242] Any dispute between States Parties involving the interpretation or application of the Paris or Brussels Conventions is to be determined by a body established thereunder, the Nuclear Energy Tribunal, for which the NEA Head of the Legal Affairs Section acts as registrar. **2.103**

The influence of the regional Paris/Brussels regime is apparent in the global regime, the 1963 Vienna Convention on Civil Liability for Nuclear Damage. It provides for the 'absolute and exclusive' liability of the operator and the requirement of insurance or financial security to cover that liability, with the licensing **2.104**

[238] 'SDR' means Special Drawing Rights, used by the International Monetary Fund, which calculates SDRs by reference to a basket of the currencies of the 5 most important trading nations (Japan, Germany, the UK, the US, and France). A number of international treaties stipulating monetary amounts use SDRs; see the discussion of the Civil Liability and Fund Convention regime for oil pollution damage, paras 2.90–2.95 above.

[239] Art 3(b) Brussels Supplementary Convention.

[240] For general discussion see M and M Radetzki, 'Liability of Nuclear and Other Industrial Corporations for Large Scale Accident Damage' (1997) 15:4 JENRL 366.

[241] On the causation hurdle see Bowden and Isted, 'The Sellafield Childhood Leukemia Cases 1993' (1994) 53 *Nuclear Law Bulletin* 44. The threshold of harm was the principal issue in the cases cited in n 237 above.

[242] Thus, for example, the United Kingdom has a limitation period of 30 years (20 years in respect of damage caused by lost or stolen nuclear material).

State responsible for the excess. Like the Paris/Brussels regime, liability is strict, not absolute, though the defences available are so limited as to render liability virtually absolute. The Vienna Convention was concluded under the auspices of the IAEA, which was established in 1957 to encourage and facilitate the peaceful development of nuclear power and to ensure the observance of nuclear non-proliferation safeguards; a secondary responsibility was setting health and safety standards. In practice, particularly after Chernobyl, this secondary responsibility has become a primary focus of IAEA activity.[243] IAEA standards do not have direct binding force, though they clearly make a significant contribution to nuclear safety by setting international standards against which national practice may be measured, as well as forming a benchmark upon which national and regional regulation is based.

> In summary, the following main principles are reflected in the regional and global regimes:
> a) Liability is channelled exclusively to the operators of the nuclear installations;
> b) Liability of the operator is 'absolute', ie the operator is held liable irrespective of fault;
> c) Liability is limited in amount . . . ;
> d) Liability is limited in time . . . ;
> e) The operator must maintain insurance [or] other financial security for an amount corresponding to [its] liability; if such security is insufficient, the installation State is obliged to make up the difference up to the limit of the operator's liability;
> f) Jurisdiction over actions lies exclusively with the courts of the Contracting Party in whose territory the nuclear incident occurred; [and]
> g) Non-discrimination of victims on the grounds of nationality, domicile, or residence.[244]

2.105 None of the States Parties to the Paris/Brussels Conventions are also parties to the Vienna Convention, which as at 13 April 1999 had thirty-two Contracting Parties, primarily non-nuclear States.[245] In 1988, in response to Chernobyl and the perceived need to merge the regional and international approaches, a Joint Protocol was concluded, designed to link the two regimes through reciprocal liability arrangements. This creates one expanded liability regime, with the Parties to the Joint Protocol treated as though Parties to both Conventions, with a choice of

[243] PW Birnie and AE Boyle, *International Law and the Environment* (1992) 350.

[244] 'Civil Liability for Nuclear Damage: International Framework', http://www.iaea.org/worldatom/glance/legal/liability.html.

[245] Argentina, Armenia, Belarus, Bolivia, Bosnia and Herzegovina, Brazil, Bulgaria, Cameroon, Chile, Croatia, Cuba, the Czech Republic, Egypt, Estonia, Hungary, Latvia, Lithuania, Mexico, Niger, Peru, the Philippines, Poland, the Republic of Moldova, Romania, Slovakia, Slovenia, the former Yugoslav Republic of Macedonia, Trinidad and Tobago, Ukraine, Uruguay, and Yugoslavia (Serbia and Montenegro). A further 14 States have signed but not ratified the Convention, including the Russian Federation (on 8 May 1996), Spain (6 September 1963), and the United Kingdom (11 November 1964).

law rule to determine which Convention applies to a given incident. As of 31 December 1996 there were twenty Parties to the Joint Protocol, six of whom are also Parties to the Paris/Brussels regime.[246] A major weakness of the Paris/Brussels and Vienna Conventions is the small number of States possessing nuclear facilities which are Parties to either Convention, a failing only partially addressed with the 1988 Joint Protocol. It is still the case that major nuclear States such as the United States and Japan remain outside both regimes. This has led to particularly complex liability arrangements in the provision of US technical assistance to safety programmes for the remaining sixteen Chernobyl-type reactors in the territory of the former Soviet Union. A further failing in the existing liability regime is the absence of provision for the costs of environmental clean-up, such as exist, for example, in the oil pollution claims and compensation system established by the CLC and Fund Conventions (described above at paras 2.92–2.95).

In 1997 the need to modernize and improve the liability regime for nuclear damage was recognized in the conclusion of a new Convention on Supplementary Compensation for Nuclear Damage and a Protocol to Amend the 1963 Vienna Convention on Civil Liability for Nuclear Damage.[247] The Protocol increases the limit of the operator's liability to a minimum of 300 million SDRs, while the Convention increases the amounts under the Paris/Brussels regime, in recognition of the increased capacity of the insurance market. In addition to increasing the ceiling on compensation, both the Convention and the Protocol provide for an improved definition of nuclear damage,[248] extend the geographic scope of the Vienna Convention,[249] extend the limitation period within which claims may be brought for loss of life and for personal injury,[250] and provide for the jurisdiction of the coastal State over actions incurring nuclear damage during maritime transport.[251] These mirrored provisions are necessary to preserve the harmonization of the liability regimes established in consequence of the 1988 Joint Protocol. Moreover, since over two-thirds of more than 400 nuclear power plants worldwide **2.106**

[246] Denmark, Finland, Italy, the Netherlands, Norway, and Sweden. The Convention entered into force on 27 April 1992.

[247] As of 14 November 2000 only Argentina, Morocco, and Romania had become Parties to the Protocol and to the Convention. The Protocol requires 5 ratifications, whilst the Convention will enter into force following ratification by at least 5 States with a minimum of 400,000 units of installed nuclear capacity (defined in the Convention).

[248] Art I of the Convention, and Art 2 of the Protocol, define 'nuclear damage' in far greater detail than the Paris and Vienna Conventions. Included for the first time are express references to environmental damage, measures of reinstatement, and preventive measures.

[249] Art V of the Convention, and Art 3 of the Protocol, extend compensation for nuclear damage suffered beyond the territory (and the territorial sea) of a Contracting Party, to include areas in or above maritime areas beyond the territorial sea in certain circumstances. This is echoed in the jurisdictional provisions of Art XIII of the Convention and Art 12 of the Protocol.

[250] Art 8 of the Protocol.

[251] For further discussion, see the summary at http://www.iaea.org/worldatom/glance/legal/liability.html; for earlier discussion of the key issues see NEA Issue Brief No 4 (1st revision), November 1993, at http://www.nea.fr/html/brief/brief-04.html.

are not covered by either the Paris/Brussels or Vienna Conventions, increased participation in a compatible worldwide liability regime is viewed as an acute priority. A key concern therefore is to facilitate participation in this Convention through permitting States to become party without the need to become a party to the Paris/Brussels or Vienna Conventions. The 1997 Convention thus supplements systems of national compensation established either under the Paris/Brussles or Vienna Conventions by States Parties thereto, or under national systems which comply with the Annex to the 1997 Convention which sets forth in eleven key articles general provisions analogous to the existing regional and global arrangements.

(3) *Notification, Assistance, and Nuclear Safety*

2.107 In addition to these developments in respect of liability and compensation, the Chernobyl accident led to further international regulatory activity under the auspices of the IAEA in the area of nuclear safety. In 1986 two conventions were concluded, the Convention on Early Notification of a Nuclear Accident and the Convention on Assistance in the Case of a Nuclear Accident or Radiological Emergency. Both are global in scope. Unlike the Paris/Brussels and Vienna Conventions, the Early Notification and Assistance Conventions have achieved widespread support with eighty-three Parties to the Early Notification Convention[252] and seventy-eight Parties to the Assistance Convention[253] as of 4 January 1999, including in both cases the Ukrainian SSR and the Russian Federation. The Notification Convention entered into force on 27 October 1986 and the Assistance Convention on 26 February 1987. The speed with which the treaties were concluded, and their swift entry into force, are virtually unprecedented. However, this is explained partly by the absence of detailed obligations in the Conventions.

2.108 Under the Notification Convention, States Parties are required to inform, directly or through the IAEA, those States which might be affected of any transboundary release of 'radiological safety significance', a duty to notify which also exists at customary international law.[254] Detailed information regarding the accident is to be supplied to affected States and the IAEA. The Convention does not provide an objective definition or threshold for triggering this notification obligation, nor does it require States to acquire and to use monitoring equipment; however, Article 5 of the Convention does stipulate the information required to be conveyed. The Notification Convention expressly excludes military facilities,

[252] Of the 15 EU Member States and Norway, 3 have signed but not ratified (Denmark, Norway, and Portugal) while Luxembourg is not even a signatory.

[253] All the EU Member States and Norway are Contracting Parties save for Luxembourg, which has signed but not ratified.

[254] See AE Boyle, 'Nuclear Energy and International Law: An Environmental Perspective' (1989) 60 BYIL 257.

although it is possible to make a voluntary declaration on ratification of the Convention specifically to inform of military accidents, as was done by the United Kingdom for example. The provisions of the Notification Convention have been reflected in a variety of bilateral treaty arrangements, some of which strengthen the notification provisions.[255]

The Assistance Convention provides for co-operation between States and the IAEA in the event of a nuclear accident or radiological emergency to minimize the consequences and to protect life, property, and the environment from the effects of radiological releases. Assistance may be requested of the IAEA and any other State Party, but the Convention does not impose any obligation to assist;[256] nor is there any provision requiring the preparation of joint contingency plans. Incentives for assistance are provided in the form of reimbursement of costs and of certain privileges and immunities for assisting personnel and their property. Thus, in the latter instance, the assisting State may claim immunity from any legal proceedings brought by the requesting State, and seek indemnity for proceedings brought by others. **2.109**

The IAEA has important co-ordinating and information-disseminating functions under the Convention, in recognition of the need for overall co-ordination of transboundary responses in the event of a radiological emergency. The Convention also encourages bilateral and multilateral arrangements to facilitate co-operation amongst States in providing prompt assistance. Throughout, the Convention seeks to achieve a balance between the sovereignty of the requesting State, the rights of the assisting State(s), and the interests of the international community in providing a rapid response to nuclear incidents threatening or causing transboundary harm. **2.110**

The heightened importance of the IAEA's nuclear safety role[257] is well illustrated by the conclusion of a Nuclear Safety Convention under IAEA auspices in 1994.[258] It builds on soft law guidance contained in the IAEA Safety Fundamentals document 'The Safety of Nuclear Installations'. The Convention sets benchmark standards for the siting, design, construction, and operation **2.111**

[255] For example, in 1988–89 the UK concluded agreements with Norway, the Netherlands, and Denmark which require notification of an accident or activity of 'radiological safety significance' likely to have transboundary effects and of abnormal levels of radiation registered in the notifying State even if not caused by release from facilities or activities in the territory of the notifying State. There are also detailed provisions regarding the exchange of information. See Woodliffe, 'Chernobyl: Four Years On' (1990) 39 ICLQ 461, 464. See also EC Directive 87/600, which provides for the early exchange of information in the event of a radiological emergency.

[256] 'In short, [assistance] is not obligatory, it need not be sought, and it cannot be given without consent': Birnie and Boyle, n 243 above, 367.

[257] Nuclear safety is also an aspect of the work of the NEA, which since 1973 has operated a Committee on the Safety of Nuclear Installations.

[258] In force 24 October 1996: as of 12 April 1999 there were 50 Contracting Parties to the Convention, including Norway and the 15 EU Member States.

of nuclear installations, the adequacy of human and financial resources, the assessment and verification of safety, quality assurance, and emergency preparedness.[259] Peer review of national reports on implementation is the key control mechanism under this treaty, which entered into force on 24 October 1996. Such national reports are a useful source of information on national nuclear regimes.[260]

F. Energy and Environment Issues[261]

(1) Introduction

2.112 There is a potentially vast number of international treaties and instruments which bear on some aspect of energy activities, ranging from access to energy resources[262] through to the conduct of energy activities[263] and finally to regulation of the

[259] See further http://www.iaea.org/worldatom/glance/legal/nukesafety.html.

[260] See, for example, the United Kingdom's report prepared pursuant to Art 5 of the Convention, in preparation for the first meeting of the conference of the parties: http://www.open.gov.uk (1 August 1998). Reports have also been prepared by, *inter alia*, Austria, Belgium, Finland, Germany, the Netherlands, and Sweden: see http://www.iaea.org/ns/nusafe/scv_nrpt.htm#Top.

[261] An excellent example of the cross-sectoral impact of international environmental law upon the minerals industry is G Pring, J Otto, and K Naito, 'Trends in International Environmental Law Affecting the Minerals Industry' (1999) 17:1 JENRL 39 (Part I, introduction and access controls) and 151 (Part II, process controls, ie mining operations, and product controls, eg waste issues). For further general discussion of both international and domestic environmental law applicable to the petroleum sector see Z Gao, 'Environmental Regulation of Oil and Gas in the Twentieth Century and Beyond: An Introduction and Overview' in Gao (ed), *Environmental Regulation of Oil and Gas* (1998).

[262] Global treaties which may be classed in this category include: the 1982 LOSC (see above); the 1992 Convention on Biological Diversity, 31 ILM (1992) 818; the 1971 Ramsar Convention on Wetlands of International Importance Especially as Wildfowl Habitat, 11 ILM (1972) 969; and the 1972 World Heritage Convention, 11 ILM (1972) 1358. Regionally there is the 1979 Berne Convention on Conservation of European Wildlife and Habitat, (1979) ETS 104.

[263] In addition to the treaties listed above in n 262 may be added the 1991 Espoo Convention on Environmental Impact Assessment in a Transboundary Context, 30 ILM (1991) 800, and the recently concluded (1998) Aarhus Convention on Access to Information, Public Participation in Decision-Making and Access to Justice in Environmental Matters, available at http://www.unece.org/. Both apply to a wide range of energy activities and installations, including nuclear and large power plants and dams. See further paras 2.113–2.115 below. The 1992 Convention on the Transboundary Effects of Industrial Accidents, adopted under the auspices of the UNECE, applies to industrial accidents with transboundary effect arising from hazardous activities. However, the impact of this Convention on energy activities in Europe is limited by the exclusions contained within Art 2(2), which places outside the scope of application of the Convention nuclear accidents, dam failures, accidents arising from sea-bed exploration and exploitation, and spills of oil or other harmful substances at sea.

[264] In addition to GATT 1994, considered further below, other examples not considered here are the global 1989 Basel Convention on the Transboundary Movement of Hazardous Wastes and their Disposal, and the regional 1991 Bamako Convention, which covers the African continent. Only the latter conclusively applies to radioactive waste movement and disposal (which is prohibited).

movement and sale of the end product.[264] These categories are not mutually exclusive. For example, EIA procedures may be required both as an *ex ante* procedure before operations commence and subsequently as further plant and machinery is required through the operational phase of the energy activity in question to final reclamation/decommissioning. Whilst it is not possible exhaustively to explore all international instruments bearing upon energy activities, four key areas are explored below on the basis of their application to a wide range of energy activities. These are: the international regulation of environmental impact assessment and access to environmental information, air pollution, climate change, and, in the following section, energy trade and investment.

(2) *Environmental Impact Assessment and Access to Environmental Information*

The concept of environmental impact assessment (EIA) was pioneered by the United States in the 1970 National Environmental Policy Act (NEPA).[265] The impact assessment model of environmental law has spread widely. Writing in 1990 Robinson observed that: **2.113**

> jurisdictions in some thirty-five major geographic regions are today covered by EIA procedures. These governments are re-tooling their decision-making to encourage ecologically sound development.[266]

One example of the spread of the EIA in the European context is Directive 85/337/EEC on assessment of the effects of certain public and private projects on the environment.[267] This divides projects into Annex I (compulsory EIA) and Annex II (EIA is dependent on whether significant environmental effects will occur according to the nature, size, and location of the project). A number of energy projects are covered by Annex I, including the construction and decommissioning of nuclear power stations, and construction of large power plants and dams. Certain offshore oil and gas operations are likewise covered by the

---

[265] 42 USC 4321. Pub.L. 91–190 (1970).

[266] In J Owen Saunders (ed), *Legal Aspects of Sustainable Development* (1990) 22. For country summaries see A Gilpin, *Environmental Impact Assessment: Cutting edge for the twentieth-first century* (1995).

[267] [1985] OJ L 175/40, as amended by Directive 97/11/EC [1997] OJ L 73. See DG XI's home page for an introduction to the EIA activities of the EC at http://www.europa.eu.int/comm/dg11/eia/home.htm. Also relevant is Directive 90/313/EEC on Access to Environmental Information, designed to grant public access to information on the environment held by public authorities or government controlled bodies with public responsibility for the environment. Environmental 'information' is interpreted broadly and must be made available to individuals without requiring justification. Answers must be provided within a specified time, and there is a right of appeal where information is denied. The Directive also calls for periodic reports by Member States on the state of the environment. The Directive filled a distinct gap in most Member States. Like the EIA directive, there is a regional UNECE treaty (not yet in force), the 1998 Aarhus Convention on Access to Information, public participation in decision-making, and access to justice in environmental matters (see further the UNECE website, n 244 above; there are links to it on the DG XI website).

Directive: deep drilling, production development, and offshore pipelines. The 1997 amendments to the Directive make EIA compulsory for: projects producing more than 500 tonnes of oil or 500,000 m^3 of gas per day; pipelines for oil, gas, or chemical transportation over 800 mm in diameter and more than 40 km long; and installations for the storage of petroleum, petrochemical, or chemical products of 200,000 tonnes capacity or greater. Smaller oil and gas projects outwith Annex I may still be subject to EIA, depending on their nature, size, and location, either in accordance with (nationally) pre-determined thresholds or on a case-by-case basis. Public participation is part of the EIA exercise. For other projects, proximity to the coast or to a site designated under an EC Directive on wild birds or habitat[268] will be significant factors in assessing the impact of the proposed activity and whether EIA will be required.

2.114 In a transboundary context, EIA is required for certain projects by Parties to the 1991 Espoo Convention on Environmental Impact Assessment in a Transboundary Context.[269] Negotiated under the auspices of the United Nations Economic Commission for Europe, the Convention has been signed by the EC and all fifteen Member States.[270] Article 2(2) stipulates that:

> Each Party shall take the necessary legal, administrative or other measures to implement the provisions of this Convention, including, with respect to proposed activities listed in Appendix I ['List of Activities'[271]] that are likely to cause significant adverse transboundary impact, the establishment of an environmental impact assessment procedure that permits public participation and preparation of the environmental impact assessment documentation described in Appendix II ['Content of the Environmental Impact Assessment Documentation'].

[268] The application of the EC Directive implementing the 1992 Biodiversity Convention to offshore petroleum licensing was considered in *Greenpeace v X* [2000]. Greenpeace sought judicial review of petroleum licensing in the Atlantic frontier region on the basis, *inter alia*, of the failure to conserve whales, dolphins, and coral reefs in accordance with the terms of the EC Habitats Directive. It was argued that 'territory' within the Directive applies to the 200-mile zone and thus to petroleum licensing activities within that zone which may impact upon biological diversity.

[269] 30 ILM (1991) 800. The parties to the North American Free Trade Agreement (NAFTA), ie the United States, Canada, and Mexico, are considering adoption of a North American Agreement on Transboundary Environmental Impact Assessment (see http://www.cec.org/pubs_info_resources/law_treat_agree/pbl.cfm?varlan=english).

[270] As at 20 July 2000, 21 States and the EC had ratified the Espoo Convention. The Convention required 16 ratifications to enter into force. The first meeting of the conference of the parties took place in Oslo, 18–20 May 1998. For further information see the UNECE website at http://www.unece.org/env/eia.

[271] The 'List of Activities' is reminiscent of Annex I of the EC Directive and includes a number of energy-related activities, such as crude oil refineries, thermal power stations, and large-diameter oil and gas pipelines. See also Appendix III to the Convention, which sets forth 'General Criteria to Assist in the Determination of the Environmental Significance of Activities Not Listed in Appendix I', ie size and/or location and/or effects.

Environmental assessment is also employed by international financial institutions such as the EBRD[272] and the World Bank,[273] and is included in the ISO 14000 standards.[274] **2.115**

(3) Air Pollution

The 1979 Convention on Long-Range Transboundary Air Pollution (LRTAP)[275] is another regional agreement concluded under the auspices of the United Nations Economic Commission for Europe. Presently there are forty-seven Parties to the Agreement, including the fifteen EC Member States and the EC itself. The purpose of the Convention is to prevent, reduce, and control transboundary air pollution from both new and existing sources, thus embracing a potentially wide range of energy activities which contribute to air pollution. The framework approach of the Convention has allowed a step-by-step approach by States allowing 'agreement' at the outset even where there is no consensus regarding the concrete steps to be taken to address a particular environmental problem.[276] Initially only framework in character, a further eight protocols on monitoring and on specific air pollutants with specific reduction targets and timetables[277] have been added to the initial framework Convention, significantly expanding the scope of the Parties' commitments. **2.116**

---

[272] Environmental assessment procedures were established in 1992. Oil and gas developments, large-scale pipelines, and minerals operations require compulsory EIA under Appendix I: see 'Environmental Screening for Projects Requiring Environmental Assessment', *Environmental Procedures* (1992).

[273] Under Operational Directive 4.01. The Bank's Environment Department has published an *Environmental Assessment Sourcebook*: vol I is addressed to Policies, Procedures, and Cross-Sectoral Issues (World Bank Technical Paper Number 139, 1991) and vol III to Guidelines for Environmental Assessment of Energy and Industry Projects (World Bank Technical Paper Number 154, 1991). The Sourcebook is regularly updated. For general discussion of the development of EIA procedures within the Bank see I Shihata, 'The World Bank and the Environment: A Legal Perspective' in *The World Bank in a Changing World* (1991).

[274] For an excellent analysis of ISO 14000 from the petroleum industry perspective, see M Corash, 'Self-Incrimination and other Liabilities Potentially Arising from Environmental Audits, Reports and Disclosures' in Energy Law '96, the proceedings of the 12th biennial conference on petroleum, minerals, energy, and natural resources law of the International Bar Association.

[275] 18 ILM (1979) 1442.

[276] LRTAP is a particularly good example of this, with only 2 of the participating States (Norway and Sweden) initially convinced of the need for stringent reductions in SO_2 to prevent acid rain. See further E Fouéré, 'Emerging trends in international environmental agreements' in JE Carroll (ed), *International Environmental Diplomacy: The management and resolution of transfrontier environmental problems* (1988) ch 3, 35–6; and MA Levy, 'European Acid Rain: The Power of Tote-Board Diplomacy' in PM Haas, RO Keohane, and MA Levy (eds), *Institutions for the Earth: Sources of Effective International Environmental Protection* (1993) ch 3, 76.

[277] The 1984 Protocol on Long-term Financing of the Cooperative Programme for Monitoring and Evaluation of the Long-Range Transmission of Air Pollutants in Europe (EMEP); the 1985 Protocol on the Reduction of Sulphur Emissions or their Transboundary Fluxes by at least 30%; the 1988 Protocol concerning the Control of Emissions of Nitrogen Oxides or their Transboundary Fluxes; the 1991 Protocol on the Control of Emissions of Volatile Organic Compounds or their Transboundary Fluxes; the 1994 Protocol on Further Reduction of Sulphur Emissions; the 1998

2.117 LRTAP remains the only major regional agreement addressed to air pollution, reflecting the severity of the problem of acid rain in Europe. The regional character of the problem is reflected in its regulatory approach, which views the airspace of Europe as a shared resource, with regional co-ordination of pollution control and reduction measures. 'Long-range transboundary air pollution' is defined as pollution having effects at a distance such that 'it is not generally possible to distinguish the contributions of individual emission sources or groups of sources' (Art 1(b)). Pollution is likewise defined broadly, extending beyond harm to health and property to encompass harm to living resources, ecosystems, interference with amenities, and with legitimate uses of the environment (Art 1(a)). LRTAP imposes obligations to notify and to consult in the event of a significant risk of transboundary pollution, though these provisions are now amplified by the obligations contained in the Espoo Convention, discussed in para 2.114 above.

(4) Climate Change

2.118 In 1992 the UN Framework Convention on Climate Change[278] was signed by 155 States and by the EC against the backdrop of the United Nations Conference on Environment and Development.[279] This followed recognition by the General Assembly that the atmosphere is 'the common concern of mankind'[280] and the work of the Intergovernmental Panel on Climate Change (IPCC) in providing the scientific guidance necessary to regulate the emission of greenhouse gases on the international level. The Convention follows the General Assembly in recognizing that climate change and its adverse effects are the common concern of humankind (Preamble). The principal objective of the Convention is set out in

---

Protocol on Heavy Metals; and the 1998 Protocol on Persistent Organic Pollutants. A further protocol, known as the 'multi-effect, multi-pollutant agreement', was concluded in 1999 which sets new national emission limits on key air pollutants (SO_2, NH_3, NOx, and VOCs) to reduce acidification, eutrophication, and ozone pollution. For texts see http://www.unece.org/env/lrtap.

[278] 31 ILM (1992) 849. The Convention swiftly entered into force on 21 March 1994, and as at 7 September 2000 had 186 States Parties, including all the EC Member States, the EC, and Norway. For thorough discussion of the negotiation of the Convention and analysis of the resulting text see D Bodansky, 'The UN Framework Convention on Climate Change: A Commentary' (1993) 18 Yale Journal of International Law 451.

[279] For excellent background see J Heap, *Global Warming: the Complete Briefing* (2nd edn, 1997). Heap is Co-Chairman of the Scientific Assessment Working Group of the Intergovernmental Panel on Climate Change (IPCC). The IPCC was established in 1988 by UNEP and the WMO to provide scientific guidance on global warming as the foundation for international action to combat the adverse effects of resulting climate change. Its first report in 1990 indicated that under a 'business as usual' emissions scenario, global mean temperature would rise by 0.3 degrees Celsius per decade during the next century, causing significant climate change: IPCC, *Climate Change: the IPCC Scientific Assessment* (1990). These findings were substantially confirmed in the Second Report in 1992: IPCC, *1992 Supplement*, section II, para 2.

[280] See UN General Assembly Resolution 43/53 (1988): Protection of the Global Climate for Present and Future Generations of Mankind. For analysis of this phrase, see AE Boyle, 'International Law and the Protection of the Global Atmosphere: Concepts, Categories and Principles' in R Churchill and D Freestone (eds), *International Law and Global Climate Change* (1991).

Article 2 as 'stabilization of greenhouse gas concentrations in the atmosphere at a level that would prevent dangerous anthropogenic interference with the climate system'. Although framework in character, the Convention contains specific commitments in Article 4 addressed to all parties and, additionally, specifically addressed to developed States Parties. All parties are obliged to produce inventories of greenhouse gas sources[281] and sinks,[282] to formulate national and, where appropriate, regional programmes to reduce global warming, to co-operate in preparing for adaptation to the impacts of climate change, and to promote scientific research. Since these obligations are addressed to developing as well as developed States Parties, Article 4(1) qualifies these obligations by permitting parties to 'tak[e] into account their common but differentiated responsibilities and their specific national and regional development priorities'. No such qualification is made of the obligations for developed States Parties and other parties included in Annex I to the Convention (countries with economies in transition such as Poland) contained in Article 4(2). This sets forth the obligation to develop national policies and measures to mitigate the adverse effects of climate change, indicating that developed States Parties are to take the lead in modifying longer-term trends in anthropogenic emissions (Art 4(2)(a)).[283] Detailed reports on such policies are to be provided 'with the aim of returning individually or jointly to their 1990 levels . . . of carbon dioxide and other greenhouse gases not controlled by the Montreal Protocol'. Article 4(3) further provides that developed States Parties shall provide new and additional financial resources to meet the agreed full costs incurred by developing States Parties in complying with their Convention obligations. The financial mechanism which has operated provisionally under Article 11 of the Convention is the Global Environmental Facility, administered jointly by the World Bank as trustee, the UN Development Programme, and the UN Environment Programme.[284]

Notwithstanding the obligations contained in Article 4 FCCC, it was not until the negotiation of the 1997 Kyoto Protocol[285] that developed States Parties **2.119**

[281] Defined in Article 1 as 'any process or activity which releases a greenhouse gas, an aerosol or a precursor of a greenhouse gas into the atmosphere'. The chief greenhouse gases are carbon dioxide, nitrous oxide, methane, and tropospheric ozone. The UNFCCC also includes CFCs to the extent not already controlled by the 1987 Montreal Protocol to the 1985 Ozone Layer Convention.

[282] Defined in Article 1 as 'any process, activity or mechanism which removes a greenhouse gas, an aerosol or a precursor of a greenhouse gas from the atmosphere'.

[283] Sands refers to Article 4(2) as 'possibly the most opaque treaty language ever drafted': P Sands, *Principles of International Environmental Law* (1994) 277.

[284] The GEF provides incremental funding for projects in four key areas: biodiversity, climate change, ozone depletion (where not otherwise covered by the Multilateral Fund established under the 1987 Montreal Protocol to the 1985 Ozone Layer Convention), and international waters. For further details see http://www.gefweb.com.

[285] 37 ILM (1998) 22. For an excellent analysis see P Davies, 'Global Warming and the Kyoto Protocol' (1998) ICLQ 446; and (1998) 7:2 RECIEL *passim* (focus on climate change after the conclusion of the Kyoto Protocol).

committed themselves to explicit, unambiguous targets and timetables for the reduction of the chief greenhouse gases and to the development of international mechanisms for ensuring the fulfilment of these commitments. Adopted on 10 December 1997 at the third meeting of the Conference of the Parties under the FCCC, the Protocol has not yet entered into force.[286] Key mechanisms remain to be fleshed out, particularly the 'flexibility mechanisms', namely emissions trading, joint implementation, and the clean development mechanism, which are briefly described below. The core obligation of the Protocol is contained in Article 3(1), which states that Annex I Parties 'shall, individually or jointly, ensure that their aggregate anthropocentric carbon dioxide equivalent emissions' of specific greenhouse gases[287] 'do not exceed their assigned amounts' and that overall emissions of such Parties are reduced 'by at least 5 per cent below 1990 levels in the commitment period 2008–2012'. Thus for the first time specific targets and timetables are established for the reduction of greenhouse gases by Annex I Parties.[288]

2.120 In establishing targets, special provision is made for the EC 'bubble' to allow for joint action by EC Member States.[289] This is a form of joint implementation, for sharing the burden of reducing greenhouse gases between Annex I Parties, contemplated under Article 6 of the Protocol. Annex I countries may acquire 'emission reduction permits' resulting from projects with other Annex I Parties aimed at reducing emissions or enhancing natural carbon sinks. Such joint implementation is, however, expressly stated to be supplemental to dcmestic action to curb greenhouse gas emissions; thus it is not possible for Annex I Parties wholly to meet their Article 3 reduction commitments via this route. Nor is it possible to buy up emission reduction units to meet Article 3 commitments where a question of implementation has arisen in the course of the expert review of annual inventories.[290] Key elements of joint implementation remain to be addressed by the first meeting of the COP serving as a meeting of the Parties to the Protocol, when the Protocol enters into force. Most notably yet to be agreed are guidelines on implementation, including verification and reporting procedures. The extent to which emission reduction units may be utilized as 'supplemental to domestic actions' also requires clarification, given concerns that the flexibility of Article 6 may be used to avoid meeting Article 3 commitments through domestic measures. Not least, this raises

[286] As at 27 November 2000 there were 84 signatures to the Protocol and 31 ratifications. No Annex I Party has yet ratified, a reflection of the fact that much of the detail for implementation of the Protocol remains to be determined (see further paras 2.120–2.125 below). The Protocol will enter into force 90 days after it has been ratified by at least 55 of the Parties to the UNFCCC, including developed countries representing at least 55% of the total CO_2 emissions from this group.

[287] Six greenhouse gases are identified: carbon dioxide, methane, nitrous oxide, hydrofluorocarbons, per fluorocarbons, and sulphur hexafluoride.

[288] Some additional flexibility is afforded CEE Annex I Parties in accordance with Art 4(6) FCCC, such as the establishment of different base years.

[289] See further discussion in Davies, n 285 above.

[290] Protocol Art 6(4).

competition concerns, with the 'burden on business' perceived to be less where an Annex I Party relies extensively on emission reduction units in meeting Article 3 commitments. Where joint implementation is pursued, Article 4 provides that a failure to achieve joint emission reduction targets does not absolve Parties from the obligation to meet their own emission reduction targets, which are obliged to be set forth in the agreement.[291] Thus, whilst implementation may be joint, responsibility for non-compliance with targets is still that of the individual State, and the EC itself.

Article 12 of the Protocol establishes the clean development mechanism (CDM), the purpose of which is: **2.121**

> to assist Parties not included in Annex I in achieving sustainable development and in contributing to the ultimate objective of the Convention, and to assist Parties included in Annex I in achieving compliance with their quantified emission limitation and reduction commitments under Article 3.

Notwithstanding strong support from some Annex I Parties for a New Zealand proposal to make wealthier developing countries also subject to specific commitments,[292] the Protocol introduces no new commitments for developing States.[293] What Article 12 accomplishes is to provide a mechanism whereby joint implementation between Annex I and non-Annex I Parties may take place, with Annex I Parties implementing quantifiable emission reductions under Article 3 of the Protocol while non-Annex I Parties implement the obligations set forth in the Convention.[294] Private and/or public entities may participate in projects which are subject to certification and verification in order for emission reductions to be 'claimed'.[295] The mechanism is to be supervised by an executive board.[296] **2.122**

As with joint implementation between Annex I Parties, concerns that Article 3 commitments would be met wholly through the CDM are addressed in Article **2.123**

[291] A similar provision applies to the 'EC bubble': in the event of the failure by Member States acting jointly within the EC to meet their total combined level of emission reduction levels, individual Member States will remain responsible for the level of emissions notified in accordance with Art 4(2): see Art 4(6).

[292] Including Australia, Canada, Japan, and the USA. See further Davies, n 285 above.

[293] Art 10 of the Protocol reaffirms existing commitments under the Convention on the part of both Annex I and non-Annex I Parties.

[294] As Davies explains: 'The CDM has a dual purpose in that it enables developing countries to operate projects which result in emissions reductions and thus to contribute to the objective of the convention, and also allows Annex I countries who finance such projects through the CDM to use emission reductions attributable to such projects to reduce their own emission totals' (n 285 above, 457). This dual purpose is set forth in Art 12(3).

[295] Protocol Art 12(5). Only projects in which Parties participate voluntarily, which produce quantifiable long-term benefits related to the mitigation of climate change, and result in emission reductions over and above what would occur without such a certified project, will qualify for certification under Art 12(5).

[296] Protocol Art 12(4).

12(3)(b). This explicitly provides that certified emission reductions from such project activities may contribute to compliance with part of their Article 3 commitments (as determined by the COP).[297] A key concern for all three Kyoto mechanisms is to establish an appropriate level of reliance on these mechanisms, jointly and severally, in addition to domestic implementation. Setting a precise level would constitute a yardstick against which compliance with the supplementarity requirement could be measured. Finally, as with joint implementation, emission reductions deriving from CDM project activities must demonstrate that such reductions are additional to any which would occur in the absence of the certified project activity (Art 12(5)(c)).

2.124 Article 3 of the Protocol envisages an emissions trading system which will establish a market amongst Annex I Parties in emission credits. Thus, for example, if an Annex B Party[298] discovered that it risked exceeding its quota, it would have the option of acquiring some or all of the unused quota of another Annex B Party, thus increasing its total allowable emissions under the Protocol. However, it is left to the Conference of the Parties to define 'the relevant principles, modalities, rules and guidelines, in particular for verification, reporting and accountability for emissions trading'.[299] Nor is any time-scale for operationalizing emissions trading stated in the Protocol, though it is certainly expected to be operational during the first commitment period (2008–12). Any trading is expressed to be supplemental to domestic actions to meet reduction commitments;[300] limiting the operation of the trading to developed States further meets the concern expressed by developing States that such States would meet their quotas without implementing necessary domestic measures to reduce emissions simply through purchasing quota.

2.125 A great deal has therefore been left for determination by the first meeting of the Conference of the Parties serving as the meeting of the Parties to the Protocol (MOP1).[301] In practice, however, it is the meetings of the Conference of the Parties to the UNFCCC following upon the adoption by consensus of the Protocol at COP3 in December 1997 which have served as the focus for the implementation of the Protocol. COP4 took place in Buenos Aires in November 1998 and adopted a Plan of Action which establishes deadlines for finalizing the outstanding details of the Protocol.[302] Further work was carried out at COP5 in Bonn in autumn 1999,

[297] While emission reductions from jointly implemented projects in the period 2000–08 may be used by Annex I Parties in meeting their own emissions reduction target under the Protocol, projects from the pilot phase, which concluded in 1999, will not be eligible.

[298] The Protocol provides that Parties listed in Annex B may participate in emissions trading for the purposes of meeting their Article 3 commitments (Art 17).

[299] Protocol Art 17.

[300] Ibid.

[301] Note, however, that the first MOP will take place only after the Protocol enters into force, the provisions relating to which are contained in Art 24.

[302] The full text of the final report of COP4 is located at http://www.unfccc.int/.

focusing on the flexibility mechanisms and upon how better to promote technology transfer, one of the issues highlighted in the Action Plan. At COP4 the Parties agreed that the principal outstanding issues must be determined by COP6, which took place in late 2000 in The Hague but failed to reach agreement.

G. Energy Trade and Investment[303]

Reducing and eliminating tariff and non-tariff barriers to trade is one of the essential purposes of the GATT, as is reflected in the Preamble. Established in 1947, and applied provisionally until it was placed on a secure treaty footing in 1994 with the successful conclusion of the Uruguay Round of trade negotiations and the establishment of a World Trade Organization, GATT 1994 enjoys wide membership.[304] Its disciplines, which have evolved over more than fifty years of application, apply to trade in energy goods as for any other goods.[305] Thus the general principles of non-discrimination (the most-favoured-nation principle enshrined in Art I) and national treatment (Art III) apply, as does the general prohibition on the use of quantitative restrictions (Art IX). These are the cornerstones of the international trading system established under the GATT. Thus, for example, when imported oil was taxed more heavily than domestic oil under the United States' Superfund legislation, albeit for the environmental purpose of cleaning up contaminated sites in the US, this was successfully challenged as incompatible with the non-discrimination requirement of GATT Article I.[306] **2.126**

[303] For background on the relationship between trade and investment measures see ME Footer, 'Trade and Investment Measures in the Energy Charter Treaty' in T Waelde (ed), *The Energy Charter Treaty* (1996). The relevant provisions of the Energy Charter Treaty are discussed in Ch 4 below. On the GATT/WTO see generally JH Jackson, *The World Trading System* (2nd edn, 1997); JH Jackson, WJ Davey, and AO Sykes Jr, *Legal Problems in International Economic Relations* (3rd edn, 1995); and MJ Trebilcock and R Howse, *The Regulation of International Trade* (2nd edn, 1999).

[304] Croatia recently became the 140th member of the WTO (30 November 2000). For background see the WTO website at http://www.wto.org/.

[305] See generally the special issue of the JENRL devoted to international energy trade, vol 12, no 1, 1994, in particular D MacDougall, 'Trade in Energy and Natural Resources: The Role of GATT in Developing Countries' (1994) 12:1 JENRL 95, esp. 95–8. This issue also includes discussion of the trade and energy provisions of the 1987 Free Trade Agreement (Canada/US) and of the 1992 North American Free Trade Agreement (Canada/US/Mexico). For brief discussion of the differences between the FTA and the NAFTA in terms of trade in goods, including energy goods, as well as the basic provisions of the GATT, FTA, and NAFTA see Trebilcock and Howse, n 303 above, ch 2, 'The Basic Elements of the GATT, the Canada-US Free Trade Agreement, NAFTA and the European Union'.

[306] US Taxes on Petroleum and Certain Imported Substances, (1988) 34 BISD, reproduced in 27 ILM (1988) 1596. GATT permits only non-discriminatory product taxes on domestic and imported goods and prohibits tax discrimination between 'like products' or protectionist taxation of 'directly competitive or substitutable products' (Art III.4). It is prohibited under the GATT to tax in respect of unincorporated process and production methods (ie attempt to make the polluter pay at the point of import, rather than in the home country of production).

2.127 Likeness is assessed on the basis of the physical characteristics of the product, rather than, say, production methods, thus ruling out the possibility of lawfully distinguishing between products on the basis of (non-)polluting production processes and methods.[307]

2.128 Of course, certain exceptions are permitted under the GATT which are relevant for energy purposes, most notably Article XXI (national security)[308] and Article XX(g) (conservation of exhaustible natural resources).[309] The application of the latter was expressly considered in the *Reformulated Gasoline* case.[310] There regulations were passed pursuant to the United States' Clean Air Act, which sought to limit the harmful pollutants in reformulated gasoline. However, whilst permitting domestic refineries to establish baselines based on the actual refining practice over a previous defined period, the regulations did not afford the same flexibility to foreign refiners not already present in the US market. The latter were obliged to conform to a generally more restrictive baseline established by regulation; non-conforming gasoline was not allowed onto US markets.

2.129 This led refiners in, *inter alia*, Venezuela to pressure their Government successfully to complain to the GATT/WTO that such measures were contrary to the non-discrimination provisions of GATT Article I. The US Government sought to defend the measure arguing, *inter alia*, that it fell within the environmental exception of Article XX, which permits non-discriminatory and proportionate derogation from primary GATT rights for the protection of, *inter alia*, exhaustible natural resources (Art XX(g)). Whilst accepting that clean air falls within this definition, the US was not able to satisfy the requirements of the

---

[307] See WTO, *Report of the Panel in United States—Standards for Reformulated and Conventional Gasoline (Treatment of Imported Gasoline and Like Products of National Origin)*, 29 January 1996, reproduced at 35 ILM (1996) 274; and the Report of the Appellate Body, 20 May 1996, reproduced at 35 ILM (1996) 603.

[308] An exception which States tend to interpret broadly: see E Smith and D Cluchey, 'GATT, NAFTA and the Trade in Energy: A US Perspective' (1994) 12:1 JENRL 27, 44. For expansive interpretation of the national security exception under Article 36 [30] EC, see *Campus Oil Limited v Minister for Industry and Energy*, Case 72/83 [1984] ECR 2727. There an Irish requirement that oil importers purchase part of their supply from domestic refineries to safeguard domestic oil refining capacity was held to violate Art 28 [30] EC but was held to be justified under Art 30 [35] EC on the grounds of the national security exception.

[309] There are 4 requirements under Art XX(g) which must be met by an impugned measure in order to benefit from the Article XX protection. The measure must be non-discriminatory, 'primarily aimed at' conservation of resources, enforced in conjunction with restrictions on domestic products or consumption, and aimed at conserving natural resources within the jurisdiction. See further the WTO Committee on Trade and Environment, Note by the Secretariat, *GATT/WTO Dispute Settlement Practice Relating to Article XX, Paragraphs (b), (d) and (g) of GATT*, WT/CTE/W/53, 30 July 1997.

Also of potential relevance to the energy sector are Art XX(i) (export restrictions in support of domestic processing industry) and (j) (products in short supply) and Art XI.2(a) (critical shortage of essential product).

[310] n 307 above.

chapeau to Article XX. In the *Reformulated Gasoline* case the Appellate Body stressed that the chapeau is concerned with the application of the measure, and not the measure itself; ie that '[t]he chapeau, by its express terms, addresses, not so much the questioned measure or its specific contents as such, but rather the manner in which the measure is applied'. *Travaux préparatoires* indicate that this was the function intended for the chapeau: preventing abuses of Article XX exceptions. The case is noteworthy not only for its energy dimension, but also because it was the first dispute under the WTO to go to the Appellate Body of the DSB.[311]

In addition to trade in goods, the traditional concern of the GATT, the Uruguay Round of negotiations added Trade in Services and Trade-Related Aspects of Intellectual Property Rights (not further considered here), and an Agreement on Trade-Related Investment Measures (TRIMs).[312] The application of the latter to investment in the energy sector has been a matter of some discussion. The Agreement is concerned mainly (and narrowly) with the trade-related effects of investment measures. Article 2.1 provides that WTO members shall not apply any TRIM which is inconsistent with national treatment (Art II.4) nor with Article XI (prohibition on quantitative restrictions). However, 'TRIM' is not defined; instead, the Agreement provides an illustrative list which encompasses local content requirements, trade balancing requirements, foreign exchange restrictions, and domestic sales requirements. It does not apply to trade in services. International negotiations were also underway within the OECD to conclude a broader multilateral agreement on investment (MAI) but so far these have met with failure. This is largely owing to concerns regarding the scope of the MAI's provisions and their impact on domestic regulation of, *inter alia*, the environment. Instead the issue is expected to be taken up within the GATT/WTO. Thus further international regulation of cross-border investment may be anticipated. **2.130**

H. Conclusion

The purpose of this chapter has been to provide an overview of the general rules and principles of public international law which have a bearing on the regional and national regulation of energy activities, discussion of which follows below. It has only been possible to provide an outline of the breadth and depth of international regulation of relevance to the energy sector. Nonetheless, it is possible to make some general predictions as to the trends which will emerge in the international regulation of energy activities in the coming years. The first is the overlap between energy activities and other areas of international regulatory concern. **2.131**

[311] See CA Valenstein and D Hembrey, 'The WTO Gasoline Dispute: A Case Study in WTO Dispute Resolution' [1996] 14:8 OGLTR 332.

[312] See the sources cited at n 303 above.

This link was observed above (see paras 2.126–2.130) in the regulation of international trade and investment, but it may also be observed in increasing transboundary litigation relying on breach of international human rights and other obligations.[313] A further key area is climate change and the developments under the Kyoto Protocol over the next few years, which will be of profound importance for the energy sector. Linked to this is the principle of sustainable development and its enduring, if diffuse, impact upon energy activities. Another feature of the international energy landscape is the retreat from nuclear energy, a relatively heavily regulated sector on the international plane, but with the transboundary movement and disposal of radioactive waste likely to be a growing issue as installations come up for decommissioning and as recycling nuclear fuel becomes more common. This retreat from nuclear sources of energy, combined with the need to reduce greenhouse gases, is likely to lead to a closer embrace of renewable sources of energy. International regulation of these sources is in its infancy, partly owing to its relative insignificance in meeting energy demand in developed countries and to the absence of significant transboundary effects.[314] One exception to this international legislative lacuna with respect to renewables is the international regulation of international watercourses, of clear significance to hydroelectric projects.[315] There is thus little doubt that public international law will continue to have significant impact upon the conduct of energy activities at the international and transboundary levels and, increasingly, within the domestic jurisdiction of States.

[313] See n 1 above. The most notable examples are the *OK Tedi* litigation in Australia arising from Broken Hill Properties' mining operations in Papua New Guinea; the *Ogoni* case arising from Shell's activities in Nigeria; and US litigation arising from Texaco's activities in Ecuador. Whilst these are primarily instances of the application of municipal systems of law, and their conflict (the arena of private international law), public international law principles have been relied upon, thus far unsuccessfully, in attempting to impose obligations of conduct on energy companies derived from international rules regulating the conduct of States.

[314] In 1981 a United Nations Conference on New and Renewable Sources of Energy took place in Nairobi, followed by the establishment of a General Assembly Committee on the Development and Utilization of New and Renewable Sources of Energy, discussed in Ch 3.

[315] In 1997 the first multilateral agreement on international watercourses was concluded under UN auspices (preceded by numerous bilateral and regional agreements relating to specific watercourses). In the same year the International Court of Justice rendered its judgment in the Gabgikovo/Nagymoros dam dispute between Hungary and Slovakia, an illustration of the transboundary effect of such energy activities: for text of the judgment see http://www.icj-cij.org/. For analysis of this and other cases involving natural resources which have appeared on the Court's docket, see R Higgins, 'Natural Resources in the Case Law of the International Court' in A Boyle and D Freestone (eds), *International Law and Sustainable Development* (1999).

Bibliography

Books and reports

Abecassis, DW, and Jarashow, RL, *Oil Pollution from Ships* (Sweet & Maxwell, 2nd edn, 1985)

Bates, JH, and Benson, C, *Marine Environmental Law* (Lloyds of London Press, 1993–)

Birnie, P, and Boyle, AE, *International Law and the Environment* (OUP, 1992)

Blake, GH *et al.* (eds), *The Peaceful Management of Transboundary Resources* (Graham & Trotman, 1995)

Brice, G, *Maritime Law of Salvage* (Sweet & Maxwell, 3rd edn, 1999)

Brownlie, I, *Principles of Public International Law* (Oxford University Press, 5th edn, 1998)

—— *The Rule of Law in International Affairs* (Nijhoff, 1998)

Brubaker, D, *Marine Pollution and International Law* (Belhaven, 1993)

Churchill, R, and Lowe, AV, *The Law of the Sea* (Manchester University Press, 3rd edn, 1999)

Dupuy, R-J, and Vignes, D (eds), *A Handbook on the New Law of the Sea* (Nijhoff, 1991), 2 volumes

Fox, H (ed), *Joint Development of Offshore Oil and Gas* (BIICL, 1989/90), 2 volumes

Gao, Z (ed), *Environmental Regulation of Oil and Gas* (Kluwer, 1998)

Gauci, G, *Oil Pollution at Sea* (Wiley, 1997)

GESAMP Reports and Studies No. 50, *Impact of oil and related chemicals and wastes on the marine environment* (1993).

Gilpin, A, *Environmental Impact Assessment: Cutting edge for the twenty-first century* (CUP, 1995)

Haas, P, Keohane, RO, and Levy, MA, (eds), *Institutions for the Earth: Sources of effective environmental protection* (MIT Press, 1993)

Harris, DJ, *Cases and Materials on International Law* (Sweet & Maxwell, 5th edn, 1998)

Heap, J, *Global Warming: the Complete Briefing* (CUP, 2nd edn, 1997)

Higgins, R, *Problems and Process: International Law and How We Use It* (Clarendon Press, 1994)

Hill, A *et al.* (eds), *Daintith and Willoughby U.K. Oil & Gas Law* (Sweet & Maxwell, 3rd edn, 1999)

Hill, C, *Maritime Law* (Lloyds of London Press, 5th edn, 1998)

van Hoof, D, *Rethinking the Sources of International Law* (Kluwer, 1983)

IOPC, *Report on the Activities of the International Oil Pollution Compensation Funds in 1998* (IOPC, 1999)

IPCC, *Climate Change: the IPCC Scientific Assessment* (1990) and Second Report, IPCC, *1992 Supplement*

Jackson, JH, *The World Trading System* (MIT Press, 2nd edn, 1997)

—— Davey, WJ, and Sykes Jr., AO, *Legal Problems in International Economic Relations* (West Publishing, 3rd edn, 1995)

Jennings, R, and Watts, A (eds), *Oppenheim's International Law*, vol. I (Longman, 9th edn, 1996)

Kasoulides, GC, *Port State Control and Jurisdiction* (Nijhoff, 1993)

Lillich, RB, and Magraw, DB (eds), *The Iran–United States Claims Tribunal: Its contribution to the law of state responsibility* (Transnational Publishers, 1998)

Lowe, AV, *Extraterritorial Jurisdiction: An Annotated Collection of Legal Materials* (Grotius Press, 1983)

McGoldrick, D, *International Relations Law of the European Union* (Longman, 1997)

Malanczuk, P, *Akehurst's Modern Introduction to International Law* (Routledge, 7th rev. edn, 1997)

Merrills, JG, *International Dispute Settlement* (Cambridge University Press, 3rd edn, 1999)

Mouri, A, *The International Law of Expropriation as Reflected in the Work of the Iran–U.S. Claims Tribunal* (Nijhoff, 1994)

Nandan, SV, Rosenne, S, and Grandy, NR (eds), *The United Nations Convention on the Law of the Sea 1982: A Commentary* (Nijhoff, 1993), 5 volumes

Ozcayir, Z, *Liability for Oil Pollution and Collision* (Lloyds of London Press, 1997)

Rothwell, DR, *The Polar Regions and the Development of International Law* (Cambridge University Press, 1996)

de la Rue, C (ed), *Liability for Damage to the Marine Environment* (Lloyds of London Press, 1993)

—— and Anderson, CB, *Shipping and the Environment* (Lloyds of London Press, 1998)

Rummel-Bulska, I, and Osafo, S (eds), *Selected Multilateral Treaties in the Field of the Environment* (UNEP, 1991)

Sand, P, *Marine Environment Law in the United Nations Environment Programme: An Emergent Eco-Regime* (Tycooly, 1988)

Sand, PH, *Lessons Learned in Global Environmental Governance* (World Resources Institute, 1990)

Sands, P, *Principles of International Environmental Law* (MUP, 1994)

Owen Saunders, J (ed), *Legal Aspects of Sustainable Development* (Canadian Institute of Resources Law, 1990)

Shaw, M, *International Law* (Cambridge University Press, 4th edn, 1997)

Schrijver, N, *Sovereignty over Natural Resources: Balancing rights and duties* (Cambridge University Press, 1997)

Trebilcock, MJ, and Howse, R, *The Regulation of International Trade* (Routledge, 2nd edn, 1999)

Vincenzi, E, *International Salvage Law* (Lloyds of London Press, 1992)

World Bank, *Environmental Assessment Sourcebook*, Vols I (World Bank Technical Paper Number 139, 1991) and III (World Bank Technical Paper Number 154, 1991), with regular updates

WTO Committee on Trade and Environment, Note by the Secretariat, *GATT/WTO Dispute Settlement Practice Relating to Article XX, Paragraphs (b), (d) and (g) of GATT*, WT/CTE/W/53, 30 July 1997

Articles and book chapters

Akehurst, M, 'Custom as a Source of International Law' (1974–5) XLVII *British Year Book of International Law* 1

Anderson, D, 'Legal Implications of the Entry into Force of the United Nations Convention on the Law of the Sea' (1995) 44:2 *International and Comparative Law Quarterly* 313

Ande, CB, 'Liability for Pollution Damage and Legal Assessment of Damage to the Marine Environment' (1993) 11:2 JENRL 105

Asante, S, 'International Law and Foreign Investment: a Reappraisal' (1988) 37:3 *International and Comparative Law Quarterly* 588

Bodansky, D, 'The UN Framework Convention on Climate Change: A Commentary' (1993) 18 *Yale Journal of International Law* 451

Bowett, D, 'Jurisdiction: Changing Patterns of Authority over Activities and Resources' (1982) 53 *British Year Book of International Law* 1

Boyle, AE, 'Marine Pollution under the Law of the Sea Convention' (1985) 79 *American Journal of International Law* 347

—— 'Nuclear Energy and International Law: An Environmental Perspective' (1989) 60 *British Year Book of International Law* 257

—— 'International Law and the Protection of the Global Atmosphere: Concepts, Categories and Principles', in R Churchill and D Freestone (eds), *International Law and Global Climate Change* (Nijhoff, 1991)

Brans, EHP, 'The Braer and the Admissibility of Claims for Pollution Damage under the 1992 Protocols to the Civil Liability and the Fund Convention' [1995] 3:4 *Environmental Liability* 61

Carver, J, and Englefield, G, 'An International Pipeline Authority: The Case for the Central Asian Pipeline Organisation' [1995] 13:8 *OGLTR* 291

Chatterjee, SK, 'The Charter of Economic Rights and Duties of States: An Evaluation 15 Years On' (1991) 40:3 *International and Comparative Law Quarterly* 669

Cheng, Bin, 'United Nations Resolutions on Outer Space: "Instant" International Customary Law' (1965) 5 *Indian Journal of International Law* 23.

Chinkin, C, 'The Challenge of Soft Law' (1989) 38 *International and Comparative Law Quarterly* 850

Corash, M, 'Self-Incrimination and Other Liabilities Potentially Arising from Environmental Audits Reports and Disclosure'. *Energy Law* '96

Davies, P, 'Global Warming and the Kyoto Protocol' (1998) 47 *International and Comparative Law Quarterly* 446

de la Fayette, L, 'The OSPAR Convention Comes into Force: Continuity and Progress' (1999) 14:2 *The International Journal of Marine and Coastal Law* 247

Footer, ME, 'Trade and Investment Measures in the Energy Charter Treaty', in T Waelde (ed), *The Energy Charter Treaty* (Kluwer, 1996)

Fouéré, E, 'Emerging Trends in International Environmental Agreements', in J E Carroll (ed), *International Environmental Diplomacy: The management and resolution of transfrontier environmental problems* (Cambridge University Press, 1988)

Gao, Z, 'Current Issues of International Law on Offshore Abandonment, with Special Reference to the United Kingdom' (1997) 28 *Ocean Development & International Law* 59

—— 'Environmental Regulation of Oil and Gas in the Twentieth Century and Beyond: An Introduction and Overview', in ibid. (ed.), *Environmental Regulation of Oil and Gas* (Kluwer, 1998)

Gardam, J, 'Energy and the Law of Armed Conflict' (1997) 15:2 *JENRL* 87

Gauci, G, 'Protection of the Marine Environment through the International Ship–Source Oil Pollution Compensation Regimes' (1999) 8:1 *Review of European Community & International Environmental Law* 29

Girvin, SD, 'The Nagasaki Spirit' [1997] 3 *Lloyd's Maritime and Commercial Law Quarterly* 321

Higgins, R, 'Abandonment of Energy Sites and Facilities: Relevant International Law' (1993) 11 *JENRL* 6

Igiehon, 'The Abandonment Controversy: From Development of International Law to the Brent Spar Incident—"Economy" Overshadowing Environmental Protection?' [1996] 7 *OGLTR* 298

Ikenna, NE, ' "International Petroleum Law" as a Distinct Legal Discipline' (1996) 8:2 *African Journal of International and Comparative Law* 428

Johnson, D, 'The Preparation of the 1958 Geneva Conference on the Law of the Sea' (1958) 8 *International and Comparative Law Quarterly* 122

Kirk, E, 'The 1996 Protocol to the London Dumping Convention and the Brent Spar' (1997) 46:4 *International and Comparative Law Quarterly* 826

Koers, AW, 'The Third United Nations Conference on the Law of the Sea: some remarks on its contribution towards the making of international law', in W P Heere (ed), *International Law and its Sources: Liber Amicorum Maarten Bos* (1989)

Levy, MA, 'European Acid Rain: The Power of Tote-Board Diplomacy', in P M Haas, R O Keohane, and M A Levy (eds), *Institutions for the Earth: Sources of Effective International Environmental Protection* (MIT Press, 1993)

MacDougall, D, 'Trade in Energy and Natural Resources: The Role of GATT in Developing Countries' (1994) 12:1 *JENRL* 95

Mann, FA, 'The Doctrine of Jurisdiction in International Law' (1964–I) 113 *Recueil de Cours* 9

Molodtsova, E, 'Nuclear Energy Law and International Environmental Law: An Integrated Approach' (1995) 13:4 *JENRL* 275

Nelson, D, 'Submarine Cables and Pipelines', in Dupuy and Vignes (eds), *A Handbook on the New Law of the Sea* (1991), Vol. 2

Norton, PM, 'Back to the Future: Expropriation and the Energy Charter Treaty', in TW Waelde, (ed), *The Energy Charter Treaty* (Kluwer, 1996)

Ong, D, 'Alternative Joint Development Regimes: A Comparison of the Malaysia/Thailand Joint Development Agreement and the Australia/Indonesia Timor Gap Zone of Cooperation Treaty' [1992] 10:8 *OGTLR* 462

—— 'Joint Development of the Spratly Islands' Marine Resources' [1993] 11:5 *OGTLR* 158

Paasivirto, E, 'Internationalization and Stabilization of Contracts versus State Sovereignty' (1989) 60 *BYBIL* 315

Patton, E, 'Gulf War: After Effects and Legal Consequences' (1993) 11:2 *JENRL* 98

Pepe, Schiano di, 'The International Oil Pollution Compensation Funds: The Transitional Period and Beyond' [1998] 6:3 *Environmental Liability* 85

Picton-Turbervill, G, 'Decommissioning of Offshore Installations—The Legal Aspects' [1998] 6 *Oil and Gas Law and Taxation Law Review* 196

Pring, G, Otto, J, and Naito, K, 'Trends in International Environmental Law Affecting the Minerals Industry' (1999) 17:1 *JENRL* 39

Redgwell, C, 'Multilateral Environmental Treaty-Making', in V Gowlland-Debbas (ed), *Multilateral Treaty-Making* (Nijhoff, 2000)

—— 'Non-Compliance Procedures and the Climate Change Convention', in B Chambers (ed), *Global Climate Governance: Inter-linkages between the Kyoto Protocol and other Multilateral Regimes* (UNU/IAS, 1998)

—— 'Compensation for Oil Pollution Damage: Quantifying Environmental Harm' (1992) *Marine Policy* 90

—— 'The Greening of Salvage Law' (1990) *Marine Policy* 142

Roggenkamp, MM, 'Petroleum Pipelines in the North Sea: Questions of Jurisdiction and Practical Status' (1998) 16:1 *JENRL* 92

Roque, HHL, 'China's Claim to the Spratly Islands under International Law' (1997) 15:3 *JENRL* 189

Salacuse, JW, 'BIT by BIT: The Growth of Bilateral Investment Treaties and their Impact on Foreign Investment in Developing Countries' (1990) 24 *International Lawyer* 655

Sas, B, 'Legal Issues in the Control of the Construction and Operation of Pipelines and the Issue of Transit in the Caspian and Black Sea Regimes' [1995] 13:7 *OGLTR* 274

Sheen, B, 'Convention on Salvage' (1983) 57 *Tulane Law Review* 1387

Shihata, I, 'The World Bank and the Environment—A Legal Perspective', in *The World Bank in a Changing World* (Nijhoff, 1991)

Side, Baines, and Young, 'Current Controls for Abandonment and Disposal of Offshore Installations at Sea' (1993) 17:5 *Marine Policy* 354

Smith E, and Cluchey, D, 'GATT, NAFTA and the Trade in Energy: A US Perspective' (1994) 12:1 *JENRL* 27

Sornorajah, M, 'Compensation for Nationalization: The Provisions in the Energy Charter Treaty', in TW Waelde, (ed), *The Energy Charter Treaty* (Kluwer, 1996)

Thomas, JA, 'New Developments in the International Legal Regime for the Offshore Oil and Gas Industry' [1994] 12:4 *OGLTR* 110

Tromans, S, 'Chicken and Egg: Marine Oil Pollution, MARPOL and Port Reception Facilities' [1996] 14:2 *OGLTR* 513

Valenstein CA, and Hembrey, D, 'The WTO Gasoline Dispute: A Case Study in WTO Dispute Resolution' [1996] 14:8 *OGLTR* 332

Van Dyke, 'Sea Shipment of Japanese Plutonium under International Law' (1993) 24 *Ocean Development and International Law* 399

—— 'Applying the Precautionary Principle to Ocean Shipments of Radioactive Waste' (1996) 27 *Ocean Development and International Law* 379

Vinogradov SV, and Wagner, JP, 'International Legal Regime for the Protection of the Marine Environment Against Operational Pollution from Offshore Petroleum Activities', in Z Gao (ed), *Environmental Regulation of Oil and Gas* (Kluwer, 1998)

Waelde, T, 'A Requiem for the New International Economic Order', in N Al-Nauimi and R Meese (eds), *International Legal Issues Arising under the United Nations Decade of International Law* (Nijhoff, 1995)

Wagner, S, 'The Oil Pollution Act of 1990: An Analysis' (1990) 21 *Journal of Maritime Law and Commerce* 569

Woodliffe, J, 'Chernobyl: Four Years On' (1990) 39 *International and Comparative Law Quarterly* 461

Websites

Climate Change Convention *http://www.unfccc.de*
DG XI *http://www.europa.eu.int/comm/dg11/*
Global Environmental Facility *http://www.gefweb.com*
IAEA *http://www.iaea.org/worldatom/*
ICJ *http://www.icj-cij.org/*
IMO *http://www.imo.org/*
NAFTA *http://www.cec.org/*
OECD's Nuclear Energy Agency *http://www.nea.fr/* (or the mirror site at *http://www.oecd.nea.org*)
OSPAR *http://www.ospar.org/*
UKOOA *http://www.oilandgas.org.uk*
UNCC *http://www.unorg.ch/uncc*
UN Department of Ocean Affairs and the Law of the Sea (DOALOS) *http://www.un.org/Depts/los/los_docs.htm#CLCL-Docs*
UN Economic Commission for Europe *http://www.unece.org/*
WTO *http://www.wto.org/*

3

INTERNATIONAL ORGANIZATIONS AND THEIR ACTIVITIES IN THE ENERGY SECTOR

Heike Krieger and Claas de Boer[1] *with Helga Steeg*

[1] The authors would like to thank Mrs Helga Steeg for her invaluable help in providing the material comprising Part I (the IEA).

A. Introduction

3.01 The purpose of this chapter is to provide an overview of the international organizations active in the energy sector. It focuses on an introduction into the structure and functioning of these organizations in order to describe the institutional framework within which international organizations contribute to the development and application of international policy and international law on energy activities.[2] The organizations' contributions are illustrated by examples of their work in the energy sector. However, a single chapter can only give an overview of the breadth of activities undertaken by these organizations.

(1) The Need for International Co-operation in an Institutionalized Framework

3.02 The origin and production of energy as well as the transportation and consumption thereof require energy regulation on an international level. Whereas some States have vast resources in oil, coal, and gas, others have a demand for these. States have to rely on other States to turn their resources into monetary advantages or to fulfil their energy needs. This interdependence makes it necessary for States to co-operate with each other.[3]

3.03 The process of production involves investment decisions in the energy-related industry. These decisions depend not only on the interest to exploit local resources but also on the local legislation applying to the investment. Not only rules on foreign investment but also different environmental regulations within different national jurisdictions strongly influence companies' decisions on location. They have a strong impact on the construction and operation of plants producing energy and comparable goods. Consequently, there is an economic interest to co-ordinate regulations with respect to the interaction between energy and environment. Provisions of international environmental law set out a substantial framework for the energy-related industry. A further need for international regulation and monitoring developed with the use of nuclear power. For security reasons, an international monitoring system is in the interest of all States.

3.04 The supply of energy brings up issues of trade and transit. Network bound energy trade across borders involves the application of national rules through the co-operation of national gas and electricity companies. However, European States

[2] See ch 2.
[3] See HG Schermers/NM Blokker, *International Institutional Law* (3rd edn, 1995), § 4, 2.

may not impede free trade within their territories. Free movement of goods and services is guaranteed by international agreements governing trade principles. However, energy issues in Europe must still be put into a broader context. Production or use of energy in one region may have an impact in a totally different region. This is now acknowledged with regard to environmental impacts of the production and use of energy. The issues concerned range from the side effects of nuclear power to the climatic consequences of accelerated deforestation by the use of tropical wood for cooking and heating in the absence of electricity. However, there is the further danger of a strong growth in demand for limited natural resources by a growing world population.[4] Therefore, energy regulation in Europe cannot be seen as distinct from global developments. European States depend not only on European but also on institutionalized international co-operation with respect to the interaction between energy, environment, and sustainable development.[5]

However, any interest in regulating energy on an international level is counteracted by the view of each State that energy is of vital national importance for a State to perform its fundamental functions. The history of economic and foreign policy reflects the tension between international co-operation and national interests. From the disputes between France and Germany, partly fought for the coal basin in Alsace Lorraine and the Ruhr area, to the Kuwait War in 1990–91 and the crisis in Chechnya, an area with oil and gas reserves, disputes concerning sovereignty over natural resources have provoked a number of wars. States in the Middle East with their specific strategic location became world powers only because of their oil reserves in the follow-up of the first oil crisis in 1974. Still, the crisis demonstrated to the industrialized Member States of the Organization for Economic Co-operation and Development (OECD) that their economic problems cannot be solved solely by national energy policies. **3.05**

(2) Legal Aspects of International Institutions

All the matters described above are of vital concern to States' long-term interests, so that they cannot be dealt with on an *ad hoc* basis. One way of securing a continuing and self-sustaining system of energy relations is to establish an institutional framework, which can provide for a forum of co-operation, consultations, and negotiations. An international organization can be defined as an association of equal States with a permanent character established by and based upon a treaty under the regime of public international law, through which the States delegate certain powers. The association pursues common goals which may differ from **3.06**

[4] See G Handl, 'Environmental Protection and Development in Third World Countries: Common Destiny, Common Responsibility', New York University Journal of International Law & Politics 20 (1988) 603.

[5] According to Art 174 EC Treaty, community policies pursue the goal to promote measures at the international level to deal with regional and worldwide environmental problems.

political intentions of Member States. Therefore, it must have its own special organs which fulfil particular functions within the organization and represent the particular intention of the organization.[6] Thus, an international organization can be considered as a subject of international law. It is capable of possessing international rights and duties, and it has the capacity to maintain its rights and duties by bringing international claims.[7] An international organization may conclude bilateral or multilateral agreements with other international organizations or with States.[8] Whether an international organization has treaty-making power depends on its constitution[9] or on other rules of the organization. Such a power must be conferred expressly or implicitly as a competence necessary to enable the organization to carry out its functions effectively.[10] International organizations have some flexibility in interpreting their powers as contained in the express provisions of the institution's treaty base in order to respond to developments that have occurred since the development of the organization.[11] This 'implied powers doctrine' means that 'a term is being read into the organization's statute not in order to modify it or add to the members' burdens, but in order to give effect to what they agreed by becoming parties to the constitutional treaty'.[12]

3.07 Organizations can be used for direct legally binding decision-making, for political consultations to mutually influence policies in Member States, for technical assistance, and for financial support. These functions determine to a large extent the institutional structure of an international organization.[13] Generally, an international organization consists of an assembly of all Member States as its supreme authority, an executive council responsible for enacting decisions and guiding the organization between the sessions of the assembly, and a secretariat in charge of the organization's administration. International organizations, as international persons with functions often analogous to those of sovereign States, require the concession of

---

[6] R Bindschedler, 'International Organisations, General Aspects', in R Bernhardt (ed), *Encyclopedia of Public International Law (EPIL)*, Inst. 5 (1983) 120; I Seidl-Hohenveldern/G Loibl, *Das Recht der Internationalen Organisationen* (6th edn, 1996) para 0105.

[7] Reparations for Injuries suffered in the Service of the United Nations ICJ Reports 1949 174/179.

[8] Vienna Convention on Treaties concluded between States and International Organizations or between International Organizations, ILM 25 (1986) 83, which had not entered into force by 2000.

[9] The term constitution is applied to international organizations by the International Law Commission (ILC), Report of the Commission, UN Doc A/5209, Yearbook of the ILC 1962, vol II, 165; however, constitution is only used in a substantive, not a formal sense. The constitution is a constituent multilateral treaty.

[10] D Bowett, *The Law of International Institutions* (4th edn, 1982) 342.

[11] 'Reparation for Injuries Suffered in the Service of the United Nations', ICJ Reports 1949, 174 (182) and Schermers/Blokker, *International Institutional Law* (3rd edn, 1995), § 232–6, 158–63.

[12] K Skubiszewski, 'Implied Powers of International Organisations', in Y Dinstein (ed), *International Law at a Time of Perplexity, Essays in Honour of Shabtai Rosenne* (1989) 860.

[13] Schermers/Blokker, *International Institutional Law* (3rd edn, 1995), § 8, 4; § 12, 7.

privileges and immunities of these organizations, their premises, their staff, and their members' representatives. Immunities are provided for in the basic constitutional text which is supplemented by a detailed agreement.[14] Apart from these multilateral agreements the organization normally concludes a special, bilateral agreement with the host State in whose territory the headquarters or other offices of the organization are located.[15] These agreements impose legal obligations on States under international law which are implemented by municipal legislation.[16] Immunities may attach to the organization as such or to the personnel. With regard to the former there are immunities from jurisdiction, inviolability of premises and archives, fiscal privileges, and freedom of communications,[17] while the latter may have immunity from the jurisdiction of municipal courts. In any event, the organization remains responsible for the consequences of its actions. The responsibility of the organization can be determined through administrative tribunals, claims commissions, arbitration clauses in contracts, or even through bilateral negotiations between States or individuals and the organization.

There are sometimes disputes about the constitutional legality of the acts of international organizations or Member States where no judicial procedure exists which could render a binding judgment. In these cases Member States might withdraw in protest or might be expelled for constantly neglecting their obligations. These consequences, however, result from a political decision and do not substitute a judicial settlement of a constitutional dispute.[18] **3.08**

International organizations can be classified according to their functions. This criterion can be considered from three points of view: the extent of co-operation it is the organization's mission to bring about, the range covered by the organization (ie is it confined to a clearly delimited field of action), and the means used to effect such co-operation.[19] Consequently, one can distinguish universal from closed organizations, special (technical) from general organizations, and intergovernmental from supranational organizations. The latter two mark the difference between the majority of organizations concerned with co-operation between the executive branches of the governments of the Member States and an organization like the EC. While the former are basically not superior to their Member States, which cannot be bound against their will, the latter has power to take decisions which bind the Member States as well as directly binding the citizens of **3.09**

[14] eg for the UN: General Convention on the Privileges and Immunities of the UN, I UNTS 15–32; Convention on the Privileges and Immunities of the Specialised Agencies, 33 UNTS 261–302.

[15] eg Headquarters Agreement between the UN and the USA, II UNTS 11–41.

[16] eg UK International Organizations (Privileges and Immunities) Act of 12 July 1950.

[17] See D Bowett, *The Law of International Institutions* (4th edn, 1982) 345–62.

[18] ibid, 363f.

[19] For detailed treatment of classification see Schermers/Blokker, *International Institutional Law* (3rd edn, 1995), § 48–65, 33–44.

those States.[20] However, the notion of 'intergovernmental organization' is also used to differentiate between organizations founded on a treaty between States (such as the FAO or the WHO) and those founded on a treaty between governments (such as the IMF or the OECD) or to emphasize the distinction from non-governmental organizations.[21]

3.10 With regard to organizations active in the energy sector, one can distinguish between organizations which have an energy mandate only (eg the IAEA), those which have comprehensive mandates which enable them by way of interpretation to deal with energy (eg the UN), and other special organizations whose mandate may allow for particular energy activities as a means to achieve the organizations' aims (eg the IMO). There are also regional organizations with either a single energy mandate or a more general one allowing for energy activities where European States do not participate: eg the Organization of Oil Exporting Countries (OPEC),[22] the Organization of Latin American Countries (OLADE), and Asia Pacific Economic Co-operation (APEC).

3.11 The framework of international institutional law provides a 'kind of superstructure over and above the society of States',[23] although States are still sovereign. Due to the political implications of public international law the framework of international energy relations has to be considered not only from a legal point of view, but also from a political perspective. Both these aspects are reflected in institutionalized relations between States. Key organizations working on energy are: the United Nations and their specialized agencies, the IAEA, the WTO, World Bank, IMF, OECD and its IEA and NEA, EBRD, the Nordic Council, CERN, the EU, and several non-governmental organizations.

B. Energy Activities within the United Nations System[24]

(1) Introduction

3.12 The UN officially came into existence on 24 October 1945 with fifty-one original Member States.[25] The Charter established six principal organs of the UN: the General Assembly, the Security Council, the Economic and Social Council, the

[20] ibid, § 58–61, 39–42.

[21] Bowett, n 17 above, 11f.; non-governmental organizations are dealt with in this chapter in paras 3.124–3.129.

[22] See *Europa Yearbook 1998* (1998) 227–31.

[23] H Mosler, The International Society as Legal Community, Recueil des cours—Academie de droit international de le Hague, 140 (1974–IV) 189.

[24] See http//:www.un.org; JP Cot/A Pellet (ed), *La charte des Nations Unies*, 2nd edn (1991); B Simma, *The Charter of the United Nations: A Commentary* (1994).

[25] The UN had 189 Member States as at November 2000. Non-Members are the Holy See and Switzerland.

Trusteeship Council, the Secretariat, and the International Court of Justice in The Hague. The regular programme budget of the UN is approved by the General Assembly biennially. The programme budget for the two-year period 2000–1 amounted to US$ 2.535 million.[26] The purposes of the UN, as set forth in the Charter, are: to maintain international peace and security; to develop friendly relations among nations; to co-operate internationally in solving international economic, social, cultural, and humanitarian problems and in promoting respect for human rights and fundamental freedoms; and to be a centre for harmonizing the actions of the nations in attaining these common ends. Neither energy nor the protection of the environment are explicitly mentioned in the Charter. However, interpreting the purposes of the UN broadly according to the doctrine of implied powers, the UN is competent to deal with energy and environment issues as part of its task to solve international economic and social problems.

Entities within the UN system are undertaking a wide range of energy activities. **3.13** The nature of the activities is mainly dictated by the mandates of the legislative or governing bodies of the entities concerned. A large number of programmes have been carried out in technical co-operation with developing countries, including advisory services, training workshops and seminars, publications, and database management. The main activities revolve around analysis and projection, financial resources and investment, institutions and capacity building, co-operation and co-ordination, information flow, field projects, and monitoring. Many of the projects and programmes were devised to respond to perceived needs of Member States or to assist specific countries, mainly developing countries or countries with economies in transition, eg those in Central and Eastern Europe.

In the context of sustainable development, environmental concerns, including **3.14** conservation and the promotion of new and renewable sources of energy, have gained prominence. Some activities have changed little over the years. They respond to such issues as ensuring the security of energy supplies and analysing current and future supply/demand requirements. In its work the UN tries to underline that the outlook on energy demand is related to probable changes in the global energy balance, with increasing use of natural gas and hydropower and declining dependency on oil and coal taking into account the increasing demand for power, particularly in developing countries. Other activities reflect emerging issues, such as increased concern about the environmental impact of the development and use of energy resources. In order to implement the UN Framework Convention on Climate Change (UNFCCC)[27] the question of how to cut greenhouse gas emissions from increased use of fossil fuels is of major importance to the UN.[28] For the last twenty years legally binding environmental standards have

[26] UN Doc A/Res/54/250 A–C, 9 February 2000.

[27] Dated 9.5.1992, ILM 31 (1992) 851; see ch 2 above.

[28] UN Doc E/1994/75, 16 June 1994.

been developed by international organizations, beginning with the UN's involvement in attempting to protect the environment in 1972, notably Principle 21 of the UN Conference on the Human Environment.[29] This effort can be seen as part of the UN's work in sponsoring law-making activities, especially through the International Law Commission.[30]

(2) The General Assembly and the Security Council

3.15 The General Assembly has a broad political mandate, being virtually coextensive with that of the UN.[31] It is the only organ with representatives from all the UN Member States. Thus, as the main deliberative organ of the UN, the General Assembly is competent to deal with energy matters. Resolutions of the General Assembly are adopted by consensus or majority vote. Each State has one vote.[32] These resolutions are not legally binding. However, they may help to prove the existence of an *opinio juris sive necessitatis,* necessary for the formation of a new rule of customary law.[33] For instance, when in 1962 the General Assembly unanimously adopted the Resolution on Permanent Sovereignty over Natural Resources, it introduced this concept into law.[34] Some General Assembly resolutions, especially in the follow-up of the United Nations Conference on Environment and Development held in Rio de Janeiro in 1992, have touched upon energy matters.[35] Furthermore, the Assembly reviews the reports of the International Atomic Energy Agency by adopting resolutions.[36]

---

[29] *UN Yearbook* 1972, 320–1; UN Conferences are temporarily convened and relate to special subjects. They are usually sponsored by the General Assembly or the ECOSOC and may lead to the adoption of a declaration or a treaty.

[30] eg Convention on the Non-navigational Uses of International Watercourses, UN Doc A/Res/51/206 of 16 January 1997.

[31] Art 10 UN Charter.

[32] Art 18 UN Charter.

[33] G Ress, 'Interpretation', in B Simma, *The Charter of the United Nations: A Commentary* (1994) para 2.

[34] UN Doc A/Res/1803 (XVII) of 14 December 1962.

[35] In Resolution 36/193 (17.12.1981) the GA endorsed the Nairobi Programme of Action for the Development and Utilization of New and Renewable Sources of Energy, approved in the UN Conference on New and Renewable Sources of Energy. In Resolution 45/209 (20.3.1991) the GA stressed the need for comprehensive national, bilateral, and multilateral measures to accelerate the exploration and development of energy resources in developing countries. It emphasized in Resolution 45/208 (25.3.1991) the need for the development of new and renewable sources of energy in accordance with the fundamental objectives of the Nairobi Programme of Action for the Development and Utilization of New and Renewable Sources of Energy. By Resolution 47/190 (16.3.1993) the GA endorsed the Rio Declaration in Environment and Development, Agenda 21 and the non-legally binding Authoritative Statement of Principles for a Global Consensus in the Management, Conservation, and Sustainable Development of All Types of Forests, adopted by the UN Conference on Environment and Development in 14.6.1992; UN Doc A/Conf.151/26, 12.8–28.9.1992.

[36] eg UN Doc A/50/9 of 1.11.1995; see paras 3.13–3.79 below.

The Security Council may deal with energy-related questions if they touch upon world peace.[37] It may be taken as a sign of the increasing conflict potential of energy and the environment that the Security Council passed a Resolution in an energy-environment context during the Gulf War in 1991. In Cease-fire Resolution 687 (8.4.1991), paragraph 16, the Council held Iraq 'liable under international law for any direct loss, damage, and depletion of natural resources, as a result of Iraq's unlawful invasion and occupation of Kuwait' in August 1990. Paragraphs 18 and 19 of this Resolution laid the institutional foundations of the United Nations Compensation Commission (UNCC). The UNCC was established in 1991 as a subsidiary organ of the Security Council. Its mandate is to receive, process, and evaluate claims and to pay compensation for losses and damages suffered by individuals, corporations, governments, and international organizations as a direct result of Iraq's invasion and occupation of Kuwait.[38] With regard to energy law, category 'E' claims are of particular importance. 'E1' claims are oil sector claims. Approximately 100 oil sector claims with a total value of US$ 40 billion have been filed with the UNCC.[39] Funds to pay the awards of compensation are drawn from the UN Compensation Fund, which receives 30 per cent of the revenues generated from the export of Iraqi petroleum and petroleum products, pursuant to Security Council Resolution 705 (1991). Since December 1996 the Compensation Fund has received 30 per cent of the revenue derived from Iraqi oil exports under the 'oil-for-food' mechanism established by Security Council Resolution 986 (1995).[40] The exact amount coming into the Fund each month depends on the quantity of oil sold by Iraq and the price of oil. The payment of awards to individual claimants commenced in 1994, and to governments and corporations in 1999. By November 2000 the Commission had paid out approximately US$9 billion to successful claimants. 3.16

The UNCC might be described as a new structure to develop State responsibility. The Council's decisions form the framework of a massive claims system 3.17

[37] Art 24 UN Charter. It is disputed in the literature whether extreme environmental hazards amount to threats to international peace (Art 39 UN Charter); see ND White, *The Law of International Organizations* (1996) 256; Summit of World Leaders, UN Doc S/23500, 31.1.1992.

[38] See Report of the Secretary-General pursuant to paragraph 19 of Security Council Resolution 687 (1991), UN Doc S/22559 (1991), and UN Doc S/Res/692 (1991). The UNCC consists of a Governing Council, composed of representatives of the 15 current members of the Security Council at any given time, a Secretariat, and commissioners, ie individual experts. Since its establishment approximately 2.6 million claims have been filed with the UNCC seeking compensation in excess of US$ 300 billion. By November 2000 the UNCC had resolved approximately 2.5 million claims awarding US$ 31 billion; see further Crook, 'The UNCC: A New Structure to Enforce State Responsibility', AJIL 87 (1993) 144–57; S Boelaert-Suominen, 'Iraqi War Reparations and the Laws of War', Austrian Journal of Public Law 50 (1996) 225–316.

[39] UN Doc S/AC.26/1997/WP.1, para 26.

[40] Extended by Security Council Resolutions 1111 (1997), 1143 (1997), 1153 (1998), 1210 (1998), 1242 (1999), 1275 (1999), 1280 (1999), 1281 (1999), 1284 (1999), 1293 (2000), and 1302 (2000).

intended to offer relief to large numbers of claimants through comparatively simple and expeditious administrative procedures. The UNCC has also contributed to issues of liability for environmental damage. Resolution 687 stated that 'direct loss, damage, including environmental damage and the depletion of natural resources, or injury to foreign governments' were compensable. Some claimants in Category 'B' claims, concerning death and serious injuries, asserted that they suffer from serious respiratory problems arising from the air pollution as a result of the burning oil fields. The panel took the view that environmental damage from burning oil wells was caused by Iraqi occupation forces and therefore compensable.[41]

(3) The Economic and Social Council (ECOSOC)

3.18 As the ECOSOC is competent to promote world co-operation on economic, social, cultural, and humanitarian problems, many energy-related activities are carried out within the ECOSOC framework.[42] The range of the Council's work makes it essential that it works through subsidiary bodies. In energy matters the various regional economic commissions are active as well as two standing committees (see paras 3.19–3.25). Moreover, pursuant to Article 63 UN Charter the ECOSOC has entered into relationship agreements with specialized agencies, thus establishing a framework for the co-ordination of energy-related activities between the UN and other specialized agencies. The intergovernmental agencies are separate, autonomous organizations. Sixteen of the agencies are known as 'specialized agencies', a term used in the UN Charter.[43] They report annually to the Economic and Social Council. The ECOSOC discusses reports on energy activities annually, but it is entitled only to make recommendations to the General Assembly and specialized agencies, not to make binding decisions.

The Economic Commission for Europe (ECE)

3.19 The regional commissions were unforeseen in the original ECOSOC framework. However, as economic and social problems vary tremendously by region these problems can be better dealt with at a regional level.[44] The ECE is one of the five regional commissions which build a forum for dialogue where agreements can be negotiated and policies harmonized.[45] The ECE can deal directly with govern-

[41] UN Doc S/AC.26/1994/1, 38.

[42] Art 62 UN Charter. The 54 ECOSOC members are elected by the General Assembly so as to reflect an equitable geographical distribution, see Art 61 UN Charter. One of the 5 permanent members has been elected since the outset and China since 1972; the ECOSOC is financed out of the regular UN budget; see FL Kirgis, 'UN ECOSOC' in R Bernhardt (ed), *EPIL*, Inst. 5 (1983) 310–14; R Lagoni, 'Economic and Social Council' in R Wolfrum (ed), *United Nations: Law, Policies and Practice* (1995) vol 1, 461–9.

[43] For details see *Europa World Yearbook 2000* (2000) 70–113.

[44] D Bowett, *The Law of International Institutions* (4th edn, 1982) 70.

[45] The ECE has 55 Member States including all the States covered in the present book. See http://www.unece.org.

ments as well as report back to the ECOSOC. Standard-setting activities in the field of transport and trade have a direct impact on enterprises. Therefore, more than seventy international professional organizations have obtained consultative status with the ECE in order to participate in its meetings.

The programmes of the ECE in energy matters are both broad and comprehensive: the ECE is concerned with fuel-related programmes and new and renewable sources of energy. It works on the interface between energy and environment through its Committee on Sustainable Energy. The programme of work also includes coal mining and utilization, electric power, and the gas industry. Energy trade, trade facilitation and infrastructure as well as electricity interconnections are part of the ECE's work.[46] The Ad Hoc Group of Experts on Extension of European Electricity Interconnection co-ordinates the activities of a project to develop possible synchronous interconnections of electric power networks in Europe for the years 2000 and 2010. An important branch concerns policy discussions and decision-making involving the Working Party on Gas with its Gas Centre and the Ad Hoc Group of Experts on Coal and Thermal Power.[47] The ECE enhances co-operation between governments, private sector, and NGOs within the ECE region. In 1994 it developed programmes for building up national and regional capacities to promote an environmental impact assessment of coal production and the use of technologies.[48] **3.20**

A step towards co-ordination and co-operation between different international organizations can be seen in the Energy Efficiency 2000 Project. This project assists Central and Eastern European countries to enhance their energy efficiency and security to ease the energy supply constraints of economic transition. It promotes the rational use, efficiency, and conservation of energy, *inter alia*, by assisting these countries in meeting their international environmental treaty obligations under the UN Framework Convention on Climate Change, for instance.[49] **3.21**

Other subsidiary bodies of ECOSOC

By Resolution 1998/46 of 31 July 1998 the Economic and Social Council decided to establish the Committee on Energy and Natural Resources for **3.22**

---

[46] Committee on New and Renewable Sources of Energy and on Energy for Development, Report of the Secretary-General on Energy Activities Within and Outside the UN System, UN Doc E/C.13/1994/4, 21.1.1994 para 8; the Secretary-General's report on energy activities is updated on a regular basis; see UN Doc E/C.13/1996/7, 6.2.1996 and UN Doc E/C.13/1998/7, 12.2.1998; UN Doc E/C.14/2000/6, 6.7.2000. For further analysis, see K Sahlgren, *Le rôle de la Commission Economique pour l'Europe (CEE) dans l'élaboration du droit international économique*, (1986).

[47] Established by the Committee on Sustainable Energy in November 1997 to succeed the former Working Party on Coal and Working Party on Electric Power.

[48] See *Yearbook of the United Nations* (1994) vol 48, 728.

[49] See http://www.ee2000.net.

Development.[50] According to its terms of reference, the new Committee is comprised of two sub-groups of twelve government-nominated experts, approved by the Economic and Social Council. One sub-group deals with issues relating to energy, the other with issues relating to water resources. The Committee meets once every two years. In order to enhance co-ordination between UN bodies dealing with energy issues the Committee has to ensure that its own work programme will be coherent with the work programme of the Commission on Sustainable Development so that it can contribute to the Commission's work.

3.23 During its second session in 2000 the Committee had on its agenda the issues of energy and the residential sector, renewable sources of energy, financial mechanisms, and economic instruments to speed up the investment in sustainable energy development, and the status of hydroelectricity generation. The discussions are predominantly based on reports of the UN Secretary-General.[51]

3.24 The Commission on Sustainable Development was established by ECOSOC Resolution 1993/207 in accordance with General Assembly Resolution 47/191. The functions of the Commission, as set out in paragraphs 3 to 5 of Resolution 47/191, relate to monitoring progress in the implementation of Agenda 21. Agenda 21 was adopted at Rio de Janeiro by the United Nations Conference on Environment and Development in 1992.[52] It is an action plan consisting of forty chapters to guide environment-related policies of governments, such as energy, agriculture, and forestry. As Agenda 21 is implemented by national governments and international organizations, such institutional means to attain co-ordination and consistency among policies are particularly necessary. The Commission is composed of fifty-three members elected from the Member States of the UN and members of the specialized agencies for a term of office of three years. The Commission meets annually. It aims to foster the link between energy and sustainable development. The Commission requested, for instance, the Secretary-General's Report on Ongoing Energy Activities in the UN System[53] and provides recommendations to the General Assembly, through the ECOSOC, on the

[50] The former Committee on Natural Resources and the Committee on New and Renewable Sources of Energy and on Energy for Development were merged into a single expert body. The latter committee had previously taken over the mandate of the Committee on the Development and Utilization of New and Renewable Sources of Energy, including the consideration of its relation to environment and development. It also retained the mandate of the Committee on Natural Resources regarding energy. For information on the former Committees' work see *inter alia*: UN Doc E/C.7/1994/10, 31.1.1994; UN Doc E/C.7/1994/11, 17.12.1993; UN Doc E/C.13/1996/3, 15.1.1996.

[51] See *inter alia*: UN Doc E/C.14/2000/8, 22.6.2000; UN Doc E/C.14/2000/9, 20.8.2000; UN Doc E/C.14/2000/4, 22.6.2000; UN Doc E/C.14/2000/5, 22.6.2000.

[52] UN Doc A/Conf.151/26, 12.8.–28.9.1992.

[53] Report of the Secretary-General on Inventory of Ongoing Energy-Related Programmes and Activities of Entities Within the UN System, on Co-ordination of Such Activities and on Arrangements Needed to Foster the Linkage between Energy and Sustainable Development Within the System, UN Doc E/CN.17/1997/7, 27.1.1997.

basis of these reports. The Nineteenth Special Session of the General Assembly recognized the need for a movement towards sustainable patterns of production, distribution, and use of energy in its programme for the further implementation of Agenda 21. In establishing the Multi-year Programme of Work for the Commission on Sustainable Development, the Special Session decided that the sectoral theme of the ninth session of the Commission in 2001 would be Atmosphere/Energy, with Energy/Transport as the economic sector.[54] To prepare for the ninth session of the Commission an Ad Hoc Open-Ended Intergovernmental Group of Experts on Energy and Sustainable Development has been established.[55]

The majority of the UN agencies and entities work in the field of energy.[56] This **3.25** leads to a duplication of efforts and an overlap of activities. The UN is increasingly aware of this situation. Co-operation in the field of energy within the UN system has been undertaken on a formal basis since 1998 by the Ad Hoc Inter-Agency Task Force in order to prepare the ninth session of the Commission on Sustainable Development. In its initial efforts the Task Force has established a common system-wide approach to energy and has facilitated communication and exchange of information on a regular basis within the United Nations system. Therefore, the Secretary-General has suggested a continuation of the Task Force or a comparable instrument in order to ensure continued co-operation on a permanent basis.[57]

(4) The Work of the UN Secretariat's Departments

In 1997 three UN Departments which worked in the economic and social field **3.26** merged: the Department for Policy Co-ordination and Sustainable Development, the Department for Economic and Social Information and Policy Analysis, and the Department for Development Support and Management Services. This provided a good opportunity to co-ordinate and thereby strengthen the activities in the energy sector. The newly created Department of Economic and Social Affairs analyses global energy trends and their impact on development and the environment, taking into account the relevant provisions of Agenda 21. It also undertakes several tasks concerning energy, such as compiling information and setting up a database on energy statistics. Statistical information on energy is

[54] UN Doc A/Res/S-19/2, 19.9.1997.

[55] UN Doc A/Res/S-19/2, 19.9.1997, para 46. For information on the work of the Group of Experts see: Agenda and proposed programme of work, UN Doc E/CN.17/ESD/2000/1, 3.2.2000 and Report of the Ad Hoc Open-ended Intergovernmental Group of Experts on Energy and Sustainable Development, UN Doc E/CN.17/2000/12, 27.3.2000.

[56] A matrix of energy-related activities is available at http://www.un.org/esa/sustdev/iaenr.htm; it is continuously updated as a reference for UN entities.

[57] Report of the Secretary-General on Co-ordination of Energy Activities within the United Nations System, UN Doc E/C.14/2000/6, 6.7.2000, para 9-11/14.

provided through such publications as the *Energy Statistics Yearbook* and *Energy Balances and Electricity Profiles*, while global energy trends are reported through the World Economic and Social Survey, which is issued annually.[58] The objectives are to guarantee a flow of universally accessible analyses of the current and the projected balance between global energy supply and demand.[59] The Energy and Transport Branch in the Department's Division for Sustainable Development handles energy-related issues supporting the Commission on Sustainable Development.

3.27 The Department focuses on operational activities, including advisory services, project formulation, and implementation, as well as organizing meetings and workshops. The Department for Development Support and Management Services, for instance, provided technical advisory services on 60 developing countries, and executed 115 energy projects in 40 developing countries, with a total budget of US$ 110 million in 1994. It assisted a number of countries, mostly in developing States, in the expansion of their indigenous oil and gas potential and in oil and gas legislation and agreements, as well as in the preparation and evaluation of competitive bidding for licences. In Europe, seminars on energy have been sponsored in the Russian Federation, Finland, and Sweden. Some countries were also assisted in setting up computerized geoscience databases, modernizing mining laws and regulations, promoting investment, and improving the small-scale mining sector.[60]

3.28 Finally, the Secretary-General serves as depository of a great number of international conventions relevant in the energy sector,[61] for instance the UNFCCC and the United Nations Convention on the Law of the Seas (UNCLOS).[62]

(5) The United Nations Development Programme (UNDP)

3.29 The UNDP is a major actor in the mobilization of financial resources for energy-related projects next to the World Bank. This stems from the UNDP's mandate: the organization was established by the GA to help developing countries to increase the wealth-producing capabilities of their natural and human resources. Among the countries benefiting from UNDP Field Programmes are those of Central and Eastern Europe. The UNDP was created in 1965 by the merger of two other UN programmes. Membership is coincident with membership of the

[58] See Report of the Secretary-General on Possibilities of Strengthening the Co-ordination of the Organizations and Bodies of the UN System in the Field of Energy Within the Framework of the Administrative Committee on Co-ordination, UN Doc A/52/175, 18.6.1997, para 23.

[59] Committee on New and Renewable Sources of Energy and on Energy for Development, Report of the Secretary-General on Energy Activities Within and Outside the UN System, UN Doc E/C.13/1994/4, 21.1.1994, para 14.

[60] *Yearbook of the United Nations* (1994) vol 48, 918.

[61] Multilateral Treaties deposited with the Secretary-General, UN Doc ST/LEG/SER.E/.

[62] UN Doc A/CONF.62/122, 7.10.1982.

UN itself.[63] The UNDP is supervised by the Executive Board; the 36 members of this body are elected by the ECOSOC from candidates representing the various regional groups, from both developing and developed countries.[64] UNDP decisions might result in resolutions of the ECOSOC or even the General Assembly. However, since the UNDP is a programme, it is a semi-autonomous agency with no independent decision-making power. Council decisions are submitted to the ECOSOC, which may accept a decision, advise changes, or pass it to the appropriate committee of the General Assembly for action when the decision is outside UNDP's mandate.[65] The Secretary-General appoints a UNDP Administrator, who is responsible for the management of the programme. The UNDP provides technological assistance in developing countries and works with more than 150 governments and 40 international agencies. The programme serves as the world's largest channel for funding and co-ordinating international technical co-operation activities.[66] Assistance is mostly non-monetary, comprising the provision of experts' services, consultancies, equipment, and fellowship for advanced studies abroad. UNDP activities are primarily financed in two ways. Fifty-eight per cent of the programme's financial requirements comes from counterpart resources furnished by the recipient countries themselves. However, the remainder is funded by voluntary contributions from Western and Eastern industrialized nations.[67]

The organization has improved the co-ordination of its projects in the energy sector by establishing an energy umbrella programme. The Sustainable Energy and Environment Division (SEED) provides the policy framework for energy and environmental activities.[68] One of the Seed units is the Energy and Atmosphere Programme (EAP). It was created with the objective of focusing UNDP supported activities in the field of energy. EAP promotes sustainable energy policies and carries forward UNDP positions. It implements the UNDP Sustainable Energy Global Programme which focuses on support for energy programme development, fundraising, and strategic initiatives. EAP identifies and implements projects funded through UNDP's Energy Account. The Energy Account is **3.30**

[63] The Consolidation of the Special Fund and the Expanded Programme of Technical Assistance in a United Nations Development Programme, UN Doc A/Res/2029 (XX), 22 November 1965; The Capacity of the United Nations Development System, UN Doc A/Res/2688 (XXV), 11 December 1970.

[64] See UN Doc A/Res/48/162, 14.1.1994, paras 21–30. Eight members come from African, 7 from Asian, 4 from East European, 5 from Latin American, and 12 from West European and other States; the term of membership is 3 years with the possibility of re-election.

[65] C Wallace, 'UNDP' in R Bernhardt (ed), *EPIL*, vol 5 (1983) 308.

[66] *Europa World Yearbook 2000* (2000) 44–6; for general analysis of the programme see J Seth, 'The Structural Evolution of the United Nations Development Programme', Indian JIL 20 (1980) 596–615.

[67] H Sahlmann/B Blank, 'UNDP' in R Wolfrum (ed), *United Nations: Law, Policies and Practice* (1995) vol 2, 1287; C Wallace, 'UNDP' in R Bernhardt (ed), *EPIL*, vol 5 (1983) 309.

[68] Further information at: http://www.undp.org/seed; visited in November 2000.

the main vehicle to support specific, country-based project activities. Through its 'Financing Energy Services for Small Scale Energy Users' (FINESSE) programme, it assists some twenty countries in Asia and Africa to promote renewable energy technologies and efficiency services to residential, commercial, agro-industrial, and institutional energy users. UNDP and the World Bank co-sponsored the Energy Sector Managing Assistance Programme (ESMAP), which renders technical assistance to governments of developing transitional economies. EAP also carries out UNDP's activities concerned with the 1987 Montreal Protocol on Substances that Deplete the Ozone Layer (Montreal Protocol).[69] The UNDP used to fund many projects through its Indicative Project Funding (IPF).[70] In 1994 there were 122 ongoing projects under UNDP IPF funding.[71] However, the UNDP Executive Board decided in its Decision 95/23 (16.6.1995) to replace the IPF with a funding modality based on programme quality (so-called Successor Arrangements) and not on fixed national funding allocations. UNDP core resources are now allocated through TRAC.[72] In 1996 an estimated US$ 43 million was expended to countries in Europe and the Commonwealth of Independent States.[73]

3.31 The Global Environment Facility (GEF) plays a significant role in funding energy projects, involving environmentally sound technology.[74] The programme is managed jointly by UNDP, the World Bank, and the UNEP. Its aim is to support developing countries in implementing projects which benefit the global, and not just the local, environment. In Agenda 21 the GEF was recognized as a vital source and was designated as the operator of the financial mechanism.[75] In 1996 the GEF energy projects cost some US$ 291 million[76] and ranged from the installation of renewable energy systems to the monitoring of greenhouse gases. The Scientific

[69] See Ch 2 above.

[70] IPF is the projected amount available for programme activities in a country over a 5-year period. The calculations are made on the basis of population, per capita gross national product, and additional criteria such as deteriorating terms of trade.

[71] This represents some US$ 104 million in UNDP funding and US$ 46 million in cost-sharing from other sources, usually national funding: Committee on New and Renewable Sources of Energy and on Energy for Development, Report of the Secretary-General on Energy Activities of the UN System, UN Doc E/C.13/1994/4, 21.1.1994, para 24.

[72] Target for Resources Assignment from the Core. Under this system, a country obtains at least a base level of resources and can receive substantially higher levels of resources by formulating high-leverage, high-impact programmes in the area of focus, particularly for activities designed to contribute to the overriding priority of poverty elimination.

[73] *Europa World Yearbook 2000* (2000), 44–6.

[74] ILM 30 (1991) 1735; ILM 33 (1994) 1273. The programme was formally established in 1991; the GEF Trust Fund was founded by a World Bank Resolution on 14 March 1991; the Member States of the EC participate in GEF. In 1994 GEF was transformed from an experimental programme into a permanent financial mechanism.

[75] Agenda 21, ch 33, para 33.14, UN Doc A/Conf.151/26, 12.8.–28.9.1992.

[76] Committee on New and Renewable Sources of Energy and on Energy for Development, Report of the Secretary-General on Energy Activities of the UN System, UN Doc E/C.13/1996/7, 6 February 1996, para 20.

and Technical Advisory Panel of the GEF has established a working group on energy mitigation strategies.[77] The following case study is an example of the GEF projects carried out by UNDP.

A GEF project to be implemented by the UNDP in Bulgaria between 1996 and **3.32**
2002 concerns the UNFCC. On 16 March 1995 Bulgaria ratified the UNFCC, which requires the Bulgarian Government to reduce greenhouse gas emissions. The Government intends to achieve this goal by implementing energy-efficiency measures. A project sponsored by the World Bank aims at mitigating greenhouse gas emissions. It concentrates its efforts on one municipality, the city of Gabrovo. Gabrovo served as a test case for designing and realizing a national programme for Bulgaria. The project results will be distributed through a municipal energy network. An Energy and Environment Office in Gabrovo is supposed to prepare a model energy policy and model energy legislation for a Bulgarian municipality. These offices will be expanded over Bulgaria. The project also supports training programmes. The targets of the programme include the reduction of energy consumption for street lighting systems in Gabrovo as well as the reduction of energy losses in the heat generation system, transmission facilities, and end uses in order to reduce greenhouse gas emissions. The project is co-financed by GEF, the Bulgarian Government, USAID, and PHARE.[78]

(6) The United Nations Environmental Programme (UNEP)

UNEP was established by the General Assembly in 1972, following recommen- **3.33**
dations of the 1972 UN Conference on the Human Environment, in Stockholm, Sweden.[79] The General Assembly, through the ECOSOC, is the supreme authority for the programme.[80] Headquartered in Nairobi, UNEP aims to maintain a constant watch on the changing state of the environment by using a wide range of data and techniques.[81] It has the mandate to advance the development and implementation of international environmental law. It provides a mechanism through which separate environmental efforts by intergovernmental, non-governmental, national, and regional bodies are interrelated. UNEP promotes environmental science by co-ordinating activities within the UN system. Many of UNEP's

[77] Further information http://www.unep.org/unep/gef; http://www.undp.org/gef and http://www.gefweg.org; visited in November 2000.

[78] http://www.undp.org/gef/bulgaria.htm. The central aim of PHARE, a financial economic aid programme, is to provide assistance for economic reform, structural adjustment, and sustainable development in Central and Eastern Europe and to help to convert centralized economies into economies based on market-oriented mechanisms; see Council Regulation EEC No 3906/89 of 18.12.1989.

[79] See *UN Yearbook* (1972) 318–27; for the institutional framework see A/Res/2997 (XXVII) of 15.12.1972, *UN Yearbook* (1972). 331–2. The programme is managed by an executive director; see also M Kilian, *Umweltschutz durch internationale Organisationen* (1987).

[80] For the programme character. See also para 3.29 (UNDP).

[81] For further information see *UN Yearbook* (1972) 323–9; http://www.unep.org.

projects are implemented in co-operation with the World Bank Group, UNDP, FAO, UNESCO, and WHO. UNEP has generated several State-of-the-Environment Reports. Under the Environment and Natural Resources Information Network, UNEP promotes a functioning information network in every developing region, including Eastern Europe, each comprising ten cross-sectoral information databases. UNEP played a significant role in preparing and conducting the United Nations Conference on Environment and Development in 1992. Agenda 21 reaffirmed UNEP's mandate and gave its Governing Council an enhanced role in the areas of policy guidance and development. In February 1997 the Governing Council, at its nineteenth session, adopted the Nairobi Declaration[82] on UNEP's future role and mandate. The 'Earth Summit + 5', a Special Session of the General Assembly to review the implementation of Agenda 21, confirmed UNEP's essential role as a global authority promoting a coherent legal and political approach to the environmental challenges of sustainable development. Subsequently, UNEP initiated an extensive process of restructuring its functions. During 1999 UNEP implemented a new functional structure reflecting the decisions of the Nairobi Declaration.

3.34 UNEP encompasses six divisions. Within the Division of Technology, Industry and Economics the Energy & Ozone Action Unit promotes good management practices and use of energy, with a focus on atmospheric impacts. A specific feature of the UNEP energy programme is the Collaborating Centre on Energy and Environment, which aids UNEP as a research and technical support unit in incorporating environmental concerns into energy planning and policy.[83] The Division of Environmental Conventions is mandated to assist the Division of Policy Development and Law in the formulation of new agreements or protocols to existing conventions. UNEP works to implement several international conventions by providing administrative support through secretariats established by multilateral conventions, including the Vienna Convention for the Protection of the Ozone Layer and its 1987 Montreal Protocol,[84] the Basel Convention on the Control of Transboundary Movements of Hazardous Wastes and their Disposal,[85] and the UNFCCC. UNEP assists countries to prepare projects for submission to GEF for funding. UNEP is funded by the regular budget of the UN and by voluntary contributions to the Environmental Fund.[86] The Fund wholly or partly finances the costs of the initiatives undertaken within the UN system, as well as programmes of general interest such as global monitoring, assessment, and data-

[82] UNEP Governing Council, Annex to Decision 19/1, 7.2.1997; see also for the text UN Doc A/S-19/5, 4.3.1997.

[83] See http://www.uccee.org.

[84] BGBl. 1988 II 901.

[85] BGBl. 1994 II 2703.

[86] The authorized budget for the two-year period 2000–1 was US$ 120 million; see *Europa World Yearbook 2000* (2000) 49.

collecting systems. Along those lines the Fund can also contribute to activities developed within other organizations.[87]

Although the work of UNEP has been of great significance in setting standards, the effort necessary in accommodating the polarized positions of north and south has undermined its effectiveness. Furthermore, UNEP has no review and supervisory functions. It can review environmental implementation in a general sense but there is no duty on States to report to UNEP on progress achieved in implementing the standards laid down by UNEP. How far the focus on the furtherance of international environmental law in the Nairobi Declaration will help to overcome the judgement that UNEP is a highly political institution[88] remains to be seen. **3.35**

(7) The International Maritime Organization (IMO)

The IMO (founded as the International Maritime Consultative Organization in 1958)[89] is a specialized agency of the UN which facilitates co-operation among governments on technical matters affecting international shipping.[90] Its main function was initially to achieve safe and efficient navigation.[91] However, after the *Torrey Canyon* disaster in 1967, when a major tanker accident polluted the sea close to the British coast, the organization became involved in a whole series of conventions concerned with the problems posed by shipping, and especially the transport of oil, to the marine environment.[92] **3.36**

The Council is the Executive Organ of the IMO. Along with the Assembly it is in charge of supervising the work of the organization. Between sessions of the Assembly the Council discharges all the functions of the organization, save the function of making recommendations to governments on maritime safety and pollution prevention, which is reserved for the Assembly by Article 15(j) of the IMO Convention. The Council is elected by the Assembly for a two-year term and encompasses thirty-two Member States. The IMO Convention stipulates that in electing the members the Assembly shall observe the following criteria: (a) eight shall be those States with the largest interest in providing international shipping services; (b) eight shall be other States with the largest interest in **3.37**

[87] PM Dupuy, 'UNEP', in R Bernhardt (ed), *EPIL*, Inst. 5 (1983) 320.

[88] ND White, *The Law of International Organizations* (1996) 257, 260.

[89] Convention on the Intergovernmental Maritime Consultative Organization, 289 UNTS 3 and 324 UNTS 553; it became the IMO in 1982 due to the changes that had meanwhile occurred in the work programme; 1276 UNTS 468 and 607 UNTS 276; 649 UNTS 334; for further information see http://www.imo.org and *IMO News*, the organization's quarterly magazine; see also MH Nordquist, *Current Maritime Issues and the International Maritime Organization* (1999).

[90] The budget appropriation for the two years 2000–1 amounted to £36.6m; as at November 2000 the IMO had 158 Member States and two Associate Members; see *Europa World Yearbook 2000* (2000) 89.

[91] Art 1 of the 1948 Convention.

[92] See Art 1 of the Convention as amended in 1982.

international seaborne trade; (c) sixteen shall be States not elected under (a) or (b) above which have special interests in maritime transport or navigation, and whose election to the Council will ensure the representation of all major geographic areas of the world.[93]

3.38 With regard to energy matters the Maritime Safety Committee,[94] the highest technical body of the organization, and the Marine Environment Protection Committee[95] are of eminent importance. Being open to all members the Maritime Safety Committee meets at least once a year and submits proposals to the Assembly and the Council on technical matters affecting shipping, such as issues regarding the carriage of dangerous goods.[96] The Marine Environment Protection Committee is IMO's main body for environmental issues and deals especially with the prevention and control of marine pollution from ships.

3.39 The organization has taken an active interest in the implementation of existing maritime conventions of which it is the depository and in the drafting of new conventions and agreements. Some of these conventions refer to the environmental consequences of energy exploitation from the sea and transport by the sea, for example the International Convention relating to Intervention on the High Sea in Cases of Oil Pollution Casualties[97] and the Protocol relating to Intervention on the High Seas in Cases of Pollution by Substances other than Oil, 1973.[98] Likewise, the adoption of the International Convention for the Prevention of Pollution from Ships, 1973, as modified by the Protocol of 1978 relating thereto (MARPOL 73/78),[99] has been supported by the IMO.[100] Following the *Exxon Valdez* disaster in Alaskan waters, the IMO concluded an International Convention on Oil Pollution Preparedness Response and Co-operation, 1990.[101] While particularly concerned with maritime safety, the Conventions on Safety of Life at Sea, 1974 (SOLAS),[102] on International Regulations for Preventing Collision at Sea, 1972,[103] and on Standards of Training, Certification, and Watchkeeping, 1978[104] also reflect envir-

---

93 Arts 16–28 of the Convention; in November 1993 the Assembly adopted an amendment to the IMO Convention which, upon entry into force, will extend the number of members to 40. The amendment will enter into force 12 months after being accepted by two-thirds of IMO Member States.

94 Arts 27–31 of the Convention.

95 Arts 37–41 of the Convention; the Maritime Environment Protection Committee was first established as a subsidiary body of the Assembly and raised to full constitutional status in 1985.

96 Arts 28–30 of the Convention.

97 Concluded on 29.11.1969, 970 UNTS 211.

98 Concluded on 2.11.1973, BGBl. 1985 II 593.

99 Concluded on 2.11.1973 and 17.2.1978 respectively, BGBl. 1982 II 2.

100 Concluded on 2.11.1973, BGBl. 1982 II 2; Protocol of 1978 Relating to the International Convention for the Prevention of Pollution from Ships, 1973, of 17.2.1978, BGBl. 1982 II 24; for a list of conventions promoted by the IMO see http://www.imo.org.

101 Concluded on 30.11.1990, ILM 30 (1991) 733ff.

102 Concluded on 1.11.1974, BGBl. 1980 II 717.

103 Concluded on 20.10.1972, BGBl. 1976 II 1017.

104 Concluded on 7.7.1978, BGBl. 1982 II 297.

onmental and thus energy concerns. The International Safety Management Code entered into force on 1 July 1998 for all oil tankers, chemical tankers, bulk carriers, gas carriers, passenger ships, and cargo high-speed craft of 500 grt and above on international voyages. The Code is intended to improve safety on international shipping and to reduce pollution from ships. Since the Code was added as a new chapter to SOLAS, the international standard for safe management of ships became mandatory for States Parties to the Convention.

The question of liability is regulated in the Convention on Civil Liability for Oil Pollution Damage, 1969,[105] the Convention on Liability in the Field of Maritime Carriage of Nuclear Material, 1971,[106] and the International Convention on Liability and Compensation for Damage in Connection with the Carriage of Hazardous and Noxious Substances (HNS) by Sea, 1996.[107] To meet the problems arising from liability, its limitation, and the compensation available under the auspices of the IMO the International Fund for Compensation for Oil Pollution Damage was established.[108] The International Oil Pollution Compensation Fund (IOPC) is an independent international organization, based at the IMO's headquarters. **3.40**

The IMO also sets out guidelines and standards for the abandonment of energy installations and structures. Article 60, para 3 of the UN Convention on the Law of the Sea (UNCLOS) refers to 'any generally accepted international standards established in this regard by the competent international organization'. No specific organization is mentioned in these terms. However, the IMO has established itself as the competent organ, although its work has hitherto been restricted to shipping matters. After co-ordination and consultation with other international organizations, on 19 October 1989 the IMO adopted Guidelines and Standards for the Removal of Offshore Installations and Structures on the Continental Shelf and in the Exclusive Economic Zone. These Guidelines state in their Preamble that the IMO 'is the competent organ to deal with the subject'. Although the IMO's competence may be questionable and the Guidelines are adopted by non-binding resolutions, the IMO provides a forum for State practice of which these Guidelines are an outcome.[109] **3.41**

---

[105] Signed 29.11.1969, 973 UNTS 3.

[106] Concluded on 17.12.1971, BGBl. 1975 II 957, 1026.

[107] Concluded on 3.5.1996, ILM 35 (1996) 1415ff. The Convention had not entered into force as at 30 September 2000.

[108] Concluded on 18.12.1971, BGBl. 1975 II 301, 320; Protocol of 1992 Amending the International Convention on the Establishment of an International Fund for Compensation of Oil Pollution Damage, 1971, BGBl. 1994 II 1150.

[109] R Higgins, 'Abandonment of Energy Sites and Structures: Relevant International Law' in IBA Section on Energy and Natural Resources Law (ed), *Energy and Resources Law '92* (1992) 260–1; see also VI Adrianov, 'The role of the International Maritime Organisation in implementing the 1982 UNCLOS', Marine Policy 1990, 121–3; K Kaasen, 'Removal of Offshore Installations' in IBA Section on Energy and Natural Resources Law (ed), *Energy and Resources Law '92* (1992) 272.

(8) Other Specialized Agencies and International Organizations in relation to the UN

3.42 (1) Within the UN system the role of energy is seen not only in relation to economic or environmental issues but also in relation to competence concerning social issues as a question of development and science. Therefore, the dissemination of environmentally sustainable and energy-efficient industrial growth is one of the priority areas of the United Nations Industrial Development Organization (UNIDO).[110] Its objective is to promote and accelerate sustainable industrial development in developing countries and economies in transition by providing a forum for representatives of governments as well as of industry. UNIDO provides assistance to these countries to acquire and apply efficient and clean technologies suited to their development process. This includes the elaboration of energy-demand surveys and advice on the elaboration and introduction of a coherent energy-pricing policy. The organization is concerned with the development and strengthening of government institutions and provides assistance in know-how and technology transfer. UNIDO is one of the implementing agencies of the Multilateral Fund for the Montreal Protocol. It is also involved in implementing the Kyoto Protocol of the UNFCCC. The organization executed a large number of energy projects in 1992, worth US$ 148.2 million.[111]

3.43 (2) With regard to its constitutional mandate in agricultural questions, the energy concerns of the Food and Agricultural Organization of the UN (FAO) concentrate on rural projects and technical support to energy issues of Third World countries.[112] The FAO mainly provides technical information, advice, and assistance by disseminating information and advising governments on policy and planning, and by developing capacity directly in the field. The energy programmes of the FAO cover: assessment and planning; wood, solar, wind, and bio-energy; rural mechanization; small hydropower systems, draught animal technology; and integration of energy sources. FAO activities in its wood energy programmes include the production of charcoal and wood-based commercial energy for industrial and rural community needs. Wood energy is one of the five areas of priority of the Tropical Forest Action Plan, launched in 1985 to address

[110] UNIDO was founded as an autonomous organization in 1967 (UN Doc A/Res/2152 (XXI), 17.11.1966) and was converted into a specialized agency by an agreement annexed to GA Res 40/180, 17.12.1985; as at October 2000 UNIDO had 169 Member States.

[111] Committee on New and Renewable Sources of Energy and on Energy for Development, Report of the Secretary-General on Energy Activities Within and Outside the UN System, UN Doc E/C.13/1994/4, para 31.

[112] BGBl. 1971 II 1033 and I UNTS 207; the FAO, established as the first specialized agency in 1945, had a membership of 180 States and the EC as at November 2000; the FAO's regular programme is financed by contributions from Member Governments. The FAO aims to alleviate malnutrition and hunger. The budget for 2000–1 was US$ 650 million. Like the UNDP much of the FAO's technical assistance programme is funded from extra-budgetary sources.

the most urgent aspects of tropical deforestation. The FAO is also monitoring developments in small- and medium-scale hydropower plants in developing countries. Part of the FAO's work involves improving knowledge of wind-energy potential, and monitoring and analysing wind-power generating systems for decentralized rural electrification schemes.[113]

(3) The activities of the World Health Organization (WHO) with regard to energy relate to its mandate in health issues and to the interaction between health and energy.[114] Therefore, activities refer on one hand to the use of new and renewable sources of energy for health, and on the other hand to the assessment and control of environmental pollution from energy sources. It focuses on the preparation of reports and evaluation of programmes as well as on providing assistance to countries by conducting training programmes. The WHO co-operates with other UN bodies in certain areas. One of these programmes is carried out as an inter-agency project on risk management of large industrial complexes and energy production systems with the International Atomic Energy Agency, UNEP, and UNIDO.[115] **3.44**

(4) The work of the World Meteorological Organization (WMO)[116] emphasizes scientific aspects of energy issues. During the period 1992–2001 the WMO will further evaluate weather and climate implications in energy matters. To this end, it has been supporting the work of the Intergovernmental Panel on Climate Change.[117] The organization continues to assume an important scientific role on matters associated with the atmosphere's water and its relation to energy issues. An example for the outcome of the organization's work is the development and testing of systems for implementing energy meteorology within national meteorological services.[118] **3.45**

[113] Committee on New and Renewable Sources of Energy and on Energy for Development, Report (n 111 above) para 44.

[114] 14 UNTS 185. The WHO was established in 1948 and has 6 regional offices. It is financed by contributions from its 191 Member States. There is an additional fund for specific projects by voluntary contributions; in 1998–9 the budget amounted to US$ 842.7m. See *Europa World Yearbook 2000* (2000) 107.

[115] Committee on New and Renewable Sources of Energy and on Energy for Development, Report (n 111 above) para 30; see further C Vignes/H Schlenzka, 'WHO' in R Bernhardt (ed), *EPIL*, Inst. 5 (1983) 406–9.

[116] 77 UNTS 143, 800 UNTS 282. It started its activities in 1951, operating in the field of meteorology, climatology, operational hydrology. The organization had 185 members as at November 2000; its main bodies are the World Meteorological Congress and the Executive Council. The assessed regular budget for the years 1996–99 was SF 255 m: see http://www.wmo.ch.; M Peeters, 'WMO' in R Bernhardt (ed), *EPIL*, Inst. 5 (1983) 416.

[117] See *Yearbook of the United Nations 1994*, vol 48, 938; see Ch 2 above.

[118] Committee on New and Renewable Sources of Energy and on Energy for Development, Report (n 111 above) para 33.

3.46 (5) Even the United Nations Educational, Scientific, and Cultural Organization (UNESCO) is active in energy matters. Together with the ECE, UNIDO, and the IAEA, UNESCO organized a World Solar Summit held at Harare in September 1996. The Summit adopted the Harare Declaration on Solar Energy and Sustainable Development, and the outline of a World Solar Programme, 1996–2005.[119]

3.47 (6) Based on the United Nations Convention on the Law of the Sea (UNCLOS) further international institutions with relevance to ocean affairs, and thus to energy issues, came into existence. In November 1994 the International Sea-Bed Authority[120] was established under Article 156 UNCLOS and the 1994 Agreement relating to the Implementation of Part XI of UNCLOS[121] as an autonomous international organization working in relationship with the UN but so far not as a specialized agency. The Authority is the organization through which States Parties to UNCLOS shall, in accordance with the regime for the sea bed and ocean floor and subsoil thereof beyond limits of national jurisdiction (the Area) established in Part XI and the Implementation Agreement, organize and control activities in the Area, in particular with a view to administering the resources of the Area. The Agreement alters a number of provisions of UNCLOS relating to deep sea-bed mining. It has to be interpreted and applied together with Part XI UNCLOS as a single instrument. The governing bodies of the Authority are the Assembly, comprising all members of the Authority, the Council, the Secretariat (Art 158 UNCLOS), the Legal and Technical Commission (Arts 163, 165 UNCLOS), and the Finance Committee. The work of the Authority focuses on regulations for the exploration of polymetallic nodules in the Area (the Mining Code). In August 1997 plans of exploration work were formally submitted to the Council by seven registered pioneer investors and approved.

3.48 (7) Likewise, the International Tribunal for the Law of the Sea was established under Annex VI of UNCLOS.[122] Its seat is at the Free and Hanseatic City of Hamburg, Germany. The Tribunal consists of 21 independent members elected by the States Parties to UNCLOS (Arts 2–8 Annex). The Tribunal is competent to judge on all disputes and all applications submitted to it in accordance with UNCLOS and all matters specifically provided for in any other agreement which confers jurisdiction on the Tribunal (Arts 20–23 Annex). The Tribunal has exclu-

[119] Report of the Secretary-General on the Follow-Up to the Previous Sessions of the Committee on New and Renewable Sources of Energy and on Energy for Development, UN E/C.13/1998/2, 12.2.1998, para 12.

[120] http://www.isa.org.jm.

[121] ILM 33 (1994) 1309ff.

[122] See further CA Fleischhauer, 'The relationship between the ICJ and the newly created International Tribunal for the Law of the Sea in Hamburg' in *Max-Planck-Yearbook of United Nations Law* 1 (1997) 327–33.

sive jurisdiction, through its Sea-bed Disputes Chamber (Arts 35–40 Annex), over disputes about activities in the international Sea-bed Area. These matters include disputes between States Parties concerning the interpretation or application of the provisions of both agreements concerning the deep sea-bed Area and disputes between States Parties, a contractor and the International Sea-Bed Authority. The Sea-Bed Disputes Chamber has jurisdiction to provide advisory opinions at the request of the Assembly or the Council of the International Sea-Bed Authority on legal questions arising in the scope of their activities.

(9) The International Atomic Energy Agency (IAEA)

Though the idea of establishing a worldwide organization dealing with the civil use of nuclear energy was mooted immediately after World War II, the proposal to establish the organization which became the IAEA was not made until 1953.[123] The Statute of the IAEA was opened for signature in 1956 and entered into force on 29 July 1957.[124] The status of the IAEA is affected by two peculiarities: within the system of the UN, the IAEA is not a specialized agency but has a duty to report to the General Assembly and the Security Council in special situations.[125] It is an independent intergovernmental organization under the aegis of the UN. Another cause affecting the situation of the IAEA is the parallel work of EURATOM. This latter point has been solved by agreement, which calls for co-operation between the two organizations.[126] **3.49**

The institutional framework of the organization consists of the General Conference in which all members are represented,[127] the Board of Governors with thirty-five members, the Staff, and various committees. In 1999 the Board of Governors adopted a resolution concerning the size and distribution of seats on the Board of Governors, by which membership of the Board was expanded from thirty-five to forty-three seats. This amendment will enter into force when all IAEA Member States have ratified it.[128] Whereas the General Conference's powers are limited mostly to administrative questions and the competence to elect members to the Board, the Board is generally competent to execute the functions of the organization. It reports to the General Conference.[129] The Agency has **3.50**

[123] 8.12.1953, GAOR, 8th Session, 470th Plenary Meeting, 450; see further DA Fischer, *History of the IAEA 1957–1995* (1997); IAEA (ed), *Ten Years after Chernobyl: What do we really know?* (1997).

[124] Statute of the International Atomic Energy Agency. Done at the Headquarters of the United Nations, on 26 October 1956, 276 UNTS 3.

[125] Art XII C of the Statute.

[126] See Commission, XXVI General Report (1992), para 721; Commission, General Report 1996, paras 486f.

[127] In 2000 the IAEA had 131 members.

[128] IAEA, GC(43)/RES/19 October 1999.

[129] Art VI of the Statute.

about 2,300 staff and its headquarters are in Vienna, Austria. The Secretariat is headed by a Director-General and is divided into six departments: Technical Co-operation, Nuclear Energy, Nuclear Safety, Nuclear Science and Application, Safeguards, and Administration. There is also a Standing Advisory Group on Safeguards Implementation, which advises the Director-General on all technical aspects of safeguards.

3.51 The IAEA has a dual budget:[130] one budget consists of contributions by Member States as determined by the Conference and covers, *inter alia*, administrative costs.[131] It amounted to US$ 221.7 million in 2000. The second budget, which is made up of voluntary contributions, is used to support financing the technical assistance and co-operation programmes, which are projected to cost US$73 million.[132]

3.52 Its main areas of activity aim to enlarge the contribution of nuclear energy to peace, health, and prosperity throughout the world; the IAEA's work should not support military purposes.[133] To ensure these aims, the Organization provides for and assists in technical co-operation and 'safeguarding'.

3.53 The major activity of the IAEA is to 'safeguard'[134] the use of nuclear materials and facilities in Agency projects and peaceful activities in the nuclear field under the Non-Proliferation Treaty (NPT).[135] Under the NPT every non-nuclear weapon State, ie one which had not exploded a nuclear device before 1 July 1967, has to conclude a safeguard agreement with the IAEA. The safeguard systems are governed by special agreement between the Agency and the State concerned. They include monitoring the whereabouts of controlled items, reviewing records, and checking nuclear facilities. Of high relevance are inspections carried out by Agency inspectors with the general consent of a State; a State is not necessarily notified in advance of the precise date. If a State does not comply or an irregularity is found, a report has to be filed with the Board. The Board may inform the General Assembly and the Security Council or impose sanctions.

3.54 Resolution 687 (1991) of the UN Security Council, which set out terms for a ceasefire in the Gulf conflict, called on Iraq unconditionally 'not to acquire or develop nuclear weapons or nuclear-weapon-usable material or any subsystems,

[130] Art XIV B of the Statute.

[131] These cover some of the staff costs of the Agency as well as costs of implementing the safeguards (see below); the scale should come close to the principles under which contributions are made to the regular budget of the United Nations: Art XIV D of the Statute.

[132] *Europa World Yearbook 2000* (2000) 76.

[133] Art II of the Statute.

[134] Art III A para 5 and XII of the Statute; see further T Lohmann, *Die rechtliche Struktur der Sicherungsmassnahmen der Internationalen Atomenergie-Organisation* (1992).

[135] The NPT of 1.7.1969, 729 UNTS 161, entered into force in 1970; in May 1995 the Review and Extension Conference of the NPT Parties agreed to extend the Treaty indefinitely.

components or any research, development, support, or manufacturing facilities'.[136] Iraq was obliged to name all locations, amounts, and types of these items. It had to put all nuclear-weapon-usable material under the exclusive control of the IAEA for custody and subsequent removal. It was also obliged to accept 'urgent on-site inspections' and the 'destruction, removal, or rendering harmless' of the listed items. The IAEA, assisted by the Special Commission on Iraq, was to inspect the nuclear facilities listed in Iraq's declarations, as well as locations designated by the Special Commission. Only in its second declaration on 27 April 1991, following further pressure from the IAEA, did Iraq admit having nuclear material and facilities other than those known to the Agency. Since then the IAEA has conducted several inspections of Iraqi facilities.[137] Iraq's responses followed a pattern of denying clandestine activities until evidence became overwhelming, and then co-operating.[138] In October 1998 IAEA reported that while there was no evidence of Iraq having produced nuclear weapons or having obtained a capability for the production of nuclear weapons, the Agency was unable to guarantee that all items had been found.

According to its Statute the IAEA has to establish standards of safety for the pro- **3.55**
tection of health and the minimization of danger to life and property.[139] The international focus on long-term health and environmental consequences is a result of a development which began with the popularity of nuclear power as a means to improve the security of energy supply following the oil crises of the 1970s. However, in Western countries the popularity of nuclear power has diminished because of concerns about the safety of nuclear plants (especially after the nuclear reactor accidents at Three Mile Island in the United States and Chernobyl in the Soviet Union), the management of nuclear waste, and the decommissioning of plants. As the latter accident had strong transboundary impacts the setting of common standards supervised by international institutions was seen as the best means of ensuring a generally accepted minimum level of environmental protection.[140] The IAEA provided the main forum for the consideration of measures made necessary by the accident, and Member States acknowledged the importance of the Agency's role in safety and radiological protection matters.[141] Among the recommendations of a review group were that the Agency should

---

[136] See para 3.16 above.

[137] See E Chauvistré, *The Implications of IAEA Inspections under Security Council Resolution 687* (1992).

[138] See http://www.iaea.or.at/worldatom/infosource/other/iraq/iraqresponse.htm. Visited in November 2000.

[139] See Arts III A para 6 and XII A para 2 of the Statute.

[140] PW Birnie/AE Boyle, *International Law and the Environment* (1992) 347–8.

[141] IAEA, 30th Conference, Special Session, GC/SPL.1/Res.1; Statement of the Group of Seven on the Implications of the Chernobyl Accident, ILM 15 (1986) 1005; G Handl, 'Après Tchernobyl: quelques réflexions sur le programme législatif multilatéral à l'ordre du jour', RGDIP 92 (1988) 5–62.

further the exchanges of information between States on safety and accident experience, work out additional safety guidelines, and strengthen its capacity to carry out safety evaluations and inspections on request.[142] Like the IMO after the *Torrey Canyon* disaster, the IAEA has obtained an environmental perspective as a result of the Chernobyl accident.[143]

3.56 For example, the Nuclear Safety Standards Programme, revised in 1988,[144] sets basic international minimum safety standards (NUSS) and guiding principles for regulating the design, construction, siting, and operation of nuclear power plants.[145] However, IAEA standards do not have binding force.[146] Only if the Agency provides materials, facilities, or services to States do Articles III A para 6, XI, and XII of the Statute authorize the IAEA to ensure through project agreements that applicable health, safety, and design standards are met. In such cases, the IAEA has the right to examine the design of equipment and facilities and check compliance with these standards, as well as the right to send inspectors. States may also voluntarily place their nuclear facilities under the standards. Even though IAEA health and safety standards are non-binding, they contribute significantly to the control of the risks of nuclear energy. The consultation of governments during the formulation stage,[147] and in some cases co-operation with specialist bodies, such as the International Committee on Radiological Protection (ICRP), guarantees their acceptance. The Agency's standards thus reflect an expert technical consensus. Therefore they present important guidelines for most States in regulating their nuclear facilities and have created a remarkable degree of harmonization.[148] The IAEA Convention on Nuclear Safety, 1994[149] is based on the technical standards contained in the Safety Fundamentals published by the IAEA in 1993.[150] To the extent that these technical standards are included in the Convention, they are binding on States Parties to the Convention.

3.57 The IAEA has also assisted States in technical matters through experts and equipment.[151] In 1987 the Waste Management Advisory Program (WAMAP) was

[142] IAEA, Summary Report on the Post Accident Review Meeting on the Chernobyl Accident (1986).

[143] See further N Pelzer, 'The impact of the Chernobyl accident on international nuclear energy law', Archiv des Voelkerrechts 25 (1987) 294–311.

[144] See IAEA Bulletin 30 (1988) 58.

[145] IAEA GC (XXXII)/Res/489.

[146] See A Boyle, 'Nuclear Energy and Environmental Law', BYIL 60 (1989) 262–5; P Szasz, *The Law and Practices of the IAEA* (1970) 679ff; and R Rainer/P Szasz, *Supplement 1* (1993) 421; for a slightly different view see G Handl, *Grenzueberschreitendes nukleares Risiko und voelkerrechtlicher Schutzanspruch* (1992) 53–4.

[147] P Szasz, *The Law and Practices of the IAEA* (1970) 672f; and R Rainer/P Szasz, *Supplement 1* (1993) 419.

[148] For a critical approach: M Kamminga, 'The IAEA Convention on Nuclear Safety', ICLQ 44 (1995) 874.

[149] Concluded on 20.9.1994, ILM 33 (1994) 1514ff.

[150] The Safety of Nuclear Installations, IAEA Safety Series No 110, 1993.

[151] See Art XI of the Statute.

established under which the Agency undertakes advisory missions in Member States. It supports the establishment of conventions covering nuclear waste disposal. The IAEA has established various institutions in Europe supporting the Agency's research and safeguards activities. The IAEA laboratories are located in Austria, while the Marine Environment Laboratory and the Centre for Theoretical Physics are situated in Monaco and in Trieste respectively.[152]

C. The Organization for Economic Co-operation and Development (OECD)

(1) Overview

The OECD is an intergovernmental organization, based in Paris, which was formed by industrialized States with market economies.[153] The organization was the reconstitution on a worldwide basis of the regional Organization for European Economic Co-operation (OEEC). Recognizing the interdependence of the industrialized world, the OECD Convention[154] calls for policies striving for the highest sustainable economic growth while maintaining financial stability. The OECD aims to contribute to sound economic expansion in Member States as well as non-Member countries in development and to promote the expansion of world trade (Art 1 of the Convention). While the OECD was above all concerned with worldwide economic growth throughout the first period, 1960/61 to 1973, the second phase was characterized by defining policies for international trade and the international monetary system. The energy crisis provoked action and reaction to its effects on Member and non-Member countries. Structural adjustment and environmental policies were added. Since the geographical changes in Central and Eastern Europe, and since the need for worldwide co-operation became evident, new members such as Poland, Hungary, the Czech Republic, South Korea, and Mexico have acceded. **3.58**

The OECD has twenty-nine Member States. It is composed of an assembly (ie the Council) consisting of representatives from all Member States, the Executive Committee of fourteen Member States, various committees, and the Secretariat.[155] The greater part of the OECD's work is carried out by about 200 specialized bodies, such as committees and working parties. The committees cover environment, energy, fisheries, and scientific and technological policy. The **3.59**

[152] See P Szasz, 'International Atomic Energy Agency' in R Bernhardt (ed), *EPIL*, Inst. 5 (1983) 56.

[153] See further H Hahn, 'OECD' in R Bernhardt (ed), *EPIL*, Inst. 5 (1983) 214–22; http://www.oecd.org.

[154] 888 UNTS 180.

[155] Arts 7–11 of the Constitution.

Council is the supreme authority of the OECD and holds the decision-making power. It consists of the representatives of each Member State and one representative from the European Commission. The Council can take decisions which bind members only if they so agree; decisions are taken by unanimity according to the principle one state one vote. The Council can help to work out principles which can be and have been adopted into national laws. Under Article 2 of its Constitution the Member States undertake to promote the efficient use of their economic resources, so the OECD has been able to develop an environmental programme. Thus it established the Environment Policy Committee in 1970[156] in which Member States discuss common problems and make recommendations for national policies. The organization has made proposals for evaluating and improving environmental quality, examines the environmental and health risks originating from chemicals, assesses the environmental implications of different means of energy production, and advises on waste disposal. The OECD has focused on finding solutions to transboundary pollution, thus developing the polluter pays principle.[157]

3.60 In response to the energy crisis the Ministerial Council proclaimed the OECD Trade Pledge, asking Member Governments to refrain from trade restriction as an answer to balance-of-payments difficulties which result from the combined effect of oil price increases and other factors such as inflation and unemployment.[158] The original declaration of 30 May 1974 has been renewed annually by the Council.

(2) The International Energy Agency (IEA)

3.61 Co-operation on energy-related matters has been conducted at the International Energy Agency (IEA) since its foundation in 1974. The IEA is the forum for coordinating the energy policies of the twenty-four industrialized countries. Apart from the organizations concerned with nuclear energy it is one of the few organizations dealing solely with energy.[159] The IEA co-operates closely with all branches of the OECD. Its activities are more fully analysed in paras 3.133–3.179 below in a case study by a former executive director of the IEA, Helga Steeg.

(3) The Nuclear Energy Agency (NEA)

3.62 The OECD Council has also established the Nuclear Energy Agency (NEA) to facilitate co-operation in these fields and to encourage the harmonization of policy

---

[156] See Resolution of the Council concerning the Renewal of the Mandate of the Environmental Policy Committee, C(99)76/Final.

[157] PW Birnie/AE Boyle, *International Law and the Environment* (1992) 72; see Ch 2 above.

[158] Declaration by the Governments of Member Countries on Co-operation on Issues of General Economic Policy, C (74) 80 (Final) Annex; see OECD, Acts of the Organization vol 14 (1974) 201.

[159] For detail see paras 3.133–3.179 below.

and practices in radioactive waste management. The NEA was founded on 17 December 1957 to further the peaceful uses of nuclear energy (Art 1 of the Statute). Originally a European agency, it has since admitted members outside Europe. Membership is now identical to that of the OECD except that New Zealand and Poland are not members. The NEA has no legal personality of its own. It is the operational arm of the OECD for one of its specific areas of action. The OECD alone has legal personality under international law. Both Member States and other States have recognized the OECD as the responsible body.[160] Moreover, the jurisdiction of the OECD Council was not affected by the establishment of the NEA. However, the NEA has restricted intra-organizational autonomy, which is acknowledged by separate topical appropriations in the OECD budget. The NEA Statute was enacted by a decision of the OECD Council (Art 19 of the Statute). Under the authority of the OECD Council the functions attributed to the NEA are discharged by the Steering Committee for Nuclear Energy, a Secretariat, and further committees (Art 2 of the Statute). The Steering Committee can take decisions, form opinions, and render recommendations (Arts 10–11 of the Statute). The Agency's main purpose is to promote international co-operation within the OECD area for the development of nuclear power for peaceful purposes through international research, development projects, and the exchange of scientific and technical experience and information (Arts 4–5 of the Statute). The Agency's work focuses on safety, waste management, and regulation of nuclear power; the mandate of the IAEA is thus considerably broader. The NEA provides a data bank which enables participating countries to share large computer programs used in reactor calculations and nuclear data applications. The NEA makes regulations for severe accidents, promotes nuclear research institutes, and regulates radioactive waste disposal as well as the operational safety of nuclear power plants. The organization monitors nuclear reactors and co-operates with countries in Central and Eastern Europe.[161] The NEA's work includes a number of field projects.

The Halden Reactor Project became an OECD project in 1958 as an experimen- **3.63**
tal heavy water reactor. It has been used for long-term testing of water reactor fuels and for research into automatic computer-based control of nuclear power stations. The project was arranged under successive agreements with participating countries from 1964 onwards under which the national institutions assumed the obligation to build and operate the plant. The reactor and the installations remained the property of the national institutions. Some 100 nuclear energy research institutions and authorities in nineteen countries support the project.[162]

[160] H Hahn, 'OECD/NEA' in R Bernhardt (ed), *EPIL*, Inst. 5 (1983) 222.
[161] See http://www.nea.fr. and *NEA Newsletter*, published twice a year.
[162] H Hahn, n 160 above, 223.

3.64 With regard to radiation protection, the NEA has secured the continuous adoption of OECD decisions in the light of radiation protection norms developed by the International Commission on Radiological Protection (ICRP). To that end, the Steering Committee for Nuclear Energy has been authorized to amend from time to time the relevant OECD enactments in order to harmonize them with the most recent requirements of the ICRP. In elaborating these standards the NEA has built close working relationships with other international and regional organizations, in particular the IAEA, the WHO, the ILO, and EURATOM. The NEA has also established a system of supervision and emergency warning in cases of undue increase in environmental activity. The NEA has sponsored and still administers two international conventions: the Paris Convention on Third-Party Liability in the Field of Nuclear Energy and the Brussels Convention supplementary to it.[163]

D. Financial and Trade Organizations

(1) The General Agreement on Tariffs and Trade (GATT) and the World Trade Organization (WTO)

3.65 The WTO is an actor within the energy field, as energy is a good within the framework of GATT. The GATT was signed in 1947.[164] It was founded within the framework of the establishment of a new economic world order to re-establish an international market place and promote free world trade, especially in reaction to the protectionism of the 1920s and 1930s. For this purpose it was decided to establish the IMF, the IBRD, and the International Trade Organization. During 1947 and 1948 the UN held a Conference on Trade and Employment in Havana with the goal of drafting a charter to establish the ITO. During this period the GATT was being negotiated in Geneva as a multilateral agreement to reduce tariffs reciprocally, in the expectation that it would be an addendum to the Havana Charter. The ITO never came into existence but the GATT was provisionally applied from 1 January 1948. Until 1995 the original Contracting Parties continuously applied the GATT so that it was more an international treaty than an international organization.[165] An

[163] Dated 29 July 1960 and dated 28 January 1964, respectively, 956 UNTS 251. Both were updated in 1982.

[164] 55 UNTS 187/308; in 1995 128 States were formal members to the GATT 1994, 13 States applied the GATT rules, 35 States were observers. See further http://www.wto.org and the official WTO newsletter *Focus*; W Benedek, *Die Rechtsordnung des GATT aus voelkerrechtlicher Sicht* (1990); H van Houtte, *The Law of International Trade* (1995) ch 3.

[165] D Bowett, *The Law of International Institutions* (4th edn, 1982) 117; ND White, *The Law of International Organizations* (1996) 40; for a classification as an international organization see G Jaenicke, 'GATT (1947)' in R Bernhardt (ed), *EPIL*, Inst. 5 (1983) 20.

institutional structure was gradually created by a series of decisions by the *contracting parties*;[166] for example a permanent secretariat servicing the GATT was financed by the *contracting parties*.[167]

The GATT has been amended on a number of occasions. In the absence of an executive decision-making organ the Contracting Parties developed as a major mechanism rounds of multilateral trade negotiations. Since the Tokyo Round (1973–79) the Contracting Parties have preferred not to amend the GATT Treaty, but to enter into supplementary treaties (side agreements), which are not always signed by all Member States. With respect to the energy context, the codes on public procurement which try to achieve liberalization of economic sectors are of particular importance. They apply to supply contracts in cases of procurement by entities under the direct or substantial control of the Contracting Parties.[168] **3.66**

The GATT only affects international trade in goods. During the Uruguay Round the States agreed to adopt a regulation, similar to the GATT, for services: the General Agreement on Trade in Services (GATS).[169] **3.67**

With the successful completion of the Uruguay Round in December 1993, the participants decided to establish the WTO. In April 1994 the Marrakech Declaration, signed by the majority of GATT Contracting Parties, endorsed the establishment of the organization.[170] The WTO encompasses the GATT 1994[171] as well as GATS and the TRIPS[172] and TRIM[173] agreements. It recognizes the importance of environmental measures and sustainable development. The WTO Ministerial Conference, composed of representatives of all Member States, convenes at least every two years (Art IV, para 1 of the Agreement establishing the World Organizations). The first meeting took place in December 1996 in Singapore. The General Council, likewise composed of representatives of **3.68**

[166] CONTRACTING PARTIES in capital letters signifies the only explicit treaty body (Art XXV, para 1 GATT).

[167] HG Schermers/NM Blokker, *International Institutional Law* (3rd edn, 1995) § 1620, 1013.

[168] 1979 Agreement on Government Procurement, OJ 1980 L 71/44, Protocol Amending the GATT Agreement, OJ 1980 L 345/2444. The Agreement on Government Procurement (1994) (GPA) was signed in Marrakesh on 15 April 1994, OJ 1994 L 336/273 and entered into force on 1 January 1996. The GPA is one of the 'plurilateral' Agreements included in Annex 4 to the Agreement Establishing the WTO, signifying that not all WTO members are bound by it; a Committee on Government Procurement was established in 1994 with, *inter alia*, the EC Member States as members.

[169] General Agreement on Trade in Services, 15.12.1994, ILM 33 (1994) 44, 1167, 1182; OJ 1994 L 336/190.

[170] ILM 33 (1994) 13, 1125, 1144; Member States as at November 2000: 140, including the EC States and 29 States which had asked to join the WTO.

[171] ILM 33 (1994) 1154; OJ 1994 L 336/11.

[172] General Agreement on Trade-Related Aspects of Intellectual Property Rights, OJ 1994 L 336/213.

[173] Agreement on Trade-Related Investment Measures, OJ 1994 L 336/100.

the Member States, conducts the functions of the Ministerial Conference in the period between conferences (Art IV, para 2 of the same Agreement). The Secretariat renders administrative assistance in accordance with regulations adopted by the Ministerial Conference (Art VI of the Agreement).

3.69 The main purposes of the GATT were to provide for a framework to establish rules for the orderly conduct of world trade, and to supply a set of instruments for the reduction of customs tariffs and other trade barriers, by enacting the basic rules of most-favoured-nation treatment, national treatment, and reduction of tariff, and non-tariff trade barriers. The WTO goals are broader in so far as the WTO Agreement recognizes the need to protect the environment and to promote sustainable development. The WTO has to administer the WTO trade agreements, provide a forum for multilateral trade negotiations, administer the trade dispute-settlement procedures, and review national trade policies. A new Committee on Trade and Development was established to identify the relationship between trade policies, environmental measures, and sustainable development.[174] Trade ministers in Marrakech also agreed to establish a WTO Committee on Trade and Environment (CTE)[175] with analytical and prescriptive functions covering all areas of the multilateral trading system: goods, services, and intellectual property. The CTE has to identify the relationship between trade and environmental measures in order to promote sustainable development, and to make recommendations on whether any modifications to the provisions of the multilateral trading system are required.[176]

3.70 Relations between the GATT/WTO system and the EC still reflect the tension between a system designed to be universal and a regional arrangement. Under the GATT regime, favourable treatment by one nation to another must generally also be applied to all other nations. However, there are exceptions to this rule. Compatibility between regional arrangements and the GATT is provided for in Article XXIV of the General Agreement on Tariffs and Trade. This provision regulates customs unions and free-trade areas. EC Member States subscribe to the aim of harmonized world trade[177] and are aware of their duties not only under EC law but also under GATT regulations.[178] The status of the EC as a GATT Contracting Party has always been uncertain, but the issue is now solved.[179] Article XI of the WTO Agreement provides that: 'The contracting parties to GATT 1947 as of the

[174] Art IV(7) of the Agreement. J Schultz, 'The GATT/WTO Committee on Trade and the Environment: Towards Environmental Reform', AJIL 89 (1995) 423–39.

[175] GATT-Doc MTN.TNC/45 (MIN) 14 April 1994; WTO-Doc WT/CTE/1, Annex I, 12 November 1996.

[176] See the CTE's Report to the Ministerial Conference WT/CTE/1, 12 November 1996; B Chaytor/M Wolkewitz, 'Participation and Priorities', RECIEL 6 (1997) 157–62.

[177] Art 110 EC Treaty.

[178] See Art 234 EC Treaty which states that this Treaty does not affect earlier treaty relations.

[179] KJ Kuilwijk, *The European Court of Justice and the GATT Dilemma* (1996) 67.

entry into force of this Agreement and the European Communities . . . shall become original Members of the WTO.' According to European Court case-law, GATT regulations only apply directly to Member States and the EC in relation to third states, not within the Community itself.[180] The Council, the Commission, and the Parliament of the EC are involved in co-operation with the WTO, co-ordinating the views of Member States.[181] The competence of the Community and the Member States in respect of the matters covered by the WTO Agreement and related agreements is based on Articles 43, 54, 57, 66, 75, 84(2), 99, 100, 100a, 113, and 235 of the EC Treaty, in conjunction with the second subparagraph of Article 228(3) of the EC Treaty.[182]

(2) The International Bank for Reconstruction and Development (World Bank/IBRD)

According to a report of the UN Secretary-General, the World Bank is the most active international organization in energy matters, with numerous lending and non-lending projects and programmes, current and planned.[183] The World Bank and the IMF were both founded by the Bretton Woods Conference.[184] In its early years the World Bank focused on the reconstruction of economies after World War II. Today it is mainly concerned with the development of economically weak States. **3.71**

The World Bank Group comprises five organizations: the IBRD, the International Development Association (IDA), the International Finance Corporation (IFC), the Multilateral Investment Guarantee Agency (MIGA), and the International Centre for Settlement of Investment Disputes (ICSID). Only members of the IMF may be considered for membership in the World Bank according to Article II(1) of the Articles of Agreement of the IBRD. Subscription to the capital stock of the Bank is based on each member's quota in the IMF, which is designed to reflect the countries' relative economic strengths. Voting rights are related to shareholdings. Each member has 250 votes plus one additional vote for **3.72**

---

[180] ECJ, 16.3.1983, Case 266/81 *SIOT v Ministero delle finanze*, ECR 731; ECJ, 12.12.1972, Case 21-24/72 *International Fruit Company NV and others v Produktschap voor groenten en fruit*, ECR 1219; K Adamantopoulos, *Das Subventionsrecht des GATT in der EWG* (1988) 108. On whether the ECJ can take GATT law into account when asked to rule on the legality or validity of Community or Member State law in the area of foreign trade policy, see: ECJ, 5.10.1994, Case 280/93 *Bundesrepublik Deutschland v Council* [1994] European Court Reports I-4973.

[181] General Report of the Commission 1996, para 703.

[182] I Macleod/I Hendry/S Hyett, *The External Relations of the European Communities* (1996) 180; see also ECJ Opinion 1/94 *Re WTO Agreement* [1994] European Court Reports I-5267.

[183] Committee on New and Renewable Sources of Energy and on Energy for Development, Report of the Secretary-General on Energy Activities Within and Outside the United Nations System, UN Doc E/C.13/1996/7, 6.2.1996, para 27.

[184] 2 UNTS 134; 606 UNTS 294; for the Bretton Woods Conference see H Coing, 'Bretton Woods Conference (1944)' in R Bernhardt (ed), *EPIL*, Inst. 5 (1983) 13.

each share of stock subscribed to (Art V(3)). Consequently, the Bank can be compared to a global co-operative owned by its members.[185] The Group of Seven (Canada, France, Germany, Italy, Japan, the United Kingdom, and the United States) hold about 45 per cent of the shares; the US is the largest shareholder with about 17 per cent. Thus the US has the power to veto any changes in the Bank's capital base and Articles of Agreement, according to Article VIII of the founding agreement, as 85 per cent of the total votes are needed to effect such a change. The Bank's power structure contrasts with the UN's 'one State, one vote' principle, leading to divergent agendas within the organizations. The Bank's Board of Executive Directors, resident at the Bank's headquarters in Washington DC, represents all members and decides upon the Bank's policies (Art V(4, 5, 9)).

3.73 The main energy task of the World Bank relates to the funding of projects by loans and investments in a whole range of energy-related activities. It makes loans where private capital is not available on reasonable terms to finance productive investments. Loans are made either directly to governments, or to private enterprises upon the guarantee of their governments.[186] Loans usually have a grace period of five years and are repayable over fifteen years or fewer. They are normally made for projects likely to offer a commercially viable rate of return.[187] The World Bank has spearheaded initiatives towards privatizing energy organizations and enterprises. Furthermore, the World Bank is concerned with energy management questions. Jointly with the UNDP it executes an Energy Sector Management Assistance Programme. The programme involves energy conservation, power loss reduction, and power utility efficiency improvement.[188] In 1999 loans for electric power and other energy operations totalled some US$ 440 million.[189]

3.74 In 2000 the World Bank Group approved support for the Chad–Cameroon Petroleum Development and Pipeline Project.[190] The Project will exploit and distribute petroleum deposits in the South of Chad. Some 300 wells in Chad's

---

[185] As at November 2000 the Bank had 181 Member States.

[186] The loans are governed by, and create rights and duties under, international law and they are registered with the UN Secretary-General pursuant to Art 102 UN Charter; the World Bank applies General Conditions Applicable to Loan and Guarantee Agreements; see H Golsong, 'IBRD' in R Bernhardt (ed), *EPIL*, Inst. 5 (1983) 62.

[187] See http://www.worldbank.org. There are two types of bank lending. The first type, referred to above, is for developing countries able to pay near-market interest rates. The money comes from investors buying bonds issued by the World Bank. The second type goes to the poorest countries, which are not creditworthy. As bonds to finance lending cannot be issued, lending is done by the IDA. IDA credits are free of interest, carry a low (0.75%) annual administrative charge, and a very long term: 35 or 40 years including 10 years' grace.

[188] Committee on New and Renewable Sources of Energy and on Energy for Development, Report (n 183 above) para 15.

[189] *Europa World Yearbook 1999* (1999) 71.

[190] World Bank News Release No. 2000/395/AFR, 6 June 2000.

southern Doba Basin are thought to hold about 900 million barrels of recoverable oil. The oil will be transported through a 1,070 km pipeline to a marine terminal off the coast of Cameroon and onto the international market. The World Bank has approved loans of US$ 39.5 million for Chad and US$ 53.4 million for Cameroon to finance their respective investments in the project. The oilfields will be developed by a consortium of oil companies. Two joint-venture pipeline companies, one for the portion situated in Cameroon and the other for the portion located in Chad, will run the export system.

The Bank has been charged by critics with adding to environmental pollution problems by lending money to massive infrastructure or industrialization projects which involve deterioration of the surrounding natural ecology and damage local communities.[191] Criticism during the UN Conference on Environment and Development in Rio de Janeiro in 1992 led to a reference to this issue in Principle 7 of the Rio Declaration.[192] In Chapter 32 of Agenda 21 it was stated that the Commission on Sustainable Development should monitor reports on the implementation of Agenda 21 from organizations, including those relating to finance.[193] Although critics still hold that the Bank's new procedures to incorporate environmental considerations into the loan decisions rarely prevent it from making a loan,[194] the Bank has introduced major reforms, establishing an Office of Environmental Affairs to provide studies of the side-effects of its policies and has introduced environment divisions in its regional offices. The GEF programme attracted particular attention as it marks a move towards co-operation between the UN and the World Bank, which have been separate since the World Bank was established in 1947. Before the GEF was created, the UN's development of an environmental competence was entirely independent of the Bank's concern with economic issues.[195] **3.75**

[191] P Sands, 'Present at the Creation: A New Development Bank for Europe in the Age for Environmental Awareness' in *American Society of International Law, Proceedings of the 84th annual meeting 1991* (1992) 89.

[192] ILM 31 (1992) 874, 877: 'the developed countries acknowledge the responsibility that they bear in the international pursuit of sustainable development in view of the pressure their societies place on the global environment and of the technologies and financial resources they command'; ND White, *The Law of International Organizations* (1996) 262. However, in the past developing countries often insisted that loan conditions should not impede their industrial development.

[193] Agenda 21, ch 38, para 13, UN Doc A/Conf.151/26, 12.8.–28.9.1992; although according to Art IV(10) only economic considerations may be deemed relevant in the IBRD's decisions, the World Bank may take into account economic consequences of political behaviour; see H Golsong, n 186 above, 58.

[194] S Guyett, 'Environment and Lending: Lessons of the World Bank, Hope for the European Bank for Reconstruction and Development', New York Journal of International Law and Politics 24 (1992) 889/905; see also Sands, n 191 above, 77–95; for a different point of view: K Piddington, 'The Role of the World Bank' in A Hurrel/B Kingsbury, *The International Politics of the Environment* (1992) 212–27.

[195] ND White, n 192 above, 261.

(3) The International Monetary Fund (IMF)

3.76 The International Monetary Fund was established by a multilateral agreement in 1945.[196] It supports international monetary co-operation, aims at the expansion and the balanced growth of international trade, promotes stability in foreign exchange, and assists in the establishment of a multilateral system of payments in respect of current transactions between members.[197]

3.77 Each member of the Fund has a quota which corresponds to its national income, its monetary reserves, and other economic indicators. The subscription of a member is equal to the quota. It is payable in Special Drawing Rights (SDR) and in the Member State's currency. An SDR is an instrument in international payments. The amount of a country's SDRs corresponds to its quota. SDRs are valued on the basis of the exchange rates of the five members who are the largest exporters.[198]

3.78 The Fund's organs are the Board of Governors, the Executive Directors, the Managing Director, and a staff. Its powers are vested in the Board of Governors. The Interim Committee of the Board of Governors, which has twenty-four members, supports the Board in reviewing the international monetary system. However, it may not take any decision. The Executive Directors are responsible for the performance of the general operations of the Fund.

3.79 In performing the above mandate the IMF acts only indirectly in energy matters. The IMF supports members requiring exceptional assistance. The Fund established two oil facilities with low conditionality as a special policy to assist members in balance of payments difficulties resulting from the initial impact of the increased costs of importing petroleum in the period 1973–76. The facilities were financed exclusively by borrowing initially only from oil-exporting countries. The IMF did this by loan agreements with these countries and subsequently channelled the resources via the oil facilities to member countries with balance of payment deficits.[199] Throughout the 1990s in regions deemed to be at risk, the IMF emphasized thorough surveillance. The granting of credits is generally connected with special programmes, in which governments pledge to stabilize their economy. Especially in Eastern Europe, IMF activities have focused on the importance of energy for national economies on the basis of various programmes: for example, restructuring the energy sector has been identified as a means to

[196] Bretton Woods Agreement, signed at Washington on 27.12.1945; entered into force on 27.12.1945. 2 UNTS 39/134; 606 UNTS 295; 726 UNTS 266. As at November 2000 the IMF had 182 members: see further http://www.imf.org.

[197] Art I of the Agreement.

[198] France, Germany, Japan, the UK, and the USA.

[199] E Denters, *Law and Policy of the IMF Conditionality* (1996) 94; J Gold, *Legal and Institutional Aspects of the International Monetary System* (1984) 64.

strengthen the national economy of the Ukraine.[200] Tax revenues in the energy sector were supposed to reduce the deficit of the state budget in Russia.[201] In Georgia state subsidies to the energy sector have been blocked.[202]

(4) The European Bank for Reconstruction and Development (EBRD)

The EBRD plays a major role in supporting the energy reforms in Central and Eastern Europe. In 1991 the EBRD was established to foster the transition towards market-oriented economies and to promote private and entrepreneurial initiative in the Central and Eastern European countries, applying the fundamental principles of multi-party democracy, the rule of law, human rights, pluralism, and market economics.[203] The political element in the Bank's mandate is unique among international financial institutions.[204] Its activities are primarily concentrated on the promotion of the private sector (Arts 2, para 1(i), 11, para 3), the strengthening of financial institutions and legal systems, and the development of the infrastructure needed to support the private sector (Art 2, para 1(iii)). The EBRD intends to safeguard the environment by a pre-loan environmental impact analysis (Art 2, para 2(vii)). This operational mandate on environmental protection and restoration is new to financial institutions. **3.80**

The EBRD has sixty members (fifty-eight countries, the European Community, and the European Investment Bank) and twenty-six countries of operations: Central and Eastern Europe and the Commonwealth of Independent States (CIS) as well as the USA and other African and Asian States (Art 3).[205] In April 1996 the Board of Governors agreed to increase the Bank's capital base to ECU 20 billion.[206] France, Germany, Italy, and the United Kingdom are the largest European shareholders with 8.5 per cent of the capital each. Outside Europe, the United States is the largest shareholder with 10 per cent. **3.81**

The powers of the EBRD are vested in a Board of Governors, representing all shareholders of the Bank. The Board of Governors has delegated powers to a Board of Directors which is responsible, *inter alia*, for establishing policies, taking decisions concerning projects, and approving the budget. The elected President carries out the operations of the Bank under the direction of the Board of **3.82**

[200] IMF Press Release 97/39, 25.8.1997.

[201] IMF Press Release 96/13, 26.3.1996.

[202] IMF Press Release 96/7, 28.2.1996.

[203] Preamble, Art 1 of the Agreement establishing the European Bank for Reconstruction and Development, OJ EC 1990 L 372 (29.5.1990).

[204] A Newburg, 'The European Bank for Reconstruction and Development' in IBA Section on Energy and Natural Resources Law (ed), *Energy and Resources Law '92* (1992) 139.

[205] The EBRD's headquarters are in London, with 24 Resident or Regional Offices in 22 of its countries of operations (Art 33).

[206] The EBRD's initial subscribed capital is ECU 10 billion (Art 4) of which 30% was paid in as at 1 September 1997. The ECU was replaced by the Euro, with an equivalent value, from 1 January 1999.

Directors. The Bank has a special department for Nuclear Safety. With regard to Agenda 21 the EBRD established an Energy Efficiency Department in 1994 to work on energy efficiency projects in Central and Eastern Europe. The Bank makes finance available for projects intended to reduce inefficiency in energy transformation and transport. The EBRD administrates the Nuclear Safety Account (NSA) and the Chernobyl Shelter Fund (CSF), in accordance with their respective Fund Rules, in order to improve safety in nuclear power plants and assist the Ukraine in repairing the Chernobyl reactor.

3.83 One of the EBRD's strengths is that it can operate in both the private and the public sector. It merges the principles and practices of merchant and development banking, providing funds for private or privatizable enterprises and for physical and financial infrastructure projects needed to support the private sector. The Bank can offer, *inter alia*, loans, equity investments, and guarantees (Art 12).[207] In 1995 the project financing for the energy and power generation sector amounted to ECU 325 million. By enabling the EBRD to withhold funds from Member States which implement policies inconsistent with Article 1, the EBRD agreements provide a mechanism for enforcing its loan conditions (Art 8, para 3).[208]

3.84 The EBRD seeks to counter the energy crisis faced by the States in Eastern Europe, largely the result of heavy dependence on the former USSR. In 1991 total exports of energy by the former republics of the USSR decreased sharply: for instance, exports of oil fell by 48 per cent. The management of the decrease in the energy supply and the associated balance of payments effects have significant implications for the economic restoration of the region. This will encompass repairing existing supply facilities, realizing existing high priority projects (transmission lines and power stations already under construction), helping countries to diversify sources of energy supply and to improve energy security, and encouraging private sector projects which liberalize the supply of energy and bring in foreign capital.[209]

3.85 The EBRD's operations are carried out through its Banking Department. Country teams ensure consistent implementation of the Bank's country strategies; these are backed up by the specialist expertise of sector teams and operations

[207] By 31 December 1996 the Bank had approved 450 projects: these involved ECU 9.96 billion of the EBRD's own funds and were expected to mobilize an additional ECU 20.1 billion. Of the approved projects, 370 had been signed, committing ECU 7.7 billion of the EBRD's own funds. 73% of total approved funding was for private sector projects. Project-related technical co-operation is a major feature of the EBRD's activities. By the end of 1996, 47 co-operation fund agreements with bilateral donors, totalling ECU 424m, had been made with the Bank for this purpose; 1,471 projects, with a total estimated cost of ECU 398m, had been committed.

[208] The Agreement further stipulates that the EBRD shall take necessary steps to ensure that the loan is used for the activities detailed in the loan agreement (Art 13, para 1(xiii)).

[209] A Newburg, n 204 above, 139–40.

support units.[210] The following case study illustrates the EBRD's work in the energy sector.

In 1993 the EBRD started activities with regard to the Russian Unified Gas Supply. Gazprom is the world's largest integrated gas producer and pipeline enterprise and provides 30 per cent of Western Europe's gas consumption. The Russian Unified Gas Supply System (EGS) was built over twenty-five years and consists of 140,000 kilometres of high-pressure pipelines. The development of the EGS was motivated by the growth in gas demand, which had increased fourfold since 1970. The focus of investment at the time was on rapid construction of new lines. Consequently, some of the pipelines and compressor stations do not satisfy today's efficiency and environmental standards. The EBRD has worked with Gazprom to identify which investments will improve the reliability of the EGS system and gas supply to Western Europe. The Bank has acted as a catalyst, attracting loans from commercial banks and export credit agencies to Gazprom to finance these improvements. Since April 1993 the EBRD has worked with a group of Russian and international consultants on a study to reassess the present condition of the EGS system and to analyse the most cost-effective means for its reconstruction and for improving the system's efficiency.[211] The study named several critical points in the EGS system. Leakage and explosions occur as a result of stress corrosion cracking and insufficient cathodic protection in the pipelines. The study also made plans for preparing mitigatory investments to avoid future accidents. As a follow-up to the study, Gazprom and the EBRD discussed the possible financing of the first high-priority investments. The aim is to finance a number of reconstruction investments throughout the EGS.[212] **3.86**

E. Other International Organizations Active in the Energy Sector

(1) Institutional Aspects of the Energy Charter Treaty[213]

The Energy Charter Treaty (ECT) is an unprecedented agreement establishing a legal framework for investment, trade, and free transit in energy among OECD countries, republics of the former Soviet Union, and countries of Eastern Europe in order to facilitate energy co-operation.[214] **3.87**

[210] For a more detailed report on the Bank's operational activities in the energy sector see http://www.ebrd.com.

[211] The study, completed in November 1995, was financed by grants from Canada, France, Norway, the United Kingdom, the Netherlands, and the United States.

[212] These investments include mobile compressor stations, improved metering stations, valve replacement, pipeline inspection programmes, and eliminating bottlenecks in pipeline corridors.

[213] Concluded on 17.12.1994, entered into force on 16 April 1998; see http://www.encharter.org.

[214] See ch 4.

3.88 In order to guarantee its implementation, the ECT provides for institutional arrangements, ie the Energy Charter Conference and a Secretariat, established as an independent international organization in Brussels in 1996.[215] The Energy Charter Conference, periodically convened, will monitor compliance with the ECT's provisions and act as a forum for East–West dialogue on energy issues. It considers and adopts programmes of work and approves the annual accounts and budgets of the Secretariat. With regard to further elaboration of legal regulations, the Conference may authorize and approve the terms of reference for the negotiation of protocols and declarations, adopt texts and amendments thereof, and consider and adopt amendments to the Treaty (Art 34 ECT). Amendments must be adopted unanimously (Art 36 ECT). A remarkable competence is provided for in Article 34, para 7 and Article 36, para 3 ECT: these enable the Charter Conference to abolish its own functions and discharge its own Secretariat. This can be seen as an effort to restrict the authority and capability of the organization because of concern in the industry that a new agency might make market interventions.[216] The ECT does not explicitly enable the organization to make legally binding decisions.

3.89 The Secretariat is to assist the Charter Conference and support the elaboration, ratification, and implementation of the ECT and its related instruments (Art 35 ECT). The Secretary-General is to be appointed by the Charter Conference for a maximum five-year period. The Secretariat is funded by the Contracting Parties according to their capacity to pay, determined in Annex B to the ECT, which may be modified. Voluntary contributions may be accepted (Art 37 ECT). To avoid duplication of the functions discharged by existing international organizations, the ECT provides in Article 34, para 4 that 'the Charter Conference through its Secretariat shall co-operate with and make as full use as possible . . . of the services and programmes of other institutions and organizations with established competence in matters related to the objectives of this Treaty'.

3.90 However, some typical characteristics of international organizations are lacking. The ECT does not explicitly transfer international or domestic legal personality on the Conference or the Secretariat nor commit States Parties to extend privileges and immunities. Nonetheless, the provisional Energy Charter Conference adopted a decision conferring domestic legal capacity on the Secretariat in Belgium, while a headquarters agreement concluded with the Belgian Government on privileges and immunities recognizes the legal personality of the Conference.[217]

---

[215] There is a general tendency for major multilateral treaties to provide for a secretariat either set up as a kind of international organization or based at an existing international organization, such as UNEP.

[216] C Bamberger, 'The Energy Charter Treaty as a Work in Progress' in T Waelde (ed), *The Energy Charter Treaty* (1996) 599.

[217] C Bamberger, n 216 above, 599.

(2) Co-operation between the Nordic Countries

Nordic co-operation is facilitated by the Nordic Council and the Nordic Council of Ministers, through Ministerial Conferences, in special organs of co-operation, and through special departments.[218] The Nordic Council was established on 20 August 1952 through legislation between Denmark, Iceland, Norway, and Sweden. Finland joined in 1955. In 1971 the Statute of the Council was made part of a Treaty.[219] The Assemblies of the Nordic States, the Faeroe Islands, Greenland, the Åland Islands, and the Governments of the countries and the Territories, are part of the co-operation process in the Nordic Council. **3.91**

The Parties of the Nordic Council aim at maintaining and enhancing co-operation, *inter alia,* in the legal, economic, and environmental fields, and concerning transport.[220] Its organs are the Plenary Assembly, the Presidium, and the Committees. The Council has eighty-seven members.[221] Committees on environmental and economic matters, including industrial and energy policy, have been established. The Nordic Council acts through recommendations[222] and statements to the Council of Ministers and to the respective governments.[223] **3.92**

The Nordic Council of Ministers was established in 1971 as a forum for co-operation between the governments of the Member States, the Faeroe and Åland Islands, and Greenland.[224] Each member has one vote in the Council. Unanimous decisions are binding on Member States. However, if an action must be approved by a Member State's parliament according to its constitution, the decision is only binding after the approval. The work of the Nordic Council of Ministers is supported by a Secretariat. A committee on energy policy, composed of officials of the Member States, has been established.[225] **3.93**

The activities of the Council of Ministers include the furtherance of economic co-operation, especially through funding research and joint projects. The Nordic **3.94**

[218] Art 40 Agreement Concerning Co-operation ('The Helsinki Treaty'), signed at Helsinki on 23.3.1962, Royal Swedish Ministry for Foreign Affairs, Nordic Council (publ.) Treaty of Co-operation between Denmark, Finland, Iceland, Norway, and Sweden (in force 1962), Stockholm 1962, amended on 13.2.1971, 11.3.1974, 15.6.1983, and 6.5.1985. See A Berg, *Der Nordische Rat und der Nordische Ministerrat* (1988) 307–29.

[219] Arts 44–59 of the Treaty.

[220] Arts 6, 12, 19, 21, 31 of the Treaty.

[221] Arts 50, 52, 47 of the Treaty. The parliamentary assemblies of the countries and the islands elect members: Denmark elects 16, Finland 18, Iceland 7, Norway and Sweden 20 each, and the Faeroe Islands, the Åland Islands, and Greenland, 2 each.

[222] Art 56 of the Treaty.

[223] The delegations of the countries and the autonomous territories bear their own expenses. Common expenses of the Council are covered by contributions through the delegations of the Member States; these contributions are determined by the Assembly of the Presidium: Art 58 of the Treaty.

[224] Arts 60–7 of the Treaty.

[225] See Art 61 of the Treaty; A Berg, n 218 above, 284.

Investment Bank was established in 1975 in order to support the implementation of investment projects.[226] The Council's main areas of activity include energy in a wider sense as well as the financial support of petroleum extraction. In the area of environmental protection, special emphasis is put on co-operation in the energy field leading to the reduction of pollution. Nordic co-operation also supports the development of renewable energy sources. The Baltic States are supported by the Nordic Council of Ministers as well as by the Council in their efforts to make the use of energy more efficient, and to improve and implement the safety standards of nuclear power plants.[227]

(3) The European Organization for Nuclear Research (CERN)[228]

3.95 The work of international organizations is not confined to policy issues of economic or environmental interest, nor to technical and financial assistance. Some organizations exist solely to undertake research on energy matters. CERN is not only a centre for scientific co-operation, but also an organization offering services in science and research. The Organization is based on the Treaty with Financial Protocol of 1 July1953,[229] which entered into force on 29 September 1954.[230]

3.96 CERN is devoted exclusively to scientific and non-military research. The research results must be published. The Organization operates international laboratories for research on high-energy particles, situated on the border of Switzerland and France. CERN is also involved in international co-operation, especially in the fields of theoretical nuclear physics, the support of scientists, collaboration with research institutions, and work in the field of cosmic rays.[231] Initially, the Organization set up and operated a proton synchrotron for energies above ten giga-electronvolts, and a synchro-cyclotron capable of accelerating protons up to about 600 million electronvolts, as well as the necessary structures for research and administration. A proton synchrotron for energies of about 500 giga-electronvolts is now in operation.

3.97 The Organization consists of a Council and a Director-General for each Laboratory, assisted by a staff.[232] It has legal personality in the metropolitan terri-

---

[226] It has capital of 2,400 million IMF Special Drawing Rights.

[227] See *Europa World Yearbook 2000* (2000) 222–5.

[228] The European Organization for Nuclear Research has retained the acronym CERN from its predecessor, the *Conseil Européen pour la Recherche Nucléaire.*

[229] The Convention for the Establishment of a European Organization for Nuclear Research, signed at Paris on 1 July 1953: 200 UNTS 149. Major amendments made in 1967 entered into force on 17.1.1971: 808 UNTS 300/330.

[230] Its seat is in Geneva. The members are Austria, Belgium, Denmark, Germany, France, Finland, Greece, Hungary, Italy, the Netherlands, Norway, Poland, Slovakia, Sweden, Switzerland, the Czech Republic, and the UK.

[231] Art II of the Convention; see also H Hahn, 'European Organization for Nuclear Research' in 6 *EPIL* (1983) 189.

[232] Art IV of the Convention.

tories of Member States.[233] In case of disputes concerning the application or interpretation of the Convention, the Council is to offer good offices; if the dispute is not settled, it may be submitted to the International Court of Justice, according to Article XI of the Convention. The competence of the Council includes determining the Organization's policy in scientific, technical, and administrative matters, approving the programmes of activities, adopting the budget for the programmes, and determining the financial arrangements of the Organization in accordance with the Financial Protocol. The Directors-General are chief executive officers and legal representatives of the Organization in respect of the Laboratories under their control. Article VI of the Convention stipulates that the responsibilities of the Directors-General are international and are therefore not to be influenced by individual States.

F. Energy Activities within the European Union

(1) Introduction

The lack of a comprehensive European energy policy was reflected in the division of the European organizations and in Member States' insistence on their own national policy in major areas of energy matters.[234] Despite the integration process in the Union, the fragmentation of competence in energy matters continues, although standardization in this field has been discussed for a long time.[235] In 1995 the Commission published a White Paper on the energy policy of the European Union.[236] However, it is not the legal basis of a comprehensive framework; rather it is a political statement based on the competence which the founding treaties gave to the Communities and the Organs.[237] It may lead to the adoption of a structured and comprehensive body of legal instruments in the field of energy. It has to be borne in mind, though, that these instruments will have their legal basis not in the White Paper itself, but in the treaties establishing the Union. The White Paper led the European Council to adopt a resolution which calls for a comprehensive approach to energy policy: the aims of competitiveness, safeguarding energy supplies, and environmental protection have to be brought together in accordance with the principle of subsidiarity and the objective of economic and social cohesion.[238] **3.98**

233 Art IX of the Convention.

234 R Lukes, 'Energierecht' in Dauses, *Handbuch des EG-Wirtschaftsrechts* (1997) paras 2, 6.

235 See Report of the Commission, *The Common Market on Energy* (May 1988), Commission Document (88) 328 final.

236 European Commission, *An Energy Policy for the European Union, White Paper of the European Commission* (1995), COM (95) 682.

237 White Paper of the European Commission, COM (95) 682 fin, paras 10, 15.

238 Resolution of the Council, 8.7.1996, OJ 1996 C 224/1.

(2) Institutional Overview

3.99 The European Union is based on the European Communities, the Foreign and Security Policy, and Co-operation in the Areas of Justice and Home Affairs, as established by the Treaty on European Union.[239] The European Communities comprise the European Coal and Steel Community, the European Economic Community, which was renamed by the Treaty on European Union in 1992 as the European Community, and the European Atomic Energy Community. The European Economic Community and the European Atomic Energy Community were established by the Treaties of Rome in 1957.[240] The founding Treaties have been amended several times. Of high relevance are the changes imposed by the Treaty of Maastricht, affecting the institutional framework of the three Communities. The revision of the Treaty by the Treaty of Amsterdam of 2 October 1997 brought further changes.[241] The main innovations of the Amsterdam Treaty may be presented under four principal headings: freedom, security, and justice; the Union and the citizen; common foreign and security policy; and the Union's institutions.[242]

3.100 The European Union aims, *inter alia,* to promote economic and social progress and to establish a common international identity. The European Council, comprising the heads of States and Governments of the Member States,[243] gives the EU 'impetus for its development' and sets 'general political guidelines'.[244]

3.101 Each of the Communities has legal personality.[245] Thus the Communities already participate in the activities of the WTO[246] and the UN,[247] and they are party to the UNFCC.[248] The legal personality of the European Union, however, was not established by the Amsterdam Treaty. Instead, Articles 24 and 38 of the EU Treaty

[239] Title I, Art A, Treaty on European Union of 7.2.1992: OJ 1992 C 191, 224 (ILM 31 (1992) 247), entered into force on 1.11.1993. Cited as the TEU or the Treaty of Maastricht; commonly referred to as the Three Pillars.

[240] European Coal and Steel Community: 18.4.1951: 261 UNTS 140, entered into force on 23.7.1952. The Treaty expires on 23.7.2002: Art 97 ECSC Treaty. European Economic Community and European Atomic Energy Community: 25.3.1957: 298 UNTS 11/167, entered into force on 1.1.1958. The original members were Belgium, France, the Federal Republic of Germany, Italy, Luxembourg, and the Netherlands. Denmark, Ireland, and the United Kingdom joined on 1.1.1973, and Greece on 1.1.1981. With effect from 1.2.1985 Greenland ended its membership, having entered while under Danish rule. Portugal and Spain joined on 1.1.1986, Austria, Finland, and Sweden on 1.1.1995.

[241] For the Text of the Treaty see http://europa.eu.int/eur-lex/en/treaties/dat/eu_cons_treaty_en.pdf or OJ EC 1997 C 340; the Treaty entered into force on 1 May 1999.

[242] See further S Langrish, 'The Treaty of Amsterdam: Selected Highlights', *European Law Review* 23 (1998) 3–19.

[243] Member States of the European Union are the same as those of the Communities.

[244] Art 4 EU Treaty.

[245] See Art 6 ECSC Treaty; Art 184 EURATOM Treaty; Art 281 EC Treaty.

[246] See above, paras 3.65–3.70.

[247] See Commission, General Report, paras 675–8, 699–733; see also paras 3.12–3.57 above.

[248] See H Steeg, 'Energie und Umwelt', *Recht der Energiewirtschaft* 1998, 129–33.

introduced a procedure by which the Council may authorize the Presidency, on a case-by-case basis, by unanimity, to negotiate agreements with third States or international organizations if this is necessary for the implementation of Title V (Common Foreign and Security Policy) or Title VI (Police or Judicial Co-operation in Criminal Matters). Therefore, the Council may conclude an agreement on behalf of the Union. Thus limited legal personality will implicitly be conferred on the Union when the EU has concluded the first agreement.[249]

The Communities are bound together by a common institutional framework, including the European Parliament, Commission, Council, and Court of Justice. The organs of the Communities have various functions in energy matters. Depending on the competence on which an activity is based, those functions vary. Basically, the Commission, the Council, the Parliament, the Court of Justice, and the Court of Auditors perform special functions related to energy law. **3.102**

The European Parliament consists of 626 representatives of the peoples of the Member States.[250] Members are elected directly by citizens of the Union who are resident in a Member State.[251] The Parliament has a Presidency, Parliamentary Groups, Committees, Delegations, and a General Secretariat.[252] The Parliament is based in Strasbourg, but some sessions are held and committee work done in Brussels; the General Secretariat is located in Luxembourg. The Parliament's competences were limited for a long time, extending largely to consultation, supervision, and budgetary questions. The European Parliament has gained importance since the Single European Act[253] and the Treaty of Maastricht. Under Article 192 EC Treaty, the Parliament may request the Commission to submit a proposal on any matter on which it believes a Community act to be necessary. It must be consulted on the nomination of members of the Commission and the Court of Auditors. The Parliament has the right to approve or veto the composition of the Commission as a whole.[254] Supervisory functions of the Parliament include the right to ask questions of the Commission, which the latter must answer,[255] and the appointment of an Ombudsperson.[256] The Parliament may also bring **3.103**

[249] S Langrish, n 242 above, 13f.

[250] Art 189 EC Treaty. Currently, Germany is represented by 99 members, France, the UK, and Italy by 87 each, Spain by 64, the Netherlands by 31, Belgium, Greece, and Portugal by 25 each, Sweden by 22, Austria by 21, Denmark and Finland by 16 each, Ireland by 15, and Luxembourg by 6.

[251] P Craig/G De Burca, *EC Law* (1995) 59; see Council Directive 93/109 (1993) OJ L 329/34, which regulates the right to vote in Parliament elections; see also Resolution of Parliament (1994) OJ C 44/159 implementing the decision.

[252] M Ungerer in Lenz (ed), *EG-Handbuch Recht im Binnenmarkt* (2nd edn, 1994) 24.

[253] Of 28.2.1986, entered into force on 1.7.1987; OJ EC 1987 L 169.

[254] Art 214 EC Treaty.

[255] Art 197 EC Treaty, Art 23 ECSC Treaty, Art 110 EURATOM Treaty.

[256] Art 195 EC Treaty, Art 20d ECSC Treaty, Art 107d EURATOM Treaty.

proceedings before the Court of Justice[257] and intervene without having to show a special interest.[258] With the Amsterdam Treaty the European Parliament enlarged its role as a co-legislator with the Council. The co-decision procedure of Article 251 EC Treaty has been extended and simplified by dropping the third reading. Where conciliation is unsuccessful, the proposed instrument will be dropped (see further para 3.113 below).

3.104 The Commission has twenty members, one acting as President and two as Vice-Presidents. Member States appoint a President after consulting the Parliament. Members of the Commission are appointed by Member States after consultation with the President to be. Not more than two members have the same nationality. In respect of performing their functions, they are independent from governments and other bodies.[259] If a Commission member is no longer able to perform his task or commits a grave offence the member can be removed from office by the Court of Justice. The Commission has several Directorates General which deal with special subjects as provided by the Treaties, including a special Directorate General for Energy (DG Energy & Transport).[260] Directorate General Environment is concerned with the environment, nuclear safety, and civil protection. The Commission publishes a report on the activities of the Communities annually.[261] This report sets out the latest developments in energy matters as well as all other fields of Community activity related to this field. The Commission's general competences are in all matters affecting energy. It ensures the application of the Treaties of the Union and of the Communities, and the provisions enacted by the organs. The Commission gives recommendations or opinions as provided by the Treaties or as it deems necessary. It may adopt decisions as far as it is competent, and it participates in decisions of the Council and Parliament. It exercises those functions which are conferred on it by the Council.[262] The Commission's right of initiative was strengthened by the Amsterdam Treaty, *inter alia*, through the creation of new policies or areas of action (employment, health).

3.105 The Council of Europe[263] is the principal decision-making organ. It co-ordinates the policies of the Members regarding economic matters, and delegates imple-

---

[257] Art 232 EC Treaty.

[258] Art 37 Statute of the Court of Justice; see *Roquette Frères v Council* (1980) ECR 3333.

[259] Art 213 EC Treaty, Art 9 ECSC Treaty, Art 126 EURATOM Treaty.

[260] The present Commissioner responsible for Energy & Transport is Loyola de Palacio. On an irregular basis, DG Energy & Transport publishes *Energy In Europe*, a journal which covers energy policies and trends in the European Community; see: http://europa.eu.int/comm/energy/en/etf_1_en.html.

[261] General Report on the Activities of the European Union, as provided for in Art 212 EC Treaty, Art 17 ECSC Treaty, Art 125 EURATOM Treaty.

[262] Art 211 EC Treaty.

[263] Until the Treaty of Maastricht entered into force, this body was known as the Council of Ministers.

mentation to the Commission. It may also oversee implementation.[264] Each Member State is represented by one minister in the Council, according to the subject to be dealt with. Unless the EC Treaty provides otherwise Council decisions are made by a majority of its members. If a qualified majority is necessary, the members' votes have different weights, corresponding loosely to the size of each Member State.[265] The number of Commissioners and the voting weights of Member States within the Council will need adjustment for the next enlargement of the Union.

A Court of Auditors was established to monitor the finances of the three Communities.[266] This Court, composed of members totally independent in the performance of their duties, is responsible for carrying out the audit and examines the accounts of all revenue and expenditure.[267] **3.106**

The Court of Justice secures the observance of law in the interpretation and application of the Treaties of the Communities.[268] It consists of thirteen judges who may sit in plenary or in chambers.[269] It has jurisdiction to give preliminary rulings concerning the interpretation and validity of acts by the institutions.[270] The Commission is authorized to bring before the Court a Member State which has failed to fulfil an obligation under the Treaty.[271] There is the possibility for indirect review of regulations.[272] The Court also has jurisdiction over non-contractual Community liability.[273] With regard to action for annulment or failure to act, part of the Court's jurisdiction has been transferred to the Court of First Instance. **3.107**

In 1988 the Court of First Instance was established to relieve some of the burden on the Court of Justice.[274] It has fifteen members. The jurisdiction of the Court of First Instance is constrained by Article 255 EC Treaty, and by Council Decision 88/591,[275] which established the Court. It has jurisdiction over actions brought by Member States or Community institutions. The Council invested the Court of First Instance with further competences in relation to staff cases and in actions brought against a Community institution by natural or legal persons under Articles 230 or 232 of the Treaty relating to the implementation of competition rules applicable to undertakings. In addition to these cases, the Council conferred **3.108**

[264] Art 202 EC Treaty.
[265] Art 205 EC Treaty.
[266] Arts 246–8 EC Treaty, Chapter V ECSC Treaty, Section V EURATOM Treaty, as inserted by the Treaty of Maastricht.
[267] Arts 246, 248 EC Treaty, Art 45a, c ECSC Treaty, Art 160a, c EURATOM Treaty.
[268] Art 220 EC Treaty, Art 31 ECSC Treaty, Art 136 EURATOM Treaty.
[269] Art 221 EC Treaty.
[270] Art 234 EC Treaty.
[271] Art 226 EC Treaty.
[272] Art 241 EC Treaty.
[273] Arts 235, 288 EC Treaty.
[274] Art 225 EC Treaty, Art 32d ECSC Treaty, Art 140a EURATOM Treaty.
[275] OJ 1988 L 319 1.

jurisdiction on the Court of First Instance in all other actions brought by non-privileged applicants under Articles 230, 232, and 235, and under Article 238 of the Treaty where the jurisdiction of the Court may be based on an arbitration clause in a contract concluded on behalf of the Community. It has no jurisdiction in preliminary rulings.[276] Any party to an action before the Court of First Instance has an automatic right of appeal to the European Court on a point of law.

(3) The European Community (EC)

3.109 In the EC the energy field is regulated by primary law (the Treaty provisions) and secondary law, ie regulations, directives, decisions, and recommendations.[277] While regulations are directly applicable, directives must generally be implemented by Member States but are binding as to the result to be achieved. Decisions, being acts affecting individuals, are binding on those whom they address. Some authors hold that a distinction between direct effect and direct applicability must be drawn.[278] All regulations are directly applicable. Some directives may not be directly effective. Thus a directive requires a Member State to take implementing measures. However, the national court must ensure that the implementing measure is consistent with the meaning of the directive as interpreted by the European Court.[279]

3.110 Whereas the 1957 Treaty founding the EEC did not mention energy matters, there were activities of the Community in related fields.[280] Competences were based on Article 100 EEC Treaty, which provided for EEC competence in matters affecting the functioning of the Common Market; according to Article 235 EEC Treaty, Community organs could act if deemed necessary for the Common Market, even when no competence was expressly provided by the Treaty. In addition, Articles 30–7 and 59–66 ('free movement of goods and services'),[281] Articles 85, 86, and 90, para 2 (rules on competition),[282] Articles 92–4 ('subsidies') and

[276] Art 225, para 1 EC Treaty.

[277] Art 249 EC Treaty; see further P Craig/G De Burca, *EC Law* (1995) 96–102.

[278] Winter, 'Direct Applicability and Direct Effect', Common Market Law Review 9 (1972) 425–38.

[279] ECJ Case 40/69 *Hauptzollamt Hamburg Oberelbe v Bollmann* [1970] European Court Reports 69, 80; S Weatherill/P Beaumont, *EC Law* (2nd edn, 1995) 344f.

[280] Directives on energy-related activities included those on the reduction of air pollution, Directive 70/220/EEC, 20.3.1970 (OJ L 76, 6.4.1970), Directive 80/779/EEC (OJ L 229, 20.8.1980), Directive 82/884/EEC, 3.12.1982 (OJ L 328, 31.12.1982), and Directive 85/203/EEC, 7.3.1985 (OJ L 87, 27.3.1985). See A Bleckmann/S Pieper in C Lenz (ed), *EG-Handbuch Recht im Binnenmarkt* (2nd edn, 1994) 681–3, 686–9.

[281] It has been unclear whether electricity is a service or a good; the practice of EC organs seems to favour the latter view: see R Lukes, 'Energierecht' in Dauses, *Handbuch des EG-Wirtschaftsrechts* (1997) para 64.

[282] See R Lukes, 'Die europäische Energiecharta', *Europäische Zeitschrift für Wirtschaftsrecht* 1992 401.

Articles 100–2 ('harmonization') of the EEC Treaty applied to various matters relating to energy.[283]

Based on the provisions of the Single European Act,[284] the Treaty of Maastricht introduced further competences in energy-related matters. According to Article 3 lit u EC Treaty, the EC may act in the field of energy in accordance with the Treaty. Furthermore, the EC is to support the development of trans-European networks, including those supplying energy (Art 154 EC Treaty). Subject to this provision are electricity lines and pipes for the distribution of gaseous and liquid energy resources.[285] Although this provision applies only to EC Member States, the term trans-European emphasizes the need to develop networks covering the whole of Europe.[286] Co-operation agreements in the form of treaties are governed by Article 300 EC Treaty, which involves the participation of the Council, the Commission, and the Parliament.[287] The aim of this co-operation is to establish a comprehensive network with special emphasis on the connection of insular or remote regions to the central areas of the Communities.[288] Further competences relating to energy matters include a common policy on transport (Art 3 lit f EC Treaty) and a policy in the sphere of the environmental (Art 174, Art 3 lit l EC Treaty).[289] In Article 174 EC Treaty the efficient use of natural resources has been identified as one of the most important means of achieving environmental protection. While the EC has been actively regulating these specific matters, no comprehensive, legally binding approach in the energy sector has yet been achieved.[290] 3.111

Corresponding to these different competences, there is a variety of legislative procedures in the Community. The procedures used in energy matters depend upon the legal basis of the decisions, although the Amsterdam Treaty enlarged the importance of the co-decision procedure. While matters based on the competence on environmental policy, except for the general programmes of action, have so far been decided by the Council with a qualified majority after hearing the Economic and Social Council under the co-operation procedure,[291] Article 175 EC Treaty now refers to Article 251 EC Treaty, ie the co-decision procedure. Actions based 3.112

283 See R Lukes, 'Energierecht' (n 281 above) para 50.

284 Dated 28.2.1986, OJ EC 1987 L 169 1.

285 A Frohnmeyer, 'Art. 129b' in Grabitz/Hilf (eds), *Kommentar zur Europäischen Union* (1997) para 5.

286 ibid, para 1. The Community is competent to co-operate with third countries on networks: Art 129c, para (3); see also the case study on GazProm, para 3.86 above.

287 A Frohnmeyer, above n 285, para 21.

288 Art 155, para (2) EC Treaty; this serves to clarify Art 158 EC Treaty; see A Frohnmeyer, n 285 above, para 16.

289 With the Single European Act, OJ EC 1987 L 169, 29.6.1987, entered into force on 1 July 1987, competence in the field of the environment was explicitly included in EEC law.

290 For fuller discussion of the extent of EC regulatory activity in the energy sector, see Ch 5 below. The EC is also a party to the Energy Charter Treaty: see further Ch 4 below.

291 Arts 130s (1), 130r, 189c EC Treaty (pre-Amsterdam Treaty).

on the competence of trans-European networks include the creation of guidelines, financial support for realizing these, and action necessary for the inter-operability of networks, especially standardizing technical norms. The Council decides on the guidelines in accordance with the co-decision procedure.[292] In addition, this procedure is used to determine general programmes of action in environmental matters.[293] Although guidelines are deemed to be legal acts, they need to be modified into one of the forms mentioned in Article 249 EC Treaty to be executed: in this field this will usually be a decision.

3.113 The Council receives proposals from the Commission and obtains opinions from the Parliament. It adopts a common position by a qualified majority on a proposal, and this is communicated to the Parliament. If the Parliament approves or remains inactive for three months the Council adopts the act according to the common position. If the European Parliament rejects the common position by an absolute majority of its component members, the proposed act is to be deemed not to have been adopted. However, the Council provides for a Conciliation Committee if the Parliament proposes amendments to the common position by an absolute majority of its component members and the Council does not approve all the amendments. The Conciliation Committee, made up of members of both organs, has the task to agree on a joint text. In case this does not happen, the Council may confirm the common position with qualified majority unless the Parliament rejects the text with absolute majority. If a joint text is agreed on in the Committee it has to be adopted in Parliament with absolute majority of the votes cast; the Council has to decide with qualified majority. In case one of the organs does not agree, the proposal is considered to be not adopted. This procedure can be considered to be a manifestation of the growing weight of the Parliament in the decision-making process of the EC.

3.114 Activities concerning inter-operability and financial support are governed by the simpler co-operation procedure, as they are merely technical. In all cases the Economic and Social Council and the Committee of the Regions[294] must be heard. Should an action affect the territory of a Member State, this State must consent.

3.115 Secondary legislation includes the regulation of information on the import and export of oil and by-products,[295] the management of crises due to shortages of crude oil,[296] the regulation of the price of gas and electricity,[297] the transportation

[292] Arts 155, para (1), 156, 251 EC Treaty.

[293] Art 175(3) EC Treaty.

[294] These organs have advisory status: Arts 257–62, 263–5 EC Treaty.

[295] Regulations 1055/72 EEC, 18.5.1972 (OJ L 120/3), 338/75 EEC, 13.2.1975 (OJ 1975, 45/1), 1893/79 EEC, 28.8.1979 (OJ 1979, L 220/1, OJ 1979, L 297, OJ 1990, L 133).

[296] Directive (OJ 1973, L 228/1), Regulation of 20.12.1985 (OJ 1985, L 350).

[297] Directive 91/296/EEC, 31.5.1991 (OJ 1991, L 147/37).

of gas and electricity,[298] rules for the internal electricity market,[299] and for the internal market in natural gas.[300]

(4) The European Coal and Steel Community (ECSC)

The basis of the ECSC is the Common Market, which prohibits tariffs, non-tariff barriers, quotas, actions resulting in discrimination against producers, buyers, and sellers, subsidies, and other measures which affect the market.[301] The ECSC aims at a regular distribution of energy, control of prices, the improvement of labour standards, inter-State co-operation, and generation of energy.[302] To achieve these aims, the ECSC collects information, defines common goals, supports investments, and secures competition.[303] Financial support can be given to companies through credits and guarantees.[304] **3.116**

Secondary law related to coal under the ECSC Treaty has been limited. Of importance is the approval of subsidies granted by Member States by the ECSC, which reflect the diminishing demand in the hard coal sector. The Commission must be notified in advance of the granting of subsidies. France, Germany, the United Kingdom, Spain, and Portugal were allowed to subsidize their respective coal industries. However, the level of subsidies has been reduced.[305] **3.117**

The Treaty provided for the High Authority, the Consultative Committee, the Assembly, the Special Council of Ministers, and the Court of Justice.[306] The High Authority[307] of the Community, since 1967 identical with the Commission,[308] issues decisions, recommendations, and opinions.[309] The Commission may collect information in order to achieve the aims of the organization. It may also levy penalties on companies not complying.[310] Interventions should be applied only **3.118**

[298] Directive 90/547/EEC of 29.10.1990 (OJ 1990, L 313/30), Directive on the transit of electricity through large networks, Directive 91/296/EEC of 31.5.1991 (OJ 1991, L 147), Directive on the transit of gas; see R Lukes, n 283 above, para 102.

[299] European Parliament and Council Directive 96/92/EC of 19.12.1996 concerning common rules for the internal market in electricity (OJ 1997, L 027).

[300] OJ 1998, L 204.

[301] Arts 1, 2, 4 ECSC Treaty; the term coal is defined in the Appendix to the Treaty.

[302] Art 3 ECSC Treaty; on control of prices see Arts 60–4.

[303] Art 5 ECSC Treaty.

[304] R Lukes, n 283 above, para 14.

[305] Decision 3632/93/ECSC; OJ L 329, 30.12.1993, Commission, *General Report 1996*, para 374.

[306] 2nd Title ECSC Treaty; the Consultative Committee was attached to the Commission, Art 18 ECSC Treaty.

[307] Art 46 ECSC Treaty.

[308] Merger Treaty, 1965 (Treaty Establishing a Single Council and a Single Commission of the European Communities) which entered into force in 1967, OJ EC 152 (1967) 2.

[309] Art 14 ECSC Treaty; Decisions are binding in all their details, whereas recommendations are binding with respect to the objectives which they specify; however, the choice of appropriate means to attain this objective is left to those to whom the recommendation is directed. Opinions are not binding.

[310] Art 47 ECSC Treaty.

indirectly in co-operation with Member States.[311] In case of a decreasing demand for coal the Commission may impose quotas on production taking into account the views of the Consultative Committee and with the agreement of the Council.[312] In case of a shortage the Council may, possibly on the initiative of the Commission, decide unanimously on the priority of the use of coal and the distribution of the resources of the Community.[313]

3.119 The Consultative Committee has advisory functions. It is attached to the Commission.[314] It has eighty-four members who represent producers, workers, consumers, and dealers in the coal and steel industry. The Budget for the fiscal year 2000 of the ECSC amounts to EUR 178 million.[315] The Commission has allocated EUR 25 million to research projects relating to coal.[316] According to Article 97 ECSC Treaty, the Treaty expires on 23 July 2002.

(5) The European Atomic Community

3.120 The European Atomic Community (EURATOM) was established to support the rapid development of the non-military nuclear industries in the Member States and to establish good relations in this field with other countries. In order to reach these aims, EURATOM supports research, establishes safety norms and oversees their implementation, facilitates investments, and secures and monitors distribution of fissionable material;[317] the establishment of the Common Market is also relevant.[318] The aims of EURATOM mean that it must co-operate closely with industry, the scientific community, and other international organizations.[319] It shares its institutional framework with the other Communities. The Council and the Commission issue regulations, directives, decisions, recommendations, and opinions.[320]

3.121 EURATOM has its own safeguarding system[321] which is executed by the EURATOM Safeguards Directorate, whose headquarters are in Luxembourg.[322]

---

[311] Art 57 ECSC Treaty.

[312] Art 58 ECSC Treaty.

[313] Art 59 ECSC Treaty.

[314] Arts 18, 19 ECSC Treaty.

[315] Bulletin EU 12-1999, Section 1.6.5.

[316] Bulletin EU 12-1999, Section 1.5.6.

[317] Arts 1, 2 EURATOM Treaty.

[318] R Lukes, 'Energierecht' in Dauses, *Handbuch des EG-Wirtschaftsrechts* (1997) para 22.

[319] Arts 201, 206 EURATOM Treaty call for close co-operation with OECD and enables EURATOM to conclude treaties with States and international organizations.

[320] Art 161 EURATOM Treaty.

[321] Title II, Chapter VII EURATOM Treaty.

[322] See FC Dominioni, 'The Role and Tasks of EURATOM in the Field of Peaceful Uses of Nuclear Energy' in European Commission, DG XVII, *Energy in Europe*, vol 26 (December 1995) 33–6, 35.

Safeguarding means ensuring that special fissionable materials and services by the Agency are used only for civil purposes. Because of the need to co-ordinate work with the International Atomic Energy Agency (IAEA), the organization, its Member States, and the IAEA concluded a co-operation agreement.[323] The EURATOM safeguards system does not apply to materials intended for defence.[324] EURATOM has a property right on special fissionable materials.[325] Secondary legislation imposes safety standards for the general population as well as for workers.[326] Security is another regulated aspect.[327]

Fulfilling, *inter alia*, its duty to promote nuclear research, the Commission has established Framework Programmes for Research, Technological Development, and Demonstration. For example, the Fourth Framework Programme (1994–98) included research and development on radioprotection, the plutonium cycle, storage, reactor safety, and various safeguard measures. Another area of research is fusion: Sweden, Switzerland, and the then Member States established the Joint European Torus in operation since 1993. EURATOM has also become a partner of the International Thermonuclear Experimental Reactor Agreement.[328] **3.122**

The Organization and its activities are financed by the EC budget.[329] The Organization is also authorized to raise loans in order to support its research and investment activities. **3.123**

G. Non-Governmental Organizations (NGOs)

An influential development with regard to international organizations has been the increasing participation of non-governmental organizations, breaking the monopoly once enjoyed by States in favour of representation of non-State interests. Various non-governmental organizations support the European States in **3.124**

323 1.12.1975, OJ L 329 28; see paras 3.49–3.57 above.

324 Art 84 EURATOM Treaty.

325 Art 2 lit f, Chapter VIII EURATOM Treaty; this excludes all materials for defence purposes: Arts 86, 84 EURATOM Treaty.

326 Directive 80/836/EURATOM, OJ 11, 221/59; Directive 84/467/EURATOM, 3.9.1984, OJ 1984, L 265/4.

327 Fissionable materials are controlled by Regulation 3227/76/EURATOM, 290/90/EURATOM OJ L 363, 31.12.1976; direct inspections of book-keeping and the material itself in institutions handling these materials, such as power plants, are mandated, as well as the examination of data transmitted by those institutions.

328 See FC Dominioni, n 322 above, 33–6.

329 Expenditure on the safeguards system was proposed to be 15,787,000 ECU in 1997: General Report 1996, 425; see Voegelaar, 'European Atomic Energy Community' in R Bernhardt (ed), *EPIL*, Inst. 6 (1983) 111.

their law-making and implementing activities, promoting the influence of societal forces.[330] According to a definition used by the ECOSOC, an NGO is an international organization not established by intergovernmental agreement but which may accept members designated by government authorities. An NGO shall be of representative character, shall express the views of major sections of the population, and shall cover, where possible, a substantial number of countries in different regions of the world.[331] Securing the representation of non-State entities has been achieved in various ways. First, there is the device of 'associate membership'. Prime examples are the OECD and the WMO. Secondly, observer status may be granted. This allows a non-State entity to submit documents or speak in debate, though without the right to vote.[332] According to Article 71 of the UN Charter, the ECOSOC may make suitable arrangements for consultation with NGOs which deal with matters falling within its competence. Numerous special organs of the UN maintain consultative arrangements with international NGOs, which are regulated by resolutions of the General Assembly (UNEP) or of ECOSOC (UNDP) and rules of procedure or directives of the special organs (UNEP/UNDP). Some specialized agencies maintain formalized consultative relationships with NGOs which are based on special provisions in their constitutions (eg Art 26 IMO Constitution).

3.125 The following NGOs are of particular importance for the energy infrastructure in Europe. Nordel was established in 1963 and is composed of senior representatives of the electricity industries of Denmark, Finland, Iceland, Norway, and Sweden. Nordel aims at enhancing co-operation in the field of electricity. Special regard is given to technical co-operation. Nordel also maintains contact with other organizations and entities in the energy sector and disseminates information with regard to its work. Nordel is composed of a Secretariat, an Executive Board, and an Annual Meeting. It also has two permanent committees. The System Committee is responsible for technical system matters of a long-term nature, and the Operations Committee occupies itself with the day-to-day operation of the technical framework. The Executive Board implements the decisions of the Annual Meeting. A Secretariat supports the association and implements its decisions. The Union for the Co-ordination of Transmission of Electricity (UCTE) represents the mainland European electricity companies. It was founded in 1951 as an

[330] See Report of the Secretary-General on the Follow-Up to the Previous Sessions of the Committee on New and Renewable Sources of Energy and on Energy for Development, UN E/C.13/1998/2, 12 February 1998, para 24. On NGOs see S Hobe, 'Global Challenges to Statehood: The Increasingly Important Role of International Nongovernmental Organisations', Indiana Journal of Global Legal Studies (1998), 191–209; K Huefner, 'Non-Governmental Organisations' in R Wolfrum (ed), *United Nations: Law, Policies and Practice* (1995) vol 2, 927–35.

[331] UN Doc E/Res/1296 (XLIV), 23.5.1968. For more detail see *Yearbook of International Organisations 1989–90*, Appendix 3: Types of Organisations.

[332] D Bowett, *The Law of International Institutions* (4th edn, 1982) 397.

advisory body to further the exchange of information on electricity trade and to help carry out co-operative projects. Both organizations function as networks for electricity interchanges. While the electricity systems of UCTE's member companies in Western Europe are linked by synchronous frequency interconnection, the eastern part of Denmark, Norway, Sweden, and Finland are synchronous with Nordel. In England and Wales the power pool is operated by the National Grid Company.[333]

EUROGAS, the European Union of the Natural Gas Industry, was founded in 1990 as a non-profit-making international association under Belgian law.[334] Its members are the national representative bodies of the natural gas companies in Europe. EUROGAS represents the views of the natural gas industries to international organizations, especially to the European Union, and to the public. It is engaged in the development of the industry in the technical, scientific, legal, and economic fields. Through a common Secretariat, EUROGAS is connected to MARCOGAZ, which supports the harmonization of technical standards of the European gas supply industry. The International Association of Oil & Gas Producers, formerly known as the E&P Forum, has been representing the oil and gas industry before law-making authorities since its establishment in 1974. It represents the industry's views on operating standards and performance to governmental bodies and the public. It also takes into account social, environmental, and political issues with regard to the energy field. The International Association of Oil & Gas Producers is a non-governmental organization with consultative status in the IMO.[335] **3.126**

Eurofores, the European Forum for Renewable Energy Sources, was established as an independent non-profit-making organization in order to improve communication in the renewable energy sector.[336] Members are either organizations or individuals. It raises public awareness about renewable energy, and provides information to the European Union institutions, as well as to national governments and agencies. **3.127**

The International Standards Organization (ISO)[337] is a worldwide federation of national standards bodies from 100 countries. Only one body for each country is accepted for membership. It was established in 1947 and aims at promoting the development of standardization and related activities in order to facilitate **3.128**

[333] M Roggenkamp, 'Networkbound Energy Trade in Europe', Journal of Energy and Natural Resources Law 12 (1994) 60f.

[334] EUROGAS Secretariat, Avenue Palmerston, 4, 1000 Brussels (Belgium).

[335] See para 3.124 above.

[336] Secretariat Brussels, c/o European Parliament, Rue Wiertz, Office D3 11E158, B-1047 Brussels, Tel: +322 2845771/7771—Fax: +322 2849771; Secretariat Madrid, Avda. de Burgos 48, Bajo B, E-28036 Madrid, Tel: +3491 383 33 39—Fax: +3491 383 31 59.

[337] See http://www.iso.ch.

international trade in goods, services, and technology transfer. The activities of the ISO result in international agreements being published as International Standards. It has technical liaisons with the specialized UN agencies, such as the WHO, the FAO, and the IAEA. In 1994, for example, it had three technical activities related to energy: it worked on standardization in the field of solar energy use (ISO/TC 180), on establishing standards for hydrogen distribution chains, storage infrastructures, and fuelling facilities (ISO/TC 197), and on technical energy systems (ISO/TC 203). Because of increasing demand for standardized methods of comparing different energy sources, the Committee on Technical Energy Systems was created in 1991. Economic comparisons between different energy options are not always possible because future prices of fuel and equipment are not known. Comparison based on analysis in energy terms is often the only valid method. Commonly accepted definitions are desirable for describing energy systems so as to be able to compare different sectors of the industry, as well as to establish methods of arriving at criteria for comparisons. There is also a growing demand for standardized information, energy declarations, and products and processes.[338]

3.129 The increasing relevance of non-governmental organizations as well as of multinational enterprises in international relations is particularly evident in the energy sector. The development of legal regulations for these participants is a necessary future task for the law of international organizations.[339]

H. General Conclusions

3.130 Three kinds of organizations are active in the energy sector. First, organizations explicitly concerned with energy: either restricted to nuclear energy like the IAEA, the NEA, EURATOM, and CERN, or concerned with energy in general like the Energy Charter Treaty institutions and the IEA. The last is a model organization for energy concerns, and is treated in detail in section I below. Secondly, organizations like the UN, the OECD, and the Nordic Council have a broad mandate which enables them to deal with energy issues by way of interpretation of their

[338] Committee on New and Renewable Sources of Energy and on Energy for Development, Report of the Secretary-General on Energy Activities Within and Outside the UN System, UN Doc E/C.13/1994/4, 21.1.1994, paras 54–5.

[339] This was made clear by the Brent Spar incident in 1995 involving the environmental group Greenpeace. British Shell intended to sink the 45,000-tonne oil storage platform in the North Sea although it was said to be loaded with toxic and radioactive sludge. This swiftly gave rise to campaigns in the UK and Europe spearheaded by Greenpeace which led to a consumer boycott in Germany, the Netherlands, Britain, and other countries. In September 1995, however, Greenpeace conceded that its assertion that the oil platform contained 5,000 tonnes of crude oil mixed with radioactive waste and other contaminants had been incorrect. Greenpeace issued a public apology to Shell. A study showed that most of the waste—68,000 tonnes of concrete ballast—was chemically similar to rust, while 30 tonnes was low-level radioactive waste.

constitutive instruments. Thirdly, organizations with a special mandate may undertake particular energy-related activities as a means to attain their particular aims (UNDP, UNEP, IMO, and other specialized agencies). Thus the IMO, for instance, is competent to deal with energy in connection with shipping, and the UNDP is competent to support development projects in the energy sector. Environmental competences are particularly connected with competences in energy, since production, transportation, and utilization thereof are major causes of environmental pollution.

Actions taken by international organizations can be distinguished as follows: **3.131** adopting general policies (eg UN bodies, the OECD, the IAEA), legislative functions (eg the ECE, the IMO, the IAEA, and the EC), technical, scientific, and general project assistance (eg UNIDO, UNEP, the IAEA, the OECD/NEA), and funding (eg the World Bank/GEF, and the EBRD). Looking at these activities it becomes evident that the mandates of international organizations in the energy sector, except for the supranational EC, do not significantly influence national competences. Only supranational or specialized organizations (the EC, IAEA, and IEA) have legally relevant competences, sometimes restricting the sovereignty of their Member States. Other organizations' activities are restricted to making non-binding policy decisions. Therefore, the legislative functions of organizations in energy matters are also more limited than, for instance, in the environmental sector. Above all, the co-ordination of activities is still minimal. Without formal co-ordinating mechanisms there is no regular and consistent exchange of information. Even if co-operation is increasing it is still not evident how systematic the mode of co-operation is and how far it can work as a possible ground for future actions. To avoid unnecessary overlap when performing activities in the field of energy should be a predominant aim for international institutions in the years to come.[340]

Some voices advocate a worldwide energy institution. In 1997 the UN Secretary- **3.132** General, for instance, underlined the gaps in the existing UN structure, no organization having overall responsibility for dealing comprehensively with energy. He suggested filling the gap by including energy in the mandate of a restructured and revitalized UNIDO.[341] However, the fact that such ideas have so far borne no fruit is based on the different interests of energy-producing and consuming countries, different concepts of the respective roles of government policies and the market and different concepts of foreign investment policies, and of the role of the financial sector. In addition, the question remains whether it will be efficient to merge existing organizations, such as the IAEA, OECD, and IEA, into a new universal institution.

[340] As indicated, for instance, in Art 34, para 4 ECT.

[341] Renewing the United Nations: A Programme for Reform, Report of the Secretary-General, UN Doc A/51/950, 14 .7.1997, para 88.

I. The International Energy Agency (IEA)—Description and Practical Experiences: a Case Study

By Helga Steeg

(*Former Executive Director of the International Energy Agency, Paris*)

(1) *General Objectives and Structure*

History and origins

3.133 The establishment of the International Energy Agency in 1974 resulted from the reaction of the OECD countries to two geopolitical and economic situations: the vulnerability of these countries in the oil and economic sector, and the growing geopolitical strength of the oil-producing countries. These latter countries were able to cut their production from 20.8 million barrels per day (mbd) to 15.8 mbd and oil prices were increased from US$ 2.59 to US$ 11.65 per barrel. The market for oil was governed by fear and uncertainty about further shortages and drastic price increases. There were reactions on the exchange rate markets; for example Ministers of Finance were urged not to resort to 'beggar my neighbour' policies through competitive devaluation of currencies, and Ministers of Trade pledged not to use new trade restrictions through the OECD Trade Pledge, demanding a stand-still on restrictions. There were various meetings and discussions in the OECD on how to deal with the energy sector as such. But no agreement could be reached, because the OECD Council—the decision-making board of this organization—decides by unanimity if options and positions differ. In December 1973 the Secretary of State of the United States of America, Henry Kissinger, in a speech before the Pilgrimage Society in London, suggested the establishment of a new institutional co-operation based on solidarity. International negotiations concluded with the signing of the International Energy Programme (IEP) on 18 November 1974.

Legal characters of the International Energy Programme

3.134 The IEP—as amended to 7 August 1992—is the constituent instrument of the IEA. It is regarded by Richard Scott, former legal adviser to the IEA, as an international agreement according to the Vienna Convention on the Law of the Treaties.[342] Article 67, para 1 reads: 'Each signatory State shall no later than 1 May 1975 notify the Government of Belgium that, having complied with its constitutional procedures, it consents to be bound by this Agreement'. This of course means ratification by the constitutional bodies. The English, French, and German texts are equally authentic (Art 76). Annexed to the IEP is the definition

[342] R Scott, *IEA, The First Twenty Years*, vol 1 (1994) 63.

of oil reserves. However, the IEP does not create national law; the obligations of Member States are international ones, requiring separate national actions.

From its beginning the main objective of the IEA's co-operation has been energy security, together with the other two E's: economic growth and protection of the environment. My definition of energy security is: diversified supplies of energy being available at affordable prices to help economies to grow.[343] Energy security means short- and long-term energy policies, energy research, and development. Fields of IEA activities are: emergency preparedness against short-term supply disruptions, development of long-term energy policies, energy research and development, energy and environment, and co-operation with non-Member States. The institutional set-up differs between oil security—emergency preparedness—and the other activities in terms of commitments and voting. It is therefore necessary to explain the structure as well as the institutional relation to the OECD. **3.135**

Membership and organization of the Secretariat

Today the IEA has twenty-four members, that is to say all OECD members except Iceland. There were fifteen signatory States; others joined later. France, Finland, and Hungary were the latest acceding members, in 1992 and 1997 respectively. Norway has acceded under a special agreement in reference to the emergency system, discussed in Chapter 11 below. **3.136**

Regarding new members, the IEP stipulates in Article 71 that the agreement is open for accession by any member of the OECD able and willing to meet the requirements of the Programme. This Article became especially significant after the change in geopolitics. A number of Central and East European States want to join the IEA—Poland, Hungary, the Czech Republic; South Korea has also expressed interest. Negotiations are underway. The main issue to be settled is the obligation of the IEA emergency stock requirement. However, it seems that this will be solved in the future. Mexico, the Czech Republic, Poland, and South Korea have already become members of the OECD. With regard to Mexico the IEA negotiations have not yet begun. In April 1994 Mexico applied for accession to the IEA; negotiations are now on hold, with no domestic consensus yet owing to the constitutional reservation of Mexican energy resources to the Mexican State. Generally speaking, the process of enlarging both the OECD and IEA membership continues, and future developments may be expected. **3.137**

The IEA has developed a system of co-operation with non-Member States. Those are described under the section on outreach (paras 3.174–3.175 below), and include Russia, China, and India. The IEP contains a specific Article dealing with the EU: Article 72 says that the Agreement shall be open for accession by the European Communities and that the Agreement shall in no way impede the **3.138**

[343] This author's definition used in many speeches and IEA Governing Board documents.

further implementation of the Treaties establishing the European Communities. In practice the European Commission participates in all meetings without having a voting right. The Commission has suggested a formal accession of the EC to the IEA, but discussions within the Union have not led to agreement yet. Points of discussion are: who is to represent the EU, the Presidency or the Commission?; who will have the voting rights on behalf of the EU?; what is the role of national policies to implement IEA decisions?; does the EU speak with one voice (today each Member can speak)? Also, the accession has implications for the IEP, because voting rights are allotted in the IEP, which would mean changing the IEP or finding a compromise in tacit practical terms, for instance that neither of the large members can block a vote without the support of one or more smaller members. The issue is unresolved for the time being in the OECD as well as in the IEA.

Powers of the Governing Board and voting rights

3.139 One of the most important characteristics of the IEA is its voting rights system. Other than in the OECD, voting is by a majority in a number of cases. The background of this fact is the experience in the first oil crisis when the OECD Council could not reach agreement. The founding fathers wanted to create an agency which could achieve quick and efficient international co-operation, particularly necessary in times of crisis.

3.140 The Governing Board (GB), composed of one or more ministers or their delegates from each participating country (Art 50 of the IEP), is the supreme institutional body of the IEA. Article 51 describes the functions by which it can adopt decisions and make recommendations necessary for the proper functioning of the IEP. As far as voting is concerned, Articles 61 and 62 foresee four different voting systems: unanimity, simple majority, and two cases of qualified majority voting.

3.141 The IEP allots to each country general voting weights, three per country, and consumption voting weights, based on oil consumption in 1973 and related to a percentage of the oil consumption for the group as a whole (voting weights are eg: USA 44, Japan 14, Germany 8, United Kingdom and France 6, Italy and Canada 4). Combined voting weights—the sum of general and oil consumption weights—total 66. Majority voting requires 60 per cent of the total combined voting weights and 50 per cent of the general voting weights cast. There are two special voting systems related to the emergency system.

3.142 The IEP—apart from emergency—requires a simple majority for decisions on the management of the programme of work and budget, on procedural questions, and recommendations. Unanimity is required for all other decisions, particularly those imposing new obligations.[344]

[344] R Scott, n 342 above, 184ff.

In practice the GB acts in the overwhelming majority of cases by consensus. However, in recent history the minority voting was necessary to adopt the programme of work and the budget for 1994. Each country presented its position; the legal adviser counted the different voting rights necessary as described above; and the Chairman of the GB then declared that the necessary votes had been cast. This voting structure, in spite of its limited use, has been extremely helpful for the efficient functioning of the Agency. The risk of not voting with the majority but nevertheless being bound by the decision, for instance as far as the budget is concerned, helped to find a consensus in many other cases. The more the OECD and the IEA are enlarged, the more the combination of majority and unanimous voting systems will be required. **3.143**

The Secretariat is composed of an Executive Director and staff foreseen in the budget. The Executive Director (ED) is appointed by the GB upon the proposal or with the concurrence of the Secretary General of the OECD. In the case of the first ED the Secretary General proposed Dr Lantzke; in the case of Helga Steeg and Robert Priddle—present ED—the proposals came from the Chairman of the GB with the concurrence of the Secretary General. This concurrence is the result of the institutional relationship between the IEA and the OECD as laid down in the OECD Council Decision of 15 November 1974. **3.144**

Institutional relationship with the OECD

The institutional relationship between the OECD and the IEA is unique, and stems from the historical background. While the IEP is an international treaty, the OECD Council Decision on the Establishment of the Agency regulates in Article 1 of the Council Decision: 'An International Energy Agency (following called the "Agency") is hereby established as an autonomous body within the framework of the Organisation.' The Council Decision then repeats a large number of the Articles of the IEP. Article 4 is especially important, mentioning that the GB shall be the body from which all acts of the Agency derive. Article 10 is so constructed that the IEA's budget forms part of Part II of the OECD's budget, but the GB decides on the IEA's budget. The latter is then submitted to the Council for adoption by agreement of Member States of the Agency, voting in the GB to submit the proposals to the Council. This means in practice that countries which vote in the GB against the budget—as in the 1994 budget—cannot vote in the OECD Council in spite of its requirement for unanimity. Nevertheless, they are bound by the GB decision adopted. In such cases the unanimity rule of the OECD Council does not apply. **3.145**

There are also rules regarding the personnel of the Agency. They are members of the OECD Secretariat, even though they are responsible to and report to the organs of the Agency. It is clear that these provisions assure the autonomy of the Agency even though a field of unspecified niches exists, meaning that it has been **3.146** necessary for the Secretary General of the OECD and the Executive Director of the IEA to work together closely.

3.147 The persons in charge understood that it was up to them to solve controversies between the two Secretariats and not refer to the Member States as arbitrators. In practice this was how co-operation functioned smoothly.

Financing of the IEA

3.148 Article 64 of the IEP provides for the sharing of expenses among Member States according to a scale of contributions within the administrative framework of the OECD. The IEA uses the financial services of the OECD. The rules of elaborating the scale of contributions to the IEA can be amended by the Governing Board acting by a majority (Art 64, para 1). If the oil-related votes should be changed, this may come up in the future. These rules are not subject to formal amendments by the OECD Council without explicit tacit acceptance by the Governing Board. In practice financial co-operation between the competent OECD offices and the IEA has been very close. OECD auditors examine IEA financial transactions. Finally, Article 65 of the IEP allows for special activities carried out by two or more participating countries. This procedure has been used in particular for co-operation in the technology field. Another procedure which has been used in the past is granting voluntary contributions for particular purposes. Acceptance must be decided by the Governing Board. Examples were contributions of this nature after the breakdown of the former command economies. Co-operation started with the newly evolving States at their request to share the IEA's experience in energy policies and practices.

(2) Subjects and Objectives of the IEA's Activities

3.149 In the forefront of the creation of the IEA was the establishment of the emergency system, but other aims were transparency in markets, reduction of Members' vulnerability through long-term energy programmes, co-operation in developing new energy technologies, and co-operation with the outside world, as well as energy and environment. The emphasis has shifted from time to time, but all these activities are still relevant in the IEA's programme of work.

The emergency system

3.150 The emergency system's basis is laid down in the IEP, the decisions of the GB dating from 11 July 1984 and 22 February 1995. Many GB decisions were taken in the meantime either referring to specific crisis situations—as in 1979–80 relating to the Iran–Iraq conflict and war, and in 1990–91 relating to the Kuwait crisis and war. Also the technical and practical application of the emergency system was further developed.

The sharing system

The IEP, the basic document, differentiates between the obligations of Member States to have at their disposal policy instruments and the activation of the system for the group as a whole. The policy instruments are oil stocks to sustain consumption equal to at least ninety days of net oil imports—originally—, and a programme of contingent oil-demand restraint measures. The oil-stocks commitment may also be satisfied by fuel-switching capacity and/or stand-by oil production. In order to activate the system conditions, the group must sustain or reasonably expect to sustain a reduction of the daily rate of its oil supplies at least by the equivalent of 7 per cent or 12 per cent of the average daily rate of its final consumption during the base period. Member States will have to take differing actions depending on the severity of the situation. When a shortfall of oil available to the group is identified, allocation rights and obligations are calculated on the basis of permissible consumption—eg domestic oil production plus net available imports taking into account the country's demand restraint reduced by the country's oil reserves.[345] The country having the right to supply receives additional imports by countries with supply obligations. There is also the possibility of a supply shortfall for a single country.[346] As for procedure, Article 19 of the IEP lays down that the IEA Secretariat shall make a finding, when a reduction of oil supplies has occurred or can reasonably be expected to occur. The Secretariat shall establish the amount of the reduction for each participating country and for the group. The Secretariat is to consult with oil companies. Within fifteen days the GB can either confirm the finding or decide by a special majority[347] not to activate the emergency measure. **3.151**

This provision was concluded in the IEP for two reasons: first to achieve quick actions, and secondly to keep the political surveillance of the system—in other words, to combine technical and political objectives. Once the activation of the sharing system was achieved, the critical redirection of oil cargoes is to be handled by oil companies whose representatives are working closely with the Secretariat at the site in Paris. **3.152**

With the enlargement of the EU, voting powers have changed. It is still a pending question whether in an emergency situation the EU might dominate, by outvoting other important IEA countries. However, if the activation has been confirmed, the operation of the oil sharing is physically redirected through cooperation between the Secretariat, national sharing organizations, and the oil companies. The oil companies offer to redirect their cargoes on a voluntary basis to the countries with allocation rights. Despite the voluntary efforts of the industry, additional efforts are required: Member States will establish what further **3.153**

[345] ibid, ch III.
[346] ibid, vol 2 (1995).
[347] ibid.

measures are needed and how they will be implemented. These might include direct instructions from individual governments to companies. This provision was negotiated later than the IEP. The intention was to satisfy certain Member States who wanted a price element included in the allocation procedure. The goal that the oil-sharing system was to deal with physical shortages only, and was not to be a market intervention mechanism like the commodity-type agreements or exchange-rate interventions, was controversial. The mentioned version is a compromise not tested so far.

3.154 Finally, in order to satisfy antitrust legislation, the US Congress and the EU Commission have granted waivers (US Energy Policy and Conservation Act, renewal of the exemption from Article 85 of the EEC Treaty in 1994). These waivers are subject to periodical renewals, which have at times posed problems in the US, but have always finally been granted.

3.155 Two comments should be made here: first, the actual redirection of oil supplies is not a new development in the IEP; it was used as long ago as 1918 by the US and its European allies to cope with an oil shortage. Standard Oil of New Jersey and Royal Dutch Shell managed the shortage.[348] Secondly, the sharing system has never been activated although in 1981 and 1990 preparations were made in case the activation would be necessary.

3.156 The emergency sharing system is undoubtedly a strong interventionist scheme, which means a heavy-handed system, both at national and international level. But it has certainly proven so far to calm down markets, which looked to the IEA to use it, if it became necessary. This was an important element at the end of the Iran–Iraq war when it was feared that the Strait of Hormuz might be closed.

Stock draw

3.157 Since the beginning of the 1980s, intensive discussions and negotiations have taken place with the objective of using stocks earlier and more effectively.

3.158 It was argued, especially by the USA, that the IEA should have at its disposal the means to react to a shortfall below the 7 per cent shortage level. Furthermore, the USA wanted to lessen, not to abandon, pressure on reverting to the sharing system automatically. This was hotly debated. The outcome was the Governing Board decisions of 1984 and 1995. The policy and process of the Kuwait crisis, where only stock draw was implemented, hastened the achievement of a new agreement.

3.159 The GB decisions of 1984 and 1995 clearly spell out the importance of the sharing system, but make stock draw in supply disruptions equally important. This means that the circumstances of the disruption will direct the measures to be

[348] R Scott, above n 342, vol 2.

taken. In the sharing system, the Secretariat—eg the Executive Director—has the executive function of activating the trigger to start the sharing system, while in the stock draw procedure the Member States decide in the GB, as a matter of policy, which measures should be implemented. The two GB decisions foresee a clear preference for stock draw; nevertheless, the sharing system can still be activated if the crisis is severe. The new system was developed step by step.

The GB decision of 1984 describes the need for an agreed policy regarding stock draw in supply disruptions, based on experience with previous supply disruptions. In recent years the ability of many countries to use stocks had increased significantly, specifically in the USA, a number of European countries, and Japan. The 1984 decision established a consultation procedure according to which all countries must take action to restore the supply and demand balance; some countries may engage in co-ordinated stock draw, others may undertake complimentary actions, and a third group both. The GB takes the results of these positions into account in reaching its overall decision. This procedure is called CERM.[349] **3.160**

The GB decision in 1995, stating the intention to enhance the flexibility and effectiveness of the IEP and CERM, led to the agreement that IEA measures in response to a crisis should be tailored to specific circumstances, should underpin the efficient functioning of the oil market, and should minimize damage to Member States. Consistent with the IEP, the GB would normally first give consideration to a step-by-step process. Another important element was introduced: even in times of crisis, markets should remain unconstrained by price controls or restrictions other than those consistent with the implementation of IEA emergency measures. Voluntary measures should also be encouraged. **3.161**

The emergency measures were designed in the first instance to foster co-operation in solidarity among Member States in times of crisis: they are to share economic hardship together. Also bad experiences with too much government intervention in the 1970s (price controls, trade restrictions, subsidies) led to a more market-oriented approach by the IEA. **3.162**

The Kuwait crisis

The more market-oriented approach was clearly demonstrated during the Kuwait crisis. Despite a numerical shortfall of 7 per cent, the IEP measures were not triggered nor was stock draw enacted before the outbreak of war. The shortfall was the consequence of the decision by the United Nations Security Council to impose sanctions. The situation of oil supply and demand was intensively monitored through the IEA reporting mechanism (countries and oil companies). There were high company stocks and large cargoes on the sea at the time of the invasion. The IEA said throughout the crisis in its public announcements that its Member States **3.163**

[349] CERM: Co-ordinated Emergency Response Measures.

were prepared to use the IEP instruments and/or to stock draw if the need were to arise. Finally the co-ordinated stock draw, being activated and practised on the day of the outbreak of war, was intended to fence off possible reactions by the oil markets if major oil-producing installations were damaged, which fortunately was not the case. During the deliberations of the IEA countries EU Members took a very active part: the Chairman of the GB at that time was from Germany, and was followed by two British Chairmen. The EU Commission also participated in all discussions.

3.164 Some voices, both from within and without the IEA membership, advocated an earlier stock draw to bring prices down. Debates were held in the USA as well as in the EU. Prices fluctuated from week to week. It was noticeable that the likelihood of whether or not Iraq would leave Kuwait influenced market developments. The slogan at the time was 'peace week or war week'. Money was lost when oil sales were based on the weekly assumption, which turned out to be wrong. In my view, an early stock draw was neither necessary nor appropriate, because the IEA system is designed to deal with physical shortages as the underlying factor for price increases. From the day of the invasion to the outbreak of war there was never a real deficit in the oil demand and supply balance. Companies used their stocks at the beginning, governments appealed for a decrease in oil demand or loosened restrictions for refineries; switching to gas—where possible—took place. Last but not least, there was a considerable production increase by OPEC countries and also to some extent in the North Sea. The lessons of the Kuwait crisis were taken into account in the 1995 decision of the GB with the establishment of flexibility and tailoring the emergency reaction to the specific type of a supply disruption crisis.

3.165 The emergency response potential of IEA countries is described by the IEA.[350] In the future the IEA will, as in the past, inform and co-operate with non-IEA countries whenever appropriate and practical.

3.166 The case of Norway deserves special mention. A special agreement was negotiated which does not bind this country in legal terms to the application of the emergency measures. This has to be seen against the background of Norway's political situation. Not wanting to transfer sovereignty over its energy reserves to an international organization, Norway requested this exception at its accession, and the Member States agreed. Norway has twice turned down the proposal to join the EU. In the IEA Norway fully co-operated on a voluntary basis during the Kuwait crisis by increasing its oil production.

[350] OECD/IEA, *Oil Supply Security: Response Potential of IEA Countries* (1995).

Transparency of markets

A large and ever-increasing number of IEA analyses and publications exist, which have helped to bring about transparency, which did not exist in 1973. The most widely used report is the monthly oil market report, describing supply and demand of oil in the past, particularly in the previous month, and forecasting into the very near future (the next quarter and the following year). These monthly reports are always subject to revisions as developments occur. Other subjects of periodical statistics include coal, gas, prices, taxes, etc. One important example is a publication on the role of governments in energy.[351] The IEA does not undertake long-term energy planning. All the forecasts of the 1970s were overturned by developments. Therefore scenarios on the basis of certain assumptions are developed in order to justify factors which may either individually or in combination influence the energy situation. The IEA calls them outlooks. Over the years the IEA has become an authority in statistics and analyses, which are used worldwide by governments, institutions, and companies. Details of the most recent outlook are dealt with in paras 3.178–3.179 below. **3.167**

Long-term co-operation

Here again the IEP describes, although in much more general terms, the field of activities: conservation, and development of alternative sources of energy such as domestic oil, coal, natural gas, nuclear energy, and hydroelectric power. Specific fields of energy research and development, such as coal technology, solar energy, radioactive waste management, controlled thermonuclear fusion, production of hydrogen from water, nuclear safety, waste heat utilization, conservation of energy, municipal and industrial waste utilization for energy conservation, and some general energy system analysis (Art 42) also deserve mention. **3.168**

The catalogue of activities embraces almost all activities which are still relevant today although with different priorities. The IEP does not specify activities in relation to the protection of the environment; however, it provides that alternative sources of energy should be developed through standards of environmental protection. **3.169**

In 1977 a long-term co-operation programme was developed, which spells out in detail the activities pursued either nationally or in co-operation. Its most important element is the conduct of annual country reviews, whose purpose is to monitor national policies through a political (not legal) procedure, helping to develop IEA policies in accordance with national changes of policies and circumstances. In 1993 the GB adopted the 'Shared Goals',[352] which emphasize free and open **3.170**

[351] OECD/IEA, *The Role of IEA Governments in Energy* (1996).

[352] The IEA's 'Shared Goals' are used for country reviews and in IEA Governing Body documents.

markets, environmental protection, global interdependence, free and open trade, and undistorted energy prices as well as co-operation between all energy market participants. The 'Shared Goals' have not abolished the long-term programme completely, because the latter is more detailed, but where there is contradiction the 'Shared Goals' prevail. One important example is subsidies in coal and other sectors. Within the framework of the long-term co-operation, recent work has been conducted on gas security,[353] electricity, and the environment.[354] The 1996 Review of Energy Policies of IEA countries has focused on economic liberalization and structural reforms, involving the withdrawal of governments as players in energy markets. Obviously, these reforms differ from country to country in extent, timing, and results. The experimental stage has not yet been completed. However, chances and risks exist. The developments arising from the creation of the internal EU market and the globalization of world energy markets have forced governments to change their policies. The IEA work contributes to a better understanding of the issues.

3.171 The implications of the environmental debate concerning energy policies has led to increasing IEA contributions to the international debate. The IEA Executive Directors addressed the Rio and Berlin Conferences on the Climate Change Convention, and the conference of the participating countries in Japan in December 1997 as well as the subsequent conferences. The production of publications continues. Member States agree that environmentally sustainable provision and use of energy is vital to the achievement of the 'Shared Goals'. The implementation of the obligations negotiated in Kyoto 1997 as laid down in the Kyoto Protocol are the subject of discussions and analysis within the members of the IEA. The IEA has embarked on intensive work in order to assist them in defining their policies. National policy mixes, the severity of measures as well as the implications for the energy sector and the economies as a whole demand bold decisions of energy policy-makers. The task is of a long-term nature but changes in the energy sector must begin now. Yet the IEA remains a forum for discussion and negotiation of comparable policies.

Co-operation in Research and Development

3.172 The Co-operation in Research and Development (R&D) is another success story, not always receiving the necessary attention and support by Member States. But today it has a high priority in coping with the environmental challenge in energy

[353] OECD/IEA, *The IEA Natural Gas Security Study* (1995); id, *The Asia Gas Study* (1996); id, *Regulatory Reform in Mexico's Natural Gas Sector* (1996).

[354] OECD/IEA, *Electricity Supply Industry* (1994); id, *Electricity in European Economics in Transition* (1994); id, *Energy Policies of IEA Countries, 1996, 1997, 1998, 1999 Reviews* (1996) 17ff; id, *Climate Change Policy Initiatives*, vols 1 and 2 (1994); id, *Energy Policies in IEA Countries*, Electricity reform 1997, Oil in power generation 1997, International coal trade 1997, Indicators of Energy Use and Efficiency 1997 (1997) 31ff.; and id, *Energy Use and Efficiency* (1997).

policy and practice. There are more than forty international agreements, called implementing agreements, establishing the collaboration project in formal terms, identifying and legally committing the participants to the project, fixing their contributions and benefits, and assigning responsibility for the project. Since 1991 non-Member States can also be admitted by a decision of the GB. Such decisions have been taken in order to share work in the technology field with the outside world, not by the transfer of technology, but by means of co-operative activities.[355]

Subjects for international R&D co-operation vary widely. They include energy efficiency, the production and use of coal, oil, and gas, decreasing emissions, nuclear energy and fusion, renewable energies, energy systems and processes, and information. Whereas the industry was initially reluctant to participate, now several examples and ways are known to include industry. *Energy Technologies for the 21st Century* is the most recent publication.[356] **3.173**

Co-operation with non-Member States

Since the confrontational period of the 1970s and early 1980s, the IEA has engaged in a number of different activities. These include country reviews for selected countries—either important consumers or producers (Russia, East European countries, South Korea, and others)—or conferences, seminars on specific issues, including seminars with producing countries conducted at a high technical level. The question was raised whether countries could become Members of the IEA without being Members of the OECD. The answer is no. The IEA should not become a UN-type organization because it might lose its effectiveness. Nevertheless, there are various modes of tailor-made co-operation, which the author believes will widen in the future. **3.174**

For instance, special co-operation agreements between the IEA and Russia and China have been signed, forming the basis for detailed fields of practical work. At the ministerial level, the Chinese Minister of Energy participated in a special meeting with the IEA ministers. This is evidence of the growing outreach to non-Member States by the IEA. **3.175**

(3) Conclusions

In conclusion, the IEA has proved to be an effective working organization, embracing regions and countries which are democracies and adhere to a market economy, the common ground of the OECD. **3.176**

355 R Scott, n 342 above, 274ff.
356 OECD/IEA (1997).

3.177 The IEA has established itself as an authority on energy among both Member and non-Member States. Its field of activities has enlarged over the years and it has flexibly adjusted its work to the changing conditions of energy markets and political developments.

3.178 As to the future, the organization will assess possible future developments in both the near and the long term. These outlooks are not predictions. Briefly, the results are the following.[357] Growth in energy demand will continue to be much larger in the South, particularly in Asia and Latin America. The demand on world energy resources, especially fossil fuels, will decrease, as far as the OECD countries are concerned, below 50 per cent of world demand, while the share of developing countries will increase from about 28 per cent to 40 per cent. This means less impact of OECD activities than has previously been the case. The supply situation is seen in the following way: reserves will extend for a considerable number of years, coal and gas reserves longer than oil. However, two kinds of risks have to be taken into account. The bulk of known and more easily developed oil reserves can be found in the Gulf countries. The Gulf area remains politically volatile. Short-term political disruptions cannot be excluded. In the longer term the issue is whether the necessary investments will come about in time and volume. This means providing the necessary finance as well as opening up the reserves for foreign participation and technology transfer. Developments since the end of the 1980s have shown a considerable increase in the use of fossil fuel reserves in non-OPEC countries. Whether this will continue is debatable.[358] The risks have to be clearly seen and policy-makers must take them into account. A report commissioned by the Trilateral Commission in 1996 spells this out clearly.[359] The IEA, with its short-term and long-term responsibilities, will have to play its role in the future, either for the activation of its emergency programme and in case of unforeseen short-term disruptions, or in the long-term for providing political and technical assistance to avoid supply and demand imbalances. This will remain an important and difficult issue for energy politicians. It is no longer debated that economic growth for the future must be placed on a sustainable basis. No clear concept is stated for the practice. However, energy sectors will have to shoulder a critical burden, if not the most critical one, to bring the objectives about. Therefore the IEA will have to contribute in a very sustainable way.

3.179 The developments of the years 1999 and 2000 have demonstrated what was said earlier about the potential political risks in the oil sector. The first element was the renewed coherence of OPEC countries to push the oil price up from US$ 18 per barrel to over US$ 30. This led to the release of 30 million barrels from the Strategic Reserve of the United States, which was not followed by any other

[357] id, *International Energy Agency: World Energy Outlook 1998* (1996).
[358] JV Mitchell/P Beck/M Grubb, *The New Geopolitics of Energy* (1996).
[359] Martin/Imai/Steeg, *Maintaining Energy Security in a Global Context* (1996).

member of the IEA. The GB of the organization concluded on 4 October 'that the crude oil available to market is sufficient to meet current demand and a small surplus for stockbuilding. But because stocks are generally low and there are some regional imbalances in product stocks, there is unusual volatility in the short term, and current high oil prices, if sustained, could jeopardize global economic growth. The GB confirmed the availability of security stocks in IEA countries and their readiness for use in the event of significant supply disruption. The second element is the extremely dangerous political situation in the Near East which has brought the price temporarily up to US$ 38. Dialogue continues between the world's producers and consumers. In conclusion, the recent events bring to the forefront of the political agenda the vulnerability of the energy sector and especially the oil sector. The role of the IEA is of paramount importance for its members and beyond.

Bibliography

Bernhardt, Rudolf (ed), *Encyclopedia of Public International Law*, Vol. 5, *International Organisations in General, Universal International Organisations and Co-operation* (Amsterdam: New-Holland, 1983)

Bowett, Derek, *The Law of International Organisations*, 4th edn (London: Stevens Sons, 1982)

von Burchard, Friedrich, and Eckert, Lutz, *Natural Gas and EU Energy Law* (Baden-Baden: Nomos Verlagsgesellschaft, 1995)

Craig, Paul, and De Búrca, Graínne, *EC Law* (Oxford: Clarendon Press, 1995)

Directorate-General for Energy, Commission of the European Communities, *Energy in Europe* (published irregularly)

Dupuy-Jean, René (ed), *Manuel sur les organisations internationales/A Handbook on International Organisations* (The Hague: Martinus Nijhoff Publishers, 1988)

Energy in Europe, *Energy Policies and Trends in the European Community* (Luxembourg, No. 16, 1990)

Europa Publishing Ltd, *The Europa World Yearbook* (London, published annually)

Lucas, Alistair R, and Tilleman, William A, *Environmental Law and the Energy Sector: Europe and North America* (Oxford: Oxford University Press, 1995)

Pelzer, Norbert (ed), Im Auftrag der Deutschen Landesgruppe in der Association Internationale du Droit Nucléaire (AIDN)/International Nuclear Law Association (INLA) e.V., *Schnittpunkte nationalen und internationalen Atomrechts (Intersections of National and International Nuclear Law)*, Tagungsbericht der AIDN/INLA Regionaltagung am 8. und 9. September 1996 in Meissen (Baden-Baden: Nomos-Verlagsgesellschaft, 1997)

Schermers, Henry G, and Blokker, Niels M, *International Institutional Law*, 3rd edn (Dordrecht: Martinus Nijhoff Publishers, 1995)

Seidl-Hohenveldern, Ignaz, and Loibl, Georg, *Das Recht der Internationalen Organisationen einschliesslich der Supranationalen Gemeinschaften*, 6th edn (Koeln: Heymanns, 1996)

United Nations (UN Department of Public Information, New York, Geneva), *Yearbook of the United Nations* (published annually)

Weatherill, Stephen, and Beaumont, Paul, *EC Law*, 2nd edn (London: Penguin Group, 1995)

White, ND, *The Law of International Organisations* (Manchester: Manchester University Press, 1996)

Wolfrum, Rüdiger (ed), *United Nations: Law, Policies and Practice* (Munich: Beck, 1995)

4

THE ENERGY CHARTER TREATY

*Craig Bamberger, Jan Linehan, and Thomas Waelde**

A. Introduction

The Energy Charter Treaty (ECT) is unique as a multilateral treaty. It is limited in scope to the energy sector, and establishes within that sector legal rights and obligations with respect to a broad range of investment, trade, and other subjects such as the transit of energy goods, competition, the environment, access to capital markets, and transfer of technology, and in most cases provides for the enforcement of those rights and obligations. The purpose of the Treaty, as described in its Article 2, is to 'establish a legal framework in order to promote long-term co-operation in the energy field, based on complementarities and mutual benefits, in accordance with the objectives and principles of the [European Energy] Charter'. **4.01**

With respect to investment, the Treaty follows up on ideas originally conceived by John Maynard Keynes in the 1940s (the Havana Charter) and reflected in heretofore largely non-binding declarations and guidelines on foreign investment, and **4.02**

* The authors of Chapter 4 gratefully acknowledge the contribution of Mr Adnan Amkhan, the present Legal Adviser of the Energy Charter Secretariat, who reviewed a draft of the chapter and offered detailed comments. Of course, Mr Amkhan is in no way accountable for the views expressed in the chapter.

it set the stage for the unsuccessful efforts within the Organization for Economic Co-operation and Development (OECD) to agree a non-sectoral 'Multilateral Agreement on Investment', the so-called 'MAI'. A distinctive feature of the ECT is that its main investment obligations can be enforced by private parties against non-complying States through binding international arbitration. This enforcement is available not only against non-complying Eastern countries, but also against OECD States and the European Communities.

4.03 The opening for signature of the ECT in Lisbon on 17 December 1994 marked the end of the first four-and-a-half-year phase of the Treaty's development. This was a period of arduous negotiations among more than fifty States and the European Communities, set in motion by the June 1990 suggestion of Prime Minister Ruud Lubbers of the Netherlands that energy co-operation could help stimulate economic recovery in Eastern Europe and the former Soviet Union (FSU). In April 1998 a second phase of the ECT's history drew to a close, as the Treaty entered into force following the achievement of the thirty ratifications[1] required for its entry into force. This second phase witnessed the development of functioning ECT institutions on a provisional basis, and the intensive pursuit of further trade and investment negotiations that were mandated for this period by the Treaty. While the negotiations for a new investment instrument remain unfinished, in the foreseeable future there will inevitably be (with one major exception) less focus on negotiations for new instruments.

4.04 The exception concerns efforts to facilitate the unimpeded transit of energy goods across national borders, a subject that has become perhaps the central focus of the Energy Charter Secretariat and Conference in the Treaty's third phase. This third phase could in other respects prove a complex and challenging one in which some Treaty signatories—including important participants such as the Russian Federation—continue to apply the Treaty only provisionally even though it has entered into force for the great majority of signatories.

4.05 The ECT and its origins have been discussed comprehensively elsewhere.[2] This chapter briefly explains the Treaty's origins; describes the Treaty's main features

[1] As of 23 November 2000 the European Communities and the following 41 States had deposited instruments of ratification, approval, or accession: Albania, Armenia, Austria, Azerbaijan, Belgium, Bulgaria, Croatia, Cyprus, the Czech Republic, Denmark, Estonia, Finland, France, Georgia, Germany, Greece, Hungary, Ireland, Italy, Kazakhstan, Kyrgyztan, Latvia, Liechtenstein, Lithuania, Luxembourg, Moldova, Mongolia, the Netherlands, Portugal, Romania, Slovakia, Slovenia, Spain, Sweden, Switzerland, Tajikistan, the Former Yugoslav Republic of Macedonia, Turkmenistan, Ukraine, the United Kingdom, and Uzbekistan. Signatories to the Treaty, for whom the Treaty was not yet in force, were: Australia, Belarus, Bosnia-Herzegovina, Iceland, Japan, Malta, Norway, Poland, the Russian Federation, and Turkey. Bosnia-Herzegovina, Poland, and Turkey had completed parliamentary ratification.

[2] See eg TW Waelde (ed), *The Energy Charter Treaty: An East-West Gateway for Investment and Trade* (Kluwer Law International, 1996) (hereinafter cited as 'Waelde'). The book contains 27 contributions on the background, history, and major issues of the Treaty, as well as the full text of the

and its effects; provides an update on recent developments; and casts an inquisitive eye on the Treaty's future. In the process, it offers fresh commentary on several issues that may be of special interest to European readers.

B. Origins of the Energy Charter Treaty

(1) *The 1991 European Energy Charter*

The ECT was preceded by the European Energy Charter, a declaration not constituting a binding international Treaty (and thereunder expressly 'not eligible for registration under Article 102 of the UN Charter'), adopted and signed on 17 December 1991 at The Hague, which represents the first formal step in the ECT process. The Charter and Treaty were initiated in reaction to the collapse of the former Soviet Union (FSU). In 1990, Prime Minister Lubbers called for a 'European Energy Charter' to serve as a political and legal foundation for East–West co-operation, the idea being to support a transition to market economy status and to enhance political stability throughout Europe by promoting Eastern economic development. Western energy dependence and security of supply would be safeguarded by the creation of a privileged relationship of investment and trade between East and West. The East would provide investment security, and this would trigger investment inflows, which in turn would build up the Eastern economies and supply energy to the West. Liberated from regulatory hindrance, Western finance and technology would flow eastward and Eastern products westward. **4.06**

This idea was welcomed by the European Council, which invited the Commission of the European Communities to study how best to implement such co-operation. In February 1991 the Commission proposed the concept of a European Energy Charter. Following discussion of the Commission's proposal in the Council of the European Communities, the European Union invited the other countries of Western and Eastern Europe, the FSU, and the non-European members of the OECD to attend a conference in Brussels in July 1991 to launch negotiations on the European Energy Charter. The United States soon joined the negotiations, and Canada, Australia, and Japan followed suit. **4.07**

European Energy Charter, the Energy Charter Treaty, the Protocol on Energy Efficiency and Related Environmental Aspects, and the main Decisions and Understandings of the Final Act. For an account of the Treaty's origins, see J Doré, *Negotiating the Energy Charter Treaty*, ch 5. For a detailed description of the ECT see C Bamberger, *An Overview of the Energy Charter Treaty*, ch 1. The Charter text and a list of signatories current as of 1 October 1996, as well as the ECT text, a summary of its provisions, a list of its signatories, and other relevant information can also be found in *The Energy Charter Treaty and Related Documents*, published in 1996 by the Energy Charter Secretariat. For current information (updated regularly) from the Energy Charter Secretariat: http://www.encharter.org/ (where the text of the Treaty is available for downloading; the text plus commentary is also available from the Australian Ministry of Foreign Affairs: http://www.austlii.edu.au/au/other/dfat/).

4.08 The Charter that was negotiated in this first conference consists of: a statement of major principles that the signatories declare they wish to pursue, a set of guidelines or signposts for the subsequent negotiation of a 'Basic Agreement', later to become the 'Energy Charter Treaty', and a set of 'Protocols'. The Charter was able to be less qualified than the ultimate Treaty on a number of issues, since it was seen primarily as a non-binding declaration of policy and good will. However, the Charter is not without significance in interpreting the ECT, since the ECT's Preamble makes clear that the Treaty is intended to provide the basis for implementing the principles contained in the Charter.

(2) Negotiation of the Energy Charter Treaty

4.09 By the time the legally non-binding Charter had been agreed, negotiations were already underway on a treaty—the ECT—to implement the objectives and principles of the Charter. Although initiated with a sense of urgency, the negotiations encountered numerous obstacles that included not only East–West issues but also intra-OECD disagreements, which effectively prolonged the negotiating process to more than three years. In retrospect, this was a relatively modest period within which to complete a treaty of such scope, complexity, novelty, and political sensitivity among so many parties with divergent interests. Ultimately, the leadership of the European Energy Charter Conference in which the negotiations were held, faced with the growing impatience not only of the European Commission, which had been providing financial and other support to the Conference, but also of many other negotiating parties, and struggling to hold together a temporary Secretariat, took a daring decision to set a deadline for the end of the negotiations. This succeeded in producing meaningful Treaty commitments, which were accepted by most of the participants in the Conference.

4.10 A major turn in the negotiations, opening the way for this successful gamble, came when the negotiating Conference was unable to agree to apply to the 'pre-investment' stage, on a legally binding basis, the 'national treatment' standard that had been accepted in the negotiations as a treaty standard for investments already made. The Russian Federation and other transitional countries lacked experience in applying this standard and thus, unlike many OECD countries, had no legislation denying national treatment, in sensitive areas, with respect to the making of new investments; they were not prepared to let those OECD countries 'grandfather' their own restrictive practices until they had a chance to catch up. That led, at the initiative of the European Union, to the deferral of this subject to a 'second-phase' negotiation of a 'Supplementary Treaty', mandated by the ECT, and encompassing issues of privatization and de-monopolization.[3]

[3] The application of a legally binding 'most-favoured-nation' (MFN) standard to the pre-investment stage was likewise deferred.

The ECT remained open for signature for six months from 17 December 1994; by the time it closed for signature, it had been signed by forty-nine States and the European Communities.[4] The signatories include almost all the countries of Europe and all the republics of the FSU, as well as Australia and Japan. Of the signatories to the non-binding 1991 European Energy Charter, only Canada and the United States did not sign the ECT.[5] **4.11**

C. Main Features of the Treaty

Although the ECT covers a broad range of energy-related subjects, its principal provisions are those regulating energy investment, trade, and—in a novel and unique manner—the transit of energy goods through States which are Parties to the Treaty. **4.12**

(1) Investment Protection and Dispute Resolution

The ECT's investment provisions are the logical culmination of efforts made over the last fifty years to create multilateral investment rules, including: the Havana Charter of 1948; the ultimately abortive 1976–91 efforts to create a UN Code of Conduct on Transnational Corporations; several wholly or largely non-binding instruments (International Labour Organization, International Chamber of Commerce, Draft Convention, the OECD Codes and Instruments, the World Bank Guidelines); the 1966 International Centre for Settlement of Investment Disputes (ICSID) Convention,[6] which recognized the creation by State-investor agreements of individual rights against States—a precursor of Article 26 of the ECT—under international law; the 1986 Multilateral Guarantee Agency Convention,[7] providing arbitral/procedural and investment insurance facilities; the Lomé Conventions, in particular Lomé III;[8] the investment provisions of the United States–Canada Free-Trade Agreement[9] and the North American Free-Trade Agreement (NAFTA);[10] the Colonia Protocol of the Mercosur Agreement;[11] and especially the increasingly numerous bilateral investment treaties (BITs).[12] **4.13**

---

[4] The ECT remains open for possible accession on terms to be approved by the parties. The former Yugoslav Republic of Macedonia and Mongolia have already acceded.

[5] An account of the US's reasons for not signing is given in Waelde (1996a) ch 9.

[6] 4 ILM 532 (1965).

[7] 24 ILM 1598 (1985).

[8] 29 ILM 783 (1990).

[9] 27 ILM 281 (1988).

[10] 32 ILM 289, 605 (1993).

[11] The Treaty establishing MERCOSUR is at 30 ILM 1041 (1991) and the Additional Protocol on the Institutional Structure of Mercosur is at 34 ILM 1244 (1995); see A Parra, 'Provisions on the Settlement of Investment Disputes in Modern Investment Laws, Bilateral Investment Treaties and Multilateral Instruments Investment', 12 *ICSID Rev.* 287 (1997).

[12] The ECT's investment provisions are compared with those of the BITs in Waelde (1996a) ch 14.

4.14 The foreign investment regime of the Treaty is characterized by the distinction between pre-investment (the stage of 'making investments' and the issue of access conditions), and post-investment (when the risk is assumed and the 'hostage' effect arises). While the ECT contains not only a 'hard' regime for post-investment but also some binding rules with regard to the pre-investment stage (and there is an area of overlap between the two stages), the Treaty for the greater part establishes a 'soft' pre-investment regime characterized by 'best efforts' formulations, pending the outcome of the mandated second-phase investment negotiations. Those negotiations are discussed below; here we will concentrate on the post-investment regime, which includes mainly 'hard law' obligations enforceable by international arbitration.

Scope and definitions

4.15 The ECT's principal investment provisions are contained in Part III of the Treaty. The scope of the investment protection is shaped by the definitions in paragraphs (5) and (6) of Article 1. Investments are defined as 'every kind of asset, owned or controlled directly or indirectly by an Investor'. There follows in the Article 1(6) definition a non-exclusive list mentioning, among other things, tangible and intangible and movable and immovable property, 'a company or business enterprise' or an equity (eg shareholding) or debt interest therein, claims under contracts associated with an investment, intellectual property, 'Returns' (including profits, dividends, interest, capital gains, royalty payments, various fees, and payments in kind), and rights to undertake 'Economic Activity in the Energy Sector'. The definition states that changes in the form of investments do not affect their character as investments.

4.16 This definition further stipulates that the term 'Investment' refers to any investment 'associated with an Economic Activity in the Energy Sector', the definition of which employs the term 'Energy Materials and Products'. Those products are defined in Article 1(4) by means of item references to the Harmonized System of the Customs Co-operation Council and the Combined Nomenclature of the European Communities. The Treaty's Annex EM, which contains these item references, generally encompasses coal, electrical energy, natural gas, nuclear energy materials, petroleum and petroleum products, fuel wood, and charcoal. The designation of petroleum products excludes some petrochemicals that are within the item references for petroleum products. The term 'Economic Activity in the Energy Sector' is defined to mean 'an economic activity concerning the exploration, extraction, refining, production, storage, land transport,[13] transmission, distribution, trade, marketing, or sale' of the items covered by the definition of 'Energy Materials and Products', except that fuel wood, charcoal, and the distribu-

[13] ie not including marine transport.

tion of heat to multiple premises are excluded from the definition for investment purposes. It will be observed that the extension of the definition of 'Investment' to investments (ie assets) 'associated with' an 'Economic Activity in the Energy Sector' attenuates the sectoral restriction of the Treaty's protections and dispute resolution mechanisms; it can provide a basis for claiming coverage, for example, with respect to otherwise uncovered petrochemical facilities within an oil refinery complex, or maritime transportation that is 'associated with' a covered on-land investment.

In Article 1(7), 'Investors' are defined simply as natural persons having the citizenship or nationality of or permanently residing in a Contracting Party 'in accordance with its applicable law', and as companies or other entities organized 'in accordance with the [applicable] law'. The term thus has a broad scope but acquires policy substance only by its specific use in reference to investments. **4.17**

Absolute minimum standard of treatment

The key Article 10 on 'Promotion, Protection and Treatment of Investments' begins, in paragraph (1), with general statements concerning the favourable conditions that Contracting Parties must maintain for investments by investors of other Contracting Parties. These provisions are intended to ensure an absolute minimum standard of treatment such as has been established in BIT practice, based to a considerable extent on developments in international law. Paragraph (1) of the Article consists of five sentences, the first two of which explicitly refer to the making of investments. The first sentence obliges each Contracting Party, 'in accordance with the provisions of this Treaty', to 'encourage and create stable, equitable, favourable and transparent conditions' for the making of investments, while the second sentence adds that such conditions 'shall include a commitment to accord at all times to Investments of Investors . . . fair and equitable treatment'. **4.18**

The next two sentences provide that 'such investments' shall: 'also enjoy the most constant protection'; in no way be impaired in their management, maintenance, use, enjoyment, or disposal by 'unreasonable or discriminatory measures'; and 'in no case be accorded treatment less favourable than that required by international law, including Treaty obligations'. An Understanding in the Final Act of the European Energy Charter Conference indicates that the reference to 'Treaty obligations' does not include 'decisions taken by international organisations, even if they are legally binding, or treaties which entered into force before 1 January 1970'.[14] **4.19**

[14] The reference to decisions of international organizations was intended to preclude ECT dispute settlement with regard to the OECD Codes; the 1970 cut-off was intended to exclude older US treaties of 'Friendship, Commerce and Navigation'. Another provision establishing a minimum level of treatment is in para (12) of Art 10, obliging each Contracting Party to 'ensure that its domestic law provides effective means for the assertion of claims and the enforcement of rights with respect to investments, investment agreements, and investment authorisations'.

Internationalization of contracts

4.20 Then comes a provision in paragraph (1) of Article 10 which can make it a violation of a Contracting Party's obligations under the ECT to breach an investment agreement: 'Each Contracting Party shall observe any obligations it has entered into with an Investor or an Investment[15] of an Investor of any other Contracting Party'. The negotiating parties were given an opportunity to opt out of dispute resolution with regard to this obligation: Articles 26 and 27 allow the Contracting Parties listed in the Treaty's Annex IA to preclude ECT dispute settlement for breaches of the obligation, and Australia, Canada, Hungary, and Norway have elected to be listed in Annex IA.

The national/MFN treatment standard

4.21 The important paragraph (7) of Article 10 establishes, as a post-investment standard for the treatment of investment, the better of national or most-favoured-nation (MFN) treatment. This standard applies not only to the investments of investors of other Contracting Parties, but also to 'their related activities including management, maintenance, use, enjoyment or disposal'.

4.22 The key concept of 'national treatment', with its implication of non-discrimination, raises considerable interpretative challenges. Discrimination can take many forms, and existing and evolving European Communities law (competition, energy, and State aids in particular) provides numerous examples of discriminatory practices that can exist in law or be encouraged, facilitated, or tolerated by Governments. The concept has a trade law meaning that is fairly well understood in that context, but there are fewer precedents for its application in investment law.

4.23 Special problems can arise in applying the national treatment standard to a Contracting Party within which sub-units exercise autonomy.[16] If a sub-unit discriminates against investors of another sub-unit of the same State, it is not always clear what 'national treatment' in this context means.[17] Although the same problems in principle attend the obligations of multi-State international organizations such as the European Communities, they are mitigated by the fact that the Member States are themselves ECT signatories and so directly bound by the Treaty's obligations.

---

[15] Art 1(6) defines 'investment' to include every kind of asset, including a 'company or business enterprise'; thus, this provision of Art 10(1) applies to host country agreements with domestic subsidiaries of foreign investors. On the 'internationalization of contracts' (or 'sanctity of contracts') provision in the ECT, see E Paasivirta, in Waelde (1996a); see also T Waelde and G. Ndi, 'Stabilising International Investment Commitments', 31 Tex Int'l LJ 215–68 (1996b).

[16] Art 23 of the ECT makes each Contracting Party responsible for Treaty compliance by its sub-units, and allows invocation of Treaty dispute settlement provisions in respect of measures taken by those sub-units.

[17] The NAFTA addresses this problem, in Art 1102.3, by defining 'national treatment' in terms of the most favourable treatment accorded by a US State or Canadian Province.

The 'national treatment' principle becomes more complex when it is applied to public companies or private companies vested with 'special or exclusive privileges'.[18] The ECT duties of States to ensure Treaty-compliant conduct by such enterprises, transposed from relevant GATT provisions such as Article XVII, approaches a duty of enterprises with monopoly control over essential facilities or otherwise dominant market power not to abuse such power by discriminating against foreign competitors. The interplay of the Treaty's investment conditions and its creation of State responsibilities of effective regulation of such enterprises moves in the direction of a concept of State responsibility to impose and implement competition law, similar to that under Article 86 of the Treaty of Rome.[19] **4.24**

Likewise, questions can arise as to application of the trade law-based MFN principle to specific negotiations between resource-owning Governments or State enterprises and foreign investors. For example, can a company making a new investment—or an established company—request, by application of the MFN clause, the same financial treatment (consisting of the particular combination of royalties, income taxes, privileged State participation, and other levies) which was negotiated before or after with another company, and possibly ratified by legislation? Resource exploration and development licences may be negotiated, taking into account the particular geological, commercial, and bargaining context, and the application of the MFN principle could be seen to undermine the negotiating freedom of the parties concerned.[20] Be that as it may, worthy of note in this context is an Understanding to the ECT as a whole, contained in the Final Act of the negotiating Conference, that derogations from MFN treatment 'are not intended to cover measures which are specific to an Investor or group of Investors, rather than applying generally'.[21] **4.25**

A limitation on the national/MFN treatment principle, sought by the United States, is indicated by paragraph (8), which notes that the 'modalities of application' of paragraph (7) in relation to programmes of grants, financial assistance, or contracts for energy technology research and development, are 'reserved for' the 'second-phase' Supplementary Treaty; up-to-date reporting on such programmes is required by paragraph (9). **4.26**

[18] Art 22 of the ECT obliges Contracting Parties to ensure that such entities, in certain activities, behave in a manner consistent with, or refrain from acting in a manner inconsistent with, ECT obligations.

[19] For this reading of the interplay of Part III with Art 22 of the ECT, see T Waelde and P Wouters, 'State Responsibility in a Liberalised World Economy: State, Privileged and Subnational Authorities', 27 Neth Ybk Int'l 143 (1996).

[20] On this issue, see T Waelde, 'International Investment under the 1994 Energy Charter Treaty', 29 JWT 5 (1995).

[21] This concept was borrowed from Art 2 of the WTO Agreement on Subsidies and Countervailing Measures, which sets out principles for determining whether a subsidy is 'specific to an enterprise or industry or group of enterprises or industries'.

4.27 In addition, a European Energy Charter Conference Decision which has been incorporated into the Treaty allows the Russian Federation to require legislative approval for the leasing of federal property by companies with foreign participation, subject to an obligation not to discriminate between investors of different parties; and Bulgaria has been allowed to claim (in the Treaty's Annex T) with regard to Article 10(7) a 'transitional' exception concerning land ownership.[22]

4.28 Also, paragraph (10) specifies that the Treaty's standard of the better of national or MFN treatment shall not apply to the protection of intellectual property (which is within the Treaty's definition of 'Investment'). Instead, the treatment to be accorded with regard to intellectual property 'shall be as specified in the corresponding provisions of the applicable international agreements for the protection of Intellectual Property rights to which the respective Contracting Parties are parties'. This allows the Contracting Parties to maintain their existing exceptions to national/MFN treatment under the relevant intellectual property rights agreements.

4.29 There is an Understanding to Article 10 and to certain other provisions of the Treaty, sought by the United States, which acknowledges the permissibility of restraints on 'programmes which provide for public loans, grants, guarantees or insurance for facilitating trade or investment abroad', on the ground that these are not 'connected with Investment or related activities of Investors from other Contracting Parties' in the 'Area' of the restraining party.

Key persons

4.30 Article 11 first obliges a Contracting Party to 'examine in good faith' requests by investors of another Contracting Party and 'key personnel' employed by them, or by the entity which constitutes their investment, to enter and remain in connection with the making or the subsequent conduct of an investment. It then requires the host Contracting Party to allow the employment of key persons, provided that they have been permitted to enter, stay, and work and that the employment conforms to the permission granted.

Freedom to transfer funds

4.31 Each Contracting Party is obliged by Article 14 to guarantee the free transfer of funds with respect to investments, both into and out of its 'Area', without delay and in a freely convertible currency (ie a currency that is widely traded and used internationally) at the market rate of exchange for spot transactions. A non-

[22] It is noteworthy that there are only these few, limited exceptions to the 'post-investment' Treaty standard. Since the ECT does not permit reservations, these represent the full scope of the derogations allowed from the national treatment/MFN investment obligations imposed under the Treaty.

exclusive list of covered transfers mentions initial and additional capital, 'Returns', payments under a contract, unspent earnings and other remuneration of personnel, proceeds from a sale or liquidation, dispute settlement proceeds, and compensation of expropriation or other losses.

Article 14 contains three exceptions. First, a Contracting Party may protect creditors' rights, ensure compliance with securities laws, and ensure the satisfaction of judgments, all subject to the requirements of equity, non-discrimination, and good faith. Secondly, there is an opt-out for FSU Republics as concerns transfers among themselves, provided that investments of the investors of other Contracting Parties must be accorded the better of MFN or national treatment. Finally, returns-in-kind (eg exports of crude oil pursuant to a production-sharing agreement) may be restricted by the host country in circumstances where the GATT allows export restrictions, except that such returns must be allowed in accordance with the provisions of any written agreement that the foreign investor or its domestic subsidiary has with the host State.[23] **4.32**

Exception for Russian investors

Article 14 is also subject to two Decisions annexed to the Final Act of the negotiating Conference, the more significant of which applies exclusively to those FSU Republics which elected by 1 July 1995 to be subject to it. This Decision allows restrictions by such a State 'on movement of capital by its own investors', subject to several conditions aimed at protecting the rights of investors of other Contracting Parties and narrowing the scope of the exception; in fact, only the Russian Federation made such an election. The intention behind this Decision is to exclude a right of the domestic investor of such a State to request certain transfers (even where that investor is a business entity that qualifies as the investment of an investor of another Contracting Party) without foreclosing the right of the foreign investor itself to make the same request. **4.33**

Preservation of EU investor rights

The Decision is subject to an exchange of letters between Russia and the European Union, aimed at avoiding any curtailment of the rights otherwise available to the EU and its Member States under their 24 June 1994 Partnership and Cooperation Agreement (PCA) with Russia.[24] The exchange of letters was considered necessary because Article 105 of the PCA expressly provides for the PCA's inapplicability in areas covered by the ECT. Yet its payments transfer protections[25] **4.34**

---

[23] The negotiating Conference decided not to include an express let-out for balance of payments difficulties; cf Art VII, s 3 of the Articles of Agreement of the International Monetary Fund.

[24] See Council and Commission Decision of 30 October 1997, 97/800 ECSC, EC, EURATOM; for a full text of the agreement: OJ L 327 of 28 November 1997.

[25] The PCA's transfer provisions are directed mainly at inward capital flows related to the making of an investment.

are considered by the EU to be preferable to those of the ECT. Although Article 16 of the ECT contains rules designed to ensure that an investor will enjoy the most favourable treatment available to him under any treaty, the EU was apparently concerned that the rule contained in Article 105 PCA might negate those in Article 16. Interestingly, since the Conference Decision concerning Article 14 leaves intact the ECT's MFN obligation (indeed, the Decision reasserts such an obligation) there is a question whether the investors of other ECT Contracting Parties are entitled to treatment by Russia at least as favourable as that which Russia accords investors of the European Union through the PCA.

Subrogation

4.35 The host State Contracting Party is required by Article 15 to recognize the assignment of rights and claims and the ability to pursue them, where another Contracting Party or an agency thereof makes a payment under an indemnity or guarantee in respect of an investment, and the indemnifying party is entitled to the rights accorded the indemnified party under the ECT. In the case of investor-Contracting Party dispute settlement, the payments under an insurance or guarantee contract will not operate to excuse the host Contracting Party as concerns damages.

Nationalization/confiscation

4.36 Investment is protected against nationalization/confiscation (with a reference to confiscatory taxation) under the 'Hull rule', the Western position in the 1970s debate on compensation standards.[26] Articles 12 and 13 deal with compensation for expropriations and for other losses such as those caused by armed conflict, a state of national emergency, civil disturbance, or similar events. Under Article 13, no Contracting Party may nationalize or expropriate, or subject to one or more measures having equivalent effect, the investment of the investor of another Contracting Party, except: for a public purpose; on a non-discriminatory basis; in accordance with due process of law; and when accompanied by prompt, adequate, and effective compensation (amounting to fair market value immediately before the expropriation or impending expropriation became known in such a way as to affect the investment's value, and with interest to the date of payment). The investor is entitled to have the fair market value expressed in a freely convertible currency on the basis of the market exchange rate at the time the expropriation became known. Further, the expropriating Contracting Party must afford a right to prompt review of the issues raised. The expropriation article has significant current implications: first, it could be construed to cover expropriation by exorbitant

[26] See the chapters in Waelde (1996a) by M Sornarajah and P Norton.

regulation, eg in environmental matters;[27] secondly, it also covers, in spite of the very restrictive treatment of tax matters in the Treaty discussed below, confiscatory taxation.[28]

Where Article 13 on expropriation is inapplicable, Article 12 requires the host Contracting Party to accord to an investor of another Contracting Party whose investment suffers a loss due to war or other armed conflict, state of national emergency, civil disturbance, or other similar event, the better of national and MFN treatment as regards restitution, indemnification, compensation, or other settlement. In addition, prompt, adequate, and effective restitution or compensation is required where, in such a situation, the investor suffers a loss from requisitioning of its investment, or a destruction thereof 'which was not required by the necessity of the situation'. **4.37**

Host State's right to deny benefits

Article 17 allows a Contracting Party to deny the advantages of Part III to an entity owned or controlled by investors of a non-Contracting Party and lacking substantial business activities in the Contracting Party where it is organized; or to an investment of an investor of a non-Contracting Party State with which the host State does not maintain diplomatic relations, or as to which the host State maintains prohibitory legal measures. In light of the former provision, an investor based outside of the Contracting Parties to the ECT will need to employ an entity that not only is based in a Contracting Party, but also conducts substantial business activities there, in order to enjoy the legal protections afforded by the ECT. **4.38**

Arbitration of disputes

The Treaty's dispute resolution provisions that correspond to the Part III investment provisions are in Part V, which is comprised of three articles, two of which (Arts 26 and 27) establish investment dispute settlement mechanisms, and the third (Art 28) limits access to one of those mechanisms.[29] **4.39**

Compulsory arbitration of private investor disputes

Perhaps the most important aspect of the ECT's investment regime is the Treaty's provision for compulsory arbitration against Governments at the option of foreign investors, for alleged breaches of the Treaty's investment protections, **4.40**

[27] For an extended discussion: T Waelde, 'ECT and Sustainable Development', in F Weiss (ed), *Economic Development with a Human Face* (Kluwer, 1998) 223.

[28] See T Waelde, 'UK Windfall Profits Tax and Confiscatory Taxation', vol 2 (1997), On-Line Journal of the Centre for Petroleum and Mineral Law and Policy, www.dundee.ac.uk/petroleumlaw/—forthcoming in Nw J Int'l L

[29] See the chapters in Waelde (1996a) by K Vandevelde and J Paulsson; T Waelde, 'Investment Arbitration Under the Energy Charter Treaty', 12 J Int'l Arb 429 (1996).

without the need for a specific arbitral 'compromis'.[30] Article 26 provides for the resolution of disputes between a Contracting Party and an investor of a different Contracting Party 'relating to an Investment of the latter in the Area of the former, which concern an alleged breach of an obligation of the former under Part III. . .' It gives an investor the choice to submit an unresolved dispute, following a failure to resolve the dispute by negotiation: to the fora of the host State; in accordance with some other previously agreed procedure; or, for binding arbitration, to the investor's preference among ICSID; a forum established under the rules of the United Nations Commission on International Trade Law (UNCITRAL); or to a proceeding of the Arbitration Institute of the Stockholm Chamber of Commerce.

4.41 Article 26(3)(a) states that 'each Contracting Party hereby gives its unconditional consent to the submission of a dispute to international arbitration or conciliation in accordance with the provisions [of the Article]'. It also contains several technical provisions to ensure the sufficiency of Contracting Parties' consent to arbitration. Paragraph (8) requires that each Contracting Party carry out without delay any arbitral award, and that it make provision for the effective enforcement of such awards; it also provides that an arbitration award concerning a measure of a sub-national Government or authority shall allow for the payment of monetary damages in lieu of another remedy.

4.42 Furthermore, paragraph 5(b) of Article 26 allows the investor to require that an arbitration be held in a State that is a party to the New York Convention on the Recognition and Enforcement of Foreign Arbitral Awards.[31] The effect is that the provisions of that Convention will apply to the enforcement of the award in the State where the arbitration is held, and the award will be recognized and enforced in other States Parties to the Convention.

4.43 However, paragraph (3)(b) provides an exception which allows Contracting Parties to deny unconditional consent to ICSID, UNCITRAL, or Stockholm arbitration in the situation where an investor 'has previously submitted the dispute' to the domestic fora of the host State or under another previously agreed procedure; twenty-five States and the European Communities are currently listed in Annex ID as denying such consent, although it should be noted that their respective policies and practices differ widely concerning the extent to which a dispute may proceed in the domestic fora. Contracting Parties listed in Annex ID are required, by the time of their deposit of an instrument of ratification, acceptance,

[30] For the significant precursor practice in modern BITs and in ch XI of the NAFTA, see n 14 above.

[31] 4 ILM 532 (1965). The Convention can also be found (with introduction by R Brand) in II, S Zamora and R Brand, *Basic Documents of International Economic Law* 975 (CCH International, Chicago, 1990).

approval or accession, to provide a written statement of their policies and practices in this regard.[32]

State–State arbitration

Article 27 provides for binding State–State arbitration (at The Hague, unless the parties decide otherwise), by an *ad hoc* tribunal, of disputes 'concerning the application or interpretation' of the ECT. Unlike Article 26 on investor dispute resolution, Article 27 is not limited to investment disputes arising under Part III of the Treaty, although the Article 27 arbitral procedures are excluded by Article 28 from application to trade-related disputes arising under Article 5 ('Trade Related Investment Measures'); Articles 6 ('Competition') and 19 ('Environmental Aspects') likewise are not subject to Article 27 arbitration.[33] **4.44**

Initially, Contracting Parties are obliged to endeavour to settle State–State disputes through diplomatic channels, but if a dispute has not been resolved within a reasonable period of time either party to the dispute may submit it to arbitration. Article 27 then: prescribes procedures for the constitution of a panel; specifies applicability of the rules of UNCITRAL in the absence of a contrary decision by the parties or the arbitrators; and calls upon the panel to decide the dispute in accordance with the Treaty 'and applicable rules and principles of international law'. **4.45**

Where, in State–State arbitration, a measure of a regional or local Government is found not to be in conformity with the Treaty, those Contracting Parties listed in the ECT's Annex P may invoke the procedures of that Annex (which have been based on language in the World Trade Organization Agreement's Understanding on Rules and Procedures Governing the Settlement of Disputes), providing for Charter Conference authorization to the injured party to suspend such of its Treaty obligations to the offending party 'as [the Contracting Party] considers equivalent to those denied. . .' Two federal States are listed in Annex P: Australia and Canada. **4.46**

Exceptions

The ECT allows for a number of exceptions from the rights and obligations provided for therein. While many of these exceptions apply not only to the Treaty's investment protections but also to other rights and obligations, they are mentioned below because of their importance in the investment context. **4.47**

[32] These declarations are provided to the Energy Charter Secretariat, from which copies can be obtained.

[33] See ECT Arts 6(7) and 27(2). Art 27 arbitration may, however, be available for transit matters: see Bamberger in Waelde (1996a) n 4, p 8, and T Waelde (1996c) n 26.

Tax article

4.48 One of the purposes of Article 21 on taxation was to avoid having the benefits of bilateral tax treaties shared by ECT parties under that Treaty's MFN provisions. However, in their efforts to achieve that goal the negotiators went so far as to specify that except as otherwise provided in this tax article (with some limited scope for application of the non-discrimination principle, and with full application of Article 13 on 'Expropriation' and thus some scope for notions of 'confiscatory taxation'), nothing in the Treaty creates rights or imposes obligations with regard to a Contracting Party's domestic tax laws (or its international tax agreements), and they further stipulated that the tax article will prevail over any other Treaty provision in case of inconsistency between them.

4.49 This may have some unfortunate effects on other parts of the Treaty. As one example, with respect to the very important Treaty requirement that Contracting Parties observe their obligations entered into with investors or their subsidiaries, Article 21 raises a question about the value of that protection in a situation where the host State imposes a tax in violation of an investment agreement.[34]

General exceptions

4.50 Most of these exceptions, set out in Article 24, found their inspiration in the exceptions from trade rules that are contained in the GATT: (i) scarcity of 'Energy Materials and Products' due to causes beyond the control of the Contracting Party; the exception is subject to a condition of consistency with the principle that 'all other Contracting Parties are entitled to an equitable share of the international supply. . .'; (ii) measures to benefit aboriginal or socially or economically disadvantaged investors; (iii) measures considered necessary for the protection of 'essential security interests'; (iv) measures considered necessary with regard to nuclear non-proliferation; and (v) measures considered necessary for the maintenance of public order.[35] As often throughout the Energy Charter Treaty's investment regime, these provisions rely, for investment principles, on concepts and practices developed in the context of international trade law; while the significant difference between trade and investment needs to be taken into account when dealing with virtually identical language, this may be indicative of a growing convergence between international trade and investment law.

[34] However, if a breach of a tax stabilization clause were seen as a 'taking' of a contractually established proprietary right, the property protection of Art 13 would arguably not be excluded by Art 21(1).

[35] Art 24(2)(i) also contains an exception for measures 'necessary to protect human, animal or plant life or health', but this exception cannot be claimed with respect to the investment protections in Part III of the Treaty.

It should be noted that these general exceptions do not apply to the nationalization/confiscation protections in Articles 12–13 (nor to the Treaty's trade rules under Article 29, discussed below). **4.51**

'Transitional' arrangements

Although Article 32 sets out arrangements under which Contracting Parties that are among twenty-four specified 'economies-in-transition' are eligible for temporary exceptions from obligations under certain provisions of the ECT, the exceptions actually claimed, which were recorded in Annex T of the Treaty, proved surprisingly modest. The principal investment exception claimed by certain 'transitional' countries was from the Treaty's requirement that, in the interest of transparency, Contracting Parties establish 'official enquiry points' through which investors can obtain information. As noted in section E(2) below, few of these exceptions remain applicable today. **4.52**

Certain multilateral agreements

Finally, there are exceptions from the requirement for preferences that Contracting Parties accord within the context of free-trade areas, customs unions, co-operation agreements among the FSU Republics, or 'Economic Integration Agreements'.[36] **4.53**

'Economic Integration Agreements'

The provisions concerning 'Economic Integration Agreements' warrant special discussion, in light of the importance attached to them by the European Union in the course of the ECT negotiations. Paragraph (2) of Article 25 defines 'Economic Integration Agreement' (EIA) to mean an agreement 'substantially liberalizing *inter alia* trade and investment, by providing for the absence or elimination of substantially all discrimination between or among parties thereto. . .'; the definition comprehends liberalization of investment, and arguably further differs in principle from GATT Article XXIV(8)(b) in that it does not require full sectoral trade liberalization. Paragraph (1) provides that a Contracting Party need not extend, under the ECT's MFN provisions, to another Contracting Party that is not a party to the EIA, any preferential treatment enjoyed under the EIA among the parties to it. **4.54**

The EIA provisions were a highly contentious subject in the ECT negotiations; in subsequently explaining its decision not to sign the Treaty, the US cited Article 25 as one of its objections. The EU initially proposed an EIA clause applying to national as well as MFN treatment, but this was withdrawn because of widespread opposition, and the paragraph (2) test for qualification as an EIA was also made more stringent. **4.55**

[36] See Arts 24(4) and 25.

4.56 Since the exception created by Article 25 applies only to MFN and not to national treatment, it affects only preferences that a party to an EIA such as an EU State extends to a non-EU State,[37] which it does not extend domestically; such preferences are likely to be quite limited as concerns investment. Moreover, the EIA Article excuses the EIA State only from extending MFN treatment to other Contracting Parties; yet Article 24, dealing with MFN treatment of preferences accorded within free-trade areas and customs unions,[38] contains an exception only as concerns the investors of another Contracting Party, suggesting a possible distinction between an exception for benefits to investors and an exception for benefits to Contracting Parties.

4.57 Annexed to the Final Act of the negotiating Conference and incorporated by reference into the Treaty is a Decision, agreed between the EU and the US as part of the Article 25 negotiations. This Decision, drawn from Article 48 of the EC Treaty and jurisprudence of the European Court of Justice, provides that an investment of an investor of a Contracting Party which is not a party to an EIA or a member of a free-trade area or customs union shall nonetheless be entitled to treatment accorded under such EIA, free-trade agreement, or customs union, where the investment:

(a) has its registered office, central administration, or principal place of business in the Area of a party to that EIA or member of that free-trade area or customs union; or
(b) if it only has its registered office in that Area, has an effective and continuous link with the economy of one of the parties to that EIA or member of that free-trade area or customs union.

4.58 In addition, in a Declaration with respect to Article 25 that is included in the Conference's Final Act, the European Communities and their Member States recall the provisions of Article 48 of the EC Treaty according national treatment as to the right of establishment to certain kinds of firms present in the Community. They say that 'the application of Article 25 [of the ECT] . . . will only allow those derogations necessary to safeguard the preferential treatment resulting from the wider process of economic integration . . .' Also relevant is the Final Act Understanding, alluded to above, to the effect that derogations from MFN treatment are intended to be limited to measures of general applicability.

The trade provisions[39]

4.59 A major element of the ECT is that it subjects the trade of Contracting Parties that are not parties to the GATT, such as the FSU Republics, to rules of the 1947 GATT, both in those countries' relations with GATT countries and in their

[37] Except on the basis of an association agreement or in the process of accession.
[38] Art 24(4).
[39] An in-depth discussion of the ECT's trade provisions can be found in Waelde (1996a) ch 21.

relations with one another. The provisions to this effect, which are set out in Article 29 of the ECT, are said to be 'interim' ones, but this is so only in the sense that they apply 'while any Contracting Party is not a party to the GATT and Related Instruments'. (As explained in section E(3) below, a Trade Amendment to the ECT, not yet in force but which provides for provisional application, brings these provisions into conformity with the results of the GATT Uruguay Round.)

Under Article 29(2), applying provisions of the 1947 GATT to trade involving non-GATT countries, these provisions will govern trade in 'Energy Materials and Products'[40] between any two ECT Contracting Parties where either of them is not a GATT Party, or if a GATT Party, is not party to a GATT-related instrument that is relevant to such trade. The applicable 1947 GATT provisions are indicated through a list of the inapplicable ones; the negotiating Conference maximized the application of the 1947 GATT insofar as was practicable. A potential exception which was allowed for trade between FSU Republics, which could instead be governed by an agreement between them, ceased to be available as of December 1999. However, the specified GATT provisions will not govern trade between ECT Contracting Parties that are either party to the 1947 GATT or 'party' to 'GATT 1994', and to the relevant GATT-related instruments. **4.60**

The 'exceptions and rules'

Annex G to the ECT sets out the provisions of the 1947 GATT and its related instruments that will not apply to trade covered by Article 29(2), ie the exceptions. Any 1947 GATT provisions not listed there will apply to such trade. Article 29(2)(a) stipulates that these provisions govern, 'as applied on 1 March 1994 and practised with regard to Energy Materials and Products by parties to GATT 1947 among themselves...' **4.61**

Article 29(2)(a), while imposing 1947 GATT rules on trade involving non-GATT parties, is 'subject to the exceptions and rules provided for in Annex G'. Annex G, entitled 'Exceptions and Rules Governing the Application of the GATT and Related Instruments', after setting out the provisions of the 1947 GATT and its related instruments that will not apply to trade covered by Article 29(2), calls for adherence to GATT provisions in examining balance of payments measures of non-GATT countries, and stipulates notifications to the Energy Charter Secretariat by such countries in cases where applicable GATT provisions call for notifications to the GATT. **4.62**

[40] See the definition in section C(1) above.

Dispute resolution

4.63 Disputes between Contracting Parties over compliance with the applicable 1947 GATT provisions are subject to resolution under procedures set out in the Treaty's Annex D, drafted using as a point of departure what was then the 'Dunkel text' Uruguay Round dispute settlement procedures, which were subsequently modified in the course of their adoption as part of the WTO Agreement. Where a dispute resolution panel concludes that a measure of a Contracting Party fails to comply with the governing ECT provisions, it may recommend that the offending Contracting Party alter or abandon the measure. The panel's report is subject to adoption by the Charter Conference, acting by a vote of three-fourths of those present and voting (and at least a simple majority of the Contracting Parties). Where the offending Party fails to comply with the panel's ruling or recommendation, the Charter Conference may by the same vote authorize the injured Party to suspend ECT trade obligations to the other Party 'which the injured Party considers equivalent in the circumstances'. There are further provisions for the review of the level of obligations proposed to be suspended.

4.64 There are exceptions from these dispute settlement procedures both for disputes arising under the agreements between FSU Republics that are referred to above, and for those arising under agreements establishing free-trade agreements or customs unions as described in Article XXIV of the GATT.

EU–FSU nuclear trade

4.65 Paragraph (4) of Annex G covers nuclear trade, an issue which during the ECT negotiations was an especially hard-fought subject between the EU and the Russian Federation; indeed, so difficult was this subject to resolve that on 16 December 1994 it became necessary to adjourn the ceremonial meeting in Lisbon at which the text of the ECT was to be adopted by the negotiating Conference, in order to allow time for overnight negotiations (on this and on several lesser issues of Treaty interpretation).

4.66 Paragraph (4) provides: 'Trade in nuclear materials may be governed by agreements referred to in the Declarations related to this paragraph contained in the Final Act of the European Energy Charter Conference'. Article VI.7 of the Final Act contains six joint declarations of the European Communities with Russia and five other republics of the FSU, in each case stating that trade in nuclear materials between them 'shall be governed' (or 'exclusively governed') by certain other agreements, or that those other agreements 'shall exclusively continue to apply'. In the case of Russia, the governing provisions are those of Article 22 of the EU–Russia PCA. As a result of the last-minute EU–Russia negotiations, a joint memorandum was agreed, recalling the EU's stated policy on nuclear materials import quotas, confirming applicability of the PCA's national treatment provisions to imports of nuclear material from Russia, and looking toward future review of the subject. Upon reconvening the Lisbon meeting, the Conference Chairman took note of the joint memorandum, which at the request of Russia and the Communities was to be annexed to the report of the Conference session, and stated that it was clear that as far as the ECT is concerned, 'nuclear trade will be governed by Article 29(2)(a), Annex G and the joint declarations, concerning the implementation of the GATT rules by reference'.

A question not addressed in the Treaty is whether the GATT-like trade dispute settlement provisions in the Treaty's Annex D, which apply to 'disputes regarding compliance with provisions applicable to trade' under Article 29, are available for disputes arising under the EU–Russia PCA and other agreements identified in the six declarations contained in the Final Act. In other words, do the statements in the Final Act declarations, that the nuclear trade shall be governed by the PCA or other specified agreements, make compliance with those agreements a right protected by the ECT? The Final Act/Conference Decision adopting the Trade Amendment contains a Declaration by the EU and Russia which indicates that they regard such trade as exclusively covered by the PCA.[41] **4.67**

Trade-related investment measures

Of interest to foreign investors is the ECT's GATT-like discouragement of trade-related measures (TRIMs), ie measures imposing 'local content requirements' or 'trade balancing requirements'. Article 5 forbids all Contracting Parties from imposing any TRIM that is inconsistent with Article III or XI of the GATT. This specifically includes investment measures that would: require the purchase of goods of domestic origin or from a domestic source; impose limits on the purchase or use of imported goods; restrict, or link with its exports, the imports of products which an enterprise uses in local production; limit imports by restricting access to foreign exchange; or impose limits on exports, through a link to the volume or value of local production or in another manner.[42] TRIMs forbidden by Article 5 are subject to Article 26 investment arbitration (Art 10(11)). **4.68**

[41] 'The Russian Federation has raised the issue of trade in nuclear materials. The Russian Federation and the EU agreed that the Partnership and Co-operation Agreement between the Russian Federation, the European Union and its Member States, which entered into force on 1 December 1997, is the appropriate framework to deal with this issue, as confirmed in the conclusions of 27 January 1998 Co-operation Council.'

[42] There is an exception intended to allow TRIMs involving a 'rule of origin' as a condition of product eligibility for export promotion, foreign aid, government procurement, or preferential tariff or quota programmes; and pre-existing TRIMs may be temporarily maintained, subject to specified notification and phase-out requirements. On the ECT's TRIMs provisions, see the chapter in Waelde (1996a) by M Footer.

(2) The Transit Rules

4.69 Most of the oil and gas resources in the FSU are located in remote regions with difficult access to consuming areas (Siberia, Azerbaijan, Kazakhstan, Turkmenistan). Transit is therefore a subject on which a meaningful energy treaty can have substantial impact, and it is closely linked to investment. Article 7 of the ECT, dealing with this subject, contains the Treaty's most unique provisions, imposing unprecedented rights and obligations as concerns the transit of energy goods through a State that is Party to the Treaty.[43] Its potential relevance was highlighted during the dispute in early 1996 between Russia and Ukraine over Druzhba oil pipeline charges, when a Russian Deputy Minister, appearing before the State Duma, reportedly threatened to invoke the article.[44]

Definitions

4.70 In Article 7, 'Transit' refers to 'carriage through the Area of a Contracting Party, or to or from port facilities in its Area for loading or unloading, of Energy Materials and Products originating in the Area of another state and destined for the Area of a third state, so long as either the other state or the third state is a Contracting Party'. The term has a secondary meaning: it also covers carriage originating in and destined for the same Contracting Party, where the goods pass through another Contracting Party, unless the parties concerned have opted out of this provision by listing themselves in the ECT's Annex N; only Canada and the United States have done so. The terms 'originating in' and 'destined for' are undefined.

4.71 'Energy Transport Facilities' are fixed facilities specifically for handling 'Energy Materials and Products'; a non-exclusive list of such facilities mentions high-pressure gas transmission pipelines, high-voltage electric transmission grids and lines, crude oil transmission pipelines, coal slurry pipelines, and oil product pipelines.

Rules

4.72 Paragraph (1) obliges each Contracting Party to 'take the necessary measures to facilitate' transit 'consistent with the principle of freedom of transit' (a reference to Art V of the GATT) and on a non-discriminatory, reasonable basis.

---

[43] The EC Transit Directive (OJ L 147/37 of 12/6/91 at 37; OJ L 313 of 133/11 1990 at 30) can be viewed as a precursor to Art 7 of the Treaty see F von Burchard and L Eckert, *Natural Gas and EU Energy Law* (Nomos, Baden-Baden, 1995). Further analysis of the transit provisions in the EC Transit Directive and the Energy Charter Treaty can be found in Waelde (1996a) ch 22; and M Roggenkamp, 'Transit of Network Bound Energy: A New Phenomenon', 19 *World Competition* 2 (1995).

[44] BBC *Monitoring Summary of World Broadcasts,* 19 February 1996. See also 'Energy Transit, the Multilateral Challenge', Energy Charter Secretariat paper submitted to the 'G8' Ministerial Meeting, Moscow, April 1998 with ideas about expanding Art 7 of the Treaty through multilateral arrangements.

Paragraph (2) is a 'soft law' obligation to 'encourage relevant entities to co-operate' in modernizing, developing, operating, and facilitating the interconnection of 'Energy Transport Facilities', and in measures to mitigate the effects of interruptions in the supply of energy goods. **4.73**

In paragraph (3) each Contracting Party undertakes that, unless an existing international agreement provides otherwise, its 'provisions' relating to the transport of covered energy goods and to the use of fixed energy transport facilities shall treat energy goods that are in transit through that Contracting Party's 'Area' no less favourably than they treat any other such goods originating in or destined for that 'Area'. **4.74**

Paragraph (4) indicates that if transit via fixed facilities cannot be achieved on commercial terms, Contracting Parties 'shall not place obstacles in the way of new capacity being established, except as may be provided in applicable legislation which is consistent with paragraph (1)'. An Understanding to this paragraph in the Final Act of the negotiating Conference observes that legislation on environmental protection, land use, safety, or technical standards would qualify under this language. Paragraph (4) of Article 7 is subject to the ECT's 'transitional arrangements', providing for temporary exceptions that the 'economies-in-transition' were allowed to take from specific provisions of the ECT; such exceptions, which are listed in Annex T to the Treaty, are described below. Paragraph (4) of the 'Transit' article was the object of exceptions on the part of several countries, but only Bulgaria continues to maintain such an exception. **4.75**

Under paragraph (5) of Article 7 the transit State is not obliged to permit construction or modification of new transport facilities or to allow new or additional transit through existing ones, where it demonstrates to the other Contracting Parties concerned that such development would endanger the security or efficiency of its energy systems, including the security of supply. However, subject to paragraphs (6) and (7), the Contracting Parties 'shall . . . secure established flows . . .'. **4.76**

Paragraphs (6) and (7) are the Article's most operationally relevant provisions. Paragraph (6) provides that the transit State 'shall not, in the event of a dispute over any matter arising from that Transit, interrupt or reduce, permit any entity subject to its control to interrupt or reduce, or require any entity subject to its jurisdiction to interrupt or reduce the existing flow' of energy goods prior to the conclusion of the dispute resolution procedures set out in paragraph (7), except where specifically allowed to do so by a relevant agreement or where permitted to do so by a conciliator appointed under paragraph (7). **4.77**

Paragraph (7), which only applies following the exhaustion of all other dispute resolution remedies previously agreed to between the concerned Contracting Parties or between the concerned entities, allows a Contracting Party to the dispute to require the Energy Charter Secretary-General, who heads the Secretariat **4.78** that supports the Energy Charter Conference, to appoint a conciliator. If the conciliator fails to secure agreement within sixty days, 'he shall recommend a resolution and shall decide the interim tariffs and other terms and conditions to be observed . . . until the dispute is resolved.'[45] Paragraph (7)(d) states that the Contracting Parties 'undertake to observe and ensure that the entities under their control or jurisdiction observe' the conciliator's decision for twelve months, unless the dispute is resolved sooner. Paragraph (7)(f) calls upon the Charter Conference to 'adopt standard provisions concerning the conduct of conciliation and the compensation of conciliators'.[46]

4.79 Paragraph (8) stipulates that nothing in Article 7 shall derogate from international law, including existing international agreements, and specifically from rules concerning submarine cables and pipelines.[47]

4.80 Paragraph (9) notes that the Article is not to be interpreted to require any Contracting Party to take any measure with respect to a particular type of fixed energy transport facility that is not already in existence in that country; however, it clarifies that this is not intended to excuse the Contracting Party from its paragraph (4) obligation to refrain from placing obstacles in the way of new capacity being established.

Obligations of the European Communities

4.81 The fact that the European Communities are Contracting Parties to the ECT, separately from their members, presents some interesting issues in the context of this Article, especially as concerns its paragraph (6)–(7) operational provisions. The obligations under the Article fall on the 'Contracting Parties', ie the Communities as such as well as their individual Member States. However, the obligations under the Article pertain to 'Transit', which refers in its primary definition to carriage originating in 'another state' and destined for a 'third state', phrasing that could be read to imply that the transit in question occurs through an individual State.

---

[45] The 'conciliator' therefore acts, at least with respect to the determination of interim tariffs, not just as a conciliator, ie an expert to 'encourage' a solution, but rather as an arbitrator with dispute settlement powers see: T Waelde (1996c) n 26.

[46] Such rules were in fact adopted by the Conference at its second meeting in December 1998; they vest the conciliator with substantial procedural discretion and provide for the conciliator to record his recommendation or decision, with a statement of reasons therefor, if the parties fail to reach agreement within the time provided for in the Treaty and the rules. See Summary Record of the Second Meeting of the Energy Charter Conference (CC 137).

[47] There was an exchange of Notes between Norway and the United Kingdom in June 1995 establishing that Art 7 does not affect their respective positions concerning pipelines originating in one such State and lying on the continental shelf in the other State. On the law relating to submarine pipelines, see W Wiese, *Grenzüeberschreitende Landrohrleitungen und seeverlegte Rohrleitungen im Völkerrecht* (Duncker & Humblot, Berlin, 1997).

This raises questions as to what are the obligations of the Communities when a disruption of transit is threatened. For example, as concerns enforcement of a conciliator's decision against a transit State within the EU, when are the Communities required under paragraph (7)(d) of Article 7 to 'observe and ensure that the entities under their . . . jurisdiction observe any interim decision' of a conciliator concerning tariffs, terms, or conditions? Does this obligation pertain only when the carriage of energy goods is from and destined for non-Member States, and through the territories of the European Communities' States as if they were one State, implying that the internal law of the Community is a special regime prevailing over the Energy Charter Treaty when no non-Community signatories are involved? Or does it apply to the Communities whenever such a dispute affects carriage through one of their Member States? Note that under the latter interpretation, the Article's obligations could apply to the European Communities not only with respect to disputes involving carriage of energy goods through States external to the European Communities, but also to those involving carriage through the Communities' own individual Member States. One can hypothesize other cases, where goods originate in or are destined for EU States, that pose similarly difficult questions of European Community responsibility. **4.82**

(3) Other Features of the Treaty

The ECT contains comparatively 'soft' provisions on several energy-related subjects such as competition[48] (procedures for consultation between competition authorities), the environment[49] (hortatory commitments of good environmental practice), access to capital[50] (a best-efforts obligation to promote it), and transfer of technology[51] (no obstacles should be imposed). However, it also contains 'hard law' commitments, noted above, concerning compliance by sub-federal political units[52] and State obligations regarding Treaty compliance by their State enterprises and other delegates of State power.[53] **4.83**

Article 33(1) provides that the Energy Charter Conference may authorize 'Protocols' (treaties which ECT Parties may elect, but are not required, to participate in) and 'Declarations' (non-binding instruments) 'in order to pursue the objectives and principles' of the European Energy Charter; Article 13(a) says that a Protocol complements, supplements, extends, or amplifies the provisions of the Treaty sectorally, or by category of activity, or with reference to co-operation envisaged in the European Energy Charter. In fact, the Protocol on 'Energy **4.84**

[48] Art 6. See the chapter in Waelde (1996a) by K Holmes.

[49] Art 19. See the chapter in Waelde (1996a) by C Shine; see also Waelde in F Weiss, above n 27.

[50] Art 9.

[51] Art 8.

[52] Art 23.

[53] Art 22.

Efficiency and Related Environmental Aspects' opened for signature along with the ECT and was signed by all signatories of the ECT; it entered into force on 16 April 1998.[54] Moreover, a decision has been made to direct the Conference's energy transit efforts towards negotiation of a Protocol. Other possible Protocols or Declarations have also been considered.

D. Direct Effect of the Treaty

4.85 The Treaty provides a range of means by which it can be enforced. The option of investor-State arbitration under Article 26 in respect of disputes concerning the investment chapter without the need first to exhaust local remedies is clearly an important feature of the Treaty. The Contracting Party home State of an investor may also invoke the arbitration clause in Article 27 in respect of such disputes. Action to deal with alleged breaches of other provisions of the Treaty can only be taken by a Contracting Party in accordance with the mechanism provided under the Treaty. In this respect the general provision for resolving State–State disputes in Article 27 will not apply to disputes concerning, for example, the articles on an interim trade regime, which has its own dispute resolution mechanism.

4.86 While the Treaty provides these mechanisms to deal with disputes, a national of a Contracting Party may prefer to invoke the Treaty before national courts, or an issue of interpretation of, or compliance with, the Treaty may otherwise come before such courts. In this context it will be important to consider whether the Treaty has 'direct effect'[55] within the relevant legal system. This will require an examination of the constitutional situation in each Contracting Party. As the European Communities are also Parties to the Treaty, the situation under Community law in respect of the direct effect of 'mixed agreements', such as the Treaty, also needs to be examined.[56] It will also be necessary to determine whether

[54] As of 23 November 2000 the following 40 States and the European Communities had deposited instruments of ratification or approval: Albania, Armenia, Austria, Azerbaijan, Belgium, Bulgaria, Croatia, Cyprus, the Czech Republic, Denmark, Estonia, Finland, France, Germany, Greece, Hungary, Ireland, Italy, Kazakhstan, Kyrgyztan, Latvia, Liechtenstein, Lithuania, Luxembourg, the former Yugoslav Republic of Macedonia, Moldova, Mongolia, the Netherlands, Portugal, Romania, Slovakia, Slovenia, Spain, Sweden, Switzerland, Tajikistan, Turkmenistan, Ukraine, the United Kingdom, and Uzbekistan.

[55] There is a large volume of literature on the effect of treaties in domestic legal systems. See eg FG Jacobs and S Roberts (eds), *The Effect of Treaties in Domestic Law* (Sweet & Maxwell, 1987); J Jackson, 'Status of Treaties in Domestic Legal Systems: A Policy Analysis' (1992) 86 *AJIL*, 310; EU Petersmann, National Constitutions and International Economic Law, 1–52) in H Meinhard and H-U Petersmann, *National Constitutions and Int'l Economic Law* (Kluwer Deventer, 1993), R Brand, 'Direct Effect of International Economic Law in United States and the European Union', Nw J Int'l L For present purposes, terminological differences concerning 'direct effect', 'direct applicability', and 'self-executing' (the last used in the context of the United States) can be ignored.

[56] See generally I Macleod, ID Hendry, and S Hyett, *The External Relations of the European Communities* (Clarendon, 1996) 133.

the Treaty itself or parts of it are regarded as meeting whatever the relevant test is for direct effect.[57] The investment regime of the Treaty (Part III) together with related provisions that clarify, explain, restrict, or extend Part III (eg Arts 22 and 23) is perhaps the likeliest candidate for direct effect. The coverage of Part III by the Article 26 investment arbitration mechanism indicates that, with respect to Part III, no further implementing legislative action was considered necessary.[58] The situation is very different for the mainly hortatory environmental and competition articles, where the explicit exclusion of the Article 26 investment arbitration method indicates that the Treaty's intention is not to make these articles justiciable in any way.

It is likely that in many Contracting Parties some of the provisions in the Treaty would be regarded as having a direct effect and could be invoked in national courts.[59] In the case of the European Communities and most Member States this seems to be the case, at least in respect of the investment provisions.[60] **4.87**

[57] For example, the European Court of Justice has enunciated a simple test: '[a] provision in an international agreement concluded by the Community with non-member countries must be regarded as being directly applicable when, regard being had to its wording and the purpose and nature of the Agreement and nature itself, the provision contains a clear and precise obligation which is not subject, in its implementation or effects, to the adoption of any subsequent measure.' *Demirel v Stadt Schwäbisch Gmünd* [1987] ECR 3719, pr 14; Case C-18/90, *Office National de l'Emploi v Kziber* [1991] ECR 1–199, pr 15. However, this test leaves a wide margin of appreciation to the Court in its characterization of such agreements and the factors that it takes into account require careful examination in each case.

[58] Also relevant is the Understanding to Art 26(2)(a) included in the Final Act, which makes it clear that the reference to an Investor being able to resort to local courts and administrative tribunals does not require a Contracting Party to enact Part III of the Treaty into its domestic law.

[59] For example, it has been said that in the Russian legal system international law is conferred a special status. William E Butler, *The Russian Law of Treaties* (Simmons & Hill, 1997) 26. On the other hand, an examination of the legal situation in some potential Contracting Parties excludes direct application, eg Australia; see *Dietrich* v *The Queen* (1992) 177 CLR 292 at 305.

[60] For an argument advocating an extensive direct effect of the Treaty's investment regime see T Waelde, 'International Investment under the 1994 Energy Charter Treaty', 29 J.W.T. 5–72 (1995). The argument is mainly that the Part III investment regime obligations are specific enough: that the use of the Art 26 investor-State arbitration indicates the Treaty's intention to create individual rights and direct legal impact and that the specific considerations that have kept the GATT rules from being granted direct effect (reciprocity and the nature of intergovernmental trade negotiations excluding the involvement of private parties, judges, and arbitrators) are absent. There is a strong element of preparation of transition economies for closer economic relations with the EU—in the case of the East European countries even a pre-accession element—which seems to have been a decisive factor for the European Court of Justice to assume direct effect of international trade treaties of the Community. See also MK Omalu, *Direct Effect of International Economic Agreements in the European Community: The Case of the Energy Charter Treaty* (Kluwer, London, 1999). It also should be noted that the European Communities, in making the required declaration concerning their listing in Annex ID in respect of the investment provisions of the Treaty, stated that the European Court of Justice has the power to rule on the Treaty, which could provide support for direct application.

E. Activity during the ECT's Second Phase

4.88 Since the opening of the ECT for signature in December 1994, the Energy Charter Conference and Secretariat have been given organizational form and substance, initially on a provisional basis; the Secretariat has proceeded to implement the Treaty; and, meanwhile, several second-phase negotiations envisaged by the Treaty have approached or reach fruition.

(1) The Institutional Arrangements

4.89 All Treaty signatories and any States acceding before its entry into force accepted the provisional application of the institutional provisions set out in Part VII, to the extent consistent with their laws and regulations, regardless of whether they applied the legal disciplines of the Treaty on a provisional basis.[61] The immediate consequence was that the Provisional Energy Charter Conference and a Secretariat to serve it were created. The Provisional Charter Conference met nine times before it was terminated by the entry into force of the Energy Charter Treaty on 16 April 1998. The (permanent) Energy Charter Conference meets on a regular basis.

4.90 The Treaty gives the Energy Charter Conference (referred to as the Charter Conference), which comprises the Contracting Parties to the Treaty, clearly defined powers and functions. These are set out in Article 34 and the voting regime for decision-making is described in Article 36. Among the powers and functions given to the Conference are to: carry out the duties assigned to it by the Treaty and any Protocols; keep under review and facilitate the implementation of the principles of the Charter and the provisions of the Treaty and any Protocols; facilitate in accordance with the Treaty and any Protocols the co-ordination of appropriate general measures to carry out the principles of the 1991 European Energy Charter; and encourage co-operative efforts aimed at facilitating and promoting market-oriented reforms and the modernization of energy sectors in those countries of Central and Eastern Europe and the FSU undergoing economic transition.

4.91 The Charter Conference is also given specific tasks, such as developing additional elements for the several dispute resolution mechanisms in the Treaty, for example the Rules for the Conciliation of Transit Disputes under Article 7, which were adopted in December 1998. In addition, the Charter Conference has certain tasks under the Energy Efficiency Protocol, such as developing implementing procedures. It also has the usual functions given to a Conference of Contracting Parties of adopting new instruments; approving accessions; and tending to the 'house-

[61] See Art 45(2)(c).

keeping' side of an international Secretariat, eg approving work programmes and budgets.

The Provisional Charter Conference and the Charter Conference have so far combined the roles of a negotiation forum for the development of the new instruments mandated under the Treaty (on trade and admission of investment) and an 'oversight body' for the Treaty. Much of the work of the Provisional Conference was devoted to the normal start-up tasks associated with establishing a Conference of Contracting Parties and an international Secretariat. As the Treaty does not come under the umbrella of a larger international organization such as the United Nations or the Organization for Economic Co-operation and Development, there were no pre-determined models for Rules of Procedure, Staff Regulations and Rules, etc. The Provisional Charter Conference and the Charter Conference have also been involved in considering matters relating to the implementation of the Treaty, including the exceptions granted to countries in transition, progress towards ratification, and requests to accede to the Treaty. **4.92**

From an operational or functional point of view, it is open to the Conference to decide how it approaches its working methods and what subsidiary bodies it wishes to establish. With the entry into force of the Treaty and the finalization of the current round of negotiations, the Conference could be expected to consider new organizational or working arrangements. A step in this direction was the creation (see F(1) below) of a Working Group on Transit. **4.93**

The Secretariat which serves the Charter Conference is small by international standards, particularly when regard is had to the broad scope of the Treaty. This reflects the original intention of the negotiators that the Charter Conference and Secretariat should not duplicate the work of other international organizations. The Treaty provides a specific direction to the Charter Conference 'through the Secretariat . . . [to] co-operate with and make as full a use as possible, consistently with economy and efficiency, of the services and programmes of other institutions and organizations with established competence in matters related to the Treaty'.[62] The Treaty also provides for periodic reviews of the Secretariat.[63] The practical realization of this direction to co-operate will be vital to the future of the Treaty. **4.94**

(2) Treaty Implementation

In the period of provisional application, much attention predictably was focused on encouraging signatories to ratify the Treaty. Moreover, regular reviews of the 'transitional' exceptions have succeeded in the early phase-out of most exceptions before the 1 July 2001 expiry date set in the Treaty. Many countries that had **4.95**

[62] Art 34(4).
[63] See Art 34(7).

transitional periods to bring their laws into conformity with certain provisions in the Treaty have in fact done so before the deadlines prescribed in Annex T.[64]

4.96 The peer review mechanisms in the Treaty also afford an important vehicle for implementation of other parts of the Treaty. Over the last few years, the reviews of the exceptions to MFN and national treatment in respect of the admission of investment under the dual track of the review mechanism in Article 10(9) and the negotiations for a Supplementary Treaty have developed into an important transparency exercise. One issue confronting the Secretariat and the Charter Conference is the implementation of the trade-related rules. This is clearly resource-intensive for a small Secretariat and attention will have to be given to making the implementation of this part of the Treaty viable. Some major efforts to implement the Treaty have been undertaken and financed through the EC Phare programme, following earlier Synergy, Phare, and Tacis projects to explain the Treaty and support its ratification. These technical assistance projects concern mainly an examination of an (Eastern) Member State's legal and institutional regime to identify issues of compliance with Treaty obligations and the provision of advisory services for enhancing Treaty compliance.[65]

(3) The Second-Phase Negotiations

Investment

4.97 As noted above, the application to the pre-investment stage of legally binding national and MFN treatment standards was deferred to a second phase of ECT negotiations; this was to be accomplished in a 'Supplementary Treaty'. Paragraphs (2) and (3) of ECT Article 10 therefore provide only for a 'best efforts' ECT commitment to accord the better of national or MFN treatment to investors of other Contracting Parties with regard to the making of investments. Paragraph (4) of Article 10 expressly contemplates the 'second-phase' investment treaty, negotiations towards which were required to commence by 1 January 1995 with a view to concluding it by 1 January 1998. It was recognized that the full three years would be needed in order to address the exceptions that participants in the negotiations would claim from the Treaty's general principles.

4.98 An Understanding in the Final Act stated that the 'second-phase' treaty was to include provisions relating to privatization and de-monopolization: the purpose of such provisions would not be to require privatization or de-monopolization, but rather to prescribe how the treaty would apply in case they occurred, with a goal

[64] See Summary Record of the Fourth Meeting of the Energy Charter Conference (CC 162), which notes that, save for 1 exception maintained by Bulgaria, the remaining transitional non-compliance has very limited impact on business in the energy sector. However, one Contracting Party, Armenia, has been granted additional suspensions with respect to Arts 6(5) and 20(3).

[65] For information on Phare, Tacis see: http://www.europa.eu.int/comm/.

of minimizing disincentives to undertake such activities while applying the disciplines of the treaty to their results.

In the meantime, paragraphs (5), (6), and (9) of Article 10 establish 'best-efforts' obligations of standstill and liberalization as concerns the making of investments, and require up-to-date reporting of all measures which do not comply with the standard of the better of national or MFN treatment. **4.99**

As envisaged in paragraph (4) of Article 10, the negotiations for the Supplementary Treaty were 'concluded' in December 1997. However, at that time the European Union indicated that it was not satisfied with one element of the package, namely the inclusion of some OECD countries in the Annex providing for exceptions to national treatment in case of privatizations. Two subsequent sessions of the formal adoption Conference revealed that there were other issues still to be resolved. Substantial progress was made in these sessions in resolving the issues. However, the EU indicated in June 1998 that it was not yet in a position to adopt the text, given 'serious hesitations at a political level' in some Member States. This reflects domestic pressure from, among others, labour and environmental interests, to be heard more fully before negotiations were concluded on agreements liberalizing investment.[66] **4.100**

The text under consideration contains the following elements: a legally binding obligation to accord the better of national or MFN treatment, subject only to existing discriminatory measures listed in an Annex and to any reservations concerning privatization listed in a separate Annex. The basic treatment obligation is subject to a number of Understandings and Decisions. The text has been drafted on the assumption that it in effect 'incorporates' the new standard of treatment into the Treaty. **4.101**

Given the strong opposition of three countries (Australia, Iceland, and Norway) to the application of investor-State dispute resolution provisions of the Treaty to the rights and obligations provided for in the Supplementary Treaty, the text provides that the Charter Conference may agree to reservations in this area by these countries. The negotiators also accepted that there may need to be a further elaboration of the dispute resolution mechanisms in the Treaty in the future. An authoritative assessment of the utility and viability of the Supplementary Treaty will have to await the adoption of the final package. However, given that substantive negotiations have been concluded on the basic provisions, it is possible to **4.102**

[66] There are significant parallels with the negotiations for a Multilateral Agreement on Investment (MAI) held within the OECD and which stalled in early 1998, reportedly due in part to labour, environmental, and cultural sector lobbying; see Guy de Jonquieres, *Financial Times*, 30 April 1998; the MAI negotiations were suspended in December 1998. Much of the environmental opposition was due to concern that the MAI's investment protection, in particular its expropriation rules (which are similar to those of the ECT), could be used to characterize environmental regulation as an 'expropriation', triggering compensation claims or as discrimination against foreign investors.

note that the acceptance of the concept of legal controls on the treatment of admission of investment is positive. On the negative side, the fact that broad reservations in respect of privatization have been taken by most of the FSU has the potential to undermine, in the context of future privatizations, the standstill on new exceptions to the treatment standard which is at the core of the Supplementary Treaty. In this context, investors must hope that the strong review mechanisms included in the package will discourage discriminatory behaviour.

Trade

4.103 The ECT also provides for several second-phase trade negotiations. Articles 29(6), 30, and 31 call for negotiations on, respectively: the introduction of a legally binding standstill on import and export tariffs; incorporation of the results of the Uruguay Round; and extending coverage of trade rules to energy-related equipment.

4.104 In April 1998 an Amendment to the Trade-Related Provisions of the Energy Charter Treaty was adopted which 'updates' the 1947 GATT regime to the World Trade Organization (WTO); it deals with each of the three issues on which negotiations were mandated.[67] While the Amendment is unlikely to enter into force for some years, it is important because it provides for provisional application. Moreover, the Charter Conference has decided that the Secretariat should develop an implementation system for the trade-related rules based on the regime in the Trade Amendment.[68] However, until the Amendment is applicable between all countries, which either on a definitive or a provisional basis apply the trade rules in Article 29 of the Treaty, the regime in the Treaty will continue to be relevant.[69]

---

[67] The Amendment includes provisions which ensure a so-called 'dynamic approach' to keep the trade regime up-to-date with developments in the WTO.

[68] The Secretariat was 'invited to develop the elements for one implementation system based on the regime in the Trade Amendment. In particular, where the Trade Amendment foresees notification requirements and procedures, including with regard to Understanding 2 to the Amendment, they would follow WTO practice, provided that duplication of notifications with the WTO did not occur. Furthermore, in developing dispute settlement rules and procedures WTO rules of procedure and practice would be followed and the roster of panellists to be adopted by the Conference would be drawn up in accordance with Article 3 of the Amendment. Finally, whenever necessary to maintain the principle of harmonious implementation of trade-related rules based on WTO practice, appropriate rules of procedure should include the elements necessary to achieve that aim': Summary Record of First Energy Charter Conference/International Conference, 23–4 April 1998 (CC 124).

[69] The existence of two regimes, with the complication of provisional application, seems likely to continue well into the future; for example, the Russian Federation, which applies the Treaty on a provisional basis, has declared that it will not apply the Amendment on a provisional basis, while the European Communities, which are a Contracting Party and have exclusive competence in this area, have indicated that they will apply the Amendment on a provisional basis. The presumption is that the Amendment will be applied on a provisional basis unless a contrary declaration is made within 90 days of the adoption of the Amendment.

On the question of a tariff standstill, it became apparent in late 1997 that there was no consensus in favour of such a provision. Accordingly, the Amendment 're-iterates' the best endeavours tariff commitment contained in Article 29 of the Treaty for 'Energy Materials and Products' and extends this to 'Energy-Related Equipment'. The Amendment also provides for a future Conference decision that would move items to the level of a legally binding tariff commitment based on applied tariff rates. Such a decision, which would require a unanimous vote, would involve moving items from one set of Annexes to another and is intended to obviate the need for formal amendment. It is not clear whether this mechanism will be used. There seems to be reluctance on the part of non-WTO Members to accept binding commitments before their accession to the WTO. However, the Conference is required under Understanding No. 3 to conduct an annual review of the possibility of moving items to a legally binding level and this could provide the impetus for change in the position of non-WTO Members. **4.105**

The Amendment also reflects the position of several WTO countries (and, late in the negotiations, non-WTO countries) that their tariff commitments should be at their WTO bound rate. The Amendment provides for a Conference decision to list such countries in special Annexes. The question of listing was regarded in the negotiations as essentially political, and it was assumed that only a few countries would require listing. However, late in the negotiations it became apparent that other countries wished to be listed. In the case of non-WTO Members that may wish to be listed, Understanding No. 2 provides that any concession offered formally in the process of accession to the WTO is to be treated as a commitment under the ECT and thus transitionally binding until WTO membership. To deal with the possibility that a signatory to the Treaty may not be applying the Amendment and may not be listed in the appropriate Annexes when the Conference takes a decision to move items to a legally binding tariff commitment, provision is made for 'opting out' of such a decision. **4.106**

The Amendment's provisions incorporating the Uruguay Round results follow the same approach as Article 29 and Annex G of the Treaty, which are replaced and updated. Under the Amendment, most of the substantive provisions of the WTO's Multilateral Agreements on Trade in Goods (Annex 1A to the WTO Agreement) are applicable. The rules of the Agreements apply, except those rules that are listed in Annex W as not applicable. The application of this Agreement is subject to additional rules and modifications, which appear in Annex W. The Annex 'disapplies', among others: the tariff provisions; a number of unrelated agreements; and almost all developing country-related provisions, except those permitting the granting of preferential tariffs. **4.107**

Under the 1998 Amendment the dispute resolution procedure in Annex D will also be 'closer' to the DSU (Dispute Settlement Understanding) in the WTO **4.108** and panels will be guided by the interpretations given to the WTO Agreement within the framework of that Agreement. There is also scope for non-violation complaints. However, it was necessary to exclude the institutional provisions of the WTO and the WTO dispute resolution mechanism (the DSU).[70]

4.109 The Amendment represents a significant advance in ensuring compatibility with the WTO regime. Also, under the Agreement, the updated trade regime will apply to more than seventy categories of 'Energy-Related Equipment', another important development of the regime.

F. The ECT's New Phase

4.110 It is unfortunate that the Energy Charter Treaty, following its entry into force in April 1998, did not have an opportunity to sail smoothly into a new, third phase. Interested readers can look elsewhere for information on the tempest over management of the Energy Charter Secretariat, which disrupted the transition.[71] Suffice it to say that with the replacement of a Secretary-General at the start of the year 2000, the ECT now has an opportunity to make a fresh start on this leg of its still promising journey.

4.111 Two particular aspects of the trip ahead warrant comment here. First, note should be taken of the very ambitious effort that is being made to devise legal instruments that can reduce impediments to the transit of energy goods across borders; as mentioned above, this promises to become the key focus of ECT attention over at least the coming months. But secondly, a word also needs to be said about the tricky shoals that lie ahead, in the form of continued provisional application of the Treaty by some of its signatories, especially the Russian Federation.

(1) Transit Negotiations

4.112 Following the consideration of energy transit issues at the meeting of G8 Energy Ministers in Moscow on 1 April 1998 (in the lead-up to the 1 May 1998 Birmingham Summit), the Energy Charter Conference later that month decided to constitute a Working Group on Transit.[72] The view presented to the G8 Ministers in a paper contributed by the Energy Charter Secretariat was that energy consuming areas faced increasing dependence on imported energy, while new producers were emerging in often landlocked areas, so that larger volumes of

[70] Thus, the Amendment did not incorporate the WTO Agreement's provisions for automatic adoption of panel reports or for appellate review.

[71] On this subject see, eg, Financial Times East European Energy Report, June 1999; EU Energy Policy, June 1999; B Mitchener, Wall Street Journal Europe, 7 December 1999; D Buchan, *Financial Times*, 15 November and 7 December 1999, and 26 January 2000; B Mitchener and P Shisken, *Wall Street Journal Europe*, 15 February 2000.

[72] Summary Record of First Meeting of the Energy Charter Conference (CC 124).

energy would have to cross borders. Although the ECT already addresses energy transit, and does so in an innovative and ground-breaking way, more needed to be done. Future investment would depend on investor confidence, and any transit system needs multilateral agreement on a stronger framework for unhindered transit investment and commercial operation. Governments therefore should play a proactive role by initiating consultations toward such a regime.

The Working Group's efforts during 1998–99 led, in December 1999, to a mandate to it from the Charter Conference formally to commence negotiation of a legally binding Transit Protocol to the ECT, in order to ensure unimpeded transit, promote more efficient use of transit infrastructure, and facilitate transit investment, with a view to concluding negotiations, if possible, by the end of the year 2000.[73] The basic issues to be addressed would include 'sanctity' of transit for oil, gas, electricity, and other forms of energy; transparent and non-discriminatory access (but excluding mandatory third party access) and prompt and effective dispute settlement. **4.113**

By the time of the Sixth Meeting of the Energy Charter Conference in December 2000, substantial progress had been made in drafting both a potentially binding Transit Protocol, and non-binding model transit agreements. The draft Protocol would include not only general obligations and guidelines such as on the enforceability of transit agreements and prohibition of the taking of energy goods in transit, but also specific commitments on transit capacity utilization or construction, liability, tariffs, charges, standards, metering and measuring, and actions in case of transit disruptions. Among the institutional provisions would be those on implementation and compliance, and conciliation and arbitration. The Secretariat was proposing to the Conference, at the Sixth Meeting, that negotiations on the Transit Protocol continue into 2001, with the intention of completing them in the first half of the year and opening the Protocol for signature in December 2001. **4.114**

A Transit Protocol of this scope would constitute a significant elaboration upon Article 7 and other provisions of the ECT. Its preparation requires imaginative conceptualization and considerable drafting skill to ensure its functional compatibility with the existing ECT provisions. A complicating factor, at least in the near term, is the provisional application of the ECT by some countries. **4.115**

(2) Provisional Application

Following its entry into force, the ECT is applied provisionally by a number of signatories, including the Russian Federation. On the surface, the ECT's Article **4.116**

[73] Summary Record of the Fourth Meeting of the Energy Charter Conference (CC 162). The Working Group also informed the Conference of its progress in preparing, in parallel, related non-binding model agreements, guidelines, and codes of conduct for energy transit projects, which the Conference had mandated earlier.

45 on provisional application is a bold and ambitious undertaking. However, provisional application of the ECT involves a number of uncertainties.

4.117 'Provisional application' of course refers to a Treaty signatory's commitment to apply a Treaty, in whole or in part, before completion of the ratification process; Article 25 of the Vienna Convention on the Law of Treaties allows for provisional application, which can create obligations beyond those that Article 18 of the Convention already imposes to 'refrain from acts which would defeat the object and purpose' of a Treaty. In States whose Parliament has not been asked to consent to provisional application, such a commitment normally rests on the actual or implied authority of the executive branch, the scope of which is often not clear, and which may be especially problematic as concerns the acceptance of legally binding dispute resolution mechanisms.[74]

4.118 Article 45 of the ECT provides in paragraph (1) that each signatory will apply the entire Treaty provisionally pending its entry into force, but only 'to the extent that such provisional application is not inconsistent with its constitution, laws or regulations'. However, paragraph (2) of that Article says that a signatory 'may, when signing' declare that it 'is not able to accept provisional application', in which case the signatory shall only be obliged to apply provisionally the Treaty's provisions concerning institutional arrangements (as distinct from its substantive obligations), and then only insofar as that 'is not inconsistent with its laws and regulations'; a signatory so electing, and its investors, are not entitled to claim the benefits of provisional application under paragraph (1). The following six States, for which the Treaty is not yet in force, were among those who made such declarations when they signed the ECT: Australia, Iceland, Japan, Malta, Norway, and Poland.[75]

4.119 These provisions raise a number of questions of interpretation, among which are the following. What is the function of the opting-out declaration, given the con-

[74] Of course, the 1947 GATT remained in provisional application throughout its history. For differing views on the consequences compare K Dam, *The GATT: Law and the International Economic Organisation* (U. of Chicago, 1970) at 341–4 with J Jackson, *World Trade and the Law of GATT* (The Michie Company, 1969) at 60–3. For an earlier analysis of provisional application see UN, *Report of the Secretary-General, Examples of Precedents of Provisional Application Pending Their Entry into Force of Multilateral Treaties*, A/AC.138/68, 12 June 1973; Art 7 of the 1994 Amendment to the Law of the Sea Convention used a similar method of provisional application, 33 ILM 1309, 1994.

[75] Provisional application may be terminated on 60 days' notice by a signatory that has decided not to become a Contracting Party. Where a signatory which has been applying the Treaty's substantive obligations provisionally in accordance with paragraph (1) of Art 45 terminates such application, paragraph (3)(b) of the Article obliges it for 20 years thereafter to accord the Treaty's investment protections under Parts III and V to investments that were made during provisional application; this obligation does not apply, however, to those States which elected to be listed in the Treaty's Annex PA, namely the Czech Republic, Germany, Hungary, Lithuania, Poland, and the Slovak Republic.

ditionality of the provisional application obligation? Specifically, where the existing legislation of a Treaty signatory conflicts with the Treaty's substantive provisions so as to make that signatory's compliance with the Treaty virtually impossible, was the signatory under an obligation at the time of signing to declare itself 'not able to accept provisional application', or is it instead entitled to simply rely on the conditionality language attached to the provisional application commitment? If a signatory follows the latter course, may its investors—unlike the investors of signatories actually making a declaration—claim the benefits of provisional application? If the opting-out declaration is viewed as mandatory under some circumstances, to what extent must a signatory have been unable to apply various provisions of the Treaty with respect to its relevant legislative or other measures, before the obligation to make such a declaration was triggered?

Even if it is assumed that a signatory acted properly in not making the opting-out declaration, it could prove extremely difficult to pass judgement on the extent to which the provisions of the Treaty are inconsistent with a particular signatory's constitution, laws, or regulations. One question that might arise is whether the fact that a State's constitution puts certain Treaty commitments beyond the authority of its executive means that those Treaty commitments are themselves inconsistent with the State's constitution; in other words, assuming that there is no inconsistent law or regulation, could the State be in violation of the Treaty because the State can constitutionally undertake certain Treaty commitments, even though the executive lacked the domestic authority to undertake the commitments? **4.120**

The complexity of these issues is illustrated by the possibility of having, in the context of the Treaty's important Article 7 on transit, a dispute involving a threatened disruption in the flow of energy along a chain of countries including both States for which the Treaty is in force and others that have either declined provisional application or else asserted some legal impediment to their obligation to do so. **4.121**

While provisional application has been a common practice in intergovernmental agreements for several decades, a novel feature of the Energy Charter Treaty is the combination of the vesting, by Article 26 of the Treaty, of direct arbitration rights against Governments in private parties, with Article 45 on provisional application. The question is whether the very signature of the Treaty, without ratification, makes submission to international arbitration effective on the basis of provisional application. **4.122**

Thomas Waelde has argued[76] that the signature of the Treaty should be viewed, in light of Articles 26 and 45, as the irrevocable promise of a Government to **4.123**

[76] (1996c) n 29.

arbitrate, which is accepted by a plaintiff's formal request for arbitration; this assumption could only be rebutted if the signatory Government did not have constitutional and legal authority to enter into arbitration agreements with foreign private parties. The signatory Government would therefore have to prove, between signature and ratification, that its internal law did not give it sufficient authority. Provisional application, the argument goes, would thereby make the arbitration provision effective for most Governments, as there seems to be little evidence for constraints in national law limiting the implied or explicit authority of Governments to enter into arbitration agreements.

4.124 These issues will continue to be relevant, potentially affecting not only those signatories that apply the Treaty on a provisional basis, but also those for which the Treaty is in force. While such mixed regimes are not unheard of, the implications for investors and for the strong compliance mechanisms contained in the Treaty are unclear.

G. Conclusions

4.125 The Energy Charter Treaty is, together with NAFTA, the major multilateral treaty pioneering the extensive use of legal methods increasingly characteristic of global economic regulation. Imbued by the philosophy of economic liberalism, to which the Treaty's Preamble makes explicit reference, it breaks away from the pattern of multilateral trade agreements by making Governments directly accountable to aggrieved investors before non-national tribunals for important duties specified in the Treaty. It also pushes the concept of State responsibility further than in traditional international law by formulating a concept of State responsibility for regulating private enterprises.[77] Similarly, it develops a right of energy transit far beyond the classical confines of the Barcelona Convention,[78] following here the trail blazed by the European Communities' Transit Directive. As such, it is arguably the most innovative of the modern international economic treaties. The logic of the Treaty's underlying philosophy will call for greater implementation in national law, and direct effect through application by national regulators and courts could be a principal avenue to achieve this.

4.126 One should not forget that the initiative underlying the Treaty was to create an East–West European legal framework. This original intention—first diluted by the entry of the US into the negotiations—is now re-emerging as the core membership of the Treaty encompasses Western and Eastern Europe; continued interest from non-European OECD countries, such as Australia and Japan, need not

[77] See Art 7(6) (on transit disruptions) and 22 (on State and privileged enterprises).

[78] Barcelona Transit Convention, published in M Hudson, *International Legislation*, vol 1 (1919–21) nos 41 and 41a.

deflect this progression. To the contrary, countries and regions with close energy-related links to the EU (the Mediterranean/Maghreb; the Gulf; Africa; Asia; Latin America) might well be induced either to join the Energy Charter Treaty or to negotiate similar multilateral treaties, primarily with the EU. The Treaty's content is as marked by the modern practice of bilateral investment agreements, NAFTA, and WTO practice as it is by the internal European Communities' single market and energy law, notably the Transit, Internal Energy Market and Hydrocarbons Licensing Directives, Articles 81 and 82 EC Treaty on competition law, and notions of special responsibility incumbent on State and private enterprises with a publicly privileged but dominant market position. With Russia's ratification being far from certain, the Treaty currently fulfils a role in assisting the East European countries to move towards their envisaged accession to the EU and in preparing the other countries of the FSU for closer economic association with the EU. After all, the EU was the international actor which largely initiated, promoted, supported, and funded the ECT project.

This close proximity to the EU is not without problems. One wonders to what extent this Treaty, with an independent Secretariat and Conference, can become a self-sustaining international arrangement able to survive independent of the European Union. There is a public perception that the ECT is a key instrument of EU policy towards the East, and it is perhaps not surprising that the Treaty is still widely, and incorrectly, called the 'European' Energy Charter Treaty. One may question whether this proximity will allow the Energy Charter process to evolve outside of the flows of EU energy and Eastern policy. **4.127**

The Treaty also represents, in the area of energy law, a significant development. Since the time of the American Standard Oil Monopoly, lack of transparency, positions of legally privileged market power, and discrimination—in licensing, access, and tariff-making—have been core issues of energy law in a market economy. The Treaty now transposes efforts at national regulation into the Treaty, albeit in a diluted form. **4.128**

The Treaty provokes another observation about the interrelationship between international investment law (characterized by traditional doctrine, bilateral and multilateral treaties, and a series of well known arbitral awards) and international trade law (characterized by the GATT/WTO agreements and their increasingly significant dispute settlement by panel practice). In common understanding, trade and investment law differ significantly: trade law is about short-term commercial transactions, mainly the import and export of goods, and is governed mainly by intergovernmental trade diplomacy, while investment law is about the long-term commitment of capital, and governed mainly by capital exporting State-sponsored protection against host-State originated actions. But with so many textual imports from trade to investment law, one wonders if we are not **4.129** witnessing some convergence between trade and investment law concerns, concepts, and procedures. It is perhaps not surprising that there had been an idea of moving the MAI negotiations to the WTO, and that the WTO has placed investment matters on its agenda.[79] Investment and trade are now closely interrelated. Long-term trade relations acquire investment aspects and trade restrictions can seriously undermine the viability of foreign investors. National protectionism can use the same instruments—abuse of economic and environmental regulation, taxation, State aid, procurement policies—directed against foreign trade as against a foreign investor. It is therefore entirely imaginable that in the future one may seek to interpret identical language in investment treaties by referring to the interpretation and application of such terms in the negotiation and dispute settlement practice of international trade law. With a paradigm shift away from mere protection by the home State of investors and traders to the legal architecture of a liberal global economy goes a co-ordinated use of trade and investment law methods to achieve the same objective: a global level playing field for activities in competitive markets.

Bibliography

Andrews-Speed, P, 'The Energy Charter Treaty: Its Importance to Western European Energy Companies', 9 *OGTLR* 373 (1996)

—— and Waelde, T, 'Will the Energy Charter Treaty Help International Energy Investors', 5 *Transnat'l Corp.* 31 (1996)

—— Bamberger, C, Luciani, G, and Waelde, T with an Introduction by P Schuetterle, 'The Energy Charter Treaty: A Fresh Start for the East-West Energy Business', Centre for European Policy Studies, Report No. 5, June 1997

Axelrod, R, 'The European Energy Charter Treaty', 24 *Energy Policy* 497 (1996)

Bamberger, C, *The Energy Charter Treaty: A Description of its Provisions* (IEA/OECD, 1994)

Baragona, K, and Butler, R, 'Transit Rights Under the Energy Charter Treaty', 62 *Petroleum Economist* 2 (1997)

Brazell, L, 'Draft Energy Charter Treaty', 12 *J.Energy & Nat.Res.L.* 299 (1994)

Doré, J, and DeBauw, R, *The Energy Charter Treaty: Origins, Aims and Prospects* (Royal Institute of International Affairs, 1995)

Fatouros, A, 'Transit—Energy Charter Treaty', *Rev. Hell. Dr. Int'l* 185 (1997)

Liesen, R, 'Transit Under the Energy Charter Treaty', 17 *J. Energy & Nat.Res.L.* (1999)

Nihoul, P, and Smeers, Y, 'Energy Transit Principles in the Context of the Energy Charter Treaty, Report by Directorate-General XVII of European Communities, April 1977

Omalu, MK, *NAFTA and the Energy Charter: Compliance with Implementation and Effectiveness of International Investment Agreements* (Kluwer Law International, 1999)

Paasivirta, E, 'The EU and the Energy Sector: The Case of the Energy Charter Treaty', in M Koskenniemi (ed), *International Law Aspects of the EU* (Kluwer, 1998) 197

[79] Witness the creation of the Working Group on the Relationship between Trade and Investment by the WTO's 1996 Singapore Ministerial Meeting.

Papioannou, A, 'Security of Energy Supply: The Approach in the European Union and the Contribution of the Energy Charter Treaty', 2 *Maastricht J Europ. & Comp.L.* 34 (1995)

Roggenkamp, MM, 'Transit of Network Bound Energy: A New Phenomenon?', 19 *World Competition* 2 (1995)

—— 'Transit of Network Bound Energy—The European Experience' in T Waelde, *The Energy Charter Treaty, Gateway for East-West Investment & Trade* (Kluwer, 1996)

Swaak-Goldman, O, 'The Dispute Resolution Procedures of the Energy Charter Treaty: Made to Measure', 6 *American Rev. Int'l Arb.* (Parker School/Columbia, 1995) 317

—— 'The Energy Charter Treaty and Trade: A guide to the labyrinth', 30 *J.W.T.* 116 (1996)

Waelde, T, 'International Investment Under the 1994 Energy Charter Treaty', 29 *J.W.T.* 5 (1995)

Waelde, T (ed), *The Energy Charter Treaty, Gateway for East-West Investment & Trade* (Kluwer, 1996a)

—— and Ndi, G, 'Stabilising International Investment Commitments', 31 *Tex. Int'l L.J.* 215 (1996b)

—— 'Investment Arbitration Under the Energy Charter Treaty', 12 *J. Int'l Arb.* 429 (1996c)

—— and Wouters, P, 'State Responsibility in a Liberalised World Economy: State, Privileged and Subnational Authorities', 27 *Neth.Ybk Int'l L* 143 (1996d)

Waelde, T, 'Energy Charter Treaty and Sustainable Development', in F Weiss (ed), *Economic Development with a Human Face* (Kluwer, 1998) 223

5

EC ENERGY LAW

Eugene Daniel Cross, Leigh Hancher, and Piet Jan Slot

A. Introduction

This chapter focuses on the development of law and policy relating to the establishment of an internal market in energy pursuant to the Treaty Establishing the European Community ('EC Treaty'),[1] and secondary legislation adopted thereunder. While noting the other institutions of European integration, it does not dwell on the institutional dimension or procedural matters. Instead, this chapter describes and analyses the substance of EC law relating to energy, its function within the context of the European market, and its correlation with European energy policy. **5.01**

[1] The consolidated version of the Treaty Establishing the European Community, as amended by the Treaty of Amsterdam, can be found in the Official Journal (OJ) at OJ C-340/173 (1997). This chapter uses the terms 'European Union' and 'European Community' and their related constructs interchangeably; hence references are made to Community law, Community policy, as well as to EC law and the EC Treaty.

5.02 This chapter is divided into several parts, beginning with the historical background to European energy collaboration and followed by extensive sections on the relevant Treaty rules and secondary legislation. It focuses on key legal issues and judicial doctrines relating to the energy sector, such as the treatment of public service obligations, security of supply, preferential tariffs, long-term contracts, cross-subsidization, and the essential facilities doctrine. It also surveys and analyses the expanding body of EC energy-related legislation as well as the agenda for future reform.

B. The Development of a Treaty and Policy Framework

5.03 In contrast to the first half of the twentieth century, when law was often used by nations as an instrument for the exclusion of foreign goods, services, persons, and capital, the period since the Second World War can be characterized, *inter alia*, by the efforts of Western powers to build a new world order designed to promote free and fair trade subject to the rule of law. Addressing Europe's special needs, the leaders of the movement for European integration sought to construct a supranational legal regime where law would function as an instrument of market, and ultimately political, integration.

5.04 Because of Europe's great need for energy in the post-War reconstruction, European policy-makers focused on the energy sector as an area for urgent development of common policies and co-ordinated action.[2] This is reflected in the fact that two of the three treaties dating from the 1950s are specifically directed at the energy sector.

5.05 The Treaty of Paris, signed in 1951, founded a supranational coal regime for a fifty-year period through the establishment of the European Coal and Steel Community (ECSC),[3] while the EURATOM Treaty, signed in 1957, created the European Atomic Energy Community.[4] These new institutions were made responsible for a common coal and nuclear policy as part of a sectoral approach to integration.

[2] See Comité Intergouvernemental créé par la Conférence de Messine, *Rapport des Chefs de Délégation aux Ministres des Affaires Etrangères* (1956) (the 'Spaak Report'); see also L Armand, 'Some aspects of the European energy problem: suggestions for collective action' (OEEC 1955); OEEC, 'Europe's growing needs of energy—How can they be met?' (OEEC 1956).

[3] Treaty Establishing the European Coal and Steel Community, 18 April 1951, 261 UNTS 167, as amended by the Treaty of Amsterdam, OJ C 340/01 (1997) [hereinafter ECSC Treaty]. This Treaty lapses in 2002.

[4] Treaty Establishing the European Atomic Energy Community, 25 March 1957, 298 UNTS 167, as amended by the Treaty of Amsterdam, OJ C 340/01 (1997).

The Treaty of Rome, which came into effect in conjunction with the EURATOM Treaty on 1 January 1958, is a more general instrument of economic integration.[5] It established the European Economic Community (EEC) as a new legal regime designed to create a common market conducted in accordance with open market principles, rules on competition, and an external commercial policy. In a few areas, the EEC Treaty provides for additional powers mandating a common policy, such as for agriculture and transport. The EEC Treaty did not, however, include provisions on a common energy policy since it was thought that the task had largely been dealt with: coal was viewed as the common policy of the present and nuclear that of the future.[6] **5.06**

Although the need to establish an integrated energy market can be clearly derived from the 1957 Treaties, the period of 1958–72 is notable for the lack of development of an effective common policy for energy.[7] This should not be attributed to neglect of the topic: European energy policy was one of the most discussed topics in the mid-1960s, and energy experts at that time were aware of Europe's increasing import dependence, of the potential market power of Middle East oil suppliers, and of the risk of a fuel shortage by the mid-1970s.[8] As early as 1968, the Community established a regime for compulsory oil stocks, which remains in place today in a more exacting form.[9] Nevertheless, Member State policies were based mainly on the availability of inexpensive oil supplies from outside of Europe and on different strategies regarding nuclear development. In their review of Community action during this period, Hassan and Duncan concluded: **5.07**

> Emphasis . . . had been placed upon the need to harmonise national policies, and to establish a competitive, integrated energy sector. Even with respect to these aims, however, all available evidence . . . suggests the period as a whole witnessed a retreat

[5] Treaty Establishing the European Economic Community, 25 March 1957, 248 UNTS 91, as amended by the Treaty of Amsterdam, OJ C 340/01 (1997).

[6] N Lucas, *Energy and the European Communities* (1977) 14–16.

[7] For another review of Community energy policy from 1957 to the mid-1980s see T Daintith and L Hancher, *Energy Strategy in Europe: The Legal Framework* (1986). For statements of early Community energy policy, see European Commission, *Première orientation pour une politique énergétique communautaire* (1968); 'Necessary Progress in Community Energy Policy', COM(72) 1200 (Oct 1972); 'Guidelines and Priority Actions under the Community Energy Policy', SEC(73) 1481 (Apr 1973) (the above statements also set forth in the Bulletin of the European Communities: Supplements 12/68, 11/72, and 6/73).

[8] See eg E Schumacher, 'The Struggle for a European Energy Policy', vol 2, no 3, J. Com. Mark. Studies 199, 203, 205 (1964).

[9] Council Directive 68/414/EEC, OJ L 308 (1968), as amended by Council Directive 72/425/EEC of 19 December 1972 amending the Council Directive of 20 December 1968 imposing a requirement on EEC Member States to maintain minimum stocks of crude oil and/or petroleum products, OJ L 291/154 (1972) (raising the minimum national requirements for compulsory oil stockholdings from 65 days to 90 days of inland consumption). This 1972 Oil Stocks Directive was repealed as of 31 December 1999 pursuant to Council Directive 98/93/EC of 14 December 1998 amending Directive 68/414/EEC imposing an obligation on EEC Member States to maintain minimum stocks of crude oil and/or petroleum products, OJ L 358/2 (1998).

away from rather than progress towards the goal of market integration in the Community's energy policy.[10]

5.08 The response of the Member States to the oil crisis of 1973 was to protect national interests, although it prompted the Member States and the Community to reconsider the urgent need for a common energy policy. They agreed upon particular policies and initiatives required to achieve Community objectives, such as a desired energy balance. The Council adopted some additional directives and decisions: on maintaining emergency stocks of fuel at power stations,[11] on restrictions on the use of fuels in power stations,[12] on additional measures on oil supplies,[13] as well as an array of recommendations on the rational use of energy.[14] Yet, in hindsight, commentators question whether the 'flood of paper resolutions' produced any genuine economic results.[15]

5.09 As pointed out at the time by energy experts within the Commission:

> [E]ven when the broad lines of Community energy policy are approved . . . they are, for the most part, exhortatory rather than binding on the Member States. . . . [and] are achieved not by Community fiat but by requesting the co-operation of the Member States.[16]

5.10 In a 1981 communication to the Council, the Commission expressed its frustration at the lack of progress:

> In the course of recent years the European Council has repeatedly declared the need for the Community to face up to the energy challenge. . . . But it has not led to the implementation of an overall strategy comprising action by the Community, Member States and producers and consumers. The inadequacy and inconsistency of the action taken in the wake of these expressions of political will can only be deplored.[17]

---

[10] J Hassan and A Duncan, 'Integrating Energy: the Problems of Developing an Energy Policy in the European Communities', 23 J Eur. Econ. Hist. 159, 166 (1994).

[11] Council Directive 75/339/EEC of 20 May 1975 obliging the Member States to maintain minimum stocks of fossil fuel at thermal power stations, OJ 1975 L 153/35.

[12] Council Directives 75/404 and 405/EEC, OJ 1975 L 178/24, 26 (requiring the pre-authorization by competent governmental authorities in the Member States for various contracts and construction projects involving natural gas or fuel oil in electricity production). Directive 75/404/EEC (involving natural gas restrictions) was repealed by Council Directive 91/148/EEC, OJ 1991 L 75/52.

[13] Council Directive 73/238/EEC on measures to mitigate the effects of difficulties in the supply of crude oil and petroleum products, OJ 1973 L 228; Council Decision 77/706/EEC on the setting of a Community target for a reduction in the consumption of primary sources of energy in the event of difficulties in the supply of crude oil and petroleum products, OJ 1977 L 292/9.

[14] See n 313 below.

[15] Hassan and Duncan, n 10 above, 164.

[16] G Brondel and N Morton, 'The European Community—An Energy Perspective', Ann. Rev. Energy, vol 2, 343, 344 (1977).

[17] Commission of the European Communities, 'The Development of an Energy Strategy for the Community', COM(81) 540 final.

A boost to the integration process was achieved in 1987 with the entry into force of the Single European Act.[18] The SEA amended all three Treaties, but the most important of these changes were made to the EEC Treaty. Article 8A (now Art 14) established the objective of an 'internal market'[19] by the end of 1992, and Article 100A (now Art 95) established a legal basis for related legislation to be adopted on a qualified majority (as opposed to a unanimity) basis in co-operation with the European Parliament.[20] The Commission used the internal market programme as the basis for its broad legislative initiative in the electricity and gas sectors,[21] which it coupled with attempts at more vigorous enforcement of the EC Treaty rules on competition and free movement of goods.[22] **5.11**

The Treaty on European Union, signed in Maastricht on 7 February 1992,[23] further amended the EEC Treaty in many important ways. But, once again, no specific provisions on energy were included except for Article 3(t) (now Art 3(u)), which lists measures in the 'spheres of energy, civil protection and tourism' as one of the Community's common policies or activities, and Article 129b (now Art 154) on trans-European networks.[24] The latter offers a financing **5.12**

[18] OJ L 169 (1987).

[19] An 'internal market' is defined in Art 14 of the EU Treaty as 'an area without internal frontiers in which the free movement of goods, persons, services and capital is ensured in accordance with [the] Treaty'.

[20] There are a variety of procedures for the adoption of EC legislation. For directives adopted or proposed in connection with the Commission's programme for an internal energy market, the co-operative legislative procedure under Art 251 (ex Art 189b) of the Treaty has been used. This procedure involves the three institutions with legislative powers—the Commission, the European Parliament, and the Council—as well as advisory bodies such as the Economic and Social Committee. An alternative procedure appropriate for the energy sector is available under Article 86(3) (ex Art 90(3)), which allows the Commission to issue directives or decisions on its own. This was used successfully to introduce a liberalization measure for the telecommunications sector. In the early 1990s the Commission threatened to use its powers under Art 86 (ex Art 90) in the energy sector, and had in fact planned in the summer of 1991 to issue two such directives to require the removal of exclusive rights to produce, import, transmit, and distribute electricity and gas. These drafts were withdrawn prior to publication due to political opposition.

[21] In pursuit of the internal market, the European Commission targeted the energy sector with an action plan first announced in a 1988 working document, COM(88) 238 final (2 May 1988). In February 1992 the Commission formally submitted a framework and set of common rules for the completion of the internal market in electricity and gas: Proposal for a Council Directive concerning common rules for the internal market in electricity, OJ C 65/04, and natural gas, OJ C 65/13 (1992). As indicated in its explanatory memorandum, COM(91) 548 final (21 Feb 1992), the main feature of the proposal was three 'new agents for change': (i) the abolition of special and exclusive rights in order to allow market entry; (ii) the 'unbundling' or administrative separation of the functions of production, transmission, distribution, and supply; and (iii) a qualified but compulsory obligation on owners of transmission and distribution grids to offer access to third parties in return for payment of reasonable compensation.

[22] See paras 5.50, 5.52–5.79 below.

[23] Treaty on European Union, OJ C 224 1 (1992), 31 ILM 247.

[24] Art 154 (ex Art 129b) has formed the basis for various proposals relating to trans-European Networks (TEN) in the energy sector. See eg COM(93) 685 final (1994). Under the TEN initiative, electricity and gas transmission interconnections have been prioritized and entitled to funding under various financing mechanisms. See European Commission, 'Trans-European energy

mechanism to correct the legacy of grid networks that reflect segmented markets.[25] The EU Treaty also contained a Declaration on Civil Protection, Energy and Tourism whereby the Commission declared that Community action in these spheres would be based on the present Treaty provisions, and whereby the Conference declared that the question of introducing new Treaty titles in these spheres would be made on the basis of a Commission report submitted by 1996.[26]

5.13 The Treaty of Amsterdam,[27] signed in 1997 and ratified by all Member States as of 1 May 1999, further amended the Treaty framework.[28] It contains a Protocol relating to the application of the principle of subsidiarity and an article relating to 'services of general economic interest', both of which have some general relevance to the allocation of powers between the Community and the Member States in the field of energy. However, neither appears to herald any substantial shift in powers back to the Member States. On one hand, the Protocol confirms that the Community institutions shall not go beyond what is necessary to achieve the objectives of the Treaty, that the Community must legislate only to the extent necessary, and that Community action should be as simple as possible. On the other hand, Member States in the exercise of their competencies must, in accordance with their long-standing obligations under Article 10 (ex Article 5) of the Treaty, take all appropriate measures to ensure fulfilment of their obligations under the Treaty, and should abstain from any measure which could jeopardize the attainment of the objectives of the Treaty.

networks: policy and actions of the European Community' (1997); Decision No 1254/96/EC of the European Parliament and of the Court of Justice of 5 June 1996 laying down a series of guidelines for the Trans-European Networks, OJ 1996 L 161/147, as amended by Decision No 1047/97, OJ 1997 L 152/12; Regulation 1655/1999 of the European Parliament and of the Council of 19 July 1999 amending Regulation 2236/95 laying down general rules for the granting of Community financial aid in the field of trans-European networks, OJ 1999 L 197/1. These actions have been funded in part by the European Investment Bank (EIB), the Community's financing arm, which has been active in financing energy investment for over 40 years. See EIB, 'Securing Europe's Energy', [1999–2] EIB Information No 101/102. The TEN initiative has been criticized by some utilities as being unduly interventionist.

[25] In its report, 'Electricity and Natural Gas Transmission Infrastructures in the Community', SEC(92) 533 final (Brussels 1992), 1, the European Commission observed: 'The present configuration of the electrical and gas systems is essentially the result of the policies aimed at achieving maximum self-sufficiency in energy followed at the national level. . . . The transportation networks for electricity and natural gas have . . . been designed and developed with a view to the national dimension, a situation which is not compatible with the achievement of an internal market . . .'

[26] In addition, the Treaty on European Union scheduled the convening of a further intergovernmental conference, beginning in 1996, and indicated some of the main points of the agenda.

[27] Treaty of Amsterdam amending the Treaty on European Union, the Treaties Establishing the European Communities and Certain Related Acts, OJ C 340/01 (1997).

[28] For further explanation on the background and institutional structure of the European Union see N Blokker and T Heukels, 'The European Union: Historical Origins and Institutional Challenges' in T Heukels and N Blokker (eds), *The European Union after Amsterdam: A Legal Analysis* (1998).

While it seems clear that the lack of a special chapter on energy in the Treaty has hindered progress in the past to some degree,[29] there has been disagreement over whether this situation should be remedied through a Treaty amendment. The Commission on occasion has been prepared to admit to a certain deficiency in the current position: in a 1995 energy policy paper it stated: 'As far as the Community framework is concerned . . . the coherent development of policy instruments is hindered by the absence of clear responsibilities for energy policy at Community level'.[30] This position may reflect the forcefulness of the opposition directed against the Commission's proposed directives published in 1992 for the internal market in electricity and gas.[31] For example, in expressing opposition to this set of proposals, the European Parliament's energy committee pointed out that, among various 'legal problems', there was no chapter in the Treaty specifically devoted to energy and no Community energy policy and that: **5.14**

> any development of the energy system towards further integration . . . and further liberalisation will necessarily be linked to the implementation of a common energy policy based on *ad hoc* provisions to be inserted into the Maastricht Treaty.[32]

Within the Commission itself, there have been differences of opinion on the need for a special chapter on energy. During the debate over the possible contents of the proposed directives on common rules for the internal market in electricity and gas, advocates of Treaty amendment were often opposed by competition law experts, who pointed out that the basic principles of the Treaty are clear, and that a special chapter on energy was asked for by the defenders of the status quo, not by advocates of the internal market.[33] However, subsequent to the political **5.15**

[29] See D Swann, *The Economics of the Common Market* 242 (6th edn, 1988) (describing four main reasons for the lack of progress towards a common energy policy). See also N Lucas, n 6 above, 15–16.

[30] European Commission, 'For a European Union Energy Policy', 8, COM(94) 659 final, 11 Nov 1995 ('Green Paper').

[31] Proposal for a Council Directive concerning common rules for the internal market in electricity, OJ C 65/04, and natural gas, OJ C 65/13 (1992) and the related explanatory memorandum, COM(91) 548 final.

[32] Draft Report, European Parliament's Committee on Energy, Research and Technology (C Desama rapporteur) (16 Feb 1993). The suggestion made in the draft report was that the Commission should confine its activities to areas such as the harmonization of rules relating to environmental protection, taxation, cost transparency, and the definition of public service obligations. This report served as a vehicle for a set of legislative counter-proposals. See paras 5.253–5.254 below.

[33] See eg C Ehlermann, 'Role of the European Commission as Regards National Energy Policies', vol 12, No 3, J. Energy & Nat. Res. L. 342, 346–7 (1994). ('It is . . . totally wrong to justify the status quo by the lack of a special chapter on energy in the EC Treaty. Such a chapter is neither necessary nor, in my view, desirable.')

agreements on these directives,[34] much of the heat of the early debate[35] over the Community's powers to enact such measures seems to have dissipated.

5.16 The key directives for the internal energy market are now in place, and they have unleashed market and regulatory dynamics that are still unfolding across greater Europe. The implementation deadlines for the Electricity and Gas Directives were 19 February 1999 and 10 August 2000, respectively, with a few exceptions.[36] In response to the internal market programme, Member States have put forth new and proposed energy legislation at a relatively rapid pace. Moreover, these internal market directives, and related guidance from the Commission, are actively being implemented through greater Europe via the process of screening and alignment of the energy regimes of the Central and Eastern European countries (CEECs) and Cyprus with the requirements of the EU's *acquis communautaire*.[37]

5.17 Nevertheless, it is clear that the key directives for the internal energy market are framework measures designed to allow a substantial degree of diversity among the national energy regimes. And it is equally clear from the first and second harmonization reports on the Electricity Directive[38] and the initial reports of the regular biannual meetings of European energy regulators[39] that much work still remains to be done in completing the internal energy market.

[34] Directive 96/92/EC of the European Parliament and of the Council concerning common rules for the internal market in electricity, OJ L 27/20 (1997) [hereinafter the 'Electricity Directive']; Directive 98/30/EC of the European Parliament and of the Council of 22 June 1998 concerning common rules for the internal market in natural gas, OJ L 204/1 (1998) [hereinafter the 'Gas Directive'].

[35] See H Jarass, *Europäisches Energierecht: Bestand-Fortentwicklung-Umweltschultz* (1996); R Scholz and S Langer, *Europäischer Binnenmarkt und Energiepolitik* (1992); but cf House of Lords, Select Committee on the European Communities, *Structure of the Single Market for Energy*, Session 1992–93, 17th Report (not raising issue of Community's power to make energy legislation).

[36] Belgium, Greece, and the Republic of Ireland were given an additional 1 year, 2 years, and 1 year, respectively, to apply the obligations under the Electricity Directive. Moreover, certain transitional regimes and derogations notified to and approved by the Commission may also be applied on a case-by-case basis. For example, in July 1999 the Commission partially approved a transitional regime notified by Luxembourg in order to modify the accounting obligations of the Luxembourg power company CEGEDEL under Art 14(3) of the Directive. Comm. Dec. 1999/793/EC, OJ 1999 L 319/12. It also approved until the end of 2003 a German notification relating to lignite production in the eastern *Länder* subject to several specific conditions. Comm. Dec. 1999/794/EC, OJ 1999 L 319/18.

[37] For an inquiry into the scope and function of the *acquis communautaire* see S Weatherill, 'Safeguarding the *Acquis Communautaire*' in T Heukels, N Blokker, and M Brus (eds), *The European Union after Amsterdam: A Legal Analysis* (1998).

[38] European Commission, [First] Report to the Council and the European Parliament on Harmonisation Requirements; European Commission, Second Report to the Council and the European Parliament on Harmonisation Requirements, SEC(99) 470. These reports have been made pursuant to Art 25 of the Electricity Directive.

[39] See eg Report of the First Forum of European Electricity Regulation, Florence, February 1998; Report of the Second Forum of European Electricity Regulation, Florence, 8–9 October 1998.

Coupled to this process of liberalization and integration of the energy markets across greater Europe, the Commission (sometimes acting in conjunction with the European Parliament) has turned its attention to development of new legislative proposals,[40] programmes,[41] policy documents,[42] and other regulatory instruments[43] which are designed to develop the legal and policy framework relating to the promotion of renewable energy sources, combined heat and power (CHP), district heating, and energy efficiency. Some of these measures are occasionally defended in part as a 'counterweight' to competition in the energy sector or, perhaps in a similar vein, as measures necessary to ensure a 'level playing field' for the market participants. Other justifications in such cases include references to the other two pillars of Community energy policy, security of supply and environmental protection, as well as to concepts relating to employment, trade, and technology policies. These efforts appear to be contributing, *inter alia*, to the acceptance and articulation by the Council of a more developed and balanced Community energy policy and strategy, designed also to help meet European commitments under international environmental law and to allay concerns relating to the threat of climate change, the need for emission reductions, and other environmental concerns.[44] At the same time, continued opposition to a number of proposed EC directives, such as those relating to a Community framework for energy taxation **5.18**

[40] See eg Proposal for a Council Directive on incineration of waste, COM(98) 558; Proposal for a Council Directive restructuring the Community framework for the taxation of energy products, COM(97) 30 final; Amended proposal for a Council Directive to introduce rational planning techniques in the electricity and gas sectors, COM(97) 69 final, OJ C 180/37 (1997); Amended proposal for a Council Directive introducing a tax on carbon dioxide emissions and energy, COM(95) 172 final; see also European Parliament, Resolution on the Commission's White Paper on an Energy Policy for the European Union, COM(95) 682 (calling on the Commission to investigate various actions and measures to promote renewable energy sources, CHP, decentralized generation, and energy efficiency).

[41] European Commission, Strengthening Environmental Integration within Community Energy Policy, COM(98) 571; Amended proposal for a Decision adopting a multiannual programme for promotion of renewable energy sources (1998–2002), see COM(99) 212 final.

[42] See eg European Commission, Energy Efficiency in the European Community: Towards a Strategy for the Rational Use of Energy, COM(98) 246 final; A Community strategy to promote combined heat and power (CHP) and to dismantle barriers to its development, COM(97) 514 final; Energy for the future: renewable sources of energy, White Paper for a Community strategy and action plan, COM(97) 599 final; Climate Change: The EU Approach for Kyoto, COM(97) 481 final; The energy dimension of climate change, COM(97) 196 final; An overall view of energy policy and actions COM(97) 167 final; An Energy Policy for the European Union (White Paper), OJ C 224/01 (1996); For a European Union Energy Policy (Green Paper), COM(94) 659 final (Brussels 1995).

[43] Communication from the Commission and European Parliament on Environmental Agreements, COM(96) 561 final.

[44] See eg Council Resolution of 7 December 1998 on energy efficiency in the European Community, OJ (1998) C 394/1; Council Resolution of 8 June 1998 on renewable sources of energy, OJ C 198/1 (1998); Council Resolution of 18 December 1997 on a Community strategy to promote combined heat and power, OJ C 4/1 (1998); Council Resolution of 27 June 1997 on renewable sources of energy, OJ C 210/1 (1997).

and to rational planning techniques in the electricity and gas sectors,[45] reveal the continued lack of a common energy policy in several key respects.

C. The Treaty Rules and the Energy Sector

5.19 There are five main points to be made about the application of the EC Treaty to the energy sector. First, energy products, including electricity and gas, have been held to be goods that are subject to the rules on free movement of goods as set out in Articles 28–31 (ex Arts 30–37) of the Treaty.[46] Secondly, firms operating in the energy sector are subject to the rules on competition as set out in Articles 81–82 (ex Arts 85–86),[47] Article 86 (ex Art 90), and related secondary legislation. Thirdly, the Treaty rules on right of establishment and the free movement of services and capital would seem to be applicable to the energy sector and have formed the basis for certain infringement proceedings involving national measures designed to control, *inter alia*, the acquisition of certain energy enterprises.[48] The fourth, and perhaps most important, point is that the general rules on free movement and competition are subject to exceptions in the Treaty which may be construed in such a way that the energy sector is treated as a special case and may not be subject to the normal or full application of these rules in specific cases. A final general point about the EC Treaty rules is that the provisions on State aids, namely Articles 87–88 (ex Arts 92–93), as well as State aid rules under the ECSC Treaty, are applicable to the energy sector and form an important part of the Commission's practice and the jurisprudence of the European Court of Justice (ECJ).[49]

[45] Proposal for a Council Directive restructuring the Community framework for the taxation of energy products, COM(97) 30 final; Amended proposal for a Council Directive to introduce rational planning techniques in the electricity and gas sectors, COM(97) 69 final, OJ C 180/37 (1997); Amended proposal for a Council Directive introducing a tax on carbon dioxide emissions and energy, COM(95) 172 final.

[46] See Case C-393/92 *Almelo v Energiebedrijf Ijsselmij* [1994] ECR I-1477 (para 28); see also Case C-158/94 *Commission v Italian Republic* [1997] ECR I-5789.

[47] See eg *Almelo v Energiebedrijf Ijsselmij*, n 46 above (holding that the EC competition rules apply to Dutch energy distributors); *Ijsselcentrale* Com Dec 91/50, OJ L 28/32 (1991) (relating to contractual restrictions on power imports and exports in the Netherlands); *Jahrhundertvertrag* Case No IV/33.151, OJ C 159/7 (1990) (relating to coal/electricity subsidy arrangements in Germany); *Scottish Nuclear* Case No IV/33.473, OJ L 178/31 (1991) ; and *Pêgo* decisions, OJ C 265/3 (1993) (relating to long-term power purchase agreements in Scotland and Portugal, respectively) and the *Grangevielle* case, see European Commission, 22nd Report on Competition Policy, COM(93) 643 final (Dec 1993) § 142 (relating to a minor price-fixing agreement between the French and Italian utilities, EdF and ENEL).

[48] See European Commission, IP/99/583 (announcing infringement proceedings against France and several other Member States for alleged restrictions on freedom of capital movements).

[49] See L Hancher, T Ottervanger, and P Slot, *EC State Aids* (2nd edn 1999); L Hancher, 'EC State Aids and Energy' [1995] 2 OGLTR 62–72; P Slot, 'Energy and Competition', 31 CMLR 511 (1994).

In the sections below, the general principles of the EC Treaty and their application to the energy sector are explained in detail. It should be noted, however, that the relative paucity of ECJ jurisprudence and Commission decisions directly addressing certain areas of the energy sector in the past has presented a challenge to those confronted with implementation or compliance issues. Interpretation has required in some instances a degree of extrapolation based on a review of standards applied to somewhat analogous industries, such as telecommunications, broadcasting, ports, transport, and postal services. Some principles can also be derived from reports of cases in which the parties have agreed to amend the offending practice and settle the case prior to its full development. With this in mind, the following section evaluate the powers afforded by the Treaty to effect energy reform towards a more open market and the extent to which these powers have been exercised. **5.20**

(1) Free Movement of Goods

Overview

The rules on free movement of goods[50] are set forth in Articles 28–31 (ex Arts 30–37) of the EC Treaty. Articles 28–29 (ex Arts 30–34) purport to guarantee free movement of goods by prohibiting quantitative restrictions on imports and exports (and all measures having equivalent effect). As is well known, the ECJ has interpreted 'quantitative restrictions' very widely, so as to cover all measures capable of hindering, directly or indirectly, actually or potentially, inter-Community trade.[51] There are, however, certain exceptions to these rules, including: (i) the problematic 'public security' exception set forth in Article 30 (ex Art 36), which allows Member States to prohibit or restrict imports or exports on grounds which include the maintenance of public security, as long as this is not a means of arbitrary discrimination or disguised restriction on trade between Member States; and (ii) the 'rule of reason' exception developed through jurisprudence for the application of Article 28 (ex Art 30) (eg to reflect environmental concerns). **5.21**

Article 28

Article 28 (ex Art 30) applies not only to provisions directed solely at imports: it also applies to national rules that affect domestic and imported goods, but put the former at an advantage. For example, in *Cullet v Leclerc*[52] the ECJ interpreted this **5.22**

[50] For a definition of goods for purposes of Art 30, see Case C-2/90 *Commission v Belgium* [1992] ECR I-4431 (holding that non-recyclable waste constituted goods). Inclusion of electricity as a 'good' was confirmed by the ECJ in *Almelo v Energiebedrijf Ijsselmij* n 46 above, para 28, and in Case C-158/94 *Commission v Italy* [1997] ECR I-5789, para 17 (citing in both cases Case 6/64 *Costa v ENEL* [1964] ECR 585).

[51] Case 8/74 *Procureur du Roi v Dassonville* [1974] ECR 837. The case-law with respect to exports, however, is more restricted. See L Hancher, *EC Electricity Law* (1992) 29–31.

[52] Case 231/83 [1985] ECR 315.

Article to cover national minimum price regulations for petrol where these prices were fixed at a level that operated to put imported products at a disadvantage *vis-à-vis* domestic products. In this case, minimum prices were fixed on the basis of national products, thus depriving imported products of any competitive advantage.

Article 29

5.23 Article 29 (ex Art 34) addresses quantitative measures restricting exports and measures having equivalent effect. A simple export ban or quota would fall under this Article and would only be justifiable if the Member State could invoke Article 30 (ex Art 36), discussed below.[53] The position of measures having equivalent effect to such bans or quotas on exports is rather more complex. It is possible to draw a distinction between those measures having a direct effect on export levels and those having an indirect effect.

5.24 Measures restricting exports such as licences, controls, and certificates would belong to the former category and would be contrary to Article 29 if not similarly imposed on domestic products. Even if the licence is granted automatically and without conditions, it must still be considered as a measure having equivalent effect to a quantitative restriction on exports. Measures restricting the categories of persons entitled to export may also be implicated by Article 29.

5.25 Measures that have only an indirect effect on export levels are especially problematic. The ECJ has generally required that the measure in question have as its specific object or effect the restriction of exports. In other words, the concern is with measures that discriminate in favour of goods intended for domestic markets against exports so as to favour national production. Thus, an obligation to supply electricity or gas to a national purchaser first (before allowing export) would probably be contrary to Article 29 if the effect of the measure was an implicit export ban. Although the case never got as far as the ECJ, a provision in the relevant Dutch gas legislation conferring a right of first option on the State-controlled gas supplier, Gasunie, to purchase all gas won on the Dutch continental shelf, was considered by the Commission to be in conflict with this Article. At the same time, Council Directive 94/22 on 'hydrocarbons licensing', discussed below in paras 5.232–5.252, specifically recognizes the rights of Member States to decide when and to what extent their hydrocarbon resources can be opened up to exploration and production.

Exemptions

5.26 Member States can continue to impose restrictions on import or export if these restrictions can be justified either under Article 30 (ex Art 36) or under the 'rule of

[53] See Case C-5/94 *Hedley Lomas* [1996] ECR I-2553.

reason' approach under Article 28. For restrictions on energy, including electricity, the most important exemption in Article 30 is that relating to public security. Restrictions in order to guarantee continuity or regularity of supply or to protect the environment may be justified under the 'rule of reason approach', provided of course that the measure in question is applied without distinction to domestic and imported (or exported) goods alike.[54] In all cases, exemptions can only be applied if the Member State can show that the particular measure is objectively necessary to achieve the results being sought and that there is no other less restrictive means of achieving this objective. This is known as the proportionality test.

Article 30 and security of supply

For the Community as a whole, there are good reasons for geopolitical concerns about energy supply: it presently imports about 80 per cent of its oil, 40 per cent of its natural gas, and about one-third of its coal. Overall external energy dependency of the Community currently stands at about 50 per cent, and by 2020 this could well increase to as much as 70 per cent, 80 per cent, and 90 per cent for natural gas, coal, and oil respectively[55] if appropriate measures are not taken. The risks associated with this type of dependency were clearly demonstrated during the oil crises of the 1970s, when the Community and its Member States were required, *inter alia*, to implement emergency arrangements developed under the auspices of the Organization for Economic Co-operation and Development (OECD) and the International Energy Agency (IEA). Although the oil and gas markets are generally stable, geopolitical concerns continue to underlie the Community's energy strategy. **5.27**

These concerns become relevant in legal terms whenever a government seeks to develop or expand indigenous resources and its measures are scrutinized under the basic principles of the Treaty. As is usually the case with the major exceptions to the basic rules of the Treaty, the problem is not whether security of supply as such constitutes an objective justification, but rather to what extent it does so. The main exception is the exception from Articles 28 and 29 (ex Arts 30 and 34), but similar exceptions may arise in the context of Article 43 (ex Art 52) on the right of establishment, Article 56 (ex Art 73b) on the freedom of capital movements,[56] as well as the competition rules as set forth in Articles 81–86 (ex Arts 85, 86, and 90). **5.28**

In the mid-1980s the ECJ set an important precedent for the security of supply doctrine in the energy sector when it examined the meaning of the term 'public **5.29**

[54] Case C-2/90 *Commission v Belgium* [1992] ECR I-4431 para 34.

[55] European Commission, 'An Overall View of Energy Policy and Actions', COM(97) 167, final, at 2 (citing European Commission, 'European Energy to 2020: A scenario approach' (1996)).

[56] See European Commission, Communication of the Commission on Certain Legal Aspects Concerning Intra-EU Investment, OJ (1997) C 220/15.

security' of Article 30 (ex Article 36) in the context of Irish requirements on oil importers. The famous *Campus Oil* case[57] involved a challenge by the oil companies against an order of the Irish Government requiring them to purchase about 35 per cent of their supplies at pre-determined prices from the only (State-owned) Irish oil refinery. Without these compulsory purchases, it was claimed, the refinery would have to close, and the Republic of Ireland would have been totally dependent on imported supplies of petroleum products. The ECJ ruled that while the requirement was contrary to Article 28 (ex Art 30) it could be excused in such circumstances under Article 30 (ex Art 36) provided that the compulsory purchases were the minimum necessary to ensure the continued operation of the refinery. Although the ECJ acknowledged that various measures had been taken at Community level to deal with oil shortages, the ECJ found that these were insufficient to give Ireland the 'unconditional assurance that supplies will in any event be maintained at least at a level sufficient to meet minimum needs'.[58] Moreover, the ECJ showed its willingness to accept a Member State's reliance on Article 30 (ex Art 36) to justify 'appropriate complementary measures' even if such measures involve elements of economic policy not normally allowed under that Article:

> It should be added that to come within the ambit of [Article 30], the rules in question must be justified by objective circumstances corresponding to the needs of public security. Once that justification has been established, the fact that the rules are of such a nature as to make it possible to achieve, in addition to the objectives covered by the concept of public security, other objectives of an economic nature which the Member State may also seek to achieve, does not exclude the application of [Article 30].[59]

5.30 This statement, coupled with the ECJ's treatment of the proportionality test as well as its acceptance of the fixing of the selling price, surprised some commentators and gave rise to the view that national governments and the industry could rely on the *Campus* judgment.[60] Indeed, in 1997 the Irish Government once again

[57] Case 72/83 *Campus Oil Ltd v Minister of Industry and Energy* [1984] ECR 2727.

[58] ibid, para 31.

[59] ibid, para 36.

[60] See P Oliver, *Free Movement of Goods in the European Community* (3rd edn, 1996) 200–1 and n 2 ('This judgment, which might be regarded as a serious blow for the prospect of creating a common energy policy, did not go uncriticized'); L Gormley, *Prohibiting restrictions on trade within the EEC* (1985) 134–9, 138 ('[I]t would seem that a Member State could torpedo the Community [resource-sharing] scheme'); J Minor, 'Current Survey', 9 Eur. LR 340–4 (1984) ('The present decision . . . confirms that Member States are accorded a certain margin of discretion to determine their own requirements in these spheres'); see also K Mortelmans, CMLR 696–713, 713 (1984) ('The activism of this Court is dangerous . . .'); *but* cf C Ehlermann, 'Die rechlichen Instrumentarien zur Verwirklichung eines Gemeinsamen Marktes nach dem EWG-Vertrag', 28, 39–41, in R Lukes (ed), *Ein EWG-Binninmarkt für Elektrizität: Realität oder Utopie* (1988).

renewed the measures used to control the acquisition, supply, distribution, or marketing of petroleum oils in the Republic of Ireland.[61]

The contours of the 'public security' exception of Article 30 (ex Art 36) were further defined in *Commission v Greece*,[62] an Article 226 (ex Art 169) infringement action, in which the Commission challenged the natural oil refinery monopoly and its exclusive import and commercialization rights.[63] In this case, the ECJ summarily dismissed the claim of the Greek Government that security of supply necessitated the exclusive rights. It stated that the Government had not demonstrated that without these rights the natural refineries would not be able to sell their products on the market at competitive prices.[64] Although the ECJ recognized that the contested measure contributed towards ensuring that Greece was supplied with petroleum products at all times, the Government failed to convince the ECJ that the measure was essential to achieve these ends, particularly since the production capacity of the country's two refineries exceeded the country's minimum needs in a period of crisis.[65] **5.31**

Some efforts have been made by the Commission to regulate national measures seeking to ensure security of supply. In a 1990 working document that provided some informal guidelines,[66] the Commission announced that it would compile an inventory of national energy measures which had security of supply as their objective, particularly in relation to State aids and fiscal provisions. For the electricity market, the Commission also proposed an immediate freeze on long-term subsidies and requirement agreements at present levels. It subsequently announced that Member States should protect no more than 20 per cent of electricity production on security of supply grounds, and that this figure should be reduced to 15 per cent as soon as possible.[67] It also included the rule in the **5.32**

---

[61] The Petroleum Oils (Regulation or Control of Acquisition, Supply, Distribution or Marketing) (Continuance) Order 1997. This continued the previous Order (entitled the 'Petroleum Oils (Regulation or Control of Acquisition, Supply, Distribution or Marketing) Order 1983 (SI No 1 of 1983)'), issued under subsection (1) of section 2 of the Fuels (Control of Supplies) Act 1971 (No 3 of 1971) (as amended by the Fuels (Control of Supplies) Act 1982 (No 18 of 1982)) declaring that the Government is of the opinion that the exigencies of the common good necessitate the regulation or control by the Minister for Industry and Energy on behalf of the State of the acquisition, supply, distribution, or marketing of petroleum oils.

[62] Case C-347/88, 1990 ECR 1-4747 paras 41–4.

[63] Case C-347/88 *Commission v Hellenic Republic* [1990] ECR I-4747.

[64] ibid, para 49.

[65] P Oliver, above n 60, 202.

[66] SEC(90) 1248, Brussels, 14 September 1990.

[67] See L Brittan, 'Competition in the European Community's Electricity and Gas Markets', Speech/91/40, London, 18 April 1991 ('We will move to a Community security of supply system as the internal market takes hold .... What we say for the time being, though, is that Member States should protect no more than 20% of electricity on security of supply grounds. This figure should come down to 15% as soon as possible. . .'); see also Answer to Written Question E-600/93, OJ 1994 C 310/3 (stating that the Commission would not count support for renewable energies towards the limit of 20%).

Electricity Directive, the final version of which includes a 15 per cent figure.[68] More recently, pursuant to its 1999 work programme, the Commission issued its long-awaited communication on security of EU natural gas supply (COM(99) 571 final). In December 2000, it issued a Green Paper on security of EU energy supply, which includes an overall strategy to strengthen the security of supply.

Article 31

5.33 Article 31 (ex Art 37) on State trading monopolies requires Member States to 'adjust' (rather than abolish) monopolies of a commercial character so as to end discrimination between nationals of Member States regarding the conditions under which goods are procured or marketed.[69] This Treaty provision was originally designed to enable the Member States to retain until the end of the transitional period (31 December 1969 for the six original Member States) existing import or export restrictions linked to State monopolies, a particularly sensitive topic. However, it has given rise to various questions of interpretation.[70]

5.34 The 1997 ruling of the ECJ in Case C-157/94 *Commission v the Netherlands* indicates that the mere existence of exclusive import rights is in itself contrary to Article 31 (ex Art 37).[71] In that case, the Dutch Government argued that only the discriminatory exercise of exclusive import rights by the Dutch electricity grid operator, SEP, would be prohibited by this Article, not the mere holding of the rights. But the ECJ held that free movement is impeded by the very existence of exclusive import rights since economic operators of other Member States are thereby deprived of the possibility of offering their products to the customers of their choice in the Member State concerned. It was irrelevant that all electricity for public supply, whether domestically produced or imported, had to pass through the grid and that final users in the Netherlands were all supplied under the same conditions. In addition, the ECJ indicated that it is not necessary that the exclusive right to import a given product relate to all imports: it is sufficient if those rights relate to a proportion of imports such that the monopoly can have an 'appreciable influence on imports'.[72]

---

[68] Directive 96/92/EC, OJ 1997 L 27/20, Art 8(4); see para 5.265 below.

[69] Art 31(1) (ex Art 37(1)) provides: 'Member States shall adjust any State monopolies of a commercial character so as to ensure that no discrimination regarding the conditions under which goods are procured and marketed exists between nationals of Member States.' In its judgment in *Bodson*, Case 30/87 [1988] ECR 2479, para 13, the Court of Justice held that this Treaty provision applies to situations in which national authorities are in a position to control, direct, or appreciably influence trade between Member States through a body established for that purpose or a delegated monopoly. See also *Almelo* [1994] ECR I-1477, paras 29–32 (describing related jurisprudence and holding that Art 31 (ex Art 37) did not apply in proceedings involving a privately negotiated contract between a regional electricity distributor and local distributors).

[70] P Oliver, n 60 above, 345–52 (referring to its 'obscure clarity' and citing extensive literature on the subject).

[71] Case C-157/94 *Commission v the Netherlands* [1997] ECR I-5699, paras 21–3.

[72] ibid, para 18.

Nevertheless, the ECJ dismissed the Commission applications in this and the other joined cases on exclusive rights to import and export in the electricity and gas sectors[73] on the basis of Article 86(2) (ex Art 90(2)) of the Treaty,[74] which affords such suppliers some degree of protection from the application of the prohibitions of the Treaty. While the rules of Article 86 (ex Art 90) are quite complex (they are discussed in further detail below) it is worth considering for the moment that the application of the principles of free movement and competition—cornerstones of a market economy—to *mixed economies* has been problematic. The Treaty rules were simply not designed for the complex task of weeding out illegitimate from legitimate State intervention, particularly intervention by State-owned firms or even private firms entrusted with public service functions. Instead, the Treaty strikes a series of uneasy compromises. Essentially it treats such intervention as inevitable but tries to minimize its impact on free trade. This compromise is perhaps most apparent in Article 86(1) (ex Art 90(1)), which allows Member States to grant special or exclusive rights, including monopoly rights, to public or private firms (unless this would be in conflict with other Treaty rules). Hence, Member States retain some degree of discretion in this field. Because many Member States have placed various public service obligations on energy utilities, such as the duty to supply, such suppliers have sought to rely upon provisions such as Article 86(2) (ex Art 90(2)) to argue for a tempering of the application of the prohibitions of the Treaty. **5.35**

(2) The Rules on Competition

The economic advantages of competition in the marketplace are well accepted. As stated by the OECD: 'In conditions of effective competition, rivals have equal opportunity to compete for business on the basis and quality of their outputs, and resource deployment follows market success in meeting consumer demand at the lowest possible costs.'[75] The traditional school of economists therefore recommends governmental intervention to prevent, among other things, the undue acquisition of market power through organized cartels or other collusive practices designed to achieve or abuse a dominant position in the market. Nevertheless, there is still much debate over the ultimate and direct goals of competition policy, particularly as to how to balance its effects on efficiency and equity.[76] **5.36**

[73] Joined Cases C-156–160/94, [1997] ECR I-5699, I-5789, I-5815, and I-5851.

[74] Art 86(2) (ex Art 90(2)) provides that where such firms have been entrusted with 'the operation of services of general economic interest' the application of the Treaty may be suspended if this would 'obstruct the performance, in law or in fact, of the particular tasks assigned to them'.

[75] See D Goyder, *EEC Competition Law* (1988) 12 (quoting OECD, *Competition and Trade Policies: Their Interaction* (1984); see also D Goyder, *EC Competition Law* (3rd edn, 1998) 9–10.

[76] See generally C Ehlermann and L Laudati (eds), *European Competition Law Annual 1997: The objectives of competition policy* (1998).

5.37 The development of Community competition policy has constituted a great challenge for Europe: in the 1950s most Member States lacked competition laws based on the prohibition principle and therefore had no direct point of reference for the development of Community competition policy.[77] Thus, a completely new policy had to be created on a Community scale in order to serve two complex functions: the integration of national markets into a single economic area and the development of competition as the driving force of the economy.[78] There is a perception that the former objective—that of market integration—was traditionally regarded as more important within the Community than that of promoting competition *per se*.[79] However, given that the EU market is now more closely integrated than in the past, there is an inevitable and proper questioning of the proper balancing of these objectives.

5.38 In terms of EC Treaty provisions, the basic principle on competition is formulated in Article 3(g) of the Treaty, which requires the Community to promote a 'system ensuring that competition in the internal market is not distorted'. Moreover, the last sentence of Article 4 (ex Art 3A(2)) stipulates that general economic policies shall be in accordance with the principle of an open market economy with free competition. The Treaty rules on competition, set forth in Articles 81–82 (ex Arts 85–86) and related secondary legislation, are primarily addressed to undertakings, although Member States are also under a duty not to distort competition.[80] Article 86 (ex Art 90) provides rules regarding public enterprises and enterprises with exclusive or special rights. These rules and their general applicability to the energy sector are discussed below.[81]

The prohibition system of Article 81

5.39 Article 81 (ex Art 85) prohibits agreements, decisions, and concerted practices by undertakings which may affect trade between the Member States and which have as their object or effect the prevention, restriction, or distortion of competition. The provision gives an enunciative list of such practices: price-fixing, limiting or

[77] Neither Italy nor Luxembourg had competition laws, and Belgium and the Netherlands had a system of controlling abuses that allowed illegal agreements to be penalized from the date on which the infringement was recorded by the respective national competition authority.

[78] See European Commission, 'White Paper on Modernisation of the Rules Implementing Articles 85 and 86 of the EC Treaty', OJ 1999 C 132/1, 6.

[79] See eg P Massey, 'Reform of EC Competition Law: Substance, Procedure and Institutions' in B Hawk (ed), *International Antitrust Law and Policy* (1997) 91–123, 91.

[80] See eg Case 13/77 *Inno v Atab* [1977] ECR 2115; Case 267/86 *Van Eyke v Aspa* [1988] ECR 4769.

[81] For additional guidance on the application and enforcement of the competition rules, as well as proposals for reform, see the European Commission's 1999 White Paper on the Modernisation of the Rules Implementing Arts 85 and 86 of the EC Treaty, OJ 1999 C 132/1 and the Commission's Proposal for a Council Regulation Implementing Articles 81 and 82 of the Treaty, COM (2000), 582 final.

controlling production, market, technical development, or investment, sharing of markets or sources of supply, applying dissimilar conditions to equivalent transactions (discrimination), and tying. The prohibition only applies if all the conditions of Article 81(1) are met. This does not mean that every clause of an agreement would have to be implicated by all these criteria: it is sufficient if one or more of the clauses meets the criterion that trade between the Member States is affected.[82] However, only the clauses that restrict competition are prohibited.[83]

The criterion 'affecting trade between the Member States' is mainly designed to allocate jurisdiction to the Community rather than the Member States. It is sufficient for an agreement to affect trade between Member States if it has a direct or indirect, actual or potential effect.[84] Agreements whose effects are confined within a single Member State will fall within the exclusive jurisdiction of the Member State concerned except where its effects constitute a threshold for the commercial actions by companies from other Member States.[85] **5.40**

The criterion 'distortion of competition' is fulfilled when the agreement aims to restrict competition even if it does not achieve these aims. If such an object is absent, the distortive effects will have to be demonstrated.[86] Again, however, the ECJ has ruled that the actual or potential effects must be assessed. In order to establish such effects, a careful analysis of the economic and legal context of the agreement in question is required. Many Commission decisions show that this involves a thorough and well reasoned evaluation of the facts. **5.41**

Article 81(2) states that agreements contrary to the first paragraph are automatically void. The ECJ has held that only the individual clauses of the agreement which are prohibited by Article 81(1) will be null and void.[87] Contractual provisions that are not affected by Article 81(1) are not assessed under Community law. The ECJ has also ruled that the effect of the nullity of some clauses on the rest of the agreement is a matter of national law. As a consequence of this case-law, the Commission, when applying Article 81(1), will declare the actions, practices, or clauses which constitute an infringement of this prohibition. **5.42**

---

[82] Case 193/83 *Windsurfing v Commission*, [1986] ECR 611 para 96.

[83] Whether this leads to the nullity of the agreement concerned is a matter of national law. National courts must assess whether an agreement with clauses contrary to Art 81(1) (ex Art 85(1)) can be converted into a valid agreement.

[84] Cases 56 and 58/64 *Consten and Grundig v Commission* [1966] ECR 299. In this case, the ECJ ruled that it is not a question of whether or not trade is negatively affected. Even if the agreement would lead to an increase of trade between the Member States, it could infringe Art 81(1) (ex Art 85(1)).

[85] Case 8/72 *Vereniging van Cement Handelaren VCH v Commission* [1972] ECR 997.

[86] Case 56/65 *Société Technique Minière v Maschinenbau Ulm* [1966] ECR 235.

[87] ibid.

5.43 Article 81(3) provides for an *individual* exemption from the prohibition of the first paragraph. Even though some agreements are contrary to the basic prohibition, they may nevertheless on balance have a positive effect for the economy. The exemption can only be granted if four cumulative conditions are met.

5.44 The first two conditions are positive:

—the agreement must contribute to improving the production or distribution of goods or to promoting technical progress;
—the agreement must allow consumers a fair share of the resulting benefit.

5.45 The last two conditions are negative:

—the agreements must not impose on the undertakings concerned restrictions that are not indispensable to the attainment of these objectives;
—the agreements must not afford such undertakings the possibility of eliminating competition in respect of a substantial part of the products in question.

5.46 Two important individual exemptions in the energy sector are represented by the decision on the German *Jahrhundertvertrag* (century contract) and the decision on the International Energy Agency (IEA) arrangements. In the *Jahrhundertvertrag* decision, the Commission exempted a set of agreements under which German electricity generating utilities and industrial producers of electricity had undertaken to purchase a specific amount of German coal up to 1995.[88] The agreements formed part of an overall plan to support the German coal industry. Since the price of German coal is substantially higher than price levels on the world market, the other part of the plan consisted of subsidies and the restriction of imports from third countries. The whole plan was supported by a special fund financed through a levy called the *Kohlepfenning*, which was paid by the final consumer. The approval of these agreements under Article 81(3) was quite extraordinary and can only be understood in the very specific context of the dire situation of the German coal industry. In its decision on the IEA arrangements, the Commission renewed its approval (until 31 December 2003) of an arrangement which the oil companies had concluded between them to implement the IEA emergency scheme.[89] The arrangements provide for an exchange of data and information that would normally be considered to infringe Article 81(1) but was accepted because of the very specific circumstances.

[88] Decision of 22 December 1992 relating to a proceeding under Art 85 of the Treaty and Art 65 of the ECSC Treaty, OJ 1993, L 50/14.

[89] Commission Decision 94/153/EC of 21 February 1994 relating to a proceeding under Art 85 of the EC Treaty CIV/30.525—International Energy Agency, OJ L 68/35 (1994).

Block exemptions

The application of Article 81(3) is presently the sole competence of the Commission.[90] This exclusive competence, combined with an extensive interpretation of the basic prohibition of Article 81(1), created a situation wherein the Commission found itself flooded with notifications for an individual exemption. In order to cope with this mass of notifications the Council of Ministers has adopted a series of enabling regulations to provide the Commission with a clearly circumscribed mandate to enact certain block exemptions.[91] As reported in mid-1999, there are five block exemptions for vertical and technology transfer agreements adopted on the basis of Council Regulation 19 of 1965. A well known example is the block exemption on exclusive distribution agreements.[92] There are also block exemptions for certain horizontal agreements, and a 1999 regulation on vertical agreements.[93] 5.47

The notification system of Regulation 17[94]

It may be apparent from the above description of the rules for individual exemptions that clear procedures are needed for granting them. This is one of the functions of Regulation 17, adopted in 1962. According to Article 4(1) of the Regulation, agreements must be notified in order to qualify for an exemption. Notified agreements may be exempted from the day of notification. In view of the sanction of nullity, it is important to notify agreements before they enter into force. Notification also provides protection against the imposition of fines. Not every agreement must be notified in order to qualify for an individual exemption. Article 4(2) exempts certain specified agreements, including those which are confined to a single Member State. 5.48

Article 2 of Regulation 17 also provides for the possibility that agreements can receive a 'negative clearance'. This is a decision by the Commission that an 5.49

[90] The Community's highly centralized system of prior notification and the Commission's 'monopoly' over the granting of exemptions was once again criticized by the Commission in its 1999 White Paper on reform of the competition rules. See European Commission, 'White Paper on Modernisation of the Rules Implementing Arts 85 and 86 of the EC Treaty', OJ 1999 C 132/1.

[91] Council Regulation 19/65/EEC on the application of Art 85(3) of the Treaty to certain categories of agreements and concerted practices, [1965] OJ Special Edition 354, as amended by Regulation (EC) No 1215/1999, OJ 1999 L 148/1; Council Regulation 2821/71/EEC, OJ 1971 L 285/1, as amended by Council Regulation 2473/72/EEC; Council Regulation 1534/91/EEC, OJ 1991 L 143/1.

[92] Reg 67/67, [1969] OJ Special Edition 10, subsequently replaced by Council Regulation 1983/83/EEC, OJ 1983 L 173/1, as amended by Commission Regulation 1582/97, OJ 1997 L 214/2.

[93] Comm Reg No 2790/1999/EC of 22 December 1999 on the application of Art 81(3) of the Treaty to categories of vertical agreements and concerted practices, OJ 1999 L 336/21.

[94] Council Reg No 17 of 6 February 1962 implementing Arts 85 and 86 of the Treaty, [1962] OJ 13/204 (Special English Edition 1959–62 P 87).

agreement does not infringe Article 81. Such a decision will be preferred by the undertakings concerned as it puts them outside the ambit of the competition rules.

5.50 When parties request an official decision, the Commission, pursuant to Article 19(3) of Regulation 17, must publish a summary of the case and invite comments from third parties. It may also do so in case the parties have not asked for an official decision, if the case is considered to be of sufficient importance. In the latter case, this publication is the main source of information about such agreements.[95] There have been several such important publications in the energy sector, including the following: (i) the Notice on the Pêgo power station in Portugal,[96] where the original twenty-eight-year exclusive power purchase contract was modified upon the insistence of the Commission; (ii) the Notice on the British Gas plc Network Code, which concerned the important arrangements for access to British Gas network and provides important information about the conditions for TPA;[97] (iii) Notices on the REN/Turbogas arrangement[98] relating to the reduction in the term of exclusivity in a twenty-five-year power purchase agreement; (iv) the modification of ISAB Energy's power purchase agreement;[99] and (v) the decision on Scottish Nuclear/British Nuclear Fuels relating to the provision and management of nuclear fuel assemblies.[100]

5.51 The different positions the Commission may take pursuant to a notification may be summarized as follows.

(i) It may decide that the agreement is not caught by the prohibition of Article 81(1) and give a negative clearance. It may do so in the form of a formal or an informal decision.

(ii) It may decide that the agreement is caught by the prohibition of Article 81(1) but proceed to give an exemption. Again, the exemption may be a formal or an informal decision.

(iii) It may decide that the agreement is prohibited by Article 81(1) and cannot be exempted. This may also be done by a formal or informal decision. In this situation, the prohibition of Article 81(1) applies from the moment the agreement came into force.[101]

---

[95] Other informational sources are the Commission's press releases and its case summaries in its annual report on competition policy.

[96] OJ 1993, C 265/3 (concluded by comfort letter).

[97] OJ 1996, C 93/5; European Commission, XXVIth Report on Competition Policy 1996, 136–7 (concluded by comfort letter).

[98] OJ 1996, C 118/7; European Commission, XXVIth Report on Competition Policy 1996, 134–5 (concluded by comfort letter).

[99] OJ 1996, C 138/3 (concluded by comfort letter).

[100] OJ 1996, C 89/6 (concluded by comfort letter).

[101] Only the 'old agreements' (already in existence on 22 Feb 1962) cannot be declared to infringe Article 81(1) (ex Article 85(1)) with retroactive effect: Case 13/61 *De Geus v Bosch* [1962] ECR 91.

Article 82 and market definition

Competition may be distorted not only by agreements, but by the abuse of dominant positions. Article 82 (ex Art 86) seeks to address this problem. It should be noted that having a dominant position as such is not prohibited, just the abuse. The distinction between dominance and abuse can be very minimal: commercial practices that are perfectly legitimate under normal market conditions may not be allowed once the undertaking has a dominant position. Apart from Article 86(2) (ex Art 90(2)), there is no possibility for an exemption from this Article. There is, however, the possibility of applying for a negative clearance under Article 2 of Regulation 17. **5.52**

Article 82 enumerates several forms of abuse: directly or indirectly imposing unfair purchase or selling prices; limiting production, markets, or technical development; discrimination; and tying. Many other forms of abuse have been condemned in ECJ judgments and in Commission decisions and notices. In the context of addressing postal sector practices, for example, the Commission has stated that 'another type of possible abuse involves seriously inefficient service and failing to take advantage of technical developments'.[102] Similarly, in a case involving the right to extend natural gas networks in France, the Commission investigated Gaz de France (GdF) and the French State under Article 82 on the basis of the 'underperforming monopoly' theory.[103] The Commission has also identified certain cross-subsidization practices likely to distort competition under Article 82, such as 'subsidising activities [in markets] open to competition by allocating . . . costs to reserved markets'.[104] **5.53**

The application of Article 82 normally involves defining the relevant product (or service) markets and the geographical market in order to establish dominance. The function of this market definition process is to determine whether there are firms in the market that can check the ability of those firms whose conduct is questioned to raise prices to non-competitive levels. **5.54**

The relevant geographical market is defined by taking into account the competitive conditions as they result from distances, transport costs, special or exclusive rights, local consumer preferences, and other relevant factors.[105] This is often a **5.55**

[102] Commission Notice on the application of the competition rules to the postal sector and on the assessment of certain State measures relating to postal services, OJ C 39/2 (1998) para 2.7.

[103] IP/99/291 (citing Case C-41/90 *Höfner and Elser v Macrotron* [1991] ECR I-1979). The Commission's investigation of GdF was dropped after the adoption of French Decree 99-278 of 12 April 1999, JO 14 April 1999, 5483, which is designed to allow Ministry-approved operators to offer natural gas distribution services in municipal areas not presently connected to the natural gas network.

[104] Commission Notice (n 102 above) 3.3. For further analysis of EC law relating to cross-subsidization, see paras 5.134–5.144 below.

[105] See Commission Notice on the definition of relevant market for purposes of Community competition law, OJ C 372/5 (1997); see also Art 9(7) of the Merger Regulation, which sets forth a general standard for the definition of geographic markets.

very fact-specific analysis. In determining the geographical scope of electricity markets, for example, the Commission may consider the seasonal variations in imports and exports, the existence of transmission bottlenecks, the use of cross-border transit fees, any differences in transmission frequencies, differences in electricity taxation, differences in various regulatory conditions such as reserve capacity requirements, and other barriers to cross-border trade arising out of environmental policies. The Commission may even consider the prevalence of cross-border mergers in the region as an indication that a physical presence on the national market is required in order to achieve significant sales. In addition to purely economic criteria, some commentators have observed that undisclosed non-economic factors may also shape the way a geographic market is defined, particularly when referrals of the case are at issue.[106] The geographical market may coincide with national boundaries, but this is not a general rule. In merger cases involving the energy sector, for example, there have been several cases where the Commission has identified concerns about the reinforcement of dominant positions in specific regional or local markets.[107] Other energy-related markets have been identified as pan-European, but not yet global, such as the market for power-generation equipment. This can be explained by customer preferences for 'home-based' suppliers which are able to offer speedy repair in case of equipment breakdown. In general, as the European market becomes increasingly liberalized, geographic markets will continue to expand to more regularly cover regional markets that overlap national boundaries.

5.56 The relevant product or service market is mainly defined on the basis of the substitutability or interchangeability of the products or services involved. If there is very low substitutability, the product will be considered a market apart. In the *United Brands* case,[108] for example, the question was whether bananas constituted a separate market or were part of a larger market for fresh fruit. The ECJ considered the organoleptical and consumer preferences, which showed that there was a separate market for bananas. In merger cases involving the energy utilities, the Commission has characterized the markets for electricity, gas, and district heating as separate markets with very limited capability for substitution in the specific circumstances of certain non-liberalized markets. For example, in approving an acquisition involving the dominant Belgian electricity and gas companies, Distrigaz and Electrabel, in 1994, the Commission defined the gas and electricity

[106] T Kauper, 'The Problem of Market Definition under EC Competition Law' in B Hawk (ed), *International Antitrust Law and Policy* (1997) 239–305, 293.

[107] See eg IP/99/197 (approving modified merger plans between Total and Petrofina, while referring to the French competition authorities the issue of concentration of petroleum storage infrastructure in the southern part of France); IP/99/387 (identifying concern with, *inter alia*, the effect of proposed merger of Exxon and Mobil on competition in the retail motor fuel sector in the north-west of Scotland).

[108] Case 27/76 *United Brands v Commission* [1978] ECR 207.

markets as separate markets 'because of the very imperfect capability for substitution existing between these two sources of energy'.[109] In explaining its decision, the Commission also indicated that other factors, such as the role of public enterprises and the existence of price-setting mechanisms in Belgium, would be taken into account in assessing the market impact:

> Taking into account the low capability for substitution between gas and electricity, and the resulting absence of direct market overlap between the two sources of energy, either at the level of the industrial customers or at the level of the domestic consumption, the Commission has reached the conclusion that the operation would not further strengthen the dominating positions already acquired on the gas and electricity markets. It has, however, noted that there is some capability for substitution as regards the domestic utilisation. Nevertheless, those gas and electricity sales to the consumers will continue to be made by the public inter-communal companies. Furthermore, the prices and terms of sale to the consumer will continue to be fixed by the public authorities.[110]

In other merger cases involving the electricity sector, the Commission has observed a distinction between exclusive uses of electricity (eg lighting, and certain chemical reactions) and non-exclusive uses for which there is potential substitutability (eg heating and traction).[111] However, even in the case of the production of heat, the Commission has characterized the substitutability as 'very imperfect', citing the higher costs of electricity for the production of heat. It is not clear from these statements whether the Commission has taken into account different methods of cost allocation between heat and electricity production in CHP units. Rather, the Commission has observed simply that 'substitutability could take place only over a long period of time because it involves different choices of equipment, according to the source of energy chosen'. **5.57**

In a 1999 case, the Commission approved a proposed acquisition of the Berlin gas and district heating supplier, GASAG, by two larger energy enterprises, one of which was involved in CHP operations in Germany. In explaining its decision, the Commission stated: **5.58**

> The Commission's investigation has shown that substitutability between gas and district heating is very limited. The decision about the heating system is usually made prior to construction or modernisation of a building. In Berlin, new constructions are planned in areas that are not connected to existing district heating networks. Only a few districts offer the possibility to choose between gas and district heating.

Similarly, in other merger cases, the Commission has noted the very limited substitutability for purposes of space heating between electricity and light fuel oil. **5.59**

---

[109] IP/94/805.

[110] ibid (translation from the French original).

[111] Comm Dec of 2/6/98 on Case No IV/M.931, Neste/IVO, OJ 1998 C 218/4.

Because initial choices in heating methods in buildings are related to and influence other investment choices, such as insulation, ventilation, and the heating network itself, the Commission has observed that changes of heating methods take place only in connection with renovation of buildings.

5.60 Once the markets are defined, the market share must be assessed. A market share of more than 50 per cent creates a refutable presumption that there is a dominant position.[112] This presumption will be difficult to refute in case of market shares substantially over 50 per cent. When undertakings have a market share of less than 50 per cent, additional elements, such as barriers to entry, will be needed to find a dominant position. A dominant position may also be constituted by more than one undertaking if such undertakings are connected by common elements such as the use of standard contracts.[113] However, in the *Kali und Salz* decision, wherein the ECJ annulled a Commission decision regarding a collective dominant position on the part of two undertakings in the potash market, the ECJ determined that a market share of 60 per cent, subdivided into shares of 23 per cent and 37 per cent after a concentration, does not of itself point conclusively to a collective dominant position.[114]

Merger control

5.61 As indicated above, Article 82 has also been used by the Commission to address situations where an undertaking with a dominant position has acquired or is seeking to acquire another company in the same market.[115] Thus, the acquisition of another firm in the same market by a firm with a dominant position is considered to constitute an abuse. The Community's merger control regulation establishes a system of prior notification for concentrations with a Community dimension.[116] Under this regulation the Commission must ascertain that concentrations will not create or strengthen a dominant position as a result of which effective competition would be significantly impeded in the common market or any substantial part of

[112] Case C-62/86 *AKZO v Commission* [1991] ECR I-3359.

[113] See Comm Dec, French West Africa Shipowners, OJ 1992 L 134; Case C-393/92 *Almelo v Ijsselcentrale* [1994] ECR I-1508.

[114] Joined Cases C-68/94 and C-30/95 *France and Others v Commission* [1998] ECR I-1375 para 226. See further Venit, 'Two Steps Forward and No Steps Back: Economic analysis and oligopolistic dominance after *Kali & Salz*', vol 35, No 5 CMLR (1998) 1101–34.

[115] Case 5/72 *Europeemballage and Continental Can v Commission* [1973] ECR 215.

[116] See Consolidated Text of Council Regulation 4064/89, OJ 1989 L 385, OJ 1990 L 257, as amended by Council Regulation 1310/97, OJ 1997 L 180/1, which amendments entered in force on 1 March 1998. The amended regulation provides quantitative thresholds and criteria defining which concentrations have a 'Community dimension', *inter alia*: '(a) the combined aggregate worldwide turnover of all the undertakings concerned is more than 2500 million euro; (b) in each of at least 3 Member States, the combined aggregate turnover of all the undertakings is more than 100 million euro. . . .' For an example of a prior notification of a concentration in the energy sector see Case No IV/M.1536 *Wind/Enel STC*, OJ 1999 C 162/6.

it. Failure to notify is subject to a fine.[117] Generally speaking, competence within the area of merger control is shared between the Commission and the Member States, such that the Commission examines very large transactions with a perceived impact on cross-border trade, whereas concentrations of a more local dimension are assessed by competition authorities at the national or provincial level.

The merger control regulation has had only limited relevance to the European energy utility sector due to its organization primarily within national boundaries. But because the concentration of the energy utility sector is a logical response to the onset of competition, it is likely that the frequency of application of the merger control rules to this sector will continue to increase. The Commission has used its powers in a few merger cases involving energy utilities to negotiate adjustments to the proposed transactions in a way that helps to ensure a more desirable ownership and structural framework in the electricity and gas markets than might otherwise develop under private transactions. **5.62**

For example, in its 1994 review of the proposed merger between the dominant Belgian electricity and gas companies, Distrigaz and Tractebel, the Commission insisted on the creation of a separate and more independent company to carry out natural gas sales to power producers with facilities of 15 MW or more.[118] Similarly, in a 1998 case involving the Finnish electricity market, the Commission expressed concern that a proposed concentration between two Finnish companies, IVO and Neste, could serve to strengthen their dominant position on the market for wholesale sales of electricity in Finland.[119] Once again, the concern was that the merged entity would have a strong position in both the power and natural gas markets, given Neste's majority ownership of the dominant natural gas supplier, Gasum. The Commission approved the transaction following a commitment by the parties to divest their controlling share to a non-controlling 25 per cent stake. In subsequent proceedings in the European Parliament, the Commission then pointed to this case as an indication of its 'commitment to use the Merger Regulation to ascertain that the electricity markets are not foreclosed through private initiatives'.[120] **5.63**

The Commission has also acknowledged a trend towards increased diversification by companies with monopoly positions in electricity generation, which it has **5.64**

[117] See eg Commission Decision 1999/459/EC of 10 February 1999 imposing fines for failing to notify and for putting into effect 3 concentrations in breach of Articles 4 and 7(1) of Council Regulation No 4064/89/EEC (Case IV/M.969 *AP Moller*); see also the related Opinion of the Advisory Committee on Concentrations, OJ 1999 C 201/4.

[118] Prior notice of a concentration, Case No IV/M.493, OJ 1994 C 222/4 (involving restructuring and ownership changes in the Belgian gas and electricity sectors). For a discussion of structure of the Belgian electricity and gas sector in connection with this case, see E Cross, *Electric Utility Regulation in the European Union* (1996) 108.

[119] Case No IV/M.931, Neste/IVO, OJ 1998 C 218.4.

[120] OJ 1998 C 118/69 (answer by Mr Van Miert).

attributed to the need of such utilities to offset potential loss of revenue resulting from the gradual introduction of competition into the market.[121] As pointed out by the Commission, such practices are not contrary to Community law, provided that the relevant rules on separate accounts for separate businesses are followed. In the words of the Commission, the aim of such legislative provisions on unbundling and transparency of accounts is 'to avoid discrimination, predatory prices, and other distortions of competition'.[122] Again, this seems to reflect an approach whereby investments by energy utilities are not subject to the level of governmental scrutiny one might have found in the past under regimes based upon traditional rate-of-return regulation.

Article 86

5.65 As observed above,[123] Article 86 (ex Art 90) is designed to strike a balance between the principles of free and undistorted competition and the State interests in maintaining exclusive rights and services of general interest. This article has three paragraphs, each of which has given rise to difficult issues of interpretation.

5.66 The first paragraph of Article 86 reiterates the obligations contained in the general provisions of the Treaty insofar as they relate to the behaviour of the governments of the Member States *vis-à-vis* public undertakings.[124] On the one hand, Member States are allowed to establish public undertakings and exclusive and special rights. On the other hand, they must observe the rules of the Treaty, in particular the rules on free movement and competition. This balance was clearly established by the ECJ in the *France v Commission*[125] judgment relating to the regulation of telecommunication terminal equipment as well as in the *Höfner*[126] case, relating to German executive recruitment services. In the former case, the ECJ specifically rejected the argument that Member States were free to create legal monopolies and that the Commission could not interfere with the maintenance of special and exclusive rights [previously] assigned to such undertakings. The ECJ stated: 'even though that article presupposes the existence of undertakings which have certain special or exclusive rights, it does not follow that all the special or exclusive rights are necessarily compatible with the Treaty. That depends on different rules to which [Article 86(1)] refers.'

---

[121] OJ 1999 C 50/128 (answer by Mr Van Miert).

[122] OJ 1998 C 118/69 (answer by Mr Van Miert).

[123] See above para 5.38.

[124] Article 86(1) provides: 'In the case of public undertakings and undertakings to which Member States grant special or exclusive rights, Member States shall neither enact nor maintain in force any measure contrary to the rules contained in this Treaty, in particular to those rules provided for in Article 12 and Articles 81 to 89.'

[125] Case C-202/88 *France v Commission (Telecommunications)* [1991] ECR I-1223.

[126] Case C-41/90 *Höfner and Elser v Macrotron* [1991] ECR I-1979.

The operation of the first paragraph of Article 86 is, however, subject to the special exception set forth in the second paragraph of Article 86; a provision that is, in the words of the ECJ, designed to 'reconcile the Member States' interests in using certain undertakings, in particular in the public sector, as an instrument of economic or fiscal policy with the Community's interest in ensuring compliance with the rules on competition and the preservation of the unity of the Common Market'.[127] **5.67**

Probably the most important question concerning Article 86(1) is whether the Member States have an unlimited discretion in establishing public undertakings and exclusive and special rights. It is now established case-law that Member States have no unlimited discretion in this respect. In establishing legal monopolies, Member States must not create a situation in which the operation of the monopoly has the necessary consequence of contravening the Treaty rules.[128] The *Höfner* case and the *Port of Genoa*[129] case provide clear examples of such situations. **5.68**

The second paragraph of Article 86 provides an exception both for the governments concerned and the undertakings involved. As for governments, this Treaty provision allows them to impose obligations on public undertakings or undertakings entrusted with the operation of services of general economic interest which would otherwise be prohibited by the Treaty. A first point of clarification of this provision concerns the word 'entrusted'. In the *GVL*[130] judgment the ECJ ruled that this must be clearly expressed by a governmental legislative measure. In fact, the assignment of such specific tasks on energy utilities may now follow from secondary Community legislation: for example, pursuant to Article 3(2) of both the Electricity Directive and the Gas Directive, which relate to the imposition of public service obligations on energy undertakings. **5.69**

The scope of the exception of Article 86(2) has been clarified in several judgments of the ECJ. In the *Corbeau*[131] and *Almelo*[132] judgments the ECJ defined the extent of the exception and the national policy objectives which may justify its application. In the 1997 cases on import and export rights,[133] the ECJ specified the concept of necessity which is implied in the words: 'insofar as the application of such rules does not obstruct the performance, in law or in fact, of the particular tasks **5.70**

[127] Case C-202/88 *France v Commission (Telecommunications)* [1991] ECR I-1223, at para 12.

[128] See D Edward and M Hoskins, 'Article 90: Deregulation and EC Law. Reflections arising from the XVI FIDE Conference', vol 32, No 1, CMLR (1995) 157–86.

[129] Case C-179/90 *Merci convenzionali porto di Genova v Siderurgica Gabrielli* [1991] ECR I-5889 (holding that Article 90(1), in conjunction with the other Treaty rules, precluded the conferral of exclusive rights to organize dock work and require recourse to a dock-work company formed exclusively of national workers).

[130] Case 7/82 *GVL v Commission*, [1983] ECR 483.

[131] Case C-320/91 [1993] ECR I-2533.

[132] Case C-393/92 [1994] ECR I-1477.

[133] Joined Cases C-156–160/94 [1997] ECR I-5699, I-5789, I-5815, and I-5851.

assigned to them.' According to the ECJ, the test is a relative rather than an absolute one. The test is whether, in the absence of the rights, it would not be possible for the undertaking to perform the particular tasks, defined by reference to the obligations and constraints to which it is subject. But, according to the ECJ: 'It is not necessary that the survival of the undertaking itself be threatened.'[134] In other words, the undertaking must be able to perform its tasks under economically acceptable conditions, which presumably would imply a normal rate of return on capital invested.

5.71 The second element of the ECJ's analysis in the 1997 cases on exclusive import/export rights is the definition of the burden of proof. Member States do not, positively, have to prove that no other conceivable measure, which by definition would be hypothetical, could enable the tasks to be performed under the same conditions. In paragraphs 54 and 55 of the case involving the Netherlands, the ECJ summarized the arguments put forward by the Dutch Government that elimination of the exclusive right would involve substantial changes in the way the system is run, in particular with regard to the obligation to contribute through planning to the proper functioning of the system on the basis of costs that are as low as possible and run in a socially responsible manner. The Court concluded that the Commission had not established that the granting of exclusive rights went further than was necessary. The Court's rule on the burden of proof therefore seems to leave a wide margin of discretion for the Member States.

5.72 The third element in the discussion of Article 86(2) was the clarification of the concept of the development of trade, which must not be affected to such an extent as would be contrary to the interests of the Community. The 1997 cases on export/import rights represent the first time that the ECJ itself has pronounced on this element of Article 86(2).[135] The ECJ noted that the Commission had not provided an explanation to demonstrate that, because of the exclusive rights, the development of intra-Community trade had been affected to an extent contrary to the interests of the Community.[136] According to the ECJ, the Commission should have defined the Community interest in relation to which the development of trade must be assessed. The ECJ also referred to the possibility for the Commission to apply the third paragraph of Article 86, and noted further that such a definition was particularly necessary since the only Community measure directly concerned with trade in electricity, the Directive on electricity transit,[137] states in its preamble that there is an increasing trade in electricity. According to the ECJ, since the Commission did not challenge other rights relating to trans-

[134] Case C-157/94 *The Netherlands v Commission* [1997] ECR I-5699, para 43.

[135] There is a brief statement on this point in the Commission's Decision in *Ijsselcentrale*, OJ 1991 L 28/32.

[136] Case C-157/94, [1997] ECR I-5699, para 67.

[137] Council Directive 90/547/EEC, OJ 1990 L 313/30, as amended.

mission and distribution, it therefore should have shown how, in the absence of a common policy, trade would have been possible having regard in particular to the existing capacity and arrangements for transmission and distribution.[138]

The ECJ's judgment in the case against France contains an interesting paragraph on the question of which obligations can be taken into account for the application of Article 86(2). The French Government argued that both EdF and GdF also had special obligations regarding the environment and regional policy. The Court observed that such obligations could only be taken into account when they are specific to those undertakings and to their business. It found that the Government had not demonstrated that these obligations went beyond mere compliance with general law. The Court also found that EdF and GdF are not under an obligation to seek to secure the most competitive tariffs and the lowest cost for the community. **5.73**

The exception for the undertakings under Article 86(2) derives from the exception for the governments, but it is not necessarily of the same breadth. According to the words of Article 86(2), the application of the competition rules would have to obstruct the performance, in law or in fact, of the particular tasks assigned to such undertakings. This distinction is clearly laid down in the ECJ's judgment in the *ERT* judgment.[139] **5.74**

It is important to make a distinction between the justification for the government measures and the conduct of the undertakings concerned when applying Article 86(2). In line with *Crespelle*,[140] it could be argued that a government measure would only infringe Article 86(1) and (2) when the undertaking acting pursuant to that measure would also necessarily infringe the competition rules as set forth in Articles 81 or 82. Conversely, this means that the actions of the undertaking are not necessarily covered by the exemption granted to government measures under Article 86(2). It will then, normally, be up to the undertaking to prove that its conduct also satisfies the test of Article 86(2). In this context, it should also be noted that it is with good reason that the government may be allowed more discretion under Article 86(2) than the undertaking. Government acts establishing public service obligations are necessarily intended for a longer period of time and cannot therefore be completely fine-tuned to a specific period of the business cycle. They may also address more than one single undertaking, and thus can concern companies with different cost structures. **5.75**

As indicated above, when Member States establish public service obligations pursuant to the directives for the internal market for electricity and gas, they have to **5.76**

[138] Case C-157/94 [1997] ECR I-5699, para 71.
[139] Case C-260/89 [1991] ECR I-2925.
[140] Case C-323/93 *Societé Civile (Crespelle)* [1994] ECR I-5097.

notify such obligations to the Commission. The directives do not specify what the Commission is supposed to do after the notification. In view of the reference to Article 86 (ex Art 90) in these Articles, one would expect the Commission to verify the compatibility of the public service obligations with this provision. Arguably, the Commission's task is to verify whether the public service obligations meet the standard laid down in the ECJ's case-law on Article 86(1), as suggested above. Furthermore, the proper fulfilment of Member State obligations under the Transparency Directive,[141] as well as full observance of the rules on unbundling and transparency of accounts provided for in the Electricity and Gas Directives,[142] may facilitate such verification.

5.77 A clear example of a situation where the exception for the governmental measure did not coincide with the exception for undertakings is provided in the application of the ECJ's ruling in the *Almelo* case by the Court of Appeal in Arnhem in the Netherlands.[143] That Court denied the exception, pointing out that the undertaking had not established sufficient evidence that it could not perform its special tasks.

5.78 Moreover, it should be noted that the exception of Article 86(2) has direct effect.[144] This means that undertakings may rely on this exception without the necessity of prior notification to the Commission as required by the rules of Regulation 17. However, if the exception is denied by national courts or arbitrators and the agreements have not been notified, they will be subject to the sanction of nullity according to Article 81(2) (ex Art 85(2)). It may therefore be a more prudent course to notify.

5.79 Finally, the third paragraph of Article 86 relates to the powers of the Commission. This provision has also been clarified in the case-law of the ECJ. In the 1991 decision in *France v Commission*, involving a challenge to the Commission Directive 88/301/EEC on competition in the market for telecommunications terminal equipment, the ECJ ruled that the Commission is empowered to enact directives specifying the obligations arising from the Treaty which are binding on the

[141] Commission Directive 80/723/EEC of 25 June 1980 on the transparency of financial relations between the Member States and public undertakings, OJ 1980 L 195, as amended by Commission Directive 85/413/EEC, OJ 1985 L 229 and Commission Directive 93/84/EEC, OJ 1993 L 254. The Commission is considering another amendment to this proposal which is intended to address the situation of incumbents in newly liberalized markets. See K Soukop, 'Commission proposes change to Transparency Directive', 1999, No 2, Competition Policy Newsletter (June 1999).

[142] Arts 13–15 of the directive on the internal market for electricity and Arts 12–13 of the directive on the internal market for natural gas. It should be noted that similar rules apply in the telecommunications sector. Furthermore, the relevant EC secondary legislation provides for supervision of the accounts by the national authorities.

[143] See the annotation by L Hancher in 34 CMLR 1997, 1509ff.

[144] See Case C-260/89 *ERT v DEP* [1991] ECR I-2925.

Member States *vis-à-vis* public undertakings referred to in that Article.[145] This is a specific power conferred on the Commission, to be distinguished from the general power for the Council under Article 95 (ex Art100a) for harmonization and the Commission's power under Article 226 (ex Art 169) to enforce Community law against the Member States.[146] In the 1992 judgment in *Netherlands v Commission*, involving an exclusive franchise for delivery of letters under 550 grams, the ECJ confirmed the Commission's power to address individual decisions addressed against Member States.[147] However, the Court specified that, even though the decision was addressed to the Member State, the Commission was under an obligation to respect the rights of the defence, including the right to be heard.[148] The Commission's decisions addressed to public undertakings and to undertakings with exclusive or special rights have to be based on the provisions of Regulation 17 or the sector-specific regulations.

(3) *State Aids*

The EC Treaty provisions on State aids set forth in Articles 87–88 (ex Arts 92–93), together with the State aid rules under the ECSC Treaty, form an important part of the Commission's practice and the case-law of the ECJ.[149] The Commission must regularly review notifications of such State aid made by the Member States, and its caseload involving State aid to the energy sector appears to be increasing. This can be attributed at least in part to the response of government to the effects (or requirements) of energy liberalization whereby governments have been taking special measures, *inter alia*, to require the transfer of selected utility assets, to protect or compensate energy utilities for 'stranded costs' or 'stranded investments' associated with the liberalization, and to protect or promote certain forms of energy production affected by the liberalization.[150] Moreover, the Commission has clarified and expanded its definition of existing State aid so as to require notification by the Member States of measures that were not originally State aid but which have become aid due to the evolution of the market.[151] **5.80**

[145] Case C-202/88 *France v Commission (Telecommunications)* [1991] ECR I-1223, para 14.

[146] ibid, para 25.

[147] Joined Cases C-48/90 and 66/90, *Netherlands v Commission* [1992] ECR I-565, paras 27–39.

[148] ibid, paras 37, 53.

[149] See L Hancher, T Ottervanger, and PJ Slot, *EC State Aids* (1999); L Hancher, 'EC State Aids and Energy' [1995] 2 OGLTR 62–72; P Slot, 'Energy and Competition', 31 CMLR 511 (1994).

[150] See eg Commission Decision 1999/791/EC of 8 July 1999 concerning the application of the United Kingdom of Great Britain and Northern Ireland for a transitional regime under Art 24 of Directive 96/92/EC of the European Parliament and of the Council concerning common rules for the internal market in electricity, and accompanying decisions regarding the applications of France, Luxembourg, Germany, Austria, the Netherlands, Spain, and Denmark, OJ 1999 L 319.

[151] See Council Regulation (EC) No 659/1999 of 22 March 1999 laying down detailed rules for the application of Art 93 of the EC Treaty, OJ 1999 L 83/1 (defining 'existing aid' as 'aid which is deemed to be an existing aid because it can be established that at the time it was put into effect it did not constitute an aid, and subsequently became an aid due to the evolution of the common

5.81 State aid involving the national energy industries takes myriad forms, and State aid cases have involved almost all types of energy sources and many types of activities, ranging from oil refineries[152] to nuclear plants to the supply of district heat. Various Member States have supported their domestic coal industry by promoting or requiring arrangements with the electricity industry, which are designed to ensure the use of domestic coal at prices well above the marginal import price. Funding under these subsidy arrangements is vetted by the Commission on a regular basis pursuant to the ECSC Treaty and the codes on coal aid,[153] whereas contracts for additional purchases of coal between coal mines and electricity generators have been assessed under the EC competition rules for their effect on competition and trade in electricity, as in the cases involving the German *Jahrhundertvertrag.*[154]

5.82 Other State aid cases under the EC Treaty rules have involved aid to energy consumers (through tax concessions, preferential tariffs, or contracts), grants to support power plant projects,[155] extensions to natural gas pipelines,[156] support for certain types of energy production such as alternative or indigenous energy sources,[157] and

market and without having been altered by the Member State. Where certain measures become aid following the liberalisation of an activity by Community law, such measures shall not be considered as existing aid after the date fixed for liberalisation').

[152] See eg Comm Dec 77/260/EEC of 22 March 1977 concerning aid planned by the Belgian Government towards the extension of capacity of an oil refinery at Antwerp, OJ 1977 L 80/23.

[153] See eg Comm Dec 1999/451/ECSC of 4 May 1999 on the granting by Spain of aid to the coal industry in 1999, OJ L 177/27 (1999); Comm Dec 1999/299/ECSC of 22 December 1998 on German aid to the coal industry for 1999, OJ L 117/44 (1999); Comm Dec 1999/299/ECSC of 2 December 1998 on German aid to the coal industry for 1998, OJ L 109/14 (1999); see also Comm Dec 3632/93/ECSC, OJ L 329/12 (1993); and Comm Dec 93/66/ECSC, OJ L 21/33 (1993) (approving earlier financial measures to support the German coal industry). Under the competition rules of the EC Treaty, the European Commission reviewed aspects of the German coal-subsidy arrangements affecting German electricity producers.

[154] In its Notice on the *Jahrhundertvertrag*, Case No IV/33.151, OJ C 159/7 (1990), the Commission stipulated that the agreement between the parties was not a State measure, and that it 'seems to justify exemption under Art 81(3) (ex Art 85(3)) under certain conditions' because it benefited consumers and the general public by safeguarding supplies and hence 'improv[ed] the generating and distribution of electricity' (para 9). The Commission therefore granted a temporary authorization.

[155] See eg OJ C 203/15 (1993) (approving German State aid (DM 600 million) to VEBA for the construction of a 800 MW lignite-fired plant at Schkopa).

[156] OJ 1995 C 290/13–14 (approving aid of MECU 9.76 to extend the Spanish natural gas grid in inland areas where aid intensity was restricted to under 30%).

[157] See eg Case 59/97 (ex NN 82/97), Commission Notice concerning investment grants of Brandenburg for the preferential use of brown coal, OJ C 381/5 (1997); Commission Communication concerning State aid to the French coal industry, C 99/9 (1999); European Commission, Press Release IP/96/1199 regarding aid to the peat industry in Ireland (finding that there is no trade between Member States in peat for energy production and therefore no State aid under the EC Treaty); Case N 1037/95, OJ C 188 (1996) regarding the Danish 'Energy 2000' action plan (raising no objections to Danish purchase and selling-price guarantees which created incentives for alternative energy sources and energy efficiency); Case N 1027/95, OJ C 215 (1996) and Case N 469/96, OJ C 339 (1996) (approving German *Länder* guidelines for promotion of energy savings

proposed amendments to national electricity laws.[158] The Commission has traditionally taken a strict approach to aid for refinery conversion,[159] or for the promotion of the offshore oil supply industry.[160] In most of these cases, it was considered that the developments in question could have been brought about by ordinary market forces. The Commission has also occasionally investigated alleged subsidies for nuclear power plants.[161] In late 1998 the Commission stated that it had no evidence of subsidies for nuclear plants that were incompatible with Community law, but that it was examining another complaint in this regard.[162]

The substantive rules and policies applicable to State aid within the energy sector are not always clear, but the general principles are embodied within a number of Commission documents called frameworks, notifications, or communications,[163] as well as the case-law and decisions. Policies are also set out in the Commission's annual reports on competition policy. With respect to State aid for environmental protection, the Commission issued guidelines in 1994, and these have been under review in the light of market liberalization trends. The procedural rules for State aid had been almost entirely the creation of the ECJ until 1999 when a procedural regulation was put in place.[164] **5.83**

and renewable energy); Commission Decision 97/542/EC of 18 December 1996 on tax exemptions for biofuels in France, OJ L 222/26 (1997) (holding that French tax exemptions were incompatible with Article 87 (ex Article 92)).

[158] See eg European Commission, Press Release IP/95/439 (deciding that State aid rules did not apply to a proposed amendment to the Danish Electricity Act to allow electric utilities to earn profits through commercial activities or cost reductions).

[159] See European Commission, XIth and XIIth Reports on Competition Policy, 1981 and 1982 pts 220 and 194 respectively.

[160] See European Commission, 6th Report on Competition Policy, 1976, pts 219–21 and IXth Report on Competition Policy, 1979, pts 162–4; see also Commission Notice concerning a proposal by the French Government to grant aid to the steel companies, Usinor/Sacilor, for non-steel activities carried out by a number of its subsidiaries, including CFEM offshore oil, OJ 1988 C 297/7.

[161] See Cross, n 118 above, 47 (quoting OJ 1993 C 327/31).

[162] OJ 1999 C 135/85 (Answer of 1 October 1998 to Written Question E-2650/98).

[163] See eg European Commission, *Competition law in the European Communities*, vol IIA: *Rules applicable to State aids* (1995); National Regional Aid, OJ 1998 C 74/9; Commission Communication on State aid elements in sales of land and buildings by public authorities, OJ 1997 C 209/3; Multisectoral framework on regional aid for large investment projects, OJ 1998 C 107/7; Community Guidelines on State aid for rescuing and restructuring firms in difficulty, OJ 1997 C 283/2; Community Framework for State aid for research and development, OJ 1996 C 45/5; Community Guidelines on State aid for environmental protection, OJ 1994 C 72/3; Commission Communication to the Member States regarding the application of Arts 92 and 93 EC and of Art 5 of Commission Directive 80/723/EEC to public undertakings in the manufacturing sector, OJ 1993 C 307/3; and Commission Communication on the accumulation of aids for different purposes, OJ 1985 C 3/2.

[164] Council Regulation (EC) No 659/1999 of 22 March 1999 laying down detailed rules for the application of Art 93 of the EC Treaty, OJ 1999 L 83/1. For an analysis of this Regulation, see A Sinnaeve and P Slot, 'The new Regulation on State Aid Procedures', vol 36, No 6, CMLR 1153–94 (1999).

Substantive rules

The broad concept of State aid

5.84 Article 87(1) EC provides that State aid is incompatible with the common market, save as otherwise provided in the EC Treaty, if it distorts or threatens to distort competition by favouring certain undertakings or the production of certain goods, in so far as it affects trade between Member States. General measures taken by a Member State within the framework of its economic policy which benefit *all* undertakings within the Member State concerned remain in principle outside the scope of Article 87(1) as these measures do not favour *certain undertakings* or the production of *certain goods*.

5.85 The ECJ has consistently held that the concept of 'aid' is not limited to directly financial measures, such as the provision of a capital subsidy,[165] but includes any other intervention involving State resources that, although provided in a different form, might produce the same economic benefit for a particular undertaking. In the 1993 case of *Sloman Neptune*[166] the ECJ made clear that any benefit granted directly or indirectly out of State resources is to be regarded as a State aid. This means that a very broad range of benefits are covered by the scope of Article 87, including: direct subsidies, interest subsidies, capital injections, grants, interest-free or low-interest loans, asset revaluations, compensation for government-imposed financial burdens, the foregoing of recovery of receivables, preferential terms, price reductions, public supply contracts, reduction in social security charges, State guarantees, State participation in capital tax concessions, tax exemptions, and the foregoing of State revenue. A basic test to identify State aids is to determine whether the measure provides an undertaking with an economic advantage that it would not have obtained under normal market conditions.[167] Thus, for example, if a government required the sale or transfer of electricity transmission lines from a State-owned utility to another company, but established the transfer price of such assets either above or below market value, the government would effectively be granting an economic advantage to one of the two companies in such a way that the transfer might contain elements of State aid.[168]

5.86 The aid must be effected by a Member State or through State resources. Thus, privileged low-interest loans granted to certain municipal energy utilities by a bank wholly owned by the Italian State, for example, would fall within the State aid rules, even if the interest rates did not derive directly from the State budget.[169]

[165] Case 30/59 *De Gezamenlijke Steenkolenmijnen in Limburg v High Authority* [1961] ECR 1, 19; Case C-387/92 *Banco Exterior de España v Ayuntamiento de Valencia* [1994] ECR I-877, para 13.

[166] Joined Cases C-72/91 and C-73/91 *Sloman Neptune* [1993] ECR I-887.

[167] Case C-387/92, n 165 above, para 13.

[168] See OJ 1999 C 245/5.

[169] See OJ 1999 C 220/14 (Commission's appraisal of a complaint about Italian laws 488/96, 142/90, and 549/95).

In such a case the State aid element would be the difference between the interest rate theoretically applicable to the undertaking (on the basis of its expected risk) and the one actually charged for the loans by the State-owned entity.

The ECJ has made it clear that actions by 'public undertakings'[170] established or appointed by a State can invoke the EC State aid rules. In the words of the ECJ: in determining whether a measure is to be regarded as State aid, 'no distinction should be drawn between cases where aid is granted directly by the State and cases where it is granted by public or private undertakings established or appointed by the State'.[171] Therefore it can be argued that any flow of funds or assets between two public undertakings has to be considered as involving State resources.[172] **5.87**

Similarly, preferences or benefits granted by public undertakings to certain private customers can also involve State aid. In other words, State aid may involve subsidy schemes not only *to* the energy sector but also *through* the energy sector. For example, preferential energy tariffs set by a State-owned or State-controlled firm to a particular customer or category of customers may be caught by Article 87(1) as a form of 'downstream aid'.[173] Thus, in a 1988 decision by the ECJ, the preferential tariff accorded to the fertilizer industry by the partially State-controlled gas supplier in the Netherlands, Gasunie, was held to be State aid.[174] Similarly, as a result of an investigation conducted in 1988, the Commission required the French power supplier, EdF, to increase its electricity tariffs to a particular aluminium producer by 10 per cent annually in the last three years of a long-term supply contract. **5.88**

Moreover, in countries where energy utilities are subject to a system of promotion of certain forms of energy, the *impact* of introducing generally applicable measures such as new energy taxes on the benefits accruing to energy enterprises under such promotion systems may also be regarded as a possible form of State aid. For example, as a result of the introduction of a new German electricity tax on 1 April 1999, the Commission subsequently opened an investigation under the State aid rules as to the impact of the new tax on the feed-in price paid to electricity producers using renewable energy sources pursuant to German legislation on the **5.89**

[170] For a definition of 'public undertakings' see Commission Directive 80/723/EEC of 25 June 1980 on the transparency of financial relations between the Member States and public undertakings, OJ 1980 L 195, as amended by Commission Directive 85/413/EEC, OJ 1985 L 229 and Commission Directive 93/84/EEC, OJ 1993 L 254. Under the 1999 Notice for a draft Directive amending Directive 80/723/EEC, the term 'public undertakings' means 'any undertaking over which the public authorities may exercise directly or indirectly a dominant influence by virtue of their ownership of it, their financial participation therein, or the rules which govern it': OJ 1999 C 377/2.

[171] Case C-305/98 [1991] ECR I-1603.

[172] See OJ 1999 C 245/5.

[173] See Hancher, Ottervanger, and Slot, n 149 above, 193, 200–4.

[174] See Joined Cases 67, 68, and 70/85 *Kwekerij Gebroeders van der Kooy v Commission* [1988] ECR 219, discussed further in paras 5.99–5.100 below.

feed-in of electricity from such sources.[175] In so doing, the Commission pointed out that its investigation was confined to the increase in the price resulting from the electricity tax and did not concern the previous feed-in price, or the electricity tax itself, which had been previously notified and approved by the Commission. In other words, the *impact* of such measures on other promotion schemes in the energy sector may also have to be notified by Member States to the Commission in addition to their notification of the general measures themselves.

Selectivity

5.90 The prohibition of Article 87 does not apply if all undertakings within a Member State benefit from assistance, without any distinction being made between them. In other words, general measures of economic policy, such as the lowering of the tax rate applicable to corporate profits, remain in principle outside the scope of Article 87, as such measures would not favour certain undertakings or the production of certain goods. The distinction between general and specific measures is not always easy to apply. Thus, the Italian reduction in the rate of social security contributions was deemed to constitute State aid because it benefited the Italian textile industry disproportionately.[176] An example of a case of selectivity in the granting of benefits to the energy utility sector can be found in Italy, where eligibility for particular benefits was made dependent on the legal status of an undertaking (only for former public undertakings transformed into joint stock companies) and on the nature of shareholders (only for undertakings with majority public shareholders and minority private shareholders).[177]

Effect on competition

5.91 The granting of benefits must result in a distortion of competition in order to be caught by Article 87(1). The Commission has formulated the test as follows: whether the measure 'distorts or threatens to distort competition [by providing] an economic advantage to certain undertakings *vis-à-vis* their competitors'.[178] For this purpose it is necessary to consider whether the aid strengthens the position of the beneficiary enterprise compared with other enterprises operating in the same line of trade.[179] However, it is not necessary for the Commission to produce a full-fledged analysis of the relevant product and geographical market along the lines of the analysis required by the Treaty rules on competition (Art 81 and especially Art 82).[180] Nevertheless, the Commission must produce something more than a statement that competition has been or may be distorted. Moreover, the Commission

---

175 Press Release IP/99/667.

176 Case 173/73 *Italy v Commission* [1974] ECR 709.

177 See OJ 1999 C 220/14.

178 OJ 1999 C 220/15.

179 Case 730/79 *Philip Morris Holland v Commission* [1980] ECR 2690.

180 ibid.

must establish that the aid would have an impact on trade between the Member States.[181] For example, in the case of the Italian measures referred to above, the Commission argued that the privileged low-interest loans and other benefits to local public undertakings affected trade in so far as they prejudiced the ability of foreign companies bidding for local concessions in Italy, since local public undertakings benefiting from the scheme could bid at more competitive prices than national or foreign undertakings not benefiting from the aid. Moreover, in cases where eligibility for the aid scheme is based on the nature of the shareholders (eg aid for utilities with majority public shareholdings only) the Commission can identify the possible deterrence on cross-border acquisitions, since companies from other Member States would not invest in the new public energy utilities in Italy if such investment meant that the acquired companies would not be eligible for the aid (or would lose the benefits of the aid).

The market economy investor principle

An important concept for distinguishing between benefits granted by governments which are prohibited by Article 87(1), and those which are not, is the market economy investor principle.[182] This analytical approach was especially developed in the context of government participation in the capital of enterprises.[183] According to this principle, government actions which take place under market terms and conditions do not give rise to the application of Article 87(1). In such cases, if the provision of funds by the State is similar to that of a private company acting based on commercial considerations, such action will not be considered as aid.[184] **5.92**

Aids compatible with the Common Market: Article 87(2)

Article 87(2) lists three specific types of State aid, of an exceptional nature, which *shall* be compatible with the Common Market: **5.93**

—aid having a social character, granted to *individual consumers*, provided that such aid is granted without discrimination related to the origin of the products concerned;

[181] Case 248/84 *Germany v Commission* [1987] ECR 4013; Case T-214/95 *Vlaamse Gewest v Commission* [1998] ECR II-717.

[182] See generally G Abbamonte, 'The Market Economy Investor Principle: A Legal Analysis of an Economic Problem', 4 ECLR 258–68 (1996).

[183] Case 318/82 *Netherlands and Leeuwarder Papierwarenfabriek v Commission* [1985] ECR 824.

[184] See Case C–56/93 *Belgium v Commission* [1996] ECR I-767 (finding that the Dutch gas supplier, Gasunie, acted as a private company based on commercial considerations and holding that price concessions to Dutch ammonia producers did not constitute State aid); see also Commission Communication to the Member States regarding the application of Arts 92 and 93 EEC and of Art 5 of Commission Directive 80/723/EEC to public enterprises in the manufacturing sector, OJ 1993 C 307/5.

—aid to make good damage caused by natural disasters or exceptional occurrences;
—aid granted to the economy of certain areas of the Federal Republic of Germany affected by the division of Germany, in so far as such aid is required in order to compensate for the economic disadvantages caused by the division.

5.94 The word 'shall' is taken to imply that the Commission has no discretion to decide whether these 'compatibility clauses' would apply.[185] However, over the years the Commission has demonstrated reluctance to apply the exemptions set out in this Article. Subsequent to German reunification in 1990, the Commission took the position that State aid to areas in the former Federal Republic of Germany would no longer be dealt with under Article 87(2)(c), but rather under Article 87(3)(a).[186]

Aids which may be compatible with the Common Market: Article 87(3)

5.95 Article 87(3) lists five categories of aids which, in the discretion of the Commission, *may* be exempted. It is important to note that this provision, as an exemption from the general principles of the Treaty, has been interpreted in a restrictive manner. Thus, in its judgment in *Philip Morris*,[187] the ECJ supported the Commission interpretation that State aids can only be allowed to the extent that they are necessary for the achievement of objectives accepted under Article 87(3). In summary, the requirements are as follows:

(i) the aid must promote or further a project which is in the Community interest as a whole;
(ii) the aid must be necessary for the achievement of this result, and the objective could not have been obtained in the absence of this measure; and
(iii) the duration, intensity, and scope of the aid must be proportionate to the importance of the intended result.[188]

5.96 The Commission has indicated that schemes for energy saving and for diversifying energy resources may be exempt as important projects of common interest.[189] The Commission has ruled, however, that a particular aid scheme cannot be considered in the 'common European interest' if it represents specific aid for a single company in a particular sector.[190] At the same time, a project carried out by only one Member State may be sufficient to justify aid where it contributes to wider

[185] Case 730/79, *Philip Morris Holland v Commission* [1980] ECR 2690.
[186] See XXth Report on Competition Policy, para 178.
[187] Case 730/79, n 185 above.
[188] See European Commission, XIIth Report on Competition Policy, 160 (1983).
[189] European Commission, VIIth Report on Competition Policy, pts 250–4, 255, 256; IXth Report on Competition Policy, pt 186; XIth Competition Report, pt 221; and XIIth Competition Report, pt 161.
[190] See Commission Decision 89/254 on aid which the Belgian government proposed to grant to Belgian Shell, OJ 1989 L 106/34.

Community goals. For example, in its Decision on the British Non-Fossil Fuel Levy, the Commission considered that measures designed to sustain the British nuclear sector in the context of the British electricity privatization and restructuring would contribute to security of supply and supply diversity, both of which were in the common European interest.[191]

In State aid Case N 13/92, the Commission approved governmental investment for a lignite-fired power station in Schkopau, Saxony-Anhalt, using locally mined lignite.[192] The construction of the 800 MW station by Veba Kraftwerke Ruhr is subsidized by DM 600 million (out of a total estimated cost of DM 2.7 billion) to cover part of the extra cost of the lignite station in comparison to the conventional coal-fired station that the operator originally intended to build on the site. The Commission considered the subsidy was justifiable on environmental and technological grounds, given that the continuation of active lignite mining would facilitate the extensive reclamation work needed in old lignite workings and that the advanced power station would have technological spin-offs.[193] **5.97**

Article 87(3)(c)

Pursuant to Article 87(3)(c), aid may be compatible with the Common Market if it facilitates the development of certain economic *activities*, where such aid does not adversely affect trading conditions to an extent contrary to the common interest. Various types of aid can be brought under this exemption. **5.98**

Cases on preferential energy tariffs

The significance of the Treaty provisions on State aids for the energy sector was demonstrated by a set of cases[194] decided by the ECJ regarding the natural gas tariffs charged by the Dutch gas supplier, Gasunie.[195] At the time of the decisions, the level of State ownership and influence over gas pricing decisions by the Netherlands government was deemed sufficient by the European Commission **5.99**

---

[191] See European Commission, Press Release, IP/90/267 (March 1990); XXth Report on Competition Policy, 258.

[192] State aid case N 13/92, OJ 1992 C 203/15.

[193] See European Commission, Press Release, 'State Aid for German Lignite Power Station' (IP/92/609, 22 July 1992).

[194] Joined Cases 67/68 and 70/84 *Kwekerij Gebroeders van der Kooy* [1988] ECR 219; Case C-169/84 *Société CdF Chimie azote et Fertilisants et al v Commission* [1990] ECR I-3083; and Case C-56/93 *Belgium v Commission* [1996] ECR I-767.

[195] The relationship between the Dutch gas supplier, Gasunie, and the Dutch nitrate fertilizer manufacturing industry occupied the attention of affected interests, Member States, the Commission, and the Court, on State aid grounds, for more than a decade. Natural gas is the chief raw material and represents 90% of the cost in the manufacture of ammonia. Ammonia is, in turn, the chief constituent in the manufacture of nitrate fertilizers. In effect, gas represents about 70% of the cost of production.

and the ECJ to implicate the State aid rules in several challenges to Gasunie's tariff structure.[196]

5.100 The 1988 decision in *Kwekerij Gebroeders van der Kooy*[197] involved a challenge to the tariffs charged to Dutch horticultural growers using heated glasshouses. The Netherlands government argued that lowered tariffs were necessary to keep such growers from switching from gas to coal heating, which would have caused more air pollution. Because coal prices were falling, the argument was made that Gasunie had to lower its contract price for gas supplies to these growers. However, the ECJ essentially found that the price level was lower than was necessary to prevent the switch to coal and that there was no need for Gasunie to align its general horticultural tariff on the equilibrium price for the least efficient type of holding. The ECJ took the view that, at least in the medium term, the position of these holdings would inevitably become marginal, so that it was not commercially justified for Gasunie to fix its horticultural tariff by reference to such undertakings.

5.101 However, in the 1996 decision *Belgium v Commission*,[198] involving the special gas tariffs ('tariff F') charged to Dutch nitrate fertilizer producers, the ECJ found nothing to support a conclusion that Gasunie had behaved differently from any other private undertaking in normal market conditions.

5.102 The application of the State aid rules to preferential pricing schemes is also demonstrated by a set of Commission investigations of the French electricity supplier EdF in the late 1980s. In an investigation of possible aid elements in a twenty-five-year electricity supply contract between the developers of a new aluminium smelter and EdF, whereby EdF also had an arrangement to take a share of the future profits of the smelter, the Commission made a detailed verification of the electricity pricing schedules as well as of forecasts for future aluminium prices. It concluded that the electricity price to be paid by the smelter was below even the marginal cost of production, and it therefore required that EdF's guaranteed minimum price be increased by 10 per cent for the years 1997 to 1999 in order to remove any State aid elements in the arrangement. In another case involving a ten-year power supply contract between EdF and a plant producing metallic alloys in Dunkirk, the Commission seemed to apply the test of whether a private in-

---

[196] At the time of these cases, 40% of Nederlandse Gasunie NV was owned by Staatsmijnen (wholly owned by the Netherlands State), and 10% by the Netherlands State and by the two private oil companies. It was administered by a board consisting of 8 members, 1 of whom was appointed by the Minister of Economic Affairs, 3 by the Staatsmijnen, and 2 by each of the private oil companies. Gas prices are set by the Board of Directors, acting by a 75% majority, and prices and delivery conditions for the supply of gas to public distributors and to other parties were subject to the approval of the Minister of Economic Affairs.

[197] [1988] ECR 219.

[198] [1996] ECR I-767, sometimes referred to as the 'Tariff F' Case.

vestor would enter into such a commercial contract, and it approved the contract following its receipt of an assurance from EdF that at the end of the contract the new plant would be paying the same electricity tariff as any other similar industrial consumer.

While the facts and context of the above cases are complex, some tentative conclusions can be offered regarding energy pricing and the State aid rules. Prices lower than the regular, listed energy tariffs of enterprises which are controlled by governments are justified in one or more of the following circumstances: **5.103**

—if such lower tariffs are the result of real cost savings such as volume discounts;
—to the extent that they form part of a general tariff applicable for the entire industry;
—to the extent that the action of the government or the government-controlled enterprise constitutes normal market behaviour (sometimes referred to as the market economy investor principle);
—if such lower tariffs serve an objective that is recognized in Community law and to the extent that they are necessary and proportionate.[199]

It is also useful to note that a deliberate foregoing of profits does not automatically constitute State aid. The market economy investor principle serves as a shield against rash judgements in this respect.[200] Moreover, in *Belgium v Commission* the ECJ endorsed the view that the commercial behaviour may be guided by the desire for an appropriate payback on the money invested. Together with the application of the market economy investor principle, the principle of non-discrimination will be the main standard of reference. Customers in similar markets and conditions must be given similar tariffs. **5.104**

Even if the above conclusions are comforting for those involved in commercial actions in State-controlled public utilities, there is nevertheless a concern on the procedural level, given that new State aids must be notified to the Commission and that failure to notify results in the (at least temporary) illegality of such measures.[201] In practice, however, notification may not always be an attractive option as governments may be less willing to subject themselves to the judgment of the Commission. This may leave the utility in the unenviable position of being caught between a reluctant, unco-operative government and the possibilities of challenges against tariffs not being cleared by the Commission under the market economy investor principle or otherwise under the rules on State aids. On the other hand, this position is hardly different from the situation under the competition rules, with which companies **5.105**

[199] P Slot, 'Regulation of Prices in the Energy Sector of the EC', vol 15, No 3 JERL (1997) 263–82, 281.

[200] See generally G Abbamonte, 'The Market Economy Investor Principle: A Legal Analysis of an Economic Problem', 4 ECLR 258–68 (1996).

[201] It should be noted that that illegality can be cured by the Commission's approval of the aid.

have learned to cope. Contrary to the situation under the EC competition rules, however, the awareness that energy tariffs may be subject to supervision by the Commission is a relatively recent development.

(4) Special Topics in EC Energy Law

Long-term contracts

5.106 Nearly all demand for gas in the EC is covered by long-term contracts with take-or-pay provisions. Such contracts are of two main types: depletion contracts and supplies contracts. The latter usually involve an agreement to supply a fixed volume of gas over a number of years, usually up to twenty-five years, while a depletion contract generally involves the purchase of the entire output from one gas field. The production usually involves a period of build-up, followed by a number of years at a constant rate—known as the plateau—and then a decline period. A long-term contract ensures the purchaser a steady and reliable supply of gas and ensures the producer a guaranteed outlet for its production. Take-or-pay provisions have been a common feature of both supply and depletion contracts: the supplier is assured of cash-flow that enables it to invest in production and/or transport facilities. It is argued that long-term take-or-pay contracts contribute to the realization of upstream gas investments, especially in the case of non-EC gas producers. Without these contracts the huge amount of finance of new gas investments may not become available and the security of supply could be jeopardized. At the same time, if gas to gas competition is to become a reality, then gas must be made available for new entrants and existing pipeline capacity must not be devoted entirely to shipping gas under existing contracts.

5.107 While new supplies of gas for continental Europe will probably come onstream in the first decade of the twenty-first century, *inter alia,* from the Bacton interconnector and from new fields being developed in Russia, new market entrants must have access not only to pipelines but also to customers. If the latter are tied to existing suppliers, such as gas merchant companies, through 'back-to-back' contracts concluded by gas merchant/transmission companies with distributors, they will not be able to shop around for new gas. The Commission estimates that approximately 75 per cent of all take-or-pay obligations are covered by such back-to-back contracts.

5.108 These back-to-back contracts usually, although not necessarily, take the form of exclusive supply and exclusive purchase commitments: the gas merchant company appoints a gas distributor to be the exclusive supplier in a particular area, usually for domestic and commercial consumers, while the distribution company undertakes to purchase exclusively from that gas supply company.

5.109 Neither back-to-back contracts nor long-term contracts with minimum guaranteed offtakes at a set price are illegal *per se* under EC law. Nevertheless, they might well be seen to restrict competition within the meaning of Article 81(1), and would therefore have to be notified, and either granted negative clearance or an exemption under Article 81(3), in order to establish their legitimacy. In fact few such contracts have been formally notified in the gas sector, although the Commission did consider the issue, albeit indirectly, in relation to the Distrigaz merger in 1993.

The Commission has addressed the legality of long-term supply contracts in the electricity sector in *Pêgo*[202] and in *Scottish Nuclear*.[203] Exclusive supply provisions have also been examined by the Commission in *Shotton*[204] and *Industrial Gases*.[205] In each of these cases the Commission eventually granted an exemption under Article 81(3). Nevertheless, it is difficult to distil any general rules from these precedents, especially, for example, with respect to more mature gas markets, where investments have long been depreciated and the parties have arguably recovered all their sunk costs. It remains to be seen whether such long-term contracts can be approved for security or continuity of supply reasons, either under Article 81(3) or eventually under Article 86(2). **5.110**

In the *Almelo* case[206] the ECJ held that the exclusive supply and purchase contracts concluded between the Dutch regional and local suppliers of electricity were contrary to both Articles 81 and 82 (ex Arts 85 and 86) and as they had not been notified, the position under Article 81(3) (ex Art 85(3)) was irrelevant. The ECJ did, however, consider that Article 86(2) (ex Art 90(2)) was applicable in principle, but left it to the national court to establish on the facts whether the exemption was necessary to allow the regional distributors to fulfil their public service obligations. While gas supply differs from electricity in certain respects—it can be stored and it can usually be substituted by other fuels, the distribution companies are still under public supply obligations to ensure reliable and cheap supplies to their customers. Whether this will legitimate long-term supply contracts that are often in the range of fifteen to twenty years, or other forms of requirements contracts, remains to be decided definitively by the ECJ. **5.111**

The Commission has had the opportunity to examine at least one agreement notified to it concerning a gas transportation contract: the Gas Interconnector Agreement.[207] This agreement related to a joint venture (JV) arrangement between nine gas companies for the construction and operation of a United Kingdom–Belgium sub-sea gas interconnection and it was cleared by a comfort letter in May 1995. The interconnector is the first pipeline link between the UK **5.112**

[202] OJ C 265/3 (1993).
[203] Comm Dec 91/329, OJ (1991) L 178/31.
[204] OJ C 106/3 (1990).
[205] European Commission, *XIXth Report on Competition Policy*.
[206] [1994] ECR I-1477.
[207] European Commission, *XXVth Report on Competition Policy*, 125–6.

and the Continental gas markets. It provides for a forward flow facility as well as a smaller reverse flow facility, ie from South to North, which could be gradually expanded upon further investment. The process leading up to the conclusion of the JV was seen to be open and transparent—all interested companies were invited to participate and there was no indication that any single company was excluded from the possibility of participating in the Interconnector by way of booking equity (shares to be funded) and/or transport capacity in the facility. All final JV participants in fact booked both. The project funding would be secured by take-or-pay contracts of twenty years' duration under which the tariffs would relate to the capacity booked by the participants under their respective transport agreements with the JV company, Interconnector UK Ltd.

5.113 The Commission regarded the project to be pro-competitive because: (a) it would open up competition in markets that had hitherto been isolated; and (b) there were sufficient possibilities for third parties to acquire, on freely negotiated terms, access to transport capacity on the Interconnector. Capacity holders will be free to provide the capacity to others by way of assignment or sublease. The length of the agreements was also considered to be justified in the circumstances of the case. Nevertheless, the Commission took the view that Article 81(1) (ex Art 85(1)) applied because certain provisions allow the JV company to market transport capacity, thereby leading to joint selling by the JV partners. Although such joint selling would only occur in limited circumstances this was not unimportant given that the parties to the JV would have 100 per cent of the relevant market for transport of piped gas across the Channel. The Commission was particularly keen to ensure that once demand for reverse flow capacity increased the JV arrangements would operate in such a way that this demand would be fully met.

5.114 This important notification illustrates the way in which the Commission takes a favourable view of agreements which lead to the opening up of the Community gas market, even if some elements of the agreement restrict competition and even if the agreements are of a long-term nature. It was obviously of key importance to the Commission that third parties could negotiate access at least by purchasing capacity rights from the parties to the JV. The Commission did not seem to require that access should be available *per se*. This seems a sensible compromise solution given that the financing of the scheme was dependent on the parties electing to book and use the full capacity of the pipeline. The Interconnector Agreement will obviously serve as a useful precedent to reassure those involved in long-term infrastructure projects that take-or-pay clauses, and arrangements leading to a full take-up of capacity, are acceptable to the Commission.

5.115 Regarding long-term contracts in the electricity sector, the Commission presented its views in 1999 in its second harmonization report on the Electricity Directive, which addressed the practice of long-term capacity reservations on cross-border interconnections.[208] Further guidance on Commission practices on adjustments to the duration of long-term contracts can be found in *European Night Services*,[209] where the Court of First Instance annulled a Commission decision by which it attempted to limit an agreement on rail services to a period of eight years. The Court reasoned that 'the length of time required to ensure a proper return on . . . investment is necessarily an essential factor to be taken into account when determining the duration of an exemption'.[210]

Essential facilities

Although the Electricity and Gas Directives require the Member States to take the necessary measures to organize access by third parties to electricity and natural gas networks,[211] certain access issues will continue to be subject to the Treaty competition rules. In this respect, should energy pipelines or transmission lines be deemed an 'essential facility', then third parties may have certain limited rights to demand access to those energy networks. These rights may be particularly relevant, for example, for parties seeking access to energy networks either not subject to EC legislation on network access, such as district heating or certain oil and gas production networks, or subject only to systems for negotiated access as opposed to regulated access. **5.116**

Much attention has been devoted in the literature on EC competition law to the development of the 'essential facility' doctrine—a concept borrowed originally from US antitrust law and transplanted to European soil, largely by the Commission. Following a series of Commission decisions, discussed below, the ECJ and the Court of First Instance have clarified the limits of the doctrine in more recent decisions such as *Bronner v Mediaprint*[212] and *European Night Services*.[213] In the 1998 *Bronner* decision, involving a refusal by the Austrian newspaper group Mediaprint to grant access to its delivery network, the ECJ made it clear that such a refusal could only be abusive if access to the distribution system in question were '*indispensable*' to carrying out the applicant's business. This ruling implies that a facility would not be deemed 'essential' unless there is no other way to enter the downstream market and it is impossible or unreasonably difficult **5.117**

[208] Second Report to the Council and the European Parliament on Harmonisation Requirements, SEC(99) 470.

[209] Joined Cases T-374/94, T-375/94, T-384/94, and T-388/94 *European Night Services v Commission* [1998] ECR II-3141.

[210] ibid, 229.

[211] For a discussion of the organization of system access under the Electricity and Gas Directives, see paras 5.267–5.273, 5.287–5.290 below.

[212] Case C-7/97 *Oscar Bronner v Mediaprint* [1998] ECR I-7791.

[213] Joined Cases T-374/94, T-375/94, T-384/94, and T-388/94 *European Night Services v Commission* [1998] ECR II-3141.

to replicate the facility in question. A different definition of the concept was provided in *European Night Services* by the Court of First Instance.[214]

5.118 The essential facilities concept was originally developed by American courts as a means of identifying refusals to deal by a monopolist who owns or controls a facility, access to which is essential for a potential competitor.[215] Its importance to network-bound energy sectors is immediately apparent, and indeed in the landmark 1973 *Otter Tail* case the US Supreme Court ruled that Otter Tail, an integrated electricity utility, was obliged to 'wheel' wholesale power supplied by another company to two municipalities which sought to engage in the retail distribution of power.[216]

5.119 Definitions of an 'essential facility' have varied. Ritter *et al.* have observed that the Commission has intervened in cases of arbitrary or discriminatory refusal of access:

> —if the third party depends on the use of the infrastructure or facilities for supplying his customers and building his own infrastructure is not a reasonable alternative;
> —if the third party satisfies objectively justified criteria for admission;
> —if the capacity of the infrastructure is adequate to carry the additional traffic, having due regard to space and capacity restraints and to the . . . operator's own requirements to provide supplies during periods of peak demand and its other long-term commitments, without recognising, however, any 'grandfathered' or 'historical' rights;
> —if the traffic for which a licence to use the infrastructure is sought satisfies the relevant technical standards . . .;
> —if the party seeking access is prepared to pay the operator adequate compensation; and
> —if the request is reasonable—which involves balancing the interests of the operator, security of supply and the public interest in competition and free trade in goods and services within the Common Market . . .[217]

5.120 In general, these or similar criteria are used by courts or other enforcement bodies to determine whether an obligation should be imposed on a 'dominant' firm to share its assets with competitors in order to enable them to compete.

---

[214] ibid, paras 208–9 (ruling that 'a product or service cannot be considered necessary or essential unless there is no real or potential substitute', and further that infrastructure, products, or services may be regarded as 'necessary' or 'essential' for entry to the relevant market only if they are not 'interchangeable' and if 'by reason of their special characteristics—in particular the prohibitive cost of and/or time reasonably required for reproducing them—there are no viable alternatives available to potential competitors of the [undertaking holding the essential facility], which are thereby excluded from the market').

[215] For an interpretation of the US essential facilities doctrine before the ECJ, see the opinion of Advocate General Jacobs in the *Bronner* case, Case-7/97 [1998] ECR I-7791, para 47 and cases and materials cited therein.

[216] See L Hancher and P Trepte, 13 Eur. Comp. LR 149–60 (1992); R Lock, 2 Util. L. Rev. 18 (1991).

[217] L Ritter, W Braun, and F Rawlinson, *European Competition Law: a Practitioner's Guide* (2nd edn, 2000) 383 (footnotes omitted).

The use of Articles 81 and especially 82 of the EC Treaty to require the owner/operator of an infrastructure facility to grant access to third parties or competitors became apparent in a series of at least six Commission decisions. A review of these cases shows the potential reach of the doctrine to the energy sector. **5.121**

In the case of *Sabena*[218] the Commission held that the Belgian airline Sabena had abused its dominant position in the market for the supply of computerized flight reservation services in Belgium. It refused the air carrier London European access to the Sabena-managed Saphir reservation system for the Brussels–Luton route. The Commission based its decision on the assessment that Sabena's computerized reservation system was an essential facility in the Belgian market: access to the Saphir system was essential for any company wishing to compete with companies active on the Brussels–Luton route (paragraph 14). **5.122**

In *Aer Lingus*[219] the Commission held that the Irish airline Aer Lingus had abused its dominant position by refusing to interline with the airline British Midland. The Commission pointed out that both the refusal to grant new interline facilities and the withdrawal of existing interline facilities might hinder the maintenance or development of competition. **5.123**

In its *Sealink* (*'Holyhead I'*) decision[220] the Commission reasoned that Article 82 (ex Art 86) was infringed where a dominant undertaking which both owned or controlled and used an essential facility, ie a facility or infrastructure without access to which competitors could not provide services to their customers, placed its competitors at a competitive disadvantage by refusing them access to that facility or granting them access only on less favourable terms than those which it gave to its own services. **5.124**

The Commission relied upon the *ERT* judgment[221] in which the ECJ had made it clear that Article 82 (ex Art 86) prohibited an undertaking which was dominant in one market from discriminating in its favour in a related market. The Commission considered the harbour operator SHL and the ferry operator SSL to be a single economic entity and the markets on which they operated to be related. Against this background, it held that the owner of an essential facility who used his power in one market in order to strengthen his position in a related market, in particular by granting his competitor access to that related market on less favourable terms than those of his own services, infringed Article 82 (ex Article 86) where a competitive disadvantage was imposed upon his competitor without objective justification. **5.125**

---

218 OJ (1988) L 317/47.
219 OJ (1992) L 96/34.
220 [1992] 5 CMLR 255.
221 Case C-260/89 *ERT v DEP* [1991] ECR I-2925, para 37.

5.126 In its *Sealink 'Holyhead II'* decision[222] the Commission considered a request for interim measures as part of a complaint by the marine cargo carrier Sea Containers Ltd (SC). It alleged that Stena Sealink Ports (SSP), which as SHL's successor owned and operated the port of Holyhead, had infringed Article 82 (ex Art 86) by denying SC access to the port which was essential for SC's plans to provide a fast ferry service through the central corridor between the United Kingdom and Ireland. The Commission recalled *Holyhead I* and added that these principles also applied when the competitor seeking access to the essential facility was a new entrant into the relevant market.

5.127 In the *Rødby* decision[223] the Commission ordered the Member State Denmark to bring to an end its infringement of Article 86(1) (ex Art 90(1)) in conjunction with Article 82 (ex Art 86). This infraction was committed, first, by the Danish Transport Minister's refusal to allow the shipping company Euro-Port A/S to build a private commercial port in the immediate vicinity of the port of Rødby, and secondly, by the same Minister's refusal to allow the same company to operate from the existing public port of Rødby. In particular, the Commission pointed out (in paras 15–16) that there were no technical obstacles for the applicant companies' access to the port and that the argument of market saturation was invalid because even in such a situation competition could result in advantages for consumers such as an improvement in the quality of products or services offered or a reduction in prices.

5.128 Finally, in the *Port of Roscoff* case the Irish Continental Group (ICG) had applied to CCI Morlaix, the operator of the port, for access to the Port of Roscoff for the purpose of commencing a ferry service between Ireland and Brittany, France. Negotiations between the parties broke down, and ICG complained to the Commission, which in turn concluded that the behaviour of CCI Morlaix constituted an unjustified refusal of supply and that the port in question was the only one capable of providing adequate facilities for ferry services between Brittany and Ireland. By way of interim measures it obliged CCI Morlaix to allow ICG access for the summer season, pending a final Commission decision. In its 25th Report on Competition Policy, the Commission noted that interim measures are not justified merely to allow a new entrant into the market. The Commission considered that the Irish ferry operator had been led to believe that it could begin operations and that CCI Morlaix was largely responsible for the situation which developed as a result.[224]

[222] OJ (1994) L 15/8.
[223] OJ (1994) L 55/52.
[224] European Commission, XXVth Report on Competition Policy, 121.

Article 82 (ex Art 86) was also interpreted in the *Magill*[225] case, concerning an appeal brought by the Irish television station, RTE, and an independent television publications company (ITP) which published television programme schedules, against a ruling of the Court of First Instance made in 1991. The latter court had upheld a Commission decision[226] that the Irish television companies together with the BBC were in breach of Article 82 (ex Art 86) because they had refused to supply the schedules to a small independent publisher. In their defence, the broadcasters claimed that the material was their property and, at the material time, was protected under copyright legislation. **5.129**

The ECJ found that in such a situation as existed in relation to *Magill*, the television companies enjoyed a *de facto* monopoly over the information used to compile listings for television programmes. The refusal to grant a licence to reproduce the copyrighted material forms part of the author's rights, and cannot in itself constitute abuse of a dominant position. Nevertheless, in exceptional circumstances that refusal could constitute abusive conduct (para 50). The Court found that such exceptional circumstances pertained in this case: the appellants were the only source of information and their refusal to supply it to Magill prevented the appearance of a new product, which the appellants did not offer, and for which there was an evident consumer demand. The ECJ did not accept that there was any justification for this refusal (paras 54–5). Finally, by refusing to grant access to the raw material indispensable for the compilation of the weekly guide, the appellants were in fact reserving to themselves a secondary market by excluding all competition on that market. A further interpretation of *Magill* was subsequently made by the ECJ in its 1998 *Bronner* decision.[227] **5.130**

Until recently, the Commission has had little to say about the terms and conditions of access to those facilities which it has deemed—implicitly or explicitly—to be essential. It has been left to the parties to negotiate a sensible solution. The Commission decision in *Eurotunnel* (OJ 1994 L 354/66) seems to go further, however, and has provoked controversy. Although the Commission granted an exemption in respect of the agreement between the Eurotunnel operating companies and the British and French railway companies, it also imposed certain conditions designed to ensure access on favourable conditions and at peak hours to the facility by other railway undertakings. This decision was quashed by the Court of First Instance in Joined Cases T79/95 and T80/95 *SNCF* and *BR v Commission*.[227a] The Court found that the Commission had not properly **5.131**

[225] Joined Cases C-241/91P and C-242/91P *Radio Telefis Eireann (RTE) and Independent Television Publications v Commission* [1995] ECR I-743.

[226] Commission Decision 89/205/EEC relating to a procedure under Art 86 of the EEC Treaty (IV/31.851– Magill, TV Guide/ITP, BBC, and PTE, OJ 1989 L 78/43).

[227] *Bronner* [1998] ECR I-7791, paras 40–1.

[227a] [1996] ECR II-1491.

understood the relevant terms of the contract between Eurotunnel and the two railway undertakings and had therefore misapplied both Articles 81(1) and 81(3) (ex Arts 85(1) and 85(3)).

5.132 The price of access is also not usually addressed. Indeed, the Commission has traditionally stressed its reluctance to become involved in regulating pricing or tariff issues, except where, as in the *Zaventem*[228] and *HOV* decisions,[229] clear discrimination against competitors can be substantiated.[230]

5.133 Whether the conduct condemned under Article 82 as a prima facie abuse is either anti-competitive or exploitative, it will still be possible for the dominant firm to legitimize its conduct through objective justifications. In this respect it may well be important to consider whether a firm can rely on a defence based on 'business justification' or 'competition on the basis of performance' or whether the concept of objective justification is rather a special defence based on the general principles of Community law.

Cross-subsidization

5.134 Cross-subsidization is a complex subject. It can generally be identified as occurring when an undertaking supports one of its activities or a segment of activity at the expense of another.[231] The Commission has produced several definitions of the concept,[232] most recently in its Notice on the application of the competition rules to the postal sector.[233]

5.135 The Commission's Notices on the application of the competition rules to the postal sector (1997) and to telecommunications (1991) indicate that unfair cross-subsidization could result when profits are diverted from reserved markets (markets protected by exclusive rights or other special rights) to markets under competition, or when costs are unfairly allocated in such a way that the reserved

---

228 OJ (1995) L 216/8.

229 European Commission, XXIIIrd Report on Competition Policy.

230 The Electricity and Gas Directives do not offer much guidance on access pricing either, beyond recalling that the transmission system operators can refuse access if there is no capacity on the system or if this would interfere with the performance of their public service obligations. The Gas Directive suggests that if the operator lacks capacity and the new entrant is willing to pay for capacity expansion, then the necessary enhancements may be required. Similar provisions were deleted from earlier drafts of the Electricity measure.

231 See G Abbamonte, 'Cross-subsidisation and Community Competition Rules: Efficient Pricing v Equity?', vol 23, No 5, Eur. LR 414–33, 414 (1998); L Hancher and J Bundia Sierra, 'Cross-subsidization and EC Law', vol 35, CMLR 901–45 (1998).

232 See Communication on the Application of the Competition Rules to Telecommunications, OJ 1991 C 233/2; Communication on the Application of Arts 92 and 93 EC and Art 5 of Commission Directive 80/723/EEC to Public Undertakings in the Manufacturing Sector, OJ 1993 C 307/3.

233 OJ 1998 C 39/2, para 3.1 ('Cross-subsidisation means that an undertaking bears or allocates all or part of the costs of its activity in one geographical or product market to its activity in another geographical or product market.').

market is bearing most of the joint or common costs. Although the directives on the internal market for electricity and for gas require separation of accounts, neither directive prescribes any particular method for allocating such costs.

Cross-subsidization from reserved to competitive markets could fall within the framework of the Treaty rules on State aid if all the tests of Article 87 (ex Art 92) are met, and in particular if the cross-subsidization is funded either directly or indirectly from State resources.[234] Examples are a direct subsidy or grant or a tax reduction for the benefit of a particular undertaking. Thus, a tax reduction intended to compensate public service obligations imposed under French law on the French Post Office had to be examined under the State aid rules, as had the allegation by a competitor that the proceeds from the tax reduction were also being used to benefit the French Post Office's competitive activities. The Court of First Instance and the ECJ both ruled that the State aid in question could be justified under Article 86(2) (ex Art 90(2)) as long as the aid in question was below the costs of the public service obligations resulting from the monopoly activities.[235] **5.136**

Furthermore, where a State-owned company cross-subsidizes a subsidiary, the provision of resources can be seen as a form of aid. In Case C-39/94 *SFEI v La Poste*,[236] the ECJ held that the provision of logistical and commercial assistance by a public undertaking to its subsidiaries, which are governed by private law and carry on an activity open to free competition, is capable of constituting State aid if the remuneration received in return is less than that which would have been demanded under normal market conditions. The concept of aid within the meaning of Article 87 of the Treaty encompasses not only positive benefits, such as subsidies, but also interventions which, in various forms, mitigate the charges normally included in the budget of an undertaking and which, without therefore being subsidies in the strict sense of the word, are of the same character and have the same effect.[237] **5.137**

The Commission subsequently adopted a decision in October 1998 confirming that no aid was involved. Following the ECJ's ruling in the *La Poste* decision, the Commission considered the application of the market economy investor principle[238] to the alleged cross-subsidization practices of the French Post Office to its subsidiary, Chronopost. In a long and complex decision, the Commission applied a modified version of the market-investor test in order to determine whether aid **5.138**

---

234 See para 5.85 above.

235 Case T-106/95 *FFSA v Commission* [1997] ECR II-229; Case T-95/94 *Sytraval and Brink's France v Commission* [1995] ECR II-2651; Case C-367/95P *Commission v Sytraval and Brink's France* [1998] ECR I-1719.

236 [1996] ECR I-3947.

237 Hancher and Bundia Sierra, above n 231, 930.

238 See generally G Abbamonte, 'The Market Economy Investor Principle: A Legal Analysis of an Economic Problem', 4 ECLR 258–68 (1996).

was involved.[239] It rejected the argument of the competing private courier firms that: (i) Chronopost should have been apportioned the full costs of setting up an equivalent infrastructure to that operated by La Poste, and (ii) strategic considerations and other synergies should not be taken into consideration where the incumbent firm enjoys a legal monopoly over the reserved market. The Commission held that the correct test was to determine whether the transactions between La Poste and Chronopost were similar to those which would occur in a private group of undertakings, where, for example, one of the group enjoyed a monopoly as a result of exclusive rights. In this respect it had to be borne in mind that such intra-group transactions would not be based on 'arm's length' market prices. The Commission therefore concluded that prices for goods and services exchanged within the same group would be free from any subsidy element if the prices were calculated on the basis of total costs involved, plus a return on capital. In fact, the prices charged to Chronopost covered only variable costs, not all of its total fixed costs, at least in the first two years of its existence. The Commission found that this would be normal practice for a new commercial activity during the start-up phase. As it transpired that the company subsequently covered all its costs, the logistical and commercial support to Chronopost was ruled to have been provided on normal market conditions. No element of aid was involved.[240]

5.139 This decision recognizes that any cost-based test under Article 87 (ex Art 92) should not automatically be the same as under Article 82 (ex Art 86). But by allowing prices to be set, albeit for a limited period at a level which covers average variable costs only, the Commission has in effect endorsed a practice of allocating a large proportion of common fixed costs to a reserved market as a normal market practice. Thus, State-owned or controlled companies in the energy field which misallocate costs so that their prices in competitive markets (eg by loading common costs on reserved, domestic markets) are kept artificially low for a substantial period of time could well be subject to the rules on State aid.

5.140 Where companies are neither State-owned or controlled nor benefit indirectly or directly from State resources, but the prices they charge for competitive goods and services are kept artificially low, then the only EC Treaty rule which might apply is Article 82 (ex Art 86). Again, assuming that the company in question is dominant in its relevant market, for example because it holds an exclusive right to supply domestic customers, such pricing policies may well amount to abuse if they are (i) predatory or (ii) discriminatory. The company could be seen to be abusing its position on a dominant market (eg the reserved market) by charging artificially low or discriminatory prices on an ancillary, competitive market (eg for eligible consumers who can choose their suppliers). The tests of predation and discrimi-

[239] Commission Decision of 9 Oct 1997.

[240] Hancher and Bundia Sierra, above n 231, 936–7.

nation are both highly complex and the jurisprudence of the European courts is by no means clear-cut on either practice, however.

The general rule is that prices charged by a dominant firm which do not cover its average variable costs are presumed to be predatory.[241] Prices that cover the latter costs but are below average total costs may be predatory if the Commission or a complainant can establish a predatory intent to drive a competitor out of the market.[242] However, in a number of its recent Notices on the application of the competition rules to regulated sectors such as post and telecommunications, the Commission appears to deviate from the standard predation test. It argues that where prices are less than average total costs and are part of an anticompetitive plan, this may be sufficient proof of predation.[243] **5.141**

Price discrimination, that is, charging different prices or tariffs to customers with the same or similar demand characteristics, can also be condemned under Article 82 (ex Art 86), if it can be established that such prices cannot be objectively justified. Price differentiation is not problematic, however. Article 82(c) (ex Art 86(c)) has traditionally been concerned with distortions of competition between customers, and so selective price discrimination has rarely been condemned unless it has been linked with some other abusive practice. Further, charging different prices to one's own subsidiary has not traditionally been seen as discriminatory. In the 1997 case of *Deutsche Bahn*[244] the Court of First Instance appears to have upheld the Commission's decision applying Article 82(c) (ex Art 86(c)) in a situation where in fact different prices were charged to independent parties as compared to the (lower) prices charged to a subsidiary. **5.142**

Indirect taxation

The use of tax instruments in the energy sector gives rise to complex legal issues under EC law. Customs duties and excise duties, as well as discriminatory forms or rates of indirect taxation that put imports at a disadvantage, can form one of the most obvious barriers to free movement. Differences in the indirect tax regimes also give rise to distortions of competition because these will lead to distortions in the final price charged for particular forms of energy. Nevertheless, some forms of fiscal instruments may be required to provide an incentive to use certain environmentally friendly fuels or processes as opposed to more polluting ones. **5.143**

Community law seeks to deal with the elimination of these barriers and distortions through the application of the Treaty primary rules set forth in Articles **5.144**

[241] See Case C-62/86 *Akzo Chemie v Commission* [1991] ECR I-3439, para 71.
[242] ibid, para 72.
[243] See OJ 1998 C 265/18, at para 110 *et seq.*
[244] Case T-229/94 *Deutsche Bahn v Commission* [1997] ECR II-1689.

23–24 and Article 90 (ex Arts 10–17 and Art 95) as well as through harmonization measures adopted under Article 93 (ex Art 99) and other EC secondary legislation. With respect to EC legislation, however, the progress seems to be slow, as a series of Commission proposals on taxation of energy products has not yet been accepted by the Council. For example, since 1991 the Commission made various unsuccessful attempts to introduce a carbon dioxide tax.[245] These proposals were not only aimed at the harmonization of taxation, but were also part of an overall strategy for stabilizing carbon dioxide emissions in the Community at 1990 levels by the year 2000.[246] In 1997 the Commission made another proposal designed to introduce a new system of taxation for all energy products. [247]

5.145 At the same time, there seems to be a general dissatisfaction with the current overall policies for energy and environmental taxes applying to the energy sector in the EU, both within the Commission and among external observers.[248] As noted in the Commission's Report on the harmonization of the laws of the Member States relating to turnover taxes:

> In the Commission's opinion the current arrangements . . . are difficult to operate and do not provide for a coherent approach, whether from a social, environmental or fiscal point of view. Their revision should therefore be addressed in the context of the common system of VAT while following in the first instance the general lines adhered to for that exercise.[249]

5.146 Excise duties on mineral oils and petroleum products have been subject to some limited harmonization. However, in its White Paper on an Energy Policy, the Commission noted:

> Excise duties on mineral oils, which are a major source of government revenue, vary significantly between Member States. Comparable excise duties have not been introduced for other energy products, at a Community level, and the Commission will analyse whether it is necessary to extend the excise duties on mineral oils to cover competing energy products.[250]

---

[245] See Proposal for a Council Directive introducing a tax on carbon dioxide emissions and energy, OJ C 196/01 (1992); Amended proposal for a Council Directive introducing a tax on carbon dioxide and emissions, COM(95) 172 final; see also M Düerkop, 'Trade and Environment: International trade law aspects of the proposed EC Directive introducing a tax on carbon dioxide emissions and energy', vol 31, no 4, CMLR (1994).

[246] For policy aspects of the carbon dioxide tax, see J Matláry, *Energy Policy in the European Union* (1997) 68–71.

[247] Proposal for a Council Directive restructuring the Community framework for the taxation on energy products, COM(97) 30 final.

[248] See eg K Deketelaere, 'European Environmental Tax Policy: Proposal for a Policy Vision and a Legal Framework' [1996] Eur. Env. LR 9–15.

[249] European Commission, Report on the harmonisation of the laws of the Member States relating to turn-over taxes—Common system of value added tax: uniform basis of assessment, COM(97) 559 final, 22.

[250] European Commission, White Paper on an Energy Policy for the European Union, COM(95) 682 final, 18.

The Commission also observed: 5.147

> The difference between minimum rates and real rates set by governments is now so big, notably in respect of motor fuels, that any adjustment of the minimum rates in order to influence the market and improve convergence of excise duties will have to be of substantial nature. Seen from an energy viewpoint, the removal of distortions resulting from a lack of approximation of Member States' effective rates, particularly on motor fuels, will have to be taken into account when considering a future fiscal structure on energy products.[251]

In the absence of Community legislation, barriers and distortions arising from the various national taxation schemes are considered under the primary Treaty rules, such as Articles 23–24 (ex Arts 9–10) and Article 90 (ex Art 95). Articles 23 and 24 establish the Community's customs union and prohibit (between Member States) customs duties on imports and exports and all charges having equivalent effect.[252] But these Articles would have little effect in practice if a Member State could still put imported goods at a disadvantage even after they have crossed the frontier or border, for example by subjecting them to discriminatory taxation. The aim of Article 90 (ex Art 95) is to prevent this from happening.[253] In other words, it aims to guarantee complete neutrality between products, irrespective of their origin. 5.148

It is important to stress that these two sets of Articles are mutually exclusive. They both deal with the imposition of a fiscal levy by the State. Articles 23–24 (customs duties and charges with equivalent effect) only apply if those duties or charges are levied by the reason of the goods crossing a border, are levied at the time of or because of importation, and are levied exclusively on imported products. Article 90 will apply where the charge in question forms part of a general system of internal taxation.[254] 5.149

The difference between the two sets of provisions is best represented by the case-law on parafiscal levies, special levies imposed on certain goods the proceeds of which are used to subsidize or otherwise support domestic goods. If the levy in question is imposed on domestic and imported goods alike it will have to be dealt with under Article 90. If the levy on the domestic goods is reimbursed in full to domestic producers, or if the support or other finance is exclusively provided for domestic products, then it will be dealt with under Articles 23–24. However, if 5.150

[251] ibid, para 62.

[252] The ECJ has interpreted this prohibition expansively. See Case 24/68 *Commission v Italy* [1969] ECR 193.

[253] Art 90 (ex Art 95) provides: 'No Member State shall impose, directly or indirectly, on the products of other Member States any internal taxation of any kind in excess of that imposed directly or indirectly on similar domestic products. Furthermore, no Member State shall impose on the products of other Member States any internal taxation of such a nature as to afford indirect protection to other products.'

[254] Case C-90/94 *Haahr Petroleum Ltd v Åbenrå Havn and Others* [1997] ECR 1-4085, para 19.

the importers also receive some share of the support, the system would be dealt with under Article 90.

5.151 The ECJ considered the compatibility of a special parafiscal charge on petroleum products levied in favour of the French Energy Saving Agency in Cases C-78–83/90, *Compagnie Commerciale de l'Ouest v Receveur Principal des Douanes de la Pallice.*[255] In this instance the ECJ had to deal with a question regarding parafiscal charges levied upon the release for consumption of certain petroleum products, which applied without distinction to domestic and imported products and was intended for the benefit of a public body, the Energy Saving Agency, which had to use its funds to finance measures to encourage energy savings and the rational use of inadequately exploited energy sources. The independent importers and distributors argued that their position was different from that of French refiners, as far as imports were concerned, and despite the fact that the contested charges were applied without distinction to all the products concerned, imported products were the only ones affected. In its ruling, the ECJ made clear the boundary between the relevant Articles:

> A parafiscal charge applied under the same conditions as regards its collection to both domestic and imported products, the revenue from which is used for the benefit of domestic products only, so that the advantages accruing from it *fully* offset the charge borne by those products, constitutes a charge having an effect equivalent to customs duties prohibited by [Article 23 (ex Article 12)] of the EEC Treaty. If, on the other hand, those advantages *only partly* offset the charge borne by domestic products, the charge in question constitutes discriminatory taxation prohibited by [Article 90 (ex Article 95)] of the Treaty. Such a parafiscal charge, being governed by [Article 23 (ex Article 12)] *et seq.* or [Article 90 (ex Article 95)] of the Treaty, is not governed by [Article 28 (ex Article 30)] thereof.

5.152 The principles set out in Articles 23–24 and Article 90 are of particular importance in the energy sector, especially in regard to assessing the legality of various national fiscal measures designed to promote environmental policy goals. This is well illustrated by the 1998 case of *Outokumpu Oy,*[256] involving a Finnish excise duty levied on certain sources of energy including electricity. Persons producing electricity in Finland by nuclear or water power or who receive electricity from the Community or import it from outside the Community were liable to pay the duty. Imported electricity was subject to a flat rate of duty calculated to correspond with the average rate levied on electricity produced in Finland. However, domestic levies were further adjusted to allow for reductions if the electricity was produced from peat or natural gas.

5.153 A Finnish company imported electricity from Sweden and was charged the flat rate of excise duty on those imports. The Finnish importer challenged the legality

[255] [1992] ECR I-1847.
[256] Case C-213/96 [1998] ECR I-1777.

of the levy and claimed that it was a charge having equivalent effect to a customs duty or alternatively that it was a discriminatory duty within the meaning of Article 90 (ex Art 95).

In addressing this legal issue, the ECJ noted first that the excise duty at issue was part of a general system of taxation and not a customs duty. The fact that the duty was payable on importation did not provide a sufficient basis for the conclusion that it was a customs duty. **5.154**

However, the Finnish importer observed that, according to the case-law, in order to form part of a general system of internal taxes, the charges imposed on imported products must be imposed on domestic products and imported products at the same marketing stage, and the chargeable event must be identical for both classes of products. **5.155**

The ECJ ruled that no difference arose from the fact that imported electricity is taxed at the time of importation and electricity of domestic origin at the time of production, since in view of the characteristics of electricity, the marketing stage is the same for both operations, ie when the electricity enters the national distribution network. **5.156**

The Finnish company also argued that the duty was not imposed on imported and domestic products according to the same criteria and without reference to their origin. The duty was levied on electricity of domestic origin at different rates depending on whether it was produced by nuclear or water power, whereas imported electricity was taxed as an end product exclusively, at a flat rate, irrespective of the method of production. **5.157**

The ECJ ruled that the fact that the origin of the goods determines the amount of duty cannot remove it from the scope of Article 90 (ex Art 95). Consequently the duty of the type at issue was found to be internal taxation within the meaning of Article 90 (ex Art 95) and not a charge having equivalent effect to a customs duty within the meaning of Articles 23–24 (ex Arts 9 and 12). The ECJ then considered whether Article 90 (ex Art 95) restricted the freedom of Member States to apply a different rate of tax to electricity depending on how it was produced. It confirmed that Member States were free to establish a tax system which differentiates between products on the basis of objective criteria. Such differentiation is compatible with Community law only if it pursues objectives which are themselves compatible with the requirements of the Treaty, such as environmental objectives. **5.158**

The ECJ went on to consider whether the differentiation at issue was compatible with the prohibition on discrimination in Article 90 (ex Art 95). The imported electricity was subject to a flat-rate duty, whatever its method of production, which was higher than the lowest duty charged on electricity of domestic origin. The ECJ refused to accept the Finnish government's argument that the origin and **5.159** method of production of imported electricity could not be determined once it had entered the distribution network so that the differential rates applicable to electricity of domestic origin could not be applied to imported electricity. Practical difficulties cannot justify the application of discriminatory internal taxation systems. The Finnish legislation did not even give the importer the opportunity of demonstrating that the electricity imported by him was produced by a particular method in order to qualify for the rate applicable to electricity of domestic origin by the same method. The ECJ therefore ruled that Article 95 precluded a national tax which imposed a flat rate of tax on imported products but allowed variations on domestic production depending on the method of its production.

5.160 In summary, Articles 23–24 and Article 90 are of considerable importance in the energy sector, in particular with regard to parafiscal taxes and their legality and to environmental taxes. Customs duties and charges of equivalent effect are illegal *per se*, whatever their effect and purpose, as an absolute prohibition. Article 90(1) allows more scope for national measures provided these are not discriminatory. The dividing or border line between these two sets of provisions is not always easy to determine, but as the 1998 Finnish electricity case illustrates, this is an important aspect of determining the legality of a particular measure.

(5) Harmonization

5.161 The harmonization (or approximation) of law is an activity provided for in the various subject matters covered by the Treaty,[257] and it should also be seen as complementary to the general prohibitive articles of the Treaty. In general, the need for harmonization arises from the fact that the diverse legal requirements and technical standards applicable within the Member States can impede the proper functioning of the Common Market.

5.162 The entry into force of the Single European Act in 1987 had a significant impact on the rules on harmonization of law. Prior to this Act, Article 100 (now Art 95) was the normal starting point for harmonization efforts. For specific matters, specific Treaty provisions such as Articles 43 and 99 (now Arts 37 and 93) would apply. In case of uncertainty or a dispute a combined legal basis would be used. Article 235 (now Art 308) was used for matters not specifically covered in the Treaty, such as those concerning the environment.

5.163 The Single European Act introduced three important new elements to the harmonization of law. The first was Articles 100A and 100B (now Art 95), which were drafted with a view to significantly expediting the completion of the internal

[257] See eg Art 3(h) (listing approximation of the laws of the Member States as an activity of the Community).

market.[258] The second was the title on environment, which provides for a policy to be carried out largely through the enactment of Community legislation.[259] The third was Article 118A (now Art 138), which provides the Community with the power to introduce measures in the field of labour conditions. One of the results of the Single European Act was to bring the question of the proper legal basis for Community legislation to the fore.[260]

Harmonization methods

Different methods of harmonization have been developed to address the different areas of legislation. Distinctions have been made, for example, between total harmonization, optional harmonization, partial harmonization, minimum harmonization, and alternative harmonization.[261] In some cases a single directive uses different methods of harmonization.[262] **5.164**

Total harmonization

Total harmonization occurs when a directive provides for no derogation, except for the safeguard measures. In such a case the system of the directive is determinative. Total harmonization was the preferred method in the early days of the Community's harmonization programme, when it was still uncertain whether and to what extent directives could provide for specific and detailed provisions eliminating the technical barriers to trade. Until the end of 1974, for example, thirty out of a total of seventy Acts involving harmonization of laws embodied total harmonization.[263] Subsequently, total harmonization has been restricted to the harmonization of product standards in cases where Article 100 is used as the legal basis.[264] The difficulty with total harmonization is that it provides Member States with insufficient flexibility and insufficient powers to regulate at the national level.[265] **5.165**

---

[258] See P Kapteyn and P VerLoren van Themaat, *Introduction to the Law of the European Communities* (3rd edn, 1998) 779–83; Case C-350/92 *Spain v Council* [1995] ECR I-1985. But cf R Scholz and S Langer, *Europäischer Binnenmarkt und Energiepolitik* (1992) 299, 156ff. The limits of Art 95 (ex Art 100A) are those of the other Treaty provisions such as Arts 5 and 167 (ex Arts 3B and 223) and the constituent elements of the concept of the internal market.

[259] See eg R Lane, 'New Community Competencies under the Maastricht Treaty', 30 CMLR 967 (1993); LJ Krämer, 'Environmental protection and Article 30 EEC Treaty', 30 CMLR 111 (1994).

[260] See R Barents, 'The internal market unlimited: Some observations on the legal basis of Community legislation', 30 CMLR 85 (1993); X Debroux, 'La choix de la base juridique dans l'action environmentale de L'Union europeénne', CDE 1995, 383ff.

[261] See P Slot, 'Harmonisation', vol 21, No 5, Eur. LR 378–97 (1996).

[262] See eg OJ 1980 L 229/11. Further examples in P Slot, *Technical and administrative obstacles to trade in the EEC* (1975).

[263] ibid.

[264] See HG Sevenster, *Milieubeleid en Gemeenschapsrecht: het interne juridische kader en de praktijk* (1992) 65; R Lauwaars and J Maarleveld, *Harmonisatie van wetgeving in Europesa Organisaties* ch 4 (1987); C Twitchett (ed), *Harmonisation in the EEC* (1981).

[265] A Mattera, *Le Marché Unique Europeén* (1990) 180–1.

Optional harmonization

5.166 Optional harmonization is present whenever a directive provides a producer of goods with the option to follow either the harmonized or the national rules. Goods traded across the borders of Member States, however, will have to meet the harmonized standards or the standards of the country of destination. Some directives leave the option to the Member States, such as Directive 74/63/EEC.[266] Optional harmonization was the favourite method in the early 1970s after the Commission received too many objections to its total harmonization programme. Subsequently, the method has been used for the harmonization of product standards on the basis of Article 94 (ex Art 100).[267]

Partial harmonization

5.167 In this case the harmonized rule applies only to cross-border transactions. As in optional harmonization, two sets of rules are present: one for intra-Community trade and one for domestic trade. The method of partial harmonization is rarely used because Community standards are usually sought for more than trans-border movements.[268]

Minimum harmonization

5.168 Minimum harmonization is used to establish rules at the Community level, while allowing Member States to provide more stringent rules at the national level. This method of harmonization has become more prevalent as the Community has expanded its regulatory activities beyond the elimination of trade barriers to areas such as environmental and consumer protection. It became apparent that common action could only be achieved if the aspirations were pitched at a level acceptable to all Member States. It became particularly important after the adoption of the Single European Act, which included a new title on the protection of the environment. Many harmonization Acts now use minimum harmonization.[269] This method received a further boost with the adoption of a new title on consumer protection in the Maastricht Treaty.

5.169 The very nature of minimum harmonization, which allows for upward flexibility at the national level, raises interesting questions about equal competitive conditions for both the producers of imported and nationally produced goods. Minimum harmonization may lead to unequal conditions of competition or, in other words, to reverse discrimination. Whether Member States will actually

---

[266] OJ 1974 L 38/31, Art 3, para 2.

[267] See Sevenster, n 264 above; see also J Curall, 'Some Aspects of the Relation between Articles 30–36 and Article 100 of the EEC Treaty with a closer look at optional harmonisation', YEL, 1984, 169ff.

[268] See Council Directives 79/7, OJ 1979 L 6/24 and 86/378, OJ 1986 L 225/40 on equal treatment.

[269] Sevenster, n 264 above.

exercise the option to enact more stringent rules will depend on the national policy priorities and the characteristics of the national industries. Thus countries with a strong priority for the protection of the environment and an important national industry may find it politically feasible to enact higher standards. The problems associated with higher national standards tend to diminish as market integration proceeds.

An interesting question is whether national higher standards can be applied to imported products. As demonstrated in the *Gallaher*[270] judgment, this is not allowed if and when the directive provides that products conforming to the minimum standard of the directive have to be accepted. However, if such a clause is absent, then the application of the national measure setting higher standards on imported products must be assessed according to the principles of Article 36. This interpretation seems to be confirmed by principles expressed in the provisions of Articles 95(4) and 176 (ex Arts 100A(4) and 130T). **5.170**

Alternative harmonization

Some directives provide for alternative methods of harmonization to achieve the objectives pursued. Such directives allow Member States to choose between alternatives. One example is Council Directive 76/464/EEC of 4 May 1976 on pollution caused by certain dangerous substances discharged into the aquatic environment of the Community.[271] Another example is Directive 89/428/EEC on the reduction and eventual elimination of pollution caused by waste from the titanium dioxide industry,[272] which provides in Article 8 for the possibility to opt for qualitative objectives rather than emission standards. **5.171**

The 'new approach' to harmonization: setting technical standards

In the early 1980s the Commission came to the conclusion that efforts to achieve harmonization of technical standards within the Community were not producing satisfactory results. One of the solutions offered to deal with this problem was to make greater use of the standards, codes, and technical norms established by the relevant normalization institutions and organizations, such as the CEN and CENELEC, as well as other European and worldwide organizations.[273] Along these lines, a 'new approach' to technical harmonization was adopted by the **5.172**

[270] Case C-11/92 *R v Secretary of State for Health, ex parte Gallaher Ltd* [1994] 3 CMLR 179, with an annotation in 31 CMLRev 165 (1994).

[271] OJ 1976 L 129/23.

[272] OJ 1989 L 201/56.

[273] The principal European standards organizations are the Comité Européen de Normalisation (CEN), the Comité Européen de Normalisation Electrotechnique (CENELEC), and the European Telecommunications Standards Institute (ETSI).

Council in a Resolution of 7 May 1985,[274] which provided a framework for the issuance of new directives based on the following four principles:

—legislative harmonization is limited to the adoption of essential safety requirements;
—safety standards are to be based on technical specifications of the European standardization organizations;
—technical specifications are not obligatory but may be adhered to voluntarily; and
—national authorities are obliged to recognize that products manufactured in accordance with harmonized standards are presumed to conform to the 'essential requirements' established by the directives.

5.173 Hence, numerous directives have been issued on the basis of the new approach, including an important series of energy labelling directives,[275] as well as directives on gas appliances and hot water boilers.[276] Additional Community measures have also been adopted to abolish barriers caused by the reluctance of Member States to accept the test results and certificates issued in other Member States.[277] Moreover, the Community has adopted various reporting obligations pursuant to Directive 98/34, laying down a procedure for the provision of information in the

[274] OJ 1985 C 136/1. For further discussion of the 'new approach' see S Farr, *Harmonisation of Technical Standards in the EC* (1996).

[275] Council Directive 92/75/EEC of 22/9/92 on the indication by labelling and standard product information of the consumption of energy and other resources by household appliances, OJ L 297/16; Commission Directive 94/2/EC of 21/1/94 implementing Council Directive 92/75/EEC with respect to energy labelling of household electric refrigerators, freezers, and combinations thereof, OJ L 45/1; Directive 96/57/EC of 3/9/96 of the European Parliament and of the Council of 3/9/96 on energy efficiency requirements for household electric refrigerators, freezers, and combinations thereof, OJ L 236/36; Commission Directive 95/13/EC of 23/5/95 implementing Council Directive 92/75/EEC with regard to energy labelling of household electric tumble dryers, OJ L 136/28; Commission Directive 96/60/EC of 18/10/96 implementing Council Directive 92/75/EEC with regard to energy labelling of household combined washer-dryers, OJ L 266/2; Commission Directive 96/89/EC of 17/12/96 amending Directive 95/12/EC implementing Council Directive 92/75/EEC with regard to energy labelling of household washing machines, OJ L 338/85; Commission Directive 97/17/EC of 7/5/97 implementing Council Directive 92/75/EEC with regard to energy labelling of household dishwashers, OJ L 118/2; Commission Directive 98/11/EC of 27/1/98 implementing Council Directive 92/75/EEC with regard to energy labelling of household lamps, OJ L 71/1.

[276] See eg Council Directive 90/396/EEC of 29 June 1990 on the approximation of the laws of Member States relating to gas appliances burning gaseous fuels, OJ 1990 L 196/15, as amended by Council Directive 93/68, OJ 1993 L 220; Council Directive 82/130/EEC concerning electrical equipment for use in potentially explosive atmospheres in mines susceptible to fire damp, OJ 1982 L 59; Council Directive 92/42/EEC on efficiency requirements for new hot-water boilers fired with liquid or gaseous fuels, OJ 1992 L 167/77, amended by Council Directive 93/63, OJ 1993 L 20; see also Commission Communication on the framework of the implementation of Council Directive 90/396/EEC of 29 June 1990, OJ 1999 C 133/4 (setting forth the references and ratification dates of the harmonized standards).

[277] Council Resolution of 21 Dec 1989 on a global approach to conformity assessment, OJ C 10/1 (1990).

field of technical standards and regulations.[278] Breach of the obligation to notify a national technical regulation or standard renders it inapplicable such that it would be unenforceable against individuals in national courts.[279] The case-law of the ECJ on this point is, however, distinct from its case-law on the horizontal direct effect of directives.[280]

In the energy field, the work of standardization covers five activities: the production and transmission of electricity, the oil sector, gas supply, renewable energy, and energy efficiency. With respect to the harmonization of energy-related standards within the construction industry, an important Community measure is Directive 89/106 on the approximation of laws, regulations, and administrative provisions of the Member States relating to construction products. The general purpose of this Directive is to create the conditions for a harmonized system of technical standards in the construction industry[281] and to eliminate obstacles to intra-Community trade in such products.[282] As noted by the Commission in its 1998 Communication on energy efficiency,[283] the development of harmonized standards under this Directive for products such as thermal insulation, windows, heat emitters, and roof renovation products can lead to the adoption of informational standards relating to the energy economy and heat retention properties of products. These are often achieved through Commission Decisions on mandates for harmonized standards.[284] These Decisions may set forth the procedure for **5.174**

[278] Directive 98/34/EC of 20 July 1998 laying down a procedure for the provision of information in the field of technical standards and regulations, OJ 1998 L 217/18.

[279] See Case C-194/94 *CIA Security International v Signalson and Securitel* [1996] ECR I-2201 (holding that a breach of the obligation to notify a Belgian technical standard on security systems rendered the standard inapplicable and could not be relied upon by defendants in a libel action). See also Commission Communication concerning the non-respect of certain provisions of Council Directive 83/189/EEC, OJ 1986 C 245/5 (stating that non-compliance with notification procedure would have the effect that the technical regulation is unenforceable against third parties in the legal system of the Member State).

[280] 'Editorial comment on the incidental effect of directives', vol 24, Eur. LR (1999) 1–2.

[281] Council Directive 89/106/EEC, OJ 1989 L 40/12, as amended by Directive 93/68/EEC, OJ 1993 L 220/1, requires the Member States to enforce laws, regulations, and administrative provisions that will ensure that construction products will satisfy the *essential requirements*, as listed in the Directive. These essential requirements provide the basis for the preparation of harmonized standards at European level for construction products, which includes any product 'produced for incorporation in a permanent manner in construction works, including both buildings and civil engineering works'. The essential requirements are set forth in the Annex and relate to: mechanical resistance and stability, safety in case of fire, hygiene, health and environment, safety in use, protection against noise, and energy economy and heat retention. The 'heat retention' requirement is a general requirement that the 'construction works and its heating, cooling and ventilation installations must be designed and built in such a way that the amount of energy required in use shall be low, having regard to the climatic conditions of the location and the occupants'.

[282] OJ 1999 C 142/105 (Answer to written question E-3114/98) (16 Oct 1998).

[283] COM(98) 246 final.

[284] See eg Commission Decision 98/436/EC of 22 June 1998 on the procedure for attesting conformity of construction products pursuant to Article 20(2) of Council Directive 89/106/EEC as regards roof coverings, roof lights, roof windows, and ancillary products, OJ 1998 L 194.

attesting the conformity of products (ie whether intervention by an approved certification body is required).[285]

Pre-emption of Member State law

5.175 When Community legislation does not 'occupy the field', Member States remain competent to adopt their own national measures at least to some degree. Such a situation is illustrated by the *Campus Oil* case, discussed above.[286] In that judgment the ECJ performed a detailed review of whether the objective of the Irish Government, namely to secure an effective national oil supply, was sufficiently provided for by the Community legislation at issue. The Court reached the conclusion that this was not the case: the relevant Community legislation did not occupy the field, and Ireland was not pre-empted from adopting additional measures, given its need to ensure the security of oil supply.

5.176 If Community legislation is found to be exhaustive (or fully 'occupying the field'), the question is then concerned with the method of harmonization that has been used. In cases of total harmonization, no derogation by national rules is permitted, except for safeguard measures provided for in the directive. In cases of partial, alternative, optional, or minimum harmonization, national rules may derogate from the norms prescribed in the directive within the permitted boundaries. Practice has shown that the concept of exhaustion is often confused with that of total harmonization.[287]

(6) Assessment of the Treaty Rules

5.177 As suggested above, a range of opinions has been expressed regarding the potency of the Treaty as an instrument for achieving energy reform. These differences of opinion undoubtedly reflect different views of opinion regarding the objectives of such reform. For example, in 1991 the head of the Commission's competition directorate, Sir Leon Brittan, called the Treaty a 'marvellous instrument' in that it provides both clear and flexible rules for the promotion of trade and competition and for the elimination of anti-competitive practices.[288] In contrast, other early

Commission Decision 1999/471/EC of 29 June 1999 on the procedure for attesting the conformity of construction products pursuant to Art 20(2) of Council Directive 89/106/EEC as regards space heating appliances, OJ 1999 L 184/37.

[285] ibid.

[286] Case 72/83 *Campus Oil v Minister for Industry and Energy* [1984] ECR 2727; [1984] 3 CMLR 544.

[287] See eg Case 169/89 *Gourmetterie van den Burg* [1990] I-ECR 2143, para 9 (referring to total harmonization instead of the concept of exhaustion of a directive). For further analysis of pre-emption doctrine and principles see E Cross, 'Pre-emption of Member State Law in the European Economic Community', 29 CMLR 447–72 (1992).

[288] L Brittan, 'Competition in the European Community's Electricity and Gas Markets', text of speech/91/40 (London, 18 April 1991). Sir Leon summarized the objectives in the electricity and gas sectors as follows: 'Consumers should have a choice of suppliers, suppliers should be able to

commentators on the programme for the internal energy market have observed, perhaps cautiously, that the EC legal framework is not ideally suited to the simultaneous realization of the complex task of reconciling energy market integration with other EC energy policy objectives, such as environmental protection and security of supply.[289]

Considering the development of the case-law since the programme for an internal energy market was announced, there seems to be substantial evidence of the continued non-application of the prohibitions of the Treaty to the energy sector, either as a result of non-enforcement or by virtue of the application of the exceptions to such prohibitions. In other words, while the potential applicability of the Treaty to the energy sector has perhaps been easy to argue in recent years, the actual application thereto to effect change appears to be limited to relatively few and minor instances. Of course, it is more difficult to assess the extent to which the mere threat of the application of the Treaty rules has affected the behaviour of the players in the energy markets—much as one might not appreciate an alert watchdog which does not bark in the night. More recent investigations by the Commission, such as the challenges to Gaz de France's monopoly over the extension of gas supply areas, have clearly been supported by the earlier development of case-law favourable to the carrying out of such enforcement actions and appear to have led to some regulatory reform at the national level. Similarly, the Commission's threats on increased Treaty enforcement may have helped to fulfil its ambitions regarding legislation for the internal market in energy, the subject to which we now turn. **5.178**

D. EC Secondary Legislation

(1) Legislation Covering More than one Energy Subsector

Transparency regulation

In assessing the functions and objectives of the Community's energy legislation, it should be kept in mind that the Community's traditional posture towards the national regulatory regimes in the utility sector was akin to a state of 'benign neglect', which left the Commission with an 'information deficit' regarding these regimes.[290] Hence, a major element of the legislative programme for an internal **5.179**

deliver their production through someone else's network, state subsidies should be transparent and limited and there should be no barriers to trade between the Community's Member States.'

[289] See L Hancher, 'A Single European Energy Market: Rhetoric or Reality?', vol 11, No 2, Energy LJ 217–41, 218 (1990); see also RIIA and SPRU, *A Single European Market in Energy* (1989) (criticizing policy-related aspects of the programme); F McGowan, 'The Single Energy Market and Energy Policy Conflicting Agendas', *Energy Policy* (Dec 1989).

[290] See L Hancher, 'The Single European Act: Will it make a difference to trade in electricity?', ESC conference proceedings, 5 Oct 1989 (Geneva, 1989) 8–9.

energy market can be seen as an attempt to develop disclosure and reporting obligations so as to enable effective monitoring at Community level.

5.180 The importance of this regulatory function is increasingly being appreciated and understood. 'Transparency regulation' can be designed to reveal the criteria by which the industry operates, the organizational structure and functioning of integrated enterprises, the relationships between the various industry players, and the basis and formation of industry costs and prices. This process enables the consumer, the industry participants, the regulatory authorities, and other concerned parties to make more rational business or regulatory decisions based on a clearer view of the market, rather than on a clouded, shielded one.

5.181 By seeking additional 'transparency rules' applicable to the electricity and gas sectors during the past decade, the Commission has substantially augmented the framework of Community measures that serve to promote information flow about the energy sector.[291] The most conspicuous examples are the directives that are clearly labelled as such: namely, the directive on price transparency and the directive on transparency of financial relations between Member States and public undertakings.[292] However, most of the existing directives relating to the electricity and gas sectors also contain disclosure or notification obligations of one sort or another, and therefore such directives can also be said to have a transparency function. For example, the directives on cross-border transit in electricity and gas require the institution of certain reporting obligations to the Commission in respect of contract requests and negotiations for cross-border transit on high-voltage wires and high-pressure pipelines. The electricity and gas directives require the institution of a system of reporting by the Member States to the Commission on public service obligations (PSOs) and other matters. The public procurement directive requires disclosure of information on bidding procedures, criteria, and awards in the utilities sector. EU environmental measures, such as the directives on environmental impact assessments,[293] on exchanges of pollution

[291] The Commission previously developed a number of transparency measures in the oil sector. See eg Council Directive 76/491/EEC of 22 April 1999 concerning information and consultation on the prices of crude oil and petroleum products in the Community, OJ L 140 (1976). On 22 April 1999 this Directive was repealed and replaced with Council Decision 1999/280/EC regarding a Community procedure for information and consultation on crude oil supply costs and the consumer prices of petroleum products, OJ L 110/8 (1999). In addition, Council Regulation 2964/95/EC of 20 December 1995, OJ 1995 L 310/5 introduced registration for crude oil imports and deliveries in the Community.

[292] Commission Directive 80/723/EEC, OJ L 195/35 (1980) on transparency of financial relations between Member States and public undertakings, as amended by Commission Directive 85/413/EEC, OJ L 229/20 (1985), and Commission Directive 93/84/EEC, OJ L 254/16 (1993). The Commission has proposed further amendments to this Directive to extend the rules on analytical accounts to all company operations in both reserved and non-reserved sectors and to companies receiving subsidies for rendering services of general economic interest.

[293] Council Directive 97/11/EC of 3 March 1997 amending Directive 85/337/EEC on the assessment of the effects of certain public and private power projects on the environment, OJ L 73/5.

information,[294] on emissions reduction,[295] and on a monitoring mechanism for Community greenhouse gas emissions,[296] are clearly designed to require the disclosure of information on environmental matters in the production of energy. Other Community measures extend disclosure and reporting requirements on energy-related matters ranging from energy investment projects[297] to containers for liquids.[298]

The Price Transparency Directive

The formation of prices is, of course, a significant aspect of the way in which an industry conducts itself and is a common subject of energy regulation. In its 1989 report on 'Transparency of Consumer Energy Prices', the Commission stated that 'price transparency should enable consumers to check whether the prices charged reflect fair conditions of competition'.[299] Moreover: **5.182**

> [w]hen energy prices are not transparent, they are capable of containing elements of State Aid unauthorised by the Commission or covering up anti-competitive practices by undertakings in breach of Community rules on competition.[300]

However, despite a long-standing concern with this subject, the Commission had difficulty reaching agreement on binding obligations in this area.[301] **5.183**

---

294 Council Decision 97/101/EC of 27 January 1997 establishing a reciprocal exchange of information and data from networks and individual stations measuring ambient air pollution within the Member States, OJ L 35/14.

295 Directive 1999/30/EC of 22 April 1999 relating to limit values for sulphur dioxide, nitrogen dioxide and oxides of nitrogen, particulate matter, and lead in ambient air, OJ 1999 L 163/41, Art 8 (on public information) and Arts 3, 5, 9, and 12 (on Member State reporting duties to the Commission); Council Directive 1999/32/EC of 26 April 1999 relating to a reduction in the sulphur content of certain liquid fuels and amending Directive 93/12/EEC, OJ 1994 L 121/13.

296 Council Decision 99/296/EC of 26 April 1999 amending Decision 93/389/EEC for a monitoring mechanism of Community carbon dioxide and other greenhouse gas emissions, OJ 1999 L 117/35.

297 Council Regulation 736/96 of 22 April 1996 on notifying the Commission of investment projects of interest in the petroleum, natural gas, and electricity sectors.

298 Council Directive 85/339/EEC of 27 June 1985 on containers of liquid for human consumption, OJ L 176/18, Art 6, Annex II (requiring Member States to send reports on measures taken on the particulars of energy consumed in the manufacture of containers).

299 Commission of the European Communities, 'Transparency of Consumer Energy Prices', COM(89) 123 final, 7 March 1989, at 4.1 (emphasis in original). In this communication from the Commission, the Commission concluded, *inter alia*, that there is 'a price transparency problem for sales of electricity in excess of 24 GWh/per year', which it characterized as 'unacceptable in view of the impending completion of the internal market': ibid.

300 ibid; see further Seventeenth Report from Select Committee on the European Communities, Session 1992–93, *Structure of the Single Market for Energy*, House of Lords Paper 56, 47 (testimony of Mr Nicholas Argyris describing the Price Transparency Directive as introducing 'a system of information to the Commission which then on the basis of that information publishes as it were marker prices for certain categories of consumers').

301 In 1981 and 1983, the Council adopted non-binding recommendations regarding tariff structures for electricity and gas respectively; see Council Recommendation 81/924/EEC of 29 October 1981 on electricity tariff structures in the Community, OJ 1981 L 337/12; Council Recommendation 83/230/EEC of 21 April 1983 on methods of forming natural gas prices and

5.184 The Price Transparency Directive relates to a procedure to improve the transparency of electricity and gas prices charged to industrial end-users.[302] Article 1 of the Directive requires the Member States to take the necessary steps to ensure that undertakings which supply electricity or gas to industrial end-users communicate certain information to the Statistical Office of the European Community (SOEC) on a periodic basis. The information reported under this Directive falls into three categories: (i) prices and terms of sale to industrial end-users, (ii) the price systems in use, and (iii) a breakdown of consumers and corresponding volume of consumption. The SOEC regularly publishes some of the information reported, but only in an aggregated form that does not enable individual commercial transactions to be identified.[303] Among other things, the data indicate general 'geographical price differentials', although, as the Commission has observed, these could be due to a combination of five factors: (i) differences in taxation and other levies, (ii) tariff policy, (iii) differences in costs (fixed and variable), (iv) other subsidies not energy-related (eg those paid to support other public services such as public transport), and (v) efficiency of economic operation.[304] The data also indicate certain countries and cities with relatively high 'price ratios' between small and large industrial consumers.

The Transit Directives

5.185 Another subject of EC legislation is the transit of electricity and gas across borders. The Electricity Transit Directive was adopted on 29 October 1990, and the Gas

tariffs in the Community, OJ L 123/40 (1983); see also European Commission, 'Application of the Community's energy pricing principles in the Member States', COM(84) 490 final (18 September 1984). Several subsequent attempts to adopt a proposed Council resolution on the implementation of the recommendations failed to secure the necessary votes in the Council. See European Commission, 'Transparency of Consumer Energy Prices', COM(89) 123 final, 1.1 (7 March 1989). These difficulties took place despite studies showing problems with price transparency in the Community. See ibid, 4.1 ('There is a price transparency problem for sales of electricity in excess of 24 GWh/per year'); see also Bureau Europeén des Unions de Consommateurs (European Consumers Organization), *Water, Electricity and Gas Undertakings: Terms of Supply*, 418 (1985) (report to the European Commission, citing a 'serious imbalance between the rights and obligations of the parties involved, to the detriment of the consumer' and a 'great lack of transparency').

[302] Council Directive 90/377/EEC, OJ 1990 L 185/1.

[303] See eg Eurostat, 'Statistics in Focus: Energy and Industry', [1998] No 26 (electricity prices for EU industry on 1 July 1998). In testimony before a committee of the British House of Lords in late 1992, the Director-General of the Commission's energy section described the system effected by the Directive as follows: 'a system of information to the Commission which then on the basis of that information publishes as it were marker prices for certain categories of consumers'. 17th Report from Select Committee on the European Communities, Sess. 1992–93, *Structure of the Single Market for Energy*, House of Lords Paper 56, 47 (testimony of N Argyris).

[304] Commission of the European Communities, *A Report from the Commission to the Council, the European Parliament, and the Economic and Social Committee on the Operation of Directive 90/377/EEC*, COM(93) 666 final (1993).

Transit Directive was adopted on 31 May 1991. The effective date was 1 July 1991 for the former and 1 July 1992 for the latter.[305]

The general purpose of these two Transit Directives, read together, is to increase electricity and gas transfers between grids and to reduce obstacles to the exchange of electricity and gas by 'making the transit . . . through grids compulsory'.[306] In the case of electricity, the grids concerned are the high-voltage transmission lines, and in the case of gas, the grids concerned are the high-pressure transmission pipelines. **5.186**

Taking the example of the Electricity Transit Directive, the Member States must 'take the measures necessary to *facilitate* transit of electricity' (Art 1), although they are not required to compel transit. The Directive defines transit to cover transactions in which: (i) the grid originates or has its final destination in the Community, and (ii) at least one internal border (ie an intra-Community border between two Member States) is crossed.[307] Electricity distribution grids are explicitly excluded from the scope of the Directive (Art 2(1)(a)). An Annex to the Directive lists the transmission grids and grid operators covered, and this has been updated periodically to add new entities. [308] **5.187**

The Directive requires contracts for transit to be negotiated between the entities responsible for the grids concerned, and where appropriate with the entities responsible for importing and exporting electricity. The conditions of transit must be non-discriminatory and fair. There is a reporting system to help the Commission monitor the negotiation and conclusion (or lack thereof) of contracts for transit (of more than one year's duration).[309] Entities may request that conditions of transit be subject to conciliation by a body set up and chaired by the **5.188**

[305] The Transit Directives have been implemented through a variety of legal mechanisms, ranging from decrees (Greece), statutory instruments (United Kingdom and Ireland), licence modifications (United Kingdom), and official agreements published in official gazettes (Denmark and the Netherlands).

[306] Recital 9, Electricity Transit Directive; Recital 13, Gas Transit Directive. The Directives define 'transit' to cover transactions in which: (i) the grid originates or has its final destination in the Community, and (ii) at least one internal border (ie an intra-Community border between two Member States) is crossed: Art 2(1)(b) and (c).

[307] Council Directive 90/547, Art 2(1)(b) and (c).

[308] See eg Commission Directive 98/75/EC updating the list of entities covered by Directive 90/547/EEC on the transit of electricity through transmission grids, OJ L 276/9.

[309] More specifically, Art 3(3) of the Transit Directive requires the Member States to take measures to ensure that the grid operators under their jurisdiction do the following without delay: (i) report any request for a transit contract of a minimum of one year's duration, (ii) open negotiations regarding such requests, (iii) report the conclusion of transit contracts, and (iv) report the reasons for failure of the negotiations to result in the conclusion of a contract within 12 months following the request. This information must be reported to the Commission and to the national authorities concerned.

Commission. A Committee of Experts on the Transit of Electricity between Grids has been established under a Commission Decision of 4 March 1992.[310]

5.189 The Electricity Transit Directive did little more than formalize existing arrangements to manage exchanges between existing utilities. Nevertheless, it clearly removed any doubts as to the legality of 'back-to-back' contracts in the sector where, for example, country A, wishing to deliver electricity to the grid network in country C through country B's high-transmission network system, would first have to sell its electricity to country B's utilities, who would in turn sell it at its own price to the grid company in country C. Given, however, that the Directive contained no rules on the calculation of the transport fee, the grid companies are still in a position to extract a high monopoly rent for transit access to their facilities, unless they otherwise agree.

5.190 The Gas Transit Directive is very similar to its electricity counterpart, except that it applies to all contracts, irrespective of their duration. Continued opposition at the national level to the Gas Transit Directive delayed the setting up of the Experts Committee and the utilization of these procedures.[311]

Legislation on the rational use of energy (and energy efficiency)

Background

5.191 In 1974, at the start of the energy crisis, the Community launched a programme on the rational use of energy.[312] This resulted in a series of EC recommendations and directives relating, *inter alia*, to the heat sector and the rational use of heat.[313]

5.192 For example, under Council Recommendation 77/714/EEC (OJ 295/5), Member States were invited to create advisory bodies/committees to be responsible for giving an opinion on all measures to increase efficiency in the supply of

[310] Commission Decision 92/167/EEC on the setting up of a Committee of Experts on the Transit of Electricity between Grids, OJ 1992 L 74/43 (1992). This Decision was amended by the Act of Accession of Austria, Finland, and Sweden, and by Commission Decision 97/559/EC, OJ 1997 L 230/18 (making the term of office renewable once).

[311] Commission Decision 95/539/EC on the setting up of a Committee of Experts on the Transit of Natural Gas through Grids, OJ 1995 L 304. The list of Members of the Experts' Committee is published at OJ 1996 C 222, as amended OJ 1997 C 93, as amended OJ 1999 C 214/5.

[312] See European Commission, 'Rational Utilisation of Energy', OJ 1975 C 152/5.

[313] Council Recommendation 76/492/EEC of 4/5/76 on the rational use of energy by promoting the thermal insulation of buildings, OJ L 140/11 (1976); Council Recommendation 76/493/EEC of 4/5/76 on the rational use of energy in the heating systems of existing buildings, OJ L 140/12 (1976); Council Recommendation 77/712/EEC of 25/10/77 on the regulating of space heating, the production of domestic hot water, and the metering of heat in new buildings, OJ L 295/1 (1977); Council Recommendation 77/713/EEC of 25/10/77 on the rational use of energy in industrial undertakings, OJ L 295/3 (1977); Council Recommendation 77/714/EEC of 25/10/77 on the creation in the Member States of advisory bodies or committees to promote combined heat and power production and the exploitation of residual heat, OJ L 295/5 (1977); Council Recommendation 80/823/EEC of 29/7/80 on the rational use of energy in industrial enterprises.

heat for industry and to promote the use of remote heat supply systems. Almost all Member States have set up such advisory bodies.

Directive 78/170/EEC (OJ L 52/32), as amended by Council Directive 82/855/EEC (OJ L 378), requires Member States to take all necessary measures to ensure that all new heat generators for space heating and/or the production of hot water in new or existing non-industrial buildings comply with (economically justifiable) minimum performance requirements (Art 1 (as amended)). This requires the adoption of measures on the inspection and certification of certain heat generators, as well as measures to make compulsory the use of insulation in certain buildings and heating systems. Under the 1982 amendments, *inter alia*, a detailed code of practice for the inspection procedure was annexed to this Directive. **5.193**

Under the 1988 Construction Products Directive,[314] Member States are obliged to enforce laws, regulations, and administrative provisions to ensure that construction products[315] will satisfy the *essential requirements*,[316] as listed in the Directive. These essential requirements provide the basis for the preparation of harmonized standards at European level for construction products. The primary aim of this Directive is to eliminate technical obstacles to intra-Community trade in such products and to create the conditions for a harmonized system of technical standards in the construction industry. The Directive stipulates that such products may only be put on the market if they are 'fit for intended use', a notion defined in relation to the essential requirements. It also stipulates that 'fitness for intended use' is to be assessed with special reference to harmonized technical specifications adopted on mandates given by the Commission. For example, Commission Decision 98/436/EC of 22 June 1998 covers roof coverings and calls for a harmonized standard to be drawn up by the European Committee for Standardization (CEN).[317] Alternatively, Commission Decisions may specify different systems of attesting the conformity of certain products, such as was done for the class of space heating appliances.[318] **5.194**

[314] Council Directive 89/106/EEC of 21 December 1988 on the approximation of laws, regulations, and administrative provisions of the Member States relating to construction products, OJ L 40/12, as amended by Council Directive 93/68/EEC of 22 July 1993, OJ L 220/1.

[315] Defined as any product which is produced for incorporation in a permanent manner in construction works, including both buildings and civil engineering works.

[316] These essential requirements relate to mechanical resistance and stability, safety in case of fire, hygiene, health and environment, safety in use, protection against noise, energy economy, and heat retention. The heat retention requirement is a general requirement that the 'construction works and its heating, cooling and ventilation installations must be designed and built in such a way that the amount of energy required in use shall be low, having regard to the climatic conditions of the location and the occupants'.

[317] Commission Decision 98/436/EC of 22 June 1988 on the procedure for attesting the conformity of construction products pursuant to Art 20(2) of Council Directive 89/106/EEC as regards roof coverings, roof lights, roof windows, and ancillary products, OJ L 194/30.

[318] Commission Decision 1999/471/EC of 29 June 1999 on the procedure for attesting the conformity of construction products pursuant to Art 20(2) of Council Directive 89/106/EEC as regards space heating appliances, OJ 1999 L 184/37.

Subsequent legislation on energy efficiency

5.195 In its 1998 Communication on energy efficiency,[319] the Commission reviewed the various existing and proposed measures in the field. This Communication describes, *inter alia*, the important initiatives for new or amended EC secondary legislation in the field, including: (i) the modified draft directive to introduce rational planning techniques in the electricity and gas distribution sectors, (ii) a review and proposed strengthening of Council Directive 93/76 to Limit Carbon Dioxide Emissions by improving energy efficiency, (iii) the proposed revision of the Directive 88/609 on limits of emissions of pollutants from large combustion plants, and (iv) the concept of a possible directive on energy management to promote energy efficiency in the public sector, such that public bodies would set examples of best practices. A related Commission action plan relating to energy efficiency was announced in 2000.[320]

5.196 The principal focus of the Community's activities in this area has been the SAVE programme (see Council Decision 91/565/EEC, OJ L 307/34), which was renewed in late 1996 (SAVE II) with an indicative budget of ECU 45 million for five years (Council Decision 96/737, OJ L 335/50).[321] SAVE provides support for pilot actions and dissemination of information in the areas of appliances, buildings, heat pumps, CHP, demand-side management, education and training, industry, and transport.

5.197 Under the auspices of the SAVE programme, Directive 93/76/EEC (OJ L 237/28) was adopted to help attain Community and Member State objectives in reducing carbon dioxide emissions and promoting the rational use of energy. Under this Directive, Member States are required to draw up and implement programmes in the six programme areas:

—energy certification of buildings;
—billing of heating, air conditioning, and hot water costs on the basis of actual consumption;
—third-party financing for energy efficiency investments in the public sector;
—thermal insulation of new buildings;
—regular inspection of heating installations with an output of more than 15 KW;
—energy audits of undertakings with high energy consumption.

[319] European Commission, Energy Efficiency in the European Community: Towards a strategy for the rational use of energy, COM(98) 246 final.

[320] Communication from the Commission to the Council, the European Parliament, the Economic and Social Committee and the Committee of the Regions—Action Plan to improve energy efficiency in the European Community, COM(2000), 247 final.

[321] Under the co-decision procedure (Art 175) in June 1999 the Commission submitted an amended proposal for a Decision adopting a multiannual programme for promotion of energy efficiency (1998–2002), following proposed amendments adopted in March 1999 by the European Parliament. See COM(99) 211 final.

This Directive allows considerable flexibility as to the choice of implementation instruments. The programmes can be implemented in a variety of ways, including laws, regulations, administrative and economic instruments, education, and voluntary agreements whose impact can be objectively assessed. In addition, Member States are allowed to determine the scope of the programmes on the basis of 'potential improvements in energy efficiency, cost-effectiveness, technical feasibility and environmental impact'. Member States are required to communicate to the Commission such laws or other measures which they adopt in the field covered by the Directive (Art 10). Moreover, under Article 9 Member States must report every two years on the results of these measures and on the choices they have made in their package of measures. **5.198**

The Commission wants to strengthen this Directive in order to enhance its impact. In its 1998 Communication on energy efficiency, it promised to propose a directive to amend Directive 93/76/EEC. More specifically, it has suggested amendments regarding energy certification of buildings (to include existing as well as new buildings), further standards for installation of insulation, and proposals for inspections and energy audits. **5.199**

An extensive legislative programme covering energy efficiency labelling of household appliances was developed in the 1990s, beginning with a framework Directive (Council Directive 92/75/EEC, OJ L 297/16) and an implementing Directive issued by the Commission (Commission Directive 94/2/EC, OJ L 45/1). Member States are required to take measures to ensure that the relevant suppliers and dealers under their jurisdiction would fulfil such energy labelling rules, and they must notify such measures to the Commission. **5.200**

This labelling programme has been extended to a variety of household electrical appliances such as refrigerators and freezers (Directive 96/57/EC, OJ L 236/36). This model was followed by negotiated agreements for household washing machines and televisions. There are also Commission Directives relating to energy labelling of household lamps (Directive 98/11/EC), household dishwashers (Directive 97/69/EC), household washing machines (Directive 96/89/EC), and household combined washer-dryers (Directive 96/60/EC). Electric ovens are covered under Directive 79/531/EEC until a revised implementing Directive is passed (see Art 13 of Directive 92/75/EEC). Energy efficiency standards are presently being developed for electric water heaters and air conditioners. Under these Directives, Member States are required to adopt the necessary measures and to inform the Commission about them immediately. There has been some delay in the transposition of these labelling directives by the Member States.[322] **5.201**

[322] See Fifteenth Annual Report on the monitoring of the application of Community law, OJ C 250 (1998).

5.202 Other measures noted by the Commission in its 1998 Communication on energy efficiency include the proposed directive to introduce rational planning techniques to the electricity and gas sectors[323] and proposed amendments to Directive 88/609 on the limitation of certain air pollutants from large combustion plants.[324] Regarding the former, the Commission has found political support within the European Parliament but not sufficient support within the Council. Regarding the latter, in July 1998 the Commission presented its proposal to amend Directive 88/609.[325] The Commission has proposed amendments to introduce limit values that are twice as strict as the current values as of 1 January 2000. It is claimed that this revision would encourage CHP use in new large combustion plants.

5.203 Council Directive 96/61/EC concerns integrated pollution prevention and control (OJ L 257/26) and applies to many types of installations, including combustion installations over 50 MW. Article 3 of this Directive requires Member States to take the necessary measures to provide that the competent authorities ensure that such installations are operated in such a way that, among other requirements, energy is used efficiently and no significant pollution is caused. The Directive also requires Member States to institute a permitting system according to the specific requirements set forth in the Directive. This would apply to CHP and other electricity production installations over 50 MW.

Legislation relating to procurement in the energy sector

5.204 The Community rules on procurement for utilities (operating in the network industries of electricity, gas, water, energy, telecommunications, and transport) form an integral part of the Community's wider regime, which aims at creating and securing an internal procurement market in Europe. This type of regulation is applied to the acquisition of works, goods, and services for public consumption. The function of procurement regulation in general is to help guarantee efficiency and good value for money, as well as to avoid the misuse of public funds. It has also been observed that 'public markets have traditionally been characterised by low import penetration resulting from the use of public procurement to support national industry, and that this has presented a serious obstacle to completing the single market'.[326]

5.205 Although directives on procurement for works and for public supplies were originally adopted in 1971 and 1977 respectively, the utilities sector was excluded

[323] Amended Proposal for a Council Directive to introduce rational planning techniques in the electricity and gas sectors, COM(97) 69 final.

[324] Council Directive 88/609, OJ 1988 L 336/1, is designed to limit emissions from sulphur dioxide, nitrogen oxide, and dust.

[325] Proposal for a Council Directive amending Directive 88/609 on the limitation of emissions of certain pollutants into the air from large combustion plants, COM(98) 415 final.

[326] S Arrowsmith, 'Deregulation of Utilities Procurement in the Changing Economy: Towards a Principled Approach?', vol 7, Eur. Comp. LR 420–9, 420 (1997).

from their scope. Following modernization of the original regime during 1988 and 1989, the procurement regime was also extended to 'contracting entities' engaged in relevant activities in the energy sector in 1990 with the adoption of Council Directive 90/531.[327]

This latter measure was amended and expanded to include procurement of services in the utilities sector with the adoption of Council Directive 93/38, known as the Utilities Directive.[328] This measure was to be implemented into national law by July 1994 in the majority of the Member States. As part of its programme of procurement regulatory reform the Council also adopted a Directive on enforcement and remedies in 1989.[329] This formed the basis for specialized 'remedies' regulation in the utility sector. **5.206**

The Community procurement rules are currently in development. Based on a Commission 'Green Paper' of November 1996,[330] which elicited comments from interested parties, the Commission published a Communication on the subject in March 1998, which set out findings and proposed actions.[331] **5.207**

When considering the rules on procurement in the energy sector, it is also necessary to bear in mind the GATT/WTO General Agreement on Procurement, which entered into effect on 1 January 1996. Furthermore, Article 36 of the Utilities Directive provides for a 'preference rule' in certain cases for goods originating in the Community over and above those originating from third countries. The application of this rule is tempered when third countries have signed bilateral agreements providing for equivalent access for Community undertakings to their procurement markets. **5.208**

A number of monographs and specialized journals deal with the detailed application of the Community procurement regime for public works, supplies, and services.[332] As the rules for the utility sector, including the energy sector, are substantially based on the 'general' regime, reference to this literature is advisable for those readers who wish to study the Community procurement regime in any **5.209**

[327] OJ 1990 L 297/1.

[328] OJ 1993 L 199/84, as amended by Directive 94/22/EEC, OJ 1994 L 164/3, and Directive 98/4/EC, OJ 1998 L 101/1.

[329] Council Directive 89/665 co-ordinating the laws, regulations, and administrative provisions relating to the application of the review procedures to the award of public supply and public works contracts, OJ 1989 L 395/33.

[330] European Commission, Public Procurement in the European Union: Exploring the Way Forward, COM(96) 583 final.

[331] COM(98) 143. For an analysis of the Commission's 1998 Communication, see S Arrowsmith, 'The Community's Legal Framework on Public Procurement: "The Way Forward" At Last?', vol 36, CMLR 13–49 (1999). For the text of the proposed new directive co-ordinating procurement procedures, see COM(2000) 276 final/2.

[332] See S Arrowsmith, *The Law of Public and Utilities Procurement* (1996); P Trepte, *Public Procurement in the EC* (1993); Brown, 'The Extension of the Public Procurement Rules for Utilities', 30 CMLR 721–48 (1993); see also the Public Procurement Law Rev. (1992 to present).

detail. The following sections summarize the rules as they apply to the energy sector and discuss some of the more important rules as well as the way in which they have been interpreted in the Community courts.

5.210 Public sector procurement practices came under close scrutiny by the Commission first in the early 1970s, and then again in the early 1980s as part of the more general exercise leading to the publication of the 1985 *White Book on the Internal Market*. Extension of the existing rules to the energy sector, along with other utility sectors, had been complicated not only by national government resistance to intervention in their privileged relationships with companies active in these sectors, but also by the diverse legal forms which such companies assumed throughout the Community. Many utilities were either in semi-public or private ownership and therefore a solution had to be devised to take account of the mix of public and private ownership in these sectors. The Commission sought to develop a concept 'which addresses the procurement problems in terms which transcend the public/private distinction and permit situations which are in substance to be treated the same regardless of differences in legal form'.[333] The heart of the problem—as expressed in Recital 14 of the original Directive 90/531—lay in the fact that entities operating in the utilities sectors did not purchase on the basis of Community-wide competition because of the closed nature of the markets in which they operate:

> due to the existence of special or exclusive rights granted by the national authorities, concerning the supply to, provision or operation of networks for providing the service concerned or the exploitation of a given geographical area for a particular purpose.

5.211 In other words, the national authorities were able to use their discretionary powers to award licences in such a way as to promote domestic preferences.

5.212 According to the Community regime, contracting entities—whether public or private—are subject to three sets of common rules: the common rules on technical specifications and standards, common advertising rules, and common criteria for the qualification, selection, and award of contracts. The aims of these three sets of rules are: to ensure transparency so that contractors throughout the Community are given an opportunity to bid for major public contracts; to secure non-discrimination, so that all tenderers are treated on a fair basis; and to promote standardization on the basis of harmonized procurement rules concerning timetables, tender notices, specifications, and award criteria.

5.213 These three sets of common rules form the basis of both the general regime for public works, supplies, and services, as well as of the specific rules for the utilities sector. Nevertheless, due to the more diverse nature of the utilities sector, these

[333] Commission Explanatory Memorandum, COM(88) 377 final, para 7.

rules are applied with somewhat more flexibility than the rules applying under the general regime. The relationship between the specialized rules for the utilities sector and those applying more generally is regulated by Article 45/3 of Directive 93/38 such that contracts falling within the scope of this Directive do not fall within the provisions of the general regime.[334]

Council Directive 93/38 applies to contracting entities which: (a) are public authorities and public undertakings and exercise one of the relevant activities listed in Article 2(2); (b) are not public authorities or public undertakings, but have as one of their activities any of those referred to in paragraph 2 or any combination thereof and operate on the basis of special or exclusive rights granted by a competent authority of a Member State. **5.214**

The terms 'public authority' and 'public undertaking' are further defined in Article 2. Article 2(2) defines the relevant activities as including, *inter alia*: **5.215**

> the provision or operation of fixed networks intended to provide a service to the public in connection with the production, transport or distribution of . . . electricity . . . gas or heat; or
> the supply of . . . electricity, gas or heat to such networks; [or]
> the exploitation of a geographical area for the purpose of . . . exploring for or extracting oil, gas, coal or other solid fuels, . . .

Article 2(3) defines special or exclusive rights as rights: **5.216**

> deriving from authorisations granted by a competent authority of the Member State concerned, by law, regulation, or administrative action, having as their result the reservation for one or more entities of the exploitation of [one of the covered utility activities].

In particular, a contracting entity shall be considered to enjoy such rights where it enjoys special privileges in planning law or where the entity supplies electricity or gas to a network which is itself operated by an entity which enjoys special or exclusive rights. These definitions are supplemented by lists contained in Annexes I–X. The meaning of 'special rights' in the context of the procurement regime has been considered by the ECJ in Case *R v HM Treasury, ex parte British Telecommunications plc*.[335] **5.217**

Because the scope of the procurement rules for the energy sector is potentially wide, a major practical difficulty lies in determining what is covered by the regime. It is not confined to conventional utilities such as those producing energy and/or supplying it through a network, but also extends to companies engaged in the exploitation of natural resources, including hydrocarbons and solid fuels, as long as they do so on the basis of special or exclusive rights. Companies engaged **5.218**

[334] See further Case 247/89 *Commission v Portugal* [1991] ECR I-3659 (interpreting Art 2(2)(b)(ii) of Council Directive 90/531/EEC).

[335] Case C-302/94 [1996] ECR I-6417.

in hydrocarbons exploration and production are also potentially subject to the Community procurement rules, and it was for this reason that a special exemption procedure was included in Article 3 for this latter group. This procedure is discussed below in paras 5.222–5.223. Furthermore, the definition of a contracting entity extends to firms which supply fixed networks, so that a private generator supplying a grid operator which itself operates on the basis of exclusive or special rights is also brought within the scope of the Directive.

Exempted transactions

5.219 The Directive specifically exempts certain types of transactions as well as certain types of undertakings. Among the exempted transactions are contracts of contracting entities awarded for purposes other than the pursuit of relevant activities or for the pursuit of such activities in a non-Member State (Art 6). This must not involve the physical use of a network or a geographical area within the Community, however. Where, for example, an electricity utility is also involved in the supply of cable television, the Directive will not apply to its award of contracts in this latter field. Article 6(3) empowers the Commission to publish lists of activities that it considers to be covered by this exclusion.

5.220 The Directive also does not extend to fuel purchasing. Article 9(b) excludes contracts that the contracting entity awards for the supply of energy or fuels for the production of energy. As both the Preamble and Article 9(2) make clear, however, the Council is to re-examine this exemption at a later date.

5.221 Article 10 exempts contracts declared to be secret by the Member States, where their execution must be accompanied by special security measures, or where the protection of the basic security interests of the State so requires.

5.222 Contracts below certain thresholds are also excluded. The threshold for public works contracts is EUR 5 million, and for public supplies and services contracts, EUR 400,000. The Directive provides that contracts may not be split up to circumvent the rules, and lays down complex requirements aimed at aggregating the value of all relevant supplies, works, and services in order to determine whether the valuation thresholds are reached (Art 14).

Exempted undertakings

5.223 The Directive provides two exemptions for certain categories of undertakings. First, the supply of water, electricity, gas, or heat to public networks by contracting entities other than public authorities does not come within the scope of the Directive if that supply is only a marginal part of the entity's overall activities. Secondly, Article 3 provides a limited exemption procedure for firms engaged in oil, gas, or coal exploration where the Member State responsible for granting the relevant authorizations agrees to respect certain conditions in their procedures for allocating licences or concessions. Article 3 has now been amended by Article 12 of Council Directive 94/22 on 'hydrocarbons licensing', discussed below in paras 5.232–5.252. Where the Member State in question has complied with the provisions of this latter Directive, contracting entities engaged in oil and gas exploration and production will not be subject to the procurement rules in full. The alternative or parallel procedure under Article 3 of the Utilities Directive is still of relevance to companies whose activities do not fall within the scope of Directive 94/22, ie companies exploring for and producing coal and other solid fuels.

Prior to the entry into force of Directive 94/22, Article 3 of the Utilities Directive provided that Member States could request that exploitation of geographical areas for the purpose of exploring for or extracting oil, gas, coal, or other solid fuels was not to be considered as an activity defined in Article 2(2)(b)(i) and that entities would not be considered as operating under special or exclusive rights within the meaning of Article 2(3)(b) by virtue of carrying on one or more of these activities provided that certain conditions were satisfied with respect to the relevant national provisions concerning such activities. These conditions are set out in Article 3(1)(a)–(e). They include the requirement that authorizations to exploit a geographical area are open to other entities under the same conditions as for the contracting entities; that technical and financial capabilities of entities to engage in particular activities are established prior to any evaluation of the merits of competing authorizations; that authorization is granted on the basis of objective criteria concerning the way in which the activities are to be carried out; and that such criteria are established and published prior to the requests and applied in a non-discriminatory manner; that all conditions and requirements concerning the carrying out and termination of the activity shall also be established and made available in advance; and finally that contracting entities shall not be required to provide any information on their actual or intended sources of procurement. A Council minute attached to the Directive makes it clear that all the relevant criteria referred to in Article 3(1) should be published. **5.224**

Even if an exemption is obtained, Article 3(2) still requires Member States to ensure that contracting entities: **5.225**

(a) [observe] the principles of non-discrimination and competitive procurement in respect of the award of supplies, works and service contracts, in particular as regards the information which the entity makes available to undertakings concerning its procurement intentions;
(b) [communicate] to the Commission, under [defined] conditions . . ., information relating to the award of contracts.

The exact scope of Article 3(2) is not entirely clear, in that it does not indicate what, if any, procedures should be followed to ensure the principles that it stipulates. Most contracting entities that are formally exempted from the strict rules of the Directive have nevertheless opted to 'shadow' its provisions to avoid possible problems. It should be noted that even if the contracting entities are exempted **5.226** from the major procedural rules, their contracting procedures are still subject to review in accordance with the 'Remedies Directive'. The amendments introduced by Article 12 of Directive 94/22 did not alter this situation.

5.227 The common rules to be applied to procurement by contracting entities are laid down in Title III (technical specifications and standards); Title IV (procedures for advertising of contracts); and Title V (qualification and selection of candidates and award of contracts). These rules generally mirror the common rules established under Directives 93/36, 93/37, and 93/50 establishing the general regime, but Directive 93/38 allows a certain degree of additional flexibility.

5.228 Article 13 requires the adoption of European specifications wherever they exist. Contracting entities may, however, establish further complementary specifications, but these should as far as possible indicate performance requirements as opposed to design characteristics. Contracting entities in any event remain subject to the general principles of Community law concerning the non-discriminatory use and application of technical standards.[336] In the absence of European specifications, the technical specifications should be defined as far as possible by reference to other standards having currency within the Community.

5.229 The Utilities Directive allows considerable flexibility to contracting entities to choose the type of procedure they wish to follow in considering tenders, providing that a call for competition has been made. Under the open procedure, all interested parties are invited to tender for the contract. Under the restricted procedure, the utility invites tenders from a selected short-list drawn up after advertising the contract. The negotiated procedure entitles the utilities to negotiate terms with one or more contractors, selected after advertising the contract. The negotiated procedure is by far the preferred procedure in the utility sector. In addition, Article 30 of the Directive provides for a pre-qualification system that allows the utility to establish and draw from a pool of approved contractors.

5.230 A particularly problematic area is the scope which a contracting entity enjoys to enter into 'post-tender' negotiations with competing tenderers following the submission of a bid. A statement regarding Article 20 of the Directive was published in 1994,[337] the legal status of which is uncertain. The statement permits discussions aimed at clarifying the tender, but prohibits negotiations on fundamental aspects of the contract, in particular prices. If significant changes are made to the contract requirements or specifications following the closing of the tender procedure, the utility should probably cancel the award procedure and start again.[338] However, if the post-tender discussions are primarily aimed at 'clarification', this

[336] Case 45/85 *Commission v Ireland* ('*Dundalk*') [1988] ECR 4929.
[337] OJ 1994 L 111/14.
[338] Case C-87/94 *Commission v Belgium* [1996] ECR I-2043 (involving tenders for public bus services and fuel consumption calculations).

should be acceptable provided that all tenderers are given the same opportunity to revise their bids. If they are not given this chance, then the principle of equal opportunity is infringed.[339]

The call for competition can be dispensed with and negotiated procedures commenced in a variety of situations, as stipulated in Article 20(2), although they must still observe the principles of non-discrimination. These include, for example, cases where there is an absence of tenders in response to a prior call for competition, provided that the original contract conditions have not substantially changed, cases of extreme urgency, or importantly for contracts awarded on the basis of a framework agreement, as defined in Article 1(4) and further dealt with in Article 5. Utilities can enter into a framework agreement under which they can 'call off' supplies or services from time to time on terms and conditions set out in the framework. Provided that the framework agreement is itself put out to tender, there is no need to invite tenders for subsequent individual orders. Article 5(4) provides that the framework agreement must not be misused to hinder competition. **5.231**

Any exemptions to the rules in the Directive must be interpreted narrowly. The Court has in particular stressed that the exemption for technical or artistic reasons or reasons connected with protection of exclusive rights—an exemption often used by a utility seeking highly specialized services or goods for which there is only one practicable source of supply—must be construed narrowly and will only be available in exceptional circumstances where there is no actual or potential competition to the appointed contractor.[340] **5.232**

(2) Legislation in the Upstream Hydrocarbons Sector

The Commission's 1988 Working Document on the Internal Energy Market recognized that the oil market was in general international in its scope and subject to competition. However, it expressed concern about the conditions for access to the exploration and production of hydrocarbons, particularly in the Member States with the largest reserves. The Commission drew attention to the fact that access was not always made available on a non-discriminatory basis: national licensing conditions favoured national producers and, even if the licensing system was more open, the terms and conditions of the licences were often awarded so as to protect local content providers. The Commission initially attempted to tackle these problems in Article 3 of the Utilities Directive of 1990, now codified as **5.233**

[339] Case C-243/89 *Commission v Denmark* [1993] ECR I-3353 ('*Storebaelt* case'), involving Danish content clause in procurement for bridge project and holding that the duty to observe the principle of equal treatment lies at the heart of Council Directive 71/305/EEC.

[340] Case C-57/94 *Commission v Italy* [1995] ECR I-1249; Case C-328/92 *Commission v Spain* [1994] ECR I-1569.

Council Directive 93/38,[341] discussed above. Article 3 provided that the Utilities Directive would not apply to contracting entities engaged in the exploration and production of hydrocarbons if the Member State could satisfy the Commission that its licensing system operated in a non-discriminatory fashion.

5.234 The 'alternative regime' in the Utilities Directive could not be used to remove all barriers to entry created by national licensing systems governing exploration and production. In certain regimes, licences were allocated on an entirely discretionary basis without any open competition. In others, national State-owned or controlled companies enjoyed extensive exclusive and special rights, either to reserved acreage or by mandatory inclusion into licensing groups. Finally the Commission suspected that certain countries were using their licensing regimes to control the final destination of products. Furthermore, it was at the discretion of the Member State to apply for the 'alternative regime' under the Utilities Directive. If they chose not to do so, they were under no obligation to amend their licensing regimes, and the oil and gas exploration and production companies had no choice but to apply the Community procurement rules, discussed above.

5.235 To remedy this situation and provide for a minimal level of harmonization of the conditions attaching to upstream activities across the Member States, the Commission proposed the adoption of a separate directive in 1991.[342] The primary aims of the early drafts of the directive on hydrocarbons licensing were to:

—establish a certain level of harmonization in licences so that all companies established in the EC could enjoy equal access to exploration/production activities onshore and offshore on an equal basis;

—remove anti-competitive restrictions in existing licences while permitting restrictions necessary for optimal resource management and depletion policies; and

—limit the restrictive effect of previously granted authorizations, especially those which conferred almost indefinite monopoly rights to explore and exploit certain geographical areas on a single national firm. This last objective proved particularly contentious and was eventually dropped almost entirely (see below).

5.236 In the final version, Directive 94/22 on hydrocarbons licensing[343] guarantees that the decision whether or not to open up a national reserve to exploitation remains a matter for the individual Member State (Recital 4 and Art 2(1)), but having made that decision the national licensing systems must follow the principles elaborated, albeit at a general level, in the remainder of the Directive (Art 2(2)).

---

[341] OJ 1993 L 199/84, as amended by Directive 94/22/EEC, OJ 1994 L 164/3, and Directive 98/4/EC, OJ 1998 L 101/1.

[342] See COM(92) 110 final.

[343] Council Directive 94/22/EC on conditions for granting and using authorizations for the prospection, exploration, and production of hydrocarbons, OJ 1994 L 164/3.

Entities that are effectively controlled by third countries or third-country nationals, however, may be refused access on grounds of national security.

The Directive is essentially a framework measure that lays down the general principles on which the national regimes should be based. Article 3 requires Member States to take the necessary measures to ensure that authorizations for the granting of exclusive rights to carry out activities relating to the prospection, exploration, and production of hydrocarbons are granted under open conditions. This means that Member States can either choose 'licensing rounds' under which they invite applications from interested entities, or if individual entities can apply for an authorization at any time, to publish a notice in the Official Journal of the EC that an application has been received. Other interested parties should have at least ninety days to submit an application (Art 3(2)(a) and (b)). Obviously only countries with significant reserves will be interested in going to the trouble of organizing licensing rounds. The second procedure, however, ensures that competitive access to smaller reserves, usually exploited on an ad hoc basis, will also be possible. Many notices have now been issued under the Article 3(2)(b) procedures. **5.237**

The Directive focuses on 'authorizations', which are defined in Article 1(3) as: **5.238**

> any law, regulation, administrative or contractual provision or instrument . . . by which the competent authorities of a Member State entitle an entity to exercise . . . the exclusive right to prospect or explore for, or produce hydrocarbons in a geographical area.

Not every authorization must be subject to competitive procedures. In any event, authorizations granted on a non-exclusive basis need not be made under the procedures laid down in Article 3(2). Prospection licences are often not exclusive, for example. Certain technical matters which may require an administrative act on the part of the competent licensing authorities, such as a change of name or ownership of an existing authorization holder, or the prolongation of an existing authorization, need not be part of a competitive procedure (see Art 3(5)). **5.239**

Article 4 deals with the size of the geographical areas which are to be subject to the procedures laid down in Article 3(2), the duration of the authorization, and the period for which entities may enjoy exclusive rights to perform authorized activities. This Article only stipulates very general criteria for defining such geographical areas, duration, and periods of exclusivity, however, and Member States have a substantial margin of discretion in their implementation. **5.240**

Article 5 lists the criteria by which authorizations should be granted. These are enumerated in Article 1(a), technical and financial capability of the entities, and 1(b), the way in which they propose to carry out the activity in question. The relevant authorizations may be granted by way of auction, so that the price which the entity is prepared to pay for the authorization may also be a relevant criterion. If **5.241** the application of the above criteria does not produce a final choice of applicant, then additional selection criteria may be used as long as these are objective and non-discriminatory.

5.242 The competent authorities are entitled in appraising applications to take account of the applicant's previous track record, but proven performance in the Member State will not be a valid criterion as this will inevitably lead to discrimination against out-of-State entities.

5.243 Article 5 also recognizes that Member States may determine the composition of an entity to which they grant an authorization, but only if they do so on the basis of objective and non-discriminatory criteria. An operator may also be determined on the same basis. All relevant licensing criteria must be drawn up and published in advance in the Official Journal of the EC, but if these details have been published in a national official journal, then a simple reference to the latter in the Official Journal will suffice.

5.244 The conditions and requirements concerning the exercise or termination of the activity in question (further referred to in Article 5(2)) must also be made available in advance to interested parties. These conditions must be applied in a non-discriminatory manner. An entity whose application for an authorization is unsuccessful has the right to a reasoned decision.

5.245 Article 6 also governs these conditions, but is expressed in negative terms. Member States are forbidden from laying down conditions, and Article 6 determines what Member States may not do with respect to licensing conditions. Of importance is Article 6(3), which deals with State participation, for example, through the vehicle of a management company.

5.246 Article 6(3) contains complex rules on State participation in hydrocarbon production. It has not been uncommon in several Member States for governments to compel private operators to accept the inclusion of a State-owned participant in their activities as part of the conditions of a licensing award. The legality of the compulsory inclusion of such an enterprise under primary law is not entirely free from doubt. Compulsory participation may interfere with the right of establishment, guaranteed by Article 43 (ex Art 52) of the EC Treaty.[344] This Article has traditionally been interpreted more narrowly than the other freedoms: the ECJ has interpreted it as primarily a prohibition on discrimination.[345] As long as domestic and non-domestic companies are treated alike, this Article is not breached. In additional case-law, however, the ECJ has expanded its interpretation of this

---

[344] Art 43 (ex Art 52) of the Treaty provides in part: '[R]estrictions on the freedom of establishment of nationals of a Member State in the territory of another Member State shall be prohibited'.

[345] Case 2/74 *Reyners v Belgium* [1974] ECR 631; Case 71/76 *Thieffry v Conseil de l'ordre des avocats de la Cour de Paris* [1977] ECR 765.

Article to suggest that it prohibits any direct or indirect restriction on the effective exercise of the freedom of establishment.[346]

Nevertheless, it remains unclear whether the restrictions at issue in these cases were contrary to Article 43 of the Treaty because they in fact resulted in a form of indirect discrimination. It therefore remains questionable whether a national measure, such as a provision in the relevant laws or regulations on exploration or production that reserves a share in a certain activity to a State-owned or controlled enterprise, could be said to result in indirect discrimination if the measure was applied to all firms equally. On the other hand, these same measures reserve certain activities to a nationally owned or controlled company, thus limiting access to a certain part of the national market to competitors, whatever their place of establishment. Unfortunately, it is not yet clear from the ECJ's case-law whether and to what extent Article 43 guarantees market access such that any national rule limiting such access would *prima facie* conflict with this Article and could only be justified either under one of the explicit exceptions listed in Article 46 or under a rule-of-reason type test. **5.247**

In any event, Article 6(3) of the Directive assumes that State participation is not of itself contrary to Article 43 of the Treaty, but it then attempts to delimit any potential discrimination that might flow from the fact of State participation. In particular, it requires that the 'State' company shall only assume rights and obligations in proportion to its participation. Thus, if the State participates for 40 per cent in the profits of production, then its voting rights and its participation in company boards should be limited accordingly. Secondly, Article 6(3) seeks to prevent State participation being used as a means to influence procurement. Hence, the State or its legal representative must not be party to information nor exercise any voting rights on decisions regarding sources of procurement for entities. In addition, Article 6(3) provides that Member States shall put in place arrangements requiring the State participant to erect a 'Chinese wall' where a company acts as both licence holder on its own account and manager of the State's participation. It must guarantee that there is no flow of information between these two functions and must keep separate accounts for both sets of activities. This 'Chinese wall' can, however, be crossed if the legal person responsible for managing the State's participation engages the part of the legal person that holds the authorization as a consultant. Information necessary to perform such consultancy activities can be permissibly passed 'over the wall'. **5.248**

The Commission originally intended that the Directive should have retroactive effect so that individual authorizations, such as that granted to the Italian State **5.249**

[346] Case C-19/92 *Kraus v Land Baden-Württemberg* [1993] ECR I-1663; Case C-55/94 *Gebhard v Consiglio dell'Ordine degli Advocati e Procuratoni di Milano* [1995] ECR I-4165 (involving freedom to provide legal services).

energy holding company ENI, would no longer be indefinite and would no longer extend to the entire output of a field. The attempt to alter existing rights on a retroactive basis was firmly resisted by both the industry and the Member States. In the final version, Article 7 provides that any legal, regulatory, or administrative provision which reserves to a single entity the right to obtain authorizations in a specific geographical area was to be abolished before 1 January 1997. This means that the underlying regimes must be abolished, but does not seem to require that authorizations granted under those regimes be modified.

5.250 Article 8 is a reciprocity provision that governs the situation where competitive access is not made available on a reciprocal basis in third countries. Member States should notify the Commission of any general difficulties encountered by entities in gaining access to reserves in third countries. If the Commission establishes that a third country is not granting Community entities access to the relevant activities on a comparable basis to that which their own national companies enjoy within the Community, then the Commission may submit proposals to the Community for the appropriate mandate for negotiation with a view to obtaining comparable competitive opportunities for Community entities. The Council shall decide on the basis of qualified majority. Individual measures can be proposed by the Commission to the Council to allow one or more Member States to refuse an authorization to an entity that is effectively controlled by a third country and/or nationals from that country.

5.251 Articles 9 and 10 contain reporting requirements. Member States must publish annual reports on the areas that have been opened up to the activities covered by the Directive, the authorizations granted, and the entities holding those authorizations. In addition, the competent authorities for issuing licences and any subsequent changes must be notified to the Commission.

5.252 Article 12 forms a 'bridge' with the rules on procurement in the utilities sector. As discussed above, the Directive on Procurement contains an 'alternative' or parallel procedure, which allows Member States to notify their oil and gas (and indeed coal) licensing regimes to the Commission with a view to obtaining an exemption for certain contracting entities from the substantive rules in the Directive. Article 12 provides in essence that once a Member State has complied with the exemption procedure, then the conditions in Article 3 of Directive 90/531 (now Directive 93/38) are considered to be satisfied.

5.253 It should be noted that Article 12 uses the term 'compliance', and not merely adoption or implementation. This suggests that the exemption will only be available once it is established that the Directive is implemented correctly and in full in the Member State in question. Unlike Article 3 of Directive 90/531, however, this later Directive does not envisage any mechanism by which the Commission can screen the relevant national provisions in advance. If the Commission is of the view that a Member State has not properly implemented the Directive on hydrocarbons licensing but has exempted the relevant contracting entities from the national rules implementing the Community procurement regime, then it will have to initiate Treaty infringement proceedings for both sets of Directives. It is perhaps understandable that several Member States have sought to consult informally with the Commission to ensure that the proposed changes to their national licensing regimes do in fact comply with the Directive on hydrocarbons licensing. Furthermore, it should be noted that even if the exemption applies, the contracting entities involved are not entirely free from the rigours of the Community procurement regime—they must continue to respect certain obligations.

Finally, Article 13 of the Directive is unusual in that it grants a specific derogation **5.254** to Denmark with respect to Articles 3 and 5 for new authorizations granted by Denmark before 31 December 2012 in respect of areas to be relinquished on 8 July 2012, upon the expiration of the authorization issued to the Danish firm AP Møller. The new authorizations must be granted on the basis of objective and non-discriminatory principles. Although the European Parliament protested at the inclusion of this derogation, the Council was only prepared to concede that it would not create any precedent for other Member States.

(3) The Electricity Directive

Background and aims

The Electricity Directive was adopted in late 1996, and entered into force in **5.255** February 1997.[347] Its adoption marked the end of almost eight years of difficult negotiations during which a large number of compromises were eventually reached and accepted by the Commission.[348]

[347] European Parliament and Council Directive 96/92 concerning common rules for the internal electricity market, OJ L 27 (30 Jan 1997). For a country-by-country analysis of national electricity legislation in light of the Electricity Directive, see 'Electricity Liberalisation in Europe: Law and Commentary' [1998] OGLTR, Special Issue (Sep 1998).

[348] In February 1992 the Commission formally submitted a framework and set of common rules for the completion of the internal market in electricity and gas. Proposal for a Council Directive concerning common rules for the internal market in electricity, OJ C 65/04, and natural gas, OJ C 65/13 (1992). The formal submission of the proposed directives met with strong opposition from a number of interest groups including consumer groups. See eg Eurelectric, 'The Outlook for Europe's Electricity Market' (conference proceedings of 17 March 1992, Brussels) (1992). Within 10 months, on 30 November 1992, the Council passed a resolution urging the Commission to consider modifications to the proposed directives. See *Agence Europe*, No 5869 (2 December 1992). In its conclusions the Council stressed that obstacles to the internal market still had to be removed and that fresh progress had to be made. The Council outlined 6 principles for the internal market: security of supply, environmental protection, protection of small consumers, transparency and non-discrimination, recognition of the differences between national systems, and the need for transitional provisions. Additional opposition to the Commission's original proposals within the EC institutional framework was expressed several months later in a report issued by the European Parliament's Committee on Energy, Research, and Technology, see draft report of the Committee (C Desama, rapporteur) (16 Feb 1993) and in an opinion issued by the Economic and Social

5.256 The most important of these compromises includes the introduction of the 'Single Buyer' (SB) model, as proposed by the French government in 1994. Although the Commission itself expressed severe doubts as to the legality of the concept in its Working Paper of March 1995,[349] further subsequent amendments to the draft directive, particularly with a view to strengthening the regulatory framework within which the SB would operate, paved the way to the eventual incorporation of the model into the Directive. The broad aims of the Directive are reflected in the 39 Recitals to the detailed Articles. Recital 9 provides that electricity undertakings must be able to operate, without prejudice to compliance with public service obligations, with a view to achieving a competitive market in electricity, but Recitals 10 and 11 recognize both the structural differences in the Member States and the different systems for regulating the sector and in accordance with the principle of subsidiarity the need to confine the provisions of the Directive to general principles, the detailed implementation of which should be left to the Member States. Recital 34 states that due to the diversity of structures and the special characteristics of systems in Member States, there should be different options for system access. Finally, the last Recital admits that while the Directive constitutes a further phase of liberalization, once it has been put into effect certain obstacles to electricity will nevertheless remain in place. Thus, proposals for improving the operation of the internal electricity market may be made in the light of experience. Unlike earlier drafts, there is no firm commitment to introducing a further or final stage of market liberalization.

Organization of the sector

5.257 Article 3 sets out the general rules for the organization of the sector. It provides first that Member States must ensure that electricity undertakings are operated in accordance with the principles of the Directive, with a view to achieving a competitive market in electricity. The two approaches to system access referred to in Articles 17 and 18 must lead to equivalent economic results, a directly comparable level of opening of markets, and a directly comparable degree of access to electricity markets.

5.258 Article 3(2) recognizes that Member States, with due regard to Article 86 of the EC Treaty, may impose public service obligations on these undertakings, which may relate to security, including security of supply, regularity, quality and prices of

Committee, OJ C 73/31 (1993). In November 1993 the European Parliament, on the basis of Mr Desama's report, expressed its opinion by issuing what was essentially a set of extensive counter-proposals. In the light of this opposition, the Commission retreated from its position and developed a set of amended proposals in conjunction with the European Parliament. See Amended Proposal for a European Parliament and Council Directive concerning common rules for the internal market in electricity, COM(93) 643 final, OJ C 123/1; (and in natural gas) OJ C 123/26 (1994).

[349] European Commission, Working Paper of 22 March 1995.

supplies, and environmental protection. Such obligations must be clearly defined, transparent, non-discriminatory, and verifiable. Examples of such obligations are an obligation for a distribution company to supply all customers of similar types at an equal price per KWh, or to purchase electricity produced using renewable energy sources. As a means of carrying out these public service obligations, the Member States can implement long-term planning. Member States must notify public service obligations to the Commission, which will check that they are appropriate and in proportion.

Importantly, Article 3(3) provides that Member States may decide not to apply the provisions of Articles 5 and 6 (rules on generation), 17 and 18 (rules on system access), and 21 (rules on direct lines) if the application of those provisions would obstruct the performance, in law or in fact, of public service obligations, but only insofar as the development of trade is not adversely affected to an extent contrary to the interest of the Community. It is suggested that Member States may rely upon Article 3(3) in individual cases only: they may not suspend the operation of the above Articles on a general basis. Furthermore, the last sentence of Article 3(3), which stresses that the Community interest includes competition with regard to eligible customers, suggests that Member States cannot suspend the operation of these various provisions if this would interfere with the minimum level of market opening guaranteed by Article 19 (see below). **5.259**

Generation

The Directive left much of the Commission's proposals in place with regard to competition in generation. New generation can be either licensed or approved subject to a tendering procedure (Art 4). The latter procedure would provide Member States with greater scope for central planning. Article 5, which covers licensing, gives a non-exhaustive list of criteria which may be applied to approving new market entrants. Independent power producers, as defined (albeit somewhat confusingly) in Article 2(4), must always be eligible for authorization procedures: they do not need to wait until a tendering round is organized. **5.260**

Given that Article 3(3) also allows the Member States to engage in long-term planning and to impose vaguely defined public service obligations as part of their licensing procedure, there can be no guarantee that new entrants will compete on a level playing field. Member States will presumably remain entitled to determine via long-term planning whether certain types of generation are permissible or not, and it is conceivable that they may use public-interest type arguments to impose some sort of cap on the amount of independent generation that can be licensed. **5.261**

The tendering procedure (Art 6) also leaves a lot to be desired, especially when this is coupled to a system based on the single buyer model (as defined in Art 2(23)). Article 6(2) allows the transmission system operator to estimate the generation **5.262** and transmission capacity needs for each system. As discussed below, the Directive does not impose any clear separation of the activities of the single buyer and the transmission operator. Although an independent body must supervise the tendering procedure, the decision when to open a tender for new capacity, as well as the amount needed, rests with the major player in the centralized systems.

5.263 New market entrants are therefore not assured of an easy passage into a market, whether through the licensing or the tendering procedure. The articles leave much scope for divergence in implementation in the various Member States, many of which already have overcapacity in electricity supply.

Transmission system operation

5.264 The Directive contains rules on the operation of the transmission system. In particular, Member States will be required to appoint a system operator (SO) who will be responsible, *inter alia,* for drawing up clear technical rules on interconnection which must be notified to the Commission in accordance with Article 8 of Council Directive 83/189 (Art 7(2)). The SO will also be responsible for managing energy flows, securing ancillary services, and guaranteeing security of supply. It must not discriminate between system users or classes of system users, particularly in favour of its own subsidiaries or shareholders.

5.265 Significantly, Article 7(6) requires that the SO is functionally unbundled from generation and distribution activities so that the management of these activities is separated and separate accounts are published. Unfortunately, however, there is no clear stipulation in the Directive that the Single Buyer functions should be kept separate from those of the transmission functions of the SO. Article 7(6) refers to the separation of the SO from 'other activities', while Article 15 requires that an SB in a vertically integrated company must operate separately from generation and distribution activities. Article 2(23) defines the SB, and indicates that the SB will be responsible for the unified management of the transmission system and/or electricity trading. This lack of clarity is particularly unfortunate as it could mean that the SB will have considerable weight in determining the economic side of dispatch, with the SO in such a system only dealing with technical matters. Article 8 entrusts responsibility of technical dispatch to the SO, while Article 8(2) also implies that economic dispatch could be entrusted to the SO.

5.266 If an electricity market is to function properly, both technical and economic dispatch must be taken out of the hands of those currently responsible for electricity generation and trading. The Directive makes no mention at all of pooling systems or any other form of trading mechanism: it is left to the discretion of the individual Member States whether or not they wish to adopt such a mechanism. Indeed, Article 8(2) seems to imply that any rules on economic dispatch may take other factors besides economic precedence of available installations into account. A Member State may require in any event that the SO give priority to dispatching generating installations using renewable energy sources or waste or producing combined heat and power. The term 'renewable energy' is not defined but probably does not include either hydro or nuclear power. The Commission itself has admitted that the priority dispatch mechanism provided in the Directive appears to be of limited use in the absence of accompanying financial measures.

Finally, for reasons of security of supply, a Member State can direct that priority **5.267** be given to the dispatch of generating installations using indigenous primary energy fuel sources, to an extent not exceeding in any calendar year 15 per cent of the overall primary energy necessary to produce the electricity consumed in the Member State concerned (Art 8(4)). However, the Commission does not envisage that this provision should be used to justify the refusal of access to the network for electricity produced from other sources. This provision will be of some assistance to those countries that have only one uneconomic fuel to support, such as coal or peat (eg Ireland) but it will obviously be of limited value to those which subsidize more than one fuel, who will find themselves quickly over the 15 per cent threshold. Nevertheless, there are, of course, other ways in which domestic fuels could be supported, for example through subsidization. Any form of subsidy whether direct or indirect would have to be granted in accordance with the EC or ECSC rules on State aid.

Articles 10 to 12 deal with the operation of distribution systems. Article 10 recognizes that an obligation to supply can be placed on distribution customers and **5.268** the tariff for such supplies can be regulated. Distribution system operators will be subject to obligations generally similar to those imposed upon the transmission system operators.

System access

Member States may choose between an SB model of system access (Art 18) and **5.269** the negotiated third party access model (Art 17). Under the latter, SOs are now required to publish indicative prices for the use of the transmission/distribution system. Member States can also opt for regulated access, giving eligible customers a right of access, on the basis of published tariffs. With regard to the SB system, Member States also have a choice as to whether to impose an obligation on the SB to buy all electricity to be transported through the system. If no such obligation is imposed, then access rights for 'eligibles' must be available on a negotiated basis, and on the basis of a published tariff. In all cases, access to the system can be refused if there is insufficient capacity or if this threatens the performance of public supply obligations. The Directive does not oblige the SO to create new capacity where there is a lack of capacity.

5.270 The question of who is 'eligible' to request access in the terms of either Article 17 or 18 was not finally determined in the Directive, and there is no longer any definition of this term in Article 2. Again, major differences of opinion as to who should be deemed eligible frustrated negotiations on the Directive, particularly as the French government was adamant that distributors should not be included in the definition, but that this category should be restricted to large consumers. As a result, a complex compromise has been written into Article 19. This Article aims to guarantee that both the SB and TPA systems should lead to an equivalent level of market access based on final consumers consuming more than 40 GWh per year. The calculations will be performed by the Commission based on Member State returns. This share is to be progressively opened after three years to 20 GWh and after six years to 9 GWh. Attempts to lower these thresholds to 5 GWh and 1 GWh failed.

5.271 Member States can specify which types of customers—ie final consumers and/or distribution companies—can gain access provided all final consumers over 100 GWh are included. This figure refers to a consumption site basis and includes self-generation but does not refer to the cumulative consumption of a group holding. At the same time distributors, even if not designated as eligible customers, must have access to supply the volume consumed by such customers. Hence the distribution supplier can seek access to the extent of the eligible customer's entitlement. Criteria defining eligibility must be published. Given that Article 3 requires that the two systems of access must lead to equivalent economic results, the threshold levels stipulated in Article 19 must be taken as absolute minima. It therefore seems that a Member State cannot invoke public service criteria—as very loosely defined in Article 3—to deny access if this would prevent the degree of market opening required by Article 19.

5.272 It should be recalled that Article 3 also provides that Member States may not decide to apply Articles 5, 6, 17, 18, and 20 (direct lines) if to do so would obstruct the performance of obligations of general economic interest subject to the Community interest. The latter phrase must surely be interpreted in the light of the thresholds set out in Article 19 as well as the general principles of Community law. Hence it is unlikely that Member States could justify a blanket suspension of the rights provided under Articles 5, 6, 17, 18, and 20: only individual cases should justify exemption.

5.273 Eligible customers can contract to purchase electricity supply from independent producers inside their territory as well as from producers and other supply undertakings outside their territory. Trade between different systems—TPA or SB—will be possible where the customer is eligible in both systems. If a customer is eligible in only one system and access is refused, the Commission may require the refusing system to give access at the request of the Member State where the eligible customer is located. Despite the original intention behind the provision to ensure that electricity trade is not only one-way, ie from closed to open systems, this provision is likely to have the opposite effect. It will probably only assist customers in more liberal States since these countries are more likely to meet the requests than a closed system. The question arises, however, as to whether the more liberalized State could choose to make the request if the exporting State did not allow an equivalent level of access. In this way the more liberalized Member State could protect its own market from exports from closed systems. Obviously much depends on whether the gradual approach to liberalization, the SB system, and the rules in the Directive are themselves in conformity with the Treaty rules of free movement of goods. It remains to be seen whether the European courts will take the view that the criteria imposed by the Directive as well as the gradual approach to market opening conform with the basic rules on free movement.[350]

Article 19 also provides that the Commission is to review the working of this system and report on the possible disequilibrium in the market some four and a half years after the measure has entered into force. According to the Council Declaration appended to the Directive, the outcome of the review should not, however, undermine the status of the Article. **5.274**

It also remains to be seen to what extent imported supply can be preferred to independent generation, or vice versa, in reaching the thresholds laid down in Article 19. If a Member State can demonstrate that final consumers consuming more than 40 GWh per year can buy directly from independents so that there is no scope for imported supplies, would this provide a valid ground in Community law for restricting such imports? **5.275**

Stranded assets

Article 24 of the Directive stipulates that the Commission can authorize the Member States to adopt transitional measures that derogate from some of the Directive's provisions, in order to allow them to be able to respect commitments or guarantees of operation granted before the Directive enters into force. In 1998 it was reported that thirteen Member States claimed the need for transitional regimes in the electricity sector.[351] However, when the Commission received the notifications of the Member States for transitional measures in the meaning of Article 24 of the Directive, it quickly became apparent that the majority of Member States wished to cope with the question of stranded costs by introducing financing mechanisms, rather than measures derogating from the Directive. **5.276**

[350] For further analysis of the reciprocity provision in the Directive as well as of some national examples see A Johnson, 'Maintaining the Balance of Power: Liberalisation, Reciprocity and Electricity in the European Community', vol 17, No 2, J Energy & Nat. Res. L 121–50 (1999).

[351] Europe Energy, 27 November 1998, 21.

Insofar as these financing mechanisms are based on taxes or levies on electricity produced or sold, they involve State resources within the meaning of the State aid rules of the EC Treaty. The Commission appears to have taken a strict approach to the application of this Article in its first eight decisions made in July 1999, whereby it determined that most of the notified measures did not constitute derogations from the Directive and had instead to be analysed under the rules on State aid.[352] The Commission did grant limited derogations for specific transitional measures, however, in the case of Germany and Luxembourg.

Conclusion

5.277 The Electricity Directive has become a complex measure: it is perhaps illustrative of a new breed of Community measures which, in deference to subsidiarity principles, allow Member States to pursue a common result—in this case to ensure a certain level of market opening—but in very different ways. This will mean that implementation of the Directive at national level will have to be carefully monitored to ensure that each system is in fact capable of delivering the necessary results. Many of the Directive's provisions are defined in vague terms so that there appears to be substantial scope for divergent interpretation and implementation. Nevertheless, it has been an important stimulus for significant market and regulatory dynamics that are still unfolding across greater Europe.

(4) The Gas Directive

Background and scope

5.278 The plans to liberalize the Community's gas market initially proceeded in parallel with those for the electricity market, with initial proposals for an internal market for natural gas also being first published in the Official Journal in February 1992. Little progress was made on this proposal, and on 11 February 1994 the Commission forwarded an amended proposal to the Council and the European Parliament.[353] Given the obstacles to achieving any consensus whatsoever on either the electricity or the gas drafts, the Energy Council of November 1994 decided to split the dossier and accept that work would first focus on the Electricity Directive. Following the successful adoption of this measure in 1996, the Irish Presidency circulated a draft gas directive in October 1996, largely modelled on the provisions of the Electricity Directive. This draft was subject to a variety of amendments, and a number of compromises had to be made before a qualified

[352] See eg Commission Decision 1999/791/EC of 8 July 1999 concerning the application of the United Kingdom of Great Britain and Northern Ireland for a transitional regime under Article 24 of Directive 96/92/EC of the European Parliament and of the Council concerning common rules for the internal market in electricity, and accompanying decisions regarding the applications of France, Luxembourg, Germany, Austria, the Netherlands, Spain, and Denmark, OJ 1999 L 319.

[353] COM(93) 643 final.

majority could be obtained in the Council. The Directive was finally adopted on 22 June 1998, and the Member States were given two years to transpose it into national regimes.[354]

The Directive establishes common rules for the transmission and storage of natural gas, distribution, and supply. It lays down rules relating to the organization and functioning of the natural gas sector (including liquified natural gas), access to the market, the criteria and procedures applicable to the granting of relevant authorization, and the operation of systems. **5.279**

Article 3(1) provides that Member States shall ensure, on the basis of their institutional organization and with due regard to the principle of subsidiarity, that, without prejudice to Article 3(2), natural gas undertakings are operated on commercial principles, with a view to achieving a competitive market in natural gas, and shall not discriminate between these undertakings as regards either rights or obligations. **5.280**

Article 3(2) almost replicates its counterpart in the Electricity Directive, recognizing that Member States can impose public service obligations which may relate to security, including security of supply, regularity, quality and price of supplies, and environmental protection. These obligations must be clearly defined, transparent, non-discriminatory, and verifiable, and they (and any revisions) must be published and notified to the Commission. Member States also have the option to introduce long-term planning as a means of carrying out public service obligations. **5.281**

Article 3(3) provides for an exemption from the application of the authorization procedure set out in Article 4 insofar as the construction of new facilities would obstruct the performance of the obligations imposed on natural gas undertakings in the general economic interest and insofar as the development of trade would not be affected to such an extent as was contrary to the interests of the Community. This is of course an application of Article 90(2) EC. **5.282**

Article 4 deals with authorizations for the construction and operation of transmission, storage, and distribution facilities as well as LNG facilities. If such a system of authorization is introduced it must be based on non-discriminatory criteria which are to be made public within six months after the entry into force of the Directive. Any refusal to grant an authorization must be capable of appeal. **5.283**

Transmission and storage

Unlike the Electricity Directive there is no requirement that these functions should be unbundled in any way from other functions in a vertically or horizontally **5.284**

[354] OJ L 204/1 (1998).

integrated utility. The transmission undertaking must operate its part of the integrated system in a secure, reliable, and efficient manner, with due regard to the environment. It must not discriminate between users or classes of users of the system, particularly in favour of its subsidiaries or shareholders.

5.285 Technical rules establishing the minimum design and operational requirements for connection to the system of LNG facilities, storage facilities, directly connected consumers' equipment, other transmission or distribution systems, and direct lines must be developed and made available. They must also be notified to the Commission in accordance with Article 8 of Council Directive 83/189. These requirements shall ensure the interoperability of systems and shall be objective and non-discriminatory. Transmission undertakings must provide any other transmission or distribution system operator with sufficient information to ensure that the transport of gas can take place in a manner compatible with secure and efficient operation of the interconnected system.

5.286 This provision does not appear to provide for any form of interconnection with or access to storage facilities. Each transmission undertaking must preserve the confidentiality of any commercially sensitive information it obtains from other systems or system users (Art 8).

5.287 Chapter IV deals with distribution and supply. Article 9 provides that distribution undertakings can be placed under public service duties to ensure supply to all customers in a given area or a certain class or both. The tariff for such supplies may be regulated and may ensure equal treatment for all customers concerned. Distribution undertakings must maintain and develop a secure and reliable system, with due regard to the environment, and must refrain from discrimination between users or in favour of its own subsidiaries or shareholders.

5.288 Chapter V deals with unbundling and transparency of accounts, and although it is phrased in similar terms to the equivalent provisions in the Electricity Directive, it is not so far-reaching. Article 13 provides that accounts must be drawn up and submitted and published (in accordance with the provisions of Council Directive 78/660). Integrated gas companies must, for internal accounting purposes, keep separate accounts for their different functions as if they were separate undertakings, and they must specify the rules for allocation of assets and liabilities, and expenditure and income. Member States can determine which authorities should have access to these accounts. The dispute settlement authority referred to in Article 21(2) should have such access.

System access

5.289 There is no Single Buyer model as such, but Member States can choose between a system of negotiated access (Art 15) or regulated access (Art 16) or both. In the case of negotiated access, natural gas undertakings and eligible customers inside or outside the territory covered by the system must be able to negotiate access to the system so as to conclude supply contracts with each other on the basis of voluntary commercial agreements. Access contracts must be negotiated with the relevant transmission and/or distribution undertaking. However, in contrast to rules for negotiated access under the Electricity Directive, there is no requirement to publish indicative tariffs. Regulated access (Art 16) will be available to natural gas undertakings, supply undertakings, and eligible customers both inside and outside the territory covered by the system, on the basis of published tariffs.

In both cases, transmission and distribution operators can refuse access to the system where this would prevent them carrying out public service obligations or where they do not have capacity or on the basis of serious economic and financial difficulties with take-or-pay contracts. Duly substantiated reasons must be given for such a refusal. **5.290**

Article 23 refers to access to upstream pipelines, defined in Article 2(2) as pipelines constructed and/or operated as part of gas or oil production processes. The Member States must provide for regimes allowing third parties to have access to such pipelines unless they are being used for local production operations. Article 23 sets out a number of reasons which may be taken into account when justifying a refusal of access, but this list does not appear to be exhaustive. **5.291**

Article 18—modelled on the Electricity Directive—reflects and attempts to deal with market opening. Article 18(3) provides for an opening of the market equal to at least 20 per cent of the total annual gas consumption of the national gas market. This minimum percentage shall increase to 28 per cent five years after the entry into force of the Directive and to 33 per cent ten years after the entry into force of the Directive. However, the Directive also incorporates qualitative rules: eligible consumers must include final customers consuming more than 25 million cubic metres of gas per year and gas-fired power generators, irrespective of their annual consumption (to be reduced to 15 million cubic metres after five years and to 5 million after ten years). If the last category is too large, however, the Member State can introduce a threshold of eligibility for combined heat and power generators, which is not lower than the 25 million cubic metre threshold. Lastly, if the definition of eligible customers would result in a greater market opening of more than 30 per cent (increasing to 38 per cent and then 43 per cent after first five and then ten years), then the qualitative definition of eligible consumer can be changed and the thresholds raised. It should be noted that for emergent markets these gradual percentages only apply after the expiration of the derogation referred to in Article 26(2). **5.292**

Other provisions

5.293 Article 21 deals with dispute resolution. Competent authorities which are independent from the undertakings must be designated to settle disputes relating to the contracts and negotiations in question and must have the power to settle such disputes. As with the Electricity Directive, cross-border disputes must be resolved by the authority covering the system of the system operator that refuses access to its system. Member States must create appropriate and efficient mechanisms for regulation, control, and transparency so as to avoid any abuse of a dominant position, including predatory behaviour. These mechanisms should in particular take account of Article 82 (ex Art 86) EC Treaty.

5.294 Chapter VII contains some important final provisions. Article 24 is identical in wording to its equivalent in the Electricity Directive and allows Member States to take safeguard measures in the event of a sudden crisis in the energy market. Such a crisis is not a purely 'economic crisis'—it must threaten the physical safety and security of persons, apparatus, and installations or system integrity. Safeguard measures must be notified to the Commission, which may also be given the power to direct the Member State to amend or abolish these measures if they distort competition or adversely affect trade.

Take-or-pay contracts

5.295 Article 25 deals with the counterpart to stranded assets in the electricity sector—the problems created for those who have concluded take-or-pay contracts which oblige them to purchase a minimum offtake at a guaranteed price under changed market conditions.[355] The Article will allow the Member States concerned by these problems to apply to the Commission for a transitional regime, which in effect will allow them to suspend access to the system as required under Articles 15 or 16. The Article envisages that this regime will apply to contracts concluded before and after the Directive entered into force, but the conditions for derogation for new contracts are much stricter. The Directive does not require that such contracts be actually modified.

5.296 Article 26 introduces the concept of an emergent market, defined in Article 2 as a market in a Member State in which the first long-term gas supply contract is in effect for less than ten years on the date the Directive enters into force. Where implementation of the Directive would cause problems in a geographically limited area, in particular where a new infrastructure (ie less than ten years old) is being built to introduce gas onto the market, then derogations can be introduced to Articles 4, 18, and 20 of the Directive. These derogations may also apply if a

[355] For further analysis see M Brothwood, 'The EU Gas Directive and Take or Pay Contracts', 8 OGLTR 318–21 (Aug 1998).

Member State is not directly connected to the interconnected system of another Member State and has only one main external supplier: that is, a supplier having more than 75 per cent of the market.

(5) *Legislation on the Heat Sector and CHP*

As discussed above in paras 5.190–5.191, early efforts to develop EC legislation in the heat sector were undertaken at the start of the 1973 energy crisis as part of the Community programme on the rational use of energy.[356] This resulted in a series of EC recommendations relating, *inter alia*, to the heat sector and the rational use of heat.[357] **5.297**

Other directives relevant to the heat sector have been issued subsequently pursuant to the Community's programmes of harmonization and standardization.[358] These efforts extend to areas such as the regulation of construction products, wherein a harmonization directive[359] obliges Member States to enforce laws, regulations, and administrative provisions which will ensure that construction products will satisfy the essential requirements as listed in this Directive, such as those on heat retention.[360] These essential requirements provide the basis for the preparation of harmonized standards at European level for construction products. **5.298**

---

356 See European Commission, 'Rational Utilisation of Energy', OJ C 152/5 (9 July 1975); M Davis and A Colling, 'District Heating and the Energy Policy of the EEC' in W Orchard and A Sherratt (eds), *Combined Heat and Power: Whole City Heating, Planning Tomorrow's Energy Economy* (1980) 91–109.

357 See eg Council Recommendation 76/492/EEC of 4 May 1976 on the rational use of energy by promoting the thermal insulation of buildings, OJ L 140/11 (1976) (making recommendations regarding the installation and use of various regulating and metering devices for the heating systems of existing buildings, office and residential); Council Recommendation 77/712/EEC of 25/10/77 on the regulating of space heating, the production of domestic hot water, and the metering of heat in new buildings, OJ L 295/1 (1977) (recommending that Member States implement measures on installation of automatic programming and regulating devices); Council Recommendation 77/714/EEC of 25/10/77 on the creation in the Member States of advisory bodies or committees to promote combined heat and power production and the exploitation of residual heat, OJ L 295/5 (1977) (inviting Member States to create advisory bodies/committees to be responsible for giving an opinion on all measures to increase efficiency in supply of heat for industry and to promote use of remote heat supply systems, and inviting a regular exchange of views at Community level); and Council Recommendation 77/713/EEC of 25/10/77 on the rational use of energy in industrial undertakings.

358 See eg Directive 90/396 on the approximation of the laws of Member States relating to gas appliances burning gaseous fuels, OJ 1990 L 196, as amended by Directive 93/68, OJ 1993 L 220; Directive 92/42 on efficiency requirements for new hot-water boilers fired with liquid or gaseous fuels, OJ 1992 L 167/77, as amended by Directive 93/63, OJ 1993 L 20.

359 Council Directive 89/106/EEC of 21 December 1988 on the approximation of laws, regulations, and administrative provisions of the Member States relating to construction products, OJ L 40/12, as amended by Council Directive 93/68/EEC of 22 July 1993, OJ L 220/1.

360 The 'heat retention' requirement is a general requirement that the 'construction works and heating, cooling and ventilation installations must be designed and built in such a way that the amount of energy required in use shall be low, having regard to the climatic conditions of the location and the occupants'.

5.299 The Electricity and Gas Directives do not directly address the heat sector, although they contain a few rules which implicate in some way the legal frameworks for heat production using either CHP units or HOB (heat-only boiler) units. These rules include the following:

—rules allowing the possible creation of 'priority rights' in central electricity dispatch for electricity produced from CHP, waste, or renewable energy sources (found in the Electricity Directive, Arts 8(3) and 11(3));
—rules on authorization of independent producers (found in the Electricity Directive, Arts 3–6), which indicate that such producers should always be eligible for an authorization procedure (Art 6(6));
—rules on access to gas or electricity networks that implicate CHP producers (found in Electricity Directive, Art 20, and Gas Directive, Art 18(2)); and
—rules allowing the imposition of standard (and perhaps preferential) tariffs for certain classes of customers (eg heat producers using natural gas as a fuel in HOB or CHP units) (found in the Gas Directive, Art 9).

5.300 Article 18(2) of the Gas Directive obliges Member States to take measures to designate gas-fired power generators as eligible customers for purposes of access to gas networks, but also allows Member States to regulate CHP producers by introducing a threshold of eligibility, which may not exceed the level envisaged for other final customers. Any such threshold must be notified to the Commission. The concern here was to prevent industrial undertakings with small amounts of CHP capacity from becoming eligible customers before the scheduled market opening would otherwise allow them. Efforts have been made by supporters of CHP to amend this rule, but these efforts have not yet been successful.

5.301 With respect to the priority dispatch mechanism envisaged under Articles 8(3) and 11(3) of the Electricity Directive, the Commission has observed in informal communications that in certain circumstances (ie with respect to power from CHP plants supplying heat to domestic heat consumers) the Member States may be allowed to establish a support mechanism for non-competitive CHP plants so as to avoid the disconnection of domestic heat consumers. However, the Commission views the situation differently for industrial CHP (in contrast to 'municipal CHP') which it sees as less likely to require a major investment in heat infrastructure and more likely to be installed because of its economic attractiveness (ie competitiveness). Hence, the Commission has stated that in such circumstances it sees less justification for support measures for industrial CHP going beyond the priority dispatch mechanism of Article 8(3).

5.302 In addition to the rules listed above, the Electricity and Gas Directives contain provisions on unbundling accounts of integrated undertakings, including rules on unbundling of non-electricity and non-gas activities respectively, which seem to implicate the accounting for some activities in the heat sector (Arts 13–14

Electricity Directive, Arts 12–13 Gas Directive). Moreover, both Directives provide that grid operators shall not discriminate between system users or classes of system users, particularly in favour of their related undertakings (Art 7 Electricity Directive, Art 7 Gas Directive).

There appear to be no mandatory provisions in EC secondary legislation regarding the authorization of other types of heat producers (non-CHP producers). However, this does not necessarily mean that a licensing regime applicable to the district heating sector should draw a distinction between CHP producers and other types of heat producers. If the same criteria are used for both CHP and non-CHP producers of heat, the criteria set forth in the Electricity Directive could therefore be viewed as the minimum criteria in this respect. If it is necessary to conduct a legal assessment of any public service obligations or other restrictions on the market entry of non-CHP heat producers (such as monopoly rights for a single heat producer/supplier), then this would take place under the applicable rules on competition, rather than under the standards of the Electricity Directive. The Electricity and Gas Directives do not directly address the licensing of other undertakings in the heat sector (such as heat distributors). **5.303**

A Community strategy on CHP was developed during the 1990s. In 1995 the European Parliament called upon the Commission to publish as quickly as possible its Communication on co-generation and to make proposals to encourage the use of CHP and to eliminate existing barriers.[361] Two years later, in late 1997, the Commission issued its Communication, and the Council quickly followed suit with a resolution on a Community strategy to promote CHP.[362] In general, the Council accepted the usefulness of an indicative target of doubling CHP in the Community by the year 2010, but it stressed that the main responsibility lies with the Member States. At the same time, it noted that additional measures may be necessary to support CHP, and it emphasized that the Community and the Member States should actively promote CHP use by stimulating and removing barriers to this market. **5.304**

(6) Legislation on Renewable Energy Sources

While EC legislation on the rational use of energy, CHP, and the heat sector dates back at least to the mid-1970s, the development of common rules and support for the promotion of renewable energy sources is really a subject of more recent attention by the Community institutions. In the early 1990s, for example, it was clear that the Commission's ability to assess the situation for penetration of **5.305**

[361] European Parliament, 'Resolution on the Commission's White Paper on an Energy Policy of the European Union', COM(95) 682.

[362] OJ C 4/01 (1998).

renewable energy sources in the Member States was in need of improvement.[363] During the late 1990s both the Commission and the European Parliament developed their proposals for new EC legislation on renewable energy, including a proposed directive on common rules for the feed-in to the grid of electricity produced using renewable energy sources. Following much debate, the Commission published in May 2000 a new proposal for a directive on promotion of renewables (COM (2000), 279 final). The Commission has also been reconsidering the role of energy taxation (and possible exemptions therefrom) and of other forms of State aid in the promotion of alternative sources of energy.

5.306 The Electricity Directive makes only scant explicit reference to electricity production using renewable energy sources. Articles 8(3) and 11(3) allow Member States to require the system operator, when dispatching generating installations, to give priority to generating installations using renewable energy sources or waste or producing CHP. This is merely an option for Member States to consider, and its use would constitute an exception to the normal rule that the dispatching of generating installations shall take place on the basis of criteria which take into account the economic precedence of electricity (Art 8(2)).

5.307 The European Commission has stated that where Member States have recourse to the priority dispatch mechanism referred to in Article 8(3) and support is limited to such mechanism, no issue as to the compatibility of any given support scheme with the Directive should arise. However, the mechanism itself appears to be of limited use, and it would probably require additional measures to effect a significant proactive programme in favour of such alternative energy sources. If the Member States do adopt support mechanisms for renewables and/or CHP that go beyond Article 8(3), the Commission will examine such mechanisms on a case-by-case basis.

5.308 While allowing electricity production using renewable energy sources, CHP, or waste to be prioritized in the dispatching of generating installations, the Directive gives no indication as to their financing, which would have to be determined at the national level as part of the implementation process. Any such financing would have to be compatible with the Treaty's provisions on State aid. The Commission has indicated in some published guidelines on the implementation of the Electricity Directive that it would be likely to analyse any such schemes

[363] See OJ C 164/12 (1991) ('The Commission is aware that the restricted availability of reliable means of assessment causes the part played by renewable energy sources . . . to be underestimated'); see also OJ C 130/23 (1991) (announcing a Commission study for 1991). Similarly, in early 1991 the Commission admitted that it only had information from 4 Member States (Germany, Denmark, Italy, and Spain) regarding schemes to remunerate private producers of renewable energy: OJ C 248/19 (answer given by Cardoso e Cunha to a written question by an MEP). For a review of the Commission's efforts up to 1997 see H van Steen, 'Towards a Community strategy for renewable energy sources' in European Commission, Energy in Europe, No 28 (July 1997).

using different points of view, taking into account its guidelines on State aid for environmental purposes as well as other sources of EC law, especially the Electricity Directive.

The older piece of (non-binding) legislation in this area is the 1988 Council recommendation to promote co-operation between public utilities and autoproducers of electricity using renewables, CHP, or waste energies.[364] Following the adoption of this recommendation, all the EU Member States have introduced legal measures or administrative practices of one type or another to establish certain duties or obligations on utilities in this regard. A variety of regulatory instruments and approaches have been utilized, and there are many lessons to be drawn from this experience.[365] **5.309**

Other activities for the promotion of renewable sources of energy are conducted under the Altener Programme, which is an ongoing multi-year framework for the Community funding of a series of studies, training, information activities, and other appropriate measures aimed at implementing Community objectives and action plans for renewable energy sources. The 1993 Council Decision (93/500/EEC, OJ L 235/41) required Member States to 'endeavour to contribute in their energy policies to the limitation of carbon dioxide emissions by taking into account the Community's indicative objectives' as set out in the Directive (Art 1). Under the renewal of this programme in May 1998 (Council Decision 98/352/EC, OJ L 159/53) the Member States are not specifically obliged to adopt measures.[366] **5.310**

---

[364] Council Recommendation 88/611, OJ L 335/29 (1988), to promote co-operation between public utilities and auto-producers of electricity. This measure was based upon the concepts and practices advanced in the United States pursuant to the federal PURPA legislation of a decade earlier. This is indicated, among other things, by the use of the term 'public utility', defined as an undertaking whose principal objective is the generation, transmission, and/or distribution of electricity for supply to third parties (id, n 8). This recommendation states that Member States 'should provide a framework for co-operation' through the introduction of standard contract criteria on a voluntary basis or, if necessary, through specific legal or administrative provisions. According to this recommendation, reimbursement for electricity sales by such producers to the public supply system should:

—be based primarily on long-term average avoided costs;
—correspond to variable avoided costs (mainly savings in fuel costs);
—guarantee the auto-producer additional reimbursement to the extent that he enables the public supply network to make savings in investment costs in the generation or purchase of electricity;
—regarding purchases *from* the public supply network, the recommendation states that auto-producers should be treated in the same way as comparable purchasers who have no means of auto-production and according to rules framed to be as transparent as possible.

[365] See E Cross, *Legal Frameworks for the Promotion of Wind Energy and Other Renewable Energy Sources in the EU Member States* (1997).

[366] In June 1999, under the co-decision procedure (Art 175), the Commission submitted an amended proposal for a Decision adopting a multiannual programme for promotion of renewable energy sources (1998–2002), following proposed amendments adopted in March 1999 by the European Parliament. See COM(99) 212 final.

(7) Consumer Protection Legislation in the Energy Sector

5.311 The Community's consumer policy has been under development in recent years, as evidenced by a new Treaty article on consumer protection, as well as the adoption in 1999 of a general Community framework for activities in favour of consumers,[367] and a 1999 Council Resolution on the subject.[368]

5.312 Article 22 of both the Electricity and Gas Directives require Member States to create 'mechanisms for regulation, control and transparency so as to avoid any abuse of dominant position, in particular to the detriment of consumers . . .', and state that Member States shall have particular regard to Article 82 (ex Art 86) of the EC Treaty. However, EC law does not otherwise provide any template or blueprint for national regulation of consumer protection in the energy utilities sector. Instead, the Community has relied on disclosure and transparency measures to provide information that can be used by consumers, such as the information resulting from the directive on price transparency. Moreover, it could be argued that the common rules on network access in the Electricity and Gas Directives are basically designed to increase consumer choice.

5.313 Another measure which is arguably pro-consumer is the Directive on Product Liability,[369] which expressly includes electricity in the definition of products subject to its provisions. In theory, the imposition of strict liability standards should create a greater incentive on electric utilities to minimize 'defects' in electricity supply and to provide warnings where necessary so as to reduce the costs of accidents. Concerns about human exposure to electromagnetic radiation, such as that emitted from high-voltage power lines, is also a subject of Community legislation.[370]

5.314 The creation of new independent regulatory authorities for the electricity and gas sectors in some Member States may lead to better systems of consumer protection in the Community. This is because the level of consumer protection is likely to be higher in jurisdictions where an independent regulator sets and enforces service standards for utility performance, and where consumer organizations have been provided with statutory rights and duties designed to ensure close access to the information and decision-making processes of the independent regulator, as com-

[367] Decision 283/1999/EC of the European Parliament and the Council of 25 January 1999 establishing a general framework for Community activities in favour of consumers, OJ 1999 L 34/1.

[368] Council Resolution of 28 June 1999 on Community consumer policy 1999 to 2001, OJ 1999 C 206/1.

[369] Council Directive 85/374/EEC on the approximation of the laws, regulations, and administrative provisions of the Member States concerning liability for defective products, OJ 1985 L 210/29, as amended by Directive 1999/34/EC of the European Parliament and of the Council of 10 May 1999, OJ 1999 L 141/20.

[370] Council Recommendation on the limitation of exposure of the general public to electromagnetic fields (0 Hz–300 GHz), adopted 12 July 1999.

pared to jurisdictions where consumer rights are determined by utilities under standard consumer contracts.

E. Summary and Conclusions

Although the need to establish an integrated energy market can clearly be derived from the 1957 Treaty of Rome, the political will to take on this mantle at Community level has been relatively slow to develop, despite (or because of) the vital nature of energy in a unified market. The Commission's willingness to pursue the programme for an internal energy market, first announced in 1988, has led to some significant legal developments during the 1990s, both in terms of case-law precedent and energy legislation. **5.315**

While the potential applicability of the Treaty to the energy sector has perhaps been easy to argue in recent years, however, the actual application to effect actual change is still rather limited. Perhaps most telling is that more than forty years after the signing of the Treaty of Rome, the ECJ rejected the Commission's effort to dismantle through Treaty enforcement the long-standing legal barriers to electricity and gas imports and exports in several Member States. It is, however, difficult to assess the extent to which the mere threat of the application of the Treaty rules has been a driver for change within the national energy regimes, both in terms of the behaviour of the market players and with respect to facilitating the Commission's ambitions regarding legislation to promote and implement the internal market in energy. **5.316**

The Community's legislative programme of the 1990s has certainly had more measurable results. There are now a series of important energy-related directives in place which must be implemented by the Member States and which have unleashed market and regulatory dynamics that are still unfolding. But much remains to be done in terms of new Community energy legislation. The development of common rules for the promotion of renewable energy sources, CHP, and energy efficiency is currently much debated. In this context, there are also complex issues regarding energy taxation and subsidization to be addressed more fully. At the same time, opposition to a number of proposed directives, for example those relating to rational planning techniques in the electricity and gas sectors and a Community framework for energy taxation, reveals the continued lack of a common energy policy in several key respects. **5.317**

It is sometimes convenient to treat EC energy law in a sort of vacuum, monitoring and assessing only the activities and results at Community level. In reality, the main regulatory game is played at the national level, and there are complex interactions between Community and national regulatory activities. While the internal market directives have been a stimulus to new legislation, there are at least **5.318** some indications that the directives were more reactive or imitative, rather than proactive or seminal, in nature. For example, it is clear that the efforts of the British government to regulate for competition in the electricity sector profoundly influenced the debate in the EC, not the other way around. Moreover, there was some degree of influence from the years of experience with regulatory reform in the United States.

5.319 Thus, in assessing the dynamics and impact of European energy liberalization in the 1990s and beyond, historians and others should endeavour to understand the fuller picture of the economic and legal realities, including the dynamics of national energy reform. New national energy legislation has been adopted (and proposed) at an ever-increasing pace in Europe for the past decade. This includes new energy laws in almost all the Member States, as well as in the countries of Central and Eastern Europe. In a few instances, the national measures seem designed to counteract the function of the internal market directives, for example by mandating long-term contracts in the network-bound energy sector and by establishing 'blocking provisions' against electricity trade from non-liberalized countries.

5.320 The structural and regulatory changes within the electricity and gas sectors during the past decade appear to be far more profound and significant than those of the previous four decades. Present indications, however, are that a wave of industry consolidation may have been unleashed as companies are seeking to position themselves against the forces (or suggestions) of competition. Rather than unbundling, European energy companies can logically be expected to seek far greater concentration. Hence, the results of the modest legal reform efforts at Community level are still far from being complete or obvious.

5.321 Some patterns in regulatory developments do seem to have been established. The Community's use of framework legislation for hydrocarbons licensing and for common rules for the internal market in electricity and gas is designed to allow a substantial degree of diversity among the national energy regimes. This ensures that the work on the continued harmonization and convergence of European energy law and policy shall remain a task for the indefinite future.

Part III

NATIONAL REGULATION OF THE ENERGY SECTOR

6

ENERGY LAW IN DENMARK

Anita Rønne

A. Introduction

(1) The Danish Energy Resource Base

6.01 Danish energy consumption is covered by domestic oil and natural gas resources, coal supplies, and domestic renewable energy sources such as waste, straw, woodchips, wind, and biogas. Denmark has neither hydropower at any big scale nor nuclear power production.

6.02 It was not until 1972 that Denmark became an oil-producing nation; gas production commenced in 1984. Since 1991, Denmark has been self-sufficient in oil and natural gas, and is in fact a net exporter of oil and gas; but it imports all coal used for electricity production. In 1997, Denmark became self-sufficient in energy. In some years Denmark imports considerable electricity while in other years electricity is exported. This variation is due to changes in precipitation in Norway and Sweden leading to fluctuations in the availability of hydropower in those countries.

6.03 The present production of oil and natural gas covers about 134 per cent of the total gross energy consumption. In 2000 all crude oil and all natural gas production came from the sixteen oil and gas fields in the North Sea; in the years to come further oil and gas fields will be developed. After the UK and Norway, Denmark is the biggest oil producer in Western Europe, and North Sea oil and gas reserves will make Denmark self-sufficient in these fuels well into this millennium. There exists one offshore oil pipeline to shore and two offshore gas pipelines, two gas storage facilities, and a country-wide gas transmission and distribution system.

6.04 Denmark has been a pioneering country in renewable energy matters, in using energy efficiently, and in promoting combined heat and power production (CHP). Production of renewable energy has become steadily more important and represented 9 per cent of the total gross energy production in 1997.[1] Pursuant to the latest energy action plan,[2] the Government has decided to work for an annual increase in the use of renewable energy by an average of 1 per cent per annum, until the year 2030. This implies that renewable energy will constitute approximately 35 per cent of the gross energy consumption in 2030. District heating covers 49 per cent of the energy demand for space heating and 70 per cent of district heating production is based upon combined heat and power production.

[1] cf *Danish Oil and Gas Production 2000*, the Energy Agency.

[2] *Energy 21, The Danish Government's Action Plan for Energy*, Danish Ministry for Environment and Energy, Apr 1996.

(2) The Energy Policy Objectives

Governmental intervention in the Danish energy industry is relatively recent. **6.05** Until the first energy crisis in 1973, energy regulation in Denmark reflected a situation characterized by sufficient and cheap oil supplies and limited awareness about the environmental impact of energy consumption and different fuel sources. Energy legislation was rare and mainly dealt with safety matters. An exception was the Subsoil Act which was adopted as early as 1932.

During the economic growth of the late 1950s and 1960s Denmark became heavily dependent on imported oil in order to meet its primary energy requirements, **6.06** and the massive increases in oil prices and the oil embargoes in 1973 and 1979 had a serious effect on Danish society. It became evident that the energy sector could not be left to unrestrained market forces, and that direct action had to be taken in order to develop an energy policy. Since then Denmark has developed a tradition of implementing vigorous energy policies with broad political support and involving a broad range of actors: energy companies, industry, local associations, municipalities, research institutions, and consumers. The implementation of these energy policies has resulted in a drop in energy consumption, coinciding with a radical change in fuel consumption patterns.

The main goal of the first energy strategy, the '*Danish Energy Policy 1976*',[3] became the security of energy supplies to safeguard Denmark during international **6.07** energy crises such as that of 1973–74. This was to be accomplished through programmes designed to promote flexibility in energy supply patterns, to reduce dependence on oil, and to enlarge fuel stocks. In seeking to resolve these problems, the Government and industry undertook a series of comprehensive decisions and actions. First of all, the exploitation of indigenous oil and natural gas resources began, and in 1979 it was decided to set up an extensive natural gas network so that natural gas could be used in Denmark. The second major initiative was the conversion of the electric power plants from oil to coal, and the third energy policy decision related to the displacement of oil as a heating source in private houses and as energy for production purposes in the manufacturing industries. Consequently, a nation-wide heat planning scheme was launched, actively involving the regional and local authorities as well as the energy supply companies. This is a success story, as the result of the initiatives taken shows that the regulation largely attained the goal set at the time: to secure energy supply and to reduce the consumption of oil.

With the necessity to put a higher priority on energy issues followed also many **6.08** new administrative tasks, and during the 1970s considerable growth of public administration, legislation, and changes of authority took place. While the 1970s

[3] *Dansk energipolitik*, Handelsministeriet (*Danish Energy Policy*, Ministry of Trade, May 1976).

was a decade of development, where the political and legal framework for the energy sector was outlined, the 1980s were characterized by the implementation of these initiatives. The second energy plan, '*Energy 81*',[4] built further on the priorities dealt with in the previous plan given the drastic price rises in energy following the oil embargoes in 1979–80, but it also emphasized socio-economic and environmental considerations.

6.09 In the late 1980s and early 1990s, the focus gradually shifted from supply security considerations, minimization of energy service costs, and local environmental effects, to wider environmental considerations, notably the goal of achieving long-term sustainable development on a national as well as a global level. In 1988, the Danish Government presented its Action Plan on Environment and Development[5] as a follow-up to the recommendations set forth in the report from the World Commission on Environment and Development, the 'Brundtland Report'. The change in priorities in the Danish energy policy targets is reflected in the plan of action *'Energy 2000'* which the Minister of Energy submitted in April 1990,[6] introducing the goal of sustainable development of the energy sector; this involved the reduction of greenhouse gas emissions, notably carbon dioxide, by explicit targets, and focusing on savings in energy consumption, increased efficiency of the supply system, conversion to cleaner sources of energy, construction of small-scale combined power and heating plants, and on research and development.[7] At the same time a big deficit in the Danish Natural Gas Project (see below, section D) has meant that this deficit is a permanent element of consideration in connection with the drawing up of the energy policy.[8] *Denmark Energy Futures*, a discussion paper published in December 1995, contains a technical analysis of future scenarios for energy consumption and supply in Denmark.[9]

---

[4] *Energiplan 81*, Energiministeriet, Nov 1981 (*Energy Plan 81*, Ministry of Energy).

[5] Plan on Environment and Development, Danish Government, 1988.

[6] *Energy 2000, A Plan of Action for Sustainable Development*, Danish Ministry of Energy, Apr 1990.

[7] For further details see Anita Rønne in 'Monopoly and Competition in Energy Supply, Denmark', Journal of Energy and Natural Resources Law, International Bar Association, Dec 1989 Supplement, 67–77; and in 'Coal and Fuel Choices in Denmark', Journal of Energy and Natural Resources Law, 1989, vol 7, no 4, 275–85, and *Re-regulation of Danish Energy Supply* in Suum Cuique—legal studies from the University of Copenhagen Law Faculty, ed Peter Blume, Ditlev Tamm, and Vibeke Vindeløv, Jurist-og Økonomforbundets Forlag, 1993.

[8] In 1979 it was decided to construct a country-wide natural gas grid, based on supplies from the Danish part of the North Sea. It was implemented within 5 years. Ongoing evaluation of project developments has been considered essential and has implied several changes over the years. A natural gas report dating from 1989 concluded that the natural gas project would show a deficit of DKK 32bn; cf Naturgasprojektets økonomi (The Economy of the Natural Gas Project), Report from the working group set up by the Minister of Energy, Nov 1989, 13 (a deficit on the project as such of DKK 6.8bn at current value plus indirect subsidization of the project through the exemption from energy taxes accorded to the natural gas project to the extent of DKK 25bn).

[9] *Denmark's Energy Futures*, Danish Energy Agency, Copenhagen, 1996.

The development within the European Union of integrating energy markets has brought a need for a new foundation for energy policy to ensure that overall environmental objectives can be maintained under the new market conditions. Simultaneously, in the international energy market cross-border trade in electricity and gas is assuming new forms and energy company ownership and alliances are undergoing change. Because of these new international challenges the fourth of the energy strategies, '*Energy 21*', was prepared in 1996,[10] which lays down the energy policy agenda for the years to come. It is highlighted that the major environmental challenge is to achieve convergence of emissions of industrialized countries to a globally sustainable level. In connection with the approval of the action plan, the Government decided to work for an international agreement on a 50 per cent reduction of CO_2 emissions from industrialized countries by 2030, compared with 1990 levels. '*Energy 21*' aims at fulfilling this goal. The plan sets out the framework for a number of initiatives, focusing especially on reducing the requirements for resources through improvement of energy intensity and the impact on the environment from the energy sector by enhanced use of renewables. In March 1997, the Government banned new or renovated power capacity based on coal. Power generated by coal will consequently be phased out as coal-based plants wear out. This decision confirms the determination to meet reduction targets in the shorter term and the long-term aim of achieving a sustainable energy supply. One of the major cornerstones in the new energy policy plan is to reform the legal and economic framework of the Danish energy sector to ensure that long-term considerations can be maintained effectively. **6.10**

As can be noted, Danish energy policy (and that of many other countries) has in its short life seen several major changes of direction. **6.11**

(3) Introduction to the Danish Legal System

Denmark, Greenland, and the Faroe Islands together constitute the Kingdom of Denmark. Both Greenland and the Faroe Islands from 1979 and 1948 respectively have had autonomous status through their own home rule arrangements, which have established a framework for extensive self-government and where legislative power is delegated to local parliaments (see section A(4) below). **6.12**

The present Danish Constitution dates from 1849, and it abolished the absolute monarchy and made Denmark a constitutional monarchy with three separate powers: the legislature, the executive, and the judiciary. The Constitution was last revised in 1953 as Law No. 169 of 5 June 1953.[11] Legislative power is vested in **6.13**

---

[10] *Energy 21*, The Danish Government's Action Plan for Energy, Danish Ministry of Environment and Energy, Apr 1996.

[11] An introduction to a general survey of the basic principles of Danish law written in English is given in *Danish Law in a European Perspective*, edited by Dahl, Melchior, Rehof, and Tamm. This highlights that the Nordic legal systems are now recognized as a separate legal family, distinct from

(the King and) the Parliament (Art 3). The Parliament (*Folketinget*) is a single chamber and is authorized to delegate its law-making competence to the administration except where the Constitution demands that Parliament shall itself issue the rules in question.

6.14 Executive power is vested in (the King and) the Government. Public administration is divided between the State (central administration) and local Governments (municipalities). State Government administration is divided into a number of Ministries and, pursuant to Article 14 of the Constitution, the Government decides on the organizational structure. A Ministry typically consists of a department and a number of agencies, organized hierarchically in the sense that the Minister/Department can instruct the agencies and decisions made by agencies can be brought to the Department which has an obligation to reconsider the decision. In addition to Ministries there exist a number of administrative bodies, boards, or tribunals, which to a certain extent are independent.

6.15 An increasing part of the administration is handled by municipalities. Pursuant to Article 82 of the Constitution, the municipalities have the right to manage their own affairs independently but subject to State supervision. The activities of a municipality are restricted to a certain local area and managed by representatives elected among the citizens within this area. Denmark is divided into 275 municipalities and fourteen counties. There is no general legislation describing the tasks of the municipalities but one of the traditional areas is energy supply. Counties and municipalities are subject to the supervision of the Minister of the Interior.

6.16 Judicial power belongs to the courts which, unlike the system in a number of other European countries, are not specialized but are competent for all cases: civil, criminal, administrative, and constitutional. The independence of the courts is guaranteed by the Constitution (Art 64). The highest court in Denmark is the Supreme Court. There are two courts of appeal or high courts and 82 lower courts. Section 63 of the Constitution guarantees judicial review of administrative decisions taken by public authorities. The Constitution does not explicitly grant a right of judicial review of the constitutionality of Acts of Parliament. Nevertheless, it has been maintained, and in 1999 was confirmed by judgment,[12] that the courts may review the compatibility between the Constitution and statutes passed by Parliament. This right of judicial review, however, has been handled with considerable restraint.

6.17 As already indicated, Denmark has no specially designated administrative courts: disputes between the public authorities and the citizens are dealt with by the

both civil law and common law, although it must be admitted that there has been a considerable influence from continental legal thinking, especially from France and Germany. The influence of Roman law is, however, limited: ibid, 35.

[12] See Judgment of the Supreme Court of 19 Feb 1999.

ordinary courts. It is, however, characteristic of Danish administrative law that quasi-judicial boards of appeal in many fields are inserted between the normal administrative authorities (Ministries) and the courts. A great number of such boards are established by statute, including those for energy activities (see paras 6.36–6.41 below).

Statutes passed by the Danish Parliament are the most important source of Danish law. On the basis of a parliamentary delegation, the administration issues regulations, which in most cases are called orders. In addition, the administration issues a number of circulars and instructions which may be issued by a superior authority directed to a subordinate authority without any special statutory authority. The courts also play an important role in the forming of the law, although precedent is not given the same importance as in Anglo-American law. A special feature of the legal method of interpreting statutes is the importance attached to preparatory works. Other sources of law besides statute, secondary legislation, and precedent are analogy, custom, and academic writing.[13] **6.18**

Another important principle of the Constitution is Article 73, which protects private positions and provides that no one can be deprived of his property unless it is found to be necessary to the 'public interest' and then only by statute and provided that full compensation is paid. Finally, Article 19 provides that the Danish Government may not enter into any binding international obligation which requires domestic implementation or is of major importance, unless prior approval has been granted by Parliament. **6.19**

(4) The Realm: Greenland and the Faroe Islands

As mentioned above, the Danish Constitution states in Article 1 that it applies to all parts of the Realm. This includes continental Denmark, the Faroe Islands, and Greenland. Both the Faroe Islands and Greenland have their own home rule arrangements, established by a special statute adopted by the Danish Parliament: the Home Rule Act of the Faroe Islands of 23 March 1948, and the Home Rule Act of Greenland of 29 November 1978. These two Acts, though not quite identical, are based on the same model of local autonomy and have established a framework for extensive self-government, where legislative and administrative powers on specific matters are transferred to the Home Rule Authorities. **6.20**

It should be highlighted that when Denmark joined the EC on 1 January 1973, the Faroe Islands were given the option to remain outside, which they chose to do. On the other hand, Greenland had to join the EC in 1973 together with continental Denmark, but was later given the option to leave the Communities, which Greenland chose to do in 1984. From a legal point of view, this has created a **6.21**

[13] A guide to the different legal sources, including the Danish, can be found in English in *Information Sources in Law,* ed Jules Winterton and Elizabeth M Moys, London 1997.

strange situation in which one part of the Realm (continental Denmark) is a full member of the European Union, while the other two parts are not.

6.22 Authority over natural resources was transferred to the Faroese authorities in 1992. Since then several new acts on oil and gas exploration have been adopted by the Faroese Parliament.[14] Following the agreement between the United Kingdom and Denmark/Faroe Islands on a maritime limitation of a disputed area between the Faroes and the Shetland Isles,[15] the first licensing round took place in the summer of 2000.

6.23 A special mineral resources regime was included in the Home Rule Act for Greenland in 1979. Pursuant to the Act on Mineral Resources in Greenland,[16] and subsequent agreements between the Prime Minister of Denmark and the Premier of Greenland, the main elements of this regime are:

—Danish recognition of the Greenlandic people's fundamental rights over mineral resources;
—joint decision power and veto rights in resource matters;
—the establishment of a joint Danish/Greenlandic Mineral Resource Council, composed of five Danish parliamentary members and five Greenlandic members. The chairman is appointed by the Queen of Denmark for a term of four years on the joint recommendation of the Danish and Greenland authorities and it has been customary to appoint the Premier of Greenland as chairman;
—division of incomes from natural resource activities between Denmark and Greenland; and
—the administration of mineral resources in Greenland from 1 July 1998.

6.24 The rest of this chapter focuses solely on the regulation of energy activities in continental Denmark.

(5) The Regulatory Instruments

6.25 To ensure consistency with Government policy, a whole range of different instruments has been utilized. Among these are:

—direct participation by the State or municipalities;
—statutory regulation of norms;
—licence systems;
—planning systems;
—economic means, such as taxes, subsidies, guarantees;

---

[14] Acts No 179 of 21 Oct 1993 on Preliminary Surveys and No 31 of 16 Mar 1998 on Hydrocarbon Activities.

[15] cf Order No 57 of 21 July 1999.

[16] cf Act No 335 of 6 June 1991 on Mineral Resources in Greenland, cf Consolidated Act No 368 of 18 June 1998.

—didactic means, such as information and consultancy schemes; and
—co-operation through negotiation systems and agreements.

The result has, however, been the development of a rather complicated organizational structure as well as confusion of different regulatory instruments, making it difficult to get an overview of the legal regulation. **6.26**

The energy supply has long been characterized by division into sectors, with the individual supply sector being regulated individually by statutes as the need arose and in response to different problems. Today, Denmark has acts on the exploration and exploitation of the subsoil, oil pipelines, the supply of natural gas, the supply of electricity, the supply of heat, renewables, and so on. Several of these sets of rules are highly complicated, but the acts are connected by a fairly uniform purpose: to ensure the most efficient use of energy, to develop domestic energy resources, and to develop multi-source energy supplies with a more or less explicitly expressed consideration of the environment. **6.27**

Another aspect of the regulatory instruments is the use of many atypical types of regulations, such as Letters and Precepts, which are binding not only on the local Governments, but also on the supply companies and, indirectly, the consumers. This is problematic because it results in a substantial part of regulation which cannot be found in statutory law, nor is it promulgated generally. In addition, agreements at both the political and the administrative levels are used extensively. **6.28**

Further, there are many different types of supply companies: electricity companies, district heating companies, and gas companies. They all compete for the same consumers, each of them establishing their own administrative machinery. Energy supply networks are increasing the co-production of heat and power at combined heat and power plants. CHP supply from large-scale plants is being further developed and local district heating plants converted to CHP based on natural gas, waste, and biomass. It is therefore expected that the number of companies will decrease in future. In this connection the design of the organization calls for a closer examination, as it is neither desirable nor rational to employ companies, partnerships, and associations. The last complicating factor to be highlighted is that the central and local Governments are performing different functions, first as regulatory and planning authorities looking after social interests, and secondly as supply companies with a more commercial orientation. **6.29**

The need for an overall revision of the rules has been recognized by the Government and reform work was launched in 1997 to consider and make recommendations for the future legal regulation and structure of the industry. Although the initial plan was to prepare a common Energy Act this idea was later abandoned because of major differences in the operational structures of the various sectors and consequently the different needs for regulation. In June 1999, **6.30**

Parliament adopted acts for reform of the electricity sector which came into force on 30 December 1999. Negotiations for the reform of the natural gas and heat sectors continued during the spring of 2000. A new Act on Natural Gas Supply and a revised Heat Supply Act followed in May 2000.

(6) The Administrative and Regulatory Authorities

Historical developments

6.31 As a consequence of the first oil crisis, administrative responsibility for the energy sector was transferred in March 1974 from the Danish Ministry of Transportation to the Ministry of Industry and Trade, which was already responsible for supply issues in the case of a state of emergency. Public control of the energy sector was gathered under a new Energy Agency in 1976, under the umbrella of the Ministry of Industry and Trade, whereas matters connected to research and development within the energy sector were vested with the Research Institute, 'Riso'.

6.32 The second oil crisis resulted in the establishment of a Ministry of Energy in 1979 by transferring the energy department from the Ministry of Industry and Trade along with responsibility for the Energy Agency and Riso.

6.33 In September 1994, the Danish Government decided to merge the Ministry of Energy and the Ministry of Environment into the Ministry for Environment and Energy. This reflected an increasing awareness of the links between the environment and energy use, and the factual change of a move away from heavy investments in the energy infrastructure to a focus on the operation and supervision of the sector. Riso was transferred to the new Ministry of Research.

Ministry for Environment and Energy

6.34 The Ministry for Environment and Energy consists of the Department, four agencies, and three research institutes. The relationship between the Ministry and its agencies is defined in separate orders.[17] The Department is led by a politically elected Minister and a permanent secretary who is a civil servant. The Department acts as the secretariat for the Minister whereas the implementation of the Government's energy policy is carried out by an Energy Agency. Furthermore, two Price Commissions for Energy were established under the umbrella of the Ministry of Business and Industry. However, those commissions were merged into a single regulator, the Energy Supervisory Board, as from 30 December 1999.

[17] cf Consolidated Act No 263 of 27 Apr 1989 on Energy Policy Actions, as amended by Act No 1076 of 20 Dec 1995, Order No 364 of 9 June 1993, and Order No 1194 of 29 Dec 1999 (in force 15 July 2000); cf Order No 652 of 23 June 2000 on the Responsibilities of the Energy Agency.

The Energy Agency

The Energy Agency was established in 1976 and is responsible for the implementation of the Government's energy policy and for the overall planning of power, heat, and natural gas supplies in Denmark. In the oil and gas area the Agency is responsible for the supervision of exploration and production activities and handles questions related to health and safety, approval of development plans, and the grant of licences. In addition, the Agency prepares and administers energy legislation, manages a range of financial support schemes, and collects statistics and data on energy production, supply, and consumption. It also carries out analysis and assessments of developments, prepares action plans for the energy sector, and acts as an appeal instance for municipality decisions in heat supply matters. **6.35**

The Energy Regulator

In Denmark prices and supply conditions for electricity, gas, and heat have been regulated by two price commissions since the 1970s: the Electricity Price Commission and the Gas and Heat Price Commission. Control of part of the network-bound energy industry has thus been separated from the policy-making Ministry for more than twenty years. These commissions, however, enjoyed only political independence, not independence from utility interests. The composition and the appointment criteria of the Price Commissions were determined in primary legislation, and represented various social interests with half of the members independent of energy utility interests and representing legal and technical knowledge and consumer interests; the remainder were appointed at the recommendation of organizations, companies, and municipalities from the supply side.[18] The Price Commissions had a common secretariat placed in the Competition Authority and control of the regulators was implemented through a special recourse system according to which any decisions could be appealed to an **6.36**

[18] The Electricity Price Commission consisted of a chairman and 11 members formally appointed by the Minister for Environment and Energy. The chairman and 5 members must be independent of utility or municipal interests and represent legal, economic, accounting, and technical expertise and major and minor consumer interests. The other 6 members were appointed at the recommendation of the Association of Electricity Supply Companies (3), the Association of District Heating Companies (1), the Union of Municipalities (1), and the two big municipalities jointly—Copenhagen and Frederiksberg (1); cf the Electricity Supply Act 1976 s 11.

The Gas and Heat Price Commission consisted of a chairman and 13 members. The chairman and 7 members must be independent of utility or municipal interests and represent consumer interests and necessary expertise. The other 6 members were appointed at the recommendation of the Association of Electricity Supply Companies (1), the Association of District Heating Companies (1), the natural gas companies jointly (1), the Union of Municipalities (1), and Copenhagen and Frederiksberg (1); cf the Heat Supply Act s 22. Both Commissions in fact had the same chairman (an economist), vice chairman (a lawyer), and technical expert (an engineer).

independent Competition Appeals Tribunal.[19] The main tasks of the Commissions were to approve prices and supply conditions for electricity, gas, and heat, deal with complaints from consumers, and compel changes in such prices and conditions if necessary. The secretariat also handled a notification system for both electricity and district heating and gas, with all companies obliged to report prices, budgets, accounts, delivery conditions, and so on, and which was open to the public.

6.37 Although all members of the Price Commissions were appointed by the Minister for Environment and Energy, the Minister could not influence the decisions of the Price Commissions. The regulators were thus independent from the political system because the appointment and delegation of authority was statutorily fixed and not limited in time. This implied that Parliament had to adopt new legislation in order to change the situation, which was needed in order to fulfil the requirements of the Electricity Directive.

6.38 As an element of the adopted reform of the electricity sector, a new Energy Supervisory Board has now been established and has functioned from 30 December 1999.[20] The new Board is replacing the Electricity Price Commission and the Gas and Heat Price Commission, and fulfils the special sector-specific supervisory and complaints function in relation to the energy sector. One of the major changes is that all members are independent of commercial interests as well as from the political system: Electricity Act 1999 (EA) sections 78 and 79. The Board consists of a chairman and six members who must represent legal, economic, commercial, environmental, and technological expertise. At least one member must fulfil the conditions for becoming a judge in the High Court. The members are appointed for four years by the Minister for Environment and Energy, but are to act independently from the Minister in their daily work. The Minister cannot change the decisions of the Board nor can the members be removed within their term of appointment. The decisions taken by the Energy Supervisory Board can be appealed to a special Energy Complaints Board:[21] EA section 89.

6.39 The Energy Supervisory Board has not only taken over the tasks of the previous energy price commissions, but is actively to provide the sectors with incentives to co-operate and improve efficiency. Moreover, the Board must also assess more technical matters and restrictive practices due to the opening up of access to the system.

[19] The Tribunal has 3 members: a President who must be qualified to be a judge of the Supreme Court and 2 members, with legal and economic expertise respectively. All members shall be independent of commercial interests. Tribunal decisions can be appealed to the normal civil courts.

[20] cf Order No 1126 of 29 Dec 1999. See also Order No 163 of 26 Feb 2000 on the responsibilities of the Energy Supervisory Board.

[21] As established by the Act on State Subsidies to Defray the Cost of CO_2 Charges of Certain Companies with Considerable Energy Consumption, cf Consolidated Act No 846 of 17 Nov 1997.

The supervisory control applies to around 350 companies from the heating sector and 300 from the electricity sector. It should be added that the formal regulator has always been supported by the control implemented within the companies themselves through the owners, which in Denmark are mainly the end-consumers, either directly or through their citizenship of a municipality. Such owners of course have a natural interest in keeping prices and expenses as low as possible. 6.40

Both the Competition Authority and the Energy Agency are to provide the Energy Supervisory Board with secretarial services. 6.41

B. Exploration for and Production of Oil and Natural Gas

(1) Introduction

As early as 1932 it was established in Denmark's first Subsoil Act that raw materials such as oil and natural gas in the Danish subsoil belong to the State of Denmark. At this time, the Act only included the land and territorial sea. Following the Danish ratification of the 1958 Geneva Convention on the Continental Shelf on 31 May 1963, sovereignty was claimed over the Danish continental shelf area in June 1963.[22] 6.42

It was considered that Danish legislation, which was not expressly limited to the land and territorial sea, hereafter also applied to exploration and exploitation activities on the continental shelf, but in order to eliminate any doubt it was proposed to introduce separate and joint regulation of activities to be carried out on the continental shelf. Consequently, the Act on the Continental Shelf was adopted in 1971.[23] This Act states that 'the natural resources of the Danish Continental Shelf are the property of the State of Denmark and may only be explored or exploited by others under a concession or a permit' (section 1). Likewise 6.43

[22] Cf Royal Order No 259 of 7 June 1963 'Danish sovereignty with respect to exploration and exploitation of natural resources is exercised to the part of the continental shelf which pursuant to the signed convention in Geneva of 29 April 1958 on the Continental Shelf . . . belongs to the Danish State', s 1. Pursuant to s 3, a licence is required to explore and exploit the natural resources in the shelf, pursuant to the Subsoil Act.

[23] Cf Act No 259 of 9 June 1971 with later amendments, cf Consolidated Act No 182 of 1 May 1979. In the Act on the Continental Shelf, it is also stated that 'Danish law shall apply to installations . . . and in safety zones around'. Further amendments have been made to the Act by Acts No 484 of 12 June 1996, No 187 of 12 Mar 1997, No 317 of 3 June 1998 and Act No 1276 of 20 Dec 2000. Because of the adoption of special legislation, such as the Subsoil Act No 293 of 10 June 1981 and the Act on Certain Marine Installations No 292 of 10 June 1981 which apply also to the continental shelf, the Act on the Continental Shelf has lost a lot of its initial importance. Denmark has not ratified the Law of the Sea Convention (primarily because the continental shelfs around the Faroe Islands and Greenland have not been finally settled) but has claimed an Exclusive Economic Zone by Act No 411 of 22 May 1996.

the Subsoil Act[24] determines that 'this Act shall also apply to the Danish Continental Shelf Area' (section 1) and further that the 'raw materials . . . belong to the Danish State' (section 2). The Danish State thus claims ownership of the natural resources in the subsoil of both the Danish land and territorial sea and the continental shelf area. It has thus exceeded its rights in international law, which only empowers a State with functional jurisdiction over the continental shelf ('sovereign rights' but not sovereignty).[25]

6.44 The Subsoil Act of 1932 did not include all the natural resources of the subsoil, but limited its scope to the resources that had not been produced commercially before 23 February 1932, on which date the law came into force. The excluded resources were, among others, stone, gravel, sand, lime, chalk, peat, clay, and lignite. These resources were later regulated by an Act on Raw Materials of 1972[26] which also included a licence system. This regulatory framework, however, is not further analysed in this chapter.

6.45 The first licence was issued in 1935 and, following various licensee changes, was replaced by a licence to the Danish shipowner A.P. Møller (now Mærsk Oil and Gas AS) in 1962. This licence, operated by the Danish Underground Consortium (DUC), was expanded to include the continental shelf area in 1963. Thus control of Danish territory on- and offshore to explore and produce hydrocarbons was, until January 1982, in the hands of only one licensee. However, following relinquishments of part of the Danish area in 1984, new licences were issued (see below, para 6.79).

6.46 Denmark became an oil-producing nation in 1972. Since 1991 the level of production has met the demand and has increasingly provided the basis for export. With respect to natural gas, Denmark commenced production in 1984 and, in addition to covering its own supply needs, Denmark has during the last ten years been able to export gas to Sweden and Germany. In 1998, Danish oil and gas production came from thirteen oilfields (Dan, Gorm, Skjold, Rolf, Kraka, Dagmar, Regnar, Valdemar, Svend, Siri, Halfdan, South-Arne, and Lulita) and from the Tyra, Roar, and Harald gasfields.[27] The Svend, Harald, Siri, South-Arne and Lulita fields are situated in the northern part of the Central Graben, while all other fields are situated in the southern region of the Central Graben. Total oil production in 2000 amounted to 21.1 million cubic metres. Gross gas production amounted to 11.3 billion nm^3 in 2000, of which some was re-injected and used as fuel. Thus, net gas production amounted to 7.1 billion nm^3 in 2000.[28]

[24] cf Consolidated Act No 552 of 29 June 1995, ss 1(3) and 2.
[25] See Ch 2 above on International law.
[26] cf Act No 285 of 7 June 1972, now Consolidated Act No 569 of 30 June 1997.
[27] *Danish Oil and Gas Production 2000*, the Energy Agency.
[28] ibid.

Mærsk Oil and Gas AS was in charge of recovery from all fields until 1999, but this production monopoly ceased when new licensees commenced production.[29]

(2) *The Subsoil Act*

Denmark established a legal framework for exploration and production of natural resources in 1932. This Act was amended in 1950 and again in 1971 following the above-mentioned Act on the Continental Shelf which, in addition to proclaiming the rights of the Danish State over natural resources on the Danish continental shelf, determined that the rules in the Subsoil Act would apply to these activities. The Subsoil Act was totally revised by the adoption of a new Subsoil Act in 1981 which constituted an important part of Denmark's energy goals of optimizing the use of Danish raw materials in accordance with the needs of its society, and expediting self-sufficiency in energy by increasing the exploration for and production of oil and natural gas from the Danish subsoil. The legal reform included an agreement of 19 May 1981 between the Danish Government and A.P. Møller, amending A.P. Møller's exclusive oil and gas licence over the entire Danish onshore and offshore areas, and several key pieces of legislation passed by the Danish *Folketing* (Parliament). **6.47**

In addition to Act No 293 of 10 June 1981, on the Use of the Danish Subsoil (the Subsoil Act), there was adopted: Act No 291 of 10 June 1981, on Establishment and Utilization of a Pipeline for Transportation of Crude Oil and Condensate (the Pipeline Act), Act No 292 of 10 June 1981, on Certain Marine Installations (the Marine Installations Act), and Act No 175 of 28 April 1982, concerning Taxation of Income Originating from Production of Hydrocarbons in Denmark (the Hydrocarbons Taxation Act). Within this whole new legal regime for the oil and gas sector, it should be emphasized that it is the Subsoil Act that establishes the central framework for oil and gas activities during all the different stages while the other acts are more or less linked to it as special conditions for the performance of the activities. **6.47A**

In order to implement the EC Licensing Directive (94/22), it has been necessary to amend the Danish Subsoil Act in 1995.[30] Pursuant to the Directive Member States have to ensure that there is no discrimination between entities as regards access to and exercise of prospection, exploration, and production of hydrocarbons. Moreover, licences must be granted on the basis of objective and justified conditions. Consequently, criteria which gave preferential status to the Danish State **6.47B**

[29] The Danish Underground Consortium (DUC) and the Statoil group handle recovery from the Lulita field, while the other fields are operated by DUC alone. The Statoil group has commenced production from the Siri field and the Amerada Hess group from the South Arne field.

[30] Act No 293 of 10 June 1981 on the Use of the Danish Subsoil, amended by Act No 310 of 17 May 1995. A Consolidated Act which includes the amendments has been issued as No 552 of 29 June 1995, as amended by Act No 447 of 31 May 2000 on Amendments to certain environmental Acts (implementation of the Aarhus Convention).

and to national companies had to be abandoned together with special purchase rights of the State to oil and natural gas.

6.48 Furthermore, the revised Act creates the basis of a more flexible system for the granting of licences through the implementation of an 'open door' procedure; and it introduces the possibility of extending the exploration phase to more than ten years. Finally, amendments include the implementation of the Directive on Environmental Impact Assessment (85/337 as amended) and the international IMO guidelines on removal of offshore installations after abandonment (see Chapter 2 above). The amendments were adopted by the Danish Parliament on 18 May 1995, and came into force on 1 July 1995.

6.49 The Subsoil Act merely lays down the framework within which operations under an exploration and production licence are to be carried out. The more specific terms are included in the issued licences and published in advance by the Ministry for Environment and Energy in the form of a 'Model Licence for Exploration for and Production of Hydrocarbons' attached to a general Invitation Letter to the public, outlining the main criteria for obtaining a licence. There have been five rounds, and each has had a separate Model Licence and Invitation Letter, reflecting different external conditions for the round, eg low oil prices, increased competition for international investments in oil and gas exploration activities, or the fact that it is known that the blocks may contain parts of discoveries already made.

6.50 Both onshore and offshore operations are governed by a single set of Model Licence terms. The economic differences between operating offshore and onshore in Denmark are not considered of such significance as to justify different licence regimes. Thus it has been taken into account that the rate of taxation of onshore fields is effectively heavier because of low investments and a corresponding limited right of hydrocarbon deductions.

6.51 The provisions in the Model Licence are standard terms in the sense that they are not subject to negotiation with the applicant oil companies. Prior to the implementation of the Licensing Directive, before the opening of the fifth round, a limited number of the provisions were negotiated, eg the area covered by the licence, the extent of work obligations, the size of the State's interest in the licence, as well as the obligation to train public employees in oil and natural gas operations, and to involve Danish institutions in research projects. In other words, even in the older licences the vast majority of the Model Licence provisions were standard terms. Due to the requirements of the Licensing Directive that the conditions under which licences are granted must be published and known in advance by all entities taking part in the licensing procedure and be applied in a non-discriminatory manner, the licensing authorities are no longer allowed to negotiate with the applicants in order to increase the specific bid, eg in respect of the extent of work obligations or the level of State participation. However, although there is no negotiation as such, it is still necessary for certain terms to be fixed individually. This applies to the area covered by the licence, the exact duration of the exploration period, the offered work obligations, and other issues that cannot be settled until the content of all applications is known.

Considerations of space here preclude a detailed description of the Model Licence. Some of the rights and obligations are described below. **6.52**

(3) The Licence System

The central element of the Subsoil Act (SA) is the establishment of a licensing system permitting private and State-owned companies to explore for and produce hydrocarbons under the control and influence of the Government through the Ministry for Environment and Energy and the Energy Agency. The basic concept is that each licensee will enjoy, for a certain period and within a delimited area, an exclusive right to explore for and produce, and an ownership interest in, the natural resources won and saved. In return, the licensees must pay duties and commit themselves to certain obligations in carrying out their activities. **6.53**

It should be highlighted that under Danish law there is considered to be no legal difference between a concession, a licence, a permission, and a permit. All these are looked upon as public administrative decisions (as opposed to contracts) and the exact phrase is often chosen at random. However, one could say that 'concession' is the more old-fashioned term and seldom used today in Denmark. The translation of the basis for the activities of Mærsk Oil and Gas is 'concession', whereas the Subsoil Act uses 'permission' and the Model developed by the Ministry is called a 'licence'. Consequently, one cannot classify the arrangement or base any legal consequences, nor determine the rights of the licensee, on the title alone. It is always necessary to analyse the regulatory framework, the negotiations conducted, the appropriate expectations derived from this process, the assumptions on which the licence is based, and the strength of the public interests involved. **6.54**

Among the licence obligations is the requirement that all essential arrangements concerning the operations of licensees are subject to official approval. Thus, under the Subsoil Act, a separate consent—which may be granted in the form of either standard or individual terms—is required for the commencement of the most essential stages of the operations. The system has several advantages for the State. First and foremost, regulation can be adjusted to the specific circumstances and immediate need, which is of particular importance taking into consideration the long duration of the licences and the fast development of technological and safety issues. Moreover, the licence procedure ensures that the licensees, both before commencing their operations and later when approvals for subsequent stages are sought, pass important information to the State. Beyond this, general rules of **6.55** reporting give the State a broad right to receive information from the licensees. Prior to the implementation of the Licensing Directive, competition between licence applicants also strengthened the State's negotiating hand, and gave the basis for adjusting the licence terms in accordance with the expectations for each individual licence area to be offered for licensing.

6.56 The extensive control of activities as complex as oil and natural gas exploration makes heavy demands on both the State and the oil companies, and to a large extent it is assumed that, through consultation and to some extent even negotiation, the parties will arrive at an optimal arrangement for each venture. For this reason the licensing system established was referred to as the 'negotiation system'.[31] However, now that the discretionary powers of the public authorities have become much more restricted, such a characterization no longer properly reflects the current situation.

6.57 The need for public control of oil and natural gas activities is based primarily on overall economic considerations, but other reasons—especially safety concerns—also justify such control. The activities are carried out under difficult working conditions. Weather and a combination of technical and financial requirements will typically subject operations to considerable time pressure, resulting in an increased risk of accidents. Within limits this risk may be reduced by controlling the manner in which a particular project is to be carried out. The State has chosen to become involved in these decisions in order to emphasize safety considerations to a larger extent than might be dictated by operating on economic considerations alone.

Procedures for granting licences

6.58 The Subsoil Act provides the basis for a flexible system of granting licences and prescribes in this connection certain procedures that have to be followed (section 12). It requires that the Parliamentary Committee on Energy be informed of the areas and the general licence conditions before a round is announced or an order for an 'open-door' procedure is issued (SA section 12(2)).

6.59 The Minister may refrain from granting a licence on the basis of the applications which have been received (SA section 12(2)(3)). Such a reservation is within the scope of the Licensing Directive as long as the applicant is informed about the reason if so requested. The Danish Subsoil Act includes a rule about the obligations of the Parliamentary Committee on Energy, and if the Committee cannot accept the granting of a licence, they shall inform the Minister of the reasons, if the Minister so requests (section 6(3)). However, the obligations of the Minister

[31] cf 'The Legal Framework for Exploration for and Production of Oil and Natural Gas in Denmark' by Anita Rønne and Michael Budtz, Journal of Energy and Natural Resources Law, 1985, 153–67.

towards an applicant does not follow, from this Act, but from the general Act on Public Administration, which settles that all administrative decisions must include a justification if not meeting the request of the party.

Today, licences can be granted in four ways.

Bidding rounds

The most common method, introduced in 1981, is to grant licences during bidding rounds and following a public invitation to apply. The invitation must be published in *Statstidende* (the Danish Official Gazette) and in the Official Journal of the European Communities at least ninety days before the closing date for applications. **6.60**

Mini rounds

Changes to the Subsoil Act in 1995 introduced alternative procedures for granting licences. One of the new procedures is that of the 'mini round'. Thus, if an application for a licence for an area is submitted without a public invitation having been issued, and the Minister for Environment and Energy judges that the application should be considered, the Minister shall publish a notice of the application in *Statstidende* and in the Official Journal of the European Communities. Other interested entities shall have a time limit of at least ninety days following this publication to submit their application. At the very least, the notices must state that sole rights to explore for and produce hydrocarbons can be applied for, which areas can be applied for or are applied for, when licences are expected to be granted, and where information on conditions, etc, can be obtained. All interested entities must be notified of any alterations to the conditions. **6.61**

Open-door procedure

For situations in which neither of these two procedures is considered appropriate, a new 'open-door' procedure has been implemented. Pursuant to the Licensing Directive Article 3.3, it is a precondition for the use of this method that the area is available on a permanent basis, has previously been subject to an authorization procedure, or has been relinquished by a licensee. As the whole Danish on- and offshore area has been included in previous licensing rounds and then relinquished by A.P. Møller this method can be applied immediately. The Minister for Environment and Energy has chosen to do so. **6.62**

The Subsoil Act states that licences may be granted within more closely defined areas and if appropriate within a more closely defined period of time. The implementation of this procedure shall take place by a specific ministerial order, which cannot take effect until a notice of the implementation of the procedure has been published in the Official Journal of the European Communities. That notification must specify, at the very least, the areas which may be applied for, and **6.63** where further information on conditions can be obtained. Changes to the conditions must be communicated in the same manner.[32]

6.64 The open-door procedure was introduced in 1997. Under this procedure, applications are invited for all open areas east of 6°15′ East longitude, including Danish onshore areas, every year from 2 January to 30 September. The procedure is intended to provide an incentive for oil companies with novel exploration ideas for areas where exploration has not yet led to any oil or gas discoveries. Applications are considered and licences awarded in the order in which they are received.

6.65 At the end of 1998, the Danish Energy Agency evaluated the open-door procedure. It concluded that the procedure works as intended, and has motivated oil companies to resume exploration, even in areas where no oil or gas discoveries have been made as yet. The Minister for Environment and Energy has therefore decided to retain the procedure in its present form.

Adjoining-block procedure

6.66 The fourth possibility is that the Minister for Environment and Energy may grant licences for a contiguous area without implementing the above procedures when justified by geological or production considerations. In such cases, the holder of a licence for any contiguous area shall be given the opportunity to apply, and must have sufficient time to do so, and access to information regarding the conditions which will apply to such licences.

Criteria for obtaining a licence

6.67 Following the implementation of the Licensing Directive, the selection criteria have been changed and are now limited in their scope. They may now only concern: the applicant's technical knowledge and economic background, and the exploration activities which the applicant intends to carry out, or the method by which the applicant intends to carry out production in the area in question. In assessing applicants the Minister may, in addition to the selection criteria, take account of any lack of efficiency or failure to meet commitments with regard to previous licences (SA, section 12a). It is a requirement that all criteria are published together with the invitations to apply, and that any changes to these criteria are published in a corresponding manner. The criteria were all included in the general Invitation Letter on the Fifth Danish Licensing Round in September 1997 (see its point 3). The Minister for Environment and Energy may, in addition, determine that the size of the sum which the applicants offer to pay when the

[32] A notification of the open-door procedure was published in ECT No C 49/23 of 19 Feb 1997, and in Denmark as Order No 169 of 24 Feb 1997.

licence is granted shall be included in the selection criteria. This principle, however, has not yet been applied in Denmark as a selection criterion.

If two or more applicants for the same area are considered to be equally qualified after evaluation of the above selection criteria, the Minister may stipulate other relevant, objective, and non-discriminatory selection criteria with a view to making the final choice between the applicants (SA, section 12a). Such additional criteria and the subsequent procedure for their application were included in the Invitation Letter for the fifth round (cf point 6), and concerned a supplementary offer to increase the State-owned company DONG Efterforskning og Produktion's predetermined 20 per cent share during the production phase (the so-called sliding scale). **6.68**

It is still open to the Minister to stipulate that the composition of the licensee group of companies or the selection of operator should be determined by the Minister, as long as the decision is based on one of the above mentioned criteria (SA, section 12a, subsections 5 and 6). The Invitation Letter for the fifth round states that applications are invited from both individual companies and groups of companies, and that the preferred operator for the group of companies must be stated separately. However, it also indicated that the authorities will only intervene if the applications cover shares of more or less than 80 per cent, because one of the licence conditions is that the State-owned company DONG Efterforskning og Produktion AS will hold a 20 per cent share of all licences. Likewise it is only if the companies disagree about the appointment of the operator that the Energy Agency reserves the right to appoint the operator on the basis of the applicants' qualifications (see points 4 and 5). **6.69**

Types of licence

In relation to hydrocarbon activities, the Subsoil Act distinguishes between two main types of licence: a preliminary investigation licence and a combined exploration and production licence. **6.70**

The preliminary investigation licence authorizes initial investigations, such as seismic, geological, and geochemical surveys, to be conducted in order to map an area and to make a preliminary evaluation of the possibility of finding hydrocarbons there. The licence does not give its holders exclusive rights, and it carries no assurance of an entitlement of preference at a later time to an exploration and production licence (SA, section 3). **6.71**

The combined exploration and production licence authorizes all activities necessary for exploration for and production of hydrocarbons. Contrary to the preliminary investigation licence, this licence grants an exclusive right of exploration and production, although it should be emphasized that the actual commencement of production is subject to further permissions or approvals (SA, sections 5 and 13). **6.72**

Thus the licensee must receive approval of a development plan, including preparations for production and necessary facilities therefore (section 10), which enables the Minister for Environment and Energy to insist on a particular mode of transportation and on connection to an existing or future pipeline system. On this basis, the Minister grants a separate production permit specifying, for intervals of at least six months, the quantity that may be produced (section 15). In addition to the principal licence, a separate approval is necessary for each individual project carried out from time to time in connection with such undertakings (section 28).

6.73 A third type of licence is the separate licence required for the establishment and operation of pipeline systems (section 17).

6.74 Finally, the Subsoil Act includes rules for licences for storage purposes (section 23), and for scientific investigations (section 24).

Issued licences

The DAPCO licence

6.75 The first licence to explore for oil and gas (as well as salt and other natural resources) was issued to an American citizen, F.F. Ravlin, in 1935. He established a company called the Danish American Prospecting Company (DAPCO) and transferred the licence thereto. In 1940 the company was taken over by Gulf, which held the licence until 1957. During the following two years ESSO became the licensee until the licence was relinquished in 1959.

The A.P. Møller licence

6.76 In 1962 a new licence was granted to the shipowner A.P. Møller, which vested the rights in a separate A.P. Møller company, Mærsk Oil and Gas AS. Over the years, A.P. Møller has involved different multinational oil companies in the activities under the licence, today operated by the Danish Underground Consortium (DUC), a joint venture by A.P. Møller, Shell, and Texaco.

6.77 Although this issuance followed a three-year period with no licensees, the terms of the licence were not tightened, but remained very liberal. Following the oil crises in 1973 and 1979 and the serious implications for the Danish economy, the licence was revised through negotiations between the Government and DUC, and resulted in two agreements, in 1976 and 1981. The 1976 Agreement established the foundation for the later decision on production of natural gas and defined the roles of DUC as producer and of the new State-owned company, the National Oil and Gas Company of Denmark (DONG), as sole importer. The 1981 Agreement radically changed the original terms of the licence, one of the major changes being that over a few years Mærsk Oil and Gas relinquished nearly all of the Danish territory: 50 per cent in 1982, 25 per cent in 1984, and the remaining area in 1986, retaining only areas in the North Sea, where exploration and production activities were in progress, and a 'contiguous area' of about 1 per cent of the original licence area, corresponding to nine blocks of an average area of 212.5 square kilometres in the south-western sector of the North Sea. With respect to the contiguous area, 25 per cent of the area was relinquished on 1 January 2000 and a further 25 per cent must be relinquished by 1 January 2005. Another important change includes the requirement to produce working programmes including specification of concrete activities.

In 2012, A.P. Møller's licence will expire. In a protocol that was attached to the licence in 1962, the licensee was promised negotiations on the question of activities after the expiry of the licence, so that negotiations on possible continuation of the activities, and on what terms, should be opened well in advance. The Licensing Directive 94/22 contains a transitional arrangement which means that Denmark can live up to the obligations of the promise, while the Government's bargaining position remains unaffected. **6.78**

The first to fifth licensing rounds

The gradual relinquishment of areas by Mærsk Oil and Gas has enabled new oil companies to be invited to Denmark. Licensing rounds were held in 1984, 1986, 1989, 1995, and 1998, resulting in the issuance of more than seventy licences. Around forty-two licences are presently in force.[33] **6.79**

(4) Licence Terms

Terms relating to area and time

The Danish area is divided into blocks, whose size is approximately 212 square kilometres. In principle, the licence grants an exclusive right to explore for and produce hydrocarbons within the relevant area. However, this exclusive right is limited in certain respects, as others may obtain a licence relating to the same area to carry out preliminary investigations for hydrocarbons (eg by seismic surveys) or to explore for and produce other raw materials, establish pipelines, and carry out scientific investigations. **6.80**

Blocks awarded in the first five rounds have been subject to a licence term of thirty-six years: an exploration period of six years and a production period of thirty years. Neither the term nor the boundaries of the licence area are irrevocably fixed, however. Under special circumstances the exploration period may be extended by as much as two years at a time, up to a maximum of ten years. The last revision of the Subsoil Act allows for the possibility of extending the exploration phase to more than ten years in exceptional cases (section 13). In special cases even the production period may be prolonged. **6.81**

[33] In addition to the Mærsk Oil and Gas licence, 2 licences derive from the 2nd round, and 4 from the 3rd round; 3 were issued between the 3rd and 4th rounds, 9 from the 4th round, 17 from the 5th round, and 6 by the open-door procedure.

6.82 Upon the expiration of the exploration period, the licence area is reduced to cover only those areas in which the licensee has demonstrated the presence of producible hydrocarbons (SA, section 13 and the Model Licence (ML), section 5).

Work programme

6.83 In Denmark, the grant of a licence is conditional upon an oil company undertaking a specific work programme. The content of that programme is determined by negotiation with the applicants and constitutes an appendix to each licence.

6.84 The work programme may be considered as part of the consideration the licensee must pay for the licence: if the work obligations are not met, the licensee must pay an amount corresponding to what the performance of those obligations would have cost, unless the Minister for Environment and Energy grants a complete or partial exemption (SA, section 32 and ML, section 36(2)). The work programme will typically oblige the licensee to carry out seismic surveys and to drill exploratory wells, and will usually state the time period within which such works must be completed. The work programme relates exclusively to the exploration phase.

6.85 If hydrocarbons are discovered, the licensee must submit a new plan, referred to as an evaluation programme, for the further works necessary to ascertain whether a commercially producible accumulation has been found (ML, section 4), as well as a time schedule for carrying out those works within the exploration period. The results of the evaluation programme form the basis of the thirty-year licence extension for the purpose of production, and for which a special development plan and production permits must be obtained.

State participation

6.86 The State became directly involved in exploration and production activities during the 1980s. State participation is carried out by the State-owned limited company DONG Efterforskning og Produktion AS, a wholly owned subsidiary of the National Oil and Gas Company of Denmark AS (DONG). State participation has been introduced in all new licences, but the State-owned company does not have control of production, as it holds only up to 20 per cent participation rights. If producible discoveries are made, DONG Efterforskning og Produktion AS has in some licences an option to increase its share up to a maximum of 50 per cent, according to a negotiated sliding scale based on the magnitude of production.

6.87 Today, DONG Efterforskning og Produktion AS participates in all licences on an equal footing with other participants, but in the first and second rounds (1984 and 1986 respectively) and partly in the third round, this applied only in principle as there was the crucial exception that the company was supported through the exploration phase on the basis of the 'carried interest' principle, ie the other participants were required to pay DONG Efterforskning og Produktion AS's share of the exploration costs. If producible discoveries were made and the licence was extended by a thirty-year production period, DONG Efterforskning og Produktion AS's payment obligation was triggered and the company, on an equal basis with the other participants, was to pay a share of the costs of development and production, corresponding to its share of the licence (SA, section 8 and ML, section 13). Costs already incurred during the exploration period were not to be reimbursed by DONG Efterforskning og Produktion AS, because of, *inter alia*, the availability to the licensees of deductions under the Hydrocarbons Taxation Act.

In order to implement the EC Licensing Directive (94/22) which prescribes common rules on granting oil and gas licences and on their terms, the Danish Subsoil Act of 1981 was amended in 1995. State participation now in principle takes place under the same conditions which apply to a private licensee. If the State or a company owned by the State participates in the activities under a licence granted after 1 July 1995, the manner in which the voting rights are exercised may not prevent the management decisions of the licensee being based on commercial principles. Moreover, the State or the company owned by the State may not receive information on, or exercise any voting rights in, decisions on the licensee's choice of sources of procurement. Furthermore, the State or the company owned by the State shall not, together with one or more Danish public participants, exercise majority voting rights in other decisions concerning the activities (SA, section 8). **6.88**

However, the 1995 Subsoil Act also states that it may be laid down as a condition for a licence that any decisions by a licensee which are not in conformity with conditions regarding the safeguarding of resource considerations or the economic interests of the Danish State shall not bind the company or person responsible for the State participation, if it notifies the other licensees that it is opposed to the decision before a fixed deadline. The right to oppose a decision shall, if the occasion arises, be exercised, especially in relation to investment decisions and to the licensee's obligation to choose suppliers in a non-discriminatory manner. **6.89**

If participation by the State is exercised by a company owned by the State which also holds licences, or interests in them acquired on another basis, the main rule is that the company shall keep specific accounts for the activities in respect of each of these categories of interest, and ensure that there is no flow of information from the part of the company exercising the State participation to the part of the company which has acquired interests in licences acquired on another basis. The Minister for Environment and Energy may lay down further regulations concerning these issues. **6.90**

If the licence is held by at least two companies jointly, the Model Licence requires that their co-operation be regulated in a separate Joint Operating Agreement (ML, section 18) subject to the approval of the Ministry for Environment and **6.91**

Energy. The central concept of this agreement is the establishment of an Operating Committee with a representative from each member of the joint venture having voting rights corresponding to its share of the licence. The Committee governs all joint affairs, although the executive function is vested in an operator appointed by the joint enterprise and approved by the Ministry. The operating agreement contains detailed provisions concerning both the rights and obligations of the operator with respect to the other participants and the reciprocal legal relationships between all the participants. The Ministry for Environment and Energy has developed a draft joint operating agreement for each round which serves as the basis of negotiations between the oil companies and DONG Efterforskning og Produktion AS.

6.92 Government policy was originally aimed at facilitating the development of DONG Efterforskning og Produktion AS as an operator for several joint ventures. However, a kind of privatization was introduced in the second round in 1986, when a Danish operator company Danop was created in which DONG formed a partnership with a private company consisting of twenty major Danish private enterprises, each partner having a 50 per cent ownership. Both the State-owned company and the group of private companies are parties to the joint venture with other, typically foreign, companies, whereas the joint operator company participates in the joint venture as an observer without any percentage interest with a view to taking over the operation of the licence either from the start or to taking it over from a foreign operator at a later stage during the exploration phase or at the beginning of the development or production phase. One of the purposes of this initiative was to establish a suitable framework for promoting collaboration between the State-owned company and a number of Danish private companies and to provide the best basis for developing Danish expertise in the offshore area, but it also illustrates a shift in policy as to the State's role in this sector. In January 2000, however, DONG acquired the full ownership of Danop, following 15 years of operation.

Disposal

6.93 Although the licensee in principle has the right to decide freely where and when it will dispose of its own production, the Danish State can to some extent require disposal of part of the recovered oil and natural gas. For licences granted before 1 January 1995, the State may control the disposition of approximately two-thirds of production by utilizing all the options, which may also be exercised independently. Moreover, the State, by virtue of its participation rights, will take a share of the production proportionate to its share of each individual licence.

More specifically the State may, with respect to crude oil: **6.94**

a) exercise an option to purchase up to 50 per cent of production from licences issued in the first, second and third rounds pursuant to section 19 of the Subsoil Act. In the Mærsk Oil and Gas licence the amount is fixed at up to 40 per cent, but on condition that Mærsk Oil and Gas is entitled to repurchase a declining share of the hydrocarbons until 1 January 1990 (the 1981 Agreement, sections 11 and 12);
b) require that royalty be paid in kind pursuant to section 18 of the Subsoil Act, section 12 of the Model Licence, and the 1976 Agreement, clause 7;
c) require that the 5 per cent profit element to be paid by new licensees pursuant to the Pipeline Act be made in the form of crude oil (section 3(4) of that Act).

With respect to natural gas: **6.95**

a) the State may require that royalty be paid in kind pursuant to the Subsoil Act, section 18, the Model Licence, section 12, and the 1976 Agreement, clause 7;
b) the licensee has an obligation to offer to the State, on commercial terms, all natural gas to be produced before negotiations are initiated with other purchasers (Model Licence, section 28, and the 1976 Agreement, clause 3);
c) if no contract is concluded between the State and the licensee the State may exercise a right of first refusal on quantities that can be utilized in Denmark, on the terms obtainable from other purchasers (Model Licence, section 29, and the 1976 Agreement, clause 3).

For licences issued after 1 January 1995 the State has no purchase rights to oil nor is this requirement included in the licences with respect to gas. Moreover, it should be added that the royalty has not been imposed from the third and later rounds, and the profit element of 5 per cent in the Pipeline Act has not been levied on licences outside the Central Graben in the North Sea. This means that in reality there are now no restrictions on the disposal of oil and gas by licensees of the fouth and fifth rounds or of open-door licences. **6.96**

To date, the Danish State has enjoyed a *de facto* monopoly over domestic natural gas resources: Danish Underground Consortium (DUC) is the only producer on Danish territory and DONG the only purchaser. However, this will change in the near future. In 1979, DONG entered into the first gas contract with DUC for the purchase of 55 billion cubic metres of natural gas over the period 1984–2008. To secure the necessary supply for a growing market, DONG completed contracts for further purchases, in 1989 for 38 billion cubic metres of natural gas and in 1993 covering all DUC gas production.[34] In 1998 DONG concluded a contract with Amerada Hess to purchase gas produced from the South Arne field. **6.97**

[34] Further information in 'Current Development', Journal of Energy and Natural Resources Law, vol 7, no 4, 1989.

Financial terms

6.98 Consistent with international practice, various financial terms are imposed on licensees in return for their licence, partly to guarantee the State a fair economic benefit from licence operations, and partly to serve as an incentive to the licensees to undertake exploration, to commence production if hydrocarbons are discovered, and to relinquish areas that prove unproductive. The Danish Model Licence is based on a system of various fees and taxes. The most important are next described.

Miscellaneous fees

6.99 To cover the administrative costs of negotiating and issuing exploration and production licences, applicants in the first round paid a fee of DKK 100,000 upon filing an application and DKK 500,000 upon issuance of the licence. In the second round these amounts were raised to DKK 250,000 and DKK 1,000,000 respectively, but later reduced significantly. In the fourth round, for instance, the fees amounted to DKK 25,000 and 100,000 respectively.

Royalties

6.100 If production is commenced, a royalty can be charged, calculated on the basis of the value of the produced substances, without deduction for production costs. A royalty is levied on the Mærsk Oil and Gas licence and licences issued in the first and second rounds. Whereas the royalty in the former mentioned licence is set at a flat 8.5 per cent for offshore production (cf licence Section 10), the royalty for licences issued in the first and second rounds is calculated on a graduated basis in order to decrease the burden on small fields. A low rate is thus charged for an initial quantity interval; the rate then increases with respect to production exceeding that interval in accordance with a marginal sliding scale. The system corresponds in principle to a graduated personal income tax scale. If the production from a deposit is below 72,500 cubic metres (5,000 barrels per day), the rate is 2 per cent. For production within the range 72,500 and 290,000 cubic metres (20,000 barrels per day), a royalty of 8 per cent is charged, and for production above that level the rate is 16 per cent.

6.101 A royalty is charged whether production is profitable or not, so the royalty itself might determine whether a field—particularly a smaller one and/or one requiring heavy investment—will be developed at all. It also might affect the date on which a field is shut in. This fact has been thoroughly considered in developing the terms of the Model Licence, since exploration activities in the Danish sector of the North Sea have so far located only relatively small deposits. The rates are equivalent for oil and natural gas, and the sliding scale is not intended to be an incentive to the companies to adjust production in relation to the intervals of the scale. Furthermore, it was intended to set the level of the royalty to correspond with that applying to current licensees, also bearing in mind the royalty rates applicable elsewhere within the oil industry.

Royalties are calculated every calendar quarter for first and second round licences and every six months for the Mærsk Oil and Gas licence on the basis of the value of the produced hydrocarbons. In principle, the stated value should reflect the real market price. Should the Minister for Environment and Energy determine that it fails to do so, he is entitled to assess the value of the production in question. If a norm price is established for recovered hydrocarbons according to the Hydrocarbons Taxation Act (see below) the value will always be assessed on that basis. **6.102**

Since 1972, a total of about DKK 11.4 billion (in 1998 prices) has been paid by way of royalties on the oil and natural gas produced from the North Sea.[35] **6.103**

Pipeline duty

In addition to the fees and the royalty, licensees are required to pay a fee for pipeline transportation of crude oil and condensate produced, including an obligation to pay the capital and operating costs associated with the use of the pipeline as well as a profit element of 5 per cent of the value of the crude oil transported. The 5 per cent fee is also applicable under certain circumstances when transportation via the pipeline is not taking place (see section C below). **6.104**

Hydrocarbons tax

Previously, companies recovering hydrocarbons in Denmark were subject only to the general corporation tax requirements. According to the Hydrocarbons Taxation Act[36] the existing corporation tax provisions to a large extent continue to apply to the production of oil and natural gas, with certain exceptions. **6.105**

Income from hydrocarbon activities is to be calculated separately, according to the 'ring-fence principle', eg losses originating from activities other than those relating to hydrocarbons cannot be deducted in the calculation of corporation tax on hydrocarbon-source income. Losses from hydrocarbon activities may, however, be deducted from income from other activities. The ring-fence principle thus applies in only one direction. It is possible, however, to carry losses from the production of hydrocarbons forward for fifteen years, compared to the five-year period usually applied in Denmark. **6.106**

---

[35] See *Oil and Gas Production in Denmark 1998*, the Energy Agency, ch 6.

[36] Act No 175 of 28 Apr 1982, cf Consolidated Act No 792 of 29 Sep 1993 with later amendments. See also 'The Legal Framework for Exploration for and Production of Oil and Natural Gas in Denmark' by Anita Rønne and Michael Budtz, Journal of Energy and Natural Resources Law, 1985, 153–67.

6.107 Exploration costs may be deducted at the time they are incurred. If the licensee has not yet started production and thus has not made a profit, such losses may, as mentioned above, be deducted from other activities. The licensee may choose instead to make the deduction over five years at 20 per cent per year, beginning when production commences.

6.108 The Act also authorizes the application of norm prices to production in calculating the income of corporations recovering oil and natural gas. According to the applicable rules, income arising from the sale of hydrocarbons is usually calculated on the basis of invoice sales prices. But in the case of affiliated buyers and sellers, it may be necessary for the assessment authorities to determine whether the invoiced prices correspond to the market price. This work is both time-consuming and difficult. It can be facilitated by means of the procedure in which a board of experts appointed by the Minister for Environment and Energy may, as required, set norm prices corresponding to the market price that would apply between independent parties.

6.109 Although production from the North Sea commenced in 1972, the DUC companies did not become liable to pay corporate tax until the beginning of the 1980s. Since 1992, the Danish corporate tax rate has been 34 per cent. By the end of 1998, State revenue from corporate tax payments totalled about DKK 14.8 billion in 1998 prices.[37] With effect from 1 January 1999, the corporate tax rate was reduced to 32 per cent. Originally, this bill proposed to lower corporate tax for all commercial activities except for offshore oil and gas activities. However, due to heavy objections from the Danish oil industry, the Government gave up this idea.

6.110 The hydrocarbon tax is calculated on the same basis as corporation tax, with the following exceptions.

6.111 The income is calculated field by field. This means, for example, that loss from the development of one field cannot be deducted from the profit realized from another. This ring-fence definition is thus narrower than the one used in calculating corporation tax, as discussed above. The calculation of income on a field-by-field basis results in advanced payment of tax; the State thus realizes its share of the income from the production of oil and natural gas earlier than would otherwise be the case.

a) The provisions concerning transfers to investment funds, investment tax credit, advance depreciation, and writing down of inventories are not applicable in the calculation of hydrocarbon tax.
b) A hydrocarbon deduction, corresponding to 25 per cent each year for ten years of the sum of investments incurred, is applicable in addition to the normal allowances for the field in question.

---

[37] See *Oil and Gas Production in Denmark 1998*, Energy Agency, ch 6.

c) The figure on which the hydrocarbon tax is payable is calculated by first adding the incomes of the taxpayer resulting from the profitable fields. All exploration costs are then deducted from this total income. The taxpayer also deducts the corporation taxes assessed for the tax year in question. A hydrocarbon tax of 70 per cent is then assessed against the income figure so derived.

The objective of the hydrocarbons taxation was to levy a special tax on extraordinarily high profits, and the system is designed so that the average rate of taxation increases in step with increased returns on investments. The Danish marginal rate of taxation is a little lower than those in effect in the United Kingdom and Norway. Fields requiring relatively large investments, eg marginal fields, enjoy a lesser tax rate because of the hydrocarbon deduction, whereas the tax on fields in which production is high in relation to investment will be heavier. In the event of real price rises for oil and natural gas, the State's share of the total income will increase; conversely, a decrease in real prices will result in a lighter taxation of income from oil (because of the deduction rules). **6.112**

Hydrocarbons tax only became payable for a few years at the beginning of the 1980s, with total hydrocarbon tax payments amounting to some DKK 0.8 billion in 1998 prices. In the light of the investments and crude oil prices expected for the next few years, it is considered unlikely that hydrocarbon tax can be levied (because of the deduction rules). **6.113**

Enforcement and dispute resolution

The Minister for Environment and Energy may under certain qualified conditions revoke a licence (SA, section 30). These conditions concern non-compliance with provisions, misleading information in a licence application, and bankruptcy. However, it is underlined that if the matter can be remedied by the licensee, it should be allowed to do so within a specific time limit before revocation can take place. **6.114**

Penalties (fines or 'simple' detention for between seven days and six months) may be imposed on anyone who performs activities without having obtained the required licences, who does not provide the required information or omits to submit samples, or who disregards directions issued in pursuance of the Subsoil Act or secondary legislation (SA, section 38). Moreover, distress may be levied for non-payment of any taxes or fees (SA, section 39). **6.115**

Any dispute is subject to Danish law and Danish courts, although a dispute can be resolved by arbitration if the parties agree (SA, section 31 and ML, section 40). **6.116**

(5) Environmental Issues

Environmental impact assessment

6.117 The EC Council Directive on the Effects of Certain Private and Public Projects on the Environment (1985/337) was implemented in Denmark in the form of amendments to the Danish Subsoil Act in 1995 (projects on the territorial sea and the continental shelf) and the Continental Shelf Act in 1997 (projects involving the installation of pipelines for transporting oil and gas from one country to another across the Danish continental shelf). Thus, prior to the launching of the projects defined in the Subsoil Act, provided that the relevant projects are deemed to have a significant impact on the environment, an assessment of the effects on the environment must be made, accompanied by the necessary measures to ensure that the party seeking approval of such a project submits the information required for making the assessment (SA, section 28a). The environmental impact assessment must have been carried out before any approvals are granted under the Subsoil Act. The projects covered are, among others, production installations in a development plan pursuant to SA, section 10, pipelines pursuant to section 17, and separate works pursuant to section 28. However, in general the requirement does not apply to licences for preliminary investigations such as seismic surveys and licences for exploration and production, as these are not sufficient in themselves to allow the licensee to commence concrete projects.

6.118 The amendments made to the Subsoil Act in 1995 authorize the Minister for Environment and Energy to lay down more detailed regulations as to which projects are to be covered by the Act and which minimum information and investigations are required to make an environmental impact assessment. In addition, the Minister may lay down regulations regarding the notification and consultation of the public as well as the authorities and organizations concerned. No general rules were, however, prepared for the submission of environmental impact assessments in connection with the amendment of the Subsoil Act. In 1997, the EC Council Directive underwent changes (1997/11/EC), although they do not affect the tenor of the 1985 Directive. The changes have already been applied to projects in the Danish part of the North Sea.[38] The amendments to the Danish Continental Shelf Act introduced in 1997 also include a provision aimed at implementing the

[38] The companies developing the Siri and South Arne fields have made environmental impact assessments for both field developments according to the rules laid down in the amended Directive. These environmental impact assessments were prepared in close co-operation between the energy and environmental authorities and the oil companies, and a reference group was set up, composed of representatives of the Danish Energy Agency, the National Forest and Nature Agency, and the Danish Environmental Protection Agency, which monitored the work and offered advice to the companies. Likewise, a reference group was appointed in connection with DONG Naturgas AS's preparation of an environmental impact assessment for the gas pipeline connecting the South Arne field with the west coast of Jutland. As the gas pipeline was to continue over land, the reference group also co-operated with the authorities in Ribe County.

amended Council Directive, so that projects for the installation of pipelines to transport hydrocarbons across the Danish continental shelf and to transport hydrocarbons over the continental shelf to the Danish coast are subject to an environmental impact assessment. On this basis, the environmental effects of establishing Europipe II were assessed, the first environmental impact assessment made for a pipeline transporting hydrocarbons across the Danish continental shelf.

According to a new notification procedure, the aim of which is to give the public an opportunity to express an opinion, the Danish Energy Agency must insert a notice in three national newspapers, announcing that an environmental impact assessment (EIA) has been made for the development of a specific field, and that the environmental impact assessment will be made available to the public at five of Denmark's largest libraries for the following two-month period. In addition, a non-technical summary should be made available at the Danish Energy Agency. **6.119**

On land, the EC Council Directive is implemented in the general Planning Act No 518 of 11 June 2000 as amended, which states that the regional plan must contain guidelines for projects likely to affect the environment significantly, and that these guidelines when adopted must be accompanied by an environmental assessment of the project (section 6). The Minister for Environment and Energy has issued specific regulations on EIA projects Order No 428 of 2 June 1999, which includes lists of projects that are subject to an EIA, either always or under special circumstances. The Aarhus Convention on Public Access to Appeals has been implemented by Act No 447 of 31 May 2000, as an amendment to the Subsoil Act, section 37a, the Continental Shelf Act, section 6a, and the Electricity Supply Act, section 89 a. **6.120**

Abandonment

The Subsoil Act, section 33 determines that a licence shall include detailed rules concerning steps to be taken in regard to installations established by the licensee when the licence terminates, together with the handling of installations which have fulfilled their purpose. The Minister for Environment and Energy can demand total or partial removal. **6.121**

Pursuant to Model Licence, section 37, the Danish State is entitled to take over without compensation all or part of any installations intended for long-term use within the licence area, if the licence is terminated. In this respect, the licensee is obliged to ensure that the facilities are located within the area and can be assigned to the State in a proper condition. If the licensee fails to comply with these obligations it is obliged to compensate for any losses. These rules also apply in the case of abandonment of installations. **6.122**

The Agency may also require the licensee to remove all or part of any installations, whether they belong to the licensee or to any other party, according to a time **6.123** schedule fixed by the Danish Energy Agency. As from 1997, an additional requirement was included in the licences that a licence holder must submit a plan for discontinuing the use of all installations etc (a winding-up plan) subject to approval by the Energy Agency before the termination or abandonment of the installation. This plan shall set out the procedure for removing the installations that the State does not wish to take over, in whole or in part. The winding-up plan shall also include information about and an assessment of the environmental impact and safety aspects of the plan, as well as a time schedule for its implementation. The Energy Agency may lay down detailed guidelines for the content of the plan.

6.124 The Energy Agency may at any time require the licensee to take any other measures necessary to prevent the facilities from posing any risk or inconvenience. If the licensee fails to comply with such a requirement, the Agency shall be entitled, without further notice, to have the necessary measures taken on the licensee's account and at its risk in every respect. The licensee shall indemnify the State against any third-party claims for compensation from the State resulting from such removal or preventive measures.

Safety

6.125 Environmental matters relating to offshore installations are regulated primarily by the Act on the Marine Environment[39] and the Act on Certain Marine Installations.[40] The obligations of the National Agency for Environmental Protection relate primarily to discharges from platforms and their effect on the surrounding environment, as well as preparedness to contain oil spills. The obligations of the Energy Agency relate mainly to the design, equipment, and operation of platforms. Co-operation between the two agencies ensures co-ordinated efforts. The Marine Installations Act covers all marine installations being used for exploration, production, and transportation, as well as any other facilities closely and permanently connected with such activities. The typical objects of regulation under the Act are drilling platforms, pipelines, and storage installations, while such things as supply ships, seismographic ships, and tank vessels are not covered.

6.126 The Marine Installations Act is intended to gather the relevant safety regulations into a single, comprehensive set of rules as well as to provide a concentration and co-ordination of supervisory functions. Thus, the Act empowers the Minister for Environment and Energy to issue rules regarding safety, health, and the environment in relation to marine installations. Although the authority to enforce compliance with the Act and rules promulgated thereunder is vested in the Minister for Environment and Energy (sections 9 *et seq*) those carrying out the regulated activities are independently obliged to ensure, through internal control, that the safety requirements are observed (sections 4 and 6). As the title indicates, the Act

[39] Now Act No 476 of 30 June 1993 with later amendments.

[40] Act No 292 of 10 June 1981.

only governs offshore activities: exploration and exploitation onshore is governed by the same set of safety regulations applicable to other kinds of land-based industrial activities.

Following the acceleration in the exploration and production of hydrocarbons from Danish territory, an extensive set of regulations and procedures has been introduced to ensure minimum intervention in the surrounding physical environment. Under environmental legislation, all drilling is subject to the regulation and approval of environmental agencies. This legislation controls the type and quantity of permissible discharge to the surroundings as well as compulsory emergency procedures for dealing with potential oil leaks. **6.127**

Liability

Pursuant to the Subsoil Act, the licensee is liable for 'accidental' damage caused.[41] Liability is strict and unlimited (SA, section 35). This liability provision must be considered together with the Model Licence, which states that oil companies jointly holding a licence are jointly and severally liable for claims arising under the Subsoil Act. Thus, even if the activities are in principle conducted by one member of the group (the operator), strict liability extends to the other participant as well. **6.128**

It follows from the broad wording of the Subsoil Act that: **6.129**

a) liability encompasses all types of damage, not only pollution, in relation to third parties as well as in relation to employees, other parties to licence-related contracts, etc;
b) liability may arise during preliminary investigations, exploration, or production; and
c) damages may be claimed from the licensee, regardless of whether the injury is caused by him or by an independent contractor.

Neither the wording of the Act nor the comments to it precisely define the scope of this strict liability. **6.130**

The damages claimed against the licensee may be reduced or eliminated if the victim intentionally or by gross negligence contributed to the injury (SA, section 35(2)). The licensee is thus in principle liable for all damage, regardless of its cause, subject to the limiting principle that there must be equivalence between the injury and the activities carried out by the licensee. **6.131**

(6) Current Developments and Future Trends

As will be learned from section H below, Denmark has adopted a new regulatory framework for a carbon dioxide tax system on onshore activities. As the offshore **6.132**

[41] In all essentials the provision corresponds to s 10 of the 1950 Subsoil Act, under which, however, the damages claim related only to injuries to the property of third parties.

industry is also responsible for carbon dioxide emissions, the question as to whether the offshore industry should be subject to a carbon dioxide tax is currently under consideration. The Model Licence, section 39 includes a provision which determines that the licence shall not restrict the State's general right to levy taxes or its authority to issue general provisions concerning specific aspects of exploration and production activities. This presumably means that a carbon dioxide tax could be levied on both existing and future licensees. Also the hydrocarbons taxation regime is subject to discussions for the time being.

C. Transportation of Oil (Offshore)

(1) Introduction

6.133 On 1 May 1984 the Danish pipeline to transport oil from the North Sea to the East coast of Jutland was completed.[42] It is owned and operated by DONG Olierør AS, a subsidiary of the National Oil and Gas Company of Denmark AS (DONG). Transportation of crude oil from the fields in the Danish part of the North Sea was previously made by sea-going vessels using a buoy system. Investigations showed, however, that pipeline transportation had several advantages in that offtake, and thus production, is not delayed by bad weather, and it is possible to develop some of the smaller fields which, taken separately, would not be profitable enough to justify production costs.

(2) The Pipeline Act

6.134 The Pipeline Act[43] is part of the legislative foundation on which the regulation of the oil and natural gas activities in the North Sea is based. While the Subsoil Act and the Marine Installations Act lay down the framework for such activities generally, the Pipeline Act is more specialized. It alone contains provisions concerning the establishment of a pipeline for the transportation of crude oil, and imposes obligations upon the licensees concerning their use of the pipeline. The Pipeline Act is a legislative phenomenon peculiar to Denmark: other countries typically leave to the licensees the control of such installations and the right to negotiate the terms of and payment for their use.

6.135 In order to optimize the use of the pipeline the Act imposes upon licensees producing crude oil from the Danish sector of the continental shelf in the North Sea an obligation to connect their production plants to the main pipeline. However, only crude oil intended for refining or sale in Denmark need be transported through the pipeline, although the payment obligation mentioned in the follow-

[42] In 1998 the capacity of DONG's pipeline from the Gorm field to shore was expanded to 270,000 barrels per day.

[43] Act No 291 of 10 June 1981, as amended by Act No 254 of 8 June 1983 and Act No 432 of 10 June 1997.

ing still applies. In special cases the Minister may grant exemptions from the obligation to connect (section 2(3)). DONG has a corresponding transport obligation, subject to such limitations as are a consequence of the capacity of the pipeline. In practice this means that the State-owned company holds a *de facto* transport monopoly. According to the Pipeline Act, many of the specific rights and obligations of DONG and the producers—apart from those relating to payment—are contained, not in the Act itself, but in a transportation agreement. Nevertheless, it is clear that the producers' obligations with respect to transportation and the payment therefore are more extensive than is the case in, for example, Norway and the UK.

Producers liable to connect shall pay to DONG a pipeline duty consisting of three elements: a) reimbursement of DONG's installation expenses, b) reimbursement of DONG's operational expenses, and c) a profit element of 5 per cent of the value of the licensee's production. The value of the produced hydrocarbons is calculated in the same way as the royalty (see section B(4) above). If the royalty is not included in the licence terms, the calculation shall be based on section 10 of the Model Licence for the first round (1984). The more detailed rules for payment are now set out in an order issued by the Ministry of Energy.[44] For fields not covered by the Act, ie outside the North Sea, the Model Licence prescribes a corresponding obligation to connect to pipelines either installed by the State or the use of which is required by the State (section 27). The same applies to the transportation of natural gas. In all cases, however, the Minister for Environment and Energy may grant exemptions from this obligation if connection is considered uneconomical or inappropriate. **6.136**

The State-owned company DONG Olierør AS owns the oil pipeline and pays an annual tax to the State (section 3a). Since 1992, 95 per cent of the income has come from the 5 per cent profit element. In 1998, the pipeline tariff payments made by DONG Olierør AS amounted to DKK 310 million, a 30 per cent decline compared to 1997. Up to and including 1998, the pipeline tariff payments yielded revenue for the Danish State of about DKK 4.3 billion in 1998 prices.[45] **6.137**

The Pipeline Act was amended in 1997.[46] The background to the revision was the expectation that the capacity of the existing oil pipeline would not be sufficient to transport oil from both the existing producing fields and future fields. The amendment is intended to enable licensees to use an offshore loading system in conveying oil from Danish offshore fields to shore in those cases where the operator is exempted from the duty to connect its facilities to the oil pipeline. However, an exemption is granted if the operator pays the Danish State a fee of 5 per cent of **6.138**

44 Order No 212 of 21 Mar 2000, concerning payment for transportation of crude oil.
45 See *Oil and Gas Production in Denmark 1998*, Energy Agency, ch 6.
46 Act No 432 of 10 June 1997.

the value of the crude oil and condensate produced, which equals the fee payable for using the oil pipeline. In other words, the 5 per cent profit element for transportation has now in principle become a general tax on oil production.

6.139 With regard to crude oil no further restrictions apart from taxes affect access to the market. There are no controls of imports and exports, and no control of prices. Neither are there any subsidies. Refining and distribution are in the hands of private sector companies, and there is no special public control except in relation to the environment and emergencies.

D. Transportation and Distribution of Natural Gas

(1) Background of the Danish Natural Gas Supply System

6.140 In 1979 the Danish Parliament took the formal decision to construct a natural gas grid,[47] based on supplies from the Danish part of the North Sea and driven by considerations regarding security of supply after the oil crises. Five years later, on 1 October 1984, a country-wide offshore and onshore transmission system of pipelines, including a gas treatment plant, storage facilities, belt crossing, and a number of 'off-take' stations were inaugurated.[48] Within the big network systems in Denmark, the natural gas sector is thus the youngest, and was implemented over a short period of time. The natural gas system as a whole was at that time the largest single project in Denmark, and not surprisingly ongoing evaluation of project developments has been considered essential and has resulted in several changes over the years. Basically, the decision to set up a country-wide natural gas network is welcome. Nevertheless, the way in which it was implemented gives rise to criticism, as it resulted in a speeded-up planning process and complicated decision-making structures without the concomitant economic responsibility. Important prior conditions for the economy of the project in the 1979 recommendation have also changed, however, and one of the more important ones was the expectation of a price level for oil of 12 US$/barrel in 1978 prices, corresponding to approximately 29 US$/barrel in 1997 prices. As is well known, however, from the middle of the 1980s for the following fifteen years oil prices were significantly lower.

6.141 The Danish gas market is based upon a contract in 1979 with Danish Underground Consortium (DUC, then structured as A.P. Møller 30 per cent, Shell 40 per cent, Chevron 15 per cent, and Texaco 15 per cent, and today structured as A.P. Møller 39 per cent, Shell 46 per cent, and Texaco 15 per cent) and

[47] Act No 232 of 8 June 1979 on Construction of a Natural Gas Supply System.

[48] In 1998, DONG laid a new gas pipeline in the North Sea for transporting gas from the South Arne field via the Harald field to the gas processing facilities at Nybro.

the State-owned National Oil and Gas Company of Denmark (DONG) for 55 billion cubic metres of gas for the period 1984–2009.

When it all started in 1979 there were no natural gas customers. The old town gas system had been closed down almost entirely, and the potential customers (private, commercial, and industrial) were using light or heavy fuel oil. Export contracts were concluded with Sweden and Germany for about 25 per cent of the annual take in the DUC contract, thus reducing the need for a rapid build-up of the domestic market, and the electricity sector was also used for balancing surplus gas. Furthermore, a temporary supply contract was concluded with Germany with deliveries from Germany during 1982–84, with the aim to introduce natural gas supply in the Southern part of Jutland and Funen before the supplies from the Danish sector came onstream. This enabled a smoother introduction of natural gas. Deliveries from the North Sea began in 1984, and since 1986 Denmark has been a net exporter of natural gas. **6.142**

It was politically agreed that the implementation of such a huge project as the natural gas network, which had to take place within a very short space of time, had to be subject to public control and guidance in order to secure an optimal utilization of these heavy investments. Furthermore, one of the political conditions for introducing natural gas at all was that it should be left to local authorities to distribute and sell the gas to the consumer as they had done for many years regarding electricity, water, district heating, and town gas for cooking. Therefore the responsibility of the project was vested with the Government and the municipalities and, simultaneously with the decision to construct a natural gas system, Parliament adopted a Heat Supply Act.[49] This Act provides the framework for the use of natural gas for heating purposes in the way that through a heat planning system it was to be decided which energy source was to be used within the respective area. Taking socio-economic considerations as its starting point, the heat planning should be carried out by the municipalities and counties and in co-operation between the energy authorities and the supply companies. **6.143**

The adoption of the Natural Gas Directive has been the impetus for major changes in the organization and regulation of the Danish natural gas sector. A reform is being implemented. It must therefore be emphasized that the Danish gas industry is still undergoing changes. In order to understand those changes and the new market conditions, the developments must be seen in their historical context. **6.144**

Organization

Organizationally, the natural gas supply was divided in two segments: (i) transmission, storage, and export on one side (in 1979 import was also included) and (ii) distribution on the other. Whereas the State-owned company DONG AS was **6.145**

[49] Act No 258 of 8 June 1979 with later amendments.

responsible for the former, five regional municipally owned gas companies were charged with the latter: Hovedstadens Naturgasselskab (HNG), Naturgas Sjælland (NGSJ), Naturgas Fyn (NGF), Naturgas Syd (NGS), and Naturgas Midt-Nord (NGMN) (and where the names are indicated the region where the company is supplying natural gas). In 1984 the activities of DONG were transferred to its subsidiary the Danish Natural Gas Company (Dansk Naturgas), which changed its name to DONG Naturgas in July 1999. DONG Naturgas has recently taken over two regional companies, see further below, under (2).

6.146 Under a commercial contract between the producer DUC and DONG Naturgas, natural gas is purchased from the North Sea production centre and transported ashore in an offshore pipeline owned by DONG Naturgas. At this time DUC is the only producer of natural gas in the Danish part of the North Sea. In addition to the 55 billion cubic metres of gas over the period 1984–2009, further contracts have been entered into between the same two parties, in 1989 for another 38 billion cubic metres during 1989–2012 and in 1993 for a variable volume (the entire volume of gas offered for sale by DUC with deliveries starting in 1997). DONG Naturgas decided to construct an additional offshore pipeline from the North Sea in order to take gas from some minor Danish gas fields and to increase the long-term security of supply, and facilitating collaboration with either Norway or the United Kingdom. The construction of the pipeline was completed in 1999, and has been put into operation.

6.147 DONG Naturgas is responsible for the main transmission within Denmark. DONG Naturgas sells and has until now been the sole supplier of natural gas to the regional distribution companies and to the municipalities of Copenhagen and Frederiksberg. In addition, DONG Naturgas, in co-operation with the regional distribution companies, sells natural gas to large industrial customers and to small-scale combined heat and power plants. Finally, DONG Naturgas has entered into purchase contracts with the large power plants.

6.148 The distribution system is owned and operated by the five regional natural gas companies, each of which is owned by several municipalities within each region. The supply areas are defined as the geographical borders of the region and in effect local monopolies prevail. The five regional companies were established by means of agreements between the participating municipalities, and organized as partnerships (limited liability companies) with a board of directors subject to supervision by the Ministry of Internal Affairs. The regional natural gas companies are thus legal persons with independent legal personality. Conditions of ownership and liabilities are governed by the articles of the company, which must be approved pursuant to the Act on Management of the Municipalities. Municipalities within a region are 100 per cent jointly and severally liable for loans raised by the natural gas company.

The State as the owner of DONG has paid in a share capital of DKK 1.8 billion which today, inclusive of interest, is equivalent to DKK 8–9 billion. DONG Naturgas and DONG have during the last few years been able to show a surplus, so that the company has been paying a dividend to the State as well as general company tax. This is expected to continue in the coming years. **6.149**

The gas distribution companies are, however, heavily in debt due to several circumstances. It was assumed that the municipalities would have invested a large part of the necessary capital requirement, but in fact only 1 per cent of the capital was financed this way. The rest of the capital has been covered by loans for which the municipalities have issued common guarantees. This has put a strain on the project's economy through higher financing costs. In 1990, with a view to ensuring better financial management of the companies, in accordance with the Heat Supply Act, the regional companies were ordered to limit their borrowing in the form of a loan framework for the individual companies. Moreover, during the implementation of the project it transpired that the investments and operational costs of the regional companies had been underestimated. Furthermore, the basis of calculation of the natural gas project assumed that there would be an obligation for consumers to connect to the natural gas grid. However, the Heat Supply Act did not contain any centrally established obligation but only allowed the municipalities to apply such an obligation. While most municipalities introduced such an obligation for new buildings, very few applied it in the case of existing buildings. Thus getting new customers connected was slower than assumed, while district heating plants and block heating plants were connected later than estimated. **6.150**

As the regional companies are non-profit companies, prices can only reflect 'justified' costs, as determined by the Price Commission (see A(6) above). The risk that the companies could not pay interest and repayments on their already large, growing debts would have been great, if the Government had not given the regional natural gas companies preferential treatment by exempting natural gas from taxes. The Government has thus provided an effective annual subsidy which increased to almost DKK 3 billion in 1996 through the tax exemptions and in this way financed the debts. **6.151**

Relationship between DONG and the regional companies

In 1979 no agreements as to the regulation of the relationship between DONG and the regional companies had been entered into. Until 1987 the main principle for the collaboration between DONG Naturgas and the five regional companies was the interrelated finances of all gas companies: the companies shared expenditure from the project equally based on the idea that the whole natural gas project from platform to consumer was one project. It was then realized that this principle did not constitute a viable basis for the most efficient and cost-effective implementation of the project. 'One project' meant that it was left to the distributor, **6.152** the regional company, to decide to what extent distribution pipelines should be built, the financial consequences of which had to be shared by the other regional companies and the wholesaler (the State-owned company) without these other companies having any influence on deciding those investments.

6.153 Following a request from the Minister of Energy, a revised agreement of 4 June 1987—the '4 June Agreement' between DONG Naturgas and the regional companies—provides that each natural gas company got independent finances, which means that the individual company carries responsibility for its own construction and operational expenditure and thus for its own economic transactions. The natural gas project is therefore no longer one, but six projects, one for each company. The division of the Danish gas market is settled in the contract and DONG Naturgas is burdened with the main part of the risk connected with major changes in consumer prices of energy which follows from different external factors like oil prices, depreciation of the dollar, and alterations of taxes.

6.154 DONG Naturgas has an obligation to supply to the regional companies though the amount cannot exceed 2.6 billion cubic metres a year. In September 1998 a new contract was entered into for additional amounts.

6.155 As was the custom at the time, the contract between DONG Naturgas and DUC is based on a take-or-pay principle. This means that there is an obligation either to take the gas or alternatively to pay for it. According to the '4 June Agreement', however, this obligation is not imposed on the regional companies. The sole rights of DONG Naturgas to negotiate, transport, and store natural gas is the assurance that DONG Naturgas may sell the gas on the Danish market. However, the Gas Directive (98/30/EC) of 22 June 1998 implies that this safeguard will be abandoned in the future, because the market must be open to competing companies.

6.156 The agreement of 4 June 1987 stipulates the gas prices from DONG Naturgas to the regional companies and the level of the prices to the end-consumer which the regional companies can obtain. Hereby is ensured that the sale is carried out according to equal national guidelines as foreseen in the legislation. The so-called transmission prices are the same for all the regional companies dependent on to which customer group it is resold. In addition, the individual regional company has to pay a capacity duty to DONG Naturgas which is calculated on the basis of the maximum purchase per hour in the individual year by each regional company. The agreement means that DONG Naturgas has a considerable influence on the establishment of tariffs for all consumers.

Financial support

6.157 When natural gas was introduced in 1979, Denmark was almost entirely dependent on imported fuels. The economic rationale for the gas project was based upon substitution prices for the energy sources replaced, that is, the high oil prices at the time.

The general fall in oil prices in the middle of the 1980s placed the gas project and the other collective heat supply systems in a difficult economic situation. The falls in the rate of exchange of the dollar and the price of crude oil weakened the competitiveness of the collective heating systems with the prospect of a slow pace of connection to the supply systems if initiatives were not taken to counteract this.

In connection with tightening finance policy, in 1985/86 the Government decided to raise energy taxes considerably with a view to equalizing the price decrease of oil products and coal on consumption in households. In this way the overall energy policy could be maintained at the same time as improving the revenue of the gas companies. Had the Government not given the regional natural gas companies preferential treatment by exempting natural gas from taxes, the risk that the companies would be unable to pay interest and repayments on their already large, growing debts would have been great. **6.158**

As a consequence of the expected increase in the preferential tax as a result of the companies' increasing sales of natural gas, the Parliament adopted a new Act on Natural Gas Charges in June 1997.[50] Natural gas is thus subject to a tax of 75 per cent of the charge levied on oil. At the same time, subsidies in terms of basic allowance will be made available for the repayment of the regional companies' debt. The fundamental terms for natural gas customers will remain unchanged, with gas prices linked to oil prices according to the same main principles as today. This change was approved by the European Commission in August 1998. **6.159**

(2) The Natural Gas Reform

As a first step to meet the EU liberalization requirement of the natural gas sector, the Danish Government requested DONG Naturgas and the regional gas distribution companies to start negotiations on revision of the natural gas contract terms on delivery. As part of this process the Danish Government, in a letter of 16 December 1998, offered to take over the regional gas companies, including the debts and the paying of goodwill. However, by the expiry of the time limit of 1 March 1999, only one company—Naturgas Syd—had accepted the offer. Negotiations have continued between the parties on a reform of the gas sector and on 23 June 1999 an agreement on the future organization of the natural gas market and on the economic support was reached between the Danish Government and the two major regional gas distribution companies: Hovedstadens Naturgasselskab (HNG) and Naturgas Midt-Nord (NGMN). The two other regional companies, Naturgas Sjælland (NGSJ) and Naturgas Fyn (NGF), are not parties but the agreement is designed so that it is possible for these two companies to join in the future. **6.160**

[50] cf Consolidated Act No 887 of 3 Oct 1996, as amended by Act No 443 of 10 June 1997, and further amended by Act No 957 of 20 Dec 1999.

6.161 The agreement establishes the framework for a reduction of the financial support to the natural gas sector such that the current energy tax on natural gas of about 80 per cent of the tax levied on oil products continues[51] but further State aid will disappeared as from 1 January 2000. It is presumed that the debts of the companies are to be paid by 2014 and that the two companies will vest operational responsibilities in a common holding company in order to get out of debt at the same time and to co-ordinate operations more closely and thereby more efficiently. Moreover, the roles of the gas companies will change. Following the opening of the natural gas market, DONG Naturgas will have full responsibilities for gas sales to consumers, who will get open market access, whereas HNG and NGMN shall function as grid and supply obligation companies, which are responsible for operating the grid and for offering gas supplies to all consumers in the supply area who cannot freely choose their gas supplier or do not wish to do so. The latest development is that DONG Naturgas takes over Naturgas Sjælland from 2001. Consequently only Naturgas Fyn stands by itself.

6.162 The reform does not involve any changes with respect to ownership of the companies. It is also presumed that shares will remain in public ownership, and consequently any assignment is subject to approval by the State. The regional companies will still continue as non-profit companies, and cannot engage in commercial activities.

6.163 The Government entered into a political agreement on 22 March 2000 with the Liberal, Conservative, Socialist People's, Centre Democrats, and Christian People's Parties on a reform follow-up. This establishes the framework and principles for the implementation of the EC Gas Directive and the overall framework for the future development of the heat supply sector.

6.164 The legal follow-up to the agreement includes a new contract between DONG Naturgas and the regional companies to replace the agreement of 4 June 1987 (the '4 June Agreement') and a new Natural Gas Act. The main principles of the contract were previously agreed on 11 February 2000 between DONG and HNG and MN. A number of major customers will be transferred to DONG from the regional companies as the latter will not participate in the open and competitive gas market.

6.165 With respect to the new Gas Act, a draft bill was published for comments on 18 January 2000. A Bill was presented to Parliament on 29 March 2000 (No 239) and was adopted as Act No 449 of 31 May 2000. It entered into force on 1 July 2000. This legal reform is considered to ensure the implementation of the EC Gas Directive.

[51] The Government, however, raised the tax on natural gas from 1 January 2000 to approximately 85% of the tax on oil products.

(3) The Natural Gas Supply Act 1972

The Natural Gas Supply Act No 294 of 7 June 1972[52] is a very brief Act of nine sections. The most important principle is that a licence is required to import, sell, transport, or store gas regardless of the form in and the place from which the natural gas is brought to the Danish market (section 1(1)). Local distribution of natural gas is, however, not covered by the Act (section 1(2)). A licence may be granted in the form of a sole rights licence for a specific period (section 1(1)). **6.166**

Issued licences

Only one licence has been issued: the sole rights licence to DONG Naturgas to import, sell, transport, and store natural gas in Denmark until 2012.[53] The heavy investments and the long time-scale were highlighted as the reasons for issuing just one licence with exclusive rights and covering the whole country. The licence was granted on 12 June 1979 and transferred to a DONG subsidiary, Dansk Naturgas, in 1984 following the approval of the Minister pursuant to section 3(3). The company is now DONG Naturgas. The licence was changed in 1994 to abolish the monopoly of imports so as not to exclude others from performing the same task.[54] **6.167**

Licence terms

If the licence is granted in the form of a sole rights licence—as the one to DONG Naturgas—the Act includes a list of licence terms which apply (section 3). The list is not exhaustive, but describes only the minimum content of the licence. Thus the Act states generally in section 3(2) that the Minister may lay down further conditions, as in fact happened for DONG Naturgas's licence. According to the preparatory works of the Bill, the licence shall stipulate directly what the licence covers and the extent of the supply obligation of the licensee. **6.168**

The exclusive rights cover the right to sell, transport, and store natural gas (and from 1979–94 also the right to import); these activities are further defined in an annex to the licence. It is stated that the expression 'sale' covers every sale where delivery takes place in Denmark, except a first-time sale of natural gas produced in the area covered by the licence, and sale in gas phase at a pressure of less than sixteen bars. The term 'transportation' includes every type of transport of natural gas within the area covered by the licence, except: piped transmission between production plants for natural gas in Danish territory, transportation in consignments by air or sea from other countries, the Faroe Islands, and Greenland to a Danish port or airport, or transportation of natural gas in gas phase at a pressure of less **6.169**

[52] As amended by Act No 255 of 6 Aug 1983.
[53] The licence is published as Order No 269 of 18 June 1979.
[54] See Order No 341 of 4 May 1994.

than sixteen bars. Finally, 'storage' means any form of storage of natural gas, except storage in producible oil- and gasfields, where the storage is an element of the exploitation of these fields, and storage in gas phase at a pressure of less than sixteen bars. Storage is thus defined in a negative way.

6.170 As already indicated, neither the Act nor the licence cover local distribution of natural gas. The licence, however, includes a condition in section 1(2) that the licensee may make direct deliveries to major consumers, possibly via the pipesystems of local distribution companies, by agreement with these. The scope of this provision has caused several conflicts between DONG Naturgas and the regional companies.

6.171 The geographical area of the licence is the whole Kingdom of Denmark: the land, the territorial sea, and the safety zones around installations on the continental shelf. The Faroe Islands and Greenland are excluded. The licence is granted for a period from 12 June 1979 to 8 July 2012 and will thus expire at the same time as the A.P. Møller production licence (see B above). The licence period may be extended, and at the very latest by the year 2010 (two years before expiry) negotiations shall be entered into between the Minister and the licensee. However, this time limit is no longer relevant.

6.172 Public control and supervision is carried out through several requirements. The licence is first of all conditional upon the Minister's approval of the articles of association of the licensee and these may not be amended without the consent of the Minister (Act, section 3 and licence, section 4).

6.173 The development plans for the construction of transmission systems for natural gas and for the initiation and maintenance of the supply are also subject to approval by the Minister. The same requirement applies to major alterations of existing installations and specific time limits for implementation of the plans can be set (Act, section 3 and licence, section 5). A rather special condition is that transport agreements with third parties are also subject to the approval of the Minister. In this connection there is a special obligation on DONG Naturgas to transport natural gas as determined by the Minister on condition that the transport will take place on commercial conditions (licence, section 7).

6.174 The activities are subject to public supervision by the Energy Agency,[55] the costs of which shall be refunded to the State by the licensee (Act, section 3 and licence, section 8). The licensee must give the Minister and the supervisory authorities full access to all information regarding the activities, including the right to obtain copies of material.

6.175 The licensee is obliged to carry out the activities so as not to risk personal injury or damage to another person's property, pollution, or deleterious effects on plant

[55] cf Order No 364 of 9 June 1993.

and animal life. Finally, the licensee must comply with the orders given by the Minister with a view to ensuring a satisfactory execution of the supply activities, including orders regarding the establishment of co-operation with other firms within the energy supply sector, regarding measures to counteract any supply failure, and regarding its supply obligation having regard to the existing supply options for natural gas (licence, section 6). If any damage occurs as a consequence of the licence activities, the licensee is liable even if the damage was accidental. However, the compensation may be reduced or even abandoned if the injured party contributed to the damage through repeated or gross negligence (Act, section 7).

The Natural Gas Supply Act determines that the licence shall specify what shall happen to the installations established by the licensee in the event of the expiry, surrender, or forfeiture of the licence (section 5). In section 18 of the licence it is settled that the State is entitled to take over, partly or wholly, real property, pipelines, and any other installations at their book value. If the State does not want to make use of this right, the Minister may instead demand that part or all of a plant must be removed within twenty-four months. **6.176**

Disagreements between the Minister and the licensee about the forfeiture, take-over, or removal of installations are finally settled by a board of arbitration consisting of three members, and which shall base its decision on Danish law. All other disagreements shall be finally decided by the Minister for Environment and Energy (licence, section 19). **6.177**

The licensee is subject to Danish legislation and orders at all times, and is not relieved of the obligation to obtain permissions required pursuant to other legislation (licence, section 3). Although it is said in the licence, section 3, that the licence is subject to the rules of the Treaty on the European Economic Community, the licence nevertheless included a provision in section 13 obliging the licensee to use Danish goods and services if technically and financially competitive. This requirement was, however, abandoned by the Minister by letter of 27 November 1991. It is finally stated that the Minister in addition to the existing rules at his own discretion may lay down general regulations regarding the establishment and operation of transmission plants for natural gas in the national interest (licence section 3(3)). **6.178**

The Heat Supply Act on Gas Prices

Rules for the natural gas prices that DONG Naturgas, and the regional gas companies can obtain from the Danish consumers were until 1 July 2000 found in the Heat Supply Act, section 20[55a]. In the prices can be included necessary expenses **6.179**

[55a] cf Act No 382 of 13 June 1990, as amended.

for fuel, wages and salaries, and other operation costs, administration and marketing, interest paid on loan capital and deficits previously incurred in connection with the establishment and major expansion of the supply systems. In addition the gas companies may include operational depreciation and, subject to the approval of the regulator—earlier the Gas and Heat Price Commission, but from 30 December 1999 the Energy Supervisory Board—allocations to reinvestment funds and interest paid on contribution capital in accordance with regulations laid down by the Minister for Environment and Energy. It is permitted to stipulate different prices for individual consumers, groups of consumers and geographical areas. But the prices of natural gas may not exceed the consumer prices including government taxes of a corresponding quantity of gas oil.

6.180 The Minister for Environment and Energy can, in accordance with section 20, and after referring to a Parliamentary Committee, lay down rules for the price setting of natural gas to customers consuming more than 300.000 m^3 of natural gas per year. In the case that consumers in accordance with the heat supply planning are obliged to use natural gas, the prices shall be notified to the price regulator, which has the power to direct a change in price or supply conditions.

6.181 Any price and other supply conditions shall be notified to the price regulator unless an exemption is granted (cf section 21). If not duly notified they are invalid. This provision is supplemented by Order No 610 of 27 August 1990 where among other things certain time limits are set for the notification. The price regulator has the power to direct a change in prices or supply conditions if the regulator finds that the terms are unreasonable, exceeds the maximum price pursuant to section 21 or is deemed to lead to an uneconomic use of energy contrary to the public interest. It is, however, a requirement that the regulator first seeks to obtain the requested result through negotiations, cf section 21. As for consumers who buy more than 300.000 m^3 of natural gas per year, the prices are confidential and the regulator cannot issue an order about changing the supply conditions. The regulator is further described above in paragraphs 6.31–6.41.

6.182 Pursuant to the Heat Supply Act, section 29, the Minister has the power to direct the further development of the natural gas network and the extent of the obligation to supply. Among other things, this implies a decision about construction or the obligation to supply within a specific area and within certain time limits, or that an already planned development has to be changed or limited. It can also be decided that the natural gas company has to start the preparation of supply plans and in this connection orders can be given as to the degree of details and ways of preparing the plans. The Minister can furthermore control the costs of the natural gas companies. This regulation can be implemented according to general regulations or individually towards a company, and in this connection natural gas companies are, upon request, obligated to furnish the Minister with the information he may deem necessary for exercising his powers.

Another way of public control is the fact that the Minister can set rules as to limiting the borrowing by regional natural gas companies and as to settling the companies' debts, cf section 30. This means of control is further detailed in a special ministerial Order No 864 of 6 December 1998. **6.183**

(4) The Natural Gas Supply Act 2000

The new Natural Gas Supply Act came into force on 1 July 2000. It introduced completely new market conditions. The main objectives are to ensure that the Danish natural gas supply is organized and implemented in accordance with considerations of security of supply, the national economy, the environment, and consumer protection (section 1(1)). It is emphasized that within the terms of the stated objective, the Act is to ensure consumers access to inexpensive natural gas. Thus the targets are equivalent to those included in the new Electricity Act. However, there remains one major difference—the aim of consumer influence on the administration of the assets of the electricity sector does not apply to the gas sector. Within this framework there is a focus on promotion of sustainable utilization of energy, including by means of energy savings, while ensuring efficient use of financial resources and creating competition in the markets for trade in natural gas (section 1(2)). **6.184**

A new concept in the gas legislation is the distinction between grid activity and supply activity, and the separation of tasks regarding public commitments and commercial activities. In contradiction to the old Act, the new Gas Act also regulates distribution, including transmission, distribution, supply, and storage of natural gas. It covers both the land territory and the territorial sea, the exclusive economic zone, and the continental shelf area (section 2). The Minister, however, has the power to exempt certain minor installations and activities from the provisions of the Act (section 2(3)). **6.185**

The Minister for Environment and Energy is, as previously, obliged to inform a special Parliamentary Committee on Energy Policy on all important issues connected to natural gas supply in Denmark (section 4). **6.186**

The Act is to be supplemented by secondary legislation, and some has already been issued. **6.187**

The licence system

A decisive result of the gas reform is that DONG's exclusive licence is abandoned in order to open up the market for new companies. A main element of the Act is therefore the introduction of a licence system for activities related to transmission, distribution, supply of customers who cannot choose their supplier, LNG facilities, and storage (sections 10, 16, and 24). Thus the new Act includes more licence requirements than the previous one. **6.188**

6.189 Moreover, new construction projects for transmission grids and major changes in the existing installations are also conditional upon obtaining a licence (section 13). Finally, it is necessary to apply for a special licence from the Minister in order to establish direct lines (section 17).

Procedures for granting licences

6.190 With respect to the award procedure no special requirements are set for the issuance of gas licences. It is, however, a general requirement that licences can only be issued to applicants which are found to have the necessary expertise and economic background (section 28). For all types of licences the Minister is empowered to request a fee from the applicants to cover costs connected to the administrative decisions on the applications.

6.191 The new Gas Act determines that those companies already performing activities are allowed to continue their business as long as the companies apply for the necessary licences within the time-limit set by the Minister, and subject to the condition that the companies obey the provisions of the Act concerning the activity in question (section 60(2)).

6.192 With respect to the grant of a licence to establish direct lines, the applicant must have been refused access to the system, and the refusal reviewed unsuccessfully by the Energy Supervisory Board (section 17(2)). Moreover, licences for new construction projects for transmission grids and major changes in the existing installations can only be granted if the applicant is in a position to document that there is sufficient need for the development (section 13).

6.193 As mentioned above, the Minister for Environment and Energy must inform a special Parliamentary Committee on Energy Policy on all important issues connected to natural gas supply in Denmark. However, it is not anticipated that this requirement applies to the specific licences. The consultation procedure is thus less comprehensive than the one applying to the upstream oil and gas sectors.

The licence terms

6.194 The licences will only cover a delimited area and will last for at least twenty years (apart from the licence to LNG facilities which is of no relevance in Denmark). The supply licence, however, will only be valid for a shorter period but at least for five years. The maximum period a licence can last is not fixed in the Act, but is expected to be in the licences.

6.195 The Act imposes explicit obligations that will always apply to licensees, and mentions certain terms that at the discretion of the Minister can be included in a licence. Moreover, there is a general authority for the Minister to include other objective and non-discriminatory conditions (section 28(2)). It should be noticed that new licence terms can be set following a period of five years and subsequent to a one-year notice (section 31).

With respect to the holders of licences for transmission, the licensees are to ensure adequate and efficient transportation of natural gas with accompanying services, including maintenance, conversion, and developing of the supply grid in the supply area to the necessary degree, offer the necessary supply capacity, and maintain the physical regulation of the system (section 12). Further regulation can be issued by the Minister. A transmission company must also as necessary connect distribution grids and customers, ensure the quality of the delivered gas and the security of supplies, co-operate with other transmission companies in Denmark and abroad with a view to an efficient exchange of natural gas, draw up plans for future demand for transmission capacity, and ensure sufficient quantities of natural gas in the total supply system in order to maintain the physical balance within the grid. Further regulation can be issued by the Minister (section 12). **6.196**

A distribution company must likewise ensure adequate and efficient transportation of natural gas with accompanying services, including maintenance, conversion, and developing the supply grid in the supply area to the necessary degree (section 11). The grids are to be operated as a public infrastructure, placed at the disposal of all users of the system on objective, non-discriminatory terms (sections 7, 18, and 23). A distribution company must connect customers to the distribution grid as necessary (section 14). Further rules can be issued by the Minister. Distribution companies shall promote the use of natural gas in order to reduce environmental impact and offer consulting services with respect to energy conservation (section 14(1)). The Minister can lay down rules concerning the obligation of the distribution companies to map gas consumption and to plan and ensure that energy savings are implemented (section 14(3)). **6.197**

Some companies have supply commitments to customers within an area designated for natural gas supply. These companies must also promote the use of natural gas in order to reduce environmental impact (section 26(2)), and offer consulting services with respect to energy conservation (section 27(1)). **6.198**

The Minister for Environment and Energy has also the power to decide that the transmission and distribution companies in co-operation shall initiate research and development with a view to efficient energy application, environmental improvements, and safety with respect to natural gas use. The Minister can lay down rules concerning the preparation of activity plans and the approval of these (Natural Gas Supply Act, section 11(3)). **6.199**

As far as storage is concerned, a storage company shall measure gas supplies to and from the storage, provide users with necessary information about measurement, and offer the necessary storage capacity so that the transmission companies can ensure security of supply (section 15). The Minister can issue further rules on **6.200** the task and the necessary storage capacity that must be available for emergencies.

6.201 With respect to unbundling, all natural gas companies are obliged to keep separate accounts for transmission, distribution, and storage activities, and where relevant keep separate accounts for non-core activities (section 47).

6.202 A licence for construction projects for transmission grids and major changes in the existing installations, LNG facilities, or direct lines can be conditional upon specific terms related to the construction and operation of the grid (sections 13, 16, and 17(3)).

6.203 The Act includes authority for the Minister to expropriate property for the purpose of establishing the transmission system for natural gas, as long as it is in the public interest (section 55). Like previously, the activities are subject to public supervision carried out by the Energy Agency, the costs of which shall be refunded to the State by the licensee (section 30). The licence is likewise excepted from legal proceedings and can be neither directly nor indirectly transferred to others without approval by the Minister of the conditions for such a transfer (section 32). To ensure that the transportation system can remain public property, the State has by the new Act obtained a right of pre-emption to the distribution grid (section 33). The price will be fixed on ordinary market terms. If a local authority makes a profit when a natural gas company is sold, this will be set off against the general State subsidy to the local authority. This will ensure that assets built up in the natural gas companies with State subsidies will return to the State if the company is sold.

6.204 If the conditions laid down are repeatedly not complied with, if incorrect or misleading information is provided in a licence application, or if the licensee goes into liquidation or goes bankrupt, the consequence is that the licence can be forfeited (section 33). If a matter can be remedied by the licensee, the Minister can lay down a time limit which allows the licensee to fullfil his obligations. As to the decision to withdraw a licence due to non-compliance or misleading information, it has to be taken by the courts.

Market opening

6.205 Generally, everybody has the right upon payment to be supplied by natural gas either via an offer by a supply-committed company or to choose the supplier if eligible (section 7). Natural gas companies and eligible customers have the right upon payment to make use of transmission and distribution grids for the transportation of natural gas and to utilize storage facilities, when necessary for efficient access (section 18).

The Act includes rules on the gradual opening of the market that follows the minimum requirements of the Gas Directive. The market opening was 30 per cent on 1 July 2000, increasing to 38 per cent and 43 per cent from 1 August 2003 and 2008, respectively (section 8). The Minister for Environment and Energy can issue further regulation about which natural gas customers have the right to choose their supplier. **6.206**

The power stations, the major decentralized CHP plants, and the major industries will be able freely to choose their gas supplier, whereas the regional gas distribution companies will not be covered because this would have the consequence that public companies would compete with each other. However, it should be noted that because of long-term supply contracts the real market opening will be more modest than the percentages stated. The intention is that the regional companies will be able to continue distribution activities and the supply of minor customers whereas DONG will be in charge of supply activities subject to competition. **6.207**

The principle of negotiated TPA will apply to access to the transmission network and storage, whereas regulated access will apply to the distribution grid (sections 19 and 20). Prices and conditions for transportation in the transmission grid are subject to negotiation, but the transmission company must publish the commercial main conditions at the latest one year after the Act came into effect and then once a year. A request for transportation shall be addressed to the transmission company by whose grid the gas is to be transported. Negotiations with applicants for transportation must be initiated without undue delay. **6.208**

Prices and conditions for transportation in the distribution grid are set by the distribution companies according to regulated prices which shall be published (section 20). A request for transportation shall be addressed to the distribution company by whose grid the gas is to be transported. The distribution company must provide applicants with access to transportation without undue delay. The distribution companies must without undue delay initiate negotiations with other distribution companies on prices and conditions for transportation of gas through the grid of the company to other distribution grids. **6.209**

Prices and conditions for the storage of natural gas are likewise subject to negotiation, and a request shall be addressed to the storage company in whose storage facility the gas is to be stored. Negotiations with applicants for storage must be initiated without undue delay. **6.210**

The transmission companies, in co-operation with the distribution and storage companies, set the rules for the use of the grids and storage, which must be objective and non-discriminating and accessible for users and potential users of the said installations (section 23). The rules must be forwarded to the Minister for Environment and Energy. **6.211**

6.212 The Minister for Environment and Energy is authorized to lay down rules for access to upstream pipelines after the matter has been presented to the Energy Policy Committee of the *Folketing* (section 21). It is intended to provide the same access to upstream pipelines as to the transmission grid in step with Denmark's neighbouring countries providing similar access.

6.213 A request can be refused if there is a lack of capacity, if the quality of the gas delivered and supply security cannot be ensured, or there are not sufficient gas quantities to maintain the physical balance in the grid, or because of serious economic and financial problems with contractual take-or-pay conditions (section 18(3)). Any refusal must be justified. If a natural gas company gets or expects to get into serious economic and financial problems because of contractual take-or-pay obligations, it can apply for an interim exception from the rules on access to the grid (section 22). The Minister can issue more detailed rules.

Price regulation

6.214 To safeguard consumers' rights to natural gas supply, the licensees will be obliged to connect and supply customers in areas designated for natural gas supply pursuant to heat planning. The maximum price provisions for natural gas will be continued in the new legislation for clients who do not have market access, and prices are therefore still subject to public regulation with the exemption of supplies to customers covered by the market opening (sections 7, 9, 36, and 37). As indicated above, payment for transportation through the transmission grid will take place following negotiations between the companies involved, on a commercial basis, and have to be notified to the Energy Supervisory Board to ensure that DONG does not abuse its monopoly position. Payment for transportation through the distribution grid is based on a cost-based tariff system, where the client pays the same price irrespective of the place of delivery. The tariff is differentiated according to the way in which the systems are utilized, and is also to be notified to the Energy Supervisory Board.

6.215 The natural gas companies will continue to be self-sustainable or 'non-profit' companies, and thus remain not liable for taxation. However, a benchmarking system is introduced in order to create an incentive for rationalization and increased efficiency (section 37(3)). This system is to be controlled by the new Energy Supervisory Board (sections 40, 41, and section A(6) above).

(5) Conclusion

6.216 As can be understood from the above, the gas sector is in a phase of transition. It is one of the youngest sectors within the energy industry, and characterized by a far more limited number of market players than for instance the electricity sector. Furthermore, the next decade will continue to be bound by long-term contracts which seemed necessary at the time in order to guarantee the big investments.

Consequently, we will not expect the gas sector to change overnight. Nevertheless, it should be emphasized that an important process has been initiated which cannot be stopped. Liberalization is introduced gradually, and within a rather limited period this sector will also be subject to competition. However, there will still be an important role to play for the authorities in order to guarantee that DONG's monopoly situation is not misused, and that environmental considerations and consumer protection are ensured. The latest development is that Parliament is considering further amendment to the Gas Act in the light of the EU Commission's latest proposal for changes to the market directives.

E. Heat Supply

(1) Introduction

During the last twenty years, the structure of the heat supply system has changed **6.217** considerably, with a shift away from individual oil burners towards collective systems such as district heating and natural gas. Whereas piped supply amounted to 25 per cent in 1980, it increased to 65 per cent in 1998. As discussed above, the natural gas grid had to be started from scratch, whereas district heating already had a long tradition in Denmark, although a large expansion of the network was required.

The development of the Danish supply system has implied comprehensive public **6.218** planning and co-operation between the Government, the municipalities, the production companies, and the distributors. A confirmation of successful planning is the fact that energy consumption for heating purposes has declined from 234,653 TJ in 1980 to 198,249 TJ in 1998, although the area to be heated has increased by around 20 per cent.[56]

District heating is defined as space and water heating of a number of buildings **6.219** from a central plant, delivered to the consumers as hot water through an insulated double pipeline system. It dates back to the beginning of the twentieth century. In the 1920s the first district heating networks were established in Denmark in the largest towns where there were possibilities of exploiting surplus heat from the electric utilities. Since the building boom in the 1950s and 1960s, district heating has been the predominant form of heat supply in Danish cities. The large expansion of district heating in the 1960s was based primarily on oil, but after the energy crises in the 1970s many district heating plants converted to coal. Throughout the 1980s environmental considerations became gradually more predominant in energy supply policy. With the 1986 CHP agreement, the stage was set for the expansion of electricity capacity in the 1990s, and Energy 2000 and the new Heat Supply Act of 1990 initiated a planning process under which district heating plants are to convert to small-scale CHP production and use

[56] Energy Statistics 1998, Danish Energy Agency.

environmentally benign fuels.[57] A number of district heating plants may, however, continue the present biomass-based district heating production for another couple of years, and then convert to biomass CHP.

6.220 Today district heating production covers close to 50 per cent of energy consumption for space heating against 30 per cent in 1980.[58] In a comparative context the equivalent figures for oil are 22 per cent against 61 per cent, whereas natural gas covers 18 per cent but was developed much later. Seventy per cent of district heating production is now based on CHP of which small-scale CHP accounted for about 20 per cent in 1994.

(2) Structure of the Industry

6.221 Denmark is supplied by about 430 independent district heating companies. Most of these are owned either by the consumers or by the municipalities. The utilities have very different sizes. The smallest companies have a supply area including about fifty consumers whereas the biggest supply several hundred thousand. District heating is primarily concentrated in the cities where the number (and concentration) of consumers is higher. Almost all the district heating companies are members of *Danske Fjernvarmeværkers Forening* (Danish District Heating Association). The main tasks of the Association are to serve as a technical platform for exchange of know-how, to represent its members in relation to the public authorities, to deal with problems in connection with common tariffs, and to promote technological developments.

6.222 Most district heating companies both produce and supply heat. In some cases, however, heat is bought from another producer: a power station, manufacturing enterprise, or a refuse incineration plant. The major cities in Denmark have a high penetration of district heating supplied by large power plants, whereas the district heating generated in small and medium-sized towns is mainly based on natural gas. The average connection rate in district heating areas is 82 per cent and is still increasing.[59] District heating has proved to be very flexible regarding the use of different fuels. As indicated above, in the early years lignite and coal were burned. Because of convenience and the low prices, fuel oil was then used for several decades, but since the oil crisis a wide spectrum of solid fuels and waste heat sources have provided energy for the Danish district heating supply.[60] District heat is supplied from CHP plants owned by the electricity companies, and small-

[57] See 'Re-regulation of the Danish Energy Supply', by Anita Rønne in *Suum Quique*, Copenhagen, 1993, 273ff; and 'The Legal Dimension of Sustainable Development with the Emphasis on the Energy Sector', by Anita Rønne in *Law and Ecology*, Copenhagen, 1994, 64.

[58] cf *Energy in Denmark 1998*, Danish Energy Agency, 9.

[59] *Combined Heat and Power in Denmark*, Danish Energy Agency, 1998.

[60] For further information, see *District Heating in Denmark*, published by the Danish Ministry of Energy (1987).

scale CHP plants and conventional heating plants mainly owned by the district heating companies.

(3) The Heat Supply Act

The legal framework was established by the adoption of the Heat Supply Act in 1979.[61] Since then, Denmark has been implementing a systematic heat planning process to reduce oil dependence and to introduce natural gas into the Danish energy supply system. Thus a unique feature of the Danish energy system is the very detailed regulation of the heat supply structure, broken down to the level of the individual consumer. The actual planning is the concern of municipalities and previously also the counties, which work out local and regional heat plans for the use of district heating, natural gas, or other energy forms, subject to governmental control and influence by the Ministry for Environment and Energy. This influence has however, also been reduced following the Energy Reform in 2000. The Act has been revised several times, and replaced by a new Heat Supply Act in 1990 and followed by more changes as late as in July 2000. Parallel to these Acts, the regulation of the area has been widely based on voluntary agreements concluded between the Government and the energy sector, especially during the 1980s. One major accomplishment is that the voluntary agreements in the heating and electricity sectors supplementing the underlying legislation have made a great contribution to promoting small- as well as large-scale CHP production in Denmark for the last fifteen years (see E(5) below). **6.223**

The political agreement of 22 March 2000 on an energy reform follow-up included the framework for the future development of the heat supply sector, and has now been implemented through an amendment to the Heat Supply Act. In contradiction to the electricity and natural gas sectors, competition will not be introduced in the heat supply sector. One reason for this is that the heat supply network is not a connected grid thereby creating the possibility of free trade, another is that planning as to which form of supply and fuel is to be utilized has been determined locally and the corresponding investments already made. Moreover, it is not considered environmentally acceptable that more polluting fuels could outdo less polluting fuel sources. Some legal amendments have, however, been considered appropriate in order to modernize the Act and to include some consequential changes due to the adoption of the new Electricity and Gas Acts. The changes **6.223A**

[61] The Heat Supply Act No 258 of 8 June 1979 was replaced by the Heat Supply Act No 382 of 6 June 1990, later amended by Act No 327 of 14 May 1992, Act No 96 of 9 Feb 1994, Act No 213 of 29 Mar 1995, Act No 436 of 10 June 1997, Act No 379 of 2 June 1999, and Act No 451 of 31 May 2000, see Consolidated Act No 772 of 24 July 2000. The Act is elaborated by secondary legislation, the most important being Order No 139 of 3 Mar 1991, concerning approval of projects for collective heat supply undertakings, and Order No 196 of 22 Mar 1991, concerning decisions as to connection to collective heat supply plants, now replaced by Orders No 582 and 581 of 22 June 2000, respectively.

concern transfer of regulation of the natural gas sector to the Natural Gas Supply Act, the settlement of heat prices, including the introduction of a benchmarking system and some obligations of a public service nature, some restrictions on the transfer of ownership and finally control by the Energy Supervisory Board.

6.224 The objective of the Heat Supply Act is to secure the most economic and environmentally friendly use of energy for heating, and to reduce dependence on oil with a view to promoting combined production of heat and electricity as far as possible (section 1).[62] The new Heat Supply Act of 1990 was adopted as part of the Government's anti-bureaucratic plan, and its main purpose was to decentralize the exercise of public authority within the area of heat supply. The most important feature of the Act was to exclude the counties from participation in heat planning and to abandon centralized approval of heat supply plans. Consequently, one of the major purposes of the amendments is to place a greater responsibility upon the municipalities. Even so, the State has reserved for itself the possibility for great influence and control. It is a characteristic feature of the Act that whenever authority is delegated to the municipal level, the power to interfere with the decision-making remains with the Ministry for Environment and Energy (sections 3, 4, 5, 7, 9, 11, 12, 13, 14, and 15). However, the central control has been further reduced in the recent amendments to the Act, see below under (4).

6.225 The Heat Supply Act imposes State price control (Part 4) and the principle of non-profit of heat supply is maintained also following the implementation of the energy reform 2000.

(4) The Planning System

6.226 Nationwide, most Danish heat planning has taken place according to the Heat Supply Act 1979, and all Danish counties and municipalities have carried out heat planning according to the following model. As part of general heat planning, county councils prepared regional heat plans in co-operation with the local councils, containing plans for the delimitation of supply zones, the structure of supply systems, and the distribution of natural gas and local energy sources (straw, waste, and woodchips) for the district heating plants, including district heating stations of all sizes. The plan in question regulated the heat supply methods to be given future priority, and as competition in supply systems is economically wasteful, the plan virtually provided a monopoly of a specific energy supply. In this way the Ministry for Environment and Energy could determine that planning must be based on specified principles.

6.227 The regional heat plans were ultimately subject to approval by the Ministry for Environment and Energy. Following this approval, the plans provided the framework for heat planning in the 275 municipalities, where the local councils were to

[62] The objective was expanded in 1990 to include environmental considerations.

decide on the final delimitation of zones and supply systems. Planning was carried out in close co-operation with the utilities in question: the district heating plants, natural gas companies, and electric power stations. It also accommodated comprehensive public hearing and information phases.

The creation of the heat planning system was inspired by the physical planning system. The State defined the overall framework for activities at regional level, where in turn the scene was set for more detailed planning activities at regional and municipal level. The heat planning system, which is described in the Heat Supply Act 1979, included four main phases: **6.228**

—a mapping phase in which the status of the existing heat supply and heat demand were described (status/basic data);
—a proposal phase in which future options for the development of the heat supply were outlined (opportunities/surveys);
—a planning phase in which cost options were identified and decisions on main projects and the general development were taken (decision/firming up); and
—a project phase in which the planned and approved projects were implemented (implementation/plant installation).

In the planning process, one of the initial subjects of interest was the problem of deciding on zones for collective heat supply, ie natural gas or district heating. Another important subject was the structural change towards the increased use of domestic energy sources (natural gas and local energy sources) in existing district heating plants. To accelerate the planning process heat planning was divided into two phases. The first phase of the heat planning programme, 'interim' or 'partial' planning, enabled the rapid introduction of natural gas into the building sector and considerable expansion of the use of surplus heat from power stations and industry, both of which significantly reduced the use of oil. Interim planning was primarily concerned with supply for medium-sized and large towns, areas with a relatively large and concentrated heating requirement. An essential reason for the speedy procedure was the decision to introduce natural gas from the Danish part of the North Sea to the Danish energy supply system from 1984 onwards. However, as early as 1982, a supply of natural gas was established in parts of Southern Jutland based on natural gas from the Federal Republic of Germany. The second phase of the heat planning process, general heat planning (which is also completed), required all energy forms to be investigated and covered the whole country, towns as well as less densely populated areas. New issues emerging after the adoption of the heating plans are dealt with in amendments and revisions. **6.229**

Following the revision of the Heat Supply Act in 1990 a follow-up phase was initiated, where heat plans were adjusted and new initiatives taken where necessary. **6.230**

In recent years domestic fuels have been strongly promoted in heat planning. Because of the low price of coal compared with other energy forms, a number of **6.231** district heating plants were altered to use this form of energy instead of oil. However, an agreement was reached on 13 April 1984 between the Government and the Social Democratic Party to provide first priority for the utilization of domestic fuels, including natural gas, in future heat planning, thus preventing the collective heat supply undertakings from converting to coal. In continuance of this, the Ministry for Environment and Energy issued specific guidelines for heat planning (pursuant to the Heat Supply Act, section 3), requesting local councils to give special emphasis to the application of indigenous energy sources and not to consider conversion to coal in areas where either natural gas or local sources of energy were available.

6.232 The use of local sources of energy has also been encouraged by a number of new environmental developments in the agricultural sector, such as the 1985 prohibition against field burning of straw as from 1990, and directions for the storage of manure. Furthermore, the Danish Parliament adopted substantially improved financial conditions in order to ease the establishment and reorganization of collective heating systems based on domestic resources. It should be emphasized that an important element of the promotion of indigenous energy sources is exemption from energy duty.

6.233 The express intent of the agreement between the Government and the Social Democratic Party of June 1986 is to secure the increased use of domestic fuels and to increase the co-production of heat and electricity. Hence the establishment of decentralized CHP plants is of special concern in heat planning. In order to prevent the erosion of the financial foundation of district heating or natural gas, the Government has forbidden the installation of electric heating in new buildings in areas where collective heating systems are available.

6.234 Following the latest amendment of the Heat Supply Act in July 2000, the planning procedures have been simplified and decentralized in the way that the final approval of a new project can be issued by the municipalities without previous submission to the central authorities. A 'call-in' provision has been introduced instead.

Public requirements

6.235 When seen in relation to the heavy investment and operating costs of the supply system, some intervention by the public authorities is imperative. Accordingly, several means of compulsion are vested in the Ministry for Environment and Energy and in the local councils.

6.236 First, the Ministry for Environment and Energy can issue specified principles on which the local planning must be based (sections 3 and 5). Secondly, the establishment of new collective heat supply undertakings and major alterations of existing plants are subject to approval (section 4). Thirdly, the municipalities may instruct existing plants to carry out an approved construction project within a specified time limit (section 6(3)), to adapt their production plants to the use of specified forms of energy, and last but not least, to use specific forms of energy (section 7(1)).

The municipalities may also require new or existing buildings within areas planned for district heating or natural gas to be connected to the collective heat supply plant, in which case consumers must take steps to be connected within a certain time limit, among other things taking into consideration the natural pace of replacing existing heating installations (sections 11 and 12). Compulsory connection to the networks can be compensated through subsidies under certain conditions, eg if heat prices rise as a result (section 12). **6.237**

Furthermore, installation of specified heating systems in new or existing buildings may be forbidden under section 14. This power has been used eg for the installation of electric heating in new buildings located in areas where collective heating systems were available. **6.238**

As part of the amendments due to the energy reform, the heat supply companies are to perform certain so-called public service obligations by for example, increasing the number of households connected to district heating networks, by advising consumers about energy savings within heating, and by research activities (section 29). Another important change has the purpose of maintaining consumer ownership of and influence in the heat sector and to increase consumer representation in the boards of the companies not owned by either municipalities or by the end-consumer (section 23 e–k). The later mentioned rules resemble those of the Electricity Act 1999. **6.239**

Procedures

The Minister for Environment and Energy must inform the Parliamentary Energy Committee of the more important measures which are planned (section 3(3)). **6.240**

Price control

All activities, and prices, are subject to public supervision. The Heat Supply Act lays down the basic parameters for heat pricing, stipulating that heat supplies must be priced according to actual costs, on a non-profit basis. As a point of departure the non-profit principle of the Heat Supply Act is maintained also under the reformed system (section 20). However, the regulatory framework is supplemented in order to develop a more cost effective operation by introducing a maximum limit for the cost-based heat prices that will be based upon an efficiently operated heat plant by way of comparing several key figures for efficiency (benchmarking) (section 20a). To promote the utilization of renewable energy and **6.241** surplus heat, private sector producers will be allowed to make profits, however, combined by the introduction of ceilings in prices for heat or fuel in order to protect customers financially (section 20b). Cost and tariffs are to be submitted to the national regulator in charge of administering the rules for energy pricing—until the end of 1999 the Gas and Heat Price Commission but now replaced by the Energy Supervisory Board (see section A(6) above).

(5) Agreements to Use Certain Fuel Sources

6.242 Parallel to the Heat Supply Act, development of the area has been widely influenced by 'voluntary' agreements concluded between the government and the energy sector, especially in the 1980s. They have made a great contribution to promoting small- as well as large-scale CHP production in Denmark for the last 15 years. Because of the low price of coal compared with other energy forms, a number of district heating plants were altered to use this form of energy instead of oil. However, the first political agreement was reached on 13 April 1984 to provide first priority for the utilization of domestic fuels including natural gas in future heat planning, thus preventing the collective heat supply undertakings from converting to coal. Another political agreement of June 1986 secured an increases use of domestic fuels and increased co-production of heat and electricity. In 1990, it was agreed politically that approximately 300 district heating plants outside the large combined heat and power areas of the big cities should be converted to CHP plants based on natural gas, biomass or waste incineration during the 1990s, with the expected result of adding about 1,200 MW generating capacity by the end of 1998.

6.243 The CHP conversion programme was divided into three phases up to 1998, each phase focusing on conversion of a specific group of district heating plants according to socio-economic conversion costs. The general criteria of conversion to be met by the municipalities and the district heating companies were to choose natural gas-fired CHP if the plant was situated in a natural gas supply area, to purchase heat from an existing CHP plant when situated in the vicinity of areas already supplied with co-generated heat, and to choose biofuels if the plant was located outside areas supplied with natural gas or co-generated heat, thus choosing the environmentally best fuel source and production form whenever possible.

(6) Current Developments and Future Trends

6.244 As already indicated, the overall framework for the future development of the heat supply sector has been agreed and implemented in 2000. Consequently, major changes to the legal framework are not foreseen in the near future. The heat supply sector has been subject to comprehensive and detailed central planning over a period of 20 years, but the heat supply network is now completed and therefore the role of the public authorities is reduced to adjusting plans and supervision.

F. Electricity Supply

(1) Introduction

Electric energy was introduced in Denmark as early as 1891,[63] but until the energy crisis in 1973–74 there was practically no Government intervention in the electricity sector except for reasons of safety. Although electricity consumption in Denmark has increased constantly since the introduction of electricity, the increase has been considered inevitable, a development governed by socio-economic factors which should not be interfered with as long as the electricity industry was able to meet requirement in a sufficient way. And the sector proved its competence and capacity, as two of the main features of the Danish electricity supply have for a long time been security of supply and low production prices. Even after the adoption of the first Electricity Supply Act in 1976, which vested a strong governmental influence with the central administrative system, the power was not utilized extensively, and the Government's role in the electricity sector has been much less significant than in other energy sectors. In other words, the utilities were given considerable discretion as to, among other issues, selecting the form of fuel to be utilized—at least until the end of the 1980s. **6.245**

The last decade of the twentieth century has, however, seen a comprehensive change of policy, and new market conditions, due first to environmental impact considerations but later also to the introduction of competition into the supply industry. In a modern society the production of electricity has environmental and economic consequences such that only efficient electricity use and efficient utilization of production capacity is acceptable. Electricity consumption cannot be seen in isolation, but forms part of the total pattern of energy consumption. In the light of this, it is not surprising that the electricity sector has been subject to increasing Government intervention. State regulation has developed rapidly due to the growing emphasis on energy conservation and environmental protection, and the Danish Government has put restrictions on the use of fuels, imposed taxes on coal and oil products, and increasingly required combined production of electricity and heat. **6.246**

Competition in electricity generation started slowly with the establishment of a growing number of small non-utility generators, in the form of decentralized CHP plants and wind turbines. It was, however, the adoption of the internal market within the European Union that accelerated the new process towards an emerging competitive market in Denmark. The first steps in the opening of the **6.247**

[63] *Elektricitetens Aarhundrede. Dansk elforsynings historie* (The Century of Electricity. The History of Danish Electricity), by Birgitte Wistoft, Flemming Petersen, and Harriet M Hansen, Association of Danish Electric Utilities, 1991.

Danish electricity market were taken by a revision of the Electricity Supply Act 1976 which came into effect on 1 January 1998. In June 1999, however, a completely new Electricity Act was adopted by the Danish Parliament and, apart from one chapter on environmentally benign electricity production, this Act came into force on 30 December 1999. The latter mentioned chapter came into force on 1 November 2000. From the same dates the Electricity Supply Act 1976 as amended was abandoned. It is thus a characteristic feature of the present Danish electricity sector that it is undergoing profound changes—a process which will undoubtedly continue in the years to come.

6.248 The electricity generation capacity in Denmark by the end of 1998 has been calculated to be around 11,800 MW, of which generation by utilities accounts for 9,340 MW and generation by non-utilities for 2,430 MW. Wind turbines are increasingly being built—684 by utilities and 4,524 by non-utilities, and accounting for 238 MW and 1,205 MW respectively. The total electricity sold to consumers in Denmark in 1998 amounted to 32,441 GWh and the residential sector, industry, and the service sector each account for a little less than one-third of total consumption. It is noteworthy that even though economic growth was 3.5 per cent from 1996 to 1997, the sale of electricity decreased a little.[64]

6.249 The average electricity price before taxes is around 0.41 DKK/KWh. In international terms, Denmark thus has low electricity prices before taxes. For household consumers, however, the price almost triples to 1.16 DKK/KWh as electricity is subject to five different tax elements:

—a special electricity tax of 0.46 DKK/KWh (which will increase gradually to 0.52 DKK/KWh in 2002),
—a carbon dioxide tax of 0.10 DKK/KWh,
—a sulphur tax of 0.09 DKK/KWh which in the year 2000 increased to 0.13 DKK/KWh,
—payment to an energy conservation fund of 0.06 DKK/KWh, and
—25 per cent VAT.[65]

6.250 In general, VAT-registered consumers (private enterprise) have most taxes on electricity for processing purposes reimbursed. However, the share of reimbursed carbon dioxide tax depends on the type of end-use and on whether an agreement has been entered into on energy conservation measures.

6.251 Electricity generation in Denmark mainly takes place in large, central, combined heat and power plants (CHP) fuelled by coal. Prior to the oil crisis in 1973, oil was used for generating 80 per cent of the total electricity production in Denmark,

[64] *Electricity Supply in Denmark, 1998, Statistics,* Association of Danish Electric Utilities, 5, 27 and 35.

[65] ibid, 8.

and coal for just 20 per cent. Ten years later, a planned conversion to coal as the main generating fuel had been carried out so thoroughly that coal powered 92 per cent of the Danish electricity generation. This massive conversion took place in a period of 4 per cent average growth in power consumption, and was primarily due to the economic incentive for the transition from oil to coal, and the desire for greater security of supply. The fuel switch was made possible by the power plants having a substantial surplus capacity during the period, and the possibility of importing power via the expanded transmission grid from Sweden, Norway, and the Federal Republic of Germany. These factors all made it technically possible to retire power plants from operation during rebuilding. It should be noted that the conversion took place on purely commercial terms and with no subsidies at all. In this respect, the aggressive strategy pursued by the power plants in purchasing coal, and the rather liberal Government approach to the environmental impact problems in connection with the use of coal, were of great importance.

Natural gas is increasingly being used for electricity production, even in larger **6.252** power plants, and an increasing share of generation stems from local CHP units and wind turbines, built partly within the umbrella of the utilities, partly as independent power producers (IPP). In 1996, the generation of non-utility generators increased 32 per cent in comparison to the previous year, and 97 per cent of private generation was sold to the utilities. Wind turbines accounted for 17.9 per cent of total non-utility generation. The share of local CHP stations and industrial auto-producers was 65.4 per cent and 16.7 per cent respectively.[66] There are no legal limitations to private power generation in Denmark apart from the licence requirement (see below).

Denmark has always had limited hydropower production, but today it amounts **6.253** to just about 1 per cent of the total electricity production. In the 1970s the use of nuclear power produced in Denmark was an element of Danish energy policy. In principle, the legal basis was established by the adoption of the Act on Compensation for Damages caused by Nuclear Power,[67] and the Act on Safety and Environmental Factors relating to Nuclear Plants,[68] but the building of nuclear power stations did not in fact begin, in spite of political consent and severe pressure from the power stations and manufacturing industry. On the contrary, implementation of the programme was virtually abandoned by Parliament resolutions on Public Planning, Excluding Nuclear Power, and Abolition of Land Reservations for the Nuclear Power Stations (of 29 March and 30 April 1985). As a result of this, nuclear power plays no part in the planning of the present or future energy supply in Denmark.

[66] *Electricity Supply in Denmark, 1996*, Association of Electric Utilities, 19.
[67] Act No 332 of 19 June 1974.
[68] Act No 244 of 12 May 1976.

(2) Structure of the Industry

6.254 The Danish electricity supply industry is characterized by a large number of companies in vertical integrated ownership and the absence of State-owned companies. Electricity supply in Denmark has always involved the consumer and had a decentralized industry, originating in small local utilities with their own generation units. The municipalities and rural consumer-organized transformer associations, and later on co-operative distribution companies, formed the basis of power production and distribution. In 1935, the number of electricity supplying companies reached its maximum of about 500 per 3.5 million inhabitants. Today the number has been reduced to about 100 for a population of some 5 million.

6.255 It should be noted that the Danish electricity sector has been undergoing profound changes in the last few years and that frequent mergers into bigger utilities are taking place. The municipalities are still heavily involved in electricity supply, as just under half of the distribution companies are owned by municipalities and a similar number by co-operatives owned by the local consumers within the supply area. Ownership is automatic and follows the property. One major distributing utility is a limited company in which municipalities are the main shareholders. The distribution companies own and operate the network at 10/20 kV and low voltage, and the distributing utilities within a region are owners of the regional generation utility. Electricity has until recently been solely bought from this regional generation plant and from independent power producers in the geographical supply area. However, this situation will probably change in the future.

6.256 Most generation takes place at eighteen power stations, formerly owned by ten power companies, which during Summer 2000 merged into two companies—one operating in Eastern Denmark and one in the West. Both companies, ELSAM and E2, are organized as legally independent companies but, as mentioned above, owned and operated jointly by the regional distribution companies in the local area. These regional generation utilities own and operate the network at 50/60 kV and to some degree at 132/150 kV.

6.257 The Danish electricity system is divided into two separate grids. There are plans to connect east and west Denmark, but no concrete action has been implemented yet. Denmark has, however, interconnected electricity systems with Sweden, Norway, and Germany and has a long tradition of extensive co-operation in power exchange. Previously, the utilities co-operated within ELKRAFT, while the Jylland-Fyn (Jutland-Funen) production companies form the ELSAM power pool. ELSAM and ELKRAFT owned and operated the transmission grid at 400 kV-level, the interconnection abroad, and part of the 132/150 kV network, in addition to co-ordinating electricity trade with other countries, long-term system planning, electricity and combined heat and power production, the expansion of the power plants, and the purchase of fuels.

However, as a consequence of an amendment[69] to the old Electricity Supply Act 1976, and the European Commission's electricity market directive, restructuring has taken place. The amended Electricity Supply Act 1976 introduced three functions of the electricity supply industry: production, system operator/transmission, and distribution, and required unbundling in terms of cost accounting and managerial functions. **6.258**

The Jutland-Funen electricity supply industry decided to divide the three functions into an independent legal entity and to transfer all ELSAM's transmission activities to a new company, Eltra. Eltra took over the entire transmission network in Jutland and on Funen, the international interconnections, and the tasks to be performed by the 'transmission system operator'. The Minister for Environment and Energy approved the partial transfer of ELSAM's licence in December 1997, and appointed Eltra pursuant to section 3a of the Electricity Supply Act 1976 as amended, as the transmission system operator in the Jutland-Funen area. Eltra is established as a partnership and is owned by the distribution companies in the area. **6.259**

The utilities in the Eastern part of Denmark decided to establish a separate division within the ELKRAFT Company, and the Minister appointed ELKRAFT System as the transmission system operator for that region. The production utilities then merged into one company, E2, and decided to restructure their business into a system operator company and a transmission company, ELKRAFT System and ELKRAFT Transmission. The system operator has continued the activities associated with the ELKRAFT System's system operator licence. The transmission company own the 400 kV transmission grid and the interconnections with Germany and Sweden previously owned by ELKRAFT. The two new companies were set up in 2000 to meet the requirements of the new Electricity Supply Act 1999. **6.260**

It should be highlighted that Nord Pool[70] and Eltra began a joint venture of power trade in Jutland/Funen in July 1999, and that power trade began the following year in October in Eastern Denmark. **6.261**

Nearly all production and distribution companies co-operate within the Association of Danish Energy Utilities, an association which deals with topics **6.262**

[69] By Act No 486 of 12 June 1996, which entered into force on 1 Jan 1998

[70] Norway established a power pool in 1993. In 1996 this was expanded into a joint electricity exchange for Norway and Sweden. Today, Nord Pool is owned equally by the two State-owned companies Statnett SF and Svenska Kraftnät. As of 1 July 1998, Finland was integrated in the Norwegian-Swedish electricity market. Today, Danish electricity companies trade in the Nordic power pool.

of common interest for the members and acts as spokesperson in dealings with authorities and the public.

(3) The Legislative Framework

6.263 Following the oil crisis in 1973/74 and in the light of the plans of the electricity utilities at that time of introducing nuclear power, the first Bill on Electricity Supply was presented to Parliament in 1974. The Act was adopted as Act No 54 of 25 February 1976, and came into force on 1 January 1977, introducing among other things a licensing system and price regulation of electricity supply activities. Since then twelve amendments[71] have been passed by the Danish Parliament. The last amendment is most noteworthy: it provided for implementation in part of the Electricity Directive 96/22/EC and was put into force as of 1 January 1998. However, neither the existing licensing system for power stations and grids nor the 'non-profit' system of the Danish Electricity Supply Act, which covered distribution, generation, transmission, and sales, was changed on that occasion.

6.264 Subsequently, the Government initiated a reform of the electricity and heating area to assess whether legislation or other initiatives were desirable and to draw up rules for the electricity sector in the period up to the renewal of the electricity licences. Many of the licences were due to expire in 1998, and were consequently extended for a short period until the end of 1999. On 3 March 1999, the Danish Government concluded an agreement with the major opposition parties on a legislative reform of the electricity sector. This agreement was the result of several months of political debate. It outlines the framework of new legislation defining the future organization of the electricity market, the opening of the electricity market, and how to protect the environment in the coming liberalized electricity market in a probably unique way.

6.265 The political agreement was implemented in June 1999 by the adoption of five new Acts, of which the new Act on Electricity Supply No 375 of 2 June 1999 and the Act No 376 on Carbon Dioxide Quotas for Electricity Production are the most interesting. The other three Acts concern changing subsidies, the calculation of prices of renewables, and introducing the new common energy regulator in the heating sector.[72] On 17 November 1999, a supplementary political agreement was concluded between the majority of the parties in Parliament to determine the framework of the economic conditions for the electricity generators when the

[71] Act No 54 of 25 Feb 1976 as amended by Act No 818 of 19 Dec 1989, Act No 327 of 14 May 1992, Act No 328 of 14 May 1992, Act No 329 of 14 May 1992, Act No 445 of 30 June 1993, Act No 95 of 9 Feb 1994, Act No 35 of 18 Jan 1995, Act No 409 of 14 June 1995, Act No 1088 of 20 Dec 1995, Act No 486 of 12 June 1996 (all included in Consolidated Act No 632 of 1 July 1996), Act No 189 of 12 Mar 1997, and Act No 89 of 10 Feb 1998.

[72] Act No 375 of 2 June 1999 on Electricity Supply, Act No 376 of 2 June 1999 on CO_2 Quotas for Electricity Production, Act No 377 of 2 June 1999 on Amendments of the Act on Subsidies for Electricity Production and Act No 379 of 2 June 1999 on Amendments of the Heat Supply Act.

market is liberalized. The political agreement was implemented by an amendment to the new Electricity Supply Act by Act No 1110 of 29 December 1999 and secures the financial foundation of the plants in the transition period (debts and take-or-pay commitments) and conditions of payment for environment-friendly electricity generation at existing power plants. By a special Order No 1126 of 29 December 1999, the new Electricity Act 1999 as amended entered into force, apart from the rules on PSO (environmentally benign electricity production) which had to await the approval of the European Union Commission and came into force as of 1 November 2000. Likewise the amendments to the Heat Supply Act came into force. The Act on Carbon Dioxide Quotas was put into effect as from 15 July 2000. The political agreement of 22 March 2000 includes a follow-up to the electricity reform and establishes the framework for the further use of biomass in electricity generation, settlement of the costs of prioritized production, the energy savings area and the Green Energy Market. This was implemented through an amendment to the Electricity Act No 448 of 31 May 2000.

Below, the old Electricity Act is presented before the new Act is analysed. It is im- **6.266** portant to know the main principles of the old regime in order to appreciate the new developments. Moreover, the new Electricity Act 1999 includes several of the elements of the Electricity Act 1976.

(4) Electricity Supply Act 1976

The central element of the first Electricity Supply Act was the introduction of a li- **6.267** censing system (section 3).[73] A licence granted by the Ministry was a precondition for the production, transmission, or distribution of electricity. These licensing requirements, however, did not include pure distribution or activities from power plants less than 25 MW and transmission systems less than 100 kV. Moreover, new construction projects and future capacity developments were also conditional upon Government consent (section 5(1)(5)). Amendments in 1996 introduced a new type of licence for the transmission system operator (section 3a). With respect to the award procedure only, special conditions were set to the issuance of an exclusive licence for nuclear power production (section 4) which needed parliamentary approval.

Those companies which prior to the adoption of the Electricity Supply Act in **6.268** 1976 carried on electricity supply activities were granted a right to obtain a licence as long as they declared a willingness to comply with the terms provided in the Act, especially section 5, and provided that the applicant's articles of association

[73] See further 'Coal and Fuel Choices in Denmark', section 2, by Anita Rønne, Journal of Energy and Natural Resources Law, vol 7, no 4, 1989.

did not contradict any provisions of the Act. A formality was, however, a requirement of submitting an application for a licence (section 17).

Issued licences

6.269 Licences were issued to all utilities in operation at the time where the Electricity Supply Act came into force[74] and to ELSAM and ELKRAFT to import and export electricity. Most of these licences were granted during 1977–80 and ran until the end of 1999. In addition, Eltra and ELSAM System were granted licences as transmission system operators, likewise until the end of 1999. Finally, licences were issued during the 1990s to enterprises producing electricity for their own consumption or in connection with the conversion to CHP. For example, one licence was granted to the oil company Shell in order to produce electricity for its refinery, and another to Dansk Salt. These two licences have no supply area, and excess production is sold to the network.

Licence terms

6.270 The basic concept of the licence was that each licensee company would enjoy, for at least twenty years and within a delimited area, a right to supply electricity, and a corresponding obligation to deliver electricity as directed by the authorities. The rights were not exclusive, but for a long time there existed *de facto* monopolies within geographical areas. Competition in electricity production and distribution could occur, and was growing due to the building of wind turbines and small combined heat and power plants, constructed either by the power companies or privately. With respect to nuclear energy the Electricity Supply Act required a licence to be exclusive (section 4) but no licence was ever issued.

6.271 Most licences were issued in the period from 1977 to 1982 for the minimum period at that time—20 years, which was supposed to reflect the lifetime of a plant. Consequently, many licences were close to expiring in 1998. At this time, however, the Minister for Environment and Energy had initiated but not completed a programme of reform of the legal framework in order to implement the Electricity Directive. To extend the licences for a limited period to allow time for finalizing the reform, the Ministry passed an amendment to the Act in February 1998. Accordingly, the minimum licence period was changed to two years (section 3). There was no maximum limit to the duration of a licence.

6.272 The Act imposed obligations upon the licensees that would always apply, but section 5(2) imposed additional terms if the special circumstances of the relevant supplier so indicated or the aim was to supplement in specific fields. Regarding the system operator licence, the Minister could likewise issue more detailed regu-

[74] Nordjyllandsværket, Vestkraft, Midtkraft, SønderJyllands Højspændingsværk, Fynsværket, Københavns Belysningsvæsen, Sjællandske Kraftværker, Østkraft, Skærbækværket.

lations requiring that these tasks were separated from other activities in management and accounting, and concerning the performance of these tasks (section 3(6) and (7)).

The content of each licence is generally alike. Pursuant to section 5 of the Act, a list of obligations is always imposed on the licensees, including approval of their statutes and any change to them; that the licensee should supply power as directed by the Minister, and that the commencement or alteration of construction works of new facilities were to be approved by the Minister. Finally, a licensee could be required (for payment) to place his transmission grid at the disposal of the system operator. **6.273**

Public control is primarily implemented through the licence obligation to submit various information and to prepare detailed plans for capacity developments. This requirement enables planning for the whole electricity supply of the country in such a way that the Government has been able to consider electricity supply planning in correlation with other energy planning. **6.274**

Operational requirements and agreements

The Ministry was, to a significant extent, entitled to influence the operations of the licensees. Pursuant to section 13, the Ministry could order the utilities: to construct their production plants in such a way that prescribed forms of energy could be used and the highest energy efficiency achieved; to use certain forms of energy; and to maintain certain stocks of fuel. For instance, the Minister for Environment and Energy used this provision to ban coal use in new power stations in March 1997. The ban implied that no new coal-fired power or heat plants would be approved. **6.275**

Although the public authorities had the power to regulate activities fairly extensively, co-operation has been preferred when adjustments have been found to be necessary. Hence the power companies have entered into several agreements with the Ministry and the State-owned company dealing with energy supply, especially during the 1980s. **6.276**

Direct action was taken by Government in requesting the power companies to purchase gas quantities from DONG Naturgas AS, a wholly owned subsidiary of DONG AS, for which there was no other market. The surplus gas agreement formed part of a political settlement of 13 April 1984 between the Government and the Social Democratic Party on strengthening the natural gas project. The reason for this move was that the connection rate to the natural gas grid was below expectation; industrial enterprises in particular were reluctant. Because of DONG's contractual commitments, an alternative sale was needed. **6.277**

6.278 As part of the policy to promote the utilization of local resources, ELSAM and ELKRAFT entered into an agreement in December 1985 with the Minister of Energy, concerning increased use of renewable and indigenous sources in electricity production. The utilities committed themselves to establish large wind turbines and wind-power farms, totalling at least 100 MW before 1991—equivalent to double the capacity installed during the previous five years. A second agreement concerning the same capacity was entered into in 1990, supplemented by a ministerial order requiring the installation of additional 200 MW by 2000. Finally, an agreement was reached in 1997 to develop further 750 MW wind power offshore by the year 2008 (see section G below).

6.279 Another agreement was reached on 6 June 1986 between the Government and the Social Democratic Party, subsequently approved by the electricity utilities, on future development of generation capacity. According to this agreement a number of small-scale CHP plants based on indigenous fuels (natural gas, waste, biogas, or biomass) with a total generating capacity of 450 MW were to be built by 1995. This was only partly implemented, but it paved the way for a 1990 Parliamentary agreement on a CHP Conversion Programme, according to which all small and medium-sized district heating plants should convert either to small-scale CHP or to biomass before 1998.

6.280 Another Government initiative was a letter of February 1989, requesting the power companies to revise their planning of future development in order to give first priority to less polluting fuels and to increase the utilization of natural gas.

6.281 In order to increase the use of biomass, an agreement was entered into in 1993 and revised in 1997. The utilities were obliged to use 1.2 Mt of straw, 200,000 tonnes of woodchips, and 200,000 tonnes of either straw or woodchips annually by the year 2000. The Biomass Agreement of 14 June 1993, as amended, seeks to maintain the utilization of biomass. Before the end of 2003, two to three large biomass plants should be established. The aim is to make use of the tendering instrument to bring down costs as much as possible.

6.282 It would be misleading to call these agreements 'voluntary', for contractual freedom is an illusion. First, several of the agreements follow a political agreement which explicitly prescribes the expected outcome. This means that the system is supported by a political majority. Secondly, the administrative power contained in the Act regarding the use of a specific form of energy actually amounts to a threat of unilateral fixing.

6.283 The use of agreements as a mechanism of public regulation brings into focus legal issues which the general law of contracts and of public administration is not suited to solve, and which are far removed from the traditional essence of these legal fields. Consequently, development does present its problems.

The use of agreements gives the State a double possibility for regulation: both as party to an agreement, and as legislator. The process may be difficult to perceive and control wherever a regulation takes part through agreements to which the demands of form, content, and publication are limited. The result seems to be a tendency to give in on many fundamental values of law and legal principles, which have been developed through an extensive legal tradition. The extent to which one may frown upon the use of agreements depends partly upon the mutual strength of the parties and their professionalism. **6.284**

Price control

The supply of electricity in Denmark since 1977 has been based on a non-profit system, where prices must reflect the cost of supplying the individual customer. The inevitable profits or losses must be transferred to the next accounting year, resulting in electricity price decreases or increases. **6.285**

The pricing was strictly regulated by the Electricity Supply Act, section 9, which laid down general rules for both wholesale and retail tariff formulation, which were further defined in secondary legislation and by the practice of the then Electricity Price Commission (see section A(6) above). The Act identified the main cost elements where the maximum price was to cover 'necessary expenses for fuel, wages, and other operational costs, administration and sales costs, operational depreciation and interest paid on loan capital'. In addition—if adopted by the Price Commission—the companies could include in their prices 'allocations to re-investment funds and interest paid on contribution capital'. Very important in this respect were guidelines on prices and supply conditions issued by the Association of Electricity Companies and District Heating Companies and approved by the Electricity Price Commission. **6.286**

Prices and conditions of supply had to be notified to the Price Commission and published. They were valid on the date of notification but the Commission could compel changes and also treated complaints from consumers. The practice of the Commission was to allow profits only when they reflected results of rationalization in the electricity generating company. It was further provided that in the case of CHP the split between the costs of generation of electricity and of heat should be made fairly based on reasonable operational principles. It was also part of the pricing structure that all consumers should participate in the costs of generating electricity from renewable energy sources and in the cost of maintaining systems to secure supplies (section 9f). This meant that any extra costs of generating electricity in this way would be included in the total cost, from which the electricity sale price was calculated. **6.287**

Any non-core activity (activities other than electricity supply) had to be carried out by separate companies, and side activities had to be somehow connected to **6.288** the electricity supply. These rules were recently tightened as a consequence of one former Danish electricity generating company (SEAS) getting into severe financial trouble over side investments *inter alia* in large glasshouses for raising tomatoes, the intention being to use the surplus heat from the electricity generation to heat the glasshouses.

6.289 To overcome market access problems, the utilities have been forced to purchase power from small privately owned power production companies at fixed buy-back rates. In principle the prices have been long-term marginal costs of the electricity system, for wind turbines formulated as 85 per cent of the sales price to domestic consumers.

System access

6.290 The Electricity Supply Act was fundamentally amended in May 1996 in order to regulate access to the network. The new rules came into force on 1 January 1998, following the completion of the notification procedure at the European Commission.

6.291 In connection with the Nordic liberalization (see Chapter 11 below) there was no regulation governing access to the Danish electricity market. However, a decision by the Danish Competition Council of 28 February 1996 stated that due to lack of rules on network access in the Electricity Supply Act, grid-owners were obliged to negotiate access to the grid with everybody that requested access. Therefore, the Minister for Environment and Energy deemed it necessary specifically to regulate market access in the Act, primarily to secure the future of Danish environmental policy. On one hand this model would open the market, on the other hand it made it possible to conduct a national Danish environmental and energy policy at the same time as introducing competition gradually.

6.292 The amendment to the Electricity Supply Act consisted of three main elements, all inspired, and present within the framework of, the Electricity Directive. First, end-users of more than 100 GWh in consumption per year per site and distributors (and generators) of more than 100 GWh in sales per year got market access and therefore the ability to enter into agreements for the supply or purchase of electricity from another Danish electricity generating utility or from an electricity generating utility abroad (section 9d). If unreasonable requirements were made in negotiation for net access the Price Commission, at that time, could issue an order to the electricity supply business to enter into an agreement on terms currently applicable in similar agreements.

6.293 Only six consumers were eligible for access in the same category, namely Staalvalsevaerket (a steel plant), Aalborg Portland (a cement factory), Novo Nordisk (a pharmaceutical company), Shell Rafinaderiet (a refinery), Statoil Rafinaderiet (a refinery), and Cheminova (a chemical plant). The small number of qualifying enterprises has probably also meant that pressure from the industry to liberalize has been relatively limited.

Secondly, according to the Act, it would not be a distortion of competition if the electricity supply utility was fulfilling its obligations under section 9 of the Act to secure a number of public service obligations (PSOs). PSOs are political and administrative orders imposed on the electric utilities to ensure supply security, technical quality, and balance in the supply, necessary transmission capacity, sufficient reserves and minimum capacity in fuel stores, the protection of consumers (including the right to receive a supply and the right to be connected to a distribution system), and environmental considerations (including, very importantly, the supply of electricity from non-central CHPs and from electricity generating plants using renewable fuels or renewable energy. Two examples are the obligations to purchase electricity from IPPs at regulated prices and to build and operate wind turbines and biomass-fired power stations). **6.294**

These types of public service obligations had to be given priority by the system operators and were sold back to all consumers at regulated prices. The funds were recovered from all consumers in Denmark through an obligation for all consumers to purchase a fair share of 'green' electricity, or alternatively to pay a fair share of the costs. Other more traditional public service obligations, such as costs related to the obligation to supply and to maintain security and quality, were covered by a special charge paid by all consumers. **6.295**

The last element to be highlighted in the amending Act was the system operator: the rules here closely resemble those of the Directive. The system operators were also given tasks relating to public service obligations. **6.296**

(5) Electricity Supply Act 1999

The Electricity Supply Act 1999 has as its main target to ensure that electricity supply is organized and implemented in accordance with considerations of security of supply, the national economy, the environment, and consumer protection (section 1(1)). This objective is not very different from the aim of the old Electricity Act, but consideration of the consumers is accentuated. Thus the new Act emphasizes that within the terms of the stated objective, the Act is to ensure consumers access to inexpensive electricity and continue to provide them with influence over the administration of the assets of the electricity sector. There is still a strong focus on the promotion of environmentally friendly use of energy, by (*inter alia*) savings in electricity consumption, co-generation of heat and power, and the use of renewable sources of energy and environmentally friendly fuels (section 1(2)). However, it is now emphasized that this promotion shall also ensure efficient use of financial resources and the creation of competition in the markets for the production of and trade in electricity. **6.297**

6.298 Administrative responsibilities in this connection fall within the sphere of the Ministry for Environment and Energy and the Energy Agency and, in contrast to the Heat Supply Act, the administrative powers are not delegated to local authorities. The Act lays down the legal framework of public control. Most important in this respect is a licensing system for most electricity and supply activities, market opening and grid access, unbundling of activities, consumer influence, prioritized sale of environmentally benign electricity, public regulation of electricity prices, and the appointment of a new Energy Supervisory Board.

6.299 In principle, the Electricity Supply Act covers all forms of electricity activities: production, transport, trade, and supply of electricity (section 2(1)) but the Minister for Environment and Energy may decide that small installations or small-scale activities shall be wholly or partly exempted from the provisions of the Act (section 2(4)). Rules on safety, emissions, taxes, subsidies, etc are contained in separate Acts. The Act applies on land as well as offshore in territorial waters and within the exclusive economic zone—the latter relevant to offshore plants using energy from water, waves, and wind, with accessory cables (sections 2(2) and 13).

The licence system

6.300 Today all activities connected to electricity supply are subject to licensing: production, transmission and grid activities, system operation, and supply (sections 10, 13(2), 19, 23, 27, and 33). The new Electricity Act thus expands the licence requirement by including also the sole distribution of electricity and transmission systems less than 100 kV—activities that previously were exempted. Minor production activities from power plants less than 25 MW are, however, still excluded from the general licence requirement (section 10(1)). The limit of 25 MW was introduced in the old Electricity Act 1976 and chosen at the time, partly because the practice then was to construct far bigger plants, and partly because this limit was identical to the size that needed approval according to the rules on special polluting industry of the Environmental Protection Act then in force. The Act no longer includes rules on establishment of nuclear power stations (section 11(4)).

6.301 It should be highlighted that the Danish State alone is entitled to use energy from water and wind in territorial waters and in the exclusive economic zone (section 13(1)), and there is a requirement to obtain a special permit of the Minister for Environment and Energy to perform preliminary surveys, and to use energy from water and wind offshore (section 13(2)). Onshore activities connected to the establishment of wind turbines are regulated by the Act on Renewables.

6.302 New construction projects for electricity production and transmission grids designed for voltages of more than 100 kv and major changes in the existing installations are further conditional upon obtaining permission (sections 11, 16, and

21). The limit of 100 kv is chosen as a natural delimitation between distribution and transmission, because transmission grids normally have a voltage of 120 kv and distribution grids no more than 60 kv.

Procedures for granting licences

With respect to the award procedure only special conditions are set for the issuance of a licence for preliminary surveys and the use of energy from water and wind offshore (section 14). A special tendering procedure has thus been established, resembling in part the procedure that applies to oil and gas exploration and production (see section B(3) above). Two procedures can be utilized by the Minister for Environment and Energy—public invitation to tender pursuant to rules determined by the Minister (a bidding round) or the publication of an application received whereupon other interested parties are invited to submit an application (open-door procedure)—the difference being by whom the initiative is taken. This procedure should give all interested parties equal access and conditions. Existing plants established pursuant to the previous rules are exempted from these tender requirements (section 18). **6.303**

The Act also includes authority for the Minister for Environment and Energy to issue rules concerning the procedures for granting permissions for construction projects and major changes in existing production plants (section 11(3)). **6.304**

Like the old Act of 1976, the new Electricity Supply Act determines that those companies which carried on electricity supply activities prior to the adoption of the new Act are granted a right to get a licence as long as they declare that they will comply with the terms provided in the Act and the licence, and provided the statutes of the applicant do not contradict any provisions of the Act or other rules and subject to the approval by the Minister. In addition, the company must fulfil the requirements for being granted a licence (section 97(1)). **6.305**

A very important provision is that the new Act includes requirements concerning organizational issues. It is a precondition that all assets and owner shares in other companies are transferred and owned directly by the grid companies (section 97(2)). This rule is intended to ensure that the assets accumulated in the production companies, which by the new Act are no longer subject to price regulation based on the 'non-profit' system, will still benefit the consumers. The Minister for Environment and Energy may under special circumstances make an exemption from these rules (section 97(3)). **6.306**

As a formality, however, an application for a licence must be submitted within a specific time limit, set at 1 March 2000. Special guidelines have been issued by the Energy Agency on the licence application. During this transition period from the expiry of the old licences until new licences are issued the company is entitled to continue its activities (section 98). **6.307**

6.308 Parliament is ensured some control by the Act, as the Minister for Environment and Energy is obliged to keep a special Parliamentary Committee on Energy informed about all essential circumstances relating to electricity supply (section 3).

The licence terms

6.309 The basic concept of the licence is that each licensee company will enjoy within a delimited area a right to perform the defined activities for at least twenty years, and has in return some corresponding obligations. This applies to licences for production, transmission and grid activities, and system operation. Licences have a minimum term, but not a maximum. With respect to supply-committed activity, the licence term is fixed at only five years, and cannot be either shorter or longer. As for licences for utilizing energy from water and wind, no period has been indicated (sections 10(2), 13(5), 19(2), 27(2), and 33(2)).

6.310 The Act imposes explicit obligations upon the licensees that will always apply. It also includes specific provisions that can be applied at the discretion of the Minister (sections 12, 13(4), 23(3), 50(2), and 59(3)). Finally, there is a more general authority for the Minister to set additional terms in licences (section 50). However, this power is restricted to special cases to fulfil the objectives of the Act and which are justified by the special circumstances of the relevant company.[75] This latter possibility is similar to the rule in the old Electricity Supply Act, but whereas this possibility was only applicable to new electricity supply undertakings, the rule on licence terms in the new Electricity Supply Act 1999 applies also to companies already in operation. It has been added that terms may also be laid down in order to comply with EC rules and recommendations in the area. It should be noted that the licence terms can be changed after five years upon advance notice of one year (section 51).

6.311 Licences are exempt from legal proceedings and may neither directly nor indirectly be transferred to any other party without ministerial approval (section 53). Any licence can, however, be withdrawn if the licence conditions are repeatedly breached, if incorrect or misleading information is provided in a licence application, or in the event that the licensee enters into liquidation or bankruptcy (section 54). The licensee must also accept public supervision and pay the expenses related thereto (section 51).

Market opening

6.312 Everyone in Denmark has the right to be supplied with electricity upon payment on transparent, objective, reasonable, and uniform terms (section 6). Consumers

[75] According to the general remarks to the Bill on Electricity Supply 1976 the option is considered to be rather limited, and it is stated that the possibility of applying other conditions is not as wide as the authorization in the Natural Gas Supply Act.

are thus entitled to delivery of electricity by means of a supply offer from a supply-committed enterprise. From 1 January 2003 all consumers—industrial as well as private—can freely choose their electricity supplier (section 7). Today only a few consumers (with an annual consumption of 100 GWh) have a free choice, but the opening of the market for consumers will advance gradually. From 1 April 2000 consumers with an annual consumption of more than 10 GWh have had a free choice of supplier, and from the beginning of the year 2001 consumers with an annual consumption of more than 1 GWh were included.

This time-frame gives the companies the necessary time to establish the measuring and control system needed to service about 3 million consumers in a new way. In order to ensure that all consumers can have electricity supplies on reasonable conditions both before and after full market opening has been implemented in 2002, a number of electricity companies are levied with a 'supply commitment'. These companies must guarantee supply to consumers who could not from the start buy electricity on the market and those who do not wish to use their new freedom to choose suppliers (sections 34 and 6). **6.313**

Organization

The new Electricity Act opens up the industry for increased competition, and therefore new company regulations had to be introduced. First and foremost, areas which will continue to be a natural monopoly are separated from more competitive activities. Competition will be possible within both production and trading companies, which in the future will be run as ordinary commercial companies. CHP plants will, however, continue to be subject to supply commitments to heat consumers and a special price control for heat supplies. **6.314**

In the new structure the present distribution companies will be replaced by grid companies and supply obligation companies. The electricity transmission grid is to be operated as a public infrastructure, and placed at the disposal of all users of the electricity system on objective, non-discriminatory terms (sections 24 and 73). The owners of the grid companies will not have any returns (sections 69 and 70(4)) and the grid and its control are to be managed independently of production and trade interests (section 47). Vertical integration is to be discouraged to ensure effective competition and production and trading companies may not own more than 15 per cent of the grid, supply obligation, or system-responsible companies (section 38). In the future the equity interests in the power plants and in the grid, which are owned by the present distribution companies, are to be placed in the grid companies (section 97(2)). **6.315**

The fact that the sector is owned from 'below' by municipalities and consumers through the distribution companies is not changed, but to ensure that the assets are not risked through competitive activities when companies split off **6.316** subsidiaries, ownership of the assets is placed in the grid company (section 97(2)). The consumers' interests are safeguarded by a requirement that elected consumer representatives have a dominating influence on the running of the grid company (section 40). The overall responsibility for the electricity grid will be placed in an independent system-responsible company, which is to secure co-ordination of the total system (section 28). The company is to be non-profit and two public representatives, appointed by the Minister, should be on the management board to control the activities of the company (sections 32 and 71). The State has a pre-emptive right if the present owners wish to sell their shares in the transmission lines (section 35). To protect smaller consumers, some companies will get a licence to be supply obligation companies. These companies are to ensure that all consumers are offered a standard package of energy and energy-saving services supplied on reasonable conditions (section 34). Directly or indirectly elected consumer representatives shall have a minimum of one-third of the voting rights at their disposal (section 43).

6.317 Supply obligation companies and grid companies may continue with their present owners. In the future, however, it will be demanded that commercial activities in the supply obligation companies are separated from the grid activities, to secure the division between monopoly and business activities (section 47).

Environmentally benign electricity production

6.318 In order to develop renewable energy production in the future, all electricity consumers in Denmark will have to buy an increasing share of electricity produced from renewable energy sources (section 8). First a quota is determined: the political agreement requires that 20 per cent of electricity consumption must be covered by renewables in 2003. The Minister has now informed the public that the 'green market' will come into effect as of 1 January 2002. Simultaneously the aim is to secure fair conditions for the many private consumers who have invested in wind power during the years. Those rules came into effect as from 1 November 2000 following the approval of the EU Commission.

6.319 A competitive mechanism has been developed to ensure that the development of renewable energy is as cost effective as possible. The producers of renewable energy are to sell their electricity on a special renewable energy market—RE market—and a certification of renewable energy electricity is therefore introduced. The producers will receive RE certificates equal to the quantity of certified electricity they produce (section 60). The market price of the RE certificates should help provide a secure and stable demand for renewable energy. These RE certificates are bought by the supply obligation companies/consumers who will then be able to prove that they have fulfilled their RE electricity minimum quota (section 62). Consumers and companies who do not fulfil their quota are to pay a fine which will be used to continue developing renewable energy (section 63).

The parties have agreed to implement various transitional schemes until the special RE market has been finally established. This is to ensure fair depreciation terms for private individuals who have already invested in renewable energy plants and to ensure that the development of renewable energy plants does not stop in the interim period (sections 59, 65, and 66). **6.320**

(6) Carbon Dioxide Framework

Through a number of international agreements Denmark has committed herself to reducing, *inter alia*, the emission of carbon dioxide. As a consequence of the Community's commitment to the UN climate panel on stabilization of greenhouse gas emissions in the year 2000 compared with 1990, Denmark has committed herself, to the EU, to a 5 per cent reduction of such emissions within this period. Furthermore, Denmark has agreed a national target of reducing carbon dioxide emissions by 20 per cent in the year 2005 compared with 1988, as shown by a number of parliamentary decisions during the years 1990–97 as well as the Government's energy action plans Energy 2000 and Energy 21. **6.321**

Denmark has already made a considerable effort to reduce carbon dioxide emissions, *inter alia* through energy savings, increased application of CHP and renewable energy, as well as very efficient power plants using natural gas. The electricity sector has a key role to play in relation to fulfilling international environmental commitments, and this is the background for the decision to determine an annual ceiling for total carbon dioxide emissions from the electricity sector by Act No 376 of 2 June 1999 on Carbon Dioxide Quotas for Electricity Production. Denmark is the first country to take such a step. The Act came into force as of 15 July 2000, cf Order No 628 of 23 June 2000. **6.322**

In principle all electricity is covered by the Act, but from the starting phase renewables and small decentralized CHP facilities will be exempt. The ceiling reduces gradually and it should ensure that carbon dioxide emissions from the electricity sector will decrease by 20 million tonnes a year between 2000 and 2003 (section 2). In the year 2000 the ceiling was established at 2.3 million tonnes. It will be decreased by 1 million tonnes each year. The carbon dioxide ceiling means that each production company, including the two production co-operations, is allocated an annual quota of the gas which they are allowed to emit (section 3). The first quotas were announced on 15 December 2000, and the following years will be by 1 July each year, following consultation with the addressees. No consideration is taken of ownership—be it national or foreign—as long as the installation is situated on Danish territory. **6.323**

The use of quota systems is well known in Denmark. For a number of years the sulphur dioxide and nitrous oxide emissions of power plants have been regulated through quotas based on Executive Order No 885 of 18 December 1991 on the **6.324** limitation of emission of sulphur dioxide and nitrogen oxides from power plants as amended by Executive Order No 321 of 4 June 1998. This quota scheme allowed flexibility for the electricity sector as the power plants themselves have been able, to a large extent, to choose technology and location when new flue gas cleaning plants were to be built.

6.325 If the annual carbon dioxide quota is exceeded, the production companies must pay the State the sum of DKK 40/tonne of gas in the years 2000–03 (section 13). Any revenue from this tax is to be used for energy saving purposes. Within 2001 the framework for the subsequent years must be settled.

6.326 The system is to be flexible so that companies can benefit from the advantages of electricity exchange with other Nordic countries. Thus quotas not fully used can be transferred to the following year. For this reason, the companies will be able to save emission permits in a 'carbon dioxide bank' so that less use of quotas in one year may lead to a corresponding increase of the quota during the following year (section 5).

6.327 The carbon dioxide quota system prepares for the Kyoto Mechanisms of the Kyoto Protocol—international trade in quotas as well as the project-based mechanisms Joint Implementation and Clean Development Mechanism. The carbon dioxide quotas and the savings may thus be transferred (section 6). Against the background that the more specific guidelines for the application of the Kyoto Protocol under the UN Climate Convention are to be agreed upon, the political parties have agreed that before 2001 they must discuss the ceiling for carbon dioxide emissions from the electricity sector for 2003 and onwards.

6.328 Electricity producers covered by this Act are required every year, no later than 31 March, to report to the Minister for Environment and Energy on the previous year's electricity production, utilized heat production, fuel consumption, and carbon dioxide emissions for each electricity generating plant (section 8). The principles and the individual elements in the quota system are to be made more detailed, but this has not happened yet.

(7) Independent Energy Supervisory Board

6.329 An independent Energy Supervisory Board has been established in order to create a sector-specific inspection and appeals function in relation to the energy sector (section 78). It is to be characterized by neutrality: all members must be independent from the industry as well as from the political system. It must represent expertise in the areas of legal, economic business, environmental, and technical knowledge (section 79). The Board replaces the Electricity Price Commission and the Gas and Heat Price Commission, and its decision can be appealed to the Energy Complaint Board (section 89, and see A(6) above).

(8) Conclusion

The electricity sector is in a phase of transition. The Electricity Act of nearly twenty-five years ago has been replaced by a completely new legal regime providing for fresh regulation not only of the activities, but also of the market players. It is therefore important to notice that the organization has not yet crystallized into an overall picture of the situation, and we can expect a whole range of mergers. **6.330**

A comparison with the old system will show that the licence requirement has been expanded to cover the distribution sector and all the newly defined activities and thus categories of companies. Thus in principle everything will in future be subject to licensing: production, transmission and grid activities, system operation, and supply. The public influence on operation has been substituted by the setting of carbon dioxide quotas, and the maintenance of certain stocks of fuel is now vested in the system operator. Regarding price control and the non-profit system, this regulation shall only apply to the grid activities, while production and trade will be subject to competition. **6.331**

Finally, it should be noted that the industry is critical of the reform programme, especially the new organization structure. Thus the reform programme may be challenged in court. **6.332**

G. Renewable Energy

(1) Introduction

In recent years Denmark has introduced a range of programmes and policies designed to accelerate and ensure the development and use of renewable energy. In a historical context, the high priority placed on renewable sources was due to an unstable energy market with the prospect of increasing energy prices. Society had a desire to save fuel and money and to ensure security of supply. Today, however, with adequate supplies and fuel prices at low levels, environmental concerns and this sector's suitability to small communities have become the main reasons for giving priority to the development and use of renewable energy sources. Renewable energy technology is considered a possible alternative to conventional energy production based on fossil fuels, since it results in reduced emissions of sulphur dioxide, nitrogen oxides, and carbon dioxide. In this context the development of renewable energy technology is not only of domestic value: in the global perspective Danish renewable energy technology may prove an environmentally positive alternative to traditional energy production, especially in small isolated communities. **6.333**

To help advance technological development as much as possible, sizeable public subsidies have been provided and remarkable results have been achieved, such as **6.334** reduced prices of installations and improved efficiency of individual technologies. The long-term objective is to make these resources economically competitive with conventional energy sources, and in fact the economy and efficiency of renewable energy installations has in recent years improved considerably.

(2) Development of the Various Renewables

6.335 The long-term aim is the development of an energy system in which an increasing proportion of the energy consumption is covered by renewable energy. On the basis of the initiatives already launched, it was estimated that domestic renewable energy will contribute some 12–14 per cent of the total gross energy consumption by 2005. Because the development has taken place more quickly than anticipated, this result will in fact be achieved earlier. The Government has expressed the intention to continue development at an average annual rate of 1 per cent. By the year 2030 it is therefore predicted that renewables will increase to 5.500 MW (of which 4.000 MW is expected to come from offshore wind turbines) corresponding to a share of about 35 per cent of the total gross energy consumption, and 50 per cent of electricity production.[76]

6.336 In the short term, the development of renewable energy is expected to take place primarily by increasing the use of biomass and wind power. The burning of straw, wood, and solid wastes in district heating plants and small-scale CHP production moved quickly from the experimental stage to large-scale development, supported by the exemption of such resources from energy taxes, and environmental policies, as for instance the 1985 prohibition against field burning of straw from 1990 in order to use that resource. Such initiatives also contribute to local solutions to environmental problems, and are encouraged in district heating plants by the improvement of the financing conditions for the establishment and reorganization of the systems.

6.337 Wind energy has received major support in the form of research, Government testing and certification, grants, and electricity tax rebates, as well as large-scale development and other support by utilities. As a result, Danish wind turbine production has undergone a dramatic technological development, and Danish wind turbines must be considered as leading on the world market with regard to technical quality. Costs have continued to decline and have now approached competitive levels. Due to this, the Government has already reduced grants for wind turbines. The most recent large wind turbines are so competitive today that the use of electricity from wind turbines is one of the cheapest ways of reducing carbon dioxide emissions from power production. The electricity companies are still supporting the development of this resource, and they have entered into several agreements with the Ministry for Environment and Energy, committing

[76] *Energy 21*, Danish Energy Agency, 1996, 39.

themselves to establish large wind turbines, totalling a certain amount MW within specific time limits (see F(5) above).

The most economical way is still to erect wind turbines on land. However, resources on land are limited when housing and nature and landscape considerations are taken into account, and as wind conditions at sea are considerably better than at sites on land, wind turbines are now constructed offshore, and are expected to become competitive in step with the development of technology. The off-shore wind-turbine Orders obligate power companies to establish 750 MW wind power off-shore before the end of 2008. **6.388**

Biogas derived from animal waste is a large potential resource and is also receiving research support and grants. Changed environmental protection regulations for animal manure storage have increased economic incentives for biogas, but the technical and economical barriers involved are still large. In order to overcome some of these technical problems, the Government continues to fund research and grants to encourage their further development. The implementation of the Biomass Agreement of 1993 means that the use of biomass for energy purposes will be increased from 50 PJ[77] to some 75 PJ a year before the end of 2000. Biomass was expected to comprise almost 10 per cent of the total consumption of fuel in the year 2000. The Agreement was revised in 1997 to extend the time limit for implementation. The main part of the exploitation of biomass has taken place in plants which only produce heat, but the objective of the development in recent years has been to increase the use of biomass in power-producing plants. This has partly been achieved by increasing the use of straw and chips in power plants, partly through the conversion of waste heating installations to power production, and partly by the development of combined heat and power technologies for smaller district heating plants. According to the new agreement, the target that 1.5 million tonnes biomass is to be used annually is to be met by the end of 2005. The parties included in the agreement will secure the economic basis for establishing two to three big biomass plants by the end of 2003. In order to cut costs as much as possible, when securing construction of subsequent plants it is aimed to issue calls for tenders. **6.339**

The Government has taken other initiatives to promote the use of renewable energy. These are dealt with above under sections E and F, along with related matters such as small electricity producers, the use of combined heat and power production, and district heating. On the legal front there have also been some developments. The need for statutory protection of wind access was demonstrated by the increasing number of wind turbines. Consequently, the Government adopted new legislation which introduced a kind of licensing system, so that approval **6.340**

[77] PJ = Petajoule. 1 million tonnes oil equivalents = 41,4868 PJ.

from the Ministry for Environment and Energy must be obtained prior to the construction of a wind turbine.

(3) Wind

6.341 The development of wind energy started in the 1890s. With no other natural energy sources (no waterfalls for hydropower, no coal, no known oil and gas resources, etc) it was natural that Denmark wanted to implement wind technology as a basis for electrification. The shortage of imported fossil fuels during World Wars I and II and the oil embargoes of 1973 and 1979 provided further powerful incentives for using wind energy for electricity production. However, it was environmental concerns that set the stage for the present era of wind power. Denmark has some of the highest per capita carbon dioxide emissions in the world, and the prospect of climate change is the main reason for the present focus on wind energy use.

6.342 Total electricity production from wind turbines in 1997 amounted to 1,932 GWh (384 GWh from utility-owned turbines and 1,548 GWh from privately owned turbines). This equals 6 per cent of total electricity consumption in Denmark. At the end of 1998 the contribution of renewable energy to the total gross energy consumption was calculated at close to 10 per cent.[78] According to the Danish Association of Energy Utilities, 4,784 turbines with a capacity of 1,129 MW were connected to the grid at the end of 1997.[79] Different groups own wind turbines: private individuals, private co-operatives, and electricity utilities. In addition, wind turbines are owned by a few private industrial enterprises and municipalities. In 1996 the Danish Government's new Plan of Action—*Energy 21*—was published, and an important issue is that the Government set a national target for reducing carbon dioxide emissions in the atmosphere by 20 per cent from their 1988 levels before 2005. In the longer term, Denmark is willing to accept the reduction targets that follow from the Kyoto Protocol and strives to reduce its carbon dioxide emissions to half their 1990 levels by 2030.

6.343 In order to provide individual households outside areas with district heating and natural gas supplies with better opportunities to contribute to the use of cleaner energy, the Government has supported the development of small wind turbines (household turbines) producing electricity for heat and power. The small wind turbines are seen as a supplement to the general development of wind power.

The regulatory framework for wind energy

6.344 From the very first policies in the late 1970s different forms of direct subsidies and regulatory incentives have been implemented to develop the construction of wind turbines.

[78] *Energy Statistics 1998*, Danish Energy Agency: Total energy consumption 854,760 TJ and renewable energy 77,477 TJ.

[79] *Wind Power in Denmark—Technology, Policies and Results*, Danish Energy Agency, 1998, 5.

The Government has entered into several political agreements and agreements with the electric utilities on the further expansion of wind energy. Thus in 1985 an agreement was reached between the Government and the Danish electricity utilities, committing the utilities to installing 100 MW of wind turbines over a five-year period. This agreement was fully implemented by the end of 1992. A second 100 MW agreement between Government and utilities, entered into in 1990, was finally implemented in 1996. According to an Executive Order from the Government, a third utility phase of an additional 200 MW was to be installed by 2000. These three phases focused primarily on land-based wind turbines, but two offshore MW demonstration wind farms (Vindeby and Tunø Knob) are also the result of the agreements between the Government and the utilities. On 29 September 1997, a new agreement was entered into with the Danish utilities to develop 750 MW more offshore wind power by the year 2008. This is expected to be produced at five wind farms, which together will produce 8 per cent of Denmark's consumption of electricity (see F(5) above). **6.345**

Secondly, the Act on the Use of Renewable Energy was amended in 1990 to include a new system of approvals to support the further development of wind power.[80] The Danish approval scheme for wind turbines was established to fulfil a common desire expressed by wind-turbine manufacturers, owners, and authorities for a coherent set of rules for approval of turbines installed in Denmark. An approval is partly based on the type of the turbine and partly on a certified quality system which, as a minimum, describes the production and installation of the turbine. Today all manufacturers have an ISO 9000 quality system. **6.346**

A set of rules has been developed and adopted in *Teknisk Grundlag for Typegodkendelse og Certificering af Vindmøller i Danmark* (Technical Criteria for Type Approval and Certification of Wind Turbines in Denmark). In the future the recommendations are to be replaced by IEC or CENELEC standards, and the technical criteria are to be harmonized on a European level. **6.347**

The Danish public research and development institution, Riso, is authorized by the Danish Energy Agency to issue approvals or type-approvals for wind turbines, including the tests and measurements required for the approvals. Today, the market for these services has been liberalized, and private enterprises can be authorized to perform type-approvals, certifications, and tests and measurements. This market is open to international competition and several foreign enterprises are active.[81] The new Electricity Supply Act 1999 includes rules on the establishment of off-shore wind power plants in sections 13–18. Utilizing energy from water **6.348**

[80] See Act No 302 of 16 May 1990 section 10a and Order No 270 of 2 May 1991 on Type Approval and Certification of Wind Turbines.

[81] For a description of the different type of approvals see *Wind Power in Denmark—Technology, Policies and Results*, Danish Energy Agency, 1998.

and wind off-shore is thus subject to a new licence system based on tendering procedure.

6.349 Finally the Government has demanded that municipalities integrate plans for future wind turbine siting into local zoning plans to ensure that an adequate number of new sites for wind turbines can be found to reach the target of 1,500 MW installed by the year 2005. Plans were finalized in many municipalities by 1 July 1995, but the planning procedure has continued to ensure that all municipalities comply. Spatial planning establishes a framework for siting wind turbines on open land, and balances the interest of wind energy against other interests, including the way in which existing urban features and landscapes can best be protected. Previously, the installation of land-based wind turbines required no specific environmental assessment. The balancing of the interests of wind-energy use against other interests in open land was usually contained in the legislation on each area. Today, environmental assessments are more often required for wind farms and clusters of wind turbines.

Financial incentives for developing wind energy

6.350 In 1979, the Government introduced a renewable energy programme that included installation and reduction subsidies. An installation subsidy of 30 per cent of total project costs was granted to wind turbines. As the industry matured and wind turbine prices started to decrease, the installation subsidy was gradually reduced until it was finally abolished in 1989. A total of 2,567 turbines received installation subsidies of DKK 275.72 million in current prices between 1979 and 1989.[82]

6.351 Direct production subsidies have continued to be granted in different versions over the years. Prior to the energy reform of 1999, a production subsidy of DKK 0.27/KWh was granted to private wind-turbine owners. There were limitations on the wind-farm developments to which the above incentives apply. Power utilities received DKK 0.10/KWh in subsidy as reimbursement of the general carbon dioxide tax on electricity. Also in this respect certain limitations applied. Favourable taxation schemes have likewise been used to stimulate private wind turbine installations. These taxation schemes have changed over time. Today, income from wind turbines is taxed by and large like other income.

6.352 The Danish Government has sponsored several research and development programmes on wind energy over the years. Today, Government-sponsored research and development on wind energy comprises two programmes: the Energy Research Programme (EEP) and the Renewable Energy Development Programme (UVE). As part of the latter, the Danish Energy Agency partly finances the Test Station for Wind Turbines at Risø National Laboratory.

[82] *Wind Power in Denmark—Technology, Policies and Results*, Danish Energy Agency, 1998.

Payment for wind-generated electricity

The electric utilities are obliged to receive and pay for wind-generated electricity from private producers; different agreements have existed over the years. Since 1993 the payment for wind-generated electricity has been related to the utilities' production and distribution costs. However the rules of price settlement were changed by Act No 378, 2 June 1999, amendments to the Act on Utilisation of Renewable Energy Sources on a temporary scheme which implies that the subsidy will be financed through the electricity prices. Power utilities are obliged to pay wind-turbine owners a KWh rate of 85 per cent of the sales price to ordinary consumers with annual electricity consumption of 20.000 kWh exclusive of charges. In addition, a surcharge of DKK 0.27 per kWh shall be granted. Wind energy plants owned by electricity companies receive a surcharge of only DKK 0.10 per kWh. **6.353**

H. Environmental Issues

Environmental and energy policies have become closely interrelated and the emphasis on the strain placed on the environment has resulted in a number of initiatives to save and use energy more efficiently, to replace the polluting forms of energy and increase the development of alternative energy resources, and to reduce emissions. **6.354**

Denmark has been one of the strongest voices urging the need for industrialized countries to strengthen commitments and agree on substantial reductions of emissions of carbon dioxide and other greenhouse gases. In 1990, the Danish Government took up the challenge by deciding to reduce emissions of carbon dioxide from the energy and transport sectors by 20 per cent in 2005 compared to 1988. Apart from this national reduction target, Denmark also committed itself to stabilizing emissions of greenhouse gases at the 1990 level by the year 2000 within the framework of the Climate Convention. Denmark ratified the Climate Convention on 21 December 1993 and signed the Kyoto Protocol on 1 May 1998. Moreover, as a contribution to the overall stabilization of carbon dioxide emissions from European Union countries by the year 2000, Denmark is also committed to achieving a 5 per cent reduction by 2000 as compared to the 1990 level. **6.355**

Some environmental issues were touched upon under the various sections above, but the focus here is on more general issues such as energy tax systems, subsidies, reduction of emissions, and energy-saving initiatives. However, considerations of space prevent a detailed description of the wide range of programmes and legislation that Denmark has adopted in order to support sustainable development of the energy sector. Consequently this section can only present a kaleidoscope picture of the relevant area. **6.356**

(1) Energy Taxes

6.357 Energy is heavily taxed in Denmark, although the history of energy taxes is no more than twenty years old. It is a complicated system as the regulation is frequently changed and reimbursement takes place according to different support schemes. It would be beyond the scope of this book to give a detailed description of the regimes for energy taxes, and consequently only a brief outline is given to indicate the structure.

6.358 The first energy taxes were introduced on electricity and light and heavy fuel oil in 1978, to be followed by taxes on coal in 1982, and on natural gas in 1996. The introduction of this tax system was primarily intended to create an incentive for energy savings as well as to provide guidance on choices to favour more environmentally friendly fuel sources and ensuring connection to collective energy systems.

6.359 Following the 1990 energy plan, *Energy 2000*, a packet of new Acts was approved, introducing a carbon dioxide tax and a number of subsidy schemes and recycling some of the revenue for various energy-saving measures: see Act on a Carbon Dioxide Tax on certain Energy Products, Act on Change of Tax on certain Oil Products, Act on Tax on Coal, Lignite, and Coke etc, Act on Tax on Electricity and Act on Tax on Natural Gas, of 21 December 1991. The Act implementing a carbon dioxide tax on oil, coal, and gas, reflecting growing concern about global environmental problems. The tax is paid by households and the public sector, while industry and the commercial sector were originally entitled to a 50 per cent or more refund. This Act entered into force on 15 May 1992 for households and the public sector, and on 1 January 1993 for industry and the commercial sector.

6.360 A general tax reform phased in during the period 1994–98 has the aim of introducing a gradual shift of the weight of the tax system away from taxing earned income towards taxing the consumption of scarce resources and pressure on the environment. The tax reform involves a gradual increase of green taxes, primarily in the household sector, and the main increase in energy taxes was for coal and electricity. The tax reform's increases in green taxes do not apply to energy use by enterprises, except energy used for space heating.

6.361 The Danish energy tax has also been revised so as to improve energy efficiency in industry. The legislation which entered into force in January 1996 introduced different carbon tax rates in the industry for room heating, heavy processes, and light processes. The tax rates were gradually increased from 1996 to 2000. All revenue raised by the tax will be recycled to the industry through extended possibilities for investment grants and through a reduction of the social security contribution paid by the employers. A number of energy-intensive companies will receive a reimbursement, provided they agree to implement energy efficiency measures under agreements negotiated between the individual companies and the Energy Agency. If the companies do not fulfil the agreements, reimbursements already paid will have to be returned and the tax will be imposed in full. Together, the energy and the carbon tax on room heating will gradually be increased to the same level as for households. The rates for light and heavy processes are somewhat lower. A sulphur dioxide tax has also been introduced.[83]

Total electricity taxation amounts to around 65 per cent of the total price for a household consumer, and the taxes consist of five elements: 1) an energy tax; 2) a carbon dioxide tax; 3) VAT; 4) a tax related to sulphur dioxide emissions; and 5) an energy conservation tax. Electricity tax is paid by the end-user; fuel used for electricity generation is not taxed. On the other hand, fuel for heat generation is taxed, and consequently there has to be a split between fuels for electricity and fuels for heat in CHP stations. The rate of the energy tax in 1998 was 0.46 DKK per KWh. The tax is paid by all consumers, but for VAT-registered consumers the entire tax is reimbursed for electricity for processing and 70 per cent of the tax for electricity for heat purposes until 1998. **6.362**

The carbon dioxide tax is based on externality costs of 100 DKK per tonne of gas. It should be noted that this cost element is also paid by end-users and does not differ with the source of electricity generation. The rate is 0.10 DKK per KWh, paid by all consumers. However, a share is reimbursed for VAT-registered consumers, the share depending on the type of end-use and on whether a negotiated agreement has been made on energy conservation measures. Also, this reimbursement has been declining. **6.363**

The rate of VAT is 25 per cent, and is paid by all consumers. However, for VAT-registered consumers the entire tax is reimbursed. With respect to tax related to sulphur dioxide emissions the rate was increased from 0.09 to 0.13 DKK per KWh in the year 2000. The payment of an energy conservation tax amounts to 0.06 DKK/KWh. **6.364**

A tax on natural gas was introduced in 1996 of DKK 0.01 per cubic metre, and natural gas also became liable to the carbon dioxide tax. The tax on natural gas increased considerably from 1998. As of January 2000, the tax amounted to DKK 1.60 per cubic metre. It is intended to raise the rate to match the tax on oil. The difference in tax level does not affect consumers, only the earnings of the utilities. **6.365**

[83] Consolidated Act No 887 of 3 Oct 1996 on Natural Gas Charges as amended by Act No 443 of 10 June 1997 and Act No 957 of 20 Dec 1999; Consolidated Act No 689 of 17 Sep 1998 on Electricity Charges; Consolidated Act No 701 of 28 Sep 1998 on Energy Charges on Certain Oil Products; Consolidated Act No 702 of 28 Sep 1998 on Coal Charges; and Consolidated Act No 643 of 27 Aug 1998 on Carbon Dioxide Charges of Certain Energy Products.

(2) Subsidies

6.366 Since 1981 Government subsidies have been granted for renewable energy at an almost constant level of about US$ 21.4 million per year. About 40 per cent of these have been given as general subsidies covering up to 30 per cent of investment cost for the purchase of equipment approved by one of the test stations for renewable energy (test stations for wind, solar energy, biomass, and heat pumps). Subsidies have now been eliminated completely or partially (eg subsidies for biomass burners for district heating and wind energy have been reduced from 30 per cent to 0 per cent) following the successful achievement of market penetration.

6.367 Funds have been granted for pilot or demonstration projects, and used to bring several technologies to market maturity, starting with wind farms, continuing with large district heating stations for wood and straw, and large biogas plants. The focus is now on biomass-based co-generation and gasification, and the development of new technologies in renewable energy, among others wave energy and offshore wind turbines.

6.368 Conversion of coal-fired district heating plants to combined heat and power plants based on natural gas, waste, or biomass, and the use of biomass in areas not supplied by natural gas, large existing combined heat and power plants, or heat from waste incineration has also been encouraged.[84] Subsidies of up to 50 per cent of investment can be obtained, but typical grants are in the range of 15 per cent to 25 per cent of investment. Subsidies amount to some US$ 7.1 million annually. This subsidy scheme also enables subsidies to be granted for service pipes, both in existing biomass-based CHP districts and district heating networks planning to convert to biomass-based CHP and in connection with completely new biomass-based CHP supply networks.

6.369 The Act on State Subsidies for Conversion of Older Dwellings to CHP of 3 January 1992 grants subsidies for installation of water-borne central heating in dwellings erected before 1950, motivated by connection to CHP-supplied district heating networks (mainly in the centres of the large cities), totalling up to US$ 214 million over ten years. The estimated impact is the connection of around 65,000 dwellings. Apart from the carbon dioxide and energy savings obtained by changing to CHP-derived heat, conversion also contributes to lower sulphur and nitrogen oxide emission levels in the cities.

6.370 Another initiative is to have existing buildings with electric heating converted to district or natural gas heating. This conversion will promote electricity savings and better utilization of the district heating and natural gas networks. Conversion is

[84] Act No 3 of 3 Jan 1992 on State Subsidies for the Promotion of CHP Plants and Exploitation of Biomass Fuels.

advantageous both from a general socio-economic point of view and environmentally. Conversion from electric heating to district or natural gas heating requires substantial investment in the buildings in question for installation of a central heating system. To overcome this barrier to conversion, a State subsidy system has been established. Electrically heated buildings for use in industry and trade can receive subsidies for conversion to central heating by means of the general subsidy scheme for energy savings in industry. In 1995, the Act on State Subsidies for Conversion of Electrically Heated Buildings was passed, which enables subsidies to be given for the installation of central heating in electrically heated dwellings and public buildings in areas not presently supplied with district heating or natural gas. The immediate substitute will be oil heating, but additional subsidies may be given to convert to biomass heating, etc. This grant scheme for supporting conversion from electrical heating to central heating (especially in combination with renewable energy) amounts to US$ 8.6 million annually.

A subsidy scheme was established in 1997 for the installation of district or natural gas heating in electrically heated dwellings and public buildings. The subsidy is managed by a committee composed of representatives of consumers, interest groups, utility companies, and the Government: the Electricity Savings Fund. Members are appointed by the Minister for Environment and Energy. The fund is also charged with granting subsidies to promote energy efficiency in electrical appliances in dwellings and public institutions. US$ 7.1 million was set aside for the scheme in 1997. Since 1998, the scheme is financed by a fixed amount of US$ 0.0086 per KWh sold. The potential for conversion of electrically heated buildings is estimated to be about 50,000 buildings in areas supplied with district heating or natural gas and about 25,000 buildings in areas not supplied by these sources. **6.371**

As an element of the Carbon Dioxide Acts, a subsidy was granted for CHP plants based on natural gas or renewable energy. The subsidy is to compensate for the carbon dioxide tax levied on the consumer's electricity price, rather than on the main fuel (coal) used for electricity production. An additional subsidy could be obtained for electricity produced by wind turbines or from biomass. **6.372**

(3) Reduction of Emissions

The environmental effects of energy supply and use have been a growing concern in Denmark and have become a more integral part of Danish energy policies. In May 1984, the Government passed an Act for Reduction of Emissions of Sulphur Oxides, aiming at a reduction of 50 per cent by 1995. For power plants, the requirement calls for a gradual reduction of 42 per cent from the 1980 level of sulphur oxide emission by 1995. In 1989 Parliament adopted new legislation for a further 20 per cent reduction of sulphur emissions by 2005. The Act includes **6.373** restrictions of nitrogen oxide emissions, aiming at a 50 per cent reduction by 2005, compared to 1980.

6.374 Every year the quotas are announced for the following eight years, those for the first four years being final and those for the subsequent four years being preliminary. The quotas have continuously been tightened, and are set on the basis of negotiations between the Energy Agency, the Agency for Environmental Protection, the Association of Counties, the municipality of Copenhagen, and the electric utilities.

6.375 The Act has now been replaced by a ministerial order issued pursuant to the general Act on Environmental Protection, but the principle of setting annual quotas for the emission level is still the same.[85]

6.376 Further reduction of the environmental impact caused by electricity production is also obtained through the replacement of old, inefficient, and heavily polluting units, introduction of flue-gas cleaning, the building of wind turbines and decentralized CHP plants, and electricity conservation, etc.

6.377 Environmental concerns about open-air straw burning and the disposal of solid and animal wastes have been important reasons behind their increased use as energy resources.

(4) Energy Savings and Conservation

6.378 As a part of the political Agreement of 3 March 1999 between the Danish Government and the major opposition parties on a legislative reform of the electricity sector, the Government committed itself to draft new energy-saving legislation before the end of 1999 with a view to ensuring more coherent prioritization of efforts to achieve the greatest possible environmental benefits. In accordance with the Agreement, any profit from the payments received from power stations for exceeding carbon dioxide quotas for electricity production must be used for energy-saving purposes.

6.379 Subsequent to the adoption of the new Electricity Supply Act the actors have better-defined roles in relation to savings by virtue of the clearer distinction between monopoly services in grid companies and commercial services in supply obligation and trading companies. The purpose is to establish a framework that will ensure a clear division of tasks and prioritization between the various public energy-saving activities and the best possible utilization of local and popular engagement in these activities.

[85] Order No 885 of 18 Dec 1991 on Limitation of Emissions of Sulphur Oxides and Nitrogen Oxides from Power Plants, as amended by Order No 321 of 4 June 1998, issued pursuant to the Act on Environmental Protection (No 358 of 6 June 1991, cf Consolidated Act No 698 of 22 Sep 1998 as amended).

As part of the process, the Energy Agency published a discussion paper in October 1999 on its preliminary proposals for issues to be included in the new legislation, and a draft bill was published for comments on 18 January 2000. An Act on Encouragement of Saving in Energy Consumption was passed on 26 May 2000 as Act No 450 of 31 May 2000 and came into force 1 July 2000. 6.380

The Act lays down general principles for the way in which energy saving action is to be prioritized, including creating the possibility of obtaining a broad, secure data basis concerning energy consumption, etc. The Act introduces a number of new measures into the area of energy savings and the existing measures are further developed. There will be a multi-pronged effort which aims broadly at the different forms of energy consumption (electricity, district heating, natural gas, oil, etc) and a number of different sectors which consume energy: households, public institutions, business enterprises, and transport. The measures are combined into a holistic view in order to deal with the different factors of importance for energy consumption, including technical (technological development, design, etc) and domestic factors (making energy consumption visible, influencing consumers' behaviour). In this field, public authorities will show the way by means of demonstration projects. 6.381

Labelling and auditing

The Danish Parliament adopted an Act empowering the Minister for Environment and Energy to set efficiency standards for electrical appliances and other equipment system, for informing consumers of the electricity consumption of various appliances, and for facilitating easy comparisons between competing products. Denmark has thus developed an extensive scheme for energy labelling of appliances in addition to implementing the EC Directives for efficiency standards for refrigerators and freezers, adopted in 1996.[86] 6.382

For manufacturing companies and the public and private service sectors, it is foreseen that standards will be introduced not only for refrigerators and freezers, washing machines, and dishwashers, but also office equipment, lighting, electric motors, process ventilation, pumps, boilers, and technical insulation. 6.383

As part of *Energy 21*, new legislation was introduced aiming at promoting energy and water savings in buildings. This requires that all buildings from 1997 onwards must be energy labelled and that owners draw up an energy plan. Modernized consultancy services regarding building energy plans and energy conservation are supporting these efforts. 6.384

Since 1981, a scheme for auditing existing buildings has been in force, involving the identification of measures with less than eight to ten years' simple pay-back 6.385

[86] Order No 1067 of 18 Dec 1997 and Order No 1014 of 28 May 1994.

time (in consumer prices). The audits are offered by State-authorized energy consultants. Following the implementation of all measures identified, an energy certificate is issued. In the period 1981–84 heating inspection was combined with a grant scheme. In the first year of the scheme, a heating inspection was a precondition for a Government subsidy for heat-saving measures. Thereafter, heating inspection was a subsidized option, and in the last period of the grant scheme heating inspections received 80–100 per cent subsidies. Since 1985, the provision of a heating inspection report or an energy certificate has been mandatory when a building changes hands (although no sanctions were specified). For small buildings of less than 1,500 square metres energy labelling when the building is sold became mandatory from 1997. The label makes it easier for potential buyers to compare buildings and to evaluate their energy consumption.

6.386 As proposed in *Energy 21*, a new subsidy scheme and an Electricity Saving Fund[87] were established in 1997 with the aim of granting subsidies for the development and implementation of energy-efficient appliances and products, especially in dwellings and the public sector. Subsidies are also given to convert electrical heating in dwellings to central heating based on natural gas or district heating. Subsidies amounted to US$ 6.4 million per year and have now been granted also for marketing and procurement of energy-efficient products. The Fund is administered by an independent board.

Building Regulations

6.387 The regulation of new buildings has been tightened in several steps. The Building Regulations of 1977 introduced stricter insulation requirements from 1979. In 1985, the Regulations for small buildings were modified to allow flexible solutions within a limit for heating and ventilation (in terms of maximum net heating requirement per square metre, among other things the intention being to encourage increased use of passive solar concepts). As decided in the previous energy action plan *Energy 2000*, a new Code was introduced, which will cut an additional 25 per cent of net heating demand, reducing it to about 70 KWh per square metres per year.

6.388 The Code also limits electricity consumption for ventilation and will enforce low-temperature heating systems in order to increase the efficiency of various heat-supply systems, such as district heating systems, condensing boilers, solar energy, and heat pumps. The new Code entered into force in May 1995. A planned further reduction to halve the present level, to 45 KWh per square metre, is scheduled to enter into force around the year 2005. Development work by building companies and research institutions to this end is being pursued. Buildings respecting this limit through combined exploitation of passive solar techniques, insulation, and coated glazing are already being built.

[87] Act No 1209 of 27 Dec 1996.

Other initiatives

Another initiative is aimed at getting central and local Government authorities to pursue a more energy-conscious buying policy, especially with respect to electrical equipment and appliances. Information on energy consumption of the best products on the market is distributed to the public purchasers. **6.389**

The Government has, moreover, improved incentives to implement energy conservation in public buildings. Among other things, this has been achieved by ensuring that a proportion of money saved on the energy bill can be used for other purposes. **6.390**

Since 1992, energy management and annual reporting on energy consumption have been mandatory in every building used by the State (central administration and State institutions, defence, and State-owned entities such as the railways). Local energy managers must be appointed in every institution. A special consultancy service for energy audits and assistance, computer programs, etc are offered to managers. Co-ordinated purchases of office equipment of high energy standards are encouraged. **6.391**

An information campaign targeted at owners, lessees, and users of luxury holiday homes in the tourist sector has been launched to ensure that consideration is paid to energy consumption in connection with the installation and use of installations with a high energy consumption (jacuzzis, swimming pools, solaria, etc). **6.392**

The Danish power distribution companies have established extensive information and consultancy schemes, recognized as a related activity by the regulatory authorities. Most companies are involved in local information activities directed towards consumers and educational institutions and offer a certain basic package of consultancy on electricity savings free of charge. Other initiatives include arrangements with stores and electricians to supply low-energy light bulbs to consumers funded via the electricity bill, schemes for distributing low-energy bulbs to all their customers free of charge, or for buying back old, inefficient appliances when new, efficient ones are sold. A large project for determining methods to be used for implementing integrated resource planning (least-cost planning) has been carried out by the sector, in the framework of the EU's SAVE Programme. **6.393**

A campaign run by some power companies for replacement of electrical appliances (particularly refrigerators, freezers, and low-energy lighting) will be expanded into longer or permanent schemes and campaigns covering consumers throughout the country. The schemes can also be expanded to cover other types of appliances. Danish power companies have carried out a successful country-wide replacement campaign for freezers. Possibly more country-wide campaigns will be carried out in the future for other types of appliances. **6.394**

6.395 Individual metering of the electricity, district heating, gas, and water resources used in buildings has become mandatory in new buildings from 1996 and in existing buildings from 1997, and informative electricity bills for households and for customers in the public and private service sectors have also been introduced.

I. Conclusion

6.396 At the dawn of the new millennium, the Danish energy sector is experiencing major changes. Danish energy policy has in its short life seen several major changes of direction. However, the prospects for the energy sector on the threshold of the twenty-first century are more turbulent than ever, and it is beyond doubt that the coming years will bring fundamental innovations in the way in which energy is bought, sold, produced, transported, and regulated at the local, regional, and global levels.

6.397 As indicated, Government intervention in the Danish energy industry is a relatively recent phenomenon. The oil crises of the 1970s were the milestone for the new political and regulatory era. During the economic growth in the late 1950s and 1960s, Denmark had become heavily dependent on imported oil in order to meet its primary energy requirements, and the massive increases in oil prices and the oil embargoes in 1973 and 1979 had a serious effect on Danish society. It became evident that the energy sector could not be left to free market forces. Since then Denmark has developed a tradition of implementing vigorous energy policies with broad political support and involving a broad range of actors: energy companies, industry, associations, municipalities, research institutions, and consumers. The result was that one of the most distinctive features of energy supply in the decade between the mid-1970s and the mid-1980s became the high levels of public intervention, influence, and control. While the 1970s was a decade of development, when the political and legal frameworks for the energy sector were outlined, the 1980s can be characterized by the implementation of these initiatives.

6.398 In the late 1980s and early 1990s major economic investment has been made in an energy infrastructure. Energy planning since then has therefore involved adjustments and adaptations to current developments rather than major comprehensive project decisions. Gradually, the focus has shifted from supply security to wider environmental considerations, notably the goal of achieving long-term sustainable development on the national as well as the global level. Environmental and energy policies have thus become more closely interrelated and the emphasis on the strain placed on the environment has resulted in a number of initiatives, focusing especially on reducing the requirements for resources through improvement of energy intensity and the impact on the environment from the energy sector by enhanced use of renewable energy.

At the same time another shift of perspective has been demonstrated in energy policy, influenced by the new wave of deregulation, privatization, liberalization, and globalization. To Denmark, the development within the European Union of integrating energy markets still has a great impact on developments. It brought a need for a new foundation of energy policy to ensure that overall environmental objectives can be maintained under the new market conditions. In 1999, the Danish Parliament adopted a legislative reform for the electricity sector which includes a new Electricity Act, changes to the Act on Utilization of Renewable Energy, and a new Act which introduces a framework for the reduction of carbon dioxide emissions. In the summer of 2000 a second part of the energy reform was implemented by the adoption of a new Natural Gas Act, an Act on Energy Savings, and amendments to the Heat Supply Act. The purpose of these initiatives is to open the energy markets while ensuring that the environment is also safeguarded in the coming liberalized electricity and gas markets, that renewable energy is developed, and that Denmark can fulfil its international environmental commitments. **6.399**

There is no reason to believe that public intervention in the Danish energy sector is declining, and no significant deregulation trends can be observed. Likewise, privatization measures have had a marginal impact on the energy sector in Denmark. In Denmark, it is more to the point to talk about reregulatory moves in energy law, because public involvement has not been reduced by those recent initiatives. On the contrary, it is tempting to say that regulation is increasing and becoming even stricter than before, and that executive power is centralized rather than decentralized. For example, the Electricity Supply Act of 1976 has eighteen articles, whereas the Act of 1999 has 107! Likewise, the current Natural Gas Act has only nine articles, whereas the new draft bill includes sixty-four. To this must be added the high number of reservations and authorities to issue more detailed rules in secondary legislation. **6.400**

Climate is a key issue in Denmark. The Climate Convention was ratified on 21 December 1993 and the Kyoto Protocol signed on 1 May 1998, and it is evident that Denmark takes its international commitments very seriously. The Danish Government has been one of the strongest voices urging industrialized countries to strengthen commitments and to agree substantial reductions of emissions of carbon dioxide and other greenhouse gases. Denmark took the lead at a very early stage and showed that it is possible to reduce both energy consumption and the environmental impact of the energy system. It has pioneered the use of renewable energy, using energy efficiently, and the promotion of CHP systems. **6.401**

As early as 1990, the Danish Government took up the climate challenge by deciding to reduce emissions of carbon dioxide from the energy and transport sectors by 20 per cent in 2005 compared to 1988. Denmark has also committed itself to stabilizing emissions of greenhouse gases at the 1990 level by the year 2000. **6.402**

Denmark has received public criticism of the solitary course taken with respect to, say, making commitments to reduce carbon dioxide emissions. However, time has shown that small countries like Denmark can lead the way in order to create the basis for wider acceptance and willingness to implement measures and make commitments to avoid or at least reduce vulnerability to climate change.

6.403 In conclusion, we are not faced with a stable and static field of law! On the contrary, energy law is constantly marked by dramatic changes. Although most regulation of energy supply dates back no more than twenty-five years, there have been several shifts of political course, which have all had major legal implications. There is no reason to believe that this situation will change in the third millennium. This is one of the exciting challenges for energy law!

Bibliography

Policy documents and statistics

Report on Nature and the Environment 1999, Ministry for Environment and Energy

Energy in Denmark 1998, Danish Energy Agency

Danish Oil and Gas Production 1998, Energy Agency

Wind Power in Denmark—Technology, Policies and Results, Danish Energy Agency, 1998

Combined Heat and Power in Denmark, Danish Energy Agency, 1998

Energy Statistics 1997 and 1998, Energy Agency

Electricity Supply in Denmark 1996 and 1997, Statistics, Association of Danish Electric Utilities

Energy 21, Action Plan for Energy 1996, Danish Ministry for Environment and Energy, April 1996

Denmark's Energy Futures, Danish Energy Agency, Copenhagen, 1996

Energy 2000, A Plan of Action for Sustainable Development, Danish Ministry of Energy, April 1990

Action Plan on Environment and Development, Danish Government, 1988

District Heating in Denmark, Danish Ministry of Energy, 1987

Energiplan 81, Energiministeriet, november 1981. (Energy Plan 1981, Danish Ministry of Energy, November 1981)

Dansk energipolitik, 1976, Handelsministeriet, maj 1976. (Danish Energy Policy, 1976, Ministry of Trade, May 1976)

Dansk Olie og Naturgas (DONG) *Annual Reports*

DONG *Reports to the Danish Parliament*

Energinyt (Energy News) Energy Agency (5 issues per year)

Articles and literature

Dahl, Melchior, Rehof, and Tamm (eds), *Danish Law in a European Perspective,* GadJura, Copenhagen, 1996

Hahn-Pedersen, *A.P. Møller og den danske olie* (*A.P. Møller and Danish Oil*), Albertslund, Schultz Information, 1997

Bent Ole Gram Morgensen, *Elforsyning. Afvejning af hensyn til en sektor på vej mod det indre marked* (*Electricity Supply: Balancing concerns in a sector on its way towards the internal market*) Copenhagen, Jurist og Økonomforbundets Forlag, 1998

Rüdiger, Mogens, *DONG og energien* (*DONG and Energy*) Handelshøjskolens Forlag, Århus, 1998

Rønne, Anita, 'Alternative Approaches to Regulatory Agency Structures and Powers: Eastern and Western Europe', Journal of Energy and Natural Resources Law, February 1997, 41–50

—— 'The Legal Dimension of Sustainable Development with the Emphasis on the Energy Sector', Law and Ecology, Copenhagen, 1994, 54–65

—— 'Re-regulation of Danish Energy Supply', in *Suum Cuique—Legal studies from the University of Copenhagen Law Faculty*, ed Peter Blume, Ditlev Tamm, and Vibeke Vindeløv, Jurist- og Økonomforbundets Forlag, Copenhagen, 1993, 271–82. Also published in Danish in 1991 by same publisher, 308–16

—— Blume, Peter, and Christensen, Peter, 'Retlig regulering—teknik og metode' ('Legal Regulation—Mode and methods') Akademisk Forlag, Holstebro, 1990, 97–114 and 197–248

—— 'Monopoly and Competition in Energy Supply, Denmark', Journal of Energy and Natural Resources Law, London, December 1989 Supplement, 67–77

—— 'Coal and Fuel Choices in Denmark', Journal of Energy and Natural Resources Law, London, 1989, Vol. 7, No 4, 275–85

—— 'Current Development', Journal of Energy and Natural Resources Law, various volumes

—— 'Olie og naturgas: Mellem offentlig ret og privat ret' ('Oil and Natural Gas: Between public and private law') Retsvidenskabeligt Institut B, Yearly Report 1988, 15–27

—— 'Offentlig regulering af olie- og naturgasvirksomheden i Danmark' ('Public Regulation of Oil and Natural Gas Activities in Denmark') MARIUS No 149, 1988, The Nordic Institute of Maritime Law, Oslo

—— and Budtz, Michael, 'The Legal Framework for Exploration for and Production of Oil and Natural Gas in Denmark', Journal of Energy and Natural Resources Law, London, 1985, 153–67, also published in Danish in UfR 1984, Copenhagen, 369–79

Winterton, Jules, and Moys, Elizabeth M. (eds), *Information Sources in Law*, London, 1997

Wistofte, Birgitte, Petersen, Flemming, and Hansen, Harriet M. (eds), *Elektricitetens Aarhundrede: Dansk elforsynings historie* (The Century of Electricity: The history of Danish electricity supply) vol 1 1891–1940, vol 2 1940–92)

Legislation

A Consolidated Act is an official promulgation of the basic Act with the incorporation of subsequent amendments.

General

Act No 254 of 8 June 1983 on Dansk Olie og Naturgas (DONG)

Consolidated Act No 263 of 27 April 1989 on Energy Policy Actions, as amended by Act No 1076 of 20 December 1995

Order No 652 of 23 June 2000 on the Responsibilities of the Energy Agency
Order No 1011 of 9 November 2000 on Amendments to Order on Delegation of Tasks to the Energy Agency
Order No 163 of 26 February 2000 on the Responsibilities of the Energy Supervisory Board

Exploration and production of oil and natural gas

Royal Order No 259 of 7 June 1963 on Danish Sovereignty of the Continental Shelf
Act No 259 of 9 June 1971 on the Continental Shelf, Consolidated Act No 182 of 1 May 1979, as amended by Act No 484 of 12 June 1996, Act No 187 of 12 March 1997, and Act No 1276 of 20 December 2000
Act No 411 of 22 May 1996 on Exclusive Economic Zones
Act No 293 of 10 June 1981 on the Use of the Danish Subsoil
Act No 310 of 17 May 1995 on Amendment of the Act on the Use of the Danish Subsoil
Consolidated Act No 552 of 29 June 1995 on the Use of the Danish Subsoil
Act No 447 of 31 May 2000 on Amendments to certain environmental Acts (implementation of the Aarhus convention)
Order No 169 of 24 February 1997 on certain areas in Denmark that are available for consecutive issuance of licences to explore for and exploit hydrocarbons, see also ECT No C 49/23 of 19 February 1997
Act No 292 of 10 June 1981 on Certain Marine Installations
Act No 175 of 28 April 1982 on Taxation of revenues in connection with Hydrocarbon Production in Denmark, Consolidated Act No 792 of 29 September 1993 with later amendments
Act No 285 of 7 June 1972, see Consolidated Act No 569 of 30 June 1997 on Raw Materials
Act No 476 of 30 June 1993 on the Marine Environment with later amendments
Act No 577 of 29 November 1978 on the Home Rule of Greenland
Act No 335 of 6 June 1991 on Mineral Resources in Greenland, Consolidated Act No 368 of 18 June 1998
Act No 317 of 3 June 1998 on Amendment to the Act on Mineral Raw Material in Greenland, the Act on Protection of the Marine Environment, and the Act on the Continental Shelf (Transfer of the Administration of the Raw Material to Greenland's Home Rule)
Act No 137 of 23 March 1948 on the Home Rule of the Faroe Islands
Order No 1090 of 6 December 2000 on Access to Upstream Networks
Act No 179 of 21 October 1993 on Preliminary Surveys
Act No 31 of 16 March 1998 on Hydrocarbon Activities

Oil transportation

Act No 291 of 10 June 1981 on the Establishment and Use of a Pipeline for Transportation of Oil and Condensate, as amended by Act no 254 of 8 June 1983 and Act No 432 of 10 June 1997
Order No 181 of 30 April 1984 on Payment for Transportation of Oil and Condensate, replaced by Order No 212 of 21 March 2000

Transportation and distribution of natural gas

Act No 294 of 7 June 1972 on Natural Gas Supply
Act No 232 of 8 June 1979 on Construction of a Natural Gas Supply System
Order No 269 of 18 June 1979 on Sole Concession for the Import, Negotiation, Transport, and Storage of Natural Gas
Order No 341 of 4 May 1994 on Amendment of Order on the Sole Concession for the Import, Negotiation, Transport, and Storage of Natural Gas
Consolidated Act No 887 of 3 October 1996 on Natural Gas Charges as amended by Act No 443 of 10 June 1997 and Act No 957 of 20 December 1999
Act No 449 of 31 May 2000 on Natural Gas Supply
Order No 579 of 22 June 2000 on Calculation of the Maximum Price for Natural Gas
Order No 578 of 22 June 2000 on Natural Gas Consumers right of Choosing Supplier
Order No 731 of 31 July 2000 on Refusal of Access to the Natural Gas System due to serious economic and financial problems with contractual take-or-pay obligations
Order No 732 of 31 July 2000 on Dispute Resolution concerning Access to the Natural Gas System

Heat supply

Act No 382 of 13 June 1990 on Heat Supply, with later amendments
Act No 379 of 2 June 1999 on Act on Amendments to the Heat Supply Act
Act No 451 of 31 May on Amendments to the Heat Supply Act
Consolidated Act No 772 of 24 July 2000
Order No 582 of 22 June 2000 on Heat Planning and Appraisal of Projects for Collective Heat Supply Plants
Order No 581 of 22 June 2000 on Connection to Collective Heat Supply Plants

Electricity supply

Act No 332 of 19 June 1974 on Compensation for Damage caused by Nuclear Power
Act No 244 of 12 May 1976 on Safety and Environmental Factors relating to Nuclear Plants
Act No 54 of 25 February 1976 on Electricity Supply, see Consolidated Act No 632 of 1 July 1996 as amended by Act No 189 of 12 March 1997 and Act No 89 of 10 February 1998
Act No 375 of 2 June 1999 on Electricity Supply
Act No 1110 of 29 December 1999 on Amendments to the Act on Electricity Supply
Act No 448 of 31 May 2000 on Amendments to the Act on Electricity Supply
Act No 1277 of 20 December 2000 on Amendments to the Act on Electricity Supply and Act on Subsidies to Electricity Production
Order No 1126 of 29 December 1999 on Enforcement of the Act on Electricity Supply, Act on Amendments to the Act on Electricity Supply and Act on Amendments to the Act on Heat Supply
Act No 376 of 2 June 1999 on Carbon Dioxide Quotas for Electricity Production
Order No 628 of 23 June 2000 on enforcement of Act on Carbon Dioxide Quotas and Amendments to the Act on Electricity Supply

Act No 377 of 2 June 1999 on Amendments to the Act on Subsidies for Electricity Production

Order No 92 of 11 February 1999 on Access to the Electricity Supply Grid System

Order No 814 of 28 August on Amendments to Order on Access to the Electricity Supply Grid System

Consolidated Act No 689 of 17 September 1998 on Electricity Charges

Consolidated Act No 701 of 28 September 1998 on Energy Charges on Certain Oil Products

Consolidated Act No 702 of 28 September 1998 on Coal Charges

Renewable energy

Consolidated Act No 692 of 25 August 1999 on Utilization of Renewable Energy

Act No 378 of 2 June 1999 on Amendments of the Act on the Utilization of Renewable Energy

Order No 270 of 2 May 1991 on Type Approval and Certification of Wind Turbines

Act No 450 of 31 May 2000 on Encouragement of Saving in Energy Consumption

Consolidated Act No 643 of 27 August 1998 on Carbon Dioxide Charges of Certain Energy Products

Consolidated Act No 846 of 17 November 1997 on State Subsidies to Defray the Costs of Carbon Dioxide Charges of Certain Companies with a Considerable Energy Consumption

Consolidated Act No 754 of 28 September 1999 on State Subsidies for Product-Oriented Energy Savings

Act No 92 of 11 February 1999 on Subsidies for Energy Savings etc in Companies

Act No 3 of 3 January 1992 on State Subsidies for the Promotion of CHP Plants and Exploitation of Biomass Fuels

Act No 1209 of 27 December 1996 on the Electricity Saving Fund

Order No 885 of 18 December 1991 on Limitation of Emissions of Sulphur Oxides and Nitrogen Oxides from Power Plants, as amended by Order No 321 of 4 June 1998

Consolidated Act No 698 of 22 September 1998 on Environmental Protection, as amended

Websites

Part I

Climate Change Convention *http://www.unfccc.de*

EU Commission

http://www.europa.eu.int/comm/dgs/internal_market

http://www.europa.eu.int/comm/dgs/energy_transport

http://www.europa.eu.int/comm/dgs/competition

http://www.europa.eu.int/comm/dgs/environment

Energy Charter Secretariat *http://www.encharter.org*

Global Environmental Facility *http://www.gefweb.com*

IAEA *http://www.iaea.org/worldatom*

ICJ *http://www.icj-cij.org*

IMO *http://www.imo.org*
NAFTA *http://www.cec.org*
OECD's Nuclear Energy Agency *http://www.nea.fr* (or the mirror site at *http://www.oecd.nea.org*)
OSPAR *http://www.ospar.org*
UN Economic Commission for Europe *http://www.unece.org*
UN Department of Ocean Affairs and the Law of the Sea (DOLAOS) *http://www.un.org/Depts/los/los_docs.htm#CLCL-Docs*
WTO *http://www.wto.org*

Part II

Denmark

Danish Energy Agency *http://www.ens.dk*
DONG *http://www.dong.dk*
Association of Danish Energy Companies *http://www.danskenergi.dk*
The A.P. Moller Group *http://www.maersk.com*
The Law Faculty, University of Copenhagen *http://www.jur.ku.dk*

France

Ministry of Economy, Finance and Industry *http://www.industrie.gouv.fr*
Commissariat à l'énergie atomique *http://www.cea.fr*
Electricité de France *http://www.edf.fr*
Electricity regulatory commission *http://www.cre.fr*
French environment and energy conservation agency *http://www.ademe.fr*
Gaz du France *http://www.gdf.fr*
General nuclear materials company *http://www.cogema.com*
National agency for radioactive waste management *http://www.andra.fr*
National centre of scientific research *http://www.crns.fr*

Germany

Bundesministerium für Wirtschaft und Technologie *http://www.bmwi.de*
Bundesministerium für Umwelt, Naturschutz und Reaktorsicherheit *http://www.bmu.de*
Bundesministerium für Bildung und Forschung *http://www.bmbf.de*
Bundeskartellamt (federal competition authority) *http://www.bundeskartellamt.de*
Association of German electricity suppliers *http://www.strom.de* (Many links!)
Association of local enterprises *http://www.vku.de*
High-tension grids *http://www.dvg-heidelberg.de*
Bundesverband der deutschen Gas- und Wasserwirtschaft e.V. *http://www.bgw.de*
Ruhrgas *http://www.ruhrgas.de*
Mining and Technology *http://www.rag.de*
Institut für deutsches und europäisches Wirtschafts-, Wettbewerbs- und Energierecht (Freie Universität Berlin) *http://www.fu-berlin.de/iww/*
Institut für Energierecht an der Universität zu Köln *http://www.uni-koeln.de/jur-fak/instenr/*
Institut für Berg- und Energirecht *http://www.ruhr-uni-bochum.de/ibe/*

Italy

The Authority for electricity and gas *http://www.autorita.energia.it*
The Ministry for Industry and Trade *http://www.minindustria.it*
ENEA—The Governmental Agency for New Technologies, Energy and the Environment *http://www.enea.it*

Netherlands

The Dutch Ministry of Economic Affairs *http://www.minez.nl*
The Office for Energy Regulation *http://www.dte.nl*
The Netherlands Competition Authority *http://www.nma-org.nl*
Amsterdam Power Exchange *http://www.apx.nl*

Norway

Ministry of Petroleum and Energy *http://www.oed.dep.no*
The Nordic Power Exchange *http://www.nordpool.no*
Nordic Institute of Maritime Law *http://www.ub.uio.no/ujur/instbib*

Spain

Ministry for Economy *http://www.mineco.es*

United Kingdom

The Department of Trade and Industry *http://www.dti.gov.uk*
UK Offshore Operators Association (UKOOA) *http://www.oilandgas.org.uk*
The CEPMLP Internet Journal *http://www.dundee.ac.uk/cepmlp/journal/*

7

ENERGY LAW IN FRANCE

Fabienne Helvin

A. Introduction

(1) General Remarks

The French conception of energy policy described in this chapter seems to be more comprehensive than that of most European countries, for it encompasses rational use of energy and fiscal instruments. France was first induced to rationalize energy use, efficiency, and conservation after the Second World War because of a temporary energy shortage. These efforts intensified after the oil crisis in 1974. **7.01**

The first Act dealing with energy conservation was passed in 1948, and a new and stronger political impulse was given to energy efficiency and energy savings from 1974 onwards, through new acts and the founding of new public bodies. Taxation has been used to enforce energy policy, deter the use of imported sources of energy, encourage rational use of energy, and increase economic competitiveness of low-emission energies. Thus, tax policy on energy goods and energy production is described in detail in this chapter.

7.02 Another difference lies in the description of electricity generation. Ninety-two per cent of electricity produced in France in 1997 was from wind energy, hydropower, and nuclear energy without emitting greenhouse gas. Therefore nuclear power, hydropower, and wind energy are presented under 'electricity generation'. French law on combined heat and power (CHP), geothermal resources, biofuels, solar energy, and wood-based energy are described as partly or totally used for heat generation and are not included in electricity generation.

(2) *Overview of Energy in France*

7.03 France's total consumption of primary energy amounted to 229.3 million tonnes of oil equivalent (Mtoe) in 1995, after correction for climatic variations, and was approximately equal to that of 1994. Final consumption was also stable at 191.6 Mtoe. In real terms, total consumption increased by 1.7 per cent to 226.3 Mtoe. Although weather conditions were mild in 1995, 1994 was even milder, which explains the slight increase in real energy consumption.

7.04 France is endowed with few fossil fuel resources. Coal output is falling due to the closure of unprofitable mines. Oil and gas production is declining steadily. Although nuclear power is the main domestic energy resource, 85 per cent of the natural uranium needed is imported. Strategic risks have been spread more evenly by diversifying hydrocarbon supplies. The massive conversion from oil to electricity and gas in industry and in the tertiary-residential sector cut back the proportion of petroleum products in final energy consumption from 69 per cent in 1973 to 43 per cent in 1989. As a result, France is now less vulnerable to an oil crisis.

7.05 In 1995, domestic energy production increased by 2 per cent and amounted to 116.2 Mtoe, due to an increase in nuclear power production (+4.8 per cent) which over-compensated for the decrease in hydroelectric production. Nuclear power was the largest component of domestic production at approximately 76 per cent in 1995, ahead of hydropower at 16 per cent. In 1995 there were fifty-four active pressurized reactors, with another four under construction. In 1995 nuclear and hydropower energy production together represented more than 100 Mtoe. France's self-sufficiency rate doubled between 1973 (22.5 per cent) and 1990 (47.8 per cent) and reached 51.4 per cent in 1995.

After correction for climatic variations, 41 per cent of total primary energy consumption was accounted for by oil, which is now predominantly used in transport. Electricity[1] accounts for 37.6 per cent of total final consumption. Electricity intensity (the ratio of demand to gross domestic product) has risen steadily since 1973, at a much faster rate than in the other IEA countries, although in absolute terms it remained well below the IEA average. Electricity consumption reached 401.2 TWh in 1995, and 45.1 per cent of the total final consumption was accounted for the commercial/residential sector, 28 per cent for industry, 25.3 per cent for transport, and 1.6 per cent for agriculture. 7.06

Energy intensity[2] was low compared with IEA averages. Carbon intensity[3] was also low, due to both the low energy intensity and the relatively small share of fossil fuel in total primary energy supply. France is one of the industrialized countries with the lowest carbon intensity, along with Japan. 7.07

Nuclear generation and energy saving represented nearly 100 Mtoe, higher than oil production in Kuwait. Under the current estimate, approximately 35 Mtoe or 17 per cent of total consumption has been saved annually through energy conservation policy measures in force since 1973. Renewable energy sources account for 21.6 per cent of the total primary energy production (9.4 per cent, excluding hydropower). Wood-based energy is widely used in France: in 1994, France accounted for 36.5 per cent of primary wood-based energy produced in Europe (Sweden excluded), according to Eurostat. 7.08

(3) Administrative and Regulatory Framework

Parliament

Parliament controls Government action through votes, debates, question-time sessions, and hearings. A proposed Act of Parliament is voted on by the National Assembly and the Senate, the Prime Minister having the power to override a Senate's negative vote by using the Mixed Committee procedure. Formed by an equal number of Senators and Deputies, the Mixed Committee tries to reach an agreement between the two Assemblies; if the procedure is unsuccessful the Bill is examined again by the National Assembly, whose final vote overrides the Senate's committees. Most Bills introduced into Parliament emanate from the Government and are examined by the *Conseil d'Etat* prior to their introduction. The Parliamentary Office for the Assessment of Scientific and Technological Choices currently oversees governmental energy policy. In 1998, a Senate 7.09

[1] Primary electricity = nuclear power production + hydropower production − imports + exports.

[2] Energy intensity is measured both in total primary energy supply per unit of GDP and per capita and in total final consumption per unit of GDP and per capita (3.8 toe per inhabitant compared with 4.9 for total IEA).

[3] Carbon intensity is defined as CO_2 emissions per unit of GDP and per capita.

commission of inquiry on energy policy issued a report stating that the use of nuclear energy was 'unavoidable' to ensure safety of supply and France's independence. Parliament can also ask the Government to issue surveys and reports, such as the 1996 report on diesel consumption. Five Members of Parliament sit on the Gas and Electricity Superior Council which advises the Government on any major reform project.

7.10 A debate on nuclear energy research takes place every year with the adoption of the Finance Bill, which includes the voting of CEA (*Commissariat à l'énergie atomique*, Atomic Energy Commission) subsidies. Specific debates on nuclear power issues were held in 1981, 1989, and 1993, and Members of Parliament expressed a broad consensus on nuclear energy use. Furthermore, various Acts were passed to define a complete legal framework to regulate nuclear material use, such as an Act passed in 1952 and later codified in the Public Health Code regulating the use of radioactive elements. The responsibility regime defined in the nuclear domain by the Special Responsibility Act 1968[4] is more binding than the one established under French civil law.[5] In 2006 the Parliament will rule on future nuclear waste disposal and, to provide the legislature with the necessary information, research on nuclear waste management was authorized by the Research on Nuclear Waste Management Act. Three options are being studied: transmutation, deep underground disposal sites, and conditioning for long-term storage.

Government

Energy policy

7.11 The President of the Republic is elected for a seven-year term. He 'ensures the regular functioning of public power',[6] appoints the Prime Minister,[7] and may also, for instance, dissolve the National Assembly, launch a referendum, or make appropriate decisions in a major crisis. The Prime Minister implements the President's political guidelines, provided both of them belong to the same political majority.

7.12 The Prime Minister monitors the Government action,[8] while the Government 'determines . . . the National policy'.[9] The Prime Minister has 'the power to regulate', which means that to be put into effect, a decree must be signed by the Prime Minister.

[4] No 68-943 (30.10.1968).

[5] A descendant of Roman law, French civil law is the branch of law that pertains to suits outside of criminal practice, pertaining to the rights and duties of persons in contracts, property, etc. Civil law is traditionally separated from administrative law. There is no exact equivalent to the British notion of 'common law' in French legal tradition.

[6] French Constitution, Art 5.

[7] ibid, Art 8.

[8] ibid, Art 21.

[9] ibid, Art 20.

The Ministry for Industry formulates and implements energy policy, and is vested with powers of supervision over the activities and operations of State-owned energy companies and public bodies. Under the Minister's authority, two directorates and a Council are in charge of policy implementation. The DGEMP (Directorate General for Energy and Raw Materials) is responsible for the policy dealing with monitoring the supply and use of energy and mineral raw materials, for ensuring security of supply for energy and raw materials, managing fossil fuel and mineral resources, promoting international co-operation in energy and mining, and boosting the competitiveness of products and industries in the energy and raw materials sector. It supervises the public bodies dealing with energy and raw materials. **7.13**

The DSIN (French Nuclear Regulatory Directorate) is mainly in charge of studying, defining, and implementing nuclear safety policy. **7.14**

The Gas and Electricity Superior Council was created by the Gas and Electricity Nationalization Act 1946[10] to advise the Government on energy matters. Members of Parliament, civil servants and representatives of local authorities, consumer associations, Chambers of Commerce, and industrial sectors consuming large amounts of electricity all sit on the Council. They advise on Bills and projects for decrees, and may establish working groups to investigate specific questions at the request of the Minister for Industry. The Ministries of Environment, Health, and the Interior can make decisions about energy policy, depending on their field of expertise. **7.15**

In the provinces the Prefects represent the Government and co-ordinate local State services, implementing ministerial policy. The Government appoints a Prefect in each of the 95 *départements*[11] in Metropolitan France (the DOM), and in the 'local territorial authorities'. Each Prefect is appointed by the Government and can be dismissed at will. **7.16**

The twenty-two DRIRE (Regional Directorates for Industry, Research, and Environment) are part of the local State services, cover each of the administrative **7.17**

[10] No 46-628 (8.04.1946).

[11] A *département* is a small part of the national territory created during the French Revolution. There are 22 regions, each composed of several *départements*. The Prefect representing the State in the *département* where the capital of the region sits is also the representative of the State in the region. He is therefore Prefect of both the department and the region. DOM-TOM stands for Overseas Departments and Territories. The Overseas Departments are: Guadeloupe, Martinique, French Guyana, and Réunion; the Overseas Territories are: the Wallis and Futuna Islands, French Polynesia, and New Caledonia. Each DOM is both a region and a department. Each DOM-TOM is governed by special Acts and/or decrees adapting French right to their particular situation. For instance, a new agreement signed in May 1998 by the Government and the New Caledonian main political parties stipulated that energy policy and mining legislation should be modified in the years to come to take into consideration Caledonian customary law. In addition, Saint-Pierre-et-Miquelon and Mayotte are 'territorial local authorities' which have been given a special status but are also considered part of the DOM-TOM.

regions in France, and are responsible for licensing the construction and operation of energy facilities, including some aspects of nuclear licensing. They monitor pollution and audit combustion plants. They report to the Prefect and the Ministries for Industry, the Environment, and Research.

7.18 There are about 36,000 municipalities in France. The municipal council 'governs the municipality's affairs', and is therefore empowered to make strategic decisions. The Mayor is the council majority leader, rules over the council, and prepares and implements council decisions.

7.19 Public accountants keep the State, public institutions', and local authorities' accounts. They are trained and appointed by, and work under the authority of, the Ministry of Finance. They implement public financial management Acts and decrees and comply with financial directives issued by the Ministry of Finance. They certify that financial decisions are made under due process of law. They are personally and financially liable for wrong decisions, for instance neglecting to collect revenue or unduly paying for expenditure. Their accounts are audited by the French Audit Court. For historical reasons, the CEA has no public accountant.

Institutions governing nuclear policy

7.20 The President of the Republic 'is the guarantor of national independence and territorial integrity' (1958 Constitution, Art 5). Hence, he rules over the Nuclear Foreign Policy Council formed in 1976 to decide on policy applied to exporting nuclear technology, equipment, and sensitive nuclear material. The Prime Minister and the Ministers for Industry, Foreign Trade, Foreign Affairs, Research, Defence, Finance, and Energy sit on this Council, along with the CEA Administrator General.

7.21 The Prime Minister supervises CEA activities and presides over four Standing Committees dealing with the nuclear domain.

7.22 The Interdepartmental Committee for nuclear safety adopts or prepares general measures concerning nuclear policy and co-ordinates research programmes undertaken by several ministerial departments. The Committee studies the governmental position on nuclear safety in international negotiations. It co-ordinates the protection of persons and property against hazards or nuisances created by the building, exploitation, and decommissioning of nuclear facilities. It examines radiation protection measures protecting the public and the nuclear facilities' staff, and prepares decisions to be implemented in case of radiological accident and the legislation applied to radioactive and non-radioactive effluents. It is empowered to examine the safety and control of nuclear materials, including artificial radioactive elements and waste. It also studies the means of storage and transformation of natural or artificial radioactive substances. The Ministers of Health, the Interior, Defence, and Industry sit on the Committee. A General Secretariat prepares Committee decisions.

The General Secretariat of National Defence assists the Prime Minister in steering defence policy, including nuclear safety measures in defence facilities. **7.23**

The Interdepartmental Technical Committee for EURATOM studies decisions and directives prepared by Euratom, and ensures their implementation. **7.24**

The Atomic Energy Committee, part of the CEA, is chaired by the Prime Minister and was initially set up to supervise CEA activities and be the Government's standing advisory committee on nuclear energy. The Atomic Energy Committee approves the CEA research programme and the CEA budget. A High Commissioner is appointed by the Government from amongst the Atomic Energy Committee members to advise the CEA on research and development. **7.25**

Furthermore, two major interdepartmental committees have been set up to advise the Government on major decisions. An Interdepartmental Commission for Basic Nuclear Facilities is called on to advise on each application for construction or modification of an INB (*Installations nucléaires de base*, Basic Nuclear Facilities) and on each draft order or Bill. The Prime Minister appoints the Committee chairman, chosen from within the *Conseil d'Etat*, and the Committee's Permanent Secretary. The Deputy Chairman is the CEA High Commissioner. The Prime Minister also appoints the twenty-nine Committee members representing relevant Ministries and public bodies. **7.26**

Application files and inquiry results are compiled by the Permanent Secretary in reports submitted to the Committee. Experts can testify to the Committee if necessary. To advise the Government on minor projects, a Standing Committee has been set up, including the Committee Chairman, Deputy Chairman, Permanent Secretary and nine representatives of several Ministries chosen by the President. **7.27**

The High Council on Nuclear Safety and Information was created in 1973 and reformed in 1987 to include trade union representatives, Members of Parliament, conservationist associations, experts, and Ministry representatives. The Council examines all matters involving nuclear safety and public information, issues guidelines to toughen nuclear safety standards, and submits proposals to the Ministries of Industry and Environment. **7.28**

The Minister for Industry is empowered to supervise nuclear energy production and industrial applications. The DGEMP supervises CEA development activities and studies the technical, international, and legal evolution of the nuclear domain. Under the authority of the Ministries for Industry and for the Environment, the DSIN is empowered to draft technical legislation and orders on nuclear safety and to conduct on-site safety inspections. DSIN relies on the Superior Council of Nuclear Safety and Information and on standing committees of experts which study the technical safety problems involved in the building, starting up, running, and decommissioning of nuclear facilities. **7.29**

7.30 The Ministry for Industry's High Commissioner for Defence[12] advises the Ministry on nuclear material safety, protection, and transport. He rules over the Safety of Nuclear Material Transport Committee which is called on to advise on applications requesting authorization to transport nuclear materials.

7.31 The Ministry for the Environment steers anti-pollution policy, supervises the Water Agencies' activities in the provinces, scrutinizes impact assessment studies compiled before the building of a nuclear facility, and controls classified facilities, which do not include the largest nuclear facilities, or *installations nucléaires de base*. The Ministries of the Environment, Industry, and Research supervise ANDRA (*Agence nationale des déchets radioactifs*, National Agency for Radioactive Waste Management) activities. According to the Classified Facilities Act 1976, the Ministry of the Environment rules over the High Council of Classified Facilities. In regions where nuclear facilities have been built, a nuclear division was created within the DRIRE to participate in the control of nuclear facilities.

The Ministry of Health formulates and implements public health policy, including measures to protect the population against nuclear risks, and supervises OPRI activities.

7.32 The Minister of the Interior's DSC (Directorate for Public Safety) and its local services define emergency plans protecting populations and co-ordinate the measures to be implemented in case of nuclear accident. The DSC local services are under the Prefect's authority.

7.33 The Minister of Transport rules over the Interdepartmental Committee of Hazardous Material Transport. Created in 1941, this Committee meets four times a year and controls transport by road, rail, and canal. Transport of nuclear materials by sea is supervised by the General Directorate of the Navy. In its political programme, the Government pledged to increase the independence of institutions controlling nuclear energy production and has been examining various solutions which might lead to the introduction of a new Act into Parliament.

The judiciary

7.34 The separation of the executive and the judiciary is described in Title VIII of the 1958 Constitution. The Constitutional Council was set up to perform a judicial review of the constitutionality of voted laws prior to the law publication. Such a review can also be performed by administrative and ordinary court systems through the 'exception' procedure.

7.35 The *Cour de Cassation* is the highest court in the ordinary court system and was created in 1790 to unify jurisprudence. The commercial section of the Cour de Cassation and the Court of Appeal of Paris rule on competition complaints.

[12] In France there is one High Commissioner for Defence in each Ministry.

The *Conseil d'Etat* (Council of State) was set up during the French Revolution to 'draft Bills and resolve disputes arising in administrative matters'. The five 'administrative sections'[13] of the Conseil d'Etat are consulted on Bills, draft ordinances, and important decrees. One 'litigation section' sits as a jurisdiction and is the highest court in the administrative court system. French citizens personally aggrieved by an administrative decision submit a complaint to an administrative court (*tribunal administratif*), which usually hears the case in the first instance. Appeal lies in administrative appellate courts (*cour administrative d'appel*, created in 1987) and finally to the Conseil d'Etat. The distinction between public and private law is defined by the Dispute Court (*tribunal des conflits*), which makes a final decision. The administrative judge investigates the issue submitted to him, may quash the decision, and if necessary award financial compensation to the aggrieved citizen. Hence, French administrative right stems from three sources: legislation (for instance, acts defining civil servant obligations or public service in transport), administrative rules and decisions, and administrative jurisprudence. **7.36**

Administrative and legal instruments

Legislation and regulations are organized in a strict hierarchy, described in the following section. This hierarchy is binding, for one act can only be modified or abolished by another, one decree of the *Conseil d'Etat* by another one, a decree by another decree, and so on. In the French tradition, a distinction is made between regulations and individual decisions which apply to every French citizen, and those which apply only to a list of persons or companies. **7.37**

Legislation and executive rules: the hierarchy

The written Constitution is the superior rule and primary source of legal authority in the French State. Just as the Constitution of 4 October 1958 is enforceable in court, so are the Declarations of Human Rights of 1789 and 1946 included in its Preamble. **7.38**

Next in the hierarchy come regularly ratified and published treaties which are superior to national law[14] provided reciprocity is granted by other States Parties to the Treaty. **7.39**

Following treaties are organic laws, listed in the Constitution. They are superior to national law and describe public powers organization, such as Member of Parliament statute or due process of writing and voting Finance Acts. Organic laws are adopted through a special procedure which forbids the Government from overriding a Senate vote by using the 'mixed Committee' procedure. **7.40**

---

[13] Interior, Finance, Social Issues, Public Works, and Legal Surveys and Reports.

[14] Art 55 of the Constitution.

7.41 Legislation is voted on by Parliament, which is the only source of new law, contrary to the British tradition. However, an exception is defined in Article 38 of the Constitution.[15]

7.42 According to Article 34 of the Constitution, the law determines the 'fundamental principles' and 'the rules applicable' to a list of subjects to be determined by the legislator. For instance, the legislative branch can levy and collect all taxes of any kind, and define legal voting procedures, nationalization procedure, categories of public bodies, civil servants' statutory guarantees, civil liberties, nationality, property, and crimes and misdemeanours.

7.43 Article 37 of the Constitution states: 'Matters not ruled by law are the domain of the executive'. According to Article 34 of the Constitution, a decree issued to implement an act must pronounce rules within the bounds of law. In contrast, a decree dealing with matters belonging in the Government's domain is an ' Article 37 decree' and gives the executive branch more latitude. The decree defining the 'energy-saving hour' is an 'Article 37 decree'.

7.44 The former Third and Fourth Republics (1875–1940 and 1946–58 respectively) had a different balance of powers, in which Parliament could intervene in any matter. An excess of detailed and therefore often inapplicable acts encouraged the drafters of the 1958 Constitution to narrow the law's domain to a list. The Government may declare inadmissible a parliamentary proposition dealing with a matter belonging in the executive domain. When combined, Articles 34 and 37 imply that acts are exceptional, whereas decrees and governmental orders are the most common kind of text to be found in modern French law.

7.45 Decrees which must be signed by the President of the Republic to be valid are listed in the Constitution. Decrees must be adopted by the Cabinet if they are deemed politically important or if an act requires it. The President of the EDF[16] is appointed through a 'Cabinet decree' (*décret en Conseil des Ministres*). Cabinet decrees are signed by the President of the Republic and the Prime Minister.

7.46 Apart from these 'President of the Republic' and 'Cabinet' decrees, all decrees must be signed by the Prime Minister to be valid.

7.47 Theoretically, all decrees implementing acts or rulings over a matter which was adjudicated by law before October 1958 are 'Council of State' decrees drafted by the

[15] According to Art 38, the Parliament may give a limited authorization empowering the Government to take measures usually included in the law's domain. The Government drafts Article 38 Ordinances which are immediately implemented when published. However, if the Government does not introduce a ratification Bill into Parliament within the time specified in the parliamentary authorization, the ordinance lapses. When duly ratified, an ordinance becomes law and can only be modified by Parliament. For instance, an Art 38 Ordinance lifted price controls in 1986.

[16] EdF = Electricité de France, French electricity public body.

administration in charge and sent to the administrative sections of the *Conseil d'Etat* to be scrutinized before being signed by the Prime Minister. The Council of State's advice is sent to the Prime Minister. However, the legislator can decide that a Council of State decree is not necessary to implement an article and that a simple decree is enough. Drafted by the administration and signed by the Prime Minister, simple decrees are deemed inferior to Council of State decrees.

One or more Ministers may sign governmental orders within their field of expertise. These orders implement decrees. For instance, high-octane petrol components are listed in a governmental order. **7.48**

Individual decisions

The executive can grant authorizations and concessions and sign contracts. **7.49**

The administration is usually vested with a discretionary power to grant or refuse an authorization, unless an act defines the conditions in which an authorization must be granted or denied. A decision refusing the authorization must be justified in writing.[17] The authorization cannot be negotiated. **7.50**

The *Conseil d'Etat* gave the first precise definition of a concession in the case 'Gas of Bordeaux' (1906). **7.51**

A concession is an administrative contract[18] by which an administration gives a person or a firm (the concessionaire) the responsibility of performing a public service. The concessionaire manages the public service at his own expense, with or without a public subsidy, and is vested with the power to bill public service users. If the legislature allows it, public service prices may be determined by the administration, provided they enable the concessionaire to balance his accounts. All concession stipulations regarding the organization of a public service create an obligation to third parties and are deemed part of State regulations. Concessions usually list the estate which, at the end of the contract, remains the property of the State or local authority granting the concession. According to a 1993 Act,[19] every award of a concession must be preceded by a public call for tender to ensure proper competition between operators. **7.52**

Principal public bodies

The EDF, GDF, CDF,[20] and CEA were founded in 1945 and 1946. Each is a public body. **7.53**

[17] Motivation of Administrative Decisions Act No 79-587 (19.07.1979).

[18] According to the Council of State, an administrative contract is defined by its object, namely the management of a public service, and stipulations exorbitant to civil contract law.

[19] No 93-122 (29.01.1993).

[20] GdF = Gaz de France; CdF = Charbonnages (Coal) de France.

7.54 The CEA was founded by a 1945 Ordinance.[21] Its statutes were modified in the 1970s and 1980s, first to include staff representatives on the governing board and to enable the Ministries for Industry and Research to supervise the CEA's activities, and secondly to focus its duties on fundamental and applied research, nuclear safety, and military applications. Its missions are to master atomic technologies used in energy, health, defence, and industry and to consider its industrial and research partners' requirements. The French Government recently instructed CEA to explore new fields of research covering other sources of energy, such as renewables. As a public body conducting fundamental research programmes, the CEA is granted a subsidy, which stood at FF 14 billion in the Finance Act 1996.

7.55 ANDRA, the *Agence Nationale des Déchets Radioactifs* (National Agency for Radioactive Waste Management), a former CEA division, became an independent public body in 1991 and was entrusted with waste policy implementation.

7.56 OPRI, the *Office de Protection contre les Rayonnements Ionisants* (Office for Protection against Ionizing Radiation) determines radioactive contamination specifications, measuring methods, and prevention techniques.

7.57 ADEME, the *Agence Française de l'Environnement et de la Maîtrise de l'Energie* (French Environment and Energy Conservation Agency) was founded in 1990,[22] bringing together the former AFME (energy conservation agency) with two environmental agencies, ANRED (the non-nuclear waste agency) and AQA (the air quality agency). ADEME supports energy efficiency and environment conservation through twenty-two regional delegations, which study local applications for funding. The ADEME budget is financed by direct government subsidies. Most of ADEME's programmes are aimed at increasing energy efficiency and developing renewable energy sources. The total ADEME budget stood at FF 1.6 billion in 1996.

7.58 EDF, a State-owned electricity public body, was vested with a monopoly on electricity exportation, importation, and transmission by the Gas and Electricity Nationalization Act 1946. EDF is responsible for 94 per cent of the electricity generated in France. GDF has a complete monopoly on gas imports and exports, and was also granted a legal monopoly on distribution. However, the Gas and Electricity Nationalization Act 1946 excluded from nationalization existing companies distributing gas. GDF operates most of the gas transmission and distribution network, and accounts for approximately 80 per cent of gas sold to final consumers.

---

[21] Ordinance (18.10.1945) founding CEA, No 45-2563. CEA = Commissariat à l'Energie Atomique (Atomic Energy Utility).

[22] Act no 90-1130 (19.12.1990) founding ADEME.

The coal mines were nationalized by the Gas and Electricity Nationalization Act 1946. Mine owners were given compensation and State bonds were issued to finance the nationalization. The interest paid to bondholders was financed by a 0.25 per cent tax on coal sales. CDF co-ordinated and controlled mining activities throughout the French territory and ran minor exploitations, while several public bodies, called the Coalfield Mines, were created by decree to manage the largest mines. The smallest mines, if not claimed by CDF, were exploited through granted concessions. The amount of State subsidies to CDF is decided annually by the Finance Act. In 1996 the CDF subsidy amounted to FF 4.55 billion, inclusive of VAT. Part of this subsidy is devoted to balancing the CDF old age pension budget, and must therefore comply with European Directive 3632/93 ECSC on governmental aid. **7.59**

To secure coal supplies, the ATIC (*Association technique pour l'importation du charbon*, Technical Association for Coal Importations) was founded in 1944 by major coal importers, mainly CDF, EDF, SOLLAC,[23] and a professional federation of coal importers. **7.60**

State supervision over public bodies

Due to differences in the statutes of each public body, there is no set detailed pattern of ministerial authority. However, State power over the public bodies can be broadly described, and ranges from traditional State supervision to more innovative planning agreements. **7.61**

Although public bodies do not issue shares, the State is vested with shareholder powers. The State appoints the public body chairman, along with some members of the governing board. These appointees hold office for fixed periods and the Government has the power of dismissal. The public bodies are subject to governmental regulation of the prices they may charge and the means by which they may distribute their goods. Their accounts are audited by the French Audit Court. By sitting on their governing board, the State representatives control investment policy. A 1955 decree defined the State dividend and the interest rate applied to the State contribution of capital to its public bodies. The financing of EDF, GDF, and CDF major investment projects is examined by a governmental committee, the CIES (Economic and Social Investment Committee). Set up in 1955 and reformed in 1986 and 1996, the CIES does not grant loans to public bodies any more, nor subsidies, but examines the global amount of annual investments planned by public bodies vested with a legal monopoly. Representatives of relevant ministries, including the Ministries of Finance and Industry, sit on the Committee. **7.62**

[23] A French steel company.

7.63 To introduce management by objectives into public body management, the French State negotiated a contract with EDF, GDF, CEA, and ADEME which granted them more autonomy, imposed several obligations in return, and fixed a political framework allowing them to define and carry out a mid-term strategy. However, these 'planning agreements' (*contrats d'objectifs* or *contrats de plan*) do not weaken the State's supervisory powers. Each planning agreement stipulates the interest rate (5 per cent) applied to the State contribution. The dividend can be increased to take into account the public body's economic and financial performance. According to the contract stipulations, the profits are allocated to the public body (through investments and development), the State (dividend), and the consumer through an immediate price decrease and a decrease in indebtedness.

7.64 Contract stipulations can be broadly described. EDF and GDF contracts stipulate the amount of industrial investment, earnings per share, acquisitions, and selling policy, along with pricing policy and rules of competition. In the fiscal year 1993, EDF and GDF paid to the State interest on invested capital, a profit tax, and a dividend.

7.65 The State negotiated a 1993–96 planning agreement with EDF, which assigned three major objectives to the public body. First, tariffs had to decrease by 1.25 per cent per annum in real terms. EDF would also reduce by one-third the difference between tariffs and costs of supplies for individual customer categories: in 1993 household tariffs were 5 per cent below supply costs while small and medium-size business tariffs were 5 per cent above costs. This goal has not been achieved, partly because of the Government's decision to increase VAT. Secondly, EDF had to reduce indebtedness by FF 40 billion. Thirdly, EDF had to improve the quality of its service.

7.66 However, these contract stipulations did not hinder the State from increasing the financial burden on EDF. Although the VAT rate on electricity rose, EDF was not allowed to pass this additional cost on to its customers. In 1994 a new tax was levied on hydroelectricity and the State, in justifying this decision, claimed that EDF was using water to generate electricity and should therefore finance water management improvements in France.

7.67 To narrow the gap between EDF's autonomy and that of private firms, a 'partnership agreement' has been drawn up between the State and EDF to specify the rights and responsibilities of the two partners and the conduct of the partnership. The agreement was adopted by EDF's board in March 1997 and bound the State and EDF on five major subjects. EDF's public service mission is vested with a more precise definition encompassing pluri-annual programming of investments, environment-friendly measures to ensure the safety of supply, and the quality of the electricity supply, in compliance with rules on fair access to the public service.

Lower costs will result in tariff decreases, which will reach 14 per cent by 2000. EDF will develop its activities in France and abroad. The implementation of the 'partnership agreement' will also clarify financial relations between EDF and the State. As for social policy, EDF will particularly focus on restructuring employees' working hours.

As for GDF, the first planning agreement (1991–93) set up a clear framework of relations between the State and GDF. In return for autonomy and the necessary resources to implement a successful mid-term strategy, GDF agreed to increase its performance. The second agreement (1994–96) defined GDF's five challenges, namely security of supply at the least cost, the search for excellence in its basic trades to improve its quality of service, increase in sales in France and abroad, social progress, and growth in profit to finance expansion. The third agreement (1997–99) reinforced previous guidelines and focused on adapting GDF to the changing international environment. **7.68**

GDF's offerings in the domestic heating market have been changed to provide customers with both installation and energy supply. Hence, GDF has developed complementary services dealing with climatic energy engineering to improve gas energy performances. GDF's diversification in the domestic market has been closely supervised by the State. The Government established a Diversification Committee, which monitors GDF's diversification to ensure fair competition between GDF and other operators in the gas sector (equipment suppliers, installers, etc). **7.69**

As for the CEA, its contract has scheduled decreasing staff and stabilization in 1998, and set out the main lines of research until 1998, including fuel enrichment techniques, advanced PWR technologies, plutonium and spent fuel recycling, waste incineration, and nuclear fusion. **7.70**

The ADEME planning agreement stipulates the Agency's development programmes and actions in the provinces. **7.71**

(4) Taxation

Every year Parliament votes tax laws and an annual authorization to levy taxes from which revenue is entrusted to the State and local authorities. **7.72**

The general tax legislation applies to energy production. Further specific provisions adopt fiscal law to the energy sector activity; most of these are described below. Additional taxes on energy are also applied. **7.73**

In both cases, tax legislation goals are to increase fiscal revenue and deter the use of various energy sources, either those imported or those likely to damage the environment. Therefore taxation is deemed a major tool of French energy policy, mainly used to influence consumer behaviour. **7.74**

Adaptation of fiscal law to the energy sector

7.75 VAT is levied on all economic activities. As for petroleum products, the tax base is the sum of the price and the excise. To deter petroleum product consumption, a special rule forbids any tax deduction for aircraft and automobile petrol and oil purchases and limits it to 50 per cent for liquified gas petroleum, natural gas, and diesel. A VAT rate of 5.5 per cent, instead of the usual 20.6 per cent, is applied for wood to be used for heating.[24]

7.76 The professional tax, created in 1975, is levied on private firms and public bodies; its revenue is entrusted to local authorities. The tax base includes mainly investment value and staff expenditure. The percentage of staff expenditure in the tax base will decrease to favour job creations. The tax rate is set by local authority councils within a range determined by the Parliament. Departmental funds were formed to equalize professional tax revenue between municipalities and grant subsidies to the poorest ones. When the firm or public body liable for the tax belongs to the energy sector, the decision allowing the exceeding tax revenue is made by concerned municipalities instead of the department,[25] and if municipalities disagree, by a government order signed by the Minister of the Interior.

7.77 As for corporation tax, accelerated depreciation may be applied to energy saving investments in industry, reducing taxable income. Parliament approved deductions from income tax to encourage investment in the insulation of existing buildings.

7.78 According to the Finance Act 1991, a 'hydro-tax' is levied on farmers, micro-hydroplants, industrial facilities, and thermic plants using and discharging water into watercourses. EDF pays 76 per cent of the tax revenue (FF 385 million). The tax base varies with the availability of power plants, but the tax rate is monitored to compensate for these variations and to keep the amount of the tax revenue stable. The tax revenue is entrusted to a public body[26] responsible for the maintenance, upgrading, and development of inland waterways in France. Authorized minor hydropower plants are also liable. The revenue collected on hydropower from this tax is FF 2–4 million a year. In an Act passed in 1996, the tax actually collected was limited to 3 per cent of the sales figures recorded in the previous fiscal year. The tax applied to newly built dams is half the normal rate during the first ten years of the facility's exploitation. The 1996 Act also redefined the tax base calculation.

[24] Art 278bis, French Fiscal Code.

[25] Art 1648 A-I, French Tax Code.

[26] *Voies navigables de France*, Waterways of France.

Additional taxes on energy

Oil

To deter the use of imported sources of energy and to reduce pollution, the State monitored petroleum product demand through tax legislation which allowed precise supervision. Tax law had a significant impact on French domestic oil consumption. In a 1996 report, the French Committee of Petroleum Industry noted that the petroleum products market share in France would have been 16.5 points higher if the Government had evenly taxed petroleum products and electricity use. **7.79**

Since hydrocarbons are imported goods, the petroleum excise is described in the Customs Code.[27] The excise revenue amounted to 1.8 per cent of the French GDP in 1994 and to 7 per cent of total tax revenue by the end of the 1970s. It grew to 8.7 per cent in 1988, decreased slightly in 1991 to 8.1 per cent, but grew again to 9 per cent of the total tax revenue in 1993. **7.80**

The French excise on high-octane petrol was one of the highest in the fifteen-member Union. The unleaded super excise and the heavy fuels excise have been reduced to encourage their use. European Directives 92/81 and 92/82 exempted kerosene. The gap between excise imposed upon petrol and that on diesel is the largest in Europe. This tax policy has favoured diesel consumption and influenced French consumers to buy diesel engines. A seven-year plan adopted by the Government in 1998 will progressively narrow the gap between French tax legislation and that of other Member States by increasing diesel tax by FF 0.07 per year. However, due to growing public discontent over the rise of petrol prices, the Government took several fiscal measures in the autumn of 2000. The excise on household fuel was diminished by 30 per cent by the end of September 2000. In the Finance Bill 2001 drafted by the Government, introduced and debated in Parliament from October on, the FF 0.07 per litre rise on diesel excise is postponed to 2002 and the excise on 'clean' petrol is stable for the third year in a row. To prevent petrol prices from rising excessively because of crude oil price increase, the excise rates are modulated to keep the fiscal revenue of excise + VAT on petrol stable. The modulation applies when the rise in crude oil price exceeds 10 per cent. **7.81**

A few miscellaneous excise taxes are imposed on petroleum products, mainly to support research, recycling, or modernization programmes undertaken by public or private bodies. They were reformed to comply with the Single European Act. The first one finances research and development programmes undertaken by the IFP (*Institut Français du Pétrole*, French Petroleum Institute). Its rate was modified by a January 1993 decree[28] to comply with European legislation. The **7.82**

[27] Arts 265 and 266.

[28] No 93-28 (8.01.1993).

Commission (DG IV) ruled that this tax was not to be considered a State subsidy. A second excise tax is levied on petrol, high-octane petrol, and diesel sales. The tax was updated by a March 1997 decree and finances the petrol station network modernization programme implemented by the Petroleum Products Retailers Committee. Set up by a 1986 decree[29] and modified in 1987, another excise tax was levied on base oils either produced in France or imported to support ADEME's activities.

7.83 Two taxes are levied on oil production, notwithstanding taxes on corporate profit. A State tax is levied on each tonne produced but is suspended for fields brought into production since 1994. Offshore deposits are not liable to this tax. A departmental and local tax on mines (RDCM) is also levied on oil production. RDCM rates depend on whether the field came onstream prior to 1992; new production is taxed at a lower rate. Tax liabilities are offset by a system of capital cost allowances.

Gas

7.84 According to Article 226 of the French Customs Code, an excise tax is levied on gas deliveries exceeding 5 million kWh per year to one consumer (e.g. generators). Tax exemptions are granted when gas is used for household heating or as a raw material. The exemption granted to gas used for household heating is intended to favour gas use and deter the consumption of other petroleum products.

Electricity

7.85 A local electricity tax is levied on electricity generation: the tax base is equal to 80 per cent of the invoices submitted when the relevant contracts do not exceed 36 kVA, and 30 per cent of the invoices submitted when the contracts range between 36 and 250 kVA.

Nuclear

7.86 According to the Finance Act 1975, a tax is levied on nuclear power plants and the revenue generated is allocated to the relevant city councils.

Hydropower

7.87 When a dam is built on a navigable river, hydropower concessionaires are liable for a tax established by a 1994 Act[30] and equal to 4.2 centimes per KWh. Its revenue is managed by the Terrestrial Transportation Investment Fund.

Combined Heat and Power

7.88 Since 1993 CHP operators using gas have been exempted from gas and heavy fuel excise tax by the Finance Act and must declare their facilities to benefit from this exemption. They are also granted a favourable fiscal regime allowing a one-year

[29] No 86-544 (14.03.1986).

[30] Art 302bis 2A, Fiscal Code.

period of depreciation of their investment.[31] Local authorities may also reduce the local tax levied on all industrial activities on CHP plants.[32]

Miscellaneous

ADEME's budget was financed by four taxes on municipal and industrial waste, atmospheric pollution, aircraft noise, and spent oil. These taxes were levied by ADEME. Since the Finance Bill 1999 these taxes were abolished and replaced with a 'general tax on polluting activities' (TGAP in French) levied by the State. TGAP also replaced a miscellaneous tax on household waste storage. TGAP revenue allows the State to add to the amount of ADEME subsidies, and funds anti-pollution measures, energy-saving policy, and the development of renewable energy sources. Further consultation with various economic sectors is underway to extend TGAP to energy consumption under certain limits and conditions. Due to be applied in 2001, the TGAP extension will allow the State to collect several billion francs to be used to finance a reduction of unemployment. **7.89**

(5) Some Major Milestones

Before the Second World War, several acts of Parliament and governmental orders provided the major outlines of energy legislation. After the War demand for energy increased steadily due to rebuilding programmes and harsh winters. Most of the energy industry was nationalized and the newly formed public bodies helped rebuild the country. State reform came later, when the new 1958 constitution replaced the parliamentary system, which had prevailed before and after the War, with a presidential system. After the oil crisis, the State had to ensure the safety of supplies and launch a new energy conservation policy. French citizens showed a growing concern about environment conservation, and new acts were consequently passed. Denationalization and devolution reduced the State's powers. **7.90**

Before the Second World War

The first act governing energy transmission and distribution in France was passed in 1906. A second law on hydropower was approved in 1919, and some of its provisions are still in force. In 1924 the State created the *Compagnie Française des Pétroles* (French Petroleum Company), which became the Total company after the War. In 1925 a second law established a National Liquid Fuels Board. A law passed in 1928 encouraged the development of a refinery industry on French territory, and made the building up of strategic stores compulsory to avoid shortage, for instance in the case of war. **7.91**

Small local companies produced electricity. To define the general obligations of energy-producing operators to their public partners, several decrees issued **7.92**

[31] Art 39B, Fiscal Code.
[32] Art 1518, Fiscal Code.

between 1934 and 1937 regulated the content of contracts, and were the first attempt to introduce a standard contract for electricity supply.

7.93 In France the administrative law judge has the power to rule on cases between French citizens and any public body, including the State. Citizens may file a claim for damages in the administrative law court or ask the judge to quash an administrative decision, decree, or order. During the 1930s the *Conseil d'Etat* (Council of State) specifically defined public service obligations, mainly non-discriminatory access to public services for all citizens and public service continuity, the former grounding the equalization of electricity prices over all French territory, the latter justifying restrictions on the right of public service employees to take industrial action.

Nationalization of the energy industry

7.94 Due to the destruction caused by the Second World War, coupled with increasing demand, France faced an energy shortage in 1945. The Gas and Electricity Nationalization Act 1946 nationalized most of the electricity generators, but allowed production plants under 8 MW and auto production facilities to remain under private ownership. The Act also partly nationalized the gas industry. EDF was founded in 1946 and was granted ownership of the nationalized facilities and a monopoly on electricity transmission. GDF was also founded in 1946. CDF was allocated ownership of coal mines. In 1945 Frédéric Joliot-Curie advised the Government to found the CEA, to rival American research on atomic energy and follow the tradition of excellence established in France before the War. ELF (Entreprise de Lubrifiants Français, French Lubricant Company) was founded in 1945, along with the IFP, whose aim was to undertake research and development of gas and petroleum products. A 1948 law[33] defined the first legal means and guidelines for an energy conservation policy.

7.95 Between 1946 and 1958 EDF restored the grid and thermal power plants. EDF also built thirty new dams, mainly in the Alps and along the Rhône, giving France one of the most complete European hydropower networks. In 1951 GDF discovered the Lacq gas deposit, one of the largest ever found in Europe outside the Netherlands. In 1947 the CEA built Zoé, an atomic pile prototype. In 1966 EDF pioneered the world's first tidal power dam across the Rance estuary in Brittany. Energy production rose sharply to meet the needs of the French economy, where the annual growth rate averaged 5 per cent.

State reform

7.96 The new Constitution adopted in 1958 restricted Parliament's power and granted an autonomous and exclusive regulatory power to the executive branch. Hence, many earlier laws fell into the decree field and were later modified by decrees or reg-

[33] Energy Use Act No 48-400 (10.03.1948).

ulations. Another provision set up the Constitutional Council. In 1968, the Government abandoned French-produced natural uranium gas-cooled reactors and Framatome began building pressurized water reactors under Westinghouse patents. In 1971, a first major European directive defined the guidelines of fair competition in public tenders. The *Conseil d'Etat* defined new jurisprudence (*Ville Nouvelle Est*) to determine whether the balance between the benefits and losses for the nation had been properly struck when a decision was taken to build a major public facility.

The oil crisis

In 1974 France imported 77.5 per cent of its primary energy, compared to an EEC average of 55 per cent. The Lacq gas deposit was expected to run dry after 1985. Thus the oil crisis hit France harder than most other European countries. Consequently, Parliament passed the Energy Conservation Act 1974[34] and the Nationalization of Electricity in the DOM-TOM Act in 1975.[35] AFME (*Agence Française pour la Maîtrise de l'Energie*, French Energy Conservation Agency) was set up and later became ADEME (*Agence de l'Environnement et de la Maîtrise de l'Energie*, French Environment and Energy Conservation Agency). **7.97**

The Government decided to develop a network of nuclear power plants. Although uranium deposits have been discovered on French territory, France currently imports uranium, eg from Australia, to save its own resources. In 1976, COGEMA (*Compagnie Générale des Matières Nucléaires*, General Nuclear Materials Company), a CEA subsidiary, took over uranium prospecting which had been formerly entrusted to the CEA by statute. The Government also decided to develop renewable energy use. Between 1970 and 1980, the optimal utilization of hydraulic resources raised the electricity production capacity by 60 per cent. **7.98**

To curb petroleum product consumption and raise excise tax revenue, all petroleum excise taxes were increased to discourage French consumers from using their cars. In 1976 the Government merged several State-owned companies into ELF-Aquitaine, a new and larger State-controlled oil company. Thus ELF (*Entreprise de lubrifiants français*, French Lubricants Company) was able to prospect for oil in the Middle East despite the American and Anglo-Dutch presence. The oil glut of 1986 partly reduced the pressure on the French economy, but the persistent low economic growth rate remained an incentive to implement the rational use of energy measures. **7.99**

Environmental conservation

Following the Environment Act 1976,[36] a law passed in 1983 defined a new environmental impact assessment procedure, applicable to the building of public **7.100**

[34] No 74-908 (29.10.1974).
[35] No 75-622 (11.07.1975).
[36] No 76-629 (10.07.1976).

facilities, such as power plants, nuclear facilities, dams, and electricity pylons. During the 1980s the Prevention of Oil Pollution at Sea Act 1983,[37] the Forest Act 1985,[38] the Mountain Act 1985,[39] the Shore Act 1986,[40] and the Water Act 1992[41] finalized the consensus procedure and defined the conditions for environment-friendly management. In 1981 the building of a nuclear power plant in Plogoff was abandoned due to a public outcry.

7.101 Despite French and European ecologists' protest campaigns, which culminated in the July 1977 demonstration, the decision was made in 1983 to start up the fast neutron breeder reactor Super-Phénix, owned by the international consortium NERSA, which included EDF. Due to minor technical malfunctions and much political debate, Super-Phénix was shut down by a presidential decision, until another decree issued in July 1994 allowed the reactor to start up again. The Conseil d'Etat quashed this decree in March 1997 and the Government eventually decided to close Super-Phénix for financial reasons in 1998.

7.102 Meanwhile, EDF negotiated export contracts with neighbouring countries and began substituting nuclear power plants for mid-load fossil fuel plants as the capacity and availability of nuclear plants increased. The 1988 oil glut and the 1990 Gulf crisis proved the instability of the oil market, and showed that the French economy had become less sensitive to its swift changes.

Devolution and denationalization

7.103 Between 1982 and 1987, municipalities, departments, and regions were vested with the power to subsidize economic activity and freely determine the rate of several local taxes levied on energy plants, particularly the 'professional tax'.

7.104 A 1986 Ordinance[42] lifted all price controls and put an end to the ones on imported oil, which had been set up in 1925. This Ordinance also provided for the establishment of the *Conseil de la concurrence* (Competition Council). Council members are experts, civil servants, and judges chosen from within the *Conseil d'Etat*, the Supreme Court, and the Audit Court. The Council is to advise on bills and draft decrees dealing with economic competition and legal monopolies. Unfair competition practices are proscribed by the Ordinance. The Council is empowered to hear cases claiming unfair competition practices, and may impose sanctions.

7.105 In 1993 the Government sold 11 per cent of COGEMA's capital to Total. The State sold most of its Total shares in 1992 and its ELF shares in 1994 and in 1996.

[37] No 83-583 (05.07.1983).
[38] No 85-1273 (04.12.1985).
[39] No 85-30 (09.01.1985).
[40] No 86-02 (03.01.1986).
[41] No 92-3 (3.01.1992).
[42] No 86-1243 (01.12.1986).

The Reform of the Petroleum Legislation Act 1992[43] deregulated oil imports and refining. European directives were enacted by laws or decrees, particularly Directive 92/12/EEC stating the legal regime of products liable to excise taxes. State procedures have been scrutinized to simplify authorization regimes.

Since the 1986 decrease in the price of imported coal, French coal has become too expensive. CDF still sells coal on the domestic market and covers financial losses, while operating losses are financed by Government subsidies. The Government has scheduled mine closures over a twenty-year period. The last plan agreed by the trade unions in 1994 stipulated that all mines should be closed by 2005. In 1994 the Mining Code was reformed accordingly.[44] The SNET (*Société Nationale d'Electricité Thermique*, National Company of Thermal and Electricity Generation), an EDF and CDF subsidiary, took over CDF's power generation activities. In 1994 and 1995 the coal import regime was deregulated to comply with Single Market legislation, thus ending the coal import association's monopoly. **7.106**

In addition, the 'Fight against Poverty Acts'[45] gave families or persons living in precarious financial circumstances a right to public support and guaranteed their access to energy supply. Contracts signed between the State, EDF, and GDF will define the means and amount of the two public companies' contributions. Each Prefect will sign a contract with the local EDF and GDF representatives, other energy distributors, and municipalities to implement national contracts. **7.107**

Latest developments

By the end of 1996 the European Union Member States and the European Parliament had adopted Directive 96/92 EC on common rules for the internal electricity market. This Directive introduced competition through competitive bids for electricity generation, and authorization for generators to supply eligible customers. According to the subsidiarity principle, each Member State is empowered to define the term 'eligible customers' and select an electricity network manager. A dispute settlement body is to be appointed. **7.108**

Member States were required to implement the Directive before 19 February 1999, the Electricity Bill updating the French legislation and enacting the Directive was first presented to the Parliament in 1999 and finally passed in February 2000.[46] One reason for the delay, amongst others, was that the Government wished to conduct a thorough consultation, because the French general public doubted that competition would necessarily bring a decrease in prices and an increase in quality in a sector previously managed by a public service **7.109**

[43] No 92-1443 (31.12.1992).

[44] Mining Act No 94-588 (15.07.1994).

[45] No 92-722 (29.07.1992) and No 98-657 (29.07.1998).

[46] The Modernization and Development of Public Service of Electricity Act, No 2000-108 (10.02.2000).

towards which they held no ill will. The same thorough consultation is applied to the gas sector, where a Bill was adopted by the Council of Ministers in May 2000 and will soon be debated in Parliament.

B. Exploration and Production of Hydrocarbons

(1) Introduction

7.110 Oil production amounted to 2.8 million tonnes in 1994, below the peak production of 1989. The two leading producers are Essorep, which accounts for half of total oil production, and ELF (35 per cent of production).[47] Prospecting and production activities have been low, due to lower oil prices and poor prospects of discovering large volumes of commercially exploitable oil reserves. Two of the ten oil wells drilled in 1994 resulted in discoveries, and though prospecting expenditure fell by 26 per cent, drilling picked up slightly.

7.111 Production of natural gas from the Lacq deposit was at 5 bcm in 1994. The leading producer is ELF with 93 per cent of gas production. The specific provisions applied to prospecting for hydrocarbons were abolished by a 1965 decree and an Act passed in 1977.

(2) The Legal Framework

The Mining Code

7.112 Onshore and offshore exploration of French underground territory is regulated by the Mining Code, first written and published under Napoleon I, and most recently replaced by the regularly amended Mining Code of 1956. The Code applies to the exploration for and exploitation of geothermal sites and 'mines', such as oil and gas deposits, coal, and uranium.[48] Prospecting, exploitation, and transport of mineral or fossil substances on the continental shelf are governed by the same Code. Prior to any prospecting or exploitation, a public inquiry must be held to assess the environmental impact and to inform the population.

7.113 The State monitors mining activity mainly through granting concessions and prospecting permits. A concession or permit may be granted to any applicant who possesses technical and financial ability, provided the field or deposit described in the application can be prospected or exploited. The concession may be awarded to a company created under French or another European Union Member State's law.

[47] TOTALFINA brought together Total and Fina in May 1999 and later bought 94% of ELF's capital to form a new petroleum company, TotalFinaElf.

[48] Art 2 of the Mining Code contains a definition of the term 'mines' and the minerals classified as such. Oil, gas, and coal are classified as 'mines'.

The Mining Code was updated by the Mining Act 1994, which partly enacted EEC Directive 94/22. One of the decrees implementing this Act was issued in April 1995 to complete the directive enactment and set up the competitive bid procedure applying to the granting of concessions or exclusive permits. In 1998 an Act[49] implementing the Mining Code in the departments and overseas territories (DOM-TOM) was approved by Parliament to adapt the Mining Code to the particular conditions of gold mining in French Guyana. The most recent amendment to the Mining Code was issued in March 1999 and relates, amongst others, to liability for damage caused by the production of hydrocarbons and post-production mining risks. **7.114**

The Civil Code

According to Article 552 of the French Civil Code, the landowner owns the subsoil and undertakes or allows prospecting and/or production. However, the State ensures non-discriminatory and effective access to French mining resources and may therefore allow prospecting without the landowner's agreement, if the Minister for Industry grants an authorization (after consulting the landowner) or an exclusive prospecting permit. The beneficiary is liable for damage caused according to French civil law, but the prospector can disclaim responsibility if damage was caused by an external agent. As for exploitation, the granting of a concession creates a special right of ownership, distinct from the property of the land and the subsoil. Theoretically, concessions determine the fee owed by the concessionaire to the landowner, unless they are the same person. In practice, fees are determined by negotiation between the landowner and the concessionaire. The landowner of the serviant estate may also be awarded damages to compensate for easements granted to the operator. If the landowner's enjoyment of his property is precluded by the exploitation, he may demand that the land be expropriated and be awarded damages. **7.115**

No prospecting or exploitation activity can be undertaken in back yards, gardens, or within a 50-metre safety perimeter around a dwelling. **7.116**

(3) Prospecting for Hydrocarbons

Prospecting is the act of exploring a region for (coal) mines, oil or gas deposits, or other natural resources generally to be found beneath the land or the sea bed. **7.117**

The Minister for Industry may grant an authorization (after consulting with the landowner) or an exclusive prospecting permit, the former not allowing the operator to sell the mining products without the Prefect's agreement, the latter giving the operator the right to dispose of mining products. However, the operator does not need agreement to sell liquid or gaseous hydrocarbons found by **7.118**

[49] No 98-297 (21.04.1998).

prospecting. No permit is granted to an operator unless proof of his financial and technical expertise is provided to the French administration.[50] An exclusive permit is granted for five years through a competitive bid. It may be renewed twice for a total period of fifteen years.

7.119 As for hydrocarbons, the exclusive permit perimeter is reduced by half with the first extension and by a quarter with the second, unless the operator can prove exceptional circumstances. According to EEC Directive 94/22, any person may apply for a prospecting permit or a hydrocarbon concession. To ensure non-discriminatory access to the French subsoil, French legislation allows any area not already included in a prospecting permit or a concession to be permanently open and subject to an application, in contrast with other countries' practice of implementing 'round systems'. This interpretation of the Directive was published in an official notice. In April 1997, 44 per cent of exploration permits and 25 per cent of concessions had been awarded to American operators.

7.120 The Mining Act 1994 shortened the time required between the submission of an application and the awarding of a licence from over two years to less than one year. The legal framework for prospecting and production activities in France was also simplified. The number of applications has been rising significantly since the reform took effect. Although French domestic production is low, French companies have been undertaking research programmes to develop innovative technologies and ensure better technical-economic accessibility to discovered reserves.

(4) Exploitation

7.121 Exploitation is the act of using, working, or developing mines, reservoirs, deposits, or other natural resources. Before the prospecting permit expires, only the permit holder is entitled to apply for a concession. When the operator who found the mine or deposit is not granted the concession, the concession beneficiary pays him damages fixed by the decree granting the concession.

7.122 The 'concession' is the only legal regime for exploiting a mine or a hydrocarbon deposit since the Mining Act 1994. Standard specifications defined by law were attached to concessions; however, they were not detailed enough to be implemented to each concession and were adapted through negotiation between the administration and the concessionaire. These standard specifications were abolished by the law and what still retains the name of 'concession' is actually a unilateral authorization by the State to exploit the subsoil. However, the concession is granted through a competitive bid. A decree awards the concession after a thirty-day public inquiry has been held. The maximum duration of such an authorization is fifty years, which may be renewed. The operator must prove that he

[50] French Mining Code and EEC Directive 94/22.

possesses the technical and financial ability to run the exploitation, and comply with the rules in force; the State may impose additional obligations.

Prior to the Mining Act 1994, an exploitation permit was granted to an applicant for a maximum period of five years by a governmental order. These permits could be renewed twice. They are still valid, but beneficiaries must apply for concessions when the permit expires. As for petroleum products, the beneficiary of an exploitation permit must apply for a concession when production reaches 300,000 tonnes (or 300 million cubic metres of gas). **7.123**

The Contractual Procedures Act 1992[51] determined fair competitive tender procedures to be implemented in transport, telecommunication, water, and energy supply. However, these procedures do not apply to mining concessions. Nevertheless, the mine or deposit exploiter must comply with the principles of non-discrimination and fair competition in selecting sub-contractors. **7.124**

(5) *Supervision*

Prospecting for and exploiting mines and deposits are controlled by the French administration. Civil servants may conduct on-site inspections of mines and all relevant facilities and request any document, sample, or equipment needed. During the concession period, operators send an annual report stating the effects of exploitation on the soil and environment to local authorities. Exploitation must comply with labour law, particularly with staff health and safety provisions. The operator must also comply with rules protecting the environment, public health, and safety, and with the Historical Monuments Act 1913,[52] the Protection of Natural Monuments and Picturesque Sites Act 1930,[53] the Environment Act 1976, and the Water Act 1992. **7.125**

If the mine or the exploitation of deposits prejudices any legal interests, the French administration can impose new obligations on the operator to prevent any destruction. These obligations must be carried out in a specified period of time. When a Code infringement is reported by civil servants, the administration may withdraw the permit or concession. The penalties for breaching the law range from a FF 100,000 fee to two years' imprisonment.[54] **7.126**

The amended Mining Code of 1999 includes specific provision with regard to the prevention and supervision of mining, especially the procedures for ceasing mining activities. It has also created a new public authority for the prevention and **7.127**

[51] No 92-1282 (11.12.1992).
[52] 31.12.1913.
[53] 02.05.1930.
[54] Arts 140–4 of the Mining Code.

supervision of mining risks: the Agence de Prévention et de Surveillance des Risques Miniers.[55] This authority is responsible for:

(i) collecting documents for submission for the procedure for ceasing mining activities;
(ii) providing these documents to any person interested in the prevention and compensation of mining-related damage; and
(iii) participating in the preparation of measures for preventing mining risks.

7.128 Further rules on the internal organization of this authority are included in a separate regulation.[56]

(6) Liability Issues

7.129 Liability for damage which occurs as a result of the exploration and/or exploitation of 'mines' is determined by the Mining Code. Where there are no specific mining law provisions on mining damage, the Civil Code applies.

7.130 The Mining Code contains the basic principle that the explorer or operator, or in default the holder of the mining title (exploration permit or concession), is liable for damage caused by the mining activities. Since the 1999 amendment to the Mining Code such liability is no longer limited to the geographical boundaries or to the term of the licence/concession.

Liability for damage

7.131 In case of an accident in a mine or deposit, the mayor(s) and the mining engineer are required to carry out the necessary measures to eliminate hazard and prevent damage. In case of imminent danger, they may require equipment and a workforce to undertake the necessary public works.

7.132 If mining activities are carried out below residential areas or other mining works, the explorer or producer must give a guarantee to indemnify any damage.[57] Moreover, any damage to real property as a result of (past or present) mining which cannot be repaired under normal conditions will be indemnified: the owner of the damaged property can be compensated with a replacement property of equal substance and comfort.[58]

7.133 The State may be required to pay such damages if an operator is exempt from liability by virtue of a valid exemption clause. The 1994 amendment to the Mining Code has limited the extent to which these exemptions clauses can be used. In certain cases they have been declared void. Since the 1999 amendment, (i) the State's

55 Art 4, para 1 (amended) Mining Code 1999.
56 ibid, paras 2 and 4.
57 ibid, Art 74.
58 ibid, Art 75.

liability is limited to direct, substantial, and material damage which is not covered by other sources, (ii) the State acquires the rights of victims by way of subrogation, and (iii) the damage must be caused by a mining disaster (*sinistre minier*) as defined by the Mining Code.

The termination of mining activities

Upon the expiry of the mining concession all rights and obligations are taken over by the State, after the operator has undertaken any necessary works. The mining facilities also become State property when the mine or deposit can no longer be exploited, or it may be bought by the State. In the case of operator negligence or disappearance, all the contractual rights and obligations of the operator are transferred to the State. **7.134**

By the end of the exploitation, the operator must describe the effects of mining or deposit exploitation on the presence, volume, quality, accumulation, and streaming of water, assess the consequences of work on water, and notify the French administration of the measures undertaken to preserve the environment, soils, architectural artefacts, public buildings, and road solidity. The operator must rectify any nuisance and disorder created by the mine and allow for mining to be resumed later. The administration consults the relevant municipalities, hears the operator's arguments, and determines the supplementary measures to be implemented, if necessary, to conserve the agricultural land and landscape and to comply with the main provisions of the Water Act 1992. If the operator defaults, the administration undertakes the necessary measures at his expense. **7.135**

A landowner selling a piece of land previously used as a mine or deposit must inform the buyer in writing of the former use of the land and the hazards and inconvenience which might be occasioned to his knowledge by the mine. A misinformed buyer can cancel the purchase or seek damages. **7.136**

C. Transport, Storage, and Distribution of Oil

(1) Transport

In accordance with the Reform of the Petroleum Legislation Act 1992, French refiners are required to use French oil tankers to transport a minimum of 5.5 per cent of crude oil quantities delivered to oil refineries. Although the transport of petroleum products by sea has usually proved safe, pollution may be caused by wrecked sea tankers. The French administration has defined two emergency plans, *Polmar-mer* and *Polmar-terre* (marine pollution at sea and on shore) to coordinate the complex measures to be implemented in case of an oil-spill. According to international law, the polluter is liable for the damage incurred. International conventions of 1969 and 1971 established the direct liability of **7.137** shipowners, who may financially limit their liability and be reinsured through the 'Protection and Indemnity Club'. The 1971 Convention established an international liability fund.

Pipelines

7.138 The safety rules applied to transmission of petroleum through pipelines are stated in a 1989 governmental order. To protect the environment, dwellings, and industrial sites, the pipeline course must avoid the most sensitive places and, when near them, the most extreme technical precautions must be taken to prevent accidents. A public inquiry is held to determine the best course, and if private landowners affected by the facility location object to construction, a declaration of public interest is required to give the operator the right to work on private property. Damages are awarded by the property judge. The technical pipe specifications can also be toughened if the pipeline course nears a high-tension electricity line. Planting a tree or building a durable construction on land where pipelines are built is prohibited.

(2) Storage

7.139 According to the Reform of the Petroleum Legislation Act 1992, oil companies operating in the French market must declare to the State their contribution to French market supply. They must build up a store equal to one-quarter of the flow declared within the past twelve months. The CPSSP (*Comité professionnel des stocks pétroliers stratégiques*, Professional Committee of Strategic Petroleum Stocks) was established by a 1993 decree.[59] Its members are appointed by the Minister for Industry and include representatives of oil companies and the French Ministry of Budget. The storage must stand at 25 per cent of annual delivery quantities, allowing France to comply with IEA and European Union commitments, which demand the setting up of emergency stocks equal to 90 days of net imports and 90 days of consumption respectively. The DIMAH (Hydrocarbon and Raw Material Directorate), a DGEMP division, can take appropriate measures in a crisis. The drawdown of stocks will be co-ordinated by IEA, and effected by a governmental order or by decree.

7.140 French legislation divides hydrocarbons into five categories, depending on their degree of hazard, and classifies storage facilities depending on the volume of storage and the project technical specifications. The building of the largest and most hazardous storage facilities must undergo a complete consensus process, in accordance with the Environment Act 1976 and the Democratization of Public Inquiries and Environment Conservation Act 1983.[60]

[59] No 93-132 (29.01.1993).
[60] No 83-630 (12.07.1983).

The largest facilities[61] must be authorized by the Ministry for Industry, while the majority of the projects are authorized by the Prefect. The building of smaller storage facilities must be declared to the Prefect before the project can proceed. **7.141**

The operator applies to the Prefect for permission to build a facility and sends him an application file containing the exact location of the facility, an environmental impact assessment, and a hazard assessment. The Prefect holds the public inquiry, compiles all information in a final report, and summons the departmental Hygiene Committee. Before giving the Prefect an official recommendation, the Committee holds an open debate allowing the Prefect to present the final report and the operator to make a statement. Within a three-month period after the public inquirer issued his own report, the Prefect drafts a decision. The operator is notified of the draft and may, in response, issue a new statement within fifteen days. The Prefect makes the final decision, but may postpone it if information is still lacking. **7.142**

(3) Imports and Distribution

Imports

France has no major oil deposit. The aims of the Petroleum Act 1928 were twofold: to develop national oil companies and to ensure secure supplies of oil. The State gave authorizations to import oil to a limited number of companies. Granting licences allowed the State to monitor the quantities of imported petroleum products. These controls were partly lifted during the 1980s. **7.143**

The Reform of the Petroleum Legislation Act 1992 abolished earlier legislation to comply with the European Single Market. Its aims were to maintain oil-refining capacity on French territory, develop the activity of French oil companies abroad, ensure the building up of strategic stores, and maintain a French petroleum fleet and domestic market profitability. The new law enacted European Directive 92/12 EEC and stated that 'oil imports and exports, processing, transport, storage and distribution of crude oil and petroleum derivatives are unregulated, as long as they comply with the provisions of this law'. Oil companies operating on the French market must build up stores and notify the Minister for Industry of any project for building, closing, or decommissioning an oil refinery. They must comply with the safety rules in force. **7.144**

Tariffs are levied upon petroleum products in France. Articles 25 to 27 of the Amsterdam Treaty (ex Arts 12 to 29 of the Treaty of Rome) determine the tariffs to be applied in the European Union. In practice, only oil imports from North America bear the full tariff. **7.145**

[61] Over 5,000 tonnes for liquid hydrocarbons and 500 tonnes for liquified petroleum gas.

7.146 The Reform of the Petroleum Legislation Act 1992 defined three types of operators. The authorized operators may export, store, and import duty-free petroleum products from one Union Member State to another. The registered operators may store duty-free products but must keep an accurate account of deliveries received. The other operators may receive duty-free products from another Member State but must declare them to the French administration prior to shipping. To comply with European legislation, a notice published in March 1993 abolished the licences previously needed for importing or exporting petroleum products from certain countries.

7.147 European refining companies have not invested in fundamental conversion because the differential between heavy fuels and white products does not make this investment cost-effective at the moment. European companies must comply with the differential fixed by world markets, as there is in practice no import duty on these products in the Community. Furthermore, other countries have not implemented the equivalent of European and French measures against SO_2 emissions. The loss of autonomy that could result in the European refining industry would compromise the security of European supplies. A first step to restore self-sufficiency would be to take severe sanctions against dumping practices, which can be easily identified by a comparison with the prices fixed by the world market for crude oil and petroleum products. In France, the demand is moving increasingly to white products (petrol, diesel, etc) while French refineries are still producing heavy fuels, despite the conversion investment made in the 1980s.

Distribution

7.148 Prior to 1985 companies selling petroleum products to the French consumer had to comply with a 1959 rule controlling the setting up of petrol stations and other petroleum sales outlets. The Ministry for Industry awarded 'special licences' to petroleum companies to sell petroleum products to the consumer at authorized sales outlets. A non-licensed sales outlet might be authorized to sell petroleum products but was submitted to closer control on quantities needed. A first ministerial order issued in August 1981 partly lifted the controls. Since October 1985 the creation and supply of petrol stations and other sales outlets are unregulated. Nevertheless, an outlet creation must be notified to the Ministry for Industry and comply with the safety rules in force. Companies previously awarded a 'special licence' must report quantities sold in their sales network to the French administration.

7.149 As petroleum products were both expensive and strategic imported goods, the State also started to monitor prices in 1925 by controlling petrol prices. During and after the Second World War, complete control on petroleum product prices was established, particularly through an Ordinance of 1945. In 1978, controls were lifted on the prices of a few petroleum products. From June to October 1982 a complete price freeze on the whole economy was implemented, and the

Government supervised petroleum product prices through the 'inflation-fighting commitments' agreed to by oil companies. Controls were eventually lifted in January 1985 on petrol, high-octane petrol, and diesel and in December 1985 on household fuel. French price controls were completely lifted by the Ordinance of 1986.[62] A 1988 governmental order defined how oil prices should be advertised to ensure that consumers were fully informed.

D. Transmission and Distribution of Gas

(1) Institutional Framework

The State-owned Gaz de France (GDF) is a public body. It plays a major role in the supply and distribution of gas in France, due to a mandated monopoly on gas distribution, imports, and exports of natural gas. However, this mandated monopoly does not include natural gas production, which is assured by petroleum companies, with the ELF group being responsible for almost all natural gas production in France. It also does not apply to gas transmission, which is undertaken by three distinct operators, GDF, Gaz du Sud-Ouest, and the Compagnie Française du Méthane. **7.150**

GDF's functions were defined in the Gas and Electricity Nationalization Act 1946, which nationalized 84 per cent of French gas assets, and transferred their property to GDF. GDF's structure integrates purchasing, storage, transport, and distribution. GDF and EDF have grouped the distribution of gas and electricity through a shared network of sales outlets. For instance, gas and electricity invoices are sent out jointly. The State supervises GDF investment programmes and domestic pricing policy, along with import and export contracts negotiated by the public body. Since 1991 the State has also negotiated 'planning agreements' with GDF. **7.151**

(2) Transmission and Storage

Introduction

The transmission and storage system has been designed to ensure gas transmission to the final consumer in case of supply disruption or in extreme temperature conditions.[63] In 1996, the main transmission grid totalled 30,537 km. It links the production or import sites to underground storage facilities and the largest consumption areas. Besides, the public distribution network totals 125,500 km and supplies gas to 6,000 municipalities that cover three-quarters of the French population. **7.152**

[62] See para 7.104.
[63] Probability 2%.

Transmission companies

7.153 Gas transmission is in the hands of three major transmission companies. Their transmission grids account for some 75 per cent, 8 per cent, and 17 per cent of the transportation facilities. GDF supplies the north, north-central, and south-east of France with imported gas only. *Gaz du Sud-Ouest* is owned by ELF (70 per cent) and GDF (30 per cent) and supplies the south-west of France with Lacq deposit gas, which is gradually being replaced by imported gas. In central France a third transmission network is operated by *Compagnie Française du Méthane*, which is owned by GDF (50 per cent), ELF (40 per cent), and Total (10 per cent). This network sells imported gas supplied by GDF and ELF. In addition, ELF Aquitaine de Réseaux holds a concession for a very small network. Each transportation network has a regional monopoly of supply to all customers and public or industrial distributors.

The legal framework

7.154 The Gas and Electricity Nationalization Act 1946 excluded natural gas transmission from nationalization. However, gas transmission can only be undertaken by either a public body or a company with at least 30 per cent of its shares publicly owned.[64]

7.155 The transmission of gas through pipelines is based on a concession granted by the State. These pipelines are listed in a 1985 decree[65] and supply public distribution networks, other transmission facilities, underground storage facilities, and industrial clients whose annual consumption exceeds 5 million KWh. The decree does not apply to gas transmission pipelines linking deposits to gas factories and pipelines set up within the perimeters of factories, underground storage facilities, and mines. The establishment of these transmission facilities (which are categorized in the 1985 decree) can be authorized on the basis of a simpler administrative procedure.

7.156 To obtain a concession for gas transmission, the operator must send an application to the Minister for Industry, who may decide to study it further and will send it to the Prefects in charge of the relevant departments, one of them being chosen as co-ordinator.

7.157 The main transmission lines are subject to a public inquiry in accordance with the Democratization of Public Inquiries and Environment Conservation Act 1983, while small pipelines are subject to a simplified and more specific inquiry procedure. The observations from the inquiry are sent to the operator, who in response must state the follow-up measures he intends to implement. The Prefect gives a

64 According to French law, the companies do not belong to the public sector.
65 No 85-1108 (15.10.1985).

final recommendation and sends the complete file to the Minister for Industry who may grant the concession. The concession contract and attached terms of reference are authorized by a decree signed by the Prime Minister.

For local gas transmission, authorizations are given instead of concessions. Except for the terms of reference, which are replaced by a simpler form as defined in a Minister of Industry order, the file sent to the Minister for Industry is similar to that necessary for a concession application. The Minister may decide to study the application further and send it to the Prefect, who holds the public inquiry and may grant the authorization by a Prefect order. **7.158**

If private landowners affected by the facility location object to construction, a declaration of public interest is required to give the operator the right of way on private property as defined in the Act of 1906 and the Gas and Electricity Nationalization Act 1946. Damages are awarded by the property judge. A governmental order signed by the Minister in charge of energy defined technical and safety rules applicable to gas transmission. Before the facility start-up, the operator must have the administration's formal acknowledgement that safety regulations and prescriptions described in a safety assessment attached to the application have been abided by. The operator must also notify the administration of an 'intervention and surveillance plan' which defines the facility's means of surveillance and the measures intended to be implemented in case of incident or accident. **7.159**

Cross-border transit of gas

An April 1995 decree[66] enacted the 91/296 EEC directive to govern the transit of gas between major transmission networks. GDF, *Gaz du Sud-Ouest*, and *Compagnie Française du Méthane* are mentioned in the Directive's Annex and the April 1995 decree. Transit contracts must comply with rules of fair trade and allow efficient management of transmission networks and storage facilities; they must not include any unjustified restriction, jeopardize the safety of supply, or diminish the quality of service. **7.160**

Storage

To adjust a regular annual supply to a demand which is subject to wide seasonal variations, France has developed underground storage facilities with a total capacity of 115 TWh. Eleven of them are set up in aquifer layers and three in salt cavities. **7.161**

To take into account protection of the water supply and population safety, gas storage legislation established a regime of centralized ministerial authorizations. **7.162**

[66] No 95-494 (25.04.1995).

Any person may apply for an authorization. An environmental impact assessment, geological and seismic studies of the site, and technical and financial data to allow evaluation of the applicant's ability must be included in the application sent to the Minister for Industry. If the Minister decides that the application needs further study, the Prefect has the file reviewed by the local State services. The Prefect holds a public inquiry, in accordance with the Democratization of Public Inquiries and Environment Conservation Act 1983. The relevant local authorities and bodies are consulted, and have a three-month period to answer.

7.163 The use of underground cavities to store natural gas is governed by a 1958 Ordinance on underground gas storage and a 1962 decree, later updated, mainly in 1988.[67] In accordance with these texts, prospecting permits are granted by ministerial decisions and storage permits by decrees signed by the Prime Minister.

(3) Distribution

7.164 Although the Gas and Electricity Nationalization Act 1946 allocated gas distribution to GDF, it entitled the companies which already held concessions or were partly owned by public authorities to continue distributing gas. Today, almost twenty public bodies and semi-public companies are distributing gas. After the introduction of a 1996 Act,[68] a non-nationalized distributor may extend its activities to the neighbouring municipalities if they are not already supplied by another operator.

7.165 The Nationalization Act stated that the regime of public distribution of gas through pipes is determined by a concession granted by a municipality or a group of municipalities. Standard specifications state the concessionaire's obligations, and were legally binding until the adoption of the Rights and Liberties of Local Authorities Act 1982[69] which repealed them. They are still used as non-binding guidelines for the contracting parties.

7.166 However, the public service of gas distribution must ensure social cohesion and a balanced development over all French territory. According to the Act of July 1998,[70] each Prefect consults municipalities and drafts a 'public service distribution plan' covering the department. The draft plan lists municipalities not already connected to a gas distribution grid and wishing to be in the future. The plan is approved by the Minister for Energy Policy who must consider the results of an energy impact assessment, GDF's investment profitability rate, which must not be below the limit determined in a decree, and energy policy goals, namely respect of fair competition between various energy sources and development of renewable

[67] No 58-1132 (25.11.1958), No 62-1296 (06.11.1962), No 88-220 (07.03.1988).
[68] No 96-142 (21.02.1996).
[69] No 82-213 (02.03.1982).
[70] No 98-546, Art 50 (02.07.1998).

energy sources. The Gas and Electricity Superior Council may be called on for advice. Municipalities listed in the approved plan will be connected to GDF's grid. The plan is updated every three years. Municipalities excluded from the plan may award concessions to authorized private or mixed-capital companies that possess the necessary technical and financial expertise. A 1999 decree[71] determined the Act implementing procedures, namely how municipalities should express their wishes and the 'distribution plan' be drafted, approved and published, and which procedure applies to companies willing to supply the municipalities listed in the plan. A 2000 governmental order[72] published the first list of municipalities which would be part of the 'public service distribution plan'.

(4) The Liberalization Process

The EC Directive on the internal gas market provides some common rules on gas regulation and encourages liberalization. The French Government will pass new Acts and Regulations with regard to the gas market in order to increase the efficiency of the French system while preserving the public service targets and the present system's reliability, its long-term commitments, and the balance struck between its various operators. Following the Directive, all electricity producers became deemed eligible consumers, along with firms consuming more than 25 million cubic metres per site by the year 2000, then 15 million cubic metres by 2003, and 5 million by 2008. One estimates that the French market share open to competition will therefore amount to 20 per cent by 2000, 28 per cent in 2003, and 33 per cent by 2008. The downstream gas industry, namely transmission, storage, gas terminal construction, and gas sales, will be opened to new operators. However, gas distribution is a public service and the opening of the market will be limited. Operators will be protected against the risks of the 'take or pay' system. **7.167**

E. Electricity

(1) Historical Framework

The Gas and Electricity Nationalization Act 1946 transferred the ownership of all energy producing facilities whose power exceeded 8 MVA to EDF. Private producers were forbidden to exceed this limit, but energy facilities recycling waste or supplying heating networks were excepted. It permitted independent operators to generate and sell electricity as long as their production was lower than 8 MVA. It allowed electricity generation for self-consumption. EDF had a *de jure* monopoly right over the import, export, and transmission of electricity. EDF undertook electricity distribution along with 194 non-nationalized distributors. **7.168**

[71] No 99-278 (12.04.1999).
[72] 03.04.2000.

7.169 According to a 1955 decree,[73] EDF was obliged to purchase electricity from other operators at tariffs approved by the Minister of Finance, taking into account the costs EDF would have incurred to produce and supply the same amount of energy. Although the 1955 decree first aimed at counterbalancing the distribution monopoly of EDF and non-nationalized distributors, it later became an instrument to promote diversification of energy sources. However, a Minister for Industry governmental order could suspend this obligation when the current electricity supply capacity met the demand at satisfactory economic conditions of generation, transport, and distribution. In 1995 the Minister for Industry formally acknowledged the surplus of electricity production in France and suspended the purchasing obligation for three years, except for generators using CHP or renewable energy sources.

(2) The Act on the Modernization and Development of Public Electricity Services

7.170 Between 19 February 1999 and the passing of the new Act in February 2000 the electricity market was partially opened. All consumers of over 100 GWh per site were considered eligible to choose their suppliers. This concerned several hundred consumers. Five of them left EDF for another supplier. All buyers consuming between 40 GWh and 100 GWh are still exempted from the Directive's influence.[74]

7.171 The new organization established by the Act implementing the Directive consolidates public service by guaranteeing continuity, equality of treatment for each category of client, quality of service at minimum cost, and adaptation to new technologies and French society requirements. More than thirty decrees are necessary to implement the new Act.[75] In October 2000, the ones already published allowed the new French electric system to function normally. The major milestones of the new Act can be described as follows:

7.172 • The public electricity service and its obligations are defined for the first time in the law. The public service must ensure a competitive and high-quality electricity supply and implement geographic equalization of electricity prices, which principles are stated in the law for the first time. Moreover, it includes a 'right to energy' in the sense that a low electricity tariff may be applied to the most economically deprived customers. The Act guarantees that families or persons living in precarious financial circumstances will have access to electricity supply. In charge of the balanced development of electricity generation, the

[73] No 55-662 (20.05.1955).

[74] *Petroleum Economist*, December 1999, 61.

[75] Those on the Electricity Regulatory Commission (No 2000-381, 02.05.2000; No 2000-874, 07.09.2000; No 2000-894, 11.09.2000), the eligible customers (No 2000-456, 29.05.2000), the trading (No 2000-1069, 30.10.2000), and the electricity generation (No 2000-877, 07.09.2000) are published.

public service provides an auxiliary supply to eligible clients in case of breakdown. A fair and transparent procedure finances the public service obligations imposed on EDF and non-nationalized distributors.

- Following the Directive all eligible customers may choose their supplier. More than 800 clients were to be eligible in the year 2000, accounting for 30 per cent of the domestic electricity consumption, and 3,000 in 2003 (33 per cent of domestic electricity consumption). Electricity trading is authorized for electricity generators and their subsidiaries.[76] Electricity exports and imports are no longer a monopoly. Generators implementing supply contracts with eligible customers have a right to access to the public transmission and distribution networks. France has finally opted for a system of regulated third-party access. A tariff for access is proposed by the Electricity Regulatory Commission (ERC or *Commission de Régulation de l'Electricité*, CRE, in French) and decided by the State. **7.173**

- As for electricity generation, any operator can now apply for authorization from the Minister for Energy, in accordance with procedures set out in Articles 6 and 7 of the new Act. However, facilities whose power does not exceed 4.5 MW are deemed authorized if so declared. To grant an authorization, the Minister must have regard to the criteria listed in Article 9.[77] A Pluri-annual Programming of Investments (PPI) is elaborated by the Government which reports to Parliament on its implementation. If electricity generation capacities resulting from the applying and granting of generation authorization do not match the PPI prescriptions, for instance regarding primary energy sources, the Minister may decide, in order to fill the gap, to launch a competitive bid technically managed by the Electricity Regulatory Commission. **7.174**

- The 1955 decree has been abolished.[78] The new Article 10 states that EDF and the non-nationalized distributors must purchase electricity generated from renewable energy sources and energy-efficient techniques, such as CHP, provided the power generated on a site does not exceed a 12 MW maximum threshold, which will be adapted by decree to every facility category. EDF and the non-nationalized distributors must also purchase electricity generated by facilities supplying heating networks or using household waste. **7.175**

- Following the requirements of the Directive, EDF has set up separate accounts for the production, transmission, and distribution of electricity. The national **7.176**

[76] Therefore excluding affiliates.

[77] Security and safety of public electricity networks, energy sources, site selection and public domain use, energy efficiency, operator's economic, financial, and technical capabilities, public service objectives and principles as well as the objectives defined in the pluri-annual Programme of Investments (PPI), environmental conservation, implementation of labour and social law.

[78] See also above, para 7.170.

grid is managed by a new division of EDF: the Public Transmission Grid Management Division (*Gestionnaire du réseau de transport*, or GRT). The GRT is a separate entity within EDF. It manages the grid, provides for fair access, and ensures confidentiality of information whose release might jeopardize fair competition. The right to access to the national grid is ensured by the CRE.

7.177 • Regulatory powers are divided between the State and the newly created CRE.[79] The Government is responsible for defining, implementing, and controlling energy policy, public service obligations, and technical guidelines. It is also in charge of the safety and efficiency of the French electric system. The CRE[80] ensures fair competition, access, and use of public electric grids. The six Commission members were appointed in March 2000 by the Government, the presidents of the National Assembly and the Senate, and the Economic and Social Council.[81] The CRE rules over disputes between grid users and managers and imposes a penalty when rules applicable to grid access are violated. The CRE subsidies are voted in the Finance Act.

7.178 The new Electricity Act does not change the role of the social legislation applicable to the electricity sector, except that collective bargaining has been introduced. Neither has the role of the local authorities changed with regard to the grant of concessions of electricity distribution. In addition, they are given new responsibilities in connection with decreasing electricity demand.

(3) Electricity Generation

Introduction

7.179 In France the sources of electricity generation are diverse. In addition to generation on the basis of fossil fuel emitting greenhouse gases, several other sources are used which have a less polluting effect. France is characterized first and foremost by large-scale use of nuclear power. In addition power is produced on the basis of hydropower and renewable sources such as wind energy. The following paragraphs describe the legal regimes governing these four sources of electricity production.

Thermal

7.180 The production of electricity from oil-fired generators is subject to an authorization, in accordance with the new Electricity Act and a 1996 decree implementing the Energy Saving Acts 1974, 1977, and 1980.[82]

---

[79] It is most likely that upon the entry into force of the Gas Act implementing the Gas Directive, the ECR will become the Gas and Electricity Regulatory Commission.

[80] Title VI of the new Act.

[81] A consultative Council set up by Title IX of the Constitution. Representatives of various economic sectors (trade unions, family associations, professional organizations, etc) sit on this Council.

[82] No 96-156 (26.02.1996), No 74-908 (29.10.1974), No 77-804 (19.07.1977), and No 80-531 (15.07.1980).

As for coal, the five coal-fired power stations owned by CDF and later by SNET were first used to meet CDF needs; today, they mainly supply electricity to the EDF grid. The State allocated a legal monopoly over coal imports to the ATIC association until 1994 when coal imports were deregulated. ATIC had retained some of its regulatory powers, mainly the compilation and publication of coal import statistics, control of technical specifications of imported coal, and the implementation of coal quality certification defined by a 1995 decree.[83] ATIC was controlled by the Ministry for Industry, which can veto management decisions. ATIC formed a joint stock company, which took over general consulting and technical services to coal importers and traders (including ATIC members) on a market basis. No legal prescription limits coal distribution. **7.181**

Nuclear

Nuclear legislation was created and modified according to the technical evolution and development of nuclear energy in France. Many legal provisions implemented in the nuclear domain have therefore been codified in the Public Health Code and the Labour Code. Other Acts dealing with the environment apply to nuclear issues, such as the Water Act and the Atmospheric Pollution Act. In France, as in every country developing nuclear energy, the most original feature of nuclear law lies in the numerous guidelines and rules adopted at the international level, such as the Brussels and Vienna Conventions on Responsibility and the European Directive on Radiation Protection. **7.182**

The largest nuclear facilities have been subject to a Ministry-managed system of licensing and controls since 1963, while all other hazardous industrial facilities have remained under the Prefects' authority and control. This centralized procedure was left unchanged by the new Electricity Act and aims at protecting the safety of the population and of employees. New safeguards were added in 1973 to meet the nuclear development programme requirements. **7.183**

The development of the fuel cycle and electricity generation was originally carried out by the CEA. It lost its monopoly over these nuclear activities to its three main subsidiaries when new industrial operators were needed to develop the above-mentioned tasks. First, Technicatome (1972) was founded to take over the design, development, and construction of nuclear reactors. Cogema (1976) was vested with uranium mining, enrichment, uranium chemistry, production of nuclear fuel, fuel reprocessing, and engineering. Framatome took over nuclear plant construction and engineering, nuclear maintenance, and nuclear fuels. The holding company CEA-Industrie was set up to own CEA's subsidiaries' shares on behalf of the State. Cogema bought 34 per cent of Framatome's capital in 2000. **7.184**

[83] No 95-695 (09.05.1995).

7.185 IPSN, the *Institut de Protection et de Sûreté Nucléaire* (Nuclear Safety Institute), a CEA division, advises the Government on safety assessment procedures implemented in nuclear facilities. IPSN assesses the measures taken by operators to ensure safety and comply with regulations, controls and keeps an account of nuclear and radioactive materials in facilities, controls nuclear material transport, and takes part in all nuclear exercises. IPSN studies technical safety files and reports to the Standing Committee. ANDRA is entrusted with the waste policy implementation.

7.186 The Office for Protection Against Ionizing Radiation (OPRI) determines radioactive contamination specifications, measuring methods and prevention techniques. It assesses radioactivity by measuring, analysing, and quantifying dosages in environments where radioactivity might jeopardize the population's health. OPRI collects staff protection data in nuclear facilities and advises the Ministry of Labour. In accordance with the Anti-Pollution Act 1961 and the Water Act 1992, OPRI checks nuclear pollution of air and water. OPRI inspectors are under oath and examine effluents and radioactivity levels in areas neighbouring an INB (basic nuclear facility). OPRI defines staff radiation protection measures in nuclear facilities, determines measures, analyses, and dosages to assess radioactivity, and participates in the implementation of emergency plans to protect the population in case of nuclear accidents.[84] The Prime Minister had promised to separate controlling from operating functions, particularly in the nuclear sector. To prevent CEA from harbouring both, IPSN will soon be separated from the CEA and merged with several research teams from the OPRI to form a new public body, the IRSN (National Institute for Radioprotection and Nuclear Safety). A bill and a decree are being drafted to create the new IRSN.

Uranium production

7.187 The French Mining Code also applies to the production of uranium.[85] The State has no monopoly on prospecting for, or extraction of, uranium on French territory. The Minister for Industry is empowered to award mining licences, after a special public inquiry has been held, and the French Atomic Energy Authority and the General Mining Council consulted. To comply with the provisions of a 1990 governmental order, the licensed operator must gather statistical data on staff exposure to ionizing radiation and send them to the local Ministry of Industry service and to OPRI once a year. In accordance with the Mining Act 1994, the operator must provide the French administration with financial guarantees before starting or resuming a potentially hazardous mining exploitation.

---

[84] OPRI is also consulted in the authorization procedure for all medical and dental equipment using nuclear substances.

[85] See paras 7.112–7.136 for an analysis of the Mining Code.

The construction and use of nuclear facilities

The Anti-Pollution Act 1961[86] vested the Government with the power to issue decrees to rule over the construction, management, and control of the two kinds of nuclear facilities. The INB, *Installations nucléaires de base* (basic nuclear facilities), are nuclear reactors,[87] particle accelerators, and all nuclear plants.[88] Other nuclear facilities are ICPE, *installations classées pour la protection de l'environnement* (facilities deemed classified with the purpose of protecting the environment). **7.188**

According to French civil law, all construction projects must be authorized by the mayor within his jurisdiction, but the building permit concerning a nuclear facility is only granted by a decree based on a report submitted by the Ministry for Industry and signed by the Prime Minister.[89] In addition, all INBs, such as EDF nuclear power plants, must pass through two co-ordinated procedures: a preliminary procedure and a DUP, *déclaration d'utilité publique* (declaration of public interest[90]), establishing the need for the new public facility. Before granting the DUP and the building permit through two decrees, the Government must hold a public inquiry. **7.189**

The operator sends a complete application file to the DSIN, which calls on a standing group[91] to advise on the application. The DSIN also consults with the Ministries for the Environment and for Industry. The Prefect simultaneously holds a public inquiry, which is widely publicized as required in the Democratization of Public Inquiries and Environment Conservation Act 1983. An open debate is launched on the environmental impact assessment. The decree acknowledging the public interest and consequently granting the DUP is signed if the public inquiry results allow it. **7.190**

The other decree granting the building permit allows the operator to proceed within a set safety framework. A final safety report is submitted to the Ministers for Industry and the Environment for approval. It details the facility's perimeter, the safety rules binding the promoter, and the starting-up process. According to the Safety and Protection of Forest against Fire and Prevention of Major Hazards Act 1987 and its 1990 implementing decree,[92] the Minister of the Environment is also given a 'study on hazards', written from the preliminary safety report issued **7.191**

[86] Anti-Pollution Act (02.08.1961), No 61-842.

[87] Except reactors which are part of a moving vehicle.

[88] Preparation, production, and recycling of radioactive substances; preparation of nuclear fuels; isotopic separation; reprocessing of irradiated nuclear fuels; nuclear waste management; all storage facilities.

[89] In France a decree must be signed by the Prime Minister to be legally in force. Ministers countersign decrees.

[90] DUP: see below, paras 7.270–7.273.

[91] Representatives of the IPSN sit on the group.

[92] Act No 87-565 (22.07.1987) and Decree No 90-394 (11.05.1990).

by the operator and listing the measures designed to deal with accidents. DSIN compiles a file including the standing group's opinion, the Ministries' observations, and the public inquiry results. These technical data are part of the building authorization decree eventually drafted by DSIN. The Ministry of Health is consulted on the draft and its opinion is binding upon the Government. However, if the Ministry of Health does not give an opinion within a three-month period the draft decree is examined and adopted by the Cabinet, before being signed by the Prime Minister. Local information committees may be set up to follow step-by-step the building of the new facility.

7.192 The control of INBs is entrusted to Inspectors under the Ministry for Industry's authority. The DSIN is in charge of controls, along with the IPSN and OPRI, and carries out technical control of radioactive effluent. The operator must comply with several ministerial orders and ensure that the quality of facility structures, nuclear materials, and managing conditions do not jeopardize the facility's safety. The operator is also responsible for all the material supplied by his subcontractors.

7.193 According to the ICPE Act 1976,[93] the creation of a nuclear ICPE must be either formally declared or authorized, depending on the classification of the degree of hazard. Under the Minister for the Environment's authority, the Prefect may authorize the construction of an ICPE after a public inquiry has been held and the applicant's file studied. However, the Minister of the Environment makes the decision if several neighbouring regions are affected, after consulting with the High Council of Classified Facilities. The decree granting the INB building permit also authorizes the building of ICPEs set up in the INB perimeter. A 1985 Act[94] increased the penalties for infringement of the laws governing the management of a classified facility.

Environmental controls

7.194 Liquid and gaseous effluent releasing and water collecting must comply with a 1995 decree[95] which modified and finalized former decrees. Any release of radioactive liquid effluents by an INB must be authorized, along with the release of gaseous effluents which could pollute the atmosphere. The release of an ICPE built within an INB perimeter must be authorized, or simply notified if the category of release is listed in a 1953 decree.[96] The Ministers for Industry, the Environment, and Public Health sign the governmental order authorizing the

---

[93] No 76-663 (19.07.1976). ICPE (facilities deemed classified with the purpose of protecting the environment) is a wide category which encompasses all major transport and industrial facilities.

[94] No 85-661 (03.07.1985).

[95] No 95-540 (04.05.1995).

[96] No 53-578 (20.05.1953) implementing a 1917 Act establishing the legal regime for 'dangerous and unhealthy facilities'. The categories defined in the 1953 Decree are still relevant.

release; the Minister in charge of public safety is consulted. When a simple declaration is required by law, the operator sends the declaration to the three Ministers, who in return send a formal acknowledgement. According to the 1995 decree, the Ministry of Health is responsible for the control of radioactive effluent. The Minister informs the Prefect and the operator if law infringements are reported.

Emergency plans

The Safety and Protection of Forest against Fire and Prevention of Major Hazards Act 1987 consolidated earlier emergency plans and rescue procedures. Rescue preparation and organization are entrusted to the Prefect and mainly determined by the 'ORSEC plan'.[97] The Ministry of the Interior determines the safeguard measures and co-ordinates the State's, public bodies', and local authorities' rescue means throughout the French territory. **7.195**

A 1988 decree[98] implementing the Act of 1987 defined the emergency plans. Prepared by the Prefects, they detail the list of hazards, the means of intervention, and the duties of each administration and service, including those of the public bodies and local authorities. A particular intervention plan (PPI in French) describes each hazardous facility, lists the municipalities concerned, defines the measures of protection and the evacuation procedures to be carried out, and determines where the displaced population could be temporarily relocated. The plan also describes the immediate emergency measures to be carried out by the operator on behalf of the police before their intervention. The mayors and operators are notified of these plans, which are publicized in local newspapers. **7.196**

The Act also gave French citizens the right to be informed of major technological hazards and measures implemented to protect them. The operator must take part in a general information campaign describing the nuclear facility. According to a 1990 implementing decree,[99] the mayor must issue information listing the safeguard measures decided, particularly if a special intervention plan concerns his town. The mayor informs the public, who can examine the document at the town hall. Other decisions have been made to ensure the right to information about nuclear hazards. Representatives of local authorities, trade unions, and conservation associations sit on local information commissions set up near major energy production sites. In 1988 the Superior Council for Nuclear Safety and Information adopted a nuclear event scale. The same rating method was previously used for earthquake description. It allows the nuclear technicians and the public to understand the nature and seriousness of an incident. In 1994 this scale was replaced by the IAEA's scale, whose conception is similar. **7.197**

97 ORSEC is the *organisation des secours* (rescue organization plan).
98 No 88-622 (06.05.1988).
99 No 90-918 (11.10.1990).

Trade in nuclear material and equipment

7.198 France has adopted a complete body of legislation to meet the safety requirements of trade in nuclear material and equipment. To ensure safety, the French administration is empowered to control imports and exports and supervise nuclear material and facilities.

7.199 Export permits are granted in accordance with European and national regulations. Exports are authorized according to guidelines determined by the Nuclear Foreign Policy Council, headed by the President of the Republic. The Protection and Control of Nuclear Material Act 1980[100] empowered the Minister for Industry to authorize imports, exports, production, storage, use, and transport of nuclear materials.[101] Before granting the authorization, the Minister for Industry consults with the Minister for the Interior, and if necessary the Minister of Foreign Affairs (in case of exports or imports) or the Protection of Nuclear Material Transport Committee (in case of transport), along with other departments in charge. A fifteen-day period is allowed for reply, and non-reply is considered agreement. Under a predetermined threshold of nuclear material quantity, the operator need not apply for authorization but may simply notify the French administration.

Physical protection

7.200 The authorized operator must keep a precise inventory of nuclear material and ensure the protection of nuclear materials and their storage facility, room, or device. He is responsible for the protection of nuclear material during transport. Civil servants under the Minister for Industry's authority supervise stock inventory and stock lists of nuclear materials kept by the operators, and may request a supplementary inventory. They are under oath and sworn to secrecy. Prior to the transport of nuclear material, the operator sends a notice to the Minister for Industry, who grants an authorization after consulting the Minister for the Interior and the Protection of Nuclear Material Transport Committee. The Minister must be notified of any loss, theft, or hijacking of nuclear material. Non-compliance with this rule results in a penalty. In accordance with a 1981 decree[102] and a governmental order implementing the Nuclear Material Protection and Control Act 1980, IPSN is responsible for collecting the notifications and collating the data and may impose additional guidelines obliging the operator to comply with the governmental order. Thus, the quantities and storage locations of nuclear materials are known to the French administration, and nuclear materials are protected against loss, theft, dispersal, and damage.

---

[100] No 80-572 (25.07.1980), modified by No 89-434.

[101] This Act applies to plutonium, uranium, thorium, deuterium, tritium, and lithium 6.

[102] No 81-512 (12.05.1981).

The 1989 Act authorized the ratification of the International Convention on Nuclear Materials and enacted some of its provisions. It gave French courts jurisdiction over cases of infringement which take place abroad. 7.201

Radiation protection

A first decree[103] issued in 1966 established basic rules on radiation protection and entrusted the Ministry of Public Health with the protection of facility staff and the wider population against radioactivity. Two other decrees issued in 1975 and 1986[104] stated the rules to protect staff in INBs and other nuclear facilities. The enactment of EURATOM Directive 80–836 determined the annual limits of exposure to ionizing radiation to which workers could be submitted, and how effluent release into the environment should be controlled.[105] The operator is responsible for staff protection; he must comply with radiation protection guidelines applicable outside his facility and make every effort to limit the impact of the facility on the environment. To protect the health of both population and staff, a new Directive 96/29/EURATOM lays down basic safety standards against ionizing radiation. The Directive has been implemented in France on 28 March 2001 (French Official Journal 31 March 2001). OPRI is the Government's expert on radiation protection and gathers data on staff exposure in nuclear facilities. 7.202

Radioactive substances and waste management

The Public Health Code has codified most of the legislation applicable to natural or artificial radioactive elements. The preparation, import, exploitation, and use of artificial radioactive elements is entrusted to the CEA and licensed persons only (articles L[106] 636 to L 640 of the Public Health Code). The Interdepartmental Committee on Artificial Radioactive Elements is consulted in the procedure. The licence is awarded for a five-year period by the Minister of Health, or the Chairman of the Committee, depending on the hazard classification of the radio-elements. If necessary, the Minister may define additional rules for processing nuclear substances.[107] 7.203

A 1986 decree[108] lists the processes submitted to a system of licensing, namely the possession of radio-elements with a view to their sale, disposal, or use. The theft or loss of radioactive elements must be reported to the Prefect. 7.204

[103] No 66-450 (20.06.1966).

[104] No 75-306 (28.04.1975) and No 86-1103 (02.10.1986).

[105] According to the new international dosimetric system, France has converted from curies to becquerels and from rems to sieverts.

[106] In a French code, 'L' before the provision number stands for 'law' and means that the text is an Act of Parliament.

[107] Medical staff who will be exposed to non-sealed radioactive sources used for medical purposes must have either a special diploma of nuclear medicine or a diploma of radiobiology/radiopharmacy.

[108] No 86-80 (13.01.1986).

7.205 Radioactive waste is the result of a technical process, is not intended for recycling or reprocessing, and contains radioactive elements. Nuclear facilities either produce waste as a by-product, or are designed for waste management and storage. Waste management consists of storing the ultimate waste until it no longer represents a threat to the environment or public health. In contrast with effluents, which are diluted into the environment, radioactive waste is packaged to avoid dispersal and to prevent irradiation hazard. The packaging is designed to take into consideration the characteristics, concentration, and life cycle of the waste.

7.206 According to the Waste Destruction and Material Recycling Act 1975,[109] the operator producing or storing nuclear waste must ensure that waste disposal does not jeopardize the environment. The Act of 1975, updated in 1992, established the transparency of waste disposal measures. Before opening a waste storage facility, the operator or owner must provide the French administration with technical and financial guarantees. Other laws apply to waste storage facilities, such as the Anti-Pollution Act 1961, the Environment Act 1976, and the Water Act 1992. The Ministries of Public Health, Industry, Research, and the Environment are responsible for a rational waste management policy and for supervising facilities producing nuclear waste. Waste management activities must be authorized by the French administration and comply with labour, public health, and environmental legislation. Before the passing of the Research on Nuclear Waste Management Act 1991, a 1963 decree and the 1976 Act[110] stated that an authorization detailing the technical guidelines to be implemented in waste management and storage processes had to be granted prior to the building of any facility.

7.207 The Research on Nuclear Waste Management Act 1991[111] asserted that management of long-life radioactive waste must protect the environment and health and take into account the rights of future generations. The Act defined a research programme and storage conditions for highly hazardous waste in underground facilities. The programme results will be assessed by a committee whose members have been chosen from within the scientific community and the Parliamentary Office for the Assessment of Scientific and Technological Choices. In 1996 the Government authorized ANDRA to perform the authorization procedure for the building of three underground laboratories in Meuse, Haute Marne, and Vienne which will study underground layers to determine whether the sites are appropriate to store radioactive waste. The results of this research programme will be summed up in a report submitted to Parliament in 2006, fifteen years after the passing of the Research on Nuclear Waste Management Act. The Government

[109] No 75-633 (15.07.1975).

[110] Decree no 63-1228 1963 (later modified in 1973 and 1985) deals with INB and the Act 1976 with ICPE.

[111] Research on Nuclear Waste Management Act (30.12.1991), No 91-1381.

will propose, if necessary, a bill authorizing the creation of an underground storage centre of long-life nuclear waste, and determine the safety measures to be applied to this new facility.

The Research on Nuclear Waste Management Act 1991 also provided for the creation of ANDRA. Four decrees implementing the 1991 Act were issued in 1992 and 1993.[112] They determined the consensus procedure to be applied to local authorities and the population affected by an underground laboratory project, defined the procedure for creating a research laboratory to study the underground layers, stated the legal framework for the management of laboratory equipment, and dealt with ANDRA statutes. **7.208**

A research programme on nuclear waste has been undertaken by ANDRA and IPSN. In 1993 EDF, CEA, and COGEMA signed a contract outlining a clean-up programme lasting until the turn of the century. The five aims of this contract were to gather all the conditioned waste in up-to-date and safe storage facilities, to rehabilitate former interim storage sites, to improve waste management methods to significantly reduce their volume,[113] to reprocess a large share of experimental fuels, and to dismantle decommissioned facilities. **7.209**

In 1996 data on the quantities of plutonium stored on French territory were published in a Ministry of Industry White Paper. **7.210**

France enacted two stipulations of Directive 92/31 EURATOM concerning the export, import, and transportation of radioactive waste. **7.211**

Transport of nuclear material

French legislation broadly enacts IAEA's guidelines. The Hazardous Material Transport by Air, Rail, or Inland Waterways Act 1942[114] and the associated implementing decrees stated that nuclear material must be labelled and tracked through safety files. The Minister of Transport may issue notices to define the special procedures applicable to hazardous nuclear materials, with the exception of irradiated fuels, and makes his decision after consulting with the Interdepartmental Committee on Transport of Hazardous Materials. Transport safety is ensured by the definition of criteria to classify nuclear materials according to their degree of hazard. **7.212**

In accordance with governmental orders issued in 1982 and 1986, nuclear material transporters must be granted a licence by the Minister for Industry, who consults the Minister for the Interior and the Transport Protection of Nuclear **7.213**

[112] No 92-1311 (17.12.1992), No 92-1366 (29.12.1992), No 92-1391 on ANDRA (30.12.1991), and No 93-940 (16.07.1993).

[113] 30% for surface-stored waste, 50% for waste containing long-life radionuclides.

[114] 05.02.1942.

Materials Committee. The transport of irradiated fuels and nuclear materials may also be entrusted to sub-contractors, who must be granted licences by the Ministry for Industry. A new European Directive requires that transporters hire a safety expert.

7.214 Three governmental orders were issued to implement the Protection and Control of Nuclear Material Act 1980, and detailed the shipping conditions, security measures, and transport tracking procedures. Prior to shipping, French or foreign-licensed transporters must give data[115] to IPSN and the Ministry of Interior Safety Directorate. Several orders define the procedures applicable to each means of transport.

7.215 Rail and road transport of nuclear materials are notified to the National Safety Service (Ministry for the Interior) and truck contamination control procedures are notified to the OPRI. Several governmental orders define the procedures for the transport of nuclear materials by sea. Licences and shipping authorizations are granted by the Minister for the Navy. The Navigation Inspecting Directorate authorizes the embarkment of nuclear materials on board. If an accident likely to jeopardize public health or sea fauna and flora occurs, the Nucmar (Nuclear Material at Sea) plan determines the duties of each administration and public body.

7.216 Air transport of nuclear material must be authorized by the Secretary General of Civil and Commercial Aviation, except for air transporters who comply with IFAA guidelines.

Nuclear liability

7.217 France implements the Paris Convention of 1960 modified by the Brussels Convention of 1963 and two Protocols of 1982. These Protocols were enacted by a 1990 law[116] finalizing the international guidelines. Three laws passed in 1965, 1968, and 1990[117] determined the liability of nuclear facilities' operators. The financial deposit required was raised to FF 600 million. This amount can be reduced to FF 150 million if the facilities are classified as a minor level of hazard in a 1991 decree. A nuclear material transporter must deposit FF 150 million if these materials are governed by the Paris Convention provisions, and FF 1,500 million otherwise. The criminal penalties resulting from non-compliance with these financial regulations were tightened. Two laws passed in 1968 and 1988[118] determined the responsibility of shipowners transporting nuclear materials. The 1988 Act asserted shipowners' responsibility as public service contractors. France took

[115] Date, time, and place of departure and arrival, quantity and description of nuclear material.
[116] No 90-397 (11.05.1990).
[117] No 65-956 (12.11.1965) modified by Act No 68-1045 (29.11.1968) and No 88-1093 (03.12.1993).
[118] No 68-943 (30.10.1968) and No 90-448 (16.06.1990).

into consideration OECD Nuclear Committee guidelines on legal damages payable to victims.

The State finances damages exceeding the operator's liability as defined in the Brussels Convention. A decree issued in 1973 dealt with insurance and reinsurance of nuclear hazards in France. The Central Reinsurance Fund is guaranteed by the State and may assume the risk of nuclear operators' coverage. **7.218**

Non-proliferation

France adopted the safeguard system designed by IAEA to ensure non-proliferation. Thus, exported French nuclear equipment and plants cannot be used for military purposes. A 1992 Act[119] authorized ratification of the Nuclear Non-Proliferation Treaty (NPT). During the preparatory committee meetings of the NPT Extension Conference, France sat among the nuclear supplier group and agreed to reinforce the joint export control system applied to the export of nuclear materials and equipment for civilian and military use. **7.219**

Hydro

The main renewable energy source used in France to generate electricity is hydropower. It accounts for between 12 and 17 per cent of electricity generation, depending on rainfall level. Further development of hydropower is limited, for the most favourable sites have already been exploited and more precautions are being taken to preserve the environment. **7.220**

Authorizations and concessions

The French State has considered hydropower, a rare natural resource whose exploitation may damage the environment. Thus, small dams under 4,500 KW must be granted a unilateral authorization. Above this limit, concessions are granted by the State according to the Hydropower Act of 1919.[120] All administrative decisions (ie hydropower concessions and authorizations) granted in compliance with this Act are deemed authorizations as defined in Articles 6 and 7 of the new Electricity Act. Any natural or legal person from a European Union Member State may apply for an authorization or concession. France may extend this right to any person from the OECD countries which signed the multilateral investment agreement. **7.221**

French legislation determines the compulsory measures and means of control to be implemented by the operators and the administration. The procedure applicable to the award of hydropower concessions by the State is described in Article 2 of the Hydropower Act of 1919. To build a dam, the operator must send an **7.222**

[119] No 92-574 (01.07.1992).
[120] 16.10.1919.

application to the Dam Technical Standing Committee set up within the Ministry for Industry to study all projects.

7.223 The conditions for application are defined in a 1994[121] decree. The request should include various data.[122] An additional technical report includes a complete description of the dam, a detailed estimate of power production, a description of the applicant's financial situation, the list of lands to be flooded, a table of the financial settlements offered by the applicant to landowners and municipalities, the changes to be brought about by the project to the water supply in the area, and a financial breakdown of the exploitation. In 1997[123] a new decree gave the Prefect the complete monitoring of the procedure, provided the power of the proposed dam does not exceed 100 MW.

7.224 The Ministry for Industry (or the Prefect) officially acknowledges the application sent to him. The Ministry sends the complete file to the Prefect for study and to the relevant Ministries—including the Ministry for the Environment—for advice. Within a three-month period, the Prefect summons the local State services to a conference. The Prefect sends the conference minutes to the Ministry for Industry when the Ministry is in charge. In view of the Ministries' advice and/or the conference minutes, the Minister for Industry (or the Prefect) may decide to study the application further. Then the Prefect holds an inquiry and notifies the applicant of his decision.

7.225 The Prefect holds a public inquiry, asks the applicant for any additional data needed, takes the necessary steps to inform the population, and has the files studied by the local State services, which must make a decision within two months. In accordance with the 1919 Act, the Prefect consults the local authorities.[124] A Prefect order or a decree signed by the Prime Minister and the Ministries involved grants the concession and the generation authorization required by the Electricity Act 2000. The decree may pronounce a declaration of public interest (DUP) if the results of the public inquiry are favourable. The project of works is then established by the concession beneficiary and sent to the Prefect, who has them studied by the local State services. Following this, the authorization to proceed may be granted.

Supervision and safety

7.226 Dams whose height exceeds 20 metres are deemed to be classified facilities regarding public safety. The flooding phase is carefully managed through technical

[121] No 94-894 (13.10.1994).

[122] For instance names of municipalities, lakes, streams, and rivers affected by the project, and the exact location of the project including, if necessary, the exact place where tidal energy will be used, the best estimate of works duration, and the length of the concession.

[123] Decrees no 97-1194 (19.12.1997) and No 99-225 (22.03.1999).

[124] The Chamber of Commerce, the local Committee of Agricultural Structures, the departmental Committee of Sites, and the departmental Hygiene Committee.

specifications. The operator must issue an annual report which includes data collected through video surveillance. Every ten years the operator must undergo a complete inspection of the sections of the dam which are usually under water. These inspections are carried out through diving or emptying the dam. The Large Dam Technical Study and Control Office is in charge, and issues a formal report.

Wind

Since the exploitation of wind energy is now technically mature, the Government has taken the necessary steps to develop electricity production from wind turbines. The State launched the Eole 2005 programme to encourage the building of a wind energy capacity ranging between 250 and 500 MW by 2005, without damaging the environment. The Ministry for Industry is in charge of the programme implementation, and favours the use of wind energy in areas of high electricity supply costs and abundant wind energy resources[125] in order to ensure convergence of prices in the long term. The Ministry for the Environment is empowered to reject projects which could destroy sites and fauna. Both Ministries sit on an Eole 2005 Commission set up by EDF to examine the projects. EDF will purchase electricity at the operator's price by competitive bids. Thus, each individual purchase contract binding EDF and the operator will have its own price, and the alternative local costs will be taken into account more efficiently. The first call for tender was launched in 1996, aimed at building a 50 MW capacity; the call was so successful that projects selected amounted to 77 MW. Another call for tender was limited to the Overseas Departments and Corsica, whose electricity grids are not connected to the metropolitan grid; selected projects amounted to 26 MW. To build a wind turbine, the operator must apply for a building permit and conduct an environmental impact assessment. A building permit may be granted by the Prefect. **7.227**

Research programmes are managed by ADEME whose priorities have been biofuel and wood, but might focus on wind energy in forthcoming years. **7.228**

(4) Transmission and Distribution of Electricity

Institutional framework

As EDF had a *de jure* monopoly over the import, export, and transmission of electricity, its exclusive rights to import and export electricity (and gas) were challenged by the Commission in 1994. The EC Court dismissed this application on the basis of Article 86 EC Treaty (then Art 90, para 2).[126] Nevertheless, the **7.229**

[125] Favourable sites have been listed in the North of France, Brittany, Normandy, Corsica, and in the mountains near the Mediterranean coast.
[126] See Ch 5 above on EC energy law.

import and export monopoly has now been abolished by the Electricity Act of 2000. As a result of this Act, GRT[127] is the transmission grid operator. Like EDF before it, GRT will continue to manage all energy exchanges with other major interconnected European networks. After consulting the French Electricity Regulatory Commission, the Government will issue an implementation decree which will approve the specifications of the GRT concession for transmission.

7.230 EDF does not have a complete monopoly over distribution: 5 per cent of power sold in France is distributed by 194 non-nationalized local municipality-owned or mixed private/public sector companies with shares held by the State, or by a local authority, as in Strasbourg or Grenoble. EDF holds a monopoly for the distribution of electricity throughout the rest of France. Concessions are granted by municipalities and their associations.

Transmission

7.231 Operators have a legal right of access to the GRT transmission grid. GRT is obliged to draft an annual investment plan which needs approval from the CRE. Moreover, the public transmission grid development scheme is approved biannually by the Minister for Energy, after consulting the CRE.

7.232 A 1970 decree[128] governs the building of high-tension lines but the general provisions of the laws protecting the environment and establishing consent procedures apply. All transport lines are subject to a public inquiry procedure according to the Democratization of Public Inquiries and Environment Conservation Act 1983. If private landowners affected by the location of the facility object to construction, a declaration of public interest is required to give EDF an easement over private property, as defined in the Act of 1906 and the Gas and Electricity Nationalization Act 1946. Damages are awarded by the property judge.

7.233 The Environment Act[129] obliged EDF to bury all transmission lines sited in designated environmentally sensitive areas and all low-tension lines under 63 KV in densely populated zones. However, EDF was not obliged to bury *all* low- and medium-tension lines for obvious financial reasons. A 1992 contract signed by EDF and the Government dealing with the burial of cables is being implemented at a total cost of FF 4 billion.

(5) Tariff Policy

7.234 Following the choice for regulated third-party access, the new Electricity Act 2000 provides that all transportation tariffs, applicable to the use of transmission

---

[127] GRT= Gestionnaire du Réseau de Transport, Public Grid Transport Manager; see above, para 7.176.

[128] No 70-492 (11.06.1970).

[129] No 95-101 (20.02.1995).

and distribution grids, are set by the Ministers of Finance and Energy on the basis of a proposal by the CRE.

As for electricity supply, a distinction is made between supplies to eligible and to non-eligible customers. The electricity tariffs to non-eligible customers, non-nationalized distributors, and auxiliary services in case of a breakdown are set by the Ministers of Finance and Energy after consultation with the CRE. Following free market principles, electricity prices to eligible customers are deregulated. The tariffs must reflect France's energy policy and are supervised by the DIGEC (*Direction du gaz, de l'electricité et du charbon*, Gas, Electricity and Coal Directorate), a DGEMP division. **7.235**

F. Other Renewable Energy Sources, CHP, and Energy Efficiency

(1) Introduction

The law applicable to combined heat and power (CHP), energy efficiency, and all renewable energy sources, with the exception of hydropower and wind energy, is described in this section. Technically, CHP, geothermal resources, biofuels, solar water heating, and wood-based energy are not classified as electricity generation, because they are partly or totally used for heat generation. Rational use of energy, energy efficiency, and energy conservation are deemed part of energy policy, whereas in other countries they are considered to be environmentally related measures. **7.236**

(2) Other Renewable Energy Sources

This section describes policy implemented on renewable energy sources which are not used solely to generate electricity. Wood is the main renewable energy source in France. In 1994, 715,219 TJ of primary energy was generated in France from renewable energy sources, according to Eurostat accounting methods. Wood-based primary energy accounted for 50.8 per cent of this total and hydropower for 40.9 per cent. Research programmes are managed by ADEME. These programmes range from increasing awareness among the general public to the funding of technological research and development in decentralized electricity production, biomass, geothermal, and solar heating. **7.237**

Institutional framework

Under the 1955 decree EDF was obliged to purchase electricity from private operators producing electricity from renewable energy sources. Article 10 of the new Electricity Act states that EDF and the non-nationalized distributors must purchase electricity generated from renewable energy sources and by energy-efficient techniques, such as CHP, if the power generated on a site does not exceed a 12 MW maximum threshold. A decree will determine the specific threshold for each energy. **7.238**

7.239 A tax on municipal waste was imposed in 1993, mainly to deter waste disposal, and to encourage the combustion of waste as an energy source. This tax will be eliminated in 2002.

7.240 The French Mining Code applies to geothermal resources. The authorization procedures for mining apply to geothermal exploitation. Geothermal sites are classified into high- and low-temperature sites. The Prefect is empowered to grant three-year prospecting permits and must hold a public inquiry. The Prefect also grants exploitation concessions for low-temperature sites. The beneficiary of the prospecting permit is given the exclusive right to apply for a concession during the validity of the permit. Furthermore, if prospecting proves the existence of a geothermal site, a concession is automatically granted. The concession is valid for thirty years, but can be extended for several fifteen-year periods.

7.241 Since March 1995, FF 100 million have been invested annually into the Fund for Amortization of Electrification Costs (FACE) to finance demand-side management policy and renewable-based generation projects that would avoid the costly upgrading of transmission lines. This Fund finances investments in isolated rural areas. Approximately FF 65 million have been allocated to renewable energy sources. In 1995 selected projects included the replacement of electrical heating systems in the residential sector with wood- or other fuel-based systems, and encouraging the use of highly efficient electrical appliances.

Main policy measures

7.242 France has invested in biofuels, wood, solar, and wind energy and developed a new strategy on combined heat and power (CHP).

7.243 The Government supports biofuels[130] through the funding of joint public-private sector research and by granting tax exemption. The Agriculture for Chemistry and Energy Association (AGRICE) was set up in 1994 to oversee joint State-industry bio-energy development projects and other research pertaining to new markets for agricultural products. This organization is funded by the State and oil, chemical, and agro-industrial companies. Biofuels produced in demonstration plants from crops grown on land which would otherwise be left fallow under European Union farm regulations are partially exempt from taxes applied to petroleum products.[131] The cost of the biofuels produced has been assessed by the loss of tax on substituted oil products, and rose from FF 300 million in 1994 to FF 600 million in 1995. The long-term cost-effectiveness and environmental advantages of biofuels have been questioned in an official report.

---

[130] Methyl-ester and ethanol.

[131] Revised Finance Act 1997, Art 25 (No 97-1239, 29.12.1997) and Decree No 98-309 (22.04.1998).

France's forested land area, one of the largest in Europe, covers 28 per cent of the French metropolitan territory and has been growing by 35 per cent during the last fifty years. In 1994 France accounted for 36.5 per cent of primary wood-based energy produced in Europe (excluding Sweden), according to Eurostat. In September 1994 the Ministries for Industry and Agriculture and ADEME launched a 1995–98 State-funded programme on wood-based energy, to favour the use of wood-based energy in central heating, structure the supply network, and encourage local development and employment. In 1996 competitive bids open to regions and departments selected thirty-nine wood-based energy projects totalling 45 MW. 7.244

In 1996, following the 1994 national energy and environment debate in Parliament, the Ministry for Industry launched a programme funded by several public sources to deploy 20,000 solar water-heating systems by 2000 throughout France, particularly in the DOM-TOM where the cost of supplying electricity exceeds revenues. More than 5,000 solar water-heating systems have been installed. 7.245

(3) Combined Heat and Power

The Ministries for Industry and the Environment have encouraged the development of combined heat and power (CHP) in France through attractive tariffs. Hence, the number of CHP facilities doubled between 1994 and 1995. 7.246

The Government later defined new conditions applying to EDF purchases of electricity generated by CHP. Under the new Electricity Act, which considers CHP as an energy-efficient technique, EDF and the non-nationalized distributors must purchase electricity generated from CHP if the power generated on a site does not exceed a 12 MW maximum threshold. 7.247

(4) Energy Efficiency

Net savings increased in France every year until 1990, but have failed to increase since then. The Government uses several policy instruments to increase, or at least stabilize, energy efficiency, such as taxes on fuels, subsidies for energy-efficient investment, publicly funded research and development, information and technical assistance programmes, including EDF activities to reduce electricity demand. 7.248

Institutional framework

Before the Clean Air and Rational Use of Energy Act

To induce consumers and investors to take mid-term calculations into consideration, the Government informs the public on possible savings, encourages investment in energy savings through grants or taxes levied on energy consumption, and has requested labelling and audits to be carried out. 7.249

7.250 The Energy Use Act 1948[132] gave the Government power to ensure and enforce the publication of technical specifications regarding electrical household and industrial equipment. An Advisory Committee on the Rational Use of Energy was established. The Act also set up administrative reviews of major power plant building. This administrative procedure was later abandoned.

7.251 The Energy Conservation Act 1974 forbade contract stipulations increasing energy consumption, required individual energy consumption in collective housing to be measured, and empowered the Government to determine and enforce new building and collective heating specifications. An Act passed in 1977[133] extended the Government's power to the control of imports, exports, production, retailing, and storage of energy resources. The Energy Conservation Act also stated the measures which the Government can implement through decrees in an energy shortage or an important deficit of payments, such as allocation and restriction of energy to energy-consuming activities (heating, car use, etc).

7.252 The Energy Conservation and Heat Use Act 1980 and its associated decrees encouraged the creation of heating networks through a classifying procedure which included a public inquiry and resulted in a decree signed by the Prime Minister. The procedure is implemented at the request of a local authority. In the perimeter of a classified network, local authorities were empowered to compel any new heating installation to be connected to the network. The Act also gave banks tax incentives to increase loans allocated to investment in saving energy. A decree issued in 1981 listed the facilities and equipment destined to save primary energy in the industrial, housing, and tertiary sectors and defined the facilities and equipment, favouring the substitution of petroleum products with renewable energy sources.

Clean Air and Rational Use of Energy Act 1996: rational use of energy provisions

7.253 The Clean Air and Rational Use of Energy Act[134] was passed in December 1996. Its goals were to tighten anti-pollution measures and to update the rational use of energy legislation of 1948 and 1980. The Energy Use Act 1948 was abolished. The Energy Conservation Act 1974 remained unchanged, since one of its main aims was to provide the State with necessary powers to meet an energy shortage.

7.254 The Energy Conservation and Heat Use Act 1980 was updated to include cooling networks,[135] and to limit the application of the classifying procedure to heating

[132] No 48-400 (10.03.1948), later abolished.

[133] No 77-804 (19.07.1977).

[134] No 96-1236 (30.12.1996). The new Electricity Act also includes provisions on rational use of energy. In its Art 17, it states that local authorities empowered to grant distribution concessions should promote rational use of energy, to delay or avoid extension or upgrading of distribution grids under their supervision.

[135] See Decree no 99-360 (05.05.1999) which updated the 1981 Decree implementing the 1980 Act and dealing with heating and cooling networks.

and cooling networks using primarily renewable energies, CHP, and recycled energy. Classification is now pronounced by a Prefect's order.

As for energy-related emissions, decrees determined technical specifications to be implemented in buildings and movable goods other than cars, and to compel producers and consumers to control energy consumption and emission of pollutants. Energy consumption and emissions of pollutants must be clearly advertised when selling or lending real property or movable goods, including cars. **7.255**

The new Act also states that more oxygen has to be added to the composition of petrol, diesel, domestic fuel, and high-octane petrol before the turn of the century. Under Article 24, car manufacturers and owners must take the necessary steps to reduce energy consumption and polluting emissions. Two years after the adoption of the new Act, the State and public bodies possessing more than twenty vehicles must make 20 per cent of the vehicles they purchase electric, LNG-fuelled, or gas-fuelled. In cities of more than 100,000 inhabitants, owners of public transport fleets were also given a two-year period to use vehicles fuelled with petrol containing more oxygen. To encourage the use of electric, gas-fuelled, and LNG vehicles, the new Act established fiscal incentives, such as exemptions, tax reliefs, tax refunds, and short-term fiscal depreciation. Low-emission vehicles will enjoy privileged access to roads and parking. **7.256**

Main policy measures

Since 1974 more than fifty measures have been implemented by the French Government to encourage energy savings. They range from new rules to budget subsidies and public company policy, tax incentives, and information campaigns. **7.257**

As for new texts, the periodic audit by public authorities of energy-intensive industrial installations was required, with the aim of identifying energy-saving and pollution-control investments. Efficiency standards for large industrial boilers were updated. Codes defined insulation standards for new buildings. These regulations were tightened and extended to include boilers and heating systems and were updated to implement the new Clean Air and Rational Use of Energy Act.[136] Following the adoption of European Directives the Government enacted requirements for energy labelling and efficiency[137] of refrigerators, freezers (1995), and clothes dryers (1996). Dishwasher and washing machine labelling will be introduced later. Transport policy includes non-energy policy, such as speed limits, which have reduced fuel consumption by road vehicles. New lorries with reduced fuel consumption might also be labelled. **7.258**

[136] Several decrees implemented the Act, such as No 98-817 on small boilers' efficiency (11.09.1998) and No 98-833 on control of large boilers' efficiency (16.09.1998).

[137] See Decree No 98-257 on refrigerators' efficiency (31.03.1998).

7.259 A FF 1.4 billion grant programme was set up in 1983, and ended in 1987, for large industrial projects involving energy efficiency improvements and the substitution of oil for coal. Other grants partly cover the costs of preparatory studies on energy use in new combustion plants. In 1995 the Government introduced a FF 5,000 grant for the purchase of electric vehicles during the period July 1995 to December 1996, and EDF added a FF 10,000 grant per sale to the car manufacturer or importer. Pilot programmes have already been launched in La Rochelle and Tours to observe consumer behaviour and test where to locate recharging points.

7.260 The Government supports public transport, particularly urban transport networks. ADEME assists local authorities in designing urban transport plans. Promotion of an integrated rail and road system might be subsidized if the State budget can afford it. In preparation for the future, ADEME is running a programme to improve truck and lorry efficiency. EDF is undertaking research on electrical equipment and networks. In the private sector, IFP funds research and development projects to improve engine systems using conventional fuel. It focuses on models for designing new engines, improving engine technology, post-treatment of de-pollution, and engine fuel-lubricant matching.

7.261 Fiscal law allowed accelerated depreciation for energy-saving investments in industry, and tax deductions encouraging investment in the insulation of existing buildings. However, private haulage companies still enjoy a low gas oil tax, and the 'axle tax' levied on haulage companies to finance the upgrading of roads and motorways has not been raised recently.

7.262 The Government has launched several information campaigns encouraging consumers to take into account energy savings. These *chasse au Gaspi* campaigns promoted energy-saving in general and the use of energy-efficient electrical appliances.

G. Environmental Issues

(1) Environmental Impact Assessment

7.263 Two legal procedures were set up to assess the impact of building a major facility: the classified facility procedure and the declaration of public interest. They apply to all major energy facilities. Furthermore, environmental zoning forbids major projects to be located in protected areas.

Classified facilities

7.264 A first important step to protect the environment was taken by the French Government with the Classified Facilities Act 1976.[138] Listed in a decree, these

[138] No 76-663 (19.07.1976).

ICPE facilities are broadly defined as hazardous to the environment, the neighbourhood, public health, public safety, agricultural activities, and sites and monuments. Facilities representing a major hazard are authorized by the Prefect, the others are declared, and must abide by general specifications adopted, by the Prefect, to protect the population, health, and the environment. In certain classified facilities, the use of hazardous substances must also be authorized. Before the start-up of a classified facility, the operator must offer financial guarantees to the administration.

The Prefect holds a public inquiry before granting the authorization in an order detailing technical specifications to be implemented in building and exploiting the facility, along with the necessary means of intervention in case of an accident. If the degree of hazard of a classified facility was not properly assessed when it was authorized or declared, the Ministry for the Environment can halt its exploitation for the time necessary to prevent any accident. To control the implementation of these legal prescriptions, the administration is empowered to conduct on-site inspections; the civil servants responsible are under oath and sworn to secrecy. **7.265**

Public inquiry and declaration of public interest

Public inquiry

The public inquiry precedes a declaration of public interest (DUP in French) and aims at giving to the general public accurate information on the planned facility and assessing the impact of building the facility. The inquiry records public opinions, suggestions, and proposals. The provisions of the Democratization of Public Inquiries and Environment Conservation Act 1983, as modified by the Environment Act 1995, apply to all energy facilities listed in a 1985 decree.[139] **7.266**

At the Prefect's request, the President of the local Administrative Court appoints the public inquirer chosen from a list established by a local committee. The public inquirer conducts the inquiry and can appoint experts and ask them to make a more thorough impact assessment; he must give a clear and fully argued recommendation, and may add suggestions. A committee may be appointed instead of a single inquirer if the size of the project justifies it. No person either personally or indirectly involved in the project can be appointed inquirer or committee member. **7.267**

The file sent to the Prefect by the applicant must contain the necessary information to hold the inquiry and prepare a DUP as described in a 1985 decree.[140] After being studied by the local State services and sent to the local authorities for advice, the complete project file is open for consultation to ensure public information. **7.268**

[139] Hydrocarbon pipelines, all nuclear facilities and their releases, power lines, underground storage facilities, prospecting and exploitation of hydrocarbons and geothermal deposits and sites, prospecting of mining substances, hydropower plants and dams, and all ICPE.

[140] No 85-1109 (15.10.1985).

Special registers are kept in which the public may write their observations. The inquirer or the committee issues a report, drawing conclusions and compiling information, propositions, and the operator's responses. The inquirer must give his own conclusions and send the final report to the Prefect, who in turn sends it to the President of the Administrative Court. The public has access to the report.

7.269 A national independent committee was established by the Environment Act 1995 to scrutinize every major infrastructure building planned by the State, including energy facilities. The committee holds an open public debate which may not last more than six months. The seventeen committee members are appointed by the Prime Minister for five years and mainly represent the judiciary, Parliament, local authorities, and conservationist and consumer associations. The committee chairman is chosen from within the *Conseil d'Etat.* Each project is examined by an *ad hoc* group of three to seven members who may request more information from the operator. The *ad hoc* group may recommend a supplementary study, which must be completed within two months. After the public debate, the Government may launch the public inquiry procedure and make the DUP.

Declaration of public interest and compulsory purchase orders

7.270 The DUP is described in an Ordinance of 1958,[141] later updated and codified in the Expropriation Code. The Democratization of Public Inquiries and Environment Conservation Act 1983 introduced new procedures guaranteeing environmental conservation and applying to the building of an energy facility. The DUP provides the administration with the legal ground to ask the property judge for a ruling depriving the French citizens affected by the project of their property and awarding damages. The DUP also acknowledges the 'public need' and describes the 'general interests' involved. The administrative judge scrutinizes the existence of a real 'public interest', particularly since the ruling *Ville Nouvelle Est* (1970). The State and the public bodies or private persons in charge of a public service may benefit from the procedure. The DUP decree is signed by the Prime Minister when an energy facility is at stake. The DUP is coupled with a second procedure authorizing a compulsory purchase order, necessary to deprive French citizens of their real property.

7.271 To issue the compulsory purchase order, a second and more detailed 'parcel inquiry' is held to determine precisely the land and buildings encompassed in the procedure and provide the legal ground for every individual expropriation.

7.272 The compulsory purchase order is signed by the Prefect. The properties listed are purchased and their property transferred to the State. The order is sent to the relevant landowners and landlords. However, the order does not transfer the property immediately, because only a judge can deprive the landowner of his property

[141] No 58-997 (23.10.1958).

by a ruling, according to an Act of 1810. The administrative judge has no jurisdiction over property transfer. The property judge is empowered to defend private property against State decisions and can therefore order the transfer and fix the damages. The relevant owners are notified of the judge's decision.

Environmental zoning

Before authorizing a public or private project likely to have an impact on the environment, an impact assessment must be undertaken according to the European Directive of 1985. The Directive listed the potential effects of the project to be examined, such as the impact on the population, fauna and flora, soil, water supply, weather and landscape, properties, and cultural artefacts. The Landscape Act[142] 1993 vested the State with the power to issue by decree compulsory guidelines to protect the landscape. **7.273**

(2) Air Pollution and Energy-Related Emissions

Institutional framework

Before the Clean Air and Rational Use of Energy Act 1996

Under the Environment Act 1976, DRIRE are responsible for enforcing anti-pollution measures applied on stationary sources. They must be notified of the building of any facility whose power exceeds 2 MW. They are vested with the power to license and inspect all classified installations, namely all combustion plants, boilers, and factories with fuel-burning capacities above 20 MW. These installations are subject to special regulations, some of which deal with emissions. The legal framework was finalized to incorporate an integrated pollution control approach. **7.274**

Regulations on emissions mainly concern NO_x, SO_2, particulates, and lead. The European Directive on emissions from large combustion plants was enacted in 1990 and applied to power plants whose power exceeds 50 MW. France has implemented three measures to bring about reductions of 70 per cent[143] of SO_2 emissions by 2003 and 40 per cent of NO_x by 1998. First, a 1974 decree established urban protection zones.[144] Secondly, a tax on atmospheric pollution was introduced in 1985 for classified industrial facilities and all combustion plants over 20 MW, with the aim of deterring emission of pollutants (SO_2, NO_x) in industrial processes. It was extended to particulate and VOC emissions in 1991. The tax revenue is managed by ADEME and finances State and private investments in pollution control equipment. Thirdly, limits were imposed on the sulphur content of heavy fuel oil, in coal burned in small combustion units **7.275**

[142] No 93-24 (08.01.1993).

[143] Compared to the 1980 level.

[144] Paris, Hauts-de-Seine, Seine-Saint-Denis, Val-de-Marne, Lyon, Marseilles, Lilles, and Strasbourg.

(2 MW), and on the lead content of gasoline. Various taxes are levied on low and high sulphur fuel oil, and on leaded and unleaded gasoline.

The Clean Air and Rational Use of Energy Act 1996

7.276 The Clean Air and Rational Use of Energy Act 1996 applies to energy-related emissions and all emissions putting air quality into jeopardy, except for nuclear effluents which are governed by earlier legislation. The Act empowers the State to take necessary steps to protect air quality, defines plans to be drafted to improve it, sets up emergency procedures, deals with energy-related emissions, and establishes an air quality assessment network and law enforcement process.

7.277 The State is entrusted with air quality control, in association with local authorities. Air quality objectives will be defined, along with alert thresholds and a list of polluting substances whose discharge into the atmosphere constitutes a health hazard for the population.

7.278 Each Prefect in charge of a region must prepare a regional plan for air quality to determine objectives for air quality in particularly sensitive areas. An inventory of polluting emissions and an assessment of air quality must be made prior to the plan's elaboration. The Prefect consults local authorities, mainly municipalities, and committees, such as Departmental Hygiene Committees. The draft plan is open for examination by the public. The Prefect modifies the plan if public reaction and local authority recommendations require it. Each Prefect must also prepare a plan to protect the atmosphere, to be implemented in the largest cities. The Prefect consults the municipality, holds a public inquiry to consult and inform the citizens, and modifies the plan if the inquiry results and local authority recommendations require it.

7.279 When pollution exceeds alert thresholds, the Prefect informs the public and takes the necessary steps to curb the magnitude and effects of the pollution. If the Prefect decides to restrict or forbid the use of cars, the public are given free public transport. The new Act modifies the Domestic Transport Act[145] 1982 so that urban transport plans respect air quality requirements. An air quality assessment network was deployed throughout the French territory.

7.280 To prevent pollution and achieve the objectives defined in each plan to protect the atmosphere, the authorities in charge of police must take measures including, for instance, the restriction or suspension of road traffic, or the suspension of plant activity, if one or several plants are the source of pollution. Civil servants in the Ministries of Finance, the Environment, and Industry are authorized to enforce the new law, for instance by conducting on-site inspections, and taking samples and documents. The Prefect will officially ask any offender to comply with legal provisions within a fixed period of time. Further non-compliance will result in

[145] No 82-1153 (30.12.1982).

penalties and allow the Prefect to take the necessary measures at the offender's expense or order suspension of the offender's polluting activity.

Convention on Climate Change

France signed the Framework Convention on Climate Change in 1992 and ratified it in 1994. France submitted its national programme to the International Negotiating Committee, as required by the Framework Convention. Total emissions of carbon dioxide have fallen since 1990: energy-related emissions, accounting for most of the total, fell by 5 per cent between 1990 and 1993. The programme also projected the stabilization of methane emissions at their 1990 level until 2000. It forecast a 50 per cent cut in NO_X emissions, and a 25 per cent reduction in both SO_X and VOC emissions. These forecasts take into account recent measures, such as tax increases, stricter thermal insulation for new buildings, incentives to promote the use of wood, promotion of fuel-efficient and low- or zero-emission vehicles, and voluntary commitments by industry. The responsibilities of the Interdepartmental Committee on Electric Vehicles have been broadened to cover other vehicles. The Committee has set up a task force of officials from the relevant Ministries, namely Industry, Transport, Environment, and Housing. **7.281**

To reach these goals, major public bodies carry out research programmes. EDF is focusing on modelling atmospheric pollution, and the CNRS (*Centre national de la recherche scientifique*, National Centre of Scientific Research) is running the 'Ecotech' programme investigating socio-economic factors affecting energy use. In the private sector, IFP is developing low-emission engine and motor systems. **7.282**

An interdepartmental Standing Committee was set up in 1992 to co-ordinate policy on climatic change. In 1996 surveys showed that carbon emissions per capita had reached the low point of 1.7 tonnes, while the European Union average was 2.3 tonnes. **7.283**

(3) Pollution at Sea and Oil Transmission

Although the transport of petroleum products by sea has usually proved safe, the 1978 *Amoco Cadiz* wreck caused major pollution of the Brittany coast. Hence, the French administration has defined two emergency plans, *Polmar-Mer* and *Polmar-Terre* (marine pollution at sea and on shore) to co-ordinate the complex measures to be implemented in case of an oil-spill. The Polmar plans were defined by a 1978 Prime Ministerial guideline, and listed the means of protection available and the zones to be protected in priority to prevent an ecological disaster and clean up the consequences of any oil-spill. The plans are carried out under the Prefect's authority. **7.284**

The mayor is vested with the power of ruling over the shore, and must therefore inform the public and forbid access to the sea in the case of an oil-spill. The mayor **7.285** may be involved in the anti-pollution plan with the State's local administration, which can prove costly for the municipal budget. These direct financial burdens, supported by the State and the local authorities, must be added to the direct economic losses (damaged nets and fishing boats, for instance) and to indirect economic losses to marine activities (fishing, tourism, etc) or activities using sea water (such as cooling power plants) caused by marine pollution.

H. Conclusions

(1) *General Observations*

7.286 Energy law in France must meet both the challenges inherent in the French economy and foreign policy goals: almost no fossil energy resources, a mild climate, a relatively widespread population, increasing demand for energy supply (traditionally met under the State's close supervision), and new demand for both environmental conservation and quality of service.

7.287 Public bodies and State-owned companies have been established, and legislation provided the necessary procedures to obtain consensus from the population concerned, to ensure the best quality of service and implementation of the tightest safety measures, and to encourage the use of new technologies to save energy or produce it from renewable energy sources.

7.288 France has undergone some deregulation, particularly in the petroleum sector. Since the 1970s Standing Committees within the administration have been established to co-ordinate the relevant ministerial actions, and they increasingly involve citizens' representatives in decision-making. Now Parliament commonly scrutinizes Government decisions and evaluates results. The European Directives will bring about a cautious deregulation of the energy market, diminishing the role of the public bodies entrusted with energy management. A relatively new instrument is likely to play a role in French energy policy: regulatory authorities. They will be established, according to the French legal tradition, with a back-up of specific laws and decrees.

(2) *Future Developments*

7.289 The main feature of French energy policy is undoubtedly the 11 December 1997 Kyoto Protocol, which ratification was authorized by the French Parliament in July 2000. The goal set for France was to keep greenhouse gas emissions stable over the Protocol period. Since about 87 per cent of electricity is generated in France without greenhouse gas emissions, thanks to the use of nuclear power, hydropower and soon wind energy, the Government must find a way to decrease pollution in the transport and building sectors to fulfil the French commitments.

This will prove difficult. For instance, considerable investments are necessary to transfer a significant part of the goods transport from lorries to trains.

Growing public concern about the environment will also be a major feature of the future energy policy, particularly in electricity generation and transmission. **7.290**

Although French public opinion remains strongly in favour of the use of nuclear power in opinion polls, local associations vehemently ask for more information on neighbouring nuclear facilities and demand independent check-ups for the populations. The building of future underground laboratories studying underground storage of nuclear waste was criticized. To protect bird colonies and nesting territories and to keep picturesque landscapes untouched, ecologists locally protested against the deployment of wind turbines. Micro hydropower plants were also repelled by local protesters who argued that they would bring as much disturbance to river fauna and flora as large dams for a meagre electricity output. **7.291**

As for transmission, the Prime Minister abandoned the building of high-tension power lines over the Pyrenees to protect the bear's natural habitat, although the high-tension lines between France and Spain are suffering from congestion. In January 2000 the old tanker *Erika* sank near the Brittany coast, causing another oil-spill which triggered a public outcry and a new debate on oil transportation. **7.292**

The Government response was twofold. On the national level, the Land Planning and Sustainable Development Act 1999[146] was passed. It required the drawing up of collective service plans. The State draws up the collective service plans dealing, amongst other things, with energy and transport. Local authorities and associations, *inter alia*, are called on to advise on the plan provisions, and the State carefully takes into consideration the economic development projects implemented on the European territory. The collective service plan on energy will determine the goals of renewable energy sources exploitation and rational use of energy policy. The plan will assess the regional energy needs, generation and energy saving potential, and energy transmission needs. The plan will also determine how the State and the local authorities will favour energy efficiency and renewable energy use. The evolution of energy transmission facilities will be programmed. The plans are in the making. The typical French policy mix of planification, dialogue, and State intervention was preferred to a market-driven approach. **7.293**

As for oil-spills, international support is necessary to implement a more tightened policy. The French Ministry of Transport objectives during the French Presidency of the European Community (second semester 2000) were to convince EU Member States to strengthen the controls on ships mooring in European harbours and to abandon as quickly as possible the use of simple hull ships. France also asked the International Maritime Organization to strengthen safety **7.294**

[146] No 99-533 (25.06.1999).

specifications, particularly for ships transporting hazardous materials. The income generated by increasing oil prices will be partly used to increase research and development efforts in exploration and production of hydrocarbons, but nothing so far has gone towards the improvement of petroleum product transport by sea. In November 2000, another wreck of a ship transporting hazardous chemicals off the French coast underlined the necessity to speed up reforms and extend the reinsurance mechanism established in oil transport by sea to other hazardous materials.

7.295 The only non-polluting energy is the one not generated. Unfortunately, the decrease of oil prices from 1986 on had hindered the implementation of strong energy saving and energy efficiency policies. The recent rise in oil prices jeopardizes economic growth but favours new energy efficiency measures and makes a few renewable energies, like wind energy, less unprofitable. So far, the markets could not determine a 'fair' oil price, allowing worldwide prosperity, safe oil transport, and development of alternative energies. Since the world economy is still heavily dependent on oil, a constant dialogue between oil producers and consumers is necessary, along with the political stability usually provided by democratic political regimes.

Bibliography

ADEME, *Annual Report* (in French)
Annales des Mines, *Energy in France and in the World—Annual Survey* (summary in English)
CEA, COGEMA, FRAMATOME, EDF, GDF, CDF, *Annual Report* (in English)
DGEMP, Energy survey division, *Energy 2010*, general report (perspectives énergétiques de la France à l'horizon 2010) (in English)
—— Energy survey division, *Energy Key Facts and Figures* (1994) (in French)
—— *Report on Energy Policy* (document d'orientation sur la politique énergétique), 1993.
—— *Energy Statistics Yearbook* (in French)
—— *Nuclear Energy in 110 Questions* (in English), 1997
—— *Annual Tables on Energy Consumption in France* (in French)
—— *Annual Report* (in French)
—— and DHYCA, *Petroleum Industry in France* (1995) (annual report in French)
—— and DHYCA, *Monthly Report* (statistics, survey by country, in French)
—— and DIGEC, *Annual Report* (in French, introduction in English)
—— and DIGEC, *Key Figures of Electricity Generation in France* (1995) (in French)
—— and DIGEC, *Statistics on Gas Industry* (in French)
DGSI (General Directorate for Industrial Strategy, a division of the French Ministry of Industry), *Energy Consumption in Industry—Annual Survey* (in French)

Bibliography on administrative law (in French)

Prosper Weil, Le droit administratif français, collection 'Que sais-je?'
Long–Weil–Braibant–Devolde, Les grands arrêts de la jurisprudence administrative
Guy Braibant, Le droit administratif français, collection 'Presses de la fondation nationale des sciences politiques'

Articles in English

Blanchard, P, 'French Electricity Sector: ECJ Decision on Monopolies for the Import and Export of Electricity', *Journal of Energy & Natural Resources Law*, vol 17, No 3, 265–80
Cagniart, C-H, *The Electricity Directive: French Implementation in Progress, Oil and Gas Law & Taxation Review*, 1999, 217–20
Laffont, Jean-Jacques, 'The French Electricity Industry', in *International Comparisons of Electricity Regulation*, Cambridge Univ Press, 406–56
Lauriol, Thierry, 'Exploitation of Hydrocarbons in France: Legislation and Taxation', *Oil and Gas Law & Taxation Review*, 1990, vol 8, No 6, 178–81
—— and Alice Rouaud, 'Public Procurement in the Energy Field in France', *Oil and Gas Law & Taxation Review*, vol 14, No 1, 32–7
Verkhovskoy, Pierre, 'The Privatisation of Elf Aquitaine', *Oil and Gas Law & Taxation Review*, vol 12, No 3, 75–81

Legislation

1906 First Act on energy transmission and distribution
1919 Hydropower Act (16.10.1919)
1925 Control on petroleum product prices (abolished in 1986)
1928 Petroleum Act (02.05.1930 abolished in 1992)
1942 Hazardous Material Transport by Air, Railroad or Inland Waterways Act
1945 Ordinance founding CEA [No 45-2563, 18.10.1945] (a public body dealing with atomic energy research)
1946 Gas and Electricity Nationalization Act [No 46-628, 08.04.1946]
1948 Rational Use of Energy Act [No 48-400, 10.03.1948] (abolished in 1996)
1955 Implementation Decree of Nationalization Act [No 55-662, 20.05.1955] (EDF and non-nationalized distributors buy electricity generated from renewables by other operators)
1958 Ordinance on Declaration of the Public Interest [No 58-997, 23.10.1958]
1958 Ordinance on Underground Gas Storage [No 58-1132, 25.11.1958] (updated in 1962 [No 62-1296 (06.11.1962) and 1988 [No 88-220 (07.03.1988)])
1961 Anti-Pollution Act [No 61-842, 02.08.1961] (the Government determines through decrees rules applicable to the construction, management, and control of nuclear facilities)
1965 First Act on responsibilities of nuclear facility operators [No 65-956, 12.11.1965] (updated 1968 and 1990 [Nos 68-1045 (29.11.1968) and 88-1093 (03.12.1993)], respectively)
1966 First decree [No 66-450] establishing the radiation protection basic rules and entrusting the Ministry of Public Health with protection of facility staff and population

1970 Decree No 70-492 governs the building of high-tension lines
1974 Energy Conservation Act [No 74-908, 29.10.1974]
1975 Nationalization of Electricity in Overseas Territories [No 75-622, 11.07.1975]
1976 ICPE Act [No 76-663, 19.07.1976] (facilities deemed classified for the purpose of protecting the environment)
1976 Environment Act [No 76-629, 10.07.1976]
1980 Energy Conservation and Heat Use Act [No 80-842, 15.07.1980]
1980 Protection and Control of Nuclear Materials Act [No 80-531, 25.07.1980]
1982 Rights and Liberties of Local Authorities Act [No 82-213, 02.03.1982] (standard specifications drawn up by the State were applicable to concessionaires of local authorities until this Act repealed them, including in the energy sector)
1983 Democratization of Public Inquiries Act [No 83-630, 12.07.1983] (ensure a better participation of the general public in public inquiries)
1983 Prevention of Oil Pollution at Sea Act [No 83-583, 05.07.1983]
1985 Forest Act [No 85-1273, 04.12.1985]
1985 Mountain Act (the building of energy facilities must abide by their provisions) [No 85-30, 09.01.1985]
1986 Ordinance lifting all price controls, including in the energy sector [No 86-1243, 01.12.1986]
1987 Safety of Forests Act [No 87-565, 22.07.1987]
1990 Act creating ADEME [No 90-1130, 19.12.1990] (Environment and Energy Conservation Agency)
1991 Research on Nuclear Waste Management Act [No 91-1381, 30.12.1991] (also formed a new public body, ANDRA, dealing with nuclear waste management)
1992 Reform of the Petroleum Legislation Act [No 92-1443, 31.12.1992] (petroleum sector is deregulated)
1992 Water Act [No 92-3, 03.01.1992] (applies to facilities using river water, such as power plants)
1992 Fight Against Poverty Act [No 92-722, 29.07.1992] (right to public support for families living in precarious financial circumstances, including guarantee to energy supply)
1994 Mining Act (adapting the legislation to the closing of French mines) [No 94-588, 02.08.1994]
1995 Environment Act [No 95-101, 20.02.1995]
1995 Decree [No 95-494, 25.04.1995] enacting Directive 91/296 on transit of gas
1996 Clean Air and Rational Use of Energy Act [No 96-1236, 30.12.1996]
1996 Act [No 96-142, 21.02.1996] (a non-nationalized distributor may extend its gas-distributing activities to neighbouring municipalities)
1998 Act setting up the 'public service distribution plan' of gas (Art 50) [No 98-546, 02.07.1998]
2000 Electricity Act [No 2000-108, 10.02.2000] and implementation Decrees

8

ENERGY LAW IN GERMANY

Dr Johann-Christian Pielow and Dr Hans-Martin Koopmann

A. Introduction

8.01 The economic relevance of the energy sector in Europe and in the Federal Republic of Germany is evident.[1] German *per capita* consumption (176 gigajoules in 1997) is the fourth largest in the EU after that of the Benelux countries.[2] In recent years, however, the total consumption of primary energy sources has been steadily declining (from 14,912 petojoule in 1990 to 14,490 petajoule in 1997). Among the most important energy sources, mineral oil holds the first place with a share of 39.5 per cent, followed by natural gas (20.6 per cent), brown and hard coal (11.1 and 14.1 per cent respectively), and nuclear energy (12.8 per cent). Remaining energy sources such as water, wind, and wood constitute approximately 2.0 per cent of the total consumption of primary energy.[3]

8.02 Steadily growing consumption by the transport sector[4] has overtaken (decreasing) industrial consumption[5] as the most significant consumer of energy.[6] As a consequence of the structural changes in Germany's energy sector, especially from East German brown coal and hard coal to mineral oil, natural gas, and nuclear energy, carbon dioxide emissions caused by the use of primary energy sources fell approximately 17.4 per cent during the period from 1985 to 1997.[7] Energy prices have demonstrated a slight downward trend, for example from 0.082 (1990) to 0.078 Euro/kWh of electricity in 1997 for industrial consumers.[8] The recent liberalization of the German energy supply sector (see section E below) has put electricity prices under pressure, especially for large industrial consumers.[9] National efforts to save and conserve energy have been relatively successful. From 1973 to 1994 the gross national product grew more than 55 per cent whilst energy consumption increased by only 7.4 per cent.

---

[1] See for example: HK Schneider, *Energie*, in *Handbuch der Wirtschaftswissenschaften (HdWW)*, vol 2, 1980, 362; from a economic point of view see further: A Dittmann, *Energiewirtschaft*, 1998; J Hensing, W Pfaffenberger, and others (eds), *Energiewirtschaft: Einführung in Theorie und Politik*, 1998; W Pfaffenberger, *Elektrizitätswirtschaft*, 1993; D Winje and D Witt, *Energiewirtschaft*, 1992. As to the economic and technical details of the German energy sector see for example: Leonh Müller, *Handbuch der Elektrizitätswirtschaft: technische, wirtschaftliche und rechtliche Grundlagen*, 1998; G Bischoff and W Gocht (eds), *Das Energiehandbuch*, 4th edn, 1981; D Schmitt and H Heck (eds), *Handbuch Energie*, 1990.

[2] See: *Energie Daten 1995—Nationale und internationale Entwicklung*, edited by the Federal Ministry of Economy and Technology.

[3] ibid, 1997/98, fig 4.

[4] From 25.2% in 1990 to 27.0% in 1996.

[5] From 31.5% in 1990 to 24.9% in 1996.

[6] *Energie Daten*, see n 2 above, fig 5.

[7] ibid, fig 9: from 1.045 million tonnes in 1985 to 863 million tonnes in 1997.

[8] ibid, fig 27.2.

[9] In the meanwhile discounts of between 15 and 20% are possible: cf *Frankfurter Allgemeine Zeitung*, no 43, 20 February 1999, 13–14.

Germany is highly dependent on the import of primary energy sources. There is plenty of hard coal (mainly situated in the Ruhr region and in Saarland) and brown coal (situated between the River Rhine and the city of Aachen as well as in the Länder of Saxony and Saxony-Anhalt) but only some natural gas and a little mineral oil. Deposits of crude oil and mineral gas are mainly situated in Northern Germany and the adjacent North Sea coastal area. In 1996 extraction of deep-mined hard coal was 48.2 million tonnes, while surface-mined brown coal provided about 189 million tonnes. In 1995 the national extraction of crude oil was less than 3 million tonnes;[10] the national extraction of natural gas was approximately 19,121,000 million cbms, ie 21 per cent of the total consumption with the remaining 79 per cent imported mainly from Russia (37 per cent), the Netherlands (26 per cent), and Norway (14 per cent).[11] **8.03**

German generation of electricity was estimated at approximately 547,000 million kWh in 1997. More than 65 per cent is produced on the basis of heat by coal and increasingly gas and some oil-fired power plants, with the balance generated from the nineteen remaining nuclear power plants (30 per cent) and about 5 per cent from other sources, such as hydropower.[12] **8.04**

(1) A Brief Historical Overview

The history of network-bound energy supply (electricity and gas)[13] began with private initiatives rather than state activities. In 1826 the first two gas supply systems were installed by the British Imperial Continental Gas Association in Hanover and Berlin. These were based on private law contracts with the local authorities; the first electricity supply contract was concluded between the Deutsche Edison-Gesellschaft (a licensee of Thomas Alva Edison's American company) and the City of Berlin in 1884. These contracts already comprised typical elements of present-day concession contracts (see paragraph 8.28 below). Increasingly, larger cities in particular became engaged in the energy sector through their own companies (*kommunale Versorgungsunternehmen*). Different motivations were responsible for this development, such as unsatisfactory private activities and the **8.05**

[10] Imports in 1996: about 103 million tons, mainly from the former Soviet Union (25.4%), Norway (21.3%), the UK (17.4%), Libya (11.9%), Saudi-Arabia (5.4%) and Algeria (4.8%).

[11] On the other hand, crude oil extraction by German companies abroad was more than 17 million tonnes in 1995. The respective amount of natural gas was nearly 3.4 million cbms. Source: *Verlag* Glückauf (ed), *Jahrbuch Bergbau und Energie 1997* 276f, 1092, 1100. As to the legal background of the extraction of mineral oil in the German North Sea coastal area, see for example PJ Tettinger, *Erdölförderung im Wattenmeer*, 1993.

[12] Regionally these figures may vary according to the energy profile of the individual Länder.

[13] For more details see: H-U Evers, *Das Recht der Energieversorgung*, 2nd edn, 1983, 21ff.; W Löwer, *Energieversorgung zwischen Staat, Gemeinde und Wirtschaft*, 1989, 33ff.; W Wesener, *Energieversorgung und Energieversorgungskonzepte*, 1986, 7f.; W Fischer (ed), *Die Geschichte der Stromversorgung*, 1992; recently: G Hermes, *Staatliche Infrastrukturverantwortung*, 1998, § 13; ED Cross, *Electric utility regulation in the European Union—a country by country guide*, 1996, 127ff.

necessity to control monopolies, but the primary motivation was the financial interest in the profitable exploitation of new technologies. In 1911 less than 30 per cent of the gas enterprises were in private ownership. In the electricity sector, the private share was only 25 per cent. In rural areas, however, municipalities remained dependent on private co-operation, being generally unable themselves to meet the considerable financial requirements of a suitable supply system. Not only the municipalities, but also private and mixed public-private companies performed the supply task. During the First World War, the former Reich and the Länder also acted as entrepreneurs in the energy market.[14]

8.06 In parallel with further technical developments, such as the long-distance transport of electricity by high-tension grids and energy production close to extraction sites of hard coal, brown coal, and water, large supraregional enterprises were founded. In consequence of the more economic operation of new and larger power plants, a radical process of concentration and monopolization took place. This development initiated a lively political debate on the regulation of the energy industry, a task hitherto performed by the municipalities on the sole legal basis of the public ways (eg roads) necessary for the supply network. Nevertheless, it took until 1935 for the first legal framework regulating the sector as a whole to be established.[15] As a political compromise, the new law respected existing structures of the energy industry and assigned a system of control mechanisms to the Reich's Minister of the Economy. Proposals to nationalize the sector, however, remained unsuccessful.

8.07 The German Energy Act of 1935 remained in force substantially unchanged until the liberalization of the German energy sector in 1998. In the meantime an historic milestone was the federal competition law of 27 July 1957.[16] However, in order to preserve traditional 'area monopolies', monopoly contracts between the energy supply companies (*Demarkationsverträge*), and between such companies and the municipalities (*Konzessionsverträge*), were exempted from the central prohibitions of this act.[17]

8.08 The most relevant historical development concerning upstream activities is the Federal Mining Act (*Bundesberggesetz*) of 13 August 1980.[18] It replaced the more heterogeneous mining laws of the Länder (see section C(3) below). The mining

[14] See sections B(1) and (2) below for a discussion of the legislative and administrative competencies of the Bund (federation) and the Länder (regional states) in Germany.

[15] *Gesetz zur Förderung der Energiewirtschaft* of 13 December 1935 *(EnWG)* of 13 December 1935, published in *Reichsgesetzblatt* (RGBl), part I, 1451.

[16] *Gesetz gegen Wettbewerbsbeschränkungen—GWB*, published in *Bundesgesetzblatt* 1957, part I, 1081.

[17] Which were: no agreements against competition and no horizontal or vertical contracts. See also para 8.106 below.

[18] *Bundesgesetzblatt* 1980, part I, 1310. Latest substantial change by the Act of 12 February 1990, *Bundesgesetzblatt* 1990, part I, 215.

industry suffered severe problems when more and more mines where shut down as a consequence of stronger competition in the international coal market. (Legal aspects of necessary coal subsidies are dealt with in section C(2) below.)

The beginning of the peaceful use of nuclear energy followed the American 'Atoms for Peace' policy in the early 1950s. Commercial use for electricity production commenced in the early 1970s.[19] The lack of acceptance among German society and—as a result—spectacular cases before the federal courts led to stagnation, with some projected power stations abandoned while still under construction (eg the fast breeder reactor in Kalkar) and others switched off (eg the high-temperature reactor in Hamm-Uentrop). Since the problem of nuclear waste management is still unsolved, recent political tendencies are towards opting out of the entire nuclear energy programme (*Ausstieg aus der Atomenergie*). See further section D(6) below. **8.09**

Last but not least, the process of reunifying Germany entailed severe consequences while harmonizing East German energy law. These are addressed where relevant in the following sections. **8.10**

(2) *Structure of the Energy Industry*[20]

Due to these heterogeneous historic developments, it is not surprising that industry structures vary widely from sector to sector. **8.11**

Energy supply entities (*Energieversorgungsunternehmen*) are concerned with the production, transport, and/or supply of electricity. There are three levels.[21] On the first level there are presently eight 'compound entities' (*Verbundunternehmen*). These major supply companies develop, maintain, and connect the supraregional high-tension grids (360/220 kV) and run the central power plants, with occasional co-operation in these fields. Compound entities are frequently vertically integrated utilities.[22] This means that one and the same utility produces, transports, and often also distributes electricity. As a rule, distribution takes place to the regional and local utilities. The second level concerns the supply of local utilities and consumers predominantly in rural areas. It consists of approximately eighty regional utilities which supply a large number of municipalities. Only in rare cases will second-level utilities produce their own energy instead of purchasing their **8.12**

[19] For an overview see for example Bender/Sparwasser/Engel, *Umweltrecht*, 3rd edn 1995, 425; M Kloepfer, *Umweltrecht*, 2nd edn 1998, 1020ff.

[20] The structure of the coal industry is dealt with in section C below.

[21] For an overview see: Vereinigung Deutscher Elektrizitätswerke, VDEW (ed), *Strommarkt Deutschland* 1996, 1997; ED Cross, *Electric utility regulation in the European Union—a country by country guide*, 1996, 130ff.

[22] The most important company is RWE Energie AG; other Verbundunternehmen are: Energie Baden-Württemberg (EBW), Bayernwerk AG, Berliner Kraft- und Licht AG (BEWAG), Hamburgische Electricitätswerke AG (HEW), PreussenElektra AG, Vereinigte Energiewerke AG (VEAG), and VEW Energie AG.

electricity from the first level of supply. The third level comprises the approximately 900 local utilities which are concerned with supplying the population of their respective municipalities. Third-level utilities often also deliver gas, heat, water, public transport, and waste services.

8.13 First- and second-level utilities are predominantly private limited companies (*Aktiengesellschaft*: AG, or *Gesellschaft mit beschränkter Haftung: GmbH*), though Länder and municipalities frequently hold shares and enjoy voting rights. Third-level utilities either belong to the municipal administration or consist of private limited companies owned by the municipalities, sometimes in co-operation with private shareholders. Independent electricity producers also exist especially in the field of renewable energy sources (section F(1) below).

8.14 The organization of network-bound gas supply follows basically the same structure as the electricity sector: compound entities which also run the import business,[23] regional utilities, and local suppliers. At the third level there are numerous companies which also deal with electricity. Besides these structures, some companies concentrate exclusively on upstream activities.

8.15 The actual structures of the electricity and the gas industry with its more than 1,000 utilities are expected to change considerably during the coming years as a consequence of the liberalization of these sectors.

8.16 Traditionally companies in the oil sector are privately owned, whether engaged in upstream or downstream activities. The players on the market are German (for example the ARAL AG, VEBA OEL, RWE-DEA groups), foreign (AGIP, BP, Elf), and multinational (Esso/Exxon, Mobil, Shell).

8.17 The involvement of the State in the energy sector differs as much from sector to sector as do the structures of the respective industries. Most remarkably, due to the federal structure of the German State, there are no uniform and specialized regulatory bodies as is the case, for example, in the United Kingdom (eg Offer, Ofgas) or in the German telecommunications sector.[24] Production and supply activities are as a rule subject to the supervision of the Ministries of the Economy of the Länder and, occasionally, specialized authorities (such as mining authorities in Northrhine Westphalia and Saxony). In the process of liberalizing network-bound energy supply, supplementary supervision by the competition and antitrust authorities of Bund and Länder has become increasingly important (see section E(4) below).[25]

[23] For example Bayerngas GmbH, Ruhrgas AG, Thyssengas GmbH, Verbundnetz Gas AG, Wintershall Gas GmbH (WINGAS).

[24] cf *Regulierungsbehörde für Telekommunikation und Post*, §§ 66ff of the German Telecommunications Act (*Telekommunikationsgesetz*). As to the—fruitless—discussions on creating a national energy authority see K-H Friauf, in B Börner (ed), *Beharren und Wandel im Energierecht*, 1986, 28ff with further references.

[25] cf G Kühne, *Das neue Energiewirtschaftsrecht*, in NJW 1998, 1902, 1905.

B. Constitutional Framework

Unlike the constitutions of some Member States of the European Union,[26] the German Constitution (Basic Law for the Federal Republic of Germany, *Grundgesetz für die Bundesrepublik Deutschland*, of 3 May 1949)[27] does not contain any specific reference to the energy sector. The Federal Constitutional Court, however, has ruled that safeguarding energy is a high-ranking general interest, comparable to that of one's 'daily bread'.[28] Permanent availability was called an indispensable prerequisite for the functioning of the entire economy, an 'absolute common good'.[29] Being an element of the *öffentliche Daseinsvorsorge* (literally 'public existence provision'[30]), energy supply was regarded as necessary for the individual to safeguard his/her existence in accordance with the dignity of human life (Art 1[1] of the Constitution).[31] **8.18**

Not only does the dependence of consumers and the economy on a safe and cheap energy supply require special regulation of the energy sector, it is also a consequence of the technical and economical peculiarities of this sector. Electricity and gas supply are network-bound; electricity cannot be stored; the storage of gas is possible only in a very limited way, therefore production must always be capable of meeting peak demand; and production entities and distribution grids require immense investment costs which may only take place on the basis of a sound legal framework providing for stable long-term conditions. As a consequence, public regulation of the energy sector is often held to be both necessary and justified.[32] The competent legislator is either the Federal Parliament (Bund) or the regional parliaments (Länder). In addition, their respective executive competencies are established according to the constitutional distribution of administrative competences. Each is now addressed in turn. **8.19**

[26] See Art 10 of the Irish Constitution, Art 43 of the Italian Constitution, Arts 66(2) lit d and 81 lit n of the Portugese Constitution and Art 149(1) No 25 of the Spanish Constitution.

[27] Last altered on 16 July 1998: see *BGBl* 1998 part I, 1822.

[28] Federal Constitutional Court, judgment published in *Europäische Grundrechte Zeitschift (EuGRZ)* 1995, 86, 92.

[29] Federal Constitutional Court, *BVerfGE* (report of cases), vol 30, 292, 323–4.

[30] In a narrower sense providing public utilities.

[31] Federal Constitutional Court, *BVerfGE* vol 66, 248, 258.

[32] For a survey see: D Ehlers, *Wirtschaftsaufsicht*, in Achterberg/Püttner (eds), *Besonderes Verwaltungsrecht*, vol I, 1990, section I/2, margin number 524; W Löwer, *Energieversorgung zwischen Staat, Gemeinde und Wirtschaft*, 1989; HJ Papier, *Staatliche Einwirkungen auf die Energiewirtschaft*, in Festschrift zum 125-jährigen Bestehen der juristischen Gesellschaft zu Berlin, 1984, 529ff; HD Jarass, *Formen staatlicher Einwirkung auf die Energiewirtschaft*, in Der Staat, vol 17 (1978), 507ff; H Gröner, *Die Ordnung der deutschen Elektrizitätswirtschaft*, 1975.

(1) The Distribution of Legislative Competence

8.20 Since Germany is a Federal State (see Article 20[1] of the Constitution) the distribution of competence between the Federation (Bund) and its Member States (Länder) is of particular relevance. Distribution of federal competences is found in Articles 30, 70–82 (legislative competences) and Articles 30, 83–91b (administrative competences) of the Constitution. As a rule, Article 30 assigns the exercise of State authority and the performance of State tasks to the Länder, so long as the Constitution does not provide otherwise.

8.21 The latter is the case, for example, with legislative power for the energy sector (see Article 74[1] no 11), and similarly for the peaceful production and use of nuclear energy (Article 74[1] no 11a of the Constitution), both of which involve 'concurrent legislative competence' (*konkurrierende Gesetzgebung*). This means that both Bund and Länder have the right to legislate, but with Bund legislation prevailing over Länder legislation when the Bund chooses to exercise its competence. The Bund may only use this privilege where federal legislation would contribute to harmonizing the individual legal and economic environments (Art 72[2] of the Constitution). The 'energy sector' within the meaning of Article 74(1) no 11 comprises legal regulation of the production, transformation, storage, and distribution of energy as well as energy law in a wider sense.[33]

8.22 Until now, the Bund has not fully exhausted its wide margin of possible competences within the energy sector. Some competence has remained with the Länder. While, for example, the Bund claimed for itself the regulation of basic structures of the energy sector (mainly by the Federal Energy Act—*Energiewirtschaftsgesetz*, the Federal Mining Act—*Bundesberggesetz*, and the Federal Nuclear Act—*Atomgesetz*), the Länder regulate energy-saving matters and, to some extent, the support of renewable energies. However, opinions differ on the exact extent of Länder competence; for example, whether or not Länder may pursue an independent energy policy conflicting with federal policy is a matter of continuing controversy.[34]

(2) Administrative Competence

8.23 Administrative competence is exercised by the Bund, the Länder, and the municipalities (*Gemeinden* and *Kreise*—municipalities and districts). The vast majority

[33] See K Stern, *Energierecht im Widerstreit zwischen Bundes- und Landeskompetenz*, 1988, 18, 27–8. Included in the energy sector are laws governing energy installations and their safety, State supervision, energy prices and taxes, as well as energy supply. Furthermore, Art 74(1) Nos 13 and 16 assign legislative competences concerning energy research and (energy) competition law to the Bund.

[34] KH Friauf, *Verfassungsrechtliche Grenzen einer eigenständigen Energiepolitik der Länder*, in B Börner (ed), Beharren und Wandel im Energierecht, 1986, 11ff; H Hantke, *Bundesstaatliche Fragen des Energierechts*, 1990; H Hantke, *Landesenergiegesetzgebung—Grenzen und Möglichkeiten*, in Recht der Energiewirtschaft (RdE) 1992, 105ff, 139ff, with further references.

of administrative competences are assigned to the Länder, which not only execute their own laws, but, as a rule, also execute the laws passed by the Bund 'as their own affair' (Art 83 of the Constitution), which means in their own name and responsibility. In the latter respect, the Länder are not competent to legislate, but enjoy exclusive competence to administer. Exceptions from this rule are the Bund-directed and supervised administration by the Länder (*Bundesauftragsverwaltung*—Article 85 of the Constitution) and administration through Bund-owned, ie federal, authorities (*bundeseigene Verwaltung*—Articles 86 and 87 of the Constitution). The first concept describes a situation where the Länder perform their administration under the direction and control of the Bund. The second concept means that the Bund runs its own administration in order to perform an administrative task itself.

In addition, special attention should be paid to such affairs which are 'rooted in the local community', where competence is assigned to the local governments by Article 28(2) of the Constitution. This is addressed in paragraphs 8.27–8.33 below. **8.24**

Competences of Bund and Länder

Administrative competence in respect of the energy sector lies predominantly with the Länder. The Federal Energy Act, for example, is exclusively executed by the Länder Ministries of Economy as 'their own affair'. Specific problems may occur in connection with the interpretation of the wide legal concepts used in the Federal Energy Act. Some Länder display a tendency to establish their own independent interpretation of these concepts in order to push their own political visions (especially as to the promotion of renewable energies).[35] Another example of exclusive Länder administration is the execution of the Federal Mining Act by the Länder Ministers of the Economy as higher mining authorities and subsequent authorities (for example: the middle and lower mining authorities called *Oberbergämter* and *Bergämter* in Northrhine-Westphalia and Saxony). **8.25**

A typical example of Bund-directed and supervised administration is the execution of the Federal Nuclear Act. Here, the Länder authorities are subject to numerous directives and control by the competent Federal Minister.[36] This has gained crucial relevance in the context of the heavily debated issue of the location of nuclear power plants and of final disposal sites for nuclear waste. The Federal Constitutional Court has repeatedly stressed federal rights to supervise and direct **8.26**

---

[35] See on this question H Hantke, *Bundesstaatliche Fragen des Energierechts*, 1990, 164ff; JF Baur, *Unterschiede in der Energiepolitik in der Energiepolitik der Bundesländer aus ordnungspolitischer und wirtschaftsrechtlicher Sicht*, in Recht der Energiewirtschaft (RdE) 1987, 66ff; E Hoffmann, *Die rechtliche Situation der Aufsicht über Elektrizitätsunternehmen*, ibid, 158ff.

[36] See Art 87c of the Constitution in conjunction with §24 of the Federal Nuclear Act (*Atomgesetz*).

nuclear energy policy against competing Länder ambitions.[37] Similarly, several petitions for public referenda against nuclear power stations raised at the Länder level have been held impermissible.[38]

Table 1: Administrative power as to the execution of federal energy law:

General rule: Execution by the Länder 'in their own right' (Art 83 of the Constitution)	*Explicit exceptions as to federal administrative power:*
→ 'energy law' is executed mainly by Länder authorities, → Federal administrative power is reduced to issuing general administrative rules and supervision *only* as to the accordance with the applicable *law* (Art 84[2] and [3] of the Constitution) → lack of any specific regulatory/administrative body of the Federation in the relevant context	(1) Implementation by the Länder 'for the Federation' (*Bundesauftragsverwaltun* see Art 85 of the Constitution) → example: execution of the *Nuclear Act* → The Bund may then: —issue general administrative rules, —provide for the uniform training of civil servants and appoint the heads of intermediate authorities, —give directives, —supervise the legality and the reasonableness of implementation. (2) Direct federal administration (*Bundeseigene Verwaltung*, Arts 86ff of the Constitution) → own administrative structure of the Federation (example: fiscal authorities) → not relevant in the field of energy law, there are some federal institutions as to special aspects of environmental and/or technical regulation, eg: Federal Office of the Environment (*Bundesumweltamt*); Federal Office for Radiation Protection (*Bundesamt für Strahlenschutz*).

The practical consequence is that the Länder hold the majority of *administrative/executive* power.

[37] Federal Constitutional Court, BVerfGE vol 81, 310 (*'Schneller Brüter'*); BVerfGE vol 84, 25 (*'Grube Konrad Salzgitter'*).

[38] Bavarian Constitutional Court (*Verfassungsgerichtshof*), decision published in Bayerische Verwaltungsblätter (BayVBl) 1987, 652; Northrhine-Westphalian Constitutional Court, decision published in Nordrheinwestfälische Verwaltungsblätter (NWVBl) 1987, 13; R Grawert, *Volksbegehren vor dem Verfassungsgerichtshof*, in Nordrheinwestfälische Verwaltungsblätter (NWVBl) 1987, 2ff.

Competences of the municipalities

It is commonly believed that the supply of residents with electricity and gas falls within 'affairs rooted in the local community' and thereby becomes a matter of local—and autonomous—'self-government' under the Constitution.[39] This establishes, however, only a basic administrative responsibility of the municipalities and does not automatically decide whether local bodies may perform supply tasks themselves either as a legal obligation or as an exclusive right. **8.27**

German municipalities traditionally invoked their title in public highways (ie local roads, squares etc) in order to decide freely whether to operate the local energy supply as a municipal enterprise or to delegate the supply task to a third party, eg a private or mixed public-private company. The latter alternative was realized by contractual agreements transferring the exclusive right to use the public highways for supply purposes to the respective undertaking (*Konzessionsvertrag*). This allowed the municipalities to establish monopolistic supply structures within their territories and, at the same time, to maintain their influence in the field of energy supply including the possibility of running the local energy supply at their own risk (and profit). If the task was delegated, the 'authorized' supply company was charged a substantial concession fee (*Konzessionsabgaben*) for the use of municipal roads.[40] German competition law limited these contracts *de facto* to a period of twenty years (see paragraph 8.108 below). When the 'concession contracts' between a municipality and a non-municipal supply undertaking expired, a new decision of the local government on how to operate the local energy supply (by its own activities or 'delegated' to private enterprises) was required. In particular the question arose whether, and under what conditions, the municipalities were allowed to take back (or 're-municipalize') the performance of supply tasks and take over privately built supply installations.[41] **8.28**

[39] cf Art 28(2), 1st sentence of the Constitution: 'The municipalities shall be guaranteed the right to manage all the affairs of the local community on their own responsibility within the limits set by law'. See also, for example, Art 83(1) of the Bavarian Constitution assigning 'the supply of the residents with water, [electric] light, gas, and electric power' to the municipalities. See in this context a famous judgement of the Bavarian Constitutional Court, in BayVerfGHE (report of cases) vol 10, 113, 120.

[40] The total amount of such 'concession fees' charged by all German municipalities was about 6.1 billion DM in 1995 (cf Kühne, *Das neue Energiewirtschaftsrecht*, in Neue Juristische Wochenschrift—NJW—1998, 1902, 1905) and therefore constitutes a significant post on the energy bill to be paid at the end by the consumer.

[41] The question of the proper take-over price has been much disputed in the literature. See, for example, Tettinger/Pielow, *Der Sachzeitwert als der nach wie vor maßgebliche Übernahmepreis beim Versorgerwechsel*, Bochum 1995.

8.29 This legal basis for municipal control of energy supply has never been confirmed *de iure*. The most heavily debated question is whether a municipality may derive an exclusive 'right' from the sole fact of its title to the public highways.[42]

8.30 Since the Energy Act of 1935 did not contain any reference to a specific role for the municipalities in the field of energy supply (nor does the 1998 Act), the answer to this question depends on the extent of the constitutional guarantee of local self-government and the supplementary guarantees in the individual Länder constitutions.[43] The proponents of a significant municipal influence within the energy sector maintain that the above-mentioned mechanism, as a traditional practice within German municipalities, forms a sort of 'untouchable essence' of the constitutionally guaranteed principle of local self-government. Accordingly, municipalities should be able to decide independently how to use their property and whether or not to make profits.[44] On the other hand it has to be stressed that the guarantee of local self-government in Article 28(2) of the Constitution forms only a principle of the *internal* relationship between the different (national, regional, and local) levels of public administration. It does not affect *external* relations between public bodies and private entrepreneurs. Like all other public bodies, municipalities are held to respect the fundamental rights and freedoms of private entrepreneurs and owners of supply networks. Apart from that, the principle of local self-government in Article 28(2) of the Constitution is only guaranteed 'within the limits of the law', including the ordinary Länder laws which govern the economic activities of the municipalities. Local energy supply constitutes such an economic activity. Accordingly, as an administrative court underscored recently, a municipality must perform a public task only insofar as the respective local need is not satisfied by others.[45]

---

[42] Already hesitant: ER Huber, *Wirtschaftsverwaltungsrecht*, vol I, 2nd edn, 1953, 565ff: '*détournement de pouvoir*'. The French or Spanish concept of *domaine public* or *dominio público* is almost unknown in Germany. Accordingly, to speak of a 'concession' and 'concession fees' in Germany when admitting non-municipal energy enterprises does not mean the transfer, assignment, or delegation of an original public or municipal task or responsibility, as may be the case under the 'Roman' concept of *service public* or *servicio público*.

[43] In favour of a strong position for local bodies: G Püttner, *Das Recht der kommunalen Energieversorgung*, 1967, 27; also K Stern and G Püttner, *Die Gemeindewirtschaft—Recht und Realität*, 1965, 160. Judgments: for example Bavarian Administrative Court, published in Recht der Energiewirtschaft (RdE) 1993, 15–16.

[44] See: G Püttner, *Der verfassungsrechtliche Rahmen für die Energieversorgung in Deutschland*, in Landes- und Kommunalverwaltung (LKV) 1991, 209ff; J Wieland/J Hellermann, *Der Schutz des Selbstverwaltungsrechts der Kommunen gegenüber Einschränkungen ihrer wirtschaftlichen Betätigung im nationalen und europäischen Recht*, 1995, esp 102ff.

[45] Hessian Administrative Tribunal, published in Recht der Energiewirtschaft (RdE) 1993, 143. The judgment dealt with water supply but expressively referred to energy supply as well. In the same sense regarding the energy supply see: W Löwer, *Energieversorgung zwischen Staat, Gemeinde und Wirtschaft*, 1989; summary in DVBl. 1991, 132ff; W. Löwer, *Energieversorgung und gemeindliche Selbstverwaltung*, in Recht der Energiewirtschaft (RdE) 1992, 85ff; F Ossenbühl, *Rechtliche Aspekte der Energieversorgung in den neuen Bundesländern*, in Die öffentliche Verwaltung (DÖV) 1992, 1ff.

To appreciate the complex problem of municipal competences within the energy sector, it is necessary to differentiate the stages of energy supply (production, transport, distribution), taking into account the traditional role of the municipalities.[46] Apart from some examples of local district heating systems and local power stations, municipalities have rarely contributed to the production of energy. Hence, it would be quite unreasonable to grant them an (exclusive) constitutional right to produce energy. Some tendencies towards decentralization, however, can be found in the context of the employment of alternative energy sources (especially the use of industrial waste heat for energy production—*Kraft-Wärme-Kopplung*). On the other hand, it should not be forgotten that many of the major regional companies serving the electricity market are closely connected to the municipalities by virtue of shares and voting rights.[47] From a municipal point of view, special relevance is attributed to the development of local energy supply concepts encompassing energy saving and environmental protection. Such concepts could improve the use of energy with regard to specific local structures and needs.[48] Furthermore, local planning law enables the municipalities to decide on the location of supply areas and supply installations, including supply grids.[49] **8.31**

In order to preserve municipal influence in the energy sector, local governments have been granted the right to apply a 'single buyer' system under the new Federal Energy Act of 1998 (see paragraph 8.116 below).[50] **8.32**

[46] See for example E Schmidt-Aßmann, *Kommunen und örtliche Energieversorgung*, in *Festschrift für Fabricius*, 1989, 251; PJ Tettinger, *Rechtliche Markierungen für kommunale Energiepolitik*, in Nordrhein-Westfälische Verwaltungsblätter (NWVBl.) 1989, 1ff.

[47] See D Ehlers, in Achterberg and Püttner (eds), *Besonderes Verwaltungsrecht*, vol I, 1990, 1/2, margin number 547; G Brüggemeier and R Damm, *Kommunale Einwirkung auf gemeinschaftliche Energieversorgungsunternehmen*, 1988; W Kluth, *Rechtsfragen der Beteiligung von Kommunen an Großkonzernen—Das Beispiel RWE*, in J Peter and K-U Rhein (eds), Wirtschaft und Recht, 1989, 117, with further references.

[48] As early as 1977, the Federal Government encouraged the local bodies to develop such concepts. See *Bundestags-Drucksache* (BT-Drucks)—Bulletin of the Federal Parliament—8/1357, 5. See moreover: Th Würtenberger, *Energieversorgung und gemeindliche Entwicklungsplanung*, in Wirtschaft und Verwaltung 1985, 188; W Wesener, *Energieversorgung und Energieversorgungskonzepte*, 1986. On the Länder level there are special support programmes for energy conservation, see for example, concerning Northrhine-Westphalia, G Einert, *Aktuelle Fragen der Energiepolitik in Nordrhein-Westfalen*, in Nordrhein-Westfälische Verwaltungsblätter (NWVBl) 1993, 242.

[49] See for references: RP Löhr, in Battis, Krautzberger, and Löhr, *Baugesetzbuch, Kommentar*, 3rd edn, 1991, §9, margin number 50.

[50] See further: JF Baur and K-H Friauf, *Energierechtsreform zwischen Europarecht und kommunaler Selbstverwaltung*, 1997. On similar issues in the field of telecommunication see: M Moraing, *Möglichkeiten und Grenzen kommunalwirtschaftlicher Betätigung unter besonderer Berücksichtigung der Telekommunikation*, 1995; H Pünder, *Die kommunale Betätigung auf dem Telekommunikationssektor*, in Deutsches Verwaltungsblatt (DVBl) 1997, 1353ff (in favour of a broad municipal influence); against: M Müller, *Zur verfassungsrechtlichen Problematik kommunaler Unternehmen auf dem Telekommunikationsmarkt*, in DVBl 1998, 1256ff. The Federal Constitutional Court recently refused to deal with a constitutional complaint raised by a number of municipalities (decision of 7

8.33 The above-mentioned controversy over 're-muncipalization' continued in the new East German Länder.[51] Since a safe and cheap electricity supply was very important to build up new economic structures, the final GDR Government concluded an electricity contract (*Stromvertrag*) with the three largest West German electricity suppliers in August 1990, just before Reunification. This contract was intended to safeguard energy supply and to modernize the outdated power stations and power grids through comprehensive investment.[52] Generally speaking, the electricity contract reserved the West German influence on the new reprivatized East German supply entities by virtue of a majority shareholding. The Treaty between the German Democratic Republic and the Federal Republic of Germany Establishing German Unity of 31 August 1990[53] confirmed the idea of the electricity contract and made it binding in public law. Through this regulation the East German municipalities were virtually excluded from any activity of their own within the energy supply sector. One hundred and sixty-four local governments disagreed and filed a complaint with the Federal Constitutional Court. The dispute was settled by agreement, the 'electricity compromise',[54] which allowed the East German municipalities to run their own supply enterprises. To this end parts of the reprivatized energy industry were transferred to the municipalities. As a result, a number of the larger East German cities now run their own supply businesses whilst the majority of the municipalities participate in the regional supply companies as shareholders. By allowing the compromise agreement, however, the Federal Court forfeited the opportunity to define the position of the municipalities within the energy sector.[55]

January 1999—2 BvR 929/97). The complaint was directed against § 50 of the Telecommunications Act obliging the municipalities to allow access to public streets and squares for telecommunication cables free of charge and in a non-discriminatory way. On recent questions regarding the economic activities of local governments see: D Ehlers, *Rechtsprobleme der Kommunalwirtschaft*, in DVBl 1998, 497ff; J-C Pielow, *Gemeindewirtschaft im Gegenwind ?—Zu den rechtlichen Grenzen kommunaler Wettbewerbsteilsnahme am Beispiel der Telekommunikation*, in Nordrhein-Westfälische Verwaltungsblätter (NWVBl) 1999.

[51] See for example F Ossenbühl, *Wem gehören die ehemaligen Stadtwerke in den neuen Bundesländern?* Die Öffentliche Verwaltung (DÖV) 1991, 301; G Püttner, *Zur Rückgewinnung der Stadtwerke in den neuen Ländern*, 1991; W Harms (ed), *Neuordnung der Energiewirtschaft in den ostdeutschen Ländern*, 1991.

[52] See PJ Tettinger, in R Schmidt, *Öffentliches Wirtschaftsrecht—Besonderer Teil*, part 1, § 7, margin number 10; H Reschke-Kessler, in P Kirchhof, E Klein, and H Reschke-Kessler, *Die Wiedervereiningung und damit zusammenhängende Rechtsprobleme*, 1991, 70.

[53] Published in BGBl 1990 part II, 889.

[54] Agreement settling the dispute before the Federal Constitutional Court on the structure of the energy supply in the new Länder of 22 December 1992, published as an annex to *Verband Kommunaler Unternehmen (VKU)—Nachrichtendienst*, no 536, 3 August 1993.

[55] In this context see also the judgement of the Federal Administrative Court, in BVerwGE vol 98, 273ff.

C. Mining Law

The mining industry, especially the coal industry, is one of the traditional branches of the German economy. Hard coal helped the young Federal Republic to recover from World War II whilst brown coal was more or less the only energy source for the economy in the former German Democratic Republic.[56] As in other countries, the German mining economy is presently exposed to economic and geopolitical changes ('globalization'; 'Europeanization') and thus faces strong pressure for adaptation. **8.34**

(1) The Economic Relevance of the Mining Industry

The most important deposits of hard coal are to be found in the Ruhr area in Northrhine-Westphalia, and in the Saarland. Yet geological peculiarities—especially the fact that the coal deposits are often situated at a depth of more than 1000 metres[57]—and the burden of international economic competition resulted in the fact that hard coal could no longer be extracted in an economically efficient manner. Therefore, output has drastically decreased during the past fifty years: German output of hard coal amounted to a total of only 53.1 million tonnes in 1995 whereas it was 143.2 million tonnes in 1960.[58] **8.35**

The brown coal economy has not faced comparable difficulties. The extraction of brown coal takes the form of open-cast mining in the Cologne-Aachen area as well as in the Eastern German brown coal areas around Leipzig (*Mitteldeutsches Revier*) and north-east of Dresden (*Lausitzer Revier*). A total output of 192.7 million tonnes in 1995 is used almost exclusively for energy production. Brown coal mining is expanding even though it has been vehemently criticized by ecological groups because of its large social and environmental impacts. For the same reasons, it is opposed by people living near the open-cast mines. Despite all justified concerns, brown coal and hard coal are acknowledged domestic sources of energy. Reasons for continuing with mining in Germany are the security of supply conferred with domestic resources and the export of German mining technology. Coal is still the most important primary energy resource in Germany:[59] in 1997 the suppliers generated 27 per cent of electricity from brown coal and 25 per cent from hard coal. Considering the German mining industry only from the **8.36**

[56] On the history of the German mining industry, see for example Kroker, *Zur Entwicklung des Steinkohlenbergbaus in Nordrhein-Westfalen zwischen 1945 und 1995*, in Glückauf 1996, 457ff; L Mez, M Jänicke, and J Pöschk, *Die Energiesituation in der vormaligen DDR*, 1991.

[57] See for example J Depenbrock, *Zur Nordwanderung des Steinkohlenbergbaus an der Ruhr*, in Nordrhein-Westfälische Verwaltungsblätter (NWVBl) 1987, 70ff with further references.

[58] Statistics from Verlag Glückauf (ed), *Jahrbuch 1997*.

[59] See HB Giesel, *Die deutsche Steinkohle im Wettbewerb der Energieträger*, in Glückauf 1996, 701ff.

perspective of energy law would, however, be an over-simplification of the topic. Potash and rock salt, metal ore, iron ore, and other industrial minerals[60] are undoubtedly worth extracting. Another important aspect of mining is the underground storage of radioactive and other wastes, both temporarily and permanently.

(2) Economic Structures of Coal Mining

8.37 The decline of coal mining commenced in the 1960s in the area around the Ruhr and the Saar as a consequence of economic problems concerning the exploitation and sale of German (hard) coal as well as decreasing demand for hard coal in the energy sector. Production processes have since undergone severe rationalization and concentration. Only a few private mining companies survived. In the field of hard coal mining it is in particular the Ruhrkohle AG (RAG), Essen, whose subsidiaries have diversified their activities in numerous other business sectors worldwide (for example mining and environmental technology, trade, real estate, transportation etc). In the summer of 1998 the Ruhrkohle Bergbau AG took over the former Saarbergwerke AG, Saarbrücken, and, subject to the approval of the Commission, intends to merge with the Preussag Anthrazit AG, Ibbenbüren, to become the Deutsche Steinkohle AG with a total of no more than fifteen hard coal mines. As a consequence of the 'coal compromise of Bonn' (*Bonner Kohlekompromiß*) of March 1997, it is planned to reduce the number of employees in the hard coal mining industry from nearly 80,000 today to 36,000 in 2005 without any mass dismissals.[61] In the field of brown coal mining the following undertakings are noteworthy: the Rheinbraun AG, Köln, belonging to the group of RWE AG (Essen) as well as the Lausitzer Braunkohle AG (LAUBAG) and the Vereinigte Mitteldeutsche Braunkohlewerke AG (MIBRAG), the latter two being the main successor companies of the State-owned companies of the former GDR.

8.38 As in many other European countries engaged in coal mining, the competitiveness of German hard coal and the preservation of jobs involved relies heavily on public subsidies. Under European Community law, subsidies have to be granted as measures of regional or social development in order to avoid sanctions from the European authorities.[62]

8.39 Relevant statements on the nature of public subsidies are contained in the decision of the Federal Constitutional Court concerning the 'century agreement'

[60] For details, see: Wirtschaftsvereinigung Bergbau (ed), *Bergbau Handbuch*, 5th edn, 1994, 182, 184, 200ff; see 205ff on peat cutting: ibid, 205ff; as to the extraction of uranium: ibid, 215ff, and potash salts ibid, 223ff.

[61] cf *Berliner Morgenpost* of 30 July 1998. At the end of the 1950s there were 153 mines with a total of 600,000 employees.

[62] Decision No 3632/93/ECCS of the Commission of 28 December 1993, OJ 329/12 of 30 December 1993.

(*Jahrhundertvertrag*).[63] This contract established a fund in order to make German hard coal competitive on a long-term basis. All electricity suppliers were under a statutory obligation[64] to contribute to this fund, which in turn subsidized domestic hard coal.[65] Energy suppliers were allowed to add their respective financial burdens to the consumer price of energy in the form of the 'coal penny' (*Kohlepfennig*). A constitutional complaint was raised by an individual citizen who challenged his electricity bill, in particular the increased amount due to the 'coal penny'. The Federal Constitutional Court held that the material burden of the coal penny fell on consumers, rather than the energy suppliers, and that such a burden was permissible only as a general tax. The 'coal penny' was classified by the judges as an unjustified 'special duty' (*Sonderabgabe*) so the fund system was held to violate the financial regime of the Constitution.[66]

The 'coal penny' has been replaced by direct subsidies of hard coal. After a political tug-of-war in the 'coal session' (*Kohlerunde*)[67] accompanied by serious miners' strikes, the Act Concerning Support for German Hard Coal Mining (*Steinkohlebeihilfengesetz*)[68] was passed as a part of the mentioned 'coal compromise'. Until the year 2005, financial support for hard coal mining will take place via direct federal subsidies. German coal must be used in power plants and in steel production. In addition, the subsidies cover part of the costs of inevitable mine closures. The amount of subsidies will decrease annually from DM 7,000 m in 1998 to 3,800 m by the year 2005. **8.40**

From an EC law perspective, it is still uncertain what will happen to the coal compromise after the ECSC Treaty and decision 3632/93/ECSC expire in 2002. After that date, subsidies for the coal mining industry will have to be reviewed in the light of the general provisions of Articles 92ff of the EC Treaty. Much will then depend on the interpretation of the notion of 'economic development' in Article 93 **8.41**

[63] Federal Constitutional Court, in BVerfGE vol 91, 186, 201ff; also published in Europäische Grundrechte Zeitung (EuGRZ) 1995, 86ff.

[64] Federal Act Safeguarding the Further Use of Hard Coal in the Electricity Sector (*Drittes Verstromungsgesetz*) published 17 November 1980 in: BGBl, part I, 2137.

[65] §§ 1, 2, and 8 of the former Federal Act on the Electrification of Hard Coal (*Verstromungsgesetz).*

[66] Namely Art 74, No 11 in conjunction with Arts 72, 105, and 110 of the *Grundgesetz*, cf Federal Constitutional Court, in BVerfGE, vol 91, 186, 201ff; 206) = EuGRZ 1995, 86, 91ff. As to the consequences of this ruling see for example P Lauffer, *'Steinkohlenverstromung'—Perspektiven nach dem Beschluß des Bundesverfassungsgerichts vom 11.10.1994 zum Kohlepfennig*, 1995; H Lecheler, *Der 'Kohlepfennig-Beschluß' und seine Konsequenzen*, in Neue Juristische Wochenschrift (NJW) 1995, 933ff.

[67] For details as to the parliamentary and legislative development see P Lauffer, *Neuordnung der Kohlesubventionen*, in Recht der Energiewirtschaft (RdE) 1998, 6ff.

[68] *Gesetz über Hilfen für den deutschen Steinkohlenbergbau bis zum Jahre 2005 (Steinkohlebeihilfengesetz)* 12 December 1997 (BGBl 1997 I No 85).

(3a,c) TEC. Other important issues are 'security of supply', and the concept of 'services of general economic interest' in Article 90(2) TEC.[69]

(3) Mining Law within a Federal Framework

8.42 Together with other sub-categories of the 'law of economy', the mining industry appears in the German constitution (*Grundgesetz*) as a matter of 'concurrent legislation'.[70] Therefore, the Länder have the right to legislate only 'as far as the Federation does not exercise its legislative powers'.[71] This could give rise to the assumption that the mining sector is dominated by federal legislation. However, it took many exhaustive efforts before the Federal Mining Act (*Bundesberggesetz, BBergG*) of 13 August 1980 (BGBl I, 1310) entered into force on 1 January 1982. This law suspended former Länder law.[72] The old mining rights—going back to the Middle Ages in some cases—remained effective as individual exceptions only.

8.43 Mining is not only subject to the Federal Mining Act. In addition, other laws may be relevant, such as water law, the law of waste disposal and treatment (especially in the case of underground waste disposal),[73] and directives on the approval of industrial sites (for example in the case of subterranean gas stores) as well as nuclear law in the case of the final storage of radioactive waste.

8.44 The German federal system is characterized by the fact that, in practice, the majority of legislative competence is held by the Federation (*Bund*) whereas the implementation of the laws is usually a matter for the Länder (see paragraphs 8.18–8.25 above). The same is true of mining law. In accordance with this general rule, the public authorities occupied with the execution of the Federal Mining Act are part of the administration of the Länder.[74] Generally, the hierarchy comprises three levels: the *Bergamt* (lower mining authority) and the *Oberbergamt* (middle mining authority), both specialized administrative institutions of the Länder, with the Länder ministers for economic affairs at the top of the hierarchy. The main task of the mining authorities is to supervise mining activities in accordance with the Federal Mining Act, from the search for mineral resources through to

[69] For details: P Lauffer, n 67 above, 8ff.

[70] Art 74(1) No 11 of the Constitution.

[71] For details, see section B1 above.

[72] For example, the Prussian General Mining Act (*Preußisches Allgemeines Berggesetz—ABG*) of 24 June 1865 (GS 705), which was valid throughout the Prussian areas (with some regional peculiarities). After World War II, it became Länder law in the Länder successing Prussia, for example in Northrhine-Westphalia. For details see R Willecke, *Vom Preußischen Allgemeinen Berggesetz zum Bundesberggesetz—Entwicklungstendenzen im deutschen Bergrecht*, 1988, 31.

[73] See Chr Sladek, *Versatzbergbau zwischen Umwelt- und Bergrecht: Ein Erfahrungsbericht aus der behördlichen Praxis*, in von Danwitz/Hüffer (eds), Bergbau und Umwelt, 1999.

[74] cf § 142 of the Federal Mining Act.

mine decommissioning and until no further danger exists to human life and health, the public interest, or other mines or mineral resources.[75]

The mining authorities exercise effective supervision through comprehensive administrative acts, such as: passing mining decrees;[76] the grant, refusal, and withdrawal of mining rights; the approval of operation plans; exercising the power to give individual instructions for danger prevention;[77] and the right to information from mining companies. **8.45**

(4) *The Scope of the Federal Mining Act* (Bundesberggesetz)

The scope of the Federal Mining Act includes the exploration for, extraction and processing of certain mineral resources. This includes related activities such as reclamation of the surface during mining activities and afterwards.[78] The law also applies to activities such as investigation of the subsoil, for example with regard to its suitability for the construction of subsoil (gas) stores. The Act also applies to the German continental shelf, transit pipelines, and energy-related scientific activities. **8.46**

Section 1 of the Mining Act sets forth its objectives as follows: **8.47**

> to safeguard the supply of mineral resources by regulating and supporting the exploration for, and extraction and processing of mineral resources, taking into account their particular location and the protection of such deposits by dealing economically and carefully with the ground and the soil;
> to provide for the safety of mining operations and of miners; and
> to strengthen and improve precautions against dangers to the life, health, and property of third parties and to compensate for damage.

(5) *The Legal Classification of Mineral Resources*

Section 3(1) of the Federal Mining Act defines mineral resources as being all mineral substances, solid, liquid, or gaseous, occurring in natural sedimentation or accumulations (deposits) in or on the ground, on or under the bottom of the sea, and in the sea. Mining law classifies mineral resources as *bergfrei* or *grundeigen.* Only mineral resources classified as *grundeigen* (roughly translated, land-owned) are assigned to the landowner and protected as his/her property.[79] Such property rights do not extend to mineral resources classified as *bergfrei* (free from **8.48**

---

[75] As to the relevance of the release from mining supervision from a standpoint of public order law see Ipsen/Tettinger, *Altlasten und kommunale Bauleitplanung,* 1988, 31ff, with further references.

[76] cf §§ 65ff of the Federal Mining Act.

[77] ibid, §§ 71ff.

[78] ibid, § 2(1). See eg G Kühne, *Abandonment and reclamation of energy and resource sites and facilities—what happens when the operator fails to meet its obligations ?* in Energy and Resources Law '92, 1993, 308ff.

[79] cf § 3(2) of the Federal Mining Act.

land-property by virtue of the mining law). *Grundeigen* are all mineral resources which are not classified as *bergfrei*. The Federal Mining Act contains an exhaustive catalogue of *bergfrei* mineral resources: it mentions, for example, lead, iron, gold, copper, mercury, hydrocarbons, hard and brown coal, including the natural gas occurring in connection with the coal extraction,[80] potash, rock salt, and other salts. Furthermore, *bergfrei* includes all mineral resources contained in the continental shelf and the coastal waters as well as thermal energy released by the extraction of mineral resources. Evidently, the reason this distinction is to safeguard the supply of mineral resources in the interests of the national economy independently from the consent of the individual landowner and from the actual shape of the individual real estate. Therefore, the landowner is denied access to *bergfrei* mineral resources unless mining permission is obtained (see section 6 below).[81]

8.49 On the other hand, mineral resources classified as *grundeigen* are exclusively assigned to the landowner. Such resources include basalt lava, slate, *Speckstein*, several sorts of quartz and clay, and all other non-*bergfrei* mineral resources. However, the Federal Mining Act is only applicable so long as the *grundeigen* minerals are extracted by underground mining:[82] *grundeigen* mineral resources extracted in open-cast mining do not fall within the scope of the Act. They remain assigned to the landowner; their extraction is subjected to other laws, such as the civil law, regional excavation law (*Abgrabungsrecht*), and the laws of area (*Raumordnungsrecht*) and urban (*Bauplanungsrecht*) planning law.[83]

8.50 Until 1996 the situation was different in Eastern Germany, where all mineral resources were *bergfrei*.[84] This situation was preserved[85] under the Treaty estab-

[80] As to methane in hard coal mines: P Franke, *Rechtsfragen der Methangasgewinnung aus Steinkohleflözen* in Recht der Energiewirtschaft (RdE) 1994, 1ff; G Kühne, *Rechtsfragen der Aufsuchung und Gewinnung von in Steinkohleflözen beisitzendem Methangas*, 1994.

[81] H-J Papier, in Maunz and Dürig, *Grundgesetz, Kommentar* (loose-leaf as of November 1997), Art 14, margin number 438. As to the relation of *bergfrei* mineral resources and the guarantee of property in Art 14 of the German Basic Law: Federal Administrative Court, in Zeitschrift für Bergrecht (ZfB) 101 (1960), 89, 93.

[82] § 3(4), no 2 of the Federal Mining Act.

[83] See for example: J Berkemann, *Planerische Lenkung des Abbaus von oberflächennahen Bodenschätzen*, in Deutsches Verwaltungsblatt (DVBl) 1989, 625ff. Sometimes, namely in connection with the extraction of sands and pyrites, water law applies. See in this context first of all: Federal Constitutional Court, in BVerfGE (report of cases) vol 58, 300ff (*Naßauskiesung*). See further: Federal Court of Justice (*Bundesgerichtshof*—BGH), in BGHZ (report of civil cases) vol 90, 3, 9; from recent literature: G Gaentzsch, *Rechtliche Fragen des Abbaus von Kies und Sand*, in Neue Zeitschrift für Verwaltungsrecht (NVwZ) 1998, 889ff, and M Reinhardt, *Bergrechtliche Determinanten wasserbehördlicher Entscheidungen*, in von Danwitz/Hüffer (eds), Bergbau und Umwelt, 1999.

[84] § 3 of the GDR Mining Act of 12 May 1969 (GBl I No 5, 29). For further details: U Hüffer/PJ Tettinger, *Sand und Kies als Gegenstand des Bergwerkseigentums in den neuen Bundesländern*, 1993.

[85] Constitutional objections concerning the reduced rights of property and of equality failed since they could affect the supply of the building industry with raw materials which was necessary in order to rebuild the former GDR: cf Federal Administrative Court (*Bundesverwaltungsgericht*), in BVerwGE (report of cases) vol 94, 12, 28ff. As to the similar position of the Federal Constitutional Court, see decision of 24 September 1997 (1BvR 647/91 *et al*) and BVerfGE vol 86, 382ff.

lishing Germany's unity (*Einigungsrutrog*) until the law of 15 April 1996, which upheld those stipulations in the Treaty of Unification.[86] Consequently *grundeigen* are now assigned to the landowner in the former East Germany.

(6) *Mining Permits (*Berechtsamswesen*)*

Mining permits give the right to search for and extract mineral resources. It was one of the central objectives of the *Bundesberggesetz* to clear up the confusing situation of numerous different mining rights and permissions granted under the individual regional laws of the past, some of them effective since the Middle Ages. If still relevant, ancient rights and permissions were transformed into the new types of the *Bundesberggesetz*, whilst other legal permissions which had become practically meaningless expired. Today, there are two categories of mining permissions:[87] permission to search for mineral resources in a specified location, ie an *Erlaubnis*, which means permission in a narrower sense; and a *Bewilligung*, which means 'grant' or permission in a wider sense, and *Bergwerkseigentum*, meaning 'mine property'. **8.51**

The latter two of the above belong to the same category of permission, since they basically provide the same rights, namely to search for mineral resources and to extract them. The difference between a *Bewilligung* and a *Bergwerkseigentum* is that the latter shares the legal nature of real property as to transfer and mortgage. Mining permissions come into being by virtue of a grant which requires first of all evidence of the applicant's reliability and financial capacity. Since the grant requires a proper balance between public and private interests it has been questioned whether an applicant has a *right* to be granted a mining permission when all requirements are met, or whether the competent mining authority has a discretion to refuse permission. In the light of the constitutionally guaranteed freedom of entrepreneurial activities,[88] the better view is that no such discretion exists.[89] **8.52**

The Federal Mining Act also contains criteria according to which the grant of a mining permission must be refused.[90] This is especially the case where prior public interests outweigh the interest in the search for mineral resources—a blanket **8.53**

[86] See *Gesetz zur Vereinheitlichung der Rechtsverhältnisse bei Bodenschätzen* of 15 July 1996 (BGBl I 602). Nevertheless and as a general rule, mining permissions as to *bergfreie* mineral resources, obtained under the old law, remain valid. For further details: J Berkemann, *Bergrechtsvereinheitlichung und Bestandsschutz für bestehende Bergbauberechtigungen*, in Der Betriebsberater (BB) 1996, 1450ff.

[87] cf §§ 6, 7–9 of the Federal Mining Act.

[88] Art 12(1) of the Constitution.

[89] See H Schulte, *Die Bergbauberechtigungen nach dem Regierungsentwurf für ein Bundesberggesetz*, in Zeitschrift für Bergrecht (ZfB) vol 119 (1978), 414, 419ff; Boldt/Weller, *Bundesberggesetz*, 1984, § 11, margin number 1; JD Rausch, *Umwelt- und Planungsrecht beim Bergbau*, 1990, 23–4.

[90] cf §§ 11–13 of the Federal Mining Act.

clause, which is to be interpreted in accordance with aspects of environmental protection. Regardless of the qualification of their legal nature as regards public or private law,[91] all mining permissions are constitutionally protected as private property by Article 14(1) of the Constitution.[92]

8.54 The holder of a permission to search for mineral resources (*Erlaubnis*) for commercial purposes has to pay a 'field fee' (*Feldesabgabe*), to the Land where the search is taking place.[93] However, since the costs of the search have to be taken into account in favour of the permit holder the field fee is of no significant economic relevance. The holder of a permission to search and extract (*Bewilligung* and *Bergwerkseigentum*) has to pay an 'extraction fee' (*Förderabgabe*), which gives the respective Land an interest in the economic success of the mining company.[94] This interest is 10 per cent of the average annual market value.[95]

(7) Mining Operations

8.55 German mining law clearly distinguishes between the mining permission (*Bergbauberechtigung)* as a necessary legal title (see section 6 above) and its realization by means of mining activities. For mining activity an additional permission is required which is subject to numerous requirements. For this purpose, the Federal Mining Act contains detailed provisions concerning a specific legal concept of the mining law, the 'operation plan' (*Betriebsplan*).[96]

General planning obligations and types of operation plans

8.56 Works connected with the search for, and extraction and processing of mineral reserves may only be set into operation or abandoned pursuant to an 'operation

[91] As to the phenomenon that the *Bundesberggesetz* tends to mere public law solutions, even though mining law is a cross-section of both public and private law: U Karpen, *Grundeigentum und Bergbaurechte nach dem Bundesberggesetz vom 13. 8. 1980*, in Archiv des öffentlichen Rechts (AöR), vol 106 (1981), 15ff (17); G Kühne, in Kühne/Gaentzsch (eds), *Wandel und Beharren im Bergrecht*, 1992, 49–50.

[92] *Bundesverfassungsgericht* (Federal Constitutional Court), BVerfGE *(*report of cases) vol 77, 130ff (136); vol 80, 360ff (364–5); *Oberverwaltungsgericht* (*OVG*) of Northrhine-Westphalia, in Zeitschrift für Bergrecht (ZfB), vol 11 (1990), 33ff (36); OVG of Rhineland Palatine, in Neue Zeitschrift für Verwaltungsrecht (NVwZ) 1994, 44ff; H Krüger, *Verfassungsrechtlicher Eigentumsschutz für den Bergbau*, in Festschrift für F Fabricius, 1989, 99ff; recently: G Kühne, *Bestandsschutz alten Bergwerkseigentums unter besonderer Berücksichtigung des Art. 14 GG*, 1998; as to the specific relation between mining property and street planning cf judgment of the Federal Admnistrative Court (BVerwG), in Deutsches Verwaltungsblatt (DVBl.) 1998, 895ff.

[93] § 30 of the Federal Mining Act.

[94] Federal Constitutional Court, in BVerfGE vol 72, 330, 410.

[95] § 31 of the Federal Mining Act. As to the finding of this market value, see the individual Länder decrees based on § 32 of the Act, for example the decree on the mining fees of Lower Saxony of 17 December 1981 (GVBl, 413) with later modificactions (eg version of 23 June 1992, GVBl 169). In order to siphon off—at least partly—the 'windfall profits' arising from international quotations, the *Förderabgabe* for mineral oil and gas grew to 32% of the market value (40% is the absolute limit). Thus Lower Saxony obtained considerable revenues from oil and gas.

[96] §§ 51ff of the Federal Mining Act.

plan' (*Betriebsplan*), which has to be established by the entrepreneur and approved by the competent mining authority.[97] According to the official reasons given for the Federal Mining Act, the main peculiarity of mining is its progressive character, adapting itself to the changing environment, while permanently reducing the overall reserves of mineral resources. This dynamic operation not only causes specific dangers for employees, third persons, and goods, but also has a negative effect on the land surface, where it may result in severe changes. This is particularly the case with open-cast mining. These specific circumstances require ongoing supervision of mining operations. Therefore, mining law provides for a special procedure concerning the operation plan as a means of preventive and continuous supervision.[98] Approval of the operation plan is the traditional method of supervision by the mining authorities.[99]

Different kinds of operation plans are to be distinguished:[100] **8.57**

—the *main operation plan* (*Hauptbetriebsplan*), which is compulsory for the establishment and management of a company usually for not longer than two years;[101]
—the *special operation plan* (*Sonderbetriebsplan*), providing for complementary tasks and which refers only to special parts of a company or projects with an independent significance;[102] and
—the optional *framework operation plan (Rahmenbetriebsplan)* to be provided only at the request of the mining authority. It must contain general information about the intended project and its technical implementation.[103]

Common mining practice requires a framework operation plan before a new extraction and preparation plant is built. Such a plan enables the mining authority to take into account the long-term development of a project. The framework operation plan also makes possible an early and comprehensive investigation of the environmental impact of certain plants. Therefore, the framework plan is compulsory if a project entails significant effects for the environment.[104] This legal obligation also constitutes a legislative effort to introduce the EC Directive on environmental impact assessments (EIA) into German law (see section 10 below). **8.58**

---

[97] § 51(1), first sentence of the Federal Mining Act.
[98] See H Zydeck, *Bundesberggesetz* (Materialien), 1980, 232–3.
[99] It takes the legal form of a 'preventive prohibition' (*Verbot mit Erlaubnisvorbehalt*). cf judgments of the *Oberverwaltungsgericht* (OVG) Berlin, in Zeitschrift für Bergrecht (ZfB), vol 131 (1990), 200, 209, referring to the Federal Constitutional Court, in BVerfGE vol 81, 329, 332; *Oberverwaltungsgericht* (OVG) Rhineland-Palatinate, in Natur und Recht (NuR) 1994, 45–6.
[100] cf § 52 of the Federal Mining Act. For more details see: E Schmidt-Aßmann and F Schoch, *Bergwerkseigentum und Grundeigentum im Betriebsplanverfahren*, 1994, 137ff and 173ff.
[101] cf § 52(1) of the Federal Mining Act.
[102] ibid, § 52(2) no 2.
[103] ibid, § 52(2) no 1.
[104] ibid, § 52(2a) in connection with § 57c.

Furthermore, the constitutional principle of 'environmental protection' (Article 20a of the Constitution) may require the framework operation plan to be in place even if the Mining Act does not require it.[105]

Material requirements

8.59 Operation plans must specify the scope of the intended mining activity, its technical realization, and its duration. Evidence must be given that a catalogue of further requirements is met.[106] Section 55(1) of the Federal Mining Act enumerates these requirements:

—the entrepreneur and his/her representatives must be skilled and reliable;[107]
—necessary precautions must be taken against threats to life, health, goods, employees, and other people, for example visitors, in the enterprise;
—no damage must occur to mineral resources whose protection is of public interest;
—precautionary measures must be taken to preserve the land in the interest of the safety of persons and the proper functioning of traffic;
—waste must be disposed of in accordance with the relevant laws;
—the necessary precautions for the reclamation of the land surface must be taken, to a reasonable extent;
—the safety of existing sites already in operation must not be jeopardized; and
—detrimental effects of search and extraction should not result.

8.60 The requirements for the operation plan have traditionally been concretized in legal literature and jurisprudence. While individual developments cannot be dealt with in detail here,[108] it should be noted that these individual criteria do not serve the protection of subjective rights of individuals. As a consequence, there is no standing for an individual claim based on these requirements.

8.61 Once the requirements have been met, a mining company has the right to have its operation plan approved.[109] Any damage caused by mining activity after the plan has been approved may give rise to a claim for compensation only (see section 13

[105] cf PJ Tettinger, *Gewinnung und Aufbereitung von schwefelwasserstoffhaltigem Erdgas auf einer Ferieninsel?*, 1997, 27 with further references.

[106] §§ 52(4) and 55(1) of the Federal Mining Act.

[107] This requirement does not apply to framework operation plans.

[108] For details see for example the exhaustive information in Boldt/Weller, *Bundesberggesetz*, 1984, § 55 margin nos 6ff. As to the important requirement concerning 'detrimental effects' see H Schulte, *Gemeinschädliche Einwirkungen nach § 55 BBergG*, in Festschrift für F Fabricius, 1989, 149ff.

[109] See sentence of the *Bundesverwaltungsgericht* (Federal Administrative Court—BVerwG), in Deutsches Verwaltungsblatt (DVBl.) 1996, 253 (256); from the literature for example: Piens/Schulte/Graf Vitzthum, *Bundesberggesetz*, 1983, § 51, margin no 5; Boldt/Weller, *Bundesberggesetz*, 1984, *Vor* § 50, margin no 11, and § 55, margin no 4.

below). Further claims, including seeking the termination of the mining activity, are excluded.

However, the authority competent to approve the operation plan can restrict or prohibit the search and the extraction 'as long as contravening public interests predominate'.[110] In this respect, public interest matters protected by laws other than the Federal Mining Act become relevant for the approval procedure.[111] The mining authority is only competent so long as no other authorities, eg in the field of water law, are especially and exclusively concerned with safeguarding these matters. The sphere of potential 'predominant public interests' is large. Matters of superior area planning, the law of urban planning, nature conservation, the conservation of the countryside and monument protection, protection against air pollution, noise, poisonous substances, radiation, water pollution, and the protection of tourism, as well as of the interests of the landowners affected by the respective mining project, are of special concern.[112] **8.62**

Within a balanced decision, the mining authority must investigate whether the established public interests 'predominate' over the interest in the planned extraction of mineral resources. From a macro-economic perspective the interest in the extraction of mineral resources is of great importance.[113] However, the assessment of this interest can differ considerably from case to case. The Federal Mining Act also requires the 'economical and careful dealing with the ground and the soil'—which demand must be interpreted and balanced according to the high-ranking principle of 'environmental protection' referred to in Article 20a of the Constitution. The mining authority does not exercise any final discretion; on the contrary, in case of a lawsuit its decision is subject to comprehensive judicial review.[114] **8.63**

(8) Mining and Land Ownership

An especially difficult problem concerning the underground mining of hard coal is the interface between the extraction of mineral resources and the protection of private land. As regards constitutionally protected private property (Article 14 of the Constitution) the Federal Court of Justice (*Bundesgerichtshof*) has ruled that under the Federal Mining Act 'the natural conflict between real property and mining rights must be regarded as a relationship of vertical neighbourhood with a **8.64**

---

[110] cf § 48(2), first sentence, Federal Mining Act.

[111] cf Federal Administrative Court, in BVerwGE vol 74, 315, 323.

[112] For detailed information on the spectrum of 'public interests' to be taken into account see PJ Tettinger, *Gewinnung und Aufbereitung von schwefelwasserstoffhaltigem Erdgas auf einer Ferieninsel?*, 1997, 33ff, with further references.

[113] See judgments of the Federal Administrative Court, in BVerwGE vol 74, 315, 318 and vol 81, 329, 339.

[114] See judgment of the Federal Administrative Court, in BVerwGE vol 81, 329, 345f.

mutual obligation to behave in a reasonable way'.[115] The Federal Administrative Court (*Bundesverwaltungsgericht*) has interpreted the phrase 'predominant public interests' in the Federal Mining Act[116] to be in conformity with the Constitution. Accordingly, aspects of neighbour protection are inherent in the doctrine of the 'predominant public interest', which assigns the affected landowners a subjective right and legal standing against the planned mining operation.[117] The decisive problem, however, is to find suitable parameters for an adequate balance between the mining rights and the surface of the property. This question has arisen before the Federal Constitutional Court.[118]

(9) Planning Procedure

8.65 The operator must submit the operation plan, its prolongation, supplementation, or modification, together with the respective documents to the competent authority for its approval of the planned activity. The mining authority has to involve in advance those authorities (for nature conservation, for the conservation of the countryside, for construction supervision, water authorities, etc) or local authorities whose responsibility is affected by the planned activity.[119] Especially concerning projects of regional importance, a general area planning procedure may have to be carried out. In the context of such a procedure, the proposed mining sites will be assessed individually.[120] The participation of private third parties affected by the plan is provided for in the general laws on the administrative procedure of the Länder. The question of private landowners who are potentially affected by the planned mining activity being involved in the procedure has

[115] In BGHZ (report of cases in civil law matters) vol 111, 263, 264.

[116] cf § 48(2), first sentence, of the Federal Mining Act.

[117] See judgment of the Federal Administrative Court, in BVerwGE vol 81, 329, 345f.

[118] As to decisions already passed on interim orders, see: Federal Constitutional Court, in BVerfGE vol 77, 130ff, and vol 80, 360ff. For a detailed treatise, see Schmidt-Aßmann/Schoch, *Bergwerkseigentum und Grundeigentum im Betriebsplanverfahren*, 1994; U Hüffer (ed), *Oberflächeneigentum und Bergbau*, 1994; G Gaentzsch, *Oberflächeneigentum und Bergbau aus der Sicht der höchstricchterlichen Rechtssprechung*, in Deutsches Verwaltungsblatt (DVBl) 1993, 527ff; M Beckmann, *Oberflächeneigentum und Bergbau*, in DVBl 1992, 751ff; W Hoppe, *Das Spannungsverhältnis von Bergwerkseigentum und Oberflächeneigentum im Lichte des Verfassungsrechts*, 1991. cf recently: J Glückert, *10 Jahre Streit um Cappenberg: Bestandsaufnahme des juristischen Ertrags und der offen gebliebenen Fragen (unter besonderer Berücksichtigung des Betriebsplanverfahrens)*, in von Danwitz/Hüffer (eds), Bergbau und Umwelt, 1999.

[119] Especially the participation rights of local bodies: Boldt/Weller, *Bundesberggesetz*, 1984, § 54 margin nos 8 and 11; Th Christner, *Die Beteiligung der Kommunen an der Betriebsplanzulassung nach dem Bundesberggesetz*, in Zeitschrift für Bergrecht (ZfB) vol 133 (1992), 249ff.

[120] For details see Boldt/Weller, *Bundesberggesetz* (Ergänzungsband), 1992, § 52 margin nos 71ff. As to the tension between a preceding area planning and the specific operation planning of the mining law see for example: W Erbguth, *Zulassungsverfahren des Bergrechts und Raumplanung*, in Verwaltungsarchiv (VerwArch) vol 87 (1996), 258ff; G Kühne, *Die Bedeutung der Erfordernisse der Raumordnung und Landesplanung bei bergbaulichen Vorhaben*, in Deutsches Verwaltungsblatt (DVBl) 1984, 709ff.

recently been raised in connection with the difficult relationship between mining and land ownership.[121]

(10) Environmental Impact Assessment (EIA)

With its central principles of the economic and careful use of ground and soil and the avoidance of danger to life, health, and goods of third persons resulting from mining activities, the Federal Mining Act illustrates the importance of environmental aspects. The relationship between the mining (planning) law and other fields of environmental law—for example, nature protection and planning law, water law, and the law on waste disposal and treatment—is, however, one of the most debated issues of the German public law at present, and cannot be dealt with here in detail.[122] As a rule, the general stipulations of other environmental laws are to be respected whenever the Federal Mining Act refers to 'public' or 'general' interests or contains similar blanket clauses. On the other hand, where non-mining/energy environmental provisions contain exhaustive regulation of certain matters (for example competence or procedure), they apply as well as or instead of the mining law. **8.66**

In particular and for the mining sector, EEC directive 85/337 on environmental impact assessment (EIA) of 27 June 1985[123] was implemented separately from the general EIA legislation[124] and took place within the framework of the Federal Mining Act. This was done with regard to the peculiarities of the operation planning procedure in mining law because the dynamic nature of mining had to be taken into consideration. The procedure of the framework operation plan was integrated into the *Planfeststellungsverfahren*, a standardized planning procedure of German public law concerning certain projects with special planning impact.[125] It **8.67**

[121] See section 8 above, further PJ Tettinger, *Gewinnung und Aufbereitung von schwefelwasserstoffhaltigem Erdgas auf einer Ferieninsel?*, 1997, 95ff, with more references.

[122] See in this context for example: JD Rausch, *Umwelt- und Planungsrecht beim Bergbau*, 1990; KM Rasel, *Umweltrechtliche Implikationen im Bundesberggesetz*, thesis Regensburg 1994; on the relationship between mining law and waste disposal and treatment law: Chr Sladek, *Versatzbergbau zwischen Umwelt- und Bergrecht: Ein Erfahrungsbericht aus der behördlichen Praxis*, in von Danwitz/Hüffer (eds), Bergbau und Umwelt, 1999. On the tension between mining law and environmental law, especially nature protection law, see for example: M Wilde, *Verhältnis zwischen Bergrecht und Naturschutzrecht*, in Deutsches Verwaltungsblatt (DVBl) 1998, 1321ff with further references;

[123] OJ L 175/40 of 5 July 1985.

[124] See 'Gesetz über die Umweltverträglichkeitsprüfung' (UVPG) of 12 February 1990 (BGBl I 205) with later amendments.

[125] cf § 52(2a) together with §§ 57a and 57b of the Federal Mining Act. For details see: U Gaentsch, *Die bergrechtliche Planfeststellung*, in Festschrift für H Sendler, 1991, 403ff; G Kühne, *Die Einführung der Umweltverträglichkeitsprüfung im Bergrecht*, in Umwelt- und Planungsrecht (UPR) 1989, 326ff; E Kremer, *Umweltverträglichkeitsprüfung im Bergrecht*, in Neue Zeitschrift für Verwaltungsrecht (NVwZ) 1990, 376ff; H-U von Mässenhausen, *Rahmenbetriebsplan und Umweltverträglichkeitsprüfung—Neueste Entwicklungen und Probleme*, in Zeitschrift für Bergrecht (ZfB) vol 135 (1994), 119ff; PJ Tettinger (ed), *Umweltverträglichkeitsprüfung bei Projekten des Bergbaus und der Energiewirtschaft*, 1989.

begins with an intense discussion ('scoping') of the project, the extent and method of the environmental impact assessment, and all other relevant issues involving the entrepreneur and the public authorities concerned. In the following step a hearing procedure takes place, involving the public and—eventually—any third countries affected. The draft plan must be made accessible to the public, who may raise objections. All objections have to be considered in the context of a special discussion round in order to reach a consensus. If a decision (*Planfeststellungsbeschluß*) is made it must include the expected environmental impact of the project in a summarized form. Most remarkably, all relevant administrative and legal aspects, especially concerning environmental problems, are concentrated in only one authority which is the competent mining authority. The decision precludes all later objections by third parties or by other authorities.

(11) Other Specific Planning Procedures

8.68 In exceptional cases, the required environmental impact assessment can be realized in the course of an anticipated area planning procedure (*Raumordnungsverfahren*),[126] on the Länder level. This is relevant for open-cast brown coal mining, which requires wide areas for open-cast mining operations. There is a special need for regulation in view of the enormous environmental and social impacts of this industry. Apart from special legal questions as to the reclaiming of brown coal sites after completion of the exploitation process—particularly relevant in the brown coal regions of the former GDR[127]—adequate planning instruments are indispensable. Important examples are the rules of the Northrhine-Westphalia planning law with its special instrument, the Brown Coal Planning Act (*Braunkohlenplan*) for the Rhineland brown coal area.[128] Similar rules exist in Brandenburg.[129] According to these rules brown coal committees are set up by the *Bezirksregierung* (the administrative authority of the respective Länder) and charged with the local brown coal plans. These committees are composed of representatives of the local authorities situated in the planning area, chambers of industry and commerce, employers' associations, trade unions, etc. The public must also be involved. The plans require approval by the Länder Minister who has to

[126] cf § 52(2b), 2nd sentence in conjunction with § 54 (2), 3rd sentence of the Federal Mining Act. On the consequences of federal planning reform (Bau- und Raumordnungsgesetz 1998—BauROG) in mining law, see W Hopper/W Spoerr, *Bergrecht und Raumordnung* (1999).

[127] For more details: Hüffer/Tettinger, *Braunkohlenabbau in der ehemaligen DDR und Sanierungsverpflichtungen*, 1994.

[128] See §§ 24ff of the Northrhine-Westphalian regional planning act (*Landesplanungsgesetz)*; for further details: F Schnapp, *Braunkohlenplanung in Nordrhein-Westfalen*, in Festschrift für Fabricius, 1989, 87ff.

[129] See *Gesetz zur Einführung der Regionalplanung und der Braunkohlen- und Sanierungsplanung im Land Brandenburg* of 13 May 1993 (GVBl I 170); *Verordnung über die Bildung des Braunkohlenausschusses des Landes Brandenburg* of 8 April 1992 (GVBl II 139); for Saxony, where the brown coal plan forms a specific part of the regional planning, see § 8 of the *Gesetz zur Raumordnung und zur Landesplanung des Freistaates Sachsen* of 24 June 1992 (GVBl 259).

take into consideration the requirements of long-term energy supply and the protection of the environment. The operation plans of the private mining companies must be drafted accordingly. Brown coal plans are binding on other planning authorities (for example the local governments).[130] Taking into account the severe consequences of relocating entire villages when opening a new open-cast mining site, the question has been raised whether certain important decisions concerning future exploitation activities require—besides the respective planning act of the brown coal planning authority—special justification by a parliamentary/statutory act. Recently, this question was answered in the negative by the Northrhine-Westphalia Constitutional Court (*Verfassungsgerichtshof*) in the case of the planned opening of a new and extensive open-cast mining site called *Garzweiler II.* The court held that a decision of the pluralistically composed brown coal committee offered sufficient protection of the interests involved.[131]

(12) *Implications of the Operation Plan*

Once the operation plan has been approved, the operating company is responsible for the accurate and safe operation of the mine.[132] The operating company may delegate certain powers and duties to other persons so long as they are reliable, skilled, and physically fit. Their tasks and competencies are to be continuously coordinated.[133] **8.69**

If the mining process conflicts with adjacent property and its use, the *Bundesberggesetz* contains special regulations on the cession of land, ie expropriation, and limitations for building measures. The cession of land (*Grundabtretung*) is a form of expropriation in the field of mining law.[134] It requires an application by the mining entrepreneur and must be in the public interest. It is also necessary to demonstrate that the end cannot be achieved in another reasonable, less **8.70**

[130] For more details see for example: W Erbguth, *Verfassungsrechtliche Fragen im Verhältnis Landesplanung und Braunkohlenplanung,* in Deutsches Verwaltungsblatt (DVBl) 1982, 1ff; Kamphausen, *Rechtsprobleme der Braunkohlenpläne,* in Die öffentliche Verwaltung (DÖV) 1984, 146ff. As to the relation between area/regional planning and 'mining property': W Hoppe, *Bergbauberechtigungen als verfassungskräftige Eigentumsposition und ihr Schutz gegenüber Planung,* ibid, 101ff.

[131] *Verfassungsgerichtshof Nordrhein-Westfalen,* decision of 29 April 1997, published in NWVBl 1997, 247ff (esp 251ff). As to a former judgment of the Constitutional Court (*Verfassungsgericht)* of Brandenburg of 1 June 1995, which ruled in the *opposite* sense, see Chr Degenhart, *Rechtsfragen der Braunkohlenplanung für Brandenburg,* 1996, esp 43ff (with the text of the decision at 111ff). Nevertheless, a later decision of the Brandenburg Constitutional Court of 18 June 1998 (VfGBbg 27/97) dismissed a complaint against the relevant mining planning act of 7 July 1997 intended to the village of Horno.

[132] cf § 61(1) of the Federal Mining Act.

[133] See Kirchner/Kremer, *Leitung und Beaufsichtigung eines Bergbaubetriebes,* in Zeitschrift für Bergrecht (ZfB), vol 131 (1990), 189ff.

[134] cf §§ 77ff of the Federal Mining Act. For details, see K Lange, *Grundabtretung und vorzeitige Besitzeinweisung im bergrechtlichen Betriebsplanverfahren,* in Die öffentliche Verwaltung (DÖV) 1988, 805ff.

burdensome way.[135] The fact that the extracting company is bound to the location of the mineral resources is especially relevant in this context. The public interest comprises the supply of the market with mineral products, the protection of employment, the maintenance and improvement of the economic structure, and the exploitation of mineral resources in a reasonable and systematic way. Since it is the extracting entrepreneur who benefits directly from the cession of land, it is one of the few cases of expropriation (by the State) in favour of a private person or legal entity of private law.[136]

8.71 As far as property is used in the context of mining, the Länder governments or subsequent authorities may pass decrees limiting building activities in certain areas. As in the case of the cession of land, building limitations are only permissible if the macro-economic relevance of supplying the market with mineral products or the need for an exhaustive exploitation of the mineral resources requires it in accordance with public interest.

(13) Liability

8.72 The Federal Mining Act contains specific provisions concerning the prevention of damage, liability for damage, the negative effects of mining on roads and railway tracks, and soil analysis to prevent future damage.[137] These provisions have been comprehensively treated in the literature.[138] If a third party suffers a loss there is a legal presumption that nearby mining activity caused the damage. This facilitates a plaintiff realizing his/her claim for damages before the court. Accordingly, the mining company has the burden of proof to rebut the presumption that the mine caused the damage. However, the plaintiff is not entitled to invoke this presumption if *prima facie* the damage in question was not caused by the mine.

(14) Concluding Remarks

8.73 After the EIA Directive of 27 June 1985 was incorporated into the Federal Mining Act there seemed little reason to change German mining law for the time being. Nonetheless, underground waste disposal,[139] especially the final disposal of

[135] As concerns interim legal protection against a *Grundabtretung*, see *Oberverwaltungsgericht* (OVG) of Northrhine-Westphalia, in Nordrhein-Westfälische Verwaltungsblätter (NWVBl) 1987, 78ff.

[136] As to the constitutional requirements concerning expropriation in favour of private companies, see Federal Constitutional Court, in BVerfGE vol 66, 248, 257ff.

[137] cf §§ 110ff of the Federal Mining Act.

[138] See for example: Boldt/Weller, *Bundesberggesetz*, 1984, Vor § 110; U Hüffer, *Präventive Maßnahmen im Bergschadensrecht*, in Festschrift für F Fabricius, 1989, 115ff; recently: Th von Danwitz, *Staatliche Bergaufsicht zwischen privatem Bergschadensrecht, hoheitlicher Gefahrenabwehr und Staatshaftung in den neuen Bundesländern*, 1998.

[139] In addition to the above-mentioned references: Freytag, *Der Einsatz von Rückständen im Bergbau an der Nahtstelle von Berg- und Abfallrecht*, in Natur und Recht (NuR) 1996, 1450ff.

radioactive waste and other uses of former mining sites,[140] and problems concerning treatment and liability in the case of contaminated soils (*Altlasten*) as a result of mining activities,[141] may give rise to supplementary and clarifying regulation (in the framework of nuclear, waste disposal, and other environmentally relevant law).[142]

D. Nuclear Energy

The Geman nuclear energy sector is about to undergo severe changes following the change of government on 27 September 1998. The current 'red–green' Government of Social Democrats and an alliance of former East German civil rights activists and West German environmental activists (*Bündnis 90/Die Grünen*) has underlined its determination to point the way for a withdrawal from nuclear energy production. Though withdrawal scenarios are not a new issue,[143] this is the first time that a Federal Government has promoted them. **8.74**

Soon after the federal elections, an early attempt to perform a quick phase-out failed because of substantial drawbacks: plans to replace the existing nuclear energy act, the 'federal act promoting the peaceful use of nuclear energy', by a new law 'initiating the withdrawal from nuclear energy',[144] were revoked after the new Government became fully aware of the problem that a sudden withdrawal would frustrate the constitutional property rights of both the private nuclear energy **8.75**

[140] See for example M Beckmann, *Berg-, umwelt- und planungsrechtliche Probleme der Wiedernutzbarmachung und Folgenutzung bergbaulicher Anlagen*, in Kühne/Schoch/Beckmann (eds), *Gegenwartsprobleme des Bergrechts*, 1995, 67ff. As to the judicial conflicts concerning the use of a salt mine near the North German Gorleben as a final disposal site for nuclear waste, see for example *Verwaltungsgericht* (VG—administrative tribunal) Lüneburg, in Recht der Energiewirtschaft (RdE) 1994, 186ff. In this context there are conflictive problems in the expropriation of old salt mining rights, see Av Brünneck, *Die Enteignung alter Salzrechte in Goreben*, in Recht der Energiewirtschaft (RdE) 1994, 81ff. Concerning compensation for damage caused by illegal behaviour of the mining authority in the planning process, see judgments of the *Oberlandesgericht Celle* (Superior Civil Court of Lower Saxony), in Recht der Energiewirtschaft (RdE) 1997, 32ff (claim by the Federation against Lower Saxony); RdE 1997, 118ff (claim by the future operator of the nuclear waste disposal site).

[141] Some regulations exist in the (regional and federal) waste disposal laws and in the recently adopted Federal Act on Protection Against Damaging Alteration of the Soil and on the 'Recycling' of Contaminated Soil (*Bundes-Bodenschutzgesetz*) of 17 March 1998 (BGBl I 502).

[142] As to the conflict between mining law, environmental law, and the law of supervision of industrial plants (with special regard to nuclear waste disposal) see for example: G Kühne, *Bergrechtlicher Rahmenbetriebsplan, Anlagengenehmigungsrecht und Umweltverträglichkeitsprüfung*, 1993.

[143] See already K Lange, *Rechtliche Aspekte eines 'Ausstiegs aus der Kernenergie'*, [1986] *Neue Juristische Wochenschrift*, 2459ff; P Bender, *Abschied vom 'Atomstrom'?*, [1988] *Die Öffentliche Verwaltung*, 813ff. Further documentation is provided in a periodical publication by R Lukes (ed), *Berichte über die Deutschen Atomrechts-Symposien*.

[144] cf Frankfurter Allgemeine Zeitung, 19 January 1999, 15.

companies and their shareholders. Due to amortization periods for nuclear power plants of between fifteen and twenty years, substantial claims for compensation would have been the inevitable consequence.

8.76 As another approach to accelerate the withdrawal process, the Minister of the Environment intended to prohibit the recycling (*Wiederaufbereitung*) of nuclear wastes. It was planned to force the nuclear industry to store wastes in the cooling chambers of the nuclear power plants. The underlying thought was to deny a power plant further operation as soon as its cooling capacities are exhausted. This plan failed because the recycling of German nuclear wastes traditionally takes place in Great Britain (Sellafield) and France (Le Havre). For that purpose German industry had concluded long-term agreements with British Nuclear Fuels and Cogema (F). The agreements were flanked by intergovernmental cooperation which made it virtually impossible to terminate them on short notice. On protests of the French and British governments the respective plans were cancelled.[145] Today it is clear that recycling in France and Great Britain will go on and it can be expected that the respective contracts will be fulfilled.

8.77 After these failures the new Government decided that the details of the withdrawal should be left for an agreement with the nuclear energy industry. The withdrawal target talks between the Government and the nuclear energy industry have meanwhile resulted in the so-called 'nuclear energy settlement', a voluntary agreement that could indeed give rise to fundamental changes within the German energy sector, and discussed in section (6) below.

(1) Distribution of Competence

8.78 The peaceful use of nuclear energy is within the concurrent legislative competences of the Bund and the Länder.[146] Bund legislation prevails. Administrative competence is settled separately in Article 87c of the Constitution, in the form of Bund-directed administration of the Länder (*Bundesauftragsverwaltung*):[147] administration takes place at Länder level but is substantially subjected to directives and supervision by the competent federal minister. In addition, the fact of the mere mention of the use of nuclear energy for peaceful purposes in the Constitution is regarded as constitutional approval of this energy source.[148]

145 cf Frankfurter Allgemeine Zeitung of 19 January (p. 15), 22 January (pp. 1f), and 27 January (pp. 1f), and 12 February 1999 (p. 3).

146 Article 74(1) no 11a of the Constitution was introduced by the 10th law changing the constitution in 1959. As to the concept of 'concurring competence', see section 2 above.

147 As to the term *Bundesauftragsverwaltung*, see paras 8.26 above.

148 Federal Constitutional Court, in BVerfGE vol 53, 30ff, 56.

(2) *Regulation of the Nuclear Energy Sector*

Because of the specific risks and dangers of nuclear energy, Article 2(2) of the Constitution—safeguarding the right of life and physical integrity—requires the legislator to impose comprehensive and precise regulation on nuclear energy production.[149] Necessary precautions against the typical risks must be taken (the principle of precaution) and dangers must be averted wherever they occur (the principle of protection).[150] The federal legislator passed the Nuclear Energy Act (*Atomgesetz*) to provide for precaution and protection as stipulated by the Constitution.[151] As a matter of concurrent competence it was based on Article 74(1), No 11a of the Constitution. According to its section 1, the Nuclear Energy Act shall support research, development, and the use of nuclear energy for peaceful purposes. The most important purpose of the Nuclear Energy Act, however, is the protection of life, health, and property against the damaging effects of ionizing radiation and compensation for any damage.[152] The Nuclear Energy Act itself enables the competent federal minister to issue decrees on specific nuclear matters. Accordingly, several decrees have been passed.[153] **8.79**

Another group of laws was passed in consequence of the Chernobyl disaster. In particular, the Federal Act for Nuclear Radiation Prevention (*Strahlenschutzvorsorgegesetz*) of 19 December 1986,[154] and the law establishing the Federal Agency for Radiation Protection (*Bundesamt für Strahlenschutz*) of 8 October 1989.[155] **8.80**

---

[149] ibid, vol 49, 89ff ('Kalkar'); vol 53, 30ff ('Mülheim-Kärlich'); vol 61, 82ff ('Sasbach'). Permissions according to nuclear energy law (*atomrechtliche Genehmigungen*) granted by the former GDR authorities may remain in force interimwise: cf Federal Consitutional Court, in Landes- und Kommunalverwaltung (LKV) 1994, 25, even with a view to Article 2(2) 1st sentence of the Constitution.

[150] For more details, see A Birkhofer, *Risikovorsorge in der Kerntechnik*, in Festschrift für R Lukes, 1989, 23ff.

[151] Federal Act Concerning the Peaceful Use of Nuclear Energy and Protection Against Its Dangers (*Atomgesetz—AtG*) of 23 December 1959, publication of 15 July 1985, BGBl part I, 1565), with later modifications.

[152] Federal Administrative Court, in Deutsches Verwaltungsblatt (DVBl) 1972, 678ff, 690.

[153] The most important are: Decree on the protection against damages caused by Röntgen rays (*Röntgenverordnung*) of 8 January 1987 (BGBl, part I, 114); Decree on the protection against damage caused by ionizing radiation (*Strahlenschutzverordnung*) of 13 October 1976, in the form of the publication of 30 June 1989 (BGBl, part I, 1321); both of the former decrees were last changed by a decree of 18 August 1997 (BGBl, part I, 2113); Decree on the procedures of nuclear energy law (*Atomrechtliche Verfahrensverordnung—AtVfV*) in the form of the publication of 3 February 1995 (BGBl, part I, 180).

[154] Published in BGBl, part I, 2610, last changed by an Act of 24 June 1994 (BGBl, part I, 1416).

[155] Published in BGBl, part I, 1830. As to the competencies of this agency, see ER Seidel, *Das neue Bundesamt für Strahlenschutz*, in Energiewirtschaftliche Tagesfragen 1988, 750ff. The Agency holds the permission according to former GDR law for the final disposal site of Morsleben, see Federal Administrative Court, in BVerwGE vol 90, 255ff; Federal Constitutional Court, judgment published in RdE 1994, 229–30; for a comprehensive overview of all these questions, see R Kramer and G Zerlett, *StrahlenschutzVO—Strahlenschutzvorsorgegesetz*, commentary, 3rd edn, 1990.

(3) Permissions for and Supervision of Nuclear Activities

8.81 In Germany, nuclear energy production is not a privilege of the State (there is no *service public*). The federal legislator decided to leave the sector for private performance. However, private entrepreneurs need permission to construct and to operate nuclear facilities.[156] Accordingly, one can speak of construction and operation permits. For reasons of administrative efficiency, permissions are granted gradually in the form of an uninterrupted series of sub-permits. Construction sub-permits (*Teilerrichtungsgenehmigung*) have two functions. First, they relate to specific parts of the nuclear installation which are under construction. Secondly, they contain overall approval of the whole installation as it is for the time being. So with the grant of the last construction sub-permit the entire installation is approved. The private entrepreneur then needs an operation permission which is also graduated through sub-permissions (*Teilbetriebsgenehmigungen*). These sub-permits may no longer relate to the construction of the installation and its possible deficiencies, but only to aspects of how to run the nuclear facility.[157] The Federal Administrative Court stated, metaphorically that, if the row of sub-permissions were a staircase, the competent authority could not climb back down a step already taken.[158]

8.82 All permissions must be applied for in advance.[159] The decision falls within the modified discretion of the competent Länder minister. The minister must involve any authority of the Bund, Länder or municipal level which is affected by the decision. Any disputes are settled by the competent federal minister, who will issue a directive binding on the Länder minister, whom must decide accordingly.[160]

8.83 The permission is subject to a number of fixed prerequisites.[161] Extending to both personnel and nuclear installations, the prerequisites cover the principle of precaution against damage from radiation and the principle of protection against accidents, assaults, and other third-party interference. In addition it must be scrutinized whether prevailing public interests are safeguarded, among them environmental protection. The relevant standard for all prerequisites is the 'state of science and art' (*Stand von Wissenschaft und Technik*)[162] which is the strictest of all the technical standards of German statute law. Accordingly, nuclear installations must not only use the best available technology, but also take into consider-

[156] cf § 7 of the Nuclear Act.

[157] Federal Administrative Court, in BVerwGE vol 88, 286ff, 290–1, and in: Deutsches Verwaltungsblatt (DVBl) 1993, 1151.

[158] Federal Administrative Court, in Recht der Energiewirtschaft (RdE) 1997, 62ff, 65. See further judgments in BVerwGE vol 92, 185ff; vol 88, 286ff; vol 61, 256, 265.

[159] M Ronellenfitsch, *Das atomrechtliche Genehmigungsverfahren*, 1983; Chr Degenhart, *Kernenergierecht*, 1981.

[160] cf § 7(4) of the Nuclear Act.

[161] ibid, § 7(2).

[162] ibid, § 7(2) no 3.

ation the most recent findings of nuclear science. It is not sufficient to assess only the majority opinion among nuclear scientists; rather, other opinions and the most recent developments must also be taken into consideration. If—and only if—this is done is the individual decision regarded as properly taken. At the end of the assessment procedure, an individual decision may certainly follow the majority opinion as long as other opinions have been noted and discussed appropriately. Since science and technology are in a state of continuous development it is important which version of the respective standard shall apply: it is the standard extant when the permission is granted. Subsequent developments cannot be considered further.[163] This doctrine is especially relevant if a permit is subjected to judicial review. In such case the court may not reverse the decision of the competent authority based on subsequent developments of science and technology but must review the contested decision in the light of standards extant when the decision was taken. These prerequisites are concretized by subsequent regulation, in particular, the federal decree on radiation protection (*Strahlenschutzverordnung*) which contains a number of threshold values.[164] These threshold values must represent the 'state of science and art'.

Owing to recent decisions of the Federal Administrative Court, it is now possible to explain generally how the 'state of science and art' may be implemented in the form of threshold values. As regards precaution against radiation damage it is important to specify 'harmless' radiation doses, the level of radiation below the threshold of causing cancer. However, the federal ministry in charge of the decree on radiation protection evaluated various scientific opinions and found that for the time being it is impossible to specify a threshold value below which radiation could be regarded as harmless. It therefore concluded that there is no such threshold and that the danger of cancer is related to the respective dose in a linear radiation. Consequently, the ministry took into consideration the substantial natural radiation of the terrestial environment and held that an increase of this amount by 0.3 mSv in the context of the operation of a nuclear power station would be acceptable.[165] Accordingly, 0.3 mSv was incorporated into section 45 of the decree on radiation protection as a threshold value. The Federal Administrative Court held that this was an appropriate way to approximate the 'state of science and art' through threshold values. It added, however, that because of the dynamic nature of science and technology, the Federal Government is responsible for reviewing and upgrading these threshold values in accordance with the most recent developments. **8.84**

[163] Federal Administrative Court, in Recht der Energiewirtschaft (RdE) 1998, 234ff.

[164] cf §§ 44ff of the decree on protection against damage caused by ionizing radiation (*Strahlenschutzverordnung*).

[165] Federal Administrative Court, in Recht der Energiewirtschaft (RdE) 1998, 234ff, 235.

8.85 Against the background fact that no nuclear power station has been built, approved, or even planned during the last few years, the practical relevance of these complicated legal considerations may be questioned, but the relevance is considerable. First of all, the concept of 'nuclear facilities' is broader than nuclear power stations alone. There are diverse facilities for the transport, recycling, and final disposal of nuclear wastes which are also subject to prior permission.

8.86 Another 'target' for permission requirements is the daily operation of nuclear power stations and is related to the routine upgrading of existing nuclear technology in accordance with the progress of technology.[166] The life of a nuclear power station can easily exceed forty years and it is axiomatic that the 'state of nuclear science and art' of 1960 falls short of the standard of today. Through the years, however, nuclear fuels on the market have become stronger and have required existing power plants to be adapted accordingly. On one hand, such adaptation introduces modern technology which marks clear and welcome improvement. On the other hand, it can constitute a 'significant change' (*wesentliche Änderung*) of the existing facility which might require a new 'upgrading' permission (*Änderungsgenehmigung*).[167] The routinely upgraded power station may then greatly exceed the originally applicable 'state of science and art' of, say, 1965, but fall short of that of 1999. The consequence can be paradoxical: facing the danger of not being granted the new permission, the private entrepreneur could be tempted not to upgrade his power plant and to go on with outdated technology.[168] To deny routine upgrades the necessary permission was temporarily contemplated as a means of 'cold' withdrawal from nuclear energy, especially in view of the fact that it is virtually impossible to upgrade an existing nuclear power plant to the present 'state of science and art'. However, such an opinion is ill-founded. As stressed before, the current Nuclear Energy Act intends to 'support the development and the peaceful use of nuclear energy'. As long as it is in force, no permission requirement should be transformed into a prohibition.

8.87 The use of nuclear power as an energy source has brought into being the threat of terrible disasters such as that of the Chernobyl. It has to be underlined, however, that due to Western safety standards, such events are extremely unlikely. It is nevertheless an inner conflict of nuclear regulation that the operator of a nuclear facility cannot be required to eliminate every remote theoretical risk of damage.[169] Indeed, from a certain degree of remoteness the risk becomes 'residual': it simply remains in place. The acceptance of a 'residual risk' (*Restrisko)* underlies every per-

[166] ibid, 234ff, and in RdE 1997, 62ff. See especially Th von Danwitz (ed), *Aktuelle Entwicklungen im Kernenergierecht*, 1997, dealing exclusively with this issue.

[167] cf § 7(1) of the Nuclear Act.

[168] See also H Sendler, *Das Krümmel-Urteil des BVerwG—Ein Sturm im Wasserglas?*, in Th von Danwitz (ed), n 166 above, 13ff, 24.

[169] Federal Constitutional Court, in BVerfGE vol 49, 89ff, 141ff; vol 61, 265ff, 262, 269.

mission of nuclear law. The scientific idea behind the residual risk is the 'maximum credible accident' (*Größter anzunehmender Unfall*, or *GAU*).[170] Generally speaking, a *GAU* is a theoretical assessment of what would happen if everything went wrong. A nuclear power plant must be designed in a way which makes it possible to avoid or to control such a theoretical disaster. In particular, it must be possible to switch off the reactor at any time and to keep it switched off.[171] Therefore permitting nuclear activity becomes essentially an engineering judgment. Any risk beyond this margin of credibility is residual and falls outside the *principle of precaution* stipulated by nuclear energy law.

Remarkably, the applicant for a nuclear permission is not required to make any provision for the treatment of nuclear waste. Intermediate and final storage of nuclear waste is assigned to the State.[172] In particular, the Länder are under an obligation to install intermediate storage sites which have to take over nuclear waste from the private facilities whilst the Bund is in charge of the final storage sites. Bund and Länder may delegate performance wholly or in part to third parties under certain conditions. Building and operating a final disposal site follows a special planning procedure laid down by nuclear law.[173] If radioactive waste is to be stored in the underground, for example in former salt mines, an additional planning procedure under mineral law applies.[174] **8.88**

Nuclear energy law draws a sharp distinction between permission and supervision activities. Basically, nuclear operations are supervised in accordance with the operation-type permissions granted. As a rule, nuclear supervision may not raise issues concerning the construction of nuclear facilities. It relates only to the operation guidelines applied by the staff of the nuclear power plant and to their actual application.[175] There is, however, a distinct instrument of the law of supervising nuclear operations which can directly affect the construction aspects of a nuclear facility: the 'withdrawal procedure'. In exceptional cases, supervision of the operation of a nuclear facility may reveal previously undetected deficiencies **8.89**

[170] cf § 28(3) of the federal decree on radiation protection (*Strahlenschutzverordnung*). For more details, see Federal Administrative Court, in Recht der Energiewirtschaft (RdE) 1997, 192, 195ff.

[171] cf § 7(2a) of the Nuclear Act. For permissions before 31 December 1993, see *Sicherheitskriterien für Kernkraftwerke* (safety requirements for nuclear power plants) of 21 October 1977, published by the federal minister for the interior, Federal Bulletin (*Bundesanzeiger—BAnz*) No 206 of 3 November 1977, 1ff; *Störfall-Leitlinien* (guidelines for unforeseen nuclear incidents) of 18 October 1983, published in *Beilage* 59/83 of the Federal Bulletin (BAnz) No 245 of 31 December 1983.

[172] cf § 9a of the Nuclear Act.

[173] ibid, § 9b.

[174] cf Superior Administrative Court (*Oberverwaltungsgericht*) of Lower Saxony, in Zeitschrift für Bergrecht (ZfB), vol 131 (1990), 19ff, 24, 29; EM Huntemann, *Recht der unterirdischen Endlagerung radioaktiver Abfälle*, 1989, 119ff; HW Rengeling, *Rechtsfragen zu Bundesendlagern für radioaktive Abfälle*, 1990, 19ff; U Hüffer and PJ Tettinger, *Erkundung des Salzstockes Gorleben*, 1991.

[175] Federal Administrative Court, in Recht der Energiewirtschaft (RdE) 1997, 192ff, 193.

and dangers which make it necessary to interrupt further operation. Here the competent authority can withdraw a (sub-) permission with the effect that the nuclear power station must be switched off until the deficiency is removed. The authority may also impose new conditions for the further operation of the facility.[176] In the event of extreme danger it can even shut down the facility entirely.[177] Besides the fact that the withdrawal procedure may take place at any time, regardless of any permission, the main difference from the individual permission procedures is that any subsequent interference with approved parts of a nuclear facility can result in substantial compensation claims against the State. This is especially so if the permission was withdrawn because it had been wrongly granted—and there is a tight burden of proof on the State.[178] Accordingly, the State takes a huge financial risk when deciding to withdraw a permission.

(4) Judicial Review and Access to Justice

8.90 The complicated procedures of permission and supervision have resulted in numerous disputes involving the private operators of a nuclear power plant or individuals in the vicinity. The crucial question therefore is: who can claim judicial review in respect of what?

8.91 Plainly, the private entrepreneur may contest a negative decision of the competent nuclear authority which is directly addressed to it. But third parties can also refer to the courts insofar as they are directly affected by a decision of the competent authority. This is especially so if the third party is for whatever reason deprived of the right to participate in a permission procedure, for example to be heard by the authority.[179] Going further and more generally, every procedural mistake which affects a material right of a third party opens access to the courts.[180] The respective (sub-) permissions can be challenged and declared null and void if the law is found to have been violated. In this respect, it makes no difference whether a nuclear facility was approved for the first time or in the context of a 'significant change' permission.

8.92 Besides challenging the grant of a nuclear permission a third party can also go to court to challenge the failure of the competent authority to enter the abovementioned 'withdrawal procedure'.[181] There are two ways to do so, which both

[176] cf § 17 of the Nuclear Act.

[177] ibid, § 19.

[178] ibid,§ 18. For more details, see F Ossenbühl, *Bestandsschutz und Nachrüstung von Kernkraftwerken*, 1994; S Hartung, *Die Atomaufsicht*, 1992.

[179] Federal Administrative Court, in BVerwGE vol 69, 256ff, 270; and in Deutsches Verwaltungsblatt (DVBl) 1993, 1149ff, 1150.

[180] Federal Administrative Court, in BVerwGE vol 75, 285ff, 291; and in Neue Zeitschrift für Verwaltungsrecht (NVwZ) 1993, 177–8.

[181] F Ossenbühl, *Das Krümmel-urteil des BVerwG—ein Statement aus rechtswissenschaftlicher Sicht*, in Th von Danwitz (ed), *Aktuelle Entwicklungen im Kernenergierecht*, 1997, 43ff, 44.

relate to the above-mentioned threshold values of the federal decree on radiation protection. These threshold values have a 'third-party protection' effect (*drittschützende Wirkung*) which means that a third party can go to court if he/she suffers a loss in connection with the violation of these values. First, access to justice will be granted if he/she is able to show that the threshold values were not complied with *and* that he/she is directly and adversely affected by this non-compliance.[182] Alternatively, he/she can seek to show that the threshold values no longer offer sufficient protection, being outdated or set too high.[183]

(5) *Liability and Compensation*

Liability issues can arise from many different decision making processes. If, for example, the competent authority mistakenly granted the wrong construction permit, which had to be withdrawn, and the nuclear power station—worth billions of euros—decommissioned, the State will be liable for damages.[184] The underlying thought is that the private entrepreneur must be able to rely on a permit in order to safeguard investment. On the other hand, the operator of a nuclear facility can be liable for damages caused by the facility. The Paris Convention of 29 July 1960 is relevant and embodied into the Nuclear Energy Act.[185] The amount of compensation is also dealt with in the Nuclear Energy Act.[186] **8.93**

(6) *The 'Nuclear Energy Settlement' of 14 June 2000*

On 14 June 2000, the Federal Government and the German energy supply industry concluded an agreement on a gradual and medium-term withdrawal from nuclear energy ('nuclear energy settlement')[187]—a truly unparalleled event in German postwar history. The preamble of the settlement gives a good impression of the political and economic background. An excerpt from the German text translates as follows: **8.94**

> The dispute regarding the social acceptability of nuclear energy has caused emotional discussions and severe conflicts in our country over the past decades. Notwithstanding the fact that positions are still divided with regard to the use of nuclear energy, the energy supply companies respect the decision of the federal government to bring it to an orderly end.
>
> Against this background, the federal government and the energy suppliers agree, on the one hand, to put a time limit on the further use of existing nuclear power

[182] cf Federal Administrative Court, in BVerwGE vol 61, 256ff, 263ff; vol 72, 300ff, 319ff.

[183] Federal Administrative Court, in Recht der Energiewirtschaft (RdE) 1997, 62ff, 63.

[184] cf §§ 17f of the Nuclear Act.

[185] ibid, § 25. The relevant text of the Paris Convention is published in BGBl 1976, part II, 308. See further Chapter.

[186] cf §§ 28ff of the Nuclear Act.

[187] *Vereinbarung zwischen der Bundesregierung und den Energieversorgungsunternehmen vom 14. Juni 2000*, also referred to as *Atomkompromiss*. For the time being, the text of the document is available on the 'world-wide-web', particularly on the respective 'homepages' of the Federal Government and those of the parliamentary faction of *Bündnis 90/Die Grünen*.

plants. In the meantime, on the other hand, the operation and abandonment of nuclear power plants shall go on uninterruptedly, maintaining a high level of protection and in compliance with the requirements of nuclear energy law.

Both sides shall make their contributions to the lasting implementation of this agreement. The federal government will, on the basis of this framework, draft an amendment to the nuclear energy act. Both the federal government and energy suppliers take for granted that this agreement will not result in claims for damages between the parties [. . .]

8.95 The historical developments referred to in §1 of the preamble took place in three phases, 1959–85, 1986–98, and 1998–today. During the first phase, all federal governments were in favour of nuclear energy. As stated above, §1(1) of the Nuclear Energy Act of 23 December 1959 expressly encouraged the use of nuclear energy and research and development activities in that field. It even announced public support. The original consensus was eroded during phase two in the early 1980s, following counter-movements rooted in environment and peace activist groups and the emergence of the Green Party, now *Bündnis 90/Die Grünen.* In contrast, the social democratic *SPD* remained divided on the issue for quite a while. Only after the Chernobyl disaster in 1986 had exacerbated the general fear of nuclear accidents did the issue find a stable political basis in the opposition in the federal Parliament and in the majority of the Länder governments. During the following years, a grotesque wrestling commenced between the Bund (the federal state) and several of the Länder, involving the planning, operation, and upgrade of nuclear power plants and nuclear deposit sites[188] and, more recently, transport of nuclear wastes to La Hague and Sellafield. All this resulted in numerous legal proceedings up to the Federal Administrative Court.[189] The respective decisions clearly established what was clear as a matter of public law: that the Länder would have no say in matters of nuclear energy.[190] At the end of phase two, the conflict was not settled, but the former federal Government had fortified its position by means of the constitutional division of competences between the Bund and the Länder.

8.96 Phase three was an ironic reversal of circumstances. After sixteen years, the Federal Government changed. It is beyond reasonable doubt that the new Government would have preferred just to abolish the 1959 Nuclear Energy Act and replace it with phase-out legislation. There was the necessary parliamentary majority for it. However, this way was undermined by numerous obstacles making it anything

[188] cf, for example, T von Danwitz (ed), *Aktuelle Entwicklungen im Kernergierecht,* Stuttgart etc. 1997.

[189] So, for example, the decision of 30 October 1987 (*Mülheim-Kärlich*), published in [1988] *NVwZ,* 538; the judgment of 7 June 1991 (*Obrigheim*), *BVerwGE,* vol 88, 286ff; the decision of 23 April 1996 (*Grundremmingen*), [1996] *NVwZ,* 1010, the judgment of 21 August 1996 (*Krümmel*), [1997] *NVwZ* 1997, 52.

[190] cf PJ Tettinger, *Recht der Energiewirtschaft,* in R Schmidt (ed), *Enzyklopädie der Rechts- und Staatswissenschaft: Öffentliches Wirtschaftsrecht, Teil 1,* Berlin, Heidelberg 1995, 691ff (732ff).

but advisable to take unilateral legislative steps. Existing nuclear facilities, built under the umbrella of the 1959 Nuclear Energy Act and equipped with substantial legal privileges, are to be regarded as 'property' under Article 14 of the German Constitution. Shutting them down by law could be regarded as an expropriation calling for mandatory compensation, probably amounting to billions of EUROS. It was therefore an issue of primary importance to co-ordinate the conditions of phase-out with those parties entitled to constitutional complaint, namely the energy suppliers. This is why the preamble states at the end of §3 that '[b]oth the federal Government and energy suppliers take for granted that this agreement will not result in claims for damages between the parties'.

The eventual 'nuclear energy settlement' of 14 June 2000 is a so-called 'voluntary agreement'. Its content could be roughly described as follows: with regard to each individual power station, it settles in precise terms the conditions for phasing out nuclear energy in Germany. As a rule, each nuclear power station must be switched off after having completed a life cycle of thirty-two years of commercial electricity production. However, the 'nuclear energy settlement' enables energy suppliers to switch off old power stations earlier and new ones later than that deadline. Accordingly, a power station has to be switched off after having produced a specific amount of electricity, corresponding to the estimate of electricity for the remaining years after 1 January 2000. This estimate is calculated on the basis of average annual production for individual power stations between 1990 and 1999, raised by a 'development' factor of 5.5 per cent which is due to expected technical progress or potential legal changes (*Reststrommenge*). Energy suppliers are entitled to transfer portions of a *Reststrommenge* from older power stations to more recent ones so that, in the end, some installations will be operated longer, and others less than thirty-two years. In addition to these provisions, the parties agreed to withdraw from ongoing legal proceedings related to nuclear energy. With regard to stranded investments of the past, new financial claims will not be raised. The federal Government promised, moreover, to refrain from any future impairment of or discrimination against nuclear energy, including new taxes. **8.97**

Most significantly, it is agreed that the major issues agreed upon in the 'nuclear energy settlement' shall subsequently be given the form of a federal law. In particular, the Federal Government will ensure that: **8.98**

—the original purpose of the Nuclear Energy Act, to encourage and support this kind of energy, is replaced by the objective of an orderly phase-out and a prohibition on permitting new nuclear power stations.
—the *Reststrommenge* will be established in a binding form for each nuclear power station in a new appendix to the Nuclear Energy Act.
—certain additional safety requirements will be settled in §19 of that Act.

—third party insurance (§§13ff of the Nuclear Energy Act) is raised from currently DM 500 million to DM 5 billion (EURO 2.56 billion).
—intermediate storage of nuclear wastes must take place close to the respective power stations, until the question of final storage is settled.

8.99 This ensures that the duties of energy suppliers will be of a statutory nature and has, strictly speaking, nothing to do with the voluntary 'nuclear energy settlement'.

8.100 What then is the legal relevance of the nuclear energy settlement?

—As a full-fledged voluntary agreement, the 'nuclear energy settlement' is a complete anomaly under German law,[191] which owes its existence to a unique set of circumstances, in particular a specific political deadlock unlikely to be repeated. Without doubt the new Government would have regulated straight away in the absence of such constraints upon it. In addition, the Federal Government would profit from a clearly established monopoly competence as regards the public administration of nuclear energy. Such a competence is rarely found and serves as an ideal basis for negotiations with business and industry.
—The settlement does not have legally binding force requiring neither the Federal Government to take the aforementioned procedural and legislative steps, nor requiring private energy suppliers to withdraw from current legal proceedings. In particular, it does not prevent the energy suppliers from filing a constitutional complaint against any future amendment of the Nuclear Anergy Act. It is a different question, however, whether such a complaint would be successful, now that the 'nuclear energy settlement' has been concluded. The Federal Constitutional Court would undoubtedly be influenced by the fact and terms of that agreement when dealing with the question whether the fundamental property right of energy suppliers had been violated. A different question is whether energy suppliers would be interested in challenging the 'nuclear energy settlement', since it could bring the long-desired political stability necessary for future investments.

E. The Network-Bound Electricity and Gas Supply

8.101 Following intense political debate in recent years, the law of network-bound energy supply was totally reformed in Spring 1998.[192] One reason for the reform of

[191] As to the legal relevance of voluntary agreements in Germany and in Europe, see forthcoming HM Koopmann, *Voluntary Action of Business and Industry*, London 2001, with an evaluation of the 'nuclear energy settlement' in a different context.

[192] cf *Gesetz zur Neuregelung des Energiewirtschaftsrechts* (Energy Law Reform Act) of 28 November 1997, in force since 29 April 1998, published in BGBl 1998, part I, 730.

German energy law was EC Directive 96/62 concerning common rules for the internal electricity market.[193] Injecting competition into existing industrial patterns and scaling down regulatory elements have been the key policy objectives.[194] The main problems in the controversial political debate were the conflict of policy objectives between competition and environmental protection as well as the role that municipalities and their undertakings should play in the future supply system—a problem that left its traces in the final version of the new Energy Act.

The reform basically consists of three parts:[195] a new Energy Act replaced the old law of 1935; competition privileges were suspended entirely; and related laws were modified, especially the Federal Act Concerning the Use of Renewable Energy in Electricity Supply Networks (*Stromeinspeisungsgesetz*) of 7 December 1990 (see paragraph 8.148 below).[196] The new law also applied to natural gas supply regardless of the fact that the EC directive on common rules for the internal market for gas[197] had not yet entered into force. It is intended to adapt the new Federal Energy Act to the requirements of that Directive. In the meantime general competition law applies to natural gas supply unless the new Energy Act rules otherwise. **8.102**

Even if the reform is not (yet) achieving unrestricted competition within the energy sector, it partly exceeds the requirements set out by the EC Directive on an internal market for electricity. A remarkable achievement was to avoid any tendency to over-regulate. Compared with the previous law of 1935, the new Energy Act realizes to a large extent the idea of a 'lean' regulation. Thereby it clearly contributes to the recent vision of a 'lean state, lean administration', often invoked but seldom taken seriously.[198] **8.103**

(1) Overview of the Former Legal Framework

In order to understand the new energy law an overview of the former legal framework is necessary. The traditional German legal system of network-bound energy supply was built upon a decentralized and pluralistic industry. National public monopolies such as existed in France, Italy, and Spain never existed in Germany. **8.104**

[193] OJ No L 27 (30 Jan 1997).

[194] As to details of the political reasoning behind the draft act see *Gesetzentwurf der Bundesregierung 'Entwurf eines Gesetzes zur Neuregelung des Energiewirtschaftsrechts'*, in *Deutscher Bundestag* (13th legislative session), Bundestagsdrucksache (BT-Drs) 13/7274 of 23 March 1997.

[195] For an overview of the reform, see U Büdenbender, *Energierecht nach der Energierechtsreform*, in Juristenzeitung (JZ) 1999, 62ff; M Cronenberg, *Das neue Energiewirtschaftsrecht*, in Recht der Energiewirtschaft (RdE) 1998, 85ff; G Kühne, n 199 below; G Kühne/B Scholtka, *Das neue Energiewirtschftsrecht*, in Neue Juristische Wochenschrift 1998, 1902ff; R Lukes, *Die Neuregelung de Energie-wirtschaftsrechts*, in Betriebs-Berater (BB) 1998, 1217ff.

[196] BGBl 1990 I, 2633.

[197] Of 11 May 1998, OJ L 204/1.

[198] R Lukes, *Die Neuergelung des Energiewirtschaftsrechts* in Betriebs-Berater (BB) 1998, 1217, 1222.

The system was characterized by a three-level supply system with interconnected regional and local utilities (see paragraphs 8.11ff above).[199] It was based on the Energy Act of 1935[200] and supplementary decrees as well as on specific rules within German antitrust or competition legislation.[201]

The Energy Act of 1935

8.105 According to the Preamble of the Energy Act, energy supply had to be as safe and as cheap as possible. The central objectives were achieved by a system of public supervision, controlling access to the market and, as a disputed singularity of German administrative law, maintaining an intensive investment control. Supplying utilities were obliged by law to connect to their grid and supply everyone according to uniform conditions and prices (*Anschluß- und Versorgungszwang*). This general right to supply applied to every person and legal entity within the respective supply area except those who ran their own supply devices and those consumers (generally industrial) who entered into individual supply contracts (*Sondervertragskunden*).[202] Ordinary energy supply was under the protection of a detailed system of price control based on two decrees of the federal Ministry of the Economy.[203] The conditions of supply had to comply with two ministerial decrees on general conditions of electricity and gas supply (*Allgemeine Versorgungsbedingungen*).[204]

---

[199] See also G Kühne, *The Liberalisation Process in Germany: The German Energy Act*, in ED Cross, *Electric utility regulation in the European Union—a country by country guide*, 1996, 130ff.

[200] *Gesetz zur Förderung der Energiewirtschaft—Energiewirtschaftsgesetz (EnWG)* of 13 December 1935, pubished in *Reichsgesetzblatt* (RGBl), part I, 1451. After the breakdown of the German Reich in 1945 it remained effective in accordance with Arts 123(1) and 125(1) in conjunction with Art 74(1) no 11 of the Constitution, 'insofar as is not contradictory to the Constitution'; it therefore had to be interpreted in accordance with the Constitution as a whole (*verfassungskonforme Auslegung*), and incompatible passages (for example: rules on the competent authorities of the former Reich) were invalid.

[201] §§ 103 and 103a of the *Gesetz gegen Wettbewerbsbeschränkungen* (GWB), published in BGBl 1957, part I, 1081, in its version of 20 February 1990 (BGBl I 235).

[202] As to the latter group, however, a similar right could derive from the German Civil Code (see §§ 826 and 249 of the *Bürgerliches Gesetzbuch*, BGB) and from the general rules of competition law, which concern the abuse of dominant market positions.

[203] The federal decree on the standard rates for electricity (*Bundestarifordnung Elektrizität, BTO Elt*) of 18 Dec 1989 (in BGBl, part I, 2255) concerns both regulation of the price structure and supervision of price alterations by the individual Länder Minister for the Economy. For a survey, see H Knöchel, *Die Preisaufsicht nach dem Energiewirtschaftsgesetz*, 1989. The parallel decree on the gas supply is the federal decree on the standard rates for gas (*Bundestarifordnung Gas, BTO Gas*) of 10 Feb 1959 (in BGBl part I, 46), in the form of the decree of 21 June 1979 (BGBl part I, 676). Unlike the situation in the electricity sector, energy supply entities do not need permission to raise their gas prices. This peculiarity derives from the more substantial competition of the gas supply sector leading to competitive prices.

[204] See the federal decree on general electricity supply conditions (*Verordnung über allgemeine Bedingungen für die Elektrizitätsversorgung von Tarifkunden, AVB EltV*) of 21 June 1979, published in BGBl part I, 684; and the federal decree on the general gas supply conditions (*Verordnung über allgemeine Bedingungen für die Gasversorgung von Tarifkunden, AVB GasV*) of 26 June 1979,

Competition regulation in a system of monopolies

The Energy Act of 1935 did not deal with the organization of the energy sector and left untouched the traditional structures of the energy industry. A system of complicated energy contracts excluded competition from the energy sector so that cartel concerns became the key issue of German energy law.[205] The system of 'closed supply areas' (*Gebietsmonopole* or *geschlossene Versorgungsgebiete*) functioned in a combination of two supplementary contract types. Generally speaking, an energy supplying entity entered into a 'contract of concession' (*Konzessionsvertrag*) with the municipality whose area it supplied in order to obtain the exclusive right to use municipal rights of way for the grid. The other contract type was the 'contract of demarcation' (*Demarkationsvertrag*) with other energy supplying entities, which reserved certain areas for exclusive supply by one company. Supply entities were thus excluded from direct competition by these two different contract types. **8.106**

From its entry into force on 27 July 1957, the Federal Competition Act exempted this well established system of contracts from the general guidelines of free competition.[206] These privileges, which were meant to be temporary[207] and were strongly criticized by some legal writers,[208] have mainly been justified by the technical and economic peculiarities of network-bound energy supply (lack of storage facilities; installations must be large enough to supply peak demand; high investment costs which make parallel networks unreasonable). In the same manner, the preamble of the Energy Act of 1935 spoke of the 'damaging effects of competition on the national economy'. **8.107**

published in BGBl, part I, 676. As to the interpretation of these provisions, see Hermann, Recknagel, and Schmidt-Salzer, *Kommentar zu den allgemeinen Versorgungsbedingungen für Elektrizität, Gas, Fernwärme und Wasser*, 2 vols, 1981 and 1984; KD Morell, *Verordnung über Allgemeine Bedingungen für die Gasversorgung von Tarifkunden (AVB GasV)*, loose-leaf commentary since 1989.

205 See for example: JF Baur, *Die Gebietsschutzverträge der Energieversorgungswirtschaft*, 1981; W Möschel, *Recht der Wettbewerbsbeschränkungen*, 1983, margin number 1014; E Niederleithinger, *Strommarktproblematik nach deutschem und europäischem Wettbewerbsrecht*, in R Lukes (ed), Ein EWG-Binnenmark für Elektrizität—Realität oder Utopie, 1988, 63ff; V Emmerich, *Kartellrecht*, 6th edn, 1991, 462ff; *Der kartellrechtliche Ausnahmebereich für die Versorgungswirtschaft in der Rechtsprechung*, in JF Baur (ed), Deregulierung und Regulierung durch nationales und europäisches Kartellrecht, 1994, 11ff.

206 § 103 (1) nos 1 and 2 of the Antitrust Act (*GWB*) in its former version. For a survey, see E Niederleithinger, *Die Stellung der Versorgungswirtschaft im Gesetz gegen Wettbewerbsbeschränkungen*, 1968; U Büdenbender, *Energierecht*, 1982, margin number 537, each with further references. (Key words: no agreements against competition, § 1 GWB; no horizontal agreements, § 15 GWB; no vertical agreements, § 18 GWB).

207 Cf H-U Evers, *Das Recht der Energieversorgung*, 2nd edn, 1983, 38, and S Klaue, in Immenga/Mestmäcker (eds), *Gesetz gegen Wettbewerbsbeschränkungen* (commentary), 2nd edn 1992, Vor § 103 margin no 1 at the end.

208 See for example V Emmerich, *Die deutsche Versorgungswirtschaft in der Wettbewerbsordnung der Europäischen Gemeinschaft*, in *Festschrift für v Gamm*, 1990, 581ff; R Lukes, *Die Reformdiskussion zur wettbewerbsrechtlichen Regelung der leitungsgebundenen Versorgungswirtschaft*, in Baur/Lukes (eds), Geschlossene Versorgungsgebiete, Versorgungssicherheit oder Wettbewerb, 1979, 65ff.

8.108 As a counterbalance to this exemption from free competition, later competition law reforms introduced a set of specific instruments to prevent the abuse of these electricity supply privileges.[209] In particular, under certain circumstances it was regarded as an abuse of a dominant position to refuse third-party access to a network under reasonable contractual conditions.[210] In addition, the privileges were limited to a maximum duration of twenty years,[211] on the expiration of which the contracts had to be renegotiated in order to avoid antitrust procedures. Thus closed supply areas were subjected to comprehensive revision at regular intervals, but not abolished outright.

8.109 Nevertheless these changes proved incapable of introducing substantial competition into network-bound energy supply. The competition law privileges in conjunction with the overall requirement of permissions for newcomers and the above-mentioned investment control for new supply devices resulted in practice in insurmountable barriers against penetration of the German market.[212] Because of the closed supply areas there was virtually no demand for additional (new) supplies; therefore the competent authorities saw no need to grant permissions to new suppliers. Earlier attempts by the Federal Cartel Authority (*Bundeskartellamt*) to break the closed supply areas using the Competition Act, in particular controls over the refusal of third-party access as an abuse of a dominant position, failed. This was because the courts gave priority to the requirements of a 'safe and cheap' energy supply, which could be jeopardized through disturbing the existing market conditions by transit or TPA duties.[213] In some test cases the Federal Cartel Authority also referred to the direct application of European competition rules (Arts 81 and 82 EC) and—in this context—to the case-law of the ECJ.[214] The energy law reform, however, was faster than the Court.

(2) Substantial Changes to Competition Law

8.110 Against this background, abolishing the competition law privileges must be regarded as a central pillar of the reform. A new provision in the federal competition law clearly states that the former exemptions concerning the typical monopoly

[209] Fourth reform of the Competition Act of 26 April 1980 (BGBl I 458); fifth reform of 22 December 1989, in force since 1 January 1990 (BGBl I 235). As to the political reasons motivating these reforms and more details see for example JF Baur, *Die Gebietsschutzverträge der Energieversorgungswirtschaft*, 1981, esp 44f; S Klaue, n 207 above, *Vor* § 103 margin no 2ff with many references.

[210] cf § 103(5), 2nd sentence, no 4 of the Competition Act (GWB).

[211] ibid, § 103a(1) and (4) of the Competition Act.

[212] Exception: small independent energy producers without their own networks.

[213] cf Federal Court of Justice, in BGHZ 128, 17, 33ff—*'Wingas'*; Kammergericht (Court of Appeal) Berlin, decision of 9 June 1996, in Wirtschaft und Wettbewerb (Entscheidungen) (WuW/E) OLG 5165; Kammergericht Berlin, RdE 1994, 20ff.

[214] See Federal Court of Justice, in ZIP 1997, 993ff, *City of Detmold*; Kammergericht Berlin, in WuW/E, OLG 5795ff, *City of Nordhorn*; Kammergericht Berlin, in Recht der Energiewirtschaft (RdE) 1997, 72ff, *demarcation contract Thyssengas/Ruhrgas*. See ch 5, section D4, above.

agreements within the energy sector 'shall no longer apply'.[215] Abolishing area protection is, however, no guarantee that competition will soon enter the field of energy supply, since the agreements involving energy supply entities and municipalities are still effective. But these instruments are now to be thoroughly scrutinized by the competent cartel authorities, who are obliged to apply the general provisions of German competition law.[216] In addition a new provision of the recently modified competition law stipulates that the operator of an 'infrastructure network' such as railway tracks, telecommunication, and energy supply networks, is acting 'abusively' when access to third parties is denied (similar to the American 'essential facilities doctrine').[217] The question of whether denying access constitutes abusive behaviour must be assessed in accordance with the entire legal context of the sector in question, especially with regard to the specific rules on third-party access in the new Energy Act.

The new interplay of competition law and energy law shows that the liberalization process in Germany did not impair the constitutionally guaranteed protection of private property of supply networks. Accordingly, liberalization must not result in unconditional third-party access.[218] Any regulation of third-party access must therefore not only be grounded on a proper legal basis but also take into consideration the principle of proportionality.[219] 'Common carrier' or 'pool' models were precluded because Article 14 of the Constitution provides comprehensive protection of the privately owned supply networks. A 'pool' model would be an unconstitutional interference with the protected use of one's property.[220] **8.111**

Competition law and the gas sector

The above amendments to the German Competition Act are of special importance for the gas sector as some of the main instruments of the new Energy Act—such as the rules on access (ie the application of both the system of negotiated TPA and the single-buyer system) and the need for vertically integrated undetakings to keep separate accounts—only apply to the electricity sector. All other provisions of the new Energy Act do, however, apply to gas. After the entry into force of the EC Directive concerning common rules for the internal market for gas, the **8.112**

[215] cf § 103b, 1st sentence of the *Gesetz gegen Wettbewerbsbeschränkungen* (GWB) in its version of 27 April 1998 (see BGBl I 730, 734). However, the exemptions are still in place for the water supply sector.

[216] See esp §§ 22, 26 GWB.

[217] cf § 19 (4) no 4 of the Competition Act (GWB).

[218] Some legal authors differ: G Hermes, *Staatliche Infrastrukturverantwortung*, 1998, for example holds that a network must be regarded as a *public and generally accessible* infrastructure regardless a private ownership. Such an opinion, however, conflicts with guiding principles of German law. In contrast, see J-C Pielow, *Grundstrukturen öffentlicher Versorgung*, typescript 1998, § 13.

[219] Lukes, 1220; Papier-Gutachten.

[220] See Kühne/Scholtka, *Das neue Energiewirtschaftsrecht*, in NJW 1998, 1902 (at 1906) with further references.

Energy Act is to be completed accordingly. Until then, a refusal to award third parties access to gas transportation networks has to be answered on the basis of the general rules of competition law in accordance with the specific rulings on this issue.[221] It should be kept in mind, however, that these rulings were given on the basis of the former section 103(5) second sentence number 4 of the Competition Act, ie abuse of the exception rules for the energy sector, when denying TPA without any rectification. The *Bundesgerichtshof* ruled that the Competition Act does not contain a general duty for TPA and especially no need for the grid-owner to provide specific arguments, for example possible economic disadvantages. Each single case requires a balancing of interests (*Interessenabwägung*) as a result of which TPA could be denied even if a grid-owner finally accepts the same conditions as in the offer of the concurrent supplier. There has been no ruling on gas transportation tariffs.

8.113 According to the new section 19(4) number 4 of the Competition Act, 'there is an abuse of a dominant position if a dominant enterprise denies access—against adequate remuneration—of another undertaking to its own network or other types of infrastructure, when the other entrepreneur is not able to compete within the respective market without an access to the grid. Access can be denied only by proven reasons of grid operation or 'other reasons'. Therefore, the possibility of building a separate pipeline would exclude the need for TPA. Such is not the case under the Energy Act in the case of access to the electricity grid. Further, the reasons for denying TPA under the Competition Act (§ 19(4) no 4) are wider than the respective regulations in the Energy Act. A matter of discussion is the extent to which existing 'take-or-pay' obligations can justify the denial of access.

8.114 Even if there is the possibility of applying the Competition Act within the meaning of the EC Gas Directive, 'judicial safety' for third parties would be greater if the legislator included in the Energy Act special guidelines for negotiated TPA to the gas grid and the way in which companies should keep separate accounts.[222]

8.115 Meanwhile, gas suppliers, industrial gas users and the Government are discussing a voluntary *Durchleitungsvereinbarung*, an agreement on conditions and tariffs for TPA. Compared with the electricity sector important questions need to be resolved, for example the different quality of gas from one supplier or another and the technical problems of avoiding a 'gas mix'.[223]

---

[221] Esp *Bundesgerichtshof* decision of 15.11.1994 on Wintershall Erdgas Handelshaus GmbH/Verbundnetz Gas AG; on this ruling for example: K Markert, *Die Bedeutung der BGH-Entscheidung 'Gasdurchleitung'*, in Energiewirtschaftliche Tagesfragen (ed), 400ff; by the same author: *Die Verweigerung des Zugangs zu 'wesentlichen Einrichtungen' als Problem der kartellrechtlichen Mißbrauchaufsicht*, in Wirtschaft und Wettbewerb (WuW) 1995, 560ff.

[222] For more details: H Lutz, *Durchleitung von Gas nach Inkrafttreten des Gesetzes zur Neuregelung des Energiewirtschaftsrechts und der Sechsten GWB-Novelle*, in Recht der Energiewirtschaft 1999, 102ff.

[223] See Frankfurte Allgemeine Zeitung 9 March 2000, 13.

*(3) The 1998 Energy Act (*Energiewirtschaftsgesetz*)*

The new federal Act of 24 April 1998[224] concerning electricity and gas supply, hereinafter referred to as the new Energy Act, regulates the specific rights and obligations of the electricity and gas supplying enterprises, the position of the consumer, and the supervision and control of the energy supply sector. The purpose of the law is still to ensure as safely and as cheaply as possible the network-bound supply of electricity and natural gas in the public interest. In addition, and as a result of long political debate, new emphasis is placed on balanced environmental impact.[225] This means that energy supply should meet the requirements of reasonable and energy-saving use of energy, guarantee careful and lasting exploitation of resources, and pollute the environment as little as possible. Consequently, new or alternative sources of electricity, especially the use of industrial waste heat and renewable energies, is of great importance.[226] The official reasons for the new Energy Act point out that these objectives should be pursued by competition.[227] Environmental aspects were already taken into consideration under the old Energy Act based on blanket clauses and constitutional requirements. These long-standing developments were enhanced by the environmental clause in section 1 of the new law. **8.116**

The 'energy supply entity' and permits

The concept of the 'energy supply entity' includes all enterprises 'regardless of their legal form and ownership, which supply others with electric energy or gas'.[228] As previously, the law does not distinguish between public and private law entities or between public and private ownership or responsibility. The phrase 'regardless of their legal form and ownership' also indicates that energy supply cannot be regarded as an exclusively State or public task, nor do private supply entities perform State functions. This is fundamentally different from, for example, the French model of the *concession de service public.* **8.117**

In principle, each newcomer who intends to conduct business in the energy supply sector needs a permit. Subject to the following restrictions, any person has a right to be granted a permit. First, the applicant must have the necessary personal, technical, and financial capacity. Secondly, the applicant must not substantially impair the existing supply of the supply area.[229] Permission is not required for **8.118**

[224] *Gesetz über die Elektrizitäts- und Gasversorgung (Energiewirtschaftsgesetz, EnWG)*, published in BGBl 1998, part I, 730.

[225] See § 1 of the new Energy Act.

[226] ibid, § 2(4).

[227] cf the draft reform act (*Entwurf eines Gesetzes zur Neuregelung des Energiewirtschaftsrechts*) of 23 March 1997, published in Bundestagsdrucksache (BT-Drs) 13/7274, 12.

[228] cf § 2(2) of the new Energy Act.

[229] ibid, § 3(2).

feeding electricity or gas into another network, for certain supply activities going further than the universal services (see next section), nor in cases where industrial subdivisions of the same group are inter-connected and supply each other.[230]

Obligations of energy supply entities

8.119 If an energy supply entity is responsible for supplying the territory of a certain municipality, it must supply everyone within that territory in accordance with uniform 'general supply conditions and tariffs' (*allgemeine Anschluß- und Versorgungspflicht*). The energy supplier is not however obliged to make totally unreasonable efforts. The federal Minister of Economy and Technology can pass a decree on the question of to what extent, and under what conditions, the duty of supply must be regarded as reasonable.[231] The Minister thereby defines the extent of the universal service.

8.120 Similar to the situation under the previous Energy Act, the Minister can issue decrees and regulate the general tariffs for electricity and the general supply conditions for both electricity and gas. Against this background, the old decrees remain effective.[232] The federal decree on general tariffs for electricity (*Bundestarifordnung Elektrizität, BTO Elt*) contains detailed structural guidelines, especially concerning uniform prices for obligatory supply. Electricity prices may not exceed these uniform prices without permission, which will only be granted if necessary for the individual energy supplying company on the basis of reasonable management. If the energy supplying entity is able to prove this, the permission is granted on request.[233] The decrees on general supply conditions for gas and electricity (*Allgemeine Versorgungsbedingungen Gas bzw. Elektrizität*) contain binding preformulations for electricity contracts.[234] It is worth asking, however, whether this regulation will survive in the changed environment of a competitive German energy industry.[235]

8.121 The new Energy Act also contains requirements for individual transmission grids. These must be designed and operated in accordance with the central purposes of the Act as set out in section 1 (ie a cheap, safe, and environmentally friendly energy supply). In addition the network operators must publish the technical mini-

[230] ibid, § 3(1).

[231] For details, see ibid, § 10.

[232] The decree on 'general tariffs' for gas (*Bundestarifordnung Gas*) was suspended as a part of the energy law reform.

[233] PJ Tettinger, *Administrativer Prognosespielraum bei der Strompreisgenehmigung gemäß § 12a BTO Elt?, Energiewirtschaftliche Tagesfragen* (ed) 1983, 483. The consumer has no right to bring this issue before court. See the decision of the Federal Administrative Court, published in Recht der Energiewirtschaft (RdE) 1994, 230.

[234] For a detailed treatise, see HR Ebel, *Energielieferungsverträge*, 1992.

[235] cf G Kühne, *The liberalisation process in Germany: the German Energy Act* (Energy seminar, Noordwijk a.Z. 11 May 1998).

mum requirements for connection with the transmission grid and communicate them to the competent national authority and to the European Commission. The State also has the capacity to expropriate private property necessary for energy supply objectives.[236] According to the Federal Constitutional Court, under certain conditions expropriation may even take place in favour of a private energy enterprise.[237]

The operator of a network must publish objective criteria for the feeding in of electricity from independent producers and for the use of connection lines. The criteria have to be applied in a non-discriminatory way. The transmission grid must be subjected to separate accounting. In accordance with Article 14 of the EC Directive on the Internal Market for Electricity, section 9 of the new Energy Act provides for unbundling and transparency. Electricity supply enterprises of the 'universal' service are subject to the duties of publication of annual accounts, separation of accounts for generation, transmission, and distribution activities, and specification of assets and liabilities, expenditure, and income. **8.122**

Negotiated third-party access (NTPA)

Third-party access is the central issue of the new Energy Act. For quite a while it was heavily disputed whether the opening of the networks should take place by virtue of command and control regulation or left for voluntary co-operation between the energy utilities and (industrial) consumers. Finally, the legislator opted for the latter alternative. A special option applies, however, to energy supply on the local level (see the next section). On the other hand, the new Energy Act did not adopt the system of a 'phased' opening towards competitive structures as suggested in Article 19 of the EC Directive. **8.123**

In general, network operators have to allow third-party access on conditions no worse than those applied in relation to their own, or associated companies', access. Again, the network operator is not obliged to make impossible or unreasonable (the law mentions 'operational or other reasons') efforts in this regard. There are still many doubts as to what constitute 'other reasons'. Within the formulations of the Energy Act, a network operator may deny access if the carriage of electricity produced in an environmentally friendly way (for example, electricity produced by the use of industrial waste heat (CHP), district heating, or renewable primary resources) would be jeopardized. The network operator has the burden of proof in this respect. **8.124**

Section 6(2) of the new Energy Act enables the federal Minister of Economy and Technology to regulate the necessary access agreements and to fix criteria for access prices. The Minister has not, however, made use of this power. Instead, he left **8.125**

236 cf § 12 of the Energy Act.

237 Federal Constitutional Court, in BVerfGE vol 66, 248.

the issue to the economic sectors concerned, which were given the opportunity to settle the problem themselves as a form of self-regulation. Only if their efforts prove unsuccessful would the Minister react by passing a suitable decree. Three industrial associations, the Federation of German Industries (BDI), the association of large industrial consumers (VIK), and the Association of the German Electricity Suppliers (VDEW) have reached agreement on criteria for the determination of transmission fees, the *Verbändevereinbarung* of 22 May 1998[238] which has also been approved by the Federal Cartel Authority. It contains first of all guidelines for access prices. In addition, it embodies model provisions for the necessary contracts. During negotiations it was disputed whether the prices should be 'stamp type' or 'distance type', ie whether prices should be independent from the length of carriage. The solution found was a combination of those approaches: distance tariffs apply only for high-tension carriage for more than 100 km. The *Verbändevereinbarung* agreement had to be renegotiated by 30 September 1999.[239] In the meantime, the *Verbändevereinbarung* of 22 May 1998 was replaced by the so-called '*Verbändeveinbasrung II*' of 13 December 1999.[240] The new instrument calculates transmission fees on the basis of concrete costs (*Kostenwälzungsprincip*—'principle of cost-devolution'.

8.126 Finally, the reform of the energy law brought a protection clause safeguarding the reciprocity of third-party access, especially in the field of cross-border energy selling.[241] Accordingly, access can be denied for electricity from a country if consumers from that country are not able to purchase electricity from a foreign supplier. This rule is to be renegotiated by 31 December 2006.

Optional single-buyer system on the local level

8.127 The Bundesrat (the federal representation of the Länder, something like a second chamber) and the municipalities finally succeeded in introducing an optional model in order to satisfy the special interests of local governments and their supply entities with regard to their traditional strong influence within the sector (see section A2 above). In particular, municipal suppliers were increasingly worried about their business perspectives under a system which would divide the market into commercially interesting industrial consumers to be cherry-picked by powerful competitors with supply to private households, small business con-

[238] Recht der Energiewirtschaft (RdE) 1998, vol V, XXI.

[239] For details concerning the requirements and conditions of a third-party access see U Büdenbender, *Durchleitung elektrischer Energie nach der Energierechtsreform*, in Recht der Energiewirtschaft (RdE) 1999, 1ff; M Ungemach/Th Weber, *Verfahrensfragen des Netzzugangs bei Elektrizität und Gas*, in Recht der Energiewirtschaft (RdE) 1999, 11ff (part 1).

[240] Text available on the Internet under http://www.strom.de

[241] cf Art 4 of the federal Energy Law Reform Act (*Gesetz zur Neuregelung des Energiewirtschaftsrechts*) of 28 November 1997 (BGBl 1998, part I, 730).

sumers, and the remaining commercially unattractive consumers left to the municipalities.

According to section 7(1) of the new law, energy utilities which provide a supply to all final consumers within a certain supply area (generally the municipal territory or parts of it) may opt for a 'single-buyer' system. The local enterprise is then the sole supplier within that area and, subject to authorization by the competent authority, the rules on negotiated third-party access are inapplicable. Instead, if an individual consumer is willing to use electricity from outside the supply area, the electricity supplier will purchase the electricity from the other electricity utility. The consumer and the other electricity seller must reach prior agreement on the price. The single buyer (the local supplier) may charge the consumer no more than this price but deducts a certain amount from the price paid to the third party. Accordingly, the third party pays for the carriage of the electricity. For reasons of transparency, single-buyer activities must be administered separately from production and distribution activities. **8.128**

Through the necessary licensing of the single buyer, local electricity markets will be opened to non-discriminatory access for foreign electricity. A single buyer will only receive a licence if it can guarantee 'equivalent economic results and hence a directly comparable level of opening-up of markets and a directly comparable degree of access to electricity markets' within the supply area. The legislative intention was to create a situation equivalent to the NTPA system as to transparency and accessibility. The optional single-buyer concept and the respective authorizations will expire by 31 December 2005. Further prolongation will only take place if the single-buyer system performs as satisfactorily as the NTPA system.[242] **8.129**

Critics wonder whether the single-buyer system will make a substantial difference. Municipalities should therefore think twice before choosing this option.[243] Others focus on the compatibility of the German two-model solution with the internal market Directive (the single-buyer option was originally developed as a political compromise to cope with the specific structures of the French energy market).[244] **8.130**

Further limitations on energy supply activities by the municipalities derive from the general guidelines of the Länder law on the economic activities of local governments: These stipulations require a public interest and a sufficient (financial) capacity of the acting local government. In some of the Länder there is a certain **8.131**

[242] cf § 8, third sentence of the new Energy Act.

[243] See for example M Cronenberg, *Das neue Energiewirtschaftsrecht*, in RdE 1998, 85, 87.

[244] See for example R Lukes, *Die Neuregelung des Energiewirtschaftsrechts*, in BB 1998, 1217, 1220, with further references.

principle of subsidiarity in favour of private initiative.[245] Accordingly, economic activities of the municipalities shall only take place where private performance is 'neither sufficient nor economic'.

8.132 As a specific (East) German aspect concerning the conditions of both NTPA and single-buyer mechanisms, the temporary protection clause for power generation on the basis of lignite should be mentioned.[246] It requires those who supervise grid access or (single-) buying of electricity to take into account the need for a sufficiently high level of lignite use as fuel for power production. The background is that, in the wake of German Reunification, enormous investments in the East German lignite industry were made in the expectation of marketing the electricity produced.[247]

Use of municipal property: concession contracts and concession fees

8.133 Unlike in the telecommunication sector,[248] there is no law granting the energy supplying entities a right to lay cables or pipelines underneath public highways. As already pointed out, the traditional influence of German local government within the energy supply sector was based on property, namely title to the public highways. Municipalities were able to decide independently whether to realize the energy supply by a municipal enterprise or to transfer the task by means of a concession contract (*Konzessionsvertrag*, see paragraph 8.28 above) to a third party, frequently a private or mixed private-public company. The private supplier was charged concession fees (*Konzessionsabgaben*) which formed an important source of municipal income.[249] With the opening-up of the energy market this mechanism had to be revised. The solution found in the new Energy Act must be viewed as the result of a political compromise. The right to enter into concession contracts with supply entities acting in the local area and to charge them concession fees still exists, but the traditional possibility of an exclusive contract has been abolished. Municipalities must now make their public highways available by contract and 'without discrimination' for the laying and operation of cables and pipelines for direct supply to final consumers in the local area.[250] This means that

[245] cf for example: § 108(1) of the Local Government Act of Lower Saxony, § 89 of the Bavarian Local Government Act. For details, see G Britz, *Örtliche Energieversorgung nach nationalem und europäischem Recht*, 1994; A Krebs, *Rechtliche Grundlagen und Grenzen kommunaler Elektrizitätsversorgung*, 1996—each with further references.

[246] cf Art 4 § 3 of the federal Energy Reform Act.

[247] cf G Kühne, *The liberalisation process in Germany: The German energy act, (European Energy Law seminar in Noordwijk 1998).*

[248] See § 50 of the federal Telecommunications Act (*Telekommunikationsgesetz, TKG*) of 25 July 1996 (BGBl I 1120).

[249] For further details, see PJ Tettinger, *Grundlinien des Konzessionsvertragsrechts*, in Deutsches Verwaltungsblatt (DVBl) 1991, 768ff; essential: K Stern, *Zur Problematik des energiewirtschaftlichen Konzessionsvertrags*, in Archiv des öffentlichen Rechts (AöR), vol 84 (1959), 137ff and 273ff.

[250] cf § 13(1) of the new Energy Act.

all suppliers must be granted the right to use the municipal public highways in a non-discriminatory way. Those rights can only be refused if the utility in question refuses to pay concession fees in accordance with section 14 of the Energy Act. The duration of concession contracts is limited to twenty years.

For the first time, the new regulation of the use of public (municipal) highways for **8.134** energy supply reasons makes possible the installation and operation of parallel supply networks (such as a cable for a large industrial consumer within a foreign supply area). Nevertheless one has to consider that, when stipulating the third-party access as the central instrument of competition, the new Energy Act envisages parallel networks only as an ultimate goal; even better, as an instrument to enforce bilateral TPA agreements. Thus, in practice, even where there is an option to build a parallel network, the operator of the existing network may find it easier to agree to TPA.[251]

The grant of rights to use public highways takes place in the legal form of private law **8.135** contracts, insofar as general use is not affected by the network. Temporary disruptions, especially by building activities, are not considered as affecting such use.[252]

Finally, section 14 of the new Energy Act contains detailed rules on the concession **8.136** fees (*Konzessionsabgaben*) to be charged by the municipalities for the use of public land. These fees are legally defined as 'payments made by the energy utilities in exchange for the right to supply directly final consumers in the area of the municipality with energy by using public highways for the laying and operation of supply lines'.[253] The fees are of a private law nature and cannot be considered as taxes.[254] As already mentioned, these fees are an important source of revenue for the municipalities, amounting to more than three billion euros. It is important to mention in this context that concession fees are now also payable 'for energy which is supplied to final consumers within the municipal territory by other enterprises via third-party access'.[255] This provision is intended to maintain the total amount of concession fees at pre-liberalization levels. In conjunction with subsequent legislation[256] the new Energy Act limits the concession fee to an amount

251 See background to the draft Energy Law Reform Act, in Bundestagsdrucksache (BT-Drs) 13/7274, 10ff.

252 The Federal Administrative Court affirmed this with regard to both vertical and parallel mains: BVerwGE vol 29, 248.

253 In our opinion this definition is incorrect, as there is no 'transfer' of a right to supply (in the sense of a real 'concession') but only the grant of a right to use the public highways (see also para 8.28 above).

254 They are a highly contested matter of the political and scientific discussion in Germany. cf for example J Wieland, *Die Konzessionsabgaben*, 1991, 383ff; see also G Britz, *Örtliche Energieversorgung nach nationalem und europäischem Recht*, 1994, 105ff.

255 cf § 14(3) of the new Energy Act.

256 cf the federal decree on the fees of contracts of concession (*Konzessionsabgabenveordnung, KAV*) of 9 January 1992, published in BGBl, part I, 12. See further the supplementary remarks on interpretation by the responsible federal minister, published in Recht der Energiewirtschaft (RdE) 1993, 35.

expressed in *Pfennig*[257] per kilowatt-hour. The fee may vary for the various groups of consumers and purposes taking into consideration the number of inhabitants in the municipality.

8.137 An especially difficult problem is to evaluate the take-over price of an existing supply grid, if a municipality intends to perform the relevant supply task itself, for example after the expiration of a concession contract.[258] The new Energy Act prescribes only 'the payment of a commercially appropriate price'.[259]

(4) Supervision, Planning Law, and Judicial Control

8.138 It has already been mentioned that deregulation, in addition to the injection of competition, is one *leitmotiv* of energy law reform in Germany. The sector should not be reorganized through governmental action. Instead, the necessary structural adaptations of the industry in transition from regulation to competition was left to market forces.[260]

8.139 One consequence of the deregulation effort was the abolition of the investment control contained in the former law. Nevertheless, other mechanisms of supervision have been introduced. In the context of 'unbundling' there are special duties as to transparency and accountability.[261] Additional regulatory instruments like the general supply conditions and general tariffs (for electricity) in the field of universal supply are still in force.

8.140 No special planning law for energy installations (production and transport devices) exists apart from some nuclear law provisions on the building of nuclear power stations, some mineral law provisions on coal extraction entities, and Länder law on open-cast mining. Additional planning law relevant to energy installations takes place in large-scale regional planning (*Raumplanung*).[262] It is important to note that regional planning measures do not entail obligations for private persons and enterprises. Their legal relevance lies exclusively within the public sector.

8.141 In the past some Länder used regional planning law (which widely belongs to exclusive Länder competence) as a tool against the Bund to pursue their own energy policies, especially with the aim of hindering the establishment of nuclear power

---

[257] 1 *Pfennig* = 0.01 DEM ≈ 0,005 euro.

[258] See for example: Higher Regional Court (*Oberlandesgericht*) Frankfurt, published in Recht der Energiewirtschaft (RdE) 1992, 159ff; U Hüffer, *Der Übernahmepreis in konzessionsvertraglichen Endschaftsklauseln,* in RdE 1992, 205ff; PJ Tettinger/J-C Pielow, *Der Sachzeitwert als der nach wie vor maßgebliche Übernahmepreis beim Versorgerwechsel,* 1994.

[259] cf § 13(2).

[260] cf G Kühne, *The liberalisation process in Germany: the German Energy Act,* in European Energy Law Seminar, Noordwijk a.Z. 11 May 1998, Leiden International Institute for Energy Law.

[261] cf § 7(4) and § 9 of the new Energy Act.

[262] See PJ Tettinger, in R Schmidt, *Öffentliches Wirtschaftsrecht—Besonderer Teil,* vol I, 1995, margin number 18.

stations or to enforce the establishment of decentralized power-plants on a co-generating basis.[263] The Federal Building and Development Act (*Baugesetzbuch*)[264] contains further regulation relevant for the energy sector addressing local level and urban planning.

It should be noted in this context that the draft Energy Act of 1997 contained specific provisions concerning an obligatory and specific planning procedure for high-tension grids. The former Conservative-Liberal Government, however, abolished the relevant chapter at the end of the parliamentary consultation in order to avoid the rejection of the draft act by the Bundesrat (second chamber), dominated at that time by the Social Democrat opposition. As a result of this modification the draft act did not require the express approval of the Bundesrat. The Social-Democratic opposition saw unconstitutional 'manipulation' and brought the matter before the Federal Constitutional Court where it is still pending. A final decision should contain more detail of the constitutionally guaranteed position of Länder and municipalities in the energy supply sector. **8.142**

Last but not least there are different types of public control within the network-bound energy markets.[265] **8.143**

—First, section 18(1) of the new Energy Act enables the public authority (here, the Länder Ministers for the Economy) to supervise compliance with the provisions of the Act and, if necessary, to take adequate measures in order to implement the Act[266]—a typical type of public law. Judicial review is by the administrative courts.

—On the other hand, contracts between different supply companies concerning third-party access to the grids are typical private law contracts. The entire NTPA-related contract is subject to judicial review by the civil courts.

—Finally, due to the fact that the former monopolies will retain a dominant position for a considerable time to come, the electricity and gas industries will be under close antitrust scrutiny in all aspects involving dominant positions such as merger control, abuse control with regard to pricing practices and sanctions

[263] See, for example, W Blümel, *Die Standortvorsorgeplanung für Kernkraftwerke und andere umweltrelevante Großvorhaben in der Bundesrepublik Deutschland*, in Deutsches Verwaltungsblatt (DVBl.) 1977, 301ff; J Depenbrock, *Standortvorsorge für Kraftwerke und flächenintensive Großvorhaben in Nordrhein-Westfalen*, in DVBl 1978, 17ff.

[264] From 27 August 1997, in BGBl, part I, 2141—for example: § 9(1) nos 12 and 13, concerning supply cables and pipelines within local planning acts, and § 35(1) nos 3 and 6, concerning wind and hydropower plants, no 5, concerning nuclear power plants.

[265] cf G Kühne, *The liberalisation process in Germany: the German energy act*, in European Energy Law Seminar, Noordwijk aZ 11 May 1998, Leiden International Institute for Energy Law.

[266] This type of supervision is flanked by various obligations of the entrepreneur (information, tolerate the access of private grounds, etc).

for discriminatory pricing.[267] This leads to an additional competence of the federal or Länder cartel authorities whose decisions (for example in the form of an injunction to accept NTPA)[268] are subject to judicial review by specific panels within the civil courts. Accordingly, the civil courts can be seized with access disputes in two ways.

8.144 The plurality of control mechanisms still constitutes an unresolved—and serious—problem of the new German energy law.[269] On other hand, one should take into account the specific tension between public and private law and the respective forms of judicial review which constitutes—at least under continental legal systems—something like a typical consequence of the liberalization process as a whole, and which creates similar problems in other sectors (telecommunication, broadcasting, public transport, etc). In the end, this is an important subject which requires further debates concerning the relationship and possible implementation of public law and civil or competition law solutions.

F. Energy Law and the Environment

8.145 Environmental aspects of German energy law have been dealt with occasionally in the previous sections. Nevertheless, the specific environmental relevance of the energy sector makes it necessary to deal with them separately. Evidently, energy production operates at the expense of the environment. Upstream activities diminish natural resources whilst the consumption of energy pollutes the atmosphere and accelerates climate change. The latter aspect was addressed in the United Nations Convention on Climate Change and the respective Kyoto Protocol of 11 December 1997[270] with its obligations on States to reduce emission of greenhouse gases.[271]

---

[267] In this context, § 6(1), 4th sentence of the Energy Act explicitly states that the NTPA provision has to be understood as not prejudicing the applicability of competition law on control of abuse over market dominant undertakings and on prohibition of discriminatory practices. cf G Kühne, n 265 above.

[268] As to a first test case (*ELEKTROMARK Kommunales Elektrizitätswerk Mark AG/Enron Energie GmbH*) see press communications of the Federal Cartel Authority of 23 December 1998 and 11 January 1999 (www.bundeskartellamt.de). The proceeding was suspended after accepting the TPA conditions set out by the cartel authority by the area supplier.

[269] See for example G Kühne/B Scholtka, *Das neue Energiewirtschaftsrecht*, in NJW 1998, 1902, 1908; U Büdenbender, *Energierecht nach der Energierechtsreform*, in Juristenzeitung (JZ) 1999, 62, 70f; M Ungemach/Th Weber, *Verfahrensfragen des Netzzugangs bei Elektrizität und Gas*, in Recht der Energiewirtschaft (RdE) 1999, 11ff.

[270] UN Doc FCCC/CP/1997/L.7/Add.1.

[271] See H Steeg, *Energie und Umwelt*, in Recht der Energiewirtschaft (RdE) 1998, 129ff; A Klemm, *Das Klimaprotokoll von Kyoto*, ibid, 133ff.

(1) Renewable Energy Sources and Industrial Waste Heat

The limited availability of mineral fuels, dependence on oil and gas imports, and the specific dangers of nuclear energy production are key factors influencing the development of alternative/renewable energy sources like wind, solar energy,[272] hydropower, geothermal energy, bio-mass and industrial waste heat, the individual techniques of heat recovery, and the combustion of household wastes.[273] Today the share of renewable energy in total German electricity production is still small (see section A above). Considerable growth rates in new technologies—wind energy production, for example, grew by 50 per cent between 1997 and 1998—have not changed the general trend in the renewable sector which is still clearly dominated by water energy, a traditional energy source which is certainly renewable, but not really alternative.[274] **8.146**

The Federal Government supports the European initiative to at least double the proportion of renewable energies by the year 2010. By the year 2050, the proportion of renewable energies is to be 50 per cent of total energy production.[275] These ambitious political objectives, however, should not divert attention from the fact that it will still take a good deal of progress in science and technology to achieve these targets. It is certainly clear that renewable energy sources deserve to be promoted through all possible forms of support (subsidies and tax exemptions) so long as such support does not unreasonably distort competition. Renewable energies should therefore be supported only until established in the market place.[276] **8.147**

*(2) Existing Support and the 'Feeding-in' Act (*Stromeinspeisungsgesetz*)*

German energy law reform assumes that introducing competition into the field of network-bound energy supply will provide the necessary inventive for increasing cost savings and the use of environmentally friendly technologies, for example **8.148**

[272] See *Bundestags-Drucksache* (Gazette of the Federal Parliament), No 11/2684, 29–30; No 12/7185.

[273] For a survey, see Federal Ministry for the Economy, *Erneuerbare Energien—verstärkt nutzen*, 1993.

[274] In 1998 renewable energy-based electricity generation was about 238,000 million kWh (hydopower: 161,000 million kWh; wind: 45,000 million kWh; waste combustion: 21,000 million kWh; biomass: 11,000 million kWh; photovoltaic: 200 million kWh): Frankfurter Allgemeine Zeitung, 2 March 1999, 25.

[275] See Frankfurter Allgemeine Zeitung, 2 March 1999, 25; cf *Umweltziele und Handlungsschwerpunkte in Deutschland* Federal Ministry for the Environment (ed) and *Klimaschutz und Energiepolitik*, (*4. Bericht des Arbeitskreises I 'Energieversorgung' der Interministeriellen Arbeitsgruppe 'CO_2-Reduktion'*) = Documentation no 445 of the Federal Ministry of Economy (1998).

[276] See the opinion of the Federal Government, *Förderung und Nutzung 'erneuerbarer Energiequellen' in der Bundesrepublik Deutschland* of 20 July 1988, Bundestags-Drucksache, No 11/2684, and the energy report of the Federal Government of 11 December 1991, Bundestags-Drucksache, No 12/1799, esp §§ 62ff. For further information, see G Ziller, *Forschungsförderung des Bundes im Bereich fossiler und erneuerbarer Energieträger*, in Festschrift für F Fabricius, 1989, 27ff.

combined heat and power stations.[277] The promotion of renewable energy sources and the use of industrial waste heat in the context of electricity generation are essential components of the Energy Act of 1998 (see section E3 above). The respective support mechanisms may be summarized as follows:[278]

- Electricity from industrial waste heat and renewable energy sources enjoys privileged access to the power grids in cases of limited capacity.
- If the use of electricity from industrial waste heat or renewable energies would be jeopardized, third parties can be denied access to the power grid; under the same conditions, municipalities may refuse permission to use public rights of way for parallel supply lines until the year 2005.
- New supply installations are not subject to a permitting requirement so long as they are employed outside the general supply and if primarily reliant on renewable energies or industrial waste heat.
- Consumers of universal services which engage in the production of renewable energies or the use of industrial waste heat may continue to take full advantage of such services.[279]
- When approving the general supply tariffs the competent authority has to acknowledge 'least cost-planning' considerations.[280]

8.149 As a general statement, German energy law reform is based on the assumption that the introduction of competition in the field of network-bound energy supply as such will provide the necessary incentive for increasing cost-saving and environmentally friendly technologies, for example in the form of economical and less polluting combined power stations.[281]

8.150 Another important contribution to the increased relevance of renewable energy sources—apart from direct subsidies[282]—is the federal Act of 7 December 1990.[283] Thereunder, energy suppliers must purchase electricity from renewable energy sources which has to be fed into the public supply grid.[284] The purchase rates are fixed and lie considerably above the so-called avoided costs—i.e. costs

[276] See the opinion of the Federal Government, *Förderung und Nutzung 'erneuerbarer Energiequellen' in der Bundesrepublik Deutschland* of 20 July 1988, Bundestags-Drucksache, No 11/2684, and the energy report of the Federal Government of 11 December 1991, Bundestags-Drucksache, No 12/1799, esp §§ 62ff. For further information, see G Ziller, *Forschungsförderung des Bundes im Bereich fossiler und erneuerbarer Energieträger*, in Festschrift für F Fabricius, 1989, 27ff.

[277] ibid, 85, 89–90.

[278] cf M Cronenberg, *Das neue Energiewirtschaftrsecht*, in Recht der Energiewirtschaft (RdE) 1998, 90.

[279] cf § 10(2) of the new Energy Act.

[280] ibid, § 11(1), 3rd sentence.

[281] M Cronenberg, op cit 90.

[282] As to those mechanisms see Sommerstange, 1996, 792ff.

[283] *Stromeinspeisungsgesetz, StEG* (BGBl, part I, 2633), last altered by Art 3 no 2 of the Energy Law Reform Act of 28 November 1997 (BGBl 1998, part I, 730).

[284] The Act mentions 'hydropower, wind energy, solar energy, landfill gas, sewage gas or biomass' (§ 1).

that would occur if the energy supplier had to generate the purchased electricity itself. These rates amount to at least 80 per cent (for wind energy, 90 per cent) of the average revenue per KWh from the purchase of electricity utilities to all final consumers.[285]

The Feeding-In Act pre-dates the reform of German energy law. Originally drafted against the background of the previous situation of protected supply areas, it was necessary to adapt the law to take account of liberalization. Accordingly, it is no longer the regional supplier which is in charge of purchasing the alternatively generated electricity at fixed rates but rather the operator of the regional grid of the universal supply (*allgemeine Versorgung*).[286] In addition, the following changes were made: **8.151**

- The new version of the Feeding-In Act makes a clear statement in favour of offshore wind energy. The extension of offshore sites shall be predominantly supported in the future. If the generation facility is not situated within the supply area of any network operator, the obligation to purchase the electricity shall apply to the closest network facility.
- The federal government shall encourage the electricity companies to enter into voluntary agreements as an additional measure to increase the proportion of electricity from renewable energy sources and from the use of industrial waste heat. The federal government may set out objectives to be achieved within a certain period of time.[287]
- With regard to the enormous concentration of wind energy generators in northern Germany, the Feeding-In Act now contains a complicated mechanism for compensation in favour of network operators in coastal regions. The obligation to pay for electricity from renewable energy in excess of 5 per.cent of the total KWhs sold per calendar year passes on from the network operator to the upstream system operator at the regional or compound level. In general, the obligations of the network operator shall not apply in cases of unfair hardships, particularly if the operator would be forced drastically to raise its prices for electricity transport.[288]

[285] For details, see § 3 of the Feeding-In Act. Extra costs from fulfilling the 'feeding-in' obligation can be allocated in accounts to distribution or transmission and can be included in the setting of the price for the TPA (§2, 3rd sentence of the Act).

[286] ibid, § 2.

[287] cf ibid, § 4a; as to these 'self-obligations' in the framework of a 'co-operative' energy policy see also *Empfehlung der Verbände VIK, VKU und VDEW zur Förderung der Kooperativen Kraft-Wärme-Wirtschaft (KKWW)*, in RdE 1/1999, If.

[288] For details see § 4 of the Feeding-In Act and M Cronenberg, op cit 90.

8.152 Legal issues arise in connection with the constitutional rights of the energy supply enterprises and with the financial provisions of the constitution.[289] The issue is similar to the coal penny (see section 3(2) above), viz. is the financial burden resulting from the obligation to purchase alternatively generated electricity a sort of unlawful 'special tax'? The question is still pending before the Federal Constitutional Court.[290]

The Federal Constitutional Court is, however, not the final court to deal with the legality of the German Feeding-In Act. It has now come before the European Court of Justice through an Article 234 procedure. In this respect, the German law might especially conflict with Articles 87 EC.[291]

(3) Further Legal Aspects of Employing Renewable Energy Sources

8.153 Legal problems in the use of renewable energy sources arise from the law concerning the protection of the countryside and from the civil law provisions settling the relationship of neighbours.[292] Wind energy devices in particular interfere with their surrounding environment by virtue of their appearance and noise and are subject to urban planning law.[293] Heat pumps for houses and hot water must not be operated without a permit, according to water law, if such are connected to the ground water.[294] If wastewater is used as a heat source, attention has to be

---

289 In favour of a violation of the Constitution vote: Arndt, in RdE 1995, 597ff; F Ossenbühl, in Energiewirtschaftliche Tagesfragen 1996, 94ff; H Klinger, in Festschrift für Bodo Börner, 1992, 541ff. The opposite opinion is represented by: W Hoffmann-Riem, in Die Verwaltung 1995, 425ff; R Scholz, 1995, 600ff; Studenroth, in DVBl 1995, 1216ff.

290 The court (*Amtsgericht*) of Plön filed a respective request in the Federal Constitutional Court: see Neue Juristische Wochenschrift (NJW) 1997, 591ff. In a first process the Federal Constitutional Court refused to deal with that question: see the decision in Neue Juristische Wochenschrift (NJW) 1997, 573ff. In another proceeding, the Federal Court of Justice (*Bundesgerichtshof*) held that the federal Act concerning the 'feeding-in of electricity' does not violate the constitution, judgment published in NJW 1997, 547ff. See further M Pohlmann, *Rechtsprobleme der Stromeinspeisung nach dem Stromeinspeisungsgesetz*, 1996; idem, *Der Streit um das Stromeinspeisungsgesetz vor dem Grundgesetz*, in NJW 1997, 545ff; F Ossenbühl, *Die Verfassungswidrigkeit der Vergütungsregelung des Stromeinspeisungsgesetzes*, in RdE 1997, 46ff; Chr Theobald, *Verfassungsmäßigkeit des Stromeinspeisungsgesetzes*, in NJW 1997, 550ff.

291 See S Richter, published in Pielow/López-Jurado (eds), *Deutsch-Spanische Beiträge zum Energierecht*, 1999.

292 U Battis, *Rechtsfragen der Nutzung regenerativer Energien*, in Festschrift für F Fabricius, 1989, 319ff; EM Ogiermann, *Rechtsfragen der Errichtung von Windkraftanlagen*, 1992; Federal Administrative Court, in NJW 1983, 2713 and 2718; superior administrative court of North-Rhine Westphalia, in NWVBl 1993, 174ff; superior administrative court of Lower Saxony, in RdE 1994, 18.

293 For more details see: Federal Administrative Court (*Bundesverwaltungsgericht*), in Die öffentliche Verwaltung (DÖV) 1998, 927ff; St Lühle, *Nachbarschutz gegen Windenergieanlagen*, in NJW 1998, 897ff; Chr Stenneken, *Windkraftanlagen im dedutschen Raum- und Bauplanungsrecht unter besonderer Berücksichtigung Nordrhein-Westfalens*, in Pielow/López-Jurado (eds), *Deutsch-Spanische Beiträge zum Energierecht*, 1999.

294 See § 7 of the Federal Water Act (*Wasserhaushaltsgesetz*). See also superior administrative court of Baden-Württemberg, in Baden-Württembergische Verwaltungsblätter (VBlBW) 1981, 54–5.

drawn to local wastewater law. Planning permission is required for heat pumps exceeding a certain standard of performance.[295]

The production of energy out of waste takes place first of all in the form of combustion (ie thermal exploitation of wastes).[296] Legal regulation takes place under a new federal Act (*Kreislaufwirtschafts und Abfallgesetz*)[297] which defines 'energetic' exploitation as 'the use of wastes as a substitute or alternative fuel'. This is one possible form of waste besides the extracting of non-waste substances for *recycling*.[298] After the duty to avoiding waste generation (*Abfallvermeidung*), waste exploitation/recovery must take priority over other forms of waste treatment, ie waste disposal, if it is technically possible, not unreasonably expensive, and if there is a market—existing or possible—for the extracted substances or energy.[299] The decision between recycling or energy exploitation is to be taken in accordance with environmental impact.[300] Exploitation for energy is a kind of last resort within the German waste management system in order to utilize waste as much as possible.[301] **8.154**

(4) *Energy Saving*

The reduction of energy consumption is an objective of both energy and environmental policy. Important factors in energy saving are improving the effectiveness of power plants[302] and the development of new energy-saving consumer devices, including motor vehicles. Energy saving and energy efficiency are also an important legal topic.[303] For example, Article 141 (1) of the Bavarian Constitution highlights them as a priority task of the State, its emanations, and the municipalities; similar provisions are found in the constitutions of Bremen and of the Saarland. The federal Act on energy saving of 22 July 1976[304] and derived governmental **8.155**

[295] D Gersemann, *Rechtsprobleme bei der Wärmepumpe*, in Baden-Württembergische Verwaltungsblätter (VBlBW) 1981, 383ff.

[296] As to waste combustion from the legal point of view: PJ Tettinger, in Festschrift für Fabricius, 1989, 307ff.

[297] Gesetz zur Förderung der Kreislaufwirtschaft und Sicherung der umweltverträglichen Beseitigung von Abfällen (Kreislaufwirtschafts- und Abfallgesetz—KrW-/AbfG) of 27 September 1994 (BGBl I 2705).

[298] See § 4(4) of the KrW-/AbfG.

[299] See § 5(4) first sentence of the KrW-/AbfG.

[300] See § 6 of the KrW-/AbfG, which contains further restrictions as to the thermal exploitation of wastes.

[301] See § 10(2), 3rd and 4th sentences of the KrW-/AbfG.

[302] The electricity efficiency of German coal-fired power plants shall increase from only 5% at the beginning of the century to 50% in the year 2000. Other generation sites like combined gas and heat plants are to reach an efficiency of 60%, or in the case of supplementary use for district heating purposes nearly 90%.

[303] For an overview, see R Grawert, *Gesetzliche Regelungen zur Versorgungssicherung und Energieeinsparung*, in Festschrift für F Fabricius, 1989, 335ff; E Salje, *Energieeinsparung als rechtliches Ordnungsproblem*, 1982, 674ff.

[304] *Energieeinsparungsgesetz*, published in BGBl 1976, part I, 1873, altered by Act of 20 June 1980 (BGBl, part I, 701).

decrees[305] promote energy saving in buildings. General stipulations of environmental protection law and tax law contain further approaches (see below).[306] This is in addition to regulations based on EC initiatives.[307]

8.156 Bund and Länder encourage and support-energy saving technologies by tax reductions and direct incentives. Numerous programmes exist to make the public aware of the potential inherent in energy saving. It is disputed whether, and to what extent, Länder may regulate beyond federal energy-saving regulation.[308]

(5) 'Ecological Taxes'

8.157 Taxes are generally speaking an effective tool of environmental policy. There are already numerous examples of granting tax advantages or imposing tax disadvantages on certain forms of environmentally relevant behaviour such as the taxes on low emission products/vehicles and on waste water.[309]

8.158 A further step in this direction—with focus on global climate change—is the comprehensive taxation of energy consumption including electricity. The Federal Republic has now made the first steps towards an ecological reform of the tax system. Its statutory backbone is a federal Act introducing the ecological reform of the tax system, which entered into force on 1 April 1999.[310] The underlying idea is not only to encourage internalizing environmental costs (as an expression of the polluter pays principle) otherwise visited on the 'free' environment, but also to use the revenues of the reform to promote employment through the reduction of

[305] Federal decree on the energy saving isolation of buildings (*Wärmeschutzverordnung*) of 16 August 1994 (BGBl part I, 2121), containing requirements for buildings with normal room temperatures (eg living rooms and offices), for buildings with low room temperatures (eg some warehouses), and for alterations of existing buildings.—Federal decree on heating devices and devices for industrial water (*Heizungsanlagen-Verordnung*), 4 May 1998 (BGBl, part I, 851). Federal decree on the settlement of accounts of the heating costs in accordance with the individual consumption (*Verordnung über Heizkostenabrechnung*), 20 January 1989 (BGBl, part I, 115). The Federal Act on the modernization of flats and energy saving of 12 July 1978 (BGBl, part I, 993) functions as a supplement.

[306] Especially § 5(1) of the Federal Act on the protection against harmful emissions (*Bundesimmissionsschutzgesez BImSchG*) and 2 of the first federal decree on small heating devices (*1. Bundesimmissionsschutzverordnung* of 15 July 1988, published in BGBl, 1059).

[307] See for example—concerning the obligatory information on the energy consumption of household devices—the Act for the transformation of legal Acts of the European Communities in the field of energy saving by household appliances *(Energieverbrauchskennzeichnungsgesetz)* of 1 July 1997 (BGBl, part 1, 1632) with the subsequent federal decree (*Energieverbrauchskennzeichnung von Haushaltsgeräten*) of 30 October 1997 (BGBl, part I, 2616).

[308] See for example: M Schladebach, *Landesgesetzgebung im Recht der Energieeinsparung*, in RdE 1998, 139ff; J-P Schneider, *Landesenergierecht und Grundgesetz*, 1997; see also sections 2.1. and 2.2. above for further references.

[309] See also M Kloepfer, *Umweltrecht*, 2nd edn 1998, 314ff for further references.

[310] At the first stage—others will follow––the mineral oil taxes will be raised by 0.03 Euro (heating oil 0.02 Euro) per litre, gas tax will be increased by 0.0016 Euro per KWH. A new tax of 0.01 Euro per KWH will be imposed on electricity.

labour costs. Therefore the entire project aims at finding a combined solution for the urgent contemporary problems of unemployment and climate change.

Ecological reforms are subject to severe criticism based on essentially two arguments. First, there is an inherent conflict within the concept of the reform, in particular, increasing revenues from environmental taxes in order to make labour cheaper. This contravenes the idea of creating incentives to reduce energy consumption.[311] Second, it is regarded as inconsistent and unfair to exempt certain branches of industry, as well as the use of brown coal and hard coal, from the burdens of the reform project. **8.159**

G. District Heating (*Fernwärme*)

Unlike network-bound electricity and gas supply, district heating (*Fernwärme*) does not fall within the scope of the new Energy Act. This type of energy is only suitable for short-distance transport, i.e. its source (district heating plant, industrial plant, or any other device providing for example waste heat for district heating) must be close to consumers.[312] Despite its undeniable relevance for energy saving and environmental protection, district heating does not require special regulation, since plant operators are already under a legal obligation to use waste heat themselves or to make it available to third parties that are willing to take it over.[313] Again, the district heating supplier has to supply its clients with steam, condensed or hot water as a heating source in accordance with general supply conditions, which must themselves be compatible with the federal decree on the district heating supply conditions.[314] On the other hand, the client is obliged to cover its energy demands by district heating, as far as agreed upon.[315] However, this obligation does not impair its right to use additional regenerative energy sources such as wood. **8.160**

[311] See for example M Kloepfer, op cit 315.

[312] For technical details, see G Deuster, *Die Fernwärmeversorgung*, in G Püttner (ed), Handbuch der kommunalen Wissenschaft und Praxis, 2nd edn, vol 5, 1984, 307. Recent data are published in *Bundestags-Drucksache* 12/7113.

[313] See § 5 of the federal Act on the protection against harmful emissions—*Bundesimmissionsschutzgesetz* (*BImSchG*)—in the version of 14 May 1990 (BGBl, part I, 880) with later modifications. For further details, see HD Jarass, *Bundesimmissionsschutzgesetz, Kommentar,* 4th edn, 1999, § 5, margin number 77.

[314] The *Verordnung über allgemeine Bedingungen für die Fernwärmeversorgung von Tarifkunden, AVBFernwärmeV* of 19 January 1989 (BGBl, part I, 109).

[315] As to the tacit conclusion of a contract by making use of district heating in accordance with § 2(2) *AVBFernwärmeV* and as to later charge: Higher Regional Court (*Oberlandesgericht*) of Düsseldorf, in Recht der Energiewirtschaft (RdE) 1993, 240.

H. Energy Security

(1) The Energy Safeguarding Act

8.161 The most important law on the national level is 'the federal Act safeguarding the energy supply in times of endangered or obstructed imports of crude oil, mineral oil products, or natural gas',[316] the Energy Safeguarding Act,[317] which protects energy supply against obstructions from abroad (for example by OPEC). As the long name of the statute indicates, energy supply has to be safeguarded in case of obstruction or immediate danger.[318] Measures interfering with the production, storage, transport, distribution, trade, or use of these energy sources, as well as determining price limits, or imposing comprehensive bookkeeping or registration duties may only take place in case of a market failure, which makes it impossible or unreasonable to overcome the supply disruption in a reasonable time. In such cases trade and consumption can be limited, for example by restricting the use of motor vehicles.[319] The federal Government may pass the respective decrees in advance,[320] which will enter into force as soon as the federal Government officially declares the state of supply disruption in the form of another decree.[321] This is specialized emergency law in the event of an energy crisis. In addition, there is the general emergency law designed for the state of war (*Verteidigungsfall*) or similar political crises (*Spannungsfall,* i.e. 'state of tension'), which also contains regulations concerning energy supply.[322]

(2) The Petroleum Storage Act

8.162 To prevent oil shortages on the national level, the federal Act on the minimum storage of mineral oil products from 9 September 1965[323] introduced a duty on

[316] Komplette amtl. Bezeichnung *Energiesicherungsgesetz—EnSG* from 20 December 1974 (BGBl, part I, 3681), changed by the law from 19 December 1979 (BGBl, part. I, 2305).

[317] For an overview, see R Grawert, *Gesetzliche Regelungen zur Versorgungssicherung und Energieeinsparung,* in Festschrift für F Fabricius, 1989, 335ff (341ff).

[318] See § 1 (1) of the Energy Safeguarding Act.

[319] See ibid, § 1(3).

[320] For example: Federal decree limiting the delivery of fuels in times of supply disorder from 26 April 1982 (BGBl, part. I, 520); federal decree limiting the delivery of light heating oil in times of supply disorder from 26 April 1982 (BGBl, part. I, 536); federal decree safeguarding the electricity supply in times of supply disorder—*Elektrizitätssicherungsverordnung*—from 26 April 1982 (BGBl, part I, 514); federal decree safeguarding the gas supply in times of supply disorder—*Gassicherungsverordnung*—from 26 April 1982 (BGBl, part I, 517).

[321] See § 1(3) of the Energy Safeguarding Act.

[322] The following decrees have been passed on grounds of the federal Act safeguarding the economy (*Wirtschaftssicherstellungsgesetz*): Federal decree rationing mineral oil (*Mineralölbewirtschaftungsverordnung*) from 19 April 1988 (BGBl, part. I, 530); federal decree distributing the electricity supply duties (*Elektrizitätslastverteilungsverordnung*) from 21 July 1976 (BGBl, part I, 1833), in the form of its publication from 19 April 1988 (BGBl, part I, 535); federal decree concerning the distribution of the gas supply duties (*Gaslastverteilungsverordnung*) from 21 July 1976 (BGBl, part I, 1849), in the form of its publication from 19 April 1988 (BGBl, part I, 549).

[323] Titel (BGBl, part I, 1217).

private oil importers to store a certain amount of mineral oil products. Nowadays the federal Act on the storage of mineral oil products (*Erdölbevorratungsgesetz*, ie Petroleum Storage Act) from 25 July 1978[324] obliges the importers to store the equivalent of 80 days' consumption of crude oil, mineral oil products, and related products. Domestic producers are under the additional obligation to store the equivalent of 15 days' production.[325]

(3) *The Mineral Oil Data Act*

In order to ensure Germany's compliance with its obligations arising from the international energy programme, further federal legislation[326] imposes registration duties on everyone extracting, importing, exporting, or refining crude oil or mineral oil products commercially. **8.163**

I. General Outlook

The previous sections have revealed that German energy law is a most heterogeneous subject which is always in a process of change and development. Since it extends also to constitutional law, general administrative law, competition law, environmental law, civil law, and, not least, EC law, energy law is regarded as 'cross-sectional matter'. **8.164**

Any prognosis is therefore difficult. For limited sectors of energy law, one could for example speculate on the fate of the German coal policy. Here, much depends on the outcome of the current energy target talks between the federal Government and the commercial entities involved. The EC subsidy control is also of paramount importance. The further development of nuclear energy law will depend on the current nuclear energy target talks, especially regarding the question of the disposal of nuclear wastes. **8.165**

Concerning network-bound energy supply, Germany chose a 'middle of the road approach' of negotiated third party access and single buyer system when implementing the EC directive on an internal market for electricity.[327] This solution pays tribute to specific structural and legal features of the German energy sector. Developments in the other Member States will show whether an approximation **8.166**

---

[324] BGBl, part I, 1073, now valid in the form of its publication from 8 December 1987 (BGBl, part I, 2509).

[325] cf § 25 of the Petroleum Storage Act. For the question whether the compulsory storage of mineral oil violates fundamental rights, see Federal Constitutional Court, in BVerfGE vol 30, 292ff.

[326] *Mineralöldatengesetz*, i.e. Mineral Oil Data Act, of 20 December 1988 (BGBl, part I, 2353), changed by law from 31 August 1990 (BGBl, part II, 889).

[327] G Kühne, *Incremental Regulatory Reform and Antitrust Law in the Energy Sector: the German 'Middle of the Road' Approach*, in Journal of Energy and Natural Ressources Law, Bd 14 (1996), 76ff.

of the individual systems—perhaps in the form of something like a 'pool system'—can be achieved. It can be expected that the new government will initiate changes in the new Energy Act with regard to the role of the municipalities and of renewable energy sources. There is little doubt, however, that the process of liberalization will result in comprehensive concentration developments within the energy sector. It would not be surprising if, of the approximately 1000 energy suppliers at present, only 100 will survive at the end.

8.167 The new pressure of competition will furthermore affect the composition of the so-called 'primary energy mix'. There is already a trend towards smaller, highly efficient and cost-saving gas and combination power plants. The future role of renewable energy sources will also depend on the existing privileges which provide those energy forms with the necessary economic basis. It is worth asking, however, whether these support mechanisms are reconcilable with the prerequisites of European Community law. The still somewhat unclear scope of the exemption clause of Article 90 (2) EC could gain paramount importance in this connection. The same is true for the earlier Article 7d, now Article 16.[328]

Bibliography

From the wide range of energy and mineral law literature we list the following works:

Energy Law

Baur, Jürgen F (ed.), *Reform des Energiewirtschaftsgesetzes*, Baden-Baden (Nomos) 1991; idem (ed), *Aktuelle Probleme des Energierechts*, Baden-Baden (Nomos) 1995; Ulrich Büdenbender, *Energierecht—Eine systematische Darstellung des gesamten Rechts der öffentlichen Energieversorgung*, Munich/Cologne (Technischer Verlag Resch/Verlag TÜV Rheinland) 1982; idem, *Die Kartellaufsicht über die Energiewirtschaft*, Baden-Baden (Nomos) 1995; Eugene D Cross, *Electric utility regulation in the European Union*, National Report Germany, Chichester 1996, 127 ff; Dirk Ehlers, *Das Energiewirtschaftsrecht*, in N Achterberg, and G Püttner (eds), Besonderes Verwaltungsrecht, vol I: Wirtschafts-, Bau-, Kultus- und Dienstrecht, Heidelberg (CF Müller) 1990, 188 ff; Hans-Ulrich Evers, *Das Recht der Energieversorgung*, 2nd edn, Baden-Baden (Nomos), 1983; Georg Hermes, *Staatliche Infrastrukturverantwortung (Rechtliche Grundstrukturen netzgebundener Transport- und Übertragungssysteme zwischen Daseinsvorsorge und Wettbewerbsregulierung am Beispiel der leitungsgebundenen Energieversorgung in Europa*, typescript, Freiburg i.Brsg. 1996 (to be published soon); Wolfgang Hoffmann-Riem, and Jens-Peter Schneider (eds), *Umweltpolitische Steuerung in einem liberalisierten Strommarkt*, Baden-Baden (Nomos) 1995; Uwe Hüffer, Knut Ipsen, and Peter J Tettinger (eds), *Berg- und Energierecht vor den Fragen der Gegenwart*, Festschrift für Fritz Fabricius, Stuttgart/Munich/Hanover (Boorberg) 1989; Wolfgang Löwer,

[328] See: J-C Pielow, *Grundstrukturen öffentlicher Versorgung—Grundlagen des Europäischen Gemeinschaftsrechts, des französischen und des deutschen Rechts unter besonderer Berücksichtigung der Elektrizitätswirtschaft*, 1999.

Energieversorgung zwischen Staat, Gemeinde und Wirtschaft, Cologne/Berlin/Bonn/Munich (Carl Heymanns) 1989; Peter J Tettinger, chapters *Recht der Energiewirtschaft* and *Recht des Bergbaus*, in R Schmidt (ed), Öffentliches Wirtschaftsrecht—Besonderer Teil 1, Berlin/Heidelberg a.o. (Springer) 1995 (§§ 7 and 8); see also the articles within the chapter *Energierecht*, in Jürgen F Baur, Peter-Christian Müller-Graff, and Manfred Zuleeg (eds), *Europarecht—Energierecht—Wirtschaftsrecht, Festschrift für Bodo Börner zum 70. Geburtstag*, Cologne/Berlin/Bonn/Munich (Carl Heymanns) 1992.

Systematic Commentaries to Specific Acts

Haedrich, Heinz, *Atomgesetz (Kommentar)*, 1986; Wolfgang Ludwig, and Hans Odenthal (eds), *Recht der Elektrizitäts-, Gas- und Wasserversorgung*, loose-leaf edition, last completion: December 1996, Neuwied/Berlin a.o. (Luchterhand); Wolfgang Obernolte, and Wolfgang Danner, *Energiewirtschaftsrecht*, loose-leaf edition, last completion: August 1995, Munich (Beck); Wilm Tegethoff, Ulrich Büdenbender, and Heinz Klinger, *Das Recht der öffentlichen Energieversorgung*, loose-leaf edition, last completion: October 1995, Essen (Energiewirtschaft und Technik Verlagsgesellschaft); (ed), *Aktuelle Entwicklungen im Kernenergierecht*, 1997; P Salje, *Stromeinspeisungsgesetz* [commentary to the Feed-In Act], 1999.

Journals: Recht der Energiewirtschaft (RdE); Energiewirtschaftliche Tagesfragen (et).

Mineral Law

Kühne, Gunther, and Gaentsch, Günter, *Wandel und Beharren im Bergrecht*, Baden-Baden (Nomos) 1992; Jan-Dirk Rausch, *Umwelt- und Planungsrecht beim Bergbau*, Baden-Baden (Nomos) 1990; Raimund Willecke, and G Turner, *Grundriß des Bergrechts*, 2nd edn, Berlin (Springer) 1970; Wirtschaftsvereinigung Bergbau (ed), *Das Bergbau-Handbuch*, 4th edn, Essen (Glückauf) 1983; H Zydek, *Bundesberggesetz—Materialien*, Essen (Glückauf) 1980; von Danwitz, and Hüffer (eds), Bergbau und Umwelt, 1999.

Commentaries

Boldt, Gerhard, and Weller, Herbert, *Bundesberggesetz*, 1984, and suppl vol—*Ergänzungsband*—Stuttgart/Berlin a.o. (Kohlhammer) 1992; Reinhart Piens, Hans-Wolfgang Schulte, and Stephan Graf Vitzthum, *Bundesberggesetz*, 1983.

Journals

Zeitschrift für Bergrecht (ZfB); Glückauf.

General titles in English

Cross, ED, *Electric Utility Regulation in the European Union: A Country by Country Guide*, 1996, 127 ff; G Kühne, *Monopoly and Competition in Energy Supply: Federal Republic of Germany*, in JERL 7 (1989), Supplement, 31 ff; *Incremental Regulatory Reform and Antitrust Law in the Energy Sector*: the German 'Middle of the Road' Approach, in JERL 14 (1996), 76 ff; *Jurisdiction to Enforce Competition Law in Europe: An Analysis of the European and German Legal Regimes*, in JERL 16 (1998), 68 ff; G Kühne, and

J Trealese, *The New West German Mining Law*, in Land and Water Law Review 19 (1984), 371 ff.

Key legislation

Constitutional law:

Basic law of the Federal Republic of Germany (*Grundgesetz für die Bundesrepublik Deutschland)* of 23 December 1949 (*Bundegsetzblatt*—BGBl Part I, p 1) last modified by Act of 16 July 1998 (BGBl Part I, p 1822)

Statutory law

Federal Mining Act (*Bundesberggesetz, BBergG*) of 13 August 1980 (BGBl Part I, p 1310), last modified 1990.

(Federal) Act on the (network-bound) supply with electricity and gas [energy act] (*Gesetz über die Elektrizitäts- und Gasversorgung (Energiewirtschaftsgesetz—EnWG)* of 24 April 1998 (BGBl Part I, p 730).

(Federal) Act on the peaceful use of nuclear power and the protection against its risks (Nuclear Act) (*Gesetz über die friedliche Verwendung der Kernenergie und den Schutz gegen ihre Gefahren (Atomgesetz)*) in its version of 15 July 1985 (BGBl Part I, p 1565) with later modifications.

(Federal) Act concerning the 'feeding-in' of electricity from renewable energy sources into public supply grids (*Stromeinspeisungsgesetz—StEG*) of 7 December 1990 (BGBl Part I, p 2633), lastly altered by Article 3 No. 2 of the Energy Law Reform Act of 28 November 1997 (BGBl 1998, Part I, p 730).

9

ENERGY LAW IN ITALY

Fabricio Nocera and Martha M Roggenkamp[1]

[1] This chapter is based on a text provided by Mr Luca Mezzetti of the University of Bologna.

A. Introduction

9.01 Italy depends on imports for over four-fifths of its energy supplies. There is some domestic primary energy production in Italy. Gas accounts for over half of indigenous production with the other significant contributions coming from hydropower and oil. As far as final energy consumption is concerned, oil is the most important energy resource as it accounts for over half of final consumption. Gas accounts for about a quarter of primary energy consumption. Hence, Italy is the third largest gas consumer in Europe. The demand for gas is almost equal for residential/commercial consumers and industry (some 40 per cent). The demand for electricity generation is steadily increasing. Currently, electricity consumption accounts for about 15 per cent of the final energy consumption. As nuclear energy is being phased out, about 80 per cent of electric power is generated on the basis of thermal energy, mostly oil-fired plants. Coal is also used for power generation. Besides, coal is applied as coke for steel production. Some 95 per cent of the coal used in Italy is imported.

9.02 Two major companies dominate the Italian energy sector. Since 1962 ENEL has had a monopoly over the import and supply of electricity and most (about 80 per cent) of the electricity production. The company *Ente Nazionale Idrocarburi* (or ENI) dominates the hydrocarbons sector. ENI is a vertically integrated company as it directly (or indirectly) operates the production and supply of hydrocarbons, ie oil, gas, and coal. Whereas ENI's subsidiary AGIP controls a substantial share of the gas reserves and produces almost all the gas, ENI also controls about 35 per cent of Italy's downstream oil supplies. SNAM, another wholly owned subsidiary of ENI, is responsible for the purchase, transport, and sale of most natural gas to distributors and to industrial consumers. Both ENEL and ENI are in the process of being privatized.

(1) State Organization and the Legislative Framework

State organization

9.03 Italy has been a republic since 1947. Although sovereignty is vested in the State, important powers are given to decentralized government institutions. Some regions are almost autonomous. Since the 1990s more powers have been given to the provinces, metropolitan areas, and municipalities (*comunes*).

9.04 Institutional developments began in 1972 when, in implementation of constitutional provisions, the regions were created as entities vested with legislative and administrative functions, carried out by the regional 'parliament' (*consiglio regionale*) and the regional 'government' (*Giunta Regional*). The regions may reassign certain functions within their own structure (provinces, which form a region, and municipalities or *comuni*). The State maintains *vis-à-vis* the regions a co-ordination and guidance role with a view to ensuring a harmonized overall policy.

In general, 'decentralizing' entails that, while certain basic functions are reserved to the State, a number of functions are 'delegated' to the regions (meaning that the function is still vested primarily in the State);[2] some other functions are transferred to the regions, which are thus directly entrusted to them. **9.05**

In the course of time, decentralization has evolved to the effect of entailing increased powers for the local (*stricto sensu*) entities (*comuni*) whereas provinces have lost a good deal of their traditional prerogatives. However, they have recently acquired new authority in various respects and areas. **9.06**

Legislative framework

The Italian legal system consists of primary law, the Constitution of 1946, and two categories of secondary law: *legge formale*, ie a law adopted by the parliament, and *legge sostanziale*, ie a law not adopted by the procedure typical of a *legge formale* but having the same binding nature. The latter category includes provisions which may be the object of a Legislative Decree (DLgvo), a Prime Minister's Decree (DPCM), or an inter-ministerial decree (when the competence or interest lies with the Government as a whole or with more than one Ministry), or a ministerial decree (DM), depending on the competence of a given Ministry. In certain cases (for specific or very technical matters, due to time constraints, etc) the Parliament is empowered to delegate to the Government the right to legislate. The delegation is subject to strict requirements, non-compliance with which would make the Government's provisions illegitimate. **9.07**

A Decree-Law (*Decreto-Legge*, DL) is adopted by the Government for reasons of urgency and enters into force immediately but it must be converted into a law (by the Parliament) within 60 days from entry into force. If not, it loses effect unless it is resubmitted within that deadline and with amendments (but repeated resubmission is not always welcomed by the Parliament). Besides this, a Decree of the President of the Republic (DPR) is the form in which a (substantial) law is often promulgated, normally involving the competence of the Government as a whole. The President (who has no direct legislative power) promulgates the laws adopted by the Parliament. **9.08**

[2] It also means that the State is empowered to withdraw the 'delegation' should the region fail to perform the delegated functions satisfactorily.

B. The Origins and Development of Energy law

(1) Introduction

9.09 The Italian legal system has no basic law on energy. Instead there is a wide range of regulations and public entities organizing the energy sector.

9.10 The need for energy regulation was felt in the 1930s because of the significant role energy played in the process of industrialization. Consequently, the Civil Code was amended in order to include the provision that every type of energy is to be considered a natural good.[3] This amended provision reflects the new approach of the legislator towards the energy sector.

9.11 Article 43 of the Constitution is of special importance, and applies to the energy sector in the widest meaning, including all industrial appliances. The Constitution, in giving specific recognition to the energy sector, set the premises for the creation of a legal system.

9.12 Although the origins of energy law lie at the beginning of this century, its main development started in the 1960s when several energy sector-specific statutes were adopted. The most important laws concern:

—the institution of the ENI (National Entity for Hydrocarbons) in 1953;[4]
—the search for and development of liquid and gaseous hydrocarbons in the mainland on national territory;[5]
—the institution of a national committee for nuclear energy (*Comitato Nazionale per l'Energia Nucleare* or CNEN) in 1960; replaced by the ENEA (*Comitato nazionale per la ricerca e per lo sviluppo dell'energia nucleare e delle energie alternative*) in 1982;[6] further amendments in 1991 and 1999;
—the institution of ENEL (*Ente Nazionale per l'Energia Elettrica* or National Board for Electricity) in 1962;[7]
—the possibility by ENEL to take over permits to produce hydroelectricity from local bodies and auto-producers;[8]
—the regulation of energy savings and the rational use of energy, the development of renewable energy sources and the operation of power stations generated with non-fossil fuel;[9]

[3] Art 814 Civil Code. This definition applies to all types of energy, ie natural resources as well as 'artificial energy' such as electricity. According to the law every type of energy with economic value which, to every title, could be found in nature (with the sole exception of animal energy whose enjoyment uses traditionally different techniques) is considered a good.
[4] Law of 10 February 1953, No 136.
[5] Law of 11 January 1957, No 6, then amended by Law No 613 of 24 July 1964.
[6] Law of 11 August 1960, No 933, and Law of 5 March 1982, No 84.
[7] Law of 6 December 1962, No 1643.
[8] Law of 7 August 1982, No 529.
[9] Law of 29 May 1982, No 308 and Laws No 9 and No 10 of 9 January 1991.

—the direct transformation into share companies of public-sector entities such as ENEL, ENI, IRI, and INA;[10]
—the institution of a Regulatory Authority for the electricity and gas sectors.[11]

In addition, mention should be made of the extensive economic planning that has taken place in Italy since the adoption by the Inter-Ministerial Council for Economic Planning (CIPE) of the first five-year plan (*Piano Energetico Nazionale* or PEN) in 1975 after the 1973 oil crisis. The first PEN aimed at the diversification of energy supply and energy savings. Similar goals were included in the second PEN of 1981 albeit with an increase, as nuclear power was included in order to meet the increased need for electricity. The goals of these PENs have not been reached. This is, *inter alia*, due to the financial situation of the ENEL and the political opposition to important parts of the plan.[12] Hence, the 1988 PEN (covering the period to the year 2000) included two additional goals: environmental protection and competition in energy production. A first step towards a policy on privatization and liberalization of the energy sector was taken. Laws no 9 and no 10 of 1991 give effect to the 1988 PEN and are considered to be important reform laws. **9.13**

(2) *The Role of the Constitution within the Energy Sector*

The section of the Constitution entitled 'Economic Relationship' regulates both 'public and private enterprises' (Arts 41 and 43) and 'property and ownership' (Arts 42 and 44). Both issues are of specific interest for the energy sector. **9.14**

Article 42 of the Constitution rules that property and ownership can be private or public and, subsequently, that economic commodities can belong to the State, public bodies, or private persons. Although the Constitution states that private economic enterprises are open to all, it also provides some limits for these enterprises. Private enterprises cannot be applied in such a way that they are in conflict with the social functions they have to develop.[13] As with public enterprises, it is important to note that laws should prescribe such instruments for planning and control as may be advisable for directing and co-ordinating the economic activities towards social objectives.[14] **9.15**

As in most civil law countries, the Constitution confirms that the Italian legal system is based on the principle of private ownership. Private ownership is recognized and guaranteed by laws. Consequently, private property can only be **9.16**

[10] Law of 8 August 1992, No 359.
[11] Law of 14 November 1995, No 481.
[12] L Hancher, 'The Nuclear Referenda in Italy and their Consequences' Journal of Energy and Natural Resources Law, vol 6, no 2, 1988, 137–53.
[13] Art 41 para 2 Constitution.
[14] ibid, para 3.

expropriated in the general interest and in such cases as are prescribed by law and with provisions for compensation.[15]

9.17 Article 43 of the Constitution represents the most significant provision with regard to the energy (ie electricity) sector as it provides for the nationalization of the industry. It rules that:

> For purposes of general utility the law may reserve in the first instance or transfer, by means of expropriation and payment of compensation, to the State, to public bodies, or to labour or consumers, communities, certain undertakings or categories of undertakings operating essential public services, energy sources, or exercising monopolies with the character of outstanding general interest.

9.18 In other words, nationalization is restricted to reasons of general utility and to some specific undertakings, ie undertakings operating essential public services and energy sources.

9.19 The Constitution offers two possible ways for nationalization. In the first place, certain undertakings or categories of undertakings may be reserved to the activities of the State or to other (public) bodies. In the second place, certain undertakings can be transferred by means of expropriation, and upon payment of compensation, from the State or certain (public) bodies. The latter type of nationalization is comparable to the traditional instrument of expropriation provided for by Articles 42 and 44 of the Constitution.

(3) The Institutional Framework: the Establishment of Public Utilities in the Energy Sector

Introduction

9.20 As a consequence of these Constitutional provisions, the production and supply of energy in Italy is to a large extent undertaken by public-sector enterprises. These enterprises are established and/or operated on the basis of public law. Examples are the establishment of ENI (National Entity for Hydrocarbons) for the exploration, production, and supply of hydrocarbons, the institution of the national Commission for nuclear energy (*Comitato Nazionale per l'Energia Nucleare* or CNEN), and the institution of ENEL (National Entity for Electric Energy). Since the nuclear referendum in 1987, nuclear energy has gradually been phased out. The role of the ENEA has therefore also changed: its focus is now on non-nuclear sources of energy.

9.21 In the Italian energy sector, there has been a clear movement from a trend for nationalization and public control in the 1960s and 1970s to one of privatization, liberalization, and reorganization in the 1980s and 1990s. Both trends are discussed below.

[15] Art 42, paras 2 and 3.

The Establishment of the national entity for hydrocarbons (ENI)

The National Entity for Hydrocarbons (*Ente Nazionale Idrocarburi* or ENI) was established as a public law corporation or 'public entity by law' in 1953.[16] As a public entity it had no capital by shares, but an endowment fund made up from contributions from the State. Hence it was fully owned by the State and subject in its decisions to Government instructions.[17] ENI was assigned by law to promote and carry on undertakings of national interest in the field of hydrocarbons and natural steam.[18] In addition, ENI received the exclusive right, in the area of the Upper Adriatic, to explore and exploit hydrocarbons as well as to establish and operate pipelines for the carriage of these hydrocarbons. Only the remaining national territory was open to exploration and production by other entities on the basis of private competition.[19] **9.22**

ENI does not carry out the assigned activities directly but through a number of subsidiary companies, which are wholly or partly owned by ENI. Following the exclusive functions assigned to ENI by law, it was not only assumed that ENI had the power to create these subsidiaries but also that these subsidiary companies should be controlled by ENI, or entirely delegated to public powers. In contrast with ENI, most subsidiaries were not established as public entities but as private law companies subject to the general rules on corporations in the Italian Civil Code. **9.23**

As one can easily comprehend from the letter of the law, ENI arose as a single-sector entity that could intervene solely in the sectors linked to hydrocarbons and natural steam. This scope was extended some years later as two new paragraphs were added to Article 1 of the original Act of 1957.[20] It was then ruled that ENI could promote and carry on undertakings of national interest in the chemical sector and in the sector of nuclear fuel research, production, reprocessing, and supply, as well as in the mining, exploration, and production sectors pertaining to the latter activity. Involvement in other sectors is subject to prior explicit authorization by the Minister of State Holdings and is only permitted to the extent that these activities are connected to the hydrocarbons, steam, chemical, and nuclear sectors in the sense of being instrumental or complementary thereto. In other words, ENI could expand its activities as long as there was an instrumental relationship with the basic industries. This required instrumental link, however, has not been observed in the course of the years: ENI, through the instrument of State participation, has succeeded in carrying out diversification policies. As a **9.24**

[16] Law No 136/1953.

[17] M Nicolazzi, 'Petroleum Law and Petroleum Joint Ventures in Italy', Journal of Energy and Natural Resources Law, vol 8, 1990, 39.

[18] Art 1, Law No 136/1953.

[19] Law of 11 January 1957, No 6.

[20] Law of 19 September 1967, No 1153.

consequence, the initial spectrum of activities was amplified by the addition of a great number of new enterprises unconnected with the oil-chemical sector.

9.25 Consequently, ENI can be characterized as a vertically integrated company dealing with the exploration and production of hydrocarbons as well as the processing, transportation, and supply of these energy resources.

Nationalisation in the electricity sector: The case of ENEL

Introduction

9.26 The only complete nationalization that took place concerned the electricity sector, as this was the only sector where all the elements of Article 43 of the Constitution were present at the same time, ie (i) undertakings or categories of undertakings operating essential public services, (ii) energy sources, and (iii) the existence of monopolies with the character of outstanding general interest.

9.27 Since its early developments, the Italian electricity sector was characterized by private initiative. As Italian law did not give the State or local bodies the opportunity to establish power lines, the electricity supply system was in fact developed by private undertakings. Only the generation of hydroelectricity required a Government concession. Local bodies were given the legal right, however, to supervise the utilities directly by Law no 103 of 29 March 1903. Royal Decree of 15 October 1925 which finally implemented the 1903 law provided that local utilities could be organized either through direct management or through permits to private and special corporations.[21] Consequently, in the 1930s some 90 per cent of the electricity sector was in the hands of private undertakings. After the Second World War the situation changed as politics aimed at the nationalization of the electricity sector which resulted in a Nationalization Act in 1962.[22]

The Nationalization Law

9.28 Law 1643/1962 provided the basic features of the nationalization process. Article 1 ruled that a new entity called ENEL (*Ente Nazionale per l'Energia Elettrica*) should exercise 'in the national territory the activities of production, import-export, transmission, transformation, distribution, and supply of electric energy, whatever the primary energy source'. ENEL was considered the only institution qualified to carry out all these activities. As a consequence, the property of all private enterprises undertaking activities in the electricity sector at the time, directly

[21] The opportunity to 'municipalize' the energy sector was first discussed at the beginning of 1900 under the Giolitti Government, when public utilities were managed by small private enterprises which, not being able individually to meet the market requirements, could not supply reliable, economic, and impartial service.

[22] ED Cross, *Electric Utility Regulation in the European Union* (1996) ch 5: 'Italy: Returning to private enterprise?'.

or indirectly, was completely transferred to the new public entity following payment of adequate compensation on behalf of the State.

In accordance with the nationalization law, all electricity companies were integrated into the new company ENEL.[23] The non-electricity related activities were kept out of the nationalization, and returned to the original companies. The material transfer into the new company happened gradually and was difficult because of the many economic interests and the multitude of subjects operating on the market before nationalization, who resisted the coercive privatization of the electricity sector. The parties unsuccessfully challenged the transfer before the Constitutional Court. The Court of Justice of the European Communities also upheld the Italian nationalization law, as it declared no conflict to exist between an electricity monopoly and the prohibitions imposed by the Treaty of Rome on the introduction of restraints to establishment freedom, and to the institution of new national monopolies with commercial character.[24] **9.29**

However, the nationalization law also provided for some exceptions to the nationalization requirement. Local bodies assigned with services of general interest (= municipal utilities), auto-producers generating electricity for their own need, and companies producing a limited amount of electricity (less than 15 KWh) were exempted from nationalization.[25] Following the 1970s oil crises and the need to diversify the energy sector, Law 393/1975 granted to local bodies also the right to undertake the establishment of facilities generating electricity on the basis of non-fossil fuels such as steam and waste combustion. In addition, local bodies could exercise preferential permit rights to hydroelectricity. **9.30**

However, in the 1980s the position of ENEL was again strengthened. First, Law 309/1981 enabled ENEL to create companies and joint boards with public entities and local bodies in order to carry out initiatives for energy savings, rational use of energy sources, and the realization and operation of plants for electricity generation, transmission, and distribution. Law no 308 of 29 May 1982 also gave ENEL the right to take over the exploitation of hydroelectricity where permits held by local bodies and auto-producers were due to expire. ENEL had the option to take over the facilities if they could show there would be an increase in energy and power production. **9.31**

The functions of ENEL as a public economic entity

ENEL was instituted and regulated as a public economic entity with autonomous legal personality and the function of managing electricity services (production, transmission, and supply) according to economic criteria. Consequently, labour **9.32**

[23] Art 4, para 1, Law 1643/1962.
[24] See the famous *Costa v Enel* case 6/64, ECJ 15 July 1964.
[25] Art 4, paras 5, 6, 8, Law 1643/1962.

relations were regulated by civil law provisions and on the ground of collective and individual agreements.

9.33 The qualification of ENEL as an economic public entity brought about some interesting legal consequences. First, the extent of the legal provisions applying to ENEL increased, as one should take into account both Law 1643/1962 and the general legislation. Nevertheless, ENEL could operate in a more flexible legal environment due to the fact that public entities are not subject to the normal rules of bankruptcy and company law.

9.34 Secondly, the question arose: to what extent should ENEL be autonomous? The company was awarded extensive management autonomy from the central Government. This did not result in a total lack of guidelines and public control over ENEL's activities, as it remained a public subject governed by 'the law governing public utilities', which requires the presence of a government representative on the board.

9.35 ENEL was originally forbidden to create new companies or to participate in them, with the exception of foreign companies whose main function was the import and export of electricity to and from Italy.[26] This prohibition was partially relieved in the 1980s by new provisions which allowed ENEL to participate in companies or joint boards in particular circumstances (see above). In this way, the legislator intended to increase the competence of ENEL without weakening the legal basis on which the electricity system is based: the law reserving activities of public interest to the State.

(4) The Reorganization of the Energy Sector: From Privatization to Liberalization

Introduction

9.36 In the late 1980s, after the fading of the nationalization regime and of the public presence in the economy, political forces aimed at the reorganization of the energy sector as well as the other big public entities (see paragraphs 9.09–9.13 above). The reorganization policy also resulted in some large-scale privatization operations which were not based merely on the need to improve industrial performance by increasing the role of market forces but were also driven by the need to reduce the Italian Government's budget deficits. The privatization process began in 1992 when the Government issued a decree (*decreto legge* 333 of July 11, converted into Law 359/92) concerning urgent measures for the establishment of public finances.

[26] The ground for this prohibition was fear that ENEL's entry into fields other than electricity would adversely effect the quality of service to consumers, and increase costs.

The Privatization of ENI

Following the general trend of privatization, the Government also focused on the position of ENI. The first step towards privatization was the commercialization or corporatization of ENI in 1992 when it was restructured into a joint stock company. After the establishment of ENI SpA, the Ministry of Finance placed some 64 per cent of the shares of ENI on the market. After the first offer in November 1995, three more rounds were organized in 1996, 1997, and 1998. Currently, ENI is holding a complex of companies dealing not only with energy (such as AGIP, SNAM) and the chemical industry (Enimont) but also in other sectors such as the mechanical, engineering, and tourist sectors.[27] **9.37**

ENI's energy division is vertically integrated since ENI's incorporation of AGIP on January 1998. In other words, the exploration and production of hydrocarbons is managed directly by ENI through the AGIP division. Consequently, SNAM (another ENI subsidiary) transports and distributes natural gas in Italy. Finally, AGIP Petroli is responsible for refining and distributing petroleum products. **9.38**

The Privatization of ENEL

Despite many earlier proposals regarding the reorganization of the electricity sector, the most fundamental reorganization process started when the Government issued its privatization law in1992. As a result, the public company ENEL was transformed into a joint stock limited liability company (SpA or *società per azione*) in 1993.[28] However, the process of denationalization has proven to be complex and was further complicated by political developments.[29] The political situation and subsequent general elections in 1994 interrupted the process of privatization by Minister Ciampi, leaving to the succeeding Government the matter of the reorganization of ENEL. **9.39**

In the two following years, many theories about the reorganization of the electricity sector were formulated, of which two were particularly significant. Both theories focused on the restructuring of the company before privatization and reviewed the extent to which the electricity utility should be decentralized before denationalization.[30] The first option was to keep the unitary order, thus maintaining public supervision in property and management. At the same time **9.40**

[27] Subsidiaries of ENI are, *inter alia*, Nuovo Pignone, SNAM Progetti, and Nuova Samim.

[28] Art 15 of Decree 333/ 92, as converted to Law No 359 of 8 August 1992.

[29] MM Roggenkamp, 'Implications of Privatisation, Liberalisation and Integration of Network Bound Energy Systems', Journal of Energy and Natural Resources Law, vol 15, No 1, 1997, 51–61.

[30] The outcome of this discussion is also of importance for the award of an operating concession. In case of unbundling more concessions are required. Another point of interest is the duration of the operating concession. Originally, the Government issued a proposal to award ENEL a 99-year concession. According to Decree Law 333/92 the concession is limited to 20 years.

competition could be introduced by allowing a limited number of producers other than ENEL to enter the electricity market. The second option concerned the disintegration of ENEL, both on the vertical and horizontal level, into many different enterprises. The system's efficiency could be improved through the activation of direct competition in the production sector and indirect competition in the distribution sector. Hence, the above discussion basically dealt with the extent of competition that should be introduced in the sector.[31]

9.41 The privatization of an integrated ENEL proved to be the easiest solution, as it could take place without having to solve the delicate problems linked to restructuring the industry and issuing new rules for the proper functioning of the electricity system on a disintegrated base. At the same time, though, a system based on the total integration of production, transmission, and distribution under one big private corporation is not consistent with well balanced economic development.[32] It would merely lead to a major private monopoly and not create any competition in the sector and thus deviate from the European Community's liberalization policy. Therefore it was argued that the privatization of an integrated ENEL should be made dependent on the appointment of a separate regulator.[33]

C. The Present Legal Framework: Policy of Liberalization and Decentralization

(1) The Role of Government

9.42 The privatization process that started in 1992 led to the transformation of public entities into share companies. This policy was intended to achieve many purposes, in particular the recuperation of efficiency and competitiveness, the recapitalization of strong enterprises through the use of private venture capital, and the reduction of national debt.

9.43 In 1994 and 1995 legislation was adopted which accelerated the privatization and liberalization process as the legislator provided for the transfer of State interests to

---

[31] The antitrust authorities favour the unbundling of the company and aimed at 1) a 100% reduction of State ownership (denationalization) in the generation sector, 2) a 50% denationalization of the transmission sector, and finally 3) privatizing 10% of the distribution sector. However, the Government decided to privatize ENEL as a vertically integrated company.

[32] The transition from a public enterprise to the private sector would also have a detrimental effect on the national energy policy.

[33] Law No 537 of December 1993 states that the Government should set up a regulatory authority for public services by means of a legislative decree. It should be pointed out that the privatization is in fact made dependent on the creation of such regulatory authority, while norms accelerating the privatization process were being adopted (see para 9.43). The regulator will, *inter alia*, be entitled to define the technical modifications of the service, the setting and alteration of the tariffs, and the control of the universal service obligations.

the market.[34] It should be noted, however, that direct governmental control diminished as a result of the privatization process. In order to safeguard the role of market forces and to avoid the creation of a private monopoly, the legislator also provided for the establishment of a separate regulator for the gas and electricity sector.[35] This regulator plays an important role in the entire liberalization process.

In the same period a policy of decentralization was introduced. Specific regulatory powers were delegated to lower levels of Government. This policy has changed the role of the provinces and local governments with regard to many branches of the economy. These changes have, directly and/or indirectly, affected the distribution and supply of energy. **9.44**

(2) The Regulatory Authorities

Introduction

As the extent of governmental control through public ownership in the economy ceased, the need for regulatory authorities became stronger. As a matter of fact, the privatization of public enterprises could not be properly achieved without introducing an independent body exercising regulatory and supervisory powers over these 'private' companies. However, the road towards liberalization was long, and complicated by political forces, which on ideological grounds were against the recourse to the market of public utilities. **9.45**

The Establishment of an Energy Regulator

In 1996 Law no 481 of 14 November 1995 entered into force, creating a legal framework for the establishment and operation of independent bodies supervising and regulating public services such as energy and telecommunications. These regulators are meant to take over the role of the relevant Ministries in setting prices and general regulation. Basically, all regulators are meant to achieve some strategic objectives, such as (i) the promotion of competition and efficiency, (ii) the protection of consumer interests, and (iii) the guarantee of adequate levels of service throughout Italy. A clearly defined and transparent tariff system, based on pre-set criteria, is an essential instrument for achieving the above objectives. The tariff system must take into account the financial objectives of the entities involved as well as the principles of the European Communities law and the general policy directions of the Government.[36] Besides these broad goals, the law also lays down general instructions for the establishment of these regulators.[37] **9.46**

[34] See DL 31 May 1994, No 332, converted into the Law of 8 August 1994, No 474.
[35] See Law of 14 November 1995, No 481.
[36] Art 1, Law No 481, 1995.
[37] ibid, Art 2.

9.47 The Energy Regulator is entitled:

—to advise the Government about the services that should be regulated within existing legislation, taking into account technology, market developments, and EC policy;
—to propose amendments to permits and service conditions;
—to propose the revocation of permits;
—to examine market access and competition;
—to refer anti-competitive behaviour to the Competition Authority;
—to set prices and tariffs;
—to ensure that suppliers comply with principles of transparency, equality of service, and environmental protection;
—to fine suppliers not complying with regulations and to suspend the activities of companies repeatedly violating regulations; and
—to request information and documents.

9.48 Although the regulator may propose the amendment or suspension of a permit, the final powers are still with the Minister of Industry, Commerce, and Crafts as he is entitled to award and amend permits and licences. If the Minister rejects a proposal made by the regulator, he may still ask the regulator to make a new proposal. In the case of a second rejection the Minister can require a Cabinet decision.

The Internal organization of the Regulatory Authority

9.49 The Regulatory Authority is an associate body consisting of three Commissioners, including the Chairman. All three Commissioners are nominated by the Minister of Industry and appointed by the President of Italy following a resolution of the Council of Ministers. The competent parliamentary committees are also consulted. They may withhold their consent and even block the appointment after hearings on the candidate. The Commissioners are appointed for seven years, with no possibility of reappointment. The Commissioners are public officials, subject to the duty of confidentiality while carrying out their functions.

9.50 The Commissioners are chosen from professional and competent people in the energy sector. Candidates are unsuitable if they are involved in any professional or advisory activity, managers or employees in any public or private company, charged with any other public or political function, or involved in the operation of energy enterprises. Similarly, Commissioners are not entitled, for a period of at least four years after leaving office, to be directly or indirectly involved in any consulting and employment relationship with the energy sector. The infringement of this principle is subject to a fine (except if the action amounts to a crime) of between 50 million and 500 million lira plus the amount of compensation received.

The Energy Regulator and the Competition Authority

The Energy Regulator also has the task of promoting competition in the energy sector. Hence, there is a possible conflict of interest between the Energy Regulator and the Competition Authority. The latter body was established in 1990 by Law no 287 governing the protection of competition and the market.[38] The competition law applies to 'both private and public enterprises or enterprises with widespread State participation'. An exception is made for 9.51

> enterprises entrusted with the operation of services of general interest or operate on the basis of a legal monopoly, as far as it involves the execution of their specific tasks.

Nevertheless, it should be emphasized that the Law has extended the scope of the competition law to those enterprises which, within a monopoly regime, run a public utility.[39] In other words, a direct connection is made between the aims and means of the Competition Law of 1990 and the Law on authorities regulating public utilities of 1995. In order to avoid any conflict, it is important to distinguish between the different roles and functions of each Authority. From their wording, it seems that the Law of 1995 gives the Energy Regulator the task of *promoting* competition[40] and Law 287/1990 focuses on the need to *safeguard* competition. Therefore it is important to examine more closely whether the Energy Regulator's powers are limited to the promotion of competition, and if the Competition Authority has more powers and focuses on the protection of any possible violation of competition. 9.52

The *travaux preparatoires* of Law 481/1995 suggest that all competencies for the protection of competition in the public utility sector were originally embodied in the new Regulatory Authority, thus excluding the Competition Authority. However, in the course of time some important amendments were made to the original proposal as a result of which the Competition Authority was awarded exclusive competence in the field of competition protection while the new Regulatory Authority maintained advisory powers. Hence, it can be concluded that the instruments given to the Energy Regulator are limited (proposals and advisory powers) compared to the extensive sanction and ruling powers of the Competition Authority. Moreover, both Authorities apply their powers at different stages. Whereas the new Regulatory Authority is required to examine the competitive elements of access conditions, permits and licences, and programme contracts (the preparatory phase of an activity), the ruling activity and the sanctioning powers of the Competition Authority take place in the executory phase of activity. 9.53

---

38 Law No 287 of 10 October 1990.

39 Art 8, Law 287/1990.

40 See the wording of Art 1, para 1, Law 481/1995.

The Regulatory Authority and tariffs

9.54 It should be noted, however, that the Energy Regulatory Authority has sanctioning powers in the field of setting and controlling tariffs. These powers are triggered by non-observance of the Authority's guidelines or by disobedience and infidelity in supplying the information which the Authority has the power to require in order to carry out its activity.

9.55 The Law provides that:

> the Authority has the task of fixing and/or adjusting in accordance with the market, the basic tariff, the parameters, and the other reference elements necessary to determine the tariffs, as well as the conditions for the recuperation of the general interest costs in order to guarantee the service quality and efficiency and the adequate propagation of it on the national territory, as well as the realisation of the general objectives of social character, environmental protection and efficient use of the resources, distinguishing from the tariff any tribute or improper charge.[41]

9.56 In conformity with these provisions, it has also the power to assess consumers' claims and motions concerning the observance of the quality and tariff levels. The Authority can, if necessary, impose variations on the operating conditions of the companies or correct the regulation.

(3) The Devolution of Government and its Implications for the Energy Sector

Introduction

9.57 The policy of decentralization lies behind Law no 142 of 8 June 1990, which is a framework law governing the competencies of local autonomous areas. This Law introduced important changes to the energy sector as it granted local authorities much wider powers regarding, *inter alia*, the organization and management of energy sources. It should also be noted that government devolution is not an isolated phenomenon and has to be considered within a broader legal framework. First, energy is no longer primarily regulated on a national level since it has acquired a (fully) European and international dimension. Secondly, similar events can be noticed in other sectors, particularly with regard to environmental matters. This has created some reference points, which can be helpful in order to comprehend the complex subject of energy law and regulation.

The Institutional framework

9.58 Law 142/1990 awards specific powers to both provinces and municipalities regarding energy supply. Provinces are awarded the power to exercise administrative functions of 'local interest' insofar as these concern the protection and exploitation of water and energy resources. These powers can be applied to substantial

[41] See Art 2, para 12, lett e, Law 481/1995.

parts or to the entire province.[42] The intention was to create an integrated system of functional competencies in specific (and sometimes corresponding) areas such as energy and water supply, environmental protection, and waste disposal. Municipalities can also be assigned functions in the field of gathering and distributing water and energy sources. These functions are usually delegated to the local governments where they have a principally local character, when they have to be carried out in an integrated form in a metropolitan area, or are based on economical and efficiency grounds.[43] Therefore, provision is made for the regional law, which divides administrative functions between local authorities, to assign to municipalities the necessary functions to carry out the administrative and managerial powers in the above-mentioned areas of energy and water supply, environmental protection, and waste disposal. According to this policy of decentralization, the local authority (*comune*) becomes an entity with general competencies with regard to public services, physical planning, and economic development.[44] The local entities, however, have to take into account the enhanced competences of provinces.

The Decentralization Law thus awards a pivotal role to the provinces as an intermediary between the regions and the local entities. Therefore the size of the provincial territories shall have such dimensions, in terms of width, demographic entity, and productivity, in order to allow a system of development planning enabling an economic, social, and cultural rebalancing of the regional and provincial territories.[45] The law seems to pursue the same objective with regard to the metropolitan areas, ie areas in which the largest cities and surrounding towns are integrated economically, culturally, and geographically.[46] **9.59**

The intermediary role of the provinces is illustrated by some particularly innovative provisions on planning. In fact, provinces are responsible for the determination and implementation of energy planning systems in order to achieve a consolidation process between the different levels of government, ie regions, provinces, and municipalities. According to this policy, the province becomes the fundamental institution with regard to energy planning, since the planning instruments of the provinces are meant to integrate the local and regional interests. In addition, the provinces are responsible for the implementation and execution of the aims and principles for each local situation and which are included in the **9.60**

---

[42] See Art 14, para 1, lett b of Law 142/1990.

[43] ibid, Art 19, para 1 lett e.

[44] ibid, Art 9.

[45] ibid, Art 16, para 2.

[46] ibid, Art 17. The same aim is pursued by Art 28, paras 3 and 4 which enable the regional law to exclude from the entity 'partially mountain towns', the inclusion of which would prejudice its geographical or socio-economic homogeneity, as well as including the neighbouring towns with populations of not higher than 20,000 which are an integrated part of the geographical and socio-economic system of the community.

regional planning systems. In this context the provision contained in Article 15, paragraph 4 of Law 142/1990 is fundamental. It delegates to regional law the setting of rules to guarantee the local authorities' participation in provincial co-ordination plans, which need to be checked by the region in order to establish their compliance with regional planning instructions. Article 3, paragraph 5 of Law 142/1990 reaffirms the general principle according to which local authorities and provinces contribute to the determination of the objectives of the national plans and provide for their specification and implementation.

Energy regulation at the local level

9.61 The Law no 142 of 8 June 1990, assigns to local bodies, provinces, and metropolitan areas powers concerning the organization and management of the energy sector. Whereas provinces are awarded powers with regard to the protection and exploitation of energy resources, municipalities are responsible for the gathering and distribution of energy. Although the Law assigns to the provinces the tasks of planning, co-ordination, and supervision, the direct management of energy resources is given to the municipalities. In other words, the functional competencies of the provinces necessarily include the competencies of the local entities as it is impossible to implement a complete and efficacious protection and exploitation of energy resources without taking into account the gathering and distribution of the same resources. Basically, provinces have the general task of promoting and co-ordinating the use and management (the gathering and the distribution) of different energy resources. The different use of terminology seems to be included mainly to individuate the role of the provinces and metropolitan areas (only if this last entity has been instituted).

9.62 These basic principles are confirmed by further rules in Chapters VII and VIII of Law 142/1990, which enable local authorities:

—to establish association and co-operation agreements in order to carry out, in a co-ordinated way, specific functions and services;
—to realize an associated management for one or more services (joint boards);
—to define and carry out works and planning programmes, requiring for their implementation the co-ordinated and integrated action of local authorities and regions as well as of the national government and other public bodies (programme agreements); and
—to manage public utilities through share companies with local public capital participation and, if necessary in relation to the special nature of the service, the participation of other public or private subjects.

9.63 These powers are, however, limited to the use of primary energy resources and exclude activities in the electricity sector. Nevertheless, it should be noted that the exclusion of non-electric resources should not be regarded as a limitation *per se* since most primary energy sources, in particular renewable sources, can find many uses, eg in district heating. By and large, the above rules grant wider operating and managing potentialities to local authorities as they enable the local bodies to create share companies with public and private capital.

The National Energy Plan and the role of regions and local authorities

Laws nos 9 and 10 of 1991 give effect to the 1988 National Energy Plan. Law 10/1991 is of special importance as it assigned important functions to the regions in order to increase their role and importance in conformity with Law 142/90. These regional functions relate to the funding of public support for initiatives aimed at the wise use of energy and renewable resources.[47] **9.64**

The Promotion of renewable resources and energy saving

Regions may, by agreement with local bodies and their enterprises, draw up regional energy plans aiming at the use of renewable energy sources.[48] These regional energy plans should specify: a) regional and local energy budgets; b) an overview of the available energy resources; c) the location of heating plants; d) the allocation of financial means for the establishment of new energy production plants and energy saving measures;[49] and e) procedures for the establishment of energy production plants with a capacity of 10 MW as well as hydroelectric plants. Regions also have the task of identifying suitable areas for the realization of district heating systems as well as the limits and criteria the authorities will have to observe in connecting individual households to district heating systems.[50] **9.65**

The law requires all towns with more than 50,000 inhabitants to provide specific plans on the local level for the use of renewable energy sources.[51] As for energy saving, the local authorities are also required to supervise the implementation of energy-saving measures in construction projects.[52] The mayor can order the suspension of works and/or necessary building variations to conform with the legal requirements.[53] **9.66**

Subsidies

The regions are also assigned the task of granting and supplying subsidies for: a) limiting energy consumption in the industrial, handcraft, and services sector, **9.67**

[47] D Marino and D Fontana, 'The Development of the Electricity Market in Italy: From Monopoly to Liberalisation', Oil and Gas Law and Taxation Review, 1998, 430–3.

[48] Art 5, Law 10/1991.

[49] The allocation is carried out according to a priority order relative to the percentage and absolute quantity of energy saved.

[50] Art 6, Law 10/1991.

[51] ibid, Art 5, para 5.

[52] ibid, Art 34.

[53] The mayor is also entitled to fix the terms of regularization. Non-observance involves an administrative sanction, with the enforcement of the works charged to the owner.

b) stimulating the use of renewable energy sources, and c) energy production from renewable sources in the agricultural sector. The Minister of the Treasury has the power to pass, by administrative decree, guidelines to harmonize the criteria for the assessment of applications, the procedures, and the conditions for the award of subsidies. In this specific ambit regions have only a marginal and recessive role, since their task is limited to checking the necessary prerequisites for the subsidization and to carry out the subsidy. This situation contrasts with the aim of the law that seems to assign more powers to the regions.

9.68 Nevertheless, Law no 10 identifies several types of subsidies and beneficiaries. First, subsidies can be awarded for economical-technical research in civil, industrial, or mixed projects for the production, regeneration, transport, and distribution of energy from co-generation plants. The beneficiaries are the regions, local authorities and their joint boards and associations whether directly or through their companies, enterprises or consortiums of enterprises, joint boards between enterprises, and ENEL and/or other public entities. Secondly, subsidies can be given to public and private corporations and their relative joint boards for the planning and realization of innovative plants using renewable energy sources, specific prototypes with low energy consumption, or new combustion technologies as well as initiatives using non-fossil fuels whose technology has not achieved commercial and operational maturity. Thirdly, subsidies may be given for the establishment of power plants for the production or regeneration of thermal, electric, and mechanical energy from renewable energy sources. Such subsidies can be awarded to single or associated commercial farms or heat supply companies, possibly in association with ENEL and/or municipal utility services and/or other public entities.

Energy liberalization

9.69 The above Laws contain instruments aimed not only at the rationalization of the energy system, but also at the partial liberalization of the electricity sector. Following the 1988 PEN policy objective to enhance competition in energy production, Laws 9 and 10 of 1991 also aimed at third-party electricity production from renewable resources. The above system of subsidies provides incentives with regard to sales of electricity to ENEL. A model agreement by ENEL for autoproducers was promulgated by Ministerial Decree in 1992. This model agreement defined the criteria and conditions for the production and sale by third parties. It also defined the relationship between ENEL and third-party producers, establishing precise procedures for the co-ordination of these activities.[54] However, the overall planning is in the hands of the regions and local bodies.

[54] Marino and Fontana, OGLTR 1998.

The Attribution of specific competencies in the field of energy

The most recent development concerning Government devolution is Act no 59 of 15 March 1997 (*Legge Bassanini*)[55] as implemented by Legislative Decree no 112 of 31 March 1998. Act 59/97 and Legislative Decree 112/98 enable the Government to confer specific functions and tasks on regions and local entities. It is noteworthy that for the first time the energy sector is included in the devolution programme. Although the energy sector is not listed as one of the subjects reserved to the sole competence of the State and thus excluded from attribution of powers to the Regions and local authorities,[56] Act 59/97 explicitly refers to specific functions which are excluded from attribution. The State remains responsible for: **9.70**

—research, production, transport, and distribution of energy;[57]

—planning, designing, execution, and maintenance of the main energy infrastructure such as power lines and oil and gas pipelines as long as these have been declared of national importance by a national law,[58] and

—the attribution by a national law of regulatory and supervisory powers to independent authorities,[59] as for example the Energy Regulatory Authority established by Act 481/95. The absence of 'energy' as a subject restricted to the exclusive competence of the State is thus balanced by the exclusion of the attribution to regions of considerable tasks of national importance in the regulation, control, planning, design, execution, and maintenance of infrastructures in the energy sector.

Legislative Decree 112/98 further elaborates on the functions and tasks reserved to State competence.[60] The tasks of national importance can be divided into three main categories, which are discussed below. **9.71**

The first category concerns the formulation and arrangement of technical and safety regulations. It includes (i) the definition of general technical construction criteria and essential technical regulations of production, conservation, and distribution of energy;[61] (ii) the definition of technical and marketing features of energy yield, delivery, and expenditure;[62] (iii) the use of radioactive materials;[63] and (iv) the enactment of technical regulations relating to the construction of power lines.[64] **9.72**

[55] Delegation to the Government for the contribution of functions and tasks to the regional and local entities, the reform of public administration, and administrative simplification.

[56] Art 1, para 3, Act 59/97.

[57] ibid, Art 1, para 4, lett c.

[58] ibid, lett a.

[59] ibid, Art 1, para 4.

[60] Art 29, Legislative Decree 112/98.

[61] ibid, para 2, lett c.

[62] ibid, lett d.

[63] ibid, lett f.

[64] ibid, lett g.

9.73 The second category applies to the State competencies in the field of planning and policy for the organization and management of the energy sector. The Legislative Decree specifically refers to the State's power to formulate and define the objectives of a national energy policy.[65] The State is also empowered to adopt strategic and co-ordinating measures concerning energy planning on a regional level.[66] The State also has competencies in the fields of (i) scientific energy research;[67] (ii) the import and export of energy;[68] (iii) renewable sources and energy saving as well as the regulation and award of subsidies, financial incentives, and other advantages to industry;[69] (iv) mandatory oil storage facilities;[70] (v) the execution of the natural gas plan in Southern Italy;[71] and (vi) the regulation of concessions for public watercourses for hydroelectric purposes.[72] Finally, it should be noted that the State competencies also include (i) the supply of statistical information necessary for energy planning and co-ordination with regions and local districts,[73] (ii) the definition of general targets and specific commitments to regional planning, and (iii) supervision of the National Authority of new technology, energy, and the environment (ENEA).

9.74 The third category refers to the State's powers with regard to the award of permits for the establishment and exploitation of energy facilities. Basically, the State may award permits for (i) the construction and exploitation of electricity production plants (> 300 MW), the medium- and high-voltage transmission lines, and other national energy infrastructure such as oil and gas pipelines;[74] (ii) the establishment and operation of nuclear plants, the use of ionizing radiation sources, the transportation of radioactive waste and radioactive elements, and the realization of nuclear safety provisions,[75] and (iii) the exploration, exploitation, and storage of onshore and offshore hydrocarbons.[76]

9.75 Finally, the State has the power to fix the rates to be paid by applicants for authorizations, inspections, and analyses.[77] The attribution of powers to the State is of special importance as it also indicates which competencies derive for the regions and local authorities.[78]

---

65 ibid, para 1.
66 ibid.
67 ibid, para 2, lett a.
68 ibid, lett b.
69 ibid, para 2, lett h and Art 18, letts n–o.
70 ibid, Art 29, para 2, lett m.
71 ibid, Art 29, para 2, lett n. This plan is scheduled by Art 11 of Act 784/80.
72 Art 29, para 3, Legislative Decree 112/98.
73 ibid, Art 29, para 2, lett p.
74 ibid, lett g.
75 ibid, lett i.
76 ibid, lett l.
77 ibid, lett o.
78 Art 30 of Legislative Decree 112/98.

A general attribution of energy competencies is included in Articles 29 and 31 of Legislative Decree 112/98 which attribute to the regions all administrative functions concerning energy, including those related to renewable resources, electricity, nuclear energy, oil, and gas, which are not reserved to State competence or to local authorities. The local authorities have the administrative task of supervising the policies of energy saving and the rational use of energy. **9.76**

Specific attributions of power are laid down in Article 30, paragraph 2 of Legislative Decree 112/98, which refers to capital deduction financing by public corporations and private companies as well as private/public entities of (i) the construction or re-establishment of hydroelectricity plants,[79] (ii) the construction of plants based on the concept of rational energy use, energy saving, and the development of renewable energy resources,[80] and (iii) the use of energy-saving measures in construction projects.[81] To the regions is also attributed the task of co-ordinating between the local authorities the laying down of regulations governing the planning, installation, service, and maintenance of the insulation standards of buildings,[82] and aid to local authorities for activities in the field of public information and education of people working in the energy sector.[83] Within the framework of the regional energy programmes, provinces are attributed the task of compiling and enacting plans for the promotion of renewable resources and energy saving[84] and authorizing the establishment and operation of energy-producing plants.[85] **9.77**

The above-mentioned provisions are the most recent developments with regard to the division of energy competencies between the State, the region, and local authorities. However, the provisions must be considered together with the wider body of energy legislation. **9.78**

(4) The Creation and Reform of ENEA

ENEA was created in 1982 by Law no 84 of 5 March to replace CNEN (the national nuclear energy Commission) and to expand the latter's statutory tasks relating to alternative energy sources. CNEN had been set up in 1960 and restructured in 1971, its competence remaining confined to nuclear energy. Basically, the tasks covered research and promotion, as well as inspection of nuclear safety and protection against ionizing radiation. Law no 84 of 1982 created ENEA as a governmental agency, which kept its competences in the domain of nuclear energy (with a number of specifications) but acquired new competences **9.79**

[79] Art 14, Act 10/91.
[80] Art 12, Act 10/91.
[81] ibid, Art 30.
[82] Decree of the President of the Republic, 412/93.
[83] Art 30, para 5, Legislative Decree 112/98.
[84] ibid, Art 31, para 2, lett a.
[85] ibid, lett b.

related to alternative energy sources, with the exception of hydrocarbons. These competences also covered the environmental and health aspects associated with the use of non-nuclear energy sources.[86]

9.80 A further statutory development followed in 1991 with Law no 282 of 25 August, by which ENEA was vested with competences in energy as a whole, the environmental, and technical innovations. In particular, ENEA was called upon to carry out projects, to spread know-how, to co-operate with international organizations, to give opinions, to carry out technical inquiries and checks on behalf of the Government, the regions, and local authorities, to participate in international developments of new technologies, and to promote renewable sources and the rational use of energy. It should be pointed out that, as far as initiatives in the electricity sector were concerned, ENEA was involved in joint boards for the promotion of renewable sources and the rational use of energy, and that these boards acted on the basis of agreements with ENEL.

9.81 Following the creation of the national agency for the protection of the environment (ANPA, Law no 61 of 21 January 1994) ENEA's tasks relating to inspection of nuclear safety and radiation protection were transferred to that Agency.

9.82 The ENEA statute was most recently amended at the beginning of 1999, following a delegation to the Government[87]concerning, *inter alia*, the reform of public administration at large. Although the Decree leaves the previous tasks to a largely unaffected, it should be pointed out that ENEA is now called upon to focus on research and innovation in sustainable development and protection of the environment, and to promote competition and employment in the areas concerned. A task which may be seen as a particularly important change is to act as an agency of public administration by providing advanced services in the domains of energy, the environment, and technological innovation. The relevant actions are carried out by ENEA in the framework, wherever applicable, of Italy's commitments to the European Union. Postgraduate training is also among ENEA's new tasks.

9.83 In order to accomplish its functions ENEA can negotiate agreements, set up a monitoring system of initiatives concerning energy and the environment, and finance such initiatives.

9.84 Law 282/ 91 is repealed by the Decree on ENEA 36/ 99,[88] except for Article 24 of Law 282. This provision, which addresses the relationships with ENEL, was to remain applicable until the entry into force of the provisions implementing EC Directive 96/92 on the internal electricity market. Such implementation was en-

[86] For these institutional developments, see F Nocera, 'Dal CNRN alla recente creazione dell'ENEA. Evoluzione legislativa con particolare riguardo ai compiti istitutivi in materia di sicurezza e protezione', in Rassegna Giuridica dell'ENEL, Anno XVIII, No 5, 1982.

[87] Law of 15 March 1997, No 59 ('Bassanini Law', in para 9.70 above).

[88] Art 16 of the Decree.

sured by Decree 79/99 (see section G of this chapter), which addresses ENEL's position extensively and in a new institutional and legal context. On account of ENEA's nature as a public body on the one hand, and of ENEL's privatization on the other, relations between these two entities must now be seen in the new context resulting from the latest institutional and legal developments.

D. Exploration for and Production of Hydrocarbons

(1) Introduction

The legal system on hydrocarbons in Italy has gradually developed from a system regulating aspects of hard rock mining to a modern petroleum law. Nevertheless, the legal basis for the exploration and production of subsoil minerals is still the 1927 Mining Decree and the Civil Code. The Royal Decree of 1927 states that: 'the exploration and production of mineral substances and subsoil energies, which can be industrially exploited in every form or physical condition, are regulated by the present law.'[89] It also distinguishes between two categories of mineral substances, 'mines' and 'quarries'. For the purpose of this study, the first category is more important as it includes substances like 'solid, liquid, and gaseous fuels, asphalt, and bituminous rocks'.[90] Oil and gas are also considered part of this category. As regards the ownership of the subsoil minerals, Article 826 of the Civil Code rules that 'mines' are 'part of the non-disposable patrimony of the State', ie their ownership is vested in the State. Consequently, all minerals *in situ* are considered in law to be an integral part of the mine and not the property of the private owner of the land. These subsoil minerals have no autonomous legal existence until they are separated from the mine where they are found. **9.85**

The provision that the ownership of subsoil resources is vested in the State also means that these resources are reserved for 'public use'. The use or exploitation may be carried out by the State or be entrusted to private persons who then act in the exercise of a public service. A private person can be awarded such right as a concession.[91] In Italy the State has always been closely involved in the exploration and production of hydrocarbons. As mentioned above, the right to explore and produce hydrocarbons was assigned to ENI in 1953: Article 1 of the 1953 Act assigned to ENI the task of promoting and carrying out initiatives of national interest in the hydrocarbons and natural steam sector.[92] As a consequence, ENI received an exclusive right to explore and exploit the hydrocarbon resources as **9.86**

---

[89] Art 1, Royal Decree of 29 July 1927, No 1443.

[90] ibid, Art 2.

[91] See further M Nicolazzi, 'Petroleum Law and Petroleum Joint Ventures in Italy', Journal of Energy and Natural Resources Law, vol 8, 1990, 30–50.

[92] See Law of 10 February 1953, No 136.

well as to establish and operate the pipelines for the transport and supply of hydrocarbons. However, ENI did not receive such an exclusive right for all of Italy. By the Law of 1957 ENI was assigned exclusive rights to most of the onshore territory. The five regions excepted were: Sicily, Sardinia, Trentino-Alto Adige, Friuli-Venezia Giulia, and the Valle d'Aosta. Regional mining laws govern the exploration and production of hydrocarbons in these areas. In 1967 ENI's mining rights were extended and it was made responsible for the exploration and production of hydrocarbons in the Italian territorial sea and the continental shelf adjacent thereto.[93]

9.87 Further rules regarding the exploration and production of hydrocarbons onshore and offshore were given by several Ministerial Decrees.[94] In practice, the onshore and offshore regulations did not greatly differ from each other. Therefore a specific hydrocarbons regime has developed since the end of the 1960s. Gradually, the hydrocarbons regulations have been further streamlined. The above regulations on the exploration and production of hydrocarbons were further integrated into title II of Law no 9 of 1991.[95] The 1991 Reform Law provides for the establishment of a common set of rules applicable to both onshore and offshore activities.[96] The regulations established under the earlier legislation were replaced by a Ministerial Decree.[97] The introduction of the 1991 Act has not changed the situation in the semi-autonomous regions of Sicily and Sardinia, where regional mining laws governing production onshore and in territorial waters still apply.[98]

(2) The Licensing Regime

The Distinction between permits and concessions

9.88 The Reform Law of 1991 and the earlier legislation still in force provide for a licensing regime governing prospecting, exploration, and production of hydrocarbons. The above licensing regime applies to the Italian territory outside the ENI exclusive area. ENI's subsidiary AGIP is responsible for the exploration and production of hydrocarbons within these exclusive zones.

9.89 Procedures for awarding hydrocarbons licences in the non-exclusive zones are included in Presidential Decree 484 of 18 April 1994. In order to implement the

[93] Act of 11 January 1957, No 6 provided for ENI's exclusive concession rights on the territory of Italy. This Law was amended by two different Laws: the Law of 24 July 1962, No 1072, and No 613/1967. Under the latter, the offshore areas were included.

[94] The onshore activities were included in a Ministerial Decree of 2 May 1968. A Ministerial Decree for offshore activities was given on 2 September 1967.

[95] Which integrates and modifies earlier hydrocarbons legislation.

[96] Art 13, Law No 9 of 1991.

[97] Ministerial Decree of 6 August 1991.

[98] See for Sicily: Regional Law No 30 of 20 March 1950 and Regional Decrees of 19 February 1955 (No 439) and 1 October 1956 (No 54). See for Sardinia: Regional Law No 20 of 19 December 1959. Other regional laws were abrogated by the entry into force of Law No 9 of 1991.

Hydrocarbons Licensing Directive, some amendments were made to the regime by Legislative Decree 625 of 25 November 1996. Under the latter Decree a provision was introduced to speed up permitting as it included a three-month period for the application process.

It should also be noted that Italian hydrocarbons law does not use the term 'licence'. Under Italian administrative law all State grants are, strictly speaking, to be referred to as 'concessions'. However, in practice a distinction is made in Italian hydrocarbons law between prospecting and exploration permits on one hand and production and storage concessions on the other.[99] **9.90**

Prospecting permits

The Reform Law of 1991 does not provide a definition of a 'prospecting permit'. This illustrates the limited importance of prospecting permits in the present practice. Oil companies prefer to apply directly for an exploration permit. Under the previous Offshore Petroleum Act of 1967 prospecting was defined as 'geographical, geological, or geophysical surveys in order to check the nature of sea subsoil, as to Article 2, to the end of search of liquid and gaseous hydrocarbons'.[100] The same definition of prospecting was applied to the onshore territory, ie the ENI zones.[101] **9.91**

Prospecting permits are non-exclusive and awarded for a maximum of one year. The holder of a prospecting permit must only be an individual person and does not acquire any qualified legal right as regards the award of any successive exploration permits or production concessions. A prospecting permit is awarded upon the payment of a registration fee and rent.[102] **9.92**

Exploration permits

It is current practice for companies to apply directly for an exploration permit. Exploration permits are granted by Inter-Ministerial Decree by the Minister of Industry, Trade, and Crafts, the Minister for the Environment, and the Minister for the Merchant Marine in the case of offshore areas. Before a permit is awarded, the Technical Committee for Hydrocarbons and all the regions involved are consulted. Italian natural persons and corporations and subjects of other EC Member States can apply for an exploration permit as long as they have adequate technical and financial capability. **9.93**

The Italian regime has no 'bidding rounds' or other formal procedures for the award of exploration permits. Those parts of Italian (onshore and offshore) **9.94**

[99] See M Nicolazzi, 'Petroleum Law and Petroleum Joint Ventures in Italy', JERL, 1990, 33.
[100] Art 5, Law of 21 July 1967, No 613.
[101] ibid, Art 6.
[102] Petroconsultants, World Petroleum Laws (Italy), March 1999.

territory that are not yet covered by a permit or concession may be the object of an application for a permit (or concession). All applications are published in the Official Hydrocarbons Bulletin. Other interested parties may then file their own application for the same area within a certain period of time. If there is only one application it is assessed on its own merits. If there are competing applications, the choice is made primarily on the basis of the work programme offered by each applicant. Hence, the award system is designed to promote competition and is thus in conformity with the principles of the Hydrocarbons Licensing Directive.

9.95 The holder of an exploration permit is entitled to carry out works such as drilling wells in order to identify and physically demonstrate the existence of a field. The search is successful when, through the drilling of a well, liquid or gaseous hydrocarbons are discovered.[103]

9.96 An exploration permit is exclusive and awarded for a limited area (maximum 750 square km since 1996 and 1,000 square km before 1996) which can include adjacent zones of mainland and territorial sea. The permit also has a limited duration of nine years, comprising of three periods of three years.[104] Hence, if the permit holder complies with all the duties arising from the first part of the permit, he has the right to obtain two three-year 'renewals'. After each renewal 25 per cent of the original area has to be relinquished. An exception is made for very small permit areas.

9.97 The exploration permits include an obligation to commence geological and geophysical investigations within twelve months after the grant of the permit. Similarly, drilling must commence within forty-eight months after the permit is awarded. The permit holder must also carry out a work programme according to the terms specified in the permit. The mining authority is entitled to receive the results of surveys and to approve the exploration plan and techniques for each well. Moreover, the mining authority must be informed of the mining activities and results and, within fifteen days, about the discovery of hydrocarbons.

9.98 The holder of an exploration permit is obliged to pay a registration fee and rent. The latter is paid in three parts and increases with each three-year renewal.

Production concessions

9.99 If an exploration is successful and a field is discovered, and the work programme has been carried out conscientiously, the holder of the exploration permit may apply for a production concession. A concession can be awarded if the production capacity of the discovered well justifies technically and economically the development of the field. The application must be made within 120 days of the

[103] Art 9, Law 9 of 1991.

[104] The 1998 awards provided for a duration of six years.

discovery and be accompanied by a development plan. When the above conditions are met a concession will usually be awarded to the holder of an exploration permit. Therefore the holder of the exploration permit has a specific privileged title to attain the relative concession.[105]

Concessions are awarded for a limited area (maximum 150 square km) and for a period of thirty years.[106] After twenty years the concessionaire may apply for an extension beyond the period of thirty years. Further delays of five years each may be granted if the concessionaire has fulfilled its obligations under the concession, ie has accomplished the work programme according to good oilfield practice and fulfilled all other (financial) duties arising from the concession. **9.100**

Similarly to the previous permits, the concessionaire is obliged to pay a (higher) registration fee and a rental fee per square kilometre. In addition, royalties have to be paid if the production is above a certain annual output (20,000 tonnes onshore and 50,000 tonnes offshore).[107] Whereas the royalty rates for onshore oil and gas are the same (7 per cent), the rate for offshore oil and gas differs: 4 per cent for oil and 7 per cent for gas. As from 1998 corporate income tax and a regional tax are also charged. **9.101**

Storage concession

The right to use hydrocarbon deposits for underground storage is also vested in the State. Underground storage is considered a public interest task, as are exploring and exploiting the hydrocarbons.[108] **9.102**

The State can dispose of its storage rights by granting concessions to others through the Ministry for Industry, Trade, and Crafts. In addition, ENI has an exclusive right of storage in the exclusive zones (Po valley). Currently, AGIP is the only undertaking storing gas. **9.103**

A storage concession can be awarded by the Ministry for a period of twenty years and extended for periods of ten years.[109] A storage concession and a production concession can exist next to each other. The reason is that storage concessions are basically awarded to holders of a production concession.[110] The 1996 Legislative Decree changed this situation to the extent that storage concessions can be awarded to others if a reservoir is completely exploited and the production concession has ceased. This clause introduces some competition into the market **9.104**

---

[105] See further M Nicolazzi, 35.

[106] Art 9, para 8, Law 9/91 and Art 29, Law No 613 of 21 July 1967.

[107] Cf Arts 32 and 33 of Law 613/67.

[108] Arts 1 and 3, Law No 170 of 26 April 1974.

[109] Before the 1996 legislative decree, storage concessions were awarded for 30 years. For offshore storage, the Ministry of Merchant Marine is also involved in the award procedure.

[110] Art 3, Law No 170 of 26 April 1974.

of underground storage. This clause also raises the issue of whether the holder of a storage concession takes over the responsibility and liability for abandonment from the holder of the production concession. This issue has not (yet) been solved.

The Implementation of the Hydrocarbons Licensing Directive and the position of ENI

9.105 By the Legislative Decree of 25 November 1996 a number of changes were introduced to the above regime in order to comply with the requirements of the Hydrocarbons Licensing Directive. Most importantly it changed the position of ENI in the exclusive zones in the Po valley, the Venetian plains (including the territorial waters), and the Northern Apennine foothills. It also abolished ENI's exclusive storage rights. In addition, ENI/AGIP lost its priority right for prospecting and exploration offshore.

9.106 Although ENI's rights were abolished, the Decree did enable ENI to retain some rights in areas where it had been working before 31 December 1996. The Decree provided for the following procedures:

—ENI had to cede its existing rights in the exclusive zones as from 1 January 1997;
—ENI was allowed to re-apply within a certain period to retain permits/concessions in areas where it was carrying out activities or had made investments;
—ENI had to release certain data to the Government and make other data available to interested parties (thus creating the possibility for competing permits); and
—areas not retained by ENI before the given deadline were to be made available to other applicants.

Hence, ENI/AGIP is entitled to continue most of its exploration, production and storage activities in the above-mentioned areas.

9.107 It is worth recalling case-law on the application of the 1996 Decree. The case was triggered some years ago by a recourse introduced by the Region of Sicily before the Constitutional Court, the reason for this action being the following. Two operators had applied under the Decree in point for an exploration licence to be granted by the Ministry of Industry. The licences, once granted, were published on the initiative of the Ministry in the relevant official Bulletin. This was regarded by the Region of Sicily as interference by the State with the Region's prerogatives (hence the Constitutional Court was called upon to decide on 'conflicting attributions'). The Court's decision was to the effect that publication in the Bulletin did not entail any such 'conflict' (ie no actual interference had occurred). Later on, the Region of Sicily, by a special statute, adopted a Law (no 14/2000) stipulating that granting licences for exploration on the mainland is the Region's exclusive competence.

(3) The Hydrocarbons Regime, the Environment, and Planning Law

Introduction

The exploration and production of hydrocarbons can have a considerable impact on the environment and spatial planning. The drilling of wells and the establishment of installations may harm the environment, and take up space both above and below ground. **9.108**

Environmental impact

As far as environmental impact is concerned, it is important to note that the Reform Law of 1991 provides some measures limiting the prospecting, exploration, and production of hydrocarbons in areas of particular natural interest. First, the award of a prospecting and/or exploration permit is subject to the agreement of the Minister of Environment, and of the Minister for the Merchant Navy for offshore activities. Secondly it rules that prospecting, exploration, and production of hydrocarbons is forbidden in the waters of the Gulf of Naples, Salerno, and the Egadi Islands.[111] Exploration permits are also suspended in zones classified as national parks or marine sanctuaries and they can be revoked if they seriously prejudice situations of particular environmental or archaeological-monumental interest. **9.109**

The amendments made to the hydrocarbons licensing regime in 1994 also included the implementation of the EC Directive on environmental impact assessment. Presidential Decree 484 of 18 April 1994 also incorporated procedures for the environmental impact assessment into the licensing process. **9.110**

Planning law

Under Italian law the general principle is that nothing should be built on land without specific public authorization. Violation of this principle may lead to sanctions under criminal law. Within the hydrocarbons regime a distinction can be made between installations erected on a temporary basis, and those which are more or less permanent. It is generally assumed that no public authorisation is required for temporary installations, for example the works carried out before a discovery is made. It seems that all onshore installations necessary for production have a permanent character and thus need public authorization.[112] A similar principle applies to subsoil pipelines transporting the minerals produced. **9.111**

[111] See Art 4, Law No 9 of 1991.
[112] M Nicolazzi, 38.

(4) Concluding Remarks

9.112 The hydrocarbons regime has gradually been modernized. Although the present regime is basically a competitive system, it should be noted that ENI still influences most of the upstream market. ENI's (*de facto*) production monopoly is strengthened through its vertical links with the downstream markets.

E. Imports, Storage, and Distribution of Mineral Oil and Fuels

(1) Introduction

9.113 This section deals with issues relating to downstream oil, not only oil produced in Italy but also imports of oil and the working and trading of oil and oil products. RDL no 1741 of 2 November 1933 and the implementation rule RD no1303 of 20 July 1934 regulate the activities of import, the establishment and operation of storage plants, transformation and refining plants, and fuel distribution. The transportation of oil is not within the scope of this section: due to its physical nature, oil can be transported in many different ways, like other conventional goods. While electricity and gas are network-bound, oil can be transported by pipeline or conventional carriage by land or sea (eg tankers). Transportation by pipelines requires the construction of complex linear infrastructures: these aspects are dealt with in paragraphs 9.124–9.130 below, on the natural gas sector.

(2) Imports

9.114 Imports of mineral crude oils, by-products, and residues are subject to the grant of a licence.[113] Such a licence can be either special, in the case of single imports, or general, if it relates to huge quantities of mineral lubricant oils. It is granted by the Minister of Industry, Trade and Crafts in agreement with the Minister of Finance. The duration of the licence cannot exceed 20 years for mineral crude oil and residue oil. A compulsory requirement for the awarding of a general import licence is the availability, on behalf of the applicant, of adequate technical equipment.

(3) Oil Storage and Refining

9.115 The Reform Law of 1991 also governs the establishment and operation of oil storage plants and refining installations.[114] The regulations apply to various types of plants with different technical and dimension features: a) new plants for processing mineral oil and new natural gas installations; b) new plants increasing the working capacity of existing installations; c) new storage plants for mineral oil or natural gas with a working capacity exceeding 100,000 ha; and d) new installa-

[113] Arts 1, 2, 3, RDL 2 November 1933, No 1741, and 1–11, RD 20 July 1934, No 1303.

[114] See Arts 16, 17, 18, 19 of Law 9/91 regulate these matters for the duration of the permit. Hence, the public interest declaration is only temporary.

tions increasing by more than 30 per cent the storage capacity of the above-listed plants. The establishment and operation of these installations is subject to different permits. The establishment and operation of storage plants for liquefied petroleum gas is also subject to the grant of a permit.

However, a simple authorization by the Ministry of Industry is sufficient for: a) a new plant whose processing capacity is not increasing; b) the establishment of oil storage tanks connected to the above-mentioned plants; and c) every other new installation which is smaller than those for which a permit is required. **9.116**

According to Article 17 of Law no 9 of 1991, the procedures for awarding these permits and authorizations are to be regulated by further rules, not yet issued. Article 19 of RDL 1741 of 2 November 1933 facilitates the construction of the above plants because the occupation of public or private land necessary for the construction of processing plants, storage tanks, and petrol pumps is considered to be a matter of public interest. **9.117**

(4) Fuel Distribution: The Role of the Regions

The distribution of fuel is also subject to the grant of a permit.[115] In particular, permits concern the establishment and operation of petrol pumps. They are awarded for a period of eighteen years. A requirement for the award of a permit is the applicant's technical suitability. **9.118**

After the government devolution which started in 1977[116] the regions acquired a predominant role: the regulation and grant of permits were delegated to regions and local authorities (naturally, within the ambit outlined by State directions). As a consequence of the different policies of the regions, the sector is now diversely regulated. **9.119**

F. The Gas Supply Sector

(1) The Structure of the Gas Sector

The Italian gas industry is vertically integrated and dominated by ENI. Whereas ENI/AGIP is involved in most of the domestic gas production (some 90 per cent), another subsidiary of ENI, SNAM, is responsible for the gas transmission and distribution sector. SNAM owns and operates most of the gas transmission network. Earlier provisions in the 1974 Mining Decree, providing that all gas produced offshore must first be offered for sale to ENI, were abolished by the 1991 Reform **9.120**

[115] See RDL 1741 of 2 November 1933 as specified by Art 16 of DL 745 of 26 October 1970, and further converted and amended by Law 1034 of 18 December 1970) and the implementation rule issued in DPR 1269 of 27 October 1971.

[116] See DPR 616/1977.

Law.[117] Hence, ENI/SNAM has a *de facto* monopoly on gas imports and transmission to distribution companies and large consumers like ENEL. Part of the gas distribution is in the hands of Italgas, which is partly owned by SNAM.

9.121 ENI has been in the process of privatization since 1995. This privatization process has not been accompanied by extensive proposals for liberalization. The 1991 Law only required a degree of third-party access (TPA) and the appointment of a regulator. Nevertheless, some competition is currently taking place. First, there is a limited extent of gas-to-gas competition as ENEL has been negotiating separate gas import contracts. Secondly, some pipeline competition has arisen, since Edison has been constructing a separate gas pipeline for the import of Russian gas. Nevertheless, SNAM is currently operating as a private monopoly. The implementation of the EC Gas Directive may make an important difference in this respect.

(2) Gas Transmission

The gas pipeline system

9.122 As only a limited percentage of SNAM's gas supply originates from the domestic market, most gas is imported from countries within and without the EC. SNAM has entered into long-term gas supply contracts with the Netherlands since the end of the 1960s and thereafter with Russia, Algeria, and Norway. SNAM is currently operating a network of gas pipelines of some 30,000 km, covering almost the entire country.[118]

9.123 In order to facilitate the import of gas, the Italian gas transmission system is connected to other international pipelines. SNAM holds shares in these pipelines. Algerian gas, for example, is transported through the Trans-Mediterranean Pipeline (Transmed) in which SNAM has a 50 per cent share. In addition to this southern connection, SNAM's transmission system is connected to three international pipelines in the north of Italy. Russian gas is imported through the Trans-Austria Gasleitung (TAG) operated jointly by SNAM and ÖMV. The Trans Europa Naturgas Pipeline (TENP), owned by Ruhrgas (51 per cent) and SNAM (49 per cent), carries gas from the Netherlands. Dutch gas is also transported through Transitgas, which is jointly owned by Swissgas (51 per cent), SNAM (46 per cent) and Ruhrgas (3 per cent). Through these ownership rights SNAM can exercise its *de facto* import monopoly.

---

[117] Art 9 of Law 9/91 (the National Energy Act) merely establishes that if 'Italian' gas is offered to ENI, the selling conditions should be negotiated directly between the parties.

[118] ENI *Fact Book* 1999.

The rules governing the construction of pipelines and pipeline competition

ENI/SNAM's monopoly position is (again) based on the 1953 Act establishing ENI. The construction and operation of gas pipelines falls under the general ambit of ENI. In addition, ENI has an exclusive right to construct and operate pipelines for the conveyance of indigenous gas in the exclusive zones.[119] **9.124**

The exclusive role of ENI/SNAM was further facilitated by the provision in the 1953 Act, which declared that all installations necessary to carry out the tasks assigned to ENI and/or its subsidiaries (eg SNAM) were to be considered as public utilities.[120] Therefore, the necessary installations for the transmission of gas on behalf of ENI/SNAM are declared *ex lege* as a public utility in relation to, *inter alia*, the expropriation provided for in Law no 2359 of 25 June 1865 (as amended). **9.125**

The use of public and private land

The operation and maintenance of pipelines on private land requires that the pipeline owner enter into a private law agreement with the owner of the land. The presence of such a pipeline necessarily involves certain limitations to the landowner's property rights. However, since the landowner is not completely deprived of the use of his land, purchase of the land, whether compulsory or not, is usually out of proportion and too expensive. The easement of pipelines appears therefore the most suitable possibility. An easement can be negotiated between the parties (an easement by grant) or compulsorily imposed through an expropriating decree founded on the public interest declaration of the work under Law 2359/1865. ENI/SNAM is in a favourable position as subsoil pipelines and all ancillary installations are declared public utilities by law. The Minister of Industry, at the request of ENI/SNAM, can therefore order the occupation of goods (land) necessary to accomplish the work (the construction of the pipeline) and provisionally establish the compensation and order its deposit. This provision gives ENI/SNAM an important advantage over other companies in constructing subsoil gas pipelines. **9.126**

The imposition of an easement is not necessary where a pipeline crosses public land; in fact, in this particular situation the crossing requires only a permit granted by the competent authority. The holder of the permit, however, has to pay periodic rent. **9.127**

Safety regulations

Article 24 of the 1953 Act also states that the construction and operation of pipelines for the transport of hydrocarbons (including gas) by ENI/SNAM are subject to the laws relative to the matter. This provision refers to the issue of **9.128**

119 Art 2, Law No 136 of 1953.

120 ibid, Arts 23 and 24.

technical and safety standards. There are many rules on safety, but the basic law is the Ministerial Decree of 24 November 1984. This decree regulates, amongst other issues, the minimum distances between a gas pipeline and a building and the crossing of railways and other transport infrastructure.

9.129 The establishment of gas pipelines near waterways can cause both water and soil pollution. To this end the law supplies specific technical provisions in order to prevent damage to the environment. A public authorization is required for the construction of the subsoil pipeline and this commonly includes technical rules regarding the depth of the pipeline (which must be lower than the bed of the waterway) in order to avoid damage to the pipeline resulting from changes of the riverbed.

9.130 Likewise, the removal of abandoned pipelines represents an infringement of the public land (in particular of the riverbed). Public authorization is therefore also required for the removal of pipelines.

Pipeline competition

9.131 Under Italian law there are no legal hindrances for the construction of subsoil gas pipelines. Nevertheless, it has been noted that ENI/SNAM has a clear advantage, because under the 1953 Act governing ENI, pipelines are considered to be a public utility. That pipeline competition is possible is illustrated by the establishment of a joint venture between Edison and Gazprom, which is examining the possibility of constructing a 16,000 km gas pipeline from Russia through Slovakia, Hungary, and Slovenia to northern Italy. The Italian section of the pipeline is estimated to be some 1,000 km long.

Rules governing gas transportation and gas-to-gas competition

The liberalization policy under the 1991 Reform Act

9.132 The Reform Act of 1991 introduced a limited form of third-party access (*vettoriamento*). It obliges all pipeline owners (ie SNAM and distribution companies) to transport natural gas produced in Italy to the producer's own plants or to affiliates' plants (such as those of ENI/AGIP, the Assomin Group, and Unione Petrofilera) and directly to ENEL or to other designated companies, ie municipal utilities.[121] In other words, the Law restricts the situations where TPA can be required. By limiting the designated companies to consumers such as ENEL, electricity distribution companies and producing companies, or their affiliates[122] applying the gas for their own use, the legislator has tried to avoid the establishment of direct lines

[121] See Art 12, Law 9 of 9 January 1991. As to the latter group the law actually refers to companies ruled by RD 2578 of 15 October 1925 which run an 'electricity activity' according to Art 1, para 1, Law 1643 of 6 December 1962.

[122] For a definition of the term affiliates the Law refers to Art 2359, para 1, Civil Code.

between producers and consumers. The construction of such direct lines would involve a relevant environmental impact and very high costs.

The Law also establishes some objective requirements for third-party access. First, it is limited to natural gas produced in Italy. Secondly, the gas must be adequate in terms of interchangeability, transportability, and content of noxious substances. Although the quality of third-party gas may not differ from the quality of the gas usually transported, the pipeline operator is not required to redeliver the gas shipped. The condition of interchangeability means that the shipper has the option to exchange the gas. Further limitations to TPA are the transport capacity of the pipeline, the development programmes, and the load factor of the pipeline. The pipeline owner is under no obligation to extend the pipeline capacity. **9.133**

Although Law 9/91 provides the basic framework for third-party gas carriage, the conditions and fees for access are based on negotiations between the parties involved. These negotiations are free, except that parties have to take into account adequate renumeration for the investments made, the operating costs, and the general criteria followed in the European gas markets. As long as SNAM's activities are bundled, however, it will be difficult to assess the costs of investments and transport. If parties are unable to enter into an agreement, the energy regulator, on request and after hearing the parties concerned, can establish the conditions and fees.[123] **9.134**

Except for third-party carriage, SNAM does not distinguish between a commodity price and a transportation fee. Generally, natural gas is sold according to a public tariff system, which is uniform throughout the country. Since 1994 there are three tiers of tariffs: a firm and an interruptible rate for industrial consumers and a single rate for distribution companies and municipal utilities. Each tariff is linked to a separate set of taxes. A price cap was introduced in order to stimulate productivity and service quality.[124] **9.135**

Gas-to-gas competition

The extent of competition introduced by Law no 9 of 1991 is limited indeed. It is restricted to gas produced domestically (some 30 per cent of total gas consumption). Moreover, the Act limits the number of designated companies. As the number of gas producers outside the ENI group is very limited, most of the competition comes from the electricity producers, ENEL. However, ENEL is not limiting itself to the purchase of domestic gas but is also increasing its imports. Although the 1991 Law does not provide a legal basis for access for imported gas, there are no hindrances for ENEL negotiating access with SNAM. In **9.136**

---

[123] Before 1997 tariffs were set by the *Comitato Interministeriale Prezzi* (CIP).

[124] PD Cameron, *Gas Regulation in Europe*, vol I (1995); EJC Energy, *Gas Transportation in Europe: A country by country analysis* (1997).

fact, the extent of third-party access is gradually increasing due to imports of gas by ENEL.[125]

Gas storage

9.137 Since Italy started domestic gas production in the 1950s, the number of depleted or partially depleted gas fields has gradually increased.[126] Underground gas storage was developed in 1964. The first storage fields were located near Milan,[127] and were necessary because the distance between the gas fields and the areas of consumption gradually increased, as did demand for gas in wintertime. In the 1988 National Energy Plan, the Inter-Ministerial Committee for Economic Planning proposed to increase the Italian gas storage capacity in 1992 in order to be able to cover a period of ninety days of consumption in emergency situations. These storage facilities are all operated by AGIP on behalf of SNAM.

9.138 Under the 1996 Legislative Decree, third parties can use underground storage facilities. First, storage concessions can be awarded to others besides the original producers as long as depleted reservoirs are concerned. Secondly, the Legislative Decree rules that 'unused storage capacity is given at the disposal of third parties with the prior authorization of the Minister'.[128] Obviously, third-party access to underground storage facilities is dependent on certain conditions. It should be compatible with the storage programme of the holder of the storage concession, with the foreseen developments regarding the storage deposit, and with the capacity of the transportation network. The gas injected into the storage facility will have to re-enter the network and must therefore meet the conditions of interchangeability, transportability, and content of noxious substances. As with access to the network, parties have to enter into an agreement about conditions and costs taking into account the investments, the operation costs, and the criteria followed in the European gas market.

9.139 In order to determine the unused storage capacity, holders of a storage concession have to notify the Minister each year about their storage programme for the following year. This programme must specify the volumes of gas planned for injection and withdrawal. The remaining storage capacity will be made available to third parties. Further regulations for underground storage and third-party access will be established by Ministerial Decree.

---

[125] ENI *Fact Book* (1998) 14 mentions an increase of TPA by 23.4% due to an agreement between ENEL and Algeria for import of natural gas.

[126] See also I Schong, 'Underground Gas Storage in Italy: The Juridical Regime of the Natural Gas Storage System' (1998).

[127] The first storage fields were located in Cortemaggiore (1964), Sergnano (1965), Brugherio (1966), and Ripalta (1967).

[128] Art 13, para 9, Legislative Decree 625 of 25 November 1996.

Despite the above-mentioned possibilities for access to underground storage facilities, it is doubtful to what extent it will take place. There is a shortage of capacity both in the storage facilities and the transmission networks. **9.140**

(3) Gas Distribution

SNAM supplies a considerable part of the local and regional distribution companies. It should be noted that others are not prohibited from supplying gas. Nevertheless, SNAM has a *de facto* supply monopoly in parts of Italy. Vertical integration of the gas sector is after all not limited to production (ENI/AGIP) and transmission (ENI/SNAM), but also involves distribution, as SNAM holds shares in the Italgas group,[129] which supplies some 27 per cent of the smaller consumers. However, most consumers are directly supplied by (750) municipalities or private companies. The municipalities can operate either single or jointly in groups. **9.141**

(4) Legislative Developments: Implementation of the Gas Directive

Law delegating to the Government the powers to adopt the Gas Directive

In 1999 the legislator adopted Law no 144 of 19 May 1999 in which it delegated to the Government powers to adopt provisions implementing EC Directive 98/30 on common rules for the internal market in natural gas. By contrast to the Decree implementing the EC Electricity Directive, this Law not only addresses the implementation of the Gas Directive but also various other issues such as investments and incentives to increase employment.[130] Article 41 of Law 144/99 provides guiding principles and criteria (a requirement always attached to the delegation) to be complied with on legislating in implementation of a Directive. **9.142**

On 19 May 2000 the Government issued a Legislative Decree under Law 144/99 implementing the Gas Directive.[131] Italy therefore implemented the Directive well within its deadline of 10 August 2000. The new regime is aimed at promoting liberalization of the natural gas market, in particular with regard to transport, storage, and distribution. All relevant components of the national system, including those pertaining to public service, will have to be rearranged accordingly. **9.143**

The principles and criteria provided by Law 144/999 may be summarized as follows: **9.144**

—the opening of the market must conform with rules ensuring public service, including its universality, quality, and security as well as interconnection and

[129] Of which SNAM holds 41% and private investors the remaining 51%.

[130] The implementation of EC Directive 96/92 on common rules for the electricity market is being implemented on the basis of a specific Community Law 128/98. The reason for this difference lies in the need to implement the Gas Directive before the deadline established in the Directive, which means that it would have not been possible to wait for the next Community Law to delegate.

[131] Legislative Decree 164 of 23 May 2000. The implementation date ran for one year from 23 May 1999.

interoperation of the systems. No prejudice must ensue to the powers of the Electricity and Gas Authority;

—given the increasing need for natural gas and for a higher degree of interconnection with the present European gas system, the relevant infrastructures must be ensured as a matter of urgency and not be deferred insofar as they are of public utility pursuant to the applicable laws;

—any regulatory disparity among operators and discriminatory treatment among undertakings must be eliminated. Measures must be adopted to preserve the security of supply, to promote new infrastructures for production, storage, and import, and to facilitate competitiveness and the rational use of existing infrastructures;

—if instrumental to market opening, integrated undertakings are to set up separate companies with individual accounts for import, transport, distribution, and storage in order to avoid discrimination and distortion of competition. Transparent and non-discriminatory conditions for regulated access to the gas system must be ensured; and

—measures must be adopted in order to secure the opening of the national gas market within the framework of the European markets integration. These measures are to address criteria for eligible customers on the basis of consumption per locality, and equal competitiveness conditions in the European gas market via reciprocity conditions with other EU member States.

9.145 Considering the above criteria and possible legislative and organizational developments,[132] it should be recalled that competition in the gas sector is affected by the gas fields in operation, often located in distant countries such as Russia and Algeria. Hence, the possibilities for gas-to-gas competition are structurally limited. Moreover, the gas sector in Italy is characterized by a vertical integration resulting in a *de facto* quasi-monopoly where ENI/SNAM holds a dominant position. This situation, together with fiscal advantages for natural gas, is seen as a significant obstacle to the development of both gas-to-gas and inter-fuel competition. Moreover, limiting the market opening to the 'minimum' requirement of the Directive would have an opposite effect, as it would actually reduce the 'free' market presently accessible to competitors of SNAM.

9.146 The regulatory provisions should therefore focus mainly on activities featuring a natural monopoly such as transport, distribution, and storage of natural gas. General interests could be protected by determining, on one hand, a broad threshold of eligible customers allowed to accede to the market freely, and, on the other hand, by creating separate companies for natural monopoly activities and for competitive activities, ie unbundling.

[132] Elements drawn from the annual (1998) report by the Authority for competition and the market.

It seems particularly important that the competent Regulatory Authority be able to intervene in the gas market on the same basis as in the electricity sector, and to use basically similar regulatory instruments. It is equally important that, despite the limitations referred to above, appropriate regulatory provisions be taken on access conditions to the transport grid: this would make it possible for the more efficient gas producers to enter the gas consumer market.[133] **9.147**

Legislative Decree 164/00 implementing the Gas Directive

The Gas Directive is implemented by Legislative Decree 164/00, which was approved by the Council of Ministers on 19 May 2000. When examining this Decree some provisions are of special interest. First, it departs to some extent from expectations as to the relevant antitrust provisions. This is one of the main issues of the implementing Decree, which stipulates that no single gas undertaking can represent more than 75 per cent of the total gas supply in the national network (this clearly meaning a wider choice for customers now permitted to buy gas from SNAM competitors) from January 2002 until 2010. The ceiling will have to be brought down to 61 per cent (at a rate of 2 per cent per year after 2002). From 2003 until 2010, the gas sold to final customers must not exceed 50 per cent per undertaking.[134] **9.148**

Another important issue is the qualification of eligible customers. Initially final customers consuming over 200,000 cubic metres of gas per year as well as all power generators and distributors will be eligible.[135] As of January 2003 all final customers will become eligible customers.[136] **9.149**

Thirdly, as of January 2002, dispatch and transport (activities of public interest) will be separated, via the creation of 'ad hoc' companies, from all other activities pertaining to the sector, and likewise for distribution (a public service). Storage is also, in any case, subject to unbundling from transport and delivery.[137] Distribution companies selling gas to less than 100,000 final customers shall comply with legal unbundling requirements by 1 January 2003.[138] Furthermore, provision is made (ahead of the measures for liberalization of local public services, addressed in a separate draft law) to the effect that gas distribution will be ensured by means of tenders.[139] **9.150**

[133] Currently, the extent of third party access is limited. The presence of an 'integrated operator' makes regulation more difficult and complex. For this reason and following an investigation on the gas sector, the Competition Authority strongly recommended in 1997 to establish a separate company for transport, storage and distribution on one side, and another company for import and production on the other.

[134] Art 19, paras 2 and 3.

[135] Art 22, para 1c.

[136] Art 22, para 2.

[137] Art 21, paras 1 and 2.

[138] Art 16, para 1.

[139] Art 14, para 1.

9.151 Legislative Decree 164/00 opts for regulated TPA to all facilities (transport, distribution, storage and LNG plants). Tariffs will be established by an independent authority on the basis of criteria indicated in the Decree.

9.152 Under the Decree, the Energy Regulatory Authority is entrusted with a number of powers, not only to check the liberalization process, but also to check compliance with the many requirements aiming at ensuring its effectiveness. A starting point is checking tariffs, both the consumer tariffs and the pricing of transport, distribution, and storage.

9.153 Finally, the Decree has not been adopted without criticism about certain basic issues, although some problems are linked to the intrinsic differences between the electricity and gas sectors, especially as regards the introduction of a competition mechanism which is significantly less simple in the latter sector.

9.154 In general, it is observed that while the Decree was intended to implement the Directive, the actual implementing provisions go beyond this objective, pushing the liberalization process into a thorough reform of the sector concerned, and even, according to some, exceeding the limits set out in Law 144/90 (ie in terms of principles and criteria as attached to the delegation, see para 9.144).

9.155 More specifically, the time schedule and supply ceilings established within the antitrust provisions are unexpected (being in fact the result of a last minute decision within the Government) as far as SNAM is concerned. This has given rise to discomfort within SNAM and appreciation from competitors, in both cases for understandable reasons, although the company will presumably face the challenge pragmatically. However, the opening up of the market under the recent provisions seems to affect mostly distribution and sale, whereas the impact on production and import is likely to be modest. This is of capital importance since the latter have, in their turn, a direct impact on the price of raw materials. A consequence of this is that the Authority's checks on the pricing of transport and distribution could be a difficult task, and not altogether consistent with the system in operation based on regulated access.

9.156 Practical application of the new regime is needed in order to experience pros and cons, which would make it possible to work out organizational and/or legal adjustments as the case may be.

G. The New Regime Governing the Electricity Sector: Implementation of EC Directive 96/92

(1) Introduction

The first legal developments in Italy relating to Community law on electricity date back to 1992, when a Ministerial Decree[140] was adopted to implement EEC Directive 547/90 on the transit of electricity through cross-border transmission grids. Although this Directive was more limited in scope than originally envisaged, it was still an important step towards an improvement of interconnected systems and exchanges between major European grids, by enabling national electricity boards to buy electricity from bordering and non-bordering countries. The provisions of the implementing decree reflected almost literally the Directive and put the obligation on ENEL (at the time responsible for the high-tension electric grid in Italy) to comply with those requirements, including no transit discrimination or abuse, security of supply, quality of service, etc. **9.157**

The next (and latest) important legal development concerning the electricity sector are the provisions adopted in March 1999 in order to implement EC Directive 96/92. These provisions are included in a Legislative Decree[141] and stem again from a delegation to the Government provided for in the 1995–97 'Community Law'.[142] This Law not only delegated the implementation of the Directive, but also the restructuring of all the relevant components of the national electricity system.[143] These concern mainly the powers of the Energy Regulatory Authority and the role and position of ENEL in the context of the new regime, the latter position possibly being the most complex set of provisions in Legislative Decree 79/1999. It should, however, be borne in mind that ENEL's position is closely linked to its privatization, which is not a direct consequence of the Directive, although the privatization process may only be finalized following the liberalization stipulated in the legislation implementing the Directive. The Directive's requirement of unbundled accounts therefore does not cause any dilemma for ENEL, as the Decree[144] provides for complete restructuring of the company. In fact it aims at a legal unbundling, creating separate companies for the production, distribution, and sale to eligible customers as well as to non-eligible customers who continue to be supplied by the 'local' utility. In addition, the Decree provides for the **9.158**

[140] Decree of the Ministry of Industry, of June 6 1992. The reason for a simple ministerial decree to implement the Directive is found in the 'Community Law' No 142 of 19 February 1992, which indicated such a decree as an implementing tool, given the predominantly technical contents of the subject matter.

[141] Legislative Decree of March 16 1999, No 79.

[142] Law of April 24, 1998, No 128.

[143] Art 36, Law 128 of 24 April 1998.

[144] Art 13 Decree 79/99.

exercise of ownership rights on the transmission grid, the decommissioning of nuclear power stations, and other related activities. The more specific regulatory provisions of Decree 79/99 are discussed below.

(2) Market Opening

9.159 According to the requirements of the Directive, provisions are included in the Decree[145] outlining the gradual opening of the Italian electricity market. The Decree qualifies the following categories of consumers as being eligible: (i) distribution companies delivering to customers connected to their grid, (ii) wholesale customers (confined to energy consumed by eligible customers with whom these companies have stipulated a contract), and (iii) natural or legal persons recognized by the State as having the legal capacity to purchase or sell electricity and able to choose the selling or distributing company. In order to increase progressively the opening up of the market, eligible customers are those consumers using as of January 2000 no less than 20 GWh and as from the year 2002 no less than 9 GWh.

9.160 The above system is in line with the Directive, where in fact such a gradual approach is intended to make it possible for the electricity industry to adjust to the new context on the basis of a 'flexible and ordered' process. Be that as it may, it is the basis for the creation of a dual market of free customers on the one hand, and of those bound to the purchase of electricity only from the 'local' company on the other. The weaker position of small users/customers is recognized by the Decree as it provides for certain public service obligations. The introduction of standardized tariffs in combination with the 'single buyer' specifically aim at the protection of small users/customers.

(3) Public Service Obligations

9.161 The need to strike a balance between the competition and the public service principles is one of the main features of the Decree, whereby[146] all the facets associated with liberalization are preserved on condition that obligations deriving from electricity as a public service are complied with. Such obligations include above all the application over the national territory of a standard tariff for customers other than eligible ones, ie the final customers (end-users) entitled to buy electricity exclusively from the distribution company in the territory where the customer is located ('bound' customers). The aim is to ensure security of supply as well as protection of the consumer and the environment, in the event that free competition fails to do so.

[145] ibid, Art 14.
[146] Art 1, 79/99.

(4) Price Regulation

Law no 481 of 1995 establishing the Energy Regulatory Authority also considered the question of electricity prices.[147] It particularly required uniform electricity prices for every consumer category on the whole national territory in order to guarantee equal treatment of consumers. The Regulator has the power to issue guidelines for cost identification and disaggregation of charges. Price regulation follows a system of automatic calculation mechanisms on the basis of criteria pre-set by the Regulator and linked to the state of the market. Every year by 30 September, each energy supply company has to send a proposal on new electricity prices to the Regulator, who has the power to reject or amend these proposals. The prices are published before 31 December of the same year and enter into force the following 1 January. The Regulator is therefore awarded important powers regarding the setting of prices. **9.162**

(5) Production, Import, and Export

Introduction

The Directive leaves Member States free to set out long-term planning. Subsequently, Community Law 128/98, providing the basis for the implementation of the EC Electricity Directive, holds that the Ministry for Industry, Trade, and Crafts is responsible for a secure and economical national generation system to be preserved as far as the use and supply of primary energy sources are concerned. The Decree implementing the Directive is more limited and only empowers the Ministry to issue general guidelines for the 'manager' of the transmission grid (see below) and for the managing companies of the decommissioned nuclear power stations. Nevertheless, according to Legislative Decree 112/98 the State is in any case empowered to determine the objectives and guidelines of national energy policy. This Decree stems from Law no 59 of 1997, conferring functions on regions and local entities (see above, paragraphs 9.70–9.78). **9.163**

Production

Since the 1980s there has been some competition within the production of electricity. Law 9/1981 enabled undertakings to produce electricity for their own use and for sole purchase by ENEL. Ten years later the Reform Law (Law 10/1991) also permitted third parties to generate electricity insofar as renewable resources are used. The Decree is further opening up the market as production is free and subject to authorization for the construction and operation of new installations using conventional sources. The authorization procedure for new installations will be laid down without prejudice to the provisions of Decree 112/98 (see above) and to the **9.164**

[147] Art 3, Law 481/1995.

legislation on the environmental impact assessment. The existing ENEL installations will in the meantime be transferred to the relevant companies under the new electricity regime. Finally it is ruled that from the year 2003 production or import must be limited to 50 per cent of the aggregate produced and imported in Italy.[148]

Import and export

9.165 Import and export, previously ENEL's monopoly, are now liberalized, taking into account the modalities and conditions established by the Energy Regulatory Authority for import in order to ensure sufficient transport capacity and safe operation of the grid. The Authority is also called upon to adopt standards on import from non-EU countries, to preserve its environmental and economic compatibility on conditions of reciprocity.

(6) Transmission

Introduction

9.166 Transmission is considered a natural monopoly and remains the State's prerogative. Therefore it is ruled that the shares of the transmission company are held by the Ministry of Treasury and will not be put on the market, ie privatized. In other words, after the disintegration of the vertical integrated company ENEL, the transmission lines will still be owned by ENEL. In addition, separate managers will be appointed to operate the grid and the supply system.

Network manager

9.167 A manager of the transmission grid is responsible for the transmission and delivery of electricity, and ensures compliance with any other obligation concerning security, reliability, and effectiveness, as well as the lowest possible cost of service and supply and non-discrimination among users. The manager must also ensure connection to the national transmission grid for any applicant to this effect, without prejudice to the continuity of the service and in compliance with the technical rules set up in Article 3 of the Decree. The Regulatory Authority's technical-economic conditions for access and interconnection must also be observed.

9.168 A network manager is appointed on behalf of the State on the basis of a concession regime.[149] In practice this means that ENEL will set up a joint-stock company to take over the capacity of manager, except for the ownership of the grids.

9.169 The manager's position is (in line with the Directive) independent, at least as far as the management *per se* is concerned, from other activities unassociated with the transmission system. The other features related to that position are ensured by the

[148] Arts 8 and 10 Decree 79/99.
[149] Art 3, Decree 79/99.

responsibilities mentioned above. The Energy Regulatory Authority is called upon to lay down requirements for non-discriminatory access to the grid, and the impartiality and neutrality of the transmission and delivery service. It also establishes the relevant technical rules and checks compliance. Moreover, the Authority may impose the use of electricity from renewable sources and co-generation as a priority.

The Ministry of Industry is empowered, *inter alia*, to determine the ambit of the national transmission grid, the manager's strategic and operational tasks, to grant the required concessions and to exert shareholder's rights (free of charges and in agreement with the Ministry of Treasury, which is the sole and full owner of the shares). Hence, it may be said that the powers conferred on the Ministry are limited insofar as they concern the manager's public tasks, which in fact are directly supervised by the Minister according to the concession regime. As to the form of the company represented by the manager, the Ministry's attributions are more extensive, both because Decree 79/99 could not have had certain effects on the company and for the purpose of securing the objectives of public interest to be preserved under the new regime. As to the Energy Regulatory Authority, it is seemingly left with basically technical powers, although the law creating it had provided for policy and supervision powers in this respect as a prominent feature of the Authority. **9.170**

Single buyer and market manager

Articles 4 and 5 of Decree 79/99 provide for the establishment of a 'single buyer' and a 'market manager'. The former is to set up a joint-stock company called the 'single buyer', which enters into supply contracts making available to 'bound' or non-eligible customers an uninterrupted, safe, efficient electricity supply without tariff discrimination. This is aimed at creating a public service ensuring universality, quality, and security. **9.171**

The 'market manager', however, consists of another joint-stock company, which organizes the electricity market (purchase and sale) on a neutral, transparent, objective, and competitive basis. The market regulations have to be approved by the Ministry of Industry in agreement with the Regulatory Authority. A particular feature of the system is that the market manager is competent to arrange access by producers to the grid based on 'economic merit', ie on 'economical' distribution. This does not exclude the appearance of a parallel free market for eligible customers, in respect of which the Regulatory Authority has the competence to lay down clauses and technical regulations pertaining to bilateral contracts (ie supply contracts between two market operators).[150] **9.172**

[150] Art 6, Decree 79/99.

(7) Distribution

9.173 Distribution is subject to concession.[151] Companies active upon the entry into force of Decree 79/99 (1 April 1999) are entitled to continue their distribution activities up to 31 December 2030, provided that concessions are granted by 31 March 2001. The Ministry of Industry and the Regulatory Authority will determine by a specific regulation modalities, conditions, and criteria for granting concessions after 2030. Distribution companies are obliged to connect their own grids to any applicant, without affecting continuity in the service and in compliance with rules (addressing also tariffs) adopted by the regulatory Authority. In order to rationalize distribution, only one concession may be granted for each municipality. Provision is made for the aggregation of distribution companies acting over the same territory.

(8) Alternative Resources

Renewable sources

9.174 The use of renewable energy sources in the electricity production is not a new phenomenon. Laws 9 and 10 implementing the 1988 National Energy Plan had already liberalized the production of electricity from renewable sources. In other words, the generation of electricity on the basis of renewable energy sources was not limited to ENEL, but open to any private or public person.

9.175 In order to promote the use of renewable energy sources, energy saving, and a further limitation of carbon dioxide emissions, importers and producers of energy from non-renewable sources are obliged, as of the year 2001, to introduce into the national system a percentage of energy from renewable sources. This obligation applies to power plants that are put in operation soon after the entry into force of the Decree.[152] In general, account must be taken of developments relating to compliance with the standards on limitation of polluting gas emissions, with particular regard to international commitments under the Kyoto Protocol.

Hydroelectricity

9.176 Hydroelectricity is one of the 'clean' energy resources for electricity generation. Competition in hydroelectricity is to be introduced slowly as concessions granted to ENEL expire thirty years after entry into force of the Decree.[153] New concessions are the competence of regions, pursuant to Decree 112/98. Anybody may apply for a concession, provided that organizational and financial requirements are fulfilled. In the case of succession to a previous concession holder, an increase of the energy produced as well as a plan for the environmental improvement of the

---

[151] Art 9, Decree 79/99.
[152] Art 11, Decree 79/99.
[153] ibid, Art 12.

pertinent site are to be submitted by the applicant for the purpose of the concession.

Nuclear energy

The position of ENEL

The nationalization of the electricity sector in 1962 resulted in ENEL also becoming the operator of the nuclear power stations.[154] The nationalization process also had an impact on the new Nuclear Law no1860 of 1962[155] as a distinction was made between installations intended for the production and use of nuclear energy for industrial purposes, and for electricity production (reserved to the State). The latter remained subject to the pre-existing general regime of electricity generation. The partial innovation of this regime was basically administrative, and introduced obligations for the operator of nuclear power stations, such as technical and economic capability, preparedness to dispose of radioactive waste, and financial security in case of an incident.[156] Due to its general nature, Law 1860 did not address nuclear safety and radiation protection. The issue of nuclear safety was included in other legislation developed since 1964. **9.177**

Licensing regime

Under Presidential Decree no 185 of 1964[157] all nuclear installations (including power stations) were made subject to a licensing regime for nuclear safety and radiation protection.[158] This Decree was amended in 1995 by Decree no 230, as a result of which Italian nuclear legislation was brought into line with the many Euratom Directives on radiation protection adopted in the meantime. **9.178**

Another basic legislative step was the adoption of Law no 393 in 1975 on site selection for nuclear power stations. It laid down a four-step procedure, which covered decisions ranging from the approval of a multiyear national nuclear power programme, to the choice of a precise site for a station to be built. This Law supplemented Presidential Decree 185 and was adopted mainly to address the technical and environmental requirements of nuclear sites. It also met the **9.179**

[154] It also influenced the development of Italian nuclear law which had been in preparation during those years as well as the implementation of the first Euratom Basic Standards (1959) on radiation protection.

[155] Law of December 31 1962, No 1860 on peaceful use of nuclear energy.

[156] ibid, Art 6.

[157] DPR of 13 February 1964, No 185, on the safety of plants and the protection of workers and the public against the risks arising from the peaceful use of nuclear energy.

[158] About nuclear power installations and especially the licensing regime, see F Nocera and A Di Loreto, 'Le procedure per l'autorizzazione degli impianti nucleari alla luce dell'esperienza acquisita nell'ultimo triennio' in *Ingegneria Nucleare, Rassegna bimestrale ANDIN, Anno X*, No 1, gennaio-febbraio 1969; F Nocera and C Polvani, 'Legal aspects of radiation protection in Italy' in NRPB Radiological Protection Bulletin No 9, October 1974; F Nocera and A Belli, 'Aspetti legislativi connessi alla produzione di energia elettronucleare' in *Quaderni del Giornale di Fisica*, vol I, No 2, 1976.

increased attention on environmental issues and created conditions for greater public acceptance of nuclear energy.[159]

9.180 Law no 393 was in part amended by Law no 8 of 1983[160] and gave CIPE (the Interministerial Committee on Economic Planning) some competence in the site selection procedure, previously belonging to the regions. This led to a national referendum for repeal of the relevant provisions of Law no 8/83. The success of the referendum (which did not concern the whole issue of nuclear energy but merely those particular provisions) had a much broader and above all a political impact, leading fairly soon to a 'moratorium' which in practice resulted in the phasing out of nuclear energy for electricity production.

9.181 However, it must be pointed out that, despite political events, Italian legislation relating to nuclear energy has been further developed. As of 1986, with the creation of the Ministry of the Environment,[161] a number of laws and related decrees have been or are to be adopted. Due to the implementation of EC Directives on Environmental Impact Assessment (EIA)[162] the licensing regime of nuclear installations now includes the relevant EIA procedure (see also below). Moreover, as pointed out above, Legislative Decree no 230 of 1995 implemented the many Euratom Directives.

9.182 The present standard procedure, involving many administrations and consultative bodies, for the operation of a nuclear power station contemplates two main stages: construction (subject to a clearance certificate from the Ministry of Industry) and operation. Both stages require a licence granted by the same Ministry in successive stages on the basis of successful operation tests, obviously involving nuclear fuel. These tests may not be performed before an (external) emergency plan has been approved by the Minister for the Interior. Similarly, the practical implementation of designs concerning radioactive waste disposal may not be authorized before the relevant general data have been communicated to the European Commission.[163] Inspection is carried out during construction and operation by ANPA (see above, paragraph 9.81) the Work Inspectorate (Ministry of Labour), and the local health authorities.

Decommissioning

9.183 Although the structure of the licensing regime remains unaltered under Decree 230 of 1995, the principal innovation concerns the decommissioning of nuclear

[159] See, *inter alia*, F Nocera, 'Italian law relating to the siting, construction and operation of nuclear plants. Authorisation procedure' in RT/GIU(77)1, CNEN, Rome.

[160] Law No 8 of 10 January 1983, on economic incentives to regions and municipalities making potential sites available for nuclear power stations.

[161] Law No 349 of 8 July 1986, which included provisions on damage to the environment.

[162] EC Directive 337 of 1985 as amended in 1997.

[163] See Art 37, Euratom Treaty.

installations.[164] Decommissioning was not addressed in the previous legislation. Given the developments described above, decommissioning is a very important part of the present legislation as the four Italian nuclear power stations are being decommissioned. Three installations were to be decommissioned anyway since they belonged to the first generation of nuclear power stations. The fourth and most recent one, at Caorso near Piacenza, had been in operation for many years and was closed down as a consequence of the referendum.

The decommissioning licence is granted (if necessary in more than one stage) by the Ministry of Industry, which is also empowered to impose requirements as to the state of the installation and the site on the basis of a report submitted by the operator.[165] During the decommissioning process, the requirements relating to nuclear third-party liability and financial security (which normally apply to the operation of an installation) must also be complied with, unless and until the concerned installation is excluded from the scope of the provisions adopted in conformity with the international nuclear liability regime. **9.184**

H. Energy and the Environment

(1) Introduction

Addressing the issue of 'energy and environment' makes it necessary to recall certain features of both the energy and environmental sector *per se*, since both regimes have developed along similar routes. **9.185**

The Italian energy system is based on a series of laws, regulations, etc adopted at different points in time and governing many sectors separately, which does not result in a unitary and comprehensive legal regime. Similarly, the environment has been the object of legislation dictated by circumstances rather than stemming from properly integrated planning. This also led to the proliferation of (often contradictory) legislation, as well as to difficulties in its interpretation and application. Such difficulties should be put down, *inter alia,* to different authorities (ministries) being called upon, having separate competences not necessarily and exclusively representative of the components concerned (air, soil, water, etc). **9.186**

(2) Overview of the Energy-Related Regime of Environmental Legislation

The development of this legislation by now covers well over 30 years, during which a considerable number of provisions have been adopted. Looking at examples of the **9.187**

[164] Arts 55–7.

[165] For a comprehensive analysis of Decree 230, see F Nocera, 'Il quadro normativo della sicurezza nelle attività con radiazioni ionizzanti' in CEDAM, *L'inquinamento da agenti fisici-Rumore, radiazioni e microclima* (1999).

main legal and regulatory texts also gives an idea of the 'sectoral' approach when legislating to protect the environment. In 1966 the first Law[166] on atmospheric pollution was passed; in 1973 a Law[167] addressed the preservation of health and of the environment, as well as noise, water, and atmospheric pollution in connection with industrial plants. Law 393/75 considered this last item in connection with turbo-gas power stations. A further example is the 1976 Law[168] on the protection of water from any source of pollution (discharge). In 1982 another Law[169] provided for incentives to use alternative (and less polluting) energy sources, with a view to limiting energy consumption and fostering the use of renewable sources. This might have marked a preliminary turn in energy policy as regards environmental issues, since this Law was adopted to implement the 1981 National Energy Plan (PEN), the provisions aiming to enhance the use of alternative sources, obviously having positive environmental implications. It is important to recall that this objective is also pursued in Laws 9 and 10 of 1991 which implemented the 1988 PEN, by liberalizing the production of electricity from renewable sources.

9.188 Although this abundance of legislation and related bureaucratic burdens have in practice hindered and delayed the granting of licences and concessions for the operation of energy plants, it must be acknowledged that the need to protect the environment has certainly become a fundamental feature of Italian energy law. Naturally, this characteristic is also, and understandably, due to the need to take into account the energy-environment interface issues stressed in European Community energy policy and relevant legislation.

9.189 It may be said in fact that the clear trend towards a stronger consideration of environmental issues as an indispensable facet of energy production and use, is gradually creating conditions for the two legal and regulatory threads to converge, thus reducing their 'independent' character.

(3) Environmental Impact Assessment

9.190 The adoption by the EC Council of Directive 85/337 on Environmental Impact Assessment (EIA) was a significant event as far as uniform action to protect the environment in the Community was concerned. A first consequence in Italy was the creation in 1986 of the Ministry for the Environment (by Law no 349)[170] which provided the basis for the adoption of decrees implementing certain parts of the Directive. Essential rules for environmental compatibility assessment were

---

166 Law 615 of 13 July 1966, on measures to protect against pollution of the atmosphere.
167 Law 880 of 18 December 1973, on the selection of sites for plants producing electricity.
168 Law 319 of 10 May 1976, (known as '*Legge Merli*') amended several times.
169 Law 308 of 29 May 1982.
170 See para 9.81 above.

laid down in a Decree of 1988.[171] A further Decree[172] identified certain categories of activities and installations subject to EIA and established requirements for the environmental impact analysis to be submitted by operators. In 1988 Italy also implemented the 1984 EC Directive on large combustion plants and adopted provisions on emissions control for large industrial plants covering power stations of any size.[173]

The amended EIA Directive 97/11 is reflected first in a Decree[174] (supplementing Decree 377/88) which incorporates the substance of the 1997 Directive (exception made, basically, for modifications to plant designs). A later Decree[175] laid down very technical standards relating to the required studies on the environmental impact of concerned activities and installation, bringing the Italian legislation into line with the Directive.[176] **9.191**

Despite the evident delay, Decree 348 of 1999 ensures a more consistent and comprehensive national regime for large categories of installations and activities to undergo an EIA. These activities and categories are, for example, the construction of oil and gas pipelines, storage of chemical, petrochemical, and natural gas products, thermoelectric and hydroelectric plants, solid fuel storage, and installations for treatment of irradiated fuel and radioactive waste. The reference framework for each category is structured on three levels: planning (associated with national and Community markets), design (associated with technological options for waste disposal, and proximity to other industrial activities), and environment (for a specific assessment of the impact, such as polluting factors, hydrogeological risks, etc). **9.192**

Finally, it must be recalled that a draft consolidated law comprehensively addressing environmental impact was discussed at length and has been approved by the Chamber of Deputies (not yet by the Senate). It is hoped that its final adoption and promulgation will take place in the not too distant future. **9.193**

---

[171] Prime Ministerial Decree 377 of 10 August 1988, concerning the environmental impact assessment as under Art 6 of Law 349/86, creating the Ministry for the Environment.

[172] Prime Ministerial Decree of 27 December 1988.

[173] Legislative Decree 203 of 24 May 1988. For comments on these legislative developments especially with regard to inspection, see *inter alia* F Nocera, 'La recente normativa sull'impatto ambientale-Fondamenti e rilievi interpretativi nell'ottica della vigilanza' in *La nuova legislazione ambientale* (1989).

[174] Decree of the President of the Republic of 11 February 1998.

[175] Decree of the President of the Republic of 2 September 1999, No 348.

[176] The decree was adopted in relation to Art 1 para 7 Decree No 377/88. It is recalled that the EC Directive stipulates a compulsory EIA for certain categories, while such assessment is optional (ie is left to decisions at the national level) for other categories. In Italy this is addressed by the Government's policy and co-ordination acts: an example is the Prime Minister's Decree of 3 September 1999, calling upon the regions as to the EIA procedure for categories under Annex II of the Directive.

I. Future Trends

9.194 The above legal framework needs to be considered in connection with other very important developments of the last two years. One is the reform of public administration both at 'central' and 'local' levels (decentralization of powers to regions, provinces, municipalities). This reform stems from a Law of 1997 and a Legislative Decree of 1998, restructuring the competencies among State, regions, and local authorities.[177] As a consequence, while the State maintains its competence in national energy policy and technical co-ordination among administrations, the regions and local authorities take on the 'government of energy' by acquiring several new competencies. This legislation is dealt with more in detail in paragraph 9.97 above.

9.195 The second development is a trend towards a new system which could be realized in the not too distant future, leading to simplification of the licensing procedures (broadly speaking), by creating a 'single counter': this would enable operators to apply to a single local authority, where all aspects (including protection of the environment) of the concerned activity/installation would be evaluated and relevant clearances granted. It should, however, be pointed out that the realization of a 'single counter' is not a straightforward enterprise, especially since it implies the co-ordination and then the unification of the many procedures which exist to cover the manifold aspects associated with activities to be started or installations to be operated: for example, the EIA procedure is still applicable in parallel with, rather than within, the system which should become based on the 'single counter' principle. The draft Law on environmental impact, while bringing some order into the extremely fragmented legal structure relating to the protection of the environment, should then create conditions for full implementation of such a system which is so far in operation only in a few regions.

Bibliography

Albano, R, *L'attuazione delle leggi energetiche n. 9 e n. 10 del 1991 ad un anno dalla loro emenazione: provvedimenti applicativi emanati e provvedimenti mancanti*, in *Rassegna giuridica della energia elettrica*, 1992, p 877 ff (contents of the Laws no. 9 and 10 of 1991

Ammannati, L, *Le privatizzazioni delle imprese pubbliche in Italia*, Milan, 1995 (privatization of the public sector)

Bottari, C, *Ente nazionale idrocarburi (Eni)*, in *Enciclopedia giuridica*, XII, Rome, 1989 (the evolution of legal regulation of hydrocarbons)

[177] Law of 15 March 1997, known as the 'Legge Bassanini', and Legislative Decree (implementing this law) 112 of 31 March 1998. For a thorough analysis of these institutional and legislative developments concerning the environment, see CEDAM, *Dizionario Giuridico delle Autorità Locali, ed. L Mezzetti* (1999).

Caia, G, *Il governo dell'economia*, in L Mazzarolli, G Pericu, A Romano, FA Roversi Monaco, and FG Scoca, *Diritto amministrativo*, Bologna, 1993, p 853 ff (evolution of public utilities)

—— *Stato e autonomie locali nella gestione dell'energia*, Milan, 1984 (regional and local competences in the energy sector)

Cameron, PD, *Gas Regulation in Europe*, vol I, Financial Times Energy Publishing, 1995

Cammelli, M (ed), *Energia e Regioni. Politiche istituzionali e strumenti di governo*, Bologna, 1986 (regional and local competences in the energy sector)

—— *Contenimento dei consumi energetici e sviluppo delle fonti rinnovabili di energia nella l. 29 maggio 1982, n. 308: il ruolo delle Regioni*, in *Le Regioni*, 1983, p 607 ss (energy conservation)

Carrabba, M, *Nazionalizzazione*, in *Digesto delle discipline pubblicistiche*, X, Turin, 1995

Cassesse, S, *Legge di riserva e art. 43 Cost.*, in *Giurisprudenza costituzionale*, 1960 (constitutional aspects of nationalizations)

Cavazzuti, F, *Privatizzazioni, imprenditori e mercati*, Bologna, 1996 (privatization of the public sector)

Cross, ED, 'Electric Utility Regulation in the European Union', John Wiley & Sons, 1996, ch 5: Italy: Returning to private enterprise

De Vergottini, G, *L'autorità di regolazione dei servizi pubblici e il sistema costituzionale dei pubblici poteri*, in *Rassegna giuridica della energia elettrica*, 1996 (Public Utilities regulatory authorities)

De Vergottini, G, (ed), *Localizzazione di impianti energetici e tutela dell'ambiente e della salute*, Rimini, 1988 (energy plant location)

Di Gaspare, G, *Appunti per uno studio di fattibilità della trasformazione dell'Enel s.p.a. in* public company, in S Amorosino (ed), *Le trasformazioni del diritto amministrativo*, Milan, 1995 (privatization of the public sector)

EJC Energy, Gas Transportation in Europe: A country by country analysis, 1997

Endrici, G, *Idrocarburi*, in *Enciclopedia giuridica*, XV, Rome, 1992 (the evolution of legal regulation of hydrocarbons); L Antonini, *Idrocarburi*, in *Digesto delle discipline pubblicistiche*, VIII, Turin, 1993, p 85 ff (the evolution of legal regulation of hydrocarbons)

Ferrari, E, *Funzioni statali, regionali e locali nell'attuazione della legge Bassanini n. 59 del 1997. Commento degli artt. 28–31 del d. legis. n. 112 del 1998*, in *Le Regioni*, 1998, p 587 ff (conveyance of state competences to local entities)

Galgano, F, *Pubblico e privato nella regolazione dei rapporti economici*, in *Trattato di diritto commerciale e di diritto pubblico dell'economia*, I, Padua, 1977

Gentile, GG, *L'attività regolatoria nel settore elettrico*, ibid, 1996 (Public Utilities regulatory authorities)

—— and Gonnelli, G, *Manuale di diritto dell'energia*, Milan, 1994 (constitutional aspects of nationalizations)

Guarino, G, *L'elettricità e lo Stato*, in *Atomo, Petrolio, Elettricità*, 1962 (constitutional aspects of nationalizations)

Guglielmi, G, *Idrocarburi*, in *Enciclopedia del diritto*, XIX, Milan, 1970, p 980 ff (the evolution of legal regulation of hydrocarbons)

Hancher, L, 'The Nuclear Referenda in Italy and their Consequences', Journal of Energy and Natural Resources Law, vol 6 no 2, 1988, 137–53

Marchetti, P (ed), *Le privatizzazioni in Italia: saggi, leggi e documenti*, Milan, 1995 (Privatization of the public sector)

Martino, D, and Fontana, D, *The Liberalisation of the Electricity Market in Italy*, OGLTR

Mezzetti, L, *'Funzioni' e 'materie' nell'ordinamento regionale: il giudice delle leggi si pronuncia su ambiente ed energia*, in *Sanità pubblica*, 1988, p 53 ff (regional and local competences in the energy sector)

—— *Esigenze unitarie nel settore dell'energia: condizioni di equilibrio e proporzionalità dell'intervento del legislatore statale*, in *Le Regioni*, 1992, p 1409 ff (regional and local competences in the energy sector)

—— *Diritti fondamentali e amministrazione dell'energia*, Rimini, 1990 (energy plant location)

—— (a cura di), *Dizionario Giuridico delle Autorità Locali*, CEDAM, 1999

Miele, T, *Per l'energia cade la riserva statale*, in *Guida agli enti locali—Dossier n. 1*, maggio 1998, p 127 ff (regional and local competences in the energy sector)

Motzo, G, *Aspetti costituzionali della nazionalizzazione delle imprese elettriche*, in Atomo, Petrolio, Elettricità, 1963 (constitutional aspects of nationalizations)

Nardone, C, and Pistilli, P, *Il quadro normativo delle privatizzazioni*, in *Rassegna giuridica della energia elettrica*, 1995 (privatization of the public sector)

Nicolazzi, M, 'Petroleum Law and Petroleum Joint Ventures in Italy', Journal of Energy and Natural Resources Law, vol 8, no 1, 1990, 30–50

Nocera, F, and Polvani, C, 'Legal aspects of radiation protection in Italy', in NRPB Radiological Protection Bulletin no 9, October 1974

—— and Belli, A, *Aspetti legislativi connessi alla produzione di energia elettronucleare*, in *Quaderni del Giornale di Fisica*, vol I, no 2, 1976

—— 'Italian law relating to the siting, construction and operation of nuclear plants. Authorisation procedure', in RT/GIU(77)1, CNEN, Rome

—— *Il quadro normativo della sicurezza nelle attività con radiazioni ionizzanti*, in *L'inquinamento da agenti fisici-Rumore, radiazioni e microclima*, CEDAM, 1999

—— *La recente normativa sull'impatto ambientale-Fondamenti e rilievi interpretativi nell'ottica della vigilanza*, in *La nuova legislazione ambientale*, Coll. dir. da F.R. Monaco, Maggioli, 1989

—— and Di Loreto, A, *Le procedure per l'autorizzazione degli impianti nucleari alla luce dell'esperienza acquisita nell'ultimo triennio*, in *Ingegneria Nucleare, Rassegna bimestrale* ANDIN, Anno X, no. 1, gennaio-febbraio 1969

—— *Dal CNRN alla recente creazione dell'ENEA. Evoluzione legislativa con particolare riguardo ai compiti istitutivi in materia di sicurezza e protezione*, in *Rossegna Giuridica dell'ENEL*, Anno XVIII, no 5, 1982

Pototschnig, U, *I pubblici servizi*, Padua, 1964 (on the evolution of public utilities)

Predeira, A, *Collettivizzazione*, in *Enciclopedia del diritto*, VII, Milan, 1960

Roggenkamp, MM, 'Implications of Privatisation, Liberalisation and Integration of Networkbound Energy Systems', Journal of Energy and Natural Resources Law, vol 15, no 1, 1997, 51–61

Roversi Monaco, FA, *L'attività economica pubblica*, in *Trattato di diritto commerciale e di diritto pubblico dell'economia*, I, Padua, 1977 (constitutional aspects of nationalizations)

Roversi Monaco, FA and Caia, G (eds), *Commentario alla legge 29 maggio 1982, n. 308*, in *Nuove leggi civili commentate*, 1983, p 1159 ff (energy conservation)

—— —— *Aspetti della semplificazione dei procedimenti amministrativi e del coordinamento degli interessi pubblici: insediamenti energetici ed esigenze di tutela ambientale*, in *Studi in ricordo di Enzo Capaccioli*, Milan, 1988, p 495 ff (energy plant location)

—— —— in *Nuove leggi civili commentate*, 193, p 277 ff (contents of the Laws nos 9 and 10 of 1991)

Acts and Regulations in Italy

National level

Royal Decree No 1443 of 29 July 1927 governing the exploration and production of subsoil minerals

Royal Decree Law No 1741 of 2 November 1933 as implemented by Royal Decree No 1303 of 20 July 1934 regulating the import, the establishment and the operation of storage and refining plants and the distribution of fuels

Law No 136 of 10 February 1953 establishing ENI (National Board for Hydrocarbons)

Law No 6 of 11 January 1957 as amended by Law No 1072 of 24 July 1962, Law No 613 of 21 July 1967 and Law No 1153 of 19 September 1967, governing exploration and production of hydrocarbons in those onshore and offshore areas for which ENI has not been awarded exclusive rights

Law No 933 of 11 August 1960 (as amended by Law No 1240 of 15 December 1971) establishing the National Committee for Nuclear Energy (*Comitato Nazionale per l'Energia Nucleare* or CNEN)

Law No 1643 of 6 December 1962 establishing ENEL (*Ente Nazionale per l'Energia Elettrica* or National Board for Electricity)

Law No 1860 of 31 December 1962 on peaceful use of nuclear energy

Presidential Decree No 185 of 13 February 1964 on safety of plants and protection of workers and the public against the risks arising from the peaceful use of nuclear energy, as amended by Decree No 230 of 17 March 1995 and by Decree No 241 of 26 May 2000

Decree-Law No 745 of 26 October 1970 (as amended by Law No 1034 of 18 December 1970 and implemented by DPR No 1269 of 27 October 1971), providing for a concession regime for the distribution of fuels

Law No 170 of 26 April 1974 considering underground storage as a public interest task such as exploring and exploiting hydrocarbons

Law No 393 of 2 August 1975 on site selection for nuclear power stations and on production and use of electricity, as amended by Law No 8 of 10 January 1983

Law No 319 of 10 May 1976 on protection of waters against pollution

Presidential Decree No 616 of 24 July 1977, implementing Law No 382 of 22 July 1975 on institutional arrangements of the Regions and on organization of public administration

Law No 309 of 15 June 1981 on allocation to End budget and amending Law No 1643 of 6 December 1962

Law No 84 of 5 March 1982 creating ENEA (*Comitato nazionale per la ricerca e per lo sviluppo dell'energia nucleare e delle energie alternative*) which replaced CNEN (the national committee for nuclear energy)

Law No 308 of 29 May 1982, as amended by Laws No 9 and 10 of 9 January 1991, concerning the regulation of energy savings and the rational use of energy, the development of renewable energy sources and the operation of power stations generated with non-fossil fuel, and implementing the National Energy Plan

Law No 529 of 7 August 1982 enabling ENEL to take over permits to produce hydroelectricity from local bodies and auto-producers

Law No 349 of 8 July 1986 creating the Ministry of the Environment and laying down provisions on damage to the environment

Prime Ministerial Decree No 397 of 10 August 1988 on environmental compatibility assessment and relevant procedure, as supplemented by DPR of 11 February 1998

Law No 142 of 8 June 1990 on the competencies of local autonomous areas

Law No 287 of 10 October 1990 on the protection of competition and of the markets

Law No 359 of 8 August 1992 concerning the transformation into share companies of public-sector bodies such as ENEL, ENI, IRI, INA

Law No 282 of 25 August 1991 on the eform of ENEA

Decree of the Ministry of Industry of 6 June 1992 implementing EEC Directive No 547/90 on the transit of electricity

Decree No 333 of 11 July 1992 as converted into Law No 359 of 8 August 1992 concerning urgent measures to stabalise public finances

Decree No 412 of 26 August 1993 containing provisions governing the planning, installation, service and maintenance of thermal plants in buildings for energy saving purposes

Law 537 of December 1993 providing for the establishment of a regulatory authority for public services by means of a legislative decree

Law No 61 of 21 January 1994 establishing the national agency for the protection of the environment (ANPA)

Presidential Decree No 484 of 18 April 1994 regarding procedures for the award of hydrocarbons licences in the non-exclusive zones

Law Decree No 332 of 31 May 1994, as converted into Law No 474 of 30 July 1994, issuing norms accelerating the privatisation process

Legislative Decree No 230 of 17 March 1995, implementing Euratom Directives 80/836, 84/867, 84/466, 89/618, 90/641 and 92/3 on ionizing radiation

Law No 481of 14 November 1995 establishing a Regulatory Authority for the Electricity and Gas Sectors

Legislative Decree No 625 of 25 November 1996 implementing the Hydrocarbons Licensing Directive

Law No 59 of 15 March 1997 (*Legge Bassanini*) as implemented by Legislative Decree No 112 of 31 March 1998 enabling the government to confer specific functions and tasks on Regions and local administrations

Decree No 36 of 30 January 1999 amending the ENEA statute following Law No 59 of 15 March 1997

Law No 128 of 24 April 1998 delegating to the Government powers to adopt provisions implementing EC Directive 96/92 on common rules for the internal electricity market

Legislative Decree No 79 of 16 March1999 implementing EC Directive 96/92 on electricity Law No 144 of 19 May 1999 delegating to the Government powers to adopt provisions implementing EC Directive No 98/30 on common rules for the internal market in natural gas

Legislative Decree No 164 of 23 May 2000 implementing EC Directive 98/30 on gas

Regional level

Sicily: Regional Law No 30 of 20 March 1950 on the exploration for and the production of hydrocarbons as implemented by Regional Decree No 439 of 19 February 1955 and Regional Decree No 54 of 1 October 1956

Sardinia: Regional Law No 20 of 19 December 1959 on the exploration for and the production of hydrocarbons

10

ENERGY LAW IN THE NETHERLANDS

Martha M Roggenkamp

A. Introduction

(1) Domestic Energy Sources

The Netherlands has always had domestic energy resources. For many centuries wind and coal were the most important sources of energy. Although the first windmills were constructed at the end of the Middle Ages, the use of wind energy climaxed in the seventeenth and eighteenth centuries when windmills were used for numerous industrial purposes.[1] In 1850 some 9,000 mills were operating in the Netherlands. Soon after their number decreased due to the use of steam power and the invention of the combustion engine.[2] **10.01**

[1] Important examples are the (polder) drainage mills, watermills, flour mills, and sawmills.
[2] AJ Wiggers *et al* (eds), *Grote Winkler Prins Encyclopedie*, 1977, vol 20, 174–8.

10.02 Open-cast coal mining started as early as the beginning of the twelfth century in the southern part of the Dutch province of Limburg and was gradually replaced by underground mining in the fourteenth century. The coal reserves are situated in the province of Limburg and straddle into Belgium and Germany. Several border adjustments in the nineteenth century have complicated the issue of straddling coalfields, ie the division of mining rights and ownership rights of the cross-border coalfields. These legal issues have not been resolved after the closure of the coal mines in Belgian, Germany, and the Netherlands. Negotiations about shared control of the groundwater level and the issue of liability for damages resulting from the abandoned coal mines are pending.

10.03 Through the discovery of petroleum resources, the energy situation changed at the beginning of this century. The first oil was shown to be present in the Winterswijk area (eastern Netherlands) in 1924. This was followed by the discovery of several other oilfields and minor gasfields in the following decades. However, the Dutch energy situation altered drastically as a result of the discovery of large quantities of natural gas in the Groningen area in 1959. This led to a fundamental change in Dutch energy policy as a result of which the production of coal ceased gradually. The last coal mine was closed in 1974.[3]

10.04 The present energy situation is characterized by large-scale production of natural gas onshore as well as offshore. The Groningen gasfield presently produces some 50 per cent of total Dutch gas production.[4] The vast size of the Groningen gasfield accounts for the important position of the Netherlands in the European energy market. Although the Netherlands only ranks fourth as a producer of oil in the European Community,[5] it does take a prominent position in the international oil market with regard to the import, transit, and processing of oil. Due to its strategic and central position many refineries are located near Rotterdam from which a sizeable network of crude oil pipelines as well as product pipelines runs to the hinterland in Belgium and Germany (the Ruhr area).

10.05 In addition to the above-mentioned primary energy sources, electricity production provides a major energy source. However, compared to other countries the share of electricity is relatively small due to the large-scale penetration of natural gas in the energy supply market. Although the market share of gas in the non-domestic sector is considerable, gas has an unusually high degree of penetration in the domestic sector by European standards. Some 97 per cent of all households apply gas for cooking and heating purposes. Moreover, in the Netherlands natural

[3] It is possible that new projects will be initiated if modern techniques like coal gasification (methane production) make the production of coal economically feasible.

[4] In 1998 the Groningen field produced 36,388.3 million m^3 (st). The total gas production, onshore as well as offshore, accounted for 79,905.4 million m^3 (st).

[5] Total oil production in 1998 was 2029.3 million m^3. Oil production has decreased considerably compared to the 1995 production level (= 3,209.3 million m^3).

gas is also used more extensively for electricity generation than in any other EC Member State. In addition to natural gas (49 per cent), Dutch electricity production is mainly based on generation of (imported) coal (45 per cent) and nuclear energy (6 per cent).[6] The use of so-called alternative energy sources such as wind energy, biomass, and CHP is gradually increasing.[7] However, their use is limited compared to the other sources.[8]

Finally, it should be noted that the extent of nuclear energy is limited. In the Netherlands as elsewhere nuclear energy was considered as a new and important energy source in the 1960s and 1970s. Two nuclear power plants were established. Whereas the first nuclear power plant was opened in Dodewaard in 1969 (58 MW),[9] the second and larger plant was constructed in 1973 in Borsele by the provincial electricity company in Zeeland (460 MW). Although after the first oil crisis in 1973 the Government forecast the construction of three more nuclear plants, the political situation changed drastically. The Dutch population resisted the construction of more nuclear plants. This became very clear after the outcome of the 'broad social discussion' in 1983. Social resistance increased after several nuclear disasters, most notably the Chernobyl tragedy in 1987. Consequently, it was decided to decommission the existing nuclear installations and to curtail the proposed construction of more nuclear power plants. In October 1996 it was even decided that the plant in Dodewaard would be shut down before the scheduled date of closure in 2004.[10] **10.06**

[6] In 1998 the total inland electricity production was 87,570 GWh (60,329 GWh through SEP). Production capacity is some 20,000 MW (14,000 MW through SEP). Some 11,939 GWh is imported.

[7] In 1994 renewable energy sources (CHP excluded) constituted 1% of total primary energy supply. This is considerably lower than the EU average of 4%. The major source of renewable energy is waste (= 80% of total renewable electricity in the Netherlands in 1994). Other important sources are hydropower, wind power, and solar power. See IEA 1996 Review of the Netherlands, 63. As far as CHP is concerned the situation is quite different. The share of CHP has increased considerably since the beginning of the 1990s. A surplus capacity was estimated for the end of the century.

[8] In the 1980s three hydropower plants were established in the Netherlands: Linne (near Roermond) and Alphen (Noord-Brabant) on the river Maas, and Maurik in the Nederrijn. Together they produce 35 MW which is 0.2% of the total Dutch electricity supply. Although technically other hydropower projects are feasible, their realization depends on their economic viability (Volkskrant, 21 Sept 1996).

[9] This plant was established by Common Nuclear Energy Plant Netherlands Ltd (Gemeenschappelijke Kernenergiecentrale Nederland NV). It operates mainly as a research plant and produces some 0.4% of the total electricity supply in the Netherlands.

[10] In October 1996 SEP announced that decommissioning would be commenced early 1997 and last for six years. Although the decommisioning will be finalized in 2003, the final dismantling of the plant is scheduled for some 40 years later and made dependent on the reduction of radioactivity. The cost of decommissioning is estimated at 165 million Dutch guilders. Earlier dismantling is technically possible but involves much higher costs. The closing down of the plant is a direct result of the liberalization policy of the Dutch Government. In order to compete in a European market, SEP is trying to cut down costs. Keeping this research plant open requires 70 million Dutch guilders, which is considered a high sum for research without practical impact. See *Financieel Dagblad*, 4 Oct 1996.

10.07 Taking into account the overall energy situation, it can be concluded that natural gas is the most important energy resource of the Netherlands, both as a direct energy supply and as a source for electricity supply. Although the use of alternative energy sources is limited, their role will increase as a result of the 1997 Kyoto Protocol and the need to limit carbon dioxide reductions.

(2) Administrative and Regulatory Framework

Constitutional framework

10.08 The Kingdom of the Netherlands dates from 1813 when the Napoleonic reign (1795–1813) came to an end.[11] The system of centralized government introduced by Napoleon undoubtedly influenced the new constitution of the Kingdom.[12] The constitution of 1814 established a decentralized unitary State which remained in force after the constitutional reforms in 1848 and 1983.[13] Whereas sovereignty is vested jointly in the central institutions of the State, the Constitution also gives considerable powers to the provinces and the local authorities. As a result the legislative and administrative functions can be exercised on a central, a regional (12 provinces), and/or a local level (approximately 530 municipalities). The relationship between central Government and the decentralized authorities is not hierarchical. The provinces and local authorities (municipalities) are autonomous public institutions. However, their functioning is subject to various types of central control and their regulations are of a lower order than national legislation. The Constitution does not clearly define the areas of operation. It merely states that those subjects that are matters of Government concern such as defence and foreign affairs fall outside the competence of the decentralized authorities. Through the years the central Government has gradually taken over policy areas which originally fell within the autonomous sphere of the provinces and local authorities. These shifts have usually been effected by means of central legislation.

10.09 The energy sector is a clear example of such development. Energy matters are not mentioned in the Constitution. In practice the regulation and administration of the energy sector can be dealt with on all three levels. At the end of the last century, the provinces and local authorities mainly regulated electricity and gas sup-

[11] The Kingdom of the Netherlands consisted of the present-day Netherlands and Belgium. The Treaty of Vienna of 1815 officially unified both territories.

[12] Before the French rule, the territory consisted of a number of sovereign provinces which together formed a confederation (*Republiek der Verenigde Nederlanden*).

[13] The most important constitutional reform took place in 1848 and followed (more or less) the separation of Belgium and the Netherlands in 1839. The 1848 reform introduced a system of ministerial responsibility and the Government's power to dissolve Parliament. The Constitution of 1983 comprises of eight chapters: 1) fundamental rights, 2) the Government, 3) the State General, 4) permanent advisory bodies, 5) legislation and administration, 6) administration of justice, 7) decentralization, and 8) alteration of the Constitution. It should be noted that in 1954 the Charter for the Kingdom of the Netherlands entered into force. This Charter governs the relationship between the Netherlands and its former colonies the Dutch Antilles and Aruba.

ply.[14] However, due to technical developments and the increasing importance of these products for the society as a whole, the national Government initiated central legislation. A typical example is the (partial) enactment of the first Electricity Act in 1938. Nevertheless, in the absence of autonomous powers the decentralized authorities may still have some shared powers (*medebewind*), ie they carry out a policy laid down by other (higher-ranked) Government institutions.

Regulatory instruments

The central, provincial, and local authorities all have regulatory and administrative powers. The regulatory instruments issued by these authorities have a hierarchical structure, which is outlined in the Constitution. Except for the Constitution, which does not play a direct role in the energy sector, all other types of statutory regulations are used to regulate the energy sector. The most important statutory laws are the Acts of Parliament, which are the classical laws and made by Government and Parliament together.[15] These Acts of Parliament may provide for further delegation of law-making on both the central and decentralized levels. **10.10**

On the central level further delegated legislation can be issued by Orders of Council (*Algemene Maatregelen van Bestuur*) which are made by the Government alone.[16] In addition, the Minister can issue sub-delegated legislation as ministerial regulations. On a decentralized level further regulation may be issued by the provinces, municipalities, and/or the water boards through specific secondary legislation.[17] In the case of economic regulation it is customary for an Act to consist only of outlines while the larger part of the material is left to the 'lower' (delegated) law-makers. The Dutch mining legislation is a typical example of this policy. **10.11**

[14] Co-operation of the provinces, local authorities, water boards, and private law corporations is possible on the basis of the Joint Schemes Act (*Wet Gemeenschappelijke Regelingen*) of 1984 (Stb 667). It enables the joint establishment of a separate public body with regulatory powers. Co-operation is also possible on the basis of private law agreements.

[15] Both the Government and the Second Chamber have the right to propose legislation. In practice all Bills are introduced by the Government after consultations with various advisory and professional organizations. The Bill is then discussed in the Second Chamber (ie the permanent committees). The Second Chamber and the Government can amend the Bill. Consequently, the Bill goes to the First Chamber which only has the right to reject or to pass the Bill. As long as a Bill has not passed both Chambers, the Government has always the right to withdraw a Bill. A law becomes binding once it has been ratified by the King, which takes place under the political responsibility of the minister who countersigns it.

[16] Orders of Council are considered and decided upon by the Council of Ministers (after consultation by the Council of State). They are signed by the King and one or more of the Ministers involved and are therefore also referred to as Royal Decrees.

[17] In addition to this system of territorial decentralization, Dutch constitutional law also distinguishes between various forms of functional decentralization. This means that some decentralized offices are authorized to serve particular purposes. They possess regulatory and administrative powers with regard to particular areas of functioning. A typical example is the system of water boards (*waterschappen*).

10.12 Finally, special mention should be made of the so-called covenants (*convenant*), agreements between governmental authorities and/or the Government and industry or others to achieve certain goals in a particular policy area. The legal status of these covenants is not very clear as they may vary from private to public law agreements and may have legal consequences. In other cases they can more easily be described as gentlemen's agreements. In this chapter it is important to note that covenants are often used to regulate environmental issues and matters concerning energy saving.

Administrative and regulatory authorities in the energy sector

10.13 Basically, the Minister of Economic Affairs (hereinafter the Minister) is the Government official who has the main responsibility for Dutch energy policy. In the Ministry the administration of the energy sector is managed by the Directorate General for Energy. In addition, several more or less independent branches of the Ministry monitor compliance with the (energy) law. The State Supervision of Mines (*Staatstoezicht op de Mijnen*) is a separate division of the Ministry and has the responsibility of supervising the upstream petroleum industry. It also has limited regulatory powers. In 1998 two additional divisions of the Ministry were established: the Authority monitoring compliance with the Electricity Act (*Dienst uitvoering en toezicht Elektriciteitswet* or DTe) which is a separate branch of the newly established independent Competition Authority (NMa). Upon the entry into force of the new Gas Act in August 2000 the DTe has also been given the task of monitoring compliance with the Gas Act. (Although the authority will be renamed as *Dienst uitvoering en toezicht Energie*, the abbreviation DTe remains unchanged).

10.14 In addition, a number of independent advisory bodies exist which report directly to the Minister.[18] The Mining Council (*Mijnraad*) reports directly to the Minister (on request or spontaneously) with regard to matters concerning the exploration for and production of mineral resources.[19] The General Energy Council (*Algemene Energie Raad*) is the second official body advising the Minister.[20] Their task is broader in scope as they advise the Minister on matters of energy policy, especially the relationship between energy policy and other social matters and the way in which it influences Government policy.

10.15 As the regulation and administration of the production and supply of energy are based on a sectoral approach, other Ministries deal with certain matters related to the process. This is especially true for the Minister of Town and Country

[18] In the 1970s and 1980s attempts were made to diminish the number of advisory bodies and to give the remaining bodies a proper legal basis.

[19] The first Mining Council was established in 1903. The present Mining Council is established by Act of 1 May 1970 (Stb 1970, No 169).

[20] Established by law of 1 Dec 1985 (Stb 1985, nr 287 and No 611)

Planning, Housing and Environment, and the Minister of Transport and Waterworks. However, other Ministries may also be involved. Moreover, the Ministries involved can have different, even opposite, interests, which in practice complicate the administration of the energy sector as a whole.

Regulatory framework for the energy sector

The administrative and regulatory framework of the Dutch energy sector can be characterized as a system being developed on an ad hoc basis, as a result of which it is fragmentary and modest indeed. Moreover, the downstream gas and electricity supply sector was for many decades based on private law agreements between industry and the central or local Government(s). Regulation on the national level has been slow to develop and is largely the result of a need to secure a regular supply of energy and/or developments at EC level following the Internal Energy Market Programme. Consequently, it is only at the turn of this millennium that the entire energy sector is now regulated by national laws issued by Acts of Parliament. Whereas such development of centralization can be noticed at an early stage in the upstream energy sector, the downstream sector has until recently been based on decentralized regulation and legislation. **10.16**

The oldest applicable energy law in the Netherlands is the (original) French law, the *Loi conçernant les mines, les minières, et les carrières,* which was issued in 1810 by the French Emperor Napoleon (hereinafter the Mining Act 1810).[21] The aim was to bring the most important minerals, such as coal, under the direct rule of the Crown (ie central Government). Because Napoleon considered mining an important method of stimulating industrial activity, the Mining Act of 1810 placed the regime for production of the most important minerals (the 'mines') under central regulation. When the Netherlands regained its independence in 1813, the French Act was retained 'provisionally, until further measures are taken'.[22] This Act has been applied provisionally ever since and forms the basic law for the production of onshore minerals like oil and gas. Upon discovery of the offshore petroleum resources in the early 1960s the Dutch central Government applied the sovereign rights principle of the Continental Shelf Convention and enacted the Continental Shelf Mining Act 1965 (CS Mining Act) regulating the exploration for and production of oil and gas on the Dutch continental shelf. Although the integration of onshore and offshore petroleum legislation has been discussed regularly since then, a Bill providing a modern integrated mining law was only first published in 1998. **10.17**

The (downstream) electricity sector is a clear example of a system gradually moving from decentralized regulation on the local/provincial level to a system of **10.18**

[21] Bulletin des Lois No 285. Please note that the French version is still the official text of the law.
[22] Order of General Administration of 1 Dec 1813, Stb 3.

centralized regulation. The first Electricity Act stems from 1938 and has been of limited use as only three articles entered into force.[23] Subsequently, the production and supply of electricity was for five decades based on a system of local/provincial concessions for which there was no legal basis. In 1989 the Act was replaced by a new Electricity Act which clearly illustrates the Government's changing perspective towards the energy sector after the energy crises in 1974 and 1979. Since most energy sources are limited, Dutch Government policy in the 1970s focused on the general need to secure national energy supply, *inter alia*, through the reduction of total energy demand and the diversification of energy supply.[24] A stronger role of the central Government in energy affairs was considered an essential instrument for achieving these goals. The Electricity Act 1989 acknowledges the central planning role of the Government, especially as far as production is concerned. It also introduced a limited degree of competition by way of the separation of production and distribution and a qualified obligation to offer access to the transmission lines.

10.19 Although the EC's Internal Energy Market programme of 1988 also recognizes the need to ensure security of supply, its main goal is to create a competitive energy market. The latter aspect is also recognized in the third Dutch White Paper on Energy (*Energienota*) of 1995, which differs from the previous policy documents as it outlines a complete reorganization of the energy sector based on the concepts of liberalization and privatization. New legislation, such as the Electricity Act 1998[25] and the Gas Act 2000, resulted. Although the enactment of a separate Gas Act was mentioned on several occasions in the 1960s, no such Act was ever issued. In practice, the organization of the gas industry was based on private law agreements between the Minister of Economic Affairs and the industry (Gasunie). The establishment of a Gas Act means that public statutory law will (finally) regulate the entire network-bound energy sector.

10.20 From the above it can be concluded that regulating the energy sector has not been a top priority for the Dutch government. Although there is a clear tendency towards more regulation on a national level, the process has been very slow. The EC energy liberalization programme has, directly or indirectly, been of major importance for the legislative developments in the Netherlands. Although these developments mainly concern the gas and electricity sector, the upstream sector is next discussed, followed by an examination of the downstream sector.

[23] Act of 22 Oct 1938, Stb 523.

[24] This policy is included in two Energy White Papers. The first policy document *Energienota* 1974 (Kamerstuk 13 122) was followed by another *Energienota* after the second energy crisis in 1979 (Kamerstuk 15 802). This document confirms the goals which were set out in the previous document: the diversification of energy supply and the reduction of energy demand by way of energy savings.

[25] Art 52 Electricity Act 1989 provided that an evaluation should take place before 1995.

B. Exploration for and Production of Oil and Gas

(1) Introduction

The total surface of the Netherlands territory is 41,785 square kilometres. As at 1 January 1998 a total of 58 per cent is utilized for the exploration for and production of hydrocarbons. In addition 51 per cent of the area of the Dutch continental shelf (= 57,193.4 square kilometres) is also under exploration and production. Initially a clear division could be made between the Mining Act 1810 and Mining Act 1903 applying to the onshore and the CS Mining Act. However, over the years the regulatory provisions have become more analogous. The implementation of the Utilities Directive and the Hydrocarbons Licensing Directive has strengthened this development. **10.21**

Despite several attempts and announcements about the replacement of the Mining Act of 1810 by a modern mining law, new legislation has still not been adopted, as a result of which the provisional French Act has now been in force for almost 200 years. Although a new Mining Bill was sent to Parliament in September 1998,[26] it is not certain if and when this new Mining Act will enter into force. The following is therefore based on the present situation as outlined above, with a division between onshore and offshore. At the end a brief overview will be presented of the content of the Mining Bill. **10.22**

(2) Property Rights and Mining Agreements

Sovereignty and ownership rights

Under international law States have sovereignty over their territorial energy sources. In addition, coastal States exercise sovereign rights for the purpose of exploring and exploiting their natural resources in or on the continental shelf.[27] Since mining is characterized by the separation of minerals from the land, one of the legal problems involved is the division between surface and subsoil (subsea) property rights, ie between ownership of the surface and ownership of the minerals. **10.23**

In the Netherlands mining regime a distinction must be made between the onshore and offshore regimes. The offshore regime leaves no doubt about the ownership of the offshore minerals. Article 22 CS Mining Act clearly states that 'minerals in or on the continental shelf are owned by the State'. In other words, the Dutch legislator has given a wide interpretation to the sovereign rights it has **10.24**

[26] Ontwerp Mijnbouwwet, Tweede Kamer 1998, 26219.

[27] cf 1962 United Nations General Assembly Resolution on Permanent Sovereignty over Natural Resources (UNGA Res 1803 (XVII)) and Art 2 Convention on the Continental Shelf 1958 and Art 56 para 1 Law of the Sea Convention 1982. See further chapter 2 above on international energy law.

under the Continental Shelf Convention and applied a system of domanial law as the ownership of the mineral substances has been vested in the sovereign.[28] Under the domanial law system the State is given control of the subsoil in the same manner as it has over a piece of surface land of which it holds the freehold. The State may, on the basis of this system, *inter alia*, lease, or otherwise transfer the right to exploit the subsoil.

10.25 The onshore regime is more ambiguous as it does not provide for a clear ruling of ownership rights. The Mining Act 1810 only establishes ownership rights for the post-concession period as it states that 'from the moment a concession has been granted, even to the landowner, this property (the minerals) shall be distinguished from that of the surface and shall further be considered as new property' (Art. 19 Mining Act 1810). The Mining Act 1810 contains no provisions on the ownership of subsoil minerals before the award of a concession. The confusion regarding the legal status of the minerals *in situ* can be traced back to the origins of the Mining Act of 1810. Whereas the French imperial lawyers wished to apply the domanial system and assumed that the subsoil belonged to the State, Napoleon took a different stand and applied the principles of the accession theory, which holds that the ownership of the surface also comprises ownership of the subsoil.[29] The same ambiguity is to be found in the French (and later Dutch) Acts regulating property rights.[30] Under the Dutch Civil Code, ownership of the land generally carries with it ownership of what is on and in the land (= accession system) unless either other laws do not rule otherwise or the activities take place at such a depth that the landowner has no interest in opposing them.[31] Although such a *lex specialis* could be included in the subsoil mining legislation, it is interesting to note that the Mining Act of 1810 does not provide such a clause and limits itself to the post-concession status of the minerals. However, from the absence of a pre-concession clause it cannot be concluded that the accession theory automatically applies. Some provisions in the Mining Act seem to exclude the application of the accession system. First, the Mining Act 1810 obliges all persons who wish to exploit a 'mine' to apply for of a concession. Under the accession system, however, a landowner would normally not be required to apply for a concession if subsoil

[28] A third theory is the idea that subsoil minerals are *res nullius*. This theory is less important in legal practice. See for a short overview of above theories: MM Roggenkamp, *Oil and Gas: Netherlands Law and Practice*, Chancery Law Publishing, London, 1992.

[29] BF Boekhold, *Mijnrecht*, 1912, 93–121, gives an extensive description of how the Mining Act of 1810 came about.

[30] cf Art 552 of the (French) *Code Civil* of 1804 which was translated into Art 626 Dutch Civil Code of 1838.

[31] See Art 626 Dutch Civil Code of 1838 as replaced by Art 5:20 (new) Civil Code which reads that the ownership of the land comprises, insofar as the law does not rule otherwise: a) the topsoil, b) the layers of earth beneath it, etc. Moreover, the owner of the land is (exclusively) entitled to use the space above and beneath the surface, unless activities take place at such a height or depth that the owner has no interest in opposing them (Art 5:21 (new) Civil Code).

minerals are discovered. The Mining Act also rules that a concession constitutes some 'new' ownership, even for a landowner who acquires a concession for the exploitation of a mine. Moreover, under the accession system the award of a concession to a person other than the landowner would lead to the expropriation of (subsoil) property rights. According to the Dutch Constitution expropriation may only take place in the public interest and following full compensation.[32] Although the Mining Act 1810 obliges the concessionaire to pay the landowner a compensatory sum, *redevance tréfoncière*,[33] this sum is so small in relation to the value of the minerals extracted that it cannot be considered as a full payment of compensation as required under the Constitution. These observations were confirmed by the Supreme Court in 1907 when it explicitly ruled that the Mining Act of 1810 differs from the principle of accession in the Civil Code, since the granting of a concession establishes a *propriété nouvelle* which again entitles the landowner to the form of compensation known as *redevance tréfoncière*.[34]

In the legislative process following the adoption of the Mining Act of 1810, a gradual transition can be noticed from the accession system to the system of domanial law. This transition is reflected by the increasing degree of State intervention that has been applied in the mining legislation issued in the twentieth century.[35] The above ambiguity in the onshore regime will come to a definitive end when the new Mining Act enters into force. Article 1.3 Mining Bill clearly establishes that 'minerals are owned by the State': the domanial system then finally prevails onshore as well as offshore. **10.26**

Mineral development rights and mining agreements

State sovereignty also encompasses the rights of States to choose between different systems of mineral development rights, ie the most appropriate system for exploration for and production of subsoil minerals. The Netherlands is a clear example of a situation where the classical concession system has gradually been supplemented with a licensing system based on discretionary competitive bidding and governmental control through, *inter alia*, State participation. **10.27**

The characteristics of a classical concession agreement are: (i) the award of mining rights over a vast area of acreage, (ii) for a relatively long period, and (iii) providing to the company extensive control over the schedule and manner in which the **10.28**

[32] Art 147 Constitution of 1848 and Art 14 of the revised Constitution of 1983.

[33] Arts 6 and 42 Mining Act of 1810.

[34] *Hooge Raad der Nederlanden*, 25 Oct 1907, *Weekblad van het Recht*, No 8606.

[35] FH Neiszen, *Mijnbouwpolitiek*, 's Gravenhage, 1920, 8. The degree of State intervention varies from the State demanding a share of the income, via the situation that the State restricts exploration activities during a certain period of time and decides what is to be understood by the 'proper exploitation of a mine' (Mining Act 1903), to the Continental Shelf Mining Act where the system of domain law is implemented entirely as Art 22 states that the minerals in or on the continental shelf are the property of the State.

mineral reserves are developed, whilst (iv) reserving few rights to the Sovereign except for the right to receive payment based upon production (royalty).[36] Such a concession system does not include any competitive elements.

10.29 Basically, the onshore mining regime was based on such a classical concession system. Concessions were originally negotiated between the Sovereign (Crown) and the mining company and, consequently, awarded in perpetuity for a relatively large area. The award of concessions and licences took place on a 'first come, first served' basis. Hence, the basic legislative framework for onshore exploration and production of hydrocarbons was rudimentary and did not include specific competitive elements.

10.30 The CS Mining Act, however, provided for a system of licensing rounds[37] and is therefore based on a competitive licensing system giving the Government some discretionary powers. Under a competitive bidding system licences are awarded to certain qualified bidders on the basis of competitive bids. In order to participate in the bidding process, the applicants are required to meet certain (minimum) standards. The bidding is not limited to financial grounds but also covers an applicant's ability to meet some specific (national) energy goals.

10.31 Since the 1970s the onshore concession system has gradually been influenced by the offshore regime. Currently, it can be characterized as a competitive system similar to the offshore regime. Both the onshore and offshore regimes have been supplemented with a participation or joint venture agreement in order to give the Government more control over the production activities.

10.32 The implementation of the Hydrocarbons Licensing Directive has played an important role in the evolution of Dutch mining law. As a result of the implementation of the Directive, the onshore and offshore mining regimes are now more or less the same. The Mining Bill of 1998 seems to conclude this gradual process of legislative integration.

(3) Netherlands Mining Law and the Right to Explore for and Exploit Petroleum

The scope of the mining laws

10.33 Exploration for and production of petroleum is governed by the mining legislation. It should be noted, however, that these laws have a much wider scope. The title of the Mining Act of 1810 already indicates the existence of a tripartite division of minerals: *mines*, *minières*, and *carrières*.[38] This tripartite classification of

[36] EE Smith *et al* (eds), International Petroleum Transactions, Rocky Mountain Mineral Law Foundation, Denver, 1993, chapter 5, 279–363.

[37] Art 5 CS Mining Act.

[38] Art 1 Mining Act 1810 clearly states that 'the quantities of mineral or fossil substances situated in the ground or at the surface are, with regard to the legal regulations which have been declared to apply to each of these, categorized as *mines*, *minières*, and *carrières*'.

minerals is not based on the method of extraction, but merely indicates that for each group, separate legal regimes apply.[39] A concession system applies to *mines* which includes all those minerals that are considered to be of general interest, such as gold, silver, lead, coal, and bitumen.[40] Obviously, oil and gas are not part of the classification system of the Mining Act 1810. The concession regime of the Act is nevertheless in practice applied by a wide interpretation of the term *bitumina.* When the first petroleum concession (*Schoonebeek*) was awarded in 1948 it was decided to include the wording 'bitumens such as oil and natural gas'. This clause has also been used in subsequent (but not all) petroleum concessions.

The CS Mining Act also has a wider scope than the search for and production of oil and gas as it generally applies to the exploration for and exploitation of all minerals on the Dutch continental shelf. In practice, however, the Act focuses on the exploration for and production of petroleum as the Royal Decrees implementing the provisions of the CS Mining Act explicitly limit these activities to petroleum resources. **10.34**

The Development of mining law: from a concession to a licensing system

The present regime governing both exploration and production of natural resources has developed gradually as a result of practical and political demand. For that reason two separate legal regimes govern the mining activities onshore and offshore. Moreover, it resulted into a complex system comprising of several individual mining laws and numerous implementing orders. The law currently applying can be summed up as follows: **10.35**

ONSHORE:

Public Statutory Laws
Mining Act 1810;
Mining Act 1903;
Mineral Exploration Act 1967[41]

OFFSHORE:

Public Statutory Laws
CS Mining Act 1965[42]

---

[39] Hoge Raad 25 Jan 1924, Nederlandse Jurisprudentie 1924, 593.

[40] Art 2 Mining Act 1810 states that as: '*Mines* are considered those which are known to contain, in the form of mineral veins, layers, or heaps: gold, silver, platinum, mercury, lead, iron in veins or layers, copper, tin, zinc, calamine, bismuth, cobalt, arsenic, manganese, antimony, molybdenum, graphite or other metallic substances, sulphur, coal, lignite, bitumen, alum, and sulphates having a metallic base.'

[41] *Loi conçernant les Mines, les Minières, et les Carrières* of 21 Apr 1810; *Mijnwet* 1903 of 27 Apr 1904, Stb 73; *Wet Opsporing Delfstoffen* of 3 May 1967, Stb 258. These three Acts have most recently been amended by Act of 18 Mar 1996 implementing EC Directive 94/22/EG, Stb 199.

[42] *Mijnwet Continentaal Plat* of 23 Sep 1965, Stb 428, most recently amended by Act of 18 Mar1996 implementing EC Directive 94/22/EG, Stb 1999.

Implementing Orders	*Implementing Orders*
ONSHORE:	OFFSHORE:
Mining Regulations 1964	CS Mining Regulations Royal Decree 1967 (Rules on Exploration and Production 1967); Royal Decree on the Application of Licences and Exemptions; Royal Decree 1976 (Rules on Exploration and Production 1976);
Royal Decree Onshore Concessions 1996	Royal Decree Offshore Licences 1996
Onshore Minerals Licensing Regulation 1996.[43]	CS Hydrocarbons Regulations.[44]

10.36 The most radical legislative changes appeared in the onshore regime, which, as outlined above, has developed gradually from a classical concession system to a competitive licensing regime. Whereas the Mining Act 1810 provided for a concession only for the production of *mines*, the search for minerals was free. For a long time, the landowner's consent was the only requirement for the exploration of minerals.[45] However, as a result of the large-scale exploratory activities following the discovery of the Groningen gas field in 1959, the Minerals Exploration Act (*Wet Opsporing Delfstoffen*) entered into force in 1967. Since then a drilling licence is required to search for minerals through exploratory drilling.[46] Both the Minerals Exploration Act and the Mining Act 1810 leave the Minister of Economic Affairs full discretion concerning the choice of licensee or concessionaire.[47] In the absence of a system of bidding rounds the above rules also led to a

[43] *Mijnreglement* of 21 Dec 1964, Stb 538; *Besluit van 26 maart 1996, houdende bepalingen inzake financiële voorschriften bij een concessie voor koolwaterstoffen op grond van de Mijnwet 1903 (Besluit concessies koolwaterstoffen Nederlands territoir* 1996), Stb 212; *Regeling vergunningen en concessies delfstoffen Nederlands territoir 1996*, Staatscourant of 15 May 1996, no 93.

[44] *Besluit tot Uitvoering van art. 12 Mijnwet Continentaal Plat* of 27 Apr 1967, Stb 24; *Besluit aanvragen vergunningen en ontheffingen Mijnwet continentaal plat* of 7 Feb 1967, Stb 75; *Mijnreglement Continentaal Plat* of 13 Mar 1967, Stb 158; *Besluit tot Uitvoering van art. 12 Mijnwet Continentaal Plat* of 6 Feb 1976, Stb 102, as amended by Royal Decree of 27 Jan 1995, Stb 42; *Besluit van 26 maart 1996, houdende bepalingen inzake financiële voorschriften bij een opsporings- of winningsvergunning voor koolwaterstoffen op grond van de Mijnwet continentaal plat (Besluit vergunningen koolwaterstoffen continentaal plat* 1996), Stb 212; *Regeling Vergunningen Koolwaterstoffen Continentaal Plat 1996* of 15 May 1996, Staatscourant no 93 (Continental Shelf Hydrocarbons Regulations).

[45] Art 10 Mining Act 1810.

[46] The freedom to explore remained for prospecting for minerals by means of seismic surveys, except for the period 1982–95 where oil companies also could apply for a so-called 'declaration of priority for geophysical prospecting' which was designed to give oil companies some certainty about the award of an exploration licence. The Decree governing the award of a 'declaration of priority for geophysical prospecting' was revoked as from 20 May 1995. Stc no 99 of 23 May 1995, 13.

[47] Until now it was unclear which principle predominated: 1) the freedom of the Crown to grant a concession to any suitable party or 2) the principle that the holder of a drilling licence should have the security that, if required, a concession should be awarded to the same entity. See for the old regime and the way in which the non-competitive system onshore developed: MM Roggenkamp, *Oil and Gas* (n 28 above), chapters 9 and 10.

system of 'first come, first served' as a result of which virtually no competition existed between the oil companies involved in exploring and producing petroleum on Dutch territory.

Consequently, the onshore regime of the early 1990s disagreed most with the principle of the Hydrocarbons Licensing Directive that 'steps must be taken to ensure non-discriminatory access to and pursuit of activities relating to the prospection, exploration, and production of hydrocarbons under conditions which encourage greater competition'.[48] **10.37**

In order to implement this Directive, the Government issued an Act in 1996 amending the existing mining laws.[49] Obviously most changes affect the onshore legislation. The provisions of the Mining Act 1810 which governed the award of concessions were replaced by new provisions in the Mining Act 1903.[50] As far as the onshore concession is concerned, the (French) Mining Act 1810 must now be read in conjunction with the new provisions of Articles 1 to 8m of the Mining Act 1903. The provision in the (amended) Mining Act 1903 and the (amended) Minerals Exploration Act that an application for a concession or a drilling licence has to be published in order to give other companies an equal opportunity to compete for a licence has put an end to the previous system of 'first come, first served'. **10.38**

Although the 1996 amendments to a certain extent complicate the understanding of the onshore mining regime, they clearly reflect the gradual approximation of on- and offshore licensing which has been ongoing since the 1960s. The regimes are now broadly speaking the same. Authorizations (ie a concession or a licence) are required for exploration for and production of minerals, except for seismic surveying for which only the CS Mining Act contains a (non-exclusive) licensing requirement.[51] **10.39**

The conditions under which such authorizations may be awarded are known to the applicant in advance. These conditions are included in Royal Decrees and/or Ministerial Decrees. This also reflects an important change to the onshore regime **10.40**

[48] See Directive 94/22/EC of 30 May 1994, dealt with in chapter 5 above.

[49] Act of 18 Mar 1996, Stb. 199.

[50] From the Mining Act 1810 are deleted Arts 14, 15, and 16 as well as Arts 22–31. Arts 14 and 15 held some provisions with regard to the financial capability of the entity applying for a concession. Art 16 gave the Crown the freedom to decide to which entity a concession will be awarded to. Title IV (Arts 22–31) held provisions regarding the application for a concession. As the official text of this Act is in French, any amendments have to be in French, so the new provisions are included in the Mining Act 1903 instead. The Mining Act 1903 was originally issued as an instrument to revoke a concession and/or to stimulate the concessionaire to continue regularly the exploitation of the mine. Moreover, the Mining Act 1903 provides for further regulation concerning safety and employment (= Mining Regulations 1964). See for a further discussion about the 'old' Mining Act 1903: MM Roggenkamp, *Oil and Gas* (n 28 above), 129–30.

[51] Art 2 CS Mining Act explicitly states that it is prohibited to carry out seismic surveys, to explore for, or to extract minerals from the continental shelf without a licence.

before 1996 as the Minister could in principle decide the conditions under which a concession or licence was awarded in each individual case. Although in practice the conditions of the CS Mining Act were usually followed, it left the companies with some degree of uncertainty.

10.41 Although it can be concluded that since 1996 the licensing regimes are based on the same principles, the name of the authorization still indicates whether the activity is carried out onshore or offshore. Whereas concessions and drilling licences refer to production and exploratory drilling onshore, the CS mining regime refers to reconnaissance, exploration, and production licences. The terminology also refers to another characteristic of Dutch petroleum law: the award of separate licences for exploratory drilling and production activities.[52] These licences need not necessarily be applied for, and awarded, in the above order. While an exploration licence enables the carrying out of seismic surveys, exploratory drillings are undertaken on the basis of a concession or production licence. A prerequisite for the award of a concession or production licence is, however, that an economically exploitable quantity of minerals must be demonstrated.[53] The existence of minerals is normally established through exploratory drillings. Be that as it may, a small number of 'spontaneous' production licences have been awarded without previous drillings as the applicant could otherwise demonstrate that a licensed reservoir extended into an adjoining area.[54]

Licensing award process

Introduction

10.42 Before 1996, offshore licences were awarded on the basis of licensing rounds. Such a system did not apply to the onshore regime, where the award of drilling licences and concessions was basically left to the discretionary powers of the Minister. The Hydrocarbons Licensing Directive left the Member States with the choice of two different authorization procedures: a system of licensing rounds or a bidding system.[55] Despite experiences on the continental shelf where licences were awarded in rounds at regular intervals of two or three years,[56] the legislator

---

[52] Unlike an exploration and a production licence which are both exclusive licences awarded for strictly defined areas (blocks and/or part-blocks), reconnaissance licences are non-exclusive and may cover large areas as well. Prior consent of the holder(s) of an exploration and/or production licence is required if a reconnaissance licence is to be awarded for an area where such licences have already been granted.

[53] Art 13 CS Mining Act and Art 8c Mining Act 1903.

[54] The first 'spontaneous' production licence was awarded in 1971 when the production licence for a part of block L11 adjoining block L10 was granted to Placid International Oil Ltd (Stc 1971, no 4). Since then a small number of such licences have been awarded. See eg the licence granted for part of block B18, adjoining block F3, awarded to NAM in 1985 (Stc 1985, no 182).

[55] See Art 3 Hydrocarbons Licensing Directive.

[56] See Art 5 CS Mining Act (old). The Dutch system of licensing rounds deviated from the system used in other North Sea States. See also MM Roggenkamp, *Oil and Gas* (n 28 above), 60–5.

under the new regime preferred a bidding system. The reason for this change is that after eight licensing rounds most of the Dutch territory has been licensed as a result of which only limited acreage is left for exploration and production.[57]

Application procedure

Under the new bidding regime competitive applications can be filed during a period of 13 weeks[58] after a notice has been published in the Official Gazette and the EC Official Journal stating that an exploration or drilling licence has been applied for.[59] The Minister decides about the award within 6 months after expiry of the application period.[60] The Minister may decide to close certain parts of the continental shelf for licence applications for a maximum of three years in order to allow the Government to freeze licensing temporarily if external conditions (for example, the need to revise the licensing criteria) require such practice.[61] **10.43**

Like the Hydrocarbons Licensing Directive, the amended regime identifies a number of situations where the above procedure is not required. First, the application is submitted within two years after a previous bidding procedure which, however, has not resulted in the award of a licence and the application relates to the same type of minerals and area.[62] Secondly, if the application concerns a production licence which is filed by the licence holder of a contiguous area and the application relates to the discovery of an economically exploitable quantity of minerals.[63] This situation is comparable with the award of a 'spontaneous' production licence as described above.[64] Thirdly, if it concerns the application of a production licence to which Article 13 paragraph 1 CS Mining Act applies. In other words, if the holder of an exploration licence demonstrates the existence of an economically exploitable quantity of minerals, he shall on application, submitted during the period of that licence, be granted a production licence subject to the conditions as included in the implementing orders and the territorial **10.44**

[57] Tweede Kamer 1994–95, 24 078, nr 3, p 3. The ninth licensing round has been opened since 1 April 1995. In contrast to previous rounds the Continental Shelf has remained permanently open for applications since then.

[58] By contrast to the Directive, the Dutch mining laws refer to a period of 13 weeks instead of 90 days as this fits better with the methods of the General Act on Administrative Law of 1992 (Art 4:13).

[59] Art 16a CS Mining Act and Art 5a Minerals Exploration Act. The new Art 5 Minerals Exploration Act also that the Minister issues regulations governing the procedure for application and the information an applicant has to present. Such application includes, at least, a working plan.

[60] Art 16a para 1 CS Mining Act. According to para 2, the Minister may decide once to extend this period with another three months. See also Art 5b Minerals Exploration Act.

[61] Art 5 CS Mining Act. Tweede Kamer 1994–95, 24 078, nr 3, 16–17.

[62] Art 16a para 7 CS Mining Act and Art 5a para 4 Minerals Exploration Act. See also Art 3 para 3(b) Licensing Directive.

[63] Art 16a para 6 CS Mining Act and Art 5.11 Ministerial Order 1996. See also Art 3 para 4 Licensing Directive.

[64] This situation does not apply to the onshore regime as the territory is not divided into blocks.

limitations as—possibly—included in the exploration licence.[65] The latter example follows directly from the exceptional situation that Dutch mining law requires two separate licences for exploration for and production of minerals.

10.45 In contrast with the regime applying to exploration licences, the Mining Acts do not provide a clear procedure for the application for, and the awarding of, production licences and concessions. First, it is important to note that an application for a production licence depends on the results of the exploratory drillings. In other words, an application can be made at any time during the period of an exploration/drilling licence. However, the decisive criterion for the award of a production licence/concession is the assessment of the quantity of minerals discovered.[66] The implementation of the Hydrocarbons Licensing Directive does not lead to more transparency in this respect. The situation under the old regime remains that the Government may keep the applications on file until the minerals are considered to be economically exploitable.[67] Since the Act does not contain any definitions or guidelines concerning the assessment of a reservoir's exploitability, the Minister has full discretionary powers. Consequently, it may be difficult for an applicant to assess if and when a production licence or concession will be awarded.

The Award of a licence

10.46 Although the mining laws contain some general criteria for the award of licences and concessions[68] the most important further rules are included in Royal Decrees.[69] The award of a licence or concession is basically assessed on the basis of criteria such as (i) the technical or financial capability of the applicant, (ii) the way in which applicants have operated under previous and other licences, and (iii) the way in which the applicant intends to explore or exploit the area for which an

---

[65] Art. 16a para 5 CS Mining Act. See also Art 3 para 5(b) Hydrocarbons Licensing Directive.

[66] The procedure with regard to the application for a concession is similar. Like the above, Art 8g Mining Act 1903 holds that the licensing procedure does not apply if the application relates to the development of an economically exploitable quantity of hydrocarbons situated in a contiguous area or if an adjoining area has been subject to a previous procedure without any clear result. Furthermore, the award of a concession is not made dependent on licensing procedure if the holder of a drilling licence applies for a concession as a result of the discovery of an economically exploitable quantity of hydrocarbons. Also in this respect, the onshore regime has been brought into line with the offshore legislation.

[67] In this respect the procedures governing the award of a production licence are not transparent. Furthermore, there is no specific period of time within which a production licence has to be granted. Although this situation is not directly covered by the provisions of the Directive, it could be argued that these applications for production licences, which are kept on file indefinitely, should be surrendered after a specific period of time.

[68] See Art 3 Mining Act 1903, Art 2a Minerals Exploration Act, and Art 6a CS Mining Act.

[69] *Rules on licences and concessions for minerals on Dutch territory 1996* of 15 May 1996, Stc 93, 8 and *Rules on hydrocarbons licences continental shelf 1996* of 15 May 1996, Stc 93, 11, and Royal Decree of 7 February 1967, Stb 75 concerning *rules regarding applications and exemptions following the CS Mining Act.*

application is filed. Such an appraisal is made on the basis of the work planned and/or production plans that have been submitted together with the application. If a choice has to be made between two or more applications of equal quality and standing, the Minister's decision will be made in the interest of efficient and dynamic exploration or production.

The above criteria are, although broadly speaking similar to the present regime, **10.47** exhaustive in scope and will therefore give the State less flexibility as far as licensing is concerned. However, this seems to be the consequence of the Directive's fundamental principle that licences should be awarded on an objective and non-discriminatory basis.

The Licensee

Licences and concessions are held by joint ventures.[70] The Government is usually **10.48** not involved in the establishment of these joint ventures. The mining laws generally refer to the holder of the licence or the concessionaire. The internal organization of the joint venture is regulated in a Joint Bidding Agreement which is followed by a Joint Operating Agreement. On the basis of such agreement, parties select the operator as well as the operating committee and lay down further rules regarding the joint exploration/production programmes, the division of costs and expenses, default, etc.

It can be noted, however, that the Government increasingly approaches the indi- **10.49** vidual parties of the joint venture. A striking example is the issue of liability. As a general rule parties are liable for damages and associated costs and expenses incurred in or arising out of the conduct of joint operations in proportion to their respective interests. However, following the 1996 Mining Act the existing mining laws were amended to the extent that where a licence is awarded to two or more entities, all entities are severally liable for the financial dues resulting from the licence.[71] Similar provisions were already included in the individual licences since the 1980s following the failure of a licensee to pay its State Profit Share.[72] Upon complaint, the Administrative Court ruled that the Government is entitled to include such a provision. Since these consortia are established freely without interference from the Government, as a consequence they have to accept the contested provision according to which all partners hold several liability for the financial obligations following from the licence.[73]

[70] By contrast to other systems, the Government is not in favour of 'forced marriages', ie the Government is essentially not putting together several applicants in one group.

[71] Art 23a CS Mining Act and Art 8 in conjunction with Art 10b Mining Act 1903.

[72] Tweede Kamer 1994–95, 24 078, nr 5, 10.

[73] Ruling *Afdeling Bestuursrechtspraak Raad van State* of 10 Feb 1994, *Administratiefrechtelijke Beslissingen* no 193, 536.

Onshore and offshore licence terms

10.50 The differences between the onshore concession system and the offshore licensing regime is amongst others reflected in the use of licensing terms and the obligation to publish such terms in advance. The original Mining Act 1810 obviously did not require the prior publication of such information. The Crown (later the Minister) was free to decide about terms to be included in the deed of concession (*akte van concessie*).[74] Under the influence of the CS mining regime, however, it has become customary to apply the offshore licensing regime, which is based on a system of prior knowledge of the licence terms. One of the fundamental principles of the CS Mining Act was the legislators' view that the criteria according to which a licence (most particularly a production licence) was to be awarded should be known to all applicants in advance. However, as the circumstances under which the (offshore) petroleum sector operates can change rapidly, it was also thought necessary to create a flexible licensing regime and incorporate all licence terms in an administrative order rather than an Act of Parliament.[75]

10.51 Three sets of criteria have been promulgated: the Royal Decree of 27 January 1967 (Staatsblad 24), the Royal Decree of 6 February 1976 (Staatsblad 102) as amended by the Royal Decree of 27 January 1995 (Staatsblad 102).[76] It must be noted that these regimes are not applied successively, but exist next to each other depending on the date on which the exploration licence is awarded. For an exploration licence granted in 1982, the regime of the 1976 Decree applies to both exploration and production activities. Even a production licence awarded as late as 1995 may take place under the 1967 regime as long as the exploration licence was awarded before 1976. Any other arrangement would not have given the applicants the required security.

10.52 The 1996 Mining Act brought an important change to this system because it distinguishes between financial and other licence terms. Only the financial obligations are based on a Royal Decree approved by Parliament. Hence, several Royal Decrees were issued in 1996 holding the financial terms for the award of offshore licences and onshore concessions.[77] All other licence terms which usually concern

[74] Art 7 (new) Mining Act 1903. The amended provision refers to the term 'concession' instead of the former 'deed of concession'. The difference in terminology does not have any special significance.

[75] However, a special procedure is included so as to give Parliament the opportunity to control the establishment of the licensing criteria. Art 12 para 4 CS Mining Act. A proposal for a Royal Decree has to be submitted to both Houses of Parliament. It may enter into force 30 days after submission. However, if a certain number of members of one of the two Houses of Parliament require enforcement of the Decree by law, a Bill has to be presented as soon as possible.

[76] This latter amendment deals with financial obligations only.

[77] Royal Decree of 26 Mar 1996 holding the financial obligations for concessions, Stb 213; Royal Decree of 26 Mar 1996 holding the financial obligations for the award of exploration and production licences on the continental shelf, Stb 212; Royal Decree of 26 Mar 1996 regarding depreciation, Stb 214.

matters like safety, the environment, and resource management are now given by Ministerial Order which do not require approval by Parliament.[78] The Ministerial Order's non-financial provisions regarding the environment, safety, and resource management, apply to all production licences irrespective of the date on which the exploration licence is awarded. In other words, the provisions of the 1996 Ministerial Order apply to all production licences awarded since 1996 irrespective of the award of the exploration licence. The financial terms of the licence will, however, be those of the Royal Decree, which was in force at the time the exploration licence was granted. The earlier mentioned argument that oil companies should have sufficient security with regard to the applicable licence terms, currently seems to relate to the financial conditions only.

Financial terms

Introduction

Two basic principles apply to the financial terms of a licence, namely that these **10.53** terms should be known to the licensees beforehand and that amendments to the financial terms cannot have a retroactive effect. Currently, a range of financial terms co-exists in the Royal Decrees of 1967, 1976, 1995, and, most recently, the Royal Decrees of 1996. Although the three Royal Decrees regulate the financial terms for offshore licences only, some of their principles have been applied to onshore concessions as well. This policy is confirmed by the Royal Decrees of 1996. Basically, the licence terms distinguish between (i) profit share and/or corporate income tax, (ii) royalty, and (iii) surface rentals and bonuses. Since the 1996 Mining Act, all entities are severally liable for the financial dues resulting from the licence (see above para 10.49). However, several liability only exists for the payment of royalties, surface rental, and bonuses, but not for the payment of the State profit share. If necessary, security for the payment of the latter will be required by, for example, a bank guarantee.[79]

Profit share and corporate income tax

The Royal Decree of 1967 introduced the principle of the State profit share.[80] It **10.54** rules that licence holders must pay the State at times specified in the licence, a sum fixed therein based on the profit obtained from production.[81] The size of the State's profit share may vary. Whereas the Royal Decree 1967 sets the State profit

[78] Arts 7a and 12 CS Mining Act 1996.

[79] Tweede Kamer 1994–95, 24 078, nos 10 and 11.

[80] This system was introduced before the Netherlands fiscal jurisdiction was applied to the Dutch continental shelf (Act of 30 Dec 1989, Stb 554). Since 1989 Dutch offshore fiscal jurisdiction applies to income tax, wage tax, corporate income tax, and insurance tax. Consequently, profits made by foreign companies working as contractors offshore can be taxed on the basis of Netherlands national legislation.

[81] Cf Art 11 para 1 under b CS Mining Act and Art 8a under b Mining Act 1903.

share at 50 per cent of the profit made with the licence, it was increased to 70 per cent in the Royal Decrees of 1976 and 1995. Since a licensee is obliged to keep accounts of the business in the Netherlands and the operator also is required to have an office in the Netherlands,[82] the entire profit of the offshore production is in fact attributed to the onshore establishment and therefore also assessed for corporate income tax (35 per cent).

10.55 In order to avoid double taxation, the State profit share is determined on the basis of a calculation in which the corporate income tax is deduced from the profit payable on the basis of a (positive) profit and loss account as defined in the Royal Decree.[83] The profit and loss account sets out the costs and proceeds of production, as well as reconnaissance and exploration, attributable to that year according to sound commercial practice.[84]

10.56 One of the peculiarities of the State profit share is the possibility offered by the Royal Decrees of 1967 and 1976 to increase deductible costs by a certain percentage: the 'uplift'.[85] The outcome of the latter calculation is also considered as a minimum profit to be paid to the State. As of 1 January 2001 the regime of the 1967 Royal Decree will apply again: a 50 per cent State profit share with a 10 per cent uplift.[86]

Royalties or Cijns

10.57 In addition to the State profit share, the licensees are required to pay royalties (*cijns*).[87] Whereas the State profit share is based on the profits made by the licensee, the payment of royalties refers to the value of the minerals produced.[88] Consequently some costs, such as those of transport, treatment, and storage of the minerals, are usually deducted before the well-head value is determined.[89] The

[82] Art 18 of Art II Royal Decree 1967/1976 and Art 2.6 of CS Royal Decree 1996.

[83] For example, Art 12 of Art III Royal Decree 1967 and Art 3.14 CS Royal Decree 1996.

[84] In 1994 the Ministry of Economic Affairs and the Ministry of Finance issued regulations according to which the transfer of a production licence may include financial losses attached to that licence for the purpose of calculating the State Profit Share. To be eligible to apply for the transfer of losses together with the production licence, the transfer of a production licence is restricted to a transfer in which a Dutch corporate is involved. In addition, the regulation holds a number of other requirements which have to be met in order to transfer these losses.

[85] Whereas under the regime of the Royal Decree 1967 the 'uplift' consists of a 10% elevation of the costs, the uplift is fixed to 20% of the operational expenses and 70% on depreciation under the 1976 regime. The Royal Decree of 1996, however, is limited to a 50% profit share without uplift.

[86] The Minister of Economic Affairs proposed a number of changes to the offshore financial regime in a letter of 29 May 2000, Tweede Kamer 1999–2000, 26219, nr 11.

[87] Art 11 para 1 under a CS Mining Act and Art 8a under a Mining Act 1903.

[88] The disadvantage of (fixed) royalties is that they may have a detrimental effect on profits in the case of high production costs, as for example in marginal fields. This objection has been met to some extent by levying royalties according to a sliding scale, as well as to the value according to the value at the well-head.

[89] There is a difference between the production of oil and natural gas. In general, some 10–20% of transport and other costs are deductible.

Royal Decrees provide for separate sliding scales for the calculation of royalties for the offtake of natural gas and oil. The calculation of the royalty percentage also differs according to the State's participation in the production of natural gas and/or oil (see paras 10.69–10.75 below). The royalty percentage is double the rate included in the Royal Decrees 1967/76, if the State decides not to participate in the production. Following the fall in oil prices in the early 1990s, the 1995 amendment to the 1976 Royal Decree[90] provided a minimum level on which the royalty charge could be based in order to stimulate offshore activities. When oil prices according to the IEA's publication 'Energy prices and taxes' fall below US$ 23 per barrel, licensees who exploit marginal fields will be exempted from royalty payment.[91] This means in practice that a licence holder can produce oil and/or gas from three marginal fields in one block without paying any royalties, as long as oil prices are below US$ 23 per barrel. However, when oil prices are above this level the system of Royal Decree 1976 enters into force again.[92] In order further to stimulate mining activities on the Dutch continental shelf, the Minister of Economic Affairs has decided to end the payment of royalties from offshore petroleum production as of 1 January 2001.[93]

Surface rentals and bonuses

Until recently licensees/concessionaires were also obliged to pay bonuses. Upon **10.58** the award of an (offshore) exploration licence, licensees were required until 1 July 2000 to pay the State a non-recurring bonus per square kilometre of the licence area.[94] If, thereupon, the holder of an exploration licence is not awarded a production licence, the bonus was refunded for the area the licence was applied for. In order to stimulate exploration activities offshore, the Minister of Economic Affairs decided to revoke the obligation to pay bonuses as of 1 July 2000.

Furthermore, a licensee has to pay surface rental. A surface rental is an index- **10.59** linked annual rental per square kilometre for the area for which an exploration or production licence has been granted.[95] The amount payable depends on the applicable Royal Decree as well as the type of licence. Reasons for levying surface rentals were twofold.[96] First, it is considered to be compensation for the

[90] Stb 1995, nr 42.

[91] A new para 3 is inserted into Art 3 of Art III stating that with a production level below 800,000 cubic metres, the royalty is 0. For the production of gas this exemption is set to a limit of 800 million cubic metres per year (cf Art 6 of Art III Royal Decree 1976). See also Art I under A and B of Stb 1995, 42.

[92] Stb 1995, 42, Memorie van Toelichting, 5–6.

[93] Tweede Kamer 1999–2000, 26219, no 11.

[94] Art 4 of Art II of the Royal Decrees of 1967/1976 and Art 2.2 Royal Decree No 212 of 1996.

[95] See Art 5 of Art II and Art 1 of Art III of the Royal Decrees of 1967 and 1976, as well as Arts 2.3 and 3.1 of Royal Decree No 212 of 1996. See furthermore Art 2.2. Royal Decree No 213 of 1996.

[96] See MM Roggenkamp, *Oil and Gas* (n. 28 above), 226.

Government for its obligation to supervise the activities. Secondly, it is an instrument for voluntary surrender of the licensed area. By contrast to the bonuses, surface rentals are also payable onshore. The onshore surface rental is based on the number of hectares for which a licence/concession is awarded.[97]

10.60 In addition to surface rentals, profit shares, and royalties, a number of other levies and taxes apply specifically to onshore mining activities, such as a property tax, a location payment, and a special reimbursement to landowners (the *redevance tréfoncière*).[98]

Terms relating to area and time

Duration of the licence

10.61 Since the 1980s important changes have been made regarding the duration of licences. These amendments are based on the principle that the duration of a licence should not exceed the period necessary to carry out the exploration or production. A similar principle is included in the Hydrocarbons Licensing Directive. Article 7a CS Mining Act now provides that:

> a licence for the exploration or production of hydrocarbons includes the duration of the licence, this being no longer than necessary to carry out the activities for which the licence is awarded.[99]

Under the new regime, the Minister has extended discretionary powers as the licence periods are no longer fixed in the Royal Decrees.[100] Although, in a sense, the new regime is less transparent (as an applicant does not know beforehand for how long a licence will be awarded) it also brings about a parallel with the onshore regime as amended in 1988, when an important change was made to the original system that concessions were awarded in perpetuity. As from 1988 onwards all (new) concessions are granted for the period necessary for the production of the reservoir.

10.62 Consequently, the terms relating to the area and the duration of the licence are closely related. In addition to the determination of the type of mineral(s),[101] a concession or drilling licence must specify the geographical area to which it applies.

[97] cf Art 8a under c Mining Act 1903. The concessions awarded since 1967 provide for a surface rental of NLG3 per hectare. As it is index-linked the rental amounted to NLG10.44 per hectare in 1990. Under the 1996 regime the new index-linked amount is NLG7 per 1990.

[98] See for the latter two levies: Art 8b Mining Act 1903.

[99] By its reference to hydrocarbons it marks a difference with the former system where the Act applied to minerals in general and the Royal Decree to hydrocarbons explicitly.

[100] Under the 1967 regime exploration and production licences are awarded for 15 years and 40 years respectively. Under the 1976 Decree, for example, an exploration licence will be awarded for 10 years and a production licence for 40 years.

[101] Art 4 para 1 Mining Act 1903 and Art 3 para 1 Minerals Exploration Act. Obviously a concession or licence for certain minerals cannot be granted if a similar authorization for the same type of minerals within the same geographical area already has been awarded (Art 6 Mining Act 1903).

The determined area may not exceed the area justified by the best possible exercise of the activities, from the technical and economic points of view.[102] Similarly, the time period for which a concession is awarded may not exceed the period necessary to carry out the required activities.[103] A concession can be prolonged at the request of the concessionaire if the original time period is insufficient to complete the production activities as originally scheduled in the concession.[104]

Although these amendments are important as such, their effect should not be overrated as they have no retroactive effect. The same is true for the changes based on the Hydrocarbons Licensing Directive. Hence, most major onshore concessions like the Groningen concession still rule that the concessionaire owns the 'mine' (ie the hydrocarbons) in perpetuity. **10.63**

Licence area

Since the Mining Act 1996, the duration of licences and concessions will depend on the size of the geographical area for which a licence or concession will be granted. The difference between the on- and offshore regimes lies in the way in which the licence area is defined. Whereas onshore licences/concessions are awarded for a geological unit, an area where according to geological reports minerals are to be found,[105] the Dutch continental shelf is divided into blocks of 400 square kilometres.[106] The Dutch legislator preferred blocks of a 'reasonable' size because this was better suited with its choice of a system of mandatory reduction of the licence area. Under such a relinquishment system, licence holders have to return halfway through their licence period part of the licensed area which has not been explored and thus stimulate the licensee to explore the licensed area intensively.[107] The relinquished area has to be large enough for new exploration licences **10.64**

[102] Art 4 para 1 Mining Act 1903 and Art 3 para 2 Minerals Exploration Act. See also Art 4(a) Hydrocarbons Licensing Directive.

[103] Art 4 para 3 Mining Act 1903 and Art 3 para 3 Minerals Exploration Act. Compare Article 4(b) Hydrocarbons Licensing Directive.

[104] Article 8k para 3 Mining Act 1903. In case of an extension, the Minister may, however, limit the geographical area to that part where the production has commenced but not yet completed. The Minister may always decide to terminate a concession if the concession is no longer required for proper realization of the production activities, and the concessionaire, despite repeated reminders by the Minister, has violated one of the conditions providing for such sanction.

[105] cf Minister J den Uyl, Handelingen Tweede Kamer, 17 May 1966, 1795. For the definition of the licence areas the Government is making use of the geological reports of the oil companies/applicants.

[106] The blocks are bordered by the lines of the geographic network. Their size depends on their latitude. A block of 400 square kilometres is under the geographical system 10′ latitude and 20′ longitude. Certain parts of the continental shelf have a special status as mining activities are restricted or excluded completely due to the existence of shipping routes and military training areas. Since 1986 restricted use of the excluded areas (especially the military practice areas) is possible.

[107] Under the CS mining regime which applied until 1996 all licensees have to give up after a certain period of time some 47.5% to 50% of the licensed area. Whereas under Art 2 Art II Royal Decree 1967 the period was set at 10 years, the Royal Decree of 1976 provided for a period of 6 years.

to be granted. Since the 1996 regime, however, exploration licences are only awarded for the period necessary for exploration or production of the area, as a result of which relinquishment obligations no longer exist.

10.65 Another consequence of the geometrical system is that reservoirs can extend the area for which an exploration licence has been awarded. The way in which the field will be developed depends on the situation of the adjoining acreage. If these blocks have not yet been licensed, a spontaneous production licence can be applied for. Otherwise, the licence holders have to enter into an unitization agreement with the licensees of the adjoining block or part-block.[108] The situation is complicated if the field is situated on an international border. An international unitization agreement requires the prior involvement of both governments. In the Netherlands a number of fields are situated on the border. The best known examples are the joint development of the Markham field situated on the British/Dutch border[109] and the joint petroleum production on the Dutch/German border in the Eems-Dollard or 'common area'.[110]

Work obligations

10.66 Past experiences onshore have shown the danger of awarding concessions without further instruments to enforce the production of minerals.[111] Currently, most competitive mining systems provide for instruments to encourage systematic exploration and/or production of the minerals. The CS mining regime contains several provisions safeguarding the systematic exploration and production of hydrocarbons. The above licence terms concerning the limitation of the licence area and the duration of the licence are clear examples of such provisions. Another important instrument for encouraging systematic exploration is the use of work obligations such as a work programme and a specific work commitment.[112]

10.67 Essentially, a work obligation means that the licensee is committed to drill a minimum number of wells and/or to spend a minimum amount in the licensed area

[108] See for example Art 5.4 Ministerial Order 1996.

[109] See Markham Agreement of 26 May 1992 as approved by Parliament by Act of 24 Dec 1992, Stb 673.

[110] The Agreement of Co-operation in the disputed common area, supplementary agreement of 14 May 1962, Tractatenblad 54. The exploitation of minerals in this area is complicated by the fact that the borderline is not fixed. This problem has also affected decisions about the extension of the Groningen field in Germany.

[111] Examples are the system used under the Mining Act of 1791 and the entering into force of the Mining Act 1903. Under the Mining 1810 the Government could only intervene in the exploitation of a 'mine' if a failure to exploit would constitute a threat to public safety or the continuity of supply. Art 1 (old) Mining Act 1903 enabled the Minister to summon a concessionaire to commence, resume, or regularly continue the exploitation of the 'mine' or to meet the obligations imposed on him in the deed of concession. Non-compliance could eventually lead to a public sale of the mine.

[112] In addition, licensees have a statutory obligation to report regularly about their activities to the Inspector-General of the Mines.

over a specified period of time. Statutory work commitments are included in the Royal Decrees of 1967 and 1976.[113] These commitments hold that the licensee has to start reconnaissance or exploration activities within eight months after the licence is granted and to continue these activities diligently. Under the 1967/76 regime, the licensee is further obliged to work according to a schedule of expenditures set out in the Royal Decrees.[114] The latter obligation is not included in the 1996 Ministerial Order. This Order only refers to the number of drillings a licensee has to carry our during the licence period.

Besides the statutory work commitment, the licensee also has to carry out a specific work programme. Such a work programme normally consists of a schedule of exploration or production activities.[115] As the individual work programmes are part of the application process, companies are obviously obliged to follow the programmes they have offered. Since the fifth round, the extent and quality of the work programme have been important extra-statutory requirements for the Minister of Economic Affairs when a selection had to be made from the applications submitted. The 1996 regime affirms the importance of the work programme for the bidding process.[116] This is especially true for the production plan, which replaces the Government's previous instruments concerning the disposal of minerals. By way of a production plan the Government can pursue a depletion policy. **10.68**

State participation

Introduction

Various consortia, in which several oil companies participate, produce oil and natural gas. These oil companies apply for licences, not on an individual basis, but as a joint venture on the basis of a joint bidding agreement. If the licence is awarded, the activities are carried on jointly on the basis of a Joint Operating Agreement (JOA).[117] Although the upstream sector is generally characterized by private ownership, it is important to note that the State usually participates in the **10.69**

[113] Art 8 of Art II, Royal Decree of 1967 or 1976.

[114] Under the Royal Decree of 1967 the licensee has to spend Dfl 6000 per sq km during the first 5 years and Dfl 12,000 per sq km during the next 5 years on prospecting or exploration activities. If the licensee spends more on reconnaissance and exploration during the first period, this excess may be deducted from the amounts required to be spent during the second period. Under the Royal Decree of 1976 these amounts were set at Dfl 15,000 per sq km during the first 6 years and Dfl 40,000 during the last 3 years. A specification of expenditure is to be sent to the Minister each year.

[115] Art 5a Royal Decree 1967 refers to the number of drillings to be carried out in the initial 6-year term and the order of preference for the blocks or part-blocks. Furthermore, Art 6a under d requires a production plan in which estimates are made regarding the level of production and processing.

[116] Art 3.4 of the 1996 Ministerial Order for the Continental Shelf and Art 2.5 of the 1996 Ministerial order for the Dutch territory.

[117] See also chs 13 and 11 above on the UK and Norway.

production of hydrocarbons as well. The organization of State participation in the Netherlands differs, however, from other petroleum-producing countries. First, no State oil company has been established. Secondly, the State participant is not a licence holder and is therefore not party to the joint venture.

10.70 The way in which State participation is organized stems from the discovery of the Groningen gas field in 1959 and the Government's need to develop a complete new gas supply policy. The gas policy note 'de Pous' (see below para 10.125) recognized the existence of the close relationship between production and supply. In addition to close co-ordination between production and sales of gas, the policy note considered the public supply of gas as a government task so that gas sales should not be too dependent on private suppliers. Natural gas was considered to be different from other subsoil minerals. Consequently, State participation was originally limited to the production of natural gas only.

Onshore

10.71 Legally there were no objections to State participation, as neither the Mining Act 1810 nor the Mining Act 1903 had any provisions regarding State participation or explicitly prohibiting participation by the State in petroleum production. So, when the Groningen concession was awarded in 1963, a condition was included in the deed of concession that 'the extraction of natural gas shall take place according to a co-operation agreement, approved by the Minister of Economic Affairs, between the concessionaires and the State participant'.[118] Under this co-operation agreement the parties established a partnership (*Maatschap*) in which the State has 40 per cent and the concessionaire the remaining 60 per cent of the shares.[119] The concessionaire is exploiting the reservoir for the account of the *Maatschap*. This means that the partnership decides on the actual extraction and disposal of the minerals, each according to its share in the partnership. Although the State does not participate in the concession, it can directly influence the gas production, as it is the *Maatschap* which decides on the extraction of the minerals. A similar approach has been followed in most concessions ever since.[120] In fact the Groningen concession forms the legal basis for the present system of State participation in the production of hydrocarbons in the Netherlands.[121]

---

[118] Art 11 para 1 concession 'Groningen'.

[119] This share was raised to 50% in the production of oil and gas together with the 1976 amendment to the Royal Decree concerning the execution of Art 12 of the CS Mining Act.

[120] Of all the partnerships established since 1963, the *Maatschap* 'Groningen' is the best known. Within this partnership the State holds 40% and the NAM as the concessionaire of the Groningen concession the remaining 60% of the shares.

[121] Although not all concessions granted since 1963 contain a provision with regard to State participation, the system of State participation introduced in the 'Groningen' concession has been the example for concessions awarded since then.

Offshore

The CS mining legislation is based on the same principles, except that the State does not participate through the establishment of a partnership (*Maatschap*) but through the establishment of a company with limited liability (NV or BV) within which the shares are held by the licensee and the State.[122] Further to the Royal Decrees of 1967 and 1976, the company can conclude an agreement with its shareholders to the effect that the exploitation of hydrocarbons will take place on the account and at the risk of these shareholders.[123] Many fiscal objections were put forward by the oil industry against the requirement to establish a limited liability company: Article VII Royal Decree 1967/76 enables the parties to sign a further agreement with each other according to which the company is treated as a 'cost company' only. Production then takes place on the account and at the risk of the shareholders directly, as a result of which profit share and corporate income tax is levied directly on the shareholders and not via the limited liability company. **10.72**

Extent of State participation

The extent of State participation differs as the applicable provisions vary in the individual Royal Decrees. The 1967 Decree is based on the original onshore regime of the Groningen concession, as it provides for 40 per cent State participation in the production of gas. Following the energy crisis in the 1970s the Royal Decree 1976 increased to 50 per cent the participation of the State in the production of oil and gas. Due to the interaction between the offshore and onshore regimes, most concessions awarded since 1976 have a similar provision and provide for 50 per cent State participation in the production of oil and gas. **10.73**

Since the 1990s State participation in petroleum production has again become a matter of discussion. Under the Hydrocarbons Licensing Directive the issue of State participation was important, because the State as participant could impede competition in the upstream sector. More important, however, was the decline of the price of oil, the dollar, and the rate of production (*inter alia* due to the Government's policy to concentrate on the production of small fields offshore) as a result of which profits decreased. Hence, the 1976 Royal Decree was amended in 1995 in order to reduce State participation in oil and gas production to 40 per cent.[124] **10.74**

---

[122] Art 11 para 2 CS Mining Act.

[123] Article VII Royal Decree of 1967 and 1976. The licensee and the State participant must co-operate with regard to the disposal of the petroleum extracted. The licensee and the State participant are obliged and entitled to take their share of the minerals extracted *in kind*, and have an obligation to each other under the production licence to seek modes of co-operation in the sales of the minerals and to consult with each other regularly about sales. Such co-operation is thought necessary due to the high costs involved in the sales of minerals.

[124] The request by the oil industry to expand State participation in the exploration of petroleum has not been agreed: see Stb 1995, 42.

10.75 The above principles about State participation were also included in the Mining Act 1996. Notably, the rule about State participation has for the first time been included in onshore mining legislation, an important step towards the further integration of both sectors.[125] The rules regarding State participation were implemented in the onshore and offshore Royal Decrees of 1996, ie 40 per cent State participation in the petroleum production only. However, in contrast to the previous regime, where a decision about State participation was within the discretion of the Minister of Economic Affairs, the 1996 regime involves State participation as a general rule applying to all authorizations. The State may decide not to participate in production if this would result in financial loss.[126] In practical terms the difference is insignificant: the State has basically participated in all production activities. As a result of the need to stimulate mining activities on the Dutch continental shelf, State participation has been gradually extended to exploratory activities. In 1994 it was agreed that the State could participate in exploration for oil and gas as long as these activities were carried out within the framework of a production licence. As of 1 July 2000 State participation was extended to all exploration and production activities, regardless of the type of licence. It is expected that this policy will result in a considerable increase of the exploration activities.[127]

The State Participant

10.76 The 1996 regime made no changes with regard to the State participant. Since 1989 the company *Energiebeheer Nederland* (or EBN) has always been appointed as the State participant.[128] EBN represents the State's interest in the production of a certain field and is not a licensee.[129] Following the principles of the Hydrocarbons Licensing Directive, EBN has to act on the basis of normal commercial considerations. This principle is included in the agreement between EBN and the licence holders. The State has no decision-making powers with regard to

[125] Art 8c Mining Act 1903. The concession will determine the way in which the interest of the partnership is divided. In addition to the establishment of a partnership, parties to enter into an agreement according to the concessionaire will be entitled to produce these hydrocarbons on the account of the partnership. This provision codifies the system presently used in practice.

[126] Arts 4.1 and 4.2 Royal Decree 1996.

[127] Tweede Kamer 1999–2000, 26219, No 11.

[128] Since the 1960s the State participated in the production of gas via the limited liability company NV DSM, at that time a 100% State-owned company responsible for the exploration for and production of coal. Following the decline of the coal industry, DSM gradually diversified to other sectors and the subsidiary DSM Aardgas BV was established in 1973 to administer the interests of the State in the production of gas. Following the privatization of NV DSM in 1989, the certificates of the State's shares are held by Energie Beheer Nederland (EBN), a holding company wholly owned by the State. However, as EBN lacks experience in administering the State's participation in the production of hydrocarbons, a management agreement was entered into between the State and NV DSM resulting into DSM's handling of the management of EBN.

[129] By contrast to the situation before DSM's privatization, when DSM Aardgas represented the State's participation in the production of a field and DSM Energie could be a licence holder in the same field.

the procurement activities of the limited liability company or the *Maatschap*.[130] However, it can intervene in retrospect if a procurement decision has a negative effect on government finances or depletion policy.[131]

(4) Petroleum Production and the Environment

Introduction

The fact that exploration for and production of hydrocarbons can seriously damage the environment has been known for a long time. Since the beginning of the 1900s the Mining Regulations have all contained specific provisions for the protection of health, safety, working conditions, and the environment.[132] Since the 1960s, however, a large number of laws regulating specific aspects of land use and the environment have entered into force.[133] Because of the fundamental philosophy in mining law that the organization of the mining activities includes the protection of safety and the environment, these environmental laws were originally not intended to apply to mining activities. However, it is now generally accepted that mining law is not the most suitable instrument for regulating the environmental aspects of petroleum exploration and production.[134] Consequently, the issuing of environmental and planning permits is now usually considered after the award of a concession or production licence, so a concessionaire or licensee never has a guarantee that petroleum exploration and production will actually take place. A striking example is the exploitation of the gasfield near Ameland within the concession 'Noord-Friesland'. Although the concession was awarded as early as 1969, exploitation of the natural gas field could not begin until 1982 due to the difficult process of obtaining permits.[135] **10.77**

Environmental impact assessment

One of the new environmental rules of special importance for the petroleum industry is the environmental impact assessment (EIA).[136] The importance of this **10.78**

[130] Moreover, it seems that the State only has sufficient powers under the 1976 regime to enforce decisions made by the limited liability company or *Maatschap* as under the other regimes State participation is limited to 40%.

[131] Art 4.8 para 2 CS Royal Decree 1996.

[132] The Mining Regulations are promulgated on the basis of Art 9 Mining Act 1903.

[133] These individual environmental laws have gradually been replaced by the Environment Conservation Act of 10 May 1994, Stb 1994, No 331.

[134] It should be noted that the situation offshore is different as environmental laws do not necessarily apply to the continental shelf.

[135] The planning and building permissions, finally given at the end of 1981, contain a large number of environmental conditions, which include limitation of construction to the winter season and a limitation on the height of installations. The severe local opposition is demonstrated by the fact that the local council even tried to revise the zoning plan in order to prohibit the construction of drilling rigs in nature reserve areas. *Voorzitter Afdeling Rechtspraak Raad van State*, 15 Dec 1981, *Administratiefrechtelijke Beslissingen* 1982, No 176.

[136] This instrument was for the first time specified in ch 8 of the Royal Decree of 20 May 1987, Stb 278.

instrument for the petroleum industry has increased since its introduction in the 1980s as the number of activities which are subject to a prior EIA have gradually increased to include activities such as the construction of onshore pipelines for the transportation of natural gas or oil,[137] the landing of pipelines, and the discharge of oil-contaminated cuttings from offshore installations. Other mining activities have been added, such as exploration for and production of hydrocarbons in environmentally sensitive areas.[138]

10.79 Following an amendment to the EIA Directive,[139] the CS Mining Regulations were changed in order to include a number of activities on the continental shelf for which an EIA is required.[140] Since 1999, these activities are therefore linked to a licence. Included are the establishment of offshore installations producing more than 500,000 kilograms of oil or 500,000 cubic metres of natural gas per day[141] and offshore petroleum pipelines with a diameter of 80 cm and a length of more than 40 kilometres.[142] Such a licence can be denied due to environmental reasons. The required environmental assessment is carried out on the basis of an EIA.

Mining activities in environmentally sensitive areas

10.80 Exploration for and production of petroleum in environmentally sensitive areas is gradually being restricted. The protection of the environment from mining is also clearly recognized in the Hydrocarbons Licensing Directive.[143] In the Netherlands special rules apply to the wetland area known as Waddenzee. Article 2a of the Minerals Exploration Act makes the award of a drilling licence in the Waddenzee dependent on the guidelines included in the *Planologische Kernbeslissing Waddenzee* (PKB or national planning decision) which outlines the Government's policy regarding coastal protection, land reclamation, harbours, and industrial areas as well as its policy on the exploration for and exploitation of mineral resources.[144] Licences and concessions may, for example, only be granted for large deposits and under strict conditions.[145] Areas important

[137] An EIA is also required for the construction of main pipelines for natural gas and oil which are longer than 5 kilometres in nature reserves and the wetland area.

[138] A plan indicating the intended drilling activities or the establishment of a production installation needs to be approved by the Minister of Economic Affairs.

[139] Directive 97/11/EC (OJ L73) amending EIA Directive 85/33/EEC.

[140] Royal Decree of 4 Mar 1999, Stb 1999, 116. Special provisions are included in the CS Mining Regulations since the basic environmental law does not apply to the continental shelf.

[141] Art 30a CS Mining Regulations.

[142] ibid, Art 70a.

[143] Art 6 para 2 Hydrocarbons Licensing Directive.

[144] Other important nature reserve areas are Lake IJsselmeer and Lake Markermeer which both have important functions with respect to the supply of drinking water, water management in the northern part of the Netherlands, and its function as a nature reserve area.

[145] These conditions concern, *inter alia*, the protection, conservation, and if necessary restoration of the quality of the ground, water, and air because the flora and fauna in the Waddenzee function as a nursery for wildlife.

for birds and/or seals must be avoided and no drilling fluids may be discharged into the Waddenzee.[146]

When the first national planning decision was published in 1984, the Minister of Economic Affairs also entered into a gentlemen's agreement with the oil companies involved, as a result of which all drilling activities were postponed until 10 January 1994.[147] At the expiry of the moratorium in 1994, the Government and the oil companies entered into another agreement about the use of the Waddenzee until the beginning of 1999.[148] Those companies granted a concession before the moratorium entered into force[149] are thus permitted to carry out a limited number of exploratory drillings in the wetland area. However, they are not entitled to establish any production installations in the area. In other words, the exploitation of gas discovery must take place from outside the wetland area or from the existing platform in the Zuidwal concession.[150] **10.81**

Nevertheless, no drilling activities have taken place in the area since 1994. Although the Ministry of Economic Affairs awarded the necessary permits to NAM, the Court did not accept these permits, for two reasons. First, it argued that separate EIAs were required for each individual drilling activity instead of one EIA for five drillings in five years. Secondly, the conditions for the drilling permits should be more stringent. The Court, however, did not accept the argument that exploratory drillings are contrary to the EC Birds and Habitat Directive.[151] Although the Court delayed exploratory drilling activities by the concessionaire, drilling has not been permanently denied. Be that as it may, at the urgent request of Parliament the Cabinet decided in the summer of 1999 to postpone drilling activities pending proof that there will be no harmful consequences. As this will be difficult to prove, the concessionaire has ownership rights over the minerals *in situ*, which now prove to be non-exploitable. Therefore the oil companies could **10.82**

[146] See *Nota over de hoofdlijnen van de ontwikkeling van de Waddenzee* (White paper concerning the development of the Wetland sea), Kamerstuk 13933, part e: text of the key planning decision taken after parliamentary discussion. This Note was renewed in 1993 (Eerste Kamer 1993–94, 22605, nr 114) and partially revised in 1994–95, Eerste Kamer 1994–95, 23546.

[147] *Partiële herziening van de planologische kernbeslissing Waddenzee*, 1984–85, Kamerstuk 18 220, no 13, 4.

[148] In the same period a new national planning decision entered into force.

[149] These are the concessions of Groningen, Noord-Friesland, Zuidwal, and Leeuwarden. It should be noted, however, that the offshore activities near the isle of Ameland of the Noord-Friesland concession are officially located just outside the Waddenzee and that the activities under the Zuidwal concession are officially excepted under the national planning decision.

[150] In 1995 the Zuidwal concession was amended to comply with this policy. In the amended concession only one installation is permitted in the area. See Ministerial Decree of 10 Mar 1995 published in Staatscourant of 27 Mar, no 61, 8. The policy that production installations, other than existing ones, are not permitted in the Waddenzee does also apply to the construction and landing of petroleum pipelines.

[151] Bestuursrechtbank Leeuwarden, 17 July 1998 Stc 1998, No 139.

request some type of compensation from the Government, arguing that a refusal to award a drilling permit is comparable to nationalizing the minerals.

Land subsidence

10.83 In recent years it has become clear that the production of oil and gas may lead to land subsidence which may have severe effects on the onshore environment. At the time of the first oil and gas concessions this problem had not yet been recognized and therefore no clauses were included in the deed of concession (such as the Groningen concession) on this subject. In later concessions and in the 1996 Ministerial Order[152] this matter was taken into account by including a clause to the effect that during exploitation activities regular levelling surveys and longitudinal measurements were to be made. If these show that, as a result of the exploitation, land subsidence occurs which may lead to an undesirable situation, the Minister for Economic Affairs can order measures to prevent adverse effects. These may include the discontinuation of the exploitation.

10.84 Meanwhile the holders of the Groningen concession (ie the NAM) have entered into an agreement with the provinces involved in order to prevent, limit, or repair damage caused by the subsidence of land.[153] The concessionaires have taken upon themselves the duty to pay all the costs involved.[154] A specially appointed commission decides within 45 days after receipt of the claim, by unanimous voting, which costs are eligible for compensation.[155] The agreement also states that compensation will not be sought in any other manner, which excludes actions based on the Civil Code.[156] It should be noted that the agreements are limited in scope: they apply only to damage caused by land subsidence suffered by the public authorities such as the provinces, municipalities, and water boards, and private citizens who are party to the agreement.[157] Damage suffered by private citizens not party to the agreement is not covered by the agreement; they have to claim under

[152] Art 5.5 Ministerial Order 1996.

[153] The first prognosis by NAM in 1975 assumed a drop of 30 cm in the centre of the area in the year 2025. The last prognosis in 1985, however, estimated a drop in the level of land of 60 or 70 cm.

[154] In the Groningen concession a forecast of the required amount of money was made in 1975. Of the budgeted total of 650 million guilders, 20 million was paid by 31 December 1988. In the Friesland province investigations have been carried out by the *Onderzoekscommissie bodemdaling Friesland* which was established on 16 Nov 1989, Stc 224. See parliamentary debate in 1988–89, Kamerstuk 21 108. However, this has not yet resulted in a compensation agreement such as NAM has with the province of Groningen.

[155] There is a kind of appeal body, the *College*, composed of 6 members, half appointed by the province and the other half by the concessionaire.

[156] Disputes which on the basis of the agreement cannot be adjudicated by the *College* or by civil courts, shall be submitted to arbitration at the request of the plaintiff. cf H van der Molen, Waterschapsbelangen, 1983, 429–31.

[157] According to the annual report of the Commission of 1989 25 private citizens have become party to the agreement.

the Civil Code. Such claims by private citizens have failed so far because causality between the damage and the subsidence could not be proven.

Field abandonment and removal of installations

Introduction

Finally, special mention should be made of the environmental consequences of field abandonment and the removal of abandoned installations. Since the start of large-scale petroleum activities in the 1960s, the abandonment of fields and installations has become of increasing importance both onshore and offshore. The first onshore production installation to be abandoned was in the Wassenaar field in 1988.[158] In the same period the production of several offshore fields had to be stopped. In 1999 a total of eight platforms have been removed on the Dutch continental shelf.[159] The regulatory frameworks governing the abandonment of onshore and offshore installations are not identical. In contrast with the situation onshore, the abandonment of offshore operations is governed by an international legal framework. **10.85**

Offshore

The Law of the Sea Conventions clearly recognize the environmental consequences of abandoned offshore installations. Both the 1958 Convention on the Continental Shelf (CCS) and the 1982 United Nations Law of the Sea Convention (UNCLOS) require the removal of abandoned installations. Whereas the 1958 CCS requires total removal, the 1982 UNCLOS allows partial removal if the installations are situated in very deep waters. Due to the shallow waters of the Dutch continental shelf the matter of abandonment is not as controversial as elsewhere in the North Sea. In all circumstances abandoned installations need to be removed completely.[160] The requirement of total removal is inserted almost verbatim in the CS Mining Regulations.[161] The recent ratification of the 1982 Law of the Sea Convention has not led to any amendments to this provision. **10.86**

It should also be noted that the abandonment provisions of the CS Mining Regulations are limited in scope. First, it is not clearly stated to which installations **10.87**

[158] This oilfield is part of the Rijswijk concession which was granted on 3 Jan 1955. It has been producing 7.4 million cubic metres of oil from 48 wells. The concessionaire NAM has abandoned this field entirely, removing 6 installations, 4 measuring stations and approximately 35 kilometres of pipeline. See Nammogram 15/1990, 4.

[159] See 'Oil and Gas in the Netherlands: Exploration and Production 1999', annual report of the Ministry of Economic Affairs, May 2000, 73. See Chr P Verwer, 'Abandonment and Removal of Mining Installations: Some Legal Remarks', paper delivered at OAR Conference, Aberdeen, Apr 1990, 6.

[160] See ch 2 above on international energy law.

[161] Art 68 CS Mining Regulations states that 'a mining installation no longer in use must be removed entirely'.

the obligation actually applies. Are offshore pipelines covered in the provisions? Notwithstanding the legal uncertainty, it is the general opinion that the removal obligation does not apply to abandoned pipelines, although recent practice has shown that the type of the pipeline may actually influence the decision-making process.[162]

10.88 Secondly, the CS Mining Regulations do not explicitly determine when an installation is to be considered abandoned. As the Minister of Economic Affairs may decide about the time within which the removal of the abandoned installation has to take place,[163] it seems that he also has the discretion to decide that an installation is abandoned. Ultimately the provisions of the CS Mining Regulations are limited to rules governing the safety and environmental aspects of the removal of installations.[164]

10.89 Thirdly, the CS Mining Regulations do not provide any explicit rules regarding post-removal actions to be taken by the licensee. The CS Mining Regulations seem to prohibit dumping an abandoned installation on the Dutch continental shelf as it also requires the removal of scrap or other material in the vicinity of the platform and connected with its installation. Debris has to be removed to the extent that it creates a danger to navigation or fishing. Otherwise, the dumping of offshore installations is governed by international law and the international agreements to which the Netherlands is a party.

10.90 Finally, the legislation does not include separate provisions with regard to removal costs. As removal costs can be very high and the Government has to assure payment of these costs upon abandonment when the licensees no longer have a direct interest in the field and the installation, the Minister of Economic Affairs has used its powers under Article 10 para 3(c) CS Mining Act to include a provision in the licence which obliges the licensee to put up a guarantee. Since the fifth licensing round, it is a condition of the grant of a licence that the licensee enter into a guarantee arrangement with respect to abandonment costs, in which case a model guarantee agreement for removal costs is used. The licensee has to agree to obtain a bank or other equivalent guarantee, to cover the costs of removal, at a period when at least one half of the reserves has been produced.[165] The Minister of

[162] Interdepartementale Coördinatie Commissie voor Noordzee-aangelegenheden, 'Verwijdering van pijpleidingen en kabels in de Noordzee', Nov 1988. P Peters, AHA Soons, LA Zima, 'Removal of Installations in the Exclusive Economic Zone', Netherlands Yearbook of International Law, Volume XV, 1984, 167–207. MM Roggenkamp, 'Het Juridisch Kader van Pijpleidingen in de Olie- en Gasindustrie', *Energie & Recht*, Intersentia 1999.

[163] Art 68 para 2 CS Mining Regulations.

[164] Art 68 CS Mining Regulations provides that during the removal measures must be taken to protect the safety of persons employed in the abandonment operations, of shipping, and of the fisheries and to prevent pollution of the sea. Art 69 CS Mining Regulations obliges the licensee to notify the authorities involved, such as the Inspector-General of Mines and the Director-General of Shipping and Maritime Affairs, 24 hours before the commencement of the removal.

[165] Art 2 of the Model Guarantee Agreement.

Economic Affairs shall be notified about this date at least six months before half of these produced reserves can be taken out. In this notification, account has to be given of, *inter alia*, the installation, the estimated costs of removal, and a further development plan for the field. The amount of security shall, however, never exceed the amount of removal costs estimated by the licensees. Where the licence is granted to a consortium, the guarantee is to be borne by the parties in accordance with their participating interests. The licensees shall be liable for payment of the security, except for the State participant. The security provided for is furthermore maintained by the licensees as long as and to the extent that removal of the mining installation has not been completed.[166]

Onshore

In contrast to the above, onshore legislation does not contain an explicit abandonment obligation. However, the Soil Protection Act of 1986 imposes a general obligation on all users of the (sub)soil to prevent actions being taken which may cause pollution.[167] In addition, most deeds of concession include special conditions regarding the termination of mining activities.[168] These oblige the concessionaire, on vacating a drill hole, to cut off (and remove) the pipes of the drill hole at such a depth that subsequent use of the local surface is possible. He also has to remove, after termination of the exploitation, the works made for that purpose in so far as these are not to be maintained for other purposes. If the landowner desires, the concessionaire has to bring the ground back into a state corresponding with its original use.[169] **10.91**

As the original use is often difficult to assess after a period of 30 years or longer, and the surrounding areas have usually changed as well, in practice the land will usually be restored according to the wishes of the landowner. **10.92**

The standards for land clearance are based on the Soil Protection Act,[170] as supplemented by the Environmental Protection Act, which provides for the clean-up and restoration of contaminated land.[171] The latter Act puts more emphasis on private initiative (the polluter-pays principle) and decentralization, in that provincial authorities allocate their budget for the clean-up of contaminated land. Guidelines are issued for the cleaning and restoration of land. Land needs to be restored if there is a real danger to public health and the environment, taking into account the nature and concentration of the polluting substance, the local **10.93**

166 See also Art 3.24 CS Royal Decree 1996.

167 Art 13 Soil Protection Act of 3 July 1986, Stb 374.

168 The Mining Act 1996 has not changed this system.

169 The Minister may, at the request of the proprietor (...), fix a period of time within which such compliance must take place.

170 Act of 3 July 1986, Stb 374, most recently amended on 2 Dec 1999, Stb 537.

171 Originally the Act on Soil Restoration provided clean-up rules. By the Act of 15 May 1994, Stb 331, these rules were replaced by provisions based on the Environmental Protection Act.

situation, and the condition of the soil. Hence, the authorities apply as a main principle that the ground after clearance has to be suitable for any use. It is only possible to deviate from this principle on the basis of strong technical or financial arguments. This can depend on the location; different standards apply to land reclamation in areas supplying drinking water or to farmland.

(5) Disposal of Petroleum Offshore

Introduction

10.94 Oil and natural gas produced in the Netherlands are transported mainly through pipelines to their final delivery point. Whereas crude oil is usually transported to one of the refineries in the Europoort area, all gas is supplied to the NV Nederlandse Gasunie. Until 1996 most deeds of concession as well as the Royal Decrees of 1967 and 1976 (Art 25 of Art III) determined that 'all gas produced in the Netherlands and destined for use in the Netherlands must to be delivered to the NV Nederlandse Gasunie'.[172] In addition, the Minister has a right to intervene as he may determine that the gas is essential for consumption in the Netherlands. Although the wording seems to limit the obligation to gas destined for the Netherlands, thus allowing licensees to export gas, a more restricted view has been applied in practice, giving Gasunie a first right of refusal.[173] As a direct consequence of the disposal obligation, all field-to-shore pipelines on the Dutch continental shelf are landed in the Netherlands. Because the disposal obligation was considered to be anti-competitive and contrary to the Hydrocarbons Licensing Directive, it has been removed from the 1996 Mining Act. However, the practical impact may be limited as most licences were awarded before 1996. Not many changes should therefore be expected in the offshore infrastructure. Most new fields are marginal in size. If possible these fields will be connected to existing infrastructure, mostly being 'Dutch' pipelines but possibly having a different nationality (UK or Norwegian).

The offshore pipeline system

10.95 In the early 1970s two long-distance gas pipelines were constructed offshore. First, the 178 km pipeline *Noordgastransport*, or NGT, connecting blocks L10/L11 with Uithuizen in Groningen. Secondly, the 120 km *Westgastransportleiding*,

---

[172] The Groningen concession determines more boldly that all gas produced has to be delivered to Gasunie.

[173] The narrow interpretation of the landing provision is the result of the *Placid Oil* case of 1972 when the Ministry used its powers to intervene with regard to the exploitation of the first offshore gasfield in blocks L-10/L-11. Although Placid had entered into a sales agreement with a group of German distribution companies, the Minister determined that the gas was necessary for the domestic market. Consequently the agreement was changed so that the gas could be landed in the Netherlands and delivered to Gasunie which then transported the gas to Germany. See also MM Roggenkamp, *Oil and Gas* (n 28 above), 86.

or WGT, which runs from block K13 to Den Helder. In 1983, a parallel pipeline (K15 to Den Helder) was constructed by NAM in order to transport gas of a different quality.[174] The most recent major gas pipeline is the NOGAT pipeline, which came onstream in 1992 and connects five offshore gas fields with Den Helder.[175] In the year 2000 a gasfield on the German continental shelf was connected with the NOGAT pipeline. This was the first cross-border gas pipeline on the Dutch continental shelf, not taking into account the two Norwegian transit pipelines *Zeepipe* and *NorFra*.

In addition to gas, the F3 field is also producing oil that is transported to shore by way of offshore loading.[176] All other oilfields on the Dutch continental shelf are connected to shore by pipelines. In 1982 the first offshore oil from the Helm and Helder fields was brought ashore to IJmuiden via the 60 km *Unocal* pipeline. Whereas the Hoorn field was connected to the transportation pipeline in 1983, the Haven field, also operated by Unocal, was linked to the system in 1989. In 1993 a 40 km oil pipeline connecting P15 with the Maasvlakte was constructed by Amoco. **10.96**

The legal and organizational framework

The construction and exploitation of offshore pipelines is not dependent on the grant of a separate licence. Hence, the Government has not applied its legislative powers under Article 79 para 4 UNCLOS. The CS Mining Act and the CS Mining Regulations merely apply the principle that there is a general freedom to construct submarine pipelines. Although chapter VIII CS Mining Regulations regulates the construction of 'pipelines for the exploration and production of minerals', these provisions are limited to the protection of safety and the environment. As a result of the wording of the regulations, the safety provisions do not apply directly to the construction of transit pipelines.[177] **10.97**

Be that as it may, it should be noted that the Minister can influence the use of existing pipelines through the grant of a production licence. As a production licence is awarded only if an exploitable quantity of minerals is demonstrated and, consequently, the exploitability of a field may depend on the availability of infrastructure and access to pipelines, the applicant may be required to establish a connection with an existing pipeline system. When in the 1980s Continental Netherlands Oil Company (Conoco) discovered an exploitable quantity of oil in the Kotter and Logger fields, it intended to build a separate oil pipeline from these **10.98**

174 In 1986, a short 14 km gas pipeline was constructed by BP just outside the territorial waters (block Q8 to Wijk aan Zee).

175 L2, L5, L15, and F3 are exploited by NAM and F15 by Elf Petroland.

176 *F3, Een late roeping, Shell-Venster*, July/August 1993, 9–11.

177 In practice they are applied on the basis of a Memorandum of Understanding concluded between the Dutch and Norwegian Governments.

offshore oil fields to shore in IJmuiden. The Ministry of Economic Affairs, however, refused permission as there was sufficient capacity left in the nearby Unocal oil pipeline which was designed with extra capacity to allow transport of petroleum from future discoveries. Hence, the Kotter and Logger fields were connected to the Unocal pipeline system in 1985.[178] Transport of oil from the Conoco fields is taking place on a tariffed basis, which is considered very unfavourable.

10.99 Despite the absence of a licensing regime and explicit interconnection rules, most offshore pipelines on the Dutch continental shelf operate as open-access pipelines. Nevertheless, the organizational structure may differ as some pipelines are operated directly by the joint venture holding the production licence and others by a separate pipeline company. For example, the NGT is operated by a limited liability company owned by the holders of the production licence for blocks L10/11 and the State participant EBN. The size and capacity of the NGT is larger than was originally anticipated[179] in order to facilitate third-party access to the pipeline and, consequently, lower transportation charges. The transportation charges levied by the company are based on negotiations between the parties. All users (licence holders and others) have to enter into a transportation agreement with the pipeline company. In practice, the NGT pipeline transports gas from many other fields than the original gasfield in blocks L10/L11.[180]

10.100 Although the WGT is not operated by a separate limited liability company but on the basis of a co-operation agreement between the licensees of the fields to which the pipeline was initially connected,[181] the pipeline in practice also operates as an open-access pipeline. Since the construction of WGT, many other fields[182] have been connected to this pipeline system. In the early 1990s, another Wintershall-operated pipeline was linked to WGT, the pipeline connecting the unitized British/Dutch Markham field[183] to the Dutch pipeline system.[184] This gas is

[178] In the same year, the oilfield in block P15, operated by Amoco, started to produce. In order to transport the oil to the BP refinery in Europoort, a 42 km pipeline was built to Hook of Holland.

[179] Instead of a 30-inch pipeline which would be sufficient for the transport of gas from L10/L11, DSM Aardgas BV requested the construction of a 36-inch pipeline.

[180] In 1987 only 23% of the pipeline's capacity was used by gas from L10/L11. Gas from L4, L7, P6, and K12 is also transported by Noordgastransport. See *Administratiefrechtelijke Beslissingen/NJ* 1987, no 329.

[181] A production licence for block K13 was originally granted to the Noordwinningsgroep, operated by Penzoil Nederland. At present, the pipeline is operated by Wintershall Noordzee BV which is the operator of field K13.

[182] Examples are K10 operated by Wintershall cs and K7, K8, K11, and L13 operated by NAM. Hence, the companies are in practice the same (Wintershall or NAM).

[183] It is noteworthy that the Markham field, ie block J6 and part of block J3, is the first cross-border field developed between the United Kingdom and the Netherlands. See Martha M Roggenkamp, 'The Markham Field: Joint Exploitation by the Netherlands and the United Kingdom', OGLTR, 1992, vol 10, issue 7, 193–7.

[184] A 24-inch pipeline with a length of 86 km connects the Markham field with the K13-A platform of Wintershall.

transported by Wintershall via the WGT to the Gasunie system, which then transports part of the gas directly to Germany.

The last major gas pipeline to be constructed on the Dutch continental shelf was the NOGAT pipeline, which has a capacity of more than double what is needed for the foreseeable production from the initial fields connected to the pipeline. Obviously, future connections to the pipeline system are projected.[185] Similarly to the NGT pipeline, NOGAT is operated by a limited liability company. All users have to conclude transportation agreements with the pipeline company. The tariffs charged are based on the extent to which the pipeline is used. Transportation costs will be equal for pipeline owners and third parties, and decrease as the use of the pipeline increases. On the other hand, the tariffs are designed so as to give the shareholders of NOGAT BV a fair market return for their risk. Third parties can choose between two official tariff systems.[186] Consequently, in comparison with the above-mentioned pipelines where tariffs are negotiated between parties, it seems that the NOGAT pipeline operates as an official open-access pipeline. **10.101**

(6) The Mining Bill 1998

Introduction

In November 1998 a Mining Bill was presented to Parliament. The Bill aims to integrate the provisions of the Mining Act 1810, the Mining Act 1903, the Mineral Exploration Act, and the CS Mining Act into one integrated Mining Act.[187] It therefore completes the work done in the framework of the implementation of the Hydrocarbons Licensing Directive and can be considered as the final result of a lengthy discussion about the introduction of a modern mining law which has been ongoing for many decades. Although integration of the existing rules is the most important goal, some conceptual changes were made to the mining regime as well. These developments are discussed below. **10.102**

The scope of the Mining Bill

In contrast with the present situation, the Mining Bill applies to the Dutch territory as well as the Dutch continental shelf. The Bill addresses the exploration for **10.103**

[185] A westward extension from L2 could, for example, bring in gas from fields in the D, E, J, and K blocks explored by NAM, Elf Petroland, Ultramar, and Wintershall. Also an extension eastwards from block F15 to the G block is conceivable. Gas has been discovered by NAM in block G16. Even an extension to the northwestern part of the Dutch sector of the continental shelf is possible, as NAM has discovered gas in block A18. IRO Journaal 24 Jan 1990, 17.

[186] See HG Dijkgraaf, 'The Impact of the NOGAT Pipeline on Netherlands Offshore Gas Output and Development', Financial Times North Sea Oil and Gas Conference, London, 7 June 1993, 7; and MM Roggenkamp, 'The Impact of the NOGAT Pipeline on the Netherlands Output and Development', Oil and Gas Law and Taxation Review, Nov 1993, 135–42.

[187] Tweede Kamer 1998–99, 26 219. It should be noted that in the Dutch language a distinction is made between the titles of the applicable laws, *Mijnwet* and *Mijnbouwwet*. This distinction cannot be made in the English language where both terms are translated as 'Mining Act'.

and production of minerals as well as terrestrial heat. The latter element is a new aspect of Dutch mining law.[188] Moreover, the Bill uses a more general definition of the term 'minerals':

> minerals or substances of organic origin, present in the subsoil, in a concentration or deposit which is there through natural means, in solid, liquid or gaseous form, with the exception of marsh gas, limestone, gravel, sand, clay, shells, and mixtures thereof.[189]

10.104 Another new phenomenon is the introduction of a horizontal limitation for the application of the Act. Hence, the new Mining Act only applies to the exploration and production of minerals situated more than 100 metres beneath the surface and to terrestrial heat as long as this is situated more than 500 metres below the surface.[190] It should be noted, however, that a horizontal division of mining rights is not new. The Mining Act of 1791 (preceding the Mining Act 1810) was based on a similar principle but was soon replaced by the Mining Act 1810 as landowners exploited the upper layer of soil so injudiciously that it was technically impossible for the concessionaire to start exploitation below the level of 100 feet. Although the Council of State recognizes that such a situation may appear again and therefore suggests the introduction of a 'rule of conflict', the legislator has not taken up this suggestion.

Ownership rights

10.105 The Mining Bill also gives a clear rule about the ownership of subsoil minerals *in situ*. Article 3 para 1 declares that 'minerals are owned by the State'. Hence, the domanial system applies both offshore and onshore. The ownership is transferred upon production, and not as before onshore upon the award of the concession. Under the new system of ownership any discussion about 'expropriation' by the State following the refusal of permission for exploration and production is thus avoided.

10.106 Nevertheless, licensees' exploitation rights can infringe on the ownership rights of the landowners. To facilitate matters for the licensees, the Bill states that landowners must allow licensees to carry out exploration and/or exploitation activities as long as these take place 100 metres beneath the surface and the landowners are properly compensated for any damage to their property.[191]

10.107 If a landowner objects to the establishment of installations for exploration and/or production, the Mining Bill indicates that the Laws on Hindrances in Private and

[188] Art 1 sub b Mining Bill defines terrestrial heat as 'heat present in the subsoil which originated there by natural means'.
[189] Art 1 sub a Mining Bill.
[190] Art 2 Mining Bill.
[191] Art 4 Mining Bill.

Public Law may be applied. These establish that landowners may have to tolerate the construction on their property of public works in the general interest. The Mining Bill therefore rules that installations for the exploration for and/or production of minerals, terrestrial heat, or for underground storage are public works in the general interest.[192] In practice a simplified expropriation procedure is created. However, since a landowner will not usually be able to use that part of the land where the installation is erected, the working of the Act will be limited, as case-law shows that a landowner may not be deprived of all the advantages of his property. In such case, a full expropriation procedure could be required if the landowner is not willing to co-operate, especially when taking into account that an installation for production or underground storage could be in place for many decades.

Licensing regime

As under the present regime, the Mining Bill is based on a system of authorizations and thus confirms customary practice in the Netherlands. The proposed regime is based on a competitive system, which is similar to the present mining regime. **10.108**

However, the number of types of licence has increased. An authorization is not only required for the exploration and production of minerals, but also for the exploration for and exploitation of terrestrial heat, and for underground storage of minerals.[193] It should be noted that an authorization for the disposal and piped transportation of minerals is still not required. **10.109**

The term 'exploration' is defined as 'a search for the presence of minerals (or terrestrial heat) or for additional information about these, making use of a drill hole'. Exploratory investigations which do not require the use of a drill hole are excluded. Contrary to the CS Mining Act which requires a reconnaissance licence, such prior authorization is not necessary under the new regime. In addition, the Bill requires an authorization for underground storage. **10.110**

Underground storage

Although the debate about underground storage has been ongoing for more then ten years, the first statutory provision about underground storage is now included in the Mining Bill. Underground storage is now made dependent on a special licence. The award of such a licence is not based on a competitive regime, as the **10.111**

---

192 Art 5 Mining Bill.

193 Art 6 Mining Bill. It may be decided by Royal Decree that such authorization is not required for some categories of exploration for and production of terrestrial heat (see para 2 of Art 6). Para 3 further rules that the provisions in this chapter on the exploration for and production of minerals (ie chapter 2 covering Art 6-25 on authorization for the exploration for and production of minerals and terrestrial heat) apply equally to the exploration for and production of terrestrial heat.

award of a storage licence seems mainly to concern persons having a production licence. Taking into account the long duration of production licences, the circumstances in which others can apply for a storage licence will be very limited indeed.

10.112 As storage licences will mainly be awarded for storing natural gas in depleted gasfields, a special provision is included concerning the ownership of minerals in underground storage. The ownership of stored minerals rests with the person who owned the minerals just before these were put into underground storage, or with the legal successor of the person owning the minerals just before storing them.[194] How the licensees in practice assess the ownership of stored gas is not yet clear. It seems that much will depend on metering the gas injected and withdrawn.

Provisions ensuring the proper execution of mining activities

10.113 A separate chapter of the Bill aims at ensuring that mining activities are executed properly. As a general rule the Bill declares that licensees must take all reasonable steps to prevent the mining activities (a) having an adverse effect on the environment, (b) resulting in earth movements, (c) jeopardizing safety or the systematic management of subsoil minerals and terrestrial heat.[195] The subsequent articles give further instructions about the licensee's obligations with regard to the activities mentioned.

10.114 The Environmental Protection Act applies to mining activities both underground and on the surface. Hence, the Mining Bill deviates from the original principles of the Mining 1810 and the Mining Act 1903 which were based on the idea that all aspects related to mining activities, including environmental protection, should be part of mining law. However, as the Environmental Protection Act only applies to Dutch territory (including the territorial sea), separate rules will apply to the continental shelf. Similar to the above-mentioned arrangement, the Bill requires a location licence for installation on the continental shelf. Such a licence may be denied on the basis of environmental reasons and following the outcome of an EIA.[196] In addition, the Bill contains provisions regarding the establishment and removal of installations. These rules establish a safety zone around mining installations and the removal of abandoned installations. It should be noted that similar provisions were included in the Royal Decrees implementing the CS Mining Act. Under the new regime the provisions are included in statutory law, and apply to both onshore and offshore installations. An exception is made for offshore pipelines. Article 40 Mining Bill declares that the Minister may decide that

[194] Art 3 Mining Bill. The obligation also applies to the last holder of the licence if the licence has lapsed.

[195] Art 34 Mining Bill.

[196] Art 35 Mining Bill.

abandoned pipelines on the continental shelf must be removed. Although there is no removal obligation, this is the first time that the possibility of removal has been included in Dutch law.

Another new element in the Bill is the provision regarding earth movements. The legislator recognizes that mining activities can result in earthquakes as well as subsidence. Therefore the Bill requires that measurements be carried out before, during, and for up to five years after production and storage of minerals. This obligation does not extend to offshore activities because it is not expected that earth movements following production will lead to severe damage.[197] These measurements may influence the production activities and are of importance in deciding liability in case of damage. A new provision will therefore be included in the Civil Code introducing strict liability for the licensee.[198] An Earth Movement Technical Committee is established to advise the Minister and to advise the person suffering damage from earth movements about the connection between the earth movements and the mining activities.[199] **10.115**

In order to cover liability for damage resulting from earth movements, the Minister may decide that financial security must be provided. A similar provision applies to the obligation to remove abandoned installations and (possibly) unused pipelines.[200] Additional rules regarding the environment, health, and safety may be laid down in mining regulations.[201] **10.116**

Financial provisions

Chapter five of the Mining Bill contains the financial provisions relating to exploration for and production of minerals. Separate sections deal with the payments relating to prospecting for and extracting hydrocarbons, State participation in the production of hydrocarbons, and payments and State participation in case of storage. Basically, the rules are similar to the present regime, providing for payment of a State profit share and corporate income tax, royalties, surface rentals, and bonuses. The system of State participation is also similar to the extent that it provides for a 40 per cent share of the State participant in the production activities. **10.117**

In addition, the Bill requires the holders of a storage licence to make annual payments to the State (and the province) as specified in the licence. Similarly, the provisions regarding State participation apply.[202] **10.118**

197 Art 36 Mining Bill.
198 Art 6:177 Civil Code (new).
199 Arts 98–100 Mining Bill.
200 Arts 41–3 Mining Bill.
201 Arts 44–6 Mining Bill.
202 Arts 78–9 Mining Bill.

10.119 The main difference between the Mining Bill and the present regime is the fact that the financial provisions will be included in statutory law, as a result of which the system will be less flexible. Any changes to the financial regime will require an amendment of the law, which can be time-consuming. Although the CS Mining Act provided for additional parliamentary control, enabling both Houses of Parliament to discuss amendments to the Decrees, the legislator apparently did not consider this procedure sufficient. It remains to be seen whether additional parliamentary control will counterbalance the lack of flexibility.

Concluding remarks

10.120 The Mining Bill marks the last stage in a long discussion. It provides for an integrated Mining Act which will in practice apply mostly to the exploration for and production of hydrocarbons, but also to the production of salt. As the Bill clearly aims at the integration of the onshore and offshore regimes and not is intended to substitute the old regime with a completely new and modern petroleum law, it is also envisaged that the new regime will apply immediately to most existing concessions and licences. Only concessions awarded before 1965 are exempted, because the financial provisions differ radically from the provisions in the Royal Decrees of 1967 and following. Hence, some of the most important concessions, such as Groningen, are exempted from the new mining regime.[203] The effect of the new Mining Act will therefore be more restricted than was anticipated. However, as the Groningen concession plays a crucial role in Dutch gas policy, it is not surprising that special rules apply to the production of this gasfield. Parliament has suggested that the Mining Bill and the Gas Bill should be discussed in combination. However, a combined discussion of both Bills was hindered by the need to implement the EC Gas Directive before 10 August 2000 and no such requirement exists for the Mining Bill. In addition, discussions on the Mining Bill are taking more time than was anticipated.

C. Transportation, Distribution, and Supply of Natural Gas

(1) Introduction

10.121 Until 1 August 2000 the Dutch gas transmission sector was not governed by an Act of Parliament. Statutory regulation of the gas sector was limited to the distribution sector (Energy Distribution Act) and minimum gas pricing (Natural Gas Prices Act). Government policy regarding the gas sector was mostly based on White Papers, such as the Policy Note of De Pous in 1963,[204] the Energy Notes of

[203] The other concessions are Schoonebeek, Rijswijk, Tubbergen, and Rossum-De Lutte.
[204] Tweede Kamer 1961–62, 6767.

1973/79,[205] the Gas Policy Note of 1989,[206] and the third Energy Note of 1995.[207] Before discussing the new Gas Act, an overview will be given of Dutch gas policy and regulations, as these developments largely influenced the coming into being of the new law.

Since the 1960s Dutch gas policy has been based on the assumption that national gas reserves should benefit society as a whole and guarantee domestic gas supply. The national gas transmission company NV Nederlandse Gasunie (hereinafter Gasunie) was given a key role in the purchase, transport, and sales of natural gas. Government control was effected by direct ownership control as the State was given a (direct and indirect through its State participant) share in the gas transmission company Gasunie. In addition, it was given a number of powers of approval on the basis of an agreement under private law with Gasunie, ie the right to approve the Gas Marketing Plan, the conditions and tariffs of gas supply, export prices, and gas purchasing contracts. Hence, Gasunie in fact had a monopoly position in the Dutch gas market. **10.122**

In examining the Government's marketing strategy since the 1960s it can be concluded that the Government's policy with regard to gas produced in the Netherlands has been subject to some important changes. On the basis of, *inter alia*, the presumption of rapid development of nuclear energy, the Dutch Government initially focused on the export of large quantities of gas. Due to the oil crises in the 1970s this policy changed drastically. The underlying principle followed by the Government since that time is the development of smaller gasfields, given that the Groningen field can act as a 'swing producer'. Gasunie has therefore been able to give priority to the purchasing on a commercial basis of gas produced by other, especially smaller, Dutch gasfields. This policy with regard to the development of small gasfields was reaffirmed in the Gas Policy Note of 1989,[208] the third Energy Note of 1995, and the policy discussion note 'Gas Streams' (*gasstromen*).[209] The Gas Act of 2000 is also based on the principles of the small field policy and the presumption that Gasunie will continue to play a central role in the Dutch gas market. Whether or not this policy conflicts with the Government's liberalization policy is discussed below. **10.123**

[205] Tweede Kamer 1974–75, No 13 122 (*Energienota* 1973); Tweede Kamer 1979–80, No 15 802 (*Nota Energiebeleid*).

[206] *Enkele Hoofdlijnen van het Energiebeleid Nader Bezien*, Tweede Kamer 1988–89, 21 061.

[207] Tweede Kamer 1995–96, No 24 525 (*Derde Energienota*).

[208] *Enkele Hoofdlijnen van het Energiebeleid Nader Bezien, Tweede Kamer* 1988–89, 21 061.

[209] Ministerie van Economische Zaken, Dec 1997.

(2) Gas Transmission and Distribution 1960–2000

The NV Nederlandse Gasunie

10.124 The structure of the Dutch gas industry and the key role of Gasunie within it are based on a memorandum issued by the Minister of Economic Affairs, De Pous, in 1963 after the discovery of the gasfield in Groningen in 1959.[210] The size of the Groningen field made it impossible to maintain the policy that all 'natural gas extracted and not used by the concessionaire himself should be bought and taken over by the State of the Netherlands'[211] (ie the State Gas Board, *Staatsgasbedrijf*). Although the State did not wish to apply the same principle to the Groningen concession due to the high risks and financing problems it would cause the State, it wished to be involved in the marketing of the gas since the sale of large amounts of gas could have a considerable influence on the price of oil.

10.125 The basic principle of the Gas Policy Note of De Pous was that there should be close co-ordination between the production and sales of gas, and that the public supply of gas should be seen as a Government task, so as to avoid gas sales becoming too dependent on private suppliers. As a result, a limited degree of State participation was introduced to all levels of the gas chain. In addition to State participation in the production of natural gas (via the *Maatschap*, discussed above) the State also participates in the transport and marketing of natural gas. By contrast to the State Gas Board, which was 100 per cent State-owned, the State holds only 50 per cent of the shares of the new gas company, NV Nederlandse Gasunie.

10.126 The NV Nederlandse Gasunie was established on 6 April 1963 as a public limited company, in which Shell and Esso (the holders of the Groningen concession) each hold a 25 per cent share, the Dutch State Mines (now EBN) holds another 40 per cent share (indirect State participation), and the State of the Netherlands (directly) the remaining 10 per cent share.[212] Hence, the organization of the production and supply of the Groningen gas reflects the need for a limited degree of vertical integration of the gas industry. First, the same companies are involved in the production and transport of natural gas: Shell and Esso hold the Groningen concession as well as 50 per cent shares in Gasunie. Secondly, the State participates in the production of gas through its 40 per cent share in the *Maatschap* in which the actual decisions are made about the disposal as well as the transport of gas through its 50 per cent shares (direct and indirect) of Gasunie. Although a similar structure applies to all other gas concessions/licences, it should be noted that other oil com-

[210] Tweede Kamer 1961–62, 6767 (De Pous Policy Note).

[211] cf Art 8 of the Schoonebeek concession of 3 May 1948, no 19, Stc 110.

[212] Gasunie is managed by three Managing Directors and a General Managing Director. Supervision of the management is carried out by the Board of Supervisory Directors consisting of 12 members on which representatives of both oil companies, EBN, and the Ministry of Economic Affairs have places. The Board has the right of approval of a number of management decisions with regard to, *inter alia*, contracts for import and export of natural gas and the Gas Marketing Plan.

panies may hold a concession/licence under which the connection between production and marketing is not as close as in the case of the Groningen concession.

Finally, the change in gas policy also reflected the gradual change of the gas sector from public to public/private ownership. Instead of the former State Gas Board, the gas supply is now operated by a limited liability company in which the State holds (directly and indirectly) a 50 per cent share. This means that the gas supply sector has been commercialized and partly privatized. The 'Third Energy Note' of 1995, the subsequent Note Gas Streams, and the Gas Act of 2000 can be considered as a step towards more liberalization and competition. As a result of this liberalization policy further privatization of Gasunie can be expected.[213] **10.127**

Gas transmission and the role of Gasunie

The 1963 gas policy note provided that all gas extracted in the Netherlands had to be sold to Gasunie, which would be responsible for overall Dutch gas supply as well as exports of gas.[214] As this requires a nationwide gas transportation system, the Government decided to merge the existing gas pipeline network of the State Gas Board[215] with the independent gas transportation systems of the Dutch State Mines (the State participant) and the grid of the steel company *Hoogovens*. Additional pipelines were constructed to connect all parts of the Netherlands with the existing gas transmission system. Since 1963 Gasunie has built up an extensive gas transmission system in the Netherlands with a total length of approximately 11,000 km of mainland transportation pipelines[216] and some 100,000 kilometres of distribution pipelines.[217] In order to export the Groningen gas, the Dutch transmission system was also linked to other European pipeline systems, such as the *Société Européene du Gazoduc Est-Ouest* (SEGEO),[218] transporting gas through Belgium to France, and the *Trans Europa Naturgas Pipeline GmbH*,[219] transporting gas through Germany to Basle, Switzerland, and from there across the Swiss Alps to Northern Italy.[220] **10.128**

[213] The Minister announced that the role of the State in Gasunie will be examined in due course. Tweede Kamer 26 463, No 8, 5.

[214] In the 1960s and early 1970s, however, there were operating two complementary gas export organizations: NAM/Gas Export and *Internationaal Gas Transport Maatschappij* both owned by Shell and Esso. In 1975 the tasks of both organizations were taken over by Gasunie, who since then has a *de facto* monopoly on exports.

[215] Whereas the State Gas Board had an extensive transportation network throughout a large part of the Netherlands, ie the provinces of Groningen, Friesland, Drenthe, Overijssel, Gelderland, Utrecht, South Holland, and Zeeland, the Hoogovens distributed gas from the coke furnaces in northern Holland. The DSM pipelines were situated in the province of Limburg.

[216] There are different kinds of major pipelines through the Netherlands, depending on the quality of gas, namely Groningen/low caloric gas and high caloric gas.

[217] On average the system has 56 connections per kilometer.

[218] A joint enterprise of the Belgian gas transmission company Distrigaz SA and Gaz de France.

[219] Jointly owned by Ruhrgas AG and the Italian company SNAM SpA.

[220] This pipeline system has been connected with the TRANSMED pipeline system in 1986 which transports Algerian gas to Italy.

10.129 Gasunie does not have a monopoly on the construction of gas pipelines. In the absence of a pipeline or subsoil infrastructure law, the construction and exploitation of pipelines (or other subsoil infrastructure) is basically free. The laying of pipelines is dependent on the permission of landowners to make use of their property. If landowners refuse their permission, the Law on Hindrances of Private Law may give a solution, as it enables the pipeline company to get the necessary rights of way as long as the pipeline company has been awarded a concession and a declaration that the pipeline is of public interest (see para. 10.107 above). Gasunie was awarded a general concession in 1963 for the construction and upkeep of all gas pipelines and associated works required for the transport of natural gas.[221] Consequently, Gasunie is in a favourable position as it does not have to apply for a concession in each individual case. Moreover, due to the lack of transparency in the concession system, it is doubtful whether a competing company would have been awarded a pipeline concession if so requested. It could therefore be argued that Gasunie exercised a *de facto* construction monopoly.

10.130 Until the Mining Act 1996, Gasunie did have a monopoly of the purchase of gas for domestic consumption. However, as referred to above, the obligation to sell gas to Gasunie is restricted to gas both produced in and intended for consumption in the Netherlands. Since this clause leaves the door open for gas export, some direct sales agreements have been concluded in the 1960s by Petroland,[222] holding the Leeuwarden concession,[223] and the holders of the Bergen concession.[224] These concessionaires entered into gas sales agreements with buyers in France (Gaz de France) and Germany. Subsequently, they entered into an agreement with Gasunie as a result of which the gas from the Leeuwarden and Bergen concessions was delivered to Gasunie who then supplied the buyers in France and Germany with corresponding quantities of gas from the Groningen field. A similar arrangement was made between Placid Oil and Gasunie with regard to the gas found in the K-10/L11-blocks (see above, n 173).

10.131 The above-mentioned are swap agreements rather than transit agreements, as Groningen gas is delivered to the foreign buyers instead of the gas produced by the concessionaires. Since then, however, the EC Transit Directive has entered into force, which provides for special procedures for transit of natural gas. As gas transmission in the Netherlands is not based on statutory law, the Directive has been

[221] Ministerial Order of 13 Dec 1963, No 663/1357; not a concession awarded on the basis of the mining legislation.

[222] A Dutch subsidiary of Société Nationale Elf-Acquitaine.

[223] The Leeuwarden concession was granted on 17 Feb 1969, Stc 46, to a consortium consisting of Petroland NV, Total Marine Exploitatie Maatschappij NV, Eurafrep NV, Corexland NV, and Cofraland NV by Royal Decree No 31, most recently amended on 21 Mar 1983, Stc 73.

[224] The concession was granted by Royal Decree No 14, to Amoco Netherlands Petroleum Company, Gelsenkirchener Bergwerks AG, and the Exploratie- en Productiemaatschappij Dyas NV on 1 May 1969, Stc 94.

implemented by way of a covenant between the Minister and Gasunie in which the latter states that the EC Transit Directive will be complied with.[225] In practice the Directive has had very little direct impact in the Netherlands. No transit negotiations have been notified to the EC Commission.

Gas distribution

The structure of the distribution sector

Gasunie sells most of its gas to the public distribution companies, with the exception of some large industrial users which it supplies directly. In 1999 there were approximately 30 distribution companies. As a result of some large-scale mergers following the energy liberalization process the number of distribution companies will decrease to about ten. Although the liberalization process has led to intense discussion about the need for and possibilities of privatization, most distribution companies are still owned by the provinces and municipalities. In other words, the Government has control over the energy sector through direct and/or indirect ownership interests on all three levels: production, transmission, and distribution of gas. As Gasunie only acquired a share in three distribution companies (Intergas, Obragas, and Limagas), vertical integration was (and is) almost non-existent. The main reason is that since the 1970s the distribution sector has been subject to a policy of horizontal integration.[226] Most distribution companies therefore supply gas, electricity, heat, and possibly water. A similar integration has taken place on the level of the regionally oriented association of gas and electricity distributors who have merged into a national organization called EnergieNed.[227] **10.132**

The policy of integration described above also led to changes in the legal form of the distribution companies. The public law undertakings[228] were gradually transferred into enterprises under private law such as limited liability companies (*Naamloze Vennootschap* or *NV*) in which the municipalities/provinces hold most shares.[229] This transformation constitutes a gradual commercialization of the **10.133**

[225] Agreement of 1 Jan 1992, Stc 67 of 3 Apr 1992.

[226] The organization of the energy distribution sector has been an issue of political discussion since World War II. A choice had to be made between vertical or horizontal integration. Objections to horizontal integration were merely based on the difference in production. Parliament finally opted for the horizontal integration of all energy utilities.

[227] As the result of further horizontal integration the Association of Operators of Gas Companies in the Netherlands (VEGIN) merged with similar associations of operators in the electricity, water, and heat sectors (VEEN, VEWIN, and VESTIN) to form EnergieNed. In 1999 EnergieNed's legal status changed from an association into a federation. Any energy company can become a member of this federation.

[228] *Gemeenschappelijke Dienst* (Municipal Branch) or a *Gemeenschappelijke Regeling* (Joint Arrangement) which is based on the Act regarding Arrangements between Local Authorities (*Wet houdende voorschriften met betrekking tot gemeenschappelijke regelingen*) of 1 Apr 1950, *Staatsblad* 120, amended on 20 Dec 1984, *Staatsblad* 667.

[229] Sometimes provinces also take part in a joint arrangement or a limited liability company.

sector and does facilitate further privatization of the utilities. The first attempts to privatize the distribution sectors have already been taken.[230]

Energy Distribution Act

10.134 The policy of horizontal integration and commercialization was finally codified in the Energy Distribution Act,which entered into force in 1997.[231] The scope of this Act is much more limited than initially intended, since the original idea to introduce concession areas was not included in the Act as the result of the ongoing voluntary mergers.[232]

10.135 The main tasks of the distribution companies are therefore 1) to provide a reliable energy supply at low cost, 2) to promote safety as far as use and equipment is concerned, and 3) to promote the efficient and environmentally sound use of energy.[233] In other words, the tasks of the distribution companies are restricted to the supply of energy and activities pertaining thereto.[234] Other activities are basically prohibited as these are not covered by the principle of public supply (ie at low cost) and so could lead to unfair competition. In order to ensure a reliable supply of energy at low cost, each distribution company is required to set up a consumer council advising the company about the tariffs of energy distribution.[235]

Gas distribution

10.136 Upon the entry into force of the Gas Act in August 2000, all gas companies purchased their gas from Gasunie. Since 1962 the association of energy distributors EnergieNed obtained natural gas exclusively from Gasunie on the basis of a 15-year contract. In annual negotiations about the extension of the contract, EnergieNed negotiated with Gasunie the price of gas, its quality, the quantities to

---

[230] The Minister has received a request for privatization of NV Nutsbedrijven Haarlemermeer and NV Nutsbedrijven Regio Eindhoven.

[231] Act of 14 Dec 1996, providing rules for the distribution of electricity, gas, and heat (Stb 642).

[232] As a result the original Bill (Tweede Kamer 1990–91, 22160) was necessarily amended as one of the main purposes of the Bill had already been achieved. In 1992 some 50 horizontally integrated distribution companies were supplying gas and electricity (and sometimes water and cable television) compared to the 138 gas distribution companies in 1986. The aim was to limit the number of distribution companies to 47.

[233] Art 2 Energy Distribution Act. The energy supply tariffs may include costs for the promotion of energy saving and environmental protection as long as these payments are within certain limits determined by the Minister. The Minister determines the percentage (with a maximum of 2.5%) at which these costs may be reimbursed. It is possible to differentiate between several categories of consumers (Arts 10–11 Energy Distribution Act). These provisions do not apply to Gasunie and supply from a company established outside the Netherlands (Art 15 Energy Distribution Act).

[234] Art 12 clearly defines these activities as including the supply of goods and services necessary for energy supply (at low cost), safety inspections, payment collection, the construction of supply infrastructure, and the construction and exploitation of public lighting systems and traffic regulation systems connected with electricity supply.

[235] Arts 4–9 Energy Distribution Act.

be delivered, and other terms of delivery. In addition, EnergieNed advised the gas companies about tariffs and terms of delivery with regard to the supply to end-users.[236] These terms of delivery were included in a standard contract for the delivery and supply of natural gas.[237]

This gas supply contract was considered to be almost perpetual: it was extended more or less every year and if the contract was not renewed, it nevertheless had another 15 years to run before expiry. The justification for this contract was considered to be security of supply, since Gasunie also was contractually obliged to supply as much gas as its customers required. This 15-year contract plays an important role in the present liberalization process. Negotiations about an extension of the contract broke down in 1996/1997, despite Gasunie's offer to limit the 'evergreen' contract to a period of 10 years.[238] Some distribution companies wished to negotiate on an individual basis with Gasunie about the main provisions of the contract. This resulted in some individual contracts, which contain elements reflecting the elements of a demand-driven liberalized gas market. Gasunie announced in April 2000 that it is willing to terminate these contracts as soon as the market is liberalized. **10.137**

(3) Government Control until the Entry into Force of the Gas Act

Gas Marketing Plan

From the early 1960s Dutch gas policy was mainly supply-driven. The Government's depletion policy was therefore closely connected to its supply policy. An important control mechanism is this respect is the Gas Marketing Plan, drawn up annually since 1963,[239] and which needs approval from the Minister, giving the Government an additional control mechanism. The Plan examines the supply and demand prospects of Dutch natural gas over a medium term of five years and also includes a forecast of the amount of natural gas available (the probable gas reserves) over the coming 25 years. Although the liberalized gas market will be demand-driven instead of supply-driven, as a result of which the role of planning will change, some co-ordination is still required. Hence, the Gas Marketing Plan will be (partly) substituted by an Energy Report presenting an analysis of the developments on the national and international energy markets.[240] Such a report will be made at least every fours years and shall be approved by the Minister. Its main purpose is to give guidance on the decisions to be taken by the **10.138**

[236] Due to the fact that the aforementioned contract between Gasunie and VEGIN was renegotiated in 1988 the tariffs for domestic customers have been advised unilaterally by VEGIN since Jan 1989.

[237] These standard contracts are *Aansluitvoorwaarden Gas 1979* and *Algemene Voorwaarden Gas 1979*.

[238] The previous contract ran from 1 Jan 1994–1 Jan 1997.

[239] Art 13 of the *Statuten der NV Nederlandse Gasunie.*

[240] Art 34 Gas Act.

Government. By contrast to the Gas Marketing Plan, the Energy Report focuses more on short-term policy.

Approval of tariffs and prices for natural gas

10.139 Another important instrument of Government control is the ministerial power to approve tariffs and prices. These Minister's statutory powers are very limited as the *Wet Aardgasprijzen* (hereinafter Natural Gas Prices Act)[241] only empowers the Minister of Economic Affairs to fix a minimum price for gas. It enables the Minister to intervene if he thinks that the gas price is below the market value. He may then forbid the supply of gas within or outside the Netherlands at any price lower than that which he has set. This ban applies to the delivery of gas by gas-producing companies to Gasunie.[242] If gas is supplied at a price lower than that set by the Minister, he may take physical measures to prevent further supply, thus 'turning the tap off'.[243] The State is not responsible for any damage which may occur as a result of such action.[244]

10.140 Before the entry into force of the Gas Act 2000, the Minister could also intervene in the prices set by Gasunie for the supply of gas to domestic and foreign consumers. Consequently, the Dutch Government intervened in the natural gas export contracts entered into in the 1960s with international customers such as Ruhrgas AG in Germany, Distrigaz SA in Belgium, and Gaz de France for periods of 20 to 25 years. These contracts were at fixed border prices. As a result of the oil crises the difference between gas prices on the Dutch market and the gas exported was no longer justifiable. Hence, the Dutch Government started a new round of negotiations with regard to these gas export contracts in 1980.[245] These negotiations resulted in a pricing system according to which the price of gas for export was linked to the trend in the price of oil.[246]

10.141 Before the year 2000, the Natural Gas Prices Act gave the Minister the power of 'repressive supervision' (*repressief toezicht*) as far as it concerned the supply of gas to final domestic consumers.[247] An initial distinction can be made between customers supplied directly by Gasunie and customers supplied by the gas distribution companies. For each category the price is linked to the price of the fuel to which users would logically turn if there were no natural gas. The customers supplied directly by Gasunie are large-scale users, such as industrial users and power

[241] Stb 1974, no 765.
[242] Art 2 of the Natural Gas Prices Act.
[243] Art 4 of the Natural Gas Prices Act.
[244] Art 7 of the Natural Gas Prices Act.
[245] 12 June 1980, Stc 111. These renegotiations of the gas export prices are known by the name of the Government appointed negotiator Mr Spierenburg (Royal Decree of 23 May 1980, No 18).
[246] Stc 192, 3 Oct 1980. The results of the Spierenburg negotiations were put into force by Oct 1981 after a transition period of 14 months.
[247] Art 5 of the Natural Gas Prices Act.

stations with a gas take of more than 2 million cubic metres per year. Within the other category of customers supplied by the distribution companies, a distinction was made between the industrial sector taking more than 170,000 cubic metres per year, and the small consumer sector with an annual consumption below that level.

In practice, the above categories coincided with the division in pricing zones. Whereas the first zone applied to consumers with an off-take of 170,000 cubic metres of gas per year, the last zone applied to consumers with an off-take of more than 50 million cubic metres of gas per year. The final gas tariff depended on the number of zones applying to the customer's yearly gas consumption.[248] In addition to a commodity charge based on the off-take per zone, the tariff also included a commodity price. For large industrial consumers the commodity price was calculated according to the Rotterdam market price quotation for heavy fuel oil, and is adjusted every three months, so that no time lag is involved. The price applicable to the category of small consumers (below the level of 170,000 cubic metres) is linked to the price of domestic heating oil which, before the large-scale introduction of natural gas replaced coal, was the traditional fuel.[249] For practical and historical reasons there are a number of exceptions to that structure. A typical example is the tariff system which Gasunie applies to the industrial/horticulture sector, which has been the subject of a number of judgments of the Court of Justice of the European Communities.[250] **10.142**

Since the enactment of the Natural Gas Prices Act, the Minister of Economic Affairs has intervened several times in fixing the price agreed between Gasunie and the distribution companies.[251] Although the Minister could not set the gas price himself, having only a right of approval, in practice Gasunie and EnergieNed have adjusted the price they initially agreed to the price recommended by the Minister's decision. **10.143**

In 1999 Gasunie has introduced a new tariff structure for large industrial consumers. The new system is the result of the ongoing liberalization in the gas sector and sets separate tariffs for the supply of gas and several additional services (see below). **10.144**

[248] Whereas zone B–zone E applies to industrial users, zone A is for 'small consumers'.

[249] The Dutch zoning system is discussed in greater detail in a report published by the VEGIN in the Netherlands and KOMGAS in Denmark 'Transparancy in Natural Gas Prices in Western Europe', Nov 1989.

[250] Case 169/84, *Compagnie Française de l'Azote (Cofaz) et al v Commission* [1986] ECR 408 (Cofaz I); joined Cases 67, 68, 70/84, *Kwekerij Gebroeders van der Kooy et al v Commission* [1988] E.C.R. 219; second judgment in Case 169/84, *Compagnie Française de l'Azote (Cofaz) et al v Commission* ('*Cofaz II*'). See chapter 5 above.

[251] 24 Dec 1974, Stc 251. He used his powers again in 1983 (24 Oct 1983, Stc 206); 1984 (31 Oct 1984, Stc 213) and 1985 (31 Oct 1985, Stc 212).

(4) The New Gas Act and the Liberalization Process

Introduction

10.145 On 30 March 1999 the Minister of Economic Affairs published its first Gas Bill.[252] Although some legislative attempts were made in the 1960s following the discovery of the Groningen field, the need to implement Directive 98/30/EC of 22 June concerning common rules for the internal market in natural gas ultimately triggered the legislative process. After intense debate in both Houses of Parliament, the Gas Bill was finally approved on 20 June 2000. The new Gas Act entered into force on 1 August 2000, ie just before the implementation date of 10 August 2000.[253]

10.146 Generally, the Dutch liberalization policy exceeds the requirements of the EC Directives, because the Gas Act, like the new Electricity Act, aims at a 100 per cent opening of the gas and electricity market in three separate stages. Due to these common features, the regulation of the sector is to some extent similar. The structure of the Gas Act corresponds, for example, with the Electricity Act of 25 March 1998, discussed in the next paragraph.

Market opening

10.147 For purposes of liberalization and regulation, the Dutch gas market is divided in three different consumer categories: (i) large consumers using more than 10 million cubic metres gas per year, (ii) medium-sized gas consumers using between 1 million and 10 million cubic metres of gas per year, and (iii) small consumers using less than 1 million cubic metres of gas per year. Whereas all large consumers are already free to choose their suppliers, all other consumers are captive customers who will gradually become free, obtaining the right to choose a gas supplier. Medium-sized consumers will gain this freedom on 1 January 2002, and small consumers will have similar rights as from 1 January 2004. The terms on which captive customers will become eligible may be amended by Royal Decree.[254]

10.148 Comparing the original Gas Bill with the Gas Act some important differences can be noted. These mainly concern the speed of liberalization and the requirements of market opening, ie the definition of 'small' consumers. As the Government

[252] Tweede Kamer 1998–99, 26 463.

[253] Act of 22 June 2000 on the transport and supply of gas (Gas Act), Stb 305. The legislator envisaged a phased entry into force of the Act (Stb 318). Following the entry into force of the most important parts of the Act on 1 August 2000, the provisions governing the appointment of network operators (Arts 2–9, 26, 27, and 80–84) entered into force on 1 October 2000. Subsequently, the provisions on unbundling (Arts 32–33) entered into force on 1 January 2001. Other provisions like the permanent supply licence for households will enter into force in 2003 or 2004. See Tweede Kamer 1999–2000, 26463, nr 98.

[254] Art 1 para 1 sub n and Art 1 para 1 Gas Act.

found that the electricity liberalization process developed faster than originally anticipated, so the legislator decided that the final category of gas consumers (households and other small consumers) should be able to choose their supplier as of 1 January 2004 instead of 2007. However, in practice some of these small consumers, such as greenhouse growers and CHP producers, will experience serious negative effects of the new gas pricing system following the liberalization process. Hence, it was also decided that the final category of eligible customers should be enlarged to all consumers using less than 1 million cubic metres gas per year instead of the original group consisting of households only, using less than 170,000 cubic metres of gas per year. As a result of these changes greenhouse growers are given two years' respite before they are faced with the effects of a liberalized gas market.

Until medium-sized and small consumers can freely choose their supplier, they **10.149**
will be protected by the law. The supply of gas to captive customers is made dependent upon the award of a supply licence, except for non-commercial gas supply and for foreign suppliers delivering gas to small communities in the border area. A supply licence will be awarded to applicants who can demonstrate satisfactorily that adequate provisions have been made to meet the obligation to supply gas. In practice these supply licences will be awarded to the distribution companies originally supplying gas in the respective supply areas. The holder of a supply licence is obliged to supply protected customers with gas at a fixed rate. The Minister of Economic Affairs determines maximum supply tariffs for each supplier. These tariffs may differ for each individual supplier. When determining the tariffs the Minister takes into account the importance of a regular and reliable gas supply at a reasonable rate and the effect of a supplier's management efficiency through *inter alia* gas purchasing agreements. The Minister determines the gas supply tariffs upon the information given to him by the licensees. A licensee may not charge protected customers a higher supply tariff than the rate determined by the Minister, nor supply customers outside his own supply area.

The Gas Act also introduced an additional supply licence for the period after the **10.150**
year 2004, when the market will be fully liberalized. Any supplier who wishes to supply households (consumers using less than 170,000 cubic metres of gas per year) needs a specific supply licence. This means that suppliers other than the above-mentioned distribution companies will need a licence, including traders and foreign suppliers. The Minister of Economic Affairs can award such a licence upon certain conditions. By contrast to the licence required to supply captive customers until 2004, these licences will apply to the entire territory of the Netherlands. Moreover, these licences do not include an obligation to supply: the supplier is merely obliged to use every effort to supply its customer with gas upon reasonable terms and tariffs.[255]

[255] Arts 43 and 44 Gas Act.

Network access

10.151 The Gas Act is based on a system of negotiated access to the gas grid. One of the arguments put forward for negotiated access was the fact that a system based on negotiation best suits current practice.[256] It should be noted, however, that network access in the Netherlands has been limited to (foreign) gas transmission companies such as Ruhrgas, Distrigaz, etc. Dutch consumers have not been in the position to negotiate access individually.

10.152 By contrast to a system of regulated access, where conditions and tariffs for access are issued by the Government, a system of negotiated access gives applicants less security about the possibility of access and its conditions. Nevertheless, under the Gas Act all applicants have to negotiate access directly with the operator of the gas transmission grid on the basis of indicative tariffs and conditions for the transport of gas and the supply of additional services (nTPA). Access may only be refused under certain circumstances, which are similar to those mentioned in the EC Gas Directive, such as a lack of capacity and economic difficulties resulting from take-or-pay contracts. The Director General of the competition authority (NMa) may in the latter case grant an exemption, which in turn has to be notified to the EC Commission. The Commission may review the case, and may alter NMa's decision.

10.153 The provisions of the original Gas Bill concerning access were limited to the above. Parliament feared, however, that negotiations for access could result in extremely lengthy procedures without any transportation contract being concluded. The legislator therefore amended the original access regime. As the Director General of the NMa is given a crucial role in the entire nTPA regime, it can be concluded that a system of 'regulated negotiated access' has indeed been achieved. First the Director General is involved in the process of setting the indicative tariffs. Under the current Gas Act he is required to issue specific guidelines which gas transporters have to take into account when setting up the indicative transportation tariffs. Secondly, the Director General may, at the request of one or two of the parties involved in the negotiations, fix a term within which the negotiations must be completed. If these negotiations do not result in an agreement within the term set by the Director General NMa, gas transporters shall notify the Director General of the reasons within two weeks. Thirdly, if a transportation dispute relates to conditions or tariffs or an essential related service, the Director General may impose the relevant conditions or tariffs for such period as he determines.[257]

10.154 The above provisions are intended to ensure that third parties will be served within a reasonable period of time and at reasonable tariffs. However, third par-

[256] Tweede Kamer 1998–99, 26 463, nr 3, 13.

[257] Arts 12 *et seq* Gas Act.

ties do run the risk that the outcome of a dispute settlement procedure is contrary to the provisional tariffs and conditions set by Nma. Moreover, the Director General of the NMa is put in a difficult position since he is required to act as a regulator by issuing guidelines on the basis of which gas transporters sets the indicative tariffs, yet also required to act as a dispute settlement authority for disputes regarding access. In practice this is resolved by transferring the regulatory tasks to the regulator DTe (see below).

Gasunie has already published some indicative tariffs for the benefit of the very large consumers, ie the Commodity Services System (or CSS). This tariff system has been applied as from 1 January 1999 and comprises of a commodity charge and a capacity charge. A standard supply contract is based on a one-year period and requires a premium for a period of less than one year and no discount on a period of more than one year. Until spring 2000 the standard contract was based on a five-year period. This rather lengthy period was considered to be a serious barrier to competition. **10.155**

The commodity charge is calculated as before, on the basis of a competing commodity such as oil (heavy fuel oil in case of large customers) or coal. The establishment of an independent market price is not yet envisaged. However, this situation will change if gas is to be traded on the exchange. The Amsterdam Power Exchange is at the request of the Minister currently examining the possibilities for such gas trade. **10.156**

In addition, Gasunie offers capacity services. The contractual capacity is the maximum amount of gas (expressed in cubic metres) the customer needs per hour. A distinction is made between base-load capacity and additional capacity. The base-load capacity is calculated on an hourly basis and consists of the maximum regular offtake of the consumer.[258] Base-load capacity is high in case of a continuous production process. However, the off-take of most consumers is more irregular, so the contracted base-load capacity will be rather low. Under the CSS base-load capacity is free. In other words, consumers with a high regular off-take of base-load capacity are directly remunerated by Gasunie. The difference between the contractual capacity and base-load capacity is called additional capacity and is always calculated *ex post.* Most consumers have an irregular off-take and are faced with high additional capacity for which they have to pay a capacity charge.[259] Irrespective of the type of capacity involved, all customers have to pay a distance-related transportation fee. The transportation fee is based on the assumption that there are five entry points to the Gasunie network: Noordbroek near Groningen, **10.157**

[258] The calculation of base-load capacity is based on an average yearly consumption of 8,000 hours. The total off-take per year of a given number of consumers is then divided by an average yearly consumption of 8,000 hours.

[259] If the need to contract additional capacity is limited to certain peak periods, the consumer can contract incidental capacity instead of additional capacity.

Den Helder, Maasvlakte or Rotterdam harbour, Zelzate (Belgian border) and 's Gravenvoere (near Aachen). It should be noted, however, that no gas is imported via 's Gravenvoere and Zelzate is a relatively new entry point resulting from the establishment of the UK Interconnector. Nevertheless, as a result of these entry points, the maximum transmission tariff is based on a distance of 200 km.

10.158 Basically the CSS applies to all users of the Gasunie grid, not only those who buy gas directly from Gasunie but also those who buy elsewhere and enter into a separate transportation contract with Gasunie. Following the choice for a nTPA regime, the basic rule is still 'first come, first served'. In practice third parties will be at the end of the queue. Obviously there has to be enough pipeline capacity available for the transportation of the required quantity of gas. In addition these customers will be hindered by the system of hourly balancing. Third parties transporting gas through the Gasunie system are confronted with the basic rule: hour in = hour out. This means that the amount of gas delivered into the Gasunie system and the amount of gas off-taken from the system should be in balance every hour. This is considered unfavourable in comparison with other systems that are often based on daily balancing. Moreover, this capacity must be contracted in advance. The hourly balancing system is therefore an additional barrier for third parties as they have to guarantee beforehand that a specific amount of gas will enter the grid at a specific time and that one hour later the same amount of gas will be taken out of the system. Moreover, third parties must have a gas supply contract if they apply for access to the Gasunie grid. As Gasunie cannot guarantee access to the grid at the requested time, each contract should necessarily contain an annulment clause.

10.159 As Gasunie charges high tariffs for additional and incidental capacity, the tariff system is generally considered to be favourable only for consumers taking of gas at a very regular rate. The same is true for TPA. Negotiating TPA on the basis of the above system seems to be favourable only to users who need an even capacity. Buying additional capacity, services, or commodity is relatively costly. These additional costs may remove any advantages of buying the gas from elsewhere. Whether the CSS will remain is to be seen. On 25 August 2000 the Dte published guidelines for the year 2001 on the basis of which gas transportation companies are to determine the indicative tariffs and conditions.[260] These guidelines are based on different principles from Gasunie's CSS. The guidelines require all gas transmission and storage companies to issue a number of standardised basic services for gas transmission and storage. These basic services should be such that they meet a significant part of customer demand, ie at least 75 per cent of the eligible customers' turnover. Each service entails a tariff structure or formula on the basis of which the customer can determine the costs of the service incurred. The

[260] Stc 2000, No 305.

guidelines identify three basic services: transmission services and (daily) balancing, storage of gas for third parties, and quality conversion. The latter service is only offered in so far as the gas transmission company has the necessary facilities. In practice, this is limited to Gasunie. As far as the other services are concerned, the guidelines distinguish between two types; guaranteed services or interruptible services. The tariff depends on the degree of certainty required. Deviations from the indicative tariffs are only possible in exceptional circumstances. Parties have to conclude negotiations within a reasonable period of time and notify the Director of the DTe within 14 days of the conclusion of the agreement of any deviations from the basic services and tariffs. Contracts for basic services have a minimum term of one day (in the year 2001, possibly of one month) and a maximum term of five years. In order to promote trade, companies have to provide transparent information on the available capacity. A certain minimum (20 per cent) should be reserved for capacity contracts of one year or less. Customers are not required to present a supply contract. Any unused capacity can be sold to third parties. Moreover, gas companies involved are also entitled to offer unused and available capacity to third parties ('use-or-lose-it'). Such trade in capacity may result in a separate capacity market and could be facilitated by the establishment of an independent exchange.

Since these guidelines differ in many respects from the principles under the CSS regime, the gas transmission companies have made it known that they are opposed to the way in which the DTe is carrying out its tasks. No gas company has published its indicative tariffs. Therefore it is most likely that the Director of the DTe will use its powers under the Gas Act and give these companies binding instructions regarding these indicative tariffs. Subsequently, the gas companies can start a civil procedure. **10.160**

Network access may also require the physical connection of new suppliers to the system. Since obscure technical requirements may not obstruct pipeline access, the Gas Act explicitly requires each gas transportation company to lay down objective and non-discriminatory technical rules applying to the design and exploitation of natural gas pipelines and installations. The entering into force of a European standard for high-pressure gas pipelines (PrEn 1594) will enhance the transparency of the applicable technical standards. **10.161**

Unbundling

The original Gas Bill did not require the gas companies to unbundle and to establish separate network and supply companies. Following some last-minute amendments to the Bill, the requirement of unbundling now applies to the distribution sector as a system better suited to promote competition. The parliamentary reports do not indicate why the need to appoint separate network operators is limited to the distribution grid: after all, the need to promote competition also **10.162** applies to the transmission grid. Parliament probably wishes to treat the Dutch gas transmission system similarly to the neighbouring systems in Germany and Belgium. However, as far as the main transmission grid is concerned the situation remains the same: Gasunie can maintain its role of both supplier and carrier. The Act only requires Gasunie to carry out separate bookkeeping for i) the transportation of gas through the high-pressure pipeline system and ancillary installations, and ii) the storage of gas. This obligation seems to apply to companies operating upstream pipelines as well.

10.163 Article 26 of the Gas Act requires Gasunie to save information which they know or should reasonably presume to be confidential in character unless the law provides otherwise. More specifically, Gasunie must not misuse commercially sensitive data of others obtained in negotiations about or during the performance of transport. Although this provision seems to establish Chinese walls between the transportation and the purchasing of gas, it could be argued that this division is not very tight. It does not seem to prevent the transmission company from making use of information received from a potential buyer who decides to buy gas elsewhere and then starts negotiations about access to the gas transmission networks. Gasunie, however, wants to avoid any doubts about its confidential status and established a separate office for transportation and ancillary services as of 1 April 2000.

10.164 An obligation of legal unbundling applies to the gas distribution companies.[261] As these companies are usually horizontally integrated with the electricity distribution companies, the current provision on unbundling is now in line with the Electricity Act 1998, which requires the legal unbundling of electricity transmission and supply. In practice many companies have already opted for a legal unbundling of the gas distribution sector as well (see below). Upon the entry into force of the Gas Act, all gas distribution companies are required to appoint an independent network operator upon the conditions included in the Gas Act. (These conditions are largely similar to the provisions in the Electricity Act 1998 and are discussed further below.)

Access to upstream pipelines and gas storage facilities

10.165 The Gas Directive provides rules for access to upstream pipelines and gas storage facilities. These provisions were extensively debated: some Member States argued that these facilities should be regulated on the basis of upstream legislation instead. However, a liberalized gas market cannot be achieved without access to these midstream facilities.

[261] Arts 2–9, Gas Act.

The Gas Act includes a brief provision regarding access to upstream pipelines as it merely states that the Dutch Competition Act shall apply to negotiations regarding access to upstream pipelines on the Dutch continental shelf.[262] In other words, there is negotiated access and if it seems likely that a pipeline company or gas carrier intends to abuse its dominant position a complaint can be made to the competition authority, NMa. However, following recent developments regarding the essential facilities doctrine it may be difficult to prove such abuse as the Dutch offshore regime also is based on a general freedom to construct submarine pipelines. Therefore it remains to be seen whether the Competition Act in itself is sufficient to guarantee third parties access to upstream pipelines. **10.166**

A different approach is chosen for underground gas storage. The Gas Act now applies a system of 'regulated negotiated access' to gas storage in so far as the gas companies have a dominant position.[263] More explicitly the Act states that both Gasunie and the holders of the Groningen and Bergen concessions, where the current gas storage facilities are situated, have a dominant position. In other words, access to these facilities requires indicative tariffs on the basis of guidelines issued by NMa. It is less clear on whom this obligation rests: the concessionaires who own these facilities or Gasunie, which currently is making use of them? Most likely this obligation rests on the concessionaires who have given Gasunie access to the facilities. As a consequence, an organizational division is made between third-party negotiations for transportation and for storage facilities. Such regulatory division also does not fit in with Gasunie's tariff system (CSS) which is based on the presumption that Gasunie has access to underground storage and can therefore supply additional services. **10.167**

Position of Gasunie in a liberalized gas market

The first draft of the Bill did not provide any details regarding the position of the Gasunie and its relationship with the Government. However, the Gas Act contains an additional paragraph on the systematic management of gas reservoirs within which Gasunie is given a crucial role.[264] It requires Gasunie (i) to purchase gas from the Groningen field, (ii) to purchase upon request of gas producers from other fields upon reasonable conditions and at market-value prices, and (iii) to submit annually a forecast of Dutch supply and demand for the next 20 years. This paragraph was included specifically to safeguard the Government's small-field policy and has to be considered as a public service obligation. The Minister can decide that Gasunie should be exempted temporarily from the above obligation if Gasunie would (possibly) suffer financial or economic difficulties as a result **10.168**

[262] Art 17 Gas Act.
[263] Art 18 Gas Act.
[264] Para 5.3a of the Gas Act consists of Arts 33a–33d.

of this task.[265] Further estimates of Dutch supply and demand will be included in the Energy Report. The Minister is given the explicit right to give Gasunie instructions as necessary to carry out the specific tasks given to it. Hence, since the Gas Act has entered into force the private law agreements according to which the Government can influence Gasunie's operations will finally be replaced by statutory provisions.

Supervision by the Competition Authority

10.169 The original Gas Bill did not establish a special regulator. Supervision of compliance with the Act was designated to the Dutch competition authority (NMa). This concerned all network activities. However, as a result of recent amendments the Gas Act now requires the appointment of a separate regulator. The regulator Dte is charged with the supervision of compliance with the Gas Act.[266] In addition, the Minister will supervise the gas companies' compliance with the licensing regime in order to protect captive customers. Parallel to the degree of market opening, supervision by the Minister will gradually diminish. In practice, supervision of the captive consumers may also be carried out by the authority regulating the electricity sector (DTe). Although the Gas Act explicitly gives the Director General of the NMa the task of issuing guidelines on the basis of which Gasunie has to set its indicative tariffs, this task has now been transferred to the DTe which is a separate chamber of NMa.[267]

10.170 All matters of access, however, are dealt with by NMa under the Competition Act. A complaint can also be made to NMa if a gas company is applying technical standards which obstruct connection to the network. Nma is also charged with the supervision of the offshore pipelines. If a dispute concerns a cross-border pipeline, NMa is not competent if access is denied by the pipeline company of the other State. However, the Gas Act does not give any further indications of the subsequent procedure, ie can the applicant file a complaint with the competent authority of the other State, or should the EC Commission be involved?

Conclusion

10.171 The Gas Act is an important legal document for the Dutch energy sector as it is the first statute which regulates the transmission and supply of gas. Although the original Bill was clearly drafted with the sole intention of implementing the minimum requirements of the Gas Directive, the final Gas Act is based more on principles of market opening and competition.

[265] Art 33b Gas Act.
[266] Arts 59–60 Gas Act.
[267] 'Besluit Mandaat Gaswet', Stc 2000, No 159, 22.

Nevertheless, there is still some doubt about the extent to which the new system will liberalize the gas market. The sources of gas supply are limited. In the Netherlands most gas is tied to long-term supply contracts with Gasunie. It is doubtful whether gas producers are interested in selling gas to others than Gasunie, given Gasunie's central role as resource manager in the Gas Act. Foreign resources are limited as well. Whereas Norwegian and Russian gas supplies are situated far away and the national suppliers are tied up in long-term supply contracts with Gasunie, the 'gas bubble' in the UK will soon burst, so that Britain will shortly be importing gas instead of exporting it. In addition, there is doubt about the choice of negotiated access and the tariff system proposed by Gasunie. The amendments to the first draft of the Gas Bill indicate that the Government is aware of the danger of lengthy procedures and disputes. There seems to be a tendency towards a more regulated type of access. Although the legislator has finally chosen to appoint a sector-specific regulator, it remains to be seen whether this authority has enough powers to carry out a proactive regulatory approach. After all, the experiences of countries such as the US and the UK have shown that liberalization of the gas sector requires a strong regulator and proactive regulation. The guidelines recently issued by the DTe indicate that the regulator intends to take such an active role. **10.172**

Be that as it may, some companies have turned to the possibility of pipeline competition instead of gas-to-gas competition. Delta Nutsbedrijven, for example, has constructed a separate gas pipeline from Zelzate (Belgian border) to the Europoort area through which they supply some large consumers with UK gas which is transported through the UK Interconnector. Similar projects are being discussed in other border areas. **10.173**

Nevertheless, the Gas Act is a first step towards liberalization of the Dutch gas market. It also clearly illustrates that liberalization cannot be distinguished from regulation. From an unregulated gas market, the Netherlands seems set to turn gradually to a regulated market. Considering the above-mentioned comments and experiences in other countries like the UK (see chapter 13 below) it seems obvious that more regulation can be expected. **10.174**

D. Electricity Supply

(1) The Development of the Electricity Sector

History: a process of gradual integration

The Dutch electricity sector is generally characterized by a gradual process of concentration and integration on the regional, national, and, more recently, international levels. **10.175**

10.176 Public supply of electricity started with the establishment of municipal electricity companies at the turn of the century. At that time Government policy was that: i) the generation of electricity should be free as long as this would not be contrary to the public interest, ii) the wholesale supply should be handled by the provinces, iii) the retail supply (distribution) should be managed by the municipalities who could reassign this task to the provinces again, and iv) central Government approval would only be required in special circumstances, such as the supply of electricity by large industries to third parties.

10.177 After World War I most provinces had established a regional electricity supply company.[268] Production and supply were integrated in the sense that the provincial electricity production companies usually supplied the municipal distribution companies, who subsequently supplied electricity to consumers.[269] This co-operation was facilitated by a large-scale extension of the grid as well as the interconnection of the local and regional networks.[270] In 1949, the sector was further integrated as the result of the establishment of the SEP *NV Samenwerkende Electriciteits Produktiebedrijven* (Co-operative of Electricity Generators) a limited liability company whose shares are held by the individual production companies. It aimed to enable the interconnection of production facilities as an emergency policy in case of the interruption of (regional) supply.

10.178 A further restructuring of the electricity sector was triggered by the energy crises in the 1970s. One of the main points of discussion was the structure of the production sector, either through the establishment of a national production company or through increasing co-operation of the production companies in SEP, the 'SEP plus' model. The latter model was preferred upon condition that the number of production companies would gradually be reduced. Consequently, the number of production companies decreased from fourteen in the 1980s to four in the mid-1990s: EPON (*NV Elektriciteits-Produktiemaatschappij Oost- en Noord-Nederland*), EPZ (*NV Elektriciteits-Produktiemaatschappij Zuid-Nederland*), EZH (*NV Elektriciteitsbedrijf Zuid-Holland*), and UNA (*NV Energieproduktiebedrijf UNA*). At that time the shares of these four limited liability companies were owned either by the distribution companies (as in the case of EPON and EPZ) or by various local authorities (municipalities). Although a certain degree of integration exists as far as real ownership is concerned, legally the production and

[268] The speed with which the provinces took over production activities from the municipalities differed from province to province as well as the extent to which municipalities were allowed to hold shares in the provincial limited liability company.

[269] The legal arrangements governing the management of this distribution differ from province to province. Large-scale consumers could only to a limited extent supply electricity directly from the production company. In fact it all depends on the availability of (high-voltage) power lines.

[270] This required transmission lines with a higher voltage. Instead of 10 KV, facilities to transmit at 50 KV were constructed.

distribution companies operated, and still operate, independently from each other.

The relationship between the four production companies with and within SEP is based on a co-operation agreement.[271] This has been characterized as a joint venture controlled by its parent companies together.[272] Broadly speaking, the tasks of SEP have been the same since it was established: i) negotiating the purchase of fuel for all production companies, ii) negotiating import/export agreements with foreign suppliers, iii) co-ordinating supply and demand, and iv) exploitation of the high-voltage transmission networks (380/220 KV). **10.179**

As the gradual integration of the production sector continued, the distinction between production and distribution also became more apparent. The earlier mentioned discussions regarding the organization (horizontal integration) of the distribution sector is a clear example. Separate legislation has gradually been developed for both the regulation of the production and supply of electricity and the distribution of electricity. This legislative process has been very slow. **10.180**

When the restructuring of the electricity sector was discussed at the end of the 1990s, the Government proposed a complete economic and legal integration of the four production companies into one major production company, Grootschalig Productie Bedrijf, or GPB. It was argued that only a GPB could compete in an international electricity market and deal with the existing loss-making projects as well. The four production companies could not reach agreement about the proposed restructuring. The failure to agree on co-operation will eventually lead to the liquidation of SEP, and increased competition between the four production companies who currently are faced with the issue of national or foreign take-overs and possibilities of vertical integration. **10.181**

Overview of electricity legislation before 1998

Electricity Act 1938

The first Electricity Act entered into force in 1938 after a 16-year debate in Parliament. Due to severe objections, the Act's entry into force was limited to provisions dealing with safety and the supervision of the Act.[273] The main provisions concerning the licensing regime never entered into force so that the Netherlands **10.182**

[271] The first co-operation agreement of 1949 has been amended regularly since.

[272] See also the IJsselcentrale case and ED Cross, Electric Utility Regulation in the European Union, 172. A comparison can be made with a joint venture governing oil and gas production. This joint venture is governed by a joint operating agreement. The management of the joint venture is different, however, as the upstream joint ventures are operated by one oil company appointed as such. The management of SEP is a separate legal identity.

[273] Whereas Art 1 gave a definition of electricity installation, Arts 1–13 provided for the issuance of further rules regarding safety. Art 14 dealt with the establishment of the Electricity Council (cf the above-mentioned Mining Council). Finally, Arts 15–22 regulated the supervision of the Act.

electricity sector was regulated by an incomplete Electricity Act until 1989 when the 'new' Electricity Act entered into force.

Electricity Act 1989

10.183 The 1989 Electricity Act dealt with the generation, import, transport, and supply of electricity. Distribution was part of a separate legal regime provided for by the Energy Distribution Act (see paras 10.132–10.135 above). The Electricity Act 1989 was based on a system of central Government planning. It required SEP to draw up a National Electricity Plan every two years.[274] The Plan had to be approved by the Minister of Economic Affairs and put forward long-term (20 years') supply and demand estimates, including calculations regarding total demand and required capacity as well as the level of imports and exports and the quantities to be supplied by decentralized capacity. In addition, it included a system of licensing through which the Government could exercise control of the electricity generation sector.

10.184 A licence was required for the construction and/or operation of a power station of at least 5 MW for the public supply of electricity.[275] As licensees could not engage in the supply of electricity to consumers, the Act required that production and distribution remained separate.[276] Consequently, licences could only be awarded to the four existing production companies. In addition, SEP was appointed as the designated company and was required to co-operate closely with the licensed producers.

10.185 The licensed generators had to submit all their electricity to SEP (= central production pool) before buying power back from SEP, after which they than sell to the distribution companies in the area assigned to them.[277] SEP and the licensed producers were considered jointly responsible for the reliable and efficient functioning of the national public electricity supply at the lowest possible cost and in a socially justifiable way.[278] SEP was also awarded responsibility for the transmission of electricity as it had the exclusive right to construct and operate high-voltage lines of 220 KV or more.[279]

10.186 It follows from the above that a production licence was not required for (i) the construction and/or operation of power stations generating less than 5MW, (ii) larger generators for non-public supply, and (iii) non-traditional power stations such as co-generation plants, wind-power turbines, waste incinerators, and hydroelectric

[274] Arts 15–16 Electricity Act 1989.
[275] Art 3 Electricity Act 1989.
[276] Art 4 Electricity Act 1989.
[277] Art 11 Electricity Act 1989.
[278] Art 2 Electricity Act 1989.
[279] Art 45 Electricity Act 1989.

power systems.[280] Decentralized generation by the distribution sector[281] was considered an important instrument for stimulating competition as it provided distribution companies the choice between purchasing electricity from 'traditional' producers or generating power themselves. However, as these non-licensed generators were not required to take into account the estimates of the National Electricity Plan, numerous decentralized generators (mostly co-generation or CHP) were established. This resulted in a surplus capacity during the 1990s. In order to handle the creation of surplus capacity the distribution and production companies entered into an agreement (the 'protocol') in 1996 by which the distribution companies committed themselves to continue their electricity off-take from SEP (central production power pool) for aggregate remuneration, and a commitment by SEP and the four production companies not to compete with the distribution companies in the electricity market. This agreement ran until the end of the year 2000, that is after the Electricity Act 1998 entered into force.

In order to prevent SEP from abusing its monopoly position as the sole operator of the high-voltage transmission grid, the Act provided for some competition in the transmission sector. Distribution companies and industrial consumers were given third-party access to the grid (TPA) on reasonable terms and against compensation for reasonable costs as long as there was sufficient capacity available and it involved the public supply of electricity, the import of electricity, or electricity for special large consumers.[282] Auto-producers were excluded from access to the grid. Although this system of TPA was designed to enhance competition as distribution companies were given the possibility to purchase electricity from a production company outside its area (horizontal shopping) it has never been used in practice.[283] One of the reasons for this is that distribution companies' purchasing rights were limited to electricity produced in the Netherlands. The importation of electricity was legally restricted to large industrial consumers and SEP[284] as far as it concerned electricity for public supply.[285] The Electricity Act 1989 did not **10.187**

[280] An exception was made for SEP subsidiaries (subsidiaries in which SEP participates for more than 90%) who needed a licence to construct and operate other installations.

[281] Generation by distribution companies needed the consent of SEP if the 'decentralized' plant had a capacity of more than 25 MW. Generation by a joint venture between a distribution company and others (consumers) did not require such consent.

[282] Art 47 Electricity Act 1989.

[283] One reason is that the 4 production companies basically applied the same national standard supply tariff so there was no downward pressure on the tariffs. Consequently, there was no need for horizontal shopping.

[284] SEP also needed the approval of the Minister of Economic Affairs (Art 35 Electricity Act of 1989).

[285] This applies to electricity imports at a tension of more than 500 V. The Dutch Competition Authority NMa issued a ruling in 1999 with regard to the import of electricity by Hydro Energy BV and the refusal of SEP to transport the imported electricity (Case number 650/52). Nma ruled that SEP misused its position by denying Hydro Energy BV access to the grid. The practical impact of the ruling is limited as the case concerned the Electricity Act 1989 which is no longer valid.

restrict (direct) export of electricity. In the case of an export agreement, however, there was no guarantee that the exporting (or importing) company would gain access to the grid. Any disputes about access had to be assessed by the Minister.[286]

10.188 The above limitation of import and export has been under the scrutiny of the EC Commission as well as the national courts. In addition to the above provision in the Electricity Act, cross-border electricity trade was further restricted because under the 'co-operation agreement' (*overeenkomst van samenwerking*) SEP was the only company entitled to import and export electricity. Moreover, the production companies (ie the participants in SEP) were required to impose a similar ban on the distributors in the individual supply agreements, as a result of which the distributors were unable to import directly. In the *IJsselcentrale* case, the Commission concluded that the co-operation agreement enabled SEP to control the import and export of electricity in the interest of its shareholders (ie the production companies). Such an import/export ban is contrary to Article 81(1) EC Treaty and could not be justified by Article 86(2) EC Treaty. However, the Court of Justice ruled in 1992 in the *Almelo* case that the application of an exclusive purchasing contract (excluding the import of electricity) is not caught by the provisions of Articles 81 and 82 of the EC Treaty if the restriction is necessary to enable the undertaking to perform its task in the general interest as provided for in Article 86 EC Treaty (see chapter 5 above).[287]

The 1989 Electricity Act and the distribution sector

10.189 Although the Electricity Act of 1989 intended a clear separation between production and distribution, and the distribution of electricity was basically organized by the earlier mentioned Energy Distribution Act, some provisions in the Electricity Act directly affected the distribution of electricity. Most importantly, the Electricity Act of 1989 (by contrast to the gas sector) contained a supply obligation. Each distributor is obliged to supply on request electricity to all persons in their supply area.[288] Secondly, the Act imposed on the distribution companies the duty to purchase the surplus electricity offered by auto-producers located in their supply area for a standard price (*vervangingsprijs*).[289]

10.190 The 1989 Electricity Act obliged the distribution companies to buy such surplus electricity on the basis of a standard remuneration agreement.[290] The remuneration of the distribution companies was to be 'equal to the costs . . . saved by the

[286] Art 48 Electricity Act 1989.

[287] Commission Decision 91/50/EEC of 16 Jan 1991 (*IJsselcentrale*), OJ 1991, L 228, 32; Case C-393/92 (*Almelo v IJsselmij*), CJ 1994, I-1.

[288] If the supply is considered to be unreasonable (outstanding bills and harm to the network) an exemption could be made to this supply obligation.

[289] Art 41 Electricity Act.

[290] Such a standard arrangement which has been set up by EnergieNed in consultation with SEP and possibly other organizations representing the generators.

distribution companies on average, calculated for all these companies'.[291] For renewable energy, the additional rule applied that the remuneration should be based on the method of calculation which most stimulated the aforementioned means of generating electricity.[292] As the system of remuneration was not very clear, it led to long and difficult discussions between the parties involved and procedures before the Dutch Competition Authority.

Concluding remarks

Although the 1989 Electricity Act was considered to be a modern act by the standards of that time, a number of its aims have not been fulfilled. This is especially true of the aim to introduce more competition. Moreover, the sector faced inadequate planning for new capacity, increasing production costs, and inefficient Government control. Besides, the EC's internal market policy has had more influence than anticipated by many in the 1980s. Following these developments and the required evaluation of the Electricity Act in 1995, a complete new Electricity Act entered into force in 1998.[293] **10.191**

(2) Electricity Act 1998

Introduction

The Electricity Act 1998 not only implements the EC Electricity Directive, but exceeds the EC requirements as it aims at a gradual but complete opening of the electricity market. Eventually all consumers will be able to decide individually where to purchase their electricity. In the meantime, the Act provides for the protection of captive consumers, whose supply is made dependent on a licence. Moreover, a production licence is no longer required. **10.192**

Generation

The generation of electricity is free under the regime of the Electricity Act 1998. By contrast to the previous Electricity Act, no specific licence requirements apply except permits within the framework of planning and environmental law as a result of which the same situation now exists for electricity generation as at the beginning of the 1900s. **10.193**

An end was made to the former distinction between licensed and non-licensed production or between electricity generated through 'traditional' fossil fuels and **10.194**

---

291 Art 42 para 3 Electricity Act 1989.

292 Art 42 para 4 Electricity Act 1989.

293 *Wet van 2 juli 1998, houdende regels met betrekking tot de productie, het transport en de levering van elektriciteit (Elektriciteitswet* 1998), Stb 427 as amended by Act of 3 June 1999 amending the Electricity Act of 1998 in order to give further rules with regard to the network manager and the supply of electricity to protected customers, Stb 1999, 260.

renewables. Another matter is whether these renewable energy resources can compete with the traditional fuels. After all, the Government has often financially stimulated the use of renewable energy for reasons of energy savings and environmental protection (see below).

10.195 More complicated is the position of the four production companies and SEP. The intention of the Minister to integrate the four existing electricity producers into one major production company has not been achieved (see above). As the individual producers are too small to operate independently on a competitive European market, the industry is presently confronted with (international) take-overs and mergers. Obviously the legislator foresaw this development, as the Electricity Act requires the assent of the Minister of Economic Affairs for any change of ownership of any of the four 'licensed' producers' and any of the supply and network companies until the year 2004. The Minister may withhold its assent if the ownership of shares is transferred to natural or legal persons who are not yet shareholders, ie entities other than municipalities, provinces, and distribution companies.[294] In the summer of 1999 the Minister presented a policy note including some guidelines for privatization. On the basis of these guidelines two take-over bids were assessed and approved in September 1999: the take-over of UNA by Reliant Energy (Texas) and of EZH by PreussenElektra. This is followed by the takeover of EPON by Electrabel in the beginning of 2000. Hence, foreign companies now own some 75 per cent of the traditional generation capacity.

Electricity supply

10.196 The Electricity Act envisages a gradual opening of the electricity market. The very large consumers (consumers with a total throughput capacity of more than 3*80 Ampere and a made-available capacity of more than 2 MW) are free to purchase electricity, as from the entry into force of the Act on 1 August 1998. Medium-sized consumers (consumers with a total throughput capacity of more than 3*80 A and a maximum capacity of not more than 2 MW per connection during the period between 1 August 1998 and 31 December 2001) will also be free as from 1 January 2002. Finally, the small consumers or households (consumers with a throughput capacity of not more than 3*80A during the period 1 August 1998 to 31 December 2003) will be free as from 1 January 2004.[295]

10.197 It should be noted, however, that the beginning of the liberalization process is hindered by the earlier mentioned protocol agreement of 1996 in which the distribution companies committed themselves to continue their electricity off-take from

[294] Art 92 Electricity Act.

[295] Originally the Electricity Act 1998 provided for complete market liberalization as of 1 Jan 2007. Following discussions on liberalization of the gas market, the Minister proposed to speed up liberalization. Parliament approved earlier liberalization within the framework of the implementation of the EC Gas Directive (see Art 69 Gas Act).

SEP (central production power pool) against an aggregate remuneration, and a commitment by SEP and the four production companies not to compete with the distribution companies in the electricity market. As this agreement ran until the end of the year 2000, ie after the Electricity Act of 1998 entered into force, not all parties had equal opportunities in the partly liberalized electricity market. Although this agreement is of a private nature, it should be pointed out that its legal basis lies in the Electricity Act 1998. Article 97 of the Electricity Act, which eventually did not enter into force, required that all amendments to the agreement needed the assent of the Minister (see below 10.232–10.236).

In the meantime, non-eligible consumers are protected by the Act, as it is forbidden to supply electricity to 'protected customers' without a licence.[296] The holder of a supply licence is under the obligation to supply electricity to all protected customers in its supply area for a tariff that complies with the Act.[297] A supply licence is valid until 1 January 2004, if not otherwise decided by Royal Decree, and is exclusive, as the Act prohibits licensees from supplying protected customers outside their supply area, ie in an area for which a supply licence has been granted to another supplier.[298] This limitation ceases when electricity is supplied to eligible customers. Another possible exemption concerns the electricity supply in new development areas where energy infrastructure is realized on the basis of a public tender procedure. **10.198**

A supply licence will only be granted to an applicant demonstrating satisfactorily that adequate provisions have been made to meet the obligation to supply electricity. The Ministry considers, for example, the conditions for the supply of electricity to protected customers and the handling of complaints regarding supply. Further rules for the application and award of a supply licence are presented in a separate Ministerial Order.[299] In practice, all supply licences have been awarded to those distribution companies who were engaged in the public supply of electricity and who submitted an application for a supply licence within the set time limit.[300] **10.199**

In addition to the obligation to supply, non-eligible customers are also protected by the Minister's duty to establish maximum supply tariffs. These tariffs may vary for different licence holders.[301] The Minister determines the tariffs on the basis of **10.200**

[296] Art 53 Electricity Act.

[297] Art 56 Electricity Act 1998.

[298] Art 60 para 2 Electricity Act.

[299] Art 66 Electricity Act as implemented in Ministerial Order of 29 July 1998 (*Regeling Leveringsvergunning Elektriciteitswet* 1998), Official Gazette 1998, 144, 6–7. Art 49 Electricity Act provides rules for the withdrawal of a licence.

[300] Art 95 Electricity Act 1998. The Act limits this priority right to distribution companies established before 1 July 1996.

[301] Art 57 para 1 Electricity Act. The licence holders may not charge protected customers a higher tariff than the maximum rate set by the Minister, unless an increase is necessary to stimulate the use of alternative energy as indicated in Art 10 Energy Distribution Act (Art 60 Electricity Act).

proposals made by the licence holders.[302] In doing so he must take into account the importance of reliable, renewable, efficient, and environmentally friendly and hygienic electricity supplies, including the interests of protected customers in security of electricity supplies on reasonable terms, and a price formula based on the price-cap principle.[303]

10.201 These maximum tariffs apply to the supply of electricity to protected customers. Obviously, producers and eligible consumers are free to negotiate their (individual) supply tariff. The licence holders, however, are obliged to keep separate accounts relating to the supply of protected customers and other eligible customers.

10.202 Following the parliamentary debates on the Gas Act, an additional licence is to be introduced for the supply of households after 2004. As in the provisions on gas supply, there is no explicit supply obligation but a more generally phrased obligation to make efforts to ensure the supply of electricity to small consumers on reasonable conditions and tariffs. As all suppliers are required to apply for such a licence, the group of licence holders will be extended considerably. By contrast to the licence for the supply of eligible customers, the scope of this licence is nationwide and not limited to the distribution company's original supply area.[304]

Transmission of electricity

The appointment of network managers

10.203 The Electricity Act 1998 requires a complete and legal unbundling of the production and supply of electricity and the transmission activities. This requirement differs from the more limited unbundling envisaged in the Gas Act (described above).

10.204 Consequently, the Electricity Act requires that the management and operation of the transmission system be transferred to a separate limited liability company, the network manager (or transmission system operator). Network managers, companies appointed to manage one or more networks, are appointed by the current owners of the transmission systems. An exemption can be made for networks to which a limited number of customers is or will be connected.[305] The Electricity Act also stipulates the conditions for network management. These conditions regard the transportation and connection services, imports and exports, the measurement and exchange of data, as well as co-operation between network

[302] Licensees have to send such a proposal each year before 1 October (Art 40 Electricity Act.) If such a proposal has not been sent to the Minister in time, he shall determine the tariffs on his own accord (Art 58 Electricity Act).

[303] Art 58 Electricity Act.

[304] Art 95 a–i Gas Act.

[305] Art 15 Electricity Act. Legal persons connected to the grid may not be network managers or affiliated to a network manager.

managers. The aim is to realize a balance between good quality transportation services and efficient management by the network managers.

The appointment of a network manager has to be approved by the Minister of Economic Affairs and applies for a period of ten years. Since the Act prohibits producers and suppliers from appointment as network managers, the legal unbundling of the former distribution and production companies is achieved. In practice there will be several network managers responsible for the exploitation of the entire electricity grid. As far as the high-voltage grid is concerned, the Electricity Act requires the legal entity using more than half of the circuit length (SEP) to appoint a network manager. Consequently, SEP established a subsidiary company, TenneT NV, operating the high-voltage network. The distribution companies have also appointed separate network managers.[306] However, as most distribution companies are horizontally integrated, they were faced (before the Gas Act) with the question of whether they also should apply the regime of unbundling to the gas transmission system or to disintegrate the gas and electricity supplies. **10.205**

The network managers are obliged to operate and maintain the grid, to guarantee the safety and reliability of the networks and of transport across the networks, and to construct, repair, renew, or extend the networks. They also have to maintain sufficient spare capacity for the transport of electricity, to provide third parties with a connection to the network and to carry out the transport of electricity on behalf of third parties.[307] In addition, the manager of the high-voltage network, TenneT, has the duty to make the necessary technical provisions to guarantee the transport of electricity over all networks in a safe and efficient manner. These technical provisions should also benefit the other network managers. TenneT is also charged with the transport of electricity for the benefit of third parties using the high-voltage grid for the import and export of electricity as well as the management of cross-border networks constructed by other parties (eg the projected NorNed cable).[308] **10.206**

The construction of networks

By contrast to the establishment of gas pipelines, the construction of electricity lines is not free but limited to those companies who are appointed as network managers. The construction of high voltage lines was, and still is, facilitated by the **10.207**

[306] Arts 11 et seq include further requirements for the establishment of a network manager. It should be noted that in early 2000 the Minister had not yet confirmed this appointment of these network managers as there are doubts about the independence of the network managers after privatization. Currently, these doubts remain, particularly with regard to TenneT as a result of the privatization of most of its shareholders.

[307] Art 16 Electricity Act.

[308] The NordNed cable is a new electricity cable between Norway and the Netherlands. The project was initiated by SEP and Statnett. It should be noted, however, that the construction of this cable has not yet started and that the project is treated as a stranded cost (see below).

Structure Scheme for Electricity Supply (*structuurschema electriciteitsvoorziening*).[309] The Structure Scheme is drawn up within the framework of Netherlands planning law (*Wet Ruimtelijke Ordening*). It allocates the potential sites for the high-voltage transmission lines and power stations of more than 500 MW and indicates the types of fuel choices. Since the amendment of the Act on Environmental Management (*Wet Milieubeheer*) in 1996, an EIA is required for the construction of power stations and transmission lines. In addition, the Electricity Act facilitates the construction of high-voltage transmission lines by stating that the lines designated under the above Scheme are to be considered as 'public works of common use' in order to apply the Acts on Hindrances in Private and Public Law (see above).

10.208 The construction of networks by others is limited to transmission lines with a voltage level below 0.4 KV and use below 0.1 GWh, the so-called direct lines (ie lines for limited consumers), and finally the construction of networks in development areas on the basis of a public tender procedure. Further rules regarding the construction of networks in development areas will be included in a Royal Decree.[310] Hence, the Electricity Act basically excludes the possibility of grid-to-grid competition. It can therefore be argued that the Electricity Act is not properly implementing the requirement of the Electricity Directive that Member States shall develop a licensing regime for the construction of direct lines: the provision in the Electricity Act is more limited.

Transport of electricity

10.209 The legal unbundling of network and supply activities also facilitates the choice made by the legislator to opt for a system of regulated third-party access. The regulator, on the basis of a proposal made by the network manager, sets the transmission tariff. Network managers will jointly submit proposals for the tariff structure and the transmission conditions to the regulator. In addition, each network manager will also send the regulator an individual proposal for tariffs for its own network.[311] In other words, the initiative for the development of tariffs and conditions is imposed on the network managers. Basically, the network tariffs consist of a connection charge, a transportation charge (including imports, exports, and transit of electricity) and a charge for system services.[312] The tariff is a postage stamp rate which means that it is independent of the transportation

[309] The first *Structuurschema Elektriciteitsvoorziening* was issued in 1981. A proposal for a second Structure Scheme was presented in 1992. Further amendments to this Scheme were initiated in 1993 (Tweede Kamer 1993–94, 23 424). In March 2000 the Scheme had to be amended in order to enable the establishment of a near shore wind park (Tweede Kamer 1999–2000, 27 041, no 1).

[310] A proposal for such a Decree was sent to Parliament in June 2000. It enables the construction of energy efficient networks in new development areas on the basis of a public tender procedure.

[311] Arts 25–27 Electricity Act.

[312] See also the Net Code and Tariff Code and System Code published in 1999.

distance between the connection point where the electricity is fed into the grid (the location of the supplier) and the connection point from where it is taken up (the location of the consumer). Customers can have access to the entire grid on the basis of the payment of one flat rate per contract.[313]

Upon request, a network manager is required to provide a connection to the network it manages and to make an offer for the price and the terms of electricity transportation via its network as long as sufficient capacity is available for the requested transport. The network manager shall refrain from any form of discrimination, including reservation of capacity.[314] An exception is made if transportation is required as part of the mutual assistance and support to maintain the integrity of the networks (UCTE) or on the basis of a decision of the Minister or the regulator (see below) in relation to the use of cross-border networks.[315] **10.210**

Programme responsibility

Following the abandonment of the previous system of central pooling and dispatching, the 1999 amendment to the Electricity Act included separate provisions with regard to the balancing of supply and demand of electricity, ie rules on 'programme responsibility'. Network managers need to know how much each customer needs, ie how much capacity is required in the grid, so all persons connected to the grid (customers and suppliers) are ordered to draw up or commission daily energy and transport programmes and to send these one day in advance to the network manager. These persons have financial liability for any discrepancies between the actual and expected take-up of electricity. **10.211**

For practical reasons, protected customers do not hold this responsibility. Until 2004 (or possibly 2003) the holders of the supply licence hold this responsibility. Free or eligible customers, however, are assigned programme responsibility but can decide to transfer this responsibility to third parties. It is envisaged that third parties will take over the programme responsibilities, as it is easier to balance supply and demand when large groups of customers are involved. It could even lead to substantial financial benefits, as fewer penalties will be paid for imbalances. As programme responsibility is considered a normal commercial activity, the regulator will determine rates and conditions for programme responsibility.[316] **10.212**

[313] The connection charge also includes a rate for support services. The elements for the use of the network, settlement of network losses, and settlement of transport restrictions are included in the transportation charge. See Arts 27–30 Electricity Act.

[314] Arts 23–24 Electricity Act.

[315] Art 25 in conjunction with Art 26 Electricity Act.

[316] The conditions are included in the System Code. For practical reasons an interim period is envisaged until 2001 in which a limited number of parties will hold programme responsibility.

The Regulator

10.213 Following the entering into force of the new Electricity Act the Authority monitoring compliance with Electricity Act (*Dienst uitvoering en toezicht Electriciteitswet* or DTe) was established. As mentioned before the tasks of the DTe have been extended to the supervision of the Gas Act. The DTe is appointed specifically to supervise compliance with the Act. The DTe operates on the basis of general instructions from the Minister which are laid down in policy rules. These rules are published in the Official Gazette. To enable the DTe to operate and to issue fair and objective decisions, producers, suppliers, and network managers are obliged to give all required data and information to the DTe.

10.214 The DTe operates as a department for the Dutch competition authorities (NMa) The Competition Authority may therefore assess the proposed instructions from the Minister of Economic Affairs before they are presented to the DTe. Moreover, the Director General of the Competition Authority may issue general and special instructions to the Director of the DTe if it concerns the interpretation of terms used in the Competition Act.[317] Whereas the DTe is directly involved when it concerns the implementation of the Electricity Act, a special task is given to the Competition Authority (NMa) concerning disputes relating to contracts and negotiations, in particular contracts, negotiations, refusal of access, and refusal to purchase.[318]

Import and export of electricity

10.215 Export of electricity is unrestricted, except that the manager of the high-voltage network (TenneT) has to report to the Minister any request to transport electricity from the Netherlands to another country.[319] A similar obligation applies with regard to the import of electricity. However, as Parliament wanted to avoid the possibility of countries with an over-capacity 'dumping' electricity, additional rules are included in the Act with regard to the import of electricity.

10.216 As of 1 January 2000 the Minister distinguishes several categories of Member States for the purposes of imports of electricity: (i) Member States which are completely liberalized (Germany, Finland, Norway, the UK, and Sweden), (ii) Member States which have liberalized the market to the extent required by the Electricity Directive (Austria, Italy, and Portugal), (iii) Member States which have not (yet) met the requirements of the Directive, either because their implementation efforts are too slow or insufficient (France and Luxembourg) or because their implementation date has been extended (Belgium, Greece, and Ireland), and (iv)

[317] Arts 5–8 Electricity Act.

[318] Art 51 Electricity Act, which refers directly to Art 20 para 3 Electricity Directive. The competence of Nma is limited to Dutch cases (see Art 52 Electricity Act).

[319] Art 44 Electricity Act.

Member States in a special situation, such as Spain (import level is set at 1 GWh as only these consumers are still protected under the law) and Denmark because following the appointment of the distribution companies as eligible customers only a limited number of large consumers have the freedom to import electricity.[320]

Depending on the category, TenneT is obliged to make an offer for the transport of electricity. An offer must always be made for imports from the first category. In case of the second category, consumers and suppliers consuming more than 20 GWh can import. The level is raised to 100 GWh for imports from Member States in the third category. Consumers and suppliers have to demonstrate the previous year's consumption level on the basis of a certified statement. **10.217**

Be that as it may, the Electricity Act enables the Minister to grant a dispensation. Such dispensation can only be granted if the requested import does not disrupt the balance of the electricity market. In assessing an application for dispensation, the Minister shall consider whether the prohibition of the requested transportation (ie import) is necessary and appropriate in view of its objective, and whether the prohibition would affect the development of trade to an extent which would be contrary to the interests of the Community.[321] **10.218**

Electricity trade and the establishment of the Amsterdam Power Exchange (APX)

An important instrument in the electricity liberalization process is the Amsterdam Power Exchange or APX.[322] Although the APX has been discussed in the Parliamentary debates on the Electricity Act, the Exchange's establishment and organization fall outside the direct scope of the Electricity Act. Indirectly, the above-mentioned import and export provisions are of relevance for the functioning of the APX. **10.219**

Trading on the APX started on 25 May 1999 and amounted to some 2–3 per cent of the total electricity market. The aim of APX is to facilitate spot trading in electricity. Although the APX is open to all interested parties, potential participants must pass through an accession procedure, sign a standard participation agreement, and adhere to the standard regulations. Dutch law applies to the participation agreement. In May 2000 some twenty-seven participants were admitted to the APX, including generators, distributors, trading companies (Dutch as well as foreign traders like Electrabel, Enron, and Vattenfall), and industry (DSM **10.220**

[320] Arts 44 and 45 Electricity Act as implemented in Ministerial Regulation of 25 Nov 1998 on the Import and Export of Electricity. Stc 1998, No 229, 9 most recently amended on 30 Nov 1999, Stc 1999, No 234.

[321] Art 48 Electricity Act.

[322] The APX was officially opened on 16 June 1999.

Services BV). Trades are anonymous in that the participants enter into an agreement with the APX and not directly with each other. The electricity price is determined purely by supply and demand on the exchange. Basically, electricity as a commodity is traded on one day and delivered the next day. Bids can be registered in the morning until 10 am and have to lie within a specific range which is set every week by the APX.[323] Participants have to indicate per hour the amount of electricity (MWh) they wish to buy and/or sell and against which minimum/maximum prices they will do so. This is followed by a matching procedure. Finally, at 4 pm the market clearing price and the total trade volume are announced. Under the APX agreement, all participants are obliged to supply to and take from the grid the contracted amount of electricity. The APX can provide back-up supply.

10.221 The performance of the exchange depends to a large extent on the capacity available on grid, especially the high-voltage network operated by TenneT. The APX has therefore entered into an agreement with the network managers. It is acknowledged that impediments due to actions of the system operators can result in a reduction of the available transport capacity, as a consequence of which the contracted supply volumes also need to be reduced. In addition, there may be unforeseen physical cross-border constraints as a result of which a system operator might be obliged to reduce transport capacity temporarily. The Regulations therefore exclude responsibility by APX for damage caused by constraints on the grid. Since the start of APX, the reduction of cross-border transport capacity has indeed been a problem.[324] The main reasons are the limited number of cross-border connections, the high electricity prices in the Netherlands following the abovementioned protocol agreement between the Dutch producers and distributors, and scarce unused capacity in the grids. The DTe has therefore issued special rules for the allocation of cross-border capacity.[325] Consequently, APX was awarded priority capacity APX of 250 MW; this import capacity for the APX spot market increased to an average of 900 MW in the year 2000. In order to allocate cross-border capacity fairly, the German, Belgian, and Dutch transmission operators have established an auction system. The first public sale was held in November 2000 and concerned the auctioning of import capacity for a period of three months.

10.222 Although the APX began as a spot market or day-ahead market (DAM), the aim is to establish a market in electricity futures as well. Possibly, the APX will also trade in spot gas and carbon dioxide emissions. Anticipating the futures market and other over-the-counter contracts, a Bulletin Board Trading System has been

[323] According to Art 8 of the regulations, these maximum and minimum prices are set every Friday at 3 pm.

[324] *Financieel Dagblad*, 17-6-1999.

[325] Under chapter 5.6 of Netcode the SEP is awarded priority capacity for the electricity import contracts which were concluded under the Electricity Act 1989. Thereupon capacity is reserved to the one-year contracts. Finally, capacity has been reserved for the APX.

introduced in January 2000 facilitating the development of bilateral contracts. In May 2000 eight participants were registered at the Bulletin Board Trading System.

The use of renewable energy

Apart from a policy of liberalization, the new Electricity Act has additional aims: the promotion of energy savings and the use of renewable energy. It is acknowledged that these latter developments cannot be left to the market and need further regulation and planning. **10.223**

The Energy Report

The 1998 Electricity Act requires the publication of an Energy Report giving guidance on decisions to be taken by the industry and/or the market when fuel choices have to be made. The Report is expected to take into consideration especially the importance of reliable, renewable, efficient, and environmentally clean electricity supplies and to focus on any progress achieved in the use of renewable energy resources. Hence, the Report shall include at least: **10.224**

—an analysis of developments on the national and international energy markets and the effects of these on reliable, renewable, efficient, and environmentally clean energy management;
—an analysis of changes in the use of energy sources to generate electricity and the way in and the extent to which renewable energy management is being developed;
—a summary of the intended results of the promotion of reliable, renewable, efficient, and environmentally clean energy management and the ways in which these results are to be pursued in the relevant four-year period.[326]

The first Energy Report was published in November 1999. **10.225**

The 1998 Act also obliges both producers and suppliers to promote the efficient and environmentally responsible production or use of electricity by themselves and by customers.[327] Every producer or supplier who provides an average of 10GWh per year or more shall report once every two years to the Minister how this task was implemented.[328] **10.226**

Resupply of electricity

As in the 1989 Act, a clause regarding the resupply of electricity is included. The licence holder (= distribution company) is obliged to accept an offer to supply electricity from a protected customer who generates electricity by a CHP **10.227**

[326] Art 2 Electricity Act 1998.
[327] cf Art 3 para 2 EC Electricity Directive.
[328] Art 68 Electricity Act.

station.[329] Originally this resupply clause also applied to consumers generating electricity by a hydroelectric power station, or an installation in which biomass is thermally processed without additional burning or admixture of synthetics and with conversion to electricity. In the most recent amendment to the Electricity Act, these latter producers are given permission to supply captive customers before they have become eligible in 2002 or 2004.[330] In this way the producers of alternative energy are given a head start over the other suppliers. Provisions regarding the resupply of electricity now only affect the CHP-producers. The Minister shall set the payment (tariff) for resupply for each licence holder. In determining the payments the Minister shall give consideration to the importance of reliable, renewable, efficient, and environmentally clean electricity supplies. Further rules for setting the tariffs shall be included in a Royal Decree.[331] It can be assumed that the above-mentioned dispute regarding 'avoided costs' will be part of the process for drafting such a decree which has to be taken into consideration.

10.228 It should also be noted that above provisions refer to 'protected customers'. In other words, after the market is fully liberalized there will be no obligation to resupply electricity. This will then depend on market forces, ie the commodity price and the regulated transmission tariffs.

Green certificates

10.229 The Act provides a special legal instrument to stimulate the production of renewable energy: the use of green certificates. Article 73 provides for a system of certificates, which are transferable documents showing that in a stated year a producer has generated or will generate a stated amount of renewable electricity, expressed in KWh.[332] On request, the Minister may also issue a certificate for an amount of renewable energy that has been (or will be) generated and that has been or will be transported to a supplier or customer in the Netherlands.[333] In other words, a certificate may also be awarded for electricity produced or consumed outside the Netherlands. The Minister may require a customer to use a specific number of certificates per year. If a customer fails to 'buy' a certain number of certificates per year, the Minister may impose a surcharge in the transportation tariff.[334] Further rules may be laid down in a Royal Decree and will relate to: information to be supplied to the Minister by producers, suppliers, consumers, or network managers; the manner of compliance with the system; the dealing in,

[329] Art 69 Electricity Act.

[330] Art 53 para 2 sub e Electricity Act.

[331] Art 71 Electricity Act.

[332] Renewable electricity is electricity generated by hydropower stations with a capacity of less than 15 MW or by means of wind power, solar energy, or installations in which biomass is generated.

[333] Art 74 Electricity Act.

[334] Art 76 Electricity Act.

withdrawing, registration, and retention of the certificates; the surcharge; and the payment by the network manager to the Minister of the sums obtained by applying a surcharge on the transportation rates.[335]

Under this new system, a separate market for renewable energy could be established. However, as the 1999 Energy Report has shown that the supply of sufficient renewable energy constitutes a problem in relation to increasing demand, it has been decided to postpone the introduction of green certificates until the year 2001.[336] In the absence of the implementing Royal Decree, it is too early to assess how this system will work in practice; in the meantime we have to rely on the provisions of the Electricity Act 1998. **10.230**

(3) The Electricity Sector in Transition

Introduction

The liberalization policy has a number of consequences. One consequence, which can be noted generally in the EU, is that electricity companies gradually lose their status as a public utility. Increasingly, they are treated like any other companies. For example, the sector is not longer exempt from ordinary tax law. The Electricity Act 1998 provides for the gradual levy of corporate income tax. Electricity companies will be fully taxed as from the year 2002 (or earlier, depending on the speed of liberalization).[337] Another consequence relates to the transition from a monopoly to a liberalized market and concerns the issue of stranded costs and privatization. A third consequence of the liberalization process affects the distribution sector, ie the Energy Distribution Act. **10.231**

Restructuring the electricity sector and the treatment of stranded costs

The trend that electricity companies should be treated like any other commercial entity also plays a role in the discussion about privatization. Municipalities and provinces are less interested in holding shares in electricity generation and distribution companies when they are no longer considered as a public utility. Moreover, the certainty that these utilities will be a regular and constant source of income is also gradually decreasing, especially as the sector is faced with the issue of stranded costs following the restructuring and liberalization of the sector. **10.232**

Stranded costs concern four major types of investments. First, the disintegration of SEP and the consequences for some of its long-term engagements, such as the long-term electricity import contracts concluded in 1989 and 1990, the construction and operation of the NorNed cable and the long-term take-or-pay gas contract with Norway which was entered into in 1989 and based on coal parity. **10.233**

[335] Art 77 Electricity Act.
[336] Energy Report 1999, 54.
[337] Art 89 Electricity Act.

Secondly, the future of some district heating plants, which will be too expensive to run in a liberalized market with lower electricity prices. Thirdly, the recovery of the costs of the establishment and operation of the demonstration coal gasification plant Demkolec. Finally, the protocol agreement between the four 'licensed' generators and the distributors in which the distributors agree to buy all electricity produced by the generators until the year 2000. Following Article 24 of the Electricity Directive, these issues relating to stranded costs had to be notified to the EC Commission.[338]

10.234 The Electricity Act contains some provisions regarding these non-commercial stranded costs (Arts 98–100), including the possibility of appointing a committee of three wise men to study the issue. The Herkströter Commission presented its report in December 1999. The Commission used as a guide the principle that financial compensation by the Government for stranded costs should be confined to obligations specifically encouraged by the Government. In cases where the costs would be borne by the production companies, the cost allocation formula should be based on the Agreement of Co-operation for SEP.[339] The Commission, *inter alia*, proposed that the four production companies should jointly enable SEP to bear the operational costs of the Demkolec plant until the plant is transferred to a production company or a third party. The costs of the district heating contracts should be borne by each production company's share in the total production up to a certain ceiling (NLG 1 billion). Otherwise the costs associated with district heating should be borne by the production company which undertook the relevant activity. With regard to the NorNed cable it advised that the entire agreement should be reassessed on the basis of amendments to the relevant legislation following the liberalization process. In the Commission's view the shares in the national grid company should be transferred to the State on the basis of their market value. This will strengthen the production company's ability to pay those costs. Finally it suggested that SEP should act as a liquidator and should continue to exist until the settlement process has been completed.

10.235 On 21 December 2000 Parliament agreed on the entry into force of an Act which should finally settle the termination of the Agreement on Co-operation between the Dutch electricity production companies on 1 January 2001 and its consequences for settling the stranded costs and the ownership of the high transmission grid, ie the company TenneT BV.[340] The Minister closely follows the advice of the Commission of wise men and identifies as stranded costs resulting from the

[338] The notification of the import contracts was send in too late. The Commission will assess these costs within the framework of the State aid regime. See Commission Decision of 8 July 1999, 1999/796/EC.

[339] This includes the following shareholder's division: EPON 29.5%, EPZ 28.5%, EZH 19.5%, and UNA 22.5%.

[340] Stb 607.

investments initiated by SEP before the entry force of the Electricity Directive on behalf of the four production companies all costs related to (i) outstanding loans and the dismantlement of SEP NV; (ii) the exploitation of experimental coal-gasification plant Demkolec NV; and (iii) contracts for the import of electricity and gas. The four production companies are jointly responsible for these costs, which may be divided amongst them on the basis of their share in the company SEP. In addition to costs for which the producers are directly responsible, the Act recognizes an additional category of stranded costs, ie agreements on district heating which have been concluded before the entry into force of the Electricity Act 1998. These agreements between producers and suppliers may involve costs for which compensation can be sought. The Act identifies several ways in which such compensation may be claimed. First, the Minister may decide each year for a period of ten years about a surcharge on the regulated transportation fee. These revenues will be used to cover the costs resulting from the district heating projects and the costs of purchasing the Demkolec plant. Secondly, the State will purchase all shares of the network company TenneT BV. The value of these shares is estimated at NLG 2,550,000. Although the Minister's preference was to take over 50 per cent of the shares plus one, she has yielded to Parliament and agreed to buy all the shares in TenneT on condition that the nationalization of the high transmission grid is temporary. Because of the Minister's agreement to buy all shares in TenneT, the producers have agreed to accept the arrangement offered, despite the fact that they consider parts of the Act unfavourable and unfair.

After fifty years and a gradual process of further integration SEP will finally fall **10.236** apart; the last step in the integration process, 'the creation of one major Dutch production company' has not been achieved: liberalization has finally led to disintegration.

The Distribution sector

Another transitional issue concerns the distribution sector. The Energy Distribu- **10.237** tion Act (see above paras 10.132–10.137) was amended as a result of the entry into force of the Electricity Act and the Gas Act. These amendments concerned the use of terminology and did not change the substance of the Act, except for the rules concerning competition and cross-subsidization which have been deleted as part of the liberalization process. Otherwise the Act intends to promote the efficient and environmentally friendly use of energy. However, following the liberalization process, there seems almost no need for this Act. The Ministry will therefore review the need for it and the possibility of integrating parts of the Energy Distribution Act into other legislation.[341]

[341] Energy Report 1999, 36.

E. Energy Efficiency, Conservation, and Environmental Taxes

(1) Introduction

10.238 Government policy on energy efficiency and energy conservation dates from the 1970s. The oil crises compelled the Government to consider the issues of energy saving and energy efficiency. Several measures and policy instruments were outlined in the White Papers on Energy Policy of 1974 and 1979. These policy papers focused primarily on the possibilities of energy savings in the housing, industrial, and transport sectors. The Third Energy Paper of 1995 is wider in scope and considers not only the issue of energy efficiency and energy conservation within the scenario of long-term energy supply, but also the benefits for the environment and the economy as a whole. Global warming and the need to reduce emissions of greenhouse gases are elements that have been added to the original policy on energy efficiency.

10.239 Under the Kyoto Protocol the Netherlands has to reduce greenhouse gas (carbon dioxide) emissions by 6 per cent in the years 2008–10 compared to the years 1990–5. Such a policy on emission standards is not new. The first rules regarding national emission standards were set down in a Decree belonging to the Air Pollution Act.[342] It provided for fixed standards for the concentration of sulphur dioxide and nitrogen oxide for emissions from combustion plants operating on coal, oil, and gas. These standards were further restricted by the National Environmental Policy Plans.[343]

10.240 As a general rule these environmental goals are further developed by the industry on the basis of agreements (environmental covenants) between a specific industrial sector and the Government, in which the former agrees to reduce the emissions of gases to a certain level. SEP, for example, entered into an agreement with the Government to decrease emissions of sulphur dioxide and nitrogen oxide by 12 million kilos and 25 million kilos respectively in the period between 1994 and 2000 and to reduce sulphur dioxide emissions by 90 per cent and nitrogen oxide emissions by 60 per cent in the year 2000.

10.241 The reduction of greenhouse gases is achieved not only by energy savings and efficiency, but also by the increased use of renewable energy resources. The role of renewable energy in the Electricity Act has been discussed above. The following focuses on the types of renewable energy used in the Netherlands and how they are

---

[342] Decree of 10 Apr 1987, Stb 164, implementing the Soil Protection Act. The Soil Protection Act implements EC Directive 84/360 (OJ 1984 L188/20).

[343] After the publication of the first National Environmental Plan in 1989, the Government issued its third National Environmental Plan in 1998. The environmental goals set in this plan apply until the year 2002.

used in the framework of energy saving and environmental protection. Finally, some environmental and energy taxes will be discussed. Since the Third Energy Note of 1995 such taxes have become increasingly important. These fiscal measures are an instrument for achieving energy efficiency, and the proceeds can be invested into techniques for further reducing pollution.

(2) Energy Conservation and the Environment

Introduction

Current policy on energy conservation attempts to achieve an average energy efficiency of 1.7 per cent per year. In other words, an energy efficiency improvement equivalent to one-third of energy consumption should be achieved in the next 25 years.[344] The use of renewable energy is also expected to increase by 10 per cent.[345] The promotion of renewable energy is indeed an important means to protect the environment and thus to reduce emission gases. **10.242**

The production of renewable energy or non-fossil power is to a large extent based on environmentally friendly techniques such as co-generation and wind energy plants. Although the amount of wind energy is increasing, co-generation is the most popular form of decentralized power. This is also stimulated by the large quantities of gas available in the Netherlands and the special co-generation tariffs which have been applied since 1994. Small co-generators paid the same (low) tariff as large industrial consumers.[346] This favourable situation will change in the near future when co-generators purchase their gas from Gasunie under the new tariff system, the CSS regime.[347] **10.243**

Combined heat and power

Although not considered as a renewable energy source, co-generation or combined heat and power (CHP) is a technology which leads to considerable energy savings. Under the Electricity Act 1989, the establishment of CHP was considered as an important instrument to stimulate competition with the 'licensed' producers, the traditional power producers. Distribution companies were allowed to participate in joint ventures with private firms to install generating capacity and to meet a proportion of the demand in their distribution area, as long as they bought back the privately produced electricity at prices reflecting the saved costs (see above paras 10.189–10.190). This led to a strong increase in joint ventures and decentralized CHP production. The distribution sector aimed at installing **10.244**

[344] The Action Programme on Energy Saving for 1999–2002 applied a sliding scale from 1.6% to 2% per year. See Energy Report 1999, 38.

[345] Third Energy Note 1995. The goal is to achieve an increase of 5% in the year 2010 and 10% in the year 2020. See Energy Report 1999, 41.

[346] Note that this is based on the 'old' system of zoning tariff.

[347] Energy Report 1999, 39.

some 3,850 MW of co-generation capacity in order to decrease projected carbon dioxide levels by 17.7 million tons before the year 2000. Since the Electricity Act 1998, the major driving force for the development of CHP is no longer the need to introduce competition but the Government's commitment to energy efficiency and carbon dioxide reduction.

10.245 Direct subsidies have been applied since the 1970s in order to stimulate the establishment of co-generation plants.[348] Whereas the First Memorandum on Energy Conservation aimed at an installed CHP capacity of 5,500 MW in 1990, the Second Memorandum increased the policy target to 8,000 MW installed capacity in 2000. However, in 1993 installed CHP capacity had already increased by 10 per cent to 4,000 MW. Continuation of this policy would have led to access to generated capacity of more than 2,000 MW in the year 2000 as a result of which central production plants were to be closed and/or planned capacity delayed and reduced. Hence, the policy changed drastically. The subsidies for new CHP were reduced in 1993 and totally abolished in 1995. Some elements of the tariff scheme based on the principle of 'avoided costs' were also amended in 1996 as a result of which it became less favourable to install CHP capacity. Moreover, the distribution companies entered into an agreement with the generators (the 'protocol agreement': see above) stating that the distributors would buy all electricity from the licensed generators until the year 2000. The installed CHP has thus become one of the 'stranded costs' the Government must take into account in the present liberalization process as outlined above. The Government acknowledges that special measures are required to restimulate the use of CHP.[349]

Wind energy

10.246 Despite the Netherlands tradition of wind energy, the extent of wind power has been very limited over the last decades. In 1995 wind energy capacity increased from 153 to 248 MW (some 1.2 per cent). The target is to increase capacity to 2,000 MW by the year 2010. Currently, 50 per cent of all wind power is installed by the distribution companies. Private producers generate the remaining 50 per cent. EnergieNed used to negotiate the (re)supply tariffs with the association of private producers of wind energy (Pawex). Contracts between private producers and distribution companies are now entered into on a case-by-case basis.

10.247 For many years wind energy was promoted through the Wind Energy Subsidies Order, which provided for subsidies of up to 35 per cent of project costs.[350] Following the Third Energy Note 1995 this policy was changed and substituted

[348] *Steunregeling Energiebesparing en Stromingsbronnen.*

[349] The proposed measures vary from taxes to the need to amend the transportation tariffs and the possibility of speeding up the liberalization process so that co-generators can also supply consumers directly. See Energy Report 1999, 40.

[350] See for example, *Uitvoeringsregeling windenergie 1995*, Stc 1995, nr 79.

by more fiscal measures such as the energy tax scheme (REB) and schemes for green electricity pricing (see below). The Government thinks that these tax incentives will enable renewable resources to compete with conventionally generated electricity.

The most important hindrance to the promotion of wind energy in the Netherlands is, however, the availability of suitable sites. After all, the Netherlands is a densely populated country. The construction of several wind turbines in one area to create a wind farm is often considered to be horizontal pollution and objected to by the local population. To overcome this problem an Administrative Agreement on Wind Energy Siting has been concluded between central authorities and seven provinces with the highest wind potential. These provinces will take the necessary policy measures and allocate sites in their regional planning systems to create wind energy capacity of 1,100 MW by the year 2000. In addition, the possibility of offshore sites is explored. A first 500 KW offshore project was installed in the IJsselmeer in 1994. Several wind farms are planned along the waterways. The siting of wind turbines near the shoreline is also discussed but this poses additional technical and legal problems.[351] **10.248**

Solar energy

By contrast to wind energy, the use of solar energy is mostly a stand-alone option and not connected to the grid (less than 0.1 per cent). However, projects are increasing in which homes are fitted with grid-connected photovoltaic cells.[352] In 1994 the total installed photovoltaic power was over 2 MWp. The National Research Programme for Photovoltaic Electricity has set a target of 25 MWp by 2000 and 250 MWp by 2010. **10.249**

In addition, thermal solar projects are being developed such as the '1,000 roofs project' in which the energy distribution company NUON is supporting the installation of 1,000 solar hot-water systems in a new residential area. The use of passive solar is encouraged by the Energy Performance Standard (EPS) for new buildings (see below). In view of current prices for solar hot-water systems, Government subsidies will be phased out. **10.250**

Waste and bio-mass

Waste and biomass are important renewable energy sources. They comprise 80 per cent in all renewables (CHP excluded). Waste incineration is used for electricity as well as heat production. Industrial waste (mostly waste wood) is co-fired in large coal-fired power plants. The government plans to further increase the share of wood (10 per cent) in coal-fired plants by importing biomass fuels in the form of wood **10.251**

[351] See further Energy Report 1999, 47.

[352] The size of these projects varies from 10 houses to 50–100 houses.

and charcoal. This policy will be intensified following an agreement the Minister of Economic Affairs and the Minister of Environment concluded with the owners of the coal-fired power plants in July 2000.[353] According to this agreement, the generators will give an assurance that CO_2 emissions per KWh from coal plants will be no higher than from natural gas fired plants. It is expected that important parts of the required CO_2 reduction will be achieved through the use of biomass, either through the direct firing of biomass or through special gas conversion techniques.

10.252 The Government aims to increase to 15 per cent power generated from biofuels such as landfill gas, gasification, wood, and waste combustion. The Government issued a special action programme aimed at doubling such energy output by 2000. An important legal obstacle to the use of biomass are the current emission standards.[354]

10.253 By contrast to other energy sectors, the Ministry for Housing, Physical Planning, and Environmental Management is responsible for energy production from municipal waste and industrial waste.

(3) Energy Efficiency and Conservation

Introduction

10.254 Dutch energy efficiency policy centres on the individual responsibility of user groups. User groups have to be convinced that it is worth while both economically and environmentally to save energy. Several user groups are identified such as i) the industrial sector (including the energy industry), ii) residential/commercial sector (homes and buildings), iii) the agricultural sector, and iv) the traffic and transport sector.

10.255 The policy instruments applied to stimulate energy efficiency include regulatory instruments, long-term agreements, technology developments, fiscal measures, and financial incentives. The use of long-term voluntary agreements, however, is the cornerstone of Dutch Government policy on energy efficiency. A similar trend exists for emission reduction as illustrated by the above-mentioned example of the environmental covenant between SEP and the Government.

Long-term agreements

10.256 Energy efficiency plays an important role in the industrial sector. The sector aims at an energy efficiency improvement of 20 per cent in the year 2000.[355] The aim is mainly achieved on the basis of long-term agreements. Presently, there are some

[353] Currently the four electricity generators operate seven coal-fired plants. EZH has two at the Maasvlakte, EPZ has two in Geertruidenberg and one in Borssele, UNA operates one coal-fired plant in Amsterdam, and EPON exploits another in Nijmegen.

[354] Energy Report 1999, 47.

[355] The Second Memorandum on Energy Conservation (VNEB) of 1993 identified the energy-savings policy instruments for the industrial sector up to the year 2000.

thirty voluntary long-term agreements (LTAs) on energy efficiency improvement in the industrial sector. In 1995 energy efficiency in the industrial sector had improved by 10 per cent from its 1989 level.[356] In the commercial, education, and health-care sectors there are six LTAs (with a target of 25–30 per cent energy savings) covering some 30 per cent of total energy consumption. Some nine LTAs are applied in other sectors such as the agricultural sector. The greenhouse horticultural LTA (with a target of 23 per cent energy savings) covers some 80 per cent of total energy consumption in the agricultural sector. Data show that energy efficiency improved by 10 per cent between 1989 and 1995. The first cycle of agreements have to be renewed in 2000. Although the Dutch Government plans to extend the use of voluntary agreements after the year 2000,[357] it will be limited to industries consuming less than 0.5 PJ per year. The energy-saving goals for large industrial consumers (using more than 0.5 PJ) will be based on a system of benchmarking.[358]

LTAs are also used to introduce and encourage new technologies. The extent to which new technologies can be introduced varies in the different sectors. It is expected that substantial improvement of energy efficiency can be achieved in the energy-intensive manufacturing industry (chemicals, oil, refining, etc) with new breakthrough technologies. The new LTAs will therefore focus on the development of such technologies.[359] Investment in research is further developed by tax incentives (see below). **10.257**

Standardization and regulation

Energy conservation plays an important role in the residential and commercial sector. One of the key instruments is the use of standardization policies. In the construction industry, the focus is on energy efficiency when constructing new properties. For that purpose the Energy Performance Standard (EPS) for new buildings which entered into force in 1995 was intensified in 1998 and 2000. The EPS applies to the construction of buildings and includes the use of energy-efficient infrastructure such as district heating or heat pumps. The standard is ambitious as it was designed to achieve energy savings of 15–20 per cent. Some energy-saving instruments are identified for existing buildings. Energy-saving measures include retrofitted insulation and the use of double-glazing. Recently, the Government decided to appoint special installation engineers to provide energy advice to individual households.[360] **10.258**

[356] This is the average outcome of 20 LTAs which together represent 85% of Dutch industrial energy consumption and involve almost all energy consumers.

[357] Energy Saving Policy Plan of April 1998.

[358] See Benchmark Covenant of 6 July 1999.

[359] Extra research money is earmarked for the Multi-Annual Programme on Inter-Sectoral Technologies for Manufacturing Industry (MINT).

[360] Within its policy on climate change, the Minister of Environment has allocated some NLG 50 million for this purpose.

10.259 Public education and labelling are important promotional instruments. Energy utilities and traders are encouraged to promote sales of energy-efficient equipment by means of public education and temporary premiums. Minimum efficiency standards apply to a wide range of appliances. Harmonization and standardization developments on the EC level play an important role. In order to implement some Energy Efficiency Directives, the Energy Savings Appliances Act entered into force in 1986.[361] This Act is a framework act, enabling the Government to set energy-saving standards for specific installations such as heat pumps, televisions, washing machines, and dishwashers.

Financial measures

10.260 Financial measures are used to promote energy-efficient equipment and transport: this is an important measure for promoting sustainable transport. The transport industry accounts for almost 14 per cent of total Dutch energy consumption. This share will increase due to increased mobility and economic growth. In addition to the promotion of public transport and new vehicle technology, most measures are taken in the field of fuel use and instruments to promote the purchase of energy-efficient cars and public transport. Positive incentives are included in specific income tax schemes (company bicycles, car-pooling, and teleworking) and by 'greening VAT', ie reducing VAT on the sale of environmentally friendly products.[362]

Energy taxes and environmental taxes

Introduction

10.261 Since the 1980s the Government applied specific environmental and energy taxes. Besides an environmental tax on fuels, the Government has introduced an accelerated depreciation of environmental investments (VAMIL programme), environmental levies, and energy-investment tax credit (*Energie-investeringsaftrek*), Tax-free income from green funds (*Regeling groen beleggen*), and the regulatory energy tax (*regulerende energiebelasting* or REB).

Environmental tax on fuels

10.262 The environmental tax on fuels has been applied since January 1988. Originally it was intended to be a single, transparent tax for financing environmental policy expenditure, but since 1992 the tax has been part of general revenue. The current tax regime entered into force in January 1995. Fuel was chosen as the tax base because of the 'polluter-pays' principle. The tax is based on fuel consumption in the

361 Act of 5 Feb 1986, Stb 59, most recently amended on 6 Nov 1997, Stb 10.
362 See also W Vermeend, J van der Vaart, 'Greening Taxes: The Dutch Model', Kluwer, 1998.

previous year and the energy/carbon content of the fuel (50/50) and is, *inter alia*, payable by anyone who extracts, produces, uses, or imports a certain energy resource and subsequently uses it as a fuel.[363]

The tax burden on energy-intensive industry is alleviated through special rates for the energy part of the tax. Special regimes apply for large-scale consumption of gas (consuming more than 10 million cubic metres per year) and to residual fuels.[364] Mitigation for these fuels was introduced in 1992 on pragmatic grounds, to avoid an unreasonable increase in tax burden following some earlier amendments. The relief for natural gas was considered temporary. **10.263**

VAMIL

Free depreciation of environmental investments was introduced in 1991. It is a tax instrument designed to stimulate environmental investment. Specific technologies which have not yet penetrated the market may qualify for free depreciation and are put on the 'Environment List' which is updated regularly. Free depreciation applies to some 450 types of equipment in the environmental area, including equipment for energy savings. **10.264**

Environmental levies and the energy investment tax credit

Since the 1980s the Government has issued several 'Environmental Action Plans' (*Milieu Actie Plan* or MAPs) enabling industry to enter into an environmental agreement with the Government. Within the energy sector, distribution companies have developed special MAP programmes for their supply areas. MAP II entitles distribution companies to put a levy on the electricity tariffs in the range of 0.5–2.5 per cent (average expected of 1.8 per cent). These proceeds are, for example, used to support renewables-based production and demand-side management. Continued support for renewables was achieved on the basis of the MAP 2000 plan which ran from 1997 to 2000. EnergieNed issued MAP 2000 guidelines pledging that 3.2 per cent of its electricity turnover would be generated sustainably. The Electricity Act gives a statutory basis for these MAP levies. **10.265**

The MAP levies can only be applied to captive customers. It is therefore expected that they will be abolished when all customers become eligible and free to choose their supplier. The energy investment tax credit which was introduced in 1997 is considered an alternative.[365] Under the latter regime, enterprises can discount **10.266**

[363] For an overview: ibid, 31–5.

[364] The first category pays 16 cents per GJ rather than 39 cents; the second category pays zero tax. A zero rate applies to certain fuels used in the installations where they are produced, eg blast furnaces, coke ovens, coal, and refinery gas and gaseous residuals in the petrochemical industry. Since 1997 a tax is levied on uranium 235 as part of the environmental tax on fuels used to generate electric power in nuclear installations. The tax was introduced to equalize the situation between nuclear-generated electricity and fuel-based electricity.

[365] Energy Report 1999, 36.

taxable profits by at least 40 per cent of certain energy investments up to a maximum. The energy investment tax credit is additional to normal depreciation and sometimes free depreciation is also available for environmental investments. The energy investment tax credit is limited to investments listed in the Minister of Finance's 'Energy List' which has published regularly in the Official Gazette. The Energy List enumerates specific and new means of production, including energy-saving equipment and equipment for renewable energy.[366]

Energy regulatory tax

10.267 The introduction of an energy regulatory tax was proposed in 1993 in the second National Environmental Policy Plan. The tax is intended i) to reduce carbon dioxide emissions by 1.7–2.7 Mton through decreased energy consumption, ii) to encourage energy conservation through its impact on prices, and iii) to increase the use of renewable energy.

10.268 An energy regulatory tax has been levied on small consumers since 1 January 1996. It applies to natural gas consumers of less than 170,000 cubic metres per year, low amperage electricity up to 50,000 KWh per year, and mineral oil products which are substituted for gas with ceilings comparable to the above. Through its focus on small consumers it is designed to avoid the economic costs of a unilaterally imposed energy tax on industrial energy users competing internationally.

10.269 The tax on gas is introduced in three stages with the (ultimate) effect of raising gas prices by 20–25 per cent. Electricity prices will rise by 15 per cent in a single step. Exemptions apply for the consumption of gas below 800 cubic metres (about 6 per cent of households), gas used in electricity generation and the greenhouse horticultural sector, district heating, and electricity from renewable resources. Consequently, the tax applies to most households and small to medium-sized companies. Some 40 per cent of all companies and 40 per cent of non-transport and non-feedstock energy use are covered by the tax. The environmental tax on fuels and the energy regulatory tax will together raise 2.5 per cent of total tax revenue in the Netherlands.

10.270 Although revenues from the energy regulatory tax are used to reduce direct taxes paid by households and business, it is recognized that any decrease in gas and electricity prices following the liberalization of the gas and electricity markets will be compensated by the increase in taxes.

Tax-free income from green funds

10.271 Tax-free income from green funds (*Groen Beleggen*) has applied since 1995. Private investors are not taxed on their interest or dividend income which derives from investment in certain green investment funds. These funds have to invest in certain

[366] W Vermeend, J van der Vaart, *Greening Taxes: the Dutch Model*, Kluwer, 1998, 63–9.

green projects. The aim is to encourage investment in major environmental projects, sustainable energy supplies, and environmental technology. At least 70 per cent of the total assets of the green investment fund must be invested in green projects. The designated projects are updated regularly. Basically the projects had to be new and in the Netherlands. Since 1998 a number can be developed outside the Netherlands (for example in Eastern Europe). The income tax legislation specifies which green funds (and projects) qualify as green investments. Green investments have to meet the same criteria which the Dutch central bank (*De Nederlandse Bank*) normally apply to Dutch investment and credit institutions.[367]

F. Further Developments

The Dutch energy sector is presently undergoing important changes. This is reflected by the legislative developments outlined above. Basically, the developments are the result of the EC liberalization process and concern mainly the gas and the electricity sectors. Whether or not the liberalization process will lead to more competition and opening of the energy market remains to be seen. This is especially true of the gas market. It seems that the Gas Act does not provide sufficient instruments to introduce more competition, and there is insufficient gas supply. If the Government really wishes to introduce more competition, additional legislation and regulation are required. **10.272**

By contrast to the gas and electricity sectors, there is no need to change the present mining regime and to introduce a Mining Bill. The entry into force of the new Mining Act will therefore depend on the number and extent of objections posed to the Bill. Considering the many attempts to change the mining laws, it would not be surprising if the Mining Bill were put on ice and eventually forgotten. This is even more likely since the Minister of Economic Affairs who stimulated the reform process is no longer in office. Similarly, it is doubtful whether the proposal in the Third Energy Note 1995 that all energy laws will eventually be integrated into one Energy Act will ever be achieved. It is more likely that the legislator will constantly have to issue additional rules and regulations to amend the electricity and gas laws as the liberalization process goes ahead. **10.273**

Bibliography

Ars Aequi, RR, *Speciaal nummer energierecht* (special number on energy Law), 1980, 597-
van den Berge, *De juridische situatie op energiegebied in Nederland*, SEW 1971, no 9, 539–63
Barents, R, 'Legal Aspects of Energy Policy', Journal of Energy and Natural Resources Law, 1983, vol 3 no 3, 160–76

[367] ibid, 60–3.

Bontius, GH, *Das System der leitungsgebunden Energieversorgung in den Niederlanden*, in *Neue Strukturen der Energieversorgung*, 1988, 65–85

Bouchez, L, 'Liberalisation of the Netherlands Electricity Market', Utilities Law Review, 1999, vol 10 issue 4, 152–8

Brunekreeft, G, 'The 1996 reform of the electricity supply industry in the Netherlands', Utilities Policy, 1997, vol 6 no 2, 117–26

Cameron, PD, 'Monopoly and Competition in Energy Supply: The Netherlands', Journal of Energy and Natural Resources Law, 1990, supplement, 47–66

—— and Roggenkamp, MM, 'Abandonment and reclamation of energy sites and facilities: The Netherlands', Journal of Energy and Natural Resources Law, 1992, vol 10, no 1, 21–37

Kortmann, CAJM and BovendÉert, PPT, *The Kingdom of the Netherlands: An Introduction to Dutch Constitutional Law*, 1993

Cross, ED, 'The Netherlands: Nationwide Co-operation with elements of Competition', in: *Electric Utility Regulation in the European Union*, 1996, 165–99

Deriks, M, *Das Recht der Elektrizitätsversorgung in den Niederlanden* in *Recht der Elektrizitätswirtschaft 1988*, jahrgang 49

Fitzpatrick, WW, 'Interesting Legal Aspects of the Netherlands Petroleum Regime', Oil & Gas Law and Taxation Review, 1985/1986, 312–20

Goedkoop, AG, and Veltema, AJ, 'Dutch Social security for offshore employees', Oil and Gas Law and Taxation Review, 1992, vol 10 issue 11/12, 326–31

Gonzales, HMC, 'De reorganisatie van de Nederlandse Elektriciteitsvoorziening', SEW 1988, no 9, 538–53

Hancher, L, *Sturing en energierecht in Nederland: Een blik van buitenaf*, in SEW, 1992, no 6, 566–85

Hancher, L, and Bartman, SM, *Het Wetsvoorstel Elektriciteitswet: Kanttekeningen in het licht van toekomstige marktontwikkelingen*, in *Nederlands Juristenblad*, 1998 afl 20, 905–13

Hancher, L, and Hekker, A, 'The Restructuring of the Dutch Electricity Industry: Aims and Background to 1989 Reforms', Utilities Law Review, 1991, vol 2 no 1, 12–18

Hekker, AC, *Het wetsvoorstel energiedistributie*, in *Handboek Energie en Milieu*, 1994

Huygen, AEH, *Energiebelasting*, in *Handboek Energie en Milieu*, 1993

—— *Electricity Regulation in the Netherlands: New Guide to Dutch Electricity Law*, 1995

de Keijzer, J, 'Procurement in the Energy Sector in the Netherlands', Oil and Gas Law and Taxation Review, 1996, vol. 14 issue 1, 46–50

—— 'Electricity in the Netherlands', Oil and Gas Law and Taxation Review, special issue 1998 'Electricity Liberalisation in the European Union—Law and Commentary' pp 129–147

Klemm, A, 'Das Niederlandische Elektrizitätsgesetz 1998', Energiewirtschaftliche Tagesfragen, 1999, no 49, vol 10, 700–4

de Maar, HG, *Energierecht*, 1987

North, TP, and de Wekker, P, 'Taxation of Employees on the Netherlands continental shelf', Oil and Gas Law and Taxation Review, 1992, vol 9 no 8, 239–47

Polak, MV, 'All's well that wells oil? *Ongelijke behandleing van werknemers in het voorstel van een wet arbeid mijnbouw Noordzee*, in Nederlands Juristenblad, 1992, 53–7

Roggenkamp, MM, *Oil & Gas: Netherlands Law and Practice*, 1992, 345

—— 'Health and Safety on the Dutch continental shelf', Oil and Gas Law and Taxation Review, 1991, vol 9 no 10, 312–18

—— 'The Markham Field: Joint Exploitation by the Netherlands and the United Kingdom', Oil and Gas Law and Taxation Review, 1992, vol 10, issue 7, 193–7

—— 'The Impact of the NOGAT pipeline on the Netherlands output and development', Oil and Gas Law and Taxation Review, 1993, vol 11 no 5, 135–43

—— *Het Juridisch Kader van Pijpleidingen in de Olie- en Gasindustrie*, 1999

Schierbeek, P, *Olie en Gas In Nederland en onder de Noordzee*, Monografie AMRO Bank, 1965

Vermeend, W, and van der Vaart, J, *Greening Taxes: The Dutch Model*, Kluwer, 1998

Verwer, Ch P, 'Piped Transportation in the Netherlands', 11th International Congress of Comparative Law, 1982

Legislation

Exploration and Production of Oil and Gas

Onshore

Mining Act 1810 (*Loi conçernant les Mines, les Minières, et les Carrières* of 21 April 1810) as amended by Act of 18 March 1996 implementing EC Directive 94/22/EG, Staatsblad 199

Mining Act 1903 (*Mijnwet 1903* of 27 April 1904) Staatsblad 73 as amended by Act of 18 March 1996 implementing EC Directive 94/22/EG, Staatsblad 199

Mineral Exploration Act 1967 (*Wet Opsporing Delfstoffen* of 3 May 1967) Staatsblad 258 as amended by Act of 18 March 1996 implementing EC Directive 94/22/EG, Staatsblad 199

Mining Regulations 1964 (*Mijnreglement* of 21 December 1964) Staatsblad 538

Royal Decree Onshore Concessions 1996 (*Besluit van 26 maart 1996, houdende bepalingen inzake financiële voorschriften bij een concessie voor koolwaterstoffen op grond van de Mijnwet 1903*), Staatsblad 212

Onshore Minerals Licensing Regulation 1996 (*Regeling vergunningen en concessies delfstoffen Nederlands territoir 1996*) Staatscourant of 15 May 1996, no 93)

Offshore

Continental Shelf (CS) Mining Act of 1965 (*Mijnwet Continentaal Plat* of 23 September 1965) Staatsblad 428, most recently amended by Act of 18 March 1996 implementing EC Directive 94/22/EG, Staatsblad 199

Dutch Territorial Sea Borders Act of 9 January 1985 (*Wet Grenzen Territoriale Zee*, Staatsblad 1985, 129)

CS Mining Labour Act of 1992 (*Wet Arbeid Mijnbouw Noordzee*, Staatsblad 1992, 592)

CS Mining Regulations (*Mijnreglement Continentaal Plat* of 13 March 1967) Staatsblad 158

Royal Decree of 1967 on the Exploration and Production of Petroleum (*Besluit tot Uitvoering van art. 12 Mijnwet Continentaal Plat*, 27 April 1967, Staatsblad 24)

Royal Decree of 1967 distinguishing between onshore and offshore mining jurisdiction, Staatsblad No 74

Royal Decree of 1967 on the application of licences and exemptions (*Besluit aanvragen 02*, as amended by Royal Decree of 27 January 1995, Staatsblad 42; *Vergunningen en Ontheffingen Mijnwet Continentaal Plat* of 7 February 1967 Staatsblad 75)
Royal Decree of 1976 on Exploration and Production; (*Besluit tot Uitvoering van art. 12 Mijnwet Continentaal Plat* of 6 February 1976) Staatsblad 1
Royal Decree Offshore Licences 1996 (*Besluit van 26 maart 1996, houdende bepalingen inzake financiële voorschriften bij een opsporings- of winningsvergunning voor koolwaterstoffen op grond van de Mijnwet Continentaal Plat*) Staatsblad 212
CS Hydrocarbons Regulations (*Regeling Vergunningen Koolwaterstoffen Continentaal Plat 1996* of 15 May 1996) Staatscourant No 93

Gas Supply

Natural Gas Prices Act (*Wet Aardgasprijzen*) Staatsblad 1974, No 765
Energy Distribution Act providing rules for the distribution of electricity, gas, and heat (*Wet Energiedistributie* of 14 December 1996) Staatsblad 1996, 642
Gas Act (*Wet van 22 juni 2000, houdende regels omtrent het transport en de levering van gas*) Staatsblad 2000, 305
Decree governing entry into force of the Gas Act (*Besluit 20 juli 2000, houdende vaststelling van het tijdstip van inwerkingtreding van een aantal artikelen van de Gaswet*), Staatsblad 2000, 318
Decree implementing some parts of the Gas Act (*Uitvoeringsregeling Gaswet*), Staatscourant 2000, 159
Guidelines for the year 2001 on transport and supply of natural gas (*Richtlijnen voor het jaar 2001 Gaswet*) Staatscourant 2000, 171

Electricity Supply

Electricity Act 1998 (*Wet van 2 juli 1998, houdende regels met betrekking tot de productie, het transport en de levering van elektriciteit*) Staatsblad 427 as amended by Act of 3 June 1999 amending the Electricity Act of 1998 in order to give further rules with regard to the network manager and the supply of electricity to protected customers, Staatsblad 1999, 260. Most recently amended as a result of the entry into force of Act regarding the allocation of electricity production sector (*overgongswet elektriciteitsproductiesector*), 21 December 2000, Staatsblad 607
Energy Distribution Act providing rules for the distribution of electricity, gas, and heat (*Wet Energiedistributie* of 14 December 1996) Staatsblad 1996, 642
Roles on the Electricity Supply Licence, Staatscourant 1998, 141
Regulation on transport capacity plans on the basis of Article 21 Electricity Act (*Regeling capaciteitsplannen Elektriciteitswet 1998*) Staatscourant 2000, nr 134
Rules on reciprocity (*Ministeriële regeling reciprociteit*) Staatscourant 1998, 229
Regulation containing further rules on the import and export of electricity (*Beleidsregels toewijzing importcapciteit op grond van artikel 31 Elektriciteitswet 1998*) Staatscourant 2000, 134
Rules regarding the appointment of network managers (*Beleidsregel aanwijzing netbeheerders*) Staatscourant 1999, 161

Decision regarding the tariffbase for transport and supply tariffs (*Besluit tariefdragers voor de tarieven voor transport en levering van elektriciteit*) Staatscourant 1999, 126

Decision regarding the allocation of costs (*Besluit kostenverhaal Elektriciteitswet ex artikel 85 Elektriciteitswet* 1998) Staatsblad 1998, 702

Energy Saving

Energy Savings Appliances Act of 1986 (*Wet Energiebesparing Toestellen*, Staatsblad 1986, 59) most recently amended on 6 November 1997, Staatsblad 10

Decision on the Energy Regulatory Tax (*Besluit van 23 december 1996 tot wijziging van de wet belastingen op milieugrondslag*) Staatsblad 1996, 688

11

ENERGY LAW IN NORWAY

Finn Arnesen, Ulf Hammer, Per Håkon Høisveen, Knut Kaasen, and Dagfinn Nygaard

A. Introduction

(1) Norwegian Resource Base

The energy resource base in Norway is characterized by the dominance of two energy resources, petroleum and hydroelectricity. As far as petroleum is concerned it should be noted that these resources are situated on the continental shelf off Norway, hence the exploration and production of oil and gas is a relatively new activity. These offshore resources have been developed since the 1970s. The situation of hydropower is the opposite. As Norway is a mountainous country it has made use of its waterfalls for centuries. Industrial as well as large-scale development of hydropower, however, has been developed since the beginning of the last century. **11.01**

Petroleum resources

11.02 The Norwegian petroleum resources are located on the Norwegian continental shelf. Discovered and undiscovered resources are expected to total about 12.5 billion scm oe. As of 31 December 1996 about 9.0 bn scm oe had been discovered. Of the total discovered resources 83 per cent has been found in the North Sea, 14 per cent in the Norwegian Sea, and 3 per cent in the Barents Sea. The ratio between oil and gas is approximately 50/50. Cumulative output since petroleum production began in 1971 amounts to 2.05 bn scm oe, or about 16 per cent of total expected recoverable reserves. At present rates of production, Norway's remaining discovered oil resources will last for about 14 years. The equivalent figure for gas is roughly 80 years.[1] This means that Norway will gradually develop from being mainly an oil producer in the last century to mainly a gas producer in this century.

11.03 Overall production in 1996 totalled roughly 222.1 million scm oe. Oil accounted for 175.5 m scm oe, gas for 37.4 m scm oe, and NGLs (Natural Gas Liquids) for 9.2 million scm oe. This ranks Norway as the sixth largest oil producer in the world.[2] Oil production was expected to increase slightly up to the year 2000 and then to slowly decline during the next decade, while gas production is due to double (based on sales contracts already entered into).[3]

11.04 Norway's consumption of oil represents about 200,000 barrels a day. The net export of crude oil is about 3 million barrels a day. This ranks Norway second on the list of the world's largest net exporters, after Saudi Arabia.[4] As far as gas is concerned, only negligible amounts are consumed in the domestic market. Instead, gas is exported to the European markets. At present Norway covers about 10 per cent of the total natural gas consumption in Western Europe. This ranks Norway among the world's top ten gas exporters.[5]

11.05 Gas is transported in offshore pipelines to the European markets. Six transportation systems are in operation, while four are under planning or construction.[6] The links between the transportation systems are also developing, thus forming an infrastructure of pipelines to the European continent.

11.06 Oil is mainly transported by ship to the markets. However, there are five oil or condensate pipelines in operation on the Norwegian continental shelf.[7]

[1] Fact Sheet 97, 9 and 23.
[2] ibid, 26 and 30.
[3] ibid, 26–8.
[4] ibid, 30.
[5] ibid, 34–5.
[6] ibid, 100–7.
[7] ibid, 100–7.

Summing up, Norway can best be characterized as a typical producer country. As a result the regulation and the organization of the Norwegian petroleum activities are basically designed to promote Norway's interests as a producer country. The Norwegian regulation and organization is producer (or upstream) oriented. This makes the system different from the systems in most EU countries which are consumer (or downstream) oriented. **11.07**

Electricity production and consumption

Electricity production in Norway is over 99 per cent hydro based. Norway is ranked sixth among the leading hydroelectricity producing countries in the world with a production in 1998 of 117 TWh. The real annual production often differs from the developed yearly middle production of 113,7 TWh (1998) due to changes in precipitation. As an illustration, the real annual production can differ by +/– 20 TWh from the developed yearly middle production. The total installed capacity of the Norwegian electricity system is about 27,700 MW. **11.08**

The hydroelectricity potential is estimated to about 178 TWh, including both completed developments and undeveloped rivers. The Norwegian Parliament has adopted four Protection Plans for Water Resources. 35 TWh is protected from hydroelectricity developments as a result of these protection plans. **11.09**

Conditions in Norway are favourable for the use of other renewables such as bioenergy and wind power. The production of bioenergy was about 12 TWh in 1997. Estimates show that bioenergy production can be increased considerably in the years to come. The installed capacity of wind power in 1997 was about 3.9 MW. Building of new capacity has been licensed, and several plans are now under evaluation for possible implementation later on. **11.10**

The total energy consumption in Norway in 1997 amounted to about 229 TWh. This is an increase of 6.5 per cent or 14 TWh compared to 1996. Electricity represented 47.9 per cent of net consumption, petroleum products 35.9 per cent, and bioenergy about 6 per cent. **11.11**

The consumption of electricity has shown a rapid growth in the past few years caused by a higher activity level in the Norwegian economy. The consumption in 1998 was 120,6 TWh. **11.12**

Due to the variation of precipitation from year to year, the Norwegian hydro-based electricity system is dependent on the opportunity to import and export electricity over the years. The net import in 1998 amounted to 3,6 TWh mainly from Sweden and Denmark. **11.13**

The total transmission capacity between Norway and neighbouring countries is about 3 500 MW. If utilised fully, this capacity allows about 20 TWh per year to be transported between Norway and the other Nordic countries. **11.14**

(2) Levels of Government

11.15 Norway has three levels of government: the central, regional, and local levels. On the central level the highest legislative and financial powers rest with Parliament and the highest judicial power with the Supreme Court, cf the Constitution of 17 May 1814. According to the Constitution the highest executive power formally rests with the King. According to constitutional practice, however, real executive power rests with the Cabinet. The Cabinet oversees a State hierarchy, which on the central level mainly consists of the ministries and the directorates.[8] In principle, each entity within this hierarchy can be instructed by superior entities; they are not independent State organs. In practice, directorates are established to execute the more detailed state powers within defined sectors, and they are not likely to receive more than general instructions.

11.16 As to the lower levels of government, limited legislative, executive, and financial powers have been allocated to regional and local municipalities pursuant to acts passed by Parliament. Internally, the municipalities are organized along the same principles of hierarchy as the State. Externally, they cannot be formally instructed by State organs. However, regulations passed by the municipalities must normally be presented to State organs for approval. Norway is organized as a unitary (as opposed to a federal) State.

11.17 In the Norwegian energy sector the relevant legislative and executive powers rest predominantly with the State. The Norwegian petroleum activities refer to offshore petroleum deposits, and thus a major part of the activities take place beyond the jurisdiction of the municipalities. The electricity sector is also heavily influenced by State regulation and control. However, when it comes to development of energy infrastructure on land, the municipalities execute important powers pursuant to the legislation which safeguards area planning. The Planning and Building Act constitutes the most important legislation in these respects.[9]

B. The Petroleum Sector

(1) Introduction

11.18 Exploration and production of oil and gas is governed by the Petroleum Act, hereafter called the PA. The intention of the PA is to regulate all important aspects of the petroleum activities on the Norwegian continental shelf. The regulatory emphasis of the PA is on the relationship between the authorities and the licensees. In addition, two other relationships have to be mentioned. First, the PA regulates

[8] Some State functions are also exercised on the regional and local levels of government, but we will not go into these.

[9] Act no 77 of 14 June 1985.

important aspects of the relationship between the licensee and third parties in the form of four liability regimes specially adapted to the petroleum activities. The second is the relationship between licensees and suppliers of goods and services. This relationship, however, is not regulated by the PA. The main rule in Norway—as in most other countries—is that of freedom of contract. Nevertheless, a characteristic feature of the contracting on the Norwegian continental shelf is the significant element of standard contracts and 'agreed documents'. The regulations on the bilateral level are presented as well, especially considering the so far unsuccessful striving in other jurisdictions to develop a similar concept of agreed documents.

(2) Legal and Regulatory Framework

Historic development

Norway proclaimed sovereignty over the Norwegian continental shelf regarding exploration for and exploitation of sub-sea natural resources by Royal Decree of 31 May 1963. Agreements to divide the continental shelf according to the median line principle were concluded between Norway and the UK in March 1965 and between Norway and Denmark in December of the same year.[10] So far no agreement has been reached with Russia concerning the division of the continental shelf in the Barents Sea. **11.19**

The internal legislation started with the 1963 Act.[11] The 1963 Act contained three basic principles. First, the right to submarine natural resources is vested in the State. Secondly, the King may give Norwegian or foreign persons, including legal persons, the right to explore for or exploit natural resources. Finally, the King may issue regulations concerning such activities. **11.20**

An act containing the same basic principles has been adopted concerning petroleum in the subsoil of Norwegian territory and the part of the sea bed subject to private property rights.[12] So far this act has not been of any practical significance. **11.21**

In principle, the State could have performed the petroleum activities itself in its capacity as resource owner. The alternative was to let companies perform the activities through a licence system.[13] The latter alternative was chosen, and in subsequent decrees issued pursuant to the 1963 Act a licence system was developed. **11.22**

[10] The agreement between Norway and the UK was signed in London 10 March 1965, cf St prp No 91 (1964–65). The agreement between Norway and Denmark was signed in Oslo 8 December 1965, cf St prp No 68 (1965–66).

[11] Act No 12 of 21 June 1963 relating to exploration for and exploitation of submarine natural resources. The 1963 Act is still in force: it now regulates scientific research of the seabed, and exploration for and exploitation of *other* subsea natural resources than petroleum resources.

[12] Act No 21 of 4 May 1973.

[13] The State could also have chosen an entrepreneur system or a production sharing system, but such alternatives have so far not been practised on the Norwegian continental shelf.

However, a very characteristic feature of the legal framework is the strong State participation in the activities.[14]

11.23 The starting point for the development of the licence system was the 1965 Decree, passed pursuant to the 1963 Act, section 3, in connection with the first licence round.[15] Large discoveries of oil and gas were made in 1969 (Ekofisk), which gave the Norwegian Government the incentive to stipulate tougher licence terms under the subsequent 1972 Decree.[16] Under this decree production licences were awarded which led to the discovery of several giant fields during the 1970s and the beginning of the 1980s (Statfjord, Gullfaks, Oseberg, and Troll). Eventually, a Petroleum Act was passed by the Norwegian Parliament in 1985.[17] The 1985 Act represented a continuation of the licence system and a codification of Government practice under this system. However, the purpose of the 1985 Act was also to regulate other important aspects of the petroleum activities, and in this context it introduced some novel features, among them a separate chapter on the licensee's liability for petroleum pollution damage. In 1989 a new chapter was included in the 1985 Act on compensation rules with regard to the losses Norwegian fishermen suffer as a result of the petroleum activities.[18]

11.24 The 1985 Act was replaced by a new Petroleum Act in 1996, the PA.[19] The PA introduces more flexible rules concerning, *inter alia*, the duration and geographical scope of production licences. The flexible approach is a result of the expansion of the petroleum activities to new areas, especially in the Norwegian Sea. In these areas the industry will meet larger water depths and longer distances to existing infrastructure. The PA opens more benevolent licence terms in such cases. The PA also introduces a more detailed regulation of the abandonment phase, which by the beginning of the 1990s had become an important subject in view of the shutdown of the first Norwegian petroleum fields. Apart from this, the PA basically represents a prolongation of the 1985 Act.

11.25 It should also be mentioned that several regulations were adopted pursuant to the 1985 Act, which regulated the petroleum activities in more detail. The most important ones were the petroleum regulations, adopted by Royal Decree of 14 June 1985, and the safety regulations, adopted by Royal Decree of 28 June 1985. These have now been replaced by new regulations, adopted by Royal Decrees of 27 June 1997 pursuant to the PA.

[14] See paras 11.39–11.55 below.

[15] Royal Decree of 9 April 1965 relating to exploration for and exploitation of petroleum.

[16] Royal Decree of 8 December 1972 relating to exploration for and exploitation of petroleum.

[17] Act No 11 of 22 March 1985 relating to petroleum activities.

[18] Amendment Act of 9 June 1989.

[19] Act No 72 of 29 November 1996. The preceding Government white papers are Ot prp No 43 (1995–96) and Innst O No 7 (1996–97).

Although the PA intends to regulate all important aspects of the petroleum activities, it does not preclude the application of other Norwegian laws.[20] The most important ones are the Petroleum Taxation Act, the Working Environment Act, and the Pollution Act.[21] We will on certain occasions refer back to this legislation. 11.26

Resource management

The PA establishes a framework for State management of the petroleum resources. The resource management is characterized by central planning and control. Thus, PA section 1-2 first paragraph declares that the resource management is exercised by the King pursuant to the provisions of the Act and decisions of the Norwegian Parliament.[22] The policy objectives of resource management are stated in section 1-2 second paragraph. 11.27

The Norwegian State is the owner of the sub-sea petroleum deposits. Petroleum is a limited and non-renewable resource with large revenue potential. Consequently, the main policy objective, as stated in the PA section 1-2 second paragraph, is long-term management of petroleum resources for the benefit of Norwegian society as a whole. This policy perspective is wide both as to the time-frame and as to the range of considerations. The main considerations include State revenues, public welfare and employment, Norwegian industry and industrial development, and the environment. They reflect the revenue potential and the various interests that are influenced by the petroleum activities. The basic concern of the resource management, however, is to produce as much of the petroleum in place as possible at as little cost as possible. This efficiency requirement is stated in PA section 4-1. Another important consideration is the safety aspect of the activities, which is reflected in PA sections 9-1 and 10-1. 11.28

The wide range of policy considerations has led to a high degree of Government intervention in petroleum activities. This intervention rests upon two main pillars. First, all phases of the activities are subject to direct Government control through a licence system. This means that no major activity can take place without a prior licence or approval. Licences and approvals are subject to terms for detailed—but also flexible—regulation of each licensee's activities. Thus, the general framework of the PA and the regulations passed pursuant to it is supplemented by an individual framework in the form of licence terms. 11.29

Secondly, the State regulates indirectly by organizing the activities. This organization consists of three major components: State-organized licence groups, 11.30

[20] cf PA s 1-5.

[21] Act No 35 of 13 June 1975 relating to taxation of sub-sea petroleum deposits. Act No 4 of 4 February 1977 relating to worker protection and working environment etc. Act No 6 of 13 March 1981 relating to protection against pollution and waste.

[22] In this context the term 'King' means the Norwegian Cabinet: see Introduction above.

strong State participation within the licence groups, and State organization of gas sales.

The licence system

11.31 The licence system consists in the first place of the exploration licence, the production licence, and the pipeline licence. These are the formal components of the system introduced in the 1965 and 1972 Decrees. Each licence covers separate phases of the activities. Secondly, one includes the approval of the development plan, since this approval and its connected terms in all important respects form the basis for the licensee's development of a petroleum deposit. The development plan was formally introduced in the 1985 Act, but in this regard the Act only represented a codification of Government practice. In addition the PA has recently introduced the abandonment plan and the subsequent decision by the Ministry, which have a similar function (as the approval of the development plan) in the abandonment phase.

11.32 The exploration licence is regulated by PA chapter 2. The licence is given for a limited area and for a limited period. It gives the licensee a right, but not an exclusive right, to conduct various kinds of surveys of the sea bed in order to identify the potential for possible petroleum deposits.[23] The licensee has no right to drill for petroleum, and he has no right to obtain future production licences.

11.33 The production licence is the main licence of the system, and is regulated by PA chapter 3. It gives the licensee an exclusive right to exploration, exploration drilling, and production of petroleum within a limited area and for a limited period. The licensee also becomes the owner of the petroleum when it is produced, meaning that the ownership is automatically transferred from the State to the licensee as the petroleum passes the well-head. Production licences are issued in licence rounds.[24] There has been a continuous development of licence terms from round to round, but within each round the terms are basically standard. Consequently, the regulation of the licensees' activities varies depending upon when they received their respective licences. Some standard terms have, however, been practised more or less from the beginning. These include the obligations to pay an area fee, to perform an obligatory work programme, and to enter into a joint operating agreement with the other holders of the production licence.

11.34 Although the licensee is granted certain rights within the scope of the production licence, his subsequent activities are subject to Government regulation and control. Petroleum deposits cannot be developed unless a development plan has been approved by the Ministry pursuant to PA section 4-2. The petroleum regulations

[23] The licence authorizes geological, geophysical, geochemical, and geotechnical surveys.
[24] By end 2000 there had been 16 licence rounds.

contain extensive requirements as to the contents of the plan. This makes it possible for the Government to control all important aspects of the development, including efficient recovery of the petroleum in place, the tie-in of the development to existing or future infrastructure, safety and environmental aspects, and so forth. In fact, all the various considerations under the resource management have to be taken into account at this stage, because a substantial degree of regulatory flexibility will be lost once the licensee has made his investments.[25] The subsequent Government control refers to more detailed aspects within the general framework of the approved development, the rate of production, and the fabrication, installation, and operation of individual installations. A production licence does not give the licensee the right to build and operate a pipeline for the transportation of his petroleum to the market. This activity requires a separate pipeline licence pursuant to PA section 4-3. Because of the large investments connected to the development of an infrastructure, economic efficiency normally requires that pipelines are constructed to transport petroleum from several fields. Practice in recent years has been to award the pipeline licence to all the field owners transporting petroleum through the pipeline, which means that the ownership structure of the pipeline more or less corresponds to the ownership structure of the co-mingled stream of petroleum. The purpose of the arrangement is to give the owners of the pipeline (the transporters) an incentive to charge low transportation tariffs to the owners of the petroleum (the shippers); in other words a self-regulating mechanism.[26]

Although a production licence does not give the licensee a right to obtain a **11.35** pipeline licence, it is generally understood that the licensee must have a real opportunity to ship produced petroleum to the market—by means of vessels or pipelines—at a reasonable cost. For this reason the PA and the regulations contain several provisions which authorize Government control of transportation capacity and tariffs.[27]

The final element in the licence system is the abandonment plan and the **11.36** Ministry's subsequent decision, both of which are regulated by PA chapter 5. Prior to the expiration of a production licence or a pipeline licence, or the end of use of a fixed installation operated under such licences, the licensee is required to submit an abandonment plan to the Ministry. On the basis of the abandonment plan the Ministry may choose between several decisions, with alternatives ranging from complete or partial removal to continued use for petroleum or other purposes.

[25] Investments on the Norwegian continental shelf tend to be very high due to large water depths and tough weather conditions. As to gas developments there are additional high costs connected to the development of an infrastructure of pipelines. The transportation distances from the fields to the market are becoming larger as new petroleum provinces are developed in the Norwegian Sea.

[26] The principles of this self-regulating mechanism are discussed in St meld No 46 (1986–87) 67–9.

[27] cf PA s 4-8.

11.37 The licence system basically refers to the building and operation of the installations used in petroleum activities. However, various agreements which licensees enter into with each other or with other contract parties, are also subject to Government approval pursuant to the PA or to the terms of the respective licences (including the development plan). Especially important are the unitization agreements, (PA section 4-7), the transportation and processing agreements, (PA section 4-8), and last but not least, the gas sales agreements. These approvals have become increasingly important as Norway develops into a large gas producer with connected infrastructure to the European markets. As regulatory tools these approvals naturally belong to the licence system.

Organization of petroleum activities

11.38 This organization consists of three major components: State-organized licence groups, State participation in the groups, and State organization of gas sales. In these respects the Norwegian legal framework has developed characteristic features which clearly distinguish it from other upstream-oriented frameworks. The following concentrates on these features.

State-organized licence groups

11.39 With a few exceptions in the first and second licence rounds, petroleum production licences have always been granted to groups of companies. From the third licence round, starting in 1974, these groups have been organized by the Government on the basis of individual applications from the companies. In this context the Government has also appointed an operator for each licence group, who is responsible for the practical management of licence activities on behalf of the group.

11.40 Formally, a production licence is granted to each individual company of the group. One of the standard licence terms requires the company to enter into a joint operating agreement with the other companies (of the group). From the third licence round these agreements have been made by the Ministry. The contents of the joint operating agreements has developed from licence round to licence round, but within each round the terms are basically standard. New agreements are not subject to negotiations between the Ministry and the companies, but if important changes are planned from earlier agreements, companies are invited to express their views at a hearing. In this regard the joint operating agreements are treated in the same way as the other licence terms.[28]

11.41 As to existing agreements the Ministry is in a much less flexible position. These agreements were entered into by the licensees as normally binding contracts, which means that the contracts cannot be unilaterally amended by the Ministry.

[28] See paras 11.31–11.37 above.

The licensees can of course accept amendments proposed by the Ministry, but they will normally not do so unless they benefit from such amendments. On the other hand, licensees can initiate amendments themselves, provided that there is unanimous agreement in the licence group and that they obtain the Ministry's subsequent approval. Irrespective of where the amendment initiative comes from, the joint operating agreement is not a flexible regulatory instrument.

11.42 Pipeline licences are also granted to a group of companies. In these cases, however, the companies negotiate a joint operating agreement which is subject to the Ministry's approval. There has been a general understanding that these agreements should reflect the same principles as the joint operating agreements for the production licences. Thus, even though the Ministry's involvement is less with regard to these agreements, their content has become fairly standard.

State participation in the licence groups

11.43 From the outset, the system of State-organized licence groups has been closely connected with comprehensive State participation in the groups. The Norwegian State oil company, Statoil, was established in 1972.[29] The purposes were (1) to increase State revenues; (2) to increase State influence in the activities; and (3) to increase know-how compared to what could have been achieved through the normal licence and tax systems.[30] In short, Statoil was meant to be a vehicle of the Norwegian State. Consequently, Statoil was granted a 50 per cent participating interest in all licence groups from the third licence round. The joint operating agreements contained several privileges for Statoil, including a carried interest during the exploration phase and an option to increase its participating interest if a petroleum deposit was found. In addition, the agreements contained voting rules which gave Statoil a dominant position in the decision-making process.

11.44 With effect from 1 January 1985, however, Statoil was reorganized.[31] A financial arrangement was established between Statoil and the State whereby Statoil's participating interest was split into a Statoil economic share and a State economic share, called the State Direct Financial Interest (SDFI). According to this arrangement a share of the costs accrued and a corresponding share of the revenues generated in the licence groups was directly channelled to the State. The financial privileges concerning carried interest and optional increase of participating interest should only be exercised in favour of the SDFI. Since this was only a financial arrangement between Statoil and the State, Statoil managed the SDFI in the licence groups on behalf of the State. The State itself had no formal position *vis-à-vis* the other licensees in the groups. However, as a consequence of the reorganization Statoil's dominant position in the licence groups was considerably reduced

[29] Following a decision of the Norwegian Parliament of 2 June 1972.
[30] cf St prp No 113 (1971–72) 8.
[31] Based on St meld No 73 (1983–84) and Innst S No 321 (1983–84).

through a change of the voting rules in the joint operating agreements. The latter change was given effect for all licences.[32]

11.45 Since its establishment, the financial privileges of Statoil/SDFI have gradually been reduced. By 1991 the carried interest provisions had been repealed, with effect for all production licences. In the fourteenth licence round the optional increase of Statoil's participating interest was repealed, but only with effect for licences granted in this round and onwards.[33] From the fifteenth licence round Statoil was not granted an interest in all licences. This is a consequence of Norway's implementation of the Hydrocarbons Licensing Directive.[34] According to the Directive Statoil must be treated as a normal commercial entity, which excludes any form of privilege in its favour. On the other hand, the Directive does not exclude or limit direct participation by the State. Participation can be managed by the State itself, or through a legal person (Directive Article 6). In the fifteenth licence round the latter alternative was chosen. Statoil manages the SDFI on behalf of the State, even in those licences where Statoil as a company has no participating interest. The SDFI—for its part—is represented in almost all licences.[35] This means that the SDFI is basically handled as before.

11.46 Summing up, the changes since 1985 mean that State participation has less significance than before as an instrument for State influence on the activities or as a means to acquire know-how, but it is still a very important financial instrument. As such it forms part of the 'total government take' together with taxes, royalties, and fees.

State organization of gas sales

11.47 The organization of Norwegian gas sales has developed through four phases. In the first phase gas was sold from fields where the production licence had been granted in the first and second licence rounds. The joint operating agreements under these licences were negotiated by the licensees themselves, and as a result the gas sales negotiations were conducted by the group under the leadership of the operator, who happened to be a foreign oil company.

11.48 In the second phase Statoil took a leading role in the gas sales negotiations as a result of its initial 50 per cent share in all new production licences. In the fourth licence round (1979) Statoil's leading role was formalized in the State-made joint

[32] This required the amendment of existing joint operating agreements, but the licensees accepted because the change of voting rules was for their benefit.

[33] cf St meld No 26 (1993–94) 20.

[34] Council Directive 94/22/EC on the conditions for granting and using authorizations for the prospecting, exploration, and production of hydrocarbons.

[35] In the 15th licence round the SDFI is represented in 16 out of 18 awarded licences, cf Fact Sheet 97, 14.

operating agreement. However, Statoil's leadership did not exclude the other licensees from taking part in the negotiations.

The third phase started with the ninth licence round (1985), just after the reorganization of Statoil. The new joint operating agreements introduced a gas negotiating committee for each licence consisting of Statoil and—to the extent that they had been awarded licences—the other two Norwegian companies, Norsk Hydro and Saga. The effect of this arrangement was the exclusion of foreign oil companies from the gas sales negotiations. This arrangement continued up to the fifteenth licence round. However, by that time the co-ordination of gas sales within the framework of the individual licence group had lost most of its significance.[36] **11.49**

The fourth phase started in 1987 with the establishment of a national gas negotiating committee (GFU) consisting of the three Norwegian companies, and under the leadership of Statoil. In contrast with previous gas sales arrangements this one is not related to individual gas fields. It relates to all gas resources on the Norwegian continental shelf. Consequently, the arrangement itself is not regulated in the individual licences and joint operating agreements. It is based on political guidelines adopted by Parliament in 1987, and subsequent guidelines.[37] **11.50**

According to these guidelines GFU negotiates supply contracts with foreign buyers.[38] The contracts are signed by the GFU companies as sellers. At this stage the contracts are not related to any specific field. After signature the contracts are subject to the Ministry's approval. In the next stage the Ministry allocates contract volumes between producing fields. In this context the Ministry receives advice from a special supply committee (FU) consisting of all the major gas producers, including the foreign oil companies.[39] After the allocation of contract volumes, the GFU companies transfer their contractual positions to the licensees of the producing field(s). Thus, in their capacity as GFU companies, Statoil, Norsk Hydro, and Saga operate like sales agents for the producing fields.[40] **11.51**

If certain fields are clear candidates for allocation of contract volumes already at the negotiating stage of the process, the GFU companies have in some instances invited the licensees of these fields to participate in the sales negotiations. Provided that the Ministry is notified, such participation is in accordance with the political guidelines.[41] **11.52**

---

[36] However, it should be borne in mind that the old arrangements still formally exist since they are regulated by joint operating agreements that cannot be unilaterally changed.

[37] cf St meld No 46 (1986–87) 58–65.

[38] The continental buyers are organized in a similar fashion during negotiations as the GFU.

[39] The FU was established in 1993.

[40] In addition they maintain their positions as individual licensees, and thus producers.

[41] cf St meld No 2 (1992–93) 104.

11.53 Formally, the relationship between the GFU companies is regulated by an agreement approved by the Ministry. As to the licensees of the producing fields, they are under a licence obligation to follow the political guidelines.[42]

11.54 Summing up, the organization of gas sales is characterized by an increasing element of national co-ordination. Simultaneously, the arrangement has become more or less disconnected from the licence system and the joint operating agreements.

11.55 The EC Gas Directive (Directive 96/92/EC of 22 June 1998 concerning common rules for the internal market in gas) introduces the principle of third-party access to the grid system, including upstream transmission pipelines on the Continental Shelf. In addition the European Commission has started an investigation of the Norwegian organization of gas sales through the GFU for possible violation of the EC competition rules. For the time being the Directive has not been implemented in Norway and the Commission investigation has not been concluded, but combined these developments may significantly alter the current organization of Norwegian gas sales.

Government institutions

11.56 The central governing function rests with the Ministry of Petroleum and Energy (MPE) which was established in 1978.[43] This means that the MPE has the overall responsibility for the resource management, unless otherwise decided.[44] The MPE does the preparatory work prior to the King's granting of production licences. The other major licences, approvals, consents, and decisions pursuant to the licence system are issued by the MPE. The central governing function implies that the MPE in the course of its work co-ordinates the input from several other ministries, government agencies, regional and local authorities, and various interest groups concerned, eg environmental interest groups. Of special importance is the input from the Ministry of Local Government and Regional Development, which has overall responsibility for the working environment, emergency preparedness, and safety aspects of petroleum activities.

11.57 Day-to-day control, including the more detailed approvals and consents, has been delegated to the Norwegian Petroleum Directorate (NPD), which is located in Stavanger.[45] Administratively, the NPD is subordinate to the MPE. As regards the working environment, emergency preparedness, and safety it is subordinate to the

[42] Formally, this obligation was introduced as a licence term and as a term in the joint operating agreement in the 15th licence round.

[43] Previously, petroleum matters were dealt with by a section within the Ministry of Industry and Handicraft.

[44] Resource management is dealt with in paras 11.27–11.30 above.

[45] The establishment of the NPD is based on Parliament's decision of 2 June 1972.

Ministry of Local Government and Regional Development. In the course of its work the NPD co-ordinates input from other Government agencies. Thus, at this lower level of government the NPD has a central governing function similar to that of the MPE (at the higher level).

The Norwegian model

Summing up, the Norwegian legal framework with regard to petroleum activities is based on the State's ownership of the sub-sea petroleum resources, and the general policy objective that this national resource shall be developed for the benefit of society as a whole. Since Norway is a large exporter of petroleum, the national economic interest leads to an optimization of the revenue potential from a producer's point of view. **11.58**

Although the State has chosen not to perform petroleum activities itself in its capacity as resource owner, the main characteristic features of the legal framework must be seen in the context of the State ownership. These characteristic features are the State-organized licence groups, the comprehensive State participation within the groups, the organization of gas sales, and the licence system whereby all phases and aspects of the activities are subject to State control. All these regulatory elements are characterized by strong central co-ordination by the resource owner represented by the MPE. Norway's development from mainly an oil producer to mainly a gas producer has not changed this. On the contrary, this development has led to even stronger central co-ordination than before through the national policy guidelines for gas sales and the GFU. **11.59**

Since Norway became a member of the European Economic Area (EEA), a new legal dimension has been added to the national regulation. So far this dimension has not led to any significant changes in the Norwegian model of central co-ordination. However, this may soon change as regards the organization of gas sales. **11.60**

(3) The Relationship Between the Authorities and the Licensees

Introduction

From the point of view of the authorities, five issues within the oil and gas sector require attention. There are of course no Chinese walls between these issues, and each may be split into several categories. The division does however offer a suitable angle for the discussions in this section. **11.61**

First, as the right to offshore oil and gas deposits is vested in the State, it is left to domestic law to proclaim sovereignty over the deposits and eventually to determine on what criteria others, if any, shall be given access to the deposits and activities related to extraction of oil and gas. The Norwegian regulation of this issue is addressed in paragraphs 11.68–11.75 below. **11.62**

11.63 Secondly, the performance of the activities has to be regulated. The main themes in this connection are those relating to development and operation of the oil and gas deposits, and to safety issues. These are dealt with in paragraphs 11.76–11.106 below. Two related themes will not be addressed in this section: procurement and removal.[46]

11.64 As oil and gas are vital commodities, a third issue is the marketing of produced oil and gas. Oil may be transported to the market by ships or pipelines, while marketing natural gas requires pipelines. The regulation of this issue is assessed in paragraphs 11.87–11.111 below.

11.65 A fourth issue is the allocation between the State and the oil companies of profits and/or losses accruing from the extraction of oil and gas. This allocation is done through rules on taxes and royalties.[47] These rules are complex, but a general assessment of them appears in paragraphs 11.112–11.121 below.[48]

11.66 Finally, a fifth issue is the behaviour of the actors in the market place. Key in this context are the rules on competition. However, this issue is not addressed in this chapter.[49]

11.67 The authorities' discretion as to how these issues are regulated is limited both by Norwegian law and by Norway being party to the EEA Agreement.[50] The limits following from the EEA Agreement, the most important being those that follow from the provisions on the four freedoms in general and Directives 93/38/EEC and 94/22/EC in particular, are addressed only in brief terms,[51] as the aim of this chapter is to give an overall assessment of the relationship between the authorities and the licensees, according to the specific Norwegian regime, in which the requirements of the EEA Agreement are implemented.[52]

---

[46] Removal is discussed by Ulf Hammer in section B6, below. With regard to procurement, it is sufficient to mention that the Norwegian regime complies with the requirements of EEC Council Directive 93/38.

[47] To the extent that there are losses, one could imagine State aid to (some of) the private actors. As this is not an issue in Norwegian petroleum politics, it is not addressed in the following. In this context it is sufficient to point out that if such aid is given, it will have to comply with the requirements of Arts 61 *et seq* EEA, which resemble Arts 92 *et seq* EC.

[48] The tax regime is based both on Act no 8 of 18 August 1911 relating to General Taxation and on Act no 35 of 13 June 1975 relating to Petroleum Taxation (PTA).

[49] The competition rules in question are mainly those stipulated in EC and EEA law, ie Arts 81 *et seq* EC and Arts 53 *et seq* EEA.

[50] The EEA Agreement makes Iceland, Liechtenstein, and Norway subject to substantive rules similar to those that follow from membership of the European Union as regards the four freedoms and competition.

[51] For an analysis, see ch 5 above.

[52] The EEA and EC law-related issues are horizontal in the sense that they are relevant to all the national regimes discussed in this book, and therefore analyzed separately in chapter 5.

Access to the activities

Oil and gas exploration and exploitation on the Norwegian continental shelf is organized through a licensing system, which has its legal basis in the Petroleum Act. The key licence, which gives access to the activities, is the production licence. The production licence is given pursuant to PA section 3-3, and in accordance with the procedural provisions set out in PA section 3-5.[53] Although a licence may be given to both natural and legal persons, and such persons are free to apply for licences together,[54] preference will normally be given to applications coming from a single legal or natural person.[55] For all practical purposes, this precludes applications by natural persons. **11.68**

The awarding process is mainly regulated by chapter three of the Petroleum Act. A prerequisite for the process to be initiated is that the relevant geographical area is nominated for granting of production licences (PA section 3-1). According to PA section 3-5, the Ministry shall announce the area for which applications for production licences may be submitted.[56] The announcement will be made both in the Norwegian Official Gazette (*Norsk Lysingsblad*) and in the Official Journal of the European Communities. Production licences are normally awarded in rounds, where several areas are put up for applications.[57] **11.69**

The main criteria for awarding licences must be set out in the invitation for applications, and according to PA section 3-5 third paragraph, they have to be 'relevant and objective'. What this actually means has to be decided in accordance with PA section 1-2 second paragraph and Directive 94/22, Article 5. Hence the award will be subject to an overall appraisal of the technical and financial capability of the applicants, the way in which they intend to prospect, explore, and/or bring into production the acreage covered by the licence, lack of efficiency or responsibility displayed by the applicants under previous production licences, and, where applicants are found to have equal merit, other relevant objective non-discriminatory criteria. **11.70**

However, there is an element of negotiating between the applicants and the authorities. Through this the authorities seek to ensure that the guidelines expressed in PA section 1-2,[58] as construed in the light of Directive 94/22, are implemented. **11.71**

---

[53] PA s 3-5 also reflects the procedural requirements of Directive 94/22/EC Arts 3 *et seq.*

[54] cf PA s 3-4, which presupposes group applications.

[55] If this is done, it has to be announced in the invitation for applications: EC Directive 94/22, Art 3, no 2.

[56] Production licences may also be granted without such an announcement.

[57] Licences are sometimes awarded outside rounds.

[58] The main message in PA ss 1–2 reads: 'The petroleum deposits shall be administered in a long-term perspective, for the benefit of the Norwegian society as a whole' (author's translation).

11.72 The production licence is normally assigned to a group of three to four participants, put together by the authorities. There will also usually be participation by the State.[59] This participation may, as has already been described, take two forms: indirectly through the State-owned oil company Statoil, and/or directly, referred to as SDFI.[60] However, direct participation is channelled through Statoil. Statoil competes, on equal terms, with other companies for shares in the production licences.[61] Hence the channelling of the SDFI through Statoil has as the consequence that Statoil may not have an economic interest in the licence corresponding to its share in the licence.[62] In these cases Statoil acts as a manager for the SDFI in addition to being a licensee in its own capacity. The allocation of Statoil's share in the licence between Statoil and SDFI is, as regards production licences granted after 1 September 1995, expressed in the licence itself.[63]

11.73 The State also holds a substantial part of the shares in one of the other major participants in the Norwegian oil and gas activities, Norsk Hydro. There are no known examples of the State exercising its influence over Norsk Hydro. Even though this share is less than 51 per cent, it can still be held that the company is a public undertaking in the sense of Article 59 EEA,[64] and a 'public entity' in the sense of EC Directive 94/22. This gives rise to certain problems, to which we will return in section C3 below, where the question of whether the group holding a production licence is to be considered a public undertaking in the sense of Article 59 EEA and/or Directive 93/38 is discussed.

11.74 The granting of licences is made subject to the acceptance of conditions. In this context it is sufficient to mention the work programme.[65] The completion of this entitles the licensees to an extension of the production licence for a period up to fifty years, the norm being thirty years,[66] after the expiry of the initial maximum of ten years.[67] This right to an extension, however, does not cover the whole area under the licence. According to PA section 3-9 third paragraph, the licensees will, as a general rule, have to hand back half the acreage. The size of the acreage for which an extension may be demanded is stipulated upon the award of the production licence.

---

59 See PA s 3-6.

60 The State's direct financial interest, cf Introduction, see paras 11.44–11.45 above.

61 cf Directive 94/22/EC Art 5.

62 An example is Production licence 212, where Statoil holds a 30% share. Here SDFI is also 30%, and Statoil therefore has no interest in the licence other than as a manager of SFDI.

63 For an overview of State participation in the licences granted, see Fact Sheet 97 ch 18.

64 This provision resembles Art 86 EC.

65 PA s 3-8.

66 PA s 3-9 second paragraph. See also fifth paragraph, where the ministry is given the power to grant a second extension.

67 PA s 3-9 first paragraph.

Although the production licence gives exclusive rights to exploration, drilling, and production within a specific geographical area, and although the holders become owners of the oil and gas produced,[68] they are not free to decide how the oil and gas shall be extracted and disposed of. The production licence gives access to the activities, but the performance of these activities is subject to further permissions, consents, authorizations, etc by the authorities. Hence, the production licence may be characterized as the entrance, or key, to the activities. **11.75**

Performance of the activities

General

From the licensees' point of view it is preferable that as much oil and gas as possible is produced from the deposits covered by their licence at as low a cost as possible. According to PA section 1-2, the oil and gas resources shall be administered with a long-term perspective, for the benefit of the Norwegian society as a whole. Commercial and socio-economic considerations may indicate the same solution to a given problem, but not necessarily. Deciding on the size of the installations is an example. Commercial considerations dictate that the installations are designed according to the characteristics of the deposit to be produced, ie to the needs of the licensees. Socio-economic considerations, however, may require that the installations be big enough to handle oil and gas coming from deposits covered by other licences as well. **11.76**

Another example is depletion. Here commercial considerations may dictate rapid extraction of large quantities of oil and/or gas, thus leaving more oil and/or gas in the deposit than if a lower depletion rate had been applied. Socio-economic considerations may call for a lower depletion rate, allowing for a larger total quantity to be produced from the deposit. **11.77**

Offshore oil and gas activities involve great risks not only to personnel and equipment but also to the environment. Thus, environmental aspects are a constant element in the considerations of both the authorities and the licensees. Both the licensees and the authorities will seek to reduce the environmental risks, but again commercial considerations may imply other measures and different assessments than socio-related considerations. **11.78**

Even though applying socio-economic considerations may lead to other solutions than commercial considerations, this does not imply that commercial aspects are not taken into account by the authorities. The decision to exploit the oil and gas resources through a licensing system where other entities than the State are invited to participate presupposes the possibility of profit for those engaged in the activities. This has an impact on the regulation of the activities. The balancing of **11.79**

[68] PA s 3-3.

socio-economic and commercial considerations in the licensing system, and the tools given by the licensing system for implementing these considerations, are discussed below.

Development and operation of a deposit

11.80 If the licensees want to develop a deposit, they have to submit to the MPE for approval a detailed plan for the development and operation of the deposit,[69] referred to below as a PDO. The ministerially approved PDO will reflect a blend of commercial and socio-economic (and amongst these environmental) considerations.

11.81 According to PA section 4-6, the MPE may, when warranted by substantive socio-related considerations, require that production be prepared, commenced, continued, or intensified. Thus it is not left entirely in the hands of the licensees to decide whether, or at what moment, a deposit is developed.

11.82 When developing a deposit, there will usually be a need for facilities for the handling, transportation (pipelines) etc of the oil and gas produced. The instalment and operation of such facilities needs, according to PA section 4-3, a separate licence. Where such facilities already exist, PA section 4-8 gives the MPE power to decide that the facilities may be used by parties other than the owners. The same goes for installations covered by a PDO. A prerequisite is, however, that this is warranted by considerations relating to efficient operations or socio-economic considerations, and that the MPE does not find that such use would be to the unreasonable detriment of the owners' requirements or other users of the installations or facilities. Any agreement, hence also the tariffs, concerning the use of installations and facilities covered by PA sections 4-2 and 4-3 has to be submitted to the MPE for approval. Again we see that the licencing system facilitates a balancing of commercial and socio-economic considerations, this time by providing for Government-initiated third-party access.

11.83 It should be noted that issues pertaining to the transport of oil and gas are addressed in connection with the development of a deposit, and not as a separate issue.

11.84 At the latest when approval is given according to PA section 4-2, or a licence granted pursuant to PA section 4-3, the Ministry shall also approve the production schedule (PA section 4-4). According to PA section 4-1 the recovery of oil and gas shall be conducted so that as much of the oil and gas as possible in each deposit or in several deposits in combination is produced. It is also underlined that recovery shall take place in accordance with prudent technical and sound economic principles, in a manner by which any waste of oil and gas or reservoir energy is avoided. Thus the production schedule will normally be dictated by

[69] PA s 4-2.

commercial considerations as modified by the requirement that as much of the oil and gas as possible shall be recovered. The Ministry may, however, if considerations regarding the planned management of the resources or other strong socio-related considerations so require, stipulate a production schedule which deviates from the requirements of PA section 4-1. Thus, even though commercial considerations are put in the foreground, socio-economic considerations are also relevant when stipulating the production schedule.

The approved production schedule does not give the licensees an unconditional right to produce oil and gas. The quantity that may be produced, injected, burned, or cold ventilated is stipulated for periods adapted to the deposit in question, on the basis of applications from the licensees. However, the production quantity is to be stipulated on the basis of the production schedule unless new information about the deposit, or other circumstances, warrant deviations. **11.85**

From this we see that although from a strictly legal point of view the production licence is the basis for the activities, it is the approved PDO which in fact determines the rights and obligations of the licensees during the development and operation of the deposits. It should also be noted that the approved PDO, by stipulating the main elements in the commercial assessment of the activities, also, according to general principles of Norwegian public law, limits the powers of the authorities to require or impose alterations to the plan. Section 4-4 third subparagraph of the Petroleum Act may be seen as a reflection of this. Subject to this provision the King in council may, if required by compelling socio-economic reasons, stipulate a production schedule different from the one already approved. **11.86**

Co-ordination of activities under several licences

A production licence may cover one or more blocks. The blocks are defined on the basis of geographical, not geological characteristics.[70] Hence it may happen that one deposit is covered by more than one production licence. It may also happen that a deposit is partly situated on the Norwegian continental shelf, and partly on the continental shelf of another State, eg Britain.[71] In such cases it is preferable that the deposit is developed and operated jointly by the holders of the licences, and more often than not this will also be in the interest of the licensees. The same applies where several deposits covered by different licences are best developed and operated as a single unit. **11.87**

However, the interests of the licensees holding the different licences may differ, and even if the holders of the licences are the same, their shares in the licences may differ. To prevent such situations having a detrimental effect on the development and operation of the deposit(s), PA section 4-7 obliges the licensees to use their **11.88**

---

70 PA s 3-2.

71 The fields Statfjord and Murchison are examples.

best efforts to come to an agreement concerning the joint operations. If an agreement is made, is is subject to approval by the MPE. If no agreement is made, the Ministry may decide how the activities are to be performed, and allocate the deposit. Hence, the licensees have an incentive to reach an agreement which the Ministry can approve.

11.89 Agreements concerning co-ordinated exploration drilling shall be communicated to the MPE but do not need ministerial approval.

11.90 Other forms of co-ordination of the activities under different licences than joint activities may also be called for. There may for instance be a need to co-ordinate the development of deposits in order to establish efficient transportation systems. In other terms, the management of the oil and gas resources may call for acceleration or postponement of activities. The legal basis for such orders is not PA section 4-7, but sections 4-5 and 4-6.

11.91 The co-ordination of activities under several production licences is central in relation to the transportation of natural gas, where pipelines are necessary. As has been described, the instalment and operation of pipelines needs a separate licence, pursuant to PA section 4-3. Thus the pipelines may very well serve several production licences, and the holders of the pipeline licence may not be same as the holders of the production licences. According to PA section 4-8 the Ministry may decide that the owners of installations covered by PA sections 4-2 or 4-3 shall give others access to their installations.

Landing of oil and gas

11.92 According to PA section 4-10, the King decides where and in which way landing of oil and gas shall take place. As to the question of where the oil and gas is to be landed, the power to decide this has to be executed in accordance with the requirements of the EEA Agreement, and as regards production licences issued after 1995, Directive 94/22.

11.93 In this context it is not possible to discuss this issue in any detail. However it should be pointed out that the rules of origin within the EEA, ie Protocol 4 of the Agreement, do not cover products extracted from the continental shelf, if taken literally. Hence the equivalent of Article 29 EC, Article 13 EEA, may not be applicable, cf Article 8 EEA. The applicability of Directive 94/22 is, however, not affected by this.

11.94 As regards the question of how the oil and gas is to be transported, it is necessary to differentiate between oil and gas, as it is only with respect to oil, at least at present, that there is any alternative to transportation by pipelines.

11.95 As Directive 94/22 (Art 6) allows for conditions and requirements justified by security of transport and the planned management of hydrocarbon resources, the

EEA requirements may not have any noticeable effect. Nevertheless it is quite clear that a decision to land oil and gas in Norway in order to favour Norwegian industry will constitute a breach of EEA law, provided oil and gas extracted from the continental shelf is regarded as an EEA product.

Oil and gas are vital commodities, and shortages may have a detrimental impact 11.96
on society.[72] Hence PA sections 4-11 and 4-12 give the King power to decide that the licensee shall cover national requirements, and provide transportation to Norway. The power pursuant to these sections must of course also be executed in accordance with the requirements of EEA law; therefore, the power may only be executed where justified by national security, public safety, or public health.[73] However, it seems unlikely that these provisions will be of any practical importance in the years to come, and so far they have not been applied.

Safety

A main common feature of the safety norms prescribed by acts and decrees is that 11.97
they give descriptions of general goals for safety, what we may call 'function requirements'. To a large degree this is also the case for the regulations stipulated by the Norwegian Petroleum Directorate.[74] Attached to these legislative acts are numerous guidelines that describe how the functional criteria may be complied with. The guidelines are not legally binding, but constitute a kind of 'soft law'.

The safety norms emerge through an ongoing interactive process between the 11.98
State's and the licensee's safety management, and between the prescription of/adaptation to norms and State/internal safety control.[75] Through this there is a continuous feedback to the regulatory body from the addressees of the norms. The process may be illustrated by the following diagram:

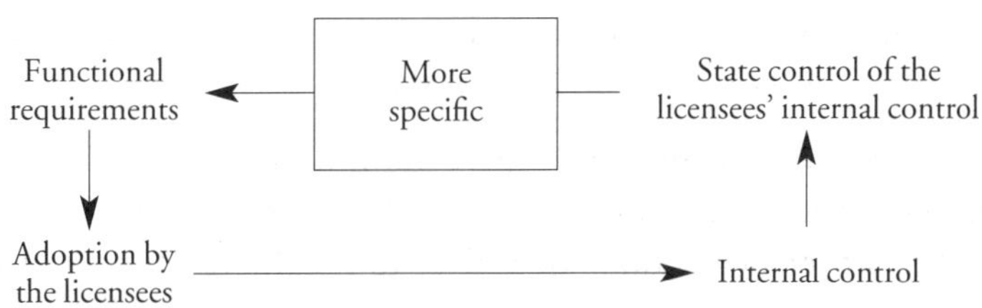

The safety regime is also characterized by the fact that all major operations need 11.99
some form of consent as to the handling of their safety issues.[76] Again we see the

[72] cf eg Case 72/83, *Campus Oil* [1984] ECR 2727.

[73] cf Art 34 EEA, which parallels Art 36 EC, provided petroleum extracted from the continental shelf qualifies as an EEA product, and Directive 94/22 Art 6.

[74] In addition to the NPD, the Norwegian Maritime Directorate acts as a regulatory supervising body in relation to oil and gas activities.

[75] See Regulation on the Licensee's Internal Control, stipulated by Royal Decree of 27 June 1997.

[76] See Regulations relating to safety etc, stipulated by Royal Decree of 27 June 1997.

application of a regulatory technique where the provisions facilitate an interplay between the regulator and the regulated. This way of regulating safety issues, through both consents given by the authorities and internal control, has worked well, and has to a certain extent been adopted in other countries.[77]

The licensing system: some general characteristics

11.100 The licensing system facilitates differentiated and flexible management of oil and gas activities. The reasons for this are as follows.

11.101 First, the question of whether or not a licence or approval should be granted is left to the discretion of the authorities. Hence, the approval may be made subject to conditions and obligations. The interrelation between approvals and conditions is an important aspect of the Norwegian licensing system, and facilitates a balancing of commercial and socio-economic considerations.

11.102 Secondly, since the companies need a licence to participate in oil and gas activities on the Norwegian continental shelf, and if they obtain a consent to proceed, they will be inclined to conform with the criteria laid down when awarding licences. Among these criteria are that any lack of efficiency or responsibility displayed by the licensees under previous production licences may lead to a new licence not being granted. Hence, the licensees will probably be more law-abiding than they would have been if they were not dependent on their good reputation among the authorities.

11.103 Thirdly, the system of licences and approvals forms a basis for a dialogue between the licensees and the authorities. This has two consequences; first, the level of competence among the authorities is increased by the information passed to them. Secondly, through this dialogue the commercial aspects of the oil and gas activities and the implementation of socio-economic objectives blends to a mix agreeable to both the authorities and the licensees.

11.104 Fourthly, the licensing system also facilitates informal governing of the activities. Because the licensees know that the authorities have the will and the power to implement different socio-economic objectives (through legislative measures and administrative acts) it is often unnecessary to take these steps: the licensees will act as desired by the authorities without being legally obliged to do so.

11.105 Finally, the authorities are to a large degree dependent on the licensees in order for the oil and gas deposits to be developed.

11.106 An overall assessment of the licensing system shows that it facilitates a legal framework for a long-term co-operation between the authorities and the licensees

[77] For a discussion, see Knut Kaasen, 'Post Piper Alpha: Some Reflections on Offshore Safety Regimes from a Norwegian Perspective', 1991 Journal of Energy and Natural Resources Law 228 *et seq*.

aimed at a performance of the oil and gas activities that is satisfactory to both parties. Thus the co-operation may be compared to a long-term joint venture. In a relationship like this, strictly legal issues play a less important part than in relationships where the regulator and the regulated are regarded, and regard themselves, as counterparts.

Marketing oil and gas

Under the licence the licensee has a right to a share in the oil and/or gas produced equalling his share in the licence. The licensee takes his share of oil in kind, and is free to dispose of it. With regard to natural gas, the system is different. Natural gas is less tangible than oil; it can be neither stored nor handled easily. Therefore, once a deposit comes onstream, there has to be a customer at the other end. To transport the gas to the buyer the licensee requires access to, and/or the creation of, an infrastructure. In addition, the licensees will need certainty as to whether their investments in the development of a deposit and/or infrastructure will be viable. Hence co-ordination is needed in order to keep costs as low as possible. **11.107**

Finally, gas-to-gas competition on the Norwegian continental shelf is regarded as having a negative impact on the planned management of the resources, and thus detrimental to the security of supply of gas to European users. One reason is that oilfields often have associated gas. In order to produce the oil, one needs customers for the gas. However, the quantities of natural gas in the deposit, or the regularity of production, may be so small that the gas has to be marketed together with gas from other deposits in order to attract customers. **11.108**

In order to take these considerations into account, the sale of gas is negotiated through the Gas Negotiation Committee (GFU), which is headed by Statoil. The GFU is responsible for preparing and conducting all negotiations on the sale of Norwegian gas. According to the Norwegian authorities, the co-ordination of gas sales is an integrated element in their management of the resources on the Norwegian continental shelf. At present the arrangement is under scrutiny by the European Commission and the EFTA Surveillance Authority, with regard to its compatibility with Article 85 EC/53 EEA and/or Article 59 (cf Art 53) EEA.[78] **11.109**

The fact that the Norwegian arrangements for marketing natural gas are being questioned by the surveillance authorities illustrates some of the peculiarities of EC law in general, and of the upstream oil and gas sector in particular. In the Netherlands, Gasunie has a legal monopoly over buying gas from Dutch deposits. It is not self-evident that the co-ordination through the GFU is any worse from a competition point of view than the Dutch arrangement. The Dutch arrangement, however, escapes the scope of Article 81 EC, but not the application of **11.110**

[78] Art 59 EEA mirrors Art 86 EC.

Articles 31 and 82 EC. As these provisions only forbid discrimination (Art 31) and abuse of a dominant position (Art 82), not the monopoly itself, the arrangement is not caught.

11.111 It remains to be seen what impact, if any, the judgments handed down by the European Court of Justice on 23 October 1997 in cases 157, 158, 159, and 160/94 will have on the assessment of the GFU arrangement.[79]

The allocation of profits and/or expenses between State and licensees

11.112 As indicated in section B1 above, the allocation between the State and the oil companies of profits and/or expenses accruing from the activities is an important issue in the regulation of the oil and gas sector. The instruments used for this allocation are several, and the result may be called 'total Government take'. This term has no legal implications, but serves to illustrate that the total revenue generated for the Government from oil and gas production is a result of several measures operating at the same time. Four elements of the total Government take are next addressed.

11.113 The first element is the area fee, cf PA section 4-9. This is calculated on the basis of a combination of the size of the licence area and the period for which the licence has been held. Thus the fee per year per square kilometre increases year by year, irrespective of the production from the licensing area. The area fee, however, only constitutes a minor element in the total Government take. The purpose of the fee is to offer an incentive to relinquish areas.

11.114 The second element is the production fee, or royalty, also based on PA section 4-9. As follows from the name, this fee is dependent on, and linked to, the production from the licence area. Not all licence areas are subject to the obligation to pay a production fee. Oil and gas extracted from deposits where the PDO is approved after 1 January 1986 are exempt from the fee. It follows from this that the production fee will fade out as an instrument for State revenue in the future.

11.115 This brings us to the third and by far the most important element in the total Government take, the tax regime. The regime consists of a combination of the general tax regime and a dedicated petroleum tax regime. This is not the place for a thorough analysis of this complex set of rules and principles, thus only some general elements will be addressed.

11.116 The first point to note is that there is a ring fence, as losses from other activities may only be deducted from the income resulting from the oil and gas activities to a limited extent: cf PTA section 3. There is however no ring fence around each licence, hence losses resulting from the activities under licence A may be deducted for the income resulting from activities under licence B.

[79] [1997] ECR I-5699.

The second point is that the income from sales of oil is assessed on the basis of so-called norm prices, stipulated by the authorities, cf PTA section 4. The norm price must reflect arm's-length transactions. As far as income from sales of natural gas is concerned, the norm price is not stipulated, although PTA section 4 provides sufficient legal basis. The reason for this is that the oil companies, in relation to natural gas, are not vertically integrated to the same extent as in relation to oil, hence the prices achieved for natural gas are thought to reflect the market price. **11.117**

The third point to note is that expenses related to the removal of installations are not deductible (PTA section 3 litra g) nor are deductions to cover future expenses for the removal of installations used in exploitation or pipeline transportation. These expenses are addressed in the separate Act no 11 of 25 April 1986 relating to the allocation of costs of removal of installations on the continental shelf.[80] The last point to be noted is that taxpayers engaged in exploitation, processing, and pipeline transportation in the areas mentioned in PTA section 1 must pay a special tax in addition to ordinary income tax, cf PTA section 5. The details in the assessment of the income on which there is a duty to pay this special tax are also given in PTA section 5. In this context it is enough to mention that the taxpayer is given an uplift. **11.118**

The fourth element in the total Government take differs from those already mentioned as its main function is not to increase State revenue, but to stimulate a reduction in emissions of carbon dioxides. Thus, according to Act no 72 of 21 December 1990 relating to CO_2 tax in the petroleum activity on the continental shelf a CO_2 tax is to be charged on the burning of petroleum and on natural gas discharged into the air, if the Storting so resolves. **11.119**

A fifth element in the total Government take is the SDFI. Originally the State participation took place as a carried interest. However, as the SDFI today, through Statoil, carries its share of the expenses accrued by the joint activities under the licence, it no longer constitutes an element in the total Government take in the sense that profits are 'taken' from the oil companies. However, the level of the State participation is significant. Hence State participation, through both Statoil and SDFI, is still an important revenue-producing measure in the Norwegian oil and gas sector. It is also worth mentioning that the State, through its participation, is directly exposed to the commercial risks of the oil and gas activities.[81] **11.120**

The rules on the allocation of profits and/or expenses between State and licensees has, because of both the instruments used and because of the intensity in which they are used, as a consequence created a situation where the State carries a considerable part of the commercial risk related to the petroleum activities. **11.121**

---

[80] See paras 11.218–11.219 below.

[81] See paras 11.38 *et seq* above.

(4) *The Relationship Between the Holders of a Licence*

General aspects

11.122 The relationship between the co-holders of a licence is governed by a set of agreements, the most important by far being the joint operating agreement (JOA). The objective of the JOA is to regulate the relationship between the participants in the same licence as far as the activities under the licence are concerned. The JOA is made by the Norwegian authorities, and acceptance of it is a prerequisite for obtaining a share in a licence for production. Thus the JOA is not really an agreement as it is not negotiated by the parties to it, nor may it be altered without the consent of the MPE. Hence, apart from governing the ad hoc co-operation between the participants in a licence, the JOA is also a part of, and closely tied to, the licensing system.

11.123 The licensing group is organized as a joint venture. The supreme body is the Joint Management Committee, on which all participants in the licence are represented. The day-to-day management is taken care of by the Operator. The Operator is nominated by the Norwegian authorities, more or less along the same lines as the nomination of the licensees. In addition there are a number of sub-committees where all the participants in the licence are represented, the most important being the Contracting Committee. Finally there is the Gas Negotiations Board of the licence, which has a subordinate role to that of the GFU. The common denominator for these committees established by or on the basis of the JOA, and for the operator, is that they are all subject to the instructions of the Joint Management Committee. Thus, from a management point of view the most important provisions of the JOA are those dealing with the decision-making process, and among these the voting rules.

The voting rules

Before the 15th licensing round

11.124 The voting rules are found in Article 2 of the standard JOA, and are drafted, as are all provisions of the agreement, by the Norwegian authorities. The voting rules give the criteria for when a proposal is adopted in the Joint Management Committee.

11.125 As to activities pursuant to licences given until the 15th licensing round, the voting rules were drafted in basically the same way. Depending on the nature of the issue, the voting rules give different criteria as to when a proposal is adopted. Even though actual votes are rare, there is often dispute as to the solution to the issues raised in the Joint Operating Committee. The reason why votes are rare is that the outcome is more or less given beforehand. Thus the voting rules will form the basis on which agreements are reached.

According to the JOA there are four categories of issues. First are the 'normal issues'. In these matters a proposal is adopted if a majority of the parties to the agreement representing a certain percentage of the licence support it. The voting rules on this level are such that no one party's single vote is necessary or sufficient to adopt a proposal. Secondly, we have the issues that have to be decided unanimously. In these matters each party, no matter how small his share in the licence, has a veto. None of these categories raise community law issues different from any other joint venture.[82] **11.126**

The common denominator for the remaining two categories is that according to Article 2.3 of the JOA they are considered to raise 'political or fundamental aspects of importance and/or might have crucial social or economic effects'. These matters are usually called section 10 issues as the wording of the JOA on this point is identical to that of section 10 of Statoil's statutes. Whether or not an issue falls into this category is left to Statoil to decide, which means that the question in the end is left to Statoil's general assembly. As all the shares in Statoil are held by the Norwegian State, this means that it is for the Minister of Petroleum and Energy to decide whether an issue is a section 10 issue or not. **11.127**

The section 10 issues fall into two categories. The first category is where the support of Statoil is sufficient when Statoil is acting according to a decision from its general assembly. The second category is often called 'qualified section 10 issues'. Here a proposal not only needs the support of Statoil, but also of another party in order to be adopted. The difference between the normal and the qualified section 10 issues lies in the character of the decisions to be made. Thus the qualified section 10 issues are expressly mentioned in the JOA. Both categories facilitate a possibility for the Norwegian Government to pursue and implement political objectives through the decisions made in the licensing group. This possibility has however to be executed in accordance with the requirements of the EEA Agreement, Article 59 EEA.[83] **11.128**

The 15th licensing round and onwards

The 15th licensing round was made subject to the provisions of Directive 94/22. Hence, the voting rules are adapted to the requirements of Article 6 of that Directive. **11.129**

The principles for the exercise of the voting right of the State are given in Directive 94/22 Article 6 no 3, second sub-paragraph. According to this provision, the vote cast by the State shall be based exclusively on transparent, objective, and non-discriminatory principles. Furthermore, the vote cast by the State shall not **11.130**

[82] There are however quite a few aspects of competition law connected to the behaviour of joint ventures as the agreements etc between the parties in a joint venture could very well infringe Art 81 EC.

[83] Art 59 EEA mirrors Art 86 EC.

prevent the decisions taken by the licence group from being based on normal commercial principles.

11.131 However, the State is barred from voting on decisions regarding sources of procurement. Nevertheless the State may veto such a decision if it does not respect conditions and requirements of a certain nature, specified in the licence. The carrying out of the decision of the licence group will amount to a breach of terms of the licence. The right to veto may therefore best be viewed as an enforcement in advance of these terms.

11.132 In decisions where the State is not barred from casting a vote, the Directive forbids the State, alone or together with one or more public entities, from exercising a majority vote.

11.133 The Norwegian State has entrusted Statoil with the management of its participation. As Statoil also participates in a number of licences in its own capacity, it is necessary to take measures to ensure that the part of Statoil which manages the state participation does not vote or become party to information on cases concerning sources of procurement. Nor may the commercial part of Statoil become party to information acquired through the management of the State's participation in licences where Statoil does not participate in its own capacity.[84] These measures, and measures relating to the technicalities resulting from Statoil's role as the manager of the State participation,[85] are not discussed here.

11.134 According to Article 6 no 3 third sub-paragraph only 'decisions . . . which would not respect the conditions and requirements, specified in the licence, regarding depletion policy and protection of the financial interests of the State' may be vetoed. We see that only certain considerations may be protected through a veto, and that as a prerequisite the conditions and requirements based on these considerations must be specified in the licence. In the 15th licensing round this prerequisite is met by section eight of the production licence, which reads:

> The licensees are obliged to adhere to the State's depletion policies and policies concerning the State's financial interest, as these are expressed in relevant laws, regulations, and documents discussed in Stortinget. If this obligation is not respected, the State or its manager may oppose a decision made by the licensees.

11.135 The right to oppose is spelled out in the Joint Operating Agreement Article 2.3, which states that:

> The State or the manager may oppose a decision by the management committee which would not respect the conditions and requirements specified in the production licence, regarding depletion policies and the State's financial interests.

[84] Art 6 no 3 second sub-para.
[85] Art 6 no 3 fourth sub-para.

The criteria for the adoption of a proposal are made up of a combination of parties and interests. The State, or to be more precise, the manager, is not defined as a party to the JOA, thus the share of the State only adds weight to the vote of Statoil, it does not count as a vote in its own capacity. In other words, the State does not have a vote in licences where Statoil also participates in its own capacity. **11.136**

The Directive requires that neither the State nor the manager exercise voting rights on decisions regarding sources of procurement to the activities. In these matters the voting right of the manager is distributed proportionally on the other parties to the licence, a solution that makes sense.[86] **11.137**

In most other cases, a decision in the management committee is reached when: **11.138**

> At least Y of the Members representing at least X% of the participating interest have voted in favour of a proposal, [provided, however, that (one or more individual company(ies)/public entity(ies)) do not constitute a quorum.].

There is no doubt that, depending on the allocation of shares in the licences, this may give rise to complicated questions, both with regard to whether the requirements of the Directive are fulfilled, and with regard to how proposals should be phrased. However, in this general context such complexities cannot be discussed. **11.139**

The problem of a limited number of actors

So far, some 220 licences have been awarded, some of which have been relinquished. The number of licensees is twenty-seven, and the number of operators sixteen. Hence cross-licence interests may prove to be a problem to the supply side of the upstream petroleum market, to the markets where the licensees act as suppliers, ie to the downstream market, and to the decisions made in each single licence. These issues raise a multitude of questions which cannot be entered into in this context. It will suffice to point at some aspects. **11.140**

The problems related to the supply side of the upstream market are linked to co-ordinated behaviour. As the licensees more often than not are in a position where their main competitors as far as the supplies needed are other licence groups where they are represented, it is not unthinkable that the licence groups tend to co-ordinate their invitations for tender. **11.141**

This problem may be addressed by Articles 53 and 54 EEA, which mirror Articles 81 and 82 EC. However, one could argue that such co-ordination enhances competition rather than limits it. It would probably also be difficult to establish whether the licensees have a dominant position or not, and whether this position is abused. **11.142**

[86] If the voting right of the State were eliminated, and disputes settled on the basis of the relative strength between the parties to the licence, this would amount to the same thing.

11.143 In the downstream market, each licensee disposes of his part of the oil produced, and the oil market is viewed as being close to a perfect market. Thus, the problem of a limited number of actors does not have repercussions in this market. As regards natural gas, the situation is to a certain extent different (see paragraphs 11.107–11.111 above).

11.144 As for the problems related to decisions made in the licence groups, they can be described as a problem of mixed interests. Although each licence group, from a strict legal point of view, is to be considered as a single entity which pursues its own commercial interests, the members of the group will also have interests in other licence groups. And, as their representation in one group does not necessarily resemble their representation in another, their views will tend to be influenced by this. This again may represent a problem to smaller licensees and to licensees who have their interests allocated in a different pattern.

The Multifaceted State

11.145 Directive 94/22 requires, as do EEA and EC law in general, that where the State is an actor in the market place, the State has to behave like any other commercial actor. It is however difficult to establish when the State is not pursuing commercial considerations, especially when the State is wearing more than one hat. In the Norwegian petroleum sector, the State is not only represented through the SDFI, but also through Statoil and, in part, Norsk Hydro. When acting through these channels, according to EEA and EC law, only commercial considerations are relevant. However, if the State acts as a regulator, and the regulation affects the free movement of goods, services etc, only considerations of a non-economic nature are relevant. As the State may to a large extent choose through which channel it may act, the requirements of the EEA Agreement boil down to little more than requirements as to form.

(5) *Third-Party Use of Production Facilities*

Introduction

11.146 In the production of oil and gas fields on the Norwegian continental shelf (NCS) it is common that infrastructure is shared between two or more fields. This is primarily to reduce investment, improve profitability, and make more fields commercial.[87]

11.147 With respect to gas, the costs of developing individual pipelines are excessive; thus most fields producing gas for transport need access to pipelines shared by several fields.[88] This is one of the reasons for pipelines being the subject of a separate

[87] Both technology and administration of projects are important means of cost reduction. The latter has resulted in a new approach to contract strategies, which is dealt with in section B8 below.

[88] Virtually all fields on the NCS produce gas for export, either as primary product (ie Troll) or associated with oil production (ie Statfjord). Not all gas is exported, a significant part is injected to enhance oil recovery and some is used for energy generation at the installations.

licence.[89] In the case of production facilities, shared use is an alternative to an independent solution. Normally this alternative is due to spare capacity being made available in existing installations offering cost savings for new fields being developed, but may also be an integral part of the original development concept.[90] In either case there will usually be two licence groups involved: one owning and one using the installations.[91] The subject of this chapter is public and private law aspects related to such third-party use of installations, as it will be referred to.[92] The groups in question are referred to as 'owners' and 'users'; the same terminology is used also for their respective fields and installations.

At the general level the Norwegian Government and the oil companies have a shared interest in third-party use of installations, as it saves development costs for the users and increases income for the owners. These potential savings and earnings for the companies should also result in a higher Government take through taxes and State participation. It is necessary to recall that the objective of the Norwegian oil policy—the oil industry shall benefit society as a whole[93]—translates into an objective of maximizing State revenue which in turn can be used for purposes prioritized by the political process.[94] However, in reality there may be differences of opinion between Government and companies on the advantages of third-party use. This may be due to different economic evaluations or other assessments of the benefits with such solutions. In paragraphs 11.168 *et seq* below the authority of Government[95] to control third-party use is reviewed. **11.148**

In a macro-economic valuation only costs related to investments in real assets and payment for production factors are relevant, which excludes items of great significance in a corporate financial valuation, such as taxes. Socio-economic or macro-economic valuations are given large weight in the governmental assessment of oil and gas projects on the NCS. **11.149**

---

[89] See paras 11.107–11.111 above.

[90] Examples of the former are the Snorre, Vigdis, and Tordis developments in the vicinity of the Statfjord and Gullfaks fields; an example of the latter is the Ekofisk field complex for which Ekofisk Centre is used by all fields in the area. A novel example is the Aasgard unitization of several independent oil and gas fields at Haltenbanken.

[91] For all practical purposes both groups will hold a production licence awarded in accordance with PA s 3-3 (see paras 11.68–11.79 above). However, it must be noted that both will often form a unitized group between two or more production licences. Whether the groups are unitized or not is irrelevant for the issues dealt with in this chapter.

[92] In the terminology of PA s 4-8, this is 'use of infrastructure by others', but here the term 'third-party use' is used.

[93] PA s 1-2.

[94] See paras 11.27–11.30 above.

[95] As from 1 January 1997 the Ministry of Petroleum and Energy exercises the authority. In the following, the terms 'Government' and 'authorities' are frequently used, as other governmental bodies may be involved, such as the Storting (PDO approvals), the Cabinet, and the Norwegian Petroleum Directorate.

11.150 The services that owners may offer to the users span a wide range. At one extreme the service is limited to transport of processed petroleum through the installations into a pipeline, while at the other extreme all activities related to the user field are conducted by the owners. Typically, the services include the processing and transport of petroleum. The rights and obligations of the parties are regulated by commercial agreements, often called Tie-In and Processing Agreements. The main contents of these are described in paragraphs 11.182 *et seq.* below.

Public law aspects

Introduction

11.151 The Petroleum Act (PA) and concomitant regulations constitute the legal means adopted to implement the objectives of Norwegian oil policy. The permits and approvals necessary for each significant step in the life of an oil or gas field from exploration through production to abandonment are described as 'the licensing system'.[96]

11.152 Formal legal decisions within this licensing system are not the only vehicle for governmental control of the industry. Most of the actual influence by Government is achieved by more informal means in a dialogue between the authorities and the licence groups. In addition general guidelines established by political decisions are also used to control the activities.[97] However, the legal instruments are important as they set an agenda for the dialogue and create an incentive for the licensees to reach agreement with the Government on how to conduct the activities. Hence, the PA also serves as a basis for informal control. This informal role of the licensing system will not be expanded on below, but it is important to be aware of it.

11.153 The legal instruments available for government control of third-party use of production installations are PA section 4-2, according to which approval of a PDO[98] is required for developing a field. Further, PA section 4-7 applies to joint operations between two or more licence groups, and PA section 4-8 directly regulates third-party use of infrastructure including production facilities. These provisions are all part of the licensing system, and vest authority in the Government both to approve and to dictate actions taken, or to be taken, by the licence groups. They all relate to the production phase in the lifetime of a field, which also comprises the planning and development of installations. The rules derived from these three provisions set various limits on how and when the authority may be exercised.

[96] See paras 11.31–11.37 above.

[97] A good example is St meld no 46 (1986–87) by which the sales organization for Norwegian gas was established, see paras 11.107–11.111 above.

[98] Plan for Development and Operation.

At a general level they also have some limitations in common. According to Norwegian public law, the Government may only exercise authority to pursue and protect relevant concerns and interests.[99] Due to the objectives for the administration of the petroleum industry there are only broad limitations on governmental authority. These may be divided into internal and external factors. The internal relate to the project or activity itself, while the external factors comprise public concerns and interests affected by the activity. **11.154**

In making decisions related to a project the Government may modify the solutions preferred by the licence groups for socio-economic reasons or even stipulate other solutions entirely. Likewise, the authorities may make alterations due to safety and environmental considerations. With respect to the socio-economic assessment of field developments, it must be emphasized that the use of existing installations has been an express objective ever since the first major development projects commenced. On the external side, factors such as the impact caused by the activity on the economy may warrant alterations to the plans made by the licence groups, or form the basis for other governmental decisions. At present, allocation of gas deliveries is the best example of this.[100] Among other external factors which the Government may take into account are the interests of fisheries and other affected businesses. **11.155**

However, the interests of the licence groups must also be given due regard: the disadvantages they suffer must be balanced against the benefits for the other interests concerned. A decision may be taken when the benefits outweigh the disadvantages; to what extent they must do so will vary with the circumstances. In this context, the licence groups have good reason to expect to proceed with their plans of development following their exploration programme and in accordance with the production licence. Thus, there must be significant weight to the conflicting concerns and interest to make significant alterations to their plans. **11.156**

The specific authority on third-party use of production facilities which follows from the relevant provisions of the PA will apply within this broad framework for governmental authority. The Government has authority to control both development concepts and the terms of agreement between the parties, discussed in paragraphs 11.158–11.167 and 11.168–11.176 below. **11.157**

Control over development concepts to enable third-party use

PA section 4-2 is a cornerstone in the licence system as PDO approval marks the transition from the exploration to the production phase in the lifetime of a field. A PDO covers all aspects related to the development concept for the field, except for any commercial agreements or other arrangements required to develop the **11.158**

[99] These limitations are reflected in PA s 10-18.
[100] See paras 11.38 *et seq.*

field. The PDO will outline the main technical features of the concept as well as safety precautions and environmental effects. The PDO will also contain an analysis of the economic and public[101] consequences of the project.[102] By the approval of the PDO, all these aspects are reviewed, and the field development plan may be modified before approval to the extent required by the public interest.

11.159 For the licensees, PDO approval is necessary to commence development and production. For the authorities the approval offers the best opportunity to influence and adjust the development concept according to the relevant internal and external factors. At this stage costs of alterations are relatively modest, allowing a reasonable amount of flexibility. Formally, the approval is granted following submission of a PDO by the licence groups. However, due to the importance of PDO approval a dialogue between the licence groups and the Government will precede this. In this process, the licence groups may alter the plan to the extent necessary to make it acceptable to the authorities.

11.160 With respect to third-party use of production installations, the importance of the PDO approval process is different between the owner and the user field. As the user field is about to be developed, PDO approval will always be necessary. The PDO approval process for the user field may lead to third-party use being chosen instead of independent development.[103] With respect to the owner field, PDO approval will only be necessary if the field is to be developed in conjunction with the user field.[104] However, during the initial approval process it may be decided to accommodate the development concept for future third-party use of the field installations.[105] In such cases, PDO approval of the owner field may increase the likelihood of future third-party use.

11.161 PA section 4-2 does not grant any authority to instruct the licence groups to take specific actions, except by terms and conditions set for the approval of a PDO. Hence, if the authorities would want to order third-party use of installations, they must rely on other provisions of the PA. Such instructions may be given pursuant to both PA sections 4-7 and 4-8. The circumstances at which these two provisions are directed are different. Neither of them has been formally invoked by the authorities to order third-party use.

---

[101] 'Public' is used here as a translation of the Norwegian word *samfunnsmessig*, a generic term for all matters related to the society as a whole.

[102] See the Petroleum Regulations ss 22–3 on the required contents.

[103] Explicit examples of this are not easy to find as these alterations will be made prior to submission, but the propensity of such solutions in the vicinity of major installations may partly be caused by the declared intent of Government to utilize existing installations.

[104] There is no need for a PDO for the owner field when the user field will utilize spare capacity in existing installations.

[105] The Heidrun and Frøy fields are both examples of fields adopted for possible future third-party use.

PA section 4-7 regulates joint operations between two or more licensees, in practice meaning licence groups. Primarily this provision obliges the groups to seek agreement on co-operation when a field extends across their licence boundaries.[106] The predecessors of PA section 4-7 only regulated these situations, but the identical section 16 in the Petroleum Act of 1985 extended the obligation to seek agreement to include also activities on several fields 'when that is obviously rational'. This obligation is the basis for the authority to instruct third-party use. It also pertains to other activities such as exploration, but this is not of interest in this context. As the obligation relates to the co-ordination of activities, it will be of relevance primarily in the planning phase prior to development of the fields. Thus, it supplements the possibilities for governmental influence in this phase offered by the PDO approval process pursuant to PA section 4-2. 11.162

When licensees in fields that could be developed jointly fail to achieve agreement 'within a reasonable time', the authorities may instruct joint development, and if necessary stipulate the terms of agreement pursuant to PA section 4-7. Hence, the authority to instruct depends on whether there is an obligation to seek agreement to develop the fields jointly, which in turn depends on the interpretation of 'when that is obviously rational' and 'reasonable time'. Of these the former phrase sets the most important limitations on the authority. The same limitations also apply on the authority to instruct third-party use of existing installations according to PA section 4-7. 11.163

The term 'obviously' requires the benefits to be clear and easily identifiable. In such cases, the licensees normally reach agreement on joint development themselves. Instructions by the authorities would only be necessary if they failed to agree on joint development. In most cases this would be due to different evaluations of the benefits gained by joint development, which will occur often due to the complexities of the petroleum industry. When these are based on sound and prudent judgement, it can hardly be claimed that joint development 'is obviously rational'. Hence, this requirement means that the authority can only order joint development in the rare cases when the objecting licensees do so for reasons other than their prudent evaluation of the benefits of joint development. In such cases, the Government will have authority to order joint development when 'reasonable time' has elapsed. This phrase is probably of no real importance; the authorities would only interfere if it were clear that the parties were not able to progress in negotiations in spite of clear benefits from a joint development. 11.164

In contrast with PA section 4-7, the exercise of the authority vested in Government by PA section 4-8 does not depend on any actions by the licensees. 11.165

[106] When two or more licences cover a field, the involved groups must be combined into one single group by a unitization agreement. These agreements are based on the JOAs stipulated by the Government. Such 'unit groups' have developed most of the fields on the NCS.

According to this provision, there are two sets of criteria for when third-party use may be ordered. First, third-party use must be 'rational' or warranted by 'public considerations'. Secondly, it must not 'unreasonably' restrain the activities of the owners of the installation or third parties with an ensured right of use, who are both referred to as 'existing users' in what follows. The wording of PA section 4-8 is primarily aimed at instructing the use of existing production facilities and pipelines. This is due to the provision originating from terms set for the first field development approvals on the NCS.

11.166 The criteria related to the reasons for an order must be seen as a reference to all relevant internal and external factors. Thus, they do not limit the authority beyond what follows from the general limitations. The criterion that the ordered third-party use shall not 'unreasonably' restrain the existing users is a more important restriction on the authority. With respect to ongoing production this criterion must be seen in the context of PA section 4-4, third paragraph. According to this provision, ongoing production may only be reduced when that is required to protect major public interests of an economic or social nature.[107] In view of this, there seems to be no realistic reason that would justify the reduction of ongoing production to benefit a new third-party user. The same would apply if owners had concrete plans to utilize any spare capacity for its own production. Hence, instructions pursuant to PA section 4-8 may in practice only be given when there is spare capacity in the installations which the owners have no immediate plans to utilize themselves. Thus, the authority will mainly serve as a means for Government to prioritize between potential third-party users.

11.167 According to PA sections 4-4, 4-5, and 4-6 the authorities may reduce production, instruct development, or prolong operations. Theoretically, these provisions may be used to schedule activities to allow for third-party use. However, all such actions will be of significant detriment to the interests of the licensees, and the benefits gained will probably never outweigh these disadvantages. Some of these provisions have been invoked, but only to further major national economic considerations.

Control over terms of agreement for third-party use

11.168 A PDO approval, according to PA section 4-2 does not comprise the commercial agreements required to develop the field. However, agreements with other licence groups must also be approved pursuant to PA sections 4-7 or 4-8.[108] In most cases approval of a PDO will be denied until such agreements are submitted for

[107] Production on the NCS was reduced in accordance with the identical s 20 fifth para in the PA of 1985 in an attempt to strengthen oil prices following the dramatic fall in prices in the mid-1980s. This was also done in 1999, to stop the sudden price drop in the spring.

[108] Until 1994 all contracts for goods and services should also be approved, but this requirement was abolished due to the EEA Treaty.

approval. This requirement for approval of agreements prior to or concomitant with the PDO does not follow from the PA but from discretionary governmental practice.

When the development depends on third-party use, the agreements between the owners and the users may in principle be approved in accordance with PA section 4-7 as a joint activity.[109] However, as PA section 4-8 specifically regulates such use, the approval will be given according to this provision. The approval will comprise all terms of the agreement, and the authorities may implement changes to any of these by conditions for approval, but when the parties have agreed this will only happen in rare instances. However, as the Ministry also has the authority to instruct on the stipulation of terms, the parties will from time to time ask it to resolve issues where agreement is not reached.[110] **11.169**

From the governmental point of view, the tariffs are the most important part of agreements on third-party use. The tariffs will determine the distribution of the savings made by the third-party use between owners and users. A high level will discourage licence groups from choosing development concepts depending on third-party use. Hence, a high level may lead to higher total field development costs and reduce the socio-economic profitability of the fields in question. The stated objective of the authorities is to ensure that the profit is not transferred to the infrastructure owners but remains with the producing field.[111] **11.170**

This objective is reflected in the stipulation in PA section 4-8 that the tariffs shall give the owners 'a reasonable profit in view of risk and investment'. This allows the authorities to reduce tariffs that would give the owners excess profits, but also ensures them a minimum tariff level. Put simply, the tariff must give a reasonable rate of return on the investments, including a premium to reflect the risk. However, determining these factors is a complex matter, particularly for third-party use of production facilities. **11.171**

With respect to pipeline transport, a set of principles for assessing a reasonable profit level is established. These were developed as part of the approval of the Zeepipe transport system, and are thus referred to as the Zeepipe principles.[112] They state that the rate shall be based on rate of return on a risk-free investment with a premium added according to the risk.[113] The investment basis is the capital expenditure for the pipeline system in question. Operational costs will be in addition to the tariff arrived at by the Zeepipe principles. For pipelines, these **11.172**

[109] Unitization agreements are approved in accordance with PA s 4-7.

[110] This is not uncommon for resolution of voting rules in unitization agreements.

[111] See *inter alia* St meld No 46 (1987–87) and St meld No 26 (1993–94).

[112] See St meld No 46 (1987–87).

[113] There are established methods for calculating both, in this case the rate used by the Government was adopted which is 7% pre-tax real rate of return.

principles have proven to be relatively easy to apply, for two reasons. First, the commercial agreements reduce the risk for the pipeline owners to a minimum; and secondly, the investments are easily defined by the scope of the pipeline project.

11.173 With respect to production facilities, neither risk nor investments are easy to determine. Third-party use may disturb production from the owner field, which could seriously impair the overall profitability for the owners. The risks of such disturbances are complex. Even if these could be assessed and a rate arrived at, establishing an investment basis for tariff calculation is an equally complex task. As the field installations are required for production in the owner field, not all investments therein may be seen as relevant. Further, and more importantly, it is questionable whether sunk costs should be attributed any relevance at all.

11.174 At present, no principles akin to the Zeepipe principles have been developed for third-party use of production facilities. In deciding a 'reasonable' level, both Government and companies have to rely on the vague criteria in PA section 4-8 and the express intention to retain the profit at the producing fields. As a consequence the authorities have been reluctant to adjust tariffs agreed by all the parties.

11.175 When the Ministry approves agreed tariffs, it endorses these as reasonable. This has raised the issue whether the authorities may at a later stage revoke the approval and adjust the tariff level. Such revocation would be to the detriment of the party who benefits from the approved tariffs, typically the owners. Hence, the criteria for revocation of decisions to the detriment of a private party must be satisfied. These criteria limit revocation to instances where major public interests suffer from the decision. In the case of tariffs these criteria would probably only be satisfied when there is a risk of permanent loss of production due to the tariff level, as when the users cannot afford to continue operations.

11.176 Finally, the Government also set the priorities between the various fields using the first major installations developed on the NCS. This was done as a consequence of the regulation of the access to pipeline transport from these installations.[114] As mentioned above, these terms are the origins of PA section 4-8.

Agreements on use of installations

The internal relationship in the licence groups

11.177 The oil activity on the NCS is conducted by licence groups, being composed of two or more licensees, ie oil companies.[115] The groups make decisions on how to

[114] Ekofisk Centre and the Norpipe pipelines to Teesside in the UK (oil) and Emden in Germany (gas).

[115] See paras 11.38 *et seq* above.

conduct their activity in accordance with the voting rules, normally by majority vote.[116]

Entering into an agreement on third-party use is for the user group analogous to the acquisition of goods and services. Hence, the ordinary majority voting rules apply. On the owner side it is argued by some that unanimous approval is required, as rental of spare capacity is outside of the purpose of a production licence group, which is to explore for and exploit petroleum within the licence area. However, this does not seem to be a viable view. The production installations and all other assets which the licence group owns are acquired for the purpose of exploration and exploitation. Consequently they are joint assets, which may be disposed of in accordance with ordinary voting rules. Thus, agreements on third-party use are also subject to majority vote in the owner group. This also follows from PA sections 4-7 and 4-8, which assumes that third-party use is an activity that may be conducted under a production licence.[117] **11.178**

As all licence groups are composed of a small number of companies, in most cases some will participate in both the owner and user groups.[118] Due to this partial identity between the groups, the voting majority in both may consist of the same companies. When there is a conflict of interest between the groups, such majority could have an undue advantage over the minority in the group where they have the lowest economic interest. For third-party use, the majority might set excessive tariffs when it has a bias on the owner side, or low tariffs when the bias is on the user side.[119] **11.179**

Issues related to conflicts of interest must be resolved based on the general private law principle of loyalty between contracting parties. A majority may violate this principle by decisions which are unduly detrimental to the minority. In Norwegian law on companies and associations, this aspect of the principle of loyalty is referred to as the principle of abuse of power.[120] In such cases the decision **11.180**

[116] The main exception is approval of the PDO, which requires individual consent. The exceptional voting rules that apply when Statoil's general assembly votes have not been used yet. See paras 11.124 *et seq* above.

[117] If third-party use was outside the purpose of the owner group, such agreement would also require the establishment of a new legal entity to conduct this business and/or amendment of the JOA.

[118] Statoil will normally participate in both, as the company was awarded an interest, typically 50%, in all production licences awarded between 1973 and 1993 (PL037–202). See paras 11.43 *et seq* above. However, Statoil has withdrawn from or transferred their interest in some of these in recent years. In these cases Statoil remains a licensee on behalf of the State Direct Financial Interest, SDFI.

[119] Conflicts of interest due to partial identity on the company level are not limited to third-party use.

[120] A licence group must in this respect be seen as an association, even though it is exempted from the Company Act. This exemption is related to the procedural requirements of the Act, and is not made to exclude the groups from relevant general principles of Norwegian law. The principle on abuse of power has been applied in several cases ranging from limited partnerships (*kommandittselskap*) to housing associations (*borettslag*), and is codified in Act No 59 of 4 June 1976 relating to Joint Stock Company, s 9-16.

may either be deemed null and void, or if that is not possible, the minority is entitled to restoration of their loss, if any. The decision need not necessarily be to the benefit to the majority, nor is it required that a gain has materialized. It is sufficient for declaring a decision invalid that it is suited to give someone an unreasonable gain at the expense of other members in the association. Furthermore, it is only required to demonstrate that the majority should have understood that the decision was of such nature.

11.181 The principle does not deny the companies the right to pursue their business objectives even if that would be to the detriment of companies in the minority. It only applies when a gain is 'unreasonable'. What would constitute such a gain has never been tested in any court or arbitration case. Hence, the actual contents of this principle within the Norwegian petroleum industry is uncertain.

The main features of the agreements

Introduction

11.182 The agreements on third-party use of production facilities, and 'Tie-In and Processing Agreements', regulate two main operational issues.[121] First, the throughput of petroleum over the owner installations and the services the owners will render to the users. Secondly, the physical connection or tie-in of the user field to the owner installations. The former relates to the commercial objective of the agreements and the latter to activities necessary to implement this objective. The following review comprises these two issues as well as the nature of the contractual obligations of the parties, with an emphasis on the throughput.

11.183 Initially it should be noted that all obligations of both owners and users terminate upon the permanent cessation of their respective operations. For the owners this will be when their field is depleted, which in most cases also will cause the users to terminate. However, in theory the owner installations may continue in operation based purely on income from third-party use.[122]

Throughput of petroleum and services rendered

11.184 The regulation of the throughput is based on two strictly defined physical points of *delivery* and *redelivery*, situated at the in- and outlets of the petroleum stream on the owner installations. At each of these points the parties have certain obligations to deliver and receive petroleum. The scope of services rendered by the owners is defined only as a *difference* in their obligations at these two points. There is no specific description of how the owners shall handle and process the petroleum.

[121] Unless otherwise stated, the description of the agreements below is based on the typical or normal regulations. There may always be individual agreements with different solutions.

[122] Heimdal is the first example of this; see also PA s 5-1 where such usage is one of several alternatives for disposing of production installations.

This structure is followed regardless of the scope of services or of whether the agreements concern the use of spare capacity in existing installations or fields being developed in conjunction. The users are obliged to deliver all petroleum produced from the user field until 'permanent cessation of production' at the delivery point. Thus, their delivery obligation comprises all commercially recoverable petroleum from the field. **11.185**

The owner's obligation to receive does not correspond with this delivery obligation, but is restricted with respect to both quantity and quality of delivered petroleum. The quantities to be received are normally based on the assumed production profile for the user field with an allowance for production in excess of expectations. Restrictions on quality may be of a discretionary nature, such as 'petroleum suitable for processing', or may stipulate specifications quantifying the contents of certain components, temperature, and pressure. The owners are only obliged to receive petroleum delivered within these restrictions and are entitled to deny receipt of excess volumes or petroleum of different quality. Hence, the owners will only receive petroleum from the users at the pace and in the state they are able to produce it if it is in accordance with their receipt obligations. **11.186**

As the volumes that can be handled on the installations are limited, the owners will limit receivable quantities to retain sufficient capacity for their own use. Quality restrictions ensure technical and commercial compatibility of the streams. Processing facilities are designed for certain qualities with which the user's petroleum must comply. Commercially, blending various streams may affect the value of the combined stream; hence there are extensive procedures for adjusting the value of the blended stream between the parties. With respect to gas, the intermingled stream must in any case satisfy the sales specifications.[123] **11.187**

Operation of oil and gas fields may be interrupted by technical malfunctions, heavy weather, and other 'unscheduled events', as well as 'scheduled' maintenance. Hence, the receipt obligation is also limited in case of temporary loss of or reduction in the handling capacity at the owner installations. In the event of such 'shut-downs' the receipt obligations will be wholly or partly suspended depending on whether there is any capacity available to the users after the requirements of the owners have been satisfied. When there are two or more user groups, their access to any remaining capacity will depend on their internal priority. These priorities are normally sequential so that the first user has first priority and so forth, but pro rata distribution of available capacity between them does also occur.[124] **11.188**

[123] For instance, due to the widespread domestic use of gas, it must be without 'objectionable odours' or not exceed a certain minimum of sulphur content.

[124] In some instances the priorities are stipulated by authorities in the approval process, see paras 11.168–11.176 above.

11.189 When the owners receive the user petroleum, the owners will normally process it.[125] Their processing obligations are defined by the quantity and quality specifications on redelivered petroleum. With respect to quantity, the owners may only redeliver what 'remains' at the outlet of their installations. Likewise the quality specifications refer in most cases only to the petroleum 'as it results from' the processing on the owners' installations. However, sometimes these incorporate specifications applicable to the transport from the owner installations. In general, the owners may only redeliver a proportionate part of the final stream; thus they do not have to compensate users with their own petroleum if quantity or quality differ from what was expected.

11.190 The users pay a tariff per unit of throughput for the services rendered by the owners.[126] Such tariffs are referred to as unit tariffs, and there are in principle two main methods for calculating them. However, as these two may be varied and combined in many forms, there are a vast number of different tariff calculations in use. Capacity fees are seldom used. Such fees are rentals for the capacity required to satisfy the owners' receipt obligation, and are common for pipeline transport.

11.191 One method to calculate a unit tariff is simply to agree upon a fixed amount per unit that covers all costs as well as profit. This amount is increased on an annual basis according to an agreed index.[127] These are easy to maintain, as they require only a minimum of adjustments, in particular if they rely on historical data rather than forecasts for throughput and escalation. Fixed-unit tariffs are today the most common. By the other main method, the unit tariff is calculated as a pro-rata share of actual costs with a profit premium.[128] The calculation of these necessitates a vast amount of work, as they rely on various forecasts and require substantial audits to verify the actual amounts. This is probably why they are now seldom used in agreements. However, pro-rata sharing of operation cost items is sometimes used in conjunction with fixed-unit tariffs.

11.192 Neither method is well suited for governmental control of the tariff level. When a fixed amount is agreed, there will be no information on how it was calculated. Thus, unless background information is given, it is only possible to make a discretionary assessment of the reasonableness of the amount. Conversely, the Government will have to deploy significant resources to control the amount of information available when pro-rata sharing is used. Even then, the final assessment of whether the tariff

[125] In some cases the petroleum is just transported through the owner installations into a pipeline grid.

[126] The units used are either barrels (bbl) or standard cubic meters (Sm^3). 1 bbl = 42 US gallons = 159 l; 1 Sm^3 = 1000 l = 6,29 bbls.

[127] The Consumer Price Index is commonly used, sometimes weighted with a petroleum price index.

[128] All capital and operational costs (Capex and Opex) plus a profit element are divided by the total units of throughput to arrive at a cost per bbl or Sm^3 as the case may be.

is reasonable will easily rest on a discretionary assessment of the profit premium. In both cases, this may be done by comparing with a 'market level'. However, in a market where there are significant opportunities for excessive pricing due to imperfect competition, this does not seem to be satisfactory. In general, the need for means of governmental control with the tariff level seems to have made little or no impact on the tariff structures stipulated in the agreements.

In general, the agreements distribute risk between the parties with a bias in favour of the owners. This is a reflection of the secondary business nature of third-party use for the owners. Their principal business objective is production of the owner field; thus they will seek to limit any potential disturbances or liabilities by third-party use as far as possible. The owners' ability to reduce their risk exposure is exacerbated by their knowledge and experience of both their field and their installations. Conversely, users must rely mostly on prognosis in assessing their needs when the agreements are made.[129] **11.193**

This bias is most pronounced in the lack of correspondence between the delivery and receipt obligations, which expose users to the risks of erroneous estimates of their needs, while it protects owners against similar risks on their side. For instance, the limitations on quantity and quality reduce the risk of disturbances to the owners' production while they may delay or otherwise restrain the production of the user field. However, this is to some extent countered by the owners assuming the financial risk for under-utilization of their installations. Due to the nature of the unit tariffs users only pay for the actual utilization of capacity. Finally, users are exposed to the risk of deficiencies in the handling of petroleum by the 'as it becomes' requirements to redelivered petroleum. **11.194**

Tie-in of user field to owner's installations

To make third-party use physically possible, the user field must be connected to the owner installations by flowlines and other means. In nearly all cases modifications must be undertaken on the owner installations, which may also require new equipment to be installed. The contractual solutions regarding responsibility for the work in the regulation of these 'tie-in' operations have changed over the years, but are now fairly uniform. **11.195**

Basically, the development of the user field comprises three elements: the user installations, the connections between the fields, and the modifications of the owner installations. The users are always responsible for all work related to the user installations, and normally also for the connection work.[130] In modern agreements **11.196**

[129] Normally the performances of installations and in particular the field reservoirs are improved over the field life. This tendency is the main reason for the large increases of Norwegian oil production over the forecasts.

[130] This will depend on whether transport between the fields is one of the services rendered by the owners, but that is seldom the case.

the owners are responsible for all work done at their installations.[131] As the modifications are incorporated into the owner installations, they will be part of the owners' property.[132]

11.197 Even though the modifications are undertaken on behalf of the users, they have in most cases no mechanisms to influence the work, apart from a stated intent that it shall be done in close co-operation with them. This lack of control is further exacerbated by the scope of work normally being defined only by vague functional criteria. This lack of control of the work exposes the users to both schedule and cost overruns.

11.198 With respect to costs, the exposure will depend on the format of payment. In the typical case, users must reimburse all costs. In these cases they have no significant control either over the performance of the work nor over costs. In view of the intense focus on costs within the industry, this is surprising. The reason may be that the owners, in particular their operator, refuse to assume any cost risks and to subject themselves to the scrutiny common in fabrication contracts.[133] In some instances a lump sum is set for the modifications, which the parties may agree to alter if the scope of work is changed.[134] In these cases, owners have the risk for cost overruns, unless users consent to increase the lump sum. This increased risk for the owners may be the reason why lump sums have not become industry practice, in spite of strong support of them as a measure to reduce modifications costs.

11.199 A general impression is that the parties have not recognized that the owners do their work on behalf of the users. Thus, their role is similar to that of a contractor, while the role in the agreements resembles that of an operator in a licence group. This does not take into account that the interest in controlling schedule and costs is not shared between owners and users in the same manner as it is between an operator and the other licensees in a group.

The Nature of the contractual obligations

11.200 There are two components in the agreements that are relevant for assessing the nature of the contractual obligations of the parties. These are the prudent operator concept and the *force majeure* clause, which both come from American law. There are no clear distinctions as to when they apply; however, this may be of limited importance as they have a similar, if not identical, legal nature.

11.201 In the agreements the standard of care for contractual performance of the duties of the parties is defined either by the prudent operator concept or by descriptions

[131] In some older agreements the users are also responsible for modification works, but this required extensive interfacing between the parties to allow the owners the necessary control over the work.

[132] The users will retain tax depreciation rights for the modification cost covered by them.

[133] See section B8 below.

[134] Vague descriptions of the work may increase the difficulties of agreeing an amount of change.

of similar legal content. According to American law, proper performance requires that the conduct at least must satisfy the 'customs in the field', but this may not always be sufficient due to new technological developments. Thus, within the limits of economic feasibility, the best available practices and technology shall be used. Similar requirements would also follow from Norwegian background law. This standard of care sets strict requirements on contractual performance of the duties. Negligent performance will constitute breach of contract.[135]

Force majeure clauses define both what constitutes a *force majeure* and the contractual effects of such events. Any event that is 'beyond the reasonable control' of the parties constitutes *force majeure*, provided that immediate notice is given and all reasonable actions to limit or prevent the consequences thereof have been taken. There is normally also a non-exhaustive list of events of such nature, including 'breakage of machinery', that are within the sphere of control of the party in question. However, these will only constitute *force majeure* if their occurrence was beyond the 'reasonable control' of the party. This must be interpreted strictly. Events that are rare, but of which there is some experience and which may be controlled by cost-effective means will not be beyond 'reasonable control'. It may be assumed that only novel or rare events whose prevention would entail excessive costs constitute *force majeure*. In general these considerations point in the direction of a strict standard of care, similar to the one that follows from the prudent operator concept. **11.202**

When there is a *force majeure* event, the party in question is relieved of any liability for failure to perform his obligations. Thus, his performance is deemed to be contractually satisfactory, in the same manner as when the standard of care is satisfied. **11.203**

The contractual implications of the *force majeure* clause go beyond those with which '*force majeure*' is associated in Norwegian background law. According to the clauses a larger range of events may constitute *force majeure*. Further, according to Norwegian general principles such events would only relieve the party from liability to pay damages, while he still would be in breach of contract. **11.204**

Comparability to pipeline agreements

Agreements on the transport of oil and gas through pipelines have the same features as those described above for agreements on the use of installations. These contractual similarities are due to the factual commonality between these two services, as both relate to the flow of petroleum owned by one party through a system owned by another. **11.205**

[135] In Norwegian law this is referred to as a performance obligation ('*omsorgsforpliktelse*').

11.206 However, pipelines are vital for the export of gas from the production facilities.[136] Furthermore, they are expensive, and access to a pipeline system is in most cases decisive for field development. Thus the main difference between the two services are found, not in the contractual terms, but in the higher level of governmental control of pipelines due to their importance for the exploitation of petroleum resources.[137]

Conclusions

11.207 Ever since the commencement of oil activities on the NCS, the Government has emphasized the need to utilize spare capacity in existing production installations to reduce the total costs of the industry.

11.208 Legally, the key instrument for implementation of this policy is the PDO approval (PA section 4-2). The PDO approval is a vital element in the licensing system and is used to control field development on the NCS, but only a few examples of this policy are reflected in PDO approvals. This may be because the licence groups decide on such concepts following a dialogue with the authorities on development alternatives. More importantly, the apparent lack of governmental control is probably due to a shared interest in such use between the licensees and Government. Both aim at maximizing profit from the activities, so both will strive to reduce costs. Hence, in most cases the governmental objectives will coincide with those of the licensees.

11.209 Commercial terms, which distort the balance between owners and users, form the major potential reason for conflicting interests between licensees and Government. However, in most cases the authorities approve the terms agreed between the parties pursuant to PA section 4-8. This indicates that any imperfections there should be in the market for third-party use have not been exploited to an extent conflicting with governmental objectives. Further, it may also demonstrate that, in the face of such technical and commercial complexity as third-party use offers, the ability for the Government to control individual solutions is limited. Hence, the Government will have to rely on increasing third-party use by general political statements. Such statements compel the licence groups to investigate such alternatives seriously in order to satisfy these particular governmental demands on prudent operations.

[136] Pipeline transport is only *required* for gas; as oil is a liquid, export of stabilized crude by tanker is often the most economical solution. However, oil normally contains amounts of associated gas larger than would be used as fuel on the field, and as flaring is not permitted pipeline transport is necessary for almost all fields.

[137] See paras 11.87–11.91 and 11.92–11.94 above.

(6) Abandonment

Introduction

The development of a petroleum field can be divided into successive phases: exploration, exploration drilling, production, and abandonment. This is also reflected in the new PA. Each phase of the development is regulated by a separate chapter in the PA. Thus, chapter 5 deals with the abandonment of installations. **11.210**

The Norwegian legislation on abandonment has developed gradually.[138] The latest legislative effort is a result of two developments: one on the national level and one on the international level. The basic question is: what is to be done with the installations after production has ceased permanently? This question is becoming more and more important on the Norwegian continental shelf. Three relatively small fields have already reached the end of production.[139] Several fields, among them the Frigg field, are rapidly approaching the end of production. At the beginning of the next century production in three of the big oilfields will close down.[140] **11.211**

The Norwegian continental shelf is characterized by deep water and severe weather conditions. This makes removal operations technically difficult and very cost-intensive. The conditions are similar to those on the UK continental shelf, but very different from those in the Mexican Gulf and most other offshore petroleum provinces. **11.212**

Some figures illustrate the magnitude of the problem. As to Norwegian installations, approximately seventy have been constructed or are under construction. A complete removal of all the installations has been estimated to cost up to NOK 50 billion.[141] **11.213**

The abandonment of installations also raises other concerns, especially relating to the safety of installations and personnel, the marine environment, and other uses of the sea. Summing up, the prospect of an increasing number of petroleum field shut-downs, combined with the complexity and variety of interests involved, call for a more comprehensive regulation of the abandonment phase. **11.214**

On the international level the abandonment phase has received increasing attention in recent years. Norway has acceded to the IMO Guidelines and has ratified the OSPAR Convention, and is thus committed to adapting its national legislation and practice to the new international framework. The PA chapter 5 is a result of this adaptation. **11.215**

[138] Abandonment was first regulated in the Royal Decree of 9 April 1965 s 50, then in the Royal Decree of 8 December 1972 section 50, and then in the Petroleum Act of 22 March 1985 s 30.

[139] North East Frigg, Odin, and Mime.

[140] Statfjord, Gullfaks, and Oseberg.

[141] The amount corresponds to GDP 5 billion. The figures are from NOU 1993: 25 14–15.

The legislation: key issues and characteristics

11.216 In principle the following main options are available once an offshore installation is disused: either to leave the installation in place or to remove the installation completely or partially. This can be called (1) the issue of removal. If the second alternative is chosen, the next issue is to decide where and how to dispose of the installation. The installation can be disposed on site, in the sea elsewhere, or on land. This can be called (2) the issue of disposal.

11.217 On this background the PA chapter 5 establishes a decision-making process based on the principle of a case-by-case evaluation. The decision-making process starts with an abandonment plan prepared by the licensee. On the basis of this plan the MPE decides on both the removal and disposal issues.[142] This allows flexible and case-specific Government control of the abandonment phase. It is important to note that this form of Government control is a characteristic feature of the licence system under the PA. As previously mentioned the abandonment plan forms a part of this licence system.[143]

11.218 Another characteristic feature is direct State participation. Generally, the Norwegian State has direct economic participation in the petroleum licences, administered by Statoil, the so-called SDFI.[144] In the abandonment phase, however, an additional dimension is added to the SDFI due to the special tax regime on removal costs. According to the Act relating to the allocation of costs of removal of installations, the Removal Cost Act, the State pays a direct share of the total costs of removal, in addition to the share incurred as a result of the SDFI. On the other hand, removal costs incurred by the individual licensees are not deductible for tax purposes. Thus, the effect of the Removal Cost Act is to exclude removal costs from the ordinary tax system. Another effect is that every abandonment case must be presented to Parliament as a budgetary matter.

11.219 The State share of the removal costs in relation to each licensee is equal to the sum of income tax paid by the licensee divided by the sum of the tax base of the licensee. Both amounts refer to the period of use of the installation by the licensee.[145] For example, if the licensee during the relevant period has paid 80 per cent of his income in taxes, the State will pay 80 per cent of the removal costs.

11.220 I will next deal with the abandonment plan and thereafter with the decision of the MPE. These issues refer to the relationship between the licensee/owner of the installation and the Government. The PA chapter 5 also deals with the relationship

[142] Ministry of Petroleum and Energy.
[143] The licence system is described in paras 11.31–11.37 above.
[144] The SDFI is discussed in paras 11.38–11.54 above.
[145] Act no 11 of 25 April 1986 relating to removal costs.

between the licensee/owner and third parties. This is the liability issue and is discussed in a separate context (together with other liability issues).[146]

The abandonment plan

The abandonment plan was formally introduced by PA chapter 5. However, an abandonment plan has been required by the MPE since the first case arose in the beginning of the 1990s. In this respect the new PA represents a codification of Government practice.[147] **11.221**

The obligation to prepare an abandonment plan rests upon the licensees of production licences and pipeline licences: PA section 5-1. This means that both production installations and pipelines are subject to the plan and the subsequent decision by the MPE. As a result of the geographical scope of PA section 1-4, installations on land that are functionally connected to the offshore activities are also subject to the plan. In respect of such installations, however, the MPE has a limited range of alternatives.[148] **11.222**

The obligation of the licensee depends upon two main events: the permanent disuse of the installations or the expiry of the licence, whichever event comes first. **11.223**

If the licence expiry comes first, and the installations may still be used, the licensee may apply for an extension of the licence instead of preparing an abandonment plan. The obligation to prepare an abandonment plan will then depend upon the outcome of the MPE's handling of the extension application. The obligation to prepare an abandonment plan also arises if a licence is surrendered by the licensee or revoked by the MPE. I will not go further into these situations in the following presentation. **11.224**

The licensee must present the plan to the MPE not earlier than five years, but not later than two years, prior to the above events. The purpose is to allow sufficient time for the MPE to handle and decide upon the plan before the events actually occur. However, the MPE may decide upon other time limits. The MPE may also exempt the licensee from the obligation to prepare the plan, or grant a partial exemption by requiring a less extensive plan. On the other hand the MPE may require additional information or even a new or modified plan. In short, the PA enables the MPE to exercise wide discretionary powers over the timing and contents of the abandonment plan. **11.225**

[146] See paras 11.236 *et seq* below.

[147] The first case was the removal of the North-East Frigg installations. The case was presented to Parliament by St prp No 36 (1994–95). The next case was the removal of the Odin installations, cf St prp No 50 (1995–96).

[148] See paras 11.228–11.232 below.

11.226 As to the contents of the plan PA section 5-1 is very general. In this regard the PA is supplemented by the petroleum regulations chapter 6, which contains the more detailed provisions. The abandonment plan shall consist of two parts; one part describing the decision alternatives and the other an impact analysis. As to the former, the licensee is obligated to present all alternatives relevant to the specific case. These alternatives may range from complete or partial removal to continued use for petroleum production, transportation purposes, or other purposes. They also include the mere abandonment of the installation in combination with future maintenance and inspections. In respect of each alternative the licensee is required to evaluate the relevant concerns with regard to technical feasibility, costs, and safety. As to the latter part of the plan the licensee must evaluate the impact of each alternative decision with regard to the marine environment, other uses of the sea, and various interests on land that might be affected by the abandonment.

11.227 Even though several alternatives must be presented and evaluated, the licensee must recommend one of them, and it is recognized that this alternative will be described in more detail than the others.[149]

The Ministry of Petroleum and Energy's decision

11.228 The licensee shall submit the abandonment plan to the MPE within the above time limits. The plan is not subject to the MPE's approval. Instead the MPE selects one of the alternatives of the licensee, but not necessarily the recommended one, and decides accordingly. In this respect the PA section 5-3 leaves a very wide margin of discretion to the MPE. However, the practice of the MPE must comply with international guidelines and conventions.

11.229 The MPE decides on both the removal issue and the disposal issue. Thus, it can choose between all the alternatives mentioned earlier. As far as the disposal issue is concerned the licensee will need separate permits from the relevant authorities responsible for the marine environment, the safety of navigation, and the safety of installations and personnel. These permits refer to the removal operation.

11.230 As to installations on land the PA limits the discretion of the MPE: PA section 5-3 sixth paragraph. In this regard the decisions available are continued use in petroleum activities, including State take-over for such purposes. The other alternatives are for other authorities to decide according to the relevant land legislation.

11.231 So far the practice of the MPE can be summarized as follows. Steel platforms to be removed and subsequently disposed of on land. Concrete structures to be removed and disposed of at sea. Pipelines and cables to be left in place. However, it

---

149 cf Ot prp No 43 (1995–96) 49–50.

must be borne in mind that the cases so far have been few and they have only involved small platforms and structures.[150]

The MPE stipulates a time limit for the licensee's implementation of the decision. PA section 5-3 designates the licensee, the owner (who may be an entity other than the licensee) and the user (if the installation is to be used for other purposes than petroleum activities) as responsible entities. In this context the term licensee also means the previous licensee if the licence has expired. However, the MPE may decide to designate only one or two as responsible entities. In this respect also the flexible case-by-case approach applies.[151] **11.232**

State take-over of installations

If the installation is to be left in place, a special alternative is State take-over of the installation pursuant to PA section 5-6. This option applies to installations permanently placed on the sea bed, but not to mobile installations.[152] Normally, State take-over is only an attractive alternative if the installation has commercial value.[153] **11.233**

The State can, however, take over the responsibility for an abandoned installation, with little or no economic value, subject to compensation from the licensee/owner of the installation. This requires an agreement between the parties (PA section 5-4 fourth paragraph). The contents of such an agreement will in all respects be a matter for negotiation between the parties. **11.234**

If the installation is placed outside the part of the sea bed subject to private property rights, ie on the continental shelf, the King decides to what extent compensation shall be given for the take-over.[154] It may choose to take over the installations without compensation. That was the only alternative in the 1985 Act. If, on the other hand, the installation is placed on land, or on the part of the sea bed subject to private property rights, the licensee can claim full compensation pursuant to Norwegian law. **11.235**

[150] cf the North-East Frigg and Odin cases.

[151] However, the MPE has to take into account IMO Guidelines Art 3.11 which imposes an obligation on the coastal State to ensure that legal title to installations and structures which have not been entirely removed from the sea bed is unambiguous, and that responsibility for maintenance and the financial ability to compensate for future damage are clearly established.

[152] The distinction between these two categories of installations is based on a functional criterion. If the installation is designed to serve only one petroleum field, the installation is permanently placed. If it is designed to serve several petroleum fields, it is mobile. cf Ot prp No 43 (1995–96) 53.

[153] This may be due to the fact that the petroleum field is not depleted, or that the pipeline can transport petroleum from other fields than the initial one(s).

[154] In this context 'King' means the Norwegian Cabinet, see para 11.15 above.

(7) Liability

Introduction

11.236 The PA contains four liability regimes dealing exclusively with petroleum activities. Section 10-9 imposes extensive vicarious liability on the licensee. Chapter 7 regulates liability for petroleum pollution. Chapter 8 has special compensation rules with regard to the losses that Norwegian fishermen suffer as a result of petroleum activities. Finally, section 5-4 regulates liability in the abandonment phase. The liability regimes are supplemented by the general rules of Norwegian tort law.[155] In addition the liability regulation in the Maritime Act (MA) and the general Pollution Act apply to certain aspects of petroleum activities.

11.237 The MA regulates tort issues related to ships and vessels, including those performing tasks in petroleum activities. The MA also regulates tort issues related to mobile drilling platforms, but not pollution resulting from leakage or discharge of petroleum during a drilling operation.[156] Such pollution is regulated by PA chapter 7. The Pollution Act regulates tort issues related to other forms of pollution than petroleum pollution. It may apply when such damage stems from petroleum activities.

11.238 The following presentation will concentrate on the special liability regimes of the PA, with emphasis on their characteristic features. It should be noted that these regimes apply when third parties suffer damage. If the injured party has a contractual relationship with the licensee the liability issues will normally be subject to a bilateral regulation that may deviate from Norwegian tort law.[157]

11.239 The liability regimes are quite different in structure, but the main responsible party is the licensee.[158] This is due to the organizational structure of Norwegian petroleum activities.[159] In practice a major part of the work is outsourced to contractors and sub-contractors. Thus, the practical work is carried out by a hierarchy of contractors, with the licence group, represented by the operator, on top. Since much of the practical work is carried out by entities other than the licence group, this may in theory dilute the responsibilities of the group and its licensees towards the State and third parties. As a result the PA prescribes that each licensee must

[155] As a main non-statutory rule liability occurs when negligence has been exercised. However, the courts have developed strict liability for hazardous and dangerous activities, which—as far as petroleum activities are concerned—would have resulted in liability in any event.

[156] MA s 507.

[157] See paras 11.306 *et seq* below on fabrication contracts. Such contracts may also regulate how the contract parties shall handle claims from a third party who has suffered a loss because of damage related to the contract work.

[158] As far as PA s 5-4 is concerned the licensee is not the only main responsible party. This provision has several characteristic features that separate it from the other liability regimes of the Act. See paras 11.259–11.268 below.

[159] Licences are normally issued to a group of licensees. One of the licensees is appointed as operator and (in this capacity) performs the petroleum activities on behalf of the licence group.

ensure that anyone working for the licence group complies with the PA, including the regulations and decisions passed pursuant to the PA.[160] This kind of overall responsibility is also reflected in the liability regulations.

This designation of the licensee as the main responsible party also has strong economic and practical reasons. Apart from the Norwegian State the licensees have the largest economic interest in petroleum activities. They are financially strong entities who are able to obtain adequate insurance cover for their activities in the open market. In these regards they will normally be in a much better position than their contractors and sub-contractors. **11.240**

Vicarious liability

PA section 10-9 regulates the liability of the licensee for damage caused by a person—legal or natural—who performs work for the licensee, ie the vicarious liability of the licensee. The scope of the liability is wide in several respects. First, the liability generally refers to damage caused to third parties as a result of petroleum activities. The term 'petroleum activity' is defined in PA section 1-6 to cover all activities connected to the development of petroleum fields on the Norwegian continental shelf. Such development can be divided into successive phases, ie exploration, exploration drilling, production, and abandonment. In each phase the term not only covers the main activities conducted offshore but also the related activities conducted on land, ie planning and building installations. To some extent the PA also applies to main activities conducted on land if they are connected to a petroleum field offshore.[161] **11.241**

As to the damage, PA section 10-9 is also generally formulated. However, in this respect the scope of the provision is limited by the application of the special liability regimes of PA chapters 7 and 8. This means that section 10-9 does not apply to losses resulting from petroleum pollution and to losses which Norwegian fishermen suffer as a result of petroleum activities.[162] **11.242**

Secondly, the licensee is liable for anyone working or performing work or services for him. This covers all kinds of contractors and sub-contractors, including the employees of such entities.[163] It is not necessary that such entities have a direct contractual relationship with the licensee as long as they are part of the hierarchy **11.243**

160 PA s 10-6.

161 The typical example is the transportation of petroleum through a pipeline from an offshore field to a terminal, which may be situated some kilometers onshore from the landing point.

162 This is stated in PA s 10-9 second paragraph with regard to petroleum pollution and in the PA s 8-1 fifth paragraph with regard to the losses suffered by Norwegian fishermen. However, the scope of s 10-9 is not restricted to the provisions of ch 8 when it comes to injuries to persons: see paras 11.251–11.258 below.

163 As to his own employees the licensee is liable under Act No 26 of 13 June 1969 relating to tort, ch 2. According to section 2-1 the employer is strictly liable when the damage is caused by negligence or wilful misconduct by an employee during his work for the employer.

of entities which performs work related to the relevant licence.[164] In this respect the vicarious liability under the PA is wider than other forms of vicarious liability under Norwegian tort law.[165]

11.244 Thirdly, the licensee's liability is independent of the type of liability incurred by the contractor. Depending on the circumstances the contractor's liability may be strict or based on negligence.

11.245 Ordinarily it is a prerequisite to vicarious liability that the underlying tortfeasor has been negligent.[166] PA section 10-9 equates the scope of the licensee's liability with the scope of the contractor's liability. Thus, the licensee becomes liable to the same extent as the contractor, and can thereby claim the same exemptions and limitations of liability. The ordinary vicarious liability provisions leave the scope of liability imposed on the vicarious party independent of the tortfeasor's liability, with the consequence that the vicarious liability may be significantly greater.

11.246 If the requisite conditions for liability of the actual tortfeasor, ie the contractor, are satisfied, contractor and licensee are jointly and severally liable towards the injured party. In this respect PA section 10-9 does not require a claim by the injured party to be directed against the licensee. If the licensee compensates the injured party, he can claim indemnity from the contractor according to Norwegian tort law. PA section 10-9 does not shield the contractor from such claims from the licensee. In short, PA section 10-9 has no channelling provisions in favour of the contractor with regard to claims by an injured party or the licensee.

Liability for petroleum pollution damage

11.247 PA chapter 7 regulates liability for petroleum pollution damage. This liability regime is in several respects different from the vicarious liability under PA section 10-9. First, the scope is regulated through a functional definition of the term 'pollution damage' (PA section 7-1). According to this definition the provisions only apply when damage or loss are caused by pollution resulting from leakage or discharge of petroleum from an installation or well, including the cost of reasonable measures taken to prevent or remedy such damage or loss. Thus, discharge of petroleum from ships transporting petroleum is not covered by chapter 7. In this respect the liability rules of MA chapter 10 apply.[167] The definition does not specify the damage or losses which may result from leakage or discharge of petroleum, or the injured parties, except that such damage or loss also includes lost fishing

[164] See paras 11.236–11.240 above.

[165] The vicarious liability under MA s 151 is one example.

[166] cf MA s 151.

[167] These are in important respects similar to those in the PA ch 7. According to MA s 191 the ship owner is strictly liable for pollution resulting from discharge of oil, including bunker oil, from the ship. The liability is channelled to the ship owner pursuant to s 193.

opportunities for fishermen. As to petroleum pollution damage, the fishermen always have to rely on chapter 7. They cannot invoke the liability regime of chapter 8.[168]

Secondly, the geographical scope is subject to special regulation in section 7-2. Here the PA focuses on where the damage occurs, and not where the damage stems from. In this respect chapter 7 differs from all the other liability regimes. Chapter 7 applies when pollution damage as defined occurs on the Norwegian continental shelf, in Norwegian territorial waters, in Norwegian internal waters, or on Norwegian territory. The installation which causes damage may be situated in those areas, but it may also be situated on the continental shelf etc of another State. PA chapter 7 also applies if the pollution damage occurs in sea areas outside the Norwegian continental shelf, but in such cases the liability regime mainly seeks to protect Norwegian interests.[169] **11.248**

Thirdly, PA section 7-3 imposes strict liability on the licensee for petroleum pollution damage. The liability of the licensee is combined with channelling provisions whereby participants in the activities are wholly or partly shielded from liability. These provisions work at two levels. If there are several participants in a licence, the injured party must direct his claim against the operator. Only if the operator fails to cover the claim may it be directed towards the other licensees. Other participants providing work or services for the licensee, ie contractors and sub-contractors, are also shielded from liability claims by the injured party (PA section 7-4). In addition, they are shielded from indemnity actions by the licensee (PA section 7-5). They can only be made liable if they, or someone in their organization, have acted wilfully or with gross negligence, and even in these cases the damages may be reduced or set aside if this is considered reasonable. **11.249**

The liability of the licensee is in principle unlimited. According to PA section 7-3, however, the courts have discretionary power to reduce the liability, partly or completely, if *force majeure* or similar events have contributed to the petroleum pollution damage. In theory, liability may also be reduced if this is considered reasonable pursuant to the general provision of section 5-2 in the Act on Torts. The latter provision is probably more important with regard to the other liability regimes of the PA, that do not have a special *force majeure* provision like the one in chapter 7.[170] **11.250**

[168] See paras 11.251 *et seq* below.

[169] In such areas ch 7 applies if damage is sustained by Norwegian vessels, Norwegian fishing gear, or Norwegian installations. However, this limitation does not apply if the damage occurs on the land or sea territory of a State which has acceded to the Nordic Convention on Environmental Protection of 19 February 1974.

[170] In comparison the liability of the ship owner for oil pollution damage is limited to a specified amount pursuant to MA s 194, cf s 195.

Compensation to Norwegian fishermen

11.251 PA chapter 8 regulates compensation to Norwegian fishermen for losses they suffer as a result of petroleum activities. Foreign fishermen cannot claim compensation pursuant to this liability regime. Its purpose is basically to ameliorate the conflict between petroleum and fishing activities on the Norwegian continental shelf. This conflict could have been solved by economic grants from the State or the licensees. Instead the legislator has chosen to solve the conflict by means of the general tort law principles adapted to the special conflict.

11.252 It follows from the above that PA chapter 8 only addresses economic losses suffered by the fishermen as a result of conflict with petroleum activities on the Norwegian continental shelf. Injuries to persons must be compensated according to Norwegian tort law or the other liability rules of the PA.[171]

11.253 There are three kinds of situations which qualify for compensation. First is the situation where fishermen have to leave some or all of their traditional fishing fields because these are occupied by the petroleum activities. Such occupation is not due to an illegal act by the licensees: they have been granted the right to operate in the relevant areas pursuant to a licence issued by the State. For this reason PA section 8-2 designates the State as the responsible party. The liability of the State is, however, limited in time. After seven years from the initial occupation of the fishing field, the State is normally not obligated to pay compensation. By this time the fishermen are expected to have adjusted their activities to the new situation. As to occupation, the licensees have no direct liability towards the fishermen pursuant to the PA. However, if the fishermen's activities are unnecessarily hindered by the activities of the licensee, the State may claim indemnification from the licensee.

11.254 The second situation is where fishermen suffer losses due to pollution and waste from the petroleum activities. In this respect PA section 8-3 imposes strict liability upon the licensee. It must be noted that this liability does not cover petroleum pollution damage. Such damage is regulated by PA chapter 7.[172] Pollution under chapter 8 includes chemicals and other toxic substances from the petroleum activities. Waste may be various kinds of debris left in the vicinity of the well or along the sailing routes of supply vessels.[173] This means that pollution and waste may stem from the activities of contractors or sub-contractors, eg the owners of supply vessels. In accordance with the general principles of the PA the licensee is

[171] cf PA s 10-9 in particular.

[172] PA ch 7 makes no distinction between fishermen and other injured parties or interests. See paras 11.247 *et seq* above.

[173] Such pollution and waste is covered by the general liability regime of the Pollution Act, but as a result of the PA chapter 8 the former act will only apply when such pollution or waste causes damage to other users of the sea. In such cases the Pollution Act s 55 imposes a strict and unlimited liability upon the owner of the installation that has caused the damage.

responsible for the activities of such entities.[174] However, such entities are not shielded from direct action by the fishermen and the licensee may claim indemnification pursuant to Norwegian tort law. This means that the channelling of liability towards the licensee is less developed in PA chapter 8 than in chapter 7.[175]

PA section 8-4 establishes joint and several liability between different licensees which deviates from general tort law principles. As to waste along sailing routes, it may be relatively easy to connect the waste to the petroleum activities, but difficult to identify the responsible licensee since a supply vessel may be serving several petroleum fields. In such cases PA section 8-4 establishes a two-step procedure. First, the fishermen have to prove—according to general tort law principles—that the waste stems from the petroleum activities. Secondly, when it comes to identifying the responsible licensees, it is only necessary to prove that the damage could have arisen from their part of the petroleum activities. In practice this means that if a supply vessel serves several petroleum fields located within a fairly limited area, all the licensees within that area are jointly and severally liable for the damage. **11.255**

Fishing losses incurred as a result of pollution and waste will typically be loss of catch or time loss (due to interrupted fishing) or loss of or damage to fishing gear. Liability is in principle unlimited. PA section 8-3 stipulates certain evidential requirements when compensation is sought for time loss.[176] **11.256**

The third kind of situation is where fishing gear is snared by installations on the sea bed, eg in pipelines or drilling wells. In this respect PA section 8-5 imposes strict and unlimited liability on the licensee. This situation resembles the one where fishing gear is caught in waste on the sea bed. However, section 8-5 refers to situations where the installation is still in use and where it is easy to identify the responsible party.[177] If the installation on the sea bed represents such a danger that fishermen have to leave the whole area, section 8-2 is applicable. We see that there are close relationships between the three liability regulations in chapter 8. **11.257**

A notable feature of the liability regime in the PA chapter 8 is the handling of fishermen's claims for compensation. As a first step the claims are handled by a special commission. Two commissions have been established, one dealing with compensation for occupation of fishing fields, and one dealing with compensation for pollution, waste, and damage caused by installations.[178] The decision of the commissions may be presented to an appeal board. Its decision may then be brought before the ordinary courts (section 8-6). **11.258**

---

174 See paras 11.236–11.240 above.

175 See paras 11.247 *et seq* above.

176 In order to claim compensation for lost fishing time in connection with locating, marking, retrieval, or bringing ashore objects, the objects shall—as a main rule—be properly marked or brought ashore and presented to the police or the port authority.

177 When the installation is abandoned s 8-5 may also apply. See paras 11.259–11.268 above.

178 cf regulations of 27 July 1990 passed pursuant to the PA.

Liability in the abandonment phase

11.259 PA section 5-4 regulates liability in the abandonment phase. There are important overlaps between this liability regime and those presented above. Nonetheless, PA section 5-4 is based on other principles, discussed below.

11.260 On the basis of the abandonment plan presented by the licensee, the MPE decides whether the installation shall be left in place or removed.[179] In the former case the MPE may decide that the installation shall be used for petroleum activities by the licensee. On behalf of the State it may also take over the installation pursuant to the PA section 5-6 and continue the petroleum activities. In such cases the liability regimes mentioned above apply.[180] The following concentrates upon the other decision alternatives. If the installation is left in place, the alternatives are uses other than for petroleum activities or abandonment. In case of removal, the alternatives are total or partial removal.

11.261 The PA section 5-3 designates the party or parties responsible for the implementation of the MPE's decision. These are the licensee, the owner (if he is not the licensee), and the user (if the installation is to be used for purposes other than petroleum activities). In this context the term licensee includes the former licensee if the licence has expired. All these entities will be responsible for the implementation of the MPE's decision, unless the MPE decides otherwise.

11.262 Alternatively, the State may take over the responsibility for abandoned installations, including future liability (PA section 5-4 fourth paragraph). This arrangement requires a special agreement between the State and the licensee/owner of the installation. It will also require compensation from the licensee/owner to the State. The extent of the compensation will—together with all other issues—be subject to negotiations.

11.263 PA section 5-4 is a very simple and general provision. It merely states that the responsible party pursuant to section 5-3 is liable for damage caused during the implementation of the MPE's decision, provided that such damage results from negligence or wilful misconduct by a responsible party.[181] Several entities may be responsible for implementing the MPE's decision pursuant to section 5-3 and thus several entities may be liable under section 5-4. In that case they are jointly and severally responsible for the economic obligations arising as a result of the liability, unless the MPE decides otherwise. The economic scope of the liability is unlimited.

---

[179] See paras 11.221–11.227 and 11.228–11.232 above.

[180] As far as the State is concerned this follows from the general provision in PA s 1-3.

[181] In fact it is not necessary to enact a liability based on negligence since this already follows from the main non-statutory rule in Norwegian tort law.

PA section 10-7 authorizes the MPE to require security from the licensees for their fulfilment of economic obligations resulting from the petroleum activities, including economic obligations towards third parties. This provision is especially important in the abandonment phase when licensees are winding up their operations. In this connection PA section 10-7 second paragraph specifies that security may also be demanded from the owner or the user of an installation if he is a responsible party pursuant to section 5-3. **11.264**

The following characteristic features of the regime can be identified so far. First, the main responsible party is not only the licensee, but may also be the owner and the user. Secondly, the number of responsible entities, and the matter of joint and several responsibility for economic obligations, may be subject to case-by-case decisions by the MPE.[182] Thirdly, there are no channelling provisions. The injured party may direct his claim against any of the parties responsible for economic obligations. The injured party may also direct his claim against contractors or subcontractors of the responsible parties on the basis of Norwegian tort law. Fourthly, the principle of strict liability prevailing elsewhere in the PA is deviated from in section 5-4. **11.265**

However, the liability regime of PA section 5-4, cf section 5-3, does not exclude the application of the other liability regimes of the Act. These apply to all phases of the petroleum activities, including the abandonment phase.[183] In this phase they are supplemented by section 5-4.[184] This implies an overlap between liability regimes. It occurs when the installation is permanently disused and the subsequent decision of the MPE (on the basis of the abandonment plan) is implemented prior to the expiry of the licence. This is a very practical situation. Due to the length of the production licences most fields will have been depleted well before the expiry of the licence. **11.266**

A few examples illustrate the overlap. Whether the installation is left in place or removed, it always needs to be decommissioned. During this operation the vicarious liability of PA section 10-9 applies. Section 10-9 also applies during the removal operation, which may entail disposal on the production site, in the sea elsewhere, or on land. If fishermen suffer economic losses due to such disposal, PA chapter 8 applies. If petroleum leaks from abandoned wells, PA chapter 7 applies. **11.267**

On this background the position of the injured parties under the PA will depend on the circumstances. If the disposal takes place prior to licence expiry, all the **11.268**

[182] In this context the MPE has to take into account the IMO Guidelines Art 3.11 which imposes an obligation on the coastal State to ensure that legal title to installations and structures which have not been entirely removed from the sea bed is unambiguous and that responsibility for maintenance and financial ability to assume liability for future damage are clearly established.

[183] Cf the definition of 'petroleum activity' in the PA, s 1-6.

[184] Cf Ot prp No 43 (1995–96) 52.

liability regimes of the PA apply. If, on the other hand, it takes place after licence expiry, only the regime of section 5-4, cf section 5-3, applies. Only the latter regime is applicable if the installation is used for purposes other than petroleum activities.[185]

11.269 The regulation of liability in the abandonment phase is thus characterized by its discriminatory approach. Although this approach has no significance in most practical cases, it can be criticized from a principal point of view.

(8) The Relationship Between the Licensees and Suppliers of Goods and Services

The legal framework for contracting on the Norwegian offshore sector

11.270 Major deliveries for offshore development projects on the Norwegian continental shelf are to a large degree based on standard contract conditions negotiated between the major operating companies and the federation of Norwegian mechanical industries. This has been the situation since 1983.[186] The development of these agreed documents was initiated by strong political pressure to bring the contracts more closely into line with Norwegian tradition than had been the case in the early days of Norwegian offshore activities. In that sense, the State's involvement in the petroleum sector included the contracts. However, over the last ten years the development of agreed documents has taken up its own momentum, and the sponsors of the standard are continuously reviewing the need for modifications. Today Norway offers the only widely used standard construction contract in the area of offshore projects; although similar documents have been developed over the last few years, they have not so far attained widespread general use.[187] The Norwegian experience thus offers an interesting example of advanced offshore construction contracting.

11.271 The main rule, in Norway as in most other jurisdictions, is the rule of freedom of contract: the parties decide themselves when, how, and with whom they want to

[185] However, in the latter circumstances (after licence expiry) the question arises whether liability rules outside the PA may apply in relation to the licensee, especially the non-statutory rule on strict liability for hazardous and dangerous activities. This question was not addressed in PA chapter 5 nor commented upon during the preparation of the Act.

[186] The development of standards started as early as the late 1970s, resulting in the first set of model and standard conditions of contract in 1983, later replaced by the NF 87 and its successor NF 92: see paras 11.275 *et seq* below.

[187] In Europe, interesting developments have taken place in the Netherlands and in the UK. The 'Standard Construction/Modification/Maintenance Contract for the oil and gas industry in the Netherlands' (January, 1993) was negotiated between two major oil companies and two major contractors operating in the Netherlands. However, the document is meant to be used for work with a maximum value of 10m Dutch guilders, and it contains alternative clauses on several issues. In the UK, the establishing of standardized conditions of contract in the offshore petroleum industry was a key recommendation of the report of the Cost Reduction Initiative for the New Era. This resulted in a series of standards issued in 1997 (covering general conditions of contract for *inter alia* construction, offshore services, well services, and design).

enter into a contract, and they can agree on any conditions. But there are obviously some modifications to this rule.

First, the conditions of a contract have to adhere to general constraints laid down in general contract law, such as the rule of contractual fairness,[188] in order to be enforceable under Norwegian law. **11.272**

Secondly, the production licences state that all activities taking place on the basis of the licence shall be governed by Norwegian law and that Norwegian contract tradition shall be observed.[189] The clause is obviously aimed at avoiding *inter alia* general conditions of contract that deviate substantially from the conditions normally used in similar contractual relationships in the Norwegian offshore sector. However, both the precise meaning and the practical implications of the clause seem unclear. **11.273**

The third modification concerns the way contracts are entered into: Norway is a member of the European Economic Area (EEA) and as such has to implement the requirements of the Procurement Directive.[190] The Directive has been implemented in Norwegian national law by a separate regulation,[191] the wording of which is close to that of the Directive. The offshore industry is subject to the regulation.[192] This implies that the petroleum industry when contracting for goods and services has to observe the procedural and material requirements of the regulation. Normally this means that contracts shall be put out for tender, and that the legitimate criteria for bid evaluation are specified in the invitation to tender.[193] Generally, the regulation did not impose any major changes on the system already practised by the operators.[194] **11.274**

[188] Act no 4 of 31 May 1918 Relating to Contracts s 36 provides that contract terms or conditions may be modified or set aside to the extent that they are considered unfair having regard to the contents of the agreement, the position of the parties, the circumstances prevailing at the time the agreement was entered into, subsequent circumstances, and circumstances in general.

[189] See eg the production licence for the 15th round (1996) item 7: 'All activities carried out under this Production Licence shall be governed by Norwegian law and be based on Norwegian contractual tradition'.

[190] Council Directive 93/38/EEC of 14 June 1993 co-ordinating the procurement procedures of entities operating in the water, energy, transport, and telecommunications sectors.

[191] Royal Decree of 16 December 1994 No 1110, in force 1 January 1995.

[192] See Royal Decree of 16 December 1994 No 1110 sect 4 No 2(a) ref sect 3 No 1(b), implementing Council Directive 93/38/EEC Art 2 No 2(b) ref No 1(b).

[193] See Royal Decree of 16 December 1994 No 1110 sec 40 and Council Directive 93/38/EEC Art 34.

[194] But the Directive and the rules on competition in the EEA Agreement caused the removal of provisions contained in the old Petroleum Act 1985 (repealed by the 1996 Act) and in the standard Joint Operating Agreements that could imply a preferential status for Norwegian suppliers.

Standard contracts and 'agreed documents'

11.275 Construction activities off the Norwegian coast are normally handled by standard documents. They govern the fabrication (and often also a major portion of the engineering) of the main components of offshore installations for the production, utilization, storage, and transportation of petroleum. The existing standard conditions of contract were negotiated between the major companies operating in the Norwegian sector[195] on one side and the Federation of Norwegian Engineering Industries (TBL) on the other. The oil companies have expressed their intention to use the document, while TBL have recommended that their members use it.[196] Thus, the Norwegian Fabrication Contract 1992 (NF 92) is an 'agreed document'.

11.276 NF 92 is extensively used within its original scope, which is 'fabrication assignments of some size for delivery to the Norwegian continental shelf'.[197] Even operating companies who did not participate in negotiating the document use it (more or less modified) for their projects. It is also increasingly being spread into other areas, such as offshore purchase orders and heavy lift contracts, onshore construction projects, and even international construction projects.

11.277 The widespread use of NF 92 has had a significant impact on this sector of contract law and contracting practices in Norway. Below, some characteristic features of NF 92 are presented.

Contract structure in development projects

11.278 Offshore development projects[198] vary in Norway like elsewhere in the world. Some common features may, however, be found.

11.279 A basic observation is that an installation is never (unless it is very small) built sequentially, starting 'at one end' and completing the various tasks in a sequential order. Instead, the installation is split into work packages which are planned and constructed in parallel. This way time is saved, and time is of the essence in this business, because the net present value of the final year of production is drastically lower than that of the first year.

---

[195] Statoil a.s., Saga Petroleum ASA, and Norsk Hydro ASA.

[196] See the Protocol to NF 92, item 1, 2nd para: 'Saga, Hydro, Statoil and the member companies of TBL intend to use NF 92 for all contracts entered into between one of the oil companies mentioned and a TBL member company'. Further, item 2 specifies that the parties at the individual application of the contract may make such adaptations 'as are appropriate in the light of the circumstances applying to each specific contract', but that such adaptations shall not entail 'fundamental changes' to the provisions on Variations and Cancellation, Delivery and Payment, Breach of Contract, and Proprietary Rights.

[197] Protocol to NF 92 item 1, 2nd para.

[198] The term commonly used for activities aimed at constructing, installing, and commissioning offshore installations (sub-sea facilities and fixed or floating platforms) for the production, processing, storage, and transportation of offshore oil and gas. See also paras 11.318 *et seq* below on likely future developments.

There are separate contracts governing each of these packages. In addition, there often are separate contracts covering functions relating to all or at least several of the packages, eg engineering and transportation. Most suppliers under all of these contracts need the help of sub-contractors to complete their tasks. Thus, there is normally a large hierarchy of contracts in a typical development project. On the top of the hierarchy, we find the oil company, which normally co-ordinates work at the lower levels. **11.280**

Lately, however, we have seen examples of a company entering into an all-inclusive main contract with a single contractor for the total platform, sub-sea installation, etc. In such cases the main contractor has to contract major parts of the necessary services, equipment, and major modules etc from other (sub-) contractors. The legal functions and problems of these sub-contracts are basically the same as those of the traditional parallel main contracts entered into by the company. But the fact that, from a practical and normally legal perspective, they are subordinate to the single main contract adds to their legal complexity. See further paras 11.324 *et seq* below. **11.281**

The close links between the different contracts and levels of the contractual hierarchy have to be reflected in the general conditions of each individual contract in the hierarchy. Important features of the documents can only be explained by reference to the fact that the individual contract does not appear in splendid isolation. It is a part of a complex and closely inter-linked family of contracts established for the purpose of completing the specified development project on schedule and within budget. **11.282**

The Norwegian Fabrication Contract 1992 (NF 92)

In Norway, the by far most frequently used set of conditions for offshore fabrication contracts is the Norwegian Fabrication Contract 1992 (NF 92). This agreed document is designed to be used for 'fabrication assignments of some size for delivery to the Norwegian continental shelf'.[199] In practice the standard is used even for small contracts and in cases involving major elements of engineering in addition to construction. When used as a basis for a main contract, NF 92 is usually also used 'back-to-back' for the sub-contracts. **11.283**

The background of NF 92 is two-fold: the experience gained by international oil companies and contractors involved in offshore construction projects, and the call for a 'Norwegian standard blend' of the various clauses resulting from this experience. Among the resulting characteristics of the document are the following. **11.284**

[199] The Protocol item 1, 2nd para.

11.285 NF 92 requires the parties to establish a professional system for administering the contract. Communication on important issues has to be very formal, there are time limits for making statements and putting forward claims, and delay may result in the claim being lost, no matter the merits of the case. This formalism is an important feature of NF 92, and it has been brought further than in most other contract forms onshore or offshore.

11.286 Some have argued that the express formalism of NF 92 creates antagonistic attitudes between the parties, and has resulted in unproductive disputes and cost-generating attitudes such as unfounded claims and unnecessary communication and documentation in day-to-day project administration. Such views form part of the background for the emergence of the partnering or alliance concepts, see paragraphs 11.318 *et seq* below.

11.287 On the other hand, others emphasize the need for contractual clarity and reliable legal tools for maintaining control of complex and diversified offshore projects, and argue that the formalism does not itself create antagonism, which results from underlying substantial problems, must be handled one way or another. The potential negative effects of the formalism can be overcome by professional administrative systems and attitudes.

11.288 The regulations on variations offer the best example of the importance attached to procedures and forms in NF 92. Therefore, we shall look into main parts of these regulations in the following section. Another issue where NF 92 offers an interesting example of advanced technique, is the regulation on risk, liability, and insurance, discussed in paragraphs 11.306 *et seq* below.

System for changing contractual obligations

11.289 Normally, what was originally contracted for under a fabrication contract is not what the company wants at the delivery date.

11.290 Several factors explain this. First, the mere fact that a long period of time usually elapses between the signing of the contract and delivery implies that things change. Technology moves ahead, the company's knowledge of its needs (eg related to the reservoir characteristics or operational aspects) deepens, safety regulations are amended, etc. Secondly, the interface between contractors working in parallel in the contract hierarchy may call for changed specifications under one contract because of unforeseen events under another (see paragraphs 11.278 *et seq* above). And thirdly and even more fundamentally, each contract is often entered into at a stage where the engineering basis for it has not yet reached sufficient completeness to allow the parties (especially the company) to spell out detailed contractual requirements.[200] Such requirements are nevertheless normally put

[200] The reason for this is the urge to get the project up and running as soon as possible in order to

into the contract, and are eventually changed to meet the needs identified in the process of completing the engineering.

The need to be able to change contract terms after the signing of the contract may be accommodated by the use of various legal tools. The most adaptable alternative is to include in the contract itself a system for changing its terms, including regulations to implement consequential changes to the contractor's compensation. Such 'variation regulation' has been included in offshore and onshore construction contracts for a long time. But the degree of detail and completeness of the system has varied a lot. The regulation contained in NF 92 is probably the most extensive to be found in any well established standard construction contract in Europe. In the following, some main factors of this regulation are presented. **11.291**

The key to understanding the variation system of NF 92 is the Variation Order (VO). This document issued by the company forms the link between a change in the contractor's obligations and the consequential change to the contract schedule and/or compensation. Thus, the issues to be examined are the circumstances under which a VO is to be issued, and the consequences of issuing it. **11.292**

The contract prescribes two fundamentally different situations in which the company shall issue a VO. First, the company has to use a VO in order unilaterally to change the obligations of the contractor. In other words, the contract vests in the company the *right* to change the contractor's obligations,[201] but subject to the company simultaneously exposing itself to the right of the contractor to claim consequential modifications on 'time or price'.[202] If a VO is not issued, these effects do not follow. Thus, the contractor is given the right to require that a VO be issued if the company presents an instruction that does not fulfil the formal criteria of a VO (see below on NF 92 Art 16). In this situation the company may choose to withdraw its informal instruction totally, the contractor's claim for a VO is thus dependent upon the company wanting to pursue the instruction. **11.293**

Secondly, in some situations the company has an *obligation* to issue a VO. These include cases of *force majeure* (affecting either of the parties), the company's default, and later amendments to laws and regulations relevant to the cost of the contractor's work.[203] The immediate purpose of the VO in such situations is not **11.294**

derive income from the investments early. See paras 11.278 *et seq* above on the reasons for splitting the work into packages that are carried out in parallel.

[201] NF 92 Art 12.1, 1st and 2nd paras. Certain—not very practical—limitations are contained in the 3rd para.

[202] However, as shown below, such consequential adjustments do not necessarily take place.

[203] The references to Art 16 in these situations are contained *inter alia* in NF 92 Arts 5.1 (amended relevant legislation), 27.1 (company default), and 28.3 (*force majeure*). Possibly, the rule also applies to unregulated cases of subsequently failed contractual assumptions (*bristende forutsetninger*), eg the situation that the ground conditions at the offshore site deviate from what was contemplated when signing the contract for the base structure of a fixed platform.

to change the contractor's obligations. Rather, the VO is used as a tool to change the contractor's *rights*, ie his compensation or the contract schedule. In other words: the VO system is used to modify the rights and obligations of both parties in situations where something has happened that according to the background law or ordinary contract law normally would call for such modification. By applying the VO system to these cases, both the conditions for such modifications and the actual modifications are positively regulated in the contract, both in terms of procedures and material rules. Little room is left for the often vague and uncertain background contract law.

11.295 Thus, the company may be *required* to issue a VO (as opposed to doing it at free will to instruct the contractor) in two different types of situations: (1) the company changes the contractor's obligations without making use of a formal VO, or (2) a situation has occurred that according to the contract shall be remedied by use of a VO. In either case there may be disagreement between the parties as to whether the situation calls for a VO, thus exposing the company to an adjustment of schedule and/or compensation. This problem is dealt with in some detail in NF 92 Article 16.

11.296 The starting point of Article 16 is that when the contractor is of the opinion that the situation calls for an adjustment to the contract schedule or his compensation under the contract, he has to request a VO to be issued by submitting a formal Variation Order Request (VOR).[204] If he fails to do so within a prescribed time limit, then he loses the right to claim that the alleged extra work for any purpose is variation work having the consequences of a VO.[205]

11.297 Having passed the barrier of a timely VOR, the company next has to evaluate the request. If it agrees a VO is issued, and everything works as if that had happened in the first instance. If the company disagrees (and still insists on the instruction being carried out), it has to make a clear statement to that effect by issuing a Disputed Variation Order (DVO). Having received a DVO, the contractor has to implement the instruction as if it had been a 'clean' VO. Two problems remain, however: how should the dispute clarified and formalized by the DVO contradicting the VOR be solved? And who should pay the cost involved in implementing the DVO until a final solution is found?

11.298 According to NF 92 the contractor at the outset has no right to compensation for work under a DVO. But he does not have to take the dispute all the way to court

[204] cf NF 92 Art 16.1, 3rd para, which specifies the form and contents of the VOR, both being important parameters considering the crucial role of the VOR.

[205] This implies that the alleged extra work is considered to form part of the original work: the contractor has to implement it without any adjustment to the compensation or the contract schedule, and he is liable for the quality of the work in the same way as if it had been included in the contract from the beginning.

or arbitration to get the money (or have the schedule revised): he can request the dispute to be provisionally decided by an 'expert' following a simple and brief procedure laid down in the contract.[206] The issue covered by this procedure is only whether the situation calls for a 'clean' VO, not the consequences if there is a basis for a VO (these have to be established according to the contract, see below). If the answer is 'VO', then the contractor shall immediately be compensated accordingly. The losing party may take the case to court within six months. Failing this he is bound by the provisional decision. Out of the existing seventy odd decisions, none has so far led to a court decision (but one has been taken to arbitration).

The contractor has to implement a VO, even if the effects of the VO on the contract price or schedule have not yet been established (NF 92 Art 15.1, 1st para). In other words, the contractor has to give away his bargaining position.[207] Thus, to maintain the original contractual balance between the parties, there is a strong call for pre-defined criteria for adjusting the contract schedule and/or price due to a VO. **11.299**

Guidelines on establishing the schedule impact of a VO are hard to define due to the unforeseeable variety of combinations that may arise. Thus, NF 92 offers only general criteria for this adjustment (Art 13.4, 1st para). This is in contrast to NTK 2000 (see paras 11.324 *et seq.* below), which provides a rigid procedural system for determining schedule effects of variations (Art 13.4). **11.300**

Price effects are simpler to pre-define. Failing agreement to another effect, the price for a VO shall be determined according to a scale of principles—moving from the mathematically accurate to the very discretionary set of factors (Art 13.2). The basic principle is that specific rates covering the type of work in question shall be used, if necessary after adjusting them to reflect that the variation work is performed under circumstances different from those envisaged when agreeing the rate. Agreeing the application of these principles may take time. Therefore the contractor shall be given preliminary compensation, which shall be considered final unless the parties agree to another sum or the contractor takes his claim for more compensation to court within six months after the VO has been issued (Art 15.2, 2nd para). **11.301**

The VO regulation contained in NF 92 has *inter alia* the following practical effects: **11.302**

[206] The main elements (cf Art 16.3) are that the expert is chosen (or 'mechanically appointed', no agreement is needed) from a pre-agreed list of persons, the parties present their case to the expert in two subsequent briefs, there is (normally) no oral hearing, and the expert's reasoned decision is handed down within 30 days following his appointment. The 'expert decisions' under the variation order clauses of NF 92 (and NF 87) are published in the periodical PetrIus (Sjørettsfondet, Oslo).

[207] This has to be so in order for the variation system to fulfil its purpose.

11.303 The regulation allows the company to adjust the contract to new demands and needs, while the contractor receives clarification of the contractual basis for his work at any time, and a procedurally and materially acceptable system for modifying his rights under the contract accordingly.

11.304 Secondly, the regulation forces the parties to identify potential disputes at an early stage. If problems are not clearly addressed within a certain time limit, they disappear, no matter their merits. In complex projects involving large organizations and enormous quantities of information and documentation, clarity is essential. Problems are better handled when relevant facts are readily at hand than later on, when reconstructing the situation may be virtually impossible and the personnel involved have scattered.

11.305 Thirdly, the regulation ensures that problems and disputes are not allowed to interfere with progress. Once the potential disagreement is identified, there are mechanisms to put it on a sidetrack for separate handling, while the work and relationship under the contract continues unobstructed. From a practical point of view, this feature of the system is crucial.

Clauses on risk, liability, and insurance

11.306 The overruling principle of the risk, liability, and insurance regulation in NF 92 is that the liability and insurance clauses are closely interlinked. All risks of damage are identified as clearly as possible and allocated to one of the parties, and this is followed up by equally clear obligations to provide insurance cover, generally to the effect that most risks are covered but normally by one insurance policy only. So the contract deviates widely from ordinary tort law considerations of causation, basis of liability for compensation, and adequacy. Instead, the system is built on the principle of 'knock for knock', ie each party carries the loss caused by damage to his own 'interest zone', no matter how the damage is caused; 'the loss stays where it hits'. In this way, the allocation of risk becomes predictable, facilitating a rational insurance system.

11.307 The risks of damage are divided into three 'interest zones', plus a fourth special zone related to the contract object.

11.308 (i) *The contractor zone.* NF 92 Article 20.1 regulates the situation where the contractor, his employees or sub-contractors, or their employees (collectively referred to as the contractor group) suffer personal injury or physical damage related to the contract work. The rule is simple: the contractor shall stand the resulting losses irrespective of whether they are caused or contributed to in any way[208] by the company or any of its employees, contractors, or subcon-

[208] The clause reads 'regardless of any form of liability, whether strict or by negligence, in whatever form, on the part of the Company Group' (Art 30.1, 1st para).

tractors or those of their employees involved in the project (collectively referred to as the company group).[209]

(ii) *The company zone.* NF 92 Article 30.2 contains regulations which mirror those found in Article 30.1 on the contractor zone. However, it should be noted that the company zone is wide: in addition to the company and its employees, it comprises all other (main) contractors than the one in question, all their subcontractors, and the employees of all of these companies. Thus the company zone covers all of the contract hierarchy (see paragraphs 11.278 *et seq* above) except the parties linked to the company via the contract in question. 11.309

(iii) *The third-party zone.* A third party suffering a loss because of damage related to the contract work can often claim compensation from the tortfeasor under ordinary tort law. The contract cannot modify this. But it can organize the way in which such claims are handled as between the parties, once the claim has been 'brought into the contractual relationship' on the basis of tort law. Basically, this is done along two separate lines of regulation: 11.310

First, some persons technically constituting 'third parties' (because they are not themselves parties to the contract) are included in the company or the contractor zone. This is the case with employees of the parties, and also with main contractors working in parallel with the actual contractor and any subcontractors: in general the total contract hierarchy. Claims for damages against these persons and companies are distributed between the parties according to (i) or (ii) above, as the case may be. 11.311

An example may illustrate the system. An employee of contractor A's subcontractor B suffers personal injury because of the negligent actions of an employee of the company. Under Norwegian law, the employer of the tortfeasor (in this case the company) is often liable to the injured employee for the resulting loss.[210] Thus, the company suffers a loss. Under the contract between company and contractor A, the injured party belongs to the contractor group. Therefore, according to Article 30.1, the contractor shall indemnify the company against the loss. In other words, the damage remains where it hit, with the contractor group represented by the contractor. 11.312

Secondly, the remaining 'genuine third parties' form a separate risk zone. Claims arising out of loss or damage suffered by anyone other than contractor group and company group in connection with the work shall at the outset be allocated to the contractor: he shall indemnify the company group—any 11.313

[209] The definitions are given in Art 1m) and u) respectively, and are more specific and extensive than the extemporation given here.

[210] See Act no 26 of 13 June 1969 relating to tort s 2-1.

member of it—against such claims. Consequently he shall not have a basis for requesting members of the company group to indemnify him against a third-party claim, even if it is caused by such members in a way that makes them liable to the third party under tort law.[211]

11.314 There is a limit of 2m NOK to this liability of the contractor. Above this limit, the company shall indemnify the contractor group, regardless of any liability on their part.[212]

11.315 (iv) *Damage to the contract object.* The contractor shall remedy damage caused to the contract object prior to delivery at his own cost and within the contract schedule, regardless of the cause of the damage.[213] But the costs involved are for all practical purposes not the risk of the contractor: they are normally covered by the construction all-risk insurance that the company shall provide (see below).

11.316 The fundamental element in insurance cover is the Construction All Risk (CAR) insurance to be provided by the company (Art 31.1). This insurance normally covers the whole project, ie all activities, parties, and objects involved regardless of how they are organized in terms of contracts. In order for the knock-for-knock system described above to operate as intended, this means that the contractor and his sub-contractors (the contractor group) have to be co-insured under the policy, and that the insurer has to waive any right of subrogation against the contractor group (Art 31.1, if).

11.317 The contractor has to provide separate liability cover for his part of the third-party liability, including specific marine insurance cover related to vessels (Art 31.2). Also, he has to establish personnel insurance covering contractor group personnel as required by applicable laws. All insurance to be provided by the contractor must give the company the right of direct action against the insurer, and the insurers shall waive all rights of subrogation against the company group. This way the insurance cannot undermine the knock-for-knock system, but will make it effective.

Trends in contract development

11.318 The parties that established the NF 92 are making efforts to establish agreed conditions for international purchases of both major and simpler equipment for the Norwegian offshore industry. The practical and commercial implications of a success in this effort would be significant.

[211] NF 92 Art 30.3, 1st para.

[212] Art 30.3, 3rd para. The same applies regarding all of the loss if it occurs after the contractor has completed his work under the contract, ie if the contract object causes damage to third parties in its lifetime (Art 30.3, if). In this way, the contractor is to a large degree protected against product liability.

[213] See Art 29.1 and 29.2, 1st para.

More importantly, from a legal point of view, one may identify other tendencies in contractual development as a reaction to a tighter economic framework for the offshore business, combined with the complexity and allegedly antagonistic effects of the traditional contracts. Two newcomers emerging from these tendencies must be mentioned: the 'alliance' contract and the 'total' contract.[214] 11.319

'Partnering' or 'alliance' contracts

The emergence of the 'partnering' or 'alliance' contract is partly based on the assumption that the traditional structures and contracts result in continuous fights over any and all issues, eg variations. To avoid this, the parties should establish a 'win-win' situation allowing each of them to maximize their profits by working together towards a common goal: establishing defined production facilities on schedule at or below a pre-agreed price. 11.320

To achieve this, the company and the main contractors to the project agree on a 'most likely cost' including profits. This sum serves as a tool for monitoring and steering the project as the work proceeds: the work of the contractors is compensated according to pre-agreed unit rates which do not include a profit element, and all payments are charged to the joint 'project account'. The amount of profit for the participants depends on whether the project account total exceeds the 'most likely cost'. If it does, the profit margin is reduced. In the worst case, all profits are lost and the parties do not even recover their net costs. However, there is a limit to this exposure: in catastrophic situations, the oil company covers the loss. On the other hand, if the project cost account is less than the 'most likely cost', the margin is a bonus to be divided between all the participants according to a pre-agreed split. The effect of this system is of course that all participants have an incentive to keep the total project cost as low as possible. 11.321

Several different approaches have been implemented in the few contracts of this type presently in operation. The tendency so far in Norway is towards the co-ordinating type of alliance or partnering, in so far as the concept is used at all. This implies that a multilateral alliance contract is put on top of the traditional individual bilateral contracts.[215] The alliance contract establishes a legal basis for exchanging information, co-ordinating the work, operating a joint project account, and distributing the final economic result between the participants. The scope of work for the alliance is limited to accomplishing all this. The impact on the clauses of the underlying individual contracts thus appears to be limited, except on technical aspects of payment, information, and co-ordination. The 11.322

---

[214] See paras 11.286 *et seq* above.

[215] The alternative to the co-ordinating alliance contract is the independent alliance, basically meaning that the alliance contract replaces the underlying bilateral contracts. This amounts to a 'joint venture' for the project, albeit differing fundamentally from ordinary contractor joint ventures in that the buyer ('company') participates in it.

commercial implications for everyone involved could on the other hand be substantive.

11.323 The parties who established NF 92 have also established an agreed standard contract to be used for the co-ordinating type of alliances.[216] Whether this or any other form of alliance contract will stand the test if major problems emerge between the parties (eg due to funds running low) remains to be seen. Indications are that partnering now tends to take the form of mere 'integrated teams' having limited contractual implications. The historic pendulum is swinging back.

'Total contracts'

11.324 Over the last few years the concept of a 'total contract' covering engineering, procurement, and construction—and often installation—of the total or a major part of an offshore installation has emerged as a means to reduce investment costs in offshore development projects. Two aspects have been focused upon: the oil company's need to rationalize and simplify the overall project control by entering into one single or very few major contracts for the total project, and its wish to make the period from project start until 'oil on deck' as short as possible (in order to maximize the net present value). In addition, new technology has become a key issue (*inter alia* advanced down-hole technology, sub-sea completion and ship-shaped hulls for floating production units—FPSOs). These trends have resulted in two typical changes compared to previous contracts: contract value has doubled or tripled (now up to 300–500 million GBP) and engineering basis at contract award is less defined.

11.325 In the prevailing competitive market, the result of these factors is that bidders run a higher risk of being unrealistically optimistic when offering firm prices for the various elements of contract work. Also, increased contract value combined with new technology and shorter contract period add up to increased general contract risk. These tendencies have contributed to cost overruns in Norwegian offshore development projects. In their search for remedies to avoid this, the parties that negotiated NF 92 have reached agreement on a new set of standard conditions of contract to be applied when contractors are invited to tender for 'total contracts' on an immature design basis.

11.326 The new standard, NTK 2000,[217] is generally quite similar to NF 92. It differs, however, in some respects, the most important being the following. First, the rise

[216] Norsk Prosjektalliansekontrakt 1996 (Norwegian Project Alliance Contract 1996) (NPA 96). This standard is presented and discussed in Kaasen, K, 'Offshore project alliancing: the aim, the constraints and the contracts', MarIus (Scandinavian Institute of Maritime Law Yearbook), 240 (1997), 141–57.

[217] Norwegian Total Contract 2000, agreed 22 March 2000 between Statoil, Norsk Hydro, and TBL NTK 2000 is the contractual basis for the two major Norwegian offshore projects that have been launched after the signature of the standard (Grane and Kvitebjørn). NTK 2000 is available (in Norwegian and English parallel texts) at Internet address *http://www.tbl.no/div/ntk/default.html.*

in contract value has led to modifications to the terms on limitation of liability for delay and defects. Secondly, NTK 2000 includes provisions to support the contractor's liquidity during the contract period in case of disputes regarding compensation. Such disputes have previously often led to tactical positioning resulting in sub-optimal performance of the contract. Thirdly, and potentially most importantly, the protocol to NTK 2000 bars the parties from establishing lump sum compensation (or target sums) for elements of contract work which at the relevant point in time have not reached a defined level of design maturity. Such elements will therefore have to be compensated on the basis of actual quantities, multiplied by pre-established norms and rates. The implication is that the contractor's exposure to competitive bidding is reduced.

C. The Electricity Sector

(1) Historical Overview

During the last decade of the nineteenth century several cities began to deliver electricity for general consumption. The first Act on electrical installations was passed in 1896. This was replaced in 1969 by a new Act on the building and operation of electrical installations. **11.327**

At the turn of the last century the consumption of electricity was limited to factories and cities. The production and distribution of electricity often originated in local communities where supply was restricted to the local area. Distribution was undertaken by a great number of public utilities, which held an exclusive right, but also had an obligation to supply the area covered by a regional concession. Tariffs were fixed by the local authorities, and normally based upon the principle of selling at cost. **11.328**

The first grid system operations took place in 1918. After World War II four units for grid system operations came into being. From 1 January 1971 a single unit was organized to cover the whole country's need for grid system operations. **11.329**

The electricity production based upon hydropower increased considerably in the second decade of the last century in order to supply the new Norwegian electrochemical and metallurgic industries. In 1998 these energy-intensive industries consumed about 28TWh. **11.330**

The rapid development of the hydropower system after World War II was carried out by public utilities and the State Power Board. This Board comprised both electricity production and the main part of the grid. Tariffs for the Board were stipulated by Parliament. **11.331**

(2) Regulatory and Organizational Framework

The Regulatory instruments

11.332 The different hydroelectricity developments permitted in the Norwegian river systems are strictly regulated either by legislation or through plenary decisions in Parliament, eg the Protection Plans for Water Resources and the Master Plan for Water Resources. The Master Plan sets out an order of priority for the consideration of individual hydroelectricity projects on the basis of economic considerations and the degree of conflict with other interests. The Master Plan is intended to ensure that those rivers which can provide the cheapest power and where the environmental impact of development are smallest are developed first. The fact that a project is approved in The Master Plan does not mean that the authorities have made an advance commitment to grant a concession pursuant to the legislation relating to watercourses.

11.333 Based upon the concession procedure the authorities must ensure that hydroelectricity resources are utilised as effectively as possible, while emphasizing the impact on the environment and on other user interests. The main acts particularly regulating hydroelectricity developments are the Industrial Concession Act of 14 December 1917[218] and the Watercourse Regulation Act of 14 December 1917. In addition, a concession is sometimes necessary in accordance with the Watercourses Act of 15 March 1940, which is the general regulation governing all sorts of exploitation of watercourses. This Act was replaced 1 January 2001 by a new Act relating to Watercourses and Ground Water based upon a proposition to Parliament.[219]

11.334 The Energy Act of 29 June 1990[220] is specifically related to the electricity and district heating supply sector and energy supply preparedness. The Energy Act was the basis for the restructuring of the Norwegian electricity market, and entered into force on 1 January 1991 based upon a proposition to Parliament.[221] As far as electricity generation, transmission, and distribution is concerned, the most relevant parts of the Energy Act are chapter 3 'Electrical Installations', chapter 4 'Trade In Electrical Energy', and chapter 2 'Procedures'.[222]

11.335 Despite high technological standards and great reliability of supply, there were weaknesses in the organization of the power supply in the pre-Energy Act period. Prices varied greatly from district to district and between various groups of con-

[218] Act no 16 of 14 December 1917 relating to the acquisition of waterfalls, mines, and other real property etc.

[219] Ot prp no 39 (1998–99) *Lov om vassdrag og grunnvann.*

[220] Act no 50 of 29 June 1990 relating to the generation, conversion, transmission, trading, and distribution of energy etc.

[221] Ot prp no 43 (1989–90) Om lov om produksjon, omforming, overføring, omsetning og fordeling av energi mm (Energiloven).

[222] PH Høisveen/PC Andersen, *Energiloven med forskrifter og kommentarer*, 2nd edn (1995).

sumers. There was little flexibility of consumption although production fluctuated considerably from year to year. Hydroelectric power stations with high development costs had been developed before cheaper ones. The high costs of developments were passed on to consumers because of the monopoly position of utilities with coverage obligations. As the electricity supply system was organized, attention focused on how far local energy needs were covered. The energy prices set by the utilities were normally an average of their development and electricity purchase costs.

The main objective of the Energy Act was to set the legal framework for making the electricity market more efficient and to achieve more flexible use of energy. The Energy Act makes a clear distinction between electricity production and trading, which are subject to competition in a market, and electricity networks, which have to be regulated and operated as monopolies. The Energy Act is based upon a system of concessions. **11.336**

Norway is contracting party to the Agreement on the European Economic Area (EEA). Article 24 of the EEA Agreement Annex IV contains specific provisions and arrangements concerning energy. Council Directive 96/92/EC of 19 December 1996 concerning common rules for the internal market in electricity is relevant to the EEA Agreement. The Directive was included in the EEA Agreement in November 1999. According to Article 3.2 of the Directive Member States may impose public service obligations on undertakings operating in the electricity sector in the general economic interest. Norway has notified the implementation of public service obligations within the meaning of Article 3.2 to the EFTA Surveillance Authority. **11.337**

The organization of the electricity market

The Energy Act sets out the framework for the organization of the electricity supply system in Norway. **11.338**

There is a dominant public ownership in the Norwegian electricity industry. The municipal ownership of the generating capacity is 56 per cent. Private ownership is some 14 per cent. Statkraft owns the remaining 30 per cent. The restructuring of the electricity sector has been carried out without any privatization. **11.339**

In order to conform with the Energy Act the State Power Board had to be restructured. As from 1 January 1992 its functions were divided into two enterprises: **11.340**

—the State Power Production Enterprise: Statkraft
—the State Grid Enterprise: Statnett.

These enterprises are regulated by the Act relating to State-owned enterprises of 30 August 1991. The State is the sole owner of Statkraft and Statnett. A State-owned enterprise has rights and obligations, is a party to agreements with **11.341** private persons and public authorities, and acts as a party in relation to courts of law and other authorities.

11.342 Statkraft is the largest hydroelectricity producer in Norway with a mean annual production of about 32 TWh. The reservoir capacity of Statkraft is about 34 TWh making up about 40 per cent of Norwegian reservoir capacity. Statkraft is the major supplier of electricity to energy-intensive industry and the wood-processing industry.

11.343 Statnett has taken over direct State ownership of 80 per cent of the grid and most of the transmission interconnections with Sweden, Finland, Russia, and Denmark. Statnett has responsibility for the superior co-ordination of the complete operation of the Norwegian power system. Statnett is responsible for the effective development and operation of the central grid system, which consists of power transmission lines, submarine cables, and substations. Through the stipulation of transport prices and rules for using the grid, Statnett shall ensure that all operators have equal access to the market.

11.344 There are a large number of electricity utilities within the Norwegian energy supply industry. The utilities are owned by one or more municipalities or counties. These utilities are organized either as municipal or inter-municipal companies, which means that the municipalities are directly liable for the financial commitments of the companies, or as limited companies or co-operative societies. Most utilities are limited companies, such companies being considered as the most effective means of organization to deal with the challenges in the electricity market. Among the production utilities there are several private industrial public limited companies with their own electricity production.

11.345 A Nordic electricity exchange—Nord Pool—is established and organized as a limited company owned 50 per cent by Statnett and 50 per cent by the Swedish Grid Company, Svänska Kraftnät. Nord Pool operates a 24-hour electricity spot market, a financial market for futures and forwards, and the Nordic Electricity Clearing.

The administrative and regulatory authorities

11.346 The Ministry of Petroleum and Energy is responsible for the management of the energy resources in Norway and for most of the administration of water resources, including administration of the Protection Plans for Water Resources. The Ministry shall ensure that the management of water resources is environmentally acceptable and profitable for the community as a whole, and improve the efficiency of electricity generation and sales as well as energy consumption.

11.347 The Ministry of Petroleum and Energy exercises the functions of the State as owner of Statkraft and Statnett.

The Ministry of the Environment is responsible for the administration of the Master Plan for Water Resources and for the administration of the system of Environmental Impact Assessments. The Ministry has a central role in the hearing process concerning applications for new hydroelectricity generation. The Directorate assigned to the Ministry of Petroleum and Energy on water resources and energy administrative matters is the Norwegian Water Resources and Energy Directorate (NVE). NVE is responsible for monitoring grid management and operations and regulates distribution and transmission tariffs. **11.348**

The Norwegian Competition Authority is responsible for competition in the electricity market in accordance with the Competition Act of 11 June 1993. **11.349**

(3) Electricity Generation

Introduction

Electricity generation is subject to two sets of regulations. The exploitation of natural resources is considered to be a national concern in Norway subject to regulation by the public authorities. One set of regulations is therefore linked to the administration of hydroelectricity resources such as waterfalls, watercourses, and hydroelectric power stations. The other set of regulations is linked to electricity as a product subject to trade. This regulation is necessary for safeguarding customer interests by ensuring that electricity is traded in a financially rational way in an efficient electricity market. **11.350**

Regulation of hydroelectricity resources

The development of hydroelectricity generation has been highly regulated and controlled by the authorities since the beginning of the last century. The State control also includes the further disposal of hydroelectric power stations.[223] **11.351**

Before a hydroelectric project can be subject to any concession procedure, the project has to be cleared within the regulatory framework of the Master Plan for Water Resources and the Protection Plan for Water Resources. **11.352**

In order to use the water for electricity production, a waterfall is required which allows the potential energy of the water to be exploited. The acquisition of rights of ownership or use of a waterfall requires a concession pursuant to the Industrial Concession Act. According to section 1 of this Act, a concession is necessary if the waterfall can provide an output exceeding 1,000 natural horsepower[224] after regulation, either alone or in conjunction with other waterfalls which it is practically **11.353**

[223] PH Høisveen, 'Rettslige rammer for salg av kraftverk', Lov og Rett 9/1996 (Universitetsforlaget).

[224] 1,000 natural horsepower = 736 KW.

and economically possible to develop together. A concession for acquisition is also needed when developed waterfalls are subject to trade.

11.354 When the Act was passed it adequately safeguarded the interests of the State and of the districts with the waterfalls and hydroelectric installations. This included: provisions on pre-emption rights, primarily for the State according to section 6 and secondarily for the district affected pursuant to section 9, the principal rule of limited duration for concessions, and the rule of reversion to the State when a concession expires according to section 2. The right of reversion means that the State takes over a waterfall and any hydroelectric installation as part of the development without compensation when the concession expires. A concession can last up to sixty years.

11.355 The Industrial Concession Act introduced mandatory conditions relating to concession fees and obligatory sales of electricity pursuant to section 2, which favoured those municipalities where the waterfalls were situated. The reason was to ensure that these districts were compensated for damage and shared in the economic benefits of hydroelectric developments.

11.356 In order to regulate production in a hydropower station during the year according to varying demand, it can be of crucial economic importance to be able to use a storage reservoir. The ownership rights to a waterfall do not include the use of water from a storage reservoir for electricity production. This requires a separate concession pursuant to section 2 of the Watercourse Regulation Act. The duration of a concession is up to sixty years. When a concession expires, the State has the right of reversion. The concession includes the right to expropriate the land needed for all the storage reservoir installations according to section 16.

11.357 The Act applies to regulatory measures which even out fluctuations in the flow in a river during a year. The licensing procedure includes questions about watercourses, the location of dams for water storage, and the electricity generating units. According to section 12 a concession must include separate regulation for the full reservoir level, the lowest operating level in the storage reservoir, and the lowest permitted inflow into the river below the reservoir.

11.358 Pursuant to section 8 a concession to regulate a watercourse will only be granted if the benefits to society are greater than the adverse effects. The environmental consequences of establishing a reservoir, for instance on the landscape and on fishing for salmon or trout, are central issues in the final evaluation made by the authorities, along with the effect on the interests of other users.

11.359 As a general rule the Watercourse Regulation Act authorizes the public authorities to prescribe similar conditions to those authorized by the Industrial Concession Act. Conditions for the benefit of nature and the environment are essential. A concession for watercourse regulation also includes a requirement to pay an annual watercourse regulation fee to the State and to the municipality in which the watercourse is situated pursuant to section 11. The fee is intended to compensate for any adverse effects of regulation.

The Watercourse Regulation Act has been essential in hydroelectric development in Norway. The Norwegian reservoir capacity is equivalent to 75 per cent of the production of one year. **11.360**

Even if the implementation of a hydroelectric project does not require the acquisition of rights over waterfalls or the regulation of a watercourse, measures necessary to exploit the hydropower potential may require a separate concession pursuant to the Watercourses Act. Such a concession is necessary pursuant to sections 104–6 if the project has adverse effects on public interests. Problems often arise in relation to salmon or trout fishing and nature conservation interests. **11.361**

According to section 126, a concession to carry out works in a watercourse will only be granted if the benefits to society are greater than the adverse effects for private and public interests. The Watercourses Act also enables the public authorities to prescribe various conditions intended to mitigate the adverse effects. **11.362**

Norwegian regulation of hydroelectric exploitation is considered to conform with its international commitments. The regulation is not affected by the Agreement on the European Economic Area (EEA) as long as regulation conforms with the general rules of the same Agreement. According to Article 125 the EEA Agreement shall in no way prejudice the rules governing the system of property ownership in Norway. **11.363**

In order to be granted a concession pursuant to one or more of the abovementioned Acts, the developer first has to notify NVE as soon as the planning of a new hydroelectricity project begins. The notification must state what installations are planned and as far as possible what the impact will be on the environment, natural resources, and society. Based on the notification and the comments, NVE must decide whether an Environmental Impact Assessment has to be carried out, and if so, stipulate an assessment programme. Such an assessment has always to be carried out if the mean annual production of the hydroelectric project exceeds 40 TWh, or if the storage reservoir exceeds 10 million cubic metres. Based upon the Environmental Impact Assessment and the hearings thereafter, NVE decides in co-operation with the Ministry of Environment whether the duty of assessment is fulfilled.[225] This stage of planning takes place in accordance with the Planning and Building Act of 14 June 1985 and Regulations for Environmental Impact Assessment of 21 May 1999. **11.364**

[225] For further discussion, see paras 11.393 *et seq* below.

11.365 The developer must send the necessary application for evaluation when the Environmental Impact Assessment has been followed up. The application must contain specifications on the technical properties of the project as well as potential damage to nature and the environment. The application is sent by NVE to the district concerned and to public agencies and non-governmental organizations for comments. When the comments have been given, the application is handled by NVE which evaluates the information compiled and presents a recommendation to the Ministry of Petroleum and Energy. The Ministry distributes the recommendation to the district and to other ministries concerned. If favourable comments are then given, the Ministry of Petroleum and Energy prepares the concession, which thereafter has to be granted by the King's Council in the form of a Royal Decree. Major projects and projects in dispute are sent to Parliament for consent before concessions can be granted by a Royal Decree.

Regulation of the electricity industry

Introduction of competition

11.366 The Energy Act introduced competition into electricity generation and trade. Increased competition has resulted in reduced costs, more efficient production, more rational investment decisions, and a more flexible system of production and trade. The market prices give all consumers the same incentives to engage in energy conservation. The introduction of a more efficient electricity market has resulted in a reduction in price differences for electricity between regions in Norway.

11.367 The introduction of competition into electricity generation and trade has not changed the basic objectives of the Norwegian energy policy. These objectives are to ensure rational use of energy resources, security of energy supply, and more equal prices for consumers. The policy intended to make the electricity market more efficient includes:

> reducing the number of electricity utilities. Vertically integrated utilities are no longer an aim. Vertically integrated utilities mix competitive and monopoly functions and are open for cross-subsidization;
> developing a sufficient number of buyers and sellers of electricity to create an extensive electricity market across traditional supply region boundaries; and
> the abolition of new long-term agreements often based upon ownership implying a right or an obligation for the distribution utility to cover all the electricity needs in its region from one special supplier.

11.368 The Energy Act was introduced because of the necessity for certain new legal instruments to make the energy market more efficient and to achieve more flexible energy use. There was also a need for a new Energy Act which gathered together all the provisions scattered among a variety of laws, making it difficult to form an overall picture of energy legislation, and to apply the legislation to the achievement of future aims in the energy sector. The general purpose of the Energy Act is stated in section 1-2: 'The Act is intended to ensure that the generation, conversion, transmission, trading, and distribution of energy are rationally carried out for the benefit of society, having regard to the public and private interests affected'.

Since the Energy Act entered into force on 1 January 1991 there has been a comprehensive and dynamic development within the electricity sector. To meet and control this development, Regulations relating to the production, conversion, transmission, trading, and distribution of energy were laid down by a Royal Decree on 7 December 1990 and revised on 10 December 1993, all in accordance with section 7-6 of the Energy Act.[226] The second revision was laid down on 18 February 1999. In addition NVE has given directives almost every year for the calculation of transmission and distribution tariffs, renewed directives concerning annual accounts, and directives for energy efficiency, all pursuant to the Regulations relating to the production, conversion, transmission, trading, and distribution of energy. The directives for calculating transmission and distribution tariffs and for annual accounts have been replaced by a Regulation for economical and technical reports, income limits for network activity, and transmission tariffs and regulations for metering, settling of accounts, and coordinated performance related to trade in electricity and invoicing of networks serviced. These Regulations were given by NVE 11 March 1999. **11.369**

Competition in the electricity market is based upon two legal provisions, deriving from chapters 3 and 4 respectively of the Energy Act: **11.370**

> The abolition of the exclusive right for electricity distributors to deliver electricity to all customers in their respective network monopoly regions;[227] and
> The introduction of an obligation to provide transport facilities to any independent energy supplier or customer who wants to trade in the region: Regulated Third-Party Access.[228]

In the pre-Energy Act legislation, all distributors of electricity needed a general concession to construct and operate any electrical installation with a voltage of 22 KV or less in their specific regions. The region concessions were exclusive as a consequence of the electricity networks being natural monopolies, and gave the distributors both the right and the duty to deliver electricity to all customers in the respective region. The exclusive right to deliver was abolished by the Energy Act. According to section 3-3 the distributors are still obliged to deliver electricity to all customers in the region who do not want to take part in the electricity market and change electricity supplier. This obligation is a counterpart to the monopoly to construct and operate the networks given in the region concessions by section **11.371**

[226] Høisveen, PH/Andersen PC, *Energiloven med forskrifter og kommentarer*, 2nd edn (1995).
[227] See s 3-3 conferred to s 3-2.
[228] See s 4-l conferred to s 4-3.

3-2. The abolition of the exclusive right to deliver electricity for the distributors implied a corresponding benefit for other suppliers and for customers who wanted to contract electricity in the market.

Trading

11.372 The Energy Act introduced a new set of regulations related to the trading concession (section 4-1). The trading concession has two aspects. All utilities engaged in trading electricity or which may find themselves in some form of monopoly situation must hold a trading concession granted by NVE. The second aspect concerning regulation of the networks as a monopoly is discussed below in the context of the transmission and distribution of electricity.[229] The first aspect of regulation of the electricity market is discussed in this section. In addition to the Energy Act authorizing market supervision, in particular through the trade concessions, the Competition Act gives the Competition Authority general powers to monitor competitive conditions in a market, and to take measures to counter restraints on competition.

11.373 One of the conditions in trading concessions obliges the concession holder to make surplus transmission capacity in the network system available to others engaged in supplying electricity and to generators and consumers of electricity. This obligation, called Regulated Third-Party Access, derives from section 4-3 which stipulates conditions for trading concessions pursuant to section 4-l. The obligation also applies when consumers buy electricity in the market or from other suppliers. The obligation applies on all network levels. There is no lower limit on the amount of electricity to be traded. The Norwegian Energy Act was the first statute anywhere to secure the rights of all customers to buy electricity in the market.

11.374 The first trading concessions were granted for a period of only two years. The next new concessions were granted for a period of three years. Trading concessions were last granted on 1 April 1999 for the period until 31 December 2001. Setting short periods for the trading concessions can be considered a disadvantage for the concession holders because of the uncertainty about future regulations. On the other hand, short concession periods have been essential for the authorities in order to control and adjust the legal means for the further development of the electricity market in the first years after the Energy Act entered into force.

Imports and exports

11.375 Export and import of electricity are regulated in chapter 4 of the Energy Act. Section 4-2 stipulates that only the State may export or import electricity without a concession. A concession is therefore required to trade in electricity with other countries. The concessions are given by the Ministry of Petroleum and Energy.

[229] See paras 11.400 *et seq* below.

The requirement for a concession based on long-term planning provides the authorities with the control needed to ensure that such trade is based on the principles of rational management of resources, environmental protection, and security of electricity supply.

Statnett, and Nord Pool as its operator, have the technical and administrative responsibility for arranging a short-term electricity exchange between Norway and **11.376**
Sweden. The responsibility is stipulated in separate concessions pursuant to section 4-2. In the concessions the short-term electricity exchange is stipulated for a duration of up to six months. There are therefore no limits on buying or selling electricity in the short-term market within such a period.

Long-term electricity exchange agreements have over the last years been entered **11.377**
into between Norwegian electricity producers and electricity producers in Denmark, Germany, and the Netherlands, and licensed pursuant to section 4-2. The agreements are mainly based on an undertaking by the Norwegian producer to export peak load electricity at an agreed price during daytime hours. In addition, spare transmission capacity is to be used for electricity exchange between the companies when appropriate, depending on the difference between the market price of electricity in Norway and the marginal costs in the system of the foreign company.

The agreements are based respectively on the three existing cables between **11.378**
Jutland in Denmark and Norway and on the development of one cable between Norway and Germany and one cable between Norway and the Netherlands. Statnett is the Norwegian co-owner of the cables that are to be laid in connection with the electricity exchange agreements.

The main opportunities for profits in these agreements lie in the co-ordination of **11.379**
the Norwegian hydroelectricity system with thermal power systems. Hydroelectric power stations can easily be big enough to cover consumption during peak periods. For technical reasons, hydroelectricity systems have larger capacity than is needed to meet domestic peak demand. Production at hydroelectric power stations can be regulated rapidly as demand fluctuates or if there are sudden unexpected changes in the electricity supply. On the other hand, water inflow is a limiting factor in the Norwegian electricity system.

Thermal power stations with sufficient capacity to cover peak consumption are **11.380**
expensive to build, and it is expensive to regulate production rapidly as demand fluctuates. On the other hand, thermal power stations can produce cheap electricity outside periods when they are operating at full capacity. Countries with systems based upon thermal electricity can reduce investments in new capacity by entering into long-term contracts based on peak-load electricity from Norway. In addition, thermal power stations can be operated more efficiently if electricity generation in Norwegian hydroelectric power stations is adjusted to meet

short-term fluctuations in demand. Unlike a hydroelectric system, a system based upon thermal electricity is not sensitive to variation due to precipitation. This means that Norway can export electricity during wet years and import electricity in dry periods.

11.381 Pursuant to section 4-3 the authorities have stipulated a duty for concession holders to procure all information needed to carry out the necessary control so that the electricity exchange functions in accordance with the agreements.

Access to the grid

11.382 Regulated Third-Party Access pursuant to the Energy Act is in accordance with the regulated system of access procedure in Article 17.4 of Directive 96/92 of 19 December 1996 concerning common rules for the internal market in electricity. Contrary to the Energy Act, there are limits to opening up the electricity markets in Article 19 of the same Directive.

11.383 The network owners cannot require special electricity measuring equipment when customers with a consumption under 0,5 GWh change electricity supplier. In addition, the ability for the network owner to charge transaction fees to the customer or the supplier was abolished from 1 January 1997 to stimulate the participation of ordinary customers in the electricity market.

11.384 The formulation of Regulated Third-Party Access as an obligation to make surplus transmission capacity available to others expresses a physical dimension in the sense that more electricity is carried through the network. This is an imprecise understanding since the electricity flows freely independent of the supplier. Instead, Regulated Third-Party Access should reflect the financial aspect expressed by the settling of accounts between the customer and the new supplier of electricity.

(4) Transmission and Distribution of Electricity

Introduction

11.385 Similar to electricity generation, electricity transmission and distribution are subject to two sets of regulation. Building and operation of electrical installations are important for both private and public interests in respect of land exploitation. In addition it is essential for the authorities to control the planning and development of the electricity system in a region for co-ordination with the national electricity system. One set of regulations is therefore linked to the administration of the building and operation of electrical installations. According to the Energy Act, transmission and distribution of electricity are natural monopolies which must be kept separate from competition in generation and trade. The other set of regulation is connected to efficient public control of the transmission and distribution networks as monopolies.

Regulation of building and operating electrical installations

Concession system

Section 3-1 of the Energy Act regulates the concessions for electrical installations. No installations for high-tension electricity may be built or operated without a concession. The same applies to alterations or extensions to existing installations. If agreements for extending electrical installations are not reached with the different affected landowners, the utility has to apply for permission to expropriate pursuant to the Real Property Expropriation Act of 23 October 1959. Such permission has to be co-ordinated with the concession for building and operating the electrical installation. **11.386**

The purpose of the concessions is to ensure that electrical installations are constructed and operated on the basis of uniform standards, which take into account socio-economic criteria and the public interest. The construction of high-tension transmission lines and transformers often has a substantial impact on the surrounding environment. It is necessary to apply for a separate concession for each electrical installation with a voltage higher than 22 kV. **11.387**

Pursuant to section 3-2 a general regional concession is required for the construction and operation of installations carrying a voltage of 22 kV or less. Thus an electricity utility which holds a regional concession does not need to apply for a concession for each separate installation under that level. Concessions for electrical installations and regional concessions are given by NVE for a period not exceeding thirty years, but can be subject to renewals. **11.388**

Various conditions may be stipulated in the concessions pursuant to section 3-4. In granting concessions for electrical installations notice must be taken whether the installation will result in rational electricity supplies, and this must if necessary be stipulated as a condition. In regional concessions conditions are laid down concerning energy efficiency and the preparation of plans for efficient energy supplies in the region. The conditions for energy efficiency are deepened in the Regulations relating to the production, conversion, transmission, trading, and distribution of energy. It can be stipulated that the concession holder must contribute neutral information and advice on efficient energy use by customers. Pursuant to these regulations NVE gave directives for energy efficiency in 1994. NVE ensures that the obligations imposed on the concession holders are fulfilled. **11.389**

These directives regulate the activity of the concession holder concerning energy efficiency. The directive stipulates what sort of energy efficiency measures the concession holder shall offer to energy consumers in the region. The concession holder has a special responsibility to provide neutral information. **11.390**

Information and guidance activities should be carried out in co-operation with other regional concession holders and operated by special regional energy **11.391** efficiency centres. The concession holders are obliged to carry out tasks connected to State programmes for energy efficiency and to use energy budgets actively to stimulate solutions based on energy-efficiency in new buildings. The energy-efficiency activities carried out by the concession holder must be reported each year to NVE. Revenues and costs from obligatory energy efficiency must be clear in the accounts of the concession holder. Pursuant to the directives on energy efficiency the concession holder can charge the costs concerning obligatory energy-efficiency activities in the region in the network tariffs to the customers.

11.392 The concession holder must be well enough informed as to the potential for energy efficiency in the supply region to be able to evaluate and, as the case may be, assist in energy-efficiency measures as an alternative to other means of coverage. Investment in energy-efficiency measures in both their own installations and those of customers should be considered on the same footing as new developments or electricity purchases in the market. When planning the cheapest ways of achieving energy coverage, concession holders should place the greatest emphasis on weighing these various possibilities against each other.[230]

Protecting the natural environment

11.393 Pursuant to section 3-4 conditions can be stipulated in the concessions aimed at preventing damage to the natural environment and the cultural heritage. The natural environment must be taken into account when installations are designed and their location chosen. Installations must do as little harm to animal and plant life as possible and fit into their surroundings as well as possible. Building sites must be properly cleared and any damage from construction work made good. However, conditions will only be stipulated if the costs involved are in reasonable proportion to the benefits.

Planning issues

11.394 An electricity utility which applies for a concession according to section 3-1 must draw up a long-term plan for the development of the electricity supply system in the region in which it operates. Concession holders are obliged to co-operate by adjusting their individual electricity supply plan to ensure conformity with each other, and the national electricity supply system.

11.395 Pursuant to section 2-1, notice must be taken of the public interests affected when plans are being prepared for new electrical installations. Electrical installations must be considered in relation to plans for the area involved as a whole. Public interests include science, culture, protection of the natural environment, open-air activities, the landscape, bird migration, industry, and the local communities affected.

[230] For further discussion, see section D(1) below.

Planners must notify the energy authorities as soon as the planning of a new electrical installation begins. The notification must state what installations are being planned and as far as possible what their impact will be on the environment, natural resources, and society. The notification must be sent when preliminary studies have been completed and the preparations for more concrete planning begin. Such notification only applies to power lines with voltages of 132 kV and over and above twenty kilometres in length. A notification is mandatory for gas-fired power stations and other combined heating and power stations with an installation of more than 10 MW. The planner has to send the notification to the proper authorities, to the district, and to public agencies and organizations for comments. **11.396**

Environmental Impact Assessment

Based upon the notification and the hearing, NVE decides whether an Environmental Impact Assessment shall be carried out. Such an assessment shall be carried out if the electrical installation is likely to have essential consequences for the environment, natural resources, and the society. NVE stipulates the possible assessment programme. Based upon the stipulated programme, the Environmental Impact Assessment must investigate the consequences of the electrical installation on the environment, natural resources, and society. The assessment shall give alternatives, and specify efforts to avert damage and disadvantages. The Environmental Impact Assessment has to be sent to NVE, the municipality, and the district authorities affected. NVE is responsible for the hearing and for arranging a public meeting. In co-operation with the Ministry of Environment, NVE thereafter decides whether the duty of assessment is fulfilled. **11.397**

The developer has to send the necessary application to NVE for evaluation, according to section 2-2, when the Environmental Impact Assessment has been carried out. Additional information may be necessary: for instance further investigation into possible alternative electricity line routes. The respective applications for watercourse concessions comprising the construction of a hydroelectric power station and for electrical installations in power stations and appurtenant electricity lines shall be sent at the same time to the energy authorities. This is necessary to ensure co-ordinated treatment of cases in accordance with the Energy Act and the legislation relating to watercourses enabling permits whenever possible to be issued at the same time. **11.398**

The application has to be sent to the municipalities and district authorities concerned for comments. At the same time the application is sent to public agencies established to safeguard the public interests and to others whom the project directly concerns. This refers principally to landowners and other holders of rights. A deadline is set for comments to NVE. Thereafter necessary surveys and hearings take place before final treatment and decision-making. All decisions in NVE **11.399** pursuant to chapter 3 are subject to a possible complaint procedure in the Ministry of Petroleum and Energy.

Regulation of the networks as monopolies

Natural Monopolies

11.400 The electricity transmission and distribution networks constitute natural monopolies. Electricity distribution may to some extent compete with the distribution of other fuels; either in the form of oil, wood, or through gas or district heating networks. However, the synergy benefits inherent in electricity networks mean that in practice distribution utilities meet no competition in the management and operation of the actual network. As natural monopolies, the networks must be subject to control and supervision by the public authorities.

11.401 The financial objective for electricity transmission and distribution ought to achieve a normal yield on capital invested, but that objective alone does not ensure cost-effective operation. However aware the boards and management of transmission and distribution companies may be of the need to act in the interests of consumers, they are not made aware of the consequences of efficiency to themselves to the same extent as managers of businesses exposed to competition.

11.402 Regulation of the networks as natural monopolies will be aimed to ensure that the transmission and distribution utilities do not abuse their power in the market to discriminate among their customers through their charges, and that efficiency and service are not restricted by their monopoly situation.

11.403 Large vertically integrated utilities do not provide the same incentives to improve efficiency as a separation of monopoly and competitive functions into different companies. Furthermore, vertical integration does not stimulate choice between coverage and selling through a market; this lessens the opportunities to compare prices and select the cheapest suppliers across regional boundaries. However, separation into different companies is not required by the Energy Act. Such separation is only a recommendation from the public authorities. In vertically integrated utilities the natural monopolies may therefore operate side-by-side with functions which have been opened for competition. In order to reduce the amount of mutual subsidization between different functions, to strengthen the financial management of vertically integrated utilities, and to regulate those parts of their operations which are natural monopolies, it has been necessary to separate the operations into independent profit centres.

Regulations regarding monopoly control

All utilities which may find themselves in any form of monopoly situation must hold a trading concession.[231] Pursuant to section 4-3 of the Energy Act, conditions can be stipulated in the trading concessions concerning the internal organization of the activities of the concession holder and his accounts. Such conditions are strengthened in the Regulations relating to the production, conversion, transmission, trading, and distribution of energy. **11.404**

The concession holder is obliged to keep accounts according to the provisions in the Companies Act of 13 June 1997, and in accordance with good accounting practice pursuant to the Accounting Act of 17 July 1998. The accounting requirement took effect from the beginning of the 1993 financial year. **11.405**

Pursuant to the Regulations relating to the production, conversion, transmission, trading, and distribution of energy, the concession holder must separate exposed business sectors and monopoly functions into distinct profit centres, with separate budgets and accounts for the respective sectors. Direct and indirect internal transfers of funds between monopoly business and other business must appear in the accounts. **11.406**

In accordance with section 4-3 of the Energy Act conditions can be laid down in the trading concessions concerning transmission and distribution tariffs. The tariffs in transmission and distribution electricity networks are based on an entry/exit fee system established in 1992. The entry/exit fee system is based on the following points: **11.407**

clearly defined access points where direct exchanges between producers, users, and network owners take place;
transmission fees (separate and independent from the electricity contracts) calculated on specific access points and independent of distances;
transmission fees in the various networks must be co-ordinated so that the customers are presented with only one united network tariff. Costs will be associated with both the entry of energy into the network and the exit out of the network;
the tariffs should as far as possible reflect the system cost of the network, and include both an energy (variable) and a load (fixed) component;
transmission fees will account for losses in the network. Marginal losses are included in the energy component and will be calculated in relation to the spot market price; and
transmission fees can be adjusted according to transmission quality. Such a condition is an important instrument to ensure that the networks and generating installations are rationally utilized.

The Regulations further provide that concession holders shall 1) set transmission and distribution tariffs so as over time to meet development and running costs **11.408**

[231] For discussion of the trading concession concerning competition in the electricity market, see paras 11.372 *et seq* above.

and provide the necessary yield on invested capital; 2) as far as possible devise tariffs which mirror the load on the network; and 3) must not discriminate between users of the network, but offer the same tariffs, adjusted to take account of differences in load, reliability of deliveries, etc.

11.409 On inquiry from customers, concession holders are obliged to provide calculations in advance of transmission tariffs. Concession holders and those seeking transmission services shall negotiate the more detailed terms and conditions for transmission. They are also obliged to provide NVE with the information necessary for the supervision of the monopoly activities. Based on this information, NVE can require the concession holders to change their tariffs and conditions pursuant to the directives. In the event of disagreement over the terms and conditions, or disputes over the calculation of transmission tariffs, decisions shall be taken by the regulator—NVE. All decisions by the regulator concerning tariff disagreements or disputes are subject to a complaint procedure in the Ministry of Petroleum and Energy.

11.410 The regulation of tariffs from 1992 to 1996 was based on the rate of return regulation. The utilities were allowed to cover all actual costs including a regulated return on the capital employed. This system clearly had severe weaknesses as there was no incentive to reduce costs and improve efficiency, nor for the necessary restructuring of the industry. By contrast there could be incentives to over-invest because of the guaranteed return on capital employed.

11.411 As of 1 January 1997 the regulator—NVE—therefore changed the system of monopoly control. Given the characteristics of the Norwegian electricity system, the following essential factors have been incorporated in establishing the revenue caps regulation:

—equal treatment of each of the network utilities,
—stability and predictability of the regulatory system through comprehensive and detailed rules,
—incentives to improve efficiency,
—incentives to rationalize the industry structure where appropriate, and
—incentives to invest only when necessary thus avoiding over-investment.

11.412 Based on the reported network costs in 1994 and 1995, revenue caps were established for each individual network utility. The costs of operating and investing in the network will have to be limited to the allowed annual revenue. The profit will be the difference between the allowed revenue and the actual network costs. Profits are allowed to vary +/− 7 percentage points around a normal return on capital employed.

11.413 The allowed revenue of each individual utility is updated annually over a five-year period, taking into account the annual forecasted inflation, the annual increase in demand for electricity, and the annual requirement for productivity growth. By using the annual increase in demand for electricity as an updating factor, detailed and time-consuming regulation of all the investment activities for the utilities is avoided.

(5) Conclusion

After the introduction of the Energy Act in 1991 the electricity industry in Norway has been through a vigorous restructuring, resulting in competition in production and trade combined with comprehensive regulation of the electricity networks. **11.414**

The main objective of the Energy Act, to make the electricity market more efficient and achieve more flexible use of energy, has in many ways been fulfilled. On the other hand, experience so far suggests that some of the regulations need to be revised in order to follow up the objectives of the Act completely. In this way the Act will also function in the best interest of all end-consumers in the electricity market. An evaluation of the Energy Act is now being undertaken by the authorities. **11.415**

At the same time it is important to remember that electricity in Norway is closely connected to the waterfalls as natural resources. The authorities demand public control through regulation of the waterfalls and the hydroelectric power stations. The combination of competition in electricity trade and heavy regulation of the electricity resources since the introduction of the Energy Act has not, however, jeopardized the restructuring of the electricity industry in any way. Privatization is therefore not an aim in the future for the Norwegian electricity sector. **11.416**

D. Energy Efficiency and Electricity Taxes

(1) Energy Efficiency

Energy efficiency has been part of the energy policy of Norway since the oil crisis in the mid-1970s. In addition to a grant scheme for energy-efficiency measures in private households, the service sector, and the industrial sector, the State has continuously financed other measures, mainly general information and training activities. The objective of energy-efficiency activities in Norway has always been to ensure the rational use of energy resources. It is also important to ensure that the measures help to reduce the adverse environmental effects of energy use. **11.417**

NVE has been responsible for the administration of governmental efforts in this field. The responsibility for practical implementation of the various measures has been delegated to institutions and organizations outside the central Government administration. The role of the Ministry of Petroleum and Energy is to ensure that **11.418**

State funds are allocated rationally, draw up a long-term strategy for energy efficiency, and evaluate changes in the use of energy-efficiency instruments. The organization of energy efficiency activities is to be restructured during 2001. Activities in NVE will be wound up. A new State agency will be established with responsibility for these activities. The supplement in the network tariffs for charging the costs concerning energy efficiency will be made compulsory by introducing a new section in the Energy Act. These resources are to be transferred to an energy fund. This fund will be managed by the new State agency. The purpose of this restructuring is increased effectiveness in energy efficiency activities.

11.419 Pursuant to the Energy Act the regional concessions contain an obligation to implement certain energy-efficiency measures.[232] The authorities are encouraging the establishment of regional centres to organize such activities.

11.420 The main barrier to greater activity in energy efficiency in Norway is lack of knowledge. Information and training, together with the introduction of new energy technology, are therefore the most important instruments available to the authorities.

11.421 Norway participates actively in international energy-efficiency work. Through the EEA Agreement, Norway takes part in the process and adopts the directives concerning labelling systems for household appliances to show energy use.

11.422 Norway has also reached an agreement on participation in the EU programmes SAVE (energy efficiency) and ALTENER (renewable energy sources).

(2) Electricity Taxes

11.423 Electricity consumption is subject to an electricity tax, which in 2000 was set at NOK 0.0894 per KWh. Manufacturing industries and mining and quarrying are exempt from the electricity tax, as are consumers in the northern part of Norway. The VAT rate on electricity is 23 per cent. The three northernmost counties of Norway are exempted from VAT on electricity.

11.424 New taxation rules for the electricity companies were introduced in 1998. One of the main objectives of the new rules is to ensure that taxation encourages the best possible use of the available resources. All electricity companies will be subject to income tax based on their annual profits as in other branches of industry. The new rules also introduce a tax on economic rent and a tax on natural resource extraction to be paid to the municipalities and districts.

[232] For further discussion, see paras 11.386–11.392 above.

E. Future Developments

With regard to the developments on the EC level it should be noted that the EC Directive on common rules for the internal market in natural gas introduces the principle of third-party access to upstream pipeline networks. As Norwegian companies own and operate thousands of kilometres of cross-border pipelines, the implementation of the Directive is a point of discussion. The Government is therefore examining the possibilities of incorporating this Directive into the EEA Agreement. **11.425**

The Government has also been assessing the organization of State participation in petroleum activities, ie the structure of the ownership of Statoil and the State's Direct Financial Interest (SDFI). On 15 December 2000 the Government submitted MPE's proposal concerning ownership of Statoil and future management of the SDFI to Parliament, cf St prp no 36 (2000–2001). The MPE proposes a partial privatization (15–25%) of Statoil. As a result the SDFI will be reorganized. It is proposed that the management of the SDFI is transferred to a new 100 per cent state owned company. The management of the SDFI will be the sole purpose of the new company. Its internal relationship with the State will be structured in a corresponding manner as today's relationship between Statoil and the State. Its external relationship with the other licensees and third parties will be that of a licensee. However, the company will not perform the function as an operator. It is not the intention of the reform to create a new Norwegian oil company. As part of the reform the MPE opens for the sale of 20 per cent of the SDFI to the companies. However, 15 per cent is reserved for Statoil, while the other companies have to compete for the remaining 5 per cent. **11.426**

A final element in the MPE's proposal is the establishment of a new state owned transportation company that shall operate the gas transportation infrastructure on the Norwegian Continental Shelf, ie all the gas pipelines and the gas terminals on land (subject to Norwegian jurisdiction). At present Statoil executes this function. However, the ownership of the pipelines and terminals will rest with the present licensees (of the pipeline licences).

It is expected that St prp nr 36 (2000–2001) will be dealt with by Parliament before Easter 2001. Then follows the practical implementation of the reform, including the introduction of Statoil on the stock exchange, the partial sale of the SDFI, and the necessary amendments to the PA. This will constitute the largest reform of the Norwegian petroleum sector since 1985. However, it will not change the main characteristic features of the legal framework.

The restructuring of the electricity industry in Norway will accelerate in the years to come. The companies involved in generation of and trade in electricity will be **11.427** subject to mergers and buy-outs. The number of such companies will therefore reduce considerably within the next few years. In this way the restructured companies will be prepared to meet increased competition in the Nordic electricity market.

Bibliography

General

Knophs oversikt over Norges rett. 11. utg. Oslo, 1998. 942 pp (comprehensive overview of Norwegian law)

Petroleum and energy law: books and articles

Arnesen, Finn, *EØS-avtalens konsekvenser for praktiseringen av det norske petroleumskonsesjonssystemet.* I: LOR 1992, 456–77 (consequences of the EEA Agreement for the operation of the Norwegian concession system)

—— An overview on Norwegian petroleum law and its compatibility with European community law. Compendium for the Erasmus course. Oslo: Sjøretten, 1993. 47 s

—— *Nytt innhold i gamle bestemmelser.* I. LoR 1996, 339–56 (new meaning to old provisions)

—— Offshore licensing in Norway: a privilege for Norwegian companies? I: JERL, vol. 13 (1995), 258–66

—— 'The adoption of the product licence directive', in Peter Christian Müller-Graf and Erling Selvig (eds), *The European economic area,* Berlin, 1997, 81–95

—— *Regulerer EØS-avtalen den norske stats utnyttelse av petroleumsforekomster?* I: TfR 1994, 424–69 (Does the EEA Agreement regulate the Norwegian Government's management of petroleum resources?)

—— *Statlig styring og EØS-rettslige skranker.* Oslo: Universitetsforlaget, 1996. 717 s. Dr. avh. (EEA-law barriers to State governance. Doctoral thesis)

Askheim, Lars Olav, *Lånefinansiering av petroleumsutvinning: risikofordeling og fleksibilitet.* 196 s. Lic. jur. Oslo: Sjørettsfondet, 1988. (Marius no 148) (loan financing of petroleum production)

Askheim, Gisvold og Tapper, *Kontrakter i petroleumsvirksomheten.* Oslo: Sjørettsfondet, 1983. 625 s. (contracts in offshore petroleum activities)

Beyer, Jebsen, Krokeide, *Scheel og Ulfstein: Borerigger i rettslig belysning.* Oslo: Sjørettsfondet, 1975 (drilling rigs from a legal perspective)

Brannsten, Erik, and Mork, Marit, *Anskaffelser og ansvar.* Oslo: Universitetsforlaget, 1998 (Iusef no 27)

Bull, Hans Jacob, Norwegian petroleum law. I: Scandinavian studies in law. 1981, 33–50.

—— *Petroleumsrett. I: Knophs oversikt 11. utg.* Oslo, 1998 (petroleum law)

—— *Tredjemannsdekninger i forsikringsforhold.* Dr. avh. Oslo: Sjørettsfondet, 1988. 598 s. (insurance cover of third parties. Doctoral thesis)

—— and Kaasen, Knut, Abandonment and reclamation of energy sites and facilities in Norway. I: JERL 1992, 37–45

Bull, Krokeide, Kaasen, Selvig og Woldseth: *Innføring i petroleumsrett 2. utg.* Oslo: Sjørettsfondet, 1982. 160 s. (Introduction to petroleum law)

Fleischer, Carl August, Off-shore activities and the emerging legal regimes. I: Defence of Northern Europe. Oslo: Europabevegelsen i Norge, 1986, 3–8

—— *Petroleumsrett.* Oslo: Universitetsforlaget, 1983. 601 s. (Petroleum law)

Gade og, Woxholth, *Offshorecertepartier i rettslig belysning.* Oslo: Sjørettsfondet, 1979. 163 s. (Offshore charter parties in a legal perspective)

Gass i Norden (*konferanse*) (1986: Trondheim) (Gas in the Nordic countries)

Gassalgskontrakter. *Foredrag holdt på seminar i Stavanger 26. april 1983.* 60 s. Oslo: Nifs, 1983. (Marius no 88) (Gas sale contracts. Paper presented at a seminar in Stavanger 26 April 1983)

Graver, Hans Petter, *Sikkerhetsregulering og reguleringsteknikk—Oljedirektoratets regulering av sikkerheten ved produksjon av petroleum.* Oslo: Sjørettsfondet, 1983. 224 s (Safety regulatory and regulation technic—The Petroleum Directorate's safety regulation of petroleum production)

Hammer, Ulf, Competition and Public Service Obligations: Two Regulatory Models in the Electricity Sector, in Peter-Christian Müller Graff and Erling Selvig (eds), *EEA–EU Relations*, Berlin Verlag 1999

—— *Tilrettelegging av kraftmarkedet. En studie i reguleringen av nettets koordinerende funksjoner.* Oslo: Cappelen 1999. (English summary: Structuring of the electricity market—A study in the regulation of the coordinating grid functions. Doctoral thesis)

—— *To EØS-rettslige studier fra kraftmarkedet.* IUSEF no 35 (Two EEA studies from the electricity market)

—— *Hovedtrekk ved organiseringen og reguleringen av kraftmarkedet.* I: LoR 1996, 390–401. (Main aspects of the organization and regulation of the electricity market)

—— *Omorganisering av kraftmarkedet.* Marius, 204. Oslo: Nifs, 1994. 101 s. (Reorganization of the electricity market)

—— Reorganization of the Norwegian electricity market. I: JERL, 1996, 95–8.

Helle, Hallvard, *Om styring og samspill ved salg av gass. Forholdet mellom myndighetene, Gassforhandlingsutvalget og de enkelte rettighetshavere ved markedsføring og salg av norsk gass.* 104 s. Oslo: Nifs, 1991. (Marius, no 183) (Regulation of gas rates)

Hjort og Meyer, *Forurensningsansvar i oljevirksomheten.* Oslo: Sjørettsfondet, 1981, 357 s. (Pollution liability in the petroleum activities)

Husebø, Egil Martin, *Oljejuss: en innføring i norsk olje- og gassrett.* Oslo: Bedriftsøkonomens forlag, 1990, 205 s. (Oil law—an introduction to Norwegian oil and gas law)

Høisveen, Per Håkon, and Per Conradi Andersen, *Energiloven: med forskrifter og kommentarer. 2. utg.* Oslo: Eget forlag, 1995, 256 s. (The Energy Act: with regulations and comments)

—— *Rettslige rammer for sag av kraftverk. Lov og Rett* 1996, 614–18. (The legal provisions for the acquisition of hydro-electric power stations)

Innføring i petroleumkontrakter. 3. b. Oslo: Nifs, 1993 (Introduction to Norwegian petroleum contracts)

Krohn, Kaasen, Lund, Rein og Sogn, *Norsk petroleumsutvinning i rettslig belysning.* Oslo: Sjørettsfondet, 1977, 650 s. (Norwegian petroleum production from a legal perspective)

Kaasen, Knut, *Kommentar til NF92.* Oslo: Universitetsforlaget, 1994, 814 s. (Comments to Norwegian fabrication contract 92)

Kaasen, Knut, Offshore cost overruns the investment. Committee report and its legal issues. Marius (Scandinavian Institute of Maritime Law, Yearbook (1999)), 247, 215–31

—— Offshore project alliances: the aim, the constraints, and the contracts. Marius 240 (1997), 141–57

—— Partnering: the emperor's new clothes? Marius 247(1999), 233–47

—— Post Piper Alpha: some reflections on offshore safety regimes from a Norwegian perspective. I. JERL, 1992, 281–9

—— Removal of offshore installations: some comments on the interaction between national and international law. I: Energy and resources law-92. London: Graham & Trotman, 1992, 266–74

—— *Sikkerhetsregulering i petroleumsvirksomheten. En rettslig studie av regelverkene om sikkerhet på norsk kontinentalsokkel.* Dr. avh. Oslo: Sjørettsfondet, 1984. 648 s. (Safety regulation of offshore petroleum activities. A study of the legal frameworks for safety regulation on the Norwegian continental shelf. Doctoral thesis)

Materialsamling i petroleumsrett. 11. utg. 478 s. Oslo, Nifs, 1997 (Petroleum law compendium, materials and documents)

Mestad, Ola, *Statoil og statleg styring og kontroll.* Oslo: Sjørettsfondet, 1985, 326 s. (Statoil and State governing and control)

Norsk gassavsetning: Rettslige hovedelementer/Are Brautaset [*et al*] Oslo, 1998. 611 pp. (Norwegian gas market—the main legal aspects)

Norwegian gas in the new Europe: how politics shape markets, ed Ole Gunnar Austvik. Oslo: Norwegian institute of international affairs, 1991, 129 s.

Norwegian petroleum law. Oslo: Sjørettsfondet, 1978

Nygaard, Dagfinn, *Andres bruk av utvinningsinnretninger.* (Lic. avh) Oslo: Sjørettsfondet, 1997, 365 s. (Use of field installations by other licence groups)

Olie og gas i Norden. Nordisk Ministerråd, 1984– (Oil and gas in the Nordic countries)

Øyehaug, Knut Erling, *Borefartøyer og jurisdiksjon.* Oslo: Sjørettsfondet, 1986, 370 s. (Drilling vessels and jurisdiction)

Petroleumsloven. Lov om petroleumsvirksomhet av 22. mars 1985: med kommentarer. Lasse Hagen *et al*, 672 s. Oslo: Tano, 1989. (The Petroleum Act of 22 March 1985 No 11 relating to petroleum activities: with comments)

Proceedings of the regional energy law seminar in Oslo; May 8–9 1984. Marius, no 94. Oslo: Nifs, 1984. 249 s.

Selvig, Erling, *Petroleumsrett til studiebruk.* 688 s. Oslo: Nifs, 1988. (Petroleum law)

—— *Petroleumsrett til studiebruk.* Utdrag. Oslo: Nifs, 1995. (Petroleum law. Abstracts)

—— *Stensilhefte i petroleumsrett.* Oslo: Sjørettsfondet, 1986, 491 s. (Petroleum law)

Stenvik Stenseth, Geir og Are, *Oljeterminhandel.* 257 s. Oslo: Sjørettsfondet, 1989. (Oil trade)

Syversen, Jan, Abandonment of oil installations: some comments on the interaction between international and national law. I: Energy law 1992.

—— Petroleum taxation in Norway. I: DNC oil now 1986.

—— *Skatt på petroleumsutvinning.* Oslo: Sjørettsfondet, 1991, 762 s. (Petroleum taxation)

Periodicals

Acts, regulations and provisions for the petroleum activities. Stavanger: Norwegian Petroleum Directorate (Annual)

Fact sheet. The energy sector and water resources in Norway. Oslo: Ministry of Petroleum and Energy (Annual overview)

Fact sheet. The Norwegian petroleum activity. Oslo: Ministry of Petroleum and Energy (Annual overview)

Marius. Oslo: Nifs, 1974– (Periodical. Publishing articles on maritime and petroleum law issues)

Petrius. Oslo: Nifs, 1995– (Expert decisions, arbitral awards and court rulings related to offshore contracts)

Legislation

Acts

Act of 14 December 1917 No 16 relating to acquisition of waterfalls, mines and other real property etc.

Act of 21 June 1963 No 12, relating to scientific research and exploration for and exploitation of subsea natural resources other than petroleum resources.

Act of 13 June 1975 No 35 governing the taxation of subsea petroleum deposits.

Act of 11 June 1976 No 79 relating to the control of products and consumer services (The Product Control Act).

Act of 4 February 1977 No 4 relating to worker protection and working environment etc.

Act of 13 March 1981 No 6, relating to protection against pollution and relating to waste.

Act of 25 April 1986 No 11 relating to the allocation of costs of removal of installations.

Act of 14 June 1985 No 77 relating to planning and building

Act of 29 June 1990 No 50 relating to the generation, conversion, transmission, trading, and distribution of energy etc

Act of 21 December 1990 No 72 relating to tax on discharge of CO_2 in connection with petroleum activities on the continental shelf.

Act of 4 June 1993 No 58 relating to general application of wage agreements etc.

Act of 29 November 1996 No 72 relating to petroleum activities.

Regulations stipulated by Royal Decree or Ministry

Regulations relating to scientific research for natural resources on the Norwegian continental shelf etc.; Royal Decree of 31 January 1969.

Regulations relating to norm price fixing; Royal Decree of 25 June 1976.

Regulations relating to safety delegates and working environment committees; Royal Decree of 29 April 1977.

Regulations for the imposition of enforcement damages; Royal Decree of 3 June 1977.

Regulations relating to prohibition against anchoring and fishing with certain gear in the Ekofisk area; Royal Decree of 14 April 1978.

Provisional regulations relating to littering and pollution caused by petroleum activities on the Norwegian continental shelf; Royal Decree of 26 October 1979.

Regulations relating to prohibition against anchoring and fishing with certain gear in the Statfjord area; Royal Decree of 15 August 1980.

Regulations relating to the governmental action control group in the event of accidents leading to or involving risks of extensive oil pollution or material damage; Royal Decree of 19 November 1982.

Regulations relating to prohibition on anchorage and on fishing with certain types of gear in the Statfjord area between the Statfjord B platform and neighbouring buoy; Royal Decree of 21 December1983.

Regulations relating to work with ionizing radiation; Royal Decree of 14 June 1985.

Regulatory supervisory activities with the safety etc in the petroleum activities on the Norwegian continental shelf; Royal Decree of 28 June 1985.

Regulations relating to prohibition on anchorage and on fishing with certain types of gear in the Statfjord area between the Statfjod C platform and neighbouring loading buoy; Royal Decree of 5 September 1986.

Regulations relating to prohibition on anchorage and on fishing with certain types of gear in the Gullfaks area between the Gullfaks A platform and neighbouring loading buoy and between the Gullfaks A platform and the subsea completed wells A-IH, A-2AH, A-3H, A-4H and A-5H; Royal Decree of 13 February 1987.

Regulations relating to safety zones etc; Royal Decree of 9 October 1987.

Regulations relating to prohibition on anchorage and on fishing with certain types of gear around/above subsea installations on Ost-Frigg; Royal Decree of 9 October 1987.

Regulations relating to prohibition on anchorage and fishing with certain types of gear in the Gullfaks area, around subsea completed well A-9H, between the Gullfaks A platform and the subsea completed well A-9H etc; Royal Decree of 22 April 1988.

Regulations relating to prohibition on anchorage and on fishing with certain types of gear around Snorre subsea installation; Royal Decree of 23 June 1989.

Regulations relating to prohibition on anchorage and fishing with certain types of gear around wellframes with manifold water injection on the Draugen field; Royal Decree of 23 June 1989.

Regulations to Chapter VI of the Petroleum Act relating to compensation to fishermen; Royal Decree of 27 July 1990.

Regulations relating to compensation to fishermen for fishing time lost; Royal Decree of 27 July 1990.

Regulations relating to worker protection and working environment in the petroleum activities; Royal Decree of 27 November 1992.

Regulations relating to the Working Environment Act Section 3, subsection 2, litera f); Royal Decree of 14 May 1993.

Regulations relating to an area with prohibition against anchoring and fishing at the Norne field; Royal Decree of 21 April 1995.

Regulations relating to an area with prohibition against anchoring and fishing at the Heidrun field; Royal Decree of 13 July 1995.

Regulations relating to an area with prohibition against anchoring and fishing around the Troll B platform; Royal Decree of 11 August 1995.

Regulations relating to genetic defects and working environment; Royal Decree of 25 August 1995.

Regulations relating to an area with prohibition against anchoring and fishing at the Asgard field; Royal Decree of 29 March 1996.

Regulations relating to an area with prohibition against anchoring and fishing at the Rimfaks, Gullveig and Gullfaks Sor fields; Royal Decree of 22 November 1996.

Regulations relating to an area with prohibition against anchoring and fishing at the Balder field; Royal Decree of 6 December 1996.

Regulations relating to the petroleum register; Royal Decree of 19 June 1997.

Regulation relating to petroleum activities; Royal Decree of 27 June 1997.

Regulations relating to safety in the petroleum activities; Royal Decree of 27 June 1997.

Regulations relating to the licensee's internal control in petroleum activities on the Norwegian continental shelf; Royal Decree of 27 June 1997.

Regulations relating to the production, conversion, transmission, trading, and distribution of energy; Royal Decree of 18 November 1999, amending the Royal Decrees of 10 December 1993 and 7 December 1990.

Regulations for Environmental Impact Assessment of 21 May 1999.

Regulations and orientation concerning safety applicable on Svalbard and the territorial waters of Svalbard

Regulations relating to safe practice in exploration and exploration drilling for petroleum deposits on Svalbard; Royal Decree of 25 March 1988.

Orientation relating to exploration and exploration drilling for petroleum deposits on Svalbard; Issued 9 October 1990.

Regulations from the Ministry of Finance

Regulations relating to use of norm price in tax assessment; Royal Decree of 17 December 1976.

Regulations relating to accounting for taxpayers engaged in petroleum production and pipeline transportation; Royal Decree of 17 December 1976.

Regulations relating to levy, payment, and settlement of installation tax etc; Royal Decree of 5 September 1980.

Regulations relating to taxation of income derived from production and pipeline transportation of petroleum; Royal Decree of 30 April 1993.

Regulations from the Ministry of Local Government and Regional Development

Regulations related to safety manning in the event of an industrial dispute on the Norwegian continental shelf; stipulated 19 March 1982.

Regulations relating to the collection of fees payable to the Treasury for supervision of the petroleum activities; stipulated 26 March 1993.

Regulations relating to asbestos; stipulated 16 August 1991.

Regulations relating to labeling, sale etc of chemicals that may be hazardous to health; stipulated 22 December1993.

Regulations from the Ministry of the Environment

Regulations relating to discharge of oil-contaminated drill cuttings; stipulated 10 June 1991.

Regulations relating to notification of acute pollution or the risk of acute pollution; stipulated 9 July 1992.

Regulations relating to labeling, sale etc of chemicals that may be hazardous to health; stipulated 22 December 1993.

12

ENERGY LAW IN SPAIN

Iñigo del Guayo

A. Introduction

(1) The Spanish Energy Resource Base

12.01 Spain is heavily dependent on foreign sources of energy.[1] There is neither oil nor natural gas within the Spanish Territory nor on its Continental Shelf. Total energy consumption amounted to 102.4 million toe in 1997. The respective significance in 1997 of the consumption of final energy excluding renewables was as follows: 3.2 per cent coal; 67 per cent oil products; 11.4 per cent natural gas; and 18.4 per cent electricity. The Spanish energy market is mostly based on the consumption of oil, which in 1997 amounted to a total figure of 56,195 toe, ie 54.9 per cent of the total consumption of primary energy. Other relevant fossil fuels are coal and natural gas, which in 1997 amounted to a consumption, respectively, of 17,921 toe (17.5 per cent) and 11,019 toe (10.8 per cent). Nuclear power climbed to 14.1 per cent of the total consumption of primary energy in 1997 (14,413 toe). There are nine nuclear power plants with a total capacity of 7,400 MW.[2] Although the level of rainfall is very low, hydroelectricity accounted for 19.4 per cent of total electricity generation in 1997 and to 3 per cent of the total primary energy consumption (3,113 toe).

12.02 Natural gas has been the primary energy with the fastest development in Spain. Natural gas demand will increase even more when the electricity generators reinforce the use of natural gas, a situation that will coincide with the full operation of the Maghreb Gas Pipeline, which was opened in November 1996.

(2) Energy Policy

12.03 The White Book on the Spanish Industry which the Government wrote in 1995 laid down the energy objectives the Government will pursue, such as i) favouring the competitiveness of the Spanish industry by means of better energy supplies; ii) encouraging energy efficiency; iii) developing new energy technologies; iv) reinforcing the competitiveness of national energy groups; v) balancing environmental protection with the diversification of energy resources; and vi) stimulating energy savings. The new Government (PP, *Partider Popular*), which took power in May 1996, has added two objectives: i) privatization of energy utilities, and ii) liberalization of the energy market.

[1] The information in this section is taken from the 1997 Annual Report of *Sedigas* (Society for the Study and Development of the Gas Industry), which in turn extracts the figures from the Secretary of State for Energy and Mineral Resources of the Spanish Ministry for Industry and Energy. See also International Energy Agency, *Energy Policies of IEA Countries* (Spain), 1996 Review, and Directorate-General for Energy, *Energy in Europe*, Special Issue (September 1996), 1996 Annual Energy Review, Part II, Spain: Summary Energy Balance, 74.

[2] i) Trillo, Cofrentes, Almaraz I and Almaraz II, owned by *Iberdrola*, ii) Vandellós II, Ascó I and Ascó II, owned by *Endesa*, iii) José Cabrera, owned by *Unión Fenosa*, and iv) Santa María de Garoña, jointly owned by *Iberdrola* and *Endesa*.

The National Energy Plan (NEP) 1991–2000 passed by the Spanish Parliament contains an ambitious Energy Efficiency and Saving Plan. Under a Ministerial Order of the 28 March 1996, the Government has established a new regulation of the Energy Saving and Efficiency Programme for the period 1995–99. Both the NEP and the Programme establish lines of subsidies for energy development projects. The Programme is organised on the base of four different schemes: i) energy saving; ii) substitution of coal and oil by natural gas; iii) substitution by renewable sources of energy, and iv) production of electricity by means of renewable energies and co-generation. During the first period of validity of the NEP, from 1991–94, experience shows that objectives have been met satisfactorily overall, with good results in the production of electricity by means of renewable energy and co-generation, but with deficient results in areas of energy saving and substitution. **12.04**

(3) *A Brief History of the Spanish Energy Sector*

After the Spanish Civil War (1936–39) the importance of the public sector within the field of energy reached grand proportions, in comparison with the relative importance of the private sector. A good example of this was the *Instituto Nacional de Industria* (The National Institute for Industry: INI) set up in the 1950s and in existence until 1995, which owned most of the energy utilities. The lack of indigenous sources of energy in Spain may also explain the strong presence of the State within the sector, due to the perception that security of supply could not be guaranteed otherwise. A phenomenon parallel to the growth of the public sector was the increase in governmental intervention in the economy, in all public and private sector business activity. In the 1960s, however, a process of economic liberalization and deregulation began slowly. This process was not accompanied by a reduction in the scale of public-sector activity. The new democratic political system set up in 1977 and 1978, and the restoration of the Monarchy in 1975, together with the application for entry into the European Communities, did push into liberalization. After the Government of the Union of the Democratic Centre (UCD) from 1977 to 1982, the Socialist Party (PSOE) took power and kept it until 1996. Due to ideological reasons, there were no plans within the Government to privatize public enterprises. However, on practical grounds a number of partial privatizations did take place from 1989 within the public energy sector (eg the gradual privatization of *Repsol*, *Endesa*, *Campsa*, and *Gas Natural*). A parallel, but distinct movement is the liberalization of the economy through deregulation. This movement began, as previously noted, during the 1960s, but gained momentum in 1986 with the Kingdom of Spain's entry into the European Community. Community law, most notably its provisions concerning State monopolies and less restricted competition, has fostered a more liberal economic environment. Given that European law calls for equal treatment for public and private-sector enterprises[3] it makes less sense for the State to maintain **12.05**

[3] Except for the companies covered by Art 86 EU Treaty (former Art 90 para 2 EC Treaty).

these enterprises. The new conservative Government, which took power in 1996, has strongly fostered policies of both privatization and liberalization.

B. Constitutional and Legal Framework of Energy Law

(1) The Spanish Constitution and Legal Order

12.06 The Spanish political system is a parliamentary monarchy. The Spanish Constitution was approved by the Spanish Parliament on 31 October 1978 and by a referendum of the Spanish people on 6 December 1978. It received the Royal Assent on 27 December 1978. It is the Basic Law and any other law is subject to its content. It was published in the Spanish Official Bulletin on 29 December 1978. The 10 titles of the Constitution deal, respectively, with the following aspects: i) fundamental rights and duties; ii) the Crown; iii) the Spanish Parliament; iv) the Government and the public administration; v) the relationship between Parliament and Government; vi) the judiciary; vii) economy and taxes; viii) the territorial distribution of powers; ix) the Constitutional Court; and x) amendments to the Constitution.

12.07 Spain is not a federal country; it is a unitary one, so that whenever its laws refer to the 'State' they mean the country as a whole, as opposed to the regions, or autonomous communities.

12.08 With regard to the legal order, a basic distinction must be drawn between central, regional, and local levels. At the central level, the main legal instruments are Parliamentary Acts, Royal Decree-Laws, Royal Legislative Decrees, Royal Decrees, and Ministerial Orders. Both Decree-Laws and Legislative Decrees are approved by the Government, but enjoy the same rank as a Parliamentary Act. According to Article 86 of the Spanish Constitution, the Government is allowed to promulgate Royal Decree-Laws only in cases of urgent and extraordinary necessity.[4] Royal Legislative Decrees are approved by the Government, in accordance with an Act of Parliament which delegates to the Government the power to enforce rules, which should have otherwise been approved by the legislature. At the regional level, the main legal instruments are Parliamentary Acts passed by Parliaments of the 17 Autonomous Communities, Decrees of the Regional Governments, and Orders of the Regional Ministers. At the local level, the main instruments are Regulations which both Municipalities and Provinces may

[4] After such promulgation, the Government must submit the Royal Decree-Law to the Parliament within 30 days. The Parliament may confirm or abrogate it. Within those 30 days, the Government may also submit to Parliament the content of the Royal Decree-Law to be passed as an Act, in accordance with the Urgent Procedure for the approval of Acts. Royal Decree-Laws cannot affect the basic institutions of the State, the rights and freedoms of its citizens, the distribution of authority between the State and the Autonomous Communities, or the electoral law.

empower in particular areas. Within the Spanish Legal Order there are decisions of Ordinary Courts (in civil, social, criminal, and administrative issues) and of the Constitutional Court, created by the Spanish Constitution.[5] The Constitutional Court has, besides the task of solving disputes between the Central Government and the Autonomous Communities, exclusive rights to repeal an Act of Parliament if it considers that such Act contravenes the Constitution.

(2) Relevant Constitutional Provisions for the Energy Sector: The Right to Property and the Freedom of Enterprise

There are a number of constitutional provisions which specifically apply to the energy sector. These provisions are part of the fundamental rights and freedoms. First, the Constitution recognizes the right to private property, subject to those social obligations which Parliamentary acts may impose.[6] Accordingly, no expropriation of private goods can occur unless there is a social interest in such expropriation, which is then subject to indemnification.[7] Even if a particular activity within the energy sector has been declared by an Act to be a public service, the shareholders of private companies operating in that area will enjoy this fundamental right. The company will continue to own those assets which it has built and which are needed for the supply of energy. In other words, assets which belong to energy utilities do not belong to the public domain, although they are specially protected in order to guarantee the continuity and regularity of the supply of energy. **12.09**

Secondly, the Constitution recognizes the freedom of enterprise within a market economy, subject, in its turn, to the exigencies imposed by the national economy and by future economic plans.[8] Article 38 of the Constitution therefore limits governmental intervention in the business of private energy companies. In addition, other Constitutional provisions have a direct impact on the development of the Spanish energy sector. These are be discussed below. **12.10**

(3) Public Undertakings

Legal framework

The Constitution authorizes the Public Administration to run commercial activities.[9] Such authorization means that the Public Administration can create public companies in whatever fields it thinks appropriate. Under this provision neither special privileges nor monopolistic rights can be awarded to those public undertakings. **12.11**

[5] Arts 159–65.
[6] Art 33, 1 and 2 Constitution.
[7] Art 33, 3 Constitution.
[8] Art 38 Constitution.
[9] Art 128, 2 (first sentence) Constitution.

12.12 The Organization and Functioning of the Public Administration of the State Act 1997[10] is applied to the Institutional Administration, that is to say, the different public entities created by the State in order properly to fulfil their tasks. They are the Autonomous Organisations (*Organismos Autónomos*) and the Public Undertakings (*Entidades Públicas Empresariales*). There are also Public Undertakings which adopt the form of a State Company (*Sociedades Mercantiles Estatales*). As to the Law relating to Public Undertakings, two issues must be clarified: the legal form to be adopted by the Undertaking (public or private form); and the particular set of laws governing its business relations with third parties (public or private law). The difference between the various legal forms is based on the structure the Undertaking chooses to adopt, as it could be of either a public nature in the case of public entities (*Organismos Autónomos* and *Entidades Públicas Empresariales*) or of a private one (*Sociedades Mercantiles Estatales*). The *Sociedades Mercantiles Estatales* are of a private nature because they have to be constituted as public limited companies, one of the forms foreseen in commercial law, and the State, or one of its Public Institutions, would have to possess the majority of its capital. The *Organismos Autómonos* are not only of a public nature but also subject to public law. The *Entidades Públicas Empresariales* are of a public nature but are subject to private law in their dealings with third parties (except when they exercise public functions, in which case they are subject to public law). The Commercial Companies are not only of a private nature (though the State has a majority stake in them) but also subject to private law.

12.13 Public Entities enjoy a certain degree of autonomy from the Government, but the Public Administration retains control by establishing provisions with which the Entity must comply, including requiring the organization to submit to rules on public accounts and taxation of its operations. A number of controls are laid down in the General Budget Act 1988.[11] First, there is control by the Accounts Court (*Tribunal de Cuentas).*[12] Secondly, the Government can control the entity by checking its efficiency records.[13] Thirdly, Parliament can have control by approval of the general State Budget, which will eventually determine the budgets of the relevant entities.[14]

Privatization in the energy sector

12.14 In the 1950s and the 60s, the importance of the public sector reached grand proportions. A good example of this importance was the National Institute for Industry (INI), set up during this era and in existence until 1995. The INI was

[10] Act No 6 of 14 April 1997.

[11] Royal Legislative Decree No 1091 of 23 September 1988.

[12] Art 136 of the Constitution and Art 132 of the General Budget Act 1988.

[13] Arts 17, no 2 and 88.

[14] Arts 48, 50, 51, and 55.

created as a holding of all State undertakings. The National Institute for Hydrocarbons (INH) was founded in 1981 and had as its aim the grouping of all the State-owned petroleum entities dispersed throughout the public sector into a single State enterprise. It became the owner of all State-owned petroleum and gas companies (such as *Campsa* and *Enagas*). The restructuring of the petroleum sector was completed in 1987 through the creation of the *Repsol* holding within the INH. *Repsol* became the parent organization for all of the INH's petroleum-related activities. Since the reorganization of 1987, the INH held 100 per cent of the shares in both *Repsol* and the gas supplier *Enagas,* the latter being the only company that remained outside the new *Repsol* holding. With the establishment of *Repsol* the Spanish Government created an integrated national company capable of operating successfully in a competitive market, and which could compete with multinational oil companies once the Spanish market was fully liberalized in 1992. Spain entered the European Communities in 1986 and the transitional period finished in 1992.[15]

The wave of privatization of the 1980s made little headway in Spain. The Socialist Government, which took power in 1982 and governed Spain until May 1996, had no plans for privatization on its platform. However, a number of privatizations were undertaken from 1989, such as the partial privatization of the petroleum company *Repsol*, one of the best known privatizations in the international financial markets. In 1989 some 25 per cent of its shares passed into private hands. A second partial privatization took place in 1995. The State still retains a stake of 10 per cent and it does not seem to have encouraged competition in the Spanish oil market. **12.15**

The INI was remodelled in 1992, when the holding was split into two: *Teneo* was formed from the profitable enterprises, and the other holding grouped those running at a deficit. The possibility of proceeding with the privatization of all or some of the component enterprises in the first group was then considered. It was a first step towards privatization, since those making profits would not help the non-profit making companies. Therefore, the remodelling would push into the privatization of the former. This tendency shown by the Socialist Government and its Ministry for Economy was obviously not born of ideological motives, but rather of practical reasons. Basically, the Treasury needed liquid assets to cover the public deficit and existing debts contracted by the Public Administration. **12.16**

[15] The creation of both the INH and *Repsol* are examples of privatization through commercialization. The INH was founded as a State company and *Repsol* as a commercial company. In both cases, therefore, the foundation meant a step forward into privatization. See, further, Roggenkamp, M, 'Implications of Deregulation, Integration and Privatisation of Networkbound Energy Systems', who identifies three types of privatizations: i) denationalization (ie transfer of State ownership to public ownership); ii) contracting out of public assignments to private firms; and iii) commercialization, which means that the management of the public tasks is carried out under private law by private law companies, notwithstanding that those companies are owned by the Government.

Privatization was an additional way for the Government to obtain income, and to reduce the public deficit. The INI's profitable companies would not receive money from the State from 1993 onwards, but the non-profitable ones would (mainly those within the military, shipbuilding and coal sectors). In order to successfully launch *Teneo*, the State assumed the debts of its component companies.

12.17 As from 31 July 1995, the INI and the INH ceased to exist and two new Public Institutions were founded.[16] On one hand was the new State Industrial Agency (AIE: *Agencia Industrial del Estado*) which took over responsibility for the non-profitable companies of INI.[17] On the other hand was the new State Company for Industrial Shares (SEPI: *Sociedad Estatal de Participaciones Industriales*) which grouped together the former *Teneo*[18] companies and the INH's companies. However, on 5 September 1997 the Government abolished the AIE, whose companies were put under the control of SEPI.[19] By means of this change, unprofitable companies of the AIE would not receive money from the State, but rather from the profitable companies of SEPI. This lack of financial help from the State led to the rapid privatization of the former AIE companies.

12.18 On 28 June 1996, the new Spanish Government announced an ambitious privatization plan, which has affected energy utilities such as *Endesa*, *Repsol*, *Gas Natural*, and *Enagas*, in which the Government still retained at that time, respectively, 39 per cent, 10 per cent, 3.5 per cent, and 9 per cent of the shares. In case of further privatization it might well be that the Government decides some golden shares should be retained, as regulated by the Privatization Act 1995.[20] However, State companies which operate within the coal sector will not be privatized (such as *Hunosa* and *Minas de Figaredo*).

(4) Public Services and the Energy Sector

12.19 The Constitution also states that 'from time to time, a Parliamentary Act may reserve to the public sector the management of essential resources or services especially those of a monopolistic nature'.[21]

12.20 There is a debate throughout the European Union on the concept of public service and, specifically, on whether a common approach to public services can be identified throughout the various legal systems of the Member States.[22] The

---

[16] As a result of the entry into force of Royal Decree-Law No 5 of 16 June 1995, later passed as an Act of Parliament: Act No 5 of 10 January 1996.

[17] There are 13 public companies within the mining, steel, shipyard, and defence sectors.

[18] *Teneo* was dissolved on the 4 July 1996 and its companies, such as *Endesa* and *Iberia*, were integrated within the SEPI.

[19] Royal Decree-Law of 5 September 1997.

[20] Act No 5 of 23 March 1995, developed by Royal Decree No 1225 of 15 September 1995.

[21] Art 128, 2 (first part of the second sentence) Constitution.

[22] See ch 5 above on EC law, section D2.

origin of this debate is Article 86 EU Treaty (former Article 90, 2 of the EC Treaty) according to which services of general economic interest may be exempted from some of the rules on free competition. The debate embraces also how public or universal service obligations can impose restrictions on the liberalization projects of the European Commission.

In Spain, a public service is just a reserved essential service, ie the Constitution substitutes the traditional expression of 'public service' for the new 'reserved essential service'. Essential service has a wider meaning than public service and in this respect it is considered that all public services are essential but not all essential services will be public services. Only those essential services reserved by an Act for the Public Administration would be, properly speaking, public services. The supply of electricity is declared by the relevant Act to be an essential service, but is not reserved for the Public Administration. Since the Constitution was approved in 1978, the Spanish Parliament has not always clearly distinguished between the expressions public service, essential service, and reserved essential service. In declaring an activity to be a public service, ie a reserved essential service, Parliament may be pursuing various aims: (i) sometimes, the only purpose of an Act declaring an activity to be a public service is to justify intensive regulation of the activity, (ii) sometimes designation as a public service tries to exclude any private initiative on the area and the public service must be carried out by a public institution; and iii) the declaration of a public service sometimes means that the Public Administration retains the concession-awarding power. Most public services can be delegated to private individuals or companies, and the Public Administration retains the title in the service but will pass on the economic management, normally under a contract: i) concessions; ii) interested management; iii) agreement with private persons (*Concierto* or Agreement); and iv) a mixed economy company. **12.21**

Parliament may declare an activity to be a reserved essential service subject to two requirements: i) the actual essentiality of the activity and ii) respect for the constitutional rights of citizens (eg school education cannot be reserved for the Public Administration). **12.22**

Reservation can be done especially in cases where the essential services are of a monopolistic nature, ie considered to be natural monopolies. Reservations operate in those sectors where the scope for competition is limited. It must be stressed that a Parliamentary Act is needed to declare that an essential service is reserved for the public sector. The constitutional rule is the freedom of enterprise in every economic sector of the country. Freedom of enterprise is a constitutional right.[23] A reservation is an exception to such freedom, which must be adopted by Parliament in so far as it affects a constitutional right. It is exclusively for the Act **12.23**

[23] See Art 38 Constitution, discussed above.

to regulate the scope and the exercise of fundamental rights.[24] However, it is unconstitutional for the Government, through statutory instruments and without authorization from Parliament, to reserve any essential service for the public administration.[25]

12.24 Whenever an essential service is reserved for the Public Administration, it is for the Administration to decide how the service will be performed. There has traditionally been an academic dispute in Spain on whether the establishment of a public service implies the constitution of a monopoly. One of the most widespread intellectual agreements in that regard was that whenever an Act declares an activity to be a public service, the relevant Public Administration would be free either to set up a public institution to carry out that activity in a monopolistic way or to delegate the management of that activity to private individuals or companies. The Public Administration could then monopolize either the responsibility for the public service together with its management (this is what happened when a monopolistic public institution was created) or only the responsibility, the management being therefore plural and private (concessionaires).

12.25 Prior to the entry of Spain within the European Communities, the Public Administration was free to choose to monopolize the management of an activity which had been declared a reserved essential service. The freedom of the Public Administration to choose how a public service should be managed was narrowed, because European law prohibits the maintenance of State monopolies of an economic nature or the creation of new ones.[26]

(5) Economic and Energy Planning

12.26 Article 131 of the Constitution states that the Spanish Parliament may approve General Economic Plans, which will have the following aims: i) to look after collective needs, ii) to harmonize and balance sectoral and regional development; and iii) to encourage the growth of the national income and the just distribution of it. Draft Plans will be made by the Government, relying on the forecasts made by the Autonomous Communities, and with the advice of trade unions, and that of professional, economic, and business organizations. No such General Economic Plan has been published by the Spanish Parliament so far. In fact, only sector plans have been produced. There have been three National Energy Plans since the path to a democratic political system started. The first was approved in 1979, the second in 1984, and the third, which is currently in force, was for the

[24] Art 53 Constitution.

[25] Art 28, 2 of the Constitution recognizes the right of strike, but states that the Act regulating its exercise must guarantee the functioning of essential services of the community during the strike (Art 37, which refers to collective conflict measures between employers and employees and the need to protect the functioning of essential services).

[26] Art 31 EU Treaty (former Art 37 EC Treaty). See also ch 5 above on EC law, section D(1).

period 1991–2000. Although Energy Plans are approved by Parliament, they are not Parliamentary Acts. The legal nature of those Plans is, therefore, uncertain. Energy Plans do not normally contain compulsory measures, but simply announce which energy policy the Government will follow in the relevant period. Most legislative measures within the energy sector are announced by the Plan. One of the most important features of energy planning in recent years is the nuclear ban of the 1984 National Energy Plan, as opposed to the construction of ten new nuclear powers plants which the 1979 NEP had envisaged.

(6) Energy and the Public Domain

Every kind of resource, whatever its form may be, is subject to the general national **12.27** interest, whether it is privately owned or belongs to a public power.[27] A Parliamentary Act may declare that a particular kind of natural resource belongs to the Public Domain (eg rivers, minerals, and hydrocarbons, such as oil and natural gas). Article 132 of the Constitution deals with those resources which are to be considered as part of the Public Domain. Among them are the tideland, beaches,[28] the territorial waters,[29] and the natural resources of the Exclusive Economic Zone[30] and of the Continental Shelf. It is for future Acts to include within the Public Domain any other resources[31] whose legal framework is based on the following principles: i) the State cannot dispose of them in any way; ii) they cannot be seized; and iii) they cannot be acquired by individuals.

(7) Energy, Central Government, and the Autonomous Communities

The Spanish Autonomous Communities

The path to Democracy in Spain was also the path to autonomy of the Regions. A **12.28** new legal framework for Regions was an essential issue within the debates which took place between 1976 and 1978, while the Parliament was writing a Constitution.

The Spanish Constitution abolished the centralized character of the Spanish State **12.29** and recognized the right to autonomy of the Regions.[32] As a result of the new constitutional provisions about the territorial organization of the State, a number of Autonomous Communities were set up. There were three Regions (Catalonia, Galicia, and the Basque Country) in 1976, when the move towards democracy started, which had previously enjoyed (from 1931 to 1936, during the

[27] Art 128, 1 Constitution.

[28] The Coasts Act 1988, Act No 22 of 28 July 1988.

[29] The Territorial Waters Act 1977, Act No 10 of 10 January 1977.

[30] The Exclusive Economic Zone Act 1978, Act No 15 of 20 February 1978.

[31] For example, the Water Act 1985, Act No 29 of 2 August 1985, developed by Royal Decree No 849 of 11 April 1986, and by Royal Decree No 927 of 29 July 1988.

[32] Art 2 Constitution.

Republican period) a high level of autonomy. This historical reason explains why they were the first Regions to have access to autonomy, once Franco died and the process towards a constitutional system started. Fourteen more Autonomous Communities were set up from the end of 1981 to February 1983: the entire Spanish territory is now divided into seventeen Autonomous Communities. There are ten Communities which comprise more than one Province: i) The Basque Country,[33] ii) Catalonia,[34] iii) Galicia,[35] iv) Andalusia,[36] v) Valencia,[37] vi) Aragón,[38] vii) Castilla-La Mancha,[39] viii) the Canary Islands,[40] ix) Extremadura,[41] and x) Castilla y León.[42] Seven Communities have territories which coincide with the territory of only one Province: i) Asturias, ii) Cantabria, iii) La Rioja, iv) Murcia, v) Navarre, vi) the Balearic Islands, and vii) Madrid.[43]

The Distribution of powers between the State and the Autonomous Communities

12.30 The distribution of powers between the State and the Autonomous Communities is laid down in Title VIII (Articles 137 to 158) of the Constitution and in the seventeen Autonomous Statutes, the latter as modified by several Spanish Parliamentary Acts. There are four general rules which monitor the relations between the State and the Autonomous Communities. There is thus a basic difference between the Spanish unitary system, as laid down by these four rules, and a federal system, in which, according to the traditional understanding, there is usually a list of competences expressly awarded to the federation, the remaining ones being in the hands of the federal states. Article 149, number 3, of the Spanish Constitution rules that:

a) those competences not expressly conferred upon the State by the Constitution may be in the hands of the Autonomous Communities whenever they are listed within the Statute of the relevant Autonomous Community;

---

33 With three Provinces: Alava, Bizkaia, and Gipuzkoa.

34 With four Provinces: Barcelona, Girona, Lleida, and Tarragona.

35 With four Provinces: La Coruña, Lugo, Ourense, and Pontevedra.

36 With eight Provinces: Almería, Cádiz, Córdoba, Granada, Huelva, Jaén, Málaga, and Sevilla.

37 With three Provinces: Alicante, Castellón, and Valencia.

38 With three Provinces: Huesca, Zaragoza, and Teruel.

39 With five Provinces: Albacete, Ciudad Real, Cuenca, Guadalajara, and Toledo.

40 With two Provinces: Las Palmas and Santa Cruz de Tenerife.

41 With two Provinces: Badajoz and Cáceres.

42 With nine Provinces: Avila, Burgos, León, Palencia, Salamanca, Segovia, Soria, Valladolid, and Zamora.

43 Besides these seventeen Autonomous Communities, there are two Towns in Africa (Ceuta and Melilla) located within the Moroccan Territory, which also enjoy a level of Autonomy, though lower than the former. Gibraltar should enjoy the same level of Autonomy as the other Spanish Autonomous Communities as soon as it comes back to the Sovereignty of the Kingdom of Spain, in accordance with UN Resolutions on the issue.

b) those competences not included within the Statute of a Community will belong to the State;
c) in the case of a conflict between the law of the State and that of an Autonomous Community in an area whose competence is shared by both, the former will prevail. It has to be stressed that this rule does not apply to those competences exclusively conferred upon the Autonomous Community;
d) State law is, in every case, supplementary to Regional law.

Some powers are awarded by the Constitution exclusively to either the State (such as international relations) or the Autonomous Communities (such as regional museums and libraries). However, many of the powers conferred upon the State by Article 149 of the Constitution are not absolutely exclusive powers on the relevant area, but rather powers which are limited to what may be considered the basic or uniform aspects of that sector, ie basic or uniform aspects to be enforced throughout the Spanish territory, and powers which are usually to be shared somehow with the Autonomous Communities. This is the case of the competence of the State on laying down the Basic Law on both environmental protection and energy and mines. On the other hand, those powers which are awarded to the Autonomous Communities by Article 148 of the Constitution are not, in many cases, exclusive powers either, but powers which have to be exercised within the general framework laid down by the State. It will be for the Autonomous Communities to develop, within that basic framework, the various central statutory provisions. This is the base for the development of Regional Policies. There is therefore wide scope for conflicts between both instances on the interpretation of what is basic and what is not. However, it is for the Spanish Parliament to state in every Act it passes what is to be considered as a basic aspect within that particular area, subject to any other powers which the Constitution or any of the seventeen Autonomous Statutes may have conferred upon the Autonomous Communities. The freedom of the Autonomous Communities to develop that Act is, therefore, narrowed. The Constitutional Court has the final word in any dispute between the State and the Autonomous Communities.[44] **12.31**

The Energy sector, the State, and the Autonomous Communities

Among the provisions of Articles 148 and 149 of the Constitution, nine refer specifically to the respective powers of the State and of the Autonomous Communities related to the energy sector. According to Article 149, 1 the State has exclusive power with regard to: **12.32**

a) the general planning of economic activities (Rule 13);
b) the legislation and regulation of and concession for hydraulic exploitation and resources, as long as the relevant waters run through more than one

[44] Art 161, 1 (lett c) and 2 of the Constitution.

Autonomous Community, as well as on electricity installations whose exploitation affects any other Community or the transport of the energy exceeds the borders of that Community (Rule 22);
c) the Basic Law for the Protection of the Environment (Rule 23); and
d) the Basic Energy and Mineral Law (Rule 25).

12.33 According to Article 148, 1 the Autonomous Communities have competence with regard to:

a) regional and town planning and housing (Rule 3);
b) public works in the interest of the community (Rule 4);
c) the execution of State environmental protection regulations (Rule 9);
d) projects, construction, and exploitation of hydraulic resources, channels, and bodies of water (Rule 10); and
e) the development of the economy of the Community within the objectives laid down by the State for the whole country (Rule 13).

12.34 Competence concerning energy is, therefore, shared by the State and the Autonomous Communities. It is for the State to lay down the Basic Law on Energy and Mines. The Autonomous Communities have the competence to develop that basic framework, and to execute within it the content of such legislation.[45]

12.35 There is no Energy Act in Spain, but several Acts of the Spanish Parliament cover specific energy sectors, such as hydrocarbons and electricity. As a matter of fact, the Parliaments of the Autonomous Communities have not yet passed any Act to rule energy issues,[46] nor have the respective Regional Governments enforced secondary legislation on the matter. The Autonomous Communities have mainly exercised their powers on energy through their authorization and concession-awarding power, in accordance with State law, and the subsidization of several programmes to promote energy saving and renewables. Three Autonomous Communities have set up Regional Energy Agencies, in order to promote various energy-efficiency programmes in that regard: i) *Ente Vasco de la Energía* (the Basque Country);[47] ii) *Instituto Catalán de la Energía* (Catalonia);[48] and iii) *Ente Regional de la Energía* (Castilla y León).[49]

---

[45] This is also the case for competence on environmental protection (Art 149, 1, Rule 23, Spanish Constitution). Some Autonomous Communities have approved their own laws in that area, and in many cases submit for previous Environmental Impact Assessment more energy installations than the State (see, for example, the Environmental Protection Act 1994 of Andalusia, Act no 7 of 18 May 1994).

[46] There are exceptions, such as the Electricity Distribution Act passed recently by the Autonomous Community of Castilla-La Mancha.

[47] Act No 9 of 24 November 1982. It has been very active in the past twelve months in order to reach an agreement with the three main energy companies which operate in the Region, an agreement which, in its turn, led to a Combined Cycle Power Plant producing gas and electricity from oil residues of a Basque refinery (*Petronor*).

[48] Act No 9 of 3 May 1991.

[49] Act No 7 of 3 December 1996.

Besides the complex structure of the Constitution with regard to the distribution of powers between the State and the Autonomous Communities, one also has to take into account that, due to historical reasons, not all the Communities were given the same level of autonomy from the first moment. Rather, there have been two speeds in the journey to self-government of the seventeen Autonomous Communities. Only five Communities (Andalusia, Catalonia, Galicia, the Basque Country, and Navarre) could develop, from the moment they were set up, the Basic Law of the State on energy and mineral activities through Regional Parliamentary Acts. The Autonomous Communities of Valencia and of the Canary Islands were soon awarded, by means of two Spanish Parliamentary Acts passed in 1982, the same powers as those five Communities. It was only in 1992[50] that the Spanish Parliament allowed the level of autonomy of the 'slow' Communities to increase and, therefore, the Statutes of some Autonomous Communities to be modified in order to include within their powers the development of the Spanish Basic Law on Energy and Mines.[51] **12.36**

Decisions of the Constitutional Court on the distribution of powers between the State and the Autonomous Communities within the energy sector

There are several decisions of the Spanish Constitutional Court in which the competence of the State on energy installations is enforced, and others by which the competences of the Regions on energy issues are recognized. **12.37**

In 1982 the Government of Catalonia gave its consent for a high-voltage grid to be constructed within the borders of the Autonomous Community. The Central Government applied for review of that decision to the Constitutional Court, which stated that the fact that the grid was within the borders of Catalonia did not mean that such grid was within its jurisdiction, because i) it is connected to the high-voltage grid of the Iberian Peninsula, ii) it may affect other Regions, and finally, iii) there is evidence that Catalonia itself will benefit from electricity which is produced out of its territory and crosses the grid.[52] **12.38**

However, there is scope for regional powers to be exercised, not only in cases of production of electricity for consumption by the producer, but also in cases of power plants whose clients are located exclusively within the borders of the Community. On 4 June 1985, the Government of the Autonomous Community of Aragón authorized the hydroelectricity generation plant 'El Pueyo' to be enlarged. The Central Government applied to the Constitutional Court for a review **12.39**

[50] Act No 9 of 23 December 1992.

[51] Ten Spanish Parliamentary Acts were passed in 1994, which modified the statutes of those ten Communities.

[52] Decision No 12 of 2 February 1984. The same doctrine is laid down in the Decision No 119 of 20 October 1986 (*the State v the Autonomous Community of Catalonia*), and Decision No 67 of 30 April 1992 (*the State v the Autonomous Community of Madrid*).

of that Decision, because it considered its competence to have been violated by the Regional Government. The main argument was that the production of the enlarged plant would exceed the threshold of 5 MW/year and that, consequently, it would have a supra-community impact. It would then be for the Spanish Ministry for Industry and Energy to award the authorization. The Constitutional Court rejected the argument of the Spanish Government because there was no rule which laid down such a threshold, and therefore, had the Court accepted that argument, the solution of the conflict would have relied upon the report of only one of the two parties. According to the Court, the Spanish Government did not give enough evidence that the enlargement of the plant would affect any other Community besides Aragon. The Court eventually stated that the competence to award the authorization was a regional one.[53]

12.40 With regard to powers on energy policy, one decision of the Spanish Constitutional Court has reinforced the position of the Central Government. On 12 September 1980, the Regional Government of the Autonomous Community of the Basque Country awarded an authorization to a refinery, Petróleos del Norte, S.A. (*Petronor*), by which it was allowed to modify the initial project and, therefore, partially to change the structure of its production. The authorization did not allow Petronor to produce more products than when it was built, but rather to produce some oil products instead of others. The Central Government of Madrid considered such authorization to invade its competences on the energy sector and asked the Constitutional Court to quash it. Before explaining the decision of the Constitutional Court, a brief explanation of the law in force at the time the conflict arose may be useful. On one hand, the construction and operation of oil refineries were regulated by Decree number 418 of 9 March 1968, and by Decree number 2232 of 20 July 1974. On the other hand, there were two National Energy Plans (1978 and 1983) in which refining activities were planned for the whole of Spain, in terms of which amount of oil products should be assigned to the Spanish market, which to importing countries, and in which plants the refining capacity should be enlarged or limited. According to Article 10 of the Statute of the Autonomous Community of the Basque Country (the Gernika Statute)[54] it has competences for both energy and industrial policy. Competences on industrial policy are wider than on energy. This explains why the Basque Government wanted its authorization to rest on its competences on industrial policy, rather than on energy. The Constitutional Court did eventually quash the regional authorization on two main grounds:[55] i) the authorization was undoubtedly within what should be considered to be part of the energy sector, and in such

[53] Decision No 74 of 14 May 1992.

[54] The Statute of the Autonomous Community of the Basque Country was approved by the Spanish Parliament as the Act No 3 of 18 December 1979.

[55] Decision No 24 of 21 February 1985.

area it is for the Autonomous Community to develop and execute of State Basic Law; ii) the amount of each oil product produced by refineries is of key importance for Spanish energy policy, and a unilateral (ie regional) variation of the conditions under which the State authorized a refinery to operate affects the whole national energy system.

(8) Energy and Local Entities

The Constitution guarantees a level of autonomy to Municipalities, Provinces, **12.41**
and Islands.[56] There are more than 8,000 Municipalities, 50 Provinces, and 11 main islands.[57] The Local Organization Act 1985[58] deals with those local entities and with other territorial entities (such as entities smaller than a Municipality and the association of Municipalities). Articles 25 and 36 of the Act list the competences, respectively, of the Governments of Municipalities and Provinces. The relevant competences for the energy sector are, in the case of Municipalities, those on i) town planning; ii) environmental protection; iii) customer protection; iv) street lighting; and v) collection and treatment of waste. With regard to Provinces, the most important competence in relation to energy is the power to elaborate plans for the extension of electricity networks throughout the Province, especially in rural areas.[59] The Local Organization Act 1985 also lists[60] those services which are reserved for the local entities, among which is heating. Originally, the Act reserved for the local entities not only heating, but also gas supply. The Hydrocarbons Act 1998 deletes the reference to gas supply in the Local Organization Act 1985. The reference to gas supply and to heating among those activities reserved for the local entities within the Local Organization Act 1985 did create a number of problems for the proper interpretation of the meaning of its wording, because the former Gas Act 1987[61] and the former Oil Act 1992,[62] both repealed by the Hydrocarbons Act 1998, empowered either the Central Public Administration or the Autonomous Communities to regulate those industries. This contradiction between the Local Organization Act 1985 and the sector Acts was the origin of several academic disputes and decisions of the Spanish Courts, to which the relevant sections of this chapter refer.

[56] Arts 140 and 141.

[57] There are 7 islands within the Autonomous Community of the Canary Islands: El Hierro, Fuerteventura, Gran Canaria, La Gomera, Lanzarote, La Palma and Tenerife and 5 islands within the Autonomous Community of the Balearic Islands: Mallorca, Menorca, Ibiza, Formentera and Cabrera.

[58] Act No 7 of 2 April 1985. It was developed by the Regulation of the Local Organization Act 1985 (1986), approved by Royal Legislative Decree No 781 of 18 April 1986.

[59] Art 28, 1, f of the Local Organization Act Regulation 1986.

[60] Art 86.

[61] Act No 10 of 15 June 1987.

[62] Act No 34 of 22 December 1992.

(9) *Administrative and Regulatory Authorities*

12.42 According to the distribution of powers between the Central Government and the Regional Governments of the seventeen existing Autonomous Communities, as stated in the Spanish Constitution, administrative powers belong either to the Central Ministry for Economy or to the Regional Departments for Industry and Energy. Three Autonomous Communities (the Basque Country, Catalonia, and Castilla y León) have set up their own Energy Institutes, for the purpose of unifying their various competences on energy issues. Within the Ministry for Economy[63] there is a Secretary of State for Economy and Energy, which has one General Directorate for Energy and Mines. Under the supervision of the Ministry for Science and Technology there are three public institutions, which deal with some energy and mineral issues: i) the Centre for Energy, Environmental, and Technology Research (CIEMAT);[64] ii) the Diversification and Saving of Energy Institute (IDAE);[65] and iii) the Spanish Geological and Mineral Technology Institute (ITGME).[66]

12.43 There were no regulatory agencies within the energy market in Spain until 1998. Even after the creation of such agencies most regulatory powers are to be exercised by the above mentioned Central and Regional Governmental Departments. However, the National Electricity System Regulation Act 1994 (NESRA)[67] set up a Commission for the National Electricity System, to which few regulatory powers over the electricity industry have been awarded. Within the Electricity Sector Act 1997, the Commission retains those powers. However, the Hydrocarbons Act 1998 put an end to this Commission, and in its place set up the new National Commission for Energy, which will have few regulatory powers in both the Electricity and Gas Markets. In addition to these institutions, there is a Tribunal for the Defence of Competition (or Competition Authority), which looks after the completion of competition rules within the Market.[68]

C. Mineral Law

(1) *General Issues on the Ownership and Exploitation of Mines*

12.44 All mines and other geological resources located in the Spanish national territory, in the territorial waters, or in the Continental Shelf are declared by Article 1, 3 of

[63] Royal Decree No 557 of 27 April 2000.
[64] Royal Decree No 221 of 14 February 1986.
[65] Royal Decree No 802 of 21 April 1986, as modified by the Royal Decree No 252, of 21 February 1997.
[66] Royal Decree No 1270 of 28 October 1988.
[67] Act No 40, of 30 December 1994.
[68] Act No 16 of 17 July 1989, as developed by Royal Decrees No 157 of 21 February 1992 and No 1080 of 11 September 1992.

the Mining Act 1973 to be part of the public domain.[69] In Spanish law there is no presumption arising from surface ownership, as is the case in some common law countries, where mines, quarries, and minerals in their original position are part and parcel of the land, and consequently the owner of surface land is entitled *prima facie* to everything beneath or within it, down to the centre of the earth.[70] On the contrary, Spanish mining law is based on the assumption that mines belong to the State.[71] Hence, the Spanish State has the exclusive right of searching for, drilling for, working, and getting minerals in the whole Spanish Territory (including the Continental Shelf, the territorial waters and the Exclusive Economic Zone). The State exercises its competences through the Ministry for Economy, and through the Spanish Geological and Mineral Technology Institute (ITGME). However, the State may authorize individuals to search for minerals and may award concessions for the exploitation of a mine. After Spain's entry into the European Communities, the Mining Act 1973 was modified in order to allow individuals and companies from other Member States belonging to the EC to enjoy the rights of the Act,[72] save for strategic minerals, which are subject to the general rules of foreign investments in Spain.

Notwithstanding the public nature of mines, the principle which inspires Spanish law on mining activities is the promotion of private initiative, giving private individuals or companies the right to apply for an authorization to search for minerals or for a concession to work a mine, save in those areas where the State has reserved this right for itself. Traditionally, Spanish mining law has tried to encourage private investment within the sector.[73] In fact, the exploitation of mines is usually done by private concessionaires, except for valuable minerals of a strategic nature, such as coal and uranium. **12.45**

(2) Classification of Mineral Resources

Article 3 of the Mining Act 1973 classifies mines and geological resources into three sections. Section A refers i) to those mineral resources which have a low economic value and the geographical area in which they are commercialized is limited and ii) to those mineral resources which are suitable to be used in the **12.46**

[69] Act No 22 of 21 July 1973. It was developed by the Royal Decree No 2857 of 25 August 1978 Art 132 of the Constitution declares the natural resources of the Exclusive Economic Zone to be also part of the public domain.

[70] In virtually all other countries (differing from the United States) valuable minerals, such as gold, silver, oil, natural gas, coal. and uranium, belong to the sovereign: Smith, EE, *et al*, 'International Petroleum Transactions', Rocky Mountain Mineral Law Foundation, Denver 1993, 228.

[71] See Arts 334, 349, and 350 of the Spanish Civil Code (1889).

[72] Royal Legislative Decree No 1303 of 28 June 1986.

[73] Act No 6 of 4 January 1977, an Act to encourage the operation of mining activities, as amended by Act No 43 of 27 December 1995, which was developed by Royal Decrees No 1167 of 2 May 1978 and 2485 of 23 December 1994. This legislation settles, among some other provisions, a number of fiscal benefits for mining companies.

construction of infrastructure and no further treatment—or a simple treatment—is needed for that purpose.[74] Section B refers to i) mineral waters; ii) thermal springs; iii) underground structures; and iv) those resources formed as a consequence of the conduct of any mining activity regulated by the Act.[75] Section C refers to all minerals and geological resources not included in the two previous sections. A new section D was created in 1980,[76] by which the following minerals ceased to be included within section C and are now subject to the special rules of section D: i) coal; ii) radioactive minerals (such as uranium);[77] iii) geothermal resources; iv) bituminous stones; and v) any other minerals or geological resources which the Government may decide in the future to be included within it.

(3) Areas of Minerals Reserved for the State

12.47 The State may reserve for itself the exploitation of a particular mineral within the whole national territory, the territorial waters, and the Continental Shelf. It may also reserve for itself in certain areas, either temporarily or definitively, the research for and working of specific minerals or of all minerals within that area. All pending applications for authorizations and concessions from private individuals or companies on the reserved area or mineral will be cancelled. However, the reserve will not affect applications made before the proposed reserved was registered in the Book of Reserves at the Ministry for Industry, nor authorizations or concessions already in operation in that area or for the particular reserved mineral. When the reservation for the State is of any of the minerals included within section D, the reserve does affect authorizations and concessions awarded for any such mineral on the same area. The research for or work on minerals within reserved areas may be done by the State itself, or its entíties, or by private companies with which the State signs a contract.

12.48 Whenever there is incompatibility between the activities carried on by former holders of authorizations or concessions on the reserved area and the activities which the new reservation brings about, the State may impose restrictions upon the businesses of the former or even decide that the authorizations and concessions are to be terminated and the installations expropriated. Even when an area has been reserved for the State, private individuals or companies can apply for authorization to search for concessions to extract minerals which remain outside the scope of the reservation. In those cases, the State may impose restrictions on the

[74] Art 3, 1, A Mining Act. See also Decree 1747/1975 of 17 July 1975, which develops this article.

[75] Art 3, 1, B Mining Act.

[76] Act No 54 of 5 November 1980, an Act to modify the Mining Act 1973, with special regard to mineral resources suitable for energy uses.

[77] The National Undertaking for Uranium (*Enusa*) was charged by the Decree No 3322 of 23 December 1971, with the task of exploiting such mineral, and supplies it to the Spanish nuclear power plants.

entitled individual or company. The reservation can be cancelled by the Government at any time, and from that moment all restrictions imposed upon companies operating in that area will come to an end.

(4) *Authorizations and Concessions*

For the exploitation of minerals resources included within sections A and B, authorization is required. As regards the minerals in section C a division needs to be made between exploration and production. The exploration for these minerals is subject to an authorization, which is given for short periods of time (one to three years) and does not create any contractual relation between the individual or company and the Public Administration. The exploitation of minerals in section C is, however, subject to a concession. A concession is awarded for thirty years, its duration may be extended, and it has the nature of an administrative contract. **12.49**

The Hydrocarbons Act 1998 deals with exploration and exploitation of petroleum (oil and natural gas). It expressly states that any problem which cannot be solved by using its provisions must be solved by referring to the Mining Act 1973. This is why the rules of section B governing the use of underground structures will apply to gas storage, since neither the Gas Act 1987 nor the Hydrocarbons Act 1998 contain detailed rules on that issue. **12.50**

With regard to mineral resources of section D, the scope for private initiative is narrowed, and, in general terms, both the searching for and the exploitation of those resources will be carried out by the State. **12.51**

The Mining Act 1973 also deals with the expiration of mining rights, which may be caused by the improper fulfilment of the duties of the concessionaire. Mining rights can be transferred, subject to a previous authorization of the Public Administration. **12.52**

(5) *Coal Production*

There are around eighty-seven enterprises within the coal sector and 26,133 employees. Coal reserves are estimated for a period of thirty-two years, based on the current consumption. Due to geological factors, the cost of extraction of Spanish coal is very expensive, and more than double the cost of imported coal (including transport costs). **12.53**

There is a strong presence of the State in the coal sector by means of Public Enterprises. The State has 100 per cent of the shares of the two major coal companies (*Hunosa* and *Minas de Figaredo*). The output of *Hunosa* represents 20 per cent of all output in Spain, and absorbs 80 per cent of all State subsidies to the coal sector. On 10 December 1986 the association of coal producers (*Carbunion*) and the electricity association (*Unesa*) created a new price framework for coal (the New Thermal Coal Contracting System) which distinguished between underground **12.54** and open-cast mine coal prices and envisaged a system of subsidies for both the production and consumption of national coal. The levy imposed on electricity bills to support the consumption of Spanish coal was administered from 1979 by the Electricity Compensation Office (OFICO), whose functions were in 1994 passed onto the Commission for the National Electricity System.[78] Due to the European Commission's Decisions of 20 December 1989 and 25 July 1990, Spain would have to have reduced compensation paid within that framework, and to have reduced payments made in any other way, by 31 December 1993. Further Decisions of the European Commission have approved the maintenance and gradual reduction of subsidies in Spain, under the ECSC Treaty and its developments.[79]

12.55 A drastic decrease in 1997 and 1998 of the amount of compensation for the consumption of national coal was envisaged by the draft protocol between the electricity companies and the Government, signed in November 1996. However, miners went on strike as soon as they heard about the content of the draft protocol, so that the Ministry for Industry and Energy finally decided not to include any changes in the existing system of compensations, and postponed any decision on the issue. After that controversy, the Electricity Sector Act 1997 allowed for the preference of using national coal, by means of Article 25. According to this Article, the Government may establish procedures compatible with the free market for generation, to achieve the operation of those units of electricity generation that use local sources of primary energy for combustion, up to a limit of 15 per cent of the total amount of primary energy necessary for producing the electricity demanded by the national market, considered over annual periods and adopting the measures necessary to avoid altering the market price.[80]

12.56 Transitional Disposition 4 of the Electricity Act 1997 addresses the problem of national coal. According to the Disposition, the Government may establish the necessary incentives to ensure that owners of energy-producing installations consume national coal at the rate fixed every year by the Ministry of Industry and Energy. This aim will, in any case, respect the limit laid down by Article 25 as from the year 2004. Those incentives may include a premium equivalent to one peseta/KWh for those generation groups which have actually consumed national coal and equivalent to the quantity actually consumed. The Budget Act 1998 established that subsidies for the consumption of national coal would not be supported by tariffs paid by consumers, but rather by a special tax on electricity consumption. This was aimed to comply with EU requirements.

[78] Transitional Disposition No 4 of the National Electricity System Regulation Act 1994.

[79] See ch 5 above on EC law, section C.

[80] Translation of Art 25 from L Pastor Ridruejo and JI González Ruiz, *Spain*, Special Issue of the Oil and Gas Law and Taxation Review on the Liberalisation of Electricity in Europe (1998), 169.

D. Oil and Gas Exploration and Exploitation

Exploration and exploitation of oil and natural gas are regulated by the Hydrocarbons Act 1998.[81] The amount of oil and natural gas production in Spain is very small. There have been few exploitations, mainly of natural gas (in the Cantabric Sea, in the Pyrenees, and in the Guadalquivir Valley), which are now depleted or almost depleted. Some of them are being transformed into gas storage. There are, however, some exploration activities. The Law related to Hydrocarbons has traditionally been more generous towards foreign investments than the Mineral Law, because the performance of exploration and exploitation activities needs expensive technology, which has not been generally available in Spain. **12.57**

Prospecting for and exploration and investigation of the existence of hydrocarbons are subject to previous authorization. Prospecting activities do not imply the use of drilling.[82] Authorizations to explore oil and gas will be awarded by means of a tender procedure.[83] The exploitation of oil or natural gas wells is subject to a concession.[84] According to the Hydrocarbons Act 1998, those companies or individuals who enjoy a concession to exploit oil or gas fields need to obtain an authorization to transport such oil and gas to storage installations or to store the gas and oil they extract. **12.58**

Spain has not developed special legislation to implement the Hydrocarbons Licensing Directive on the conditions for the awarding and use of authorizations for the exploration and exploitation of hydrocarbons.[85] It is assumed that the Hydrocarbons Act 1998 properly incorporates the Directive's aims and provisions. **12.59**

E. The Gas Supply Industry

(1) Development of the Spanish Gas Industry

A brief history of the Spanish gas industry

For more than 100 years (approximately, from 1850 to 1960) most Spanish towns have enjoyed town gas, manufactured from coal or from oil products at local factories. However, the development of the natural gas industry goes back to the end of the 1960s when natural gas was transported to Barcelona by ship and distributed in some towns of Catalonia. The company *Gas Natural* founded in **12.60**

[81] Arts 7 to 36 Hydrocarbons Act.
[82] Art 14 Hydrocarbons Act.
[83] Arts 15 to 23 Hydrocarbons Act.
[84] Arts 24 to 29 Hydrocarbons Act.
[85] Council Directive No 94/22/EC of 30 May 1994. See also the ch 5 above.

1965[86] was responsible for all the activities related to natural gas. Apparently, the new company had to face several difficulties with gas suppliers. Notwithstanding the lack of gas consumption in Spain at that time, large amounts of gas were contracted with severe *take or pay* clauses within those contracts. As a consequence of the increasing financial problems of that company, the *Empresa Nacional del Gas* (*Enagas*), a wholly State-owned company, was founded in 1972. It bought *Gas Natural* and expropriated (nationalized) the contracts that the company had made with foreign gas suppliers. From 1972 the development of the gas industry ended and *Enagas* ran at a deficit. The 1973 and 1979 oil crises, in turn, worsened the financial conditions of *Enagas* with regard to the gas supply contracts signed with Algeria.

Modern gas policy

12.61 The 1983–1992 NEP aimed at the development of natural gas in Spain. Forecasts made by the NEP could only be successful if the conflict with Algeria were to be settled. It was also assumed, as a consequence, that provisions included in the NEP depended on a healthy price policy, to make gas use attractive to consumers and to allow distribution companies to operate without financial disadvantages. After several years of discussions, Spain and Algeria signed an agreement in 1985, involving a long-term contract with advantageous clauses to both countries. All the companies operating in gas supply signed a Protocol in the summer of 1985. They all agreed on questions of geographical demarcation of the distribution sector within the business and accepted that the public undertakings *Repsol* and *Enagas* should have the basic responsibility for this sector. This was a new business for *Repsol*, which had previously been involved in the distribution of liquefied petroleum gases (butane and propane). Due to the fact that gas demand in 1987 surpassed the forecasts made in 1983 by the NEP, the first Gas Plan was issued in 1988.

12.62 The 1991–2000 NEP seeks to encourage the consumption of natural gas. For that purpose, it foresees a) the building of several new gas-fired power stations, b) the conversion of some nuclear power stations into gas-fired power stations, c) the extension of the national gas network to new regions and d) the construction of a pipeline between Hassi R'Mel (Algeria) and Córdoba (Spain). Therefore, the new NEP tries to go further than the 1983–1992 NEP and the 1988 Gas Plan, since the scenario it draws for the national overall supply of gas is more favourable in terms of gas availability and gas consumption. Consequently, a Protocol was signed on 8 June 1994 between the electricity companies and *Enagas*, according to which the former commited themselves to buying gas for electricity generation purposes from the latter.

[86] Gas Natural was founded by the company Catalana de Gas.

The acceleration in the expansion of natural gas throughout the Iberian Peninsula was remarkably high in 1997 and will make it possible to achieve higher levels of penetration in the domestic and commercial market, reaching 16.2 per cent of total sales in the year 2000. Natural gas sales in 1997 have risen by 32.7 per cent, the highest rate of progress since the natural gas business started. The market of natural gas for electricity generation has also dramatically increased in 1997 and represents 14.3 per cent of total demand of natural gas. Also in 1997, 10 power stations used natural gas for generation purposes. **12.63**

Gas supplies

Spain relies upon imports of natural gas.[87] The Spanish Gas Policy tries to diversify the sources of gas supply, by means of imports through European gas networks and by means of methane-gas tankers with subsequent re-gasification in the three LNG plants installed in Spain (Barcelona, Cartagena, and Huelva). The capacity of the LNG plants at Cartagena and Huelva have been increased and the mooring facilities of the former modified in order to receive large methane-gas tankers. In July 1995 *Enagas* agreed to purchase 40 per cent of the liquefied natural gas (LNG) production of the future plant of Trinidad and Tobago.[88] **12.64**

The improvement of the natural gas storage system is being carried out by *Enagas*. The Serrablo storage plant has been in operation since 1992 and the one situated at the Gaviota field was recently put into operation and reached full capacity between 1997 and 1998. *Enagas* is considering transforming the Marismas gas field (near the mouth of the Guadalquivir River) into an underground storage area. A protocol was signed with *Repsol* to start operating the gas fields in Cadiz Bay (*Poseidón*), which are also likely to be converted into underground storage areas. Enagas has discovered various aquifers and salt pits in different geographical areas which could also be used for storage. After implementation, the programme will make available a system of regulating storage areas which will make it possible to cover seasonal variations in demand and to dispose of a strategic capacity to cover ninety days of steady consumption in Spain. This implies counting on storage facilities for some 5,000 million cubic metres of usable gas in the year 2005. **12.65**

[87] In 1997, gas supplies were as follows: national gas: i) Marismas y Palancares (0.6%); ii) Poseidón (0.7%); iii) total national gas: 1.3%; imported gas: i) Algeria (61.6%); ii) Libya (8.6%); iii) Norway (13.3%); iv) Abu Dhabi (9.2%); v) Qatar (1.3%); other sources (4.7%); total imported gas (98.7%).

[88] The launching of this Caribbean plant took place towards the end of 1998, and will produce some 3 million tons of LNG a year, equivalent to some 12 million cubic metres of natural gas a day. It will meet approximately 20% of current Spanish natural gas requirements.

(2) The Spanish Gas Industry

Main companies

12.66 The Spanish Gas Industry has become horizontally and vertically integrated. There are twenty-two companies associated in the *Sociedad para el estudio y desarrollo de la industria del gas* (*Sedigas*). However, almost all of them are owned by the 'new' *Gas Natural* which was created in 1991 (see below)[89] and which is a private monopoly. The integration process took place between 1989 and 1995. The integration was monitored by the most important companies, ie the private *Catalana de Gas*, SA and the companies *Repsol* and *Enagas*, which before privatization were public companies under the governmental *placet. Enagas* is the owner of the gas transport network and the exclusive supplier to the Spanish market. Since 1981 the INH held 100 per cent of the shares in *Enagas.*[90] In 1987, the holding *Repsol* was created within the INH, as the parent organization for all the INH's petroleum-related activities. *Enagas* was the only company of INH which remained outside the new holding.

Horizontal and vertical integration

Horizontal integration

12.67 The most important event in 1991 and 1992 within the distribution sector of the Spanish gas market is the establishment of a new holding: *Gas Natural* which is the result of the merger of *Gas Madrid* (owned by *Repsol*) and *Catalana de Gas.* This holding holds the respective stakes of *Repsol* and *Catalana de Gas* in several distribution companies. It is easy to understand that this new company completely dominates the Spanish distribution sector. It owns thirteen distributing companies all over the country, and has a major stake in three other companies (10 per cent of *Gas Natural de Alava*, 18.7 per cent of *Gas de Euskadi*, and 35 per cent of *Gas Aragón*) which distribute gas in almost every Region of Spain, and there are no competitors. The company has also a strong presence in the Latin American Market. The main shareholders of *Gas Natural* are *Repsol* (45 per cent) and *La Caixa* (saving bank) (25 per cent).

12.68 *Enagas* was kept outside the merger, and remained as the owner and manager of the National Network, the exclusive importer and bulk gas supplier, and the gas distributor to consumers other than domestic and commercial ones (ie industrial consumers).

Vertical integration

12.69 In 1995 *Gas Natural* took 91 per cent of the shares of *Enagas.* The INH retained the remaining 9 per cent of the shares. Both *Enagas* and *Gas Natural* remain independent

[89] The new 'Gas Natural' is thus different from the one created in 1965.

[90] See paras 12.14 and 12.15 above.

in the running of their businesses. This takeover has meant an indirect privatization of the gas industry, since *Gas Natural* is a private company. The new ownership helped to put an end to the historical disputes between *Gas Natural* and *Enagas* with regard to the prices the latter, as the exclusively importer of natural gas, was charging to the gas-distributing companies. Two main reasons explain why each step of the process was taken.

First, *Enagas* had traditionally faced severe financial problems, due to the fact it was charged with the task of building up a national network. The completion of such a task requires huge investments and is high capital-cost intensive. *Enagas* has a *de facto* monopoly for the supply of gas to industrial consumers, except in the Autonomous Communities of the Basque Country and Catalonia. Yet, the amount of the supply business was not big enough to generate the revenue needed to recover those investments if gas is sold at competitive prices. On the other hand, the company agreed in the 1985 Protocol[91] to sell gas to the distributing companies at prices which should not always reflect the real delivery costs but which would guarantee the financial viability of the distributing companies. The creation of a gas market in Spain may justify some of this anti-competitive behaviour, and it may be that only vertical integration will help to create that market. **12.70**

Secondly, the European Commission has attempted since 1988 to introduce legislation in order to promote gas-to-gas competition within the European Community. The Draft Gas Directive, or Third-Party Access Directive, submitted by the Commission to the Council in 1992,[92] was a warning against the monopoly of *Enagas* since it aimed at a system in which the Spanish distributing companies and big industrial consumers would be allowed to shop around and to look for new gas suppliers other than *Enagas*. As neither Spanish law nor European Community law prohibit customers from shopping around, most of the difficulties in that regard are practical difficulties, which derive from some *de facto* monopolies and from the dominant position of certain companies in the market. The enforcement of the Directive would strengthen the position of distributing companies and big customers and would make it clearer that there is a right to access to the gas network. In view of that Draft Directive and its effects, Enagas agreed to be taken over by its biggest client, *Gas Natural*. **12.71**

The integration of the Spanish gas industry is not necessarily contrary to the principle of unbundling. Both *Enagas* and *Gas Natural* keep their independence as corporations. Moreover, unbundling does not imply a division of ownership. **12.72**

[91] See para 12.61above.

[92] This 1992 draft Directive was amended in 1993 and eventually became the 1998 Gas Directive: COM (93) 643 final: modified proposal of a Directive of the European Parliament and of the Council for the establishment of common rules for the creation of an Internal Gas and Electricity Market, made in Brussels on the 9 December 1993.

However, there is a potential threat that transparency and competition are hampered when the industry becomes integrated.

Liberalization, integration, and privatization

12.73 The changes which the Spanish gas market has recently experienced show how liberalization pushes sometimes into privatization and integration. The maturity of some European gas markets is in strong contrast with new markets which, as in Spain, still lack the infrastructure and where demand for gas is below the European average. These circumstances, together with the attempts of the European Commission to create an Internal Market for gas, may well explain why the Spanish gas industry has become an integrated one: the prospects for liberalization have forced the companies to combine their efforts in order effectively to create a gas market and to face competition from those companies which in the future will be seeking to grasp a quota of that market.[93]

12.74 On 28 June 1996 the Spanish Government announced an ambitious privatization Plan, which has affected some energy utilities, such as *Gas Natural* and *Enagas*. SEPI has already sold the 9 per cent shares it still has in *Enagas* to *Gas Natural*.

Recent Developments in the Spanish Gas Industry

12.75 Key drivers for liberalization of the gas trade in Spain are the Government and the electricity companies. The Conservative Government which took power in 1996 has a liberal approach to the regulation of strategic sectors of the economy, such as energy, transport, and telecommunications. It committed itself to the privatization and liberalization of those sectors for many years. A particularly important sector is the electricity industry. The Government also had the will to introduce a certain level of competition within the gas industry. Electricity companies want cheap supplies of natural gas, so that they can offer lower prices to the pool (see below). Big industrial consumers would also prefer energy companies to offer better electricity and gas prices.

12.76 Changes have been promoted both by the Government through legislation and by the important market players such as the holding *Gas Natural/Enagas* in association with the electricity company *Endesa*, *Repsol* in association with *Iberdrola*, *Amoco*, and EVE (*Ente Vasco de la Energia* the Basque Governmental public holding, which, among other companies, owns *Gas de Euskadi*), and the company *Gas de Asturias*, in association with *Enron*.

[93] I del Guayo, 'Privatisation, Integration and Liberalisation of the Spanish Gas Industry', Journal of Energy & Natural Resources Law, 1 (1996) 88–94.

Politically speaking there are both obstacles to and pressures for the liberalization of the market. The Government needs the support of both the Basque and Catalan Nationalist Parties, the latter having more power within the Spanish Parliament. The gas industry is dominated by Catalan capital, since the gas industry started in Barcelona in the mid 1960s. The Catalan Government tries to maintain the position of *Gas Natural*, and will threaten the central Government if it tries to go too far with the liberalization process. On the other hand, the Basque Government is the owner of *Gas de Euskadi*, through the public holding EVE. The Basque Government thinks that the natural partner of *Gas de Euskadi* is *Iberdrola*, which, in its turn, is the partner of *Repsol* in two main gas projects in Bilbao.[94] Therefore, the Basque Government is pushing the central Government to go as far as possible within the liberalization process, so that *Gas de Euskadi* can become the second gas operator in Spain. They are also considering the possibility of connecting the Basque gas pipeline system to the French network. **12.77**

(2) The Regulation of the Gas Industry

Introduction

The development of the gas industry in Spain has taken place under the Gas Act 1987,[95] which was repealed by the Hydrocarbons Act 1998, passed by the Spanish Parliament on 17 September 1998. **12.78**

Gas supply in Spain was, from the very early years of this century, a public service. The Gas Act 1987[96] retained the same idea: the production (of manufactured gas), transport, and distribution of gas, as well as every activity related to those activities, were declared by the Act to be a public service, specifically an essential service reserved for the Public Administration. However, that declaration did not mean that those activities must be carried out by a Public Undertaking; rather, the Act foresaw that activities related to gas supply would be assigned, through concessions, to either public or private companies. In the case of gas, therefore, the reservation of the public service to the Public Administration did mean that it has the concession-awarding power. **12.79**

Among the key drivers for liberalization is the Hydrocarbons Act 1998. This Act repealed and substituted a number of Acts, such as i) the Exploration for and Exploitation of Hydrocarbons Act 1974, ii) the Gas Act 1987, and iii) the Oil Act 1992. Both upstream and downstream oil and gas activities, which were previously governed by those three Acts, were after the entry into force of the Hydrocarbons Act, subject to a single Act. The Act regulates in separate Chapters **12.80**

[94] These are a combined cycle power plant and a regasification plant.
[95] See, further I del Guayo, 'Gas Regulation in Spain', *Utilities Law Review*, 2 (1991) 78–82.
[96] Act No 10, of 15 June 1987.

exploration for and exploitation of oil and gas (see above),[97] the distribution of oil products (see below),[98] and the supply of natural gas.

12.81 Articles 54 to 102 of the Hydrocarbons Act lay down the legal framework for all activities related to the supply of natural gas to consumers. Even though most of these provisions are exclusively devoted to the supply of natural gas, some provisions also apply to the supply of other gas distributed by pipelines, such as i) propane, ii) manufactured gas, iii) synthetic gas, or iv) the mixture of butane, propane, or natural gas with air for distribution. Articles 103 to 107 deal with expropriation issues and servitudes and Articles 108 to 117 with infractions and fines.

12.82 Article 54 of the Hydrocarbons Act states that the production, regasification, storage, transport, distribution, and trade (commercialization) of gas can be freely carried out by any company. The installations needed for the production, regasification, liquidization, transport, storage, and distribution of natural gas will be subject to authorization. The Act creates a new liberalized atmosphere for the gas business to be developed, but some of its provisions will hinder the birth of competition, as will some provisions which are missing. It seems that the legislator did not take into account the realities of the Spanish Market when drafting this Act: the system designed would have been appropriate for a country in which there were many gas supplies and many operators.

The Gas transmission network

The National Gas System

12.83 The Natural Gas System (NGS) comprises of (i) the Basic Network; (ii) the secondary transport networks (ie those pipelines whose pressure is between 60 and 16 *bares*); and (iii) the distribution network (ie those pipelines whose pressure is 16 *bares* or less, and all pipelines which, irrespective of their pressures, are designed to convey gas from a pipeline of the Basic Network or of the secondary transport network to a consumer); and (iv) any installation ancillary to those three kinds of installation.

12.84 In its turn, the Basic Network consists of several installations, ie the high-pressure gas pipelines (pipelines with a pressure of 60 *bares* or more), the gas liquidizing plants and the regasification plants of LNG connected to the NGS, the gas storage facilities, and the connections between the Basic Network and gas fields or gas storage in Spain, and finally the international connections between the NGS and foreign systems or storage.

[97] Arts 7 to 36.
[98] Arts 37 to 53.

Currently the Basic Network is being extended to the Ruta de la Plata pipeline (from the South to the North), which will be built in order to reinforce the coverage of the western Iberian Peninsula. It will connect Seville with Gijón, cross Extremadura from North to South, continuing through the Western side of Castilla-León, and crossing the provinces and cities of León, Zamora, and Salamanca. That gas pipeline was completed in 1998. During 1995, the Ministry for Industry and Energy, *Gas Natural* and the Autonomous Communities of Extremadura, Castilla-León, Murcia, Valencia, and Andalusia have signed draft agreements to promote gasification in these Communities. On the other hand, the basic network of the Mediterranean Arc (Cartagena-Barcelona gas pipeline) will be reinforced in order to achieve more capacity. **12.85**

There are now only five international delivery points in Spain. There are two international Pipelines (Maghreb and Pyrennees) and three regasification plants (Huelva, Cartagena, and Barcelona). This is a physical obstacle for both the diversification of gas supplies and the increase of the number of those supplies. **12.86**

The Maghreb pipeline

The Maghreb pipeline runs from Algeria via Morocco to Spain. It has a length of around 530 kilometres in Algerian territory, 545 kilometres in Moroccan territory, and 40 kilometres under the waters of the Strait of Gibraltar. The construction of this international gas pipeline was envisaged many years ago, but was not finally undertaken until after the renegotiation of the supply contracts with Algeria and the publication of the new prospects for gas consumption in Spain within the 1991–2000 NEP. **12.87**

The project formally started with a Madrid Summit on the 30 April 1991, in which the Ministers for Energy of Spain, Morocco, and Algeria took part. The Protocol then signed has brought about an extremely complex corporate structure. The construction and operation of the pipeline which crosses Algerian territory is the responsibility of *Sonatrach*, the Algerian State-owned gas supplier. As to the Moroccan and Spanish sections, *Enagas* was designated as the responsible company.[99] *Enagas* was authorized by the Moroccan Government to construct, use, and operate the Moroccan part of the pipeline.[100] Furthermore, both *Enagas* and *Sonatrach* founded a new corporation in 1992 (Europe Maghreb Pipeline Ltd: EMPL) which is owned by the users of the pipeline and which will enjoy the right of use the pipeline for twenty-five years. The Moroccan Government created a company to construct the pipeline on behalf of EMPL, which is called *Metragaz*.[101] **12.88**

[99] Enagas was awarded a concession to transport gas on the Spanish territorial waters and on the Continental Shelf by the Ministerial Order of 5 April 1994.

[100] Gas activities on the Moroccan side are normally operated by the *Societé Nationale des Produits Pétroliers*, which is wholly owned by the Moroccan State.

[101] R Piqueras, 'The Maghreb-Europe Gas Pipeline: Its Juridical Structure', Oil and Gas Law & Taxation Review, 3(1995) 95–8.

12.89 When *Gas Natural* took over *Enagas*, the assets related to the Maghreb pipeline, which were owned by *Enagas*, were segregated and placed into a new company, *Sagane*, in which the INH had 91 per cent, the remaining shares belonging to *Gas Natural. Enagas* assigned its rights in the supply contract with *Sonatrach* to *Sagane*, and the latter became subrogated in the position of *Enagas* in the agreement signed with the Moroccan Government and acquired the shares held by *Enagas* in EMPL and *Metragaz. Gas Natural* did not want to buy that part of *Enagas*'s business, due to the big financial risks which surrounded that project. Had *Gas Natural* bought those assets, the value of the shares of the company would have drastically diminished, because of the amount of debt which the Maghreb pipeline project had already incurred. The creation of *Sagane* was subject to serious criticism from Spanish left-wing parties. They alleged it was created just to make the privatization of *Enagas* more profitable for *Gas Natural. Gas Natural* was given a preferential right to take over *Sagane*, which it exercised in 1996. The Maghreb pipeline, however, is temporarily still segregated.

12.90 The pipeline has also been extended into Portugal. The companies arising from the association between *Gas Natural* and the Portuguese *Transgas* are, on the one hand, *Gasoducto Al Andalus* and *Gasoducto de Extremadura*, in which the majority share capital will be held by *Enagas* and, on the other hand, the companies *Gasoducto Campo Maior-Leiria-Braga* and *Gasoducto Braga-Tuy*, in which *Transgas* will hold a majority interest. The acquisition by *Transgas* of 27.4 per cent of the company Europe-Maghrib Pipeline Limited (EMPL), owned by the Spanish company *Sagane*, comes within this framework. *Sagane* holds the purchasing rights of the contract for the supply of Algerian gas as well as 70 per cent of *Metragaz*. This international pipeline is already in operation.[102]

The Gradual opening of the gas market

12.91 The Hydrocarbons Act identifies two types of consumers: eligible consumers and consumers subject to the tariff system. Eligible consumers are i) companies which own generation plants, providing they take part within the generation pool; ii) consumers whose annual consumption volume is higher than 10 million cubic metres. In the year 2000, the threshold is 5 million; in the year 2003, 3 million; and in the year 2008 every single consumer will be considered, irrespective of their annual consumption, as an eligible consumer.[103] The Act does not consider distributors as eligible consumers. This may conflict with Article 18(8) of the Gas Directive. It also seems clear from the wording of the Act that a particular

[102] For further information on the Maghreb pipeline, see I del Guayo, 'The Euro-Maghreb Pipeline', paper presented at the Seminar organized by the Centre for Energy, Petroleum, and Mineral Law & Policy of the University of Dundee (London, 6 November 1998).

[103] Art 60(3) and Transitional Disposition No 5, as amended by Royal Decree-Law No 6 of 6 April 2000.

company cannot add the consumption of several consumption points in order to be considered as eligible consumers. As long as these consumers cannot meet the given threshold, they are not eligible and subject to the tariff system. In other words, consumers who do not have the right to choose their supplier are subject to a system in which the tariffs are approved by the Government.

Within a period of three years, starting at the moment a consumer reaches the relevant threshold, it will be up to the consumer to choose their supplier. They can buy gas either from a distributor or from a commercializer. Commercializers are companies which buy gas to resell it to eligible consumers or to commercializers. For that purpose, they have access to the installations of other companies. Distributors are those companies which own distribution installations, ie the previous distribution companies. The Hydrocarbons Act 1998[104] states that in those areas in which a concession for distribution already exists, no authorizations will be awarded before the expiration date of such concession, with a maximum of 10 years. This will hinder the liberalization of the gas market. Such derogation is foreseen in Articles 3 and 4 of the Directive. Under the Hydrocarbons Act distributors are solely entitled to i) distribute natural gas through pipelines; and ii) build, keep, and operate those distribution installations needed for the physical delivery of gas to points of consumption. They will buy gas from transporters, in order to sell it to their tariff consumers. **12.92**

Transporters are companies which own transport pipelines, regasification plants, transport pipelines, or gas storage facilities.[105] They buy gas to re-sell it either to transporters or to those distributors which are connected to their installations (and for the purpose of selling it to Tariff Consumers). **12.93**

Access to the gas network

The Hydrocarbons Act provides for third-party access to both transport and distribution pipelines, as well as to regasification plants and storages. Access is regulated rather than negotiated. Only transporters, eligible consumers, and commercializers have access to the system. In the case of distribution pipelines, access is given to eligible consumers and commercializers. However, the wording of the Act is very obscure and it is unclear whether there is access to basic transport pipelines and to international connections to the Spanish gas system. If not then the whole aim of the Act, the liberalization of the market, will be at risk. In any case, both electricity generation plants, as long as they take part within the free generation market, and commercializers will be considered as eligible consumers in order to have access to the installations of other companies. **12.94**

[104] Transitional Disposition No 15, as amended by Royal Decree-Law No 6 of 6 April 2000.

[105] In this context one company owning only a gas storage would be considered to be a transporter.

12.95 The Government is required by the Act to lay down rules on access. Some rules on access came into force in January 1998.[106] However, these rules must soon be replaced by new ones, in accordance with the Hydrocarbons Act 1998. The obligation to allow access is imposed on two subjects: i) the concessionaires of gas pipelines belonging to the National Pipeline Network (the high-pressure network) and of pipelines connected to the National Pipeline Network which are needed to supply the consumers who have the right of access; and ii) the concessionaires of regasification plants which feed the National Pipeline Network. In other words, the obligation is basically imposed on *Gas Natural*, since, on the one hand, *Enagas*, which belongs to that company, is currently the owner of the National Pipeline Network and of the three existing LNG regasification plants and, on the other hand, those other concessionaires which may be affected by the new obligation also belong to *Gas Natural*. One may also consider the *Sociedad de Gas de Euskadi* to be included in the companies affected by the new rules. In fact, the incorporation of the Gas Transit Directive[107] into Spanish Law took place in 1995,[108] and the companies affected, ie those companies listed in the Annex, are *Gas Natural*, *Enagas*, and *Sociedad de Gas de Euskadi*. The regulation of access to the network also imposes on the concessionaires of LNG regasification plants the obligation to contract regasification services for third parties. Access must be carried out under non-discriminatory, transparent, and objective conditions. However, the Act also states some reasons for refusal of access: i) whenever access hinders the fulfilment of public service obligations; and ii) whenever access makes difficult—due to severe economic and financial difficulties—the fulfilment of long-term supply contracts.

Gas tariffs and prices

12.96 Articles 91 to 99 of the Hydrocarbons Act contain general principles governing the tariff and the price systems. The Ministry for Economy fixes tariffs both for final consumers and for access to gas services. However, the Act empowers the Government to liberalize gas tariffs fully in the future. Tariffs will be the same all over the country and will be subject to a maximum. The Council Directive number 90/377/EC, of 29 June 1990, on final gas price transparency was incorporated into Spanish law in 1996.[109]

Unbundling

12.97 The provisions on unbundling in the Hydrocarbons Act are very soft. It is not a legal unbundling, but rather an unbundling of the accounts. This means that

[106] Royal Decree No 1914 of 27 November 1997.

[107] Council Directives Nos 91/296/EC and 95/49/EC of respectively 30 May 1991 and 26 September 1995.

[108] Royal Decree No 2069 of 22 December 1995.

[109] Royal Decree No 258 of 16 February 1996.

several companies within the same group or holding of companies can carry out several activities. Therefore, the position of the holding *Gas Natural/Enagas* will not be affected by those provisions, so that it will be extremely difficult for new distributors to enter the market, and the hypothetical quota of the market for new commercializers will be very low, since the big stake of the gas business will remain in the hands of the holding.

The Regulator

The Hydrocarbons Act 1998 created the National Commission for Energy, which replaces the Electricity Commission set up in 1997, and which will supervise both the electricity and gas markets. Powers remain, however, in the case of those two Markets, in the hands of the Ministry for Economy. This means that the Commission is not a proper regulatory Body—even though it has some regulatory powers—but a consultation Body. Anti-competitive behaviour is policed by the Competition Authority. **12.98**

Competences of the State, of the Autonomous Communities, and of the local entities on gas supply

Since the beginning of the gas industry in the middle of the last century, the Public Administration has had a number of powers in this area. Gas supply was originally the exclusive competence of local authorities. In 1956, however, a Decree[110] transferred these competences to the State. The Local Organization Act 1985 expressly reserved gas supply to the competence of local entities, the reason being that, at that time, the legislator only took into account town gas. The organization of the new natural gas industry should have led to a different statement than that of the Local Organization Act 1985. In fact, both the Autonomous Communities and the State were entitled by the Gas Act 1987 to organize the distribution of gas,[111] the legal position of the local entities being weaker than under the 1985 Act. The contradiction between those two Acts could be overcome by the fact that local entities could not themselves award concessions to companies but may be awarded a concession by the State or by the Autonomous Community. Municipalities would not, then, award concessions for the supply of gas. However, they are the owners of the municipalities' territory, and companies therefore need also to obtain a licence from them to use (when necessary) public land and have to pay several taxes to local authorities. The conflict is currently being examined by the Spanish Supreme Court, to which four Municipalities have applied against the Decision of the Government of the Autonomous Community of Galicia to award concessions to *Gas Natural* in the areas of their jurisdictions. If those Municipalities succeeded, that would threaten the business of *Gas Natural* in **12.99**

[110] Decree of 27 January 1956.
[111] Art 1 Gas Act 1987.

Galicia. However, the Hydrocarbons Act 1998 expressly repeals the reference to gas supply being within the competences of local entities.

12.100 According to the Hydrocarbons Act 1998, the State retains the main powers with regard to the gas industry, because only the Ministry for Economy can award authorizations relating to fundamental aspects of the sector.[112] Therefore, the scope for the Autonomous Communities to exercise their powers is limited and reduced to the possibility of awarding authorizations for commercialization or for gas distribution within the borders of the Community.

(4) The Prospects for a Gas Commodity Market in Spain in the Light of the Hydrocarbons Act 1998

12.101 The natural gas market is basically a long-term transactions market. The liberalization of the Spanish gas market will only take place if a certain level of short-term transactions is achieved (ie spot transactions). It is difficult to see how such a spot market will emerge taking into account, on one hand, that distributors neither have access to the network—even though such a prohibition is not clear from the wording of the Act—nor can they sell gas to consumers other than tariff consumers, and on the other hand, commercializers cannot sell gas to tariff consumers.

12.102 At the very last moment of the Parliamentary Debates, a Transitional Disposition number 6 was introduced, by which every Tariff will include 'a connection and security element', which will be used to compensate all those investments made on the Basic Network, previous to the entry into force of the Act. These are the 'stranded costs' within the Gas Industry.

(5) Latest Developments

12.103 On 23 June 2000 further liberalizing measures were adopted by the Government (Royal Decree-Law number 6, of 23 June 2000): i) no shareholder can hold more than 35 per cent of the shares in *Enagas*; ii) *Enagas* becomes the System Operator and will guarantee, according with the principles of transparency, objectivity, and independence, the security of supply of the Spanish gas market and the proper co-ordination between the access, storage, transport, and distribution points; iii) by the year 2003 no operator will be allowed to supply to the market more than 70 per cent of the total gas consumed in Spain; iv) the unbundling of accounts is extended to transporters, which will have to have separate accounts for transport, regasification, and storage; v) a new tariff system will be enacted by the year 2001, which will reflect the criteria laid down by the Hydrocarbons Act 1998; vi) the threshold to be considered an eligible consumer is lowered: in the year 2000, those consumers whose annual consumption is

[112] Art 3 Hydrocarbons Act.

higher than 3 million cubic metres; in the year 2002, 1 million; in the year 2003 every single consumer will be considered, irrespective of annual consumption, as an eligible consumer; vii) the period in which distributors enjoy an exclusive right to distribute gas in a particular area is shortened, from the year 2013 to the year 2005; viii) 75 per cent of the gas coming via the pipeline from Algeria is assigned to *Enagas*, which in its turn must sell it to distributors for the tariff market; the remaining 25 per cent will be assigned to commercializers, and thence to eligible consumers.

F. The Oil Products Supply Industry

(1) Introduction

This section provides a description and an analysis of the juridical framework for 12.104 the distribution of oil products in Spain, as seen through the process of demonopolization in the oil distribution sector, which started in 1984. The main topics included herein are automotive fuels (such as gasoline), kerosene, liquified petroleum gas, and all other refinery products necessary to those sectors of the economy vital for the well-being of the nation, namely: surface, air, and maritime transport, agriculture, fishing, heating, the production of electricity, etc.

On 14 January 1993 the Oil Act 1992[113] entered into force. Its first article states, 12.105 with simple and solemn words, that 'the oil monopoly, created by the Royal Decree-Law of 28 June 1927, as modified by the Reorganization of the Oil Monopoly Act of 17 July 1947, is abolished'. In theory, this law was to provide for the last and definitive step towards a full liberalization of the oil market in Spain. Nonetheless, certain circumstances have impeded an effective and full liberalization of the market. First, it was necessary for the Government to develop this law further through a series of Royal Decrees. Some of these Decrees, in turn, imposed obstacles to the creation of a truly open market. Secondly, the law was ambiguous in its specification of various requirements concerning the sale of oil products within Spain, which meant that the liberalization was in the hands of the Government, since it was the Government which had the authority to confer or to deny the various forms of authorization necessary for a new company to enter the market. Thirdly, the law was approved seven years after Spain's entry into the European Communities, so the Government was able to create an atmosphere favourable to strengthening the position of Spanish companies within the market (especially, at that time, that of the State-owned *Repsol*) making the liberalization not quite a reality, given that the market is, in fact, already strongly cornered by a limited number of firms.

[113] Act No 34 of 22 December 1992.

12.106 The Hydrocarbons Act 1998 repealed the Oil Act 1992. A number of provisions within the 1998 Act go further down the path of liberalization. The effective liberalization of the Spanish market requires stronger action than a liberalizing law: particularly, non-discriminatory business practices on the part of those companies which, at the beginning of 1993, owned the transport infrastructure for oil products. A step in that direction was adopted by the Government in 1996, through the establishment of a third-party access system to the network,[114] a system now regulated by the Hydrocarbons Act 1998. Still, the current situation in the Spanish oil products market is an example of how the law is frequently at odds with reality.

(2) Brief History of the Oil Monopoly in Spain

An Overview

12.107 The oil monopoly in Spain has been one of the most iron-clad in Europe and has lasted for more than sixty-five years. The entire oil distribution process, from the importation level to the consumer level—including the setting of prices and conditions of sale—has traditionally been subject to numerous and complicated rules. Throughout its long existence the monopoly has gone through distinct phases, chiefly in accordance with the needs of the industry. In simplified terms, it can be stated that the monopoly has had four phases, lasting: i) from its creation in 1927 to its reorganization in 1947; ii) from 1947 to the creation of the INH in 1981; iii) from 1981 to Spain's entry into the EC, in 1986 and iv) from 1986 to the promulgation of the Oil Act 1992.[115]

From the creation of the Monopoly in 1927 to 1947

12.108 The history of the monopoly is fully linked to the history of the *Compañía Arrendataria del Monopolio de Petróleos, SA* (*Campsa*). The monopoly and *Campsa* were created in 1927. The monopoly did not exist as an independent body, but was a part of the State Budget designed to provide revenues. *Campsa* was then entrusted with the task of carrying out the duties assigned to the Monopoly. Initially, the Government had only 30 per cent of the shares in *Campsa*. Government participation grew, and after the reorganization in 1947 the Government controlled a majority of the shares. In any event, the monopoly's control over *Campsa* was always intensive and was exercised, among other ways, through a Government delegation within the company. The contract between the State and *Campsa* in 1927 had as its aim the management of all activities related to the oil industry. The creation of the monopoly involved the expropriation of all transport and distribution installations then in existence.

[114] Royal Decree-Law No 7 of 7 June 1996.

[115] A full description of these phases does not fall within the scope of this section. See, in that regard, A Correljé, 'The Spanish Oil Industry', Tinbergen Institute Research Series, 84, 1995.

From 1947 to the creation of the INH in 1981

The contract between the State and *Campsa* lasted for twenty years, during which time it became apparent that *Campsa* was unable to carry out in a satisfactory manner all of the responsibilities that had been assigned to it, although it did carry out its financial functions as well as its selling and distribution functions effectively. As a result, the Reorganization of the Oil Monopoly Act 1947[116] relieved *Campsa* of its other responsibilities which were then entrusted to other companies, chiefly to the INI and its subsidiaries, expressly created to assume, besides many other tasks within the industry field, the following responsibilities in the oil sector: importation (and the building of the necessary fleet), refining, storage, research, and exploration and exploitation of any fields discovered. Throughout the period 1947–81 various amendments were made to the 1947 Act, of which the following should be noted. **12.109**

a) regulations relating to the refining process (1968), which allowed entry into the market of two private companies: *Compañía Española de Petróleos* (*Cepsa*) and *Petróleos del Mediterráneo* (*Petromed*);
b) the creation of *Butano, SA* in 1957, which broke *Campsa*'s monopoly on liquified oil gases (being of crucial importance in Spain, given the lack of natural gas);
c) regulations governing the conditions for sale of oil products; and
d) rules governing contractual relations between the monopoly (and *Campsa*) and the various concessionaires.

The INH was created in 1981 and had as its aim the grouping of all the State-owned entities dispersed throughout the public sector into a single State enterprise. In this way, it became the owner of all State-owned oil companies: *Hispanoil*, *Butano SA*, EMP (with its four subsidiaries: *Alcudia*, EMP *distribución*, EMP *internacional*, and *Bioquímica española*), *Campsa*, and *Enagas*. **12.110**

From 1981 until the incorporation of Spain into the EC in 1986

At the end of June 1983 the Spanish Government, *Campsa*, and the Spanish refineries signed an agreement (the Protocol) which made necessary the adoption of two new acts. The Oil Importation Act 1984[117] allowed oil products to be imported by companies other than *Campsa*. Article 1 stated that, even though the monopoly would maintain its activities, individuals and companies could henceforth import oil products so long as they operated as delegates of the monopoly and under the regulations applicable to it. The Spanish Parliament also approved the Oil Sector Organization Act 1984.[118] As a result, all refineries bought shares in **12.111**

[116] Act of 17 July 1947.
[117] Act No 41 of 1 December 1984.
[118] Act No 45 of 17 December 1984.

Campsa, these being both the State's refineries and two big private refineries: *Cepsa* (*Compañía Española de Petróleos*) and *Petromed* (*Petróleos del Mediterráneo*)[119] respectively, by two Spanish banks. This partial privatization of Campsa was seen as the first step to meeting EC legal requirements concerning oil distribution, mainly Article 37 EC Treaty (now Art 31 EU Treaty)[120] which states that Member States shall progressively adjust any State monopolies of a commercial character so as to ensure that when the transitional period has ended, no discrimination regarding the conditions under which goods are produced and marketed exists between nationals of Member States. This provision shall apply to any body through which a Member State, in law or in fact, either directly or indirectly supervises, determines, or appreciably influences imports or exports between Member States. These provisions shall likewise apply to monopolies delegated by the State to others. Through its reorganization in 1984[121] *Campsa* could thereby avoid offering its services to every interested foreign company, as would have been the case from the non-discriminatory character of State monopolies within the EC.

From 1986 until the Oil Act 1992

12.112 The following information about this period is not in chronological order, but arranged according to the following criteria: i) regulations governing sales throughout the period; ii) the creation of *Repsol*; and iii) the reorganization of *Campsa* and the creation of the *Compañía Logística de Hidrocarburos, SA* (CLH), the new Spanish company entrusted with the transport and storage of oil products. An important legal step towards liberalization was the Royal Decree-Law number 5 of the 12 December 1985, which liberalized the wholesale supply of oil. Further Decrees (from 1988 to 1991) partially liberalized retail sales of oil products. According to those Decrees, new companies were allowed to establish their own petrol stations, but *Repsol*'s *de facto* monopoly hindered the business opportunities of those foreign companies wishing to operate within Spain. Hence, the legal changes were unhelpful in terms of the liberalization of the Spanish oil market because *Campsa* (that is to say, *Repsol*) kept all the existing petrol stations along the Spanish road network. The Spanish Ministry for Industry and Energy divided the Spanish market into two networks: the so-called Basic and Parallel Networks. New companies were only allowed to build

[119] BPMed was founded in 1988 with both British Petroleum and *Petromed* owning 50% of the shares. *Petromed* was owned by *Banesto*, one of the largest Spanish banks. British Petroleum bought into *Petromed* in 1991. BP Oil *España* recently completed its restructuring in Spain. The parent company has been merged with BPMed and with *Internacional Mediterránea de Comercio* (*Incomed*). Through this merger, BPMed transferred its filling stations to BP Oil *España* and, thus, a significant market share (almost 10% of the market).

[120] See ch 5 above on EC law, paras 5.36 *et seq.*

[121] Spain entered the European Communities in 1986.

new filling stations in the Parallel Network (which did not include those roads and villages with heavy traffic), whereas the already existing companies could operate along the Basic Network.

According to an official *Repsol* Report,[122] the 'transitional regulatory regime' (from 1986 to 1992): **12.113**

> was characterized by three principal features. First, EC entities were permitted to compete increasingly in the Spanish market. For instance, EC entities were allowed to import oil products into Spain up to specified maximum amounts which increased gradually between 1986 and 1 January 1992, when EC import restrictions were removed entirely. Secondly, sales of oil products were gradually liberalized. At the beginning of the transitional regime most EC oil products were sold by importers to the State, which then sold the products at prices determined by the State. These sales were liberalized on a product-by-product basis. Once liberalized, an oil product was no longer sold to the State, but through non-concessionary retail networks at a sales price determined by prices set by *Campsa* as the dominant retailer, subject only to price ceilings compatible with EC standards. Thirdly, the transitional regime required that gasoline, diesel, and certain other oil products produced by existing refineries for domestic consumption continue to be sold through the retail network consisting of privately owned stations that were operated pursuant to Government concessions (the Concessionary network).

It is clear that the transition period was not a period of excessive freedom of action for the companies, given that such freedom existed chiefly in the field of importation but not in that of sales. Moreover, the liberalization was very slow, being done on a product-by-product basis, and affected the products which were least important in the commercial sense. Finally, the distinction between the non-concessionary and concessionary networks involved considerable discrimination between businesses operating in the two networks. More than half of the filling stations in the Basic Network belong to *Repsol*, the remainder to companies such as Cepsa and BP Oil *España*; in the Parallel Network filling stations belong to various multinational companies (such as Shell, Total, Petrogal, and Agip), to *Repsol* (and its subsidiaries *Petronor* and *Campsa*), *Cepsa*, *Ertoil*, *Eserqui*, and to *Petrocat*. In contrast to other countries within the EU, there is considerable scope for the creation of new filling stations. **12.114**

The re-structuring of the oil sector was completed in 1987 through the creation of the *Repsol* holding within the INH. *Repsol* became the parent organization for all of the Institute's oil-related activities. Since 1987 the holding has consisted of five components: *Repsol-Exploración*, *Repsol-Butano*, *Repsol-Química*, *Campsa* and *Repsol-Petróleo* (with its three subsidiaries *Repsol-Distribución*, *Repsol Oil International*, and *Repsol-Derivados*). After the reorganization of 1987, the INH held 100 per cent of the shares in *Repsol*, until the creation of the public holding **12.115**

[122] *Repsol Prospectus*, 9 March 1993, 40.

SEPI in 1995, to which the INH's shares in several energy utilities were transferred. With the establishment of *Repsol*, which became the seventh largest oil company in Europe, the Spanish Government created an integrated national company which would be capable of operating successfully in a competitive market and of competing with multinational oil companies in Spain, once the Spanish market was liberalized in 1992. *Repsol* was privatized in 1989 and 1995 and the State still retains 10 per cent of the shares, the remaining shareholders being the Mexican oil company *Pemex* (5 per cent), BBVA (a Spanish Bank) (4.2 per cent), investors from the USA (18 per cent), and private shareholders (62.8 per cent).

12.116 New plans for the role of *Campsa* in the oil sector were made by *Repsol* and *Cepsa* in 1990. *Campsa* would continue only as a transport and storage company, under the name of CLH and all of the company's retail activities, including the operation of its 2,159 filling stations, would be taken over by the following refineries according to their market share in *Campsa*: *Repsol*, *Cepsa-Elf Aquitaine*, BP, *Petromed*, and *Ertoil*. The Government submitted its proposals to divide the company—and therefore its intention to award to *Campsa* and *Repsol* the vast majority of the former monopoly—to the European Commission, and the European Commission advised the Spanish Government that the project should be examined to determine whether that division was contrary to Article 85 EC Treaty (now Article 81 EU Treaty). The European Commission approved the project. This decision was adopted on 23 December 1991. The division plan was finally authorized by an Act of Parliament.[123] Furthermore, *Repsol* bought the exclusive rights to the *Campsa* brand name. The new logistical service company was named CLH, its sole business, from that point onward, to be the storage and transportation of oil products. The shareholders of CLH are *Repsol* (with a majority stake), *Cepsa-Elf Aquitaine*, BP Oil *España*, and Shell. The newly created company possesses one of the most important logistical networks in Europe: 3,258 kilometres of pipelines in operation and 150 kilometres more under construction as well as 36 tank farms. It also transports more than 30 million cubic tonnes of oil products annually. CLH bought 50 per cent of the shares of *Terquimsa*, which possesses (in Barcelona) one of the largest tank farms in Spain, and which was previously owned by *Gas Natural*. An agreement was easily reached, because *Repsol* was at that time the main shareholder in both CLH and *Gas Natural*. Through this purchase, CLH strengthened its position in the Catalan market while, for its part, *Gas Natural* has almost attained its goal of divesting itself of those of its assets which are not directly related to the gas market. CLH is quite obviously in a dominant position in the Spanish market. It will therefore need to act cautiously, lest other companies bring suit for alleged abuses of power, such abuses being forbidden by Article 82 EU Treaty. There must be, in particular, no discrimination between the users of its network or unfair contractual terms imposed on weaker clients. A real

[123] Act No 15 of 5 June 1992.

problem might arise out of access for foreign operators to the CLH transportation network and storage system. Even though CLH offers its services to every company prepared to pay for them, a barrier to foreign operators as to the use of its network still exists. Since foreign companies only operate a few outlets, only small quantities need to be transported and stored, making theirs a relatively expensive business.

(3) The Oil Act 1992

In October 1991 the Spanish Parliament began to debate a new NEP. As a result of these debates, the Minister for Industry and Energy announced that a new Act, fully liberalizing the distribution of oil products, would be adopted. The promulgation of the Act took place on 22 December 1992. In 1998, the Hydrocarbons Act 1998 was passed. Further liberalizing measures have been introduced by the latter. **12.117**

(4) The Hydrocarbons Act 1998

Articles 37 to 53 of the Hydrocarbons Act 1998 are devoted to the oil products supply industry. Article 37 deals with the general principles; Articles 39 to 44 with liquid oil products; Articles 45 to 48 with liquefied petroleum gases; and Articles 49 to 53 with security of supply issues. There is a distribution of areas of responsibility between the State and the Autonomous Communities.[124] **12.118**

According to the Oil Act 1992, individuals did not need a concession from the State—as was the case prior to its adoption—but rather a simple authorization. The aim of this authorization was essentially to verify that the applicant has enough capacity to cover his market quota. The Public Administration would also assume responsibility for consumer protection, security of supply, safety of the installations, and storage requirements. Article 37 of the Hydrocarbons Act 1998 states that the importation, exportation, refining, transport, storage, distribution, and sale of oil and oil products are free market activities, which may be carried out by those who fulfil the requirements laid down within the Act. In giving the authorization, the Government will check the conditions of the installation, and not those of the individual applicant. Nevertheless, wholesale or bulk distribution is still subject to an authorization, the awarding of which will be subject to an inspection not only of the installation, but also of the financial status of the applicant. The grant of an authorization for refining, transport, and storage installations is subject to the following conditions: a) technical and safety characteristics; b) environmental protection; and c) fulfilment of regional planning provisions. **12.119**

124 Although Art 86 of the Local Organization Act 1985 reserves for Municipalities the essential service of heating supply, the Decision of the Spanish Supreme Court of 16 September 1993 states that Municipalities cannot operate within those areas reserved for the State or for the Autonomous Communities by special legislation, such as the oil products distribution legislation.

12.120 Bulk distribution is governed by Article 42 for liquid products and Article 45 for liquefied petroleum gases. The future distributor must prove not only that it has legal, technical, and financial capacity, but also that it has enough storage capacity. Bulk distribution can be carried out throughout the country by those with authorization. The requirements relating to storage capacity and security of supply are new barriers for potential competitors. Those companies which may wish to establish themselves in Spain must invest a great amount of money in order to satisfy those requirements. Companies already functioning at the time of the liberalization do not have to make those investments, as they already had storage installations. Moreover, the transport and storage outlets are owned since the reorganization of the sector by the CLH, the successor to *Campsa. Repsol* is the owner of CLH, together with some other companies. This means that the former can easily avail itself of the services offered by the latter. However, the Government enacted a Royal Decree-Law in 1996[125] in order to introduce a system of open access by third parties to the transport network, as well as to the fixed reception and storage installations. This system is now regulated by Article 41 of the Hydrocarbons Act 1998. Access should be provided under non-discriminatory, transparent, and objective conditions. Access can only be denied in two cases: i) lack of capacity of the installation; and ii) whenever the applicant has not paid for the use of previous access services. Resale distribution is governed by Articles 43 for liquid products and Article 46 for liquefied petroleum gases.

12.121 Articles 49 to 53 are devoted to the security of supply. Every authorized wholesale operator who distributes oil products in Spain, and every enterprise which carries out any commercial activity concerning oil products not acquired from the operators regulated by the Act, will be obliged to maintain minimum security storage standards at depots. The Government will determine the quantity, form, and geographic location of that storage up to a maximum quantity based on 120 days of the company's annual sales. It will revise those limits when the international agreements so require. The Oil Act 1992 imposed upon the Government the obligation of creating a Public Entity for the constitution, maintenance, and management of the strategic reserves and of the enforcement control of the minimum security standards, an obligation which was fulfilled in 1994.[126] Within the Hydrocarbons Act 1998 there are more provisions about that Public Entity.

(5) Latest Developments

12.122 On 23 June 2000 further liberalizing measures were adopted by the Government (Royal Decree-Law number 6, of 23 June 2000): i) no shareholder can hold more than 25 per cent of the shares in CLH, and those shareholders having refining capacity cannot own more than 45 per cent of the shares in it; ii) the building of new

[125] Royal Decree-Law No 7 of 7 June 1996.

[126] Royal Decree No 2111 of 28 October 1994.

petrol stations is allowed within commercial centres; iii) the number of petrol stations which one company can have is limited; iv) an obligation to send information on prices to the Ministry is imposed upon retail distributors of oil products.

G. Electricity Law

(1) Introduction

Sources of electricity supply

The Spanish electricity generation industry is mainly based on the use of coal and nuclear, with some hydroelectricity, oil, natural gas, and renewables. Some electricity is imported from France.[127] **12.123**

The structure of the Spanish electricity industry

The Spanish electricity industry consists of around ten vertically integrated generating and distributing companies, and there is a mixture in the ownership of the industry. There are two major private companies (*Iberdrola*) and *Endesa*, together with two smaller private companies (*Unión Fenosa* and *Hidroeléctrica del Cantábrico*). *Endesa* owns three companies which operate in Catalonia (*Fecsa*, *Hidruña*, and *Enher*), other smaller companies (such as *Eléctrica del Viesgo*, *Eléctricas Reunidas de Zaragoza*, and *Saltos del Nansa*), and the *Compañía Sevillana de Electricidad* (which operates in Andalusia and Extremadura). *Endesa* has been privatized during the past few years. Yet the Government retains some of its shares. The new conservative Government did not exempt this company from its privatization plan, which was announced by the Minister for Industry and Energy in June 1996. The privatization of the company was completed in 1999. **12.124**

On 18 October 1996 the Government allowed Endesa to acquire up to 75 per cent of the shares of *Sevillana de Electricidad* and up to 100 per cent of those of *Fecsa*. Those mergers increased the value of the shares of *Endesa* and the Government will obtain bigger profits through its privatization. Both the Government of Andalusia and the Spanish Electricity Commission were opposed to that project of *Endesa*, the former because it wishes *Sevillana* to keep its regional character and the latter because of the threat to competition which may arise from that merger. The market **12.125**

[127] The net electricity generation in 1990 was as follows: 17.5% hydroelectricity; 36.7% nuclear; 34.8% national coal; 4.6% imported coal; 1.5% fuel; 0.4% natural gas; 4.5% auto-production (*Source*: NEP 1991–2000). The net electricity generation envisaged by the NEP 1991–2000 for the year 2000 was as follows: 16.4% hydroelectricity; 23.2% nuclear; 28.9% domestic coal; 5.8% imported coal; 11.3% natural gas; 4.4.% imports from Electricité de France; 10% auto-production. (*Source*: NEP 1991–2000). The electricity actually generated at 31 December 1997, was the following: 19.4% hydroelectricity; 7.9% oil products; 29.2% nuclear; 33.6% coal; 8.5% natural gas; 1.4% other sources (including biofuels, residues, and wind energy) (*Source*: Ministry for Industry and Energy).

shares in the generation and distribution sectors are, respectively, as follows: 52 per cent and 41 per cent for *Endesa* and its subsidiaries, 29 per cent and 39 per cent for *Iberdrola* and its subsidiaries, 14 per cent and 15 per cent for *Unión Fenosa* and 5 per cent and 5 per cent for *Hidroeléctrica del Cantábrico.*[128]

The Legal framework

12.126 Spanish electricity law has been subject to many changes since 1984. The regulatory framework which was in force from 1984 to 1997 was rooted in the Protocol signed by the electricity utilities and the Government in 1983. It envisaged the shift of decision-making power in favour of the Government, the nationalization of the high-voltage grid, the guarantee of the financial viability of the utilities by means of the establishment of a new tariff system, and an asset-exchange agreement among utilities and a new method of payments among them, with the aim of balancing costs within a unique tariff all over the country. As a result of this Protocol, the Unified Operation of the National Electricity System Act 1984 was approved.[129] The National Electricity System Regulation Act 1994 which replaced the 1984 Act tried to introduce some competition in the electricity sector. More changes were included in the Electricity Act 1997 implementing the EC Electricity Directive. Before discussing the current situation, an overview of the previous two electricity laws follows.

(2) The Unified Operation of the National Electricity System Act 1984

12.127 The regulation of the Spanish electricity industry has traditionally been based on the following principles: i) public and centralized planning of production capacity, ii) the unified operation of production and transport activities through a State-owned company, since 1984/1985 *Red Eléctrica de España* (REE), iii) the submission of electricity companies to public service obligations, and mainly to the obligation to supply to customers, and iv) the homogeneous conditions with which customers must be supplied, and particularly the uniformity of prices, fixed by the Government, all over the country.

12.128 The Unified Operation of the National Electricity System Act of 1984 foresaw the creation of REE, which was finally founded in 1985.[130] REE, which must be under majority public ownership (at least 50 per cent) was charged with the transport of electricity through the high-voltage grid, as well as with the central dispatching

---

[128] See G Ariño, 'Regulating Competition and Security of Supply: The Case of Spain', in L Hancher (ed), *The European Energy Market: Reconciling Competition and Security of Supply,* Series of Publications by the Academy of European Law in Trier, vol 13, Cologne 1995, 57–65; and ED Cross, 'Spain: Increasing the Role of the Government', in ED Cross, *Electric Utility Regulation in the European Union: A Country by Country Guide,* John Wiley & Sons, 1996, 205–30.

[129] Act No 49 of 26 December 1984.

[130] Royal Decree No 91 of 23 January 1985.

control.[131] The 1984 Act really nationalized the transmission grid because electricity companies which owned that kind of grid were obliged to sell it to REE, in exchange for a stake in the company (proportional to the generation assets they owned). According to Article 2 of the 1984 Act, REE had a legal monopoly on transporting electricity through high-voltage grids. REE was also empowered to give instructions to generator companies.

(3) The National Electricity System Regulation Act 1994

Introduction

In 1994 a new Act was passed: the National Electricity System Regulation Act (NESRA).[132] This Act governs all activities related to electricity supply, that is i) generation, ii) transport, iii) unified operation of the national electricity system, iv) international exchanges, and v) distribution.[133] The regulation of those activities was intended to satisfy customers' needs and would be pursued to rationalize, to increase efficiency, and to optimize those activities. The beginning of the Preamble of the Act stated: 'The fundamental objective of this Act is to guarantee the security of electricity supply at the lowest possible cost and at an appropriate quality'. **12.129**

The National Electricity System (NES)

The principles on which electricity regulation has traditionally been based in Spain, and particularly the principle of an Unified Operation of the production and transport activities, together with the kind of public intervention they bring about, explain how deep the idea of a NES was rooted in Spanish electricity law. The NES consisted of the joint activities of production, international exchanges, unified operation, transport and distribution of electricity to final customers.[134] **12.130**

The Integrated System and the Independent System

The NES consisted of two main systems: the Integrated System (IGS) and the Independent System (IPS). The IGS incorporated all currently existing installations at that time for the production, transport, and generation of electricity and all the electricity generated and traded by or through those installations in the **12.131**

[131] For many years the co-ordination of generation and transmission activities was carried out by *Unidad Eléctrica* (*Unesa*), established in 1944, which is an association of Spanish electricity utilities. In 1979 that responsibility was transferred to *Aseléctrica*, which was subject to Government control through the Delegation of the Government within it, and to which veto powers of its decisions were awarded. REE is, since 1985, in the place of *Aseléctrica*. *Unesa* groups nowadays all electricity companies, and acts as a lobbying group to protect their interests.

[132] Act No 40 of 30 December 1994.

[133] Additional Disposition No 10 foresees the regulation of commercialization of electricity.

[134] Art 9 and Preamble, No 12 National Electricity System Regulation Act 1994.

Peninsula,[135] including the electricity which was internationally traded, save both the electricity which is self-consumed and the electricity which would be generated by the IPS once it started working. The IPS would consist of the electricity which the Government might authorize to be generated by specific installations outside the IGS. Both Systems must be maintained separately, as the Act unequivocally stated that: i) the electricity generated by the IPS would not be integrated in the IGS; ii) the electricity which would be integrated into the IGS concerned all types of electricity generated in the Spanish territory and including that one which came from international exchanges, except the electricity generated by the IPS; and iii) those companies which operated in one System could not undertake activities in the other.[136] The Act provided for some exemptions to this rule of strict separation.

Centralized planning of the NES

12.132 Energy planning is a common feature within the Spanish energy policy. In the 1960s and the 1970s there was a Ministry for Planning and there have been three NEPs since the establishment of a democratic political system (1979, 1984, and 1991). Such planning has usually made wrong forecasts with regard to electricity demand, so that there has traditionally been an over-capacity on the generation side.

12.133 The NES was subject to a centralized planning power of the State. Thus, the legislator started from the assumption that the co-ordinated performance of the industry could only be achieved through electricity planning. The Autonomous Communities would take part in making those plans. It was for the Parliament to approve a plan submitted to it by the Government. The planning power had to be exercised according to the following criteria: i) security of electricity supply; ii) national and integrated management of energy resources; iii) energy-saving and demand-side management; iv) protection of the environment and of the rights of customers; and v) rational and objective payment of the costs which the companies incur.

The Integrated System as a public service

12.134 The IGS consisted of i) joint planning of the generation, international exchanges, transport, and distribution for the purposes of meeting the demand for electricity, ii) unified operation of all elements of production and transport, as well as the international exchanges of electricity, iii) economic integration of electricity, and iv) the application of a single tariff for each type of consumption of electricity.[137]

[135] There were specific provisions for the Balearic and Canary Islands, and for extra-peninsular sub-systems (such as Ceuta and Melilla): Additional Disposition No 15.

[136] See Art 9, 3, Art 11, 2, and Art 14, 1 NESRA 1994.

[137] See Art 11, 1 NESRA.

The activities to be performed within the IGS were declared by the Act to be a public service.[138] With that declaration, it tried to condense into only one expression the various powers which the Government had in order to achieve one of the main aims of the Act as a whole, which was the reliability of the system and the need for a continuous and secure electricity supply. In this regard, the IGS also guaranteed the supply of electricity to those customers who used the electricity generated by the IPS. However, neither the supply of electricity nor the performance of any activity for that final purpose (generation, transport, and distribution) were to be considered a reserved public service. 12.135

Only the unified operation of the system was expressly reserved for the Government. Thus, that declaration did not mean that the activities will be carried on by a State-owned company, save for the unified operation of the system, which was a reserved public service. On the contrary, the Act stated that the activities belonging to the IGS could be freely performed by private companies.[139] The meaning of the declaration had, therefore, nothing to do with the ownership of the companies which actually generate, transport, or supply electricity, nor with the means by which those activities would be carried out, but rather with the submission of those companies to a number of powers of the Public Administration and to a number of strict rules (stricter than for any other sector of the economic activity which the relevant Act did not declare to be a public service). Those powers and rules were summarized in Article 3: i) public planning; ii) price control; iii) the regulation of the NES as a whole, and specifically its unified operation; iv) the power to grant authorizations and to fine those companies which do not properly fulfil their obligations; v) the power to lay down minimal quality standards and to decide the level of security of supply with which the companies within the IGS must comply; vi) powers to inspect the installations; vii) the power to give instructions on the enlargement, improvement, and adaptation of the installations, so that they became suitable for a proper service, whose continuity was guaranteed. 12.136

The Unified operation of the NES

According to Article 31 of NESRA, the unified operation of the IGS was an essential service reserved for the Public Administration of the State. The management of such public service was the responsibility of a State-owned commercial company, REE, in which the State must retain a majority stake. Its main functions were to determine and control the level of security of supply of the IGS in the short and medium term, and the joint exploitation of the generation and transmission installations, in such a way that the costs of the IGS were kept to a 12.137

[138] See Art 2, 1 NESRA.
[139] See Art 2, 2 NESRA.

minimum. Both the Ministry for Industry and Energy and the Commission for the NES were empowered to lay down guidelines on the unified operation, with which the company managing it must comply. According to the Transitional Disposition number 5, REE would continue to manage the unified operation of the NES.

12.138 Notwithstanding some novelties of NESRA, the basic structure of the traditional Spanish approach to electricity regulation remained intact. Although only the activities within the IGS were subject to such Unified Operation, companies which generated electricity within the IPS were also subject to the instructions of REE.[140]

12.139 After the coming into force of the NESRA, the NES remained owner of all the energy produced, transported, and sold within the Spanish borders. Generating companies did not sell the electricity they produced to either final consumers or to distributing companies, because they had a statutory duty to sell it to REE, which in turn would supply that electricity to the distributing companies.[141] This was the so-called technical integration of electricity within the IGS.

12.140 The system would compensate each producer, according to its standard costs. This was the economic integration of the IGS, which took place under a global system of settlement and payment for all activities comprising it. Articles 15 to 20 of NESRA dealt with the economic regime of electricity activities. Those rules were basically incorporated into the Act on the Legal and Stable Framework for Electricity Costs and Prices, established in 1987.[142] Such Framework was the result of the 1983 Protocol signed by the utilities and the Government. Companies were remunerated regardless of the actual costs incurred by them, according to standard costs based on determinations by the Government of: i) generation costs; ii) transmission and distribution costs; iii) costs of the unified operation of the NES; iv) costs of demand-side management programmes developed by distributing companies; v) costs of the Commission for the NES; vi) costs resulting from the incorporation of the electricity of the IPS; and vii) other costs derived from the incorporation into the NES of electricity generated under the special regime of production (ie renewables and co-generation). The Government would calculate electricity tariffs every year in such a way that the total amount of revenues must equal the total amount of costs of the IGS. The system was envisaged to create incentives for the reduction of the costs incurred, since producers might 'beat' production standard costs and increase their profits by reducing investment and operating and maintenance costs. Distributing companies charged electricity tariffs to customers, which were approved by the Government, and the NES

[140] Art 12, 3 NESRA.
[141] See Ariño, G, n 128 above.
[142] Royal Decree No 1538 of 11 December 1987.

would redistribute them among all operators.[143] Tariffs, which were equal throughout the country according to different categories of consumers, were maximum tariffs, so that distributing companies might charge a lower rate, and they had fixed and variable elements.

The Independent system

Besides the IGS, NESRA contained a brief reference to an IPS which would be based on free market prices and contracting. Article 12 stated that the Public Administration of the State might authorize the electricity generated by specific installations to be exempted from the IGS. The Electricity Regulator had to submit a previous and non-binding report. The Government would take into account, in order to decide whether or not to award the authorization, both the criteria laid down for energy planning and the effect on the functioning of the IGS in its role as a public service supplier. Such electricity could be either internationally traded or sold to customers who fulfilled the conditions which would be established by further regulations. As an exception, such electricity could be bought from the independent generator to be incorporated in the IGS. The IGS would provide to the IPS any services which the acquisition of the electricity required and would guarantee to the users of the IPS an alternative supply of electricity, who consequently would bear the costs so generated. **12.141**

Anyone who had read the wording of Article 12 would have reached the conclusion that free entry did not exist. It involved an authorization awarded by the Government at its discretion, and not a regulated formula to govern entry, on the basis of whether or not it was deemed to be opportune. The criteria on which decisions would be based, such as the general effect of the authorizations on the functioning of the IGS, could not be effectively overseen by any Court. The IPS would need to be subject to a regulated system of authorizations, awarded according to objective and legally founded criteria. Exceptional circumstances might have arisen, such as proven over-capacity of the system, where a refusal to entry would have been fair, but in such a case sufficient and irrefutable grounds would have needed to be presented. The wording of Article 12 seemed to allow only that further developments of NESRA would have specified which planning criteria could result in the refusal of an authorization, thus making more transparent the reasons for the decision, especially when it would have differed from the Electricity Regulator's report. **12.142**

Although energy from IPS could indeed be put onto the international market,[144] free importation did not exist, as the IPS was itself subject to a discretionary authorization dependent on planning. The IPS could, however, export if there were **12.143**

[143] Cross, ED, n 128 above, 221–2.

[144] Art 13, 5 NESRA.

means of connection with enough capacity. The electricity could be put also onto the internal market. It was said[145] that the threshold might have been about 100 GWh, establishing a programme for the gradual access of minor consumers. This threshold, which in Spain would have been no more than 200 companies with 17 per cent of the national consumption, was admittedly not very ambitious, but it might well have been sufficient for testing whether competition worked or not, hence allowing the IPS to be adapted progressively to the introduction of customers with a lower threshold of consumption. Article 12 did not specify that electricity could be sold to the distributors. The incorporation of the distributor to the number of eligible buyers would have been the fastest way of transferring the profits generated through competition to the consumers. Could the existing generators and consumers be incorporated into the IPS, or only new generating installations to supply new customers? It might well be that NESRA could have been understood to exclude access by existing producers and consumers, on the basis of the negative impact of such access to the IGS, and of the wording of Article 14, 1 NESRA. Finally, electricity from the IPS could be bought by and incorporated into the IGS. It would be exceptional, not only because that is what Article 12, 1 expressly stated but also because both systems should in principle be maintained separately.

12.144 Any purchase of electricity and the following incorporation into the IGS had to be made in accordance with the principles which Article 13 NESRA laid down for international exchange of electricity. The application of those principles to the purchase of electricity made by the IGS from the IPS might have led to the following consequences: i) authorization for such incorporation could be granted following a procedure which assured competition and corresponded to the principle of awarding production units through competition; ii) REE would make that purchase if it was a short-term (spot) purchase and its aim was to optimize and support the normal functioning of the IGS, and also when the IGS as a whole guaranteed the supply of that electricity; iii) the purchase of electricity from the IPS could be made by generators of the IGS when their own installations guaranteed such supply.

12.145 According to Article 12, 3, the activities undertaken in the IPS must not prejudice the unified operation nor transport and distribution within the IGS. Whoever undertook said activities would be subject to specific instructions given to this end by REE. The strict application of this provision might have nullified the free practice of activity in the IPS, given that it was obvious that, as this practice developed, it would affect the IGS, and, if REE could give unconditional orders and instructions for the running of the IPS, it would easily cease to function. It would then have to be understood that the specific instructions referred to in Article 12, 3

[145] A Lafuente, *Cinco Días* newspaper, 17 January 1996.

should be only of a technical nature considered essential for access to the network. On the other hand, generators in the IPS were not subject to the unified operation carried out by REE.[146]

According to Article 15, 3 the activities comprised in the IPS would be compensated according to the conditions agreed upon by whoever undertook them, as well as by the buyers of electricity. Said conditions would be communicated to the Public Administration. The users of the IPS would have had to pay a complementary charge to the IGS to cover the costs which it had borne. That complementary charge included the costs of any services provided by the IGS to the IPS, and, specifically, i) the cost of auxiliary services provided for the acquisition of electricity from the IPS; ii) the cost of the guarantee of supply which the IGS provided for the IPS; and iii) the use of the transport networks, which demanded clear, objective, and non-discriminatory regulation of the conditions of access to the network.[147] Moreover, the users of the IPS must share with the customers of the IGS i) some specific, non-production related costs of the whole NES; ii) the costs of the nuclear debt; and iii) the so-called stranded costs.[148] The former were costs related to the diversification of primary sources of energy or to any other aims of the Energy Policy established for the electricity sector and related ones such as the subsidies for the consumption of national coal. **12.146**

Global assessment of NESRA 1994

The 1994 Act represented the first major legislative change in the electricity supply industry since 1984. Yet, the basic structure of the system remained unchanged. The basic structure of the regulatory framework set out by statute in 1984 with the Unified Operation of the National Electricity System Act 1984 survived despite criticism of its effectiveness and economic rationality. However, the Act introduced a number of changes in the system, directed to the creation of a more competitive and flexible market. These changes included, among others, i) unbundling, ii) competitive bidding rules, iii) access to the transmission and distribution network and iv) the basis for an independent system co-existing with the regular integrated system of public supply. **12.147**

(4) The Liberalization of the Electricity Market: the Electricity Act 1997

Introduction

Since 1996 the Government has developed an economic policy of liberalizing the traditionally regulated public sectors with two objectives: i) to comply with the requirements of liberalization adopted in the European Community in order **12.148**

[146] Art 31 and 32 NESRA.
[147] Art 12, 2 and 16, 4 NESRA.
[148] Additional Disposition No 4 and No 8.

to create a true internal market; and ii) to promote economic efficiency and the reduction of prices through competition, after the proven failure of State intervention in the economy.

12.149 The conservative Government wanted to go further along the path of liberalization and privatization of the electricity industry. On 9 October 1996 the Ministry for Industry and Energy sent a Draft Protocol to the electricity companies which tried to settle the rules governing the gradual opening of the market to competition. This Protocol was signed by the Ministry and the companies in December 1996. The basic aims of that Protocol, laying down the principles which will govern the functioning of the industry from 1998, were described by the Minister for Industry and Energy as follows:

> First, to liberalize access to primary sources of energy; secondly, to introduce competition within the generation industry; thirdly, to use the public undertaking which is charged with the task of operating the high-voltage grid not only as a guarantor of the supply but also as a Pool, whose task will be to compare the offers of the generators with the demands of the customers; and finally, to enlarge the number of customers who are entitled to choose their electricity suppliers freely. These measures will lower electricity costs. Such reduction in cost will also come from the gradual unbundling of generation, transport, and distribution companies. The unbundling will be done at an initial stage by the division of the accounts of the integrated companies, and later by requiring those companies to divest their transport and distribution activities, and therefore to create separate companies. These new principles must lead to a decrease of the level of Government intervention on prices, costs, and investments.[149]

12.150 Subsequently, the Spanish Parliament passed—in 1997 and 1998—two basic legislative measures restructuring both the electricity and the gas sectors, although to a very different extent and scope. The new Electricity Act 1997[150] (hereinafter LSE, *Ley del Sector Eléctrico*) marks the start of a revolution in electricity regulation in Spain, as it establishes the basis for a radical change in the electricity regulatory model. Like any real change, this will take time, and for this reason, a transitional period and the principle of gradual implementation of the reform have been foreseen.

12.151 Since the enactment of the LSE in November 1997, electricity regulation is characterized by three developments. First, the legislative development of the Electricity Act provides a complete reversal of the traditional electricity regulation. Secondly, the Hydrocarbons Act 1998 led to the creation of a new National Commission for Energy, and eliminated the Commission for the National Electricity System which was set up in 1994. Thirdly, new measures were taken in December 1998 providing for further liberalization at the consumer level, along

[149] ABC newspaper, 16 October 1996, 46.
[150] Act No 54 of 27 November 1997.

with a new mechanism of stranded cost recovery that allows for securitization. The following sections describe and analyse the main elements of the new electricity regime.

The Production of electricity under the Electricity Act 1997

Freedom to generate

Article 21 LSE establishes 'free entry into generation', with no compulsory planning (ie planning is just indicative) but only an authorization procedure with objective, transparent, and non-discriminatory criteria. The procedure is intended to verify the following objectives: i) safety standards, ii) environmental protection, and iii) the location of the plant and the legal, technical, and financial characteristics of the applicant. Authorization is needed for every generation installation, irrespective of whether it will be offering its energy to the pool or not. A generator may decide to remain outside the pool system, and to supply electricity directly to eligible consumers. **12.152**

The choice of the Spanish Government is in accordance with Article 4(6) of the 1996 Electricity Directive, which establishes that Member States may choose between an authorization or a tendering procedure. It provides that Member States may establish objective criteria for the grant of authorizations related also to fuel choice and in respect of public service obligation. Long-term compulsory planning is also accepted in Article 3 of the Directive. However, the LSE does not foresee compulsory planning, so that it has gone much further than the 1996 Electricity Directive. **12.153**

Special Production Regime: co-generation and renewables

Since the 1980s the Government has tried to encourage the use of renewables. The Energy Conservation Act was approved in 1980[151] and, despite the fact that this Act was repealed by the NESRA, the benefits which it introduced for the use of renewables are still in force, the last Royal Decree having been approved in 1998.[152] It envisages fiscal benefits and subsidies for those companies which operate with renewables or which are engaged in energy-efficiency projects. **12.154**

Both Article 25 of the LSE and Article 8 of the 1996 Electricity Directive accept the possibility of giving priority in the dispatch to generating installations using i) renewable energy sources or waste or producing combined heat and power, and ii) indigenous primary energy fuel sources to an extent not exceeding 15 per cent of the overall primary energy necessary to produce the electricity consumed in the national market. Besides the priority in dispatch, the LSE establishes public subsidies for renewable energy sources and co-generation. **12.155**

[151] Act No 82 of 30 December 1980.
[152] Royal Decree No 2818 of 23 December 1998.

12.156 Articles 27 to 31 of the LSE deal with the so-called Special Generating System. According to Article 27 electricity-generating activities will be regarded as generation under the special system in the following cases, when carried out in installations in which the installed capacity does not exceed 50 MW: i) auto producers using co-generation or other forms of electricity generation associated with non-electricity activities provided they involve high-energy performance; ii) when any of the non-disposable renewable energies, biomass, or any type of biological fuels are used as primary energy, provided that the owner does not carry out generating activities under the ordinary system; c) when non-renewable waste is used as primary energy. The generation of electricity from processing plants for waste from the agricultural, cattle, and services sectors having installed capacity of 25 MW or below shall also be considered as generation under the special system when there is high-energy performance.[153] These provisions of the LSE were developed by the Royal Decree no 2818 of 23 December 1998.

Hydroelectricity

12.157 The Water Act 1985 applies to the establishment of plants for the generation of hydroelectricity. In principle, the award of concessions for the exploitation of water resources is within the competence of the Water Boards, established under the Water Act 1985 in each of the Spanish river basins and which are subject to central public administration. In other cases, the competence belongs to the relevant Departments of any of the Autonomous Communities. Whenever it is within the competence of the public administration of the Central Government, and not of that of the Autonomous Communities, both concessions for the use of water and authorizations to generate electricity may be subject to a special procedure.

Nuclear electricity

12.158 One of the main features of the Spanish Electricity Industry is the nuclear ban. The 1979 NEP designated the construction of nuclear plants with a generation capacity that happened to be far above demand and with some financial costs that extraordinarily raised the price of electricity. Due to these facts, and due to the energy policy backed by the Socialist Party, the Government elected in 1982 ordered the indefinite postponement of investment in nuclear power already under construction. These investments[154] were definitively cancelled in 1984 by NESRA. Nevertheless, the ban raised a considerable debt during the period 1983–95. To cover these costs a levy has been included in electricity tariffs, which will apply for the next twenty-five years.

[153] The translation of Art 27, 1 of the LSE is taken out from L Pastor Ridruejo, and JI González Ruiz, *Spain*, Oil and Gas Law & Taxation Review, Special Issue, 1999.

[154] In the nuclear power stations of *Lemóniz, Valdecaballeros,* and *Trillo II.*

Nuclear generation is governed by the Nuclear Energy Act 1964, the Nuclear Security Council Act 1980,[155] and the LSE. The two former Acts deal mainly with safety issues, whereas the current framework for Nuclear Generation is regulated by the LSE. **12.159**

The National Undertaking for Radioactive Residues (Enresa),[156] a State-owned company, manages radioactive waste from the point of generation to final disposal, and is also responsible for dismantling nuclear power plants. It is financed through a percentage levied on the electricity tariff. **12.160**

Coal

Besides the priority in dispatch of those units of electricity generation which use local sources of primary energy for combustion, up to a limit of 15 per cent of the total amount of primary energy necessary for producing the electricity demanded by the national market, the LSE establishes public subsidies for national coal. Later—in December 1997—the General Budget Act established that coal subsidies would not be supported by the tariff but by an special tax on electricity consumption (4.864 per cent of electricity consumption). This instrument was aimed to comply with EU requirements, particularly the Decision of the European Commission no 3632 of 28 December 1993,[157] but at heart nothing has changed. **12.161**

Transmission and distribution under the Electricity Act 1997

The Infrastructure

The transmission grid consists of all electricity lines, and related installations, which have a voltage of 220 KV or higher, as well as every installation, irrespective of its voltage, which is needed for international connections with the grid. REE (*Red Eléctrica de España*) is charged with the task of operating the grid. The REE is also charged with the transit of electricity on the basis of Council Directive 90/547/EC on Electricity Transit, incorporated into Spanish law in 1993.[158] **12.162**

Article 36 of the LSE also allows companies to ask for an authorization to construct and operate transmission installations. The construction of direct lines is provided for in Article 43 of the LSE.[159] When applying for a construction authorization, a company must submit in its application i) the technical and safety conditions of the installations, ii) the fulfilment of the rules for the protection of the **12.163**

[155] Act No 25 of 29 April 1964 and Act No 15 of 22 April 1980, both as amended by the NESRA, and the LSE.

[156] Royal Decree No 1522 of 14 July 1984 and Ministerial Orders of 30 December 1988 and 1 December 1989.

[157] See ch 5 above on EC energy law.

[158] Royal Decree No 1247 of 5 March 1993. Royal Decree No 2018 of 26 December 1997, governs the transit of electricity and consumption points.

[159] Art 43 implements Art 21 of the 1996 Electricity Directive.

environment, iii) the location of the lines, and iv) their financial, legal, and technical capacity for the performance of the project.

12.164 Installations for electricity distribution are also subject to previous authorization. In no case shall such authorizations be granted as a monopoly or provide any exclusive rights.

12.165 The LSE incorporates existing rules[160] on awarding authorizations for the construction of electricity lines and on the expropriation and servitude system. Electricity activities were declared to be of public interest, which enables the Public Administration to expropriate land and other goods needed for the construction of electricity installations. Electricity companies will have to ask the public administration to declare that the construction of a particular installation is in the public interest. The urgent procedure for expropriation, established by the Expropriation Act 1954, can be followed after such a declaration has been made.

Transmission and distribution

12.166 The REE acts, under the LSE, not only as a transmission company, subject within the transmission field to competition, but also as the System Operator. It looks after the maintenance and extension of the grid and is responsible for the technical management of the System.[161] The Government will designate for each distribution area a Distribution System Operator. This activity is reserved to either Spanish or EU firms. Articles 44–51 LSE deal with electricity supply to customers, and particularly the duty to maintain the supply, regularity, and quality.[162]

Unbundling

12.167 Article 14 of the LSE requires the segregation of regulated and unregulated activities by different companies (year 2001) with separate accounts since 1997. Even so, both regulated and unregulated activities may be carried by the same company acting through subsidiaries. The 1996 Electricity Directive only requires unbundling and transparency of accounts.

Network access

12.168 According to Article 16 of the 1996 Electricity Directive, Member States are free to choose between the TPA (with negotiated or with regulated price) and the Single Buyer systems. The LSE introduces a system of regulated TPA for transmission (Article 38) and distribution (Article 42). The Government will fix access tolls. The transmission or distribution company may refuse access only where it

[160] The Electricity Expropriation Act 1966, Act No 10 of 18 March 1966, developed by Decree No 2619/1966 of 20 October 1966, and Royal Decree No 2617 of 20 October 1966.

[161] Transport activities are further regulated by Royal Decree No 2819 of 23 December 1998.

[162] Distribution activities are also further governed by the Royal Decree No 2819 of 23 December 1998.

lacks the necessary capacity. Substantiated reasons (based on the security, regularity, or quality of supply) must be given for such refusal.

Market opening and tariffs under the Electricity Act 1997

Eligible consumers

Free choice of supplier is given to 'eligible consumers'. According to the Transitory Disposition no 13 of the LSE and Article 19(2) of the 1996 Electricity Directive, they will be selected by gradual access to the market in the next years with different schedules and levels of consumption: 1998 (15 GWh and railways), 2000 (9 GWh), 2002 (5 GWh), 2004 (1 GWh), and 2007 (all consumers). Later, Royal Decree no 2820 of 23 December 1998, establishing tariffs for access as a part of the Protocol agreed with the electricity companies in September, established a new calendar for 1999 for access to the market on the following levels of consumption: January, 5 GWh; April, 3 GWh; July, 2 GWh; and October, 1 GWh. This will open the market for 42 per cent of the electricity demand (around 8,000 qualifying consumers). By means of Royal Decree-Law no 92 of 17 April 1999, from 1 July 1999 eligible consumers are those consumers supplied with a nominal tension higher than 1,000 volts. The Government is also now empowered to modify such a limit and to fix the liberalization calendar for those consumers supplied with a nominal tension of less than a thousand volts. **12.169**

Tariffs and prices

Hence, there are basically two kinds of consumers. First are eligible consumers who freely negotiate the price with the producer or traders. The LSE creates the new entity of the trading company *(comercializadores)* being one who can provide energy to eligible consumers on a free market system.[163] Second are the non-eligible consumers who are subject to the tariff system. The latter category of consumers must pay the same tariffs regardless of their location within the Spanish territory. Tariffs are fixed by the Government. Tariffs include those for generating, transmission and distribution costs, retail supply costs, the so-called permanent costs of the electricity system (costs of the National Commission for Energy, costs of the system and the market operators, and compensation for stranded costs), and diversification and security of supply costs (ie premiums to renewables, co-generation, and costs related to the nuclear ban). Eligible consumers will pay generation costs (either by reference to the pool price or as offered by a generator supplying electricity directly outside the pool) and the cost of using the transport and distribution lines. They will also bear some of the general costs of the system.[164] **12.170**

[163] Art 44 LSE. The 1996 Electricity Directive does not regulate this figure but requires in Art 19(3) that distribution companies have access to the market for the volume of electricity consumed by their customers designated as eligible within their distribution system.

[164] See further L Pastor Ridruejo, and JI González Ruiz, *Spain*, Oil and Gas Law & Taxation Review, Special Issue, 1999.

Organization of the market

Functioning of the pool system

12.171 The LSE creates an hourly generation spot market on the following basis: i) all generating companies should bring their energy to the pool; ii) the units entering the pool will receive the price offered for the last unit required at each half an hour to cover demand: this is therefore a marginal price system; iii) some units will receive a 'power guarantee' payment; and iv) the units required will receive a payment of the ancillary services.[165] The functioning of the system was further developed by Royal Decree no 2019 of 26 December 1997.

12.172 Besides the existing market at the pool, contracts between generators and consumers may exist. In comparison, Article 8(2) of the 1996 Electricity Directive only requires that the dispatching of generating installations should be determined on the basis of objective criteria approved by the Member States, taking into account the economic precedence of electricity from generating installations.

System operator and market operator

12.173 In order to guarantee the independent operation of the Electricity System, the LSE (Articles 33 and 34) created two different institutions to run it. On one hand, the market operator (*Operador del Mercado*), which receives offers, prepares the merit order, and clearing. Its name is *Compañía Operadora del Mercado Español de Electricidad, SA*. It receives and matches demand and supply bids in co-ordination with the system operator. It is also charged with the task of managing the pool and of settlement and liquidation of payments between participants. This liquidation function was developed by the Royal Decree no 2017 of 26 December 1997, on the liquidation of transport, distribution, and trade costs, permanent costs of the system, and diversification and security costs. In order to safeguard the independent functioning of the market operator, a Committee of Market Agents has been set up.

12.174 On the other hand, there is a system operator (*Operador del Sistema*) which manages the grid company, being responsible for technical management of the system. The system operator is the REE. It makes the final decision on central dispatching of generating facilities resulting from the matching of supply and offer for electricity following the economic matching determined by the market operator. It is obliged to segregate those accounts related to its transmission business from those related to its functions as system operator. It is a private company, and no shareholder can have more than 10 per cent in it, save electricity-related shareholders whose stake may reach a maximum of 40 per cent. Up to the year 2003 the Government will retain 25 per cent of the shares. However, there are neither commercial nor

[165] See Arts 11, 16.1, and 23–5 Electricity Act 1997.

technical advantages in the legal separation between market operator and a system operator and it will generate endless co-ordinating problems. Article 7(6) of the 1996 Electricity Directive only requires independence of the system operator, at least in managerial terms, from other activities not related to the transmission system. At this point it must be remembered that in Spain (since 1984, with the creation of the REE) the transmission system is independent from the generation and distribution companies.

The National Commission for Energy

Competences in electricity have traditionally been exercised by the Ministry for Industry and Energy (since May 2000, the Ministry for Economy) of the Public Administration of the State. After the coming into force of NESRA, the Ministry retained crucial functions, but the Act set up an Electricity Regulator, the Commission for the National Electricity System[166] to which some functions were assigned. The Hydrocarbons Act 1998 created a new National Commission for Energy, which replaced the Commission for the National Electricity System set up in 1994. **12.175**

The National Commission for Energy looks into the transparency and objectivity of the functioning of the electricity system. Whenever the Commission exercises public tasks it is subject to the Public Administration and Common Administrative Procedure Act 1992.[167] Other activities are governed by private law. Its Chairman, its eight Commissioners, and its Secretary are appointed by the Government, after a hearing before the Parliamentary Committee for Industry, for a period of six years. They cannot be removed, except for very special circumstances such as incapacity or conviction of a crime. There are two Consultative Bodies (one for electricity and one for hydrocarbons) which have an advisory function to the Commission, and which consist of up to a maximum of 36 and 34 members respectively, representing the public administration of the State, the Autonomous Communities, the energy companies, energy users, and other representatives of social interests and of the protection of the environment. The Chairman of the Commission is also the Chairman of the Consultative Bodies. **12.176**

Many of the functions of the Commission are of an advisory nature. In fact, it has to submit a Report on several draft regulations which the Government may elaborate on, such as regulations to develop the LSE, electricity plans, and draft rules for fixing electricity prices and the remuneration of activities of the system. However, the Commission can draft its own regulations and submit them to the Government for approval. The Commission has to give its opinion on the authorization processes for new generation or transport installations and on any issues **12.177**

[166] Arts 6–8 NESRA. See also above.
[167] Act No 30 of 26 November 1992.

which the Autonomous Communities may submit to it. It asks the public administration to sanction companies which do not properly fulfil their duties.

12.178 The Commission exercises arbitration functions among the electricity companies, particularly when resolving problems on access to the transmission and distribution networks. The decisions of the Commission can be quashed by the Minister for Economy. This right of appeal to the Public Administration shows that the National Commission for Energy is not really an independent regulatory body.

12.179 From a competition point of view, the most important function of the Commission is supervisory: to ensure that the electricity companies do not fall into anti-competitive behaviour and do not abuse their dominant position within the market.[168] The 1996 Electricity Directive only requires in Article 22 that Member States 'shall create appropriate and efficient mechanisms for regulation, control and transparency so as to avoid any abuse of dominant position, in particular to the detriment of consumers, and any predatory behaviour'.

12.180 Although the regulatory and supervisory functions of the market have been assigned to three levels (Ministry for Economy, the National Commission for Energy and the Committee of Market Agents), the majority of regulatory functions continue to fall within the Ministry for Economy, who establishes rules for functioning, grants authorizations, and fixes prices on regulated activities. However, the Ministry is not the independent regulatory entity desirable for the application of any regulatory model overseeing competition.

The Issue of 'stranded costs'

12.181 Besides the market price for generation, the LSE provides, as it is accepted in Article 24(1) of the 1996 Electricity Directive, a transitional period for the recovery of stranded costs. Thus, the recovery of 1,988,561 million pesetas (US$13 billion) has been allowed to the incumbent generators (based on a spot market price of 6 pts/KWh) in a maximum period of ten years which ends on 31 December 2007. Later, the General Budget Act of December 1998 established a reduction of stranded costs (of 257,000 million pesetas, 1.6 billion US$) and a new mechanism for its recovery which would allow for the securitization of part of those compensation rights (up to one billion pesetas). This has been a highly controversial issue. The possibility of securitization of stranded cost recognized to generating companies in the LSE as amended in December 1998 started a political debate. Both the Spanish Constitution and European Community Law have been questioned in a very politicized public debate.

[168] There is scope for conflicts between the electricity regulators and the competition watchdogs.

The starting point of the analysis must be the correct legal categorizing of the compensation of stranded costs. It is not a State aid to help companies adapt to competition, but is based on legal rights recognized in the LSE, although there is some uncertainty about their *ex-ante* quantification as transition costs depend on real market prices. 12.182

Although there are many possible methods for the quantification of stranded costs (*ex-ante* v *ex-post*, based on value of assets v based on expected revenues), in the Spanish case the quantification must respect the legal basis established in the legislation applied before the LSE, ie the Unified Operation of the National Electricity System Act 1984, the Stable Legal Framework of 1987, and NESRA 1994, which gave the companies contractual rights of revenues based on the 'stranded' costs. 12.183

As compensation for the costs of transition to competition (stranded costs or CTC) is a legal right acquired in previous legislation, its denial would violate the Spanish Constitution, which guarantees respect for property rights and the principle of legitimate confidence in the continuation of regulation. Both principles have been defended by the Spanish Constitutional Court and the European Court of Justice. 12.184

The Spanish mechanism for recovery of stranded costs complies in principle with Community law. It is a transitional measure that can be authorized by the European Commission according to Article 24(1) of the 1996 Electricity Directive, which refers to 'those member States in which commitments or guarantees of operation given before the entry into force of this Directive may not be honoured on account of the provisions of this Directive and may apply for a transitional regime'. 12.185

Regarding European State aid rules, the legal nature of Spanish compensation of stranded costs to electricity companies is as follows: they are not aids but legal rights. However, as 'State aid' is an economic concept in Community law[169] (identified by its effects: advantage without legitimate title), the Spanish method for quantifying stranded costs and its legal basis must be publicly explained. If the quantification were clearly excessive, a State aid could be identified for the excess. In any case it is necessary to point out the extreme difficulties of such an appraisal as the multiple alternatives for quantifying stranded costs require at last a judgement based on reasonableness and political acceptance. The subsidiarity principle applies both in the rhythm of the liberalization and in the transitional measures deemed necessary in each Member State. 12.186

[169] See ch 5 above on EC energy law, section D(3).

(5) *Global Assessment*

Comparison with the EC Electricity Directive

12.187 As a whole, it seems clear that the reform embodied in the LSE goes further than the requirements of the 1996 Electricity Directive, both in the choice of the wholesale competition model through a spot market and free contracting, and in the level and time schedule for opening the supply market. The time schedule for market opening was accelerated in December 1998 and April 1999.

12.188 The 1996 Electricity Directive only requires a minimum standard of rules deemed necessary to guarantee a comparable access to national electricity markets for the internal market to be feasible. The Spanish Electricity Act 1997 has chosen an ambitious path in the trend of liberalization, recognizing both the legal and the economic demands of the European Union. Undoubtedly, the most novel element of the reform is the creation of a wholesale market, which started operation on 1 January 1998. There is freedom within the pool to buy and sell electricity in and out of the spot market. That is the radical change introduced into electricity regulation by the LSE. Basically, the Spanish Electricity Act 1997 is a good law that addresses the real problems. It provides a good point of departure in the process of reform. Nevertheless, some problems are pending in the liberalization process concerning the lack of competition; these are discussed below.

Lack of competition

12.189 In the electricity sector, given its technical characteristics and its integration with other energy and industrial sectors, the new regulatory model for competition required: i) on the one hand, to organize the market in such a way that the necessary global technical operation of the electricity system as a whole is combined with a decentralized exploitation system; such combination must be achieved through free pricing and offers extended by firms; and ii) on the other hand, to implement the regulatory reform with a gradual transition which faces all transition-related problems in a competitive context—stranded costs, liberalization of primary energies, elimination of subsidies for consumers, adaptation to the production of renewable energy sources, cogeneration, etc.

12.190 One of the problems is that, in practice, there is not enough competition within the electricity market. This has been officially recognized as a part of the global assessment on the performance of the market after some months of operation. The market has worked normally since 1998, in compliance with the approved procedures, and without significant problems in security and quality of supply. From an economic point of view, the positive aspects include the opening of the market to external agents, new generation projects, the entrance of new suppliers, and the adoption of important programmes directed towards the reduction of costs in electricity companies. On the other hand, i) the fact that demand is not elastic in relation to prices, ii) the highly concentrated structure of electricity companies, and iii) the lack of competition in the electricity market were some of the negative aspects. The absence of real competition is also proven by the fact that very few consumers preferred to contract in the new market rather than retaining the traditional supply at a regulated tariff. For that reason, in September 1998 a new Protocol was agreed between the Minister of Industry and Energy and the electricity companies with the explicit aim of fostering competition. The measures of that Protocol were the following: i) a new time-scale regulating market access to qualified consumers, ii) a reduction in tariffs for access and capacity payments, iii) a decrease in general tariffs, and iv) a decrease and a new mechanism for the recovery of stranded costs (CTC) which would allow their partial securitization. In summary, there is a general feeling, even at the official level, that the Spanish electricity market technically performs well, but that in fact there is not enough competition. To foster such competition, new measures have been taken, and close control on the development of the market must be maintained.

Obstacles to the 'free entry' of generating companies

There are obstacles to the 'free entry' of generators because of the point of departure in the corporate structure (concentration in two generating companies with 80 per cent of the market and vertical integration), and because of the mix of energy sources which exists in Spain (in particular, the preferences for national coal, and the concentration of hydroelectricity energy in two generators). **12.191**

The corporate structure may lead to the existence of an oligopoly in which prices can be higher than those properly established by a competitive market. On the other hand, the vertical integration permits the existence of generation and distribution groups, all of which can restrict competition if the autonomous management of affiliates is not guaranteed. The regulation to be applied to the electricity sector, in a careful way, should defend competition. In cases of price manipulation and restrictive competitive practices, the control measures are varied. Some are already contemplated in the LSE and others may be articulated for the normal performance of the system. These latter measures should be proposed by the National Commission for Energy in its function of 'overseeing that the activities contemplated by the present Act are carried out in a free competition regime' (Article 8, 1, no 13 of the LSE). **12.192**

The second factor which can present difficulties or distort the creation of a truly competitive market in Spain is the difference in the mix of primary energy sources (hydroelectricity, nuclear, domestic coal, and natural gas). Restrictions on access to those sources may hinder competition within the electricity market. **12.193**

Obstacles to effective freedom of imports do exist, as the capacity of international networks is currently limited. The 1996 Electricity Directive requires free imports **12.194** of energy under specified conditions. Terms for its authorization are regulated, and denial is only possible when reciprocity of qualifications among the parties is not met (as foreseen in Article 19, 5 of the 1996 Electricity Directive). But, obviously, the effective freedom of imports depends upon the capacity of international networks, which is at this time quite limited. It is necessary to expand networks within the Trans-European Energy Network Programme. Until this occurs, it will also be a severe limitation to opening up the Spanish market.

12.195 Obstacles to free price-fixing in the electricity market, regarding exceptions to marginal pricing through the pool (admission of physical contracts, alteration in merit order motivated by energy policy, like preference for domestic coal, co-generation and renewable energy sources. . .) and regarding a tariff structure that still has cross-subsidies among consumers.

(6) Latest Developments

12.196 On 23 June 2000 further liberalizing measures were adopted by the Government (Royal Decree-Law number 6, of 23 June 2000); i) electricity producers whose generating capacity is higher than 40 per cent of the whole national capacity will not be allowed to increase it within 5 years (or 3 years if the capacity is higher than 20 per cent); ii) however, they may invest in new power stations if they close or divest themselves of existing ones; iii) some electricity installations of the special production regime are obliged to sell their surplus electricity to the wholesale market; iv) by the year 2003 every consumer will be an eligible consumer, and therefore free to choose a supplier; v) within the following three years there will be a reduction of tariffs (up to a maximum of 9 per cent); vi) commercializers are now allowed to buy electricity abroad and from the special production regime generators; by the year 2003 they will also be allowed to buy from ordinary generators; vii) the number of administrative requirements for exercising the right of choice of supplier is reduced; viii) the level of the costs of security of supply which consumers pay is reduced, and there is a limit to the subsidy which each generating installation can obtain from the consumption of domestic coal.

H. Energy and the Environment

(1) Constitutional and Institutional Framework

12.197 Article 45 of the Constitution entitles everybody to enjoy a healthy environment, and the public powers will therefore promote the rational exploitation of natural resources, in order to improve quality of life and to protect and restore the environment. The implementation of such environmental policy is for the Ministry for the Environment which was established on 5 May 1996. In addition, most of the Autonomous Communities have their own environment departments.

(2) Environmental Law and the Energy Sector

The Atmospheric Environment Protection Act 1972[170] lists as contaminating activities nuclear power plants and fossil fuel power plants subject to emissions control. The Directive on the Control of Emissions by Large Combustion Plants[171] was incorporated into Spanish law in 1991.[172] Almost every Spanish electricity power station is subject to that Directive, since a large combustion plant is a plant with capacity of more than 50 MW. **12.198**

An environmental impact assessment (EIA) must be carried out for the construction of many energy installations,[173] such as i) oil refineries, ii) gasification plants, iii) liquidization plants, iv) power stations of more than 300 MW, v) large dams of more than 15 metres in height, and vi) open-cast mines. **12.199**

The Autonomous Communities have competence to develop the basic framework of the State on Environmental protection.[174] Some of them have approved their own laws in that area, and in some Autonomous Communities the list of installations whose construction is subject to a previous EIA is longer and wider than the list contained in the National Act. This is the case, for example, of the Autonomous Community of Andalusia.[175] Even when the construction of a particular energy installations is not subject to a formal EIA according to national law, the impact on the environment should normally be evaluated within the procedure for the authorization of such installations (eg electricity lines,[176] gas pipelines, and underground storage facilities). **12.200**

As to water quality, environmental protection is governed by the Water Act 1985. This contains specific provisions for the protection of the environment from damage caused by mining activities.[177] **12.201**

Some other relevant laws for the protection of the environment from energy activities are the following: i) the Residues Act 1998,[178] ii) the Nuclear Energy Act 1964 and the Nuclear Security Council Act 1980, iii) the Regulation on Dumping **12.202**

---

170 Act No 38 of 22 December 1972, developed by Decree No 833 of 6 February 1975 (as amended in 1985, 1986, and 1987).

171 Council Directive No 88/609/EC of 24 November 1988.

172 Royal Decree No 646 of 22 April 1991.

173 Royal Legislative Decree No 1302 of 28 June 1986 (as modified by the Hydrocarbons Act 1998), developed by Royal Decree No 1131 of 30 September 1988.

174 Art 149, 1, Rule 23, of the Constitution.

175 The Environmental Protection Act 1994 of Andalusia, Act No 7 of 18 May 1994.

176 The Coasts Act 1988 prohibits the construction of high-voltage electricity lines on the maritime public domain (such as the tideland and beaches). However, the LSE allows, exceptionally and based on public interest needs, the Council of Ministers to permit the construction of such installations, save on beaches.

177 Royal Decree No 2994 of 15 October 1982.

178 Act No 10 of 21 April 1998.

Dangerous Substances from Onshore into the Sea,[179] and iv) the Regulation on Disturbing and Dangerous Activities,[180] insofar as the Autonomous Communities have not substituted it for regional regulations.

12.203 Furthermore, there is a Radioactive Residues Plan within the NEP[181], which is carried out by *Enresa*, with the help of the Centre for Energy, Environmental and Technical Studies (CIEMAT). The fourth general radioactive waste plan was issued in 1994. It aims principally to improve the management of low-level and medium-level radioactive waste, locate deep geological formations for high-level radioactive waste disposal and develop technology for dismantling nuclear installations.[182]

I. Future Developments

12.204 The Electricity Act 1997 applies the new competitive regulatory model inherent to new public services, with the following features: i) separation of activities which will permit the introduction of competition wherever possible, ii) free entry and free investment in competitive activities, abandoning centralized planning, iii) free contracting and competitive pricing, iv) free access to the network, the infrastructure in which competitive services are rendered, v) changing the concept of public service, as singular deliveries of 'universal services', and vi) oversight of the model by an independent regulatory body.

12.205 This new competitive regulatory model is also characterized by a new sense of regulation. Strictly speaking, the electricity sector has not been deregulated. This sector will always be regulated for various reasons: the characteristically collusive nature of its supply, the technical restrictions of the network, the need to organize the market, the natural monopolistic character of some activities, the essential service to citizens provided by electricity and gas supply, and the strategic importance to the country. But, in contrast to the previous regulatory model substituting the market, the new regulation helps to create a market; it is a new model of 'regulation for the market' which imposes responsibilities (obligatory pool, adhesion contracts, submission to the system operator, third-party access), all of which makes a market possible. During a transition period, measures for the recovery of stranded costs are taken in both the Electricity Act 1997 and the Hydrocarbons Act 1998. There will never be a perfect market but rather an imperfect and regulated one. Nevertheless, a regulated market is always better than the total absence of a market and the omnipresence of regulation. Even more: a bad market is

[179] Royal Decree No 258 of 10 March 1989.
[180] Decree No 2414 of 30 November 1961.
[181] Annex II to the NEP 1991–2000.
[182] International Energy Agency, *Energy Policies of IEA Countries* (Spain), 1996 Review, 76.

better than good regulation. A comparison between the Electricity Act 1997 and the Hydrocarbons Act 1998 is useful. Both Acts apply the new competitive regulatory model inherent to new public services, but the two Acts present a very different degree in the extent of liberalization, as shown in the definition of eligible consumers.

Bibliography

Ariño, G, 'Regulating Competition and Security of Supply: The Case of Spain', in L Hancher (ed), 'The European Energy Market: Reconciling Competition and Security of Supply', Series of Publications by the Academy of European Law in Trier, vol 13, Cologne 1995, 57–65

Correljé, A, 'The Spanish Oil Industry', Tinbergen Institute Resarch Series, 84, 1995

Cross, ED, 'Spain: Increasing the Role of the Government', in ED Cross, 'Electric Utility Regulation in the European Union: A Country by Country Guide', John Wiley & Sons, 1996, 205–30

Directorate-General for Energy, *Energy in Europe*, Special Issue (Sept 1996), 1996 Annual Energy Review, Part II, Spain: Summary Energy Balance

del Guayo, I, 'Gas Regulation in Spain', *Utilities Law Review*, 2 (1991), 78–82

—— 'Privatisation, Integration and Liberalisation of the Spanish Gas Industry', *Journal of Energy & Natural Resources Law*, 1 (1996), 88–94

International Energy Agency, *Energy Policies of IEA Countries* (Spain), 1996 Review, 76

Pastor, L, and González Ruiz, JI , *Spain*, Special Issue of the 'Oil and Gas Law and Taxation Review' on the Liberalisation of Electricity in Europe (1998), 169

Piqueras, R, 'The Maghreb-Europe Gas Pipeline: Its Juridical Structure', Oil and Gas Law & Taxation Review, 3 (1995), 95–8

Smith, EE, *et al*, 'International Petroleum Transactions', Rocky Mountain Mineral Law Foundation, Denver 1993

Legislation

1. The Spanish Civil Code (1889)
2. The Expropriation Act 1954, of 16 December 1954
3. The Nuclear Energy Act 1964, Act No 25, of 29 April 1964
4. The Atmospheric Environment Protection Act 1972, Act No 38, of 22 December 1972 (developed by Decree No 833, of 6 February 1975, as amended in 1985, 1986, and 1987)
5. Mining Act 1973, Act No 22, of 21 July 1973 (developed by Royal Decree No 2857, of 25 August 1978)
6. The Encouragement of Mining Activities Act 1977, Act No 6, of 4 January 1977 (developed by Royal Decrees Nos 1167, of 2 May 1978, and 2485, of 23 December 1994)
7. The Territorial Waters Act 1977, Act No 10, of 10 January 1977
8. The Exclusive Economic Zone Act 1978, Act No 15, of 20 February 1978
9. The Spanish Constitution 1978
10. The Nuclear Security Council Act 1980, Act No 15, of 22 April 1980

11. Act to Modify the Mining Act 1973, Act No 54, of 5 November 1980
12. The Local Organization Act 1985, Act No 7, 2 April 1985 (developed by the Regulation of the Local Organization Act 1986, approved by Royal Legislative Decree No 781, of 18 April 1986)
13. The Water Act 1985, Act No 29, of 29 August 1985 (developed by Royal Decree No 849, of 11 April 1986, and by Royal Decree No 927, of 29 July 1988)
14. The Environmental Impact Assessment Act, Royal Legislative Decree No 1302, of 28 June 1986 (developed by Royal Decree No 1131, of 30 September 1988)
15. The Coasts Act 1988, Act No 22, of 28 July 1988
16. The General Budget Act 1988, Royal Legislative Decree No 1091, of 23 September 1988
17. The Defence of Competition Act 1989, Act No 16, of 17 July 1989, as developed by Royal Decrees Nos 157, of 21 February 1992, and 1080, of 11 September 1992
18. The Public Administration and Common Administrative Procedure Act 1992, Act No 30, of 26 November 1992
19. The Privatization Act, Act No 5, of 23 March 1995 (developed by Royal Decree No 1225, of 15 September 1995)
20. The creation of SEPI Act, Act No 5, of 10 January 1996 (as amended by Royal Decree-Law of 5 September 1997)
21. The Organization and Functioning of the Public Administration of the State Act 1997, Act No 6, of 14 April 1997
22. The Electricity Act, Act No 54, of 27 November 1997
23. The Residues Act, Act No 10, of 21 April 1998
24. The Hydrocarbons Act 1998, Act No 34, of 7 October 1998

13

ENERGY LAW IN THE UNITED KINGDOM

Stephen R Dow

A. Introduction

(1) The United Kingdom

13.01 The United Kingdom of Great Britain and Northern Ireland is a complex jurisdiction, made up of three separate legal systems. The largest jurisdiction is that of England and Wales. The others, namely Scotland and Northern Ireland, are much smaller both in land mass and population. The three systems are distinct, but there is considerable overlapping legislation. The legal traditions are distinct but often similar: there is no written constitution; and each has its own independent judiciary.

13.02 There are relatively few particular difficulties caused for the energy sector by the separate jurisdictions. There are some organizational differences, but legal differences are minimal. Offshore jurisdiction, both civil and criminal, nominally divides[1] the UK continental shelf[2] into three sectors. For criminal matters, offences may be tried in any of the three jurisdictions. For civil matters, the standard rules regarding choice of law and forum apply. It is accordingly common to find English law as the law of the contract. Devolution has created greater political independence for both Scotland and Northern Ireland, but the elected bodies do not have competence to legislate in the energy sector. With respect to energy matters, the Scottish Parliament does not have jurisdiction in the field of energy matters,[3] although a sizeable proportion of hydrocarbon resources are found in the Scottish sector. Accordingly, powers related to hydrocarbon licensing remain with the Secretary of State for Trade and Industry. The coal industry, the gas supply industry, and the electricity industry are similarly unaffected. It also follows that tax revenues will not be controlled by the devolved legislative bodies.

(2) United Kingdom Energy Resource Base

13.03 The vast majority of producing hydrocarbon fields are found in the North Sea, although there is increasing exploration (and production) in the Atlantic Ocean, in

[1] Oil and Gas (Enterprise) Act 1982 ss 22, 23, and 24; see also Civil Jurisdiction (Offshore Activities) Order 1987 SI no 2197; Criminal Jurisdiction (Offshore Activities) Order 1987 SI No 2198.

[2] Continental Shelf Act 1964, implementing the Geneva Convention on the Continental Shelf 1958.

[3] Scotland Act 1998, providing powers for the Scottish Parliament after devolution.

the areas west of the Shetland Isles. Generally, gas is found in the southern North Sea, with greater quantities of oil found further north. The North Sea is becoming mature, with a number of fields approaching the end of their productive lives. Total proven reserves are around 5,000 million barrels,[4] down from some 19,000 million barrels twenty years before. At present production rates, the UK has only around five years of production remaining. Production is around 2.5 million barrels per day, which is around 3.7 per cent of total world production.

On the consumption side, UK demand is about 1.8 million barrels per day, **13.04** demonstrating that the UK is a significant net oil exporter.

Turning to natural gas, UK proven reserves are around 0.76 trillion cubic metres, **13.05** representing about 0.5 per cent of the world proven reserves. At present production levels, proven reserves would support almost nine years of production. With production of around 87 billion cubic metres annually, and demand for around 86 billion cubic metres, there is an obvious oversupply in the gas market and scope to export gas through the new interconnector to Belgium. The UK also receives gas from part of the Norwegian sector.

Turning to coal, at the end of 1997 the UK had proven reserves of 2,500 million **13.06** tonnes, representing 0.2 per cent of total world reserves. At present production levels of under 30 million tonnes (oil equivalent) annually, proven reserves will support a further fifty years of production.

The electricity industry in the UK is quite diverse in its fuel sources. Total in- **13.07** stalled capacity is around 70GW,[5] and has shown a slight rise in recent years as new combined cycle gas turbines (CCGTs) are built, and the nuclear reactor at Sizewell is taken into account. There have been closures of coal-fired plant, and reclassification of some coal-fired capacity as dual-fired (coal and gas).

The fuel mix in the electricity sector has shown a remarkable change in recent years. **13.08** Coal retains the biggest share, now around 33 per cent, followed closely by natural gas with 31 per cent. The third significant source is nuclear power, with around 26 per cent of the market. The remainder is made up of imported power (5 per cent, mainly from France); oil-fired capacity (2 per cent); hydroelectric power (1 per cent); and other sources, principally renewables (around 2 per cent). This represents a huge change over the last five years, following liberalization of the electricity generation market. As recently as 1993[6] coal provided over 50 per cent of fuel for power

[4] *DTI, Oil and Gas Reserves of the United Kingdom* (known as the Brown Book) 1999; for international comparisons of production statistics see *BP Statistical Review of World Energy* 2000. Proven reserves are those which geological and engineering information indicate with reasonable certainty can be recovered in the future from known reservoirs under existing economic and operating conditions.

[5] See DTI, *Digest of UK Energy Statistics* 1999.

[6] See DTI, *Digest of UK Energy Statistics* 1993.

generation, with gas having a 10 per cent share and oil 6 per cent. The shift in favour of gas has been remarkable in both its scale and its speed.

(3) History of the UK Resource Base

13.09 The United Kingdom is one of Europe's major energy producers, particularly since the development of offshore hydrocarbon reserves. Prior to becoming a significant oil and gas producer, the country relied heavily on its substantial (although dispersed) coal reserves. The energy picture in the United Kingdom is changing again, now that the producing areas of the North Sea are increasingly regarded as mature, although the recently discovered fields in the Atlantic Margin have provided optimism that replacement reserves will be found within UK jurisdiction to compensate for the older fields reaching the final stages of their productive lives.[7] Gas production, formerly viewed as the poorer relation of oil production, has become increasingly important, particularly following liberalization of the gas supply market, and the move towards gas-fired power generation. The opening of the UK-Continental Gas Interconnector has provided a further impetus for renewed gas production, as it signalled the end of the UK as a closed gas system.

13.10 In addition to possessing substantial quantities of hydrocarbons, the UK has considerable coal reserves. However, coal is becoming less important in the energy mix,[8] and the coal industry has seen savage cutbacks since its peak.[9] Cheaper coal imports have also seen the market for UK coal eroded, and exports have fallen.[10] The proportion of UK mined coal as a percentage of the total market for coal has fallen and continues to fall.[11] Formerly a state monopoly, coal production has been privatized,[12] and with the major purchaser of coal (the electricity industry) also privately owned, the scope for support of the coal industry by means of guaranteeing a market for UK coal is considerably reduced. Employment within the coal industry is again under threat. UK coal relies on subsidy to survive, and accordingly its future within an increasingly competitive energy market is not secure.

[7] Estimates of UK reserves vary; DTI Energy Statistics suggest there may be reserves (including probable reserves) to support thirty years of oil production and a hundred years of gas production.

[8] In 1996 coal's share of the electricity generation market fell below 40% for the first time. With the construction of additional gas-fired plant, the market share for British mined coal is likely to continue to fall; the effect of the moratorium on gas-fired power plant consents has been to reduce the rate of coal's decline.

[9] See further 'British Coal Privatisation', B Gladstone, Engineering and Mining Journal 193 (1992).

[10] Imports rose by over 400% between 1985 and 1995; exports fell by over 60%; see *DTI Digest of UK Energy Statistics.*

[11] See Gladstone n 9 above. Even before the majority of new gas-fired electricity generating plant was built, UK mined coal supplied 85.4 mt of a total coal consumption of 108.6 mt, that is 78.7%. Three years earlier UK coal supplied nearly 87% of demand.

[12] Coal Industry Act 1994.

In the electricity industry, the United Kingdom has seen both privatization and liberalization, leading to the development of a competitive market. The electricity industry has considerable overcapacity in generation, which has helped the development of the competitive market (discussed further below). In common with other UK energy industries, the electricity industry is now characterized by an absence of State control and ownership, which has implications for security of supply and particularly for diversity of supply. With the advent of the liberalized market there is a danger that insufficient attention will be paid to the requirement for diversity of fuel source—although the recent moratorium on consents for new gas fired plant may signal a renewed focus on diversity. **13.11**

(4) Historical Overview of the Energy Sector

Energy industries in the UK were, in common with many countries, started by private companies. Over time, the nature of the industries changed to being heavily State-controlled and mostly State-owned. The prevailing view was that the State could best serve the public requirement for energy by itself being the provider—such ownership and control enabled the State to guarantee supply. Accordingly, the coal industry, and the electricity industry, were taken into State ownership. The offshore hydrocarbon industry developed later and was treated differently. At the start of offshore development[13] the Government was content to take its share via taxation—there was no State participation. The first oil shock in 1973, the sudden rise in oil prices and a change of approach with the election of a Socialist Government, saw the creation of the British National Oil Company (BNOC) in 1975,[14] which took majority participation in new and existing licences. The flirtation with State ownership was short-lived, however, as its powers were cut after the election of the Thatcher Government in 1979. Deprived of its right to a majority stake in new fields, BNOC slowly declined into oblivion and eventual abolition. The Government was again content to take its share of oil revenues by means of taxation alone rather than seeking income by means of ownership. In addition, the State again lost interest in direct depletion controls. **13.12**

The gas supply industry was again treated differently. The State gas supplier, the British Gas Corporation (and its forerunner the British Gas Council) had monopoly purchase rights over all gas produced in the UK sector of the North Sea. Accordingly, no gasfield could be developed without its consent to purchase the gas, which was an indirect form of depletion control. The monopoly purchase right was abolished with the privatization of the gas supply industry in 1986, but **13.13**

[13] Following the Continental Shelf Act 1964, the onshore licensing regime under the Petroleum (Production) Act 1932 was extended offshore. Legislation now consolidated in Petroleum Act 1998.

[14] BNOC was a State company created under the Petroleum and Submarine Pipelines Act 1975. It was not a private company in which the Minister held all the shares (cf Nuclear Electric under the Electricity Act 1989).

a number of the supply contracts which arose out of that right continue to operate today (discussed further below).

13.14 The Thatcher Government oversaw a revolution in the energy industries, as the State interests were privatized. The rationale for privatization was simple: the State-owned industries were not perceived as successful. The Government thought that private enterprise could deliver energy more cheaply than the State industries—there were other reasons for privatization, but desire for cheap energy appears to be the major driver. Today, the energy industries in the United Kingdom are characterized by an absence of State ownership and control.

13.15 It is difficult to discern a comprehensive energy policy for the UK: policy has been to provide an independent regulatory framework within which the market may make decisions. There are discernable sectoral policies, but no overall strategy. The Government accordingly seeks to provide a framework of regulation, creating a culture under which persons other than the Government will ensure secure, diverse, and sustainable supplies of energy in the forms that people and businesses want, at competitive prices, having regard to the environment.[15] Where a market can be made genuinely competitive, the UK sees no need for regulation. The obvious example is the market for North Sea crude oil, where there is little or no market regulation and no attempt to control price.[16]

13.16 There remains a substantial public interest in the energy industries, as without energy the economy could not function. The UK Government does not believe that it is necessary for the State to be the energy provider, rather it sets the conditions such that others will find it attractive to enter the market and become energy suppliers. Such thinking underpins the privatization of the gas supply industry, the electricity industry, and the coal industry. The difficulty with this approach is that if Government does wish to intervene to correct a perceived market imperfection, there is often little scope for it to do so.

(5) Administrative and Regulatory Authorities

Department of Trade and Industry

13.17 With the privatization of the gas and electricity industries, the post of Energy Minister no longer merited Cabinet rank. Once its own government department, the Department of Energy is now part of the much larger Department of Trade and Industry. The Energy Minister is a junior minister. The President of the Board of Trade (the title used by the Secretary of State for Trade and Industry) represents energy interests at Cabinet level.

[15] DTI, *Oil and Gas Resources of the United Kingdom*, 1993.

[16] There is no effort by the UK Government to control production levels to influence the market price. Rather the price for UK crude, principally Brent Blend, is established by the market, the International Petroleum Exchange.

The absence of State ownership has reduced the role of the Minister considerably. He is still responsible for energy policy, essentially to create the appropriate conditions for others to supply energy. The intention of privatization was to remove the Government from the decision-making process—it has been successful in that regard. One qualification is that the privatization legislation, in particular the Gas Act and the Electricity Act,[17] allow the Minister to share powers with the independent regulator for the industry. Powers and duties under the Act are shared between the Minister and the Director,[18] although in practice the Minister delegates his authority to the Director. Whilst the practical position is clear, the Act may provide a mechanism for future government involvement, particularly in licensing decisions. The statutory position is also a clear weakening of the regulator. **13.18**

Independent industry regulators

In creating the privatization structures, the Government recognized that the energy industries are different from other sectors. The requirement to deliver energy through a single network of pipes or wires means that there will always be a need for some form of regulation of the transport of energy. In addition, monopoly sections of the supply market remained as not all consumers gained the right to choose their supplier immediately;[19] accordingly there was a need for price regulation. There was also recognition that regulatory assistance would be needed to develop competition in the market. The industry structures created at privatization were not always capable of sustaining competition. **13.19**

The Director General of Gas and Electricity Markets (the successor to the Director General of Electricity Supply and the Director of Gas Supply) is independent of Government. He is an economic regulator (technical regulation remains the province of the Minister) involved in tariffing and pricing decisions, and competition issues. Regulatory powers are given to the individual, who is guaranteed security of tenure for a fixed period of five years. Whilst appointment remains the gift of the Minister, it is clear that once in post the incumbent is not subject to ministerial control or influence. The true degree of independence is debatable, given the appointment powers of the Minister and also the legislative sharing of duties between the regulator and the Minister, but in practice the regulators have been seen to act independently. **13.20**

[17] Gas Act 1986; Gas Act 1995; Electricity Act 1989.

[18] Director General of Gas Supply; Director General of Electricity Supply. The offices created under the individual sectoral Acts have been merged to create the Office of Gas and Electricity Markets (OFGEM).

[19] Under the Gas Act (and the Electricity Act) the intention was to open the market in stages. Large users initially gained the right to choose their supplier; over time the monopoly threshold would be lowered. The UK abolished the monopoly threshold during 1998, at which point all consumers (including domestic) gained the right to choose supplier.

13.21 The coal industry is regulated by the Coal Authority, which is structured in an entirely different way to other energy regulators. The Coal Authority is the holder of the State's rights to coal,[20] which at first glance looks similar to former State company rights. The difference is that the Coal Authority is not a producer of coal. Instead it is the licensing agency acting on behalf of the State, imposing and enforcing conditions attached to licences, but as it does not engage in production there is no question of industry participants also competing with the regulator.

Other regulators

13.22 The energy industries remain subject to competition law. Accordingly, both the Office of Fair Trading, and perhaps more importantly the Competition Commission (formerly the Monopolies and Mergers Commission), retain an interest. Both have been involved in investigations of the energy industries since privatization. Their role is to investigate competitive abuses; in particular the Competition Commission must report on whether the activity in question operates against the public interest. However, it is worth noting that the Commission reports to the Secretary of State for Trade and Industry, who is under no obligation to accept its recommendations; indeed he can ignore them. The Competition Commission's role can cover general investigations, and also specific investigations of takeovers or mergers, issues discussed further below.

13.23 Other government bodies are also involved in the regulation of energy matters, in particular the Department of Environment, Transport, and the Regions (successor to the Department of the Environment) which is involved in the promotion of energy efficiency and energy saving schemes.

13.24 The energy industries are also subject to environmental regulation, with the role of the Environmental Protection Agency and other governmental bodies becoming increasingly important.

B. Exploration for and Production of Oil and Natural Gas

(1) Introduction

13.25 The UK is a significant producer and exporter of hydrocarbons, but almost all its resources are found offshore on the continental shelf. Production is characterized by the expense and difficulty of drilling and producing offshore—platforms must withstand the rigours of the winter storms of the North Sea. The province was initially developed at a time of high oil prices, which readily justified the huge outlays on infrastructure. With more recent falls in the oil price, and the maturing of the province, there has been strong emphasis on lower-cost techniques for the recovery of oil from smaller fields.

[20] Coal Industry Act 1994.

In the UK, the oil industry is fundamentally different from other energy industries, in that it has never seen the same degree of State involvement. Oil exploration and production has largely occurred without the direct involvement of a State oil company, with the exception of the short-lived British National Oil Company (BNOC).[21] Following the reduction of BNOC's role after 1979, and its subsequent abolition, together with the sale of the State's stake in British Petroleum, the UK Government has no direct ownership involvement in exploration or production of hydrocarbons. It is instead content to seek a return on its ownership of the resource by means of taxation. 13.26

(2) Development of the Hydrocarbon Industry

The first rights to explore for petroleum in the UK were granted under the Defence of the Realm Act 1914, at the start of the First World War. The Government was concerned to ensure the supply of fuel oil to its naval fleet, which had converted from coal burning. The concern was that the UK had no domestic production of oil, and might therefore be vulnerable to supply shortages. The concern led to limited domestic exploration for oil, but the greatest impact had already been felt in the Government's decision to take a stake in the Anglo-Persian Oil Company (which later became BP). Anglo-Persian had the benefit of an extensive concession in what is now Iran, and although the UK Government took majority ownership, the company never behaved as a traditional State company.[22] It operated on a commercial basis, rather than simply following the traditional State company approach of provision of service in the public interest. 13.27

(3) Development of Licensing

Licensing is inextricably linked to ownership, since clearly only the party entitled to the resource can permit another to exercise that right on his behalf. Petroleum licensing became institutionalized under the first statute dedicated to the oil industry, the Petroleum Act 1918. Whilst not affecting any existing rights,[23] a licensing system was put in place. The Act gave the State the right to enter land to search for, bore for, and get petroleum; and it created the licensing system whereby the Government could allow others to carry out those tasks on its behalf. The State could prevent unauthorized drilling as an invasion of its rights. It could therefore control wasteful or competitive drilling, a problem which plagued the United States but which has never been a serious issue in the UK. 13.28

[21] BNOC was created under the Petroleum and Submarine Pipelines Act 1975, and was an attempt by the Labour Government both to exercise greater control over sovereign resources, and to appropriate more of the rent in a time of high oil prices.

[22] It is not the intention of this chapter to rehearse the history of Anglo-Persian, which is well documented. Both *The Prize*, by Daniel Yergin, and *The Seven Sisters*, by Anthony Sampson, put the history of the company into its international context.

[23] Rights under regulations made under the Defence of the Realm Act, granted to a number of landowners to drill for hydrocarbons.

13.29 The territorial scope of the 1918 Act was limited to the UK land mass—there was no thought of the possibilities of offshore discoveries; nor was there any international precedent for claiming offshore jurisdiction. The true significance of the 1918 Act is that it represented the creation of the licensing system. However, it did not lead to any great degree of exploration. There were only a few oil strikes, and most were very small. There simply were no huge onshore fields waiting to be discovered.[24] Licences granted under the 1918 Act were, however, perpetual: despite low prospectivity a few remain in existence.

(4) Licensing and Ownership: The Petroleum Act 1998

13.30 The Government has recently taken the opportunity to consolidate legislation relating to hydrocarbon ownership and exploitation, with the passing of the Petroleum Act 1998. There has been no substantive change in the law.

13.31 The first function of the legislation is to declare the ownership of hydrocarbons to be vested in the State. Now found in section 1 of the Petroleum Act 1998, the measure can be traced back to the Petroleum (Production) Act 1934. The declaration is the most fundamental measure in UK oil and gas law. The 1998 Act vests in the Crown all petroleum in its natural condition in strata *in situ* in Great Britain,[25] together with the exclusive right to search for, bore for, and get petroleum.[26] In answer to claims that the interest in petroleum should run with the land, the Act simply declared that the State had always had rights to petroleum. No compensation was paid to landowners for loss of a resource which they had never owned. The declaratory nature of the measure is perhaps controversial, but has simply been accepted.

13.32 The definition of petroleum has caused controversy in relation to coalbed methane. Coalbed methane is adsorbed into the surface of coal. There is no doubt that in the UK coal is owned by the State (formerly vested in British Coal, now in the Coal Authority)[27] but the ownership of the methane proved more controversial. Development of a potentially valuable resource was held up by arguments over ownership, which were resolved by the declaration in the Coal Industry Act 1994 that coalbed methane fell within the definition of petroleum. Accordingly, the Coal Authority had no right to license production of coalbed methane, but the development of coalbed methane cannot go ahead without first obtaining access rights to the coal seam. Access rights must be sought from the licence holder of the coal seam or, where no licence has been issued, from the Coal Authority. Given

[24] Onshore in the UK has rarely been prospective. The only significant field is Wytch Farm on the Dorset coast, others are extremely small producers. Having said that, small operators have demonstrated that it is possible to operate low-cost onshore fields at a profit, exploiting a niche in the market which their larger competitors (with higher administration costs etc) would not be in a position to take.

[25] 'Great Britain' does not include the continental shelf, but does include the territorial sea.

[26] Petroleum Act 1998, s 1.

[27] See Coal Industry Act 1994.

that coalbed methane production must take place before the seam is mined, access rights will usually be sought from the Coal Authority.[28]

In relation to petroleum, the Crown[29] chooses not to exercise its rights itself, but rather to license others to do so on its behalf (and pay part of the rent to Government by way of taxation). The 1998 Act, consolidating the 1934 Act, permits the Crown to impose conditions on such licences. The initial measure did not, however, immediately lead to a substantial expansion of activity, but did create the basis of the licensing regime still used in the UK. **13.33**

(5) Offshore Licensing: the State's Right to Hydrocarbons

The onshore regime was effectively extended offshore by the Continental Shelf Act 1964.[30] The discovery of the Groningen field (in 1959) in the Netherlands sector of the North Sea led to the hope that discoveries would be made nearby. At that time the UK had no mechanism to license offshore activity, and accordingly when implementing the Geneva Convention on the Continental Shelf 1958, the Government took the opportunity to apply a licensing regime offshore that is to the continental shelf beyond the territorial sea. **13.34**

The same fundamental licensing model applies: the Crown has the right to issue licences; the licence is issued by the Minister subject to various conditions; and the Government appropriates part of the rent. But there is an important difference in the ownership of the resource. Onshore (including within the territorial sea) the State has an absolute right to the hydrocarbon resource. Offshore, in keeping with international law provisions,[31] the State does not claim absolute sovereignty. Rather, it claims an exclusive right to explore for and exploit hydrocarbons. No person has a better right, and the right can be defended, but it is not absolute sovereignty. The practical consequence is that the offshore licence can only transfer that right, it cannot give a right to own oil in the ground. Hydrocarbons are taken into ownership at first possession, that is at the wellhead, by means of a legal fiction known as the rule of capture.[32] Until that time there is no outright ownership. By contrast, on land there is absolute ownership and accordingly the licence can transfer ownership of oil in the ground. **13.35**

The other difference with the onshore model was the method of allocating acreage. Onshore, acreage was formerly allocated on an ad hoc basis: interested persons made applications at any time for a licence. The system has now been **13.36**

[28] Coal access agreement rights.

[29] The rights of the Crown are exercised by Government, not the Monarchy.

[30] Continental Shelf Act 1964, now partly consolidated into Petroleum Act 1998, implementing the Geneva Convention on the Continental Shelf 1958.

[31] See Geneva Convention on Continental Shelf 1958; also Brownlie, *Principles of Public International Law* (Clarendon Press, Oxford).

[32] See Daintith and Willoughby, *United Kingdom Oil and Gas Law* (Sweet and Maxwell, London).

made more regular by the creation of onshore licensing rounds. Offshore, the usual procedure is for acreage to be awarded in rounds. Periodically (often annually) the Government offers specific areas, divided into blocks, to potential licensees. In this way the Government retains a degree of control over the pace of development of natural resources, and imposes a degree of order on the process.

(6) Nature of the Licence

13.37 The licence is ultimately the link allowing the company seeking to develop resources which belong to the Crown. The licence allows the company to take over the Crown's rights, under certain conditions, and subject to various payments. A licence is essential in that a person has no right to explore for hydrocarbons even on his own land—there is separation of the ownership of mineral rights from ownership of the land.

13.38 Forsaking State ownership does not mean that the Government has forsaken all control over its resource. The terms and conditions attached to the licence mean that the Government must give approval to all works. Detailed applications for consent to drill and produce hydrocarbons are necessary; the Government retains detailed control. However, it does not have direct control over depletion rates of the resource, although the UK Government has shown a tendency to encourage development (and therefore maximize immediate tax revenues) rather than limiting the pace at which its resource endowment is used up. The Government's right to approve the reservoir development plan allows it to dictate the production rate appropriate to the public interest.

13.39 The licence is essentially a contract between the Government and the licence holder, and it transfers a State right. It is also a regulatory instrument, in that it allows the Minister to exercise various functions in the public interest. It is a strange concept that, despite being a transfer of the Crown's right to search for, bore for, and get petroleum, simply holding a licence is not enough to allow its holder to develop a hydrocarbon deposit. The Minister has to approve the work programme (including method, scope, and timing); the bare rights under a licence are essential but not extensive.

13.40 The hybrid nature of the licence leads to considerable debate as to methods of amendment, and possibilities of review of the Minister's decisions. If the licence were purely a contract, it could not be amended unilaterally. However, in the UK there have been several instances of unilateral amendment of the licence, perhaps most notably by the Petroleum and Submarine Pipelines Act 1975 with the compulsory addition of the British National Oil Company (BNOC) with a majority holding to all licence groups.[33] In the event, licences were amended by the

[33] It is important to note that BNOC was never granted a statutory monopoly. It simply took majority participation in all licences; that is, BNOC held 51% share of the licence within a contractual joint venture.

Government without formal challenge from licence holders, the absence of a challenge being most likely due to the risk of being excluded from future licence awards. Licence holders considered the disadvantages of litigation to be too high, but the illusion of the licence as a straightforward contract was shattered.

Where a regulatory element is involved, the actions of the Minister are subject to control by the courts by means of judicial review. Judicial review is by definition limited—it is not an appeal against the Minister's decision, but a method of ensuring that the Minister follows his own procedures and rules. If he fails to do so, his decision can be overturned. However, the merits of the original decision are irrelevant. There is a strong case for arguing that the decisions of the Minister[34] should be subject to judicial review. Nonetheless, there is no reported case of a licence holder having sought the intervention of the court, again perhaps due to the fear of losing out in future licensing rounds. **13.41**

(7) Types of Licence and Obligations of Licence Holders

Offshore in the UK there are two types of licence. The exploration licence is a non-exclusive right to conduct exploration activities. The licence covers a substantial area, and allows seismic and other surveys. It does not permit invasive drilling. Further, there is no guaranteed link between work done under an exploration licence and obtaining a licence to produce any hydrocarbons found. The absence of security of tenure is partly explained by the difference in scale—an exploration licence area is several times larger than a production block—and partly by the Government's historical discretion in awarding production licences. Where the Minister has wide discretion, he can take into account exploration activity in deciding who wins the more valuable production blocks. **13.42**

The production licence itself allows appraisal work, together with development and production, from a defined area (or block). The production licence is awarded over a single block, and is exclusive. The holder can prevent unauthorized intrusion into the licensed area. The block size is of fundamental importance to the operation of the industry: it is unlikely that geological structures containing hydrocarbons fall neatly within artificially drawn block lines. Accordingly one licensee may have to co-operate with his neighbour to facilitate production of the field as a single unit.[35] Where blocks are smaller, unitization is more likely. **13.43**

[34] Following the abolition of the Department of Energy, the relevant Minister is now the Secretary of State for Trade and Industry (known as the President of the Board of Trade).

[35] The Minister has power to compel unitization (of fields lying across block boundaries) in the public interest—see Petroleum (Production) (Seaward Areas) Regulations 1988 (as amended), Schedule 4 (Model Clauses).

Onshore licences

13.44 Onshore licences are rather different from offshore licences.[36] Formerly graded into three separate steps, and therefore three separate licence applications, the system was simplified following the Hydrocarbons Licensing Directive[37] to create a single-tier licence. The former Exploration Licence, Appraisal Licence, and Production Licence have been replaced by the single Production Exploration and Development Licence (PEDL).[38] The result has been a substantial reduction in the administrative costs associated with applications, although licences already in existence are not affected. Onshore activity in recent years has largely focused on coal bed methane, although the initial hopes for the development of that industry were dealt a severe blow by delays caused by the dispute over ownership of the resource.

(8) Licence Award Process and Criteria

13.45 The advertizing of acreage in rounds also offers an opportunity for the Government to impose different award criteria over time, yet still be consistent in its treatment of neighbouring acreage. UK award criteria have changed dramatically over the years, including in the early years preference to companies in joint venture with UK State companies,[39] perhaps a peculiar requirement in view of the absence of a State oil company. Some requirements, for example UK participation in procurement by licensees which is clearly discriminatory, have been substantially modified or discarded over time.

13.46 The primary criterion is to establish the technical and financial competence of the applicant. There is no doubt that hydrocarbon development is expensive—the public interest in developing State resources is best served by permitting exploitation by those best qualified. The vast majority of licence applications are made by groups of companies acting together in a joint venture,[40] primarily to spread risk and costs. The success rate for oil exploration is still quite low, so companies wish to take a small part of a number of projects rather than all of a single project. The overall returns are likely to be improved as the risk is spread.

13.47 The process begins with the publication of details of acreage on offer, published by the Minister in the Official Journal of the European Communities.[41] The

[36] See Salter, *Onshore Oil and Gas Law*, (London) Sweet and Maxwell.

[37] Hydrocarbons Licensing Directive 92/94.

[38] See Petroleum (Production) (Landward Areas) Regulations 1995.

[39] The criteria led to substantial involvement in licences for British Gas Corporation (assets later privatized under the Oil and Gas (Enterprise) Act 1982); and the National Coal Board (later British Coal).

[40] It is important to stress that a joint venture is not a partnership, and not a separate legal person. It is created by contract and has no legal personality.

[41] Publication in the Official Journal (required following the implementation of the Hydrocarbons Licensing Directive) has replaced publication in the Gazette (London, Edinburgh, Belfast) as official notice of the licensing round.

notice is the first indication of the areas on offer, although the Minister usually seeks consultation with the industry to see which blocks are the most interesting or the most prospective. The Minister will almost certainly offer a range of acreage, from the most desirable to less attractive areas. The discretionary element in the award process has previously led companies to bid for less attractive acreage—the Minister could choose to award packages of desirable acreage to those who also apply for the poorer areas. The perceived wisdom is that applying only for the best acreage may not secure all that the applicant seeks.

Applications may be invited for full blocks, or part blocks (created by surrender of acreage). An application is made for each individual block, rather than a single application for multiple blocks. **13.48**

The notice also describes the method of allocation. Usually discretionary, it will set out the criteria on which the Minister will base his decision. Formerly a wholly discretionary system, the Hydrocarbons Licensing Directive has continued the erosion of the discretionary element. The goal of the Directive is to impose transparent and non-discriminatory licence award criteria; the UK has made significant changes to the procedure, and has considered moving part of the way towards auctioning acreage. **13.49**

Cash payments may be made for acreage: in the Seventh Round the Government effectively chose a winner of a fixed price contest. There is little to commend the approach, and much to criticize. The bidders have less information about the block than the Government which sets the price. In order to attract bidders, the price will tend to be lower than the value of the block, which may be against the public interest. The decision as to the winner may be entirely arbitrary: where two groups are equally technically and financially capable, the choice is by definition arbitrary. Auctions might be one way to realize greater value to the Government, assuming that the highest bidder is sufficiently qualified. **13.50**

Each round has had a different emphasis on essentially similar award criteria. The Minister may, for example, announce that he will examine the environmental management programmes of each application; or he may give priority to those who promise to bring the field into production at the earliest date. Typically bidders will also offer to carry out various appraisal work on the block, and the Minister will usually prefer the more extensive work. **13.51**

The Eighteenth Round saw a change in the procedure. It offered a range of acreage in both mature areas (blocks and part blocks in the North Sea) and also frontier acreage (in Atlantic areas). The procedural change saw an indication of the areas which will be available in rounds in the near future, including further frontier acreage. The decision as to which blocks to offer is of critical importance in determining the attractiveness of future investment; in times of low oil prices it is **13.52** difficult to attract new investment to mature areas. Allowing companies more time to plan is one part of replacing the former discretionary approach of awarding blocks of poorer prospectivity alongside higher quality blocks to the same applicant, which is clearly in breach of the ideals of the Hydrocarbons Licensing Directive. The Nineteenth Round, covering areas in the Atlantic margin, was the subject of a successful challenge by the environmental lobby. The Minister was unable to demonstrate that account had been taken of the Habitats Directive and the Round did not proceed to a conclusion. It is clear that awards in future Rounds will be determined on the basis of criteria compatible with the Habitats Directive (essentially environment impact surveys) and Hydrocarbons Licensing Directive.

(9) Obtaining a Licence: Bidding Agreements

13.53 Applications are commonly (though there is no formal requirement) made by groups of companies who have a common interest. Membership of the group is entirely voluntary, but based on the same desire to spread risk. Companies coming together in a contractual joint venture to make a licence application will often do so in the same groupings. Choosing a co-venturer may be difficult as each company has different priorities and different interpretations of the geological data, which may make finding a common interest difficult. The bidding group may choose to regulate its internal relationship by means of a bidding agreement, although it should be borne in mind that obligations under a licence are joint and several irrespective of such internal agreement between the parties.

13.54 In choosing a co-venturer, perhaps the most important element is ensuring that the company would be acceptable to the Minister as a licensee. Technical skill and financial strength are important, as is a track record in applications and commitment to the specific criteria of the round.

13.55 The bidding agreement[42] will contain confidentiality provisions allowing the pooling of data. In the oil industry knowledge is equivalent to money and is not lightly given away. The provision prevents disclosure beyond the co-venturers. The agreement also details the areas in which the group is interested, and will usually prevent signatories joining other groups competing for the same acreage. It will restrict ability to join other groups looking at the same areas of mutual interest.

13.56 The bidding agreement will also outline the respective shares (interests) of the participants. There is no reason why the group should have equal shares—the shares are an indication of the percentage interests they wish to take in the licence (if awarded). However, a licence is awarded to a named group, without specifying the respective interests, and all obligations to the Minister are undertaken on a joint and several basis.

[42] See further Alison Huxtable, *Bidding Agreements*, in Davis (ed) *Upstream Oil and Gas Agreements*.

The agreement will further specify which company will act as operator,[43] and will determine procedures for the operating committee to decide which acreage to bid for. There will usually be weighted voting according to percentage interest ownership, and accordingly it is important to set the passmark for a proposal in such a way as to reflect the various interests. If it is set high, small percentage interest holders may have a veto; if too low, small holders may be ignored. **13.57**

The primary function of the bidding group is to determine which blocks to bid for. It will analyse data and make a decision in the operating committee. It must also determine the scope of the work programme to be offered in the bid, although usually any company which votes against the work programme will be able to escape at that point. Such a move is in the interests of the remaining members who are unlikely to want to bid with an unwilling participant. Withdrawal is unlikely to be allowed once the application is lodged. **13.58**

The agreement will usually stay in effect until the earlier of the execution of a joint operating agreement (where the bid is successful) or the date on which the licence is awarded to another group or the Minister announces that the bid is unsuccessful, or all participants agree to make no application. However, given the difficulties and costs of finding suitable co-venturers, there is a tendency to have agreements which cover the same area of mutual interest appearing in future rounds. Such a move may also hasten the trend towards standardized bidding agreements (with attendant lower transaction costs). **13.59**

(10) Obtaining a Licence: Joint Operating Agreements

The Joint Operating Agreement (JOA) creates the contractual joint venture between successful applicants for a licence. It is the method of regulating the co-venturers' relationships in exploiting the licence. The contractual joint venture is not a partnership, and has no legal personality. Crucially, it is not a separate taxable entity (although of course the individual co-venturers are liable to tax on their share of income). The UK tax regime has largely been behind the continued popularity of the joint venture, but clearly if tax rules changed it may become appropriate to create single purpose companies to exploit the resource. **13.60**

In the UK the form of the JOA[44] tends to follow that of the BNOC 5th Round Pro-Forma. As a freely negotiated contract, there is no reason why the agreements covering different fields should bear any similarity in style or form. However, with the compulsory addition of the British National Oil Company to every licence issued,[45] there was an obvious incentive to reduce transaction costs by having a **13.61**

[43] The Minister has the right to approve operators in terms of Model Clause 24; Petroleum (Production) (Seaward Areas) Regulations 1988 as amended.

[44] See further *Taylor and Winsor on Joint Operating Agreements*, Taylor and Tyne (Longman).

[45] BNOC became the majority interest holder on all new and existing licences after its creation under the Petroleum and Submarine Pipelines Act 1975.

similar joint operating agreement in each case. The details would be different, but the form would be the same, making agreement to add BNOC to each licence much easier to implement. The influence of the 5th Round Pro-Forma is still evident.

13.62 The JOA is freely negotiated between the parties, and is subject to approval under the licence by the Minister. The JOA is the constitution of the joint venture, comparable in many ways to the articles of association of a company. Its principle elements are to specify the respective ownership stakes of the parties, although the licence obligations remain joint and several. Obligations under the JOA are several, not joint, but it cannot overrule the licence. The arrangement may not always be binding against third parties, which leads to a need to add rights of recovery against co-venturers for liability in excess of the percentage interest.

13.63 The JOA will also appoint the operator, subject to the Minister's approval. The operator need not be one of the licence holders, and is frequently an associated company of one of the licensees. The JOA will list his duties, from preparation of the annual work programme and budget to reporting requirements to the non-operators. The operator is a fiduciary—he cannot exploit his position *qua* operator for profit. He simply carries out the functions of organizing or supervising all or any of the operations of searching or boring for or getting petroleum. In similar fashion, he will not be liable to the co-venturers for losses unless he is guilty of wilful misconduct. Negligence is probably insufficient: liability will only attach where there is intentional or reckless disregard of the JOA or the work programme.[46]

13.64 Controls over the operator are primarily exercised by the operating committee, representing each licensee and voting according to percentage interests. The pass-mark is again of crucial importance in balancing the interests of the group. The committee must approve all operations: where it fails to do so, the parties should consider whether it is appropriate to have a sole risk clause.

13.65 Sole risk clauses are common in JOAs, but their use is infrequent. Sole risk allows a party to elect to carry out operations which have been turned down by the operating committee; it is different from a non-consent clause allowing a party to opt out of a decision already taken. A party invoking a sole risk clause carries out the operation at his sole expense and he alone takes the benefits. It represents a significant risk for the party invoking the clause, and is restricted in its application.[47] The true impact of the clause, however, is felt where a sole risker makes a discovery, when the others may be allowed to buy back in under payment of a

[46] See further Daintith and Willoughby, *Manual of United Kingdom Oil and Gas Law.*

[47] The type of operations available may be restricted, eg to deepening wells; or new appraisal wells etc. Sole risk is unlikely to be applied to votes on construction contracts.

heavy premium.[48] The payment may be as high as ten times the sole risker's costs—the very existence of the clause therefore creates the opportunity for the minority to seek to control the group. It may be that the parties voting against the work will choose to participate at the sole risk notice stage rather than risk being excluded until the work is done, at which time re-entry is only possible on payment of the premium.[49]

The principle function of the non-operator under a JOA[50] is to pay his share of the costs as and when he is required to do so. Where there is a default, the JOA must provide a remedy. Traditionally, the remedy has been that the defaulter's share is paid by his co-venturers and the percentage interest of the defaulter is then forfeit. However, the forfeit is somewhat draconian, and accordingly the JOA may specify certain modifications to ensure that the sanction is in proportion to the loss caused—a danger in JOAs, as a small payment default could otherwise trigger forfeiture of the entire licence interest. The addition of withering provisions under which only part of the interest is forfeit at any one time; or separate mechanisms for compulsory sale of the assets followed by repayment of the amount of the default and return of the excess receipts to the defaulting party,[51] has served to reduce the risk that forfeiture clauses will be interpreted as a penalty. **13.66**

(11) Licence Terms and Conditions

The production licence is granted subject to various conditions, specified in the Model Clauses,[52] the most important of which include work programmes, and the obligation to surrender acreage. Work programmes must be approved by the Minister, who therefore has control of the speed of development of resources. It also shows the Minister how much money will be spent—the public interest is usually best served by more extensive work programmes. **13.67**

The acreage surrender obligation contained in the licence conditions requires that part of the block be returned to the Government, usually after six years. The requirement creates a powerful incentive for the licence holder to negotiate the necessary contracts,[53] perform the work, and decide which part of the acreage to retain. The Government seeks to remove any incentive to hold unused blocks. **13.68**

[48] The premium is not legally a penalty (and therefore unenforceable) but a payment made in recognition of the risk taken.

[49] See further T Winsor, *Sole Risk*, in MacDougall and Wälde (eds) *European Energy Law Selected Topics.*

[50] See further Bean, *Fiduciary Obligations and the Joint Venture.*

[51] See for example *Johnson v Jobson*, 1989 1 All ER 621, a case involving shares in a football club. The principle of equitable relief from forfeiture by compulsory sale is nonetheless compelling.

[52] See Sched 4 to the Petroleum (Production) (Seaward Areas) Regulations 1988 (as amended).

[53] A significant number of contracts will be necessary, not least of which will be the agreement with co-venturers, the joint operating agreement. Six years can prove a strict timetable to negotiate all the deals, perform the work, and decide which part of the acreage to keep.

The Minister is usually interested in early development to bring early revenue and taxation.

13.69 In addition, special conditions may be imposed where the block is close to the shore, or in another environmentally sensitive area. There is a general obligation not to flare gas except in accordance with consent given by the Minister, but further conditions to protect sensitive environments may be added to the licence.

13.70 The licence holder is also obliged to make payment to the Government, both rent for the acreage under the licence, and (in some cases)[54] royalty on the value of hydrocarbons won and saved. Royalty in kind has been abolished.

13.71 Further, the licence holder must seek the Minister's consent before selling or otherwise disposing of the ownership of either the licence itself, or the beneficial interest in the hydrocarbons won and saved. It is not surprising that the Minister seeks to control the identity of licence holders—in the absence of such controls, there would be no guarantee that the party taking the licence (and promising to carry out certain work) would actually carry out the work. Formerly the Minister only allowed a party who had performed the agreed work obligations to dispose of his interest, but now where the incoming party agrees to perform the work (and shows he has the technical and financial capability to do so) the practice has been for the Minister to give consent. It should, however, be borne in mind that the Minister has significant discretion in making his decision, and accordingly it is possible that the trend may change again.

13.72 Further, under Model Clause 28 the licence holder must unitize the field if told to do so by the Minister. In the absence of agreement, the Minister can impose unitization on the parties. There is no recorded example of a forced unitization, reflecting the belief that it is better to make even a poor bargain with the owner of a neighbouring field than to accept terms imposed by the Minister, which are simply an unknown quantity. The clause is an extremely powerful weapon—a useful threat which forces co-operation without the Minister becoming involved in practice.

13.73 The final major obligation of the licence holder is to provide such information to the Minister as he may require. The Minister therefore has access to all information from all licensees, about both production and geology. The Minister has access to a wider picture than any individual company, and is in a privileged position to judge the likely value of future acreage offers, which is particularly valuable where there is an auction of acreage. The Government has carried out a consultation process on moving to acreage auctions for mature North Sea areas, and whilst this might have great attractions (most notably that where a block is bought for

[54] Royalty has been abolished for fields obtaining development consent after March 1982. Further, with the abolition of Petroleum Revenue Tax (PRT) for fields with development consent given after March 1993, new fields are only liable to corporation tax.

cash there would be no requirement for prior submission of a work programme) it appears that the concept is unlikely to be taken any further. There was no intention to apply competitive tendering (auction) to Atlantic Ocean frontier acreage: the intent was rather to lower transaction costs in relation to seeking acreage in the mature North Sea.

(12) Abandonment Provisions

The UK has experienced some difficulty with respect to abandonment. Abandonment agreements are a recent phenomenon, as the issue has only arisen relatively recently in practice. At the time of development little thought was given to how to dismantle or remove installations, including platforms and pipelines. Recent difficult cases, in particular the Brent Spar, have focused the attention of the industry. **13.74**

At the end of the productive life of a field, the owner must deal with the infrastructure. Essentially there are three options. First, it can be dismantled and returned to shore (where it can either be broken up or perhaps reused); secondly, the structure can have the topsides removed and the remaining support toppled in place; and thirdly, the structure can be cleaned and then towed away from its site and dumped in deep water. Finding an alternative use for the structure whilst it remains on site—for example as a processing station for production from other fields—can delay a final decision. **13.75**

The UK legal regime is fundamentally based on its international law obligations, with the undoubted influence on the policy of the Brent Spar affair.[55] The legal regime is essentially quite simple, requiring that any structure in water less than 75 metres deep be entirely removed.[56] Only structures in deeper water can be subject to partial removal. The UK provisions are now found in the Petroleum Act 1998, consolidating the provisions of the original Petroleum Act 1987, which in turn builds on the UK's international obligations. The UK was party to the Geneva Convention on the Continental Shelf 1958, Article 5(5) of which envisaged the 'entire removal' of structures. At the time of its creation, the offshore oil industry was extremely limited: there was no deep-water production. The expectations of industry with regard to abandonment options have changed as the infrastructure has grown in size.[57] **13.76**

[55] It is not the intention of this chapter to cite the history of the Brent Spar abandonment. It is sufficient to say that while its owners complied fully with legal requirements, the decision to dump the structure in deep water was reversed due to public pressure.

[56] See Petroleum Act 1998; see also IMO Guidelines and Standards for the Removal of Offshore Installations and Structures on the Continental Shelf and in the Exclusive Economic Zone (1989).

[57] For example, the Troll A platform (in Norwegian sector) is over one million tonnes; there are around sixteen concrete platforms in the UK sector which will present acute technical difficulties in removing; there is also the difficult question of disturbing the cuttings pile (waste accumulated on the seabed around the platforms can include chemicals).

13.77 It is clear that the 1958 Convention proscribed toppling in place, but it is not entirely clear that it would have barred offshore deep-water dumping. Nor was it certain that 'entire removal' necessitated bringing the structure onshore: whilst it is perhaps an unlikely interpretation, deep-sea dumping might still have been allowed since that option still takes the structure off site.

13.78 However, the UK is now a party to the 1982 UN Convention on the Law of the Sea (which replaces the 1958 Convention for States, like the UK, party to both. See further ch 2 above). The 1982 Convention envisages partial removal (in practice either toppling in place or deep-sea dumping) in limited circumstances. Despite such support, partial removal remains extremely controversial, particularly from an environmental viewpoint, and also in view of difficulties associated with residual liability.

13.79 In addition to the Law of the Sea Convention, the United Kingdom is also a party to the regional OSPAR Convention.[58] The 1998 meeting of the OSPAR Convention adopted Decision 98/3 on the Disposal of Disused Offshore Installations which treats dumping or the leaving wholly or partly in place of any such installation as an exception to the basic prohibition upon such activities under the Convention. Derogations are specifically designed to meet the need to leave in place larger steel and concrete platforms in the northern North Sea, thus addressing the concerns of Norway and the United Kingdom.

13.80 Decommissioning is an issue not only for the oil companies, but also for Government and taxpayers. In the UK, abandonment costs may be set against petroleum revenue tax, which effectively means that the taxpayer bears a significant proportion of the cost.[59] The options for partial removal also leave unsolved the question of residual liability for damage caused by the sunken infrastructure. The suggestion that such liability, which would normally still attach to the owner, should be assumed by the Government is difficult to defend: there is a substantial difference between shipwrecks and deliberately sunk redundant platforms. The problem of residual liability may make the option unattractive, although the deep-sea dumping option also must face that problem.

13.81 The legal regime under the Petroleum Act 1998 allows the Minister to request the submission of an abandonment programme.[60] This is usually provided by the operator, but a wide range of parties may be served with a notice requiring submission of the programme. Such parties include owners, managers, owners of

[58] The OSPAR Convention 1992, concerning *inter alia* pollution of the North Sea, replaced the Oslo and the Paris Conventions. See further ch 2 above.

[59] Depending on the tax position of the relevant field, the taxpayer may pay around 60–70% of the total cost of abandonment. Fields with development consent prior to March 1993 are liable to PRT: fields with development consent since that date do not qualify for the relief.

[60] See Petroleum Act 1998, s 29.

interests in the joint operating agreement, and associates of such persons, and the provisions are designed to prevent anti-avoidance.[61] Former owners may be brought back, a principle consistent with the idea that he who enjoys the benefit should pay the cost.

It is of crucial importance to note that the 1998 Act allows for the possibility of partial removal. Where a platform (or other infrastructure) is not to be entirely removed, the abandonment programme must specify what provisions are to be made for ongoing maintenance.[62] **13.82**

Under the 1998 Act the Minister may accept or modify the programme;[63] where no programme is submitted he may draw up a plan and if necessary carry it out and recover the costs.[64] The plan should reflect the best practicable environmental option. **13.83**

The current difficulty for the oil industry in the UK is that it is clear following the Brent Spar controversy that merely complying with the law is no longer sufficient in practice. It is clear that there has to be a greater degree of public consultation. The UK has not yet ruled out deep-water dumping in the future (there is perhaps little option for the large concrete platforms) but equally there is a race to be second in the next phase of field abandonments. Companies are reluctant to risk exposing themselves to criticism, even where they have complied with the requirements of the legislation. **13.84**

The costs of abandonment are likely to result in an increased use of abandonment security agreements. The fundamental problem regarding abandonment costs is that there is no income from the field at the relevant time, and so agreement is required to ensure earlier payment of required funds. Traditional default provisions are simply not appropriate security, as forfeiture of a non-productive interest is no hardship. **13.85**

The alternatives are either to require payment to a fund commencing at an agreed point in the field's life, or guarantees of payment. Parent company guarantees are not available to all; there may be attendant jurisdictional problems; and not all parent companies are sufficiently creditworthy. Obtaining a guarantee from a bank with the appropriate credit rating would almost certainly be expensive. All options have an associated cost, which might make reaching agreement difficult. **13.86**

As the UK sector of the North Sea is generally regarded as a mature province, it is likely that there will be occasions in the near future to review the applicable **13.87**

[61] ibid, s 30.
[62] ibid, s 29.
[63] ibid, s 32.
[64] ibid, s 33.

regime. It is submitted that in view of the costs (and the problems over security for costs) the public interest requires additional government intervention to minimize the risk of the taxpayer being left with the problem. The anti-avoidance provisions go much of the way, but requiring proper security would improve the position of the taxpayer.

C. Transportation of Oil and Gas

(1) Transportation Agreements

13.88 The joint operating agreement (JOA) addresses the arrangements between the parties to take petroleum from the reservoir only as far as the well-head. It does not address transportation or marketing issues—to do so would almost certainly be regarded as falling within the definition of partnership,[65] ie two or more persons carrying on a business with a view to profit. The absence of joint transportation activities, and particularly joint marketing activities, is regarded as crucial in avoiding partnership and its incumbent taxation problems. Joint marketing also runs the risk of falling foul of competition regulations.[66]

13.89 It follows, however, that a number of other agreements are required by licensees. The petroleum must be taken from well-head to shore. The traditional route has been via a pipeline. Consent for the building of pipelines is required from the Minister.[67] One of the most controversial parts of pipeline consents relates to the sizing of pipes. Clearly it is in the national interest that pipes be built slightly larger than the anticipated immediate needs, to allow fields developed later to join into older pipeline networks (which minimizes pipeline proliferation and should reduce costs overall). The difficulty is that the builder of the pipeline may have to wait for any return on the 'excess' capacity, in the form of transit fees. The builder is at risk of incurring larger capital costs today but not getting the return until tomorrow. Sizing decisions are ultimately a matter for negotiation between the builders and the Government.

13.90 In the UK sector there is no government ownership of offshore pipelines. Pipelines are owned by consortia mostly made up of oil producers, particularly those with fields nearby which will utilize the pipeline. Despite each member of the consortium having only a small stake, owners have historically had little difficulty in obtaining pipeline capacity. The owner is in effect party to both sides of the negotiation. However, where a new producer requires to negotiate access there may be greater difficulty. There is provision for third-party access in the

65 See Partnership Act 1890 s 1.
66 See in particular Treaty on European Union Arts 85 and 86; Competition Act 1998.
67 Petroleum Act 1998.

terms of the Petroleum Act 1998,[68] but it is not an absolute right of access. Rather it is a restricted right of access—transport is only allowed if it can be shown that allowing such transport will not prejudice the efficient operation of the pipeline. There are obvious problems in determining the availability of sufficient capacity, discussed further below in relation to gas pipelines.

An application for access under the Act may be made to the Minister, who may issue directions regarding the existence of the right, and also volume, tariff, timing, and connection rights. As pipelines are a natural monopoly, it is of great importance that third-party access at regulated tariffs be available. In the absence of such rights, the further development of hydrocarbon resources may be restricted. The issue of access to pipelines and pipeline tariffs should not be allowed to become a barrier to new entrants seeking to develop resources. **13.91**

In addition to the statutory access mechanism, there is a voluntary code of access to infrastructure, regulating the principles of terms and conditions of access. The code, introduced following pressure from the Government (with the threat of greater legislative powers should no agreement be reached) has provided the background to third-party access rights offshore. **13.92**

A party seeking access will first attempt to negotiate terms and conditions. Assuming there is capacity in the pipe, the major stumbling block is likely to be the tariff which has become a particular problem since the abolition of Tariff Receipts Allowance.[69] The problem of negotiating with a monopolist is obvious: the monopolist will attempt to appropriate the economic rent. The existence of statutory access rights may serve to mitigate the worst effects of a poor negotiating position; the voluntary code also helps parties seeking access to overcome the inherent monopoly problem. **13.93**

(2) Particular Problems in Transport Agreements

However, perhaps the greater problem in any pipeline agreement relates to the valuation of the product. The difficulty is caused by the fact that there are many inputs of different qualities and only one output quality, in other words the pipeline will mingle the various inputs and produce a standard output. The most appropriate way to address the attendant problem of valuation is to adjust the volume of the redelivered product, although crude oil may experience more difficulties than gas in this respect as new fields may be compelled to trade production volumes at a discount. A party who inputs a product of higher quality than the **13.94**

[68] Formerly the Petroleum and Submarine Pipelines Act 1975 s 23, now see Petroleum Act 1998 Part III.

[69] Finance Act 1993. The Tariff Receipts Allowance was a tax concession given to the owner of the pipeline. The result was that the effective value of the tariff was higher than the sum paid by the party gaining access. The abolition of TRA meant that the value of the payment to the pipeline owner went down, and accordingly there was an incentive to raise tariff rates.

output specification would expect to have returned a greater volume; similarly, a party putting in a poorer quality product receives less than the input volume when the product is returned. The agreement must be capable of taking account of the changing qualities of inputs over time.

13.95 There is now the possibility of avoiding pipelines by using floating production facilities. Offshore loading simply avoids pipelines and loading difficulties, although it will clearly be relevant only to oil, not to gas. Floating production also avoids issues of co-mingling, but may mean that the oil is traded at a heavier discount as it establishes itself in the market.

13.96 Transportation agreements are also fraught with timing difficulties. It is essential to view the contract process as a chain of events, each dependent on the other. A transportation agreement is of no use if the JOA does not guarantee that there is oil at well-head to transfer to the pipe. Similarly, there is little point in transporting oil to the tanker terminal if there is no buyer for the product.

13.97 The offshore transportation system in the UK is privately owned, and mostly operated by agreement between the owners. That system takes the product from well-head to beach. With respect to oil, it can be loaded onto tankers and taken to its market anywhere in the world. With respect to gas, it will also be necessary to have onshore transport to the consumer. Ownership of the onshore system is different from that offshore, as it is a legacy of the former State-owned gas monopoly; related issues are discussed further below.

D. Coal Production

(1) Introduction

13.98 The UK coal industry is in decline, principally due to its inability to produce competitively priced coal.[70] Competition from cheaper imported coal, together with the loss of traditional customers to competing fuel sources (principally the reduction in demand for coal for power plants) are behind the decline. The overall picture for the future for UK coal is bleak, although some individual mines are still successful and profitable.

13.99 The UK coal industry provided the energy which drove the Industrial Revolution. The industry was nationalized[71] following World War II, and remained in public ownership until becoming the last of the major energy industries to be privatized by the Conservative Major Government in 1994. The privatization was different from other energy industries, in that the Government recognized it was selling a

[70] See *The Prospects for Coal—Conclusion of the Government's Coal Review* 1993, Cmnd 2235, HMSO.

[71] Coal Nationalization Act 1945.

declining industry. The sale may also have been influenced by a desire by Government to reduce the political muscle of the coal industry, and in particular of the mining unions. The privileged position of UK coal, particularly in the three decades before privatization, gave the industry enormous political power. The fall of the Conservative Heath Government in 1974 was largely due to a miners' strike; the strong reliance of the electricity industry on coal supplies gave the mining industry a very strong bargaining position. The loss of the electricity generation market to other fuels, most recently gas, has changed the nature of the mining industry.

(2) Rights to Coal

Rights to coal are vested in the State,[72] and were formerly the province of the National Coal Board (later British Coal), the State monopoly. The monopolist had an exclusive right to produce coal. In common with other State companies, the performance of the State coal monopoly was unimpressive. There was little if any incentive to control costs—emphasis was put on production. The cost was simply passed to the consumers, particularly the electricity generators. As the electricity industry was also a State monopoly, there was no real difficulty in the Government passing on costs as appropriate or paying subsidies. **13.100**

The monopolist was in a unique position, being entitled to the coal and having the right to produce it. The few independently owned coal mines were licensed by and effectively regulated by the monopolist. Creation of competition was effectively frustrated by incomers being in the position of competing with their own regulator. The assumption was that the state company would work the coal in the absence of compelling reasons to license another company. **13.101**

Following privatization, the right of ownership in coal is vested in the Coal Authority,[73] which is a licensing authority not an industry participant. The coal mines formerly owned by the State were sold separately: accordingly the 1994 Act attempts to create the conditions for competition in coal production to emerge. The difficulty with encouraging competition is that the market for coal is disappearing. The market price of coal is held down by the need to compete with imports and other fuels; the result is that expensively mined UK coal has difficulty finding a market. **13.102**

The Coal Authority effectively plays the same role as the Minister in hydrocarbon licensing, representing the public interest. The industry was privatized at the same time as the creation of the Coal Authority; again the different style of privatization shows the UK's preference for sectoral energy policy rather than a comprehensive **13.103**

---

[72] ibid, held by the Coal Authority under the Coal Industry Act 1994.

[73] Created by the Coal Industry Act 1994, the Coal Authority is a different type of industry regulator from that found in other energy industries in the UK. Independent of Government, it holds ownership rights to coal; is specifically barred from mine operation; and is obliged to operate a licensing system in the national interest.

energy strategy. In this instance, privatization took the form of selling off the assets of the former State company, British Coal, to a number of different participants.

13.104 The Coal Authority is a group of individuals (not more than eight) appointed by the Minister,[74] but independent of the Government in its operations. The Coal Authority is specifically barred from involvement in the working of coal, therefore avoiding a potential conflict of interest of the dual role of operator and regulator which British Coal had faced. The Minister may issue binding general directions to the Coal Authority,[75] but cannot give specific instructions on a particular issue. The independence of the Authority is not undermined.

13.105 The Coal Authority has the power to add conditions to licences, and is responsible for enforcement.[76] Coal production is associated with a number of different environmental problems, including pollution of rivers, acidic drainage from mines, subsidence, and waste piles. Ceasing production at a mine does not end the pollution potential.

13.106 Privatization caused some concern that the purchasers might not be able to meet the considerable environmental costs associated with mining. Liability for historical pollution is held by the Coal Authority, insofar as such liability was not transferred at privatization. Ongoing pollutants are a liability incumbent on the operator; there are a significant number of legislative measures to be taken into account,[77] and a number of different regulatory bodies can be involved depending on what is affected by the pollution.

(3) Coal Contracts with Power Generators

13.107 The coal industry became increasingly dependent on the contracts with the power generators. With the availability of imported coal, and increasing use of other fuel sources, further pressure was put on the UK coal industry. The problem is stark: the contracts directly support employment in the mining industry. If the generators do not buy coal, the coal industry may virtually disappear.

13.108 The issue came to a head after the privatization of the electricity generators. Previously, under State control, there was little difficulty in persuading (or compelling) the generators to buy expensive UK coal. The Minister could simply direct that such purchases be made by the State-owned generator. After the privatization of the generators there was no such persuasive or compulsive power, but

---

[74] Secretary of State for Trade and Industry; see Coal Industry Act 1994 s 1.

[75] ibid, s 6.

[76] ibid, ss 31 and 32; emergency enforcement powers are short-term (three months) with limited appeal routes; longer term enforcement powers require notice periods and consultation exercises.

[77] Planning controls (Town and Country Planning Acts) aside, major legislative measures include the Environmental Protection Act 1990; the Water Resources Act 1991; and the Control of Pollution Act 1994.

it is clear that the Government still sought to influence the generators to sign contracts which would support the coal industry. A range of practical measures was introduced, the most obvious being a moratorium on new gas fixed plant and the redesigning of the wholesale electricity trading arrangements. In addition the generators were no longer barred on competition grounds from taking over electricity suppliers—a measure never directly linked to several of the coal purchase contracts but one which the generators had long sought. Direct subsidies of coal would be subject to the State aids regime and the approval of the European Commission.

It is possible that generators would like to withdraw from coal generation (assuming that the decision is made purely on grounds of price rather than of diversity and security of supply) but are effectively prevented from doing so by the operation of existing coal purchase contracts. The contracts oblige the generators to purchase UK-mined coal at above prevailing world market rates—an obvious support for the coal industry. The coal contracts frequently date from the era of State control of both coal and electricity. Passing on the higher costs in a monopoly environment is simple—the consumer has no choice and no escape route. In a competitive market, passing on costs is much more difficult, if not impossible, where the purchaser has a genuine choice. The negotiation of new coal contracts as the old contracts expire over time is therefore problematic. The generators want to force down the price of coal, a condition which the coal producers cannot meet as production costs are high. Accordingly, generators are moving away from coal, and UK coal is also losing out to cheaper imported coal. **13.109**

The result is that the coal contracts have to take account of many different factors. Presently, the generators agree to pay a high price (relative to other fuels) for coal, and the volume deliverable under the contracts reduces each year. The relatively short life of the contracts makes the subsidy acceptable to the European Commission as a transition measure to a liberalized market. It is unlikely that the Commission would be prepared to sanction a further heavy subsidy for the UK coal industry in the form of an obligation on generators to buy high-cost coal for a prolonged period. **13.110**

The nature of the coal industry in the UK has changed. Now wholly privatized, and heavily dependent on the coal contracts, its future is bleak. The Government's options to intervene in the liberalized market are limited. In effect, for the UK coal industry to survive a subsidy is required, but such subsidy is unlikely to find favour with the Commission. If high-priced coal contracts are still to be used as a form of subsidy, the cost of electricity effectively rises to maintain the coal industry. Such a policy decision will be difficult for any Government, but there is an additional complication in the UK as the Government does not directly control electricity prices (see further below). To raise electricity prices to meet the **13.111** scheme's costs would require the approval of the independent regulator, who would need to be convinced that the price increase is worth paying to secure the diversity of fuel sources; even then this only applies in the price regulated section of the market. It would be even more difficult to pass on a higher cost in the unregulated market, where the buyers are large users.

13.112 Accordingly the Government is presently trying a different approach. A moratorium on further consents for gas-fired power plants has been imposed, which should prevent further erosion of coal's share of the electricity fuel market during the moratorium. The moratorium is not accompanied by any inducement to buy coal: rather, the scheme relies on the generators having little option but to purchase coal as the total demand for power cannot be met from other plants. In this way, the Government clearly hopes to avoid difficulties with either State-aids provisions, or competition provisions. It is not entirely clear that the attempt will be successful, as the moratorium is discriminatory and inhibits the development of competition in generation. The counter argument, that diversity of supply is worth paying for, is not easily reflected in the constitution of a liberalized market or the enforcing of non-discriminatory competition law and State-aids rules. A further part of the strategy for coal is to redesign the wholesale electricity market, creating a bilateral contract trading market, although it is not clear how the change will operate to benefit coal. With the new trading arrangements coming slowly into place during 2001, the moratorium has been lifted.

13.113 The difficulty with the Government's approach is that it is not guaranteed to meet its aim of supporting the UK coal industry. It may support demand for coal—at least preventing demand rapidly falling further—but the effect may be to increase imported coal volumes rather than to secure a market share for domestically mined coal. As there is no link between the coal contracts and power generators (which would attract the immediate attention of the competition authorities, in particular the European Commission) there is no direct support for UK coal. It is simply an attempt to slow down the loss of the most important market for coal.

E. Gas Supply Industry

(1) Introduction: Privatization of the Gas Supply Industry

13.114 The privatization structure encompassed in the Gas Act 1986[78] was arguably fundamentally flawed. The Act simply moved the former monopolist, the British Gas Corporation, into the private sector as British Gas plc. The privatization was a

[78] The Gas Act 1986 has since been amended by the Gas Act 1995. The substantive structure of the privatization remains—the amendments merely seek to rectify some of the problems which plagued the early years of the liberalized industry.

triumph of ideology: the Government clearly believed that introducing the potential for competition created an incentive similar to that of true competition.[79] Such a belief was short-sighted in the extreme, particularly as it was applied to an industry containing elements of natural monopoly. Further, the gas industry is one where significant investment in infrastructure is frequently required—new participants face a significant barrier to entry into the market. There is also a time factor involved for entry into the market, even if it is only the time taken for a licence application to be approved and the licence issued. The net result of the ideological influence was that the structure of the industry under the Gas Act did not directly address the fundamental issue of competition—the Government effectively handed responsibility for the later development of competition to the industry regulator. The structure created by the Government was unlikely to lead to self-sustaining competition without regulatory intervention. Having said that, it is clear that regulatory intervention in the period since privatization has served to create a competitive market in gas.

With the change of ownership, the UK gas industry none the less underwent significant change. The fundamental effect of privatization is to move an industry (or a company) out of State control. The traditional argument against privatization of energy industries is that there is a strong element of strategic importance—the economy cannot function without reliable energy industries. Governments have traditionally considered that the best way to guarantee reliability was to perform the functions themselves (or through State companies) thereby ensuring a high degree of security of supply. The Gas Act completely rejected that view, demonstrating the belief that the private sector was entirely capable of ensuring sufficient security of supply. The Government chose both to privatize the gas industry and also liberalize through the development of competition. **13.115**

From a non-political viewpoint, the greatest justification for liberalization is its potential effect on the prices charged to consumers. In a state monopoly, the State sets prices and does not have to be responsive to the needs of consumers. The State monopoly has a service mentality and not a profit motive. Financial considerations are secondary to social obligations, whether in the form of service guarantees or of subsidies. By contrast, in a privatized system the interests of shareholders become paramount. The profit motive is the primary objective. In a wholly liberalized system[80] the price is set by the interaction between buyers and sellers. **13.116**

[79] Such belief is entirely consistent with the Chicago school of thought. The problem is not with the theory itself, but with its application to the gas industry. Where there is no barrier to entry into a market, clearly the threat of competition is credible. In the case of gas, the threat is less credible.

[80] The UK gas supply industry structure after privatization did not create full competition immediately. A monopoly threshold remained—the threshold has been progressively reduced, allowing an increasing number of customers to choose their supplier, and was entirely removed in 1998. Accordingly the UK took twelve years to reach complete liberalization.

Accordingly, prevention of abuse by a monopolist is extremely important, as such abuse is clearly against the public interest. The initial structure created under the Gas Act did not properly address this issue.

13.117 From an academic view, gas privatization in the UK is perhaps best viewed as an experiment which did not work at first, but which presented tremendous challenges to modify the concept into a fully competitive structure. However, account should also be taken of the practical cost of the delay. The benefits of privatization were not felt in the UK for some years after the Gas Act, leaving a significant opportunity cost to be borne. The scale of that cost is difficult to establish, but clearly, had the privatization mechanism been designed differently, the benefits would have been delivered earlier and the opportunity cost might have been reduced.

(2) Historical Overview: Scope of the Former Monopoly in the Gas Industry

13.118 The State monopoly in the United Kingdom related only to the transmission and distribution of gas. There was no State monopoly over production—any State involvement in hydrocarbon production disappeared with the demise of the British National Oil Corporation (BNOC).

13.119 The British Gas Corporation did, however, enjoy a privileged position as a State monopoly. It owned the onshore pipeline network, and was solely responsible for the transmission of gas to consumers. Further, it owned all the gas within its pipelines—its privileges included a monopoly purchase right for all gas from the United Kingdom sector of the North Sea. Given that the UK was a closed system in gas supply (a position only changed by the opening of the Bacton-Zeebrugge Interconnector) the State company held an extremely valuable (monopoly) right. In its role as sole buyer of gas, it could also dictate the pace of development of offshore gas resources—no producer would consider making the enormous investment required to bring a field into production without being certain that the product had a buyer. Further, no bank would have advanced money to a company for the development of a field without a buyer first being in place. The State company was the only possible buyer—it either bought all the gas from a field under a depletion contract[81] or the field remained undeveloped.

13.120 The existence of the monopoly purchase right therefore effectively enabled the Government through its State companies to determine the pace of offshore gas development. Such a power is wholly separate from the Government's right to approve development plans,[82] and accordingly when the Government transferred ownership

[81] A study of the merits of depletion contracts (for the whole production from a designated field) as opposed to a supply contract (for a volume of gas of specified quality without designating the field) is beyond the scope of this chapter. Depletion contracts are now rare—it is understood that none have been signed since 1991—and liberalization is the reason behind such a shift in gas sales arrangements.

[82] See Model Clauses—Petroleum (Production) (Seaward Areas) Regulations 1988 (as amended).

of the gas supply industry (and simultaneously abolished the monopoly purchase right) its ability to control the details of offshore development was largely unaffected.

Accordingly, gas production arrangements remained unaffected by the Gas Act. **13.121** Production is an inherently competitive activity given access to pipelines, and even under the monopoly purchase arrangements there was still competition in production. The producers had to compete to sell to the monopolist in the first place—British Gas Corporation was able to exploit its position to hold down wholesale prices,[83] a practice which was also changed by the abolition of the monopoly purchase right at the time of privatization.

(3) Contracts Existing at the Time of Privatization

The privatization structure did not adequately address the issue of the contracts **13.122** under which North Sea production entered the UK pipeline network. The State monopoly had a contractual right to all gas actually produced. As the monopolist was privatized intact, its private sector successor took up the benefit of the contracts. Accordingly, on the first day following privatization, British Gas plc (BG) stood alone as a supplier. It enjoyed a contractual right to all North Sea production—there simply was no gas for anyone else to sell. There was no alternative to intervention by the industry regulator to prompt gas release to competitors, in order that supply competition could be established whilst new fields were being developed for customers other than BG. The reluctance to release gas has also contributed to the present oversupply (strictly capacity for overproduction) in the United Kingdom, in that (potential) new suppliers had to find new sources of gas to sell to consumers. Accordingly, additional gas was added to a market which had limited growth prospects outside power generation—a recipe for oversupply, price volatility, and one of the causes of the 'take or pay' problems faced by the former monopolist. As competitors have taken a greater share of the gas market, BG has seen its share decline. Its obligations under the long-term contracts with producers are unchanged, so that effectively it has to buy gas for which there is no market. The contracts typically contain a 'take or pay' clause, such that BG must pay for a minimum quantity of gas even though it has not actually taken the gas. Given that there is limited offshore storage of gas, where there is no buyer the former monopolist must simply lower its nomination volume to the producer, leaving the gas in the ground, but it still must pay for a minimum quantity.[84]

[83] Efforts by the monopolist to hold down prices paid to producers created a considerable degree of resentment, recently been felt by BGC's successor in its efforts to find a solution to the liability for oversupply under 'take or pay' contracts.

[84] The minimum quantity will vary depending on the contract. Contracts negotiated before 1986 typically had high levels of minimum take, which was to be expected given that BG then enjoyed a supply monopoly. Whether the monopolist should have foreseen the removal of the monopoly right, and the reduced minimum take in contracts leading up to 1986, is an unanswerable question—although to have done so might have been viewed as the State monopoly acting in the interests of another rather than its own interests.

(4) Transmission Monopoly

13.123 The transmission monopoly has also been criticized for leading to the restriction of competition, but it should be viewed in an entirely different light from the problems caused by ignoring issues surrounding the production contracts. Transmission is a natural monopoly, characterized by extremely high development costs and relatively low operating costs. It is generally regarded as uneconomic to allow pipelines to be built in competition with each other—it is preferable to have a single line which is subject to regulation. In that way, the fixed cost is only taken into account once in setting the tariff.

13.124 At privatization the ownership and operation of all onshore pipelines was transferred to BG. It is worth bearing in mind that the State company did not have any interests in offshore pipelines—it was only responsible for gas transmission from the beach to consumer. Its successor simply took over that role.

(5) Creation of Supply Competition

13.125 British Gas plc also took over the State company's role as a supplier. The Gas Act did not envisage full competition being established immediately, rather it set a threshold above which there would be a competitive market, but below which BG would have a monopoly supply right. The threshold was initially set at 25,000 therms per year, which only allowed the biggest consumers the right to choose their supplier. All others had to purchase gas from the former monopolist. The threshold was progressively lowered before final abolition in 1998.

13.126 The result was that the privatization mechanism created a private sector entity with tremendous power. It was no longer a statutory monopoly, but on its first day it faced no competitors. It had lost the monopoly purchase right, but remained contractually entitled to all gas being produced at the time. It had a valuable transmission monopoly, and remained the monopoly supplier to the biggest sector of the market. British Gas plc was the world's largest privately owned gas company, created virtually as a monopolist and with the profit motive driving its actions. Controlling the new company was a task for the regulator.

(6) Regulation of the Gas Supply Industry

Director General of Gas Supply

13.127 The Gas Act provided for the creation of an independent regulator, the Director General of Gas Supply. The functions of the gas regulator have now been merged with the electricity regulator, to form the Director General of Gas and Electricity Markets and his office OFGEM. The regulator has a number of functions, but is primarily concerned with overseeing the development of competition. The regulator is solely concerned with the gas supply industry—he is a single industry regulator not a general competition watchdog. The office is additional to other competition bodies in the UK (the Competition Commission, formerly the Monopolies and Mergers Commission; the Office of Fair Trading) and not a substitute. It might be thought that the function of a single industry regulator is to create conditions for competition which render his existence meaningless—to do himself out of a job—but in the gas industry that can never be the case. The pipeline network is a natural monopoly and will always require price regulation; but the regulator is also concerned with other matters, including licensing. He is primarily, but not solely, an economic regulator—he is also given administrative functions.

The first Director General, Sir James McKinnon, faced a difficult task. His office (then called the Office of Gas Supply, OFGAS) was responsible for overseeing the development of competition in an industry characterized by monopoly. In terms of the Act, powers are given to the Director General personally, a characteristic of all UK utility regulators, which perhaps surprisingly does not appear to have had any practical adverse consequences. The Director General is appointed by the Secretary of State, but is entirely independent of political influence. He is appointed for a five-year term, and cannot be removed except on grounds of incapacity or misbehaviour.[85] The term is renewable. **13.128**

The concept of an independent regulator is fundamental to the operation of the liberalized gas market. The purpose of independence is to remove political interference. Judgements are made on economic grounds, rather than for political reasons. The price of gas (to customers who must buy from the monopolist) is not subject to direct political control. The UK regulators have on the whole retained public confidence. **13.129**

The duties of the Director General are varied, perhaps reflecting the difficult position faced by the regulator. He is independent of both Government and industry, yet surprisingly dependent on both to carry out his function. He cannot function effectively without the support of his political masters, and is equally dependent on the industry to provide information on which to base his decisions. OFGAS was particularly exposed to the risk of regulatory capture, in that it was (initially at least) entirely dependent on one source (BG) for information. Given that the source was also the regulated body, OFGAS risked receiving incomplete information. Had the privatization mechanism broken up the monopolist, the Director General would have been less at the mercy of the regulated. **13.130**

[85] See Gas Act 1986 s 1. It is far from clear what constitutes 'misbehaviour', although given that a court action would be required to remove a Director General who did not accept the Minister's view of what amounted to misbehaviour, the chances of abuse are reduced.

Role of regulator

13.131 The regulator will always be involved in setting the tariff for transmission, as the activity is a natural monopoly. In the UK the tariff is set for a five-year period, and reviewed at the end of that time. The issue is extremely controversial and has recently resulted in several references to the Competition Commission, formarly the General Monopolies and Mergers Commission (MMC) because the regulator and the pipeline company were unable to come to agreement; the Competition Commission largely agreed with the Director General. The debate focuses on the return which should be earned by the pipeline company on its assets. There is a question over how pipeline assets should be valued, an issue which is of critical importance to the pipeline company as the valuation will ultimately determine the level of revenue it is allowed to earn. It is clear that the regulator is entitled to determine the valuation mechanism.

13.132 The regulator is also involved in setting the consumer price of gas in a monopoly section of the market, a role which has not entirely disappeared even after all consumers have a choice of supplier. Prices for domestic consumers will still be subject to regulatory capping. Larger gas consumers, with greater bargaining power, do not need such protection, and the price for such consumers is set by the market. Regulatory capping of domestic gas prices is scheduled to be removed during 2001, although it is likely that there will be a delay as the former monopolist still dominates that section of the market.

13.133 In creating the independent regulator, the UK adopted a system of price regulation for monopolies.[86] The idea is simple but has wide-ranging effects. The regulator sets the increase in the price which the utility may charge the consumer. The increase is restricted to a certain level (the X factor) below the rate of inflation. The effect is to provide an efficiency incentive for the utility. For example, if X were to be set equal to the rate of inflation, there would be no real revenue increase for the utility. It must therefore cut costs to remain equally profitable, bearing in mind that inflation will affect its costs while the price control prevents a corresponding rise in its revenues. The incentive is increased by allowing the utility to keep any additional efficiency savings it might make. For example, if the formula requires a 2 per cent gain to maintain profitability, but the utility manages a 5 per cent efficiency gain, the extra 3 per cent is profit for the utility shareholders.

13.134 Setting the level of the X factor is extremely important. It effectively determines how much of a potential efficiency gain belongs to the shareholders and how much belongs to the consumers in the form of reduced prices. Where it is set too low,

[86] The RPI—X formula is generally credited as the invention of Professor Stephen Littlechild, formerly the UK electricity regulator. The formula restricts product price increases to a level (the X factor) below the retail price index, a measure of inflation.

companies which can make sizeable efficiency gains can make large profits. Where it is set too high, investing in utility shares is unattractive. Utilities are traditionally viewed as safe investments earning a return on an activity which does not involve any great degree of risk. However, if the X factor is low and efficiency gains are large, the utility's share price performance may be spectacular.[87]

(7) Duties of the Director General of Gas Supply

The duties of the Director General (which as noted above are shared with the Minister, but in practice authority is wholly delegated to the Director General) are aimed at ensuring that his functions are carried out 'in the manner which he considers is best calculated'[88] to secure that all reasonable demands for gas through pipes is satisfied so far as it is economical to do so. Further, he must secure that persons authorized to supply gas are able to finance their supply activities. **13.135**

In addition, he must carry out his functions in a manner he considers best calculated to protect the interests of consumers in respect of prices charged and other terms of supply; he must promote efficiency and economy on the part of suppliers, protect the public from the dangers associated with gas supply, and have particular regard to the interests of the disabled and those of pensionable age. **13.136**

It is apparent that the duties may conflict. The function of the regulator in this respect is to balance the interests of the consumers with the interests of shareholders. He may not always be able to satisfy both. Indeed, the duties may lead to insoluble conflict. The Director General's duty to secure that suppliers can finance their activities fundamentally conflicts with his duty to protect the interests of consumers, at least in the short term. Financing activities implies a high price, whilst consumers interests may be best served by a low price. **13.137**

At a more abstract level, the duty to secure that suppliers can finance activities may lead to a conflict with the duty to promote competition. The UK gas market is mature, in that no substantial demand growth is forecast. It is conceivable that the point could be reached where there are too many suppliers, and some cannot sustain their business. It is unclear whether the Director General might be liable for failing to secure that they could finance activities—might his issuing of a licence after that given to the insolvent company lead to a claim that he should have known that such expansion of the number of suppliers was unsustainable? The conflict can equally be applied in the other direction, in that where the Director General refuses to issue a licence on the grounds that there would then be too **13.138**

[87] Arguably the UK electricity industry is a case where the X factor was set too low—share prices rose dramatically indicating that shareholders were receiving more of the benefits from privatization than they had anticipated. Consumers accordingly lost out. Similar arguments can be made concerning British Gas.

[88] Gas Act 1986, s 4 (as amended), sets out the duties of the Director General; see also Gas Act 1995; Utilities and Competition Act 1992; Utilities Act 2000.

many licence holders for all to be able to finance supply activities, he can expect to be sued by the disappointed applicant. Further, it is not entirely clear whether activities have to be financed from income from supply business, or whether the Director General is able to take into account income from diversified activities. Clearly he has no right to direct suppliers to raise finance or restructure debt, yet the logical extreme of the duty is that he is a quasi-guarantor of the supply business. Whilst it is unlikely that the Director General would interpret his role in this way, it would be open to an insolvent licence holder to invite a judge to do so. The possibility of such a claim can only increase as competition in the gas market becomes more intense, although the chances of success are probably low.

13.139 Perhaps the most powerful duty is one which appears quite benign. The duty to secure effective competition in the carrying on of activities allows a determined regulator the opportunity to examine any anti-competitive behaviour in the sector.

13.140 The duties of the Director General were modified slightly under the Gas Act 1995, to include a duty to take account of the effect on the environment. The precise impact of such a duty is not clear, although it would be entirely appropriate for the regulator to insist on the production of environmental impact statements for activities in the industry, particularly for pipelines. Such statements might increase costs, but may also focus attention on problem areas.

Duty to secure competition

13.141 A further duty to secure competition in the conveyance of gas through pipes, and in the provision of gas to areas not previously served, is also important. The duty reflects the reality of the competitive gas market, which is fundamentally dependent on the activities of the transmission company. Given that transmission is a natural monopoly, there is a need for regulation. It is a practical impossibility to have actual competition in a pipeline, but the effects of competition can be reproduced by provision of third-party access. Third-party access fundamentally seeks to break the link between ownership of the pipeline and ownership of the product within that pipe. If the pipeline owner has no interest in the supply of gas (ie no interest in the product) he is encouraged to concentrate on his own activity, namely transmission. He is not in competition with the user of the pipe. Where a pipeline company is also a supplier, it may acquire an advantage for its own supply activities by denying third-party access to others. Where the link is broken, that incentive no longer exists.

13.142 The privatization of the British Gas Corporation did not address the ramifications of that link. The potential abuse was first addressed (after a lengthy Monopolies and Mergers Commission investigation, and an investigation by the Office of Fair Trading) by the creation of 'Chinese walls' between the supply arm and the transmission arm of BG. The approach was designed to ensure that BG supply did not have an inherent advantage over its rivals—access to pipelines would be on an equal footing. It is ironic that British Gas plc later decided to break itself into component parts, and separate ownership of the supply business (Centrica) from the transmission company (TransCo), a complete reversal of its position in defending itself from attack by the competition authorities.

(8) Statutory Third-Party Access to Onshore Pipelines

The Gas Act was revolutionary in the sense that it provided a mechanism whereby any supplier could acquire third-party access rights in the face of opposition (or unreasonable tariff requests) by the pipeline company.[89] The major strength of statutory third-party access is that it provides a stronger negotiating position for the supplier seeking access, as both sides know that the failure of negotiations means that a solution may be imposed. It may be preferable to negotiate one's own bad bargain than to take the risk of inviting a regulated solution. **13.143**

In terms of the Act, a supplier can gain the right to use a pipeline belonging to the former monopolist. A supplier cannot use the provision to gain access to offshore pipes, or to privately owned pipes, although there are comparable provisions in other statutes.[90] The Act envisages that the parties will first negotiate, and requires a notice period to the pipeline company, presumably designed to allow a period of reflection. The application for access rights is made to the Director General, who can give directions as to the terms and conditions of access provided he is satisfied that giving directions would not prejudice the existing operations of the pipeline—statutory third-party access is not an unqualified right. It is, however, frequently difficult to establish when a pipeline's capacity has actually been reached: the point at which the pipe is physically full is obvious, but the point at which it is contractually full is much less obvious as each user will have a range of nominated capacity.[91] It is for the Director General to satisfy himself that there is available capacity. **13.144**

Where the Director General is satisfied that there is sufficient capacity, he may give directions as to the terms on which the supplier and the pipeline company should enter an agreement. The directions may include securing the right to convey gas during a specified period; the right to convey a specified quantity; securing **13.145**

[89] See Gas Act 1986 s 19 (as amended). Rights to use processing facilities can be acquired under the Gas Act 1995 in similar fashion.

[90] See for example Petroleum and Submarine Pipelines Act 1975 s 23; Pipelines Act 1962 s 10, Petroleum Act 1998. In addition there is a voluntary code of practice governing the principles of negotiating terms and conditions of access.

[91] One danger of having a wholly independent pipeline company is that it might try to sign as many transportation agreements as possible, in an effort to ensure that total minimum nominations are as close as possible to the pipe's total physical capacity and thus maximize revenue. This might lead to problems when nominations increase as demand rises. The problem is partly mitigated by the use of 'send or pay' provisions, guaranteeing a certain level of income for the pipeline company.

that the exercise of the right is not impeded; regulating the tariff payable; securing supplies of back-up gas in the event of the supplier's failure to input gas to the system; and securing the supplier's right to connect his own pipe to the network system.

13.146 The biggest issue in pipeline access is likely to be the tariff. Unusually, section 19 of the Gas Act gives guidance as to matters which the Director General may properly take into account in determining the tariff, providing that the tariff should reflect the cost of service and a return on capital. The Act clearly envisages that the pipeline company is entitled to make a profit from third-party access deals, although determining the level of that profit remains contentious.

13.147 It is unclear what effect the demerger of the transmission business will have on the number of applications for statutory third-party access. The provision is still essential, if only to provide suppliers with an improved bargaining position in negotiation. The unanswered question is whether the demerger will actually change the incentive on the pipeline company: if the 'Chinese walls' were truly effective, there should be no difference whatsoever.

(9) Licensing Regime for the Gas Supply Industry

13.148 The first issue in looking at the gas supply industry is to ask why licensing is necessary. Privatization is partly premised on the idea that the gas industry is no different from any other—that its strategic role can be carried out as effectively by the private sector as by the public sector.

13.149 The justification for licensing is partly strategic and partly administrative. Moving the gas industry into the private sector does not diminish its strategic value, it simply means that the private sector is considered as trustworthy to perform the essential functions as its State-owned equivalent. Given that there is a strategic value, licensing is a manner of retaining State control. The system tries to ensure that only appropriate persons are allowed to participate in the industry. Secondly, given that the gas industry is characterized by its dependence on a natural monopoly, it is essential to identify which parties will be using these pipelines. Compelling participants to hold licences is a convenient way of identifying who is in the market for pipeline services. It also provides a manner of ensuring that all participants are subject to the same rules—the licence requirements are simply minimum conditions for participation in the industry. Conditions ensure that service standards are maintained in the competitive environment, and reduce the risk that insufficiently expert (or capitalized) companies will enter the market to the detriment of security of supply.

13.150 Under the 1986 Act, British Gas plc became the public gas supplier,[92] authorized to supply gas to mainland Britain. Other suppliers were authorized under section

[92] See Gas Act 1986 s 7. The Act does not name British Gas, but in practice the company was the only public gas supplier, permitted to supply gas in mainland Britain as its authorized area. The Gas Act would have permitted regional monopolists, but this option was not taken up as it would have necessitated the break-up of BG.

8, though such authorizations were actually restricted to the right to sell to consumers with a demand level in excess of the monopoly threshold.

Types of licence

However, the Gas Act 1986 has been amended in respect of the licensing regime. The basis of regulation is unchanged, namely that any person who transports gas through pipes, or arranges for gas to be transported through pipes, or supplies gas, commits an offence unless he holds the appropriate licence. The new regime, created by the Gas Act 1995, brings the gas supply industry more clearly into line with other privatized UK utilities. The terminology changes, replacing 'authorizations' with a clear licensing procedure. More importantly, it creates new categories of licences for the industry. **13.151**

Under the new regime, the Director General has power[93] to issue three distinct types of licence, reflecting the changed characteristics of the industry. The new regime matches the prohibitions to the manner in which the system operates, extending the licensing regime to those involved in arranging transport of gas with the pipeline company. The clause is clearly aimed at intermediary gas marketers, and recognizes that future development of the UK gas market may involve new participants in this role. For example, after full liberalization of the market there is no reason why banks or supermarkets should not become involved in the gas industry. Such companies are in a strong position to exploit the opportunities offered by the liberalization of the market—they have substantial customer bases and existing payment collection systems. However, they lack expertise in the operation of the gas industry, and accordingly may choose to enter the gas market in a joint venture with a recognized expert in the field. The co-venturer would arrange for the gas to be supplied, dealing with the pipeline company, and the bank/supermarket would deal with the consumer and payment. The new licensing system is designed to cope with such radical future developments. **13.152**

The new regime abolishes the concept of the public gas supplier. In its place is created the public gas transporter, which is in practice a single entity, now operating under the name TransCo. Theoretically, a number of public gas transporters could be created by the breakup of the company into regional operations, but there does not appear to be any compelling reason to do so. There are some other holders of public gas transportation licences over small areas covering new developments, which are effectively enclaves carved out of TransCo's licence, a welcome move in removing any remaining complacency in the pipeline company's operations. It is no longer guaranteed to be able to build new pipes to new developments. **13.153**

---

[93] Again, whilst power under the Act is shared between the Secretary of State and the Director, in practice the Director is wholly reponsible.

13.154 A person cannot hold both a transport licence and the second type of licence, the supply licence.[94] Again this is in recognition of how the industry operates in practice, introducing a clear distinction between the business of supply and that of transportation. It is statutory support for the removal of any interest by the transmission company in supply; it is ensuring that suppliers compete on an equal footing at least as far as transmission costs are concerned. It is a significant move away from the structure created at privatization, and a clear recognition of the shortcomings of that structure.

13.155 The supply licence deals with the area of the industry which is most easily opened to competition. Supply is the activity of contracting with a consumer to sell the product. It does not require large investment in infrastructure: the activity has relatively low barriers to entry. The most significant legal hurdle is to satisfy the Director General that the applicant is an appropriate person to hold a licence. In the absence of a history of financial irregularities or other undesirable activities, an applicant who can demonstrate his ability to perform the activity will be likely to obtain a licence. However, as the characteristics of the market change with the lowering of the threshold, there may be an increasing need for scrutiny of applicants in order to increase the protection of the consumer. The first consumers able to choose their supplier were large users, typically well able to look after their own interests. There is a risk that small consumers may not prove so adept, although the Gas Code (created under the Gas Act 1995) requirements for suppliers should provide some additional degree of consumer protection as well as offering existing suppliers a degree of protection from cut-price but incompetent entrants to the market.

13.156 The third type of licence is the shipping licence, for those who arrange the transport of gas with the public gas transporter. It is anticipated that most suppliers will also want to hold shipping licences; however, where a supplier has no experience of the gas industry he may prefer to purchase the shipping service from a specialist company. This is perhaps the way in which organizations with strong customer links but no direct gas experience will choose to enter the fully liberalized market.

(10) Operation of the Gas Market: The Network Code

13.157 The principle reason for creating the new third licence, the shipping licence, was to reflect the way in which the gas supply market operates. The activity of dealing with the transmission company is viewed as a distinct operation, and is likely to become increasingly important as the operation of the Network Code[95] is more

[94] See Gas Act 1995 s 7(3).

[95] The Network Code essentially sets out the rules for use of the transmission network. The Code regulates the relationship of the shippers and suppliers with the transmission company. Finally implemented in April 1996, the Code represents a fundamental industry change in terms of the responsibility for balancing the system. The Code is a contract between shipper/suppliers and the pipeline company, the terms of which are approved by the regulator.

clearly understood. The Code represents a fundamental change in the way in which the pipeline system is operated. Under the State monopoly there was no real need for an equivalent of the Code, as balancing of supply and demand could readily be carried out given that there was only one supplier. As the competitive gas market gradually expanded after privatization more suppliers became involved. The physical operation of the network is perhaps more difficult (as there is no longer one person deciding where the inputs to the onshore network will be made on any particular day) and billing arrangements ever more complex as consumers changed suppliers. Identifying which supplier is to be paid by which consumer is one of the major issues of the Network Code—the issue fundamentally affects the revenue of suppliers and is therefore critical to the success (or otherwise) of the liberalized market. Removing the monopoly threshold has increased the difficulty many times over, and is one of the reasons why trials in selected areas were carried out in the run-up to full liberalization.

The question of payment of suppliers is dependent on the accuracy of metering. **13.158** At privatization, licensing arrangements were effectively divided into the industry's component activities, but perhaps surprisingly metering was not singled out as a unique sector. Instead metering remained inextricably bound to supply, that is, the supplier took over metering. There appears to have been inadequate recognition of the value and place of metering in the gas industry.

Metering is also fundamental to the operation of the Network Code. The most **13.159** striking provision of the Network Code is its implementation of the concept of daily balancing. The requirement is simple: each day, each supplier must input an equivalent amount of gas to the system as his consumers collectively withdraw. The requirement represents a defining moment in how the UK gas industry operates. It fundamentally changes the responsibility for balancing, taking it away from the pipeline company and placing the onus squarely on the supplier. Satisfying the requirement essentially involves metering.

Where a supplier is not in balance he is subject to a financial penalty. The pipeline **13.160** company (TransCo) is financially neutral in that balancing is not primarily its responsibility—it simply receives a payment for its services of moving the gas. The penalty under the Network Code is quite severe, covering costs associated with the pipeline company having to act as balancing agent of last resort, and is accordingly a strong incentive to take virtually any steps to return to balance. There are various ways in which a supplier may seek to balance his inputs with his customers' offtake. The most obvious is demand management. If all customers take a specified amount of gas each day there is no difficulty in balancing, as the supplier simply matches the volume to the contract with the producer. The problem is that such customers are rare—gas is traditionally used for space heating and accordingly demand will tend to fluctuate with the weather and temperature. The alternative is to cap demand in some way, whether by means of a price incentive (high price for gas over a certain limit) or by interruptible contract will depend on the willingness of the supplier to seek balancing by other means.

13.161 The other means of balancing are in the direct control of the supplier rather than in the hands of co-operative consumers. The Code provides for a degree of flexibility. The supplier who is short of gas (consumers' demand exceeds the supplier's expected input volume to the pipeline) has a number of options. He can buy gas from a supplier who has an excess, a course of action which will almost certainly cost him a premium on the price, but which is probably cheaper than paying the penalty. The flexibility mechanism operated by TransCo aims to make such a market less ad hoc and more predictable. Gas can also be purchased on the spot market.[96]

13.162 Alternatively, the supplier can take gas out of storage. Whilst it is not possible to store gas in any significant quantity within the pipeline network, it is possible to store gas in disused or depleted offshore fields. Excess production is pumped into the store, typically during the summer months when demand is low, and can be extracted as needed during the winter. It is likely to be essential for all suppliers to have gas held in storage to assist in the balancing requirements. The storage arrangements are dictated by the Network Code.

13.163 In similar fashion, the supplier may seek to alter the nomination made to the offshore producer selling the gas. Again there may be an additional cost involved, depending on the sales contract, but paying that cost may be preferable to paying the penalty.

13.164 If all efforts fail to cure the imbalance, the pipeline operator (TransCo) will balance the system upon payment of the penalty. The size of the penalty is crucial in determining the incentive for suppliers. Imposing a large penalty means that suppliers have a very strong incentive to take steps to avoid it. The difficulty is that as competition in the market develops, in the event that suppliers (or some suppliers) lose the ability to predict demand as their customers meters are infrequently read, a company in difficulty with balancing will spend more time arranging to correct the imbalance than in carrying out its core activity of gas supply. The biggest risk is that the threat of the penalty will make suppliers unwilling to take on certain categories of consumer. If that is the case, the development of the market will be hindered unless the scale of the penalty is reduced, or the balancing period is extended beyond one day. There are, however, no signs of change in responsibility for balancing. Equally, experience to date is that companies can

[96] The International Petroleum Exchange now offers a gas contract; development of standard terms (quality, quantity, delivery point) acceptable to industry participants has increased the attractiveness of trading in this way. Gas traded on the spot market is not for instant delivery, which means that there is still a role for the flexibility mechanism.

learn to use the various options to balance even on days of extreme demand fluctuation.

The penalty therefore effectively determines which party bears the cost of balancing supply and demand on the pipeline network. Currently the penalty is high enough to move the responsibility to suppliers. If the penalty was very low (lower than the costs of other forms of balancing measures) then responsibility would effectively move to the pipeline company—an undesirable result given that the aim of separating the functions of the industry was to ensure that the pipeline company is only involved in transit issues. **13.165**

(11) Development of the Competitive Market

It is clear that the structure of the UK gas industry created under privatization was incapable of spontaneously developing a competitive market. Since privatization tremendous progress has been achieved, and the structure of the industry has been altered by regulatory action. The biggest change has been in the relationship of the pipeline operator with the former monopolist as supplier—with the (voluntary) demerger, there is now complete separation of ownership of the respective businesses as well as operational control. **13.166**

Competition policy

In its approach to competition policy, the Government has placed a heavy emphasis on the distinction between ownership and operational control. There has been general acceptance, at least within the gas industry, that independence of management and accounting is sufficient to create the same incentive as would exist where the two businesses were separately owned. Starting with the introduction of 'Chinese walls' between the pipeline operation and the supply operation, and culminating in the demerging of the businesses, separation of the activities has underpinned the development of competition. **13.167**

If the Government had accepted the concept of divestment, it might have been seen as impliedly admitting that it erred in creating the structure for the gas industry under privatization, which admission might have been costly in political terms. The passage of time, however, reduces any potential embarrassment. Market conditions might reasonably be expected to change over time, and the Government becomes less possessive about the original structure. **13.168**

Practical measures

Over time, the Government was able to accept a number of extremely important recommendations arising out of competition investigations which helped the development of the gas supply market. Such regulatory action included the placing of an obligation on the former monopolist to publish firm price schedules. At **13.169** the very minimum, this created a starting point for consumers within the tariff market (those with demand above the monopoly threshold) to negotiate prices with other suppliers. It arguably gave an advantage to the new suppliers in seeking to win consumers from the former monopolist. Linked to that was the requirement for publication of tariffs for third-party access, again aimed at assisting suppliers to win customers. Publication of the tariff at least enabled the supplier to establish his cost base in negotiations with a potential consumer.

13.170 Another fundamental measure which developed competition in the market, but which had largely unforeseen effects, was the gas release programme. Developed in an effort to circumvent the problem of the former monopolist being contractually entitled to all gas produced from the UK sector of the North Sea, the gas release programme ensured that British Gas could not buy all the product from new fields. It was not designed to have an instantaneous effect. Its aim was long-term development of the gas market, by ensuring that there was gas for others to sell.

Needs of new suppliers

13.171 The difficulty was that the programme did not address the immediate need of the new suppliers. As outlined above, there was an incentive to bring new fields into production leading ultimately to overproduction, price volatility, and the 'take or pay' problem.

13.172 At the time, however, allowing development of new fields did not seem to be creating a problem. Indeed it solved an immediate need. It was also thought that the market for gas would increase, that is, that demand for gas would expand. The former monopolist was not particularly concerned with losing market share, as it assumed it would simply have a smaller share of a bigger market and accordingly still be selling at least an equivalent volume of gas. The anticipated increase in demand was expected to come from power generators building gas-fired plant; from the Interconnector allowing export to the vast western European gas markets; and also from increased use of natural gas as fuel for the transport sector.

13.173 In the immediate aftermath of the liberalization of the electricity industry there was a move by electricity generators towards building new plants to generate cheap electricity. Gas was viewed as a means of providing cheap power, and the newly privatized electricity companies considered building several new stations. These stations were intended as substitutes for existing, higher-cost (usually coal-fired) plant. There was tremendous expectation of a corresponding increase in demand for gas, which had formerly not been used for power generation as Governments believed it could be put to better uses.

13.174 The expected 'dash for gas' did not materialize. Many of the proposed power stations were never built, probably because they were not strictly necessary in the first place. Demand was not able to support so many new plants; substitute capacity was not needed to that extent as the generators were compelled by the coal contracts to purchase coal in any event, and would have had to continue to do so even after the gas plants were built (at least until the coal contracts expired). The effect on the gas supply market was quite dramatic, in that the expected increase in demand was much less than anticipated. This unfulfilled expectation also contributed to the oversupply of gas.

Problems of oversupply: incentive for a spot market

The oversupply problem in the UK reached a point where gas was produced with no contracted buyer. The excess gas provided the impetus for the growing spot market in the UK, although the actual market is probably better described as an ad hoc rather than a true spot market. Commodity exchange trading of gas, in the same way as oil is traded on exchange, is in its early stages and continues to develop. Sales of the excess production did, however, cause further problems for the former monopolist, in that it permitted the development of a spot price for gas. Given the oversupply, the spot price was significantly lower than the price paid for gas under the existing long-term contracts with producers, which in turn created tension within the long-term contracts. There was a price incentive to break the contracts, but the producers were not prepared to allow the suppliers (including the former monopolist) to escape. The suppliers were left to ponder whether they should buy cheap gas in the spot market and lose some of that gain under the 'take or pay' penalty in the long-term contract. In most cases there is no real quandary for the supplier as the financial penalty is equivalent to the contract price, but where the penalty is lower (for example where make-up rights can be invoked) there may be a commercial incentive to turn away from the contract and embrace the spot market. **13.175**

There is little doubt that the UK can expect to continue its experience of overproduction for some years. There will probably still be gas to sell in the developing spot market, and as exchange-based trading develops greater volumes, there is less incentive to enter long-term contracts in the future. As long as the exchange's standard terms are acceptable to the industry, and workable in practice, the trading of gas is likely to become ever closer to the trading of oil. Gas can never have a world market as it is pipeline constrained, but the principle is the same. The danger then is that financing of new gasfields becomes difficult—lenders are used to seeing gas sold before production comes onstream. Oil developments overcame the problem, but given the lack of a world market it may take longer for gas to achieve the same level of trust and acceptance by the lenders. **13.176**

F. Electricity Supply Industry

(1) Introduction

13.177 The UK electricity supply industry was privatized by the Electricity Act 1989. The Conservative Thatcher Government had considerable experience of privatizations, having been in office for almost a decade.[97] It had the benefit of lessons learned from the gas privatization. Indeed, many of the issues relevant to the gas industry discussed above are equally relevant in the electricity industry. The regulatory structure created, including the duties of the regulators, were virtually identical.

13.178 The position in Scotland is different from that in England and Wales. The market in Scotland is much smaller by volume yet geographically quite diverse. Before 1989 Scotland was served by two State companies. The companies were privatized, and liberalization was introduced in the sense that new generators and suppliers could enter the market. However, the transmission system in Scotland remains part of the two privatized former State companies; there is no separate transmission entity. There remains a link in ownership between transmission, distribution, and supply. In effect, the system consists of two vertically integrated companies, with the opportunity for other companies to establish generation businesses or supply businesses. The vertical integration link can be criticized for its potential to limit competition, but the jurisdiction is small and dealing with the issue (by means of requiring transparency and non-discrimination) is thought sufficient to deal with the problem.

13.179 Northern Ireland also has a separate electricity system, which also exhibits a degree of vertical integration. The primary difficulty in Northern Ireland is, however, at generation level; the Province is small and there are very few plants. The wholesale price of electricity is higher than in the rest of the United Kingdom, although efforts by the regulator have started to address those issues.

13.180 The major interest in the UK electricity industry is in the structure for England and Wales, which has attracted considerable comment and indeed has provided a model for reform in other jurisdictions. The following section focuses on England and Wales.

(2) Historical Overview of the Electricity Supply Industry

13.181 The State monopoly over electricity was more far-reaching than its gas equivalent. The gas monopoly did not cover production, whilst the electricity monopoly embraced all sections of the industry—generation, transmission, distribution, and

[97] Utility privatizations were a particular feature of the general privatization programme, including sale of the telecoms industry, the gas industry, and the water industry.

supply. The monopoly was in two separate stages. The most important State company, the Central Electricity Generating Board (CEGB) was responsible for generation and transmission activities. Following on from that, there were twelve regional monopolies, the Area Boards, which dealt with distribution and supply. However, the CEGB was in real control of the system, with the Area Boards subordinate.

The CEGB had watched as the gas industry was privatized, and had seen the State monopoly moved in its entirety to the private sector. There was a reasonable expectation that the same privileged treatment would be afforded to the CEGB. It was a considerable shock to the corporation that the privatization structure proposed to break it up into its constituent activities. **13.182**

In similar fashion to the gas industry, the electricity industry is characterized by a natural monopoly element. Transmission (at high voltage), together with distribution (low-voltage connection into consumer sites) are both natural monopolies, and accordingly the arguments applicable to the gas transporter are equally applicable to these activities. The crucial question is again the relationship of the natural monopoly to the supplier. As outlined above, in the gas industry linking the transmission company to a supplier led to difficulties in establishing the competitive market. The Government was not slow to learn the lesson (even if it was reluctant to acknowledge it publicly). Accordingly, the Government was no longer persuaded by the State company that break-up would lead to operational difficulty. The Government was prepared to consider (and indeed implemented) a privatization scheme to break the industry into its constituent parts. **13.183**

Generation is a fundamentally competitive activity. There is no reason why all plant need be owned by the same person—indeed, to facilitate the creation of a price mechanism and the fostering of a price incentive, it is desirable that there be a large number of generators. The Act sought to ensure that after privatization there would be a truly competitive market in generation. The UK electricity industry is characterized by an excess of generation capacity, which made the creation of a competitive market less difficult. **13.184**

Generation in the UK utilizes several different fuel sources. Diversity of fuel sources is considered beneficial, limiting dependence on any one given source and improving the security of supply. The UK generators have coal-fired plant; oil-fired plant; gas-fired plant; nuclear stations; a small amount of hydro power; and some small renewable energy projects. The Government considered it important to retain that diversity after privatization, although it would no longer be directly within State control. The difficulty is that the liberalized market does not always deliver diversity, as shown by the problems experienced in selling coal to the electricity generators. Where the State gives up ownership of generation companies it **13.185** cannot expect to retain full control over their investment policies. In particular, the strong commitment to nuclear power also required to be reassessed, although it is difficult to see why the individual private generators should share the views of Government as to the desirability of fuel diversity.

(3) Structure of the Industry After Privatization

13.186 The break-up of the CEGB therefore had to take account of several objectives. First, there was to be separation of the functions of generation and transmission. Accordingly, responsibility for transmission was given to a new company, National Grid. Secondly, the successor generation companies had to be viable while taking account of the need for diversity. The problem was the nuclear stations, which were regarded as relatively high-cost, and in particular had an unknown liability for decommissioning. The initial proposal was to create two generators. National Power would take around 70 per cent of existing generating plant, including the nuclear stations. PowerGen would take the remaining 30 per cent. The idea was that the bigger company needed the 'extra' plant to help pay for the costs of the nuclear stations. The proposal, however, was defeated by strong opposition, which clearly thought that selling the nuclear stations was not possible given the unknown decommissioning costs. Such costs are by definition unknown as Governments have not given any guidance or enacted any laws specifying precisely what is required in the decommissioning of a nuclear reactor. It is, for example, unknown whether the reactor core can be left on site, or whether it has to be removed, and if so to where.

13.187 The result was that the Government changed its mind as to the structure of the privatization of generators. It removed the nuclear stations from privatization, creating a new State-owned company (Nuclear Electric) to own and operate the plant. Nuclear Electric was not a traditional State company, but a private company registered under the Companies Acts, but with all its shares owned by the Secretary of State. It followed that no further parliamentary approval would be required for the future sale of the company.

13.188 The decision to withdraw the nuclear plants from privatization was taken relatively late. It meant that there was no time to reassess the effect on the other proposed generators, the sale of which went ahead as planned. However, this meant that there were no longer two equally strong companies in the generation market. National Power was strengthened by the removal of the nuclear stations—although there would be a third generator, Nuclear Electric, in the market.

13.189 The twelve Area Boards were also privatized as the Regional Electricity Companies (RECs). The activities of distribution and supply were, perhaps surprisingly, not separated. The RECs were put in a strong position, having monopoly distribution rights over the authorized area, together with a supply monopoly to consumers within that area whose demand was below the monopoly threshold. The RECs were also protected from takeover by means of a Government-held 'golden share', for a period of five years until 1995, allowing the companies the opportunity to develop their knowledge of the business and become more efficient. Since the expiry of the golden share there has been considerable takeover activity.

Failure to separate distribution (localized low-voltage transmission) from supply might have led to similar problems in the electricity industry as were experienced in the gas industry. The potential for abuse undoubtedly still exists, but separation of accounting to enable cross-subsidies to be identified helps avoid damage to the competitive market. However, there is no doubt that the experience in other utilities of separation of ownership of the natural monopoly element from ownership of the supply business may lead to increased pressure for reform of the RECs. Such pressure may grow after the introduction of full competition to the supply market. **13.190**

The privatization therefore resulted in the creation of a competitive generation market, but dominated by two major players. In addition there was the nuclear generator, and the opportunity for other generators to join the market. The mechanism had provided for competition from the first day of the new market—a significant improvement on the same stage in the gas industry. On the supply side, there were a series of regional monopolists serving consumers below the monopoly threshold, and the possibility of larger consumers having a choice of supplier. The Government's decision to break up the State monopoly seemed set to lead to more rapid development of competition. **13.191**

(4) Ownership of the Grid Infrastructure

The first significant alteration to the privatization structure came five years after privatization, and involved the transmission company, National Grid plc. Under the privatization mechanism the RECs had taken substantial shares in the company. However, in an effort to preserve the distinction between transmission and supply businesses, the RECs were required to divest themselves of their shares in the Grid. The same company could not own both a supply business and a stake in the high-voltage transmission business, although to date there has been no equivalent move towards separating supply from distribution. **13.192**

(5) Regulation of the Electricity Industry

In common with other utility privatizations, including gas, there is provision in the Electricity Act for the creation of an independent regulator.[98] The regulator, the Director General of Electricity Supply, is given a broadly similar range of **13.193**

[98] See Electricity Act 1989 s 1.

powers to those held by the gas regulator. The Office of Electricity Regulation (OFFER) is again charged with overseeing the development of a competitive market, although in the electricity supply industry the task was made easier by the break-up of the State monopoly. The structure was more likely to lead to self-sustaining competition.

13.194 Following the 1998 government review of the utility regulation,[99] the energy sectoral regulators were merged. The Office of Gas Supply and the Office of Electricity Regulation have jointly become the Office of Gas and Electricity Markets. The rationale behind the merger is simply that the two industries share many common threads. There is increasing convergence between the industries as more gas is used for power generation. The liberalized structure of the industries is broadly similar. Both are fundamentally dependent on a network to transport the energy. The Review eventually led to the Utilities Act 2000, which formalized the regulatory merger. The Utilities Act also gives an additional power to the Minister to give general directions to the regulator. Whilst it is possible that such a power could undermine the independence of the regulator, it is clear that the Minister has no right to intervene in a specific case. The extent of use of the power remains to be seen.

13.195 The crucial aspect of regulation is that where there is no competitive market, the independent regulator is involved in setting the tariff for the service. Accordingly, he will always be involved in setting tariffs in respect of transmission of electricity, and also the tariff in respect of distribution. Once again the emphasis is on price control rather than rate of return regulation, and again use is made of the RPI—X formula.[100] The incentive created by restricting price increases has been the central change in the way in which companies operate—State monopolies need pay little regard to price incentives, but it is the primary driver of the behaviour of private companies.

13.196 The problem which the UK has faced has been to reconcile the views of the regulator as to the size of the efficiency gain a company should make, and the size of the gain which the company has actually been able to make. Under the UK system a company keeps any gain beyond that required by the regulator. There is little doubt that shareholders have received considerable benefits as a result of the price controls being perhaps not as onerous as might have been justified. The regulator's duty to secure that licensees can finance the carrying on of their activities might justify his taking a cautious approach, but assuming that the share price performance is an indicator of the benefit accruing to the shareholder, it is clear that the

[99] DTI, *Review of Energy Sources for Power Generation*, October 1998.

[100] RPI—X seeks to mimic the effects of competition by providing a target gain. It operates by restricting price increases to a certain amount (x) less than inflation (retail price index). The effect is to restrict income, hence setting a target for efficiency gains necessary for the company to maintain profit.

companies have been able to extract much greater efficiency gains than the regulator had required. Indeed, the electricity regulator chose to re-examine the last revision to the formula in the light of the great rises in electricity company share prices immediately after his first announcement. The problem is firstly one of information—the regulator is fundamentally dependent on the companies to give him access to the required information—and secondly one of interpretation. The regulator in setting the X factor is determining how big an efficiency gain he believes the companies should be able to make. However, in doing so he is second-guessing the management of the companies, who should know the individual business better than the regulator. Accordingly there may be room for efficiency gains which the regulator does not see—not because he may be incompetent but simply because he is not involved in the day-to-day running of the business.

The electricity regulator is also involved in setting the tariff for electricity used by consumers whose annual demand is below the monopoly threshold.[101] The regulator has continued to be involved in a form of price capping for domestic consumers after full liberalization. Accordingly it may be seen that the RECs operate a largely regulated business—each has a local monopoly over distribution. Domestic consumer prices are controlled. The only segment of the market where their business is in competition with others is in supply to the non-tariff market (large consumers). **13.197**

In a similar fashion to the gas industry, the electricity regulator is required to issue annual reports. He is not directly accountable to Parliament, but his report is laid before Parliament and it is possible that a Parliamentary committee might ask him to appear before it to respond to concerns. **13.198**

(6) The Electricity Act: Licensing

The primary means of regulating the industry is by requiring participants to hold licences. Once again, it is worth asking why such a licence is required, and again the licence requirement is justified on strategic grounds. Under privatization the Government gave up ownership of the industry. Licensing is its method of retaining a degree of control in a structure where the Government can no longer influence decisions through ownership rights. The licence is also a convenient method of identifying those involved in the industry, that is, establishing who is the subject of regulation as well as being the instrument of control over that participant. **13.199**

It is an offence[102] to carry out generation, transmission, distribution, or supply activities without holding a licence issued by the Director General. Each activity has **13.200**

---

[101] Monopoly threshold is currently an annual demand of under 100kW, gradual abolition of the threshold and introduction of full competition by region will complete the competitive market. The threshold was finally removed in late 1998.

[102] See Electricity Act 1989 s 4.

its own licence,[103] although there is no direct control of vertical integration by barring the holding of more than one type of licence.[104] Together with divestment of the grid, vertical integration is instead controlled by way of general competition law, although the former approach of preventing generators taking over supply companies has recently been relaxed.

13.201 The generation licence is arguably the most important stage of the industry, as the generators establish the initial cost of electricity. Establishing competition in generation is accepted as the most powerful instrument of controlling such costs—competition is the means by which cheap generation is ensured.

Generators

13.202 The incentive for cheap generation may, however, conflict with the desire for diversity of fuel source. The 'dash for gas' immediately after privatization was one illustration of the problem. Generators have an incentive to move away from high-cost sources, even to the extent that there is heavy reliance on one particular fuel source. Currently, the cheapest form of generation of electricity is from gas, and accordingly generators will first consider building gas-fired plant. There is little sign of new or proposed investment in coal-fired or nuclear plant which is regarded as higher cost than gas. The danger is that the incentive leads to over-reliance on gas as the fuel source. If there is then a sudden rise in gas prices, or a sudden restriction in gas supply, the electricity industry would face a serious problem and inevitably the price of electricity would rise.

13.203 Generating electricity from gas may conceivably create a systemic risk. Particularly where gas demand is very high in winter, power stations must be able to guarantee their supply in order to continue to generate electricity. If generators elect to buy gas under interruptible contracts, and supply is cut off in terms of the contract as total demand for gas rises, there is a corresponding reduction in the available electricity capacity. If demand for electricity is also high there may also be insufficient capacity or a short-term rise in the price. In the event that generation becomes dominated by gas, perhaps generators should be barred from buying gas under interruptible contracts.

Transmission

13.204 The second form of licence, the transmission licence, is held by National Grid plc. It is a wholly regulated business. Similarly the RECs have monopoly licence rights over distribution within their geographical areas. The justification for the single licence is simply that it is thought to be economically inefficient to build competing

[103] The Act gives responsibility to both the Secretary of State and the Director, although in practice responsibility is wholly that of the Director.

[104] Unlike the gas supply industry, where a transporter cannot also be a supplier.

grids. Grids are characterized by having high building (sunk) costs, and relatively low ongoing (operating) costs. Accordingly, using only one grid (and allowing third-party access) removes the need to invest heavily in additional infrastructure, and has the benefits of low operating costs.

Supply

The monopoly supply business of the RECs, also a wholly regulated business, is licensed separately from the right to supply the non-tariff market (the competitive segment of the market where consumers have a choice). Such second-tier suppliers represent the only competitive area of the supply market. The market will be extended to include all consumers with the removal of the monopoly threshold. **13.205**

(7) Purpose of Licensing

Licensing is intended to control the activities of participants in the electricity supply industry. It is also intended to ensure that there is a common standard for quality of electricity, ensuring that the product is homogeneous. There is no possibility of a company competing on the ground that its electricity is in some way superior to other electricity. All electricity is identical and the only differentiation can be with respect to price. The Government is still involved in regulation of quality, safety, etc, but the liberalized market means it is not involved in establishing the price. **13.206**

Obligation to supply

The abolition of the State monopoly creates a difficult problem in relation to the traditional obligation of universal service—the obligation to supply. In the gas industry there was initially little difficulty as the monopoly remained intact, but with the advent of competition the gas industry faces the same problem. The issue is essentially who bears the obligation to supply. The Electricity Act 1989 provided[105] that the obligation should be borne by suppliers. Where a supplier holds a monopoly, bearing such a burden is entirely appropriate. However, where the monopoly is removed and there is a fully competitive market that justification is no longer available. Placing the obligation to supply on all licensed suppliers is an obvious step, but is not a complete answer as it effectively allows a consumer to elect which supplier should bear the burden. If all consumers were to choose the same supplier that might create a heavy cost to that supplier and put him at a competitive disadvantage—he is unable to focus on other business. The answer would be to create some form of rationing mechanism by which the burden is undertaken in rotation, although that is unlikely to be easy to achieve in practice. The wider question is whether the obligation to supply is compatible with the competitive market. **13.207**

[105] S 16.

Vertical integration and licensing

13.208 The single most striking feature of the UK electricity privatization is its separation of the various activities into different businesses. The mechanism was designed to avoid vertical integration (which was perceived as a problem in the gas industry). The licensing regime is designed to support that structure, although there is no absolute bar on the holding of more than one type of licence. Controls over vertical integration in the electricity industry are accordingly by means of general competition law.

13.209 With clearances to allow generators to take over RECs, and the increasing amount of generating plant owned or controlled by RECs, there is a danger that such increased vertical integration will undermine the fundamental aim of separation.

13.210 Vertical integration was not an issue in the early years of the liberalized industry, as the Government retained a 'golden share'[106] allowing it to prevent unwanted takeovers. The expiry of the 'golden share' in 1995 changed the picture, allowing the possibility of takeovers. Encouraged by the financial performance of the RECs, and the opportunity to continue such performance over the next five-year regulatory cycle, there were numerous potential buyers, although the RECs were occasionally able to mount a strong defence.

13.211 The majority of RECs are no longer independent. Most have been taken over by outside companies, which has not in itself altered the competitive structure of the market.

Vertical integration and multi-utilities

13.212 There have, however, been takeovers of some RECs by the (privatized) water utility in the same geographical area. The creation of such multi-utilities has obvious attractions in that there is an opportunity to save on the costs of dealing with consumers—for example, billing costs should be reduced. However, as the customers of the merging utilities are likely to have substantial overlap, growth potential is likely to be limited.

13.213 Multi-utilities involved in different industries do not pose the same problems for the competition authorities as are created by vertical integration. The issue of vertical integration first arose in the takeover of one REC, Manweb, by Scottish-Power. The purchaser already owned generating plant, leading to the risk that it might be tempted to sell self-generated electricity to its own supply business. The

[106] The golden share was a special voting right given to the Government to block takeovers. It allowed the company a period of time to become used to the competitive environment before it was subject to potential takeover. The share served no other purpose—it did not allow the Government to control the operation of the company, or nominate directors etc. It simply preserved the independence of the company for a set period of five years.

risk is that the transfer is not carried out at the prevailing market price. The takeover was, however, allowed to go ahead, creating a degree of vertical integration to be controlled by the imposition of various licence conditions to prevent abuses.

13.214 The Government took a completely different approach to proposed takeovers of RECs by the main generators, National Power and PowerGen. The Monopolies and Mergers Commission (now the Competition Commission) investigated the proposed takeovers and recommended that they be allowed to go ahead subject to conditions to prevent abuses. The Government, which is not bound to accept MMC recommendations, did not agree. The Secretary of State barred the proposed takeovers as incompatible with the public interest. The crucial question was control of vertical integration, and the Minister evidently considered that the best protection from abuse was separation of ownership. The strong line taken by the Government was in contrast to its earlier views, and also in contrast to its views on allowing RECs to acquire generation capacity. However, with a change of Government there was also a change of emphasis. The strong defence of the ideals of the privatization structure was not supported by the present Government, which has permitted PowerGen to acquire a supply business subject to conditions (involving capacity shedding) aimed at creating greater competition in the generation sector. Vertical integration is increasing in the industry, with the potential for abuse being controlled by licence conditions (principally the economic purchasing obligation, discussed further below), requirements for separation of accounts, and general competition law. It is debatable whether such controls are as effective as requirements for separate ownership.

Vertical integration and capacity shedding

13.215 Due to potential excessive control of the electricity pool by the main generators (discussed below), the regulator had established a programme of capacity shedding. In effect the programme forced the generators to sell plant, thereby reducing their market share and their ability to influence the pool price. Potential purchasers of the plant included the RECs. Such purchases were not initially opposed, permitting backward vertical integration. Opposition to forward vertical integration was maintained for some time (a patently ridiculous distinction) but has now been abandoned. However, where generators have expressed an interest in acquiring supply businesses, the Director and the competition regulators (including the Minister) have taken the opportunity to consider forcing additional capacity shedding.

(8) The Electricity Price: Pooling

13.216 The UK privatization created a complex arrangement for the wholesale market in electricity. The electricity pool is a consequence of the licensing regime rather than being established directly under the Act. It is a condition of licences that all generators (including co-generators selling excess power from their own sites into the network), together with all suppliers, be members of the pool. It is also a condition that all trading of electricity take place through the pool—selling outside the pool is not permitted.

13.217 The electricity pool is created by the Pooling and Settlement Agreement between all generators and all suppliers. It creates a mechanism for establishing the wholesale price of electricity, and provides the first mechanism for balancing supply and demand. It is fundamentally the means by which cheap generation is encouraged.

13.218 Electricity cannot be stored (except indirectly in pumped storage schemes). Accordingly, there must be a system to balance supply with demand—to decide which power stations run at which times. The pool tries to establish a basis for selection of power stations, by creating a ranking order based on bidded cost of generation.

Operation of the pool

13.219 The pool operates by dividing the day into 48 half-hour segments, starting at 6am. On the day before, each plant bids a quantity of electricity at a certain price for each half-hour segment. If the plant does not wish to operate in every segment, it simply does not bid for that half hour. Bids are received by the grid operator and ranked according to the price. The bids are accepted in order until the total quantity of electricity is equal to the network's forecast of demand. The price of electricity under the last accepted bid, the system marginal price, is then used as the starting point for calculation of the pool price for electricity.

13.220 Using the price of the highest accepted bid causes peculiar behaviour in the electricity pool. Where a generator wishes his plant to be accepted into the successful merit order, he has an incentive to bid low—and hope that the system marginal price is higher allowing him a greater price for the electricity. The ultimate guarantee of success in the merit order is to bid electricity at price zero. The risk then for generators is that all predicted demand is satisfied by bids at zero which would create a system marginal price of zero.

Problems in pooling

13.221 The fundamental defect of the electricity pool in the UK is the virtual duopoly enjoyed by the two major generators, National Power and PowerGen. At peak demand, total demand cannot be satisfied without the participation of the two main generators. The inherent risk in the pooling system is that a generator can identify that (in a given half hour) he will be able to make the final accepted bid, that is, that he is the marginal generator who is determining the pool price. If the identity of the marginal generator can be established in advance, then bidding behaviour can be altered accordingly. The bidder can effectively set the pool price himself. The UK has experienced considerable difficulty overcoming this potential problem, as the two main generators had the majority of market share. There has been no evidence of a cartel in operation, but given that the pool is a classic example of the economist's repeated game it is hardly surprising that the two main participants have a high degree of influence over the wholesale market.

The regulator dealt with the problem in two ways. First, the generators gave various undertakings regarding behaviour influencing the pool price; the second line of attack was the capacity shedding programme, under which the generators were compelled to sell plant and reduce market share. The corresponding increase in the number of generators, together with the reduction in the ability of the main generators to predict the identity of the marginal generator, should reduce the problem. **13.222**

The price paid to generators for electricity is not simply the system marginal price. The output price is based on the system marginal price, with the addition of a capacity charge and an uplift. The capacity charge is a reward for the availability of the generator, and its value is dependent on the loss of load probability and the value of that loss of load. In effect, it rewards power stations which are strategically placed on the network. It is unfortunate that most power stations are located some distance from demand for electricity, and that there is considerable power loss in transmission. The pricing structure is designed to reward plant built close to the location of demand. However, it is politically difficult to build a power station close to a centre of population, and the site may not be convenient for fuel supply. **13.223**

The pool operation is largely dependent on the accuracy of the forecast by the network. If the forecast is inaccurate, and demand is much higher than anticipated, there is provision for calling on stations to operate beyond the merit order. There is a special payment for out of merit running, which offers another potential opening for abuse of the system. If one of the main generators were not to bid any capacity into the system, the likelihood of demand exceeding total bid capacity is increased. The chance of additional plant being called on therefore increases, with the prospect of additional reward for the generator offering plant for out of merit running whilst he may be said to have caused the shortage in the first place. **13.224**

The perceived inadequacies of electricity pooling, together with the Government's desire to try to protect the coal mining industry, led to moves to develop a new wholesale trading system for electricity. The moratorium on gas fired plants was imposed until such a time as the new trading arrangements could be put in place. The initial timescale called for the introduction of bilateral trading markets by October 2000. The timescale has been extended largely due to the complexity of designing software to run the system, and the problems of redesigning the existing contracts for differences. It is anticipated that the bilateral **13.225** trading market will become reality late in 2001. The bilateral trading market is designed to bring together both generators and suppliers to set the price of power. One perceived defect in the pool is that it is a one-sided market, in that there are only generators involved in setting the price. Whilst the observation is frequently made, it is not strictly accurate as the suppliers are involved in the mechanism by which the demand estimate is made. As electricity is a homogeneous product the pool assumes that it is not essential for suppliers to be able to identify the plant from which power is drawn.

13.226 The New Electricity Trading Arrangements (NETA) are an effort to bring the buyers and the sellers closer together. Crucially, a contract market will also permit large users to make direct purchases from generators, which was more difficult under the pooling arrangements. NETA is intended to replace the pool. The concept is for electricity to be traded like any other commodity, and in particular to bring the spot trading of electricity and gas closer into line.

13.227 The key features of the system are that it will replace the Pooling and Settlement Agreement with a Balancing and Settlement Code. The Balancing and Settlement Code will be approved by the regulator. The code will set out the precise obligations of the licensed generators and suppliers, all of whom will be required to subscribe to the Code. Generators will no longer have to go through the pool bidding system to sell power. Instead parties will be able to enter bilateral contracts in a series of linked power markets.

13.228 The balancing requirement will be met through self dispatch of the generators. There will no longer be the same need for the centrally controlled dispatch. Each generator effectively determines when to switch the plant on, subject to system security considerations, rather than being directed to do so by the system operator (presently the National Grid Company (NGC)). Generators will be responsible under the Code for ensuring that their output matches their net contracted positions. Suppliers will be responsible for ensuring that their net contracted positions meet the total demand of their consumers. If the amount of electricity a generator or supplier physically supplies or uses within the trading period does not match its contracted position, it will have to pay a balancing charge as part of the compulsory settlement process. The setting of the balancing charge is intended to provide a strong incentive to generators and suppliers to remain in balance. If there is an imbalance, system security is maintained by the grid operator who is then entitled to pass the whole cost of balancing back to the party causing the imbalance.

13.229 There is no single price for power. Instead the price of power is freely negotiated within each individual market. The concept of setting pool price related to system marginal price is simply irrelevant to bilateral markets. The individual contract price is determined between the buyers and the sellers, in a similar fashion to negotiating contracts for differences under the pooling system. There will be several prices for electricity—each market will have its own clearing price. The cost will also be dependent on ability to balance and avoid the balancing charge.

The Balancing and Settlement Code will be administered by the NGC. The company already runs the pooling system and is in the best position to develop software to run the bilateral market. In addition, it is intended that the bilateral contracting markets will be subject to regulation by the Financial Services Authority to ensure transparent and competitive practices. **13.230**

There are to be three separate bilateral contract markets. Long-term contracts are generally regarded as those in excess of three years. It is likely that the majority of power will be traded long term, in similar fashion to the pooling system where most power is traded under contracts for differences. Long-term contracts suit the needs of generators to guarantee cash flow, and also of suppliers seeking to meet baseload demand. However, it is almost impossible to trade all power via long-term contract as the balancing of supply and demand requires great flexibility throughout the day. Long-term contracts cannot readily be matched to individual and varying demand patterns throughout each day. **13.231**

Accordingly a separate bilateral market will be established for medium-term contracts. Contracts for between six months and three years are likely to be useful to suppliers as demand patterns change—and also as their customer bases change. The competitive retail market means that suppliers no longer have the security of a monopoly customer base. If a supplier is losing retail market share, there is a strong incentive to avoid buying power from generators on a long-term basis. **13.232**

The short-term market, generally regarded as contracts under three months, allows for greater flexibility to meet fluctuating demand. For example, demand is greater in winter than summer, providing a rationale for a supplier to buy short term. Short-term contracts also help suppliers take account of gaining or losing market share. **13.233**

The problem with short-term markets is that there is less security for generators. There may be problems in financing new plant, although the maturing market and greater confidence in new technology has allowed the financing of merchant plant (a plant which sells into the market with no long-term offtake contract in place). Traditional power financing has been on the basis of offtake contracts of fifteen years or more. That will almost certainly disappear with the introduction of bilateral trading. **13.234**

Given that electricity cannot be stored, it is essential that there is a balancing mechanism for the market. Three-month contracts cannot meet the need for flexibility within the day. Accordingly there is to be a balancing market selling power for delivery within a few days, and also within the day itself to permit continuous balancing. The balancing market is to be administered by the system operator, in **13.235** similar fashion to the gas balancing market, aiming to maintain system integrity. The balancing market replaces the need for out of merit running within a pooling system.

13.236 The bilateral trading market also seeks to separate the provision of power from the provision of ancillary services. There will be a separate market for ancillary services, which allows a power plant to seek two separate revenue streams. There is conceivably a risk to system integrity by allowing generators to choose whether to trade in the ancillary services market rather than having the system operator call on generators to provide ancillary services. The Balancing and Settlement Code contains emergency provisions to allow the system operator to make demands on generators, but the intention of the market is to have a separate price for ancillary services. Given that the value of ancillary services is intimately linked to plant location on the system, there is a risk that some plants will effectively be able to set their own price. The system operator is aware of the difficulty and it is one of the reasons why the introduction of bilateral trading has been delayed. It is entirely possible that there will be regulatory intervention in the ancillary services market in the form of price caps.

13.237 The danger with the bilateral trading market is that it is unproven. There is no other example which uses bilateral trading to the same extent as is proposed under the New Electricity Trading Arrangements. It is an experiment. The intention is to put further pressure on the wholesale price of power. The criticism has been that generators have not faced enough pressure in the pool. Exposing the generators to bilateral trading is thought likely to lead to greater pressure on their costs. The ultimate effect of that is partly dependent on the degree of vertical integration allowed within the industry, and the ability of generators to force high-priced power through to their own supply companies and onto consumers. Consumer choice limits that ability provided that consumers are prepared to move supplier. The economic purchasing condition limits the ability to pass between generator and supplier within the same holding company. The solutions to the potential problems of vertical integration are in place but it remains to be seen how effectively these operate in practice.

13.238 There is one further barrier to rapid implementation of NETA. There are problems turning the existing contracts for differences (which are dependent on the pool to set the difference price) into bilateral contracts. At first glance the solution is easy—the contract for differences effectively sets a fixed price which could be turned into the contract price. In practice it is not so easy as market participants expect the bilateral prices to be lower. The renegotiation of the contracts for differences has opened up both pricing issues and contract duration issues, as most of the existing contracts for differences were set up to cover long-term bank loans.

(9) Distortions of the Generation Market

As outlined above, coal contracts cause distortion of the generation market by compelling generators to purchase fuel at higher cost than might otherwise be the case. That higher cost supports the coal industry and provides diversity of fuel sources. It is nonetheless a distortion, and as such difficult to reconcile with the aims of the liberalized market. However, perhaps a more significant distortion is caused by the non-fossil fuel levy.[107] The generation market is distorted by compelling suppliers to take a certain quantity of electricity generated from nuclear power, and also from renewable sources. The Minister is empowered under the Electricity Act[108] effectively to partition the generation market, guaranteeing a market share for nuclear power and for renewables. The cost of support for the nuclear power industry is spread between all consumers. **13.239**

(10) Nuclear Power

Nuclear power has a chequered history in the UK, with a largely admirable safety record but a generally poor record of cost over-runs and delays in commissioning new plant. The Sizewell B pressurized water reactor was the final plant commissioned in the UK, years late after a long-running public inquiry and many times over budget. The nuclear plants, most of which were privatized with the sale of British Energy,[109] are generally regarded as high-cost producers, certainly higher cost than gas. The cost of nuclear-generated electricity has been falling in recent years with improved plant performance, but there is no doubt that there is room for further improvement. The economics of nuclear power are fundamentally different from fossil fuel plants, being heavily biased towards a front-end cost and having a relatively low operating cost. The result is that nuclear plants can generally be operated profitably provided they operate as baseload. Investors have shown their belief in nuclear power by buying shares in British Energy, despite the continuing uncertainty over decommissioning costs. **13.240**

At the time of the Government decision to remove nuclear plants from the privatization, a review of the nuclear industry was promised. Reporting in 1995,[110] the review was to some extent overshadowed by the problems experienced in bringing the Sizewell project into operation on time and at cost. The review was categorical in stating that no new nuclear plants would be built entirely with public **13.241**

[107] See Electricity Act 1989 ss 32 and 33, and regulations made thereunder.

[108] Electricity Act 1989 ss 32, 33.

[109] British Energy was the successor to Nuclear Electric and Scottish Nuclear, and held all nuclear plant except the ageing Magnox reactors. The company was privatized in 1996 despite concerns over establishing the true cost of decommissioning. As outlined above, no further parliamentary approval was required for the sale.

[110] See Department of Trade and Industry, *Nuclear Review*, May 1995.

money, but did not rule out the further building of nuclear plants by private companies. It is clear, however, that the building of nuclear plants would require strong political support as well as financial muscle. Currently, the economics of building nuclear plants are not generally viewed as favourable. The additional safety requirements specified by the Atomic Energy Authority and the Nuclear Installations Inspectorate must also be taken into account.

13.242 The Government took care not to rule out the building of new nuclear plant, possibly to prevent further concerns over diversity of fuel sources. The privatization of the generators has taken the fuel decision away from Government, and although the Minister has to give a special consent[111] for the building of power stations, there is little the Government can do to influence the choice of fuel beyond refusing consent. The generators are driven by cost considerations and shareholder satisfaction—whilst diversity is clearly important to companies in the long term, it is not yet apparent that shareholders are unduly concerned.

G. Lessons from the UK Experience

13.243 The privatization programmes for gas and electricity in the UK had similar aims. The mechanisms to achieve the aims were different, but the goal of liberalizing the market, giving the consumer a choice of supplier, and crucially creating a downward pressure on costs and therefore prices, was common to both industries. The result was an entirely new operating environment. The move away from State control also involved removing State involvement in setting prices (thereby removing an instrument of social policy); removal of state involvement in investment in new infrastructure; and removal of State responsibility for energy security. Energy policy has moved away from Government being the provider of energy, towards a policy of encouraging others to provide energy in forms demanded by consumers, at prices determined by the market. The general public interest is no longer the main driver of the industry, rather the industry is driven by the needs of consumers.

13.244 It is striking that the UK has taken so long to move from a partially liberalized system to the verge of a fully liberalized market—an important lesson for those seeking to follow the UK model is that development of competition is extremely difficult. Attempts to isolate the key features of the development of liberalized energy markets in the UK must recognize that some are responses to political problems, and some are a consequence of the history of the industries.

[111] Consents required under s 36 Electricity Act 1989, and notification procedure for new power plants under Energy Act 1976.

(1) Powers of the Regulator

The key features of the UK system include the extent of powers granted to the regulator. Government and Parliament are largely excluded, and it follows that if a State is not prepared to give up direct control of its utility sectors, it should not adopt the UK model. **13.245**

(2) Licensing Matches Operations

Secondly, the licensing system is set up along the operational lines of the industry. Each activity requires a separate licence and can therefore be separately controlled. Protection of the structure created on day one of liberalization is therefore made easier. **13.246**

(3) Reliance on Contract

Thirdly, there is strong reliance on contracts between licensees. Both the Network Code and the Pooling and Settlement Agreement and its successor, the Balancing and Settlement Agreement, are contracts between the industry participants, with compulsory membership as a licence condition, and the terms of the agreement approved by the regulator. The contracts are fundamental to the operation of the industry but are not direct creations of statute. The statute alone is insufficient to create a working industry: it merely serves as the legal basis for giving up the rights of the State. It is not a detailed description of the operation of the system but a framework onto which detailed rules can be fixed. The result is that the Government is kept out, and there is an element of detailed control by the industry, subject to regulatory approval. **13.247**

(4) Regulation of Natural Monopoly

Fourthly, the natural monopoly element is strictly regulated. Control of monopoly is essential to the systems—the UK has developed towards having the natural monopoly in different ownership to the suppliers (who own the product in the pipe or wire). The exception is local distribution of electricity, although the opening of the market to full competition may conceivably lead to changes. The offshore hydrocarbons industry has developed differently, with less strict provisions regarding access to pipelines, but if there were gross abuse of the natural monopoly, further regulation would clearly be likely. **13.248**

(5) Balance of Interests: Shareholders and Consumers

Fifthly, it is clear that balancing the interests of shareholders and consumers, by means of the price control formula, is an extremely delicate task. In the event that the regulator is too strict companies may be forced out of business, and in addition he may be in breach of his duty to ensure that licensees can finance the **13.249** carrying on of activities. If he is not strict enough he is open to criticism. The problem is not one which is easily solved as it is dependent on information from the companies themselves, and interpretation of that information. It is clear that the regulator can learn from experience, and that any gain kept by the company is under threat at the following periodic review.

(6) Wholesale Market

13.250 Sixthly, the creation of a wholesale market is problematic. The gas industry is presently experiencing difficulty over its traditional long-term contracts, and there is a move towards developing a spot market. The electricity industry currently operates the pooling mechanism but has developed measures to mitigate its worst effects, and the wholesale trading arrangements are being altered to make more use of spot markets.

(7) Benefit to Consumers

13.251 Seventhly, the benefit to consumers must be tangible. Consumers are not generally interested in the structure of an industry—what matters is the final price of the product and the regularity of supply. The UK is characterized by overcapacity in both the production of gas and the generation of electricity, and supply continuity has not historically been a problem. Matters are different in other countries where shortages are common. The most important element to consumers is the price—it is doubtful if there is anything more politically sensitive than the electricity price (except perhaps the price of bread). A government which presides over large price rises is unlikely to be re-elected. Equally, a government is at risk of unpopularity where it allows utilities to take a share of the benefits which consumers perceive to be unfair. If any delay should occur to the introduction of full competition, and the utilities are perceived as benefiting from that gain, the industry (and privatization itself) will be brought into disrepute. The UK has also seen several examples of individual company directors benefiting from share options, which has tarnished the industry in the eyes of the public. To be fair, the issue is properly one of corporate governance rather than of electricity or gas law.

(8) Subsidies to be Identified

13.252 Eighthly, subsidies and inefficiencies in the industry need to be identified. Most have been removed, in order that consumers pay a true price for the product. Some subsidies remain, particularly the nuclear levy in the electricity industry, although that is being phased out. Other costs are being addressed, particularly transmission costs. The Monopolies and Mergers Commission has recently approved far-reaching changes to the method of determining the appropriate cost for gas transmission, and its ruling may have far-reaching implications for other utilities. The development of the competitive market requires that subsidies be identified and addressed in order that all participants are treated equally.

(9) Law Clear and Enforced

Ninthly, the law must be clear and must be enforced. Fearless enforcement of competition law is essential to drive out abuses and potential abuses in the energy industries. It is, for example, arguable that as transmission charges were unchanged during the MMC investigation of gas transportation, consumers are overpaying. There is no doubt that transmission charges will eventually fall—the difficulty is determining the size of that reduction. In the meantime consumers pay more for gas due to the continuing level of the tariff. **13.253**

(10) Obligation to Supply

Tenthly, the obligation to supply must be reconsidered in the light of the abolition of monopoly. The obligation will no longer be the same as under a monopoly system. It is fundamentally more difficult to identify which party bears the obligation—placing it on all suppliers does not provide a complete answer. A system to determine which individual supplier should bear the obligation is needed, although it is by no means clear why in a truly liberalized market there should continue to be an obligation to supply. At a theoretical level, it might be a casualty of the move to liberalization. **13.254**

(11) Liberalization Part of a Process

Finally, the privatization of energy industries cannot be viewed in isolation. The creation of a new entity with new incentives may have dramatic effects in other areas of the economy. In the UK, privatization of the electricity industry is likely to lead to the ultimate demise of the domestic coal industry as a volume producer. In embarking on a privatization programme a government should be aware of the implications. The most obvious implication is that it loses control of the price as an instrument of social policy—it can no longer provide cheap electricity to the population to boost standards of living. The government can no longer manipulate the energy price to affect the headline rate of inflation. The incentive to become more efficient may lead to job losses in the energy industries and to unemployment. **13.255**

It is clear that the UK energy privatizations opened a new area to the rigours of law, both regulatory and contractual. The licensing structures, and the independent regulators, are subject to the constraints of administrative law, including judicial review. The associated contracts, controlling the operation of the industry, have yet to be tested in court. The UK is an example of a country where privatization has largely worked, first because the concept has been accepted rather than challenged in court, and secondly because the balancing of the share of rewards has generally been accepted as fair. **13.256**

The UK energy industries have developed a legal framework to deal with the rigours of the competitive market. Whilst the legal structures are in place there **13.257** remains a possibility that the particular problems posed by introducing full competition might bring about practical problems which the framework will be unable to address within the short time available, in particular metering issues.

H. Conclusions

13.258 The United Kingdom energy industries are diverse. The greatest similarity is the absence of State ownership or control—the mechanisms of arriving at private ownership of hydrocarbons, coal, gas supply, and electricity supply were very different but the end result is liberalized energy markets.

13.259 Oil and gas law in the UK has developed substantially since large-scale production commenced in the mid-1970s. The legislative rules and general agreements are well developed. There is a startling lack of litigation in the industry, and a remarkable lack of State participation. The Government has been content to license the industry and collect its share of the rent. The tax system is likely to be modified in the near future, although low oil prices appear to have delayed announcement of the Government's intentions. The present system, involving corporation tax, royalty, and petroleum revenue tax for old fields, and only corporation tax for new fields, allows the UK to take advantage of being a mature province. The existing producing fields are taxed much more heavily than new, smaller, marginal fields. The UK Government can continue to collect large amounts of tax from the old fields whilst offering fiscal incentives for new field development.

13.260 The problems facing the industry are primarily related to the commercial concerns of maintaining profitability in a time of low oil prices. The move to alter the relationship between the producers and the contractors has potentially far-reaching implications for future competition in the industry. Alliancing (perhaps more properly termed gainsharing) is tending to replace the older, more adversarial contracting practices. Most obviously beneficial in construction contracts, the practice is now extending to other areas ranging from catering to helicopter flight sharing. The danger is that co-operative practices serve to restrict the number of contractors over time, to the detriment of competition. The practice has not (to date) attracted the attention of the competition authorities.

13.261 The coal industry is facing a bleak future, and even the possibility of closure. The consequence of the liberalization of energy markets is to bring into play the rigours of competition—UK coal is not best able to compete in the world market. However, the need for diversity of fuel sources in electricity generation (and recognition that diversity must be paid for) may save some of the industry from closure. However, it is difficult to be optimistic.

The gas industry has seen fundamental changes, both at privatization and subsequently as the liberalized market has developed. Its challenge is to deal with the problem of oversupply, which will only partly be mitigated by the Interconnector. Its major hope has to be expansion of demand through greater use of gas by the power generators and perhaps the transport sector. The gas market also continues to change with the development of a spot market in gas. **13.262**

The electricity industry has also seen fundamental changes. Its future challenges are to address diversity, particularly in a legal environment where the Government has no direct control; to define its relationship with the coal industry; and to decide its future structure with respect to vertical integration, taking account of trading needs. **13.263**

Overall, the striking feature of UK energy industries today is the absence of direct Government involvement. In the energy supply industries, the Government is simply a party to licences, and most responsibilities shared by the Minister and the regulator are in practice exercised by the independent regulator. The Government is content to play an overall supervisory role and keep that to a minimum, indeed its role in the regulation of the upstream hydrocarbon sector is much more noticeable than in the supply industries. **13.264**

The UK energy industries are fundamentally based on an effort to encourage competition. The goal is laudable, but the UK has taken around a decade to get close to full liberalization. Others can learn from that experience, in particular the need for strong competition law. **13.265**

The result of the energy privatization programmes in the UK has been to create arguably the most liberal energy sector in the European Union. Nonetheless, those looking on it from that viewpoint should be cautious. There are a number of areas on which the UK Government's actions can be criticized. The UK has after a decade still not established completely liberalized markets, and with the moves to save the coal industry may actually move further away from the ideal. Regulation of natural monopolies will always remain, and efforts to encourage competition will undoubtedly continue. The immediate future of regulation in the supply industries may have uncertainties in detail, but it is clear that the liberalized market has a long life ahead of it. **13.266**

Bibliography

Baldwin, R, and McCrudden, C, *Regulation and Public Law* (London, Weidenfeld and Nicolson, 1987)

Barnett, A, *Privatising European Energy: Issues and Lessons* (FT Management Report, FT Business Information, 1994)

Beesley, M (ed), *Major Issues in Regulation* (London, Institute of Economic Affairs, 1993)

Beesley, M (ed), *Regulating Utilities: The Way Forward* (London, Institute of Economic Affairs, 1994)

Brown, M, and Ridley, G (eds), *Privatisation: Current Issues* (London, Graham and Trotman, 1994)

Director General of Electricity Supply, *Annual Report*, 1991–97

Director General of Gas Supply, *Annual Report*, 1987–97

Ernst, J, *Whose Utilty?* (Open University Press, 1994)

Estrada *et al* (ed), *Natural Gas in Europe: Markets, Organisation and Politics*, (London, Pinter Publishers, 1988)

Holmes, A, *Privatising British Electricity: Restructuring and Resistance* (FT Management Report, FT Business Information, 1992)

McEldowney, J, *Electricity Industry Handbook* (London, Chancery Law Publishing, 1992)

McGowan, F, and Thomas, S, *Electricity in Europe: Inside the Utilities* (FT Management Report, FT Business Information, 1992)

Mestmacker, E (ed) *Natural Gas in the Internal Market* (London, Graham and Trotman, 1993)

Monopolies and Mergers Commission, 'Report on the Matter of the Existence or Possible Existence of a Monopoly Situation in Relation to the Supply in Great Britain of Gas through Pipelines to Persons other than Tariff Customers' Cmnd 500 (London, HMSO, 1988)

Monopolies and Mergers Commission, 'Reports under the Fair Trading Act 1973 on the Supply within Great Britain of Gas through Pipelines to Tariff and Non-Tariff Customers of the Conveyance and Storage of Gas by Public Gas Supplier' (London, HMSO, 1993)

Monopolies and Mergers Commission, 'Report under the Gas Act 1986 on the Conveyance and Storage of Gas and Fixing of Tariffs for the Supply of Gas by British Gas plc' (London, HMSO, 1993)

Ogus, A, *Regulation: Legal Form and Economic Theory* (Oxford University Press, 1994)

Peebles, M, *Evolution of the Gas Industry* (London, MacMillan, 1980)

Salter, J, *Onshore Oil and Gas Law* (London, Sweet and Maxwell)

Steel, and Heald (eds) *Privatising Public Enterprises* (London, Royal Institute of Public Administration, 1984)

Veljanovski, C (ed), *Privatisation and Competition: A Market Prospectus* (London, Institute of Economic Affairs, 1989)

—— *Regulators and the Market: An Assessment of the Growth of Regulation in the UK* (London, Institute of Economic Affairs, 1991)

Legislation

Petroleum (Production) Act 1918
Petroleum (Production) Act 1934
Coal Nationalisation Act 1945
Continental Shelf Act 1964
Control of Pollution Act 1974

Oil Taxation Act 1975
Petroleum and Submarine Pipelines Act 1975
Oil and Gas (Enterprise) Act 1982
Oil and Pipelines Act 1985
Gas Act 1986
Civil Jurisdiction (Offshore Activities) Order 1987 SI no 2197
Criminal Jurisdiction (Offshore Activities) Order 1987 SI no 2198
Petroleum Act 1987
Petroleum (Production)(Seaward Areas) Regulations 1988 (as amended)
Electricity Act 1989
Environmental Protection Act 1990
Water Resources Act 1991
Competition and Utilities Act 1992
Offshore Safety Act 1992
Coal Industry Act 1994
Gas Act 1995
Petroleum (Production)(Landward Areas) Regulations 1995
Competition Act 1998
Petroleum Act 1998 (consolidating measure)

Part IV

CONCLUSIONS

14

ENERGY LAW IN EUROPE: COMPARISONS AND CONCLUSIONS

Catherine Redgwell, Martha M Roggenkamp, Anita Rønne, and Iñigo del Guayo

A. Introduction

The purpose of this chapter is to revisit the European energy law landscape revealed in the preceding chapters from the broad perspective of all of the national legal systems considered, noting too the shaping influence of EC and international **14.01** law upon these systems. Part B examines the legislative, administrative, and organizational arrangements across the countries considered, paying particular attention to energy regulatory competence, the ownership of resources and energy entities, and regulatory approaches and methods. Part C turns to the substantive regulation of oil, gas, and coal exploration and production, followed in parts D and E by considerations of gas and electricity supply respectively. Part F addresses nuclear and renewable energy activities and energy efficiency initiatives, whilst Part G briefly visits the energy and environment interface. Part H then draws some general conclusions about the future development of energy law in Europe, privatization, liberalization, and globalization being the key trends to emerge which will clearly continue to shape energy law in Europe for decades to come.

B. Legislative, Administrative, and Organizational Systems

(1) Introduction

14.02 The energy sector is a key sector of national economies around the globe. Consequently, governments have become involved in the development of energy resources and in setting the framework within which energy markets operate. However, there is no simple formula for any energy issue—there is neither a standard energy policy nor a universal regulation model, and each State has to find a balance between energy security, economic growth, and environmental protection. It is therefore crucial to bear in mind varying national conditions, energy objectives, and needs when making a comparison of the organizational and regulatory systems of various countries.[1]

14.03 This book has considered energy law in Denmark, France, Germany, Italy, the Netherlands, Norway, Spain, and the United Kingdom. These States demonstrate significant differences in government control, influence, and resource base. For example, France, Norway, and Italy are dominated by major State-owned industries, although in the latter two countries the industry has been subject to gradual privatization. In Denmark and the Netherlands both public and private energy enterprises exist and there has been established the basis for joint decision-making, while in Germany and the United Kingdom the energy sector is mainly private but still subject to specific regulatory controls. In the UK ownership of the energy sector was previously largely in the hands of the State but has since been extensively privatized. It is therefore important to bear in mind that the pattern of public or private involvement is not a static one.

[1] Anita Rønne, 'Alternative Approaches to Regulatory Agency Structure and Powers', Journal of Energy & Natural Resources Law, vol 15, no 1, Feb 1997, 41–2.

The United Kingdom, Denmark, and Norway are net exporters of both oil and gas, while the Netherlands is a net exporter of gas only and France, Spain, Italy, and Germany are heavily dependent on imports of both. Although the exporting countries meet their energy requirements from indigenous production, they make use of very different sources. In the United Kingdom, energy consumption is based on oil, gas, coal, and nuclear power, while Norway exports all gas and bases its power production on hydro. The energy requirements of the Netherlands are met primarily by natural gas and, to a lesser extent, by imported oil and coal. Denmark on the other hand is one of the most significant developers of renewable energy together with the Netherlands but uses considerable amounts of coal, all of which is imported. France, Spain, the United Kingdom, and Germany have significant nuclear power programmes. In addition Spain and Germany are producers of coal. **14.04**

The nature and extent of public involvement in the energy sector has been subject to radical changes during the last thirty years, ranging from nationalization/expropriation following World War II, to increasingly strong Government involvement and control following the energy crises of the 1970s, to less State intervention, deregulation, the introduction of competition, and even privatization of the industry in the late 1980s and the 1990s.[2] In general, public involvement has been strongest in the grid-based industries, namely gas, electricity, and district heating, in the nuclear sector, and in those countries where the coal industry is not viable and depends largely on public support. Today there is a worldwide trend towards more liberalized energy markets, and a move away from price-fixing, State monopolies, and energy trade protection. However, not all matters may be left to the operation of market forces. A system of regulation must be maintained to ensure that a competitive market situation exists in order to operate efficiently—to prevent abuse of monopoly power and to ensure the entrance of new suppliers. Moreover, wider issues of safeguarding concerns such as energy security, suitable environmental standards, quality of supply, and energy conservation must be properly catered for. This is the function of regulation. **14.05**

(2) Policy Developments

One of the most distinctive features of the energy supply sector is the gradual change in political perspective which has occurred over the last three decades. Whereas the energy supply sector in the 1970s and 1980s was characterized by a high degree of public intervention, influence, and control as a result of the energy crises in the early seventies, a shift of perspective has been demonstrated in energy policy during the nineties. This change is influenced partly by general political **14.06**

[2] See also MM Roggenkamp, 'Implications of Privatisation, Liberalisation and Integration of Networkbound Energy Systems', Journal of Energy & Natural Resources Law, vol 15, no 1, Feb 1997, 51–61.

changes such as a rise in deregulation philosophy, increasing privatization, an emphasis on market forces and increased co-operation following the political changes in Eastern Europe, and the impact of global environmental problems. Other changes may be linked with various elements linked to the energy sector specifically. The decline in energy prices during the 1980s and the *rapprochement* between the big oil exporters in OPEC and the big energy consumers within the International Energy Agency (IEA) has led the energy market to become less volatile. Consequently, the emphasis on security of energy supplies is less dominant on the political agenda. Furthermore, the unexpected stagnation in the electricity consumption of many industrialized countries has resulted in a surplus capacity.

14.07 Developments towards a single European market have undoubtedly had a significant impact. Prior to 1986, only a few Directives had been adopted which dealt directly with energy matters, and these were largely confined to responses to the oil crisis in 1973 and the need to maintain emergency stocks of fuels. The entry into force of the Single European Act provided the basis for the European Commission to focus increased attention on the energy sector with the application of internal market concepts to this sector, within a broader package of legislative initiatives in order gradually to establish the internal energy market. These developments were observed in some detail in Chapter 5 above. The removal of trade barriers and increased competition between companies across Europe should lead to more efficiency, better customer service, and lower prices. Essential aspects of liberalization of the energy sector, be it within Europe or outside, are to minimize barriers to entry, to encourage competition in energy supply, to protect the interests of end users and consumers, and to facilitate free customer choice with respect to supply. This is a very difficult and complex task, not least because national energy markets have different structures in respect of ownership and competition.

14.08 Government responses to market liberalization and its implications for the legal regulation of energy supply systems have varied across Europe. In broad terms there is a trend towards increased regulation combined with the deployment of new legal techniques and mechanisms such as agreements and contracts, a phenomenon that could be referred to as re-regulation.[3] There is, however, no doubt that liberalization of the energy market is a sensitive issue. Countries such as Italy and Germany have been firmly committed to the type of monopoly organization which the Electricity Directive's 'single-buyer' system will allow them to retain.

[3] See *Re-regulation of the Danish Energy Sector* by Anita Rønne in *Suum Cuique—Legal Studies from the University of Copenhagen Law Faculty*, ed Peter Blume, Ditlev Tamm, and Vibeke Vindeløv, 1993, 275. See also Academic Advisory Group papers: 'Privatisation, Liberalisation and Deregulation in the Energy Industry', in Journal of Energy & Natural Resources Law, vol 14, no 1, Feb 1996.

Other countries favour a more liberalized approach and have on their own initiative taken important steps in this direction. The US was the pioneer, followed in Europe by the United Kingdom and later by the Nordic countries, particularly Norway, Sweden, and Finland. One concern for those countries pursuing a more liberal approach is the risk that less liberal countries will take advantage of a situation where trade between States is open while retaining the advantages of a monopoly in their home State.

A further sensitivity which has emerged over the last decades at both the national and international levels is the appropriate balance to be achieved between economic growth and environmental protection. The result has been increased priority afforded environmental protection and the preservation of natural resources on the domestic and international political levels. Many initiatives have built on the concept of sustainable development, a concept popularized by the 1987 Brundtland Report[4] and given more concrete expression at the 1992 United Nations Conference on Environment and Development. **14.09**

Bearing the above factors in mind, it is possible to generalize that European energy policies are in the main concerned with the development of an energy supply system which is stable, safe, flexible, efficient, low cost and, so far as possible, environmentally friendly. **14.10**

(3) Constitutional Issues

In the sense that a constitution is a single document with overriding legal force, which sets out the framework and the principal functions of the organs of government within the State, declares the principles by which those organs must operate, and guarantees the rights of the citizen, all the States considered here have a written constitution save for the United Kingdom. However, there are wide differences between these written constitutions. For example, energy matters are specifically referred to in the Spanish Constitution, whilst absent from the Italian, Danish, Norwegian, and Netherlands Constitutions where energy matters are subsumed under general legislative competences. **14.11**

A further point of distinction is that it is only Germany which possesses an explicitly federal constitutional structure, with the remaining countries based on a unitary system of government. However, in most countries the local authorities are autonomous, and the relationship with the central Government is not strictly hierarchical. This is the case for example in Denmark, France, the Netherlands, Norway, and Italy. These countries thus have many features of incipient federalism with a degree of decentralization to the regions. In Germany, responsibilities **14.12**

[4] The World Commission on Environment and Development, *Our Common Future*, Oxford 1987, named for the chair of the Commission, the then Norwegian Prime Minister Gro Harlem Brundtland.

with respect to energy are shared between the Federal Government and the sixteen Länder. For the remaining unitary States, decentralized administrative arrangements divide the State into smaller administrative regions, most commonly with two levels, a regional level of counties or provinces and a local or municipal level, and often each level is vested with different competences in respect of energy regulation. For example, the local level carries out licensing in France and heat planning in Denmark and are active participants in local energy supply as in Norway and Denmark (see further below, paras 14.29–14.30, on direct participation). A remarkable structure is the Spanish one, comprising a unitary State yet with 17 Autonomous Communities (ie Regions) enjoying a level of autonomy greater than the German Länder. A policy of decentralization has been pursued in Italy since law no 142 of 8 June 1990 granted local authorities much wider powers regarding, *inter alia*, the organization and management of energy sources. Conversely, however, the Netherlands is experiencing gradual centralization of energy regulation.

14.13 All the States considered herein except Norway are members of the European Union. Chapter 5 amply demonstrates the key impact which EC law has made upon the regulation of energy activities in the Member States. However, Norway is subject to most of the same rules through the EEA Agreement.

(4) Ownership Issues

Introduction

14.14 Property rights are one of the fundamental principles of the European legal order, with most national constitutions according property right protection and with the EC law recognizing the sovereign rights of Member States over their natural resources. When discussing the energy sector, a distinction needs to be made between ownership of energy resources and ownership of the enterprises producing and distributing energy.

Ownership of oil, gas, and coal resources

14.15 The ownership of energy resources varies according to where such resources are located, onshore or offshore. Under general international law States have permanent sovereignty over the natural resources, including energy resources, located within their territory. Hence, States are free as a matter of international law to determine whether subsoil energy resources are owned by the State (the domanial system) or by the individual landowners (the accession system). A combination of such approaches according to the resource in question is not uncommon.[5] States

[5] For details of the various system of ownership see KW Blinn *et al*, 'International Petroleum Exploration and Exploitation Agreements: Legal, Economic and Policy Aspects', Euromoney Publications, 1986, 21–31.

vary the regulatory level at which these ownership rights are regulated. Only Spain has included an explicit declaration in its Constitution that energy resources are subject to the general interest of the State, the other countries considered here regulating the issue by statute.

Although most civil law countries vest the ownership of the subsoil in the surface landowner, an exception is usually made for energy resources such as oil, gas, and coal. Hence, most countries reviewed claim State ownership of oil, gas, and coal resources onshore (Denmark, Norway, the United Kingdom, Spain and, upon adoption of the new Mining Bill, the Netherlands). In Germany, ownership of the resources is also vested in the State, but at the regional level. However, some other countries leave the issue of ownership to energy resources unresolved (the Netherlands and Italy). It should be noted that the applicable energy legislation in these countries was usually drafted in the early twentieth century; elsewhere, when replaced by modern legislation, all countries appear to opt for State ownership. 14.16

As for offshore energy resources, international law recognizes the sovereign rights of the State over the resources of the continental shelf and functional sovereign jurisdiction for the purposes of exploring and exploiting these resources. Under international law, States do not 'own' the resources but enjoy sovereignty to explore and exploit them. Nonetheless, several of the States considered here claim not only a right to regulate but also ownership of offshore oil and gas resources (eg Denmark, Norway, Spain, and the Netherlands). 14.17

Structure of industry

The organization of the energy sector, in particular the extent and form of public ownership, varies widely from country to country. Particular changes have been experienced over the past fifteen years or so, with a growing tendency to move away from the concept of integrated utilities and to introduce more competition into the electricity and gas industries in particular. These changes continue, stimulated in part by the necessity to implement key European directives in the energy field which impact upon the structure of the energy sector. 14.18

In countries such as the United Kingdom, France, Italy, and Spain most of the energy sector was nationalized by law after World War II with energy responsibilities allocated to new State-owned utilities. Today the UK energy sector has experienced extensive privatization, while the Spanish energy sector has recently undergone wholesale privatization. In contrast, the French energy sector is still dominated by major state-owned industries for oil, electricity, and gas supplies and for ownership of coal mines. These State-owned companies enjoy a virtual monopoly and are not run as commercial companies; rather, they are subject to extensive State influence notwithstanding steps towards achieving a greater degree of autonomy for the utilities. 14.19

14.20 Unlike in the United Kingdom and Spain, in Denmark and Norway the introduction of greater competition into the energy sector has not been accompanied by a privatization programme. In these countries the State and the municipalities are heavily involved in network-bound energy supply, in consequence of which public ownership is significant. For example, the whole Danish gas sector is in public ownership, with a State company controlling gas transmission, and primarily municipality-owned companies controlling gas distribution. Danish municipalities also own half of the decentralized electricity supply sector and hold a major interest in district heating. While Norway does not have a downstream gas industry, there is dominant public ownership (State and local) in the electricity sector. The central transmission system and the short-term market is operated and organized by a State-owned company, whereas distribution is operated by municipalities. This resembles the situation in the Netherlands where both public and private energy enterprises are found. Originally, branches of the Ministry were the main energy players, but these institutions were eventually commercialized as private limited companies. Nonetheless, some public ownership is retained: whereas the Dutch State owns 50 per cent of the gas transmission company Gasunie and 100 per cent in the electricity transmission company TenneT (as of 2001 and on a temporary basis) municipalities and provinces still dominate the energy distribution sector. Following the new Electricity Act and the need for new capital, the issue of privatization is presently high on the political agenda of the Netherlands.

14.21 In contrast, the energy sectors in Germany and the United Kingdom are mainly in private ownership. Germany has a highly decentralized gas and electricity system where private companies are dominant, even in the nuclear industry. This has led to a traditional emphasis upon competition law as a regulatory technique for control of a privatized sector. Gas distribution, however, is controlled by the municipalities and regional Governments also hold shares in some of the electricity generating companies.

14.22 Certainly, of all the States considered here, the United Kingdom has experienced the most significant changes in the organization of its energy industry, from widespread public ownership after World War II to the present situation of a near total absence of State ownership in the sector. The gas supply industry was privatized in 1986, followed by the restructuring of the electricity supply sector which today has no State ownership. British coal production was vested with a State monopoly until 1994, when it also was privatized. With the exception of a short period in the 1970s, the oil and gas sector has remained completely in private ownership.

(5) Organization of Public Authorities in the Energy Sector

14.23 While in all the countries considered here national parliaments play an important role in energy policy and legislation, governmental institutions for formulating and implementing energy policy vary widely between them. Such variations are the result of, *inter alia*, differences in administrative tradition, the structure of the energy sector, and the political considerations to be taken into account in energy policy-making.

Notwithstanding these variations, in general all the States considered here have found it necessary to establish a grouping within Government with responsibility for energy policy formulation. This group is most commonly led by a Minister with wide responsibilities for economic and industrial policy, reflecting the philosophy that energy is but one of many industries. Such an approach is evident in France, the United Kingdom, the Netherlands, Spain, and Germany. An alternative is to establish a separate Ministry of Energy, reflecting the perception that special attention is needed to this specific sector, at least for a period of time, and reflecting the emphasis put on energy policy. Thus Denmark created a separate Ministry of Energy following the second oil crisis in 1979. In 1994, however, it was merged with the Ministry of Environment to create the Ministry for Environment and Energy, reflecting the integration of the environmental concerns in energy matters. Norway established the Ministry of Oil and Energy in 1978, although energy was vested for a period with the Ministry of Industry and Energy. The United Kingdom once had a Ministry of Energy but following the privatization of the industries the Ministry was limited to a Minister without portfolio of Cabinet rank and energy matters included under the Ministry of Trade and Industry as a Department of Energy. As many other departments are concerned with energy policy—particularly those responsible for finance, external affairs, the environment, and technology—effective co-ordination between the various departments is very important. State activities of a commercial character are normally entrusted to State companies or public corporations. Examples are found in Norway and Denmark, but also in France and Italy. **14.24**

The fact that Government plays different roles brings the risk of mixing political and economic interests: of a conflict in functions between the State *qua* policy maker and *qua* regulator. The separation of these functions between different institutions is one mechanism employed for reducing such conflict, the potential for which arises particularly where the State retains significant ownership of the industry. A trend in the establishment of independent regulators may be observed. For some States, such as Denmark, the concept of independent sectoral regulators had been adopted in the 1970s although providing for industrial representation (50 per cent) until 2000. Danish regulators are delegated specific responsibilities by legislation which can only be revoked by new legislation. Following the Danish electricity reform of 1999 industry representation involvement has ceased and a new energy regulator has been established independent both from political and from utility interests. In the United Kingdom independent regulators for electricity and for gas have existed for more than a decade, with decision-making exercised by a Director General. Spain has had an Electricity Commission which **14.25** has recently been replaced by a national Commission for Energy covering both electricity and gas. Although organized under the central Ministry in Norway, the regulatory authority has considerable independence in its regulatory functions and is not politically appointed but comprises civil servants. Following the new Electricity Act adopted in February 2000, the French Government also established a special Electricity Regulatory Commission (*Commission de régulation de l'électricité* or CRE). In the Netherlands supervision of compliance with the Electricity Act 1998 and the Gas Act 2000 is carried out by a sector specific regulator (*Dienst toezicht en uitvoering energie* or DTe) which is an independent branch of the recently established independent Competition Authority (Nederlandse Mededingings Authoriteit or NMa). All regulators have wide authority to issue detailed general regulations or guidelines and individual administrative decisions on operations, tariffs and disputes. Control of the regulators is implemented through different 'recourse systems' implying that the decisions of the regulators can be challenged by other organs or courts.

14.26 An independent regulator assures potential investors that regulation of the industry is removed from day-to-day political control and influence, thereby providing an element of stability in a sector characterized by heavy investment over what is generally a considerable time period. A further benefit is the development of a specialized and highly professional body which can meet energy enterprises on an equal footing, and facilitate swift and cost-effective methods of dispute settlement. Other specific responsibilities may include: promoting competition and balancing the interests of the supplier and the customers; issuing licences; price regulation; quality control; monitoring compliance; co-operating with other institutions in counteracting monopolistic abuses; and publishing and gathering information.

(6) *Regulatory Instruments*

Introduction

14.27 National energy policy objectives tend to include all or most of the following: ensuring energy security, efficient and rational use of energy; facilitating competition and reducing the anti-competitive consequences of natural monopolies; protection of the environment and consumers; and minimizing cost. To ensure consistency with government policy, a whole range of regulatory instruments are employed, including:

- direct State participation
- statutory regulation
- licensing and other systems
- negotiation systems and agreements
- economic means such as taxes, subsidies, and guarantees.

14.28 Energy law is generally characterized by the integrated and mixed application of these instruments, with the result that it is often difficult to obtain an overview of the chief regulatory techniques employed. Regulation may be comprehensive, encompassing the operation of the industry as a whole with open access to the system and the protection of consumer interests in the broadest sense (eg the United Kingdom), or it may take a softer form based on a co-operative relationship between industry and national government and close relations with the municipalities which the distribution utilities serve (eg Denmark, the Netherlands and, with respect to downstream activities, Norway).

Direct participation by the State or municipalities

14.29 In addition to general involvement by governments through an administrative department, governments in the countries considered here which have indigenous production of energy resources have all engaged companies which are either fully or partly owned by the State in such development, although some just for a limited period of time. At the outset many of these companies had a status preferential to that of private parties: guaranteed participation, preferential rights to certain licence areas, deferred interest during exploration, options to increase its share during production, training, and rights to purchase oil and gas produced. Today the general picture shows a reduction of the role of the State companies. Almost all special positions have been abandoned, which has become a direct requirement following the adoption of the Hydrocarbons Licensing Directive. Consequently, those companies still extant participate on a more or less equal footing with private companies. Some companies have been reorganized, such as Statoil in Norway in 1985, while others have been completely privatized or even abolished, such as the British National Oil Corporation, privatized in 1982 and abolished in 1985.

14.30 As far as network bound industries are concerned, the rate of public participation varies considerably within the group of countries considered here. Some have integrated national systems in which a State monopoly is responsible for all parts of the activities, some have decentralized systems where a State-owned monopoly controls a certain aspect of the industry, some have extensive participation by the municipalities in some sections, others have mixed public and private ownership/co-operation or vest all activities in the private sector. The general pattern for public involvement is that the municipalities are involved in local energy supply and their activities therefore focus on distribution, whereas the State engages itself at the national level in transmission activities. In many countries, however, the electricity and gas industry is going through major changes—not least influenced by the initiatives of the European Commission.

Statutory regulation

14.31 A legislative framework for market intervention has been established for almost all sectors: oil, natural gas, coal, electricity, nuclear power, and even for renewables, eg Denmark. The division into sectors is, however, in the process of dissolution because of the integration of energy supply systems and the need for considering different issues across sectors, for instance energy consumption, environmental impact, and combined heat and electricity production. It is beyond doubt that the EC energy liberalization programme has had a big impact on legislative developments in all the States considered here.

14.32 Even with a greater reliance on market forces, parts of the network-bound industries have monopoly characteristics and must therefore be regulated. Some countries like Germany rest on the general law against abuse of monopoly situations, others bring together the utilities, industry and other consumers, and central and local governments through commissions in order to regulate prices (eg Denmark until the new legal reform) or vest these responsibilities in an independent regulator appointed either as a board or a single regulator (the United Kingdom and now Denmark following the 1999 reforms).

14.33 In addition to primary laws adopted by Parliament, more detailed regulation is found in secondary legislation issued by the central administration and administrative decisions and guidelines issued by either the same authority or the regulator.

Licences and other systems

14.34 All the countries considered provide for fuel and energy production and supply to be carried out under some kind of licence issued at the discretion of the responsible authority in either the national or regional governments and with broadly the same effect and content. These licences may be called concessions, licences, permissions, authorizations, or permits.

14.35 During the years there have been many legal discussions about how licences should be characterized or classified in the legal system. This relates to the fact that it has traditionally been assumed that a private, binding agreement gives the licensee better protection against unilateral changes of the licence content than an administrative act. However, the number and variety of views on this issue indicate that the problem is complicated and scarcely subject to resolution on the basis of a single legal formula.[6] Furthermore, one should be very careful about analysing

[6] See the discussions and various national analyses in *The Legal Character of Petroleum Licences: A Comparative Study*, ed Terence Daintith, University of Dundee, Centre for Petroleum and Mineral Law Studies and Energy and Natural Resources Committee of the International Bar Association, 1981.

the legal nature of the licence by the wording alone because historical and legal traditions may explain differences in the concept of licences. Their precise meaning must thus be derived from their specific national legal context. In some jurisdictions like Spain and Italy the use of the term 'concession' implies a pure contractual relationship, where changes, nevertheless, can be introduced unilaterally by the public administration. Permits, however, are not contracts and are set unilaterally by the State, which may also provide for future unilateral revisions of conditions. In countries such as Denmark and Norway 'concessions' seems simply to be the older term and 'licences' the more modern term for the same legal concept, which is considered to be mainly administrative in nature.

However, even if it is assumed that the licence is based upon an administrative act, the freedom of the State to adjust its terms unilaterally is restricted. First, general principles of public law require that administrative authorities take all decisions on the basis of objective, non-discriminatory and non-arbitrary considerations. The licensee is thus entitled to fairness, taking into consideration the negotiations conducted with the State, the pre-conditions on which the licence is based, and the risks and investments undertaken by the licensee.[7] The concept is further confirmed by the general principles of EC law and the adoption of the Directives on the internal market for hydrocarbons, gas, and electricity. Even if the rights of the licensee are protected, changes can sometimes be justified by the strength of the public interests involved. In this case most countries have adopted substantive constitutional guarantees for the individual companies which, among other things, implies full compensation. **14.36**

It should be highlighted that changes can be achieved through external means such as taxation. Tightening up tax provisions will itself be capable of upsetting the economic basis on which the licence is held. Against this background, it is doubtful whether classifying the licence, or parts of it, as a private binding agreement would create any real protection of the financial interests of the licensee.[8] **14.37**

Regulation based on a licence system differs depending first and foremost on the nature and type of the regulated activity. It is thus characteristic that the activity is fundamental to the function of the society as a whole, involves heavy investment, and until recently was often also classified as a natural monopoly. Extensive control is usually reserved for the Government/regulatory authority, as to whether a licence should be granted, and as to the term of the licence. **14.38**

Although the form of a licence is individual, its contents often apply to several licensees and so will be of a more general nature. Therefore many licence conditions **14.39**

---

[7] See also *The Legal Framework for Exploration for and Production of Oil and Natural Gas in Denmark*, by Anita Rønne and Michael Budtz in Journal of Energy & Natural Resources Law of International Bar Association 1985, vol 3, no 3, 168.

[8] ibid.

might as well have been issued in the form of statutory regulation. Most often the statute itself says in general that the regulatory authority may attach specific conditions to the issuance of a licence. Sometimes the statute contains complete specifications and thereby lays down for the licensing authority the contents of the licence provisions. At other times the legislation only describes the type of conditions which may or must be inserted in a licence. Generally the listing of optional and mandatory provisions is not exhaustive, but leaves the settlement of the final contents to the discretion of the licensing authority. However, the authority will always have to act within the the rule of law, within the statutory framework and the objectives of the statute. Following the adoption of the EC Directives on the internal energy market, the ability to attach conditions to a licence has been restricted.

14.40 Licences include rights as well as obligations. The rights typically allow the licensee to perform certain actions, and give some security for the investments of the licensee in the sense that the licence cannot be changed or withdrawn arbitrarily. The duties often reflect the social importance of the activity and require the licensee to perform, tolerate, or omit to do certain things.

14.41 The conditions found in a licence include the specification and delimitation of the relevant activities, the area, and the duration, which is usually rather long. Thus in Denmark oil exploration and production licences are issued for thirty-six years and electricity production licences for twenty years. The licence is strictly personal: the licensee cannot transfer or assign the licence without the consent of the regulatory organ. The State ensures that it is informed about the activities by establishing a duty to supply information, and the basis for its supervision of the activity. Licences often include an obligation to supply and the right for the public authorities to control the revenues of the licensee. Clearly, no licensee would take on these obligations without certain financial returns. The vested rights are frequently—or have been until recently—exclusive, although combined with an obligation to deliver and supply. These monopoly rights are, however, subject to change in the light of the wave of liberalization sweeping Europe.

Negotiation systems and agreements

14.42 Significant detail is provided for in national legislation and subsequent administrative decisions.[9] There has, however, been a tendency for governments to favour the use of contractual agreements rather than to apply statutory controls. The use of agreements as a mechanism for public regulation brings into focus legal issues which the general law of contract and public administration is not well suited to address, and which are far removed from the traditional essence of these legal fields. Consequently, this development does present its problems. The use of agreements

[9] See also different methods of harmonization in ch 5 D(5) above.

provides the State with potential dual control—as a party to an agreement, and as legislator. It may be difficult to understand and control where a regulation takes part through agreements of which the demands of form, content, and publication are limited. The result seems to be a tendency to give in on many fundamental values of law and legal principles, which have been developed through an extensive legal tradition. The extent to which one may frown upon the use of agreements depends partly upon the mutual strength of the parties and their professionalism.

There is as yet no overall view of the legal impact of the application of the agreement form. Energy law does not belong to the hard core of public administration law, nor are these agreements identical to those known in private law. The energy sector thus involves legal issues which must be solved by reference to both general public law and the theory of contract law. **14.43**

Economic means: taxes, subsidies, guarantees

All countries considered here make use of financial instruments to implement energy policy and to receive revenues from production activities. These include: general taxation such as corporation tax, special tax regimes such as petroleum revenue tax, royalties, area fees, energy taxes, carbon dioxide taxes, and fiscal incentives such as grants, tax credits, and subsidies. These are an important element of regulation, but space does not permit a detailed review of them in this book. **14.44**

(7) Concluding Remarks

It is difficult to draw general conclusions from the complex and varied pattern of government involvement in the energy sector. Methods of intervention which have worked well in some countries have failed in others, and both private and State-owned companies have proved that they are capable of operating efficiently. Serious distortions have been due primarily to the lack of a clear, transparent, and long-term policy and financial constraints, which have seriously impeded the enterprises' investment programmes. **14.45**

The International Energy Agency says in general that: **14.46**

> State-owned companies work well when they are strongly backed and given clear objectives by the government and then allowed freedom to manage within those objectives. They work badly when subject to heavy political interference [. . .] Control over private sector utilities works best when it is based on partnership between government and industry or is relatively light-handed, transparent and with clear goals. It works badly when the regulatory systems are complex and legalistic.[10]

It is too early to attempt to judge the success of the new liberalization arrangements, but it is obvious that the public cannot rely on competition alone. Governments are likely to retain some power over decisions on fuel choices for **14.47**

[10] *The Role of the IEA Governments in Energy*, International Energy Agency, 1992, 32–3.

power and CHP generation, the location of power plants above a certain size, security of supplies, emergencies measures, the level and diversity of gas imports, safety levels, environmental norms, and the protection of consumers. Too detailed government intervention should, however, be avoided and some scope for the initiative of producers and consumers should be allowed.

14.48 The objective of regulation, and also of competition, should be to protect the consumer while maintaining the incentive of the utility to provide cheap, high-quality services. A good regulatory system should be based on clear procedures and rules, and decisions should be based on adequate information and reasoning, and made available to those affected and the public. The key words are thus fairness, consistency, accountability, and transparency.

C. Exploration for and Production of Fossil Energy Resources: Coal, Oil, and Natural Gas

(1) Introduction

14.49 Some of the countries under review, such as the United Kingdom, produce coal as well as oil and natural gas, although production levels vary. Others, such as the Netherlands, have ceased to produce coal because costs became too high in comparison with the costs of imported coal or with the production of other energy resources such as oil and gas. Nevertheless, the legal regimes are to some extent comparable because the exploration for and the production of coal and petroleum have common features, such as the need to regulate the ownership of the subsoil resources. Moreover, some countries initially based their laws on the production of oil and gas on an older regime governing the exploration for and production of coal.

(2) Exploration for and Production of Coal

The Industry

14.50 Only three of the countries here reviewed, Germany, Spain, and the UK, still have significant coal production. French coal production is insignificant in comparison. Production is primarily for domestic consumption, particularly for electricity generation. Nonetheless a number of countries have coal-fired power stations, even where coal production has ceased (eg Denmark and the Netherlands).[11] These stations use imported coal either from future members of the EU, such as

[11] The decision to use coal for electricity production in these two countries was a result of the 1973 oil crisis and the resulting need for diversification of energy resources, rather than because of the lack of indigenous energy resources: see further ch 6 A(2) above.

Poland, or from South American or African countries, such as Colombia and South Africa.[12] Norway is the exception, neither producing nor consuming coal.

The British, German, and Spanish coal industries are in decline and these three countries have restructured their coal industries within the past fifteen years. In these countries domestic coal is both expensive, due to the costs associated with the extraction of coal which is usually located deep underground, and polluting, so that there is also a significant proportion of cheaper and/or cleaner imported coal. However, coal is still the most important primary energy resource in Germany and the brown coal industry there is actually expanding.[13] **14.51**

Ownership of coal

The laws of the three main coal-producing countries address ownership issues in three very different ways. **14.52**

The Spanish Civil Code 1889 states that mines belong to the public domain of the State, unless they are passed to private individuals or companies by means of a concession. It was then accepted that the concessionaire would become the owner, not only of the minerals it extracted, but also of the minerals *in situ*, ie the mine. Therefore there was some scope for private ownership of mines under the Spanish Civil Code.[14] Awarding the ownership of coal mines to the State is an exemption to the Roman law principle of accession, according to which the owner of the surface land is entitled to everything above and below it.[15] Various laws passed within the twentieth century in Spain (particularly the Mining Act 1973, which is still in force) introduced the public domain system, according to which mines and *in situ* minerals (eg unworked coal) belong to the State, and title to the minerals transfers to the concessionaire upon extraction.[16] The Spanish Civil Code provision giving the ownership of mines to the concessionaire is no longer in force: the mine and *in situ* minerals are under State ownership, even if the exploitation is carried out by a private concessionaire, which in turn becomes the owner of the minerals which it extracts. **14.53**

In the UK and in other common law countries, mines, quarries, and minerals in their original position are part and parcel of the land. Consequently the owner of surface land is *prima facie* entitled to everything beneath or within it, down to the centre of the earth (cf the accession system under Roman law). This principle applies even where title to the surface has been acquired by prescription, **14.54**

[12] France maintained monopoly control over coal imports until 1994: see ch 7 C(2).

[13] See ch 8.

[14] That is also the case in Italian law, because the Italian Civil Code reserves to the State the ownership of subsoil resources 'not available to the private owner of the land': see ch 9 above.

[15] This accession principle is also accepted by the French Civil Code. It does not necessarily apply to all natural resources *in situ*: see below.

[16] This is also the case under the Dutch Mining Bill 1998: see ch 10 above.

but it is subject to exceptions. At common law, gold and silver belong to the Crown, and by statute coal (together with certain associated minerals) was previously vested in the National Coal Board, and so were any minerals removed from land under a compulsory rights order for open-cast working of coal. The Coal Industry Act 1994 vested coal ownership in the Coal Authority, which is not deemed to be part of the Crown, and allowed a number of mines to be sold to private companies.[17]

14.55 The German Federal Mining Act 1980, which repealed and substituted a number of regional laws, classifies mineral resources into two categories: *bergfreie* minerals and *grundeigene* minerals. Only *grundeigene* minerals belong to the surface landowner. The reason for this distinction is the need to safeguard the supply of mineral resources, irrespective of the consent of the private landowner and the size of the property. Coal is considered to be a *bergfrei* mineral resource, so that it does not belong to the owner of the surface land, who will not have access to coal unless a mining permission is obtained. Mining rights are awarded by the Länder mining authorities.[18] Conflicts may emerge between the surface landowner and the holder of mining rights, which must be resolved according to what the Federal Court considers to be a 'vertical neighborhood relationship', in which both have an 'obligation to behave in a reasonable way'.[19]

Coal activities

14.56 In all the countries reviewed above, exploration for and exploitation of coal is subject to either a licence (the UK) or a permission (Germany), and the power of the State to oblige the surface landowner to allow mining activities to be carried out is recognized. Such an imposition will, however, bring about the necessity to pay compensation to the surface landowner for the use of its ownership. In Germany a distinction is made between a permission to search (*Erlaubnis*) and a permission to search for and extract minerals (*Bewilligung* and *Bergwerkseigentum*, the latter sharing the nature of real estate ownership, being transferable and mortgageable). A distinction also exists in Spain, where permission is needed to search (*permiso*) and a concession to extract (*concesión*). However, German law also requires, apart from these permissions, that the company asks for and obtains from the competent authority a mining operation permission. Either public or private companies carry out coal mining activities. In Spain, the vast majority of coal production is in the hands of public companies, though a few private companies do exist. In the UK mining activities have passed into the private sector, as also in Germany where mines are predominantly in the hands of private companies.

---

[17] See ch 13 D(2) above.
[18] See ch 8 C(3) above.
[19] See ch 8 C(8) above.

Coal subsidies

Following the decisive importance of coal for the industrial development of Europe, particularly in the nineteenth and the first half of the twentieth century, its production became expensive, and as a consequence, its existence became dependent on State subsidies. However, at the very heart of European integration is the prohibition on State aids which are incompatible with the internal market.[20] This is why there are specific provisions under the Treaty establishing the ECSC, which will be substituted in the year 2002 (as far as coal subsidies are concerned) by the general provisions on State aids within the Treaty of Rome. The European Commission has allowed a certain amount of financial help to be awarded to national coal production, and has sanctioned aid schemes in Germany, Spain, and the UK. However, Germany and Spain were forced to include that aid in the State budget, thus putting an end to the traditional system of charging a supplement to consumers. The old charge has now been substituted in both countries by a special tax imposed on consumers. On the other hand, the 1996 Electricity Directive allows Member States to give priority to electricity generated by domestic sources of energy, up to a ceiling of 15 per cent of the overall primary energy necessary to produce the electricity consumed in the national market, a provision designed mainly to allow coal subsidies. **14.57**

(3) Exploration for and Production of Oil and Gas

Introduction

Large-scale exploration for and production of oil and gas for the countries under consideration here takes place mainly in the North Sea. This is the case for Norway, the UK, Denmark, and to some extent the Netherlands. Whereas oil and gas reserves are found on the continental shelf only in Norway and Denmark, petroleum is also found onshore in the UK, and the Netherlands. In the Netherlands onshore gas production is much more important than offshore activities. In addition to these four countries, some oil and gasfields are found in Germany (in the north and in the North Sea), France (the Lacq field), Italy (in the Po Valley), and to a very limited extent in Spain. **14.58**

The Legal framework

There are significant differences in the legal regimes governing the exploration for and the production of oil and gas. Whereas these activities may be governed by a general Mining Code, as in France,[21] Germany,[22] and the Netherlands,[23] other **14.59**

[20] See ch 5 above.
[21] See ch 7 above.
[22] Ch 8 above.
[23] Ch 10 above.

States, such as Norway[24] and the UK,[25] have issued special petroleum laws. Spain, on the other hand, has recently issued a Hydrocarbons Act governing both upstream and downstream activities.[26] Another distinction concerns the relationship between the onshore and offshore regimes. Sometimes one regime governs both (see for example Denmark and the newly presented Dutch Mining Bill). More often two different regimes apply, one for offshore and one for onshore activity.

14.60 Onshore, exploration for and production of petroleum is generally based on a Mining Code or a Mining Act. These laws were usually drafted at the turn of the twentieth century or even earlier. The oldest mining law still in force is the French *Loi conçernant les Mines, les Minières et les Carrières* of 1810 which still applies provisionally in the Netherlands.[27] In France this law was replaced by a new Mining Code in 1956.[28] In the Netherlands the Government presented in 1998 a Mining Bill which is intended to replace the 1810 French Mining Code.

14.61 Most mining laws distinguish two or more categories of minerals to which different legal regimes apply. Usually such a distinction indicates that certain minerals are more important and need the closer scrutiny of (central) Government. The most important category generally includes silver, gold, coal, and hydrocarbons. The production of these minerals is dependent upon a concession or licence awarded by central Government. The less important minerals may be produced without direct government involvement.

14.62 Both the original French 1810 Law and the French Mining Law of 1956 divide subsoil minerals in three categories, to which different regulatory regimes apply. The most important category is *mines*. Obviously the Mining Act of 1810 did not include hydrocarbons, so the Netherlands had to apply a legal trick in order to apply the Mining Act 1810 to the production of oil and gas. Although the Italian system also distinguishes between several categories of minerals, the Royal Decree of 1927 limits itself to two categories, mines and quarries. A similar distinction is found in the German regime.[29] The *Bundesberggesetz* of 1980 (replacing the mining laws of the individual *Bundesländer*) distinguishes between *bergfreie* and *grundeigene* minerals. Whereas the latter are part of a landowner's property, the former are independent of land ownership and can only be exploited on the basis of a licence or concession.

14.63 The search for petroleum on the continental shelf of the North Sea was triggered by the discovery of the Groningen gasfield in the Netherlands in 1959. However, before starting any exploration activities, the coastal States had to establish the

[24] Ch 11 above.
[25] Ch 13 above.
[26] Ch 12 above.
[27] Ch 10 above.
[28] Ch 7 above.
[29] Ch 8 above.

necessary legal instruments. Following the conclusion of the 1958 Geneva Convention on the Continental Shelf, North Sea States first claimed the right to explore and exploit their offshore petroleum resources.

In exercising their functional jurisdiction offshore, Denmark and the UK decided to extend their onshore legislation to the continental shelf. Hence, the application of both the Danish Subsoil Act and the UK Petroleum (Production) Act was extended offshore on the basis of a Continental Shelf Act. The Netherlands and Norway decided to establish special legislation for the exploration for and exploitation of offshore natural resources. Although the Dutch Government considered applying the Mining Act 1810 to offshore mining, the Continental Shelf Mining Act was enacted instead since the legislator would have met considerable difficulties in applying the 'provisional' classical onshore regime to the requirements of offshore petroleum production. Norway, on the other hand, did not have any onshore petroleum production and thus legislated for the first time with the offshore Petroleum Act issued in 1963 (replaced by the Petroleum Acts of 1985 and 1996). 14.64

The Ownership of oil and gas

When discussing the ownership of oil and gas, a distinction should be made between the ownership of the minerals before and after production. Whereas all regimes clearly identify that the concessionaire or licensee owns the minerals upon production, some uncertainty may exist about the ownership of minerals *in situ*. The German, French, and Netherlands regimes do not explicitly declare that unworked minerals are owned by the State. In Italy the Civil Code (Art 826) reserves to the State ownership of subsoil resources which are not part of the landowner's property, so there is some uncertainty about which subsoil minerals are owned by the State and which by the landowners. 14.65

By contrast to the above regimes which apply to a large range of minerals, the UK enacted a specific Petroleum Act as early as 1918. However, as with most of the above regimes, this Act left the matter of ownership of subsoil petroleum resources unresolved. This situation changed under the Petroleum (Production) Act 1934, section 1 of which declared the ownership of the hydrocarbons to be vested in the State. As a result, no compensation had to be paid to the landowner for loss of resources.[30] Similarly, the Danish Subsoil Act of 1932 explicitly declares that all natural resources in the Danish subsoil belong to the State of Denmark to the extent the resources had not been exploited before the enactment of the Act. 14.66

[30] This element has played a role in the discussion in the Netherlands about the ownership of the natural resources *in situ*. The fact that landowners are paid compensation (albeit very small in amount) is used as an argument for the accession theory, ie that title to natural resources run with title to the land.

14.67 Offshore coastal States have sovereign rights over their natural resources. It should be noted, however, that the North Sea States interpret the extent of their offshore functional jurisdiction differently. The UK, consistent with international law, does not claim sovereignty but rather claims the right to explore and exploit the resources. Denmark and the Netherlands take a much wider view and claim that the natural resources of their continental shelves are owned by the Kingdom of Denmark and the Kingdom of the Netherlands respectively. Since Norway proclaimed sovereignty over the Norwegian continental shelf in 1963, it can be argued that Norway has also gone further than it is entitled under the 1958 Continental Shelf Convention, and now the 1982 Law of the Sea Convention, which refer only to 'sovereign rights'.

14.68 Be that as it may, the offshore petroleum regimes of all the North Sea States are based on regulation of the offshore activities by a framework Act, and further regulations which can be amended more easily if the situation so requires. Moreover, all legal systems provide for a licensing regime.

Licensing regime

Introduction

14.69 Petroleum production activities consist of several stages, generally including: a) preliminary investigations, eg seismic, geological, and geochemical surveys; b) exploratory or appraisal drilling; c) production of hydrocarbons; d) transportation and supply of petroleum to the first delivery point; and e) the abandonment and possible removal of the production installations. This final stage is discussed below with reference to environmental issues. All the countries considered here provide for (some of) these activities to be carried out under a licence or concession,[31] although the number and type of licences may differ.

Onshore

14.70 Hydrocarbons are considered to be so important that their ownership should not run with ownership of the land. A special regime applies to these resources, either a general Mining Act or a specific Petroleum Act. All regimes, however, have in common the fact that they make exploration for and/or production of these resources subject to a licence, concession, or permit.

14.71 At the outset, most hydrocarbon licences and concessions were based on the traditional concession system, and awarded for extremely long periods of time

[31] Other methods of regulating oil, gas, and mining activities such as production-sharing contracts and agreements establishing simple owner-contractor relationships, are in use in some countries. However, in Europe there is a tradition of using a licence system where private and State-owned companies are permitted to explore for and exploit natural resources: see eg Denmark, the Netherlands, Norway, and the United Kingdom.

and/or over a very large area.[32] Onshore licences were awarded on the basis of a system of 'geological units' and not on the basis of blocks and/or part blocks as is the case offshore. Notably, the first petroleum licences under the UK 1918 Petroleum Act and concessions under the Netherlands 1810 Mining Act were awarded in perpetuity. As for geographic scope, it is striking that one licence applied to the entire territory of Denmark, and was even expanded to encompass the continental shelf area in 1963. That ceased to be the case in 1982.

These concessions and licences conferred broad rights to the concessionaire or licensee and involved very few governmental control mechanisms. As these concessions or licences were often the result of individual negotiation, no competitive elements were included. The Hydrocarbons Licensing Directive of 1996 brought some important changes to the onshore petroleum regimes. In the Netherlands, for example, the onshore mining regime was virtually without any competition: basically, it was a case of first come, first served. However, since 1996 all applications for a drilling licence need to be published in order to provide others with the opportunity to submit a competing application. Although the Directive has important consequences for the Dutch onshore regime, it does not affect existing concessions, so that the effect on this regime is as yet very limited. **14.72**

Following the Hydrocarbons Licensing Directive the UK onshore system has also been amended. The former three-tier system is replaced by the single Production, Exploration, and Development Licence (PEDL). It should be noted, however, that the integration of the separate licences is not required by the Directive, although it was triggered by the Directive and the perception that the onshore licensing regime required amendment in any event. PEDLs were introduced to cut down (largely administrative) costs, reflecting a general trend conditioned by the fact that most major fields are already under development, as a result of which Government and industry must focus on smaller acreages and thus seek to reduce costs. **14.73**

Offshore

Most North Sea States provide for the award of an exploration licence, a production licence, and a pipeline or transportation licence. The last reflects the fact that the distance between the well and the first delivery point is usually far longer offshore than onshore. Preparatory activities such as seismic surveys are generally carried out on the basis of a non-exclusive licence. In contrast, the exploration and production licence is an exclusive licence which covers both exploratory drilling and production. The licence is split into an exploration period and an exploitation period. Before entering the production period, the Government must first **14.74**

[32] Ernest E Smith *et al*, *International Petroleum Transactions*, Rocky Mountain Mineral Law Foundation, Denver, Colorado, 1993.

approve a development plan. Therefore, such production licences impose a two-step approach: the UK, Norwegian, and Danish petroleum regimes are examples. The Netherlands Government has chosen a different approach and awards separate licences for prospecting, exploratory drilling, and production. Its Continental Shelf Mining Act provides for a non-exclusive reconnaissance licence for seismic survey, an exclusive exploration licence for exploratory drilling, and an exclusive production licence enabling the licensee to exploit hydrocarbons as well as to explore for them. Although these licences are not necessarily awarded in this order, a production licence will seldom be applied for directly because such a licence is only awarded where an economically viable quantity of hydrocarbons has been discovered. An exception may be made if a field straddles another block: the licensee may then apply for a 'spontaneous' production licence for the neighbouring block. Be that as it may, the practical impact is the same for both systems since production can only begin after government approval and upon proof that sufficient hydrocarbons are present.

14.75 Although the licence in its form is individual, the contents of the licence often apply to several licensees and so will be of a more general nature. In the United Kingdom a set of model clauses is attached to the individual licence, and Denmark and Norway publish a model licence for each licensing round. Therefore many licence conditions might as well have been issued by statutory regulation. Conditions always found in a licence are the specification and delimitation of the activities, the area covered, and duration, which is usually rather long. Production licences are often issued for periods of some thirty-six years (Denmark) or forty years (Netherlands). Working obligations and time schedules are also included.

14.76 Offshore licensing in all North Sea countries is based on a competitive system. Until recently licensing was based on a system of 'rounds'. The Hydrocarbons Licensing Directive brought about some change: it gives Governments the choice between a system of organized licensing rounds and an ad hoc licensing system. Whereas the first system is based on a public invitation to bid, the latter enables applications for a licence at any time, which must be published in order to give others the possibility to compete. Consequently, a more diverse picture has arisen in the North Sea area. Whereas the UK and Norway still use organized licensing rounds, the Netherlands has opted for an ad hoc system. The Netherlands is now using the ad hoc system because most of its acreage has been licensed so that only limited acreage is on offer, often consisting of relinquished acreage. Denmark has included several options in its legislation: in addition to licensing rounds, an ad hoc procedure is possible either by way of mini-rounds or through a new 'open door' procedure.

14.77 As far as offshore exploration and production is concerned, it seems that the Hydrocarbons Licensing Directive has resulted in more diverse systems. Other licensing award regimes have been adopted. This could lead to the unanticipated result that there will be less, rather than more, transparency in licensing procedures.

The Hydrocarbons Licensing Directive stipulates that the criteria for awarding a licence shall be transparent and non-discriminatory. Potential licensees should be able to ascertain the criteria before application. These criteria are usually included in regulations implementing the Act or in Model Clauses. As for the criteria, a distinction may be made between a system of licensing rounds and an ad hoc system. Governments have used this distinction to impose different criteria for each individual licensing round, according to the licensing system employed. Moreover, when indicating the acreage on offer, Governments have also indicated the applicable criteria in such notice. This system applied in all North Sea countries with some variations. Whereas the Norwegian, Danish, and UK Governments limited each round to specific acreage to which special criteria applied, the Netherlands licensing rounds were not restricted to specific blocks but covered all the remaining acreage and thus did not give detailed licensing criteria in each individual round. Since the Hydrocarbons Licensing Directive, however, different criteria cannot be applied to different rounds. One reason for this, amongst others, is that specific criteria cannot be presented for ad hoc licences. Governments seeking to apply such a licensing system are required to stipulate licence award criteria in legislation, so that applications for a licence can be made at any time. Most regimes have therefore included in their legislation the technical and financial criteria applicable to the award of a production licence. These licence provisions apply from the moment the licence is awarded. The situation is further complicated in the Netherlands by the fact that exploration and production on the Dutch continental shelf are not covered by one licence; a complicated system applies, in which the conditions for the production licence are linked to the time of the award of the exploration licence. In other words, as three different financial regimes apply, the time of the award of the exploration licence determines the regime applying to the production licence. The criteria for the award of a production licence are therefore not transparent since the legislator has not defined when and under which conditions a field is considered to be economically viable, thus leaving the award of a production licence to the exercise of ministerial discretion. **14.78**

Pipeline or transportation licence

Most North Sea States require a separate pipeline or transporation licence. Hence, a production licence does not entitle the licensees to construct and exploit a submarine pipeline. There is clearly a close relationship between the award of a production licence and that of a pipeline licence. In essence, any development plan will include some information about the transportation of the hydrocarbons to the shore. Moreover, when awarding a pipeline licence licensing authorities **14.79** usually take into account whether the applicant companies have been granted a production licence. The situation in Denmark is different as the existing offshore petroleum pipelines are constructed and operated by the Danish State-owned company DONG.

14.80 In contrast with the regimes in Norway, the UK, and Denmark, in the Netherlands a pipeline licence is not required. Its Continental Shelf Mining Act applies the traditional 'right of immersion' under the law of the sea, whereby all States have the freedom to lay submarine pipelines on the continental shelf. This is notwithstanding the fact that Article 79 of the 1982 law of the sea Convention permits the coastal State to regulate the construction and operation of submarine pipelines for the exploration and production of hydrocarbons. This power follows the functional jurisdiction of coastal States, and is exercised by Norway, Denmark, and the UK. The Dutch legislator has not made use of this enhanced coastal State jurisdiction, instead conferring a general right of immersion on the holders of a production licence. Whereas in some cases the pipelines are operated as an integral part of the production activities, in other cases separate pipeline companies have been established, as a result of which the production and transportation of petroleum has become two distinct elements. Basically, Government control is limited to instructions on the basis of the development plan and the application of competition law. However, if a pipeline company is abusing its dominant position, recourse through competition law will probably take more time than direct government control through the relevant petroleum law, as is the case in Norway and the UK. The Danish government has applied its pipeline jurisdiction extensively: it is the only North Sea country that has issued a separate law for the contruction and the operation of a single offshore pipeline, the Pipeline Act of 1981.[33] This law, provides, *inter alia*, for a detailed tariff scheme for third-party use.

14.81 It should also be noted that the Hydrocarbons Licensing Directive does not regulate this final stage of the upstream petroleum sector. There are no provisions governing the transportation and supply of petroleum to the first delivery point. By contrast, provisions regarding the use of upstream pipelines are found in the Gas Directive (see below). It seems that EC energy law leaves the issue of upstream pipelines in a regulatory grey zone inbetween upstream and downstream legislation, currently referred to as midstream legislation.

14.82 On the other hand, the Hydrocarbons Licensing Directive has led to some direct improvements in the internal energy market. Since 1996 all North Sea States have removed from their legislation any requirement that petroleum be landed within their own jurisdiction. That obstacle to the export of petroleum has thus been re-

[33] Ch 6 above.

moved from the domestic petroleum laws. It is very likely that the situation regarding the offshore pipeline infrastructure will change in the future, and that cross-border pipeline connections will be constructed in place of connections to the national pipeline systems.

Licensees and joint ventures

Petroleum licences are usually awarded to a group of companies. Governments' approaches to the establishment of these groups may vary. Whereas in the Netherlands and the UK the companies are free to decide the membership of the group, the Norwegian Government and, to a lesser extent, the Danish one may influence this process. **14.83**

The internal relationship is usually regulated by joint venture agreements, known as joint bidding and joint operating agreements. If a licence is awarded the group usually enters into a joint operating agreement (JOA). In the Netherlands and the UK, companies enter into such JOAs according to their own wishes and requirements. Although not standard-form agreements as such, JOA terms have become more or less standardized over the years owing to the number of repeat players in offshore activities, with the same companies negotiating rights and duties under the JOA. Nevertheless, contractual freedom may be limited through the exercise of governmental control, either through the requirement of Ministerial approval of the JOA, as in the UK and Denmark, or through the Ministry by way of laws and/or licensing criteria which directly influence the JOA. **14.84**

In Norway JOAs are standard agreements in the sense that the Government drafts the JOA, acceptance thereof being a prerequisite for the award of a production licence. In Denmark a proposal for a JOA is made available for the applicants, but modifications of the content are accepted by the authorities. In general the Danish authorities do not get involved in the internal relationship of the group today, whereas representation in meetings and negotiations was a part of the pattern in eg the first and second rounds. In general Norway and Denmark have employed standard agreements more frequently than the Netherlands and the UK, with Norway also requiring the use of the Standard Norwegian Fabrication Contract (NF 92) in respect of the construction of offshore installations. **14.85**

State participation

As mentioned above, the Governments of those countries reviewed here which have indigenous energy resources have engaged in the development of these resources through companies which are fully or partly owned by the State. Basically, States seek maximum control over exploration and production and to obtain maximum benefit from such activities. The extent of State participation has varied over the years: nationalisation and increased governmental control have since the mid-1980s been replaced by a trend towards privatization and liberalization. **14.86**

Following that trend, State oil companies have either been abolished or their influence and preferential positions have been severely reduced.

14.87 In order to prevent States from directly influencing the market and competition through their ownership of oil companies, the Hydrocarbons Licensing Directive gives clear instructions with regard to State participation. These provisions are of special importance for Norway, Denmark, and the Netherlands, but not for the UK whose Government no longer participates in the exploration for and production of hydrocarbons since the abolition of BNOC in the 1980s. Whereas the Norwegian and Danish States participate in the licence through a State oil company, Statoil in Norway and DONG in Denmark, the Dutch Government usually participates indirectly in the production of gas (and oil under certain circumstances) through a holding company called EBN (Energiebeheer Nederland). However, EBN is explicitly not party to the licence. In this respect the State participation of EBN in the Netherlands is comparable to the State Direct Financial Interest (SDFI) which has applied in Norway since 1985. In contradiction to Statoil in Norway, the Danish DONG has only a minority interest in the licences of 10–20 per cent.

14.88 Since the entry into force of the Hydrocarbons Licensing Directive, with its specific provisions regarding State participation, North Sea States have had to consider their domestic laws closely. The first thing to note, however, is that the Directive does not preclude the establishment of a State oil company so long as a level playing field for companies, whether national or other European, publicly or privately owned, is created. If the State participates, the Directive clearly establishes that it may only assume rights and obligations in proportion to its participation. State participation may not be used to influence the licensee's procurement activities. Special provisions apply where a State oil company is both a licence holder and the holder of the State's participation in the production. This applies to Norway, where Statoil is participating commercially in several licences and also holds the State's financial interest. With the implementation of the Directive, the role of the State oil companies Statoil and DONG has changed in that these companies are now treated in a similar way to other commercial companies. In other words, some of their previous privileges have disappeared. In Norway, Statoil therefore has no guarantee that it will always obtain an interest in a licence. To an increasing extent State participants and State oil companies are considered to be an instrument for Government profit (ie a financial instrument) rather than an instrument for Government influence in the economy of the petroleum industry.

Concluding remarks

The hydrocarbons industry is divided into an onshore and an offshore industry. A further distinction may be drawn between Northern and Southern Europe, in that although some domestic petroleum production is taking place in Italy, France, and Germany, these activities are limited in comparison with the activities in and around the North Sea. When offshore activities commenced in the 1960s both the UK and Denmark extended their onshore jurisdiction offshore. Whereas the same legislation applies to the onshore and offshore areas in Denmark, the UK has gradually developed special petroleum legislation for the offshore. Similarly, the Netherlands and Norway have developed special legislation for hydrocarbons exploration and production on the continental shelf. These laws apply to the continental shelf outside the territorial waters. The distinction between the onshore and offshore legal regimes is to some extent artificial as it suggests that different regimes may apply on each side of the borderline. **14.89**

Under the 1996 Norwegian Petroleum Act the continental shelf regime also applies to the territorial sea and to activities onshore. In the Netherlands, the licensing regime of the Continental Shelf Mining Act has to a large extent been applied to the onshore concessions. This system will finally be codified when (or if) the 1998 Mining Bill enters into force. The Netherlands will then also have one regime for both exploration for and production of hydrocarbons. Hence in both Norway and the Netherlands the offshore regime has directly influenced activities onshore, whilst for Denmark and the UK it was the onshore regime which, at least initially, conditioned offshore legal developments. Finally, it may be noted that the UK legislator has also sought to streamline some aspects of onshore and offshore energy law and policy. An example is the 1996 Pipeline Safety Regulations which apply onshore as well as offshore. Similarly, the Offshore Infrastructure Code of Practice was introduced in 1996 in order to facilitate third-party access to offshore pipelines. The liberalization process in the onshore gas sector was one of the reasons for streamlining the access procedures offshore.[34] Hence, a gradual integration of the onshore and offshore regimes is apparent in all North Sea countries. **14.90**

D. The Gas Supply System

(1) Introduction

The present European gas market is essentially the result of the discovery of the Groningen gasfield in the Netherlands in 1959. The size of the field, and the **14.91**

[34] T Daintith, G Willoughby, *United Kingdom Oil and Gas Law*, Sweet & Maxwell, loose-leaf edition, 1999, I-727. See also MM Roggenkamp, *Het Juridisch Kader van Pijpleidingen in de Olie- en Gasindustrie*, dissertation, Feb 1999, 474–5 and 487–90.

expectation that nuclear energy would soon meet domestic energy needs, led the Dutch Government to enter into export contracts in the early 1960s with Germany, Belgium, France, and Italy. In addition, the discovery of the Groningen field led to large-scale exploration in the North Sea, with major discoveries in the early 1970s on the continental shelves of Norway and the United Kingdom. The discoveries on the Danish and Dutch continental shelves are much smaller.

14.92 In consequence of these discoveries, national gas supply markets were established in the 1960s in the Netherlands, Germany, Belgium, France, and Italy. These markets are connected by a system of long-distance pipelines supplying Dutch gas (and some indigenous gas) to domestic consumers. The Danish gas market was connected to this system at a later stage by the Deudan pipeline connection between Germany and Denmark. More recently, the UK gas market became connected to the continental system with the coming into operation of the UK Interconnector between Bacton and Zeebrugge in 1998. Until then all gas from the British continental shelf was landed and used in the UK. In contrast, no gas from the Norwegian continental shelf is used for domestic purposes in Norway: in the absence of a domestic gas market, all Norwegian gas is exported. Pipelines from the Norwegian continental shelf are landed in the UK, Germany, Belgium, and France. Norwegian gas is exported not only to these North European countries, but also to Italy and Spain, which are also supplied by gas from Algeria and Libya. In addition, there is an east-west pipeline connection for gas from Russia that is sold to Germany, Austria, and France.

(2) Market Structure

Introduction

14.93 Historically, most national gas markets have been organized as legal or *de facto* monopolies, with transportation, supply, and import/export carried out by a single entity. Legal monopolies were (or are) found in the UK (British Gas), Denmark (DONG), and Italy (ENI/SNAM) with the establishment of these gas supply and transmission companies based on an exclusive concession or licence on the basis of a Gas Act or Energy Act. In France, the exclusive rights awarded to Gaz de France were limited to distribution, imports, and exports. A *de facto* monopoly existed in the Netherlands and Italy in the absence of specific gas laws governing gas supply. The situation in Germany is special: it is the only example in this book where the Government has awarded several gas supply licences as a result of which there is no monopoly and several gas transmission companies exist alongside each other. By contrast, gas distribution is monopolized at the supply level by the local communities on the basis of concession and demarcation agreements. Hence, there is a supply monopoly at the municipal level which directly influences the gas transmission sector. Moreover, in some of the States discussed in this book the gas companies were/are also vertically integrated. This is the case with Gaz de France, and was so for British Gas until the 1980s to the extent that British Gas was also involved in the production of gas. In the early 1990s the Spanish gas market was in the process of being horizontally and vertically integrated. The situation in the Netherlands and Denmark is similar to the extent that the national transmission companies supply the local and/or regional distribution companies. However, a unique feature of the Danish system is that the gas transmission system is not limited to the land territory but extends onto the continental shelf.

Public/private ownership

14.94 The gas industry has basically been a publicly owned sector, but a distinction must be made between the three different supply stages. Private companies undertake gas production, although the State may well also participate (see upstream sector). Moreover, the State has for a considerable period influenced the gas supply sector via national landing obligations in respect of gas. Although the implementation of the Hydrocarbons Licensing Directive has resulted in the abolition of such landing obligation clauses the effects are still lingering as the new regime does not affect pre-existing gas contracts. In this respect it is also important to note the establishment of the national gas negotiating committee in Norway (GFU) in 1987. This body consisting of the (then) three Norwegian oil companies is clearly the result of the Norwegian Government's intention to influence the pooling and the supply of gas produced on the Norwegian continental shelf. Consequently, it will be difficult for producers and consumers to enter into direct supply contracts. Nevertheless, despite different degrees of government control, the production sector is basically privately owned.

14.95 The transmission and distribution of gas (ie the downstream gas sector) is mainly publicly owned: the transmission companies are owned by central Governments and the distribution companies by regional and/or local Governments. However, this situation is rapidly changing. The privatization process is speeding up. Apart from the German transmission companies (which were privately owned from their inception) and the NV Nederlandse Gasunie (a public/private partnership which replaced the Dutch State Gas Board as early as 1963) the privatization process started in the 1980s. British Gas was privatized in 1986, with a similar process taking place in Spain (Enagas) nearly a decade later, in 1995. In these two countries privatization also affected the distribution companies which were also taken over by private companies. Although a trend of take-overs and mergers in the distribution sector can be noted in other States as well, it is not yet clear to what extent the distribution sector will be privatized.

14.96 There is undoubtedly a clear trend towards privatization of the gas sector. This trend is to a large extent the result of the liberalization policy of the countries reviewed (save for the UK where liberalization followed privatization) and is based on developments within the Community.[35]

(3) National Gas Markets after the 1998 Directive Establishing Common Rules for the Creation of an Internal Market for Gas

Introduction

14.97 The Gas Directive was adopted in June 1998 and had to be implemented by the Member States by 10 August 2000. The Directive requires a gradual market opening, ranging from 20 per cent in the year 2000 to 33 per cent in the year 2008. The required market opening is achieved through the appointment of eligible customers, ie those free to decide where and from whom to purchase their gas. Access to the network can be achieved either by way of negotiated third-party access (TPA) or regulated TPA. In addition, the Directive provides for access to upstream pipelines.

14.98 Furthermore, all gas companies are required to unbundle their accounts in order to provide sufficient transparency. Integrated gas companies must keep separate accounts for their different functions as if they were separate undertakings. Essentially, transmission and distribution companies have to operate on the basis of commercial principles. Each transmission undertaking is required to preserve the confidentiality of any commercially sensitive information it obtains from other systems or system users. Distribution companies may, however, be placed under public service duties in order to ensure that all customers in a given supply area will be supplied. Finally, the Directive requires Member States to appoint independent competent authorities for dispute resolution.

Market opening

14.99 Although the Directive only requires a limited market opening, it is interesting to note that a number of Member States go further than the thresholds included in the Directive. The UK, for example, already has a fully liberalized market. As provided in the Directive, the process has taken place in several stages. Larger gas consumers gradually became free to choose their supplier in the 1980s, and in the late 1990s the process started taking place at the level of individual households.

14.100 A similar process is taking place in the Netherlands as the Gas Act provides for a complete market opening in three different stages: first large consumers, then medium-sized in 2002, followed from 2004 for all consumers, including households. Non-eligible consumers and households are protected by the law via a licensing system. Until 2004, suppliers (the former distribution companies) require a licence for the supply of non-eligible customers. The suppliers then have

[35] See ch 5 above.

a duty to supply with the tariffs being set/controlled by the Minister. As of 2004 all gas suppliers (former distribution companies, foreign companies, and traders) need another licence if they wish to supply households. Under this licence there is no firm obligation to supply, but a general duty to take care of gas supply.

Similarly, the Spanish gas market is becoming fully liberalized. In 1998 a Hydrocarbons Act entered into force, replacing the former upstream and downstream hydrocarbons legislation. Hence, since 1998 an integrated hydrocarbons law exists for exploration, production, transmission, and supply. Although this Act was not drafted for the purpose of implementing the Gas Directive, it is based on similar principles so that the supply of and trade in gas is no longer limited to one company. The Spanish gas market will be opened gradually, starting with the electricity generators (as long as they are taking part in the power pool) and consumers above a certain threshold of use. The market was opened in 2000, with a target of 2003 for all consumers to be eligible and thus free to choose a supplier. 14.101

The Italian Gas Act of May 2000 provides for market opening in two stages. At first all consumers using more than 200,000 m^3 of gas per year are considered eligible. As of January 2003 all final consumers will be eligible. In Germany the situation is different. The new Federal Energy Act of 24 April 1998 has not adopted the system of a gradual market opening as suggested by the Gas Directive. Basically, all consumers are considered eligible. The law itself gives all consumers the right to negotiate access. However, it is assumed that negotiations for access will at first be limited to industrial consumers as the conditions for negotiating access and the reasons for refusing access are not very clear, thus hindering the proper functioning of the system. Nevertheless, it is likely that smaller customers and households will also enter the market as was experienced recently in the electricity sector. 14.102

The situation in France is different again. Here the process of liberalization has been very slow. It applies a minimum level of market opening. As in Spain, further stages of increasing eligibility are envisaged, though still set according to a minimum threshold of use. In consequence the French gas market will open from 20 per cent in 2000 to 33 per cent in 2008 and thus meet the minimum standard of the Directive. Transmission, storage, and gas sales will be open for new operators. 14.103

System access

The Member States reviewed have opted for different types of access. Although in the initial legislative process most Member States opted for a system of negotiated access, the final choices made are more diverse. Whereas the Netherlands, Germany and France apply a system of negotiated access, the UK and Spain apply a system of regulated access. Denmark has chosen a mixed system, ie negotiated 14.104

access for the transmission grid and regulated access for the distribution grid. In Italy and the Netherlands the negotiated TPA regime also applies to gas storage.

14.105 The Directive has also included a provision regarding access to upstream pipelines. This provision enables consumers to enter into negotiations for gas supply from all suppliers, including the offshore producers. The regulatory regime for these pipelines is different. These pipelines are usually not governed by the downstream gas laws, but by the upstream mining or petroleum laws. Consequently, these pipelines systems are not operated by the national gas company (ie the monopoly). An exception is again the Danish gas pipeline system, which extends into the North Sea. It can be assumed that the implementation of the Gas Directive, ie the choice between regulated or negotiated access, also applies to this part of the pipeline system. Be that as it may, as regards the upstream pipelines in the North Sea area it may be noted that in practice a system of open access exists. The Norwegian, the UK, and the Dutch systems consist of numerous pipelines owned by several consortia of oil companies. Access to these pipelines (resulting from the connection of newly discovered gas fields) is based on negotiations between the producer and the pipeline company/operator. A difference between the regulatory systems is the extent of Government control. Whereas the Norwegian offshore pipelines are under strict Government control, the Dutch system is virtually without such control, with the Gas Law limiting such control to the application of competition law to upstream pipelines.

14.106 In this respect it is interesting to note the UK experience of the early 1990s, which illustrates that light-handed regulation does not necessarily stimulate competition. There limited rules about access to the pipeline systems resulted in lengthy negotiations. In order to speed up the negotiations so that the requirements of the liberalized gas market could be met, the UK Government issued an Offshore Infrastructure Code of Practice in 1996, further regulating negotiation procedures.

14.107 Taking into account the experiences offshore, it can be concluded that if the aim is to introduce more competition in the gas sector, a system of negotiated access without further regulating the negotiating process is inadequate. In addition, clear rules are required for denying access. The German Energy Act, for example, merely provides that access can be denied on the basis of 'operational or other reasons', wording so vague as to leave market players in considerable uncertainly regarding the circumstances under which access may be denied.

Unbundling

14.108 The Directive only requires an administrative unbundling of the undertakings as it lays down rules concerning the accounts of the natural gas undertakings. Moreover, integrated national gas undertakings must keep separate accounts for their natural gas transmission, distribution, and storage activities and, where appropriate, consolidated accounts for non-gas activities. A balance sheet and a profit and loss account must be drawn up for each activity. The accounts for transmission and for distribution activities may be combined, however, where access to the system is on the basis of a single charge for both activities.[36] These rules may only be amended in exceptional cases.

Most Member States have included in their legislation a requirement for administrative unbundling. This trend can be noticed in most countries discussed in this book, eg Spain, Denmark, France, and Germany. Again the Netherlands has opted for a mixed system. A system of legal unbundling applies to the distribution grid and a limited degree of administrative unbundling (ie unbundling of accounts) applies to the transmission sector. The most advanced system is again to be found in the UK where network and supply activities are legally and physically unbundled. Whereas British Gas is still involved in the supply of gas, the network activities have been transferred into a separate company, Transco. It should be noted that this devolution has taken place gradually and at the initiative of British Gas. The UK chapter shows that the establishment of 'Chinese Walls' between the transmission and the supply arm was not considered as a proper guarantee against challenge from the competition authorities. Hence, British Gas itself decided to break up the company into several components. It remains to be seen if a similar trend will occur in continental Europe. **14.109**

If Governments really wish to establish a liberalized market, total physical unbundling may indeed be necessary. In practice, negotiations for access with a 'bundled' gas company seem to be a barrier for concluding agreements on access. Whatever 'Chinese walls' are established between the network operator and the supplier, there will always be some doubt about the way in which business information can or will be treated. This is so especially where no agreement can be reached over the purchase of a certain quantity of gas (eg the price) and afterwards negotiations are entered into for access to the system for the transport of other gas. **14.110**

Finally, it should be noted that examples of legal and physical unbundling are found in the electricity sector (see below). The reason for choosing a different principle for the gas sector seems somewhat arbitrary, though clearly the desire to protect national interests has played a part. Moreover, in countries like the Netherlands where the gas distribution sector is horizontally integrated with the electricity sector, the need to unbundle the gas distribution sector is more apparent as the electricity sector was already legally required to unbundle its activities. The question is whether increased horizontal integration in other Member States **14.111**

[36] Undertakings must specify in their internal accounting the rules they will follow for the allocation of assets and liabilities, expenditure and income, as well as for depreciation, in drawing up their separate accounts.

will lead to a similar result. It is highly likely that market forces will lead to a further unbundling of supply and transport activities.

Public service obligations

14.112 Article 3 of the Gas Directive states that Member States may, in the general economic interest, impose public service obligations (PSOs) on natural gas undertakings. A PSO may relate to security, regularity, quality and price of supply, and to environmental protection. From the above chapters it is clear that the concept of public service obligations is more common in southern European countries than in northern Europe. In southern Europe the concept of 'public service' is often included in the Constitution (eg Spain). In parallel with the concept of public service runs the concept of essential services, which plays a role in discussions regarding competition in network-bound sectors. The concept of essential services is outlined in the EC chapter above and is not necessarily the same as a public service, as the chapter on Spanish energy law clearly illustrates.[37]

14.113 The French, Italian, and Spanish systems have always been based on the concept of public service. This concept plays a special role in the distribution sector. In France, Act no 98-546 of 1998, for example, enables each Prefect (a representative of the State on the local level) to draft a 'public service distribution plan' listing municipalities not already connected to a gas distribution grid but wishing to be in the future. This plan is updated every three years. Gas distribution in France remains a public service and market opening will be limited. In Spain the former 1987 Gas Act also explicitly declared that the production, transmission, and distribution of gas are a public service. In this case it meant that the reservation of a public service gave the administration the power to award concessions. The new Hydrocarbons Act of 1998, however, does not include such a provision.

14.114 As previously indicated, northern Europe is less familiar with the concept of a public service obligation. In essence, gas companies and networks are considered to be public utilities providing a public service. Gas companies can thus have an advantage when land must be expropriated for the construction of gas pipelines. Such examples are found in the Netherlands and Germany.[38]

14.115 PSOs are most often applied in the distribution sector, primarily to protect the final consumer at the end of the 'gas chain'. Most interesting, therefore, is the discussion by some Member States of the application of a PSO to other stages of the gas chain. The Netherlands has imposed a PSO upon the gas company Gasunie as Gasunie is given a crucial task in national resource management, particularly in the maintenance of the small field policy. Gasunie will be under an obligation to purchase all natural gas from the small fields offshore at commercial prices.

[37] Ch 12 above.
[38] Chs 10 and 8 above.

Take or pay

Gas undertakings may refuse access to the pipeline system if such access would cause these undertakings serious economic and financial difficulties with their take-or-pay contracts (cf Articles 17 and 25 of the Gas Directive, the latter containing a derogation clause). The issue of take or pay (TOP) has rarely been discussed in the countries under review. An exception is the UK chapter above. This is not surprising as the liberalization process is much further developed in the UK than in any other Member State. Hence, some examples from the UK experience may be of importance for the other North Sea States. **14.116**

Since the introduction of the Gas Act 1986, entities other than British Gas (BG)[39] have been able to enter into supply agreements with consumers such as electricity generators, as a result of which gas-to-gas competition was introduced. In addition, an oversupply of gas was created. A further consequence was that the share of BG in the UK gas market gradually decreased and BG was thus confronted with contractual TOP clauses it could not meet, resulting eventually in litigation testing such clauses.[40] **14.117**

Until recently the situation in other North Sea countries was comparable to the situation in the UK before 1986. Except for Norway, existing production licences have been based on the assumption that all gas is to be sold to the national gas company. Hence, current Dutch and Danish gas producers supply their gas to the national gas undertaking, Gasunie or DONG respectively. Moreover, these gas supply contracts are long-term contracts, as indeed are Norwegian gas contracts. The difference may be, however, that whereas the Dutch and Danish gas contracts are mostly depletion contracts, most Norwegian gas contracts since the development of the Troll field are volume-based contracts leaving the producer some flexibility to enter into additional supply contracts with new customers. The introduction of gas-to-gas competition is therefore limited to new gas fields and will depend on the price and conditions offered by the competing gas purchasers. So far as existing gas fields are concerned, competition can only emerge if the Government or independent regulator actively interferes and decides that a certain percentage of gas should be destined for the open market, as has been the case in the UK.[41] **14.118**

Supervision and control

The Directive requires Member States to designate an independent competent authority to settle any disputes relating to negotiations on access to the system. **14.119**

39 See ch 13 above.
40 ibid.
41 ibid.

The designated authority should be independent from the administration, with Member States afforded the choice of appointing a specific supervisor or designating an existing authority such as the competition authority. However, some of the States under review have appointed the competition authorities to settle disputes relating to access negotiations, as for instance in the Netherlands and Germany. Italy and the Netherlands have appointed independent energy regulators operating separately from the Competition Authority. The German chapter clearly illustrates the role a competition authority can play in the gas (and electricity) sector. It also illustrates, however, that supervision by the competition authority can be time-consuming and inflexible. The tasks of a competition authority can be more limited in scope than those of an industry regulator, with the latter better placed to play a more active role in the liberalization process. The tentative conclusion, which can be drawn from this is that appointing the competition authority as the gas industry's watchdog is no guarantee of the establishment of a liberalized gas market; this requires the appointment of an independent regulator with more extensive powers.[42]

14.120 In practice few States have appointed specific gas regulators. The best known example is, of course, the Director General of Gas Supply under the UK Gas Act 1986, an independent regulator. Here the regulator is charged with the task of overseeing the development of competition in the gas sector. The regulator's office (Office of Gas Supply or OFGAS) is additional to other competition bodies like the Monopolies and Mergers Commission. The regulator is required actively to introduce competition in the gas sector and, in this respect, the UK has gone further than the requirements of the Directive. The tasks of the regulator are not limited to settling disputes relating to access negotiations, but also include involvement in setting tariffs for transmission and supply. The work of the independent regulator has therefore resulted in a system of price regulation for monopolies, with the possibility of price-capping acting as an incentive to industry for the introduction of greater efficiency and competition. Denmark has also had a special regulator for the gas and heating sector up till 2000.

14.121 Sometimes a regulator is established for more than one energy sector in a country. Denmark, subsequent to its energy reform and Spain are examples of this approach. Spain has thus replaced the former sectoral specific Electricity Commission with the National Commission for Energy under the Hydrocarbons Act 1998. The Commission is required to supervise both the gas and electricity markets. How powers are divided between the Ministry and the Commission is not very clear and could therefore result in a struggle for power between the authorities involved, ie the Ministry, the regulator/supervisor, and the competition authority. Denmark has also recently merged two regulators into a single body.

[42] cf the discussion in Italy about the appointment of an energy regulator versus the competition authority (ch 9 C(2) above).

(4) Concluding Remarks

The European gas industry is gradually developing from a monopoly-based to a liberalized market structure. The Gas Directive provides a minimum level for liberalization. When considering the countries under review in this book, a clear difference can be noticed between countries aiming at a larger degree of market opening and liberalization, and those which adhere to the minimum level of market opening. Although the Gas Directive provides for more limited market opening for newly established gas markets, this option has not always been used. Spain, for example, is a new gas market but has opted for complete market opening so that it goes further than the requirements of the Directive. A related issue is whether all Member States really wish to liberalize their gas market. It seems that a clear distinction can be made between countries who wish to liberalize the market and those who do not, with the latter not going beyond the minimum level of liberalization required under the Directive. **14.122**

A further difference can be noted when assessing the countries aiming at complete liberalization. This difference is based on the extent of (re)regulation of the gas market. It seems that countries like Spain and the Netherlands, which have just started the liberalization process, have included more light-handed regulation than countries that have experienced liberalization for some time, eg the UK. Whereas the (original) Dutch and Spanish regimes have included a system of licensing only temporarily in order to protect non-eligible customers, the UK system is heavily regulated and provides for licences at all stages: supply licences, transport licences, and shipping licences. The UK licensing regime, however, also developed gradually from limited regulation to the present licensing regime. Similar developments are likely in other liberalizing States. This trend will, however, very much depend on the extent to which governments really want to liberalize. **14.123**

Another matter requiring resolution is the integration of the individual systems. In the past the gas industry in each Member State was organized as a monopoly; the new European gas market, however, consists of many individual gas markets with different degrees of liberalization. As in the electricity sector, where the current focus is on the regulation of interconnectors, future policy needs to concentrate on the integration of the various systems in order to achieve a truly liberalized European gas market, with a free flow of gas and without internal borders. **14.124**

E. The Electricity Supply System

(1) Organization of the Electricity Industry

The electricity industry consists primarily of four activities: generation, transmission, distribution, and supply. Three criteria may be used to describe the organization of the electricity sector in a particular country: i) the level of integration of **14.125** the industry; ii) the ownership of the industry; and iii) the central, regional, or local allocation of regulatory powers.

14.126 Electricity companies may carry out one or more of these four activities and may be integrated, either vertically (if they carry out two or more of those activities) or horizontally (if they supply more than one natural or energy resource). The ownership of the industry may be public or private. The electricity industry may be centrally, regionally, or locally organized. The central or local character of the electricity industry does not depend exclusively on central or local allocation of regulatory powers. In order to have an accurate picture of the central or regional or local character of the electricity industry of a particular country, public ownership must also be taken into account.

Level of integration

14.127 The level of vertical or horizontal integration differs in the countries reviewed. The French and Italian electricity industries are vertically integrated. In France the electricity company is involved in generation, transmission, and distribution.[43] Since the Nationalization Law of 1962, ENEL has been charged with the tasks of importing, generating, transporting, and distributing electricity. Although the liberalization process has changed that situation to some extent, as other market players may enter the market, ENEL is still structured as a vertically integrated company.[44]

14.128 In the UK there is no vertical integration, save in Scotland and, to some extent, Northern Ireland. The activities of distribution and supply were not separated by the Electricity Act 1989. Generators have recently been allowed to take over regional electricity companies, and these increasingly own or control generating plants.[45]

14.129 A traditional feature of the German electricity sector has been the existence of a corporate structure with three levels: i) the 'compound or interconnected entities' or *Verbundunternehmen*, which are frequently vertically integrated, ii) the regional utilities, and iii) local supply entities.[46] Many of the regional and local supply entities are horizontally integrated as they deliver electricity, gas, district heating, and water. Another example of horizontal integration can be found in the Netherlands where the Government has actively pursued a policy of horizontal integration since the 1970s. For this purpose a Bill on Energy Distribution was drafted; however, as the sector started to integrate horizontally on a voluntary basis the present Energy Distribution Act does not contain any provisions on this issue.

---

[43] See ch 7 A(2) above.
[44] See ch 9 above.
[45] See ch 13 F(7) above.
[46] See ch 8 A(2) above.

Ownership

Closely related to the matter of vertical or horizontal integration is the issue of ownership. Even if the sector is not vertically or horizontally integrated, it may still be integrated through ownership. There is public and private ownership within the European electricity industry. In those countries where the existence of public ownership—to a lesser or greater extent—has been identified, there are examples of central public ownership (as in France) and of regional and local public ownership (as in Germany, Denmark, and the Netherlands). **14.130**

Examples of central public ownership are the French company Electricité de France[47] and the Norwegian companies Statkraft and Statnett. Even though there is some private ownership within the Norwegian electricity generation market (15 per cent), public ownership is dominant in both the distribution and generation sectors.[48] In Germany, Länder and municipalities frequently hold shares and enjoy voting rights in the 'compound entities' (*Verbundunternehmen*) and in the regional utilities, even though these entities adopt the form of public limited companies. In the case of the approximately 900 supply entities, these are either part of the municipal administration or adopt the form of public limited companies whose shares belong to the municipality, sometimes with the co-operation of private shareholders.[49] The Dutch electricity industry is also in public hands. Provinces and municipalities hold shares in distribution and/or generation companies which are organized as public limited companies. Until recently these distribution companies, as well as the provinces and municipalities, held the shares in the four producing companies. However, three production companies were privatized at the turn of the millenium. Until recently the transmission company was owned by the four producing companies. The central Government has decided to take over 100 per cent of the shares in the transmission company. **14.131**

In Denmark, 50 per cent of the industry is owned by the municipalities, either directly as a part of the municipality or indirectly through ownership of shares. It is an integrated sector where the distribution companies own the transmission and generation companies. The other 50 per cent is owned by co-operatives of consumers.[50] The regional distribution companies own the generation companies, from which they buy electricity and which co-operate closely. Distribution companies also own the transmission companies.[51] **14.132**

---

47 See ch 7 A(2) above.
48 See ch 11 above.
49 See ch 8 A(2) above.
50 See ch 6 above.
51 ibid.

14.133 In Spain there has traditionally been public and private ownership. The State owned the companies *Endesa* and REE.[52] Integration of this sector in Spain is limited to common ownership in the distribution and generation sectors. Transmission has been carried out since 1984 by a separate public undertaking (REE), which is being privatized under the present Conservative Government Privatization Programme.[53] There has recently been considerable takeover activity and privatization.[54]

14.134 Generally there is a tendency towards privatization. In addition to Spain and the Netherlands, a privatization policy has been pursued in Italy which has seen ENEL privatized. An example of a totally private industry is the British one, with the sole exemption of the old generation nuclear reactors (Nuclear Electric) though even here there are prospects for privatization.[55]

Allocation of powers

14.135 Some of the countries reviewed have traditionally allocated regulatory powers to central institutions (France,[56] Norway,[57] Denmark,[58] and the UK[59]). In some Nordic countries (Denmark and Norway) there are central regulatory institutions but also a high degree of local involvement in ownership.

14.136 In the Netherlands the electricity supply industry is an example of a system gradually moving from decentralized regulation on either local or provincial level to a system of centralized regulation. For fifty years (1938–89) electricity supply in the Netherlands was based on voluntary concessions at a local or provincial level, but the Electricity Act 1989 gave a stronger role to central Government, especially in the generation sector.[60] Although the new Electricity Act of 1998 is based on a system of centralized regulation and legislation, the Government's role with regard to central planning has been abandoned.

14.137 There are examples of regional powers in the electricity sector in Germany,[61] and, more recently, in Spain.[62] In Spain there are increasing regulatory powers in the hands of the seventeen Autonomous Communities. One Autonomous Community has recently passed its own Electricity Distribution Act. Nevertheless, public ownership has traditionally been of a central nature, ie State ownership.

[52] See ch 12 G(2) above.
[53] See ch 12 B and C(1) above.
[54] See ch 12 F(3) above.
[55] ibid.
[56] See ch 7 A(1) and (2) above.
[57] See ch 11 above.
[58] See ch 6 above.
[59] See ch 13 A(5) above.
[60] See ch 10 A(2) above.
[61] See ch 8 B(2) above.
[62] See ch 12 B(7) above.

Regional and local powers can also be identified in Italy, where the electricity industry is currently a complex combination of small local electricity companies, the national undertaking ENEL, and independent producers.[63]

(2) National Electricity Markets and the 1996 Directive Establishing Common Rules for the Creation of an Internal Market for Electricity

Status of implementation

All Member States have implemented the 1996 Electricity Directive: for example Spain (*Ley del Sector Eléctrico*, of 27 November 1997), Germany (*Gesetz zur Neuregelung des Energiewirtschaftsrechts*, of 28 November 1997), the Netherlands (*Elektriciteitswet*, of 2 July, 1998, amended in 1999 and 2000), Italy (Legislative Decree no 79, of 16 March 1999), and Denmark (The Act on Electricity Supply, of 2 June 1999).[64] In France the implementation of the Directive was under prolonged discussion in Parliament and was finally implemented on 10 February 2000 (Loi no 2000-18).[65] The UK's Electricity Act 1989 created such a liberalized electricity market that compatibility with the European Directive is assumed. In accordance with the Directive's provisions, Member States have legislated gradually to open up the market by means of giving freedom of choice to electricity suppliers and consumers. **14.138**

Electricity generation

Sources of electricity within the EU vary from one country to another. Whereas nuclear power is the main source of electricity in France[66]—which is also one of the largest wind energy producers[67]—Norway relies extensively upon hydroelectricity. Coal is still one of the main sources of electricity generation in many of the countries reviewed. In general terms, and with the exception of France and the UK, Member States are heavily dependent on foreign sources of energy for the generation of electricity. Denmark became self-sufficient in energy in 1997, but it still imports coal for electricity generation.[68] In the Netherlands, almost half of the total electricity generation is based on natural gas, the remaining source being imported coal.[69] **14.139**

All of the countries reviewed here share two objectives within their energy policies: diversity and security of supply. The move towards liberalization and **14.140**

[63] See ch 9 F above.
[64] This Act was passed together with four more Acts on various electricity issues: see ch 6 above.
[65] See ch 7 C(1) above.
[66] See ch 7 C(2) above.
[67] ibid.
[68] It is now reconsidering the use of coal due to its negative environmental effects, and increasing the use of natural gas and renewables: see ch 6 A(2), and fn 1 of this chapter, above.
[69] Nuclear generation amounted to 6% in 1995, but its use will decrease in the coming years: see ch 10 A(1) above.

competition may endanger those two objectives, and that is why States have taken legislative measures to overcome that risk. The countries reviewed are seeking to increase the use of renewable sources of electricity generation, with Denmark having achieved a successful 10 per cent so far.[70]

14.141 The Electricity Directive allows Member States to choose between an authorization and a tendering procedure for the construction of new generation units. Moreover, it gives freedom to Member States to introduce long-term and compulsory electricity capacity planning. The countries reviewed in this book have established, in most cases, an authorization procedure, with no compulsory planning controls. However, there is scope in the legislation recently passed to determine 'whether certain types of generation are permissible or not, and it is conceivable that they may use public-interest type arguments to impose some sort of cap on the amount of independent generation that can be licensed'.[71] This is certainly the case in Italy, where Article 36 of Legislative Decree no 79 refers to 'the Ministry for Industry and Commerce being responsible for a secure and economical rational generation system to be preserved as far as the use and supply of primary energy sources are concerned'.[72] In France, the Electricity Act implementing the Electricity Directive states that:

> authorizations to build new production facilities are awarded by the Minister in charge of energy according to the principles of transparency and fairness referred to in the Directive. However, if the generators do not propose to construct capacity according to the Government's long-term planning, a system of competitive bidding applies in order to meet the long term requirements.[73]

14.142 In the UK there is competition within the generation market, which is subject to a licensing requirement, but dominated by two players. In Denmark[73a] Germany,[74] Spain,[75] and Italy[76] electricity generation is subject to an authorization (license or permission). In the Netherlands, the Electricity Act 1998 has abolished the licensing requirement of the Electricity Act 1989 with regard to the construction and operation of power stations.[77]

14.143 In almost every country considered there are provisions within the law for the protection of national sources of electricity. The 1996 Electricity Directive has allowed Member States to give priority in the dispatching of electricity generated by domestic sources of energy, with up to 15 per cent of the overall primary energy

[70] See ch 6 above.
[71] See the EC Law ch 5, section E(3) above.
[72] See ch 9 F above.
[73] See ch 7 C(1) above.
[73a] See ch 6 F(5) above.
[74] See ch 8 E(3) above.
[75] See ch 12 D(2) above.
[76] See ch 9 F above.
[77] See ch 10 D(1) and (2) above. Planning permits are, however, required.

necessary to produce the electricity consumed in the national market. In some of the countries reviewed, such as Italy and Spain, the functioning of the generation market, ie the matching of demand and supply, has been entrusted to a market operator. The British electricity market inaugurated a pool system,[78] which example has been followed by some of the countries reviewed, such as Spain.[79]

Transmission system operation

In the UK responsibility for transmission after privatization was conferred on a new company, the National Grid. At the time National Grid was privatized, the regional electricity companies took substantial shares in it, but were afterwards asked to divest of their shares in the grid. While only the National Grid enjoys a licence for transmission, there is third-party access to it.[80] Under the new German legislation there are specific provisions on access to the transmission grid belonging to the existing *Verbundunternehmen*, which have pushed interested parties into an agreement (*Verbändevereinbarung*).[81] Electricité de France (EDF) has a *de jure* monopoly over transmission and enjoys a concession from the State in that regard.[82] To comply with the 1996 Electricity Directive, the management of the transmission grid will be entrusted to EDF, but in carrying out such task it will be independent from other EDF activities, which must also separate those accounts related to generation from those related to distribution.[83] There are two separate grids in Denmark but these grids are not yet connected, even though the country has connections with Norway, Sweden, and Germany. In the new liberalized environment, the Danish transmission grid is operated as a public infrastructure by an independent, non-profit, and system-responsible company, and the grid is placed at the disposal of all users.[84] The transmission of electricity is entrusted in the Netherlands to network managers, which are appointed for ten years by the owners of transmission systems, but only with Ministerial approval. Producers and distributors cannot be appointed as network managers. SEP (NV Samen werkende Elektriciteitsproduktie-bedrüvon) has appointed such a network manager (a subsidiary of SEP, TenneT NV) and so too have the distribution companies.[85] In Italy the operation of transmission grids will be carried out by a network manager on behalf of the State and under a concession. ENEL has been split up into several companies, with one company (with shares held by the Treasury) responsible for the national transmission grid.[86] In Spain, REE is charged with the 14.144

[78] See ch 13 F(8) above.
[79] See ch 12 G(4) above.
[80] See ch 13 F(6) above.
[81] See ch 8 E(3) above.
[82] See ch 7 C(3) above.
[83] ibid.
[84] See ch 6 above.
[85] See ch 10 D(2) above.
[86] See ch 9 F above.

task of operating the high-voltage grid, but the Electricity Act 1997 allows companies to ask for an authorization for the construction and operation of transmission installations.[87]

Access to the system

14.145 It is well known that the Electricity Directive is the result of a number of compromises, particularly with respect to the manner in which Member States may regulate access to the electricity system. The Directive offers a basic choice between TPA and a single-buyer system. Even within the former, there is still the choice between regulated and negotiated access (see the discussion of gas above).[88] As a result of the need to implement the Directive, some countries have chosen the regulated system (Spain[89] and Denmark), while others have chosen the negotiated system (Germany).[90] In the Netherlands there is regulated access, even though the initiative for the development of tariffs and conditions is in the hands of the network managers.[91] The construction of direct lines raises questions of compatibility between the Dutch Electricity Act 1998 and the Electricity Directive.[92] Italy has chosen the single-buyer system,[93] and so has Germany, but only at the local level.[94] Although the idea of a single-buyer system was conceived by French officials, the new Electricity Act has not adopted this system of access and limits the market opening to 33 per cent of the market.[95] The French Electricity Act 2000 provides for a system of regulated TPA and entrusts the Electricity Regulatory Commission with supervisory powers. In the UK there has been third-party access to the electricity networks since the Electricity Act 1989. This system inspired the regulated access system within the Electricity Directive.[96]

Distribution and supply

14.146 A common feature of the countries reviewed here is the existence of two kinds of consumers: those with the right to choose their electricity supplier and those without such right ('captive' consumers). The Electricity Directive imposed freedom of choice for a certain kind of consumer and, consequently, the gradual opening of the market. The differences among the countries reviewed depend on the timing for the full opening of the supply market. In Denmark, for example, every

[87] See ch 12 G(4) above.
[88] See also ch 5 D(3) above.
[89] See ch 12 D(2) and ch 6 F(5) above.
[90] See ch 8 E(3) above.
[91] See ch 10 D(2) above.
[92] ibid.
[93] See ch 9 F above.
[94] See ch 8 E(3) above.
[95] See ch 7 C(3) above.
[96] See ch 13 F(6) above.

single consumer will freely choose its electricity supplier by the year 2002.[97] Most of the countries reviewed confer upon distribution companies exclusive rights to supply to 'captive' consumers located within a particular distributing area.

The German *Demarkationsverträge* and *Konzessionsverträge*, which were supplementary contract types of the 'closed supply areas' system, were important obstacles to the creation of a free market in Germany within the distribution sector.[98] Substantial changes were introduced in the German Competition Law, which put an end to their exemptions thereunder.[99] Under the new German Act energy supply entities are awarded a permission to supply within a particular area.[100] Distribution activities are subject to a licence in Spain, and the Government will designate for each distribution area a distribution system operator.[101] In the UK, the regional electricity companies have monopoly distribution rights over the authorized area, together with a supply monopoly to consumers within that area whose demand is below the monopoly threshold.[102] In Italy distributors, acting under a concession, are awarded a right to supply to customers within an area, and domestic consumers do not have the right to buy electricity from suppliers other than those operating in the area where they are located.[103] The Dutch Electricity Act 1998 prohibits distributors from supplying electricity to non-eligible consumers ('protected consumers') without a licence, awarded, in its turn, to particular areas.[104] **14.147**

Unbundling

The French Electricity Act will impose the separation of the accounts of EDF in respect of generation, transmission, and distribution.[105] Unbundling is also required in Italy, according to the Legislative Decree implementing the Electricity Directive, particularly for transmission services. The Spanish Electricity Act 1997 requires the segregation of regulated and unregulated activities by different companies by the year 2001, with separate accounts since 1997. In practice both regulated and unregulated activities may be carried out by the same company acting through subsidiaries.[106] The new German Act states that electricity enterprises of 'universal service' are subject to the obligation to publish their annual accounts with separation of accounts for generation, transmission, and distribution activities, **14.148**

[97] See ch 6 above.
[98] See ch 8 E(1) above.
[99] See ch 8 E (1) and (3) above.
[100] See ch 8 E(1) above.
[101] See ch 12 G(4) above.
[102] See ch 13 F(6) above.
[103] See ch 9 F above.
[104] See ch 10 D(1) above.
[105] See ch 7 C(1) above.
[106] See ch 12 G(4) above.

and with specification of the rules for the allocation of assets and liabilities, expenditure, and income.[107] The Dutch Electricity Act 1998 requires a complete and legal unbundling of the production and supply of electricity and the transmission activities. In the UK, even though the activities of distribution and supply were not separated by the Electricity Act 1989, there is separation of accounting. The UK privatization of electricity had as one of its main objectives the separation of activities into different businesses. However, generators have recently been allowed to take over regional electricity companies, and these increasingly own or control generating plants. In Denmark, under the new legislation passed in 1999, distribution companies are being replaced, on the one hand, by grid companies and, on the other hand, by supply obligation companies. In the future, ownership may remain as at present, with municipalities or with co-operatives of consumers, but the grid must be managed independently from production and trade activities. Production and trade companies will not be allowed to own more than 15 per cent of the grid or of the supply obligation company or of the company responsible for the national grid system.[108]

Public service obligations

14.149 At the heart of the French conception of electricity supply is the idea of public service, which means i) the guarantee of continuity, ii) equality of treatment for each category of consumers, iii) quality of service at minimum cost, and iv) adaptation to new technologies and to the requirements of the French society. These basic ideas will remain under the new French Electricity Act.[109] EDF is obliged to supply electricity to any customer under certain specified conditions and cannot discriminate between customers.[110] The new Danish Electricity Act 1999 foresees the awarding of licences to supply obligation companies, in order to protect small consumers.[111] The permissions awarded in Germany to the energy supply entities include the obligation to supply to anyone within the territory of the permission.[112] This is also the case in Spain.[113] The supply of electricity is a public service in Italian law, the main consequence being the existence of a unified tariff for consumers who are not eligible. An obligation to supply non-eligible customers is also within the Dutch Electricity Act 1998.[114] There is an obligation of universal services, ie to supply, in the UK, which will raise questions about its compatibility with a competitive market.[115]

[107] See ch 8 E(3) above.
[108] See ch 6 above.
[109] See ch 7 C(1) above.
[110] See ch 7 C(3) above.
[111] See ch 6 above.
[112] See ch 8 E(3) above.
[113] See ch 12 D(2) above.
[114] See ch 10 D(1) above.
[115] See ch 13 F(7) above.

Imports and exports of electricity

There is freedom of import and export in Denmark, Germany, Spain, and the UK.[116] In the Netherlands, export freedom prevails but import is restricted and subject to the principle of reciprocity in the country of origin or of destination. The transmission system operator (TenneT) has to report to the Minister any export or import request. The Minister may ban or restrict imports from Member States who have not yet, or only to a limited extent, opened their market.[117] Imports and exports are free in Italy with some restrictions on non-EU imports but with ENEL enjoying a *de facto* monopoly; further restrictions on imports are to be introduced in 2003. In France imports and exports of electricity have been deregulated by the new Electricity Act 2000. EDF will in accordance with its transmission monopoly manage all energy flow exchanges with other major interconnected European networks. There has traditionally been power exchanges involving, in various permutations, France, the Netherlands, Denmark, Norway, and Germany. **14.150**

Electricity regulators

A specific regulatory body in the UK, the OFGEM, issues and controls the relevant licences for generation, transmission, distribution and supply. The Monopolies and Mergers Commission is involved when competition is at stake.[118] In Spain, regulatory powers are shared by the Ministry for Economy and the National Commission for Energy. However, the former retains the most important powers.[119] In France the Ministry for Industry has the power to authorize new generation capacity above a certain minimum threshold. **14.151**

The new French Electricity Act creates a regulatory body for both electricity and gas.[120] In Italy, there is an authority for both the electricity and gas markets. This authority operates separately from the competition authority.[121] An independent Energy Supervisory Board has been set up in Denmark.[122] In Germany there are no specific regulatory bodies, but strong involvement by the general competition authorities.[123] In the Netherlands there is an authority monitoring compliance with the Electricity Act and the Gas Act (Dte), which is a branch of the competition authority (NMa).[124] **14.152**

116 See chs 6, 8, 12, and 13 above.
117 See ch 10 D(2) above.
118 See ch 13 A(5) and F(5) above.
119 See ch 12 G(4) above.
120 See ch 7 C(1) above.
121 See ch 9 F above.
122 See ch 6 above.
123 See ch 8 A(2) above.
124 See ch 10 A(2) above.

F. The Use of Non-Fossil Energy Resources: Nuclear, Renewables, and Energy Efficiency

(1) Nuclear Energy

The Market

14.153 Reliance on nuclear power is highly variable amongst the States considered here. Only France, where 92 per cent of electricity is derived from nuclear and renewable sources, is experiencing growth in this sector. Nuclear power is the main domestic energy source in France which, as of 1997, had fifty-four reactors with a further four under construction, all under public ownership. Whilst this increases domestic self-sufficiency, this is offset by the requirement to import 85 per cent of the natural uranium used in the industry. Of the nuclear States considered here, only Spain is self-sufficient in uranium.

14.154 Neither Norway nor Denmark possess any operational nuclear power plants, whilst the Netherlands is in the process of decommissioning one of only two installations it ever built. A moratorium on nuclear investment since 1982 means that there are now only nine nuclear plants in Spain which are now in private ownership. In the United Kingdom nearly twenty nuclear plants are operational but no new installations are anticipated, at least not from public funds. Of these only the newer reactors were privatized in 1996 with the remaining, older Magnox reactors retained in public ownership. Public ownership has been retained in the nuclear sector in Italy, which has seen a public referendum lead to a moratorium on the further development of nuclear power and, in consequence, is decommissioning its four publicly owned nuclear installations. Following similar more recent internal debates in Germany, which has nineteen nuclear power plants in private ownership satisfying 30 per cent of electricity demand,[125] a new agreement in 2000 initiates gradual withdrawal from reliance upon nuclear energy. Best estimates are for a twenty-year time-scale for withdrawal from the sector, including the decommissioning of existing installations.[126] In any event, no new reactors have been planned or built recently in Germany owing to deep public reservations about this form of energy.

[125] Or 12.8% of total energy demand in 1997: see ch 8 above.

[126] The financial consequences of immediate withdrawal from the sector, given the substantial claims for compensation which could arise from private nuclear operators and their shareholders, have dictated a more long-term approach to this fundamental shift in energy choice. Moreover, long-term contracts have been entered into with the nuclear reprocessing facilities of British Nuclear Fuels at Sellafield in the UK and of Cogema at Le Havre in France, underpinned by intergovernmental co-operation agreements, thus preventing the implementation of proposals which would have required German nuclear operators to store nuclear waste *in situ* and prohibiting recycling.

What is striking from this brief summary is that France is the only country considered in this study which is presently increasing its nuclear capacity. The vogue for privatization, so marked in its impact on other energy sectors, is also evident in the nuclear sector. In Germany, Spain, and the United Kingdom (the latter save for the older Magnox reactors) the nuclear sector is in private hands with the privatization process only recently concluded in Spain (1999) and in the United Kingdom (1996, though provided for in the 1989 Electricity Act). In Italy and in France the nuclear sector is still in public ownership. **14.155**

Radioactive waste

A further point in common amongst nuclear States is the problem of managing radioactive waste, an inevitable by-product of nuclear energy activities. Domestic concerns have been expressed regarding radioactive waste movement and disposal and there is international opposition to the transboundary movement of hazardous materials.[127] In some States specific bodies are charged with responsibility for radioactive waste management, including ANDRA in France and NIREX in the UK. In Germany, notwithstanding that nuclear power stations are privately owned and operated, the State is responsible under the 1985 Nuclear Act for treatment and storage of radioactive waste generated. Responsibility is shared by the Bund and the Länder, with the former responsible for final storage sites and the latter charged with installing intermediate storage sites. **14.156**

In this regard deep store, including in defunct salt mines, has been considered. Both the UK and France are also actively investigating onshore deep disposal of radioactive waste, reflecting in part the fact that deep-sea disposal of even low-level radioactive waste is now impermissible under the 1972 London Convention.[128] In 1996 France selected three sites (Meuse, Haute Marne, and Vienne) where underground laboratories could be built. Feasibility studies into deep underground disposal are conducted, with a final report due in 2006. Attempts in the UK to establish a deep rock characterization facility at Drigg in Cumbria failed at the planning inquiry phase. Concerns regarding the transboundary implications of such disposal, including the potential for contamination of the Irish Sea, led to the unprecedented attendance and testimony at a planning inquiry of representatives from another State, in this case the Republic of Ireland. The possibility of a complaint to the European Commission under **14.157**

[127] This includes the transboundary movement of nuclear fuels for reprocessing. For further discussion of the international dimension of the transboundary movement and disposal of radioactive waste, see ch 2 above; on the EC dimension, see ch 5 above.

[128] In a sense these twin legal issues of removal and subsequent disposal mirror those addressed in the offshore petroleum sector in respect of decommissioning, which is addressed below. Current debate surrounds the extent of the prohibition under the London Convention, in particular whether deep-seabed disposal is ruled out.

EURATOM was also mooted, but in the event not pursued as planning consent for the facility was refused.

The development of nuclear energy in Europe

14.158 In general it is possible to detect three distinct attitudes to the development of nuclear energy in Europe, which may be broadly summarized as (i) embrace, (ii) reconsider, and (iii) abandon. The conclusion of the 1997 Kyoto Protocol to the 1992 Framework Convention on Climate Change may see a fourth phase emerging: reconsideration of the nuclear option. Clearly nuclear developments have been conditioned by external stimuli, including the energy crises of the 1970s which placed emphasis on the search for indigenous sources of energy and for non-fossil fuels, and the safety of nuclear power which accidents such as Chernobyl in 1986 called into question. Both have had particular impact on European energy choices in this sector. The risks of nuclear energy and potential liabilities are recognized. Indeed, each of the nuclear States considered here has nuclear-specific legislation which dates from the conclusion of the OECD Paris/Brussels regime for nuclear liability concluded in 1960 and 1963.

14.159 The generation of nuclear power for electricity is otherwise addressed in the relevant national legislation, such as the Nuclear Energy and Electricity (LSE) Act in Spain where, in addition to the nuclear site licence, authorization is also required under Article 21 of the LSE (which also addresses safety standards and environmental protection). In the UK the 1965 Nuclear Installations Act is the primary regulatory instrument in terms of the licensing and control of nuclear installations for liability and other purposes, but with the contribution of the plants to electricity supply and the structure of the industry regulated by the 1989 Electricity Act. In France it is primarily the Anti-Pollution Act 1961 which regulates the construction and operation of nuclear facilities, and laws enacted in 1965, 1968, and 1990 which govern liability issues. In Italy Law no 1860/62 addresses the peaceful uses of nuclear energy but it was Decree no 185 in 1964 which first addressed nuclear safety and radiation protection issues, and subjected the nuclear sector to a licensing regime (amended by Decree no 230 in 1995 further to implement EURATOM Directives).

EC law

14.160 EC law is also of importance in this sector, most notably the 1980 Basic Safety Standards Directive 80/836/EURATOM which, *inter alia*, establishes the maximum annual limits of radiation exposure for workers in the nuclear industry. Directive 96/29/EURATOM laid down new basic safety standards for workers and for the general population with an implementation deadline of 13 May 2000. Within the EC the EURATOM Treaty regulates the market for nuclear power and establishes uniform safety standards for the industry. In addition, the 1985

EIA Directive applies, and prior assessment is required for both the siting and subsequent enlargement of nuclear installations and, following the 1997 amendments to the Directive, for decommissioning.

Decommissioning of nuclear installations

As indicated above, a number of States which initially embraced nuclear energy have now reconsidered this commitment, leading not only to a moratorium on new building, but also to the decommissioning of existing nuclear installations. Italy is a good example of this process, with decommissioning addressed for the first time only in 1995. Decree 230 requires a specific decommissioning licence from the Ministry of Industry. As indicated above, with the recent amendments to the 1985 EIA Directive a prior environmental impact assessment must be carried out before decommissioning a nuclear installation located in an EC Member State. The legal regime for decommissioning is not fully settled in all of the nuclear States considered, though financial provision has been made for the future costs of decommissioning in Spain and in the United Kingdom. In Spain a special body (Enresa) has been established to address both radioactive waste management and the decommissioning of nuclear installations, and its costs are met by revenue generated from a percentage of the electricity tariff. The nuclear sector in Europe will see increasing decommissioning activity as existing nuclear installations reach the end of their operational life; closely related is the quest for a secure and cost-effective method of radioactive waste disposal. Whatever the long-term impacts of the need to reduce emissions of greenhouse gas emissions in fulfillment of climate change obligations, it is highly unlikely that a significant resurgence in nuclear electricity generation will occur in the near future. **14.161**

(2) Renewable Energy Sources

Introduction

Renewable sources of energy are those which are not depleted through exploitation, such as wind and solar power, hydroelectric power, and biofuels. Alternative sources of energy is a term employed to distinguish new from traditional energy sources such as oil, gas, and coal. Some sources will fall in both categories depending upon the method of exploitation, a good example being geothermal energy. **14.162**

With the notable exception of Denmark, where renewable energy is anticipated to contribute 35 per cent of energy supply by the year 2030 (in 1999 it was 10 per cent), renewable forms of energy remain a very small component of overall energy supply in Europe. This picture will change over the coming years, not only in response to domestic pressure for more environmentally friendly sources of energy, but also in consequence of international and EC law. As was discussed in chapter 3 **14.163** above, the implementation of the 1997 Kyoto Protocol to the 1992 United Nations Framework Convention on Climate Change will lead to increased national emphasis upon renewable forms of energy.[129]

14.164 The recent EC White Paper on Renewable Energy Sources sets a target of 12 per cent EU market penetration for renewables by the year 2010 and facilitates the development of renewables technology through its ALTERNER (renewable energy sources) and JOULE-THERMIE (energy technology) programmes.

The share of renewables in the national energy markets

14.165 The most common sources of renewable forms of energy are hydroelectric, wind, solar, waste, and biofuels. The relative importance of each (within the modest renewables total) varies from State to State; for example, hydroelectric power is of fundamental importance in Norway, where it contributes 99 per cent of electricity demand and places Norway sixth in the world in terms of the production of such energy. Biofuels also contribute to national energy consumption, amounting to 6 per cent in 1996, and wind power is also being exploited, albeit on a small scale. In Spain 19.4 per cent of total electricity generation derives from hydroelectric power, whilst in France it ranges from 12 to 17 per cent. Hydroelectric power has probably peaked in France with the exploitation of existing feasible sites and because of environmental concerns regarding such exploitation. Germany also uses more hydroelectric power than other forms of renewable energy, followed by wind power, but renewables still contribute only about 2 per cent of total primary energy consumption.[130] Without the potential for anything other than the present small-scale hydroelectric developments, Denmark relies primarily upon wind power as a source of renewable energy, but also relies extensively on biofuels, especially waste, in district heating plants. At the end of 1997 there were an estimated 4,784 wind turbines in Denmark with a total capacity of 1,129 MW; anticipated capacity in 2005 is expected to be 1,500 MW. In the Netherlands 80 per cent of renewable energy is derived from biofuels, though there are also two hydroelectric power stations. With one of the largest forested areas in Europe (28 per cent of its metropolitan land area) it is not surprising that wood-based energy is an important renewable energy source in France, accounting for 50.8 per cent of the primary energy derived from renewable sources there. Hydroelectric power runs a close second at 40.9 per cent. Furthermore, under the European Deep Geothermal Energy Programme the feasibility of an enhanced geothermal system is being assessed at Soultz-sous-Forêts, France, near the border

[129] In addition to the national chapters above, see D Zillman, ed, *The Kyoto Protocol: From Principle to Practice* (Kluwer Law International, 2001), with a number of national case studies of relevance here.

[130] See ch 8 above. It has nonetheless set an ambitious national target of 50% of total energy production from renewables by the year 2050.

with Germany. This three-year project (1998–2000) was initially a joint venture between Electricité de Strasbourg and Pfalzwerke (operating as EEIG Heat Mining) and is designed to test the feasibility of a first power plant of 5 MW. Geothermal energy is also found in Italy. The overall renewables picture in Europe is rather different from, say, that of the United States where geothermal is the largest source of non-hydro renewable energy, producing in 1998 as much electricity as wind power and solar energy combined.

The legal framework

In the countries considered in this book, legal regulation of renewables is generally effected through planning legislation in respect of the siting of the installation(s), and through electricity legislation in terms of generation, distribution, and supply issues if generating electricity; otherwise renewables are addressed under heat generation. For example, in France hydroelectric power and wind energy are regulated as part of the electricity sector, whilst other forms of renewable energy, such as biofuels, solar power, and wood-based energy, are classed as heat-generating sources. Geothermal energy is regulated under the applicable mining codes (as in Denmark, France, Italy). An environmental impact assessment (EIA) is also required for some renewables projects, a recognition of the environmental concerns to which even renewable energy projects give rise. For example, in France and the United Kingdom prior assessment is required in respect of significant wind turbine development, while under the Norwegian Environmental Impact Assessment Act of 1996 all proposed hydroelectric projects must be referred to the NVA to determine whether a prior EIA is necessary. **14.166**

Few of the States considered above have chosen to regulate renewable energy activities, whether individually or collectively, by separate statute. An exception in respect of individual (source-specific) legislation is hydroelectric power which is separately regulated in Norway,[131] France, and Spain. At the time of writing the only State to have enacted general renewables legislation is Denmark. However, the focus of its 1992 Act on the Utilization of Renewable Energy Sources (as amended) is in fact wind energy, regulating both the construction and operation of wind turbines and the cost of connection to the grid and of the electricity generated. **14.167**

[131] The 1940 Watercourses Act, currently under revision by the Watercourses Act Committee of 1994. In addition, the Norwegian system awards a concession under the Industrial Concession Act which conveys 'rights of ownership or use of a waterfall' for up to 60 years, with reversion to the State (and a right of pre-emption for the duration of the concession): ch 11 above. This is unaffected by the EEA Agreement which, *inter alia*, preserves the Norwegian system of property ownership (Art 125).

A separate market for renewables?

14.168 Additional legal measures are designed to protect the supply of renewables, in anticipation of a separate market for renewable energy. The state of the market will depend on the development of renewables within each State. Whilst hydroelectric power, where available, is well established in the market, wind and solar energy are not necessarily so well established in all of the States under consideration. Recent attention has focused on more cost-effective forms of renewable energy, such as biofuels. A common device is to oblige electricity distribution companies to accept a certain percentage of electricity supply from renewables regardless of type, and/or from particular forms of renewable energy. This is the case in the Netherlands, Germany, Denmark, France, and the UK. In the last two a tendering system has been employed as a mechanism for allocating supply contracts between renewables operators and the utilities.[132] Such support mechanisms are designed to operate until renewables sources have an established market, whereupon this obligation on licence holders will lapse. In Germany voluntary agreements by electricity companies to increase their reliance on renewable energy sources are also employed. In Denmark electricity consumers are required to obtain a fixed quota of their electricity consumption from renewables (to be 20 per cent by 2003) through the purchase of renewable energy certificates, failing which a fine is imposed with the proceeds allocated to further developing renewable energy sources.[133]

14.169 It is also envisaged that this system of green certificates will be used in the Netherlands to encourage the production of electricity from renewable forms of energy. Provided for in primary electricity legislation, such certificates stipulate the amount of electricity to be generated; the Minister may require the use of a specified number of certificates per year, with a penalty for non-compliance. In the Netherlands such certificates may be awarded in respect of electricity produced or consumed outside of the Netherlands, underscoring the emphasis on reliance on renewables irrespective of their place of origin or consumption. Used in conjunction with the obligations on licence holders indicated above, the thrust of the system is to encourage the development of a market for renewable forms of energy.

---

[132] In France a tendering system was first launched in 1996 to promote the use of wind energy. It will generate 500 MW by 2005. In the UK the 1989 Electricity Act provided for a non-fossil fuel obligation to be imposed on electricity suppliers and for 'rounds' for the allocation of funds for the development of renewables technologies considered able to contribute economically to UK energy supply by 2005. By the end of 1998 five such rounds had been held, with contracts for the supply of electricity awarded by competitive tender. See chs 7 and 13 above.

[133] Renewable energy is sold on a special renewable energy market (the RE market) with renewables producers obtaining renewable energy certificates (RE certificates) for the quantity of renewable energy produced. These RE certificates are then purchased by consumers as evidence of satisfaction of the minimum RE electricity quota.

Subsidies and energy taxes

Subsidies are another device used to encourage the development of renewables in the States under consideration, eg in the Netherlands, Denmark, Spain, France, and Germany. They also encourage energy saving and conservation. Subsidies have been employed for a variety of purposes, ranging from installation subsidies covering a percentage of the total project cost, to direct production subsidies and privileged access to power grids. Subsidies are also available for solar energy, biomass, and heat pumps to cover the cost of test stations. Like wind energy, the success of biomass fuel for district heating has led to the phasing out of subsidies in this sector as well. In France the Fund for Amortization of Electrification Costs (FACE) has been employed to encourage fuel replacement and energy efficiency, particularly in isolated local communities (a concern also in Denmark), supporting in particular renewables projects where the costly upgrading of transmission lines can be avoided. In the States considered here, some shift of emphasis away from subsidies to fiscal measures such as energy taxes and green electricity pricing is emerging, a reflection in part of emerging markets for renewables. This is well illustrated in Denmark where generous installation subsidies for wind energy development and for biomass burners for district heating have been withdrawn following the successful establishment of a market for these renewable sources of energy. Similar developments may be observed in the Netherlands. **14.170**

A further common technique is to impose a legal requirement for utilities to purchase renewable supplies, generally operated in conjunction with subsidies. Various exceptions may be available to the distributor of electricity in respect of connecting a renewable supply to the grid. For example, although in Denmark the cost of such connection is shared by the supplier and the distributor, the latter may refuse connection on the basis of disproportionate cost. **14.171**

Environment and energy taxes (both positive, eg a green tax exemption for renewable energy, and negative, eg an energy consumption tax) are employed in some States, including the Netherlands, Denmark, France, and (regionally) Spain. Energy is particularly heavily taxed in Denmark, where 60 per cent of the total cost of electricity to the consumer is attributable to taxes. Energy efficiency is encouraged through tax rebates. For example, if energy-intensive industry agrees energy efficiency measures with the Danish Energy Agency and achieves efficiency gains, a tax rebate is granted. Generally speaking, support for renewable forms of energy takes the form of a rebate on energy taxes for utilities relying on a percentage of renewable sources of supply and/or tax incentives phased out as the industry achieves independent market status. For example, in France not only are renewables granted tax advantages, such as excise tax exemption for biofuels, but reliance on renewables is being encouraged through a tax on municipal waste, first imposed in 1993 and to be phased out by 2002, to encourage waste combustion as an energy source. **14.172**

Renewables and the environment

14.173 Paradoxically, however, the chief obstacle to the development of some renewables is not financial but environmental. For example, both the Netherlands and the United Kingdom have encountered fierce local resistance to the siting of even modestly sized wind farms. To a lesser extent such difficulties have been encountered in Denmark,[134] with all three States increasingly turning their attention to offshore sites which also offer improved wind conditions. In Germany priority is also given to offshore wind energy, with the provision of a guaranteed 'feed-in' to the public supply grid. By 2030 Denmark hopes to generate 5,500 MW from wind power, 4,000 MW of which is expect to be generated from offshore sites. This encouragement of offshore development underscores the fact that, though considered an environmentally sound form of electricity generation in terms of emissions, wind farms do raise other environmental concerns, such as nuisance and loss of amenity. The same may be said of other forms of renewable energy; indeed, the October 1998 IEA report on renewables explicitly addresses the potential environmental burdens of renewable energy sources.[135] With World Energy Council estimates of future global renewables reliance in the year 2020 lying between 25 per cent (current policies) and 45 per cent (ecological scenario), not to mention the impact of the more modest EC target of 12 per cent reliance on renewables by 2010, it is clear that these environmental issues will not only persist, but are likely to intensify.

(3) Energy Efficiency, Savings, and Conservation Measures

14.174 Energy savings and efficiency and the encouragement of renewable forms of energy go hand in glove in the energy law and policy of the EC and of the States considered here. In France, it is calculated that energy conservation measures have led to a 17 per cent reduction in total energy consumption, amounting to 35 Mtoe, since they were first instituted in 1973. Whilst the initial impetus for such measures was the oil crises of the 1970s, environmental concerns at the domestic, European, and international levels have led to renewed efforts in these areas in all of the States considered. In particular, implementation of the 1997 Kyoto Protocol has encouraged States further to consider such measures not only from the perspective of energy supply (the preoccupation of the 1970s) but also from the perspectives of efficiency and environmental protection. Collectively, the Member States of the EU are committed to an 8 per cent reduction in greenhouse gases by 2008–2012.[136] Regulatory techniques for achieving these objectives vary

[134] Surmounted in part through the requirement that municipalities integrate plans for future wind turbine development within local zoning plans, most of which were finalized in 1995.

[135] A review of the positive and negative environmental implications of renewables for electricity generation was conducted by the Renewable Energy Working Party of the International Energy Agency and published as *Benign Energy? The Environmental Implications of Renewables* (IEA, 1998).

[136] See ch 5 above.

from State to State, and range from voluntary agreements between Government and specific industrial sectors, such as the use of environmental covenants in the Netherlands, to the use of carbon or energy taxes, as in Denmark.

Such measures are taken within the context of nationally set targets and timetables for achieving net gains in energy efficiency and in respect of reliance on renewables. For example, the Netherlands has set a goal of an annual average of 1.7 per cent energy efficiency, designed to produce improvement equivalent to one-third of energy consumed over the next quarter of a century. Energy savings are achieved in part through reliance on CHP, a particular feature of both Dutch and Danish energy policy. Norway has integrated energy efficiency concerns into the regional concessions for electricity installations, which contain obligations to implement energy efficiency measures. Energy efficiency is also achieved through specific agreement with industry on the targets to be achieved and through increasing consumer awareness by, *inter alia*, labelling the energy efficiency of energy-consuming household products such as washing machines and refrigerators.[137] Efficiency standards are also set for buildings in construction through building regulations and their operation (eg to decrease heat loss). In France periodic audits of energy-intensive industrial installations are required which form the basis for identifying energy-saving and pollution-control investments ranging from building insulation standards to energy efficiency standards for large boilers. **14.175**

G. Energy and the Environment

(1) Environmental Controls

The Legal framework

The environmental impact of energy activities is a matter of increasing public concern, and hence of legal regulation in the States considered here. Environmental regulation takes place in two forms: direct and indirect. Indirect regulation is found in mining codes, oil and gas and other legislation,[138] and in licence terms and conditions regulating, *inter alia*, health and safety, environmental, and resource management matters. Requirements of good oilfield practices, the avoidance of wasteful practices, prohibitions on the flaring of gas and the discharge of oily cuttings, and monitoring to safeguard against the possibility of subsidence, are but a few examples. More rigorous requirements may be imposed in respect of activities in environmentally sensitive areas, such as the Waddenzee in the **14.176**

[137] Norway has implemented directives concerned with labelling of the energy efficiency of household appliances in consequence of the EEA: see ch 11 above.

[138] Including EC law, such as Art 6(2) of the Hydrocarbons Licensing Directive; the new Electricity Directive 96/92/EC permits restrictions on authorizations for, *inter alia*, environmental conservation and energy efficiency.

Netherlands, or in national parks, marine sanctuaries, or areas of particular environmental or archaeological significance in Italy. Certain offshore areas may thus be restricted from petroleum. Special measures may also be devised to address emergencies such as oil spills. In France, which experienced the *Amoco Cadiz* oil spill disaster in 1978, oil spill contingency plans have been developed both in respect of offshore ('*Polmar mer*') and onshore ('*Polmar terre*') marine pollution. In Denmark the environmental body, the National Agency for Environmental Protection, has primary responsibility for regulating discharges from installations and oil spill emergency preparedness. Under Norwegian law, liability for petroleum pollution damage is regulated under the 1996 Petroleum Act and includes discharges of oil or gas from installations. The geographic scope is broad, encompassing all areas landwards of the outer limit of the Norwegian continental shelf, including land territory.

14.177 In general such regulation is concerned with the conduct of energy activities and their environmental impact, but does not seek directly to regulate the environment *per se*. In other words, good oilfield practices will be mandated, and limits or prohibitions on the discharge of oil and flaring of gas, but not specific ambient air or water quality standards. The latter is the remit of direct environmental regulation, generally contained in separate environmental and planning legislation. In some States general environmental legislation does not extend offshore, thus necessitating the use of traditional petroleum or other laws to regulate the environmental consequences of offshore activities. Thus, for example, the Netherlands applies the amended EIA Directive offshore through its continental shelf mining regulations, not through its basic environmental law.

Environmental Impact Assessment

14.178 Both international and EC law have had an impact, in the latter context most notably through the 1985 EIA Directive 85/33/EEC with its 1997 amendments. In implementing the Directive as amended, States are required to conduct a prior environmental impact assessment before constructing onshore pipelines for the transportation of natural oil or gas, landing pipelines, or discharging oil-contaminated cuttings from offshore platforms.[139] EIA may also be required for offshore activities on the continental shelf. For example the Netherlands Royal Decree of 4 March 1999 contains separate licensing provisions for larger offshore installations and larger/longer pipelines which pose a proportionately greater

[139] See the Netherlands Royal Decree of 20 May 1987; France had already legislated with the 1976 Environment Act requiring an EIA for, *inter alia*, the construction of power plants, nuclear facilities, dams, and electricity pylons. In 1999 a new Italian decree further implemented the 1985 Directive, addressing, *inter alia*, pipelines, thermo- and hydro-electric plants, and installations for the treatment of irridated fuels.

threat of environmental harm. Similar provisions are found in Denmark.[140] In general States require more rigorous assessment of activities to be conducted in environmentally sensitive areas both onshore and offshore, such as nature reserves and wetlands. Case-law in the Netherlands has confirmed the requirement of an EIA for each individual drilling activity in wetland areas. Other EC environmental Directives, such as the Birds and Habitats Directives, have also been invoked in environmental challenges to petroleum activities.[141]

Abandonment and removal of offshore installations

Introduction

In addition to the environmental consequences of installing and operating offshore installations, the environmental impact of the abandonment and removal of such installations has been a contentious issue, well illustrated by the controversy surrounding the disposal of the *Brent Spar* in 1995. All the States considered here are parties to the 1982 UNCLOS save for Denmark, where it is under active consideration. All the North Sea States[142] are also Parties to the 1992 Convention for the Protection for the Marine Environment of the North-East Atlantic (the OSPAR Convention). Nonetheless, practice varies regarding the extent to which precise removal obligations are addressed by legislation or otherwise, and as to the legal mechanism for ensuring that the costs of removal are borne by the operator (in an application of the polluter-pays principle). Entire removal is required for installations on the Netherlands' continental shelf and clearly stipulated in the relevant legislation, though the extent of this obligation in respect of pipelines remains to be clarified. In other cases removal obligations are established not by legislation but in policy documents, reflecting both the very different physical environments for States bordering the North Sea and differences in regulatory approaches. Thus the United Kingdom requires as a matter of policy complete removal in the shallower southern sector of the North Sea, but will consider on a case-by-case basis leaving *in situ* or only partially removing installations in the northern sector. Denmark applies a total removal obligation on the Danish continental shelf. **14.179**

Abandonment practice

Given the requirement of total removal in relatively shallow seas, it is perhaps not surprising to find that abandonment practice in the Netherlands is on the whole more discretionary, with the Minister of Economic Affairs empowered under the **14.180**

[140] Statutory amendments to the Danish Subsoil Act in 1995 and the Continental Shelf Act in 1997 give effect to the EIA Directive, an EIA being required for offshore installations and pipelines and for separate works.

[141] Invoked unsuccessfully in eg the Netherlands: see ch 10 above.

[142] The relevant regional convention for the Mediterranean Sea is the 1976 Barcelona Convention, as updated in 1996, discussed in ch 2 above.

relevant Continental Shelf Mining regulations to determine when, and if, abandonment has taken place. In Norway, Denmark, and the United Kingdom, an abandonment programme must be submitted for government approval. In Norway this applies to both installations and pipelines in the Norwegian sector, and to any land-based installations functionally connected to the offshore activities. The plan must include removal/disposal alternatives and an impact analysis of those alternatives in terms of the marine environment, other uses of the sea, and any relevant interests on land, though in practice the alternative recommended by the licensee will be more fully analysed. Similar requirements are imposed under UK legislation. Practice under the Norwegian legislation indicates that more lightweight structures are likely to require total removal and disposal on land, while larger structures will also require removal from the seabed and disposal on land. Pipelines and cables are left *in situ.* Caution must be exercised in extrapolating from Norwegian practice: at the time of writing only two structures have been considered, North East Frigg and Odin, so generalization is risky. Similar caution should be exercised in extrapolating from the UK experience, where as yet total removal has only been required in respect of the remains of the *Piper Alpha*, following the 1988 explosion disaster, and in respect of *Brent Spar.* The latter proved controversial not in respect of the removal obligation—total removal was technically and financially feasible—but in respect of the disposal. Following the well publicized opposition to deep-sea disposal mounted by Greenpeace, the *Spar* was now designated for land-based disposal (a quay extension) in Norway.

Removal permit

14.181 Whilst decisions on both the removal and the disposal issues are generally taken by one entity which approves the abandonment programme, eg the Ministry of Petroleum and Energy in Norway, or the Department of Trade and Industry in the UK, separate permission is usually needed from the relevant authorities to carry out the disposal, eg a dumping permit for disposal on the continental shelf. Title to the remains left *in situ*, in whole or in part, is left by international law for the State to determine, subject to the requirement in the IMO Guidelines that title is unambiguous and that responsibility for future maintenance, and liability for any future damage, is clearly established. In the practice of North Sea States this degree of certainty is not uniformly achieved. In Norway the MPE designates 'responsible entities' in approving an abandonment plan; in addition there is statutory provision for the possibility that the State may assume title to installations left *in situ* and, with such title, future liabilities. This is generally the case only where future financial benefit will accrue from that installation or field. By

[143] Set by agreement between the parties, ie the owner and the State, but on the continental shelf the amount of compensation (if any) is fixed by the State (1996 Petroleum Act). Under the previous 1985 Act the only possibility was to take over continental shelf installations without compensation.

agreement between the parties it is also possible for the State to take over an abandoned installation with no further commercial value, subject to the requirement that the licensee/owner of the installation pay compensation to the State.[143] Similar provisions exist in Denmark for the State to assume responsibility for installations where further commercial use is contemplated, or where the installations is abandoned, subject to the requirement that the licensee indemnify the State for loss or damage caused by an installation not passed on in 'proper condition'.

Removal costs

Nor have the States considered here uniformly addressed the costs of removal in legislation. In some States separate legislation addressing the costs of decommissioning has been enacted, such as the United Kingdom's Petroleum Act and the Norwegian Removal Cost Act, a key distinction being that in the latter the State is to pay a direct share of the total costs of removal.[144] Others have relied upon licence conditions requiring a financial guarantee, such as the Netherlands. In the United Kingdom special tax relief is accorded to current financial provision for liabilities which will be incurred in future. This is not the case in Norway where the State already directly shoulders some of the costs of decommissioning. There the proportion paid by the State bears a direct relation to the tax paid by the licensee. **14.182**

Disposal of the installations removed

Once the nature and extent of the removal obligation is ascertained, it is still necessary to address the second major legal issue in respect of the decommissioning of offshore installations: the disposal of remains wholly or partially removed. International guidance is found in the 1992 OSPAR Convention which places considerable reliance upon case-by-case evaluation by the State concerned. Whilst not formally described as an EIA, the procedures set forth for the decommissioning and disposal of offshore installations in the area covered by the 1992 OSPAR Convention are very closely analogous to this process. More recently OSPAR Decision 98/3 on the Disposal of Disused Offshore Installations, which binds States Parties to OSPAR from 9 February 1999, considers final disposal on land to be the preferred option for decommissioned offshore installations. **14.183**

Concluding remarks

From the above discussion it is clear that in future the emphasis will be on land-based disposal sites in respect of a wide range of energy activities, including the disposal of radioactive waste and of decommissioned remains of both nuclear and **14.184**

[144] See ch 11 above. At first glance this might not be perceived as a dilution of the polluter-pays principle since the Norwegian State has direct economic participation in offshore petroleum activity in consequence of the participation of Statoil and the SDFI (State Direct Financial Interest). However, the contribution of the State exceeds its liability as a direct participant in the licence.

offshore petroleum installations. This is not to overlook the environmental effects of land-based energy activities. Environmental remediation of energy sites and facilities during and upon the cessation of energy activities is common in respect of onshore oil and gas activities, and in respect of coal, the obligation generally being to restore the land to beneficial use.[145] In Germany, for example, brown coal has had a particularly significant environmental impact since it is extracted via open-cast mining methods.

(2) Transboundary Environmental Issues

14.185 All the States considered here are Parties to the 1979 ECE Treaty on Long-Range Transboundary Air Pollution (LRTAP).[146] It is not surprising therefore that all regulate emissions of key acid rain contributors, in particular sulphur dioxide and nitrogen oxide. The 1992 Climate Change Convention and the 1997 Kyoto Protocol have likewise stimulated activity towards carbon dioxide reduction. As the table produced in the introductory chapter to this work demonstrates, contributions to carbon dioxide emissions vary across Europe. Further legislative activity in this area is to be expected.[147] For example, in May 1999 the Danish Parliament passed new legislation, an Act on carbon dioxide quotas for electricity production, which obliges the electricity producers to conform with a fixed annual ceiling for carbon emissions, to be gradually reduced each year. A ceiling of 2.3 million tonnes carbon dioxide has been set for the year 2000, with subsequent annual reductions of 1 million tonnes. This requires the fixing of quotas for each electricity production company; exceeding the limit will lead to fines, the revenue from which will be used for energy-saving projects. Some degree of emission quota banking will also be permitted, not to generate a tradeable emission permit market, but to allow the transfer of unused quota from one year to the next. Emission quotas are personal and cannot be traded to other entities. Further refinements of this and other national systems under contemplation await the outcome of international discussions regarding the implementation of the flexibility mechanisms under the Kyoto Protocol (not yet in force).

H. Concluding Remarks

14.186 This book has analysed the energy sectors in a number of countries in Europe. Some trends can be noted, the most important of which is the trend towards glob-

[145] See generally (1992) 10:1 JERL (*passim*), a special issue devoted to abandonment and reclamation issues.

[146] See ch 2 above.

[147] For an overview of national implementation measures in the UK, the Netherlands, Denmark, Germany, Spain, Norway, and the EC, see the national reports available at the UNFCCC website: http://www.unfccc.de.

alization. The production and supply of energy is no longer a national issue, let alone a municipal or provincial one. Whereas at the beginning of the twentieth century energy supply was dealt with at a municipal or provincial level, it is true to say that at the beginning of the twenty-first century the issue of energy supply is necessarily dealt with on an international level, particularly a European level. Regulatory issues are also developed on a pan-national, European level. Moreover, the issue of globalization is noticeable with regard to the environmental effects of energy supply. It becomes more effective to establish common solutions for environmental and energy problems than independent national solutions

Important parts of this book have dealt with the programme for the Internal **14.187** Energy Market. These legislative developments have been discussed in terms of both their upstream and their downstream impacts. Although the Directives give Member States a choice between several regimes, national legislators are more restricted than before. Obviously, many common features are to be found in the new national energy laws. With the continuing evolution of the internal energy market, it is perhaps only a matter of time before 'Energy Law in Europe' emerges as 'European Energy Law'.

INDEX